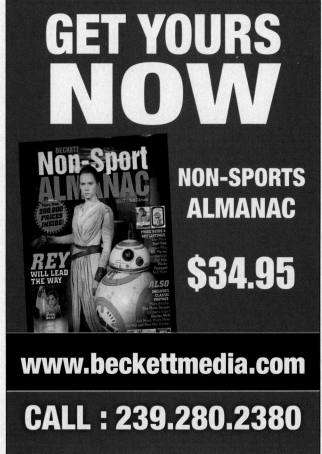

# BECKETT

# STAR WARS

## COLLECTIBLES PRICE GUIDE

### THE HOBBY'S MOST RELIABLE AND RELIED UPON SOURCE™

## FOUNDER: DR. JAMES BECKETT III

### EDITED BY MATT BIBLE WITH THE BECKETT PRICE GUIDE STAFF
#### KYLE DOBBINS - SPECIAL CONTRIBUTOR

BECKETT is a registered trademark of BECKETT MEDIA LLC, DALLAS, TEXAS
Manufactured in the United States of America | Published by Beckett Media LLC

Beckett Media LLC
4635 McEwen Dr., Dallas, TX 75244
(972) 991-6657 • beckett.com

First Printing
ISBN: 978-1-936681-31-0

# TOP 10

## STAR WARS FUNKO POP VINYL

BY MATT BIBLE

**1**

#23 DARTH MAUL (HOLOGRAPHIC)/480
(2012 SDCC EXCLUSIVE)

**2**

266B LUKE SKYWALKER (GOLD)/80
(2019 FUNKO FUNDAYS EXCLUSIVE)

**3**

14 SHADOW TROOPER/480
(2011 SDCC EXCLUSIVE)

**4**

#6B CHEWBACCA (FLOCKED)/480
(2011 SDCC EXCLUSIVE)

**5**

#24 BIGGS DARKLIGHTER/480
(2012 SDCC EXCLUSIVE)

**6**

#32 BOBA FETT DROIDS/480
(2013 SDCC EXCLUSIVE)

**7**

#501ST CLONE TROOPER/480
(2012 SDCC EXCLUSIVE)

**8**

#15 HAN SOLO STORMTROOPER/1000
(2011 ECCC EXCLUSIVE)

**9**

#16 LUKE SKYWALKER
STORMTROOPER/1000
(2011 ECCC EXCLUSIVE)

**10**

#54 PRINCESS LEIA (BOUSSH
UNMASKED)/1008
(2015 SDCC EXCLUSIVE)

# NON-SPORT
## UPDATE

## GET EIGHT ISSUES FOR
## THE PRICE OF SIX!

# Two FREE Issues
## with a 1-year
## Beckett Non-Sport Update
## subscription for
## only $30

### Limited Time Offer

**Fill out the order form below and mail it, along with your payment information, to:**

**Beckett Collectibles LLC, Lockbox # 70261, Philadelphia, PA 19176-9907**

✂ - - - - - - - - - - - - - - - - - - - - - - - - - - - - - - - - - - - - - - - - - - - - - - - - - - - - - - -

**JUST** FILL IT - CUT IT - SEND IT

## YES! Sign me up for a subscription to Beckett Non-Sport Update for only $30.00

Method of Payment ☐ Check Enclosed ☐ Credit Card ☐ Money Order ☐ Bill Me Later

Payment through Credit Card ☐ Visa ☐ MC ☐ AMEX ☐ Discover Name on Credit Card _____

Credit Card Number ☐☐☐☐☐☐☐☐☐☐☐☐☐☐☐☐ Expiration Date _____/ _____ / _____

Subscriber Name: First _____ Middle _____ Last _____

Address _____

City _____ State _____ Zip _____

Phone _____ Email _____

Signature _____ Date _____/ _____ / _____

# TOP 20

## STAR WARS TRADING CARD SETS

BY MATT BIBLE

### [1] 2017 STAR WARS STELLAR SIGNATURES

- The most premium Star Wars set ever made
- Only 100 boxes produced
- Base set limited to 40 copies

### [2] 2007 STAR WARS 30TH ANNIVERSARY

- Comprehensive in all regards (including cards of the infamous Holiday Special)
- First Harrison Ford autograph
- Huge autograph checklist that includes most of the original main cast
- Signers also include unsung heroes from behind the camera and legendary composer, John Williams
- Lots of high quality sketch cards

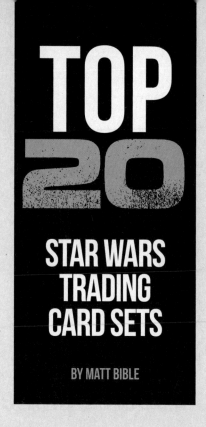

### [3] 1977 STAR WARS

- The set that started it all
- Most recognizable Star Wars set of all-time
- Still popular with a lot of fans who might not otherwise collect trading cards
- Oh, that C-3PO card!

### [4] 2015 STAR WARS MASTERWORK

- First high-end Star Wars set
- Large on-card autograph checklist
- Plenty of other premium inserts including relics
- Challenging base set.

### [5] 1993-95 STAR WARS GALAXY

- Brought Star Wars cards back after a ten-year hiatus
- Art-based approach laid groundwork for new styles of sets
- Gorgeous design and artwork

## [6] 2001 STAR WARS EVOLUTION

- First set of Star Wars trading cards to include actor autographs
- Strong autograph checklist
- Thematically spawned a sequel in 2006 and another in 2016

## [7] 1995 STAR WARS WIDEVISION

- Introduced oversized Widevision line
- Presents images as they're showcased on the big screen
- Backs contain plenty of information and production artwork
- Extensive promo card checklist

## [8] 2004 STAR WARS HERITAGE

- First set to have sketch cards from the Original Trilogy
- Old-school look and feel
- First autographs of Mark Hamill and James Earl Jones
- Retail-only LetterStickers are tough to find and still popular with set builders

## [11] 1996 STAR WARS 3-DI WIDEVISION

- One of the smallest print runs of any '90s Star Wars set
- First Star Wars cards to use 3-D technology

## [9] 1980 STAR WARS EMPIRE STRIKES BACK

- Original Trilogy set
- Three series are not as many as first film but still comprehensive as a whole with larger checklists
- Ralph McQuarrie artwork included on some cards

## [10] 2016 STAR WARS MASTERWORK

- The high-end follow-up effort to the 2015 set
- Features 80 total autograph signers
- Contains autographs of new stars Daisy Ridley and Adam Driver
- Eclectic relic cards that feature stamps and medallions

## [12] 2015 STAR WARS HIGH TEK

- Acetate designs and pattern variations make it easy to collect the set several ways
- All autographs are on-card
- Deep checklist of signers from seven films plus TV shows
- First set with a John Boyega autograph

## [13] 2013 STAR WARS JEDI LEGACY

- First pack-inserted Star Wars memorabilia cards
- Franchise's first film cel cards
- Strong autograph checklist
- Different spin on the stories of Luke Skywalker and Darth Vader

## [14] 2017 STAR WARS 40TH ANNIVERSARY

- Commemorates 40 years of Saga
- A very full 200-card base set
- Retro design to pay homage to original
- 62 different autographs including the elusive six-person booklet autograph that features Harrison Ford, Mark Hamill, Carrie Fisher, Anthony Daniels, Kenny Baker, and Peter Mayhew

## [15] 2002 STAR WARS ATTACK OF THE CLONES WIDEVISION

- Like other Widevision sets, base cards look excellent
- Large autograph checklist which includes the only autograph of Frank Oz (Yoda)

## [16] 1996 STAR WARS FINEST

- First full chromium Star Wars set outside of inserts
- Refractors make their franchise debut
- Takes an all-art approach but each artist did a nine-card group based on a similar theme

## [17] 2014 STAR WARS RETURN OF THE JEDI 3-D WIDEVISION

- Limited print run sold out quickly as online exclusive
- Autos randomly inserted as bonus
- Technology makes for a stunning base set
- Some of the greatest packaging ever for any trading card product

## [18] 2004 STAR WARS CLONE WARS

- First Star Wars sketch cards
- Cool artwork from Genndy Tartakovsky short cartoon anthology

## [19] 1977 STAR WARS WONDER BREAD

- Fresh, memorable design
- Nice alternative and complement to the original 1977 Topps set

## [20] 1996 STAR WARS SHADOWS OF THE EMPIRE

- Most cards contain character images from original Star Wars Galaxy set
- Popular with set builders

# YOUR BODY
## YOUR HOPE

**Your immune system may be the key to beating cancer.**

Immunotherapy, a new approach to cancer treatment, is bringing hope
to cancer survivors everywhere. Immunotherapy works by empowering
your body's own immune system to correctly identify and eradicate
cancer cells. This approach has been used to effectively fight many
types of cancer, with new research leading to greater hope each day.
Speak with your doctor and visit **standuptocancer.org/immunotherapy**
to learn if immunotherapy may be right for you.

Jimmy Smits, SU2C Ambassador
Photo By: Timothy White

 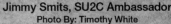

# TOP 20

## STAR WARS CERTIFIED AUTOGRAPHED CARDS

BY MATT BIBLE

**1**

2016 STAR WARS
MASTERWORK AUTOGRAPHS
DAISY RIDLEY

**2**

2007 STAR WARS
30TH ANNIVERSARY AUTOGRAPHS
HARRISON FORD

**3**

2001 STAR WARS
EVOLUTION AUTOGRAPHS
CARRIE FISHER

**4**

2004 STAR WARS
HERITAGE AUTOGRAPHS
MARK HAMILL

**5**

2004 STAR WARS
HERITAGE AUTOGRAPHS
JAMES EARL JONES

**6**

2002 STAR WARS ATTACK OF THE
CLONES WIDEVISION AUTOGRAPHS
FRANK OZ

**7**

2001 STAR WARS
EVOLUTION AUTOGRAPHS
IAN MCDIARMID

**8**

2019 STAR WARS CHROME LEGACY
PREQUEL TRILOGY AUTOGRAPHS
EWAN MCGREGOR

**9**

2016 STAR WARS ROGUE ONE
SERIES ONE AUTOGRAPHS
FELICITY JONES

**10**

2001 STAR WARS
EVOLUTION AUTOGRAPHS
BILLY DEE WILLIAMS

**11**

### 2016 STAR WARS MASTERWORK AUTOGRAPHS ADAM DRIVER

**12**

### 2006 STAR WARS EVOLUTION UPDATE AUTOGRAPHS HAYDEN CHRISTENSEN

**13**

### 2005 STAR WARS REVENGE OF THE SITH WIDEVISION AUTOGRAPHS SAMUEL L. JACKSON

**14**

### 2001 STAR WARS EVOLUTION AUTOGRAPHS ANTHONY DANIELS

**15**

### 2001 STAR WARS EVOLUTION AUTOGRAPHS KENNY BAKER

**16**

### 2007 STAR WARS 30TH ANNIVERSARY AUTOGRAPHS JOHN WILLIAMS

**17**

### 2001 STAR WARS EVOLUTION AUTOGRAPHS PETER MAYHEW

**18**

### 2010 STAR WARS EMPIRE STRIKES BACK WIDEVISION AUTOGRAPHS IRVIN KERSHNER

**19**

### 2010 STAR WARS EMPIRE STRIKES BACK 3-D WIDEVISION AUTOGRAPHS RALPH MCQUARRIE

**20**

### 2015 STAR WARS HIGH TEK AUTOGRAPHS JOHN BOYEGA

CHRISTOPHER JUE/GETTY IMAGES FOR DISNEY

# TOP 10

## VINTAGE STAR WARS ACTION FIGURES

BY KYLE DOBBINS

**1**

1977-78 STAR WARS BOBA FETT
(ROCKET FIRING PROTOTYPE)

**2**

1977-78 12-BACKS A JAWA
(VINYL CAPE)

**3**

1980-82 STAR WARS EMPIRE STRIKES
BACK FX-7 (MEDICAL DROID) PALITOY

**4**

1983 STAR WARS RETURN OF THE JEDI LUKE
SKYWALKER (JEDI KNIGHT OUTFIT) LILY LEDY

**5**

1985 STAR WARS POWER OF THE
FORCE YAK FACE

**6**

1977-78 STAR WARS 12-BACKS A DARTH
VADER (DOUBLE TELESCOPING LIGHTSABER)

**7**

1977-78 STAR WARS 12-BACKS A BEN (OBI-WAN)
KENOBI (DOUBLE TELESCOPING LIGHTSABER)

**8**

1985 STAR WARS DROIDS
VLIX GLASSLITE

**9**

1977-78 STAR WARS 21-BACKS B
BOBA FETT

**10**

1977-78 STAR WARS 12-BACKS A LUKE
SKYWALKER (DOUBLE TELESCOPING LIGHTSABER)

# TOP 10

## VINTAGE STAR WARS VEHICLES & PLAYSETS

BY KYLE DOBBINS

**1**

977-78 STAR WARS VEHICLES MILLENNIUM FALCON

**2**

1978 STAR WARS PLAYSETS CANTINA ADVENTURE SET (SEARS)

**3**

1978 STAR WARS PLAYSETS DEATH STAR SPACE STATION (KENNER)

**4**

1978 STAR WARS VEHICLES X-WING FIGHTER

**5**

1980-82 STAR WARS EMPIRE STRIKES BACK SNOWSPEEDER

**6**

1983 STAR WARS RETURN OF THE JEDI VEHICLES TIE INTERCEPTOR

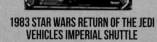

**7**

1983 STAR WARS RETURN OF THE JEDI VEHICLES IMPERIAL SHUTTLE

**8**

1980-82 STAR WARS EMPIRE STRIKES BACK AT-AT

**9**

1978 STAR WARS VEHICLES LAND SPEEDER

**10**

1983 STAR WARS RETURN OF THE JEDI VEHICLES Y-WING FIGHTER

# FROM THE BEG

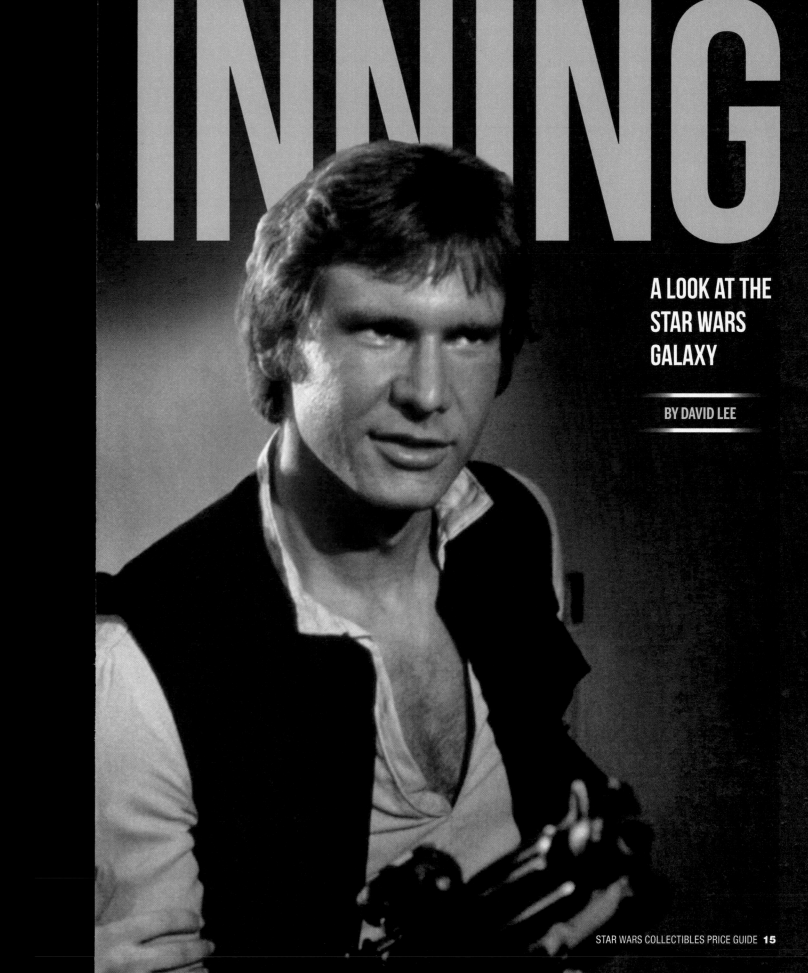

# INNING

## A LOOK AT THE STAR WARS GALAXY

BY DAVID LEE

# EPISODE I
## THE PHANTOM MENACE

**RELEASED: MAY 1999**
**BOX OFFICE: $1.027 BILLION**

The first of the prequel trilogy launched 22 years after *A New Hope*. The Trade Federation has blocked off routes to the planet Naboo, and Jedi Qui-Gon Jinn and a young Obi-Wan Kenobi are sent to negotiate. Queen Padmé Amidala is rescued, and her ship lands on Tatooine for repairs.

This is where the Jedi meet Anakin Skywalker as a young slave boy. Qui-Gon realizes his potential and similarities to an ancient prophesy of one who would bring balance to the Force.

The Sith—the mortal enemy of the Jedi—return from the shadows in the form of Darth Maul and Darth Sidious, who is pulling strings from both sides under the disguise of Naboo's Senator Palpatine.

It's evident that a war is coming, as tensions between the Republic and the Trade Federation rise. Qui-Gon trains Anakin to be a Jedi.

The Jedi are sent to Naboo to investigate the return of the Sith. Back on her home planet, Queen Amidala recruits the Gungans—underwater creatures on Naboo—to help fight the Trade Federation's invasion of the planet.

Qui-Gon and Obi-Wan battle Darth Maul in a mesmerizing lightsaber duel. Darth Maul kills Qui-Gon, but Obi-Wan cuts Maul in half, ending the Sith's resurgence.

Senator Palpatine rises to become the new Supreme Chancellor of the Senate, where he continues to manipulate the Republic and the coming Separatist movement. Obi-Wan convinces a reluctant Jedi Council to allow him to train Anakin as a Jedi.

STAR WARS EPISODE I

" AS SURELY AS ANAKIN SKYWALKER POINTS THE WAY INTO THE FUTURE OF *STAR WARS*, SO DOES *THE PHANTOM MENACE* RAISE THE CURTAIN ON THIS NEW FREEDOM FOR FILMMAKERS. AND IT'S A LOT OF FUN. GIVE ME TRANSPARENT UNDERWATER CITIES AND VAST HOLLOW SENATORIAL SPHERES ANY DAY."

– ROGER EBERT

# EPISODE II

# ATTACK OF THE CLONES

STAR WARS
EPISODE II
ATTACK OF THE CLONES

**RELEASED: MAY 2002**
**BOX OFFICE: $649.4 MILLION**

Several years removed from the events of *The Phantom Menace*, Anakin has become a talented yet arrogant young Jedi. There is a growing Separatist movement led by former Jedi Master Count Dooku. Anakin and Obi-Wan are assigned to protect Padmé Amidala, as she plans to push for the creation of an army to help the Jedi deal with the Separatists. A bounty hunter tries to kill her, and Obi-Wan investigates the origin of the would-be assassin. This leads him to the planet Kamino where he discovers that a clone army is being produced for the Republic. The bounty hunter Jango Fett serves as the army's DNA origin. Obi-Wan follows him and his young son Boba to Geonosis, where Obi-Wan discovers that Count Dooku is amassing his own army of droids.

Meanwhile, Anakin, who has stayed behind to protect Padmé, has disturbing visions of his mom suffering back on his home planet of Tatooine. He and Padmé go to save her. He discovers that she was taken by Tusken Raiders, and while he finds her, he's unable to save her. He slaughters the Tuskens and vows that he will become the most powerful Jedi ever.

Obi-Wan tells Anakin of the droid army just before he is captured on Geonosis. Supreme Chancellor Palpatine is given emergency powers to send the clones to battle the droids. Anakin and Padmé go to rescue Obi-Wan, but all three are captured. Before they are executed, the trio is rescued by a band of Jedi and clone soldiers. Anakin and Obi-Wan attempt to stop Dooku, but he overpowers them, cutting off Anakin's arm. Yoda comes to their rescue and battles Dooku, but he gets away and delivers blueprints of the Death Star to his master, Darth Sidious. This begins the Clone Wars.

> **"** *CLONES* ENDS WITH A WEDDING FOR THE FUTURE PARENTS OF LUKE AND PRINCESS LEIA. BUT IT'S THE GLIMPSE OF DARTH VADER THAT LUCAS GIVES US IN ANAKIN – TRAUMATIZED BY THE MURDER OF HIS MOTHER AND CAPABLE OF KILLING INNOCENTS – THAT REMINDS US OF THE DARK POWER *STAR WARS* EXERTED BEFORE IT BECAME A FRANCHISE."

– PETER TRAVERS, ROLLING STONE

# EPISODE III
## REVENGE OF THE SITH

### RELEASED: MAY 2005
### BOX OFFICE: $848.8 MILLION

*evenge of the Sith* takes place about three years into the Clone Wars, which have created division across the galaxy. Anakin and Obi-Wan rescue Supreme Chancellor Palpatine, who has been kidnapped by General Grievous, the leader of the droid army. The two Jedi battle Count Dooku again, and Palpatine convinces Anakin to go against the Jedi way and execute Dooku. Anakin returns to Padmé, who is now his wife. She tells him she's pregnant. Anakin begins having visions of Padmé dying in childbirth, much like the visions he had of his mother.

Palpatine, who continues to manipulate Anakin, tells him the story of Darth Sideous, a Sith Lord who learned the power to save people from death. This is a major turning point in Anakin's descent to the Dark Side, as he thinks he can learn the power to save Padmé. He discovers that Palpatine is actually a Sith Lord, which he reports to Jedi Master Mace Windu. Windu confronts Palpatine and nearly kills him, but Anakin saves him in fear of losing the ability to save Padmé.

Anakin vows to serve Palpatine, who dubs him "Darth Vader." Palpatine orders the clone soldiers to murder the Jedi during battle. Anakin leads a group of droids to massacre the rest of the Jedi at the Jedi Temple, as well as the Separatist leaders on the planet Mustafar. It's here where Obi-Wan and Anakin battle after Anakin chokes Padmé unconscious for believing she betrayed him. The battle leaves Anakin dismembered and nearly burnt to death. Palpatine transforms the Republic into the Galatic Empire. He and Yoda fight to a stalemate before Palpatine rescues Anakin and has him placed into the black, menacing Darth Vader suit. They oversee the construction of the Death Star while Obi-Wan, Yoda and Bail Organa agree to hide newborn babies Luke and Leia from the Empire. Padmé dies just after they're born.

**STAR WARS**
**EPISODE III**
**REVENGE OF THE SITH**

STAR WARS    EPISODE III    REVENGE OF THE SITH
Starring EWAN McGREGOR    NATALIE PORTMAN    HAYDEN CHRISTENSEN
IAN McDIARMID    SAMUEL L. JACKSON    CHRISTOPHER LEE
Co-starring ANTHONY DANIELS · KENNY BAKER · FRANK OZ
Music by JOHN WILLIAMS    Produced by RICK McCALLUM

Written and Directed by
GEORGE LUCAS

W W W . S T A R W A R S . C O M

"HAVING SPENT TWO SCATTERSHOT BLOCKBUSTERS WHETTING OUR APPETITE FOR THE FALL OF ANAKIN SKYWALKER, GEORGE LUCAS MAKES IT EASY TO EXPERIENCE *STAR WARS: EPISODE III – REVENGE OF THE SITH* AS A RUSH OF DELIVERANCE."

— OWEN GLIEBERMAN, ENTERTAINMENT WEEKLY

# A STAR WARS STORY

## RELEASED: MAY 2018
## BOX OFFICE: $392.9 MILLION

Another spinoff film in the expanded Star Wars storyline, Solo tells a back story of everyone's favorite "scruffy-looking nerf herder." A confident young Han and his lover, Qi'ra, bribe their way onto a transport out of Corellia. Qi'ra is captured by Imperial troopers as they are going through the gate. Han promises to find her and then joins the Imperial Navy.

Three years pass. Han meets Tobias Beckett and his small band of criminals posing as Imperial troopers during a battle. Han is arrested and thrown into a prison with "the beast," who turns out to be Chewbacca. Able to understand the wookie, Han and Chewbacca work together to escape. They convince Beckett to let them join their plan to steal a huge load of coaxium, a powerful hyperspace fuel, from Vandor-1. The plan is faulted by Cloud Riders who also try to steal the coaxium, which explodes in the attempt.

The coaxium was for crime boss Dryden Vos, so Han and Chewbacca vow to help Beckett steal another shipment. The group goes to meet Vos where Han finds Qi'ra, who has become a top lieutenant for Vos. Han reveals his plan to steal unrefined coaxium, then the group seeks help from smuggler and pilot Lando Calrissian. They reach the coaxium mines on Kessel in the Millennium Falcon, Lando's ship. After stealing enough coaxium, Han navigates the ship through the dangerous Kessel Run to avoid an Imperial blockade. Enfys, the leader of the Cloud Riders, tracks the crew and reveals they are actually rebels trying to prevent the crime bosses and the Empire from increasing their power. The two groups join forces, but Beckett betrays them. Qi'ra kills Vos as Beckett takes the coaxium for himself. Qi'ra reveals the failure to Vos' superior, Darth Maul, and takes Vos' place.

Han catches up with Beckett and shoots him before he can do the same to him. Enfys and the rebels end up with the coaxium. Han wins the Millennium Falcon from Lando in a card game. He and Chewbacca head to Tatooine for a job with a "big-shot gangster."

# ROGUE ONE
## A STAR WARS STORY

**RELEASED: DECEMBER 2016**
**BOX OFFICE: $1.056 BILLION**

A spinoff prequel story to *A New Hope*, *Rogue One* tells the story of the band of Rebels who steal the schematics of the original Death Star. Galen Erso is a scientist and engineer forced by the Empire to construct the Death Star. He's hiding with his family when Imperial weapons developer Orson Krennic finds him, wanting him to complete the Death Star. Galen's young daughter Jyn hides while her father is taken away. Family friend and Rebel leader Saw Gerrera keeps Jyn safe. Fifteen years pass. Pilot Bodhi Rook defects from the Empire and smuggles a message from Galen to Gerrera about a weakness Galen built into the Death Star.

Jyn is in an Imperial labor camp but she's freed by Rebel Cassian Andor and brought to a Rebel base. The Rebels want Jyn to find her father so they can learn more about the Death Star, however, Cassian is ordered to kill Galen. Jyn, Cassian droid K-2SO travel to Jedha and meet Chirrut Îmwe and Baze Malbus. They hook up with Gerrera, who shows Jyn the message from her father. The message instructs them to go to the planet Scarif to retrieve the Death Star schematics. Bodhi leads the group to Galen's research facility, and Cassian decides not to kill him. However, Rebel ships attach the facility, killing Galen. Krennic meets with Darth Vader and seeks his support, but Vader warns him to not allow any more breaches in security.

Jyn leads a secret mission to steal the Death Star plans on Scarif. Jyn, Cassian and K-2SO infiltrate the data tower and steal the plans during a final confrontation with Krennic. More Rebels join the fight when they learn of the mission. Bodhi, Chirrut and Baze are killed in battle, but not before completing their parts of the mission. The plans are transmitted to a Rebel ship before the Death Star destroys the base on Scarif, killing Krennic, Jyn and Cassian. Darth Vader intercepts the Rebel ship with the schematics and slaughters several Rebel soldiers. But the schematics are downloaded and quickly taken to Princess Leia on an escape ship. These events happen just before the beginning of *A New Hope*.

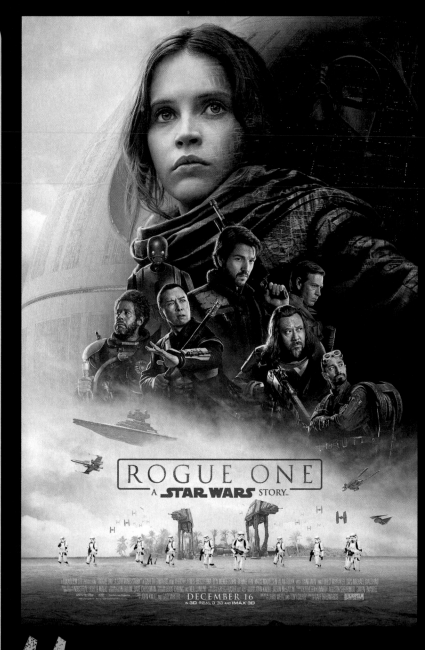

" THE INHERENT PROBLEM IN A STORY ABOUT THE SUICIDE MISSION TO STEAL THE DEATH STAR PLANS USED TO BLOW UP THE SPACE STATION AT THE END OF A NEW HOPE IS THAT WE ALREADY KNOW HOW IT ENDS. THERE'S NO SUSPENSE, NO MOMENTUS, NO STAKES."

— RENE RODRIGUEZ, MIAMI HERALD, 2016

# EPISODE IV
## A NEW HOPE

A long time ago in a galaxy far, far away...

©1977 Twentieth Century-Fox

TWENTIETH CENTURY-FOX Presents
A LUCASFILM LTD. PRODUCTION
STAR WARS
Starring MARK HAMILL  HARRISON FORD  CARRIE FISHER
PETER CUSHING
and
ALEC GUINNESS
Written and Directed by GEORGE LUCAS  Produced by GARY KURTZ  Music by JOHN WILLIAMS
PANAVISION®  PRINTS BY DE LUXE®  TECHNICOLOR®

Making Films Sound Better
DOLBY SYSTEM
Noise Reduction - High Fidelity

**RELEASED: MAY 1977**
**BOX OFFICE: $775.4 MILLION**

From the opening scene of a massive Star Destroyer passing overhead to the crazy characters in Mos Eslie Cantina, this is the film that launched a worldwide empire 40 years ago. Darth Vader captures Princess Leia, who hides the stolen plans to the Empire's Death Star in droid R2-D2. She records a message for former Jedi Obi-Wan Kenobi, who is hidden on the desert planet of Tatooine. A young Luke Skywalker buys R2-D2 and his android buddy C-3PO to work on his uncle's farm. He discovers the message, which triggers a series of events that sends Luke off on an adventure with Obi-Wan to fight the oppressive Galactic Empire and train to become a Jedi Knight.

The two meet up with the smuggler Han Solo and Chewbacca, who agree to take them to Leia's home planet of Alderaan. On the way, the entire planet is destroyed by the Death Star, demonstrating the power the Empire holds over the galaxy. After allowing themselves to be captured, Luke, Han and Chewie rescue Leia. Darth Vader battles Obi-Wan in the first lightsaber duel in the saga while the others escape. Obi-Wan sacrifices himself and becomes one with the Force, allowing him to continue to communicate with Luke.

Later, the Rebel Alliance devises a plan to destroy the Death Star using information from the stolen plans. Luke is part of the attack squadron, and maneuvers a narrow trench to reach the target. He uses the Force to focus when firing torpedoes through a small opening at the end of the trench. The Death Star explodes just as it is about to fire on the Rebel base.

❝ STRIP *STAR WARS* OF ITS OFTEN STRIKING IMAGES AND ITS HIGH-FA-LUTIN' SCIENTIFIC JARGON, AND YOU GET A STORY, CHARACTERS, AND DIALOGUE OF OVERWHELMING BANALITY, WITHOUT EVEN A 'FUTURE' CAST TO THEM. CERTAINLY THE MENTALITY AND VALUES OF THE MOVIE CAN BE DUPLICATED IN THIRD-RATE NON-SCIENCE FICTION OF ANY PLACE OR PERIOD. OH DULL NEW WORLD!"

**– JOHN SIMON, NEW YORK MAGAZINE, 1977**

# EPISODE V
## THE EMPIRE STRIKES BACK

**RELEASED: MAY 1980**
**BOX OFFICE: $538.4 MILLION**

The consensus fan favorite of the entire franchise, *The Empire Strikes Back* is also regarded by many as the best in the saga. After being forced from their base, the Rebels operate from the ice planet of Hoth. The Empire discovers their location and mounts an assault using massive AT-AT walkers. Most of the Rebels escape, and Luke goes to train with Jedi Master Yoda on Dagobah.

Han, Leia and Chewie find safety (or so they think) in the Cloud City, run by Han's former friend and fellow smuggler, Lando Calrissian. However, the band of heroes are betrayed and ambushed by Darth Vader.

His ultimate plan is to lure Luke and bring him to the Emperor. Vader freezes Han in carbonite as a test for trapping Luke. He hands Han over to the bounty hunter Boba Fett, who brings Han to the gangster Jabba the Hutt.

Vader's plan works. While training with Yoda, Luke senses his friends are in danger and goes to help, promising Yoda he will return.

Yoda knows he's not ready to face Vader, and urges Luke not to go. At the Cloud City, Luke escapes Vader's trap. After a lightsaber duel where Vader cuts Luke's hand off, Luke has nowhere to go when Vader reveals to Luke that he is his father.

It's one of the most shocking twists in Hollywood history. The family dynamic is a major factor in all the films from this point on. Lando regains control of the city, and the heroes escape in the Millennium Falcon. Luke falls into a chute to flee Vader, and his friends come back to save him.

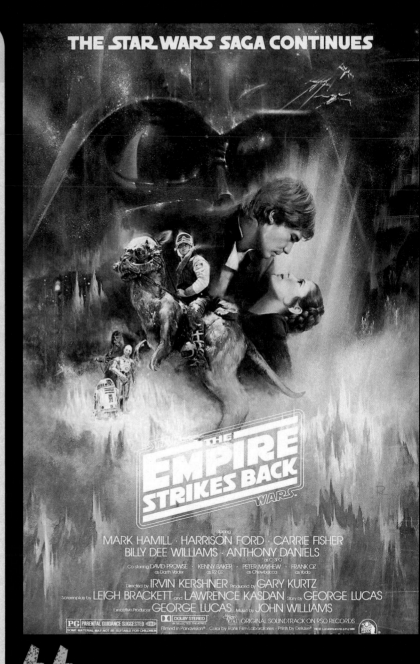

THE *STAR WARS* SAGA CONTINUES

Starring
MARK HAMILL · HARRISON FORD · CARRIE FISHER
BILLY DEE WILLIAMS · ANTHONY DANIELS
as C-3PO
Co-starring DAVID PROWSE · KENNY BAKER · PETER MAYHEW · FRANK OZ
as Darth Vader    as R2-D2    as Chewbacca    as Yoda
Directed by IRVIN KERSHNER   Produced by GARY KURTZ
Screenplay by LEIGH BRACKETT and LAWRENCE KASDAN  Story by GEORGE LUCAS
Executive Producer GEORGE LUCAS   Music by JOHN WILLIAMS

" I'M NOT SURE I'M UP FOR SEVEN MORE *STAR WARS* ADVENTURES, BUT I CAN HARDLY WAIT FOR THE NEXT ONE."

**– PAULINE KAEL, THE NEW YORKER, 1980**

# EPISODE VI
## RETURN OF THE JEDI

STAR WARS
RETURN OF THE JEDI

Starring
MARK HAMILL • HARRISON FORD • CARRIE FISHER
BILLY DEE WILLIAMS • ANTHONY DANIELS as C-3PO
Co-starring DAVID PROWSE • KENNY BAKER • PETER MAYHEW • FRANK OZ
Directed by RICHARD MARQUAND Produced by HOWARD KAZANJIAN
Story by GEORGE LUCAS Screenplay by LAWRENCE KASDAN and GEORGE LUCAS
Executive Producer GEORGE LUCAS Music by JOHN WILLIAMS

"THIRD INSTALLMENT IN THE *STAR WARS* SAGA IS A SHEER DELIGHT. SOME ROUTINE PERFORMANCES ARE COMPENSATED FOR BY INGENIOUS NEW CHARACTERS AND SPECIAL EFFECTS."

**– LEONARD MALTIN, ENTERTAINMENT WEEKLY, 1983**

### RELEASED: MAY 1983
### BOX OFFICE: $572.7 MILLION

After the defeat in *The Empire Strikes Back*, the heroes plan to rescue Han from Jabba the Hutt. Leia frees Han from the carbonite, but they are captured in the attempt. Jabba plans to execute the group. However, the heroes escape after a thrilling battle. Luke keeps his promise to Yoda, and returns to complete his training. The Jedi Master is dying, and tells Luke that when he is gone, Luke will be the last of the Jedi. Yoda confirms that Darth Vader is Luke's father, and tells Luke there is another Skywalker. Obi-Wan, talking with Luke through the Force, tells him how he hid Luke and his twin sister from Vader. Luke realizes that Leia is his sister.

Meanwhile, the Empire is constructing a new Death Star. The Rebels discover this and plan to destroy its shield generator before attacking the Death Star. Han, Luke, Leia and Chewie lead an attack on the shield generator located on the forest moon of Endor. However, Vader, sensing that Luke is with them, is prepared. The heroes get unexpected help from the Ewoks—the native creatures on the moon. Luke allows himself to be captured so that he can face Darth Vader and the Emperor, who try to turn Luke to the Dark Side.

Luke and Vader have their final battle. Luke defeats his father, cutting his hand off just as Vader had done to Luke. Luke realizes he's turning into his father, and refuses to join the Dark Side. He nearly dies at the hands of the Emperor, but Vader sacrifices himself to save his son, throwing the Emperor down a large shaft. This ultimately turns Vader back to the good side. The Death Star is destroyed and balance returns to the galaxy.

# EPISODE VII
## THE FORCE AWAKENS

**RELEASED: DECEMBER 2015**
**BOX OFFICE: $2.066 BILLION**

Continuing the *Star Wars* storyline for the first time in more than 30 years, *The Force Awakens* mixes old heroes and villains with a new generation. Luke Skywalker is in hiding. The oppressive First Order is rising to power and aims to eradicate The New Republic. They have built a mega-weapon called Starkiller Base capable of destroying an entire system of planets at once. Resistance fighter pilot Poe Dameron obtains a map reveling Luke's location and hides it in the droid BB-8. But Kylo Ren commands a band of stormtroopers that capture Poe. Poe escapes with the help of a defecting stormtrooper he names "Finn." They crash on the planet of Jakku.

Finn meets Rey, a scavenger girl who has found BB-8. The two steal the Millennium Falcon and flee after First Order pilots discover them. They are captured by Han Solo and Chewbacca, who want to take back their lost ship. The crew then sees the map in BB-8, and Han notices that it's incomplete. They find help from Maz Kanata, who assists them in getting BB-8 to the Resistance. While at Maz's cantina, Rey finds Luke's original lightsaber and has visions when she touches it.

Kylo Ren, who was once trained by Luke before turning to the Dark Side, captures Rey after he discovers she has seen the map leading to Luke. But he is unable to overpower her with the Force. Rey, who is just discovering her ability to use the Force, escapes and meets up with Han, Finn and Chewie. Han confronts Kylo Ren, who we learned is actually Han and Leia's son. Han tries to convince him to leave the Dark Side and return to his family, but Kylo Ren murders his father. Rey and Kylo Ren engage in a lightsaber duel after the heroes successfully disable Starkiller Base. Rey defeats and injures Kylo Ren. She then travels to find Luke after the map is pieced together. She hands Luke his lightsaber, indicating that he will begin training Rey as a Jedi.

> **INCOMING WRITER-DIRECTOR J.J. ABRAMS SEEMS TO HAVE HAD THE ORIGINAL THREE FILMS FIRMLY IN MIND WHEN HE EMBARKED ON THIS MONUMENTAL NEW UNDERTAKING, STRUCTURED AS A SERIES OF CLEVER IF SOMETIMES WOBBLY CALLBACKS TO A TRILOGY THAT CAPTIVATED A GLOBAL AUDIENCE AND HELPED CEMENT HOLLYWOOD'S BLOCKBUSTER PARADIGM."**

— JUSTIN CHANG, VARIETY, 2015

# EPISODE VIII
## THE LAST JEDI

**RELEASED: DECEMBER 2017**
**BOX OFFICE: $1.321 BILLION**

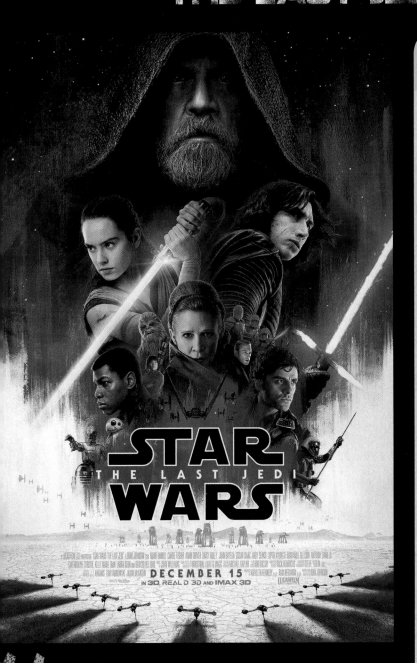

The second installment in the Star Wars sequel trilogy brought mixed reviews from critics and fans. After the destruction of Starkiller Base in The Force Awakens, the evil First Order chases Resistance forces from D'Qar. Vice Admiral Holdo reveals a plan of retreat. Defying her order, Poe, Finn, BB-8 and a mechanic named Rose plan to disable the First Order's tracking device on the main ship.

Rey, having found Luke in self-exile on the Jedi temple Ahch-To, tries to convince the Jedi master to train her and join the Resistance. Rey tells Luke of Han Solo's death at the hands of Kylo Ren. Still blaming himself for Kylo's corruption to the Dark Side, Luke refuses to join Rey. Rey and Kylo begin to connect and communicate through the Force, not understanding how it's happening. Rey is determined to convert Kylo away from the First Order and Supreme Leader Snoke.

After acquiring a master hacker to help them deactivate the tracking system, Finn, Rose and BB-8 are captured onboard Snoke's ship. Rey also lands on the ship to confront Snoke and Kylo. Snoke orders Kylo to kill Rey, but he kills Snoke in a surprise twist. He asks Rey to join him so they can rule the galaxy together. Rey refuses, and the two engage in a dramatic lightsaber battle to a draw. Admiral Holdo rams her ship into the First Order feet at light speed, allowing the rest of the Resistance to escape.

Luke finally appears during the final battle as the remnant of Resistance fighters are corned by First Order ground troops. Kylo orders all fire power to concentrate on Luke, who emerges unharmed. Kylo strikes Luke, revealing Luke is a Force projection. Luke is actually still on Ahch-To. Rey helps the rest of the Resistance escape, while Luke dies at peace to

> IT'S AS IF RIAN JOHNSON'S ASSIGNMENT WAS TO EXTEND THE FRANCHISE WITHOUT CHANGING ANYTHING FUNDAMENTAL, WHICH IS CLOSER TO THE WAY CLASSIC TELEVISION AND VINTAGE JAMES BOND MOVIES OPERATE.

— PETER DEBRUGE, VARIETY 2017

# 20 GREATEST SCENES

## Interesting ... Most Interesting

BY DAVID LEE

Ranking the top 20 greatest scenes in Star Wars film history feels a lot like facing Lord Vader himself. It can be an intimidating task, and there's no one right way to do it. Everyone is going to have different opinions, but that's what makes it fun.

We wanted to include scenes that are not only memorable, quotable and just plain cool, but also impactful and vital to the entire Star Wars saga. We included the eight feature films from the original trilogy, the three prequels, The Force Awakens and Rouge One. A scene is more than just a single moment or quote. It may be great because of the action, dialog, character or plot development, setting or all of the above. Now on to the list ...

## [20] YODA VS. COUNT DOOKU
### (ATTACK OF THE CLONES)

Yoda fights! This scene in *Attack of the Clones* isn't his only battle, but it is his first. That alone makes it impactful, and it gave fans a look at Yoda they always wanted to see. It was an awesome surprise to those who hoped they would see the Jedi Master wield his lightsaber (a small green one, of course) in the prequels.

Count Dooku, the leader of the Separatist movement, has just defeated Anakin and Obi-Wan when Yoda comes limping in with the aid of his walking stick. After failing to drop some heavy stuff on Yoda, Dooku results to Force lightning, which Yoda easily handles. Dooku then issues the line, "It is obvious that this contest cannot be decided by our knowledge of the Force, but by our skills with a lightsaber."

OK, that's kind of cheesy, but the two masters engage in a fast-paced lightsaber battle revealing Yoda's unique fighting style. He spins, jumps and flips around in a flurry of movement. We also learn in this scene that Dooku was once Yoda's apprentice.

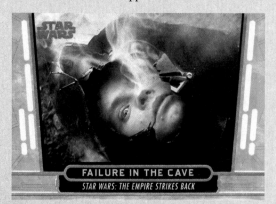

## [19] THE FAILURE AT THE CAVE
### (THE EMPIRE STRIKES BACK)

A critical failure yet major growing point in Luke's training with Yoda, this scene is as creepy as it is

meaningful and deep. Luke senses something not far away. Yoda tells him it's a place strong with the Dark Side of the Force. He tells Luke that he must go, making it obvious that it's a test Luke must face alone. There is a calm and sadness to Yoda's demeanor, as if he knows Luke will fail.

Luke: "What's in there?"

Yoda: "Only what you take with you."

Yoda warns Luke that he will not need his weapons, but he takes them anyway. Luke is caught off guard by Darth Vader (or what appears to be), and cuts his head off after a quick light saber battle. The helmet explodes to reveal Luke's face. This is some deep, creative foreshadowing, hinting at Luke's possible destiny of turning to the Dark Side to take Vader's place. At this point, it hasn't been revealed that Vader is Luke's father, so the scene is bursting with meaning.

## [18] THE BATTLE OF SCARIF
### (ROUGE ONE)

It's the climax of the mission to steal the layouts of the Empire's Death Star. The plans are protected in a larger data tower on Scarif. It's a beautiful beach setting for a battle. We've seen snow, space, desert and forest battles up to this point.

The battle includes AT-ATs stomping on the beach, tactical diversions from the Rebels, infiltration, and an awesome space battle just outside the planet's atmosphere that includes two star destroyers crashing into each other. Who doesn't want to see that?

The battle turns into a suicide mission for the diverse and unlikely group of heroes. Jyn Erso, Cassian Andor, K-2SO, Chirrut Îmwe, Baze Malbus and Bodhi Rook all die, but not before they each complete their parts of the overall mission against seemingly insurmountable odds.

THE TRASH COMPACTOR
STAR WARS: A NEW HOPE

## [17] THE TRASH COMPACTOR
### (A NEW HOPE)

Luke, Han and Chewie rescue Princess Leia, but Stormtroopers have them trapped in a corridor. Leia grabs a blaster and shoots open a hole. The group dives in one at a time and ends up in a huge trash compactor with nasty knee-high water.

There's nowhere to go, and some freaky white snake thing takes Luke under the water, releasing him as soon as the compactor is activated. The group's going to be crushed to death, but Luke calls C-3PO and R2-D2 to stop the compactor just in time. This is the first time Luke, Han, Chewie and Leia are together, so we get to see how their personalities interact. The setting of the entire scene, with Luke and Han in Stormtrooper uniforms, is one of the most memorabilia in the entire franchise.

*THE EXECUTION OF ORDER 66*

## [16] ORDER 66
### (REVENGE OF THE SITH)

This is an underrated scene but a major turning point in the rise of the Empire. Chancellor Palatine has been playing both sides the whole time, pulling the strings on the side of the Separatists and the side of the Republic under the cloak of Darth Sidious. He flips the switch with Order 66.

The Republic has created an army of clone soldiers (which preclude the Stormtroopers) spread across the galaxy fighting several battles alongside the Jedi. But when Palatine issues "Order 66" the clones, which are engineered to be completely obedient, murder the Jedi during battle. This was the beginning of the Jedi purge and cleared the way for the fast rise of the Galactic Empire.

There's an awesome moment when Yoda senses two clone soldiers about to kill him. He leaps backward and slices their heads off with one move. Also during this takeover, Anakin (now officially Darth Vader) leads an assault on the Jedi temple, which includes murdering younglings.

## [15] DARTH PLAGUEIS THE WISE
### (REVENGE OF THE SITH)

Another underrated scene, this is the final point that draws Anakin to the Dark Side. He's haunted by vivid visions of Padmé suffering and dying—visions of the future. Anakin had similar visions of his mother, whom he was not able to save.

DARTH PLAGUEIS
SITH LORD

Chancellor Palatine and Anakin are watching some kind of fancy space bubble ballet when Palatine continues to manipulate Anakin with increasing distrust in the Jedi Council. He asks Anakin if he has heard of the tragedy of Darth Plagueis the Wise, a powerful Sith Lord. Palatine says that he discovered the power to create life and keep people from dying. "The Dark Side of the Force is a pathway to many abilities some consider to be unnatural," Palatine says. Of course, Anakin is obsessed with power, so this is Palatine's final move to pull him to the Dark Side.

After telling Anakin how Darth Plagueis was killed in his sleep by his apprentice, Anakin asks, "Is it possible to learn this power?" Palatine responds, "Not from a Jedi."

Those last lines are terrific. You just know that Anakin can't resist crossing over to the Dark Side now. He wasn't able to save his mother, but now he thinks he can learn the power to save Padmé.

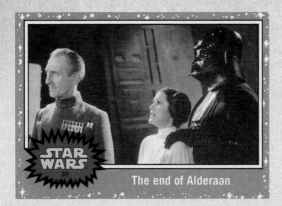

The end of Alderaan

Skirmish at the Sarlacc

## [14] THE DESTRUCTION OF ALDERAAN

### (A NEW HOPE)

This seems to be one of the more forgotten moments for a lot of Star Wars fans, but that doesn't minimize this scene's impact on the overall story. It's the first time we see the power the Empire has over the galaxy. Grand Moff Tarkin orders the biggest test for the Empire's aptly-named Death Star—destroying Princess Leia's home planet of Alderaan. Leia was just captured by Darth Vader, who is searching for Death Star plans stolen by the Rebel Alliance. She issues a great line when brought to Tarkin that reveals her personality and confidence.

"Governor Tarkin, I should have expected to find you holding Vader's leash. I recognized your foul stench when I was brought on board," she says. (Oddly, this is the only scene where Leia is forcing a British accent.)

Leia is forced to watch her planet be destroyed by one blast of the Death Star. Meanwhile, Obi-Wan and Luke are on the Millennium Falcon headed to Alderaan when Obi-Wan feels the planet's destruction. "I felt a great disturbance in the Force, as if millions of voices suddenly cried out in terror, and were suddenly silenced. I feel something terrible has happened." This illustrates the great imbalance the Empire is creating in the Force.

## [13] ESCAPING JABBA'S EXECUTION

### (RETURN OF THE JEDI)

This scene involves a lot of characters and action. It's also a major turning point for the Rebel leaders after the defeat in *The Empire Strikes Back*. Luke, Leia, Chewbacca and Lando plan to rescue Han, who has become Jabba's favorite ornament after he was frozen in Carbonite. Leia frees Han but then is taken as Jabba's slave. Jabba plans to execute Luke, Chewie and Han by

throwing them into the pit of Sarlacc where they are to be "slowly digested over a thousand years." Not sure how that works, but it doesn't sound good.

However, Luke and Lando have the escape planned. Just as Luke is forced off a plank into the pit, he turns and flips back up onto the ship as R2-D2 shoots Luke's lightsaber to him. During the battle, Leia manages to choke Jabba to death with the chain he's using to enslave her. Lando and Chewie rescue Han from sliding into the pit. Everyone's favorite bounty hunter, Boba Fett, falls into the pit after Han accidently activates his jetpack. It's an odd death for such a fan-favorite character. The band of heroes escapes and picks up R2-D2 and C-3PO on the way out of the Dune Sea.

## [12] KYLO REN MURDERS HIS FATHER

### (THE FORCE AWAKENS)

Death of Han Solo

This scene is a powerful wave of shock, sadness and intensity. We learn that Kylo Ren is Han and Leia's son, and was once trained by Luke to be a Jedi. But like his grandfather, Darth Vader, Kylo Ren is obsessed with power. This obsession turned him to the Dark Side, but he's still conflicted and feels the "pull to the Light" as he describes it.

As Han, Chewie, Finn and Rey are helping disable Starkiller Base from the inside, Han takes an opportunity to try to convince his son to return to his family.

Alone on a long bridge, Kylo Ren tells Han, "I'm being torn apart. I want to be free of this pain. I know what I have to do, but I don't know if I have the strength to do it. Will you help me?"

He takes his lightsaber as if to hand it over to his father, but suddenly ignites it through Han's body. Looking his father in the eyes, Kylo Ren simply says, "Thank you." It's an evil, cold moment, as he chooses to end his inner conflict by murdering his father. Han falls lifelessly. This could be a major character development for Kylo Ren in the up-coming two sequels.

We love the recreation done via action figures by s.w.kustoms, pictured above.

### [11] KYLO REN VS. REY ON STARKILLER BASE
(THE FORCE AWAKENS)

A lightsaber battle in the snow between the new bad guy and the new hero of the Star Wars sequels gave fans what they wanted. The battle was more like the grudge fights we saw in the original trilogy, as opposed to the acrobatic fights in the prequels. Kylo Ren reaches for his grandfather's original lightsaber that's stuck in the show. Struggling to bring it to his hand, it suddenly whips past him into Rey's hand.

It's a cool, dark setting with the glow of the sabers reflecting off the snow and their faces. The planet housing Starkiller Base is collapsing around them. Kylo Ren's anger and insecurities are apparent, but as he backs Rey up to a deep ravine, he tells her that he can show her the ways of the Force. Rey then channels the Force to overcome him, eventually slashing him across the face. This obviously sets up intriguing possibilities for the future sequels, as we later discover that Rey will train with Luke and that Supreme Leader Snoke knows Kylo Ren is ready to complete his training.

### [10] ANAKIN/DARTH VADER VS. OBI-WAN
(REVENGE OF THE SITH)

We always knew that Obi-Wan and Darth Vader likely fought when they were younger. All the prequels were building to this long duel. The fight begins with Anakin (who at this point has already been crowned "Darth Vader") force-choking a pregnant Padmé. This confirms to Obi-Wan that he has fully transitioned to the Dark Side.

The fast-paced fight between former best friends and master/student has some mesmerizing swordsmanship. The setting is the fiery, lava-filled planet of Mustafar, which creates its own element of danger. There are some parts that are a little over-the-top, but the ending is one of the best and most intense moments in the entire franchise.

Obi-Wan manages to get back to ground, keeping Anakin floating on a platform above on the lava where they were fighting. Anakin tries to leap onto the ground when his former master slices his legs off at the knees. Anakin is boiling over with pain and hate, which seems to physically change him. The lava burns him almost to a point of non-recognition. Obi-Wan has no choice but to leave his friend to die. Of course this happens just before the Emperor shows up to save Anakin and place him into the ominous life support suit he'll wear for the rest of his life.

### [9] "NO. TRY NOT. DO, OR DO NOT. THERE IS NO TRY."
(THE EMPIRE STRIKES BACK)

As Luke's training with Yoda advances, this scene brings some of the most quotable Yodaisms in the entire franchise. During his training, Luke's crashed X-Wing sinks further into the Dagobah swamp, convincing Luke that he'll never get the ship out. Yoda says that the ship is no different than anything else Luke has learned to move and manipulate with the Force.

# 20 GREATEST SCENES

"NO. TRY NOT. DO, OR DO NOT. THERE IS NO TRY."

Yoda's quick response is one of the most quoted lines in the Star Wars saga ... and is why it landed at No. 9 on our 20 Greatest Scenes list.

STAR WARS: THE EMPIRE STRIKES BACK
PREMIERE DATE: MAY 21, 1980

Luke: "Alright, I'll give it a try."

Yoda: "No. Try not. Do, or do not. There is no try."

Yoda's quick response is one of the most quoted lines in the Star Wars saga. Luke of course fails to get the entire ship out, saying it's too big. "You want the impossible," he says after Yoda gives him a lesson on how the Force works. Yoda then lifts the ship out of the swamp and places it safely on the land.

Luke: "I don't… I don't believe it."

Yoda: "That is why you fail."

Those are powerful words. It's a bit of ironic foreshadowing, too, as Luke becomes an incredibly powerful Jedi with supreme confidence in his ability to wield the Force.

HAN SOLO IS FROZEN IN CARBONITE
STAR WARS: THE EMPIRE STRIKES BACK

## [8] FROZEN IN CARBONITE
### (THE EMPIRE STRIKES BACK)

There's so much going on in and around this key scene in The Empire Strikes Back. It's pretty much the lowest point for the small band of Rebel leaders. Han, Leia and Chewie are ambushed by Darth Vader in the cloud city. Bounty hunters hired by Jabba the Hutt want Han, and Vader wants to test the carbon-freezing chamber he plans to use on Luke. Han is the guinea pig, being tortured and frozen alive in carbonite.

As he is lowered into the chamber, Leia tells him, "I love you." Han, in very Han-like fashion, calmly

responds, "I know." Han is taken to Jabba, and Vader resets the chamber to trap Luke. The iconic image of Han frozen in the large block is one of the most recognizable in the entire franchise. It's been used to create things such as ice cube trays, refrigerators and wall decals.

## [7] HAN SHOOTS FIRST
### (A NEW HOPE)

STAR WARS 162
Han Solo cornered by Greedo!
© 1977 20TH CENTURY-FOX FILM CORP. All Rights Reserved.

The Mos Eisley Cantina is loaded with crazy Star Wars characters. As Obi-Wan and Luke enter the cantina, Obi-Wan tells his new pupil, "You'll never find a more wretched hive of scum and villainy." The old and future Jedi find and agree with Han Solo (his first appearance) on a price to take them to Alderaan. Han is stopped by Greedo—one of Jabba the Hutt's bounty hunters looking to bring Han to Jabba, preferably dead. The two are sitting at a table when Han shoots Greedo from underneath the table. The camera twice shows Han slowly going for his blaster, building up tension.

This scene sparked a ton of controversy with the 1997 re-mastered edition when an initial blast from Greedo was added to the scene to try to downplay Han as a "killer." It shows Greedo's shot missing Han's head and Han shooting just a split-second after. It even resulted in popular "Han Shot First" t-shirts. Many fans didn't appreciate the scene-tampering, thinking the original captured Han's personality much better.

## [6] THE DUEL OF THE FATES
### (THE PHANTOM MENACE)

A *Phantom Menace* scene in the Top 10? Yep. While Episode I is the biggest disappointment in the movie franchise, this scene with the fierce Darth Maul wielding an intimidating double-blade lightsaber against Qui-Gon Jinn and a young Obi-Wan is fantastic. The "Duel of the Fates" music composition provides an intense backdrop throughout the fight. Darth Maul remains a mysterious and evil character in film, but we get to see his full power and ability here. No words are spoken between the combatants during the fight, which further dehumanizes Maul and paints him as relentless devil-like character.

The three meet in a hanger near the end of the movie when Maul ignites his dual-bladed lightsaber. He handles both Jedi until they are separated by an energy shield. Qui-Gon kneels to gather himself while Darth Maul paces back and forth like a caged animal. His face is full of hate. He then kills Qui-Gon while Obi-Wan watches, still trapped behind the energy shield. The young Jedi gets his revenge (not that a Jedi wants such things) when he slices Darth Maul in half.

## [5] BATTLE ON HOTH
### (THE EMPIRE STRIKES BACK)

The opening battle of *The Empire Strikes Back* takes place on the icy planet of Hoth. The Empire discovers the Alliance's Echo Base hidden on Hoth, and Darth Vader is on a personal mission to capture Luke after the Empire's defeat at the Death Star. It's an awesome and unique setting for a battle involving snow speeders, plenty of ground troops, and our first look at the giant AT-AT walkers tasked with destroying the Rebel Alliance's main power generator.

One of the iconic moments is when a Rebel snow speeder wraps a tow cable around the legs of an AT-AT, bringing it down. Luke single-handedly destroys one of the giant walkers after crashing in the snow. He harpoons up to its belly and cuts an opening with his lightsaber. He throws a grenade inside and detached his harpoon cable,

falling to the snow. The Rebels have to abandon their secret base, but manage to get large transports through the Empire blockade just outside Hoth.

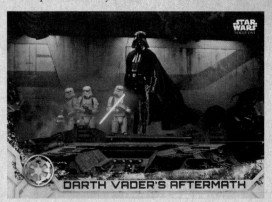

## [4] VADER ANNIHILATES REBEL SOLDIERS
### (ROUGE ONE)

Darth Vader just may be the greatest Hollywood villain of all time. This scene in *Rouge One* gave fans a glimpse of the legendary Sith Lord they always wanted. It also perfectly connects with the beginning of *A New Hope*.

After the Death Star readouts are stolen on Scarif, they're transmitted to a Rebel ship and downloaded on what resembles a floppy disc. Vader catches up to the ship and lays waste to several armed Rebel soldiers. A door jams, trapping some of the soldiers in a corridor. Vader, standing in the dark, ignites his lightsaber. The terrified solders open fire on him. We see Vader's rage and power as he effortlessly slaughters the solders.

We also realize these events happen just before the opening of *A New Hope* when Vader catches up to Princess Leia. She is handed the downloaded readouts at this scene. The Rebels narrowly escape on a smaller cargo ship. It's the same ship being chased by a Star Destroyer in the first scene of *A New Hope*.

## [3] THE TRENCH RUN
### (A NEW HOPE)

The long-shot attempt to destroy the Death Star ends with a small group of X-Wing fighters maneuvering to the end a narrow trench. Luke is among them, and ends up being the Rebels' last hope. It's a tense scene where every second counts. Meanwhile, the Death Star is moving into position to destroy the Rebel base.

Darth Vader arrives in his specially-designed TIE fighter, knocking off a few X-Wings before focusing on Luke, who is the only pilot left. Luke hears Obi-Wan tell him to

MERIDIAN TRENCH

"Use the Force, Luke" instead of relying on the computer targeting system. Luke turns off his targeting computer. The Death Star is ready to fire on the Rebel base, but Han Solo shows up in the Millennium Falcon just in time to help, which knocks Vader out of the trench.

Using the Force to focus, Luke fires a seemingly impossible torpedo shot into the narrow opening at the end of the trench, setting off the chain reaction that destroys the Death Star.

STAR WARS

The final duel

## [2] LUKE DEFEATS AND TURNS VADER

(RETURN OF THE JEDI)

It's the final showdown between Luke and Vader. Father and son. The Light and the Dark. This long scene is full of inner and outer conflict. It's Luke's ultimate struggle to see if he will bring balance back to the galaxy or take his father's place. He's determined to bring Vader back to the good side, but also is tempted to kill the Emperor. At first, Luke even refuses to fight.

During the duel, Vader senses Luke's feelings for his twin sister, who was hidden from Vader. "If you will not turn to the Dark Side, perhaps she will," he says. This is when Luke loses control and forcefully strikes his father down. He cuts Vader's hand off in symbolic fashion, just as Vader did to

him. Luke looks at the black glove covering his own robotic right hand, then at Vader's severed mechanical arm. He realizes he's turning into his father. It's a powerful moment.

The Emperor senses Luke's anger, but then Luke gathers himself and throws his lightsaber away as he says, "Never . . . I'll never turn to the Dark Side. You've failed, your Highness. I am a Jedi, like my father before me."

"So be it, Jedi," the Emperor responds as he tries to destroy Luke with Force lightning. Luke is begging his father to save him. In Vader's final act, he sacrifices himself and throws the Emperor down a deep shaft to save his son. Not only does Luke defeat Vader and survive the Emperor's test, he turns his father back to the good side. When Luke removes Vader's helmet, he reveals his father's true face—a mangled, twisted and vulnerable old man.

GREAT RIVALRIES

DARTH VADER                LUKE SKYWALKER

## [1] "NO . . . I AM YOUR FATHER."

(THE EMPIRE STRIKES BACK)

No other scene is more memorable or impactful than the ultimate twist at the end of *The Empire Strikes Back*. Bloodied and defeated, Luke is literally hanging on for his life after Darth Vader slices his hand off. With seemingly no hope left, Vader tries to persuade Luke to join the Dark Side.

Luke: "I'll never join you."

Vader: "If you only knew the power of the Dark Side. Obi-Wan never told you what happened to your father..."

Luke: "He told me enough. He told me you killed him."

Vader: "No... I am your father."

The pain in Luke's face is definite as he's unable to deny this truth. This revelation created a totally different and deeper dynamic for the entire saga. The family dynamic continues to be a core storyline from this point on, even carrying through the most recent films, *The Force Awakens* and *Rogue One*. It's also the central scene that makes *The Empire Strikes Back* a fan-favorite of the film franchise.

# THE PEOPLE'S PRINCESS

**CARRIE FISHER WAS A LOT OF THINGS TO A LOT OF PEOPLE: AN ACTRESS, A FEMINIST, A PRINCESS AND A SURVIVOR.**

**ABOVE ALL ELSE, SHE WAS A ROLE MODEL TO MILLIONS.**

BY ALLAN MUIR

# CARRIE FISHER: THE PEOPLE'S PRINCESS

For the final 40 years of her life, Carrie Fisher struggled to come to terms with the character that made her famous.

But this would have helped.

Fisher, who counted herself a proud feminist, passed away in December, 2016 at age 60, less than a month before she planned to take part in one of the many Women's Marches that took place around the world on Jan. 21. And yet she, or at least her character, was in attendance at all of them. There among the protest signs carried by the millions of marchers was one designed by artist Hayley Gilmore that pictured a defiant Princess Leia Organa with an upraised blaster declaring, "A Woman's Place Is in the Resistance." Others carried placards showing Leia with a brook-no-fools glare, or re-imagined as World War II icon Rosie the Riveter. These were more than just clever tributes from fans still processing the star's death. In fact, the message those signs delivered was clear: In the face of looming oppression, these women viewed Leia as the embodiment of hope.

> **" She was OUR princess ... and the actress who played her blurred into one gorgeous, fiercely independent and ferociously funny, take-charge woman who took our collective breath away."**
>
> **- MARK HAMILL ON CO-STAR CARRIE FISHER**

# CARRIE FISHER: THE PEOPLE'S PRINCESS

"For me, it meant carrying on Carrie's mission," her brother, Todd Fisher, told Vanity Fair of Fisher's posthumous presence at the marches. "She was a champion of women, no one can deny it...[or the] enormous influence she's had. Women around the world—women who are struggling for their identity, for their position, for equality, whatever the case may be. We started to see how many people idolized her."

It's easy to understand that attachment. The wry and fearless warrior Fisher created over five Star Wars films (six, if you count a computer-generated cameo at the end of *Rogue One*) felt completely familiar and yet was unlike anything we'd seen before. She was strong, compassionate, daring, vulnerable, charming, thoughtful, reckless, capable and the smartest person in the room. Hardly like we'd expect from a princess.

And yet, thanks to Fisher's soulful performance, she made an indelible mark, earning a place as one of the most revered characters in cinematic history as well as one of the most influential. Leia, the princess-saboteur, was the game changer: the alpha female. Without her, there'd be no Rey or Jyn Erso in the Star Wars universe. Maybe more importantly though, there'd be no Ellen Ripley (Alien), no Katniss Everdeen (The Hunger Games), no Merida (Brave), no Captain Janeway (Star Trek: Voyager) and no Buffy Summers (Buffy The Vampire Slayer).

She was the one who made anything seem possible. Even while wearing a gold metal bikini, she came to represent strength and independence to generations of women.

"In 'Star Wars,' she was our great and powerful princess — feisty, wise and full of hope in a role that was more difficult than most people might think," said creator George Lucas during a tribute to Fisher at the 2017 Star Wars Celebration in London. "She played a part that was very smart, and she was having to hold her own against two big lugs, goofballs that were screwing everything up. She was the boss. It was her war, and when I cast it, I said I want somebody young to play the part. I want somebody very young. When Carrie came in, she was that character. She was very strong, very smart, very funny, very bold, very tough, and there really wasn't much of a question. There are not very many people like her. They are one in a billion. For this particular part, it was absolutely perfect. … She wore a dress through the whole thing, but she was the toughest in the group."

"She was OUR Princess, damn it, and the actress who played her blurred into one gorgeous, fiercely independent and ferociously funny, take-charge woman who took our collective breath away," Mark Hamill added.

**" From the first film, she was just a soldier, front line and center. The only way they knew to make the character strong was to make her angry. In Return of the Jedi, she [finally got] to be more feminine, more supportive, more affectionate."**

**- CARRIE FISHER**

While others immediately appreciated Leia's impact, Fisher struggled to make peace with the role that changed her life and elevated her as an icon. ("I signed away the rights to my likeness," she joked. "Every time I look in the mirror, I have to send George a check for two bucks.") It caused her great frustration that the ground-breaking nature of her character could only have gained traction under very specific circumstances.

# CARRIE FISHER: THE PEOPLE'S PRINCESS

"Movies are dreams," she told Rolling Stone during a 1983 interview promoting the release of Return of the Jedi. "They work on you subliminally. You can play Leia as capable, independent, sensible, a soldier, a fighter, a woman in control – control being, of course, a lesser word than master. But you can [only] portray a woman who's a master and get through all the female prejudice if you have her travel in time, if you add a magical quality, if you're dealing in fairy-tale terms."

Of course, there were some who still preferred females to adhere to the more submissive stereotypes. "There are a lot of people who don't like my character in these movies," Fisher said.

"They think I'm some kind of space bitch."

Nevertheless, Fisher persisted. As did Leia, the cool and defiant princess who became a general in the films and, later, in the Star Wars Extended Universe novels, ended up ruling the entire galaxy as the New Republic Chief of State.

Lucas, to his enduring credit, understood not just the need for a fully-realized, fully independent female lead like Leia, but the dramatic potential as well. As he brought her to life with Fisher (who famously offered re-writes for Episodes V and VI after choking on George's words), they up-ended the heroic paradigm and in the process, created a template that allowed the generations that followed to view gender and heroism through a different lens.

The traditional (male) protagonists in Star Wars needed time and motivation to grow into their roles as heroes. Luke Skywalker was a frustrated farm boy searching for adventure or his purpose or anything else that would get him off the desolate rock that was his home world before he stumbled onto his destiny. Han Solo was a scoundrel who operated in the grey areas, always valuing his own hide, and his own needs, before begrudgingly learning the lesson of sacrifice.

But Leia? She was always a hero.

Raised by her adoptive father, Bail Organa, she served the people of Alderaan in the Senate while leading a clandestine campaign of espionage and sabotage to overthrow the Empire. She was fast with a blaster (we see her dropping a stormtrooper with one shot in her memorable first scene in A New Hope), tough enough to hold on to her secrets while being tortured by Darth Vader and utterly calm as she faced repeated instances of certain death.

And she was quick with the snark, too.

"Governor Tarkin," she sneered upon being brought face to face with the Death Star commander in A New Hope. "I should've expected to find you holding Vader's leash. I recognized your foul stench when I was brought on board."

But while that cool, fearless personality is part of her appeal, the key is something else entirely: It's that she never slipped into the damsel-in-distress archetype. Sure, she found herself in a few tight spots along the way—imprisoned on the Imperial starship in A New Hope or chained on Jabba's barge in Return of the Jedi— but she never needed to be rescued.

With Leia, it was simply a matter of waiting for an opportunity to extricate herself from a tough spot and then jumping back in to help the boys out of the mess they created. She was always in control, the engine of her own fate. She isn't altered by her surroundings. She forces them to change.

While Fisher admired that strength, she saw an early single-mindedness to the character.

"She has no friends, no family; her planet was blown up in seconds so all she has is a cause," Fisher told Rolling Stone. "From the first film, she was just a soldier, front line and center. The only way they knew to make the character strong was to make her angry. In Return of the Jedi, she [finally got] to be more feminine, more supportive, more affectionate."

But even as Leia grew, she didn't grow soft. In that film she took a laser blast in the arm before wiping out a squadron of Empire troops to save Han during the Battle of Endor. She also offered one of the great turn-abouts in film history, responding to Solo's declaration of love with an epic, albeit fatalistic, "I know."

That indomitable spirit carried on through her most recent appearance in The Force Awakens and The Last Jedi, where it was revealed that she had continued to lead the fight against oppression as a general with the Resistance. Older, and deeply scarred after losing her son, Ben Solo, to the dark side, she was focused on "the only thing she was ever good at" – leading the rebel forces against the First Order.

"[She's] solitary," Fisher said of Leia. "Under a lot of pressure. Committed as ever to her cause, but I would imagine feeling somewhat defeated, tired, and pissed."

Although Fisher's family gave Lucasfilm permission to use recent footage of the actress in 2019's Episode IX, company president Kathleen Kennedy said that she will not be in the final film. That means Leia's final appearance was in Star Wars: The Last Jedi. It seems certain that she had regained the spark that defined her in the original trilogy, setting Leia up for a fitting, if sadly premature, conclusion to her uniquely heroic journey.

FOREVER A
BOY

# WONDER

More than forty years ago Mark Hamill landed the role of a lifetime, and made it his own. Now in his late-60s, Hamill's Luke Skywalker is on the cusp of lighting up the silver screen again.

BY JEFF SULLIVAN

# MARK HAMILL: FOREVER A BOY WONDER

There was going to be a Luke Skywalker, that much was certain once 20th Century Fox agreed to back George Lucas' sci-fi project after several other studios passed. And there were going to be hundreds of actors trying out for the lead role. Among them was not Mark Hamill, who at the time was co-starring on the short-lived TV series *Texas Wheelers* with Gary Busey.

When the 24-year old wasn't on set, he usually found his way to Robert Englund's couch. Yes, as in the future Freddy Krueger. That is where he was, his cowboy boots by the door, three Heinekens into a six-pack, watching *The Mary Tyler Moore Show*, when Englund returned from his dual auditions for two movies that were sharing a sound stage, *Apocalypse Now* and yes, *Star Wars*, where he read for Han Solo. However, it was the role of Skywalker that made him think of the ideal fit.

In a recent interview, Englund says, "I told him, 'I think you're right for this, man. This character is like a space prince, and it's George Lucas! Mark, you've got to do this. Wow, what if you got to be in a George Lucas movie … you're the kind of actor he loves!' So, he got on the phone to his agent and the rest is history."

HAMILL AND CARRIE FISHER DURING A BREAK IN FILMING THE ORIGINAL STAR WARS.

" I told him, 'I think you're right for this, man. This character is like a space prince, and it's George Lucas! Mark, you've got to do this. Wow, what if you got to be in a George Lucas movie ... you're the kind of actor he loves!' So, he got on the phone to his agent and the rest is history."

**- ROBERT ENGLUND**

# MARK HAMILL: FOREVER A BOY WONDER

There is no debating Luke Skywalker among the most iconic characters in cinema history. Some would even rank him at the top. And that legend is only going to grow more so in the coming years and decades with another two movies remaining in the most recent trilogy. *Star Wars: Episode VIII The Last Jedi* is slated for a Dec. 15 release later this year with Hamill expected to play a significant role after just a cameo at the end of A Force Awakens.

At the time of his original casting, Hamill was a relative unknown, although as he was quick to point out, he did have 148 credits, dating back to *The Bill Cosby Show*, *General Hospital* and *The Partridge Family* as a teenager in the early-1970s. It's also worth noting that Hamill was among the few actors shooting the original *Star Wars* who felt like the film would be a success. Answering a fan's question via his always active Twitter handle, @HamillHimself, he said, "Crew was kind but thought (movie) was

'rubbish.' I kept telling them: 'We're on a winner!'"

Indeed, a winner for the ages, at the time, the highest-grossing movie of all-time. For the gig, Hamill received just $650,000, which was significantly more than his co-stars Harrison Ford and Carrie Fisher, who took in a reported $10,000 a week. However, once the film took off, writer/director Lucas gave each of them a percentage cut of the movie's profits.

By all accounts, Hamill remained grounded when that galaxy from far, far away became the talk of 1977, described by many as a gee-whiz kid. Humble and talkative (his friends at the time called him "Motor-Mouth") by nature, he spent what free time existed at the beach near his then-home in Malibu. His other hobbies included long games of Monopoly and baking cakes. Looking back on this time in 1981, on the cusp of Return of the Jedi, Hamill told People, "In Hollywood, I became an icon, like Mickey Mouse."

Still, he was more in awe than thinking he was all that, even with his own cast.

During what became a worldwide promotion

# MARK HAMILL: FOREVER A BOY WONDER

tour in 1977, Hamill spoke in England with childlike exuberance of working with such legendary actors like Alec Guinness and Peter Cushing.

"Unfortunately, I never had a scene with Peter Cushing but he was surprised because I went to work two days just to watch (him) work even though I didn't work with him," Hamill said. "But I'm a fan at heart and I had him sign a couple of posters."

Alas, for Hamill, there was another life-altering event for him in 1977, this one taking place five months before the overwhelming majority would even recognize his name, and almost costing him his life. It would also change the face of the original trilogy, literally.

In his words, to Gossip Magazine in 1978, "What happened was that I was on the wrong freeway. I was way out in the sticks somewhere and there were no cars and no traffic, thank God. I was going about 65-70 mph … I was speeding, going too fast … and what happened, I think, was that I tried to negotiate an off-ramp and lost control, tumbled over, and went off the road. I fractured

my nose and my cheek."

The near-fatal accident required three operations to his face. There have been endless rumors throughout the years on other procedures and plastic surgeries, but Hamill, who seems honest to a fault, has always denied them. In the months following the wreck, many assumed Hamill's acting career was finished, and if not for the success of *Star Wars*, it might have been.

It's also no secret that of the three stars, Ford and Fisher went on to infinitely more success post-trilogy, with the former becoming arguably the biggest star of his generation. There are probably multiple reasons for this but more times than not, the accident is cited as the primary explanation.

"Of the three of us," Hamill told People in 1978. "I've probably been most affected by the movie."

Speaking about the accident, he said, "It was the lowest point of my life. In one year I'd had the biggest breaks I'd ever had, then that. I started thinking I'd never work again."

His scars were written into *The Empire Strikes Back*

**WORKING WITH SIR ALEC GUINNESS REMAINS ONE OF HAMILL'S GREATEST ACHIEVEMENTS.**

# MARK HAMILL: FOREVER A BOY WONDER

script, with Skywalker having his face scratched in the first scene by a Wampa, although Lucas has said that wasn't the lone reason for the storyline. Still, everyone noticed Hamill looked different in the latter two movies, and no longer had that boyish look.

However, he never stopped acting, even migrating to Broadway to star in *The Elephant Man* in between the last two movies of the trilogy. Hamill also accomplished all of the goals he set for himself before turning 30 years old: star in a movie, appear in a movie nominated for an Oscar, make a million dollars and appear in a Broadway play.

Still, by the time *Return of the Jedi* released in 1983, Hamill was the first to joke about his non-star/star status. He would ask friends and family a trivia question: Name the top-billed actor in the first and third highest-grossing movies of all time.

"It's me, but even my family guesses wrong," Hamill told People in 1981. "My cousin said Richard Dreyfuss.

"I feel I haven't earned celebrity. So much of life is what you roll and where you land. I'm so much like Luke Skywalker. I guess I always will be."

Hamill stayed busy in the 32 years between appearing as Luke Skywalker, raising his three children with his wife Marilou, who he met before the release of *Star Wars* and married in December 1978 after a brief stretch of, let's call it testing out his new-found recognition.

"I had to taste groupies and fame," he said of the months after *Star Wars*. "I went to Las Vegas to date 38-year old showgirls. That was exciting for about the first 10 minutes."

There were also numerous Broadway shows, including a critically acclaimed performance in *Harrigan 'N Hart* in 1985, simulation video games, mostly sci-fi, and a bevy of voiceovers, most notably the Joker from the *Batman* animated series.

Then came the unexpected return, another trilogy, this one taking place after the original, and director J.J. Abrams most certainly, like fans around the world, wanted Han Solo, Princess Leia and Luke Skywalker to return to the Big Screen. And while Ford took some convincing, it took Hamill all of a few seconds to say yes.

"You know, we (were) all in a great place and we've all done it before, there was a beginning, a middle and end," Hamill told Rolling Stone in 2015

**BELOW: IT DIDN'T TAKE LONG FOR THE LUKE SKYWALKER FROM A FORCE AWAKENS TO FIND HIS WAY ONTO A TOY LINE SUCH AS THIS FIGURE PRODUCED BY HOT TOYS.**

# MARK HAMILL: FOREVER A BOY WONDER

**STAR WARS CELEBRITY MEANS HAMILL IS A WELCOME GUEST OF MANY, INCLUDING PRINCE CHARLES.**

just before the release of *A Force Awakens.* "You have to think about all the aspects of it because, you know, if you want to maintain a low profile, this isn't the best way to do it. [Laughs] And I sort of got into a niche where I did my voiceovers and I could do theater when I wanted to. I mean, all along the way I've been having a really great time and doing a lot of interesting stuff. It's just that people don't really pay a lot of attention."

In another interview from 2015, he added, "I spent a large part of my life putting *Star Wars* behind me so I could move on. (Returning for more films) is like taking out a pair of trousers from the back of the closet and discovering a $20 bill in the pocket."

While fans have only seen a trailer as of the spring, if nothing else, Hamill has a speaking role in The Last Jedi and more than likely, a significant role.

He has been outspoken in his disagreement of his character's direction in the movie, telling ABC News of writer-director Rian Johnson, "When I read (the screenplay), I told Rian, 'I fundamentally disagree with virtually everything you've decided about my character.' It was as shocking for me to read what Rian had written as I'm sure it will be for the audience."

Hamill also acknowledged the possibility of Skywalker going to the dark side, much like his father, Anakin/Darth Vader, and nephew, Kylo Ren.

The world awaits the answer to that question and many more this December, some 40 years after it all began, a long time ago in a galaxy far, far away, a story which has captivated the world and changed the lives of just about all involved.

Few more so than Hamill, who happened to be sitting on the right couch at the right time.

**❝ I spent a large part of my life putting Star Wars behind me so I could move on. (Returning for more films) is like taking out a pair of trousers from the back of the closet and discovering a $20 bill in the pocket."**

**- MARK HAMILL, IN A 2015 INTERVIEW**

# BELOVED IS YOU

**He's old (900 years!), green, short and speaks in bizarre, backward fashion. Even so, Yoda is one of the most admired and quoted species in the galaxy.**

BY BRYAN PETRAY

One of the most captivating aspects of the Star Wars saga is the vast collection of species, from a two-foot green omnipotent humanoid to a 16-foot, man-eating reptilian predator called "Rancor." The immeasurable imagination of George Lucas and his ability to create and bring to life so many creatures, races and personalities makes his world an irresistible attraction that has entertained generations for four decades while becoming a worldwide cultural phenomenon.

Among the nucleus of Lucas' prodigious universe is its Grand Master Jedi, Yoda, the essence of the tangible force throughout the plot. His part in the saga is paramount, yet Lucas surrenders few clues when it comes to Yoda's origin and species.

We know that Darth Sidious' early apprentice, the Sith Lord Darth Maul, with his distinctive horns, was of the Zabrak species and came from the planet Dathomir. We also know that Anakin Skywalker's young Padawan learner, Ahsoka Tano, with her elongated striped head tails, was of the Togruta order and came from the planet Shili. And Lucas so ordained that the species of the villainous Jabba the Hutt was so important that it should be included in his title.

There are more than 100 different known species and hundreds of named planets in Lucas' realm, but for his own reasons, the mastermind of the universe chose to keep us in suspense on both when it came to Grand Master Yoda.

When inquired, Lucas hasn't budged. He's been known to use the term "Yoda's species" when asked. "He's the illegitimate child of Kermit and Miss Piggy," Lucas joked in the 2002 documentary *From Puppets to Pixels: Digital Characters in 'Episode II.'*

Whatever his background, Yoda is just cool. And wise. And all-knowing. And did we mention cool?

There is no shortage of theories on Yoda's place of origin. One of the more obvious is to look to his end to perhaps find his beginning. Yoda's chosen destination for his notorious self-imposed exile was at the Outer Rim on the planet Dagobah. There he watched Luke from afar, using the force to discern that he would eventually take on his final student.

Yoda's final destination for his exile and eventual end certainly wasn't as desirable as Luke's choice on the scenic aquatic planet of Ahch-To decades later, or even Obi-Wan's exile excursion on the desolate planet Tatooine. As miserable as it seemed for Luke, Yoda seemed right at home on the snake- and swamp-ridden planet. Which might explain how Dagobah could be Yoda's home. The guess is as good as any, but alas, it's merely a guess.

What we do know is that Yoda was the most accomplished Jedi in the galaxy. Born 900 years before the Battle of Endor, he was trained by Jedi Master N'Kata Del Gormo. He went on to achieve the rank of Master Jedi at around 100 years of age and trained more than 20,000 younglings and Padawan learners over eight centuries in service to the Jedi Order.

**Even the mightiest can face overbearing adversity and fail. Yoda's flaws and failures make fans identify with him. In a way, they see themselves in Yoda. Someone who wields great power, but carries a heavy burden against a formidable foe. His fallacy makes him relatable.**

His powers were extraordinary and numerous. And his wisdom and precognition skills only scratch the surface to his full arsenal. In addition to his mastery of force acrobatics and lightsaber combat, the three-fingered Jedi legend also wielded a force shockwave, a force push as well as force absorption abilities. And under the tutelage of the spirit form of his former student, Qui-Gon Jin, Yoda also harnessed the rare ability to communicate with deceased Jedi in spirit known as the cosmic force.

With extraordinary power and abilities, it's easy to see why so many fans are infatuated with the Grand Master. His popularity is as great as his midi-chlorian count. But there's several layers to this phenomenon.

There's something to be said for a lifeform that lives for 900 years and is able to end on his own terms as Yoda did. And considering the conflict in place that he faced over those nine centuries, it's an even more impressive feat.

While Yoda's wisdom and power is legendary, he wasn't without miscue. Several of his most talented students, Count Dooku and Anakin Skywalker (to a lesser extent) fell victim to the dark side of the force. He oversaw the almost complete genocide of the Jedi Order after Supreme Chancellor Palpatine ordered the Grand Army of the Republic to execute Order 66 – branding the Jedi as traitorous and to be executed on sight.

Even the mightiest can face overbearing adversity and fail. Yoda's flaws and failures make fans identify with him. In a way, they see themselves in Yoda. Someone who wields great power, but carries a heavy burden against a formidable foe. His fallacy makes him relatable.

His unique manner of speaking, often referred to as "Yodic," using the subject-object-verb format, along with his diminutive features adds to his unfailing charm.

"Size matters not. Look at me. Judge me by my size, do you?" Yoda asked Luke Skywalker in *The Empire Strikes Back*. "And where you should not. For my ally is the force. And a powerful ally, it is." Who among us can't relate to the natural human instinct to root for the underdog?

But perhaps the biggest reason that Yoda became the saga's most beloved character is a combination of Lucas creativity, storytelling and, in his great wisdom, imparting the role to Frank Oz. The award-winning American puppeteer, also known for his work on *Sesame Street* (Cookie Monster, Bert and Grover) and *The Muppet Show* (Fozzie Bear and Miss Piggy), wowed fans as Yoda's voice and performed much of the actual puppetry work of the non-CGI incarnation of the legendary Jedi.

His work in *The Empire Strikes Back* was so widely admired that it presented a strong case to become the first puppeteer in a movie to receive an Academy Award nomination. There was a movement in Hollywood for him being considered for Best Supporting Actor, but the academy ultimately decided that a puppeteer wasn't an actor.

Regardless, Oz's role in bringing Yoda to life was brilliant. And the final product was an immensely popular character with great depth. In 2008, Yoda ranked No. 25 on Empire Magazine's list of the 100 Greatest Movie Characters of All Time, considered among unforgettable silver-screen contemporaries such as James Bond, Forrest Gump, Ferris Bueller and Indiana Jones.

As popular as he is, Yoda is still an enigma to even the most fanatical Star Wars enthusiast. Perhaps Lucas' shroud of mystery cast over one of his favorite characters was all part of a master plan of a future spin-off movie. With nearly 900 years' worth of a blank canvas, there's so much potential that could come with a telling of his full story.

# THE WISDOM OF YODA

## NINE OF YODA'S GREATEST QUOTES

**[9]** "Through the Force, things you will see. Other places. The future … the past. Old friends long gone."
– THE EMPIRE STRIKES BACK

**[8]** "Adventure. Excitement. A Jedi craves not these things."
– THE EMPIRE STRIKES BACK

**[7]** "Judge me by my size do you?"
– THE EMPIRE STRIKES BACK

**[6]** "Fear is the path to the dark side, fear leads to anger, anger leads to hate, hate leads to suffering."
– EPISODE 1 – THE PHANTOM MENACE

**[5]** "Not if anything to say about it I have."
– EPISODE III – REVENGE OF THE SITH

**[4]** "Always two there are, no more, no less. A master and an apprentice."
– EPISODE 1 – THE PHANTOM MENACE

**[3]** "That is why you fail."
– THE EMPIRE STRIKES BACK, IN RESPONSE TO LUKE SAYING "I DON'T BELIEVE IT."

**[2]** "When 900 years old you reach, look as good you will not."
– RETURN OF THE JEDI

**[1]** "Do. Or not do. There is no try."
– THE EMPIRE STRIKES BACK

# WICKED GOOD

His taste in color runs black and he's a bit of a heavy breather. It's all part of the Darth Vader aura, the most intimidating – and fascinating - presence in the Star Wars galaxy ... *and Hollywood's greatest villain.*

BY ROGER FERNANDEZ

"I had to make Darth Vader scary without the audience ever seeing his face. His character's got to go beyond that. He's done a lot of horrible things in his life that he isn't particularly proud of. Ultimately, he's just a pathetic guy who's had a very sad life."

- GEORGE LUCAS IN AN INTERVIEW WITH ROLLING STONE MAGAZINE

# DARTH VADER: WICKED GOOD

ACTORS PETER CUSHING, CARRIE FISHER AND DAVID PROWSE ON THE SET OF THE ORIGINAL STAR WARS FILM.

To loosely borrow a famous line the one-and-only Obi-Wan Kenobi used in the original *Star Wars* movie, this is the villain you're looking for.

Darth Vader, it turns out, is in fact the chosen one, the one you hate, you love, you hate to love and love to hate. No, we're not trying to work an old Jedi mind trick on you.

It's the truth. Hollywood and pop culture have never had it so good and so bad when it comes to villains, and the *Star Wars* franchise can take credit for coming up with a dream of a nightmare bad guy.

When you really think about it, the dark-mask-wearing, heavy-breathing, light-saber-wielding, wanna-conquer-the-galaxy-and-fulfill-his-destiny tough guy may be as popular and beloved as any of the heroes in the enduring saga.

Move over, Luke Skywalker, step aside Princess Leia, out of the way Han Solo, and that goes for you too, Chewbacca and Yoda — Lord Vader may have the inside track on all of them in a *Star Wars* adoration contest.

It takes a special kind of evil to get that much love.

# DARTH VADER: WICKED GOOD

## THERE IS A VADER SIGHTING ...

The world first laid eyes on this fearsome figure in the opening moments of Episode IV – the original *Star Wars* - when Vader stormed through the hallways of a starship, barking out orders, interrogating a rebel and finishing him off with one of his patented choke holds. Viewers didn't exactly know what to make of Vader, who appeared to be some type of man/robot hybrid with a booming voice and top-dog status.

And that's exactly the way Stars Wars creator George Lucas wanted it. The aim was to make the antihero an incomparable unnerving enigma. Vader proved to be a shock to the senses from the very start. The more we saw him, the more we wanted to know about him — from a safe distance, of course.

"I had to make Darth Vader scary without the audience ever seeing his face," Lucas told Rolling Stone magazine. "Basically, it's just a black mask. I said, 'How do I make that evil and scary?' I mean, he's big and black and he's got a cape and a samurai helmet, but that doesn't necessarily make people afraid of him. His character's got to go beyond that — that's how we get his impersonal way of dealing with things. He's done a lot of horrible things in his life that he isn't particularly proud of. Ultimately, he's just a pathetic guy who's had a very sad life."

THIERRY ZOCCOLAN/GETTY IMAGES

ACTOR DAVID PROWSE (SHOWN ABOVE IN AN IMAGE FROM 2013) WAS THE MAN IN THE SUIT FOR DARTH VADER WHILE JAMES EARL JONES (SHOWN BELOW) PROVIDED THE CHARACTER'S IMPOSING VOICE.

JIM SPELLMAN/GETTY IMAGES

Let's start with the character's name, which provided a hidden clue. "Darth" is a variation of dark, and "Vader" is Dutch for father. "So it's basically Dark Father," Lucas added in Rolling Stone. Little could audiences have known that Lucas had provided a sneaky hint to a planet-shaking plot twist that would rattle viewers down the line.

Now let's turn to the obvious: the look. It is the foundation for the character's popularity. The film industry had never seen anything like Vader. In Hollywood, villains were simply troublemakers who more or less looked like someone you might bump into at the grocery store, only they went about their daily life concocting sinister plans.

Perhaps, at the worst, they wore black and maybe an eyepatch, spoke with a British or Eastern European accent or sported a perpetual scowl or unsightly scar. With Vader, we didn't know whether he was chewing bubble gum or even awake, for that matter. The expression-less mask, not to mention his height and dark, flowing cape, made him that much more psychologically terrifying.

Can't forget to mention he's an expert with a lightsaber and has mastered the Force, thus he's able to wring the life out of anyone who crosses him without so much laying a finger on them. That nifty weaponry and "Force choke" gives him an aura of invincibility.

## HE'S A HEAVY BREATHER

Toss in the breathing. How many movie characters would you recognize on their breathing pattern alone? It's unmistakable, one of the most distinct and menacing sounds the film industry has ever produced. If it takes you more than a split second to identify it, perhaps you've stopped breathing. Admit it — as a *Star Wars* fan, you've tried to copy that sound, just as you've tried to emulate Vader's voice.

That voice. That sweet, full-toned, authoritative and ominous sound provided by James Earl Jones. He's the man who told us "This is CNN" and later gave sports fans goosebumps talking about baseball in a middle-of-nowhere Iowa cornfield in *Field of Dreams*. Never mind those other roles. His voice is the one that will speak for the Dark Side for eternity.

Jones admitted to The New York Times Magazine to having a little fun putting Darth Vader's voice to use off the set. Who wouldn't?

"I did that once when I was traveling cross-country," he said. "I used Darth as my handle on the CB radio.

# DARTH VADER: WICKED GOOD

The truck drivers would really freak out — for them, it was Darth Vader. I had to stop doing that."

We've got the visuals. We've got the sounds. And just to add to the sensory overload, the powers that be asked composer John Williams, the man who created the eerie *Jaws* theme, to whip up a little tune for Vader. "The Imperial March" nailed it. It's intimidating, apocalyptic and perfectly captures the unpleasant tone in all things Vader and the Empire. The song has become the unofficial anthem for anything or anyone with a despicable side.

Episode IV made it clear that Vader was a bad dude, assuming he was human, and downright cold. The more the films peeled his layers, the more we realized there was a glimmer of humanity behind the darkness. Heck, he was even a cute kid at one time and had what it took to be — spoiler alert — a dedicated Skywalker family man.

In later films, created to unveil Vader's backstory, we meet him as a young Anakin Skywalker, a slave boy thought to be the "Chosen One." The young Jedi in training was supposed to bring balance to the Force. Oops. Not quite. He's the classic case of a good kid gone bad, caught up trying to rule an entire galaxy, far, far, away. It could happen to the best of us.

In The *Empire Strikes Back*, Vader reveals himself as Luke Skywalker's father and asks the youngster to join him as the nastiest pop/son duo in the galaxy. While that reunion didn't pan out, Vader, in *Return of the Jedi,* showed compassion and proved that family always comes first when he saved Luke from the Emperor. See, he wasn't such an evildoer after all, and it's not so tough to sympathize with him.

It's impossible not to jump on the Team Vader bandwagon when he tosses the Emperor into oblivion. For all that venom and rancor early on, Vader rebounds and totally redeems himself. That's part of the attraction to the character, his transformation from a monster into a human. It's like *Beauty and the Beast* in space, only with less fur (outside of Chewie and the Ewoks), less ballroom dancing and a lot more lightsaber battles.

Few are the movie villains who can stand up to that kind of range, which is why Vader is one of best you'll ever see. An impeccable mix of visual awe and character development thrust him into the pop culture pantheon.

Vader pulled off the improbable as the poster boy for both right and wrong. No one wants to be him, yet, at the same time, everyone wants to be him. Look around the neighborhood come Halloween. His is a costume that's been in style since 1977, and it's still as hip as ever.

You'll catch him at sporting events. At Oakland Raiders home games, take a glance at the team's famed "Black Hole" section and you're sure to spot a Darth-Vader-clad fan cheering on the Silver and Black. Vader's theme song is always a go-to tune at stadiums and arenas whenever the home squad wants to take a jab at "vile" visiting teams.

Even Disneyland, "The Happiest Place on Earth," featured Vader in promotional ads. You've come a long way in popularity, and most certainly anger management, when you can make a seamless transition from aspiring to snatch power at all costs to taking a spin on the Dumbo ride. That, folks, is what you call doing a complete 180.

## HOLLYWOOD GOLD

He's such a power player that he's the equivalent of a March Madness No. 1 seed. Since 2013, StarWars.com has run an official NCAA-style bracket tournament, called "This is Madness," to determine the franchise's top character. Vader is practically a dynasty. He has dominated the Dark Side's half of the bracket, reached the final in the first four editions and won it in 2015.

Hollywood obviously has an affinity for him. Run an on-line search for the greatest movie villains of all time. Vader frequently comes up the best of the worst. *The Wizard of Oz*'s wicked witch can't hang with him, and neither can *Halloween's* Michael Myers.

When was the last time you saw Hannibal Lecter (*The Silence of the Lambs*) on a lunchbox, Norman Bates (*Psycho*) on kids' light-up shoes or Hans Gruber (*Diehard*) featured on a waffle maker? Vader is a merchandiser's dream, and everyone from toddlers to grandparents can't get enough of him. He made it chic to go against the grain in the ceaseless conflict that is good vs. evil.

The thing that makes Vader stand out in a bad bunch on earth, as out of this world as he has always been, is that deep down we can all relate to him on a certain level. That can't be said for most movie meanies.

"The first film, people didn't even know whether there was a person there," Lucas said in Rolling Stone. "They thought he was a person. They thought he was a monster or some kind of a robot. In the second film, it's revealed that he's a human being, and in the third film you find out that, yes, he's a father and a regular person like the rest of us."

Dare tell Vader he's not the most iconic ruffian the world has ever known, and you're likely to get an icy-cold stare and a calculated response that should sound familiar: "I find your lack of faith disturbing." He allowed all of us to believe that sometimes it's good to be a little bad.

# 40 GREATEST CHARACTERS

## BY RYAN CRACKNELL

**A**fter a bunch of films, a couple of television series, dozens of books and lots of other stories in other mediums, *Star Wars* has introduced an entire universe of characters. Many are icons to multiple generations. And then there's Jar Jar Binks.

Several factors go into great *Star Wars* characters. Story and personality are the big ones. These bring the emotional core that make us relate and feel a connection.

But let's be honest. Some *Star Wars* characters achieve greatness not because they make us feel but because they look cool. In a visual medium like film, an inspired design can make an impact just like a scene that brings a smile or causes our eyes to water.

With those things in mind, here are 40 of the most unforgettable *Star Wars* characters.

# 40 GREATEST CHARACTERS

## [40] MALAKILI

Malakili has the look of someone who's tough. He's a big guy without much use for shirts. His job is to look after the monstrous Rancor that resides under Jabba the Hutt's throne, gobbling up anyone who wrongs the slimy gangster. It turns out that Malakili's tough exterior is all a facade. When it comes to him and his Rancor, Malakili is all teddy bear.

## [39] WICKET

Wicket is the young hero of the Ewoks. The teddy bears with spears may get a bad rap by some who don't want their Star Wars cute and cuddly, but Wicket is different. Between all the yup-nubbing is a tough adventurer who shows little fear and lots of heart. And if your Saturday mornings in the '80s involved the Ewoks cartoon, your respect for Wicket and his adventures is probably even higher.

## [38] GREEDO

Greedo's time on the screen may be limited but his legacy is undeniable. He's part of the scum that makes the Star Wars universe so appealing. The Rodian bounty hunter looks as though he's related to the Sleestak's from *Land of the Lost.* It's in his death that Greedo's memorable status is cemented. Originally, Han shot first in their fateful meeting at the Mos Eisley Cantina. But through George Lucas' changing mind, that changed because the creator felt good guys should only protect themselves. With that, the Han Shot First movement was born, rebelling against tinkering with a classic series. And now Greedo is part of an even bigger history.

## [37] ADMIRAL ACKBAR

"It's a trap!" It's funny how one line of dialogue can make a character unforgettable. Admiral Ackbar has a lot more going for him, though. He's essentially a humanoid squid

with a uniform that would fit in at a disco. That's hard to pull off. At the center of several key battles, Admiral Ackbar has to be respected for his tactical knowledge and expertise, as well.

## [36] PADMÉ AMIDALA

Given her importance in the Star Wars saga, Padmé should rank much higher. However, the way she's introduced in the prequels, it's hard to truly get behind her. Many of her costumes are amazing. But this is Star Wars, a place with strong female leads thrive and inspire. Padmé has a few moments here and there, but many are crippled by the awkward courtship between her and her "Annie."

## [35] ASAJJ VENTRESS

Asajj Ventress is not only one of the toughest characters in the Star Wars universe, but she's also one of the scariest. Rising from a slave to apprentice of Count Dooku and bounty hunter, the dark side runs deep in the Dathomirian. Wielding a pair of lightsabers, she participated in several big battles in both the *Clone Wars* micro-series and was a central villain in the later *Clone Wars* series.

## [34] CHOPPER

Droids have provided plenty of laughs over the course of all the films and various television shows. For machines, they sometimes offer some heart that makes them endearing. A member of the crew on *Rebels,* the C1-10P droid can be a little bit cranky at times and even do things the way he wants. But Chopper sometimes shows a more playful side. In interviews, Dave Filoni, the executive producer of *Rebels,* has compared Chopper to being like a family cat much like R2-D2 is likened to a dog.

# 40 GREATEST CHARACTERS

## [33] CAPTAIN REX

The story of Captain Rex is an expansive one. It's also fairly complex. He's a central figure in *The Clone Wars*. A clone himself, he's the model trooper. By the time Rebels rolled around, Rex is much older thanks to his accelerated aging. But this simply adds more depth to his personality now that he's grizzled and gone through so much.

It can also be said now that Rex's appearances didn't stop there. Dave Filoni recently acknowledged that Rex may have been fighting for the Rebels once again on Endor during *Return of the Jedi*. Filoni has supported the idea that a noticeably older fighter among the group could indeed be Captain Rex.

## [32] SAW GERRERA

Somewhat of a militant extremist, Saw Gerrera's story is filled with personal tragedy. Although best known for his central role in *Rogue One*, he was first introduced on *The Clone Wars*. That's where his tragic origins are laid out. With several years and many battles happening between then and *Rogue One*, Gerrera continued to transform — mentally and physically. In the film, his appearance is somewhat monstrous, adding a bit of a frightening edge to his character.

## [31] JABBA THE HUTT

Unless you're one of his prisoners or part of his endless diet, being in the company of Jabba the Hutt means a never-ending party. Pre-Special Edition, Jabba was introduced by name early on as someone Han Solo was running away from. And for good reason as said slug-like creature would later go on to use him as a wall hanging. Jabba, or at least a computer-generated imposter, was later edited back into *A New Hope* but the good one is the original from *Return of the Jedi*. The slime, the laugh, the eyes — he's grotesque and disgusting. But he commands your attention, even if you're not one of his captives.

## [30] GRAND ADMIRAL THRAWN

Timothy Zahn's Star Wars novels from the early 1990s helped bring the franchise back into the mainstream. Grand Admiral Thrawn was a big reason why. Heading up the post-Vader Empire, Thrawn led by being a ruthless tactician. He's more of a thinking-person's villain than one who controlled by brute force. As part of the Expanded Universe, Thrawn was no longer part of canon for a period of time. However, he was made official again after being brought back for *Rebels*.

## [29] POE DAMERON

Introduced in *The Force Awakens*, there's still a bit to be revealed about Poe. One thing that is obvious about the Resistance X-Wing pilot is his charm. As a character, he's something of an original trilogy hybrid of Luke and Han. It's obvious that Poe has a central role in the new films, but how it plays out is still a bit of a mystery. He has some great moments, particularly alongside Finn. But, there's not quite the same dynamic depth showcased by the former Stormtrooper and Rey.

## [28] EZRA BRIDGER

Jedi apprentice with humble beginnings — where have you heard that before? While the parallel to the Skywalker lineage is obvious, Ezra Bridger's journey is a different one. The character that the animated *Rebels* revolves around, Ezra isn't your typical hero. As the show gets ready for its final run, there's a definite darkness about his destiny. That not only makes Rebels more interesting, but Ezra as well.

## [27] K-2SO

Droids aren't generally known for their emotion. They know right from wrong, black from white. K-2SO brings a level of sarcasm and feeling not normally

reserved for robots. The result is several laughs and a surprising amount of tender moments with Jynn Erso, Cassian Andor and the Rebel spies. K-2SO's imposing size and spindly arms make for a memorable look that further adds to the characterization. It's almost like the reprogrammed Imperial droid is a confused teenager or young adult coming to grips with what the future holds.

## [26] QUI-GON JINN

Make no mistake about it, Qui-Gon Jinn takes up the wise Obi Wan Kenobi role of *The Phantom Menace*. His apprentice? A young, less gray-haired version of Obi Wan. A bit of an outsider among the Jedi, he's still extremely powerful with the Force and swings a strong lightsaber. Without a lot of backstory enjoyed by so many other characters, Qui-Gon can be seen as a little too similar to the older version of Kenobi introduced in *Star Wars*.

## [25] BAZE MALBUS

Baze Malbus has a cool factor about him just for the massive gun that he carries. His appeal goes deeper, though. A member of the Guardians of the Whills, it's Baze's friendship with Chirrut Îmwe that makes him memorable. Despite not being seen on screen for long, the two have a deep connection that is both authentic and unique to the saga. Star Wars has its share of pairs, but few feel as genuine as Baze and Chirrut.

## [24] SABINE WREN

When we think of Mandalorians in Star Wars, usually the attention shifts to Boba Fett's armor. Over the course of Rebels, Sabine has made a case. She's edgy, she's tough and her role with the Man-

dalorian people is one of destiny. Sabine isn't the lead in *Rebels* but she's the type of character that a lot people have gravitated towards because of her strength. But as the show has progressed, her importance has grown in key storylines. Her strength as a leader brings a sense of destiny and promise, which only makes her more interesting to watch and follow.

## [23] LANDO CALRISSIAN

Lando's a suave, cape wearer who seems like the coolest guy ever — until he sells out his friend and becomes the Judas of the original trilogy. But Star Wars has plenty of redemption points with Lando being one of the swiftest. Bits and pieces of Lando's backstory have been worked into the films, books and comics, but perhaps his biggest claim to fame is losing the Millennium Falcon to Han Solo in a game of Sabaac.

## [22] MARA JADE

Perhaps the most prominent member of the Expanded Universe, Mara Jade was first introduced in Timothy Zahn's "Heir to the Empire." Trained by Emperor Palpatine, she shared a connection that went beyond his death. Over the course of Zahn's novels, she undergoes a major transformation in attitude. Mara Jade became a focal point of several more Star Wars books in the years that followed. Whether villain or hero, she's one of the strongest females in all of Star Wars. At least she was. With the elimination of the Expanded Universe, Mara Jade is currently not part of canon. However, like Thrawn, that could change as the revised canon grows.

## [21] KANAN JARRUS

The rugged leader of the Ghost on *Rebels,* Kanan is a Jedi who never finished his training. It could be argued that he never reached his full potential. As *Rebels* has progressed, Kanan continues to change and evolve, both physically and with his powers. Watching over and guiding Ezra, the relationship has some similarities to Obi-Wan with Anakin and later Luke. At the same time, it's different. Kanan is on his own journey of self-discovery.

## [20] JYN ERSO

Jyn Erso isn't the typical Star Wars hero. She's strong, but she's part of a team. Jyn is the central figure in *Rogue One*, but she's one in a group. She's one of many. And that's what makes her role in the franchise interesting. We learn about her backstory quickly and in a straightforward manner. Jyn is a reluctant soldier, but one nonetheless. Ultimately selfless and dedicated to the important job she has no choice but completing, she gets her big moment and a somewhat surprising sendoff.

## [19] FINN

Despite all the Stormtroopers shown on screen over the decades, few glimpses have been offered under the helmet. Because they act as a collective force, it makes it all the more impactful when FN-2187 removes his blood-marked mask to reveal the person we now know as Finn. Brave, funny, dedicated and a risk-taker, Finn is the consummate hero. And yet, there's still plenty we don't know about him — what he doesn't know about himself. A journey awaits, which should make him even more interesting by the time it's done.

## [18] DARTH MAUL

When *The Phantom Menace* arrived, Darth Maul was everywhere. And for good reason. His stare was piercing and nightmare-inducing. His skin and horns were devilish. Let's not discount the fact that he swung a double-sided lightsaber. Unfortunately, his appearance in the film was limited. The scenes were memorable, but more from Maul was needed. He was brought back for both the animated *Clone*

*Wars* and *Rebels*, which helped flesh out his character more and create a character that was interesting for more than just his look.

## [17] CHIRRUT ÎMWE

Sometimes you just have to believe. Chirrut Îmwe believed in the Force but he was no Jedi. That didn't stop him from trying to tap into its mystical powers. It'd be easy to overlook the heavily spiritual Chirrut Îmwe. He's an old, blind man who mutters to himself. What could he accomplish? Plenty. Even without Force powers, Chirrut knows how to take care of himself, even when surrounded by a mob of aggressive troopers. On top of all that, there's a quick wit, lots of humor, loyalty and caring demeanor. It's hard not to feel anything but warmth towards him.

## [16] R2-D2

Sometimes "beeps" and "boops" can go a long way in establishing a character. R2-D2 may not be a droid of many words, but he has a way of being heard. Whether he's hacking into the Death Star computers, fixing spaceships in mid-flight, carrying messages to or cutting open an Ewok net, Artoo is a resourceful little robot who brings companionship, humor and plenty of heart — even if he doesn't have one.

## [15] AHSOKA TANO

Introduced in *The Clone Wars*, Ahsoka was a Jedi Padawan working alongside Anakin. Her training paralleled her personal growth as a teenager. It was a little scary, sometimes frustrating adventure with several turning points along the way. Because we watch knowing Anakin's fate, it's also heartbreaking to see their bond form and know at some point there's going to be a breaking point.

## [14] BB-8

When the first clips of BB-8 surfaced, there was a sense

that the robot could be the next Jar-Jar Binks — a character that panders to the youngest of viewers and is nothing but obnoxious. It turns out BB-8 was all right. In fact, he was more than all right. The parallels to Artoo are obvious but they're far from identical. The spherical build of BB-8 adds a sense of innovation. His part in adventures is exciting. And his "flaming thumb" provides one of the biggest laughs of all the films.

## [12] KYLO REN

Looking to emulate the dark path of his grandfather, Darth Vader, Kylo Ren has the dark outfit and mask that makes him memorable simply by sight. For reasons not fully revealed as of yet, there is a deep-seated rage within him. Even if there is some sort of eventual redemption, it may be hard to forgive him for putting the Dark Side before family.

## [13] EMPEROR PALPATINE

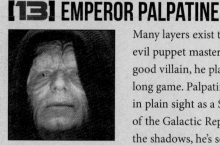

Many layers exist to this evil puppet master. Like any good villain, he plays the long game. Palpatine hides in plain sight as a Senator of the Galactic Republic. In the shadows, he's something much darker. It's Palpatine who is responsible for luring Anakin to the Dark Side and creating the monster known as Darth Vader. But much of this depth comes to light in the prequels.

Even in the original trilogy, when he's simply the Emperor, there's plenty that's frightening about him. He's old and shrivelled. He hides behind a cloak and remains largely mysterious. He shoots lightning bolts from his fingertips. And that voice, a croak that induced many a nightmare to a generation of young viewers.

## [11] GRAND MOFF TARKIN

No matter how you look at it, you can't not have strong feelings towards someone who blows up an entire planet and everyone on it. When that planet happens to belong to a beloved character like Princess Leia, clench fists are bound to happen. When it comes to film, that's a good thing. Someone's doing something right if you feel emotion, no matter if it's positive or negative.

Grand Moff Tarkin is the essence of cold and calculating. He always seems to be in deep thought, treating every breath as though it were part of a massive game of chess. He's an intelligent villain who operates on logic over emotion, bring balance to Darth Vader and terror to the Rebel Alliance.

# 40 GREATEST CHARACTERS

## [10] BOBA FETT

Boba Fett was at his coolest when the least was known about him. When he was introduced, he was something of a mystery man who had a cool outfit, awesome blaster and killer spaceship. He had a rocket pack to boot. And the job of bounty hunter? Boba Fett has that aura of cool surrounding him like an intergalactic James Dean. For the first couple of decades of Star Wars, Boba Fett was probably the coolest character in the saga. But through the Special Editions and prequels, we learned a little more about him and his origins. He can't be seen with the same mystery anymore. A less is more approach would have worked just fine for Boba Fett.

## [9] C-3PO

C-3PO isn't the most likeable character. Sometimes, the droid can be a little irritating. If he were a kid in class, he'd be the one at the front of the room with his hand up. He's the one who always tells you when you're wrong. But that's by design. Although things may revolve around the Skywalker family, C-3PO is our guide. Precision is in his programming. And sometimes, the golden robot's takes offer up some refreshing honesty the heroes might not want to hear. But it's a reflection of the danger at hand and the excitement of the stories. As far as design goes, C-3PO is impeccable. The classic golden version harkens back to Fritz Lang's black-and-white classic *Metropolis*. It adds a level of iconography for a franchise that is filled with instantly recognizable costumes and designs.

## [8] CHEWBACCA

Chewbacca is more a Wookiee of action rather than words — or growls. Primarily working as Han Solo's partner, Chewbacca is a symbol of bravery, companionship and loyalty. He may look imposing and tough (because he is), but there's a warm, cuddly side to Chewie as well that goes beyond his fur. He's a family man, one of the lone takeaways from the infamous Holiday Special.

## [7] YODA

For a small, green creature, Yoda carries quite the lightsaber. Throughout the Star Wars saga, whether it's on the big screen, TV or on the page, he's a gatekeeper of sorts for the Force. And while his power and position make him notable, it's his characterization that makes him so memorable. Most of his lines have a Yogi Berra-type of nonsense to them that actually bring forth a sense of wisdom. Yoda is funny, he's cute and, perhaps most of all, he believes in the good of life even when things are at their darkest.

## [6] REY

Who is Rey? We still don't fully know. But the glimpse that we've been given is that she's something special. Sometimes mystery works against you. In this online age, the mystery surrounding Rey, which will be fleshed out in *The Last Jedi* and Episode IX, makes for endless discussion and theories. It works to add to the mystique surrounding her. What we do know is that she's strong and resourceful. She's both serious and lends an element of humor. Even she doesn't fully grasp the power that she holds. That's a big part of her intrigue. *The Force Awakens* gave us a taste to show that she fits in with the Star Wars greats and it's exciting to root along with her.

## [5] OBI-WAN KENOBI

Introduced as the wise wizard, Ben Kenobi turned out to be so much more. His place in the saga shows the biggest change. When things start out, he's a young jedi. He's learning and still prone to mistakes. Battle after battle, big and small, there's no character that grows more over the course of the saga than Ben Kenobi, except for maybe Anakin. The dynamic with Obi-Wan is different, though. Anakin may share a similar level of loss, but Ben deals with it differently. His place on the Light Side of the Force is never in doubt. He may not be perfect, but he's a hero at every stage.

## [4] PRINCESS LEIA ORGANA

Sometimes the term "princess" brings a negative connotation in movies. Princesses have a long history of being portrayed as needing to be saved by a knight in shining armor and a perfect smile. Leia Organa is not your typical princess. Yes, Star Wars sees her getting saved by not one but two handsome gents, but over the course of the rest of the original trilogy and *The Force Awakens*, she's the one giving the orders. Leia is strong. She's comfortable giving orders, making tough decisions and getting into the thick of things. Whether that's as a diplomat, a battlefield warrior, a friend, lover or family member, it doesn't matter.

## [3] HAN SOLO

Han Solo is the kind of person many people imagine being in some sort of alternate reality. Free-spirited scoundrel, he does what he wants, when he wants. Han is handsome, funny, speaks his mind and usually gets his way. He's funny, he goes on adventures and he knows how to talk his way out of almost any tough situation. And those that he can't — he has a blaster in his holster and a Wookiee at his side. Even with the tough exterior, Han Solo has heart. He's loyal to his friends, even when it's inconvenient. Of the major Star Wars characters, Han is the closest thing we have to an everyman. He has no special powers, just skills. Flaws and all, it makes him rounded and relatable.

## [2] LUKE SKYWALKER

From a whiny desert farm boy to wise, old wizard-type, Luke Skywalker's gone through a lot of changes. A prototypical hero, he answers the call of adventure, making many important stops and discoveries along the way — including discovering that princess he kissed was actually his sister. Luke is our guidepost through the original trilogy. Early on, it looked like he was going to be one of those unbearable leads and kill everything before the Empire got the chance. In particular, it's hard not to cringe (or laugh) when we first meet him. Just listen to him sound like a three-year-old complaining to his Uncle Owen. But then things change. Destiny takes over and a champion emerges. It goes far beyond the first Death Star. In the films and adventures that follow, Luke continues to discover more about himself, his powers and responsibility — not to mention the potential dangers those bring as Light and Dark battle on inside him.

## [1] DARTH VADER/ ANAKIN SKYWALKER

Star Wars is formed around Anakin Skywalker and his descent into Darth Vader. It's a story of tragedy, rage, sadness and hope. It's the eternal struggle of good and evil played out in epic battles, iconic costumes and big moments. Because we met Anakin after we knew what he became, there's always a certain edge about his younger self. But all that lays the groundwork for the infamous villain that he would become. Even in death, he continues to influences the Dark Side through Kylo Ren. Darth Vader's menacing look matches his actions. He's a figure of strength, danger and evil — a recipe for nightmares. The movies give him several big moments, particularly when it comes to turning point battles. But Darth Vader isn't just about lightsabers and heavy breathing. He's a fleshed out and fully realized character. Between the films, TV shows, spinoff books, comics and other stories, we know who he is and how he got there. Despite all the horrible things he does, there's a certain part of us that cheers for him. So even in a universe filled with memorable characters, Vader reigns supreme.

## WHAT'S LISTED?

Products in the price guide typically:

- Are produced by licensed manufacturers
- Are widely available
- Have market activity on single items

## WHAT THE COLUMNS MEAN

The LO and HI columns reflect current retail selling ranges. The HI column on the right generally represents the full retail selling price. The LO column on the left generally represents the lowest price one would expect to find with extensive shopping.

## CONDITION

Prices in this issue reflect the highest raw condition (i.e. not professionally graded by a third party) of the card commonly found at shows, shops, online, and right out of the pack for brand new releases. This generally means NrMint to Mint condition. Action figure prices are based on Mint condition. Action figures that are loose (out-of-package) are generally sold for 50 percent of the listed price, but may list for less/more depending on popularity, condition, completeness, and market sales.

## CURRENCY

This price guide is intended to reflect the entire North American market. While not all the cards/figures are produced in the United States, they will reflect the market value in U.S. dollars.

## GLOSSARY/LEGEND

Our glossary defines terms most frequently used in the action figure/non-sports card collecting hobby. Some of these terms are common to other types of collecting. Some terms may have several meanings depending on the use and context.

| | |
|---|---|
| ALB | Album exclusive card. This indicates that a card was only available in a collector album or binder that was devoted to a certain product. |
| AU | Certified autograph |
| BB | Box bottom - A card or panel of cards on the bottom of a trading card box. |
| BI | Box incentive |
| BN | Barnes & Noble exclusive |
| BT | Box topper - A card, either regulation or jumbo-sized, that is inserted in the top of a box of trading cards. |
| C | Common card |
| CI | Case-Incentive or Case Insert - A unique card that is offered as an incentive to purchase a case (or cases) of trading cards. |
| COA | Certificate of Authenticity - A certificate issued by the manufacturer to insure a product's authenticity. |
| COR | Corrected version of an error (ERR) card |
| CT | Case-topper exclusive card |
| D23 | Disney D23 Convention |
| ECCC | Emerald City Comic Con |
| EE | Entertainment Earth exclusive - An exclusive that was offered for sale on Entertainment Earth's website. |
| EL | Extremely limited |
| ERR | Error card - A card with erroneous information, spelling, or depiction on either side of the card, most of which are not corrected by the manufacturer. |
| EXCH | Exchange card |
| FACT | Factory set exclusive |
| FLK | Flocked variant - This description applies exclusively to Funko products. |
| FOIL | holofoil |
| GCE | Galactic Convention Exclusive - This description applies specifically to Funko products. |
| GEN | General distribution - This term most usually applies to promotional cards. |
| GITD | Glow-in-the-Dark variant - This description usually applies to Funko products. |
| GS | GameStop exclusive |
| HOLO | hologram |

| | |
|---|---|
| HT | Hot Topic exclusive |
| L | Limited |
| LE | Limited Edition |
| LS | Limited Series |
| MEM | Memorabilia card |
| MET | Metallic variant - This describes a metallic version of a Funko product. |
| NNO | Unnumbered card |
| NSU | Non-Sports Update exclusive card |
| NYCC | New York Comic Con |
| OPC | O-Pee-Chee (a Canadian subsidiary of Topps) |
| R | Rare card |
| RED | Redemption card |
| SDCC | San Diego Comic Con |
| SI | Set-Incentive |
| SP | Single or Short Print - A short print is a card that was printed in less quantity compared to the other cards in the same series. |
| SR | Super Rare card |
| SWC | Star Wars Celebration |
| TW | Toy Wars exclusive |
| U | Uncommon card |
| UER | Uncorrected error |
| UNC | Uncut sheet or panel |
| UR | Ultra Rare card |
| VAR | Variation card - One of two or more cards from the same series, with the same card number, that differ from one another in some way. This sometimes occurs when the manufacturer notices an error in one or more of the cards, corrects the mistake, and then resumes the printing process. In some cases, one of the variations may be relatively scarce. |
| VAULT | This description applies specifically to Funko products and indicates a figurine that has been re-released by the company. |
| VL | Very Limited |
| VR | Very Rare card |
| WG | Walgreen's exclusive |
| WM | Walmart exclusive |

As with any publication, we appreciate reader feedback. While there are many listings, not all collectibles may be priced due to market constraints. If you have any questions, concerns, or suggestions, please contact us at: **nonsports@beckett.com**

# Action Figures and Figurines

## PRICE GUIDE

## VINTAGE

### 1977-78 Star Wars 12-Backs A

| | | | |
|---|---|---|---|
| 1 | Ben Kenobi grey hair | 1250.00 | 2500.00 |
| 2 | Ben Kenobi white hair | 1250.00 | 2500.00 |
| 3 | Ben Kenobi (w/double telescoping lightsaber) | 4000.00 | 8000.00 |
| 4 | C-3PO | 500.00 | 1000.00 |
| 5 | Chewbacca | 1000.00 | 2000.00 |
| 6 | Darth Vader | 1750.00 | 3500.00 |
| 7 | Darth Vader (w/double telescoping lightsaber) | 5000.00 | 8500.00 |
| 8 | Death Squad Commander | 450.00 | 900.00 |
| 10 | Han Solo (small head) | 1500.00 | 3000.00 |
| 12 | Jawa (plastic cape) | 5000.00 | 8500.00 |
| 13 | Luke Skywalker (blond hair) | 1500.00 | 3000.00 |
| 14 | Luke Skywalker/telescoping lightsaber | 6000.00 | 10000.00 |
| 15 | Princess Leia | 1500.00 | 3000.00 |
| 16 | R2-D2 | 1000.00 | 2000.00 |
| 17 | Stormtrooper | 500.00 | 1000.00 |

### 1977-78 Star Wars 12-Backs B

| | | | |
|---|---|---|---|
| 1 | Ben Kenobi (grey hair) | 1000.00 | 2000.00 |
| 2 | Ben Kenobi (white hair) | 1000.00 | 2000.00 |
| 4 | C-3PO | 400.00 | 750.00 |
| 5 | Chewbacca | 800.00 | 1500.00 |
| 6 | Darth Vader | 1400.00 | 2800.00 |
| 10 | Han Solo (small head) | 1200.00 | 2250.00 |
| 11 | Jawa | 625.00 | 1250.00 |
| 13 | Luke Skywalker (w/blond hair) | 1000.00 | 2000.00 |
| 16 | R2-D2 | 625.00 | 1250.00 |
| 17 | Stormtrooper | 500.00 | 850.00 |
| 18 | Tusken Raider | 500.00 | 850.00 |

### 1977-78 Star Wars 12-Backs C

| | | | |
|---|---|---|---|
| 4 | C-3PO | 400.00 | 750.00 |
| 5 | Chewbacca | 625.00 | 1250.00 |
| 6 | Darth Vader | 1000.00 | 2000.00 |
| 8 | Death Squad Commander | 450.00 | 850.00 |
| 9 | Han Solo (large head) | 850.00 | 1700.00 |
| 11 | Jawa | 600.00 | 1200.00 |
| 13 | Luke Skywalker (blond hair) | 750.00 | 1500.00 |
| 14 | Luke Skywalker (w/telescoping lightsaber) | 4000.00 | 8000.00 |
| 15 | Princess Leia | 500.00 | 1000.00 |
| 16 | R2-D2 | 500.00 | 1000.00 |
| 17 | Stormtrooper | 400.00 | 750.00 |
| 18 | Tusken Raider | 400.00 | 750.00 |

### 1977-78 Star Wars 12-Backs D

| | | | |
|---|---|---|---|
| 4 | C-3PO | 400.00 | 750.00 |
| 5 | Chewbacca | 500.00 | 1000.00 |
| 13 | Luke Skywalker (blond hair) | 500.00 | 1000.00 |
| 15 | Princess Leia | 500.00 | 1000.00 |
| 16 | R2-D2 | 500.00 | 1000.00 |

### 1977-78 Star Wars 12-Backs E

| | | | |
|---|---|---|---|
| 16 | R2-D2 | 350.00 | 850.00 |

### 1977-78 Star Wars 20-Backs A

| | | | |
|---|---|---|---|
| 1 | Ben Kenobi (white hair) | 75.00 | 150.00 |
| 2 | C-3PO | 50.00 | 100.00 |
| 3 | Chewbacca | 60.00 | 120.00 |
| 5 | Death Squad Commander | 60.00 | 120.00 |
| 9 | Han Solo (large head) | 200.00 | 350.00 |
| 10 | Jawa | 75.00 | 150.00 |
| 13 | Princess Leia | 125.00 | 225.00 |
| 18 | Stormtrooper | 50.00 | 100.00 |
| 19 | Tusken Raider | 60.00 | 120.00 |

### 1977-78 Star Wars 20-Backs B

| | | | |
|---|---|---|---|
| 5 | Chewbacca | 60.00 | 120.00 |
| 17 | Stormtrooper | 50.00 | 100.00 |
| 19 | Death Star Droid | 75.00 | 150.00 |
| 20 | Greedo | 60.00 | 120.00 |

| 21 Hammerhead | 100.00 | 200.00 |
|---|---|---|
| 22 Luke X-Wing Pilot | 125.00 | 250.00 |
| 23 Power Droid | 50.00 | 100.00 |
| 24 R5-D4 | 75.00 | 150.00 |
| 25 Snaggletooth (red) | 60.00 | 120.00 |
| 26 Walrus Man | 60.00 | 120.00 |

### 1977-78 Star Wars 20-Backs C

| 5 Chewbacca | 60.00 | 120.00 |
|---|---|---|
| 8 Death Squad Commander | 60.00 | 120.00 |
| 11 Jawa | 75.00 | 150.00 |
| 17 Stormtrooper | 50.00 | 100.00 |
| 21 Hammerhead | 100.00 | 200.00 |
| 22 Luke X-Wing Pilot | 125.00 | 250.00 |

### 1977-78 Star Wars 20-Backs D

| 11 Jawa | 75.00 | 150.00 |
|---|---|---|
| 19 Death Star Droid | 75.00 | 150.00 |
| 22 Luke X-Wing Pilot | 125.00 | 250.00 |
| 24 R5-D4 | 75.00 | 150.00 |

### 1977-78 Star Wars 20-Backs E

| 2 Ben Kenobi (white hair) | 75.00 | 150.00 |
|---|---|---|
| 5 Chewbacca | 60.00 | 120.00 |
| 6 Darth Vader | 100.00 | 200.00 |
| 8 Death Squad Commander | 60.00 | 120.00 |
| 11 Jawa | 75.00 | 150.00 |
| 13 Luke Skywalker (blond hair) | 150.00 | 300.00 |
| 15 Princess Leia | 125.00 | 225.00 |
| 17 Stormtrooper | 50.00 | 100.00 |
| 18 Tusken Raider | 60.00 | 120.00 |
| 20 Greedo | 60.00 | 120.00 |
| 21 Hammerhead | 100.00 | 200.00 |
| 22 Luke X-Wing Pilot | 125.00 | 250.00 |
| 23 Power Droid | 50.00 | 100.00 |
| 24 R5-D4 | 75.00 | 150.00 |
| 25 Snaggletooth (red) | 60.00 | 120.00 |
| 26 Walrus Man | 60.00 | 120.00 |

### 1977-78 Star Wars 20-Backs F

| 6 Darth Vader | 100.00 | 200.00 |
|---|---|---|
| 15 Princess Leia | 125.00 | 225.00 |

### 1977-78 Star Wars 20-Backs G

| 8 Death Squad Commander | 60.00 | 120.00 |
|---|---|---|
| 9 Han Solo (large head) | 200.00 | 350.00 |
| 11 Jawa | 75.00 | 150.00 |
| 13 Luke Skywalker (blond hair) | 150.00 | 300.00 |
| 18 Tusken Raider | 60.00 | 120.00 |

### 1977-78 Star Wars 20-Backs H

| 18 Tusken Raider | 60.00 | 120.00 |
|---|---|---|

### 1977-78 Star Wars 20-Backs I

| 11 Jawa | 80.00 | 150.00 |
|---|---|---|

### 1977-78 Star Wars 20-Backs J

| 11 Jawa | 80.00 | 150.00 |
|---|---|---|
| 17 Stormtrooper | 50.00 | 100.00 |
| 26 Walrus Man | 60.00 | 120.00 |

### 1977-78 Star Wars 20-Backs K

| 11 Jawa | 75.00 | 150.00 |
|---|---|---|
| 17 Stormtrooper | 50.00 | 100.00 |
| 18 Tusken Raider | 60.00 | 120.00 |

### 1977-78 Star Wars 21-Backs A1

| 2 Ben Kenobi (white hair) | 75.00 | 150.00 |
|---|---|---|
| 6 Darth Vader | 100.00 | 200.00 |
| 9 Han Solo (large head) | 350.00 | 350.00 |
| 11 Jawa | 75.00 | 150.00 |

### 1977-78 Star Wars 21-Backs A2

| 13 Luke Skywalker (blond hair) | 150.00 | 300.00 |
|---|---|---|
| 16 R2-D2 | 50.00 | 100.00 |
| 20 Greedo | 60.00 | 120.00 |
| 21 Hammerhead | 100.00 | 200.00 |
| 22 Luke X-Wing Pilot | 125.00 | 250.00 |
| 23 Power Droid | 50.00 | 100.00 |
| 24 R5-D4 | 75.00 | 150.00 |
| 25 Snaggletooth (red) | 60.00 | 120.00 |
| 26 Walrus Man | 60.00 | 120.00 |

### 1977-78 Star Wars 21-Backs B

| 4 C-3PO | 50.00 | 100.00 |
|---|---|---|
| 6 Darth Vader | 100.00 | 200.00 |
| 8 Death Squad Commander | 60.00 | 120.00 |
| 9 Han Solo (large head) | 200.00 | 350.00 |
| 13 Luke Skywalker (blond hair) | 150.00 | 300.00 |
| 15 Princess Leia | 125.00 | 225.00 |
| 16 R2-D2 | 50.00 | 100.00 |
| 18 Tusken Raider | 60.00 | 120.00 |
| 20 Greedo | 60.00 | 120.00 |
| 21 Hammerhead | 100.00 | 200.00 |
| 22 Luke X-Wing Pilot | 125.00 | 250.00 |
| 23 Power Droid | 50.00 | 100.00 |
| 24 R5-D4 | 75.00 | 150.00 |
| 25 Snaggletooth (red) | 60.00 | 120.00 |
| 26 Walrus Man | 60.00 | 120.00 |
| 27 Boba Fett | 3000.00 | 5000.00 |

### 1977-78 Star Wars 21-Backs C

| 2 Ben Kenobi (white hair) | 75.00 | 150.00 |
|---|---|---|
| 4 C-3PO | 50.00 | 100.00 |
| 5 Chewbacca | 60.00 | 120.00 |
| 6 Darth Vader | 100.00 | 200.00 |
| 8 Death Squad Commander | 60.00 | 120.00 |
| 9 Han Solo (large head) | 200.00 | 350.00 |
| 13 Luke Skywalker (blond hair) | 150.00 | 300.00 |
| 15 Princess Leia | 125.00 | 225.00 |
| 16 R2-D2 | 50.00 | 100.00 |
| 20 Greedo | 60.00 | 120.00 |
| 22 Luke X-Wing Pilot | 125.00 | 250.00 |
| 23 Power Droid | 50.00 | 100.00 |
| 25 Snaggletooth (red) | 60.00 | 120.00 |
| 26 Walrus Man | 60.00 | 120.00 |

### 1977-78 Star Wars 21-Backs D

| 13 Luke Skywalker (blond hair) | 60.00 | 300.00 |
|---|---|---|

### 1977-78 Star Wars 21-Backs E4

| 26 Walrus Man | 60.00 | 120.00 |
|---|---|---|

### 1977-78 Star Wars 21-Backs E5

| 26 Walrus Man | 60.00 | 120.00 |
|---|---|---|

| 26 Walrus Man | 60.00 | 120.00 |
|---|---|---|

## 1977-78 Star Wars (loose)

| 1a Ben Kenobi (grey hair) | 20.00 | 50.00 |
|---|---|---|
| 1b Ben Kenobi (white hair) | 20.00 | 50.00 |
| 2 Boba Fett | 25.00 | 60.00 |
| 3 C-3PO | 12.00 | 30.00 |
| 4 Chewbacca | 12.00 | 30.00 |
| 5 Darth Vader | 20.00 | 50.00 |
| 6 Death Squad Commander | 10.00 | 25.00 |
| 7 Death Star Droid | 10.00 | 25.00 |
| 8 Greedo | 12.00 | 30.00 |
| 9 Hammerhead | 12.00 | 30.00 |
| 10a Han Solo (large head) | 20.00 | 50.00 |
| 10b Han Solo (small head) | 20.00 | 50.00 |
| 11 Jawa | 15.00 | 40.00 |
| 12a Luke Skywalker (blond hair) | 20.00 | 50.00 |
| 12b Luke Skywalker (brown hair) | 20.00 | 50.00 |
| 13 Luke Skywalker X-wing | 15.00 | 40.00 |
| 14 Power Droid | 10.00 | 25.00 |
| 15 Princess Leia | 15.00 | 40.00 |
| 16 R2-D2 | 12.00 | 30.00 |
| 17 R5-D4 | 10.00 | 25.00 |
| 18a Snaggletooth blue | 75.00 | 350.00 |
| (found in cantina playset) | | |
| 18b Snaggletooth (red) | 10.00 | 25.00 |
| 19 Stormtrooper | 10.00 | 25.00 |
| 20 Tusken Raider | 10.00 | 25.00 |
| 21 Walrus Man | 10.00 | 25.00 |

## 1978 Star Wars Accessories

| 1 1977 Early Bird Package w/figures Chewbacca, Leia, Luke, R2-D2 | 1750.00 | 3000.00 |
|---|---|---|
| 2 Mini Collector's Case | 120.00 | 250.00 |

## 1978 Star Wars Accessories (loose)

| 10 Mini Collector's Case | 15.00 | 30.00 |
|---|---|---|

## 1978 Star Wars Playsets

| 1 Cantina Adventure Set/Greedo | 400.00 | 800.00 |
|---|---|---|
| Snaggletooth blue/Hammerhead#(Walrusman | | |
| 2 Creature Cantina Action | 300.00 | 600.00 |
| 3 Death Star Space Station | 600.00 | 1200.00 |
| 4 Droid Factory | 200.00 | 400.00 |
| 5 Jawa Sandcrawler (radio controlled) | 1200.00 | 3000.00 |
| 6 Land of the Jawas | 150.00 | 300.00 |

## 1978 Star Wars Playsets (loose)

| 1 Cantina Adventure Set/Greedo | 50.00 | 100.00 |
|---|---|---|
| Snaggletooth blue/Hammerhead#(Walrusman | | |
| 2 Creature Cantina Action | | |
| 3 Death Star Space Station | 75.00 | 150.00 |
| 4 Droid Factory | 30.00 | 60.00 |
| 5 Jawa Sandcrawler (radio controlled) | | |
| 6 Land of the Jawas | 30.00 | 60.00 |

## 1978 Star Wars Vehicles

| 1 Imperial Troop Transporter | 200.00 | 400.00 |
|---|---|---|
| 2 Land Speeder | 125.00 | 250.00 |
| 3 Millenium Falcon | 700.00 | 1200.00 |
| 4 Patrol Dewback | 125.00 | 250.00 |
| 5 Sonic Controlled Land Speeder | 300.00 | 600.00 |
| 6 TIE Fighter | 75.00 | 150.00 |
| 7 TIE Fighter Darth Vader | 150.00 | 300.00 |
| 8 X-Wing Fighter | 100.00 | 200.00 |

## 1978 Star Wars Vehicles (loose)

| 1 Imperial Troop Transporter | 15.00 | 30.00 |
|---|---|---|
| 2 Land Speeder | 15.00 | 30.00 |
| 3 Millenium Falcon | 75.00 | 150.00 |
| 4 Patrol Dewback | 25.00 | 50.00 |
| 5 Sonic Controlled Land Speeder | 100.00 | 200.00 |
| 6 TIE Fighter | 25.00 | 50.00 |
| 7 TIE Fighter Darth Vader | 30.00 | 60.00 |
| 8 X-Wing Fighter | 30.00 | 60.00 |

## 1979-80 Star Wars 12-inch

| 1 Ben Kenobi | 125.00 | 225.00 |
|---|---|---|
| 2 Boba Fett | 300.00 | 600.00 |
| 3 C-3PO | 125.00 | 250.00 |
| 4 Chewbacca | 100.00 | 200.00 |
| 5 Darth Vader | 150.00 | 300.00 |
| 6 Han Solo | 125.00 | 250.00 |
| 7 IG-88 | 600.00 | 1200.00 |
| 8 Jawa | 100.00 | 200.00 |
| 9 Luke Skywalker | 125.00 | 250.00 |
| 10 Princess Leia | 125.00 | 250.00 |
| 11 R2-D2 | 100.00 | 200.00 |
| 12 Stormtrooper | 200.00 | 350.00 |

## 1979-80 Star Wars 12-inch (loose)

| 1 Ben Kenobi | 50.00 | 100.00 |
|---|---|---|
| 2 Boba Fett | 150.00 | 300.00 |
| 3 C-3PO | 20.00 | 40.00 |
| 4 Chewbacca | 30.00 | 60.00 |
| 5 Darth Vader | 50.00 | 100.00 |
| 6 Han Solo | 60.00 | 120.00 |
| 7 IG-88 | 150.00 | 300.00 |
| 8 Jawa | 25.00 | 50.00 |
| 9 Luke Skywalker | 30.00 | 60.00 |
| 10 Princess Leia | 30.00 | 60.00 |
| 11 R2-D2 | 25.00 | 50.00 |
| 12 Stormtrooper | 25.00 | 50.00 |

## 1980-82 Star Wars Empire Strikes Back 21-Backs G

| 5 Ben Kenobi | 50.00 | 100.00 |
|---|---|---|
| 8 Boba Fett | 2750.00 | 5500.00 |
| 10 C-3PO | 60.00 | 120.00 |
| 12 Chewbacca | 50.00 | 100.00 |
| 14 Darth Vader | 100.00 | 200.00 |
| 15 Death Squad Commander | 150.00 | 300.00 |
| 16 Death Star Droid | 50.00 | 100.00 |
| 19 Greedo | 50.00 | 100.00 |
| 20 Hammerhead | 50.00 | 100.00 |
| 21 Han Solo (Large Head) | 60.00 | 120.00 |
| 29 Jawa | 40.00 | 80.00 |
| 37 Luke Skywalker (Blond Hair) | 100.00 | 100.00 |
| 39 Luke X-Wing Pilot | 50.00 | 100.00 |
| 40 Power Droid | 60.00 | 120.00 |
| 41 Princess Leia | 60.00 | 120.00 |
| 46 R2-D2 | 60.00 | 120.00 |

| 48 R5-D4 | | |
|---|---|---|
| 51 Sand People | 50.00 | 100.00 |
| 52 Snaggletooth (Red) | 40.00 | 80.00 |
| 54 Stormtrooper | 50.00 | 100.00 |
| 56 Walrus Man | 50.00 | 100.00 |

### 1980-82 Star Wars Empire Strikes Back 21-Backs
### H1

| 5 Ben Kenobi | 50.00 | 100.00 |
|---|---|---|
| 39 Luke X-Wing Pilot | 50.00 | 100.00 |

### 1980-82 Star Wars Empire Strikes Back 21-Backs
### H2

| 56 Walrus Man | 50.00 | 100.00 |
|---|---|---|

### 1980-82 Star Wars Empire Strikes Back 21-Backs
### I

| 8 Boba Fett | 2250.00 | 4500.00 |
|---|---|---|
| 19 Greedo | 50.00 | 100.00 |
| 20 Hammerhead | 50.00 | 100.00 |

### 1980-82 Star Wars Empire Strikes Back 31-Backs
### A

| 5 Ben Kenobi | 225.00 | 450.00 |
|---|---|---|
| 7 Bespin Security Guard (White) | 150.00 | 300.00 |
| 8 Boba Fett | 1500.00 | 3000.00 |
| 9 Bossk | 350.00 | 675.00 |
| 12 Chewbacca | 350.00 | 675.00 |
| 18 FX-7 | 300.00 | 575.00 |
| 19 Greedo | 275.00 | 550.00 |
| 21 Han Solo (Large Head) | 325.00 | 650.00 |
| 22 Han Solo (Small Head) | 325.00 | 650.00 |
| 24 Han Solo Hoth | 275.00 | 550.00 |
| 25 IG-88 | 300.00 | 600.00 |
| 27 Imperial Stormtrooper Hoth | 225.00 | 450.00 |
| 29 Jawa | 225.00 | 450.00 |
| 39 Luke X-Wing Pilot | 250.00 | 475.00 |
| 40 Power Droid | 225.00 | 450.00 |
| 46 R2-D2 | 225.00 | 450.00 |
| 48 R5-D4 | 225.00 | 450.00 |
| 52 Snaggletooth (Red) | 200.00 | 400.00 |
| 53 Star Destroyer Commander | 200.00 | 400.00 |
| 54 Stormtrooper | 175.00 | 375.00 |

### 1980-82 Star Wars Empire Strikes Back 31-Backs
### B

| 10 C-3PO | 60.00 | 120.00 |
|---|---|---|
| 14 Darth Vader | 100.00 | 200.00 |
| 16 Death Star Droid | 50.00 | 100.00 |
| 20 Hammerhead | 50.00 | 100.00 |
| 31 Lando Calrissian (Without Teeth) | 40.00 | 80.00 |
| 34 Luke Bespin (Blond Hair/Walking) | 100.00 | 200.00 |
| 37 Luke Skywalker (Blond Hair) | 100.00 | 200.00 |
| 41 Princess Leia | 60.00 | 120.00 |
| 42 Princess Leia Bespin (Flesh Neck) | 60.00 | 120.00 |
| 50 Rebel Soldier Hoth | 30.00 | 60.00 |
| 51 Sand People | 50.00 | 100.00 |
| 54 Stormtrooper | 50.00 | 100.00 |
| 56 Walrus Man | 50.00 | 100.00 |

### 1980-82 Star Wars Empire Strikes Back 31-Backs
### C

| 48 R5-D4 | 125.00 | 300.00 |
|---|---|---|

### 1980-82 Star Wars Empire Strikes Back 32-Backs
### A

| 7 Bespin Security Guard (White) | 30.00 | 60.00 |
|---|---|---|
| 8 Boba Fett | 1500.00 | 3000.00 |
| 10 C-3PO | 60.00 | 120.00 |
| 12 Chewbacca | 50.00 | 100.00 |
| 18 FX-7 | 50.00 | 100.00 |
| 24 Han Solo Hoth | 50.00 | 100.00 |
| 25 IG-88 | 60.00 | 120.00 |
| 37 Luke Skywalker (Blond Hair) | 100.00 | 200.00 |
| 41 Princess Leia | 60.00 | 120.00 |
| 50 Rebel Soldier Hoth | 30.00 | 60.00 |
| 54 Stormtrooper | 50.00 | 100.00 |
| 56 Walrus Man | 50.00 | 100.00 |

### 1980-82 Star Wars Empire Strikes Back 32-Backs
### B

| 5 Ben Kenobi | 50.00 | 100.00 |
|---|---|---|
| 9 Bossk | 200.00 | 350.00 |
| 14 Darth Vader | 100.00 | 200.00 |
| 19 Greedo | 50.00 | 100.00 |
| 21 Han Solo (Large Head) | 60.00 | 120.00 |
| 27 Imperial Stormtrooper Hoth | 60.00 | 120.00 |
| 31 Lando Calrissian (Without Teeth) | 40.00 | 80.00 |
| 33 Luke Bespin (Blond Hair/Gun Drawn) | 100.00 | 200.00 |

| 39 Luke X-Wing Pilot | 50.00 | 100.00 |
|---|---|---|
| 42 Princess Leia Bespin (Flesh Neck) | 60.00 | 120.00 |
| 46 R2-D2 | 60.00 | 120.00 |
| 53 Star Destroyer Commander | 150.00 | 300.00 |
| 58 Yoda (Orange Snake) | 75.00 | 150.00 |

### 1980-82 Star Wars Empire Strikes Back 32-Backs
### C

| 7 Bespin Security Guard (White) | 30.00 | 60.00 |
|---|---|---|
| 27 Imperial Stormtrooper Hoth | 60.00 | 120.00 |

### 1980-82 Star Wars Empire Strikes Back 41-Backs
### A

| 1 2-1B | 30.00 | 60.00 |
|---|---|---|
| 2 4-LOM | 75.00 | 150.00 |
| 3 AT-AT Commander | 30.00 | 60.00 |
| 4 AT-AT Driver | 40.00 | 80.00 |
| 5 Ben Kenobi | 50.00 | 100.00 |
| 6 Bespin Security Guard (Black) | 30.00 | 60.00 |
| 7 Bespin Security Guard (White) | 30.00 | 60.00 |
| 8 Boba Fett | 800.00 | 1700.00 |
| 9 Bossk | 50.00 | 100.00 |
| 10 C-3PO | 60.00 | 120.00 |
| 11 C-3PO (Removable Limbs) | 60.00 | 120.00 |
| 12 Chewbacca | 50.00 | 100.00 |
| 13 Cloud Car Pilot | 40.00 | 80.00 |
| 14 Darth Vader | 100.00 | 200.00 |
| 16 Death Star Droid | 50.00 | 100.00 |
| 17 Dengar | 60.00 | 120.00 |
| 18 FX-7 | 50.00 | 100.00 |
| 19 Greedo | 50.00 | 100.00 |
| 20 Hammerhead | 50.00 | 100.00 |
| 21 Han Solo (Large Head) | 60.00 | 120.00 |
| 22 Han Solo (Small Head) | 60.00 | 120.00 |
| 23 Han Solo Bespin | 60.00 | 120.00 |
| 24 Han Solo Hoth | 50.00 | 100.00 |
| 25 IG-88 | 60.00 | 120.00 |
| 26 Imperial Commander | 30.00 | 60.00 |
| 27 Imperial Stormtrooper Hoth | 60.00 | 120.00 |
| 28 Imperial TIE Fighter Pilot | 50.00 | 100.00 |
| 29 Jawa | 40.00 | 80.00 |
| 30 Lando Calrissian (With Teeth) | 40.00 | 80.00 |
| 31 Lando Calrissian (Without Teeth) | 40.00 | 80.00 |
| 32 Lobot | 40.00 | 80.00 |
| 33 Luke Bespin (Blond Hair/Gun Drawn) | 100.00 | 200.00 |
| 35 Luke Bespin (Brown Hair/Gun Drawn) | 100.00 | 200.00 |
| 36 Luke Hoth | 50.00 | 100.00 |

| | | |
|---|---:|---:|
| 37 Luke Skywalker (Blond Hair) | 50.00 | 100.00 |
| 39 Luke X-Wing Pilot | 50.00 | 100.00 |
| 40 Power Droid | 60.00 | 120.00 |
| 41 Princess Leia | 60.00 | 120.00 |
| 45 Princess Leia Hoth | 60.00 | 120.00 |
| 46 R2-D2 | 60.00 | 120.00 |
| 47 R2-D2 (Sensorscope) | 75.00 | 150.00 |
| 48 R5-D4 | | |
| 49 Rebel Commander | 40.00 | 80.00 |
| 50 Rebel Soldier Hoth | 30.00 | 60.00 |
| 51 Sand People | 50.00 | 100.00 |
| 52 Snaggletooth (Red) | 40.00 | 80.00 |
| 53 Star Destroyer Commander | 150.00 | 300.00 |
| 54 Stormtrooper | 50.00 | 100.00 |
| 56 Walrus Man | 50.00 | 100.00 |
| 58 Yoda (Orange Snake) | 75.00 | 150.00 |
| 59 Zuckuss | 50.00 | 100.00 |

### 1980-82 Star Wars Empire Strikes Back 41-Backs
#### B

| | | |
|---|---:|---:|
| 1 2-1B | 30.00 | 60.00 |
| 8 Boba Fett | 500.00 | 1000.00 |
| 9 Bossk | 50.00 | 100.00 |
| 10 C-3PO | 60.00 | 120.00 |
| 18 FX-7 | 50.00 | 100.00 |
| 21 Han Solo (Large Head) | 60.00 | 120.00 |
| 32 Lobot | 40.00 | 80.00 |
| 33 Luke Bespin (Blond Hair/Gun Drawn) | 100.00 | 200.00 |
| 39 Luke X-Wing Pilot | 50.00 | 100.00 |
| 50 Rebel Soldier Hoth | 30.00 | 60.00 |
| 54 Stormtrooper | 50.00 | 100.00 |
| 57 Yoda (Brown Snake) | 300.00 | 600.00 |
| 58 Yoda (Orange Snake) | 75.00 | 150.00 |

### 1980-82 Star Wars Empire Strikes Back 41-Backs
#### C

| | | |
|---|---:|---:|
| 4 AT-AT Driver | 40.00 | 80.00 |
| 7 Bespin Security Guard (White) | 30.00 | 60.00 |
| 12 Chewbacca | 50.00 | 100.00 |
| 24 Han Solo Hoth | 50.00 | 100.00 |
| 25 IG-88 | 60.00 | 120.00 |
| 26 Imperial Commander | 30.00 | 60.00 |
| 29 Jawa | 40.00 | 80.00 |
| 37 Luke Skywalker (Blond Hair) | 100.00 | 200.00 |

| | | |
|---|---:|---:|
| 41 Princess Leia | 60.00 | 120.00 |
| 49 Rebel Commander | 40.00 | 80.00 |
| 55 Ugnaught | 30.00 | 60.00 |
| 56 Walrus Man | 50.00 | 100.00 |

### 1980-82 Star Wars Empire Strikes Back 41-Backs
#### D

| | | |
|---|---:|---:|
| 1 2-1B | 30.00 | 60.00 |
| 8 Boba Fett | 900.00 | 1800.00 |
| 18 FX-7 | 50.00 | 100.00 |
| 21 Han Solo (Large Head) | 60.00 | 120.00 |
| 23 Han Solo Bespin | 60.00 | 120.00 |
| 27 Imperial Stormtrooper Hoth | 60.00 | 120.00 |
| 30 Lando Calrissian (With Teeth) | 40.00 | 80.00 |
| 32 Lobot | 40.00 | 80.00 |
| 35 Luke Bespin (Brown Hair/Gun Drawn) | 100.00 | 200.00 |
| 39 Luke X-Wing Pilot | 50.00 | 100.00 |
| 44 Princess Leia Bespin (Neck Painted/Front) | 60.00 | 120.00 |
| 45 Princess Leia Hoth | 60.00 | 120.00 |
| 50 Rebel Soldier Hoth | 30.00 | 60.00 |
| 54 Stormtrooper | 50.00 | 100.00 |
| 57 Yoda (Brown Snake) | 100.00 | 200.00 |
| 58 Yoda (Orange Snake) | 75.00 | 150.00 |

### 1980-82 Star Wars Empire Strikes Back 41-Backs
#### E

| | | |
|---|---:|---:|
| 4 AT-AT Driver | 40.00 | 80.00 |
| 7 Bespin Security Guard (White) | 30.00 | 60.00 |
| 10 C-3PO | 60.00 | 120.00 |
| 12 Chewbacca | 50.00 | 100.00 |
| 17 Dengar | 60.00 | 120.00 |
| 19 Greedo | 50.00 | 100.00 |
| 24 Han Solo Hoth | 50.00 | 100.00 |
| 25 IG-88 | 60.00 | 120.00 |
| 26 Imperial Commander | 30.00 | 60.00 |
| 27 Imperial Stormtrooper Hoth | 60.00 | 120.00 |
| 29 Jawa | 40.00 | 80.00 |
| 37 Luke Skywalker (Blond Hair) | 100.00 | 200.00 |
| 38 Luke Skywalker (Brown Hair) | 125.00 | 250.00 |
| 41 Princess Leia | 60.00 | 120.00 |
| 49 Rebel Commander | 40.00 | 80.00 |
| 50 Rebel Soldier Hoth | 30.00 | 60.00 |
| 51 Sand People | 50.00 | 100.00 |
| 52 Snaggletooth (Red) | 40.00 | 80.00 |
| 53 Star Destroyer Commander | 150.00 | 300.00 |
| 55 Ugnaught | 30.00 | 60.00 |
| 56 Walrus Man | 50.00 | 100.00 |

### 1980-82 Star Wars Empire Strikes Back 45-Backs
#### A

| | | |
|---|---:|---:|
| 1 2-1B | 30.00 | 60.00 |
| 2 4-LOM | 75.00 | 150.00 |
| 3 AT-AT Commander | 30.00 | 60.00 |
| 5 Ben Kenobi | 50.00 | 100.00 |
| 6 Bespin Security Guard (Black) | 30.00 | 60.00 |
| 7 Bespin Security Guard (White) | 30.00 | 60.00 |
| 9 Bossk | 50.00 | 100.00 |
| 10 C-3PO | 60.00 | 120.00 |
| 12 Chewbacca | 50.00 | 100.00 |
| 13 Cloud Car Pilot | 40.00 | 80.00 |
| 14 Darth Vader | 100.00 | 200.00 |
| 15 Death Squad Commander | 150.00 | 300.00 |
| 16 Death Star Droid | 50.00 | 100.00 |
| 19 Greedo | 50.00 | 100.00 |
| 20 Hammerhead | 50.00 | 100.00 |
| 21 Han Solo (Large Head) | 60.00 | 120.00 |
| 22 Han Solo (Small Head) | 60.00 | 120.00 |
| 23 Han Solo Bespin | 60.00 | 120.00 |
| 24 Han Solo Hoth | 50.00 | 100.00 |
| 26 Imperial Commander | 30.00 | 60.00 |
| 27 Imperial Stormtrooper Hoth | 60.00 | 120.00 |
| 28 Imperial TIE Fighter Pilot | 50.00 | 100.00 |
| 29 Jawa | 40.00 | 80.00 |
| 30 Lando Calrissian (With Teeth) | 40.00 | 80.00 |
| 32 Lobot | 40.00 | 80.00 |
| 34 Luke Bespin (Blond Hair/Walking) | 100.00 | 200.00 |
| 35 Luke Bespin (Brown Hair/Gun Drawn) | 100.00 | 200.00 |
| 36 Luke Hoth | 50.00 | 100.00 |
| 38 Luke Skywalker (Brown Hair) | 100.00 | 200.00 |
| 39 Luke X-Wing Pilot | 50.00 | 100.00 |
| 41 Princess Leia | 60.00 | 120.00 |
| 42 Princess Leia Bespin (Flesh Neck) | 200.00 | 350.00 |
| 44 Princess Leia Bespin (Neck Painted/Front) | 200.00 | 350.00 |
| 45 Princess Leia Hoth | 60.00 | 120.00 |
| 46 R2-D2 | 60.00 | 120.00 |
| 47 R2-D2 (Sensorscope) | 75.00 | 150.00 |
| 48 R5-D4 | | |
| 49 Rebel Commander | 40.00 | 80.00 |
| 50 Rebel Soldier Hoth | 30.00 | 60.00 |
| 51 Sand People | 50.00 | 100.00 |
| 52 Snaggletooth (Red) | 40.00 | 80.00 |
| 53 Star Destroyer Commander | 150.00 | 300.00 |
| 54 Stormtrooper | 50.00 | 100.00 |
| 55 Ugnaught | 30.00 | 60.00 |
| 56 Walrus Man | 50.00 | 100.00 |
| 57 Yoda (Brown Snake) | 100.00 | 200.00 |
| 59 Zuckuss | 50.00 | 100.00 |

## 1980-82 Star Wars Empire Strikes Back 45-Backs
### B

| | | | |
|---|---|---:|---:|
| 3 | AT-AT Commander | 30.00 | 60.00 |
| 6 | Bespin Security Guard (Black) | 30.00 | 60.00 |
| 14 | Darth Vader | 100.00 | 200.00 |
| 27 | Imperial Stormtrooper Hoth | 60.00 | 120.00 |
| 50 | Rebel Soldier Hoth | 30.00 | 60.00 |

## 1980-82 Star Wars Empire Strikes Back 47-Backs
### A

| | | | |
|---|---|---:|---:|
| 1 | 2-1B | 30.00 | 60.00 |
| 2 | 4-LOM | 75.00 | 150.00 |
| 3 | AT-AT Commander | 30.00 | 60.00 |
| 4 | AT-AT Driver | 40.00 | 80.00 |
| 5 | Ben Kenobi | 50.00 | 100.00 |
| 6 | Bespin Security Guard (Black) | 30.00 | 60.00 |
| 7 | Bespin Security Guard (White) | 30.00 | 60.00 |
| 8 | Boba Fett | 600.00 | 1200.00 |
| 9 | Bossk | 50.00 | 100.00 |
| 11 | C-3PO (Removable Limbs) | 60.00 | 120.00 |
| 12 | Chewbacca | 50.00 | 100.00 |
| 13 | Cloud Car Pilot | 40.00 | 80.00 |
| 14 | Darth Vader | 100.00 | 200.00 |
| 15 | Death Squad Commander | 150.00 | 300.00 |
| 16 | Death Star Droid | 50.00 | 100.00 |
| 17 | Dengar | 60.00 | 120.00 |
| 18 | FX-7 | 50.00 | 100.00 |
| 19 | Greedo | 50.00 | 100.00 |
| 20 | Hammerhead | 50.00 | 100.00 |
| 21 | Han Solo (Large Head) | 60.00 | 120.00 |
| 23 | Han Solo Bespin | 60.00 | 120.00 |
| 24 | Han Solo Hoth | 50.00 | 100.00 |
| 25 | IG-88 | 60.00 | 120.00 |
| 26 | Imperial Commander | 30.00 | 60.00 |
| 27 | Imperial Stormtrooper Hoth | 60.00 | 120.00 |
| 28 | Imperial TIE Fighter Pilot | 50.00 | 100.00 |
| 29 | Jawa | 40.00 | 80.00 |
| 30 | Lando Calrissian (With Teeth) | 40.00 | 80.00 |
| 32 | Lobot | 40.00 | 80.00 |
| 35 | Luke Bespin (Brown Hair/Gun Drawn) | 125.00 | 250.00 |
| 36 | Luke Hoth | 50.00 | 100.00 |
| 37 | Luke Skywalker (Blond Hair) | 100.00 | 200.00 |
| 38 | Luke Skywalker (Brown Hair) | 125.00 | 250.00 |
| 39 | Luke X-Wing Pilot | 50.00 | 100.00 |
| 40 | Power Droid | 60.00 | 120.00 |
| 41 | Princess Leia | 60.00 | 120.00 |
| 44 | Princess Leia Bespin (Neck Painted/Front) | | |
| 45 | Princess Leia Hoth | 60.00 | 120.00 |

| | | | |
|---|---|---:|---:|
| 47 | R2-D2 (Sensorscope) | 75.00 | 150.00 |
| 48 | R5-D4 | | |
| 49 | Rebel Commander | 40.00 | 80.00 |
| 50 | Rebel Soldier Hoth | 30.00 | 60.00 |
| 51 | Sand People | 50.00 | 100.00 |
| 52 | Snaggletooth (Red) | 40.00 | 80.00 |
| 53 | Star Destroyer Commander | 150.00 | 300.00 |
| 54 | Stormtrooper | 50.00 | 100.00 |
| 55 | Ugnaught | 30.00 | 60.00 |
| 56 | Walrus Man | 50.00 | 100.00 |
| 57 | Yoda (Brown Snake) | 100.00 | 200.00 |
| 58 | Yoda (Orange Snake) | 75.00 | 150.00 |

## 1980-82 Star Wars Empire Strikes Back 48-Backs
### A

| | | | |
|---|---|---:|---:|
| 1 | 2-1B | 30.00 | 60.00 |
| 3 | AT-AT Commander | 30.00 | 60.00 |
| 5 | Ben Kenobi | 50.00 | 100.00 |
| 6 | Bespin Security Guard (Black) | 30.00 | 60.00 |
| 7 | Bespin Security Guard (White) | 30.00 | 60.00 |
| 11 | C-3PO (Removable Limbs) | 60.00 | 120.00 |
| 12 | Chewbacca | 50.00 | 100.00 |
| 13 | Cloud Car Pilot | 40.00 | 80.00 |
| 24 | Han Solo Hoth | 50.00 | 100.00 |
| 26 | Imperial Commander | 30.00 | 60.00 |
| 27 | Imperial Stormtrooper Hoth | 60.00 | 120.00 |
| 28 | Imperial TIE Fighter Pilot | 50.00 | 100.00 |
| 36 | Luke Hoth | 50.00 | 100.00 |
| 39 | Luke X-Wing Pilot | 50.00 | 100.00 |
| 45 | Princess Leia Hoth | 60.00 | 120.00 |
| 47 | R2-D2 (Sensorscope) | 75.00 | 150.00 |
| 49 | Rebel Commander | 40.00 | 80.00 |
| 51 | Sand People | 50.00 | 100.00 |
| 52 | Snaggletooth (Red) | 40.00 | 80.00 |
| 54 | Stormtrooper | 50.00 | 100.00 |
| 59 | Zuckuss | 50.00 | 100.00 |

## 1980-82 Star Wars Empire Strikes Back 48-Backs
### B

| | | | |
|---|---|---:|---:|
| 2 | 4-LOM | 75.00 | 150.00 |
| 5 | Ben Kenobi | 50.00 | 100.00 |
| 6 | Bespin Security Guard (Black) | 30.00 | 60.00 |
| 7 | Bespin Security Guard (White) | 30.00 | 60.00 |
| 9 | Bossk | 50.00 | 100.00 |
| 11 | C-3PO (Removable Limbs) | 60.00 | 120.00 |
| 14 | Darth Vader | 100.00 | 200.00 |
| 17 | Dengar | 60.00 | 120.00 |
| 18 | FX-7 | 50.00 | 100.00 |
| 26 | Imperial Commander | 30.00 | 60.00 |
| 27 | Imperial Stormtrooper Hoth | 60.00 | 120.00 |
| 28 | Imperial TIE Fighter Pilot | 50.00 | 100.00 |
| 30 | Lando Calrissian (With Teeth) | 40.00 | 80.00 |
| 33 | Luke Bespin (Blond Hair/Gun Drawn) | 100.00 | 200.00 |
| 35 | Luke Bespin (Brown Hair/Gun Drawn) | 125.00 | 250.00 |
| 39 | Luke X-Wing Pilot | 50.00 | 100.00 |
| 49 | Rebel Commander | 40.00 | 80.00 |
| 50 | Rebel Soldier Hoth | 40.00 | 80.00 |
| 54 | Stormtrooper | 50.00 | 100.00 |
| 55 | Ugnaught | 30.00 | 60.00 |
| 57 | Yoda (Brown Snake) | 100.00 | 200.00 |
| 59 | Zuckuss | 50.00 | 100.00 |

## 1980-82 Star Wars Empire Strikes Back 48-Backs
### C

| | | | |
|---|---|---:|---:|
| 1 | 2-1B | 25.00 | 60.00 |
| 2 | 4-LOM | 80.00 | 150.00 |
| 3 | AT-AT Commander | 25.00 | 60.00 |
| 4 | AT-AT Driver | 30.00 | 80.00 |
| 5 | Ben Kenobi | 50.00 | 100.00 |
| 6 | Bespin Security Guard (Black) | 25.00 | 60.00 |
| 8 | Boba Fett | 225.00 | 450.00 |
| 9 | Bossk | 50.00 | 100.00 |
| 11 | C-3PO (Removable Limbs) | 60.00 | 120.00 |
| 12 | Chewbacca | 50.00 | 100.00 |
| 13 | Cloud Car Pilot | 40.00 | 80.00 |
| 14 | Darth Vader | 100.00 | 200.00 |
| 18 | FX-7 | 50.00 | 100.00 |
| 23 | Han Solo Bespin | 60.00 | 120.00 |
| 24 | Han Solo Hoth | 50.00 | 100.00 |
| 25 | IG-88 | 60.00 | 120.00 |
| 26 | Imperial Commander | 30.00 | 60.00 |
| 28 | Imperial TIE Fighter Pilot | 50.00 | 100.00 |
| 29 | Jawa | 40.00 | 80.00 |
| 30 | Lando Calrissian (With Teeth) | 40.00 | 80.00 |
| 32 | Lobot | 40.00 | 80.00 |
| 35 | Luke Bespin (Brown Hair/Gun Drawn) | 100.00 | 200.00 |
| 36 | Luke Hoth | 50.00 | 100.00 |
| 39 | Luke X-Wing Pilot | 50.00 | 100.00 |
| 49 | Rebel Commander | 40.00 | 80.00 |
| 50 | Rebel Soldier Hoth | 30.00 | 60.00 |
| 51 | Sand People | 50.00 | 100.00 |
| 52 | Snaggletooth (Red) | 40.00 | 80.00 |
| 53 | Star Destroyer Commander | 150.00 | 300.00 |
| 54 | Stormtrooper | 50.00 | 100.00 |
| 55 | Ugnaught | 30.00 | 60.00 |
| 57 | Yoda (Brown Snake) | 100.00 | 200.00 |
| 59 | Zuckuss | 50.00 | 100.00 |

## 1980-82 Star Wars Empire Strikes Back (loose)

| | | | |
|---|---|---:|---:|
| 1 | 2-1B | 6.00 | 12.00 |
| 2 | 4-LOM | 12.50 | 25.00 |
| 3 | AT-AT Commander | 6.00 | 12.00 |
| 4 | AT-AT Driver | 7.50 | 15.00 |
| 5a | Ben Kenobi (grey hair) | 10.00 | 20.00 |
| 5b | Ben Kenobi (white hair) | 10.00 | 20.00 |
| 6a | Bespin guard (black) | 6.00 | 12.00 |
| 6b | Bespin guard (white) | 6.00 | 12.00 |
| 7 | Boba Fett | 25.00 | 50.00 |
| 8 | Bossk | 7.50 | 15.00 |
| 9 | C-3PO | 7.50 | 15.00 |
| 10 | C-3PO (removable limbs) | 7.50 | 15.00 |
| 11 | Chewbacca | 6.00 | 12.00 |
| 12 | Cloud Car Pilot | 6.00 | 12.00 |
| 13 | Darth Vader | 10.00 | 20.00 |
| 14 | Death Squad Commander | 10.00 | 20.00 |
| 15 | Death Star Droid | 6.00 | 12.00 |
| 16 | Dengar | 6.00 | 12.00 |
| 17 | FX-7 | 6.00 | 12.00 |
| 18 | Greedo | 6.00 | 12.00 |
| 19 | Hammerhead | 6.00 | 12.00 |
| 20 | Han Solo (Bespin) | 7.50 | 15.00 |
| 21 | Han Solo (Hoth gear) | 6.00 | 12.00 |
| 22 | Han Solo (large head) | 6.00 | 12.00 |
| 23 | Han Solo (small head) | 6.00 | 12.00 |
| 24 | IG-88 | 7.50 | 15.00 |
| 25 | Imperial Commander | 6.00 | 12.00 |
| 26 | Imperial Stormtrooper | 7.50 | 15.00 |

| | | |
|---|---:|---:|
| 27 Jawa | 6.00 | 12.00 |
| 28 Lando Calrissian | 6.00 | 12.00 |
| 29 Lando Calrissian (no teeth) | 6.00 | 12.00 |
| 30 Lobot | 7.50 | 15.00 |
| 31a Luke Skywalker | 10.00 | 20.00 |
| (Bespin yellow hair tan legs) | | |
| 31b Luke Skywalker | | |
| (Bespin yellow hair brown legs) | | |
| 31c Luke Skywalker | 10.00 | 20.00 |
| (Bespin brown hair) | | |
| 31d Luke Skywalker | 12.50 | 20.00 |
| (Bespin white shirt blond hair) | | |
| 31e Luke Skywalker | 12.50 | 25.00 |
| (Bespin white shirt brown hair) | | |
| 32 Luke Skywalker (Hoth gear) | 6.00 | 12.00 |
| 33 Luke Skywalker X-wing | 6.00 | 12.00 |
| 34 Power Droid | 7.50 | 15.00 |
| 35a Princess Leia Organa | 7.50 | 15.00 |
| (Bespin flesh neck) | | |
| 35b Princess Leia Organa | 7.50 | 15.00 |
| (Bespin turtle neck) | | |
| 35c Princess Leia Organa | | |
| (Bespin gold/green neck) | | |
| 36 Leia Organa (Hoth gear) | 7.50 | 15.00 |
| 37a R2-D2 | 7.50 | 15.00 |
| 37b R2-D2 (sensorscope) | 7.50 | 15.00 |
| 38 R5-D4 | | |
| 39 Rebel Commander | 6.00 | 12.00 |
| 40 Rebel Soldier (Hoth gear) | 6.00 | 12.00 |
| 41 Snaggletooth (red) | 6.00 | 12.00 |
| 42 Stormtrooper | 6.00 | 12.00 |
| 43 TIE Fighter Pilot | 6.00 | 12.00 |
| 44 Tusken Raider | 6.00 | 12.00 |
| 45 Ugnaught | | 12.00 |
| 46 Walrusman | 6.00 | 12.00 |
| 48a Yoda (brown snake) | 7.50 | 15.00 |
| 48b Yoda (orange snake) | 7.50 | 15.00 |
| 49 Zuckuss | 6.00 | 12.00 |

### 1980-82 Star Wars Empire Strikes Back Accessories

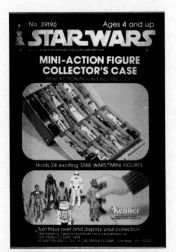

| | | |
|---|---:|---:|
| 1 Darth Vader Case | 200.00 | 350.00 |
| 2 Darth Vader Case/Boba Fett/IG88 | 200.00 | 400.00 |
| 3 Mini Collector's Case | 125.00 | 225.00 |

### 1980-82 Star Wars Empire Strikes Back Accessories (loose)

| | | |
|---|---:|---:|
| 1 Darth Vader Case | 15.00 | 30.00 |
| 2 Mini Collector's Case | 15.00 | 30.00 |

### 1980-82 Star Wars Empire Strikes Back Playsets

| | | |
|---|---:|---:|
| 1 Cloud City | 200.00 | 400.00 |
| 2 Dagobah | 125.00 | 250.00 |
| 3 Darth Vader/ Star Destroyer | 125.00 | 250.00 |
| 4 Droid Factory | 200.00 | 350.00 |
| 5 Hoth Ice Planet | 75.00 | 150.00 |
| 6 Imperial Attack Base | 125.00 | 225.00 |
| 7 Land of the Jawas | 100.00 | 200.00 |
| 8 Rebel Command Center | 100.00 | 200.00 |
| 9 Turret and Probot | 40.00 | 80.00 |

### 1980-82 Star Wars Empire Strikes Back Playsets (loose)

| | | |
|---|---:|---:|
| 1 Cloud City | 30.00 | 60.00 |
| 2 Dagobah | 25.00 | 50.00 |
| 3 Darth Vader/ Star Destroyer | 25.00 | 50.00 |
| 4 Droid Factory | 30.00 | 60.00 |
| 5 Hoth Ice Planet | 20.00 | 40.00 |
| 6 Imperial Attack Base | 30.00 | 60.00 |
| 7 Land of the Jawas | 30.00 | 60.00 |
| 8 Rebel Command Center | 30.00 | 60.00 |
| 9 Turret and Probot | 12.50 | 25.00 |

### 1980-82 Star Wars Empire Strikes Back Vehicles

| | | |
|---|---:|---:|
| 1 AT-AT | 150.00 | 300.00 |
| 2 Imperial Cruiser | 100.00 | 200.00 |
| 3 Imperial Transport | 100.00 | 200.00 |
| 4 Millenium Falcon | 250.00 | 500.00 |
| 5 Patrol Dewback | 100.00 | 200.00 |
| 6 Rebel Transport | 100.00 | 200.00 |
| 7 Scout Walker | 75.00 | 150.00 |
| 8 Slave 1 | 100.00 | 200.00 |
| 9a Snowspeeder (blue box) | 60.00 | 120.00 |
| 9b Snowspeeder (pink box) | 75.00 | 150.00 |
| 10 Tauntaun | 50.00 | 100.00 |
| 11 Tauntaun (split belly) | 60.00 | 120.00 |
| 12 TIE Fighter | 75.00 | 150.00 |
| 13 Twin Pod Cloud Car | 40.00 | 80.00 |

| | | |
|---|---:|---:|
| 14 Wampa | 150.00 | 300.00 |
| 15a X-Wing Fighter (battle damage red photo background box) | 100.00 | 200.00 |
| 15b X-Wing Fighter (battle damage landscape photo background box) | 100.00 | 200.00 |

### 1980-82 Star Wars Empire Strikes Back Vehicles (loose)

| | | |
|---|---:|---:|
| 1 AT-AT | 40.00 | 80.00 |
| 2 Imperial Cruiser | 15.00 | 30.00 |
| 3 Imperial Transport | 15.00 | 30.00 |
| 4 Millenium Falcon | 50.00 | 100.00 |
| 5 Patrol Dewback | 25.00 | 50.00 |
| 6 Rebel Transport | 15.00 | 30.00 |
| 7 Scout Walker | 15.00 | 30.00 |
| 8 Slave 1 | 60.00 | 125.00 |
| 9 Snowspeeder | 15.00 | 30.00 |
| 10 Tauntaun | 20.00 | 40.00 |
| 11 Tauntaun split belly | 25.00 | 50.00 |
| 12 TIE Fighter | 25.00 | 50.00 |
| 13 Twin Pod Cloud Car | 20.00 | 40.00 |
| 14 Wampa | 25.00 | 60.00 |
| 15 X-Wing Fighter | 30.00 | 60.00 |

### 1980 Star Wars Empire Strikes Back Micro Set

| | | |
|---|---:|---:|
| 1 Bespin Control Room/Darth Vader | 30.00 | 60.00 |
| Darth Vader lightsaber/Luke Skywalker | | |
| 2 Bespin Freeze Chamber/Boba Fett | 75.00 | 150.00 |
| Darth Vader/Han Solo in cuffs/Han Solo | | |
| 3 Bespin Gantry/Darth Vader | 40.00 | 80.00 |
| Darth Vader lightsaber/Luke Skywalker | | |
| 4 Bespin World/Boba Fett/Darth Vader | 100.00 | 200.00 |
| Darth Vader lightsaber/Han Solo carbonite | | |
| 5 Death Star Compactor/Ben Kenobi | 125.00 | 225.00 |
| Darth Vader lightsaber/Han Solo stormtrooper | | |
| 6 Death Star Escape/Chewbacca | 40.00 | 80.00 |
| Darth Vader/Luke Skywalker#{Princess Leia | | |
| 7 Death Star World/Ben Kenobi | 125.00 | 225.00 |
| Chewbacca/Darth Vader#{Darth Vader lightsaber/Han Solo#{Luke Skywalker/Luke Skywalker stormtrooper#{Princess Leia/Princess Leia holding gun#{Stormtrooper kneeling/Stormtrooper walking#{Stormtrooper firing/Stormtrooper firing u | | |
| 8 Hoth Generator Attack/AT-AT | 30.00 | 60.00 |
| AT-AT Operator/Darth Vader unpainted#{Rebel | | |
| 9 Hoth Ion Cannon/Rebel on Tauntaun | 50.00 | 100.00 |
| Rebel crouching/Rebel laying | | |
| 10 Hoth Turret Defense | 40.00 | 80.00 |
| Rebel on Tauntaun blaster#{Rebel crouching | | |
| 11 Hoth Wampa Cave/Chewbacca | 30.00 | 60.00 |
| Han Solo/Luke Skywalker hanging#{Probot/Wampa | | |
| 12 Hoth World/Hot Wampa Cave | 100.00 | 200.00 |
| Hoth Ion Cannon/Hoth Generator Attack | | |

| | | |
|---|---|---|
| 13 Imperial TIE Fighter | 50.00 | 100.00 |
| TIE Fighter Pilot | | |
| 14 Millenium Falcon/C-3PO | 150.00 | 300.00 |
| Chewbacca with wrench/Lando Calrissian#{Luke Skywalker | | |
| 15 Snowspeeder | 75.00 | 150.00 |
| X-Wing Pilot sitting#{X-Wing Pilot crouching | | |
| 16 X-Wing/X-Wing Pilot | 75.00 | 150.00 |

## 1980 Star Wars Empire Strikes Back Micro Set (loose)

| | | |
|---|---|---|
| 1 Bespin Control Room | 7.50 | 15.00 |
| 2 Bespin Freeze Chamber | 12.50 | 25.00 |
| 3 Bespin Gantry | 7.50 | 15.00 |
| 4 Bespin World | 12.50 | 25.00 |
| 5 Death Star Compactor | 12.50 | 25.00 |
| 6 Death Star Escape | 7.50 | 15.00 |
| 7 Death Star World | 12.50 | 25.00 |
| 8 Hoth Generator Attack | 7.50 | 15.00 |
| 9 Hoth Ion Cannon | 10.00 | 20.00 |
| 10 Hoth Turret Defense | 6.00 | 12.00 |
| 11 Hoth Wampa Cave | 7.50 | 15.00 |
| 12 Hoth World | 12.50 | 25.00 |
| 13 Imperial Tie Fighter | 6.00 | 12.00 |
| 14 Millenium Falcon | 12.50 | 25.00 |
| 15 Snowspeeder | 6.00 | 12.00 |
| 16 X-Wing | 7.50 | 15.00 |
| 17 AT-AT | 6.00 | 12.00 |
| 18 AT-AT Operator | .75 | 2.00 |
| 19 Ben Kenobi | 1.50 | 4.00 |
| 20 Boba Fett | .75 | 2.00 |
| 21 C-3PO | .75 | 2.00 |
| 22 Chewbacca | .75 | 2.00 |
| 23 Chewbacca (with wrench) | .75 | 2.00 |
| 24 Darth Vader | 1.25 | 3.00 |
| 25 Darth Vader (lightsaber) | 1.25 | 3.00 |
| 26 Darth Vader (unpainted) | 1.25 | 3.00 |
| 27 Han Solo | 1.25 | 3.00 |
| 28 Han Solo (carbonite) | 1.25 | 3.00 |
| 29 Han Solo (in cuffs) | 1.25 | 3.00 |
| 30 Han Solo (stormtrooper) | 1.25 | 3.00 |
| 31 Lando Calrissian | .75 | 2.00 |
| 32 Lobot | .75 | 2.00 |
| 33 Luke Skywalker | 1.25 | 3.00 |
| 34 Luke Skywalker (hanging) | 1.25 | 3.00 |
| 35 Luke Skywalker (lightsaber) | 1.25 | 3.00 |
| 36 Luke Skywalker (stormtrooper) | 1.25 | 3.00 |
| 37 Princess Leia | 1.25 | 3.00 |
| 38 Princess Leia (holding gun) | 1.25 | 3.00 |
| 39 Probot | .75 | 2.00 |
| 40 Rebel (crouching) | .75 | 2.00 |
| 41 Rebel (gun at side/unpainted) | .75 | 2.00 |
| 42 Rebel (gun on hip/unpainted) | .75 | 2.00 |
| 43 Rebel (gun on shoulder/unpainted) | .75 | 2.00 |
| 44 Rebel (gun on shoulder) | .75 | 2.00 |
| 45 Rebel (laying) | .75 | 2.00 |
| 46 Rebel (laying unpainted) | .75 | 2.00 |
| 47 Rebel (on Tauntaun) | .75 | 2.00 |
| 48 Rebel (on Tauntaun w/blaster) | .75 | 2.00 |
| 49 Rebel (w/blaster at side) | .75 | 2.00 |
| 50 Rebel (w/blaster brown) | .75 | 2.00 |
| 51 Rebel (w/blaster white) | .75 | 2.00 |
| 52 Stormtrooper | .75 | 2.00 |
| 53 Stormtrooper (firing) | .75 | 2.00 |
| 54 Stormtrooper (kneeling) | .75 | 2.00 |
| 55 Stormtrooper (on gun) | .75 | 2.00 |
| 56 Stormtrooper (walking) | .75 | 2.00 |

| | | |
|---|---|---|
| 57 TIE Fighter Pilot | .75 | 2.00 |
| 58 Turret Operator | .75 | 2.00 |
| 59 Wampa | 1.00 | 2.50 |
| 60 X-Wing Pilot | .75 | 2.00 |
| 61 X-Wing Pilot (crouching) | .75 | 2.00 |
| 62 X-Wing Pilot (sitting) | .75 | 2.00 |

## 1980 Star Wars Empire Strikes Back Mini Rigs

| | | |
|---|---|---|
| 1 CAP-2 | 10.00 | 20.00 |
| 2 INT-4 | 20.00 | 40.00 |
| 3 MLC-3 | 12.50 | 25.00 |
| 4 MTV-7 | 20.00 | 40.00 |
| 5 PDT-8 | 15.00 | 30.00 |
| 6 Tripod Laser Canon | 20.00 | 40.00 |

## 1980 Star Wars Empire Strikes Back Mini Rigs (loose)

| | | |
|---|---|---|
| 1 CAP-2 | 5.00 | 10.00 |
| 2 INT-4 | 7.50 | 15.00 |
| 3 MLC-3 | 5.00 | 10.00 |
| 4 MTV-7 | 6.00 | 12.00 |
| 5 PDT-8 | 7.50 | 15.00 |
| 6 Tripod Laser Canon | 7.50 | 15.00 |

## 1983 Star Wars Return of the Jedi 48-Backs D

| | | |
|---|---|---|
| 1 2-1B | 40.00 | 80.00 |
| 2 4-LOM | 40.00 | 80.00 |
| 5 AT-AT Commander | 25.00 | 50.00 |
| 6 AT-AT Driver | 40.00 | 80.00 |
| 8 Ben Kenobi | 30.00 | 60.00 |
| 10 Bespin Security Guard (black) | 30.00 | 60.00 |
| 11 Bespin Security Guard (white) | 30.00 | 60.00 |
| 14 Boba Fett | 300.00 | 700.00 |
| 16 Bossk | 40.00 | 80.00 |
| 18 C-3PO (removable limbs) | 40.00 | 80.00 |
| 19 Chewbacca | 40.00 | 80.00 |
| 22 Cloud Car Pilot | 30.00 | 60.00 |
| 23 Darth Vader | 60.00 | 120.00 |
| 25 Death Star Droid | 30.00 | 60.00 |
| 26 Dengar | 30.00 | 60.00 |
| 28 FX-7 | 30.00 | 60.00 |
| 31 Greedo | 40.00 | 80.00 |
| 32 Hammerhead | 25.00 | 50.00 |
| 33 Han Solo (large head) | 100.00 | 200.00 |
| 35 Han Solo (Bespin) | 60.00 | 120.00 |
| 36 Han Solo (Hoth gear) | 60.00 | 120.00 |
| 38 IG-88 | 20.00 | 40.00 |
| 39 Imperial Commander | 40.00 | 80.00 |
| 40 Imperial Stormtrooper Hoth | 40.00 | 80.00 |
| 41 Imperial TIE Fighter Pilot | 50.00 | 100.00 |
| 42 Jawa | 50.00 | 100.00 |
| 46 Lando Calrissian (with teeth) | 30.00 | 60.00 |
| 47 Lobot | 30.00 | 60.00 |
| 49 Luke Bespin (brown hair gun drawn) | 150.00 | 300.00 |
| 50 Luke Hoth | 60.00 | 120.00 |
| 55 Luke Skywalker (brown hair) | | |
| 56 Luke X-Wing Pilot | 100.00 | 200.00 |
| 61 Power Droid | 50.00 | 100.00 |
| 62 Princess Leia | 450.00 | 800.00 |
| 63 Princess Leia (Bespin neck painted front) | | |

| | | |
|---|---|---|
| 66 Princess Leia (Hoth) | 125.00 | 250.00 |
| 68 R2-D2 (sensorscope) | 40.00 | 80.00 |
| 69 R5-D4 | 50.00 | 100.00 |
| 71 Rebel Commander | 40.00 | 80.00 |
| 75 Sand People | 40.00 | 80.00 |
| 76 Snaggletooth (red) | 50.00 | 100.00 |
| 78 Star Destroyer Commander | | |
| 79 Stormtrooper | 50.00 | 100.00 |
| 82 Ugnaught | 40.00 | 80.00 |
| 83 Walrus Man | 30.00 | 60.00 |
| 86 Yoda (brown snake) | 60.00 | 120.00 |
| 88 Zuckuss | 20.00 | 40.00 |

## 1983 Star Wars Return of the Jedi 65-Backs A

| | | |
|---|---|---|
| 2 4-LOM | 40.00 | 80.00 |
| 4 Admiral Ackbar | 25.00 | 50.00 |
| 6 AT-AT Driver | 40.00 | 80.00 |
| 8 Ben Kenobi | 30.00 | 60.00 |
| 10 Bespin Security Guard (black) | 30.00 | 60.00 |
| 12 Bib Fortuna | 25.00 | 50.00 |
| 13 Biker Scout | 30.00 | 60.00 |
| 14 Boba Fett | 250.00 | 500.00 |
| 18 C-3PO (removable limbs) | 40.00 | 80.00 |
| 19 Chewbacca | 40.00 | 80.00 |
| 21 Chief Chirpa | 20.00 | 40.00 |
| 22 Cloud Car Pilot | 30.00 | 60.00 |
| 23 Darth Vader | 60.00 | 120.00 |
| 25 Death Star Droid | 30.00 | 60.00 |
| 26 Dengar | 30.00 | 60.00 |
| 27 Emperor's Royal Guard | 40.00 | 80.00 |
| 29 Gamorrean Guard | 25.00 | 50.00 |
| 30 General Madine | 20.00 | 40.00 |
| 33 Han Solo (large head) | 100.00 | 200.00 |
| 41 Imperial TIE Fighter Pilot | 50.00 | 100.00 |
| 42 Jawa | 50.00 | 100.00 |
| 43 Klaatu | 20.00 | 40.00 |
| 45 Lando Calrisian (skiff) | 25.00 | 50.00 |
| 48 Logray | 20.00 | 40.00 |
| 50 Luke Hoth | 60.00 | 120.00 |
| 51 Luke Jedi Knight (blue lightsaber) | 75.00 | 150.00 |
| 52 Luke Jedi Knight (green lightsaber) | 75.00 | 150.00 |
| 56 Luke X-Wing Pilot | 100.00 | 200.00 |
| 58 Nien Nunb | 25.00 | 50.00 |
| 64 Princess Leia (Boushh) | 40.00 | 80.00 |
| 68 R2-D2 (sensorscope) | 40.00 | 80.00 |

| | | |
|---|---|---|
| 72 Rebel Commando | 20.00 | 40.00 |
| 74 Ree-Yees | 20.00 | 40.00 |
| 77 Squid Head | 20.00 | 40.00 |
| 79 Stormtrooper | 50.00 | 100.00 |
| 84 Weequay | 20.00 | 40.00 |
| 86 Yoda (brown snake) | 60.00 | 120.00 |
| 87 Yoda (brown snake/new image) | 60.00 | 120.00 |
| 88 Zuckuss | 20.00 | 40.00 |

## 1983 Star Wars Return of the Jedi 65-Backs B

| | | |
|---|---|---|
| 1 2-1B | 40.00 | 80.00 |
| 2 4-LOM | 40.00 | 80.00 |
| 4 Admiral Ackbar | 25.00 | 50.00 |
| 5 AT-AT Commander | 25.00 | 50.00 |
| 6 AT-AT Driver | 40.00 | 80.00 |
| 8 Ben Kenobi | 30.00 | 60.00 |
| 10 Bespin Security Guard (black) | 30.00 | 60.00 |
| 12 Bib Fortuna | 25.00 | 50.00 |
| 13 Biker Scout | 30.00 | 60.00 |
| 16 Bossk | 40.00 | 80.00 |
| 18 C-3PO (removable limbs) | 40.00 | 80.00 |
| 19 Chewbacca | 40.00 | 80.00 |
| 21 Chief Chirpa | 20.00 | 40.00 |
| 22 Cloud Car Pilot | 30.00 | 60.00 |
| 23 Darth Vader | 60.00 | 120.00 |
| 24 Darth Vader (new image) | 60.00 | 120.00 |
| 25 Death Star Droid | 30.00 | 60.00 |
| 27 Emperor's Royal Guard | 40.00 | 80.00 |
| 29 Gamorrean Guard | 25.00 | 50.00 |
| 30 General Madine | 20.00 | 40.00 |
| 33 Han Solo (large head) | 100.00 | 200.00 |
| 35 Han Solo (Bespin) | 60.00 | 120.00 |
| 36 Han Solo (Hoth gear) | 60.00 | 120.00 |
| 38 IG-88 | 20.00 | 40.00 |
| 39 Imperial Commander | 40.00 | 80.00 |
| 40 Imperial Stormtrooper Hoth | 40.00 | 80.00 |
| 41 Imperial TIE Fighter Pilot | 50.00 | 100.00 |
| 42 Jawa | | |
| 43 Klaatu | 20.00 | 40.00 |
| 45 Lando Calrisian (skiff) | 25.00 | 50.00 |
| 46 Lando Calrissian (with teeth) | 30.00 | 60.00 |
| 48 Logray | 20.00 | 40.00 |
| 51 Luke Jedi Knight (blue lightsaber) | 75.00 | 150.00 |
| 53 Luke Skywalker (blond hair) | 100.00 | 200.00 |
| 56 Luke X-Wing Pilot | 100.00 | 200.00 |
| 58 Nien Nunb | 25.00 | 50.00 |
| 61 Power Droid | 50.00 | 100.00 |
| 63 Princess Leia (Bespin neck painted/front picture) | | |
| 64 Princess Leia (Boushh) | 40.00 | 80.00 |
| 66 Princess Leia (Hoth gear) | 125.00 | 250.00 |
| 68 R2-D2 (sensorscope) | 40.00 | 80.00 |
| 69 R5-D4 | 50.00 | 100.00 |
| 71 Rebel Commander | 30.00 | 60.00 |
| 72 Rebel Commando | 20.00 | 40.00 |
| 73 Rebel Soldier Hoth | 50.00 | 100.00 |
| 74 Ree-Yees | 20.00 | 40.00 |
| 75 Sand People | 40.00 | 80.00 |
| 77 Squid Head | 20.00 | 40.00 |
| 78 Star Destroyer Commander | | |
| 79 Stormtrooper | 50.00 | 100.00 |
| 82 Ugnaught | 40.00 | 80.00 |
| 84 Weequay | 20.00 | 40.00 |
| 86 Yoda (brown snake) | 60.00 | 120.00 |
| 88 Zuckuss | 20.00 | 40.00 |

## 1983 Star Wars Return of the Jedi 65-Backs C

| | | |
|---|---|---|
| 2 4-LOM | 40.00 | 80.00 |
| 4 Admiral Ackbar | 25.00 | 50.00 |
| 9 Ben Kenobi (new image) | 30.00 | 60.00 |
| 12 Bib Fortuna | 25.00 | 50.00 |
| 13 Biker Scout | 40.00 | 80.00 |
| 15 Boba Fett (new image) | 350.00 | 700.00 |
| 18 C-3PO (removable limbs) | 40.00 | 80.00 |
| 20 Chewbacca (new image) | 40.00 | 80.00 |
| 21 Chief Chirpa | 20.00 | 40.00 |
| 23 Darth Vader | 60.00 | 120.00 |
| 24 Darth Vader (new image) | 60.00 | 120.00 |
| 27 Emperor's Royal Guard | 40.00 | 80.00 |
| 29 Gamorrean Guard | 25.00 | 50.00 |
| 30 General Madine | 20.00 | 40.00 |
| 34 Han Solo (large head/new image) | 100.00 | 200.00 |
| 41 Imperial TIE Fighter Pilot | 40.00 | 80.00 |
| 42 Jawa | 50.00 | 100.00 |
| 43 Klaatu | 20.00 | 40.00 |
| 44 Klaatu (skiff) | | |
| 45 Lando Calrisian (skiff) | 25.00 | 50.00 |
| 48 Logray | 20.00 | 40.00 |
| 51 Luke Jedi Knight (blue lightsaber) | 75.00 | 150.00 |
| 52 Luke Jedi Knight (green lightsaber) | 75.00 | 150.00 |
| 58 Nien Nunb | 25.00 | 50.00 |
| 64 Princess Leia (Boushh) | 40.00 | 80.00 |
| 68 R2-D2 (sensorscope) | 40.00 | 80.00 |
| 72 Rebel Commando | 20.00 | 40.00 |
| 74 Ree-Yees | 20.00 | 40.00 |
| 77 Squid Head | 20.00 | 40.00 |
| 79 Stormtrooper | 50.00 | 100.00 |
| 84 Weequay | 20.00 | 40.00 |
| 87 Yoda (brown snake/new image) | 60.00 | 120.00 |
| 88 Zuckuss | 20.00 | 40.00 |

## 1983 Star Wars Return of the Jedi 65-Backs D

| | | |
|---|---|---|
| 1 2-1B | 40.00 | 80.00 |
| 4 Admiral Ackbar | 25.00 | 50.00 |
| 13 Biker Scout | 40.00 | 80.00 |
| 19 Chewbacca | 40.00 | 80.00 |
| 21 Chief Chirpa | 20.00 | 40.00 |
| 24 Darth Vader (new image) | 60.00 | 120.00 |
| 29 Gamorrean Guard | 25.00 | 50.00 |

## 1983 Star Wars Return of the Jedi 65-Backs E

| | | |
|---|---|---|
| 30 General Madine | 20.00 | 40.00 |

## 1983 Star Wars Return of the Jedi 77-Backs A

| | | |
|---|---|---|
| 1 2-1B | 40.00 | 80.00 |
| 2 4-LOM | 40.00 | 80.00 |
| 3 8D8 | 25.00 | 50.00 |
| 4 Admiral Ackbar | 25.00 | 50.00 |
| 5 AT-AT Commander | 25.00 | 50.00 |
| 6 AT-AT Driver | 40.00 | 80.00 |
| 7 AT-ST Driver | 20.00 | 40.00 |
| 9 Ben Kenobi (new image) | 30.00 | 60.00 |
| 10 Bespin Security Guard (black) | 30.00 | 60.00 |
| 11 Bespin Security Guard (white) | 30.00 | 60.00 |
| 12 Bib Fortuna | 25.00 | 50.00 |
| 13 Biker Scout | 40.00 | 80.00 |
| 15 Boba Fett (new image) | 350.00 | 700.00 |
| 16 Bossk | 40.00 | 80.00 |
| 17 B-Wing Pilot | 20.00 | 40.00 |
| 18 C-3PO (removable limbs) | 40.00 | 80.00 |
| 20 Chewbacca (new image) | 40.00 | 80.00 |
| 21 Chief Chirpa | 20.00 | 40.00 |
| 22 Cloud Car Pilot | 30.00 | 60.00 |
| 24 Darth Vader (new image) | 60.00 | 120.00 |
| 25 Death Star Droid | 30.00 | 60.00 |
| 26 Dengar | 30.00 | 60.00 |
| 27 Emperor's Royal Guard | 40.00 | 80.00 |
| 28 FX-7 | 30.00 | 60.00 |
| 29 Gamorrean Guard | 25.00 | 50.00 |
| 30 General Madine | 20.00 | 40.00 |
| 31 Greedo | 40.00 | 80.00 |
| 32 Hammerhead | 25.00 | 50.00 |
| 34 Han Solo (large head/new image) | 100.00 | 200.00 |
| 35 Han Solo (Bespin) | 60.00 | 120.00 |
| 36 Han Solo (Hoth gear) | 60.00 | 120.00 |
| 37 Han Solo (trench coat) | 30.00 | 60.00 |
| 38 IG-88 | 20.00 | 40.00 |
| 39 Imperial Commander | 40.00 | 80.00 |
| 40 Imperial Stormtrooper Hoth | 40.00 | 80.00 |
| 41 Imperial TIE Fighter Pilot | 50.00 | 100.00 |
| 42 Jawa | 50.00 | 100.00 |
| 43 Klaatu | 20.00 | 40.00 |
| 44 Klaatu (skiff) | 20.00 | 40.00 |
| 45 Lando Calrisian (skiff) | 25.00 | 50.00 |
| 46 Lando Calrissian (with teeth) | 30.00 | 60.00 |
| 47 Lobot | 30.00 | 60.00 |
| 48 Logray | 20.00 | 40.00 |
| 49 Luke Bespin (brown hair gun drawn) | 150.00 | 300.00 |
| 50 Luke Hoth | 60.00 | 120.00 |
| 52 Luke Jedi Knight (green lightsaber) | 75.00 | 150.00 |
| 54 Luke Skywalker (blond hair gunner) | 350.00 | 600.00 |
| 56 Luke X-Wing Pilot | 100.00 | 200.00 |

| | | |
|---|---|---|
| 58 Nien Nunb | 25.00 | 50.00 |
| 59 Nikto | 20.00 | 40.00 |
| 61 Power Droid | 50.00 | 100.00 |
| 62 Princess Leia | 450.00 | 800.00 |
| 63 Princess Leia (Bespin neck painted/front picture) | | |
| 64 Princess Leia (Boushh) | 40.00 | 80.00 |
| 65 Princess Leia (poncho) | 40.00 | 80.00 |
| 66 Princess Leia (Hoth gear) | 125.00 | 250.00 |
| 67 Prune Face | 20.00 | 40.00 |
| 68 R2-D2 (sensorscope) | 40.00 | 80.00 |
| 69 R5-D4 | 50.00 | 100.00 |
| 70 Rancor Keeper | 20.00 | 40.00 |
| 71 Rebel Commander | 30.00 | 60.00 |
| 72 Rebel Commando | 20.00 | 40.00 |
| 73 Rebel Soldier Hoth | 50.00 | 100.00 |
| 74 Ree-Yees | 20.00 | 40.00 |
| 75 Sand People | 40.00 | 80.00 |
| 76 Snaggletooth (red) | 50.00 | 100.00 |
| 77 Squid Head | 20.00 | 40.00 |
| 78 Star Destroyer Commander | | |
| 79 Stormtrooper | 50.00 | 100.00 |
| 80 Teebo | 20.00 | 40.00 |
| 81 The Emperor | 40.00 | 80.00 |
| 82 Ugnaught | 40.00 | 80.00 |
| 83 Walrus Man | 30.00 | 60.00 |
| 84 Weequay | 20.00 | 40.00 |
| 85 Wicket | 40.00 | 80.00 |
| 87 Yoda (brown snake/new image) | 60.00 | 120.00 |
| 88 Zuckuss | 20.00 | 40.00 |

## 1983 Star Wars Return of the Jedi 77-Backs B

| | | |
|---|---|---|
| 1 2-1B | 25.00 | 50.00 |
| 5 AT-AT Commander | | |
| 7 AT-ST Driver | 20.00 | 40.00 |
| 10 Bespin Security Guard (black) | 30.00 | 60.00 |
| 11 Bespin Security Guard (white) | 30.00 | 60.00 |
| 13 Biker Scout | 30.00 | 60.00 |
| 21 Chief Chirpa | 20.00 | 40.00 |
| 24 Darth Vader (new image) | 60.00 | 120.00 |
| 26 Dengar | 30.00 | 60.00 |
| 28 FX-7 | 30.00 | 60.00 |
| 29 Gamorrean Guard | 25.00 | 50.00 |
| 30 General Madine | 20.00 | 40.00 |
| 32 Hammerhead | 25.00 | 50.00 |
| 34 Han Solo (large head/new image) | 100.00 | 200.00 |
| 37 Han Solo (trench coat) | 30.00 | 60.00 |
| 41 Imperial TIE Fighter Pilot | 40.00 | 80.00 |
| 43 Klaatu | 20.00 | 40.00 |
| 49 Luke Bespin (brown hair/gun drawn) | 150.00 | 300.00 |
| 56 Luke X-Wing Pilot | 100.00 | 200.00 |
| 59 Nikto | 20.00 | 40.00 |
| 61 Power Droid | 50.00 | 100.00 |
| 65 Princess Leia (poncho) | 40.00 | 80.00 |
| 66 Princess Leia (Hoth gear) | 125.00 | 250.00 |
| 67 Prune Face | 20.00 | 40.00 |
| 70 Rancor Keeper | 20.00 | 40.00 |
| 73 Rebel Soldier Hoth | 50.00 | 100.00 |
| 74 Ree-Yees | 20.00 | 40.00 |
| 76 Snaggletooth (red) | | |
| 77 Squid Head | 20.00 | 40.00 |
| 79 Stormtrooper | 50.00 | 100.00 |
| 80 Teebo | 20.00 | 40.00 |
| 82 Ugnaught | 40.00 | 80.00 |
| 84 Weequay | 20.00 | 40.00 |

## 1983 Star Wars Return of the Jedi 79-Backs A

| | | |
|---|---|---|
| 3 8D8 | 25.00 | 50.00 |
| 6 AT-AT Driver | 40.00 | 80.00 |
| 7 AT-ST Driver | 20.00 | 40.00 |
| 9 Ben Kenobi (new image) | 30.00 | 60.00 |
| 15 Boba Fett (new image) | 275.00 | 500.00 |
| 17 B-Wing Pilot | 20.00 | 40.00 |
| 18 C-3PO (removable limbs) | 40.00 | 80.00 |
| 24 Darth Vader (new image) | 60.00 | 120.00 |
| 27 Emperor's Royal Guard | 40.00 | 80.00 |
| 29 Gamorrean Guard | 25.00 | 50.00 |
| 31 Greedo | 40.00 | 80.00 |
| 37 Han Solo Trench Coat | 30.00 | 60.00 |
| 41 Imperial TIE Fighter Pilot | 40.00 | 80.00 |
| 42 Jawa | 50.00 | 100.00 |
| 43 Klaatu | 20.00 | 40.00 |
| 44 Klaatu (skiff) | 20.00 | 40.00 |
| 45 Lando Calrisian (skiff) | 25.00 | 50.00 |
| 46 Lando Calrissian (with teeth) | 30.00 | 60.00 |
| 52 Luke Jedi Knight (green lightsaber) | 75.00 | 150.00 |
| 59 Nikto | 20.00 | 40.00 |
| 64 Princess Leia (Boushh) | 40.00 | 80.00 |
| 65 Princess Leia (poncho) | 40.00 | 80.00 |
| 67 Prune Face | 20.00 | 40.00 |
| 70 Rancor Keeper | 20.00 | 40.00 |
| 74 Ree-Yees | 20.00 | 40.00 |
| 76 Snaggletooth (red) | 50.00 | 100.00 |
| 79 Stormtrooper | 50.00 | 100.00 |
| 80 Teebo | 20.00 | 40.00 |
| 81 The Emperor | 40.00 | 80.00 |
| 82 Ugnaught | 40.00 | 80.00 |
| 83 Walrus Man | 30.00 | 60.00 |
| 85 Wicket | 40.00 | 80.00 |
| 87 Yoda (brown snake/new image) | 60.00 | 120.00 |
| 88 Zuckuss | 20.00 | 40.00 |

## 1983 Star Wars Return of the Jedi 79-Backs B

| | | |
|---|---|---|
| 3 8D8 | 25.00 | 50.00 |
| 7 AT-ST Driver | 20.00 | 40.00 |
| 12 Bib Fortuna | 25.00 | 50.00 |
| 17 B-Wing Pilot | 20.00 | 40.00 |
| 20 Chewbacca (new image) | 40.00 | 80.00 |
| 21 Chief Chirpa | 20.00 | 40.00 |
| 24 Darth Vader (new image) | 60.00 | 120.00 |
| 27 Emperor's Royal Guard | 40.00 | 80.00 |
| 29 Gamorrean Guard | 25.00 | 50.00 |
| 35 Han Solo Bespin | 60.00 | 120.00 |
| 43 Klaatu | 20.00 | 40.00 |

| | | |
|---|---|---|
| 44 Klaatu (skiff) | | |
| 45 Lando Calrisian (skiff) | 25.00 | 50.00 |
| 48 Logray | 20.00 | 40.00 |
| 52 Luke Jedi Knight (green lightsaber) | 75.00 | 150.00 |
| 56 Luke X-Wing Pilot | 100.00 | 200.00 |
| 64 Princess Leia (Boushh) | 40.00 | 80.00 |
| 65 Princess Leia (poncho) | 40.00 | 80.00 |
| 69 R5-D4 | 50.00 | 100.00 |
| 70 Rancor Keeper | 20.00 | 40.00 |
| 72 Rebel Commando | 20.00 | 40.00 |
| 74 Ree-Yees | 20.00 | 40.00 |
| 80 Teebo | 20.00 | 40.00 |
| 81 The Emperor | 40.00 | 80.00 |
| 84 Weequay | 20.00 | 40.00 |
| 85 Wicket | 40.00 | 80.00 |

## 1983 Star Wars Return of the Jedi 79-Backs C

| | | |
|---|---|---|
| 57 Lumat | 40.00 | 80.00 |
| 60 Paploo | 40.00 | 80.00 |

## 1983 Star Wars Return of the Jedi (loose)

| | | |
|---|---|---|
| 1 2-1B | 6.00 | 12.00 |
| 2 4-LOM | 12.50 | 25.00 |
| 3 8D8 | 6.00 | 12.00 |
| 4 Admiral Ackbar | 6.00 | 12.00 |
| 5 Amanaman | 60.00 | 125.00 |
| 6 AT-AT Commander | 6.00 | 12.00 |
| 7 AT-AT Driver | 7.50 | 15.00 |
| 8 AT-ST Driver | 6.00 | 12.00 |
| 9 Barada | 25.00 | 60.00 |
| 10 Ben Kenobi (blue saber) | 10.00 | 20.00 |
| 11 Ben Kenobi (gray hair) | 10.00 | 20.00 |
| 12 Ben Kenobi (white hair) | 10.00 | 20.00 |
| 13 Bespin Guard (black) | 6.00 | 12.00 |
| 14 Bespin Guard (white) | 6.00 | 12.00 |
| 15 Bib Fortuna | 5.00 | 10.00 |
| 16 Biker Scout (long mask) | 5.00 | 10.00 |
| 17 Biker Scout (short mask) | 7.50 | 15.00 |
| 18 Boba Fett | 25.00 | 50.00 |
| 19 Bossk | 7.50 | 15.00 |
| 20 B-Wing Pilot | 5.00 | 10.00 |
| 21 C-3PO (removable limbs) | 7.50 | 15.00 |
| 22 Chewbacca | 6.00 | 12.00 |
| 23 Chief Chirpa | 5.00 | 10.00 |
| 24 Cloud Car Pilot | 6.00 | 12.00 |
| 25 Darth Vader | 10.00 | 20.00 |
| 26 Death Squad Commander | 10.00 | 20.00 |
| 27 Death Star Droid | 6.00 | 12.00 |
| 28 Dengar | 6.00 | 12.00 |
| 29 Dengar (white face) | 7.50 | 15.00 |
| 30 Droopy McCool | 5.00 | 10.00 |
| 31 Emperor | 7.50 | 15.00 |
| 32 Emperors Royal Guard | 6.00 | 12.00 |
| 33 FX-7 | 6.00 | 12.00 |
| 34 Gamorrean Guard | 5.00 | 10.00 |
| 35 General Madine | 5.00 | 10.00 |
| 36 Greedo | 6.00 | 12.00 |
| 37 Hammerhead | 6.00 | 12.00 |
| 38 Han Solo | 7.50 | 15.00 |
| 39 Han Solo (Bespin) | 6.00 | 12.00 |
| 40 Han Solo (carbonite) | 80.00 | 150.00 |
| 41 Han Solo (Hoth gear) | 6.00 | 12.00 |
| 42 Han Solo (trench coat) | 6.00 | 12.00 |
| 43 IG-88 | 7.50 | 15.00 |
| 44 Imperial Commander | 6.00 | 12.00 |

| | | |
|---|---|---|
| 45 Imperial Dignitary | 20.00 | 40.00 |
| 46 Imperial Gunner | 20.00 | 40.00 |
| 47 Imperial Stormtrooper | 7.50 | 15.00 |
| 48 Imperial TIE Fighter Pilot | 6.00 | 12.00 |
| 49 Jawa | 6.00 | 12.00 |
| 50 Klaatu | 5.00 | 10.00 |
| 51 Klaatu (skiff) | 5.00 | 10.00 |
| 52 Lando Calrissian | 6.00 | 12.00 |
| 53 Lando Calrissian (skiff) | 6.00 | 12.00 |
| 54 Lobot | 7.50 | 15.00 |
| 55 Logray | 5.00 | 10.00 |
| 56 Luke Skywalker | 10.00 | 20.00 |
| 57 Luke Skywalker bespin | 10.00 | 20.00 |
| brown hair | | |
| 58 Luke Skywalker bespin | 10.00 | 20.00 |
| white shirt blond hair | | |
| 59 Luke Skywalker bespin | 12.50 | 25.00 |
| white shirt brown hair | | |
| 60 Luke Skywalker bespin | | |
| yellow hair brown legs | | |
| 61 Luke Skywalker bespin | 10.00 | 20.00 |
| yellow hair tan legs | | |
| 62 Luke Skywalker (Hoth gear) | 6.00 | 12.00 |
| 63 Luke Skywalker (stormtrooper) | 5.00 | 10.00 |
| 64 Luke Skywalker Jedi Knight (blue lightsaber) | 6.00 | 12.00 |
| 65 Luke Skywalker Jedi Knight(green lightsaber) | 10.00 | 20.00 |
| 66 Luke Skywalker X-wing | 50.00 | 100.00 |
| 67 Lumat | 10.00 | 20.00 |
| 68 Max Rebo | 5.00 | 10.00 |
| 69 Nien Nunb | 5.00 | 10.00 |
| 70 Nikto | 5.00 | 10.00 |
| 71 Paploo | 5.00 | 10.00 |
| 72 Power Droid | 5.00 | 10.00 |
| 73 Princess Leia Organa | 5.00 | 10.00 |
| 74 Princess Leia Organa | 10.00 | 20.00 |
| bespin flesh neck | | |
| 75 Princess Leia Organa bespin | 7.50 | 15.00 |
| gold neck sometimes looks green | | |
| 76 Princess Leia Organa | 7.50 | 15.00 |
| bespin turtle neck | | |
| 77 Princess Leia Organa (Boushh) | | |
| 78 Princess Leia Organa (Hoth gear) | 7.50 | 15.00 |
| 79 Princess Leia Organa (poncho) | 7.50 | 15.00 |
| 80 Prune Face | 7.50 | 15.00 |
| 81 R2-D2 sensorscope | 5.00 | 10.00 |
| 82 R5-D4 | 7.50 | 15.00 |
| 83 Rancor | 7.50 | 15.00 |
| 84 Rancor Keeper | 20.00 | 40.00 |
| 85 Rebel Commander | 5.00 | 10.00 |
| 86 Rebel Commando | 5.00 | 10.00 |
| 87 Rebel Soldier (Hoth gear) | 5.00 | 10.00 |
| 88 Ree-Yees | 6.00 | 12.00 |
| 89 Romba | 5.00 | 10.00 |
| 90 Sand People | | |
| 91 Snaggletooth (red) | 6.00 | 12.00 |
| 92 Snowtrooper | 6.00 | 12.00 |
| 93 Squid Head | 15.00 | 30.00 |
| 94 Stormtrooper | 5.00 | 10.00 |
| 95 Sy Snootles | 6.00 | 12.00 |
| 96 Teebo | 5.00 | 10.00 |
| 97 Ugnaught | 5.00 | 10.00 |
| 98 Walrusman | 5.00 | 10.00 |
| 99 Weequay | 6.00 | 12.00 |
| 100 Wicket | 5.00 | 10.00 |
| 101 Yoda (brown snake) | 7.50 | 15.00 |
| 102 Zuckuss | 6.00 | 12.00 |

## 1983 Star Wars Return of the Jedi Accessories

| | | |
|---|---|---|
| 1 C-3PO Case | 30.00 | 60.00 |
| 2 Chewy Strap | 25.00 | 50.00 |
| 3 Darth Vader Case | 75.00 | 150.00 |
| 4 Jedi Vinyl Case | 100.00 | 200.00 |
| 5 Laser Rifle Case | 40.00 | 80.00 |

## 1983 Star Wars Return of the Jedi Accessories (loose)

| | | |
|---|---|---|
| 1 C-3PO Case | 15.00 | 30.00 |
| 2 Chewy Strap | 15.00 | 30.00 |
| 3 Darth Vader Case | 15.00 | 30.00 |
| 4 Jedi Vinyl Case | 15.00 | 30.00 |
| 5 Laser Rifle Case | 15.00 | 30.00 |

## 1983 Star Wars Return of the Jedi Playsets

| | | |
|---|---|---|
| 1 Ewok Village | 100.00 | 200.00 |
| 2 Jabba The Hutt | 30.00 | 60.00 |
| Salacious Crumb | | |
| 3 Jabba The Hutt Dungeon | 75.00 | 150.00 |
| Klaatu/Nikto/8D8 | | |
| 4 Jabba The Hutt Dungeon | 300.00 | 650.00 |
| EV-9D9/Amanaman/Barada | | |

## 1983 Star Wars Return of the Jedi Playsets (loose)

| | | |
|---|---|---|
| 1 Ewok Village | 30.00 | 60.00 |
| 2 Jabba The Hutt | 15.00 | 30.00 |
| 3 Jabba The Hutt Dungeon | 20.00 | 40.00 |

## 1983 Star Wars Return of the Jedi Vehicles

| | | |
|---|---|---|
| 1 AT-AT | 150.00 | 300.00 |
| 2 B-Wing Fighter | 75.00 | 150.00 |
| 3 Ewok Assault Catapult | 25.00 | 50.00 |
| 4 Ewok Glider | 30.00 | 60.00 |
| 5 Imperial Shuttle | 250.00 | 500.00 |
| 6 Millenium Falcon | 125.00 | 250.00 |
| 7 Rancor | 150.00 | 300.00 |
| 8 Scout Walker | 50.00 | 100.00 |
| 9 Speeder Bike | 20.00 | 40.00 |
| 10 Sy Snootles and the Rebo Band | 120.00 | 250.00 |
| (w/Sy Snootles/Droopy McCool/Max Rebo) | | |
| 11 TIE Fighter (battle damage) | 40.00 | 80.00 |
| 12 TIE Interceptor | 60.00 | 120.00 |
| 13 X-Wing (battle damage) | 75.00 | 150.00 |
| 14 Y-Wing | 75.00 | 150.00 |

## 1983 Star Wars Return of the Jedi Vehicles (loose)

| | | |
|---|---|---|
| 1 AT-AT | 40.00 | 80.00 |
| 2 B-Wing Fighter | 30.00 | 60.00 |
| 3 Droopy McCool | 12.00 | 30.00 |
| 4 Ewok Assault Catapult | 15.00 | 30.00 |
| 5 Ewok Glider | 15.00 | 30.00 |
| 6 Imperial Shuttle | 30.00 | 60.00 |
| 7 Max Rebo | 8.00 | 20.00 |
| 8 Millenium Falcon | 50.00 | 100.00 |
| 9 Rancor | 30.00 | 80.00 |
| 10 Scout Walker | 15.00 | 30.00 |
| 11 Speeder Bike | 7.50 | 15.00 |
| 12 Sy Snootles | 10.00 | 25.00 |
| 13 TIE Fighter (battle damage) | 20.00 | 40.00 |
| 14 TIE Interceptor | 20.00 | 40.00 |
| 15 X-Wing (battle damage) | 30.00 | 60.00 |
| 16 Y-Wing | 30.00 | 60.00 |

## 1983 Star Wars Return of the Jedi Tri-Logo

| | | |
|---|---|---|
| 1 2-1B | 30.00 | 60.00 |
| 2 8D8 | 30.00 | 60.00 |
| 3 A-Wing Pilot | 40.00 | 80.00 |
| 4 Admiral Ackbar | 20.00 | 40.00 |
| 5 Amanaman | 100.00 | 200.00 |
| 6 Anakin Skywalker | 25.00 | 50.00 |
| 7 AT-AT Commander | 20.00 | 40.00 |
| 8 AT-ST Driver | 30.00 | 60.00 |
| 9 B-Wing Pilot | 20.00 | 40.00 |
| 10 Barada | 40.00 | 80.00 |
| 11 Ben Kenobi (blue lightsaber) | 60.00 | 120.00 |
| 12 Bespin Guard (black/ tri-logo back only) | 150.00 | 300.00 |

| | | |
|---|---|---|
| 13 Bespin Guard (white/ tri-logo back only) | 250.00 | 500.00 |
| 14 Bib Fortuna | 15.00 | 30.00 |
| 15 Biker Scout (long mask) | 30.00 | 60.00 |
| 16 Boba Fett | 350.00 | 700.00 |
| 17 Bossk | 40.00 | 80.00 |
| 18 C-3PO (removable limbs) | 40.00 | 80.00 |
| 19 Chewbacca | 40.00 | 80.00 |
| 20 Darth Vader | 75.00 | 150.00 |
| 21 Death Star Droid | 40.00 | 80.00 |
| 22 Dengar | 25.00 | 50.00 |
| 23 Emperor | 30.00 | 60.00 |
| 24 Emperors Royal Guard | 150.00 | 300.00 |
| 25 FX-7 | 30.00 | 60.00 |
| 26 Gamorrean Guard | 30.00 | 60.00 |
| 27 General Madine | 60.00 | 120.00 |
| 28 Greedo (tri-logo back only) | 60.00 | 120.00 |
| 29 Hammerhead (tri-logo back only) | 40.00 | 80.00 |
| 30 Han Solo | 75.00 | 150.00 |
| 31 Han Solo (carbonite) | 250.00 | 500.00 |
| 32 IG-88 | 100.00 | 200.00 |
| 33 Imperial Commander | 50.00 | 100.00 |
| 34 Imperial Dignitary | 125.00 | 250.00 |
| 35 Imperial Gunner | 125.00 | 250.00 |
| 36 Jawa | 500.00 | 1000.00 |
| 37 Klaatu | 15.00 | 30.00 |
| 38 Klaatu (skiff) | 25.00 | 50.00 |
| 39 Lando Calrissian | 40.00 | 80.00 |
| 40 Lando Calrissian (skiff) | 30.00 | 60.00 |
| 41 Lobot | 30.00 | 60.00 |
| 42 Luke Skywalker (Bespin) | 200.00 | 400.00 |
| 43 Luke Skywalker (gunner card) | 125.00 | 250.00 |
| 44 Luke Skywalker (Hoth gear) | 200.00 | 400.00 |
| 45 Luke Skywalker Jedi Knight | 40.00 | 80.00 |
| 46 Luke Skywalker (stormtrooper) | 150.00 | 300.00 |
| 47 Luke Skywalker (poncho) | 30.00 | 60.00 |
| 48 Luke Skywalker X-wing | 100.00 | 200.00 |
| 49 Lumat | 30.00 | 60.00 |
| 50 Nien Nunb | 50.00 | 100.00 |
| 51 Nikto | 15.00 | 30.00 |
| 52 Paploo | 15.00 | 30.00 |
| 53 Princess Leia Organa | 60.00 | 120.00 |
| 54 Princess Leia Organa (Bespin turtle neck) | 60.00 | 120.00 |
| 55 Princess Leia Organa (Boushh) | 75.00 | 150.00 |
| 56 Princess Leia Organa (poncho) | 50.00 | 100.00 |
| 57 Prune Face | 25.00 | 50.00 |
| 58a R2-D2 (sensorscope/blue background card) | 20.00 | 40.00 |
| 58b R2-D2 (sensorscope/sparks card) | 75.00 | 120.00 |
| 59 R5-D4 | 30.00 | 60.00 |
| 60 Rancor | 20.00 | 40.00 |
| 61 Rebel Soldier (Hoth gear) | 40.00 | 80.00 |
| 62 Ree-Yees | 20.00 | 40.00 |
| 63 Romba | 30.00 | 60.00 |
| 64 Snowtrooper | 30.00 | 60.00 |
| 65 Squid Head | 25.00 | 50.00 |
| 66 Stormtrooper | 100.00 | 200.00 |
| 67 TIE Fighter Pilot | 30.00 | 60.00 |
| 68 Ugnaught | 30.00 | 60.00 |
| 69 Warok | 50.00 | 100.00 |
| 70 Wicket | 40.00 | 80.00 |
| 71 Yak Face | 1200.00 | 2500.00 |
| 72a Yoda (brown snake) | 50.00 | 100.00 |
| 72b Yoda (orange snake) | 500.00 | 900.00 |

### 1985 Star Wars Droids Cartoon

| | | |
|---|---|---|
| 1 A-Wing Pilot | 250.00 | 500.00 |
| 2 Boba Fett | 1200.00 | 2500.00 |
| 3 C-3PO | 250.00 | 500.00 |
| 4 Jann Tosh | 30.00 | 60.00 |
| 5 Jord Dusat | 30.00 | 60.00 |

| | | |
|---|---|---|
| 6 Kea Moll | 30.00 | 60.00 |
| 7 Kez-Iban | 30.00 | 60.00 |
| 8 R2-D2 | 250.00 | 500.00 |
| 9 Sise Fromm | 150.00 | 300.00 |
| 10 Thall Joben | 30.00 | 60.00 |
| 11 Tig Fromm | 75.00 | 150.00 |
| 12 Uncle Gundy | 30.00 | 60.00 |

### 1985 Star Wars Droids Cartoon (loose)

| | | |
|---|---|---|
| 1 A-Wing Pilot | 40.00 | 80.00 |
| 2 Boba Fett | 125.00 | 225.00 |
| 3 C-3PO | 40.00 | 80.00 |
| 4 Jann Tosh | 15.00 | 30.00 |
| 5 Jord Dusat | 15.00 | 30.00 |
| 6 Kea Moll | 15.00 | 30.00 |
| 7 Kez-Iban | 15.00 | 30.00 |
| 8 R2-D2 | 40.00 | 80.00 |
| 9 Sise Fromm | 60.00 | 120.00 |
| 10 Thall Joben | 15.00 | 30.00 |
| 11 Tig Fromm | 40.00 | 80.00 |
| 12 Uncle Gundy | 15.00 | 30.00 |

### 1985 Star Wars Droids Cartoon Coins (loose)

| | | |
|---|---|---|
| 1 A-Wing Pilot | 4.00 | 10.00 |
| 2 Boba Fett | 12.50 | 25.00 |
| 3 C-3PO | 4.00 | 10.00 |
| 4 Jann Tosh | 4.00 | 10.00 |
| 5 Jord Dusat | 4.00 | 10.00 |
| 6 Kea Moll | 4.00 | 10.00 |
| 7 Kez-Iban | 4.00 | 10.00 |
| 8 R2-D2 | 5.00 | 12.00 |
| 9 Sise Fromm | 4.00 | 10.00 |
| 10 Thall Joben | 4.00 | 10.00 |
| 11 Tig Fromm | 4.00 | 10.00 |
| 12 Uncle Gundy | 4.00 | 10.00 |

### 1985 Star Wars Droids Cartoon Vehicles

| | | |
|---|---|---|
| 1 A-Wing Fighter | 50.00 | 100.00 |
| 2 ATL Interceptor | 50.00 | 100.00 |
| 3 Sidegunner | 30.00 | 60.00 |

### 1985 Star Wars Droids Cartoon Vehicles (loose)

| | | |
|---|---|---|
| 1 A-Wing Fighter | 25.00 | 50.00 |
| 2 ATL Interceptor | 25.00 | 50.00 |
| 3 Sidegunner | 15.00 | 30.00 |

### 1988 Star Wars Droids Cartoon Glasslite

| | |
|---|---|
| 1 C-3PO | |
| 2 Jord Dusat | |
| 3 Kea Moll | |
| 4 Kez Iban | |
| 5 R2-D2 | |
| 6 Thall Joben | |
| 7 Vlix | |

### 1988 Star Wars Droids Cartoon Glasslite Vehicles

| | |
|---|---|
| 1 Interceptor | |
| 2 Side Gunner | |

### 1985 Star Wars Ewoks Cartoons

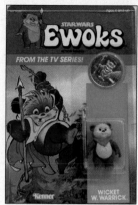

| | | |
|---|---|---|
| 1 Dulok Scout | 25.00 | 50.00 |
| 2 Dulok Shaman | 30.00 | 60.00 |
| 3 King Gorneesh | 20.00 | 40.00 |
| 4 Lady Gorneesh | 25.00 | 50.00 |
| 5 Logray | 40.00 | 80.00 |
| 6 Wicket | 50.00 | 100.00 |

### 1985 Star Wars Ewoks Cartoons (loose)

| | | |
|---|---|---|
| 1 Dulok Scout | 12.50 | 25.00 |
| 2 Dulok Shaman | 15.00 | 30.00 |
| 3 King Gorneesh | 10.00 | 20.00 |
| 4 Lady Gorneesh | 12.50 | 25.00 |
| 5 Logray | 20.00 | 40.00 |
| 6 Wicket | 25.00 | 50.00 |

### 1985 Star Wars Ewoks Cartoons Coins (loose)

| | | |
|---|---|---|
| 1 Dulok Scout | 4.00 | 10.00 |
| 2 Dulok Shaman | 4.00 | 10.00 |
| 3 King Gorneesh | 4.00 | 10.00 |
| 4 Lady Gorneesh | 4.00 | 10.00 |
| 5 Logray | 5.00 | 12.00 |
| 60 Wicket | 5.00 | 12.00 |

### 1985 Star Wars Power of the Force

| | | |
|---|---|---|
| 1 A-Wing Pilot | 50.00 | 100.00 |
| 2 Amanaman | 150.00 | 300.00 |
| 3 Anakin Skywalker | | |
| 4 AT-AT Driver | | |
| 5 AT-ST Driver | 50.00 | 100.00 |
| 6 B-Wing Pilot | 25.00 | 50.00 |
| 7 Barada | 100.00 | 250.00 |

| | | |
|---|---|---|
| 8 Ben Kenobi (blue saber) | 60.00 | 120.00 |
| 9 Biker Scout | 75.00 | 150.00 |
| 10 C-3PO (removable limbs) | 50.00 | 100.00 |
| 11 Chewbacca | 50.00 | 100.00 |
| 12 Darth Vader | 100.00 | 200.00 |
| 13 Emperor | 40.00 | 80.00 |
| 14 EV-9D9 | 175.00 | 350.00 |
| 15 Gamorrean Guard | 200.00 | 400.00 |
| 16 Han Solo (carbonite) | 150.00 | 400.00 |
| 17 Han Solo (trench coat) | 400.00 | 700.00 |
| 18 Imperial Dignitary | 50.00 | 100.00 |
| 19 Imperial Gunner | 50.00 | 100.00 |
| 20 Jawa | 50.00 | 100.00 |
| 21 Lando Calrissian | 60.00 | 120.00 |
| 22 Luke Skywalker (Hoth gear) | | |
| 23 Luke Skywalker (Jedi) | 75.00 | 150.00 |
| 24 Luke Skywalker (poncho) | 60.00 | 120.00 |
| 25 Luke Skywalker (stormtrooper) | 125.00 | 250.00 |
| 26 Luke Skywalker X-wing | 60.00 | 120.00 |
| 27 Lumat | 40.00 | 80.00 |
| 28 Nikto | 1000.00 | 1500.00 |
| 29 Paploo | 40.00 | 80.00 |
| 30 Princess Leia (poncho) | 40.00 | 80.00 |
| 31 R2-D2 (lightsaber) | 200.00 | 400.00 |
| 32 Romba | 40.00 | 80.00 |
| 33 Stormtrooper | 100.00 | 200.00 |
| 34 Teebo | 60.00 | 120.00 |
| 35 TIE Fighter Pilot | | |
| 36 Ugnaught | | |
| 37 Warok | 50.00 | 100.00 |
| 38 Wicket | 40.00 | 80.00 |
| 39 Yak Face | 3000.00 | 7000.00 |
| 40 Yoda (brown snake) | 300.00 | 600.00 |

## 1985 Star Wars Power of the Force (loose)

| | | |
|---|---|---|
| 1 A-Wing Pilot | 25.00 | 50.00 |
| 2 Amanaman | 40.00 | 80.00 |
| 3 Anakin Skywalker | 15.00 | 30.00 |
| 4 AT-AT Driver | | |
| 5 AT-ST Driver | 10.00 | 20.00 |
| 6 B-Wing Pilot | 10.00 | 20.00 |
| 7 Barada | 20.00 | 40.00 |
| 8 Ben Kenobi (blue saber) | 20.00 | 40.00 |
| 9 Biker Scout | 20.00 | 40.00 |
| 10 C-3PO (removable limbs) | 10.00 | 20.00 |
| 11 Chewbacca | 20.00 | 40.00 |
| 12 Darth Vader | 20.00 | 40.00 |
| 13 Emperor | 15.00 | 30.00 |
| 14 EV-9D9 | 25.00 | 50.00 |
| 15 Gamorrean Guard | 50.00 | 100.00 |
| 16 Han Solo (carbonite) | 100.00 | 200.00 |
| 17 Han Solo (trench coat) | 125.00 | 225.00 |
| 18 Imperial Dignitary | 30.00 | 60.00 |
| 19 Imperial Gunner | 50.00 | 100.00 |
| 20 Jawa | 20.00 | 40.00 |
| 21 Lando Calrissian | 25.00 | 50.00 |
| 22 Luke Skywalker (Hoth gear) | 25.00 | 50.00 |
| 23 Luke Skywalker (Jedi) | 25.00 | 50.00 |
| 24 Luke Skywalker (poncho) | 25.00 | 50.00 |
| 25 Luke Skywalker (stormtrooper) | 40.00 | 80.00 |
| 26 Luke Skywalker X-wing | 25.00 | 50.00 |
| 27 Lumat | 15.00 | 30.00 |
| 28 Nikto | | |
| 29 Paploo | 12.50 | 25.00 |
| 30 Princess Leia (poncho) | 20.00 | 40.00 |
| 31 R2-D2 (lightsaber) | 100.00 | 200.00 |
| 32 Romba | 15.00 | 30.00 |
| 33 Stormtrooper | 30.00 | 60.00 |
| 34 Teebo | 12.50 | 25.00 |
| 35 TIE Fighter Pilot | | |
| 36 Ugnaught | | |
| 37 Warok | 20.00 | 40.00 |
| 38 Wicket | 20.00 | 40.00 |

| | | |
|---|---|---|
| 39 Yak Face | 350.00 | 700.00 |
| 40 Yoda (brown snake) | 75.00 | 150.00 |

## 1985 Star Wars Power of the Force Coins (loose)

| | | |
|---|---|---|
| 1 A-Wing Pilot | 6.00 | 12.00 |
| 2 Amanaman | 6.00 | 12.00 |
| 3 Anakin Skywalker | 20.00 | 40.00 |
| 4 AT-AT Driver | | |
| 5 AT-ST Driver | 5.00 | 10.00 |
| 6 B-Wing Pilot | 5.00 | 10.00 |
| 7 Barada | 7.50 | 15.00 |
| 8 Ben Kenobi (blue saber) | 7.50 | 15.00 |
| 9 Biker Scout | 7.50 | 15.00 |
| 10 C-3PO (removable limbs) | 6.00 | 12.00 |
| 11 Chewbacca | 7.50 | 15.00 |
| 12 Darth Vader | 10.00 | 20.00 |
| 13 Emperor | 7.50 | 15.00 |
| 14 EV-9D9 | 7.50 | 15.00 |
| 15 Gamorrean Guard | 10.00 | 20.00 |
| 16 Han Solo (carbonite) | 10.00 | 20.00 |
| 17 Han Solo (trench coat) | 15.00 | 30.00 |
| 18 Imperial Dignitary | 7.50 | 15.00 |
| 19 Imperial Gunner | 5.00 | 10.00 |
| 20 Jawa | 10.00 | 20.00 |
| 21 Lando Calrissian | 6.00 | 12.00 |
| 22 Luke Skywalker (Hoth gear) | 10.00 | 20.00 |
| 23 Luke Skywalker (Jedi) | 10.00 | 20.00 |
| 24 Luke Skywalker (poncho) | 10.00 | 20.00 |
| 25 Luke Skywalker (stormtrooper) | 15.00 | 30.00 |
| 26 Luke Skywalker X-wing | 10.00 | 20.00 |
| 27 Lumat | 5.00 | 10.00 |
| 28 Nikto | | |
| 29 Paploo | 5.00 | 10.00 |
| 30 Princess Leia (poncho) | 7.50 | 15.00 |
| 31 R2-D2 (lightsaber) | 7.50 | 15.00 |
| 32 Romba | 5.00 | 10.00 |
| 33 Stormtrooper | 10.00 | 20.00 |
| 34 Teebo | 5.00 | 10.00 |
| 35 TIE Fighter Pilot | | |
| 36 Ugnaught | | |
| 37 Warok | 6.00 | 12.00 |
| 38 Wicket | 10.00 | 20.00 |
| 39 Yak Face | 150.00 | 300.00 |
| 40 Yoda (brown snake) | 20.00 | 40.00 |

## 1985 Star Wars Power of the Force Vehicles

| | | |
|---|---|---|
| 1 Ewok Battle Wagon | 125.00 | 250.00 |
| 2 Imperial Sniper Vehicle | 75.00 | 150.00 |
| 3 Sand Skimmer | 75.00 | 150.00 |
| 4 Security Scout | 75.00 | 150.00 |
| 5 Tattoine Skiff | 200.00 | 400.00 |

## 1985 Star Wars Power of the Force Vehicles (loose)

| | | |
|---|---|---|
| 1 Ewok Battle Wagon | 50.00 | 100.00 |
| 2 Imperial Sniper Vehicle | 30.00 | 60.00 |
| 3 Sand Skimmer | 30.00 | 60.00 |
| 4 Security Scout | 30.00 | 60.00 |
| 5 Tattoine Skiff | 100.00 | 200.00 |

## 1988 Star Wars Power of the Force Glasslite

1 C-3PO
2 Chewbacca
3 Darth Vader
4 Han Solo
5 Luke Skywalker
6 Princess Leia
7 R2-D2
8 Snowtrooper
9 Stormtrooper

## 1988 Star Wars Power of the Force Glasslite Vehicles

1 TIE Fighter
2 X-Wing Fighter

## 1988 Star Wars Uzay Savascilari Turkish Bootlegs

1a Stormtroper (Asker)(single arm band)
1b Stormtroper (Asker)(double arm band)
2 Imperial Stormtroper (Imperatorlugun Askeri)
3a AT-Driver (Surucu)(gold rocks on card)
3b AT-Driver (Surucu)(silver rocks on card)
4a Darth Vader (Kara Lider)(no dot on chest)
4b Darth Vader (Kara Lider)(dot on chest)
5a Chewbacca (Aslan Adam)(space background)
5b Chewbacca (Aslan Adam)(profile shot)
6a T E Fighter Pilot (Savas Polotu)(black boots)
6b T E Fighter Pilot (Savas Polotu)(unpainted boots)
7a See Threep (CPO)(no text on front)
7b See Threep (CPO)(text on front)
8 Death Star Droid
9 Blue Stars
10a Emperor's Royal Guard (dark red cape)
10b Emperor's Royal Guard (light red cape)
10c Emperor's Royal Guard (no cape)
11a Imperial Gunner (tan background)
11b Imperial Gunner (green background)
12a Arfive Defour (R2-D4)
12b Arfive Defour (R2-D4)(printing error)
13 Head Man
14a Artoo Detoo (R2-D2)(white scope)
14b Artoo Detoo (R2-D2)(gray scope)

## 1988 Star Wars Uzay Savascilari Turkish Bootlegs Vehicles

1 MTV-7
2 MLC-3

### 2018 Solo A Star Wars Story Force Link 2.0

| | | | |
|---|---|---|---|
| NNO | Chewbacca | 6.00 | 12.00 |
| NNO | Darth Vader | 10.00 | 20.00 |
| NNO | Emperor's Royal Guard | | |
| NNO | Han Solo | | |
| NNO | K-2SO | | |
| NNO | Kylo Ren | | |
| NNO | L3-37 | | |
| NNO | Luke Skywalker Jedi Knight | | |
| NNO | Luke Skywalker Jedi Master | | |
| NNO | Maz Kanata | | |
| NNO | Moloch | | |
| NNO | Princess Leia Organa | | |
| NNO | Qi'Ra | | |
| NNO | Quay Tolsite | | |
| NNO | Range Trooper | | |
| NNO | Rey | | |
| NNO | Rio Durant | | |
| NNO | Stormtrooper | | |
| NNO | Stormtrooper Officer | | |
| NNO | Supreme Leader Snoke | | |
| NNO | Tobias Beckett | | |
| NNO | Val | | |

### 2018 Solo A Star Wars Story Force Link 2.0 2-Packs

| | | | |
|---|---|---|---|
| NNO | C-3PO & R2-D2 | | |
| NNO | Han Solo/Chewbacca | 15.00 | 30.00 |
| NNO | Lando Calrissian/Kessel Guard | 10.00 | 20.00 |
| NNO | Qui-Gon Jinn/Darth Maul (w/probe droid) | 7.50 | 15.00 |
| NNO | Rebolt/Corellian Hound | 20.00 | 40.00 |
| NNO | Rose Tico (w/BB-8)/BB-9E | 7.50 | 15.00 |

### 2018 Solo A Star Wars Story Force Link 2.0 Creatures

| | | | |
|---|---|---|---|
| NNO | Rathtar (w/Bala-Tik) | 10.00 | 20.00 |
| NNO | Wampa (w/Luke Skywalker) | 15.00 | 30.00 |

### 2018 Solo A Star Wars Story Force Link 2.0 Multi-Packs

| | | | |
|---|---|---|---|
| NNO | Han Solo/Qi'Ra/Range Trooper/Weazel | 30.00 | 60.00 |
| (Mission on Vandor 4-Pack) | | | |

| | | | |
|---|---|---|---|
| NNO | Kylo Ren/Maz Kanata/Poe Dameron/Rey/Snowtrooper | | |
| (Last Jedi 5-Pack Entertainment Earth Exclusive) | | | |
| NNO | Starter Set (w/Han Solo) | 12.50 | 25.00 |
| NNO | Trooper 6-Pack | | |
| (2018 Targe Exclusive) | | | |

### 2018 Solo A Star Wars Story Force Link 2.0 Playsets

| | | |
|---|---|---|
| NNO | Kessel Mine Escape (w/Han Solo) | |
| NNO | Vandor-1 Heist (w/Chewbacca) | |

### 2018 Solo A Star Wars Story Force Link 2.0 Vehicles

| | | | |
|---|---|---|---|
| NNO | A-Wing Fighter (w/Tallie) | | |
| NNO | Imperial AT-DT Walker (w/Stormtrooper) | 40.00 | 80.00 |
| NNO | Kessel Run Millennium Falcon (w/Han Solo) | 50.00 | 100.00 |
| NNO | M-68 Landspeeder (w/Han Solo) | 15.00 | 30.00 |
| NNO | Swoop Bike (w/Enfys Nest) | 25.00 | 50.00 |
| NNO | TIE Fighter (w/TIE Fighter Pilot) | 30.00 | 60.00 |

# MODERN

### 2007-08 Star Wars 30th Anniversary Collection

| | | | |
|---|---|---|---|
| 1 | Darth Vader (w/30th Anniversary coin album) | 10.00 | 25.00 |
| 2 | Galactic Marine | 4.00 | 8.00 |
| 3 | Mustafar Lava Miner | 4.00 | 8.00 |
| 4 | R2-D2 | 4.00 | 8.00 |
| 5 | Obi-Wan Kenobi | 4.00 | 8.00 |
| 6 | Mace Windu | 6.00 | 12.00 |
| 7 | Airborne Trooper | 4.00 | 8.00 |
| 8 | Super Battle Droid | 4.00 | 8.00 |
| 9 | Concept Stormtrooper (McQuarrie Signature Series) | 4.00 | 8.00 |
| 10 | Rebel Honor Guard (Yavin) | 4.00 | 8.00 |
| 11 | Han Solo (smuggler) | 4.00 | 8.00 |
| 12 | Luke Skywalker (Yavin ceremony) | 4.00 | 8.00 |
| 13 | Death Star Trooper | 5.00 | 10.00 |
| 14 | Biggs Darklighter (Rebel pilot) | 4.00 | 8.00 |
| 15 | Concept Boba Fett (McQuarrie Signature Series) | 12.00 | 25.00 |

| | | | |
|---|---|---|---|
| 16 | Darth Vader (removable helmet) | 4.00 | 8.00 |
| 17 | Biggs Darklighter (academy gear) | 4.00 | 8.00 |
| 18 | Luke Skywalker (moisture farmer) | 8.00 | 15.00 |
| 19 | Jawa & LIN Droid (Tatooine scavenger) | 4.00 | 8.00 |
| 20 | Imperial Stormtrooper (Galactic Empire) | 4.00 | 8.00 |
| 21 | Concept Chewbacca (McQuarrie Signature Series) | 6.00 | 12.00 |
| 22 | M'Iiyoom Onith (Hementhe) | 5.00 | 10.00 |
| 23 | Elis Helrot (Givin) | 5.00 | 10.00 |
| 24 | Boba Fett (animated debut) | 6.00 | 12.00 |
| 25 | Luke Skywalker (Jedi Knight) | 4.00 | 8.00 |
| 26 | CZ-4 (CZ-Series droid) | 4.00 | 8.00 |
| 27 | Umpass-Stay (Klatooinian) | 4.00 | 8.00 |
| 28 | Concept Darth Vader (McQuarrie Signature Series) | 8.00 | 15.00 |
| 29 | Hermi Odle (Baragwin) | 12.00 | 25.00 |
| 30 | C-3PO & Salacious Crumb (Jabba's Servants) | 10.00 | 20.00 |
| 31 | Roron Corobb (Jedi Knight) | 6.00 | 12.00 |
| 32 | Yoda & Kybuck (Jedi Master) | 4.00 | 8.00 |
| 33 | Anakin Skywalker (Jedi Knight) | 4.00 | 8.00 |
| 34 | Darth Revan (Sith Lord) | 30.00 | 60.00 |
| 35 | Darth Malak (Sith Lord) | 15.00 | 30.00 |
| 36 | Pre-Cyborg Grievous | 20.00 | 40.00 |
| (Kaleesh warlord Qymaen jai Sheelal) | | | |
| 37 | Concept Starkiller Hero (McQuarrie Signature Series) | 4.00 | 8.00 |
| 38 | Han Solo (w/torture rack) | 10.00 | 20.00 |
| 39 | Lando Calrissian (smuggler) | 4.00 | 8.00 |
| 40 | General McQuarrie (Rebel officer) | 4.00 | 8.00 |
| 41 | 4-LOM (bounty hunter) | 4.00 | 8.00 |
| 42 | Concept Snowtrooper (McQuarrie Signature Series) | 4.00 | 8.00 |
| 43 | Romba & Graak (Ewok warriors) | 12.00 | 25.00 |
| 44 | Tycho Celchu (A-Wing pilot) | 4.00 | 8.00 |
| 45 | Anakin Skywalker (Jedi Spirit) | 10.00 | 20.00 |
| 46 | R2-D2 (w/cargo net) | 4.00 | 8.00 |
| 47 | Concept Han Solo (McQuarrie Signature Series) | 12.00 | 25.00 |
| 48 | Darth Vader (hologram) | 4.00 | 8.00 |

| | | | |
|---|---|---|---|
| 49a | Clone Trooper (7th Legion Trooper) | 4.00 | 8.00 |
| 49b | Clone Trooper (Revenge of the Sith stand/no coin) | 4.00 | 8.00 |
| 50a | Clone Trooper (Hawkbat Batallion) | 8.00 | 15.00 |
| 50b | Clone Trooper (Hawkbat Batallion) | 4.00 | 8.00 |
| Revenge of the Sith stand/no coin | | | |
| 51a | R2-B1 (astromech droid) | 4.00 | 8.00 |
| 51b | R2-B1 (Revenge of the Sith stand/no coin) | 4.00 | 8.00 |
| 52 | Naboo Soldier (Royal Naboo Army) | 6.00 | 12.00 |
| 53a | Rebel Vanguard Trooper (Star Wars: Battlefront) | 4.00 | 8.00 |
| 53b | Rebel Vanguard Trooper (Expanded Universe stand/no coin) | 4.00 | 8.00 |
| 54 | Pax Bonkik (Rodian podracer mechanic) | 4.00 | 8.00 |
| 55 | Clone Trooper (training fatigues) | 8.00 | 15.00 |
| 56a | Padme Amidala (Naboo Senator) | 4.00 | 8.00 |
| 56b | Padme Amidala (Attack of the Clones stand/no coin) | 4.00 | 8.00 |
| 57a | Jango Fett (bounty hunter) | 4.00 | 8.00 |
| 57b | Jango Fett (Attack of the Clones stand/no coin) | 10.00 | 20.00 |
| 58a | Voolvif Monn (Jedi Master) | 4.00 | 8.00 |
| 58b | Voolvif Monn (Expanded Universe stand/no coin) | 4.00 | 8.00 |
| 59 | Destroyer Droid (droideka) | 4.00 | 8.00 |
| 60 | Concept Rebel Trooper (McQuarrie Signature Series) | 4.00 | 8.00 |

### 2007-08 Star Wars 30th Anniversary Collection Battle Packs

1 Battle of Geonosis (Jango Fett/Obi-Wan Kenobi/Count Dooku/Aayla Secura) 20.00 40.00

2 Battle on Mygeeto (Galactic Marine/Ki-Adi Mundi Clone Commander Bacara/Super Battle Droid/Tri-Droid) 30.00 60.00

3 Betrayal at Bespin (Boba Fett/Chewbacca Darth Vader/Han Solo/Princess Leia) 20.00 40.00

4 Capture of Tantive IV (Darth Vader 2 Rebel Troopers/2 Stormtroopers) 20.00 40.00

5 Clone Attack on Coruscant (Clone Trooper Commander/4 Clone Troopers) 25.00 50.00

6 Droid Factory Capture (C-3PO with droid head R2-D2/Jango Fett/Anakin/Destroyer Droid) 20.00 40.00

7 Hoth Patrol (Luke Skywalker/Tauntaun/Wampa) 20.00 40.00

8 Jedi vs. Sith (Yoda/Anakin Skywalker Asajj Ventress/General Grievous/Obi-Wan) 10.00 20.00

9 Jedi vs. Sidious (Darth Sidious/Kit Fisto Mace Windu/Saesee-Tiin/Agen Kolar) 10.00 20.00

10 Jedi Training on Dagobah (Yoda/R2-D2 Luke Skywalker/Spirit of Obi-Wan/Darth Vader) 10.00 20.00

11 The Hunt for Grievous (Captain Fordo Clone Trooper Gunner/3 Clone Troopers) 30.00 60.00

## 2007-08 Star Wars 30th Anniversary Collection
### Battle Packs Exclusives

1 Ambush on Ilum (R2-D2/C-3PO/Padme/Chameleon Droids)#(2007 Target Exclusive) 30.00 60.00

2 ARC-170 Elite Squad (Astromech Droid/2 Clone pilots/2 Clone Troopers)#(2007 Target Exclusive) 50.00 100.00

3 Arena Encounter (Anakin Skywalker/Padme Amidala/Obi-Wan/Creatures)#(2007 Toys R Us Exclusive) 100.00 200.00

4 AT-RT Assault Squad (2 AT-RT's/2 AT-RT Drivers/Clone Commander)#(2007 Target Exclusive) 25.00 50.00

5 Attack on Kashyyyk (Darth Vader/2 Stormtroopers/2 Wookiee warriors)#(2008 Target Exclusive) 20.00 40.00

6 Bantha with Tusken Raiders (brown - Bantha/2 Tusken Raiders/Tusken female)#(2007 Toys R Us Exclusive) 30.00 60.00

7 Bantha with Tusken Raiders (tan - Bantha/2 Tusken Raiders/Tusken female)#(2007 Toys R Us Exclusive) 50.00 100.00

8 Battle Rancor (w/Felucian warrior)#(2008 Target Exclusive) 60.00 120.00

9 Betrayal on Felucia (Aayla Secura/4 Clone Troopers yellow)#(2007 Target Exclusive) 20.00 40.00

10 STAP Attack (2 Battle Droids/Super Battle Droid/2 STAP's)#(2008 Toys R Us Exclusive) 25.00 50.00

11 Treachery on Saleucami (Commander Neyo/Clone Trooper red/2 BARC Speeder Bikes)#(2007 Walmart Exclusive) 30.00 60.00

## 2007-08 Star Wars 30th Anniversary Collection
### Comic Packs

1 Carnor Jax & Kir Kanos (2006 Internet Exclusive)

2 Darth Vader & Rebel Officer

3 Governor Tarkin & Stormtrooper

4 Chewbacca & Han Solo

5 Quinlan Vos & Vilmarh Grahrk

6 Luke Skywalker & R2-D2

7 Obi-Wan Kenobi & ARC Trooper

8 A'sharad Hett & The Dark Woman 20.00 40.00

9 Leia Organa & Darth Vader

10 Mara Jade & Luke Skywalker 20.00 40.00

11 Anakin Skywalker & Assassin Droid

12 Baron Soontir Fel & Derek Hobbie Klivian

13 Koffi Arana & Bultar Swan

14 Lt. Jundland & Deena Shan

15 Mouse & Basso

16 Clone Commando & Super Battle Droid 30.00 60.00

NNO Obi-Wan Kenobi & Bail Organa (2007 Walmart Exclusive)

NNO Boba Fett & RA-7 Droid (Wal-Mart Exclusive) 12.00 25.00

NNO Commander Keller & Galactic Marine (2007 Walmart Exclusive)

NNO Count Dooku & Anakin Skywalker

NNO Kashyyyk Trooper & Wookiee Warrior

NNO Lando Calrissian & Stormtrooper

## 2007-08 Star Wars 30th Anniversary Collection
### Commemorative Tins

1 Episode I (Darth Maul/Anakin Skywalker Qui-Gon Ginn/R2-D9) 50.00 100.00

2 Episode II (Clone Trooper blue Anakin Skywalker/Count Dooku/Boba Fett) 20.00 40.00

3 Episode III (Yoda/Mace Windu Anakin Skywalker/Clone Trooper yellow shins)

4 Episode IV (Stormtrooper black shoulders Princess Leia/Darth Vader/C-3PO) 20.00 40.00

5 Episode V (Snowtrooper/Luke Skywalker hoth Han Solo hoth/Chewbacca hoth)

6 Episode VI (Bike Trooper/Darth Vader Princess Leia endor/Rebel Trooper) 20.00 40.00

7 The Modal Nodes Cantina Band 30.00 60.00

8 Episode II (Mace Windu/Sora Bulq/Oppo Rancisis/Zam Wesell)#(2007 K-Mart Exclusive)

9 Episode III (Commander Cody/Anakin/General Grievous/Clone Pilot)#(2007 K-Mart Exclusive)

10 Episode VI (Darth Vader/R5-J2/Biker Scout/Death Star Gunner)#(2007 K-Mart Exclusive)

## 2007-08 Star Wars 30th Anniversary Collection
### Evolutions

1 Anakin Skywalker to Darth Vader 20.00 40.00

2 Clone Trooper to Stormtrooper 20.00 40.00

3 The Sith

4 The Fett Legacy 25.00 50.00

5 The Jedi Legacy 20.00 40.00

6 The Sith Legacy

7 Vader's Secret Apprentice/Secret Apprentice/Sith Lord/Jedi Knight 30.00 75.00

## 2007-08 Star Wars 30th Anniversary Collection
### Exclusives

1 Cantina Band Member (2007 Disney Weekends Exclusive) 20.00 40.00

2 Concept General Grievous (2007 SWS Exclusive) 15.00 30.00

3 Concept Luke Skywalker (McQuarrie Signature Series) (2007 C4 & CE Exclusive) 15.00 30.00

4 Concept Obi-Wan & Yoda (McQuarrie Signature Series) (2007 SDCC Exclusive) 20.00 40.00

5 Concept R2-D2 & C-3PO (McQuarrie Signature Series) (2007 C4 & CE Exclusive) 12.00 25.00

6 Darth Vader & Incinerator Troopers (The Force Unleashed) (2008 Walmart Exclusive) 25.00 50.00

7 Emperor Palpatine & Shadow Stormtroopers (The Force Unleashed) (2008 Walmart Exclusive)

8 R2-KT (2007 Shared Exclusive) 30.00 60.00

9 Shadow Scout Trooper & Speeder Bike (2007 SDCC Exclusive) 15.00 30.00

10 Shadow Troopers 2-Pack (2008 Jedi-Con Exclusive)

11 Star Wars Collector Coin (2007 Toy Fair Exclusive)

12 Stormtrooper Commander (2008 GameStop Exclusive) 25.00 50.00

## 2007-08 Star Wars 30th Anniversary Collection
### Force Unleashed

9 Imperial EVO Trooper 8.00 15.00

10 Imperial Jumptrooper 10.00 20.00

11a Maris Brood (flesh) 15.00 30.00

11b Maris Brood (white) 10.00 20.00

12 Darth Vader (battle-damaged) 10.00 20.00

ACTION FIGURES AND FIGURINES

| 13 Rahm Kota | 20.00 | 40.00 |
|---|---|---|
| 14 Emperor's Shadow Guard | 20.00 | 40.00 |
| 15 Juno Eclipse | 10.00 | 20.00 |

## 2007-08 Star Wars 30th Anniversary Collection
### Multi-Packs

| 1 Clone Pack (Battlefront II) | | |
|---|---|---|
| (2007 Shared Exclusive) | | |
| 2 Droid Pack (Battlefront II) | 25.00 | 50.00 |
| (2007 Shared Exclusive) | | |
| 3 Clones & Commanders Gift Pack | 20.00 | 40.00 |
| (Toys R Us Exclusive) | | |
| 4 I Am Your Father's Day Gift Pack (2007 Walmart Exclusive) | | |
| 5 The Max Rebo Band Jabba's Palace Entertainers | 30.00 | 60.00 |
| (2007 Walmart Exclusive) | | |
| 6 The Max Rebo Band Jabba's Palace Musicians | 40.00 | 80.00 |
| (2007 Walmart Exclusive) | | |
| 7 Republic Elite Forces Mandalorians & Clone Troopers | | |
| (2007 Entertainment Earth Exclusive) | | |
| 8 Republic Elite Forces Mandalorians & Omega Squad | 75.00 | 150.00 |
| (2007 Entertainment Earth Exclusive) | | |

## 2007-08 Star Wars 30th Anniversary Collection
### Revenge of the Sith

| 1 Obi-Wan Kenobi | 6.00 | 12.00 |
|---|---|---|
| 2 Darth Vader | 10.00 | 20.00 |
| 3 Clone Commander (green) | 5.00 | 10.00 |
| 4 Kashyyyk Trooper | 8.00 | 15.00 |
| 5 Tri-Droid | 8.00 | 15.00 |
| 6 2-1B Surgical Droid | 6.00 | 12.00 |
| 7 Po Nudo | 8.00 | 15.00 |
| 8 Mustafar Panning Droid | 6.00 | 12.00 |

## 2007-08 Star Wars 30th Anniversary Collection
### Saga Legends

| 1 501st Legion Trooper | 8.00 | 15.00 |
|---|---|---|
| 2 Boba Fett | 15.00 | 30.00 |
| 3 C-3PO (w/battle droid head) | 6.00 | 12.00 |
| 4 Chewbacca | 6.00 | 12.00 |
| 5 Clone Trooper (AOTC) | 8.00 | 15.00 |
| 6 Clone Trooper (ROTS) | 6.00 | 12.00 |
| 7 Darth Maul | 8.00 | 15.00 |
| 8 Darth Vader | 8.00 | 15.00 |
| 9 Darth Vader (as Anakin Skywalker) | 8.00 | 15.00 |
| 10 Destroyer Droid | 6.00 | 12.00 |
| 11 General Grievous | 12.00 | 25.00 |
| 12 Obi-Wan Kenobi | 6.00 | 12.00 |
| 13 Princess Leia (Boushh disguise) | 8.00 | 15.00 |
| 14 R2-D2 (electronic) | 10.00 | 20.00 |
| 15 Saesee Tiin | 8.00 | 15.00 |

| 16 Shock Trooper | 10.00 | 20.00 |
|---|---|---|
| 17 Yoda | 8.00 | 15.00 |

## 2007-08 Star Wars 30th Anniversary Collection
### Saga Legends Battle Droid 2-Packs

| 1 Battle Droids 2-Pack I (tan infantry & commander) | 8.00 | 15.00 |
|---|---|---|
| 2 Battle Droids 2-Pack II (maroon blaster and lightsaber damage) | 8.00 | 15.00 |
| 3 Battle Droids 2-Pack III (tan blaster and lightsaber damage) | 8.00 | 15.00 |
| 4 Battle Droids 2-Pack IV (tan dirty & clean) | 8.00 | 15.00 |

## 2007-08 Star Wars 30th Anniversary Collection
### Saga Legends Fan's Choice (2007)

| 1 Biker Scout | 8.00 | 15.00 |
|---|---|---|
| 2 Biker Scout (w/Clone Wars sticker) | | |
| 3 Clone Commander (Coruscant) | 12.00 | 25.00 |
| 4 Clone Trooper Officer (red) | 8.00 | 15.00 |
| 5 Clone Trooper Officer (yellow) | 8.00 | 15.00 |
| 6 Clone Trooper Officer (green) | 10.00 | 20.00 |
| 7 Clone Trooper Officer (blue) | 6.00 | 12.00 |
| 8 Dark Trooper (Fan's Choice Figure #1) | 12.00 | 25.00 |
| 9 Imperial Officer (brown hair) | 6.00 | 12.00 |
| 10 Imperial Officer (blonde hair) | 8.00 | 15.00 |
| 11 Imperial Officer (red hair) | | |
| 12 Pit Droids 2-Pack (white) | | |
| 13 Pit Droids 2-Pack (brown) | | |
| 14 Pit Droids 2-Pack (orange) | 12.00 | 25.00 |
| 15 R4-I9 | 10.00 | 20.00 |
| 16 RA-7 | 6.00 | 12.00 |
| 17 Sandtrooper (dirty; tan shoulder) | 8.00 | 15.00 |
| 18 Sandtrooper (dirty; orange shoulder) | 10.00 | 20.00 |
| 19 Sandtrooper (clean; black shoulder) | 25.00 | 50.00 |
| 20 Sandtrooper (clean; white shoulder) | 12.00 | 25.00 |
| 21 Sandtrooper (dirty; red shoulder) | | |
| 22 TC-14 | 10.00 | 20.00 |

## 2007-08 Star Wars 30th Anniversary Collection
### Saga Legends Fan's Choice (2008)

| 1 501st Legion Trooper | | |
|---|---|---|
| 2 Commander Neyo | 10.00 | 20.00 |
| 3 Covert Ops Clone Trooper (gold coin) | 10.00 | 20.00 |
| 4 Pit Droids 2-Pack (white) | 8.00 | 15.00 |
| 5 Pit Droids 2-Pack (maroon) | 8.00 | 15.00 |
| 6 Pit Droids 2-Pack (orange) | 8.00 | 15.00 |
| 7 Shadow Stormtrooper | 12.00 | 25.00 |

| 8 Utapau Shadow Trooper | 12.00 | 25.00 |
|---|---|---|
| 9 Zev Senesca | 8.00 | 15.00 |

## 2007-08 Star Wars 30th Anniversary Collection
### Silver Coins

| 1a Darth Vader | | |
|---|---|---|
| 1b 30th Anniversary Coin Album | | |
| 2 Galactic Marine | | |
| 3 Mustafar Lava Miner | | |
| 4 R2-D2 | | |
| 5 Obi-Wan Kenobi | | |
| 6 Mace Windu | | |
| 7 Airborne Trooper | | |
| 8 Super Battle Droid | | |
| 9 Concept Stormtrooper (McQuarrie Signature Series) | | |
| 10 Rebel Honor Guard | | |
| 11 Han Solo | | |
| 12 Luke Skywalker ceremony | | |
| 13 Death Star Trooper | | |
| 14 Biggs Darklighter | | |
| 15 Concept Boba Fett (McQuarrie Signature Series) | | |
| 16 Darth Vader | | |
| 17 Biggs Darklighter | | |
| 18 Luke Skywalker tatooine | | |
| 19 Jawa & Lin Droid | | |
| 20 Imperial Stormtrooper | | |
| 21 Concept Chewbacca (McQuarrie Signature Series) | | |
| 22 M'liyoom Onith | | |
| 23 Elis Helrot | | |
| 24 Boba Fett | | |
| 25 Luke Skywalker | | |
| 26 CZ-4 | | |
| 27 Umpass-Stay | | |
| 28 Concept Darth Vader (McQuarrie Signature Series) | | |
| 29 Hermi Odle | | |
| 30 C-3PO & Salacious Crumb | | |
| 31 Roron Corobb | | |
| 32 Yoda & Kybuck | | |
| 33 Anakin Skywalker | | |
| 34 Darth Revan | | |
| 35 Darth Malak | | |
| 36 Pre-Cyborg Grievous | | |
| 37 Concept Starkiller Hero | | |
| 38 Han Solo | | |
| 39 Lando Calrissian | | |
| 40 General McQuarrie | | |
| 41 4-LOM | | |
| 42 Concept Snowtrooper (McQuarrie Signature Series) | | |
| 43 Romba & Graak | | |
| 44 Tycho Celchu | | |
| 45 Anakin Skywalker (Jedi Spirit) | | |
| 46 R2-D2 | | |
| 47 Concept Han Solo (McQuarrie Signature Series) | | |
| 48 Darth Vader (hologram) | | |
| 49 Clone Trooper (7th Legion Trooper) | | |
| 50 Clone Trooper (Hawkbat Batallion) | | |
| 51 R2-B1 | | |
| 52 Naboo Soldier | | |
| 53 Rebel Vanguard Trooper | | |
| 54 Pax Bonkin | | |
| 55 Clone Trooper (training fatigues) | | |
| 56 Padme Amidala | | |
| 57 Jango Fett | | |
| 58 Voolvif Monn | | |
| 59 Destroyer Droid | | |
| 60 Concept Rebel Trooper (McQuarrie Signature Series) | | |

## 2007-08 Star Wars 30th Anniversary Collection
### Ultimate Galactic Hunt

| | | | |
|---|---|---|---|
| 1 | Airborne Trooper | 12.00 | 25.00 |
| 2 | Biggs Darklighter (Rebel pilot) | 7.50 | 15.00 |
| 3 | Boba Fett (animated debut) | 12.00 | 25.00 |
| 4 | Concept Boba Fett (McQuarrie Signature Series) | 20.00 | 40.00 |
| 5 | Concept Chewbacca (McQuarrie Signature Series) | 15.00 | 30.00 |
| 6 | Concept Stormtrooper (McQuarrie Signature Series) | 12.00 | 25.00 |
| 7 | Darth Vader (Sith Lord) | 10.00 | 20.00 |
| 8 | Galactic Marine | 10.00 | 20.00 |
| 9 | Han Solo (smuggler) | 7.50 | 15.00 |
| 10 | Luke Skywalker (Yavin ceremony) | 6.00 | 12.00 |
| 11 | Mace Windu | 7.50 | 15.00 |
| 12 | R2-D2 | 6.00 | 12.00 |

## 2007-08 Star Wars 30th Anniversary Collection
### Ultimate Galactic Hunt Gold Coins

| | | | |
|---|---|---|---|
| 1 | Airborne Trooper | 6.00 | 12.00 |
| 2 | Biggs Darklighter | 4.00 | 8.00 |
| 3 | Boba Fett | 6.00 | 12.00 |
| 4 | Concept Boba Fett (McQuarrie Signature Series) | 10.00 | 20.00 |
| 5 | Concept Chewbacca (McQuarrie Signature Series) | 7.50 | 15.00 |
| 6 | Concept Stormtrooper (McQuarrie Signature Series) | 6.00 | 12.00 |
| 7 | Darth Vader | 5.00 | 10.00 |
| 8 | Galactic Marine | 5.00 | 10.00 |
| 9 | Han Solo | 4.00 | 8.00 |
| 10 | Luke Skywalker | 3.00 | 6.00 |
| 11 | Mace Windu | 4.00 | 8.00 |
| 12 | R2-D2 | 3.00 | 6.00 |

## 2007-08 Star Wars 30th Anniversary Collection
### Vehicles

| | | | |
|---|---|---|---|
| 1 | Aayla Secura's Jedi Starfighter | 20.00 | 40.00 |
| 2 | ARC-170 Fighter (Clone Wars) | 50.00 | 100.00 |
| 3 | AT-AP Walker | 20.00 | 40.00 |
| 4 | Anakin Skywalker's Jedi Starfighter (Coruscant) | 20.00 | 40.00 |
| 5 | Anakin Skywalker's Jedi Starfighter (Mustafar) | 20.00 | 40.00 |
| 6 | Darth Vader's Sith Starfighter | 40.00 | 80.00 |
| 7 | Darth Vader's TIE Advanced Starfighter | 30.00 | 60.00 |
| 8 | General Grievous' Starfighter | 25.00 | 50.00 |
| 9 | Hailfire Droid | 25.00 | 50.00 |
| 10 | Mace Windu's Jedi Starfighter | 15.00 | 30.00 |
| 11 | Obi-Wan's Jedi Starfighter (Coruscant) | 25.00 | 50.00 |
| 12 | Obi-Wan's Jedi Starfighter (Utapau) | 25.00 | 50.00 |
| 13 | Saesee Tiin's Jedi Starfighter | 20.00 | 40.00 |
| 14 | Sith Infiltrator | 25.00 | 50.00 |
| 15 | TIE Fighter | 15.00 | 30.00 |
| 16 | Trade Federation Armored Assault Tank (AAT) | 20.00 | 40.00 |
| 17 | V-Wing Starfighter/ spring-open wings | 50.00 | 100.00 |

## 2007-08 Star Wars 30th Anniversary Collection
### Vehicles Exclusives

| | | | |
|---|---|---|---|
| 1 | Elite TIE Inteceptor/181st Squadron TIE Pilot | 75.00 | 150.00 |
| | (Toys R Us exclusive) | | |
| 2 | Obi-Wan's Jedi Starfighter (w/hyperspace ring) | 25.00 | 50.00 |
| | (2007 Toys R Us Exclusive) | | |
| 3 | TIE Bomber (w/TIE Bomber Pilot) | 30.00 | 75.00 |
| | (2007 Target Exclusive) | | |
| 4 | TIE Fighter (w/TIE Pilot/opening cockpit and ejecting wing panels) | 25.00 | 50.00 |
| | (2007 Toys R Us Exclusive) | | |
| 5 | Y-Wing Fighter (w/Lt. Lepira & R5-F7) | 75.00 | 150.00 |
| | (2007 Toys R Us Exclusive) | | |

## 1998-99 Star Wars Action Collection

| | | | |
|---|---|---|---|
| 1 | AT-AT Driver | 15.00 | 30.00 |
| 2 | Barquin D'an | 10.00 | 20.00 |
| 3 | Chewbacca in Chains | 15.00 | 30.00 |
| 4 | Emperor Palpatine | 12.00 | 25.00 |
| 5 | Grand Moff Tarkin | 12.00 | 25.00 |
| 6 | Greedo | 15.00 | 30.00 |
| 7 | Han Solo (carbonite) | 15.00 | 30.00 |
| | (Target Exclusive) | | |
| 8 | Han Solo (Hoth) | 15.00 | 30.00 |
| 9 | Jawa | 10.00 | 20.00 |
| 10 | Luke Skywalker (ceremonial dress) | | |
| 11 | Luke Skywalker (Hoth) | 15.00 | 30.00 |
| 12 | Luke Skywalker (Jedi Knight) | 12.00 | 25.00 |
| 13 | Princess Leia (Hoth) | 12.00 | 25.00 |
| | (Service Merchandise Exclusive) | | |
| 14 | R2-D2 | 20.00 | 40.00 |
| 15 | R2-D2 (detachable utility arms) | 20.00 | 40.00 |
| 16 | R5-D4 | 15.00 | 30.00 |
| | (Walmart Exclusive) | | |
| 17 | Sandtrooper (w/droid) | 8.00 | 15.00 |
| 18 | Snowtrooper | 12.00 | 25.00 |
| 19 | Snowtrooper (blue variant) | | |
| 20 | Wicket | 20.00 | 40.00 |
| | (Walmart Exclusive) | | |
| 21 | Yoda | 20.00 | 40.00 |

## 1998-99 Star Wars Action Collection Electronic

| | | | |
|---|---|---|---|
| 1 | Boba Fett | 25.00 | 50.00 |
| | (KB Toys Exclusive) | | |
| 2 | Darth Vader | 20.00 | 40.00 |

## 1998-99 Star Wars Action Collection Multi-Packs

| | | | |
|---|---|---|---|
| 1 | C-3PO and R2-D2 2-Pack | 40.00 | 80.00 |
| 2 | Emperor Palpatine and Royal Guard 2-Pack | 20.00 | 40.00 |
| 3 | Wedge Antilles and Biggs Darklighter 2-Pack | 25.00 | 50.00 |
| | (FAO Schwarz Exclusive) | | |
| 4 | Luke (Tatooine)/Leia (Boushh)/Han (Bespin) 3-Pack | 40.00 | 80.00 |
| | (KB Toys Exclusive) | | |
| 5 | Luke/Han/Snowtrooper/AT-AT Driver Hoth 4-Pack | 60.00 | 120.00 |
| | (JC Penney Exclusive) | | |

## 1993 Star Wars Bend Ems

| | | |
|---|---|---|
| 1 Admiral Ackbar | 7.50 | 15.00 |
| 2 Ben Kenobi | 10.00 | 20.00 |
| 3 Bib Fortuna | 7.50 | 15.00 |
| 4 Boba Fett | 15.00 | 30.00 |
| 5 C-3PO | 10.00 | 20.00 |
| 6 Chewbacca | 7.50 | 15.00 |
| 7 Darth Vader | 12.50 | 25.00 |
| 8 Emperor | 10.00 | 20.00 |
| 9 Emperor's Royal Guard | 7.50 | 15.00 |
| 10 Gamorrean Guard | 7.50 | 15.00 |
| 11 Han Solo | 10.00 | 20.00 |
| 12 Lando Calrissian | 7.50 | 15.00 |
| 13 Leia Organa | 10.00 | 20.00 |
| 14 Luke Skywalker | 10.00 | 20.00 |
| 15 Luke Skywalker X-wing | 10.00 | 20.00 |
| 16 R2-D2 | 7.50 | 15.00 |
| 17 Stormtrooper | 7.50 | 15.00 |
| 18 Tusken Raider | 7.50 | 15.00 |
| 19 Wicket | 7.50 | 15.00 |
| 20 Yoda | 7.50 | 15.00 |
| 21 4-Piece A New Hope | 20.00 | 40.00 |
| (Chewbacca/Luke Skywalker/R2-D2/Tusken Raider) | | |
| 22 4-Piece Empire Strikes Back | 20.00 | 40.00 |
| (Han Solo/Darth Vader/Yoda/Lando Calrissian) | | |
| 23 4-Piece Return of the Jedi | 25.00 | 50.00 |
| (Admiral Ackbar/Boba Fett/Wicket/Bib Fortuna) | | |
| 24 4-Piece Gift Set 1 | 20.00 | 40.00 |
| (Ben Kenobi/Leia Organa/Han Solo/C-3PO) | | |
| 25 4-Piece Gift Set 2 | 20.00 | 40.00 |
| (Storm Trooper/Wicket/Yoda/Chewbacca) | | |
| 26 4-Piece Gift Set 3 | 20.00 | 40.00 |
| (Storm Trooper/R2-D2/C-3PO/Darth Vader) | | |
| 27 4-Piece Gift Set 4 | 20.00 | 40.00 |
| (Emperor/C-3PO/Luke Skywalker/Darth Vader) | | |
| 28 6-Piece Gift Set 1 | 25.00 | 50.00 |
| (Darth Vader/Stormtrooper/Luke Skywalker/R2-D2/C-3PO | | |
| 29 6-Piece Gift Set 2 | 25.00 | 50.00 |
| (Stormtrooper/Darth Vader/Emperor's Royal Guard/#(Admiral Ackbar/Lando | | |
| Calrissian/Chewbacca) | | |
| 30 8-Piece Gift Set | 25.00 | 50.00 |
| (Darth Vader/Luke Skywalker/C-3PO/Emperor/#(Stormtrooper/R2-D2/Princess | | |
| Leia/Ewok) | | |
| 31 10-Piece Gift Set | 30.00 | 60.00 |
| (R2-D2/Stormtrooper/Darth Vader/Admiral Ackbar/#(Chewbacca/Han Solo/Princess | | |
| Leia/Luke Skywalker/#(Bib Fortuna/Emperor's Royal Guard) | | |

## 2014-15 Star Wars Black Series 3.75-Inch Blue

| | | |
|---|---|---|
| 1 R5-G19 | 10.00 | 20.00 |
| 2A Luke Skywalker Hoth | 8.00 | 15.00 |
| (incorrect elbow pegs) | | |
| 2B Luke Skywalker Hoth | 8.00 | 15.00 |
| (correct elbow pegs) | | |
| 3 Darth Vader | 8.00 | 15.00 |
| (Revenge Of The Sith) | | |
| 4 Darth Malgus | 20.00 | 40.00 |
| 5 Starkiller | 20.00 | 40.00 |
| (Galen Marek) | | |
| 6 Yoda | 12.00 | 25.00 |
| (pack forward) | | |
| 7 Darth Vader | 12.00 | 25.00 |
| (Dagobah Test) | | |
| 8 Stormtrooper | 10.00 | 20.00 |
| 9 Captain Rex | 8.00 | 15.00 |
| 10 Jon Dutch Vander | 10.00 | 20.00 |
| 11 Chewbacca | 8.00 | 15.00 |
| 12 Clone Commander Wolffe | 10.00 | 20.00 |
| 13 Clone Commander Doom | 6.00 | 12.00 |
| 14 Imperial Navy Commander | 10.00 | 20.00 |
| 15 Commander Thorn | 12.00 | 25.00 |
| 16 C-3PO | 12.00 | 25.00 |
| 17 Princess Leia Organa | 10.00 | 20.00 |
| (Boushh) | | |
| 18 Mosep Binneed | 10.00 | 20.00 |
| 19 Han Solo | 20.00 | 40.00 |
| (with Carbonite Block) | | |
| 20 Jawas | 8.00 | 15.00 |

## 2014-15 Star Wars Black Series 3.75-Inch Blue Exclusives

| | | |
|---|---|---|
| 1 Battle on Endor 8-Pack | 80.00 | 150.00 |
| (Toys R Us Exclusive) | | |
| 2 Jabba's Rancor Pit | 100.00 | 200.00 |
| (Toys R Us Exclusive) | | |

## 2013-14 Star Wars Black Series 3.75-Inch Orange

| | | |
|---|---|---|
| 1 Padme Amidala | 25.00 | 50.00 |
| 2 Clone Trooper Sergeant | 6.00 | 12.00 |
| 3A Anakin Skywalker | 10.00 | 20.00 |
| (dark brown hair) | | |
| 3B Anakin Skywalker | 10.00 | 20.00 |
| (light brown hair) | | |
| 4 Biggs Darklighter | 6.00 | 12.00 |
| 5A Luke Skywalker | 8.00 | 15.00 |
| (short medal strap) | | |
| 5B Luke Skywalker | 8.00 | 15.00 |
| (long medal strap) | | |
| 6 Darth Vader | 8.00 | 15.00 |
| 7 Biker Scout | 6.00 | 12.00 |
| 8 Clone Pilot | 6.00 | 12.00 |
| 9 R2-D2 | 15.00 | 30.00 |
| 10 Pablo-Jill | 20.00 | 40.00 |
| 11 Luminara Unduli | 6.00 | 12.00 |
| 12A 41st Elite Corps Clone Trooper | | |
| (incorrect markings) | | |
| 12B 41st Elite Corps Clone Trooper | 12.50 | 25.00 |
| (correct markings) | | |
| 13 Stormtrooper | 8.00 | 15.00 |
| 14 Mara Jade | 15.00 | 30.00 |
| 15 Merumeru | 10.00 | 20.00 |
| 16 Clone Commander Neyo | 10.00 | 20.00 |

| | | |
|---|---|---|
| 17 Vizam | 8.00 | 15.00 |
| 18 Darth Plageuis | 45.00 | 90.00 |
| 19 Mace Windu | 12.00 | 25.00 |
| 20 Bastila Shan | 20.00 | 40.00 |
| 21 Luke Skywalker | 8.00 | 15.00 |
| 22 Yoda | 10.00 | 20.00 |
| 23 Toryn Farr | 10.00 | 20.00 |
| 24 Snowtrooper Commander | 8.00 | 15.00 |
| 25 Dak Ralter | 10.00 | 20.00 |
| 26 Darth Vader | 15.00 | 30.00 |
| 27 Jabba's Skiff Guard | 25.00 | 50.00 |
| 28 Ree-Yees | 20.00 | 40.00 |
| 29 Wedge Antilles | 8.00 | 15.00 |
| 31 Republic Trooper | 25.00 | 50.00 |

## 2013-14 Star Wars Black Series 3.75-Inch Orange Exclusives

| | | |
|---|---|---|
| 1 Luke Skywalker Hoth Battle Gear | 6.00 | 12.00 |
| 2 R5-D4 | | |

## 2015-18 Star Wars Black Series 3.75-Inch Red

| | | |
|---|---|---|
| NNO Admiral Ackbar | 7.50 | 15.00 |
| NNO Ahsoka Tano | 10.00 | 20.00 |
| NNO AT-ST Driver | | |
| NNO Boba Fett (prototype fatigues) | 15.00 | 30.00 |
| NNO Captain Cassian Andor | 6.00 | 12.00 |
| NNO Captain Phasma | 6.00 | 12.00 |
| NNO Chewbacca | 12.50 | 25.00 |
| NNO Darth Vader | 7.50 | 15.00 |
| NNO Elite Praetorian Guard | 15.00 | 30.00 |
| NNO Emperor's Royal Guard | 6.00 | 12.00 |
| NNO Finn (Jakku) | 10.00 | 20.00 |
| NNO First Order Stormtrooper | 6.00 | 12.00 |
| NNO First Order Stormtrooper Executioner | 6.00 | 12.00 |
| NNO Han Solo | 7.50 | 15.00 |
| NNO Han Solo (Starkiller Base) | 7.50 | 15.00 |
| NNO Imperial Death Trooper | 10.00 | 20.00 |
| NNO Kylo Ren | 7.50 | 15.00 |
| NNO Lando Calrissian | 6.00 | 12.00 |
| NNO Luke Skywalker | 6.00 | 12.00 |
| NNO Luke Skywalker (Jedi Master) | 6.00 | 12.00 |
| NNO Poe Dameron | 6.00 | 12.00 |
| NNO Ponda Baba | 6.00 | 12.00 |
| NNO Princess Leia Organa | 8.00 | 15.00 |
| NNO Princess Leia Organa (D'Qar Gown) | 15.00 | 30.00 |
| NNO Rey (Jakku) | 10.00 | 20.00 |
| NNO Rose Tico | 6.00 | 12.00 |
| NNO Sandtrooper | 7.50 | 15.00 |
| NNO Scarif Stormtrooper Squad Leader | 12.50 | 25.00 |
| NNO Sentry Droid Mark IV | | |
| NNO Sergeant Jyn Erso | 6.00 | 12.00 |
| NNO Tusken Raider | 7.50 | 15.00 |

## 2015-19 Star Wars Black Series Red Vehicles

| | | |
|---|---|---|
| 1 Special Forces TIE Fighter and Pilot Elite | 100.00 | 200.00 |
| 2 X-34 Landspeeder (w/Luke Skywalker) | | |
| 3 Rey's Speeder (Jakku) | | |
| 4 Dewback & Sandtrooper | | |
| 5 Enfys Nest's Swoop Bike | | |

## 2014-15 Star Wars Black Series 6-Inch Blue

| | | |
|---|---|---|
| 1 Sandtrooper | 15.00 | 30.00 |
| Black Pauldron | | |
| 2 Darth Vader | 12.00 | 25.00 |
| Episode VI | | |
| 3 Luke Skywalker | 25.00 | 50.00 |
| Episode VI | | |
| 4 Chewbacca | 20.00 | 40.00 |
| 5 TIE Pilot | 15.00 | 30.00 |
| 6 Yoda | 25.00 | 50.00 |
| 7 Clone Trooper Sergeant | 12.00 | 25.00 |
| 8 Obi-Wan Kenobi | 10.00 | 20.00 |
| Reissue | | |
| 9 Han Solo Stormtrooper | 12.00 | 25.00 |
| 10 Bossk | 20.00 | 40.00 |
| 11 Luke Skywalker | 12.00 | 25.00 |
| Stormtrooper | | |
| 12 Emperor Palpatine | 15.00 | 30.00 |
| 13 Clone Trooper Captain | 12.00 | 25.00 |
| 14 IG-88 | 20.00 | 40.00 |
| 15 Princess Leia | 30.00 | 60.00 |
| 16 Clone Commander Cody | 12.00 | 25.00 |

## 2014-15 Star Wars Black Series 6-Inch Blue

| | | |
|---|---|---|
| 1 Han Solo (w/Tauntaun) | 25.00 | 50.00 |
| 2 Jabba the Hutt | 25.00 | 50.00 |
| 3 Luke Skywalker (w/Wampa) | 20.00 | 40.00 |
| 4 Scout Trooper (w/Speeder Bike) | 20.00 | 40.00 |

## 2013-19 Star Wars Black Series 6-Inch Exclusives

| | | |
|---|---|---|
| NNO Admiral Ackbar & First Order Officer 2-Pack | | |
| (2017 Toys R Us Exclusive) | 10.00 | 20.00 |
| NNO Admiral Ackbar | | |
| (2017 Toys R Us Exclusive) | 15.00 | 30.00 |
| NNO Admiral Piett | | |
| (2019 Walgreens Exclusive) | 12.50 | 25.00 |
| NNO Astromech 3-Pack | | |
| (2016 Toys R Us Exclusive) | 50.00 | 100.00 |
| NNO Boba Fett (Kenner Tribute) | | |
| (2019 SDCC Exclusive) | 75.00 | 150.00 |
| NNO Boba Fett (Prototype Armor) | | |
| (2014 Walgreens Exclusive) | 25.00 | 50.00 |
| NNO Boba Fett and Han Solo in Carbonite | | |
| (2013 SDCC Exclusive) | 200.00 | 400.00 |
| NNO C-3PO | | |
| (2016 Walgreens Exclusive) | 25.00 | 50.00 |
| NNO Cantina Showdown | | |
| (2014 Toys R Us Exclusive) | 50.00 | 100.00 |
| NNO Captain Phasma (Quicksilver Baton) | | |
| (2018 Toys R Us Exclusive) | 10.00 | 20.00 |
| NNO Captain Rex | | |
| (2017 Hascon Exclusive) | 50.00 | 100.00 |
| NNO Chewbacca | | |
| (2018 Target Exclusive) | 20.00 | 40.00 |
| NNO Commander Gree | | |
| (2017 Toys R Us Exclusive) | 30.00 | 75.00 |
| NNO Commander Wolffe | | |
| (2017 Disney Store Exclusive) | 20.00 | 40.00 |
| NNO Darth Maul (Jedi Duel) | | |
| (2019 Celebration Exclusive) | 30.00 | 75.00 |
| NNO Darth Vader Emperor's Wrath | | |
| (2015 Walgreen's Exclusive) | 15.00 | 30.00 |
| NNO Elite Praetorian Guard (w/heavy blade) | | |
| (2017 Amazon Exclusive) | 20.00 | 40.00 |

| | | |
|---|---|---|
| NNO Emperor Palpatine and Throne | | |
| (2019 Amazon Exclusive) | 50.00 | 100.00 |
| NNO First Order Officer | | |
| (2017 Toys R Us Exclusive) | 10.00 | 20.00 |
| NNO First Order Snowtrooper Officer | | |
| (2015 Toys R Us Exclusive) | 15.00 | 30.00 |
| NNO First Order Stormtrooper (w/extra gear) | | |
| (2017 Amazon Exclusive) | 15.00 | 30.00 |
| NNO First Order Stormtrooper Executioner | | |
| (2017 Target Exclusive) | 10.00 | 20.00 |
| NNO First Order Stormtrooper Officer | | |
| (2015 SDCC Exclusive) | 30.00 | 75.00 |
| NNO Gamorrean Guard | | |
| (2018 Target Exclusive) | 30.00 | 75.00 |
| NNO General Veers | | |
| (2018 Walgreens Exclusive) | 10.00 | 20.00 |
| NNO Grand Admiral Thrawn | | |
| (2017 SDCC Exclusive) | 60.00 | 120.00 |
| NNO Guards 4-Pack | | |
| (2017 Barnes & Noble/GameStop Exclusive) | 60.00 | 120.00 |
| NNO Han Solo & Princess Leia Organa | | |
| (2018 International Exclusive) | 30.00 | 75.00 |
| NNO Han Solo (Exogorth Escape) | | |
| (2018 SDCC Exclusive) | 30.00 | 60.00 |
| NNO Imperial AT-ACT Driver | | |
| (2017 Target Exclusive) | 15.00 | 30.00 |
| NNO Imperial Forces 4-Pack | | |
| (2015 Entertainment Earth Exclusive) | 50.00 | 100.00 |
| NNO Imperial Hovertank Pilot | | |
| (2016 Toys R Us Exclusive) | 15.00 | 30.00 |
| NNO Imperial Jumptrooper | | |
| (2019 GameStop Exclusive) | 12.50 | 25.00 |
| NNO Imperial Shadow Squadron | | |
| (2014 Target Exclusive) | 60.00 | 120.00 |
| NNO Imperial Shock Trooper | | |
| (2015 Walmart Exclusive) | 25.00 | 50.00 |
| NNO Inferno Squad Agent | | |
| (2017 GameStop Exclusive) | 20.00 | 40.00 |
| NNO Jabba's Throne Room | | |
| (2014 SDCC Exclusive) | 100.00 | 200.00 |
| NNO Kylo Ren (throne room) | | |
| (2017 Walmart Exclusive) | 12.50 | 25.00 |
| NNO Kylo Ren (unmasked) | | |
| (2016 Celebration/SDCC Exclusive) | 30.00 | 75.00 |
| NNO Kylo Ren | | |
| (2015 Kmart Exclusive) | 15.00 | 30.00 |
| NNO Luke Skywalker (Ceremonial Outfit) | | |
| (2019 Convention Exclusive) | | |
| NNO Luke Skywalker (Death Star Escape) | | |
| (2019 Target Exclusive) | 10.00 | 20.00 |
| NNO Luke Skywalker (w/Ach-to base) | | |
| (2017 Target Exclusive) | 15.00 | 30.00 |
| NNO Luke Skywalker X-Wing Pilot | | |
| (2017 Celebration Exclusive) | 100.00 | 200.00 |
| NNO Moloch | | |
| (2018 Target Exclusive) | 30.00 | 75.00 |
| NNO Obi-Wan Kenobi (Jedi Duel) | | |
| (2019 Celebration Exclusive) | 50.00 | 100.00 |
| NNO Obi-Wan Kenobi | | |
| (2016 SDCC Exclusive) | 50.00 | 100.00 |
| NNO Obi-Wan Kenobit (Force ghost) | | |
| (2017 Walgreens Exclusive) | 10.00 | 20.00 |
| NNO Phase II Clone Trooper 4-Pack | | |
| (2016 Entertainment Earth Exclusive) | 50.00 | 100.00 |
| NNO Poe Dameron and Riot Control Stormtrooper | | |
| (2015 Target Exclusive) | 20.00 | 40.00 |
| NNO Princess Leia (Bespin Escape) | | |

| | | |
|---|---|---|
| (2018 Target Exclusive) | 10.00 | 20.00 |
| NNO Red Squadron 3-Pack | | |
| (2018 Amazon Exclusive) | 60.00 | 120.00 |
| NNO Resistance Tech Rose | | |
| (2017 Walmart Exclusive) | 7.50 | 15.00 |
| NNO Rey (Jedi Training) & Luke Skywalker (Jedi Master) 2-Pack | | |
| (2017 SDCC Exclusive) | 30.00 | 60.00 |
| NNO Rey (Starkiller Base) | | |
| (2016 Kmart Exclusive) | 12.50 | 25.00 |
| NNO Rey (w/Crait base)#[(2017 Toys R Us Exclusive) | 15.00 | 30.00 |
| NNO Rogue One 3-Pack | | |
| Imperial Death Trooper/Captain Cassian Andor/Sergeant Jyn Erso (Jedha) | | |
| (2016 Target Exclusive) | 30.00 | 75.00 |
| NNO Scarif Stormtrooper | | |
| (2016 Walmart Exclusive) | 15.00 | 30.00 |
| NNO Sergeant Jyn Erso (Eadu) | | |
| (2016 Kmart Exclusive) | 10.00 | 20.00 |
| NNO Sergeant Jyn Erso | | |
| (2016 SDCC Exclusive) | 60.00 | 120.00 |
| NNO Sith Trooper (multiple weapons) | | |
| (2019 SDCC Exclusive) | 30.00 | 60.00 |
| NNO Stormtrooper (Mimban) | | |
| (2018 Walmart Exclusive) | 15.00 | 30.00 |
| NNO Stormtrooper (w/blast accessories) | | |
| (2018 Toys R Us International Exclusive) | 50.00 | 100.00 |
| NNO Stormtrooper Evolution 4-Pack | | |
| (2015 Amazon Exclusive) | 50.00 | 100.00 |
| NNO Supreme Leader Snoke (Throne Room) | | |
| (2017 GameStop Exclusive) | 15.00 | 30.00 |
| NNO X-34 Landspeeder (w/Luke Skywalker) | | |
| (2017 SDCC Exclusive) | 50.00 | 100.00 |
| NNO Zuckuss | | |
| (2018 Disney Store Exclusive) | 12.50 | 25.00 |

## 2019 Star Wars Black Series 6-Inch Multipacks

| | | |
|---|---|---|
| NNO Droid Depot 4-Pack | 50.00 | 100.00 |
| NNO First Order 4-Pack | 60.00 | 120.00 |
| NNO Smuggler's Run 5-Pack | 50.00 | 100.00 |

## 2013-14 Star Wars Black Series 6-Inch Orange

| | | |
|---|---|---|
| 1 Luke Skywalker X-Wing Pilot | 50.00 | 100.00 |
| 2 Darth Maul | 30.00 | 60.00 |
| 3 Sandtrooper | 20.00 | 40.00 |
| 4 R2-D2 | 40.00 | 80.00 |
| 5 Princess Leia Organa (Slave attire) | 40.00 | 80.00 |
| 6 Boba Fett | 40.00 | 80.00 |
| 7 Greedo | 20.00 | 40.00 |
| 8 Han Solo | 20.00 | 40.00 |
| 9 Stormtrooper | 12.00 | 25.00 |
| 10 Obi-Wan Kenobi | 20.00 | 40.00 |
| Episode II | | |
| 11 Luke Skywalker Bespin Gear | 30.00 | 60.00 |
| 12 Anakin Skywalker | 40.00 | 80.00 |
| Episode III | | |
| 13 Clone Trooper | 12.00 | 25.00 |
| Episode II | | |

## 2015-19 Star Wars Black Series 6-Inch Red

| | | |
|---|---|---|
| 1A Finn Jakku | | |
| (Glossy Head) | 12.00 | 25.00 |
| 1B Finn Jakku | | |
| (Matte Head) | 12.00 | 25.00 |
| 2A Rey and BB-8 | | |

# ACTION FIGURES AND FIGURINES

| | | |
|---|---|---|
| (Clean) | 12.00 | 25.00 |
| 2B Rey and BB-8 | | |
| (Dirty) | 12.00 | 25.00 |
| 3 Kylo Ren | 10.00 | 20.00 |
| 4 First Order Stormtrooper | 10.00 | 20.00 |
| 5 Chewbacca | 10.00 | 20.00 |
| 6 Captain Phasma | 20.00 | 40.00 |
| 7 Poe Dameron | 10.00 | 20.00 |
| 8 Guavian Enforcer | 12.00 | 25.00 |
| 9A Constable Zuvio | | |
| (green helmet) | 10.00 | 20.00 |
| 9B Constable Zuvio | | |
| (brown helmet) | 10.00 | 20.00 |
| 10A Resistance Soldier | | |
| (green helmet) | 20.00 | 40.00 |
| 10B Resistance Soldier | | |
| (brown helmet) | 10.00 | 20.00 |
| 11 First Order TIE Fighter Pilot | 15.00 | 30.00 |
| 12 First Order Snowtrooper | 12.00 | 25.00 |
| 13 First Order General Hux | 15.00 | 30.00 |
| 14 X-Wing Pilot Asty | 15.00 | 30.00 |
| 15 Jango Fett | 10.00 | 20.00 |
| 16 First Order Flametrooper | 10.00 | 20.00 |
| 17 Finn (FN-2187) | 20.00 | 40.00 |
| 18 Han Solo | 12.00 | 25.00 |
| 19 Kanan Jarrus | 15.00 | 30.00 |
| 20 Ahsoka Tano | 20.00 | 40.00 |
| 21 Luke Skywalker | 10.00 | 20.00 |
| 22 Sergeant Jyn Erso (Jedha) | 15.00 | 30.00 |
| 23 Captain Cassian Andor (Eadu) | 10.00 | 20.00 |
| 24 K-2SO | 12.50 | 25.00 |
| 25 Imperial Death Trooper | 12.50 | 25.00 |
| 26 Kylo Ren (unmasked) | 12.50 | 25.00 |
| 27 Director Krennic | 10.00 | 20.00 |
| 28 Scarif Stormtrooper Squad Leader | 20.00 | 40.00 |
| 29 C-3PO (Resistance Base) | 10.00 | 20.00 |
| 30 Princess Leia Organa | 12.50 | 25.00 |
| 31 AT-AT Pilot/AT-AT Driver | 20.00 | 40.00 |
| 32 Obi-Wan Kenobi | 15.00 | 30.00 |
| 33 Sabine Wren | 25.00 | 50.00 |
| 34 Darth Revan | 20.00 | 40.00 |
| 35 Snowtrooper | 10.00 | 20.00 |
| 36 Chirrut Imwe | 20.00 | 40.00 |
| 37 Baze Malbus | 15.00 | 30.00 |
| 38 Imperial Royal Guard | 10.00 | 20.00 |
| 39 Lando Calrissian | 12.50 | 25.00 |
| 40 Qui-Gon Jinn | 15.00 | 30.00 |
| 41 Tusken Raider | 15.00 | 30.00 |
| 42 Hera Syndulla | 20.00 | 40.00 |
| 43 Darth Vader | 12.50 | 25.00 |
| 44 Rey (Jedi Training) | 12.50 | 25.00 |
| 45 Kylo Ren | 12.50 | 25.00 |
| 46 Luke Skywalker (Jedi Master) | 12.50 | 25.00 |
| 47 Grand Admiral Thrawn | 25.00 | 50.00 |
| 48 Stormtrooper | 15.00 | 30.00 |
| 49 Maz Kanata | 10.00 | 20.00 |
| 50 Elite Praetorian Guard | 15.00 | 30.00 |
| 51 Finn (First Order Disguise) | 10.00 | 20.00 |
| 52 General Leia Organa | 12.50 | 25.00 |
| 53 Poe Dameron | 10.00 | 20.00 |
| 54 Supreme Leader Snoke | 12.50 | 25.00 |
| 55 Rose Tico | 10.00 | 20.00 |
| 56 Jaina Solo | 20.00 | 40.00 |
| 57 DJ | 10.00 | 20.00 |
| 58 Rey | 10.00 | 20.00 |
| 59 Captain Rex | 12.50 | 25.00 |
| 60 Death Squad Commander | 15.00 | 30.00 |

| | | |
|---|---|---|
| 61 Jawa | 10.00 | 20.00 |
| 62 Han Solo | 12.50 | 25.00 |
| 63 Grand Moff Tark (w/IT-O Droid) | 20.00 | 40.00 |
| 64 Range Trooper | 10.00 | 20.00 |
| 65 Lando Calrissian | 12.50 | 25.00 |
| 66 Qi'Ra | 12.50 | 25.00 |
| 67 4-LOM | 25.00 | 50.00 |
| 68 Tobias Beckett | 20.00 | 40.00 |
| 69 Rebel Fleet Trooper | 20.00 | 40.00 |
| 70 Han Solo (Bespin) | 12.50 | 25.00 |
| 71 Val (Vandor-1) | 10.00 | 20.00 |
| 72 Imperial Patrol Trooper | 12.50 | 25.00 |
| 73 L3-37 | 12.50 | 25.00 |
| 74 Dengar | 15.00 | 30.00 |
| 75 Princess Leia Organa (Hoth) | 10.00 | 20.00 |
| 76 Lando Calrissian (Skiff) | 12.50 | 25.00 |
| 77 Rio Durant | 10.00 | 20.00 |
| 78 Han Solo (Mimban) | 15.00 | 30.00 |
| 79 Dryden Vos | 10.00 | 20.00 |
| 80 Vice Admiral Holdo | 10.00 | 20.00 |
| 81 Padme Amidala | 10.00 | 20.00 |
| 82 Mace Windu | 12.50 | 25.00 |
| 83 Battle Droid | 10.00 | 20.00 |
| 84 Chopper (C1-10P) | 12.50 | 25.00 |
| 85 Obi-Wan Kenobi (Padawan) | 12.50 | 25.00 |
| 86 Ezra Bridger | 20.00 | 40.00 |
| 87 Doctor Aphra | 15.00 | 30.00 |
| 88 BT-1 (Beetee) | 12.50 | 25.00 |
| 89 0-0-0 (Triple Zero) | 20.00 | 40.00 |
| 92 Sith Trooper | 12.50 | 25.00 |

## 2017 Star Wars Black Series 40th Anniversary 6-Inch

| | | |
|---|---|---|
| NNO Artoo Detoo | 30.00 | 60.00 |
| NNO Ben (Obi-Wan) Kenobi | 15.00 | 30.00 |
| NNO Chewbacca | 25.00 | 50.00 |
| NNO Darth Vader Legacy Pack | 30.00 | 60.00 |
| NNO Death Squad Commander | 15.00 | 30.00 |
| NNO Han Solo | 25.00 | 50.00 |
| NNO Jawa | 20.00 | 40.00 |
| NNO Luke Skywalker | 20.00 | 40.00 |
| NNO Luke Skywalker X-Wing Pilot | 120.00 | 250.00 |
| (Celebration Orlando Exclusive) | | |
| NNO Princess Leia Organa | 15.00 | 30.00 |
| NNO R5-D4 | 20.00 | 40.00 |
| (GameStop Exclusive) | | |
| NNO Sand People | 30.00 | 60.00 |
| NNO See Threepio | 25.00 | 50.00 |
| NNO Stormtrooper | 30.00 | 60.00 |

## 2017 Star Wars Black Series 40th Anniversary Titanium Series 3.75-Inch

| | | |
|---|---|---|
| 1 Darth Vader | 15.00 | 30.00 |
| 2 Obi-Wan Kenobi | 12.00 | 25.00 |
| 3 Luke Skywalker | 12.00 | 25.00 |
| 4 Princess Leia Organa | 12.00 | 25.00 |
| 5 Han Solo | 15.00 | 30.00 |

## 2019 Star Wars Black Series Archive

| | | |
|---|---|---|
| NNO Anakin Skywalker | 12.00 | 30.00 |
| NNO Boba Fett | 15.00 | 40.00 |
| NNO Bossk | 10.00 | 25.00 |
| NNO Darth Maul | 10.00 | 25.00 |
| NNO IG-88 | 8.00 | 20.00 |
| NNO Luke Skywalker (X-Wing) | 10.00 | 25.00 |
| NNO Scout Trooper | 8.00 | 20.00 |
| NNO Yoda | 12.00 | 30.00 |

## 2017-18 Star Wars Black Series Centerpieces

| | | |
|---|---|---|
| 1 Darth Vader | 30.00 | 60.00 |
| 2 Luke Skywalker | 20.00 | 40.00 |
| 3 Kylo Ren | 20.00 | 40.00 |
| 4 Rey | 30.00 | 60.00 |
| NNO Rey vs. Kylo Ren | 75.00 | 150.00 |
| (2018 SDCC Exclusive) | | |

## 2019 Star Wars Black Series Deluxe

| | | | |
|---|---|---|---|
| D1 | General Grievous | 25.00 | 50.00 |

## 2018 Star Wars Black Series Multi-Pack

| | | | |
|---|---|---|---|
| NNO | Porgs 2-Pack | 10.00 | 20.00 |

## 2013-16 Star Wars Black Series Titanium Series

| | | | |
|---|---|---|---|
| 1 | Millennium Falcon | 10.00 | 20.00 |
| 2 | Resistance X-Wing | 8.00 | 15.00 |
| 3A | Kylo Ren's Command Shuttle | 6.00 | 12.00 |
| 3B | Kylo Ren Command Shuttle (black) | 6.00 | 12.00 |
| 4 | First Order Special Forces Tie Fighter | 6.00 | 12.00 |
| 5 | Rey's Speeder (Jakku) | 10.00 | 20.00 |
| 6 | First Order Star Destroyer | 8.00 | 15.00 |
| 7 | X-Wing | 12.00 | 25.00 |
| 8 | Y-Wing | 15.00 | 30.00 |
| 9 | Luke Skywalker Landspeeder | 10.00 | 20.00 |
| 10 | Slave I | 12.00 | 25.00 |
| 11 | First Order Snowspeeder | 5.00 | 10.00 |
| 12 | Poe's X-Wing Fighter | 5.00 | 10.00 |
| 13 | First Order Tie Fighter | 4.00 | 8.00 |
| 14 | First Order Transporter | 4.00 | 8.00 |
| 15 | Tie Advanced | 5.00 | 10.00 |
| 16 | B-Wing | 12.00 | 25.00 |
| 17 | Snowspeeder | 8.00 | 15.00 |
| 18 | AT-AT | 30.00 | 60.00 |
| 19 | Jakku Landspeeder | 8.00 | 15.00 |
| 20 | A-Wing | 15.00 | 30.00 |
| 21 | Sith Infiltrator | 8.00 | 15.00 |
| 22 | Anakin Skywalker's Jedi Starfighter | 12.00 | 30.00 |
| 23 | Republic Gunship | 12.00 | 25.00 |
| 24 | Star Destroyer | 6.00 | 12.00 |
| 25 | Imperial Shuttle | 30.00 | 60.00 |
| 26 | The Ghost | 6.00 | 12.00 |
| 27 | Jango Fett's Slave I | 8.00 | 15.00 |
| 28 | Inquisitor's Tie Advanced Prototype | 6.00 | 12.00 |
| 29 | Rebel U-Wing Fighter | 8.00 | 15.00 |
| 30 | TIE Striker | 8.00 | 15.00 |
| 31 | Imperial Cargo Shuttle SW-0608 | 8.00 | 15.00 |

## 2003-05 Star Wars Clone Wars

| | | | |
|---|---|---|---|
| NNO | Anakin Skywalker | 6.00 | 12.00 |
| NNO | ARC Trooper (blue) | 5.00 | 10.00 |
| NNO | ARC Trooper (blue w/gray shoulder pad and thick blue chin paint) | 5.00 | 10.00 |
| NNO | ARC Trooper (red) | 5.00 | 10.00 |
| NNO | Yoda | 5.00 | 10.00 |
| NNO | Obi-Wan Kenobi (General of The Republic Army) | 4.00 | 8.00 |
| NNO | Durge Commander of the Seperatist Forces | 10.00 | 20.00 |
| NNO | Asajj Ventress (Sith Apprentice) | 5.00 | 10.00 |
| NNO | Mace Windu (General of the Republic Army) | 5.00 | 10.00 |
| NNO | Kit Fisto | 8.00 | 15.00 |
| NNO | Clone Trooper (facing left) | 8.00 | 15.00 |
| NNO | Clone Trooper (facing right) | 30.00 | 60.00 |
| NNO | Saesee Tiin | 8.00 | 15.00 |

## 2003-05 Star Wars Clone Wars Deluxe

| | | | |
|---|---|---|---|
| 1 | Clone Trooper (w/speeder bike) | 8.00 | 15.00 |
| 2 | Spider Droid | 6.00 | 12.00 |
| 3 | Durge (w/swoop bike) | 15.00 | 30.00 |

## 2003-05 Star Wars Clone Wars Multipacks

| | | | |
|---|---|---|---|
| NNO | Clone Trooper Army | 8.00 | 15.00 |
| NNO | Clone Trooper Army (w/blue lieutenant) | 10.00 | 20.00 |
| NNO | Clone Trooper Army (w/green sergeant) | 8.00 | 15.00 |
| NNO | Clone Trooper Army (w/red captain) | 8.00 | 15.00 |
| NNO | Clone Trooper Army (w/yellow commander) | 8.00 | 15.00 |
| NNO | Droid Army | 6.00 | 12.00 |
| NNO | Jedi Knight Army | 6.00 | 12.00 |

## 2003-05 Star Wars Clone Wars Value Packs

| | | | |
|---|---|---|---|
| NNO | Anakin Skywalker/Clone Trooper (blue) | 5.00 | 10.00 |
| NNO | ARC Trooper/Clone Trooper | 10.00 | 20.00 |
| NNO | Yoda/Clone Trooper (yellow) | 5.00 | 10.00 |

## 2003-05 Star Wars Clone Wars Vehicles

| | | | |
|---|---|---|---|
| NNO | Anakin Skywalker's Jedi Starfighter | 25.00 | 50.00 |
| NNO | Armored Assault/ Tank (AAT) | 50.00 | 100.00 |
| NNO | Command Gunship | 30.00 | 75.00 |
| NNO | Geonosian Starfighter | 15.00 | 30.00 |
| NNO | Hailfire Droid | 12.00 | 25.00 |
| NNO | Jedi Starfighter | 15.00 | 30.00 |

## 2003-05 Star Wars Clone Wars Animated Series

| | | | |
|---|---|---|---|
| NNO | Anakin Skywalker | 12.50 | 25.00 |
| NNO | Anakin Skywalker (no sleeves torn pants) | 5.00 | 12.00 |
| NNO | ARC Trooper | | |
| NNO | Asajj Ventress | 12.50 | 25.00 |
| NNO | Clone Trooper | 5.00 | 10.00 |
| NNO | Clone Trooper (blue) | 12.00 | 30.00 |
| NNO | Clone Trooper (red) | | |
| NNO | Clone Trooper (yellow) | 6.00 | 12.00 |
| NNO | Count Dooku | 5.00 | 10.00 |
| NNO | Durge | 5.00 | 10.00 |
| NNO | General Grievous | | |
| NNO | Mace Windu | 5.00 | 10.00 |
| NNO | Obi-Wan Kenobi | | |
| NNO | Yoda | | |

## 2003-05 Star Wars Clone Wars Animated Series Commemorative DVD Collection

| | | | |
|---|---|---|---|
| NNO | Volume 1 Jedi Force (Anakin Skywalker/ARC Trooper/Obi-Wan Kenobi) | 15.00 | 30.00 |
| NNO | Volume 1 Sith Attack (Asojj Ventress/Durge/General Grievous) | 12.00 | 25.00 |
| NNO | Volume 2 (Anakin Skywalker tattoo Clone Trooper/Saesee Tiin) | | |
| NNO | Volume 2 (Clone Commander Cody General Grievous/Obi-Wan Kenobi) | | |

## 2003-05 Star Wars Clone Wars Animated Series Maquettes

| | | | |
|---|---|---|---|
| NNO | ARC Trooper Captain | | |
| NNO | Anakin Skywalker | | |
| NNO | Asajj Ventress | | |
| NNO | Bariss Offee & Luminara Unduli | | |
| NNO | General Grievous | | |
| NNO | Obi-Wan Kenobi | | |
| NNO | Padme Amidala | | |
| NNO | Yoda | | |

## 2008-13 Star Wars The Clone Wars Battle Packs

| | | | |
|---|---|---|---|
| NNO | Ambush at Abregado | 30.00 | 75.00 |
| NNO | Ambush on the Vulture's Claw | 30.00 | 75.00 |
| NNO | Anti-Hailfire Droid Squad | 30.00 | 75.00 |
| NNO | ARC Troopers | 120.00 | 250.00 |
| NNO | Army of the Republic | | |
| NNO | Assault on Ryloth | 30.00 | 60.00 |
| NNO | Assault on Geonosis | 15.00 | 30.00 |
| NNO | AT-TE Assault Squad | 20.00 | 40.00 |
| NNO | Battle of Orto Plutonia | 15.00 | 30.00 |
| NNO | B'omarr Monastery Assault | 30.00 | 60.00 |
| NNO | Cad Bane's Escape | 30.00 | 60.00 |
| NNO | Capture of the Droids | 12.50 | 25.00 |
| NNO | Clone Troopers & Droids | 25.00 | 50.00 |
| NNO | Defend Kamino | 75.00 | 150.00 |
| NNO | Holocron Heist | 20.00 | 40.00 |
| NNO | Hunt for Grievous | 25.00 | 50.00 |
| NNO | Jabba's Palace | 15.00 | 30.00 |
| NNO | Jedi Showdown | 20.00 | 40.00 |
| NNO | Mandalorian Warriors | 75.00 | 150.00 |
| NNO | Republic Troopers | 30.00 | 75.00 |
| NNO | Rishi Moon Outpost Attack | 50.00 | 100.00 |
| NNO | Speeder Bike Recon | 15.00 | 30.00 |
| NNO | Stop the Zillo Beast | 20.00 | 40.00 |

## 2008-13 Star Wars The Clone Wars Battle Packs Exclusives

| | | | |
|---|---|---|---|
| 1 | Assassin Spider Droid & Clones | | |
| (Toys R Us Exclusive) | | | |
| 2 | Battle of Christophsis (ultimate) | 90.00 | 175.00 |

| | | | |
|---|---|---|---|
| (2008 Target Exclusive) | | | |
| 3 | Darth Maul Returns | 25.00 | 50.00 |
| (2012 Target Exclusive) | | | |
| 4 | Hidden Enemy (w/DVD) | 30.00 | 75.00 |
| (2010 Target Exclusive) | | | |
| 5 | Hostage Crisis (w/DVD) | 15.00 | 30.00 |
| (Target Exclusive) | | | |
| 6 | Obi-Wan & 212th Attack Battalion | 50.00 | 100.00 |
| (2008 Target Exclusive) | | | |
| 7 | Rise of Boba Fett (ultimate) | 120.00 | 250.00 |
| (2010 Toys R Us Exclusive) | | | |
| 8 | Yoda & Coruscant Guard | 30.00 | 60.00 |
| (2008 Target Exclusive) | | | |

## 2008-13 Star Wars The Clone Wars Blue and Black

| | | | |
|---|---|---|---|
| CW1 | Captain Rex | 12.50 | 25.00 |
| CW2 | Obi-Wan Kenobi | 10.00 | 20.00 |
| CW3 | Clone Commander Cody | 7.50 | 15.00 |
| CW4 | Destroyer Droid | 7.50 | 15.00 |
| CW5 | Yoda | 7.50 | 15.00 |
| CW6 | Count Dooku | 10.00 | 20.00 |
| CW7 | Anakin Skywalker | 10.00 | 20.00 |
| CW8 | Pre Vizsla | 15.00 | 30.00 |
| CW9 | Mandalorian Police Officer | 6.00 | 12.00 |
| CW10 | General Grievous | 15.00 | 30.00 |
| CW11 | Aurra Sing | 12.50 | 25.00 |
| CW12 | Captain Rex (cold weather gear) | 12.50 | 25.00 |
| CW13 | Cad Bane | 10.00 | 20.00 |
| CW14 | Clone Pilot Odd Ball | 12.50 | 25.00 |
| CW15 | Asajj Ventress | 20.00 | 40.00 |
| CW16 | Super Battle Droid | 10.00 | 20.00 |
| CW17 | Ahsoka Tano | 20.00 | 40.00 |
| CW18 | ARF Trooper | 12.50 | 25.00 |
| CW19 | Battle Droid | 10.00 | 20.00 |
| CW20 | Mace Windu | 10.00 | 20.00 |
| CW21 | Commander Gree | 15.00 | 30.00 |
| CW22 | Battle Droid Commander | 15.00 | 30.00 |
| CW23 | Kit Fisto | 10.00 | 20.00 |
| CW24 | ARF Trooper (jungle deco) | 12.50 | 25.00 |
| CW25 | Ki-Adi-Mundi | 12.50 | 25.00 |
| CW26 | Clone Trooper (flamethrower) | 15.00 | 30.00 |
| CW27 | R2-D2 | 8.00 | 15.00 |
| CW28 | Clone Pilot Goji | 15.00 | 30.00 |
| CW29 | Mandalorian Warrior | 25.00 | 50.00 |
| CW30 | R4-P17 | 10.00 | 20.00 |
| CW31 | Shaak Ti | 20.00 | 40.00 |
| CW32 | Boba Fett | 10.00 | 20.00 |
| CW33 | Embo | 15.00 | 30.00 |

| | | | |
|---|---|---|---|
| CW34 | Undead Geonosian | 7.50 | 15.00 |
| CW35 | Clone Trooper Draa | 20.00 | 40.00 |
| CW36 | Quinlan Vos | 15.00 | 30.00 |
| CW37 | Cato Parasiti | 10.00 | 20.00 |
| CW38 | Clone Commander Jet | 25.00 | 50.00 |
| CW39 | Hondo Ohnaka | 20.00 | 40.00 |
| CW40 | Obi-Wan Kenobi (new outfit) | 10.00 | 20.00 |
| CW41 | Clone Trooper Hevy (training armor) | 12.50 | 25.00 |
| CW42 | Cad Bane (w/TODO-360) | 15.00 | 30.00 |
| CW43 | R7-A7 | 12.50 | 25.00 |
| CW44 | Ahsoka (new outfit) | 60.00 | 120.00 |
| CW45 | Anakin Skywalker (new outfit) | 12.50 | 25.00 |
| CW46 | Aqua Battle Droid | 7.50 | 15.00 |
| CW47 | El-Les | 12.50 | 25.00 |
| CW48 | Clone Commander Wolffe | 30.00 | 75.00 |
| CW49 | Riot Control Clone Trooper | 25.00 | 50.00 |
| CW50 | Barriss Offee | 20.00 | 40.00 |
| CW51 | Eeth Koth | 20.00 | 40.00 |
| CW52 | Clone Commander Colt | 60.00 | 120.00 |
| CW53 | Plo Koon (cold weather gear) | 7.50 | 15.00 |
| CW54 | Saesee Tin | 25.00 | 50.00 |
| CW55 | Savage Opress (shirtless) | 12.50 | 25.00 |
| CW56 | ARF Trooper (Kamino) | 20.00 | 40.00 |
| CW57 | Stealth Ops Clone Trooper | 15.00 | 30.00 |
| CW58 | Even Piell | 25.00 | 50.00 |
| CW59 | Savage Opress (armored apprentice) | 30.00 | 60.00 |
| CW60 | Kit Fisto (cold weather gear) | 12.50 | 25.00 |
| CW61 | Seripas | 30.00 | 60.00 |
| CW62 | Captain Rex (jet propulsion pack) | 30.00 | 75.00 |
| CW63 | Chewbacca | 10.00 | 20.00 |
| CW64 | R7-D4 (Plo Koon's astromech droid) | 7.50 | 15.00 |
| CW65 | Jar Jar Binks | 10.00 | 20.00 |

## 2008-13 Star Wars The Clone Wars Blue and White

| | | | |
|---|---|---|---|
| 1 | Anakin Skywalker | | |
| 2 | Obi-Wan Kenobi | | |
| 3 | Yoda | | |
| 4 | Captain Rex | | |
| 5 | Clone Trooper | | |
| 6 | General Grievous | | |
| 7 | Battle Droid | | |
| 8 | R2-D2 | | |
| 9 | Ahsoka Tano | | |
| 10 | Clone Commander Cody | | |
| 11 | Clone Pilot Odd Ball | | |
| 12 | Super Battle Droid | 15.00 | 30.00 |
| 13 | Count Dooku | | |
| 14 | Plo Koon | 10.00 | 20.00 |
| 15 | Asajj Ventress | | |

| | | |
|---|---|---|
| 16 C-3PO | 6.00 | 12.00 |
| 17 Destroyer Droid | 7.50 | 15.00 |
| 18 IG-86 Assassin Droid | | |
| 19 Clone Trooper (212th Attack Battalion) | | |
| 20 Padme Amidala (diplomat) | | |
| 21 Clone Trooper (space gear) | | |
| 22 Magnaguard | 10.00 | 20.00 |
| 23 R3-S6 (Goldie) | | |
| 24 Jar Jar Binks | | |
| 25 Rocket Battle Droid | | |
| 26 Clone Trooper (41st Elite Corps) | 10.00 | 20.00 |
| 27 Kit Fisto | | |

## 2008-13 Star Wars The Clone Wars Darth Maul Pack

| | | |
|---|---|---|
| CW1 Anakin Skywalker (new sculpt) | 7.50 | 15.00 |
| CW2 Clone Trooper (Phase II armor) | 15.00 | 30.00 |
| CW3 Savage Opress (shirtless) | 12.50 | 25.00 |
| CW4 Cad Bane | 12.50 | 25.00 |
| CW5 Yoda | 6.00 | 12.00 |
| CW6 Plo Koon (cold weather gear) | 10.00 | 20.00 |
| CW7 Clone Commander Cody (jet propulsion pack) | 15.00 | 30.00 |
| CW8 Mace Windu | 6.00 | 12.00 |
| CW9 Chewbacca | 7.50 | 15.00 |
| CW10 Aqua Battle Droid | 7.50 | 15.00 |
| CW11 Republic Commando Boss | 12.50 | 25.00 |
| CW12 Obi-Wan Kenobi | 12.50 | 25.00 |
| CW13 Captain Rex (Phase II) | 15.00 | 30.00 |
| CW14 Aayla Secura | 15.00 | 30.00 |
| CW15 Ahsoka Tano (scuba gear) | 30.00 | 75.00 |
| CW16 Training Super Battle Droid | 10.00 | 20.00 |
| CW17 Clone Commander Wolffe (Phase II) | 25.00 | 50.00 |
| CW18 Clone Commander Fox (Phase II) | 20.00 | 40.00 |

## 2008-13 Star Wars The Clone Wars Deluxe Figures and Vehicles

| | | |
|---|---|---|
| NNO 212th Battalion Clone Troopers & Jet Backpacks | 25.00 | 50.00 |
| NNO Armored Scout Tank (w/Battle Droid) | 12.50 | 25.00 |
| NNO Armored Scout Tank (w/Tactical Droid) | 15.00 | 30.00 |
| NNO AT-RT (w/ARF Trooper Boil) | 20.00 | 40.00 |
| NNO Attack Cycle (w/General Grievous) | 15.00 | 30.00 |
| NNO Attack Recon Fighter (w/Anakin Skywalker) | 20.00 | 40.00 |
| NNO BARC Speeder (w/Commander Cody) | 15.00 | 30.00 |
| NNO BARC Speeder (w/Clone Trooper) | 15.00 | 30.00 |
| NNO BARC Speeder Bike (w/Clone Trooper Jesse) | 25.00 | 50.00 |
| NNO BARC Speeder Bike (w/Obi-Wan Kenobi) | 15.00 | 30.00 |
| NNO Can-Cell (w/Anakin Skywalker) | 15.00 | 30.00 |
| NNO Crab Droid | 20.00 | 40.00 |
| NNO Desert Skiff (w/Anakin Skywalker) | 12.50 | 25.00 |
| NNO Freeco Speeder (w/Clone Trooper) | 10.00 | 20.00 |
| NNO Freeco Speeder (w/Obi-Wan Kenobi) | 15.00 | 30.00 |
| NNO Mandalorian Speeder (w/Mandalorian Warrior) | 30.00 | 60.00 |
| NNO Naboo Star Skiff (w/Anakin Skywalker) | 15.00 | 30.00 |
| NNO Pirate Speeder Bike (w/Cad Bane) | 12.50 | 25.00 |
| NNO Republic Assault Submarine with Scuba Clone Trooper | 25.00 | 50.00 |
| NNO Republic Attack Dropship with Clone Pilot | | |
| NNO Republic Scout Speeder with ARF Trooper | 15.00 | 30.00 |
| NNO Separatist Droid Speeder with Battle Droid | 15.00 | 30.00 |
| NNO Speeder Bike with Castas | 10.00 | 20.00 |
| NNO Speeder Bike with Count Dooku | 20.00 | 40.00 |
| NNO Speeder Bike with Plo Koon | | |
| NNO Turbo Tank Support Squad | 25.00 | 50.00 |
| NNO Y-Wing Scout Bomber with Clone Trooper Pilot | 20.00 | 40.00 |

## 2008-13 Star Wars The Clone Wars Deluxe Figures and Vehicles Exclusives

| | | |
|---|---|---|
| 1 AT-RT with ARF Trooper | 25.00 | 50.00 |
| (Walmart Exclusive) | | |
| 2 BARC Speeder with Clone Trooper Buzz | 30.00 | 60.00 |
| (Walmart Exclusive) | | |
| 3 Separatist Speeder with Geonosian Warrior | 15.00 | 30.00 |
| (2011 Toys R Us Exclusive) | | |
| 4 STAP with Battle Droid | | |
| (2010 Toys R Us Exclusive) | | |

## 2008-13 Star Wars The Clone Wars Exclusives

| | | |
|---|---|---|
| 1 Captain Rex | 12.50 | 25.00 |
| (2008 Sneak Preview Mailaway Exclusive) | | |
| 2 Clone Captain Lock | 12.50 | 25.00 |
| (2011 K-Mart Exclusive) | | |
| 3 Clone Trooper: 501st Legion | 15.00 | 30.00 |
| (2008 Wal-Mart Exclusive) | | |
| 4 Clone Trooper: Senate Security | 15.00 | 30.00 |
| (2008 SDCC Exclusive) | | |

| | | |
|---|---|---|
| 5 Commander Fox | 20.00 | 40.00 |
| (2008 Target Exclusive) | | |
| 6 Commander Ponds | 25.00 | 50.00 |
| (2009 Toys R Us Exclusive) | | |
| 7 General Grievous: Holographic | 10.00 | 20.00 |
| (2008 Toys R Us Exclusive) | | |
| 8 Kul Teska | 15.00 | 30.00 |
| (2010 Toys R Us Exclusive) | | |
| 9 Nahdar Vebb | 15.00 | 30.00 |
| (2009 Mailaway Exclusive) | | |
| 10 Nikto Skiff Guard Puko Naga | 10.00 | 20.00 |
| (2010 Toys R Us Exclusive) | | |
| 11 Sgt. Bric & Galactic Battle Mat | 20.00 | 40.00 |
| (2010 Mailaway Exclusive) | | |
| 12 Stealth Operation Clone Trooper: Commander Blackout | 15.00 | 30.00 |
| (2011 Toys R Us Exclusive) | | |

## 2008-13 Star Wars The Clone Wars Red and White

| | | |
|---|---|---|
| CW1 General Grievous | 10.00 | 20.00 |
| CW2 Clone Trooper (space gear) | 15.00 | 30.00 |
| CW3 Rocket Battle Droid | 10.00 | 20.00 |
| CW4 Clone Trooper (41st Elite Corps) | 15.00 | 30.00 |
| CW5 Kit Fisto | 10.00 | 20.00 |
| CW6 Mace Windu | 10.00 | 20.00 |
| CW7 Admiral Yularen | 15.00 | 30.00 |
| CW8 Jawas | 10.00 | 20.00 |
| CW9 Commander Gree | 20.00 | 40.00 |
| CW10 ARF Trooper | 12.50 | 25.00 |
| CW11 Heavy Assault Super Battle Droid | 7.50 | 15.00 |
| CW12 Obi-Wan Kenobi (space suit) | 7.50 | 15.00 |
| CW13 4A-7 | 10.00 | 20.00 |
| CW14 Yoda | 10.00 | 20.00 |
| CW15 Whorm Loathsom | 10.00 | 20.00 |
| CW16 Commando Droid | 15.00 | 30.00 |
| CW17 Clone Trooper Echo | 20.00 | 40.00 |
| CW18 Anakin Skywalker | 7.50 | 15.00 |
| CW19 Obi-Wan Kenobi | 10.00 | 20.00 |
| CW20 Clone Trooper Denal | 20.00 | 40.00 |
| CW21 Anakin Skywalker (space suit) | 7.50 | 15.00 |
| CW22 Cad Bane | 10.00 | 20.00 |
| CW23 Ahsoka Tano (space suit) | 15.00 | 30.00 |
| CW24 Captain Rex | 12.50 | 25.00 |
| CW25 R2-D2 | 7.50 | 15.00 |
| CW26 Ahsoka Tano | 15.00 | 30.00 |
| CW27 Count Dooku | 10.00 | 20.00 |
| CW28 Commander Cody | 12.50 | 25.00 |
| CW29 Destroyer Droid | 7.50 | 15.00 |
| CW30 Luminara Unduli | 12.50 | 25.00 |
| CW31 Captain Argyus | 15.00 | 30.00 |
| CW32 Clone Commander Thire | 20.00 | 40.00 |

| | | | |
|---|---|---|---|
| CW33 | Battle Droid (AAT Driver) | 15.00 | 30.00 |
| CW34 | Matchstick | 15.00 | 30.00 |
| CW35 | Padme Amidala (adventurer suit) | 15.00 | 30.00 |
| CW36 | Clone Tank Gunner | 20.00 | 40.00 |
| CW37 | Ziro's Assassin Droid | 10.00 | 20.00 |
| CW38 | Clone Trooper Jek | 30.00 | 60.00 |
| CW39 | Commander Bly | 30.00 | 75.00 |
| CW40 | Aayla Secura | 10.00 | 20.00 |
| CW41 | Hondo Ohnaka | 30.00 | 75.00 |
| CW42 | Anakin Skywalker (cold weather gear) | 7.50 | 15.00 |
| CW43 | Thi-Sen | 15.00 | 30.00 |
| CW44 | Clone Commander Stone | 25.00 | 50.00 |
| CW45 | Darth Sidious | 75.00 | 150.00 |
| CW46 | Commander TX-20 | 20.00 | 40.00 |
| CW47 | Firefighter Droid | 25.00 | 50.00 |
| CW48 | Obi-Wan Kenobi (cold weather gear) | 10.00 | 20.00 |
| CW49 | Magnaguard (w/cape) | 20.00 | 40.00 |
| CW50 | Captain Rex (cold assault gear) | 12.50 | 25.00 |

### 2008-13 Star Wars The Clone Wars Vehicles

| | | | |
|---|---|---|---|
| NNO | Ahsoka Tano's Delta Starfighter | | |
| NNO | Anakin's Delta Starfighter | 8.00 | 15.00 |
| NNO | Anakin's Modified Jedi Starfighter | 15.00 | 40.00 |
| NNO | ARC-170 Starfighter (Imperial Shadow Squadron) | | |
| NNO | AT-AP Walker | | |
| NNO | AT-TE (All Terrain Tactical Enforcer) | | |
| NNO | Clone Turbo Tank | 150.00 | 300.00 |
| NNO | Corporate Alliance Tank Droid | 30.00 | 60.00 |
| NNO | Droid Tri-Fighter | | |
| NNO | General Grievous' Starfighter | 20.00 | 40.00 |
| NNO | Hailfire Droid (Remote Control) | 20.00 | 40.00 |
| NNO | Homing Spider Droid | 25.00 | 50.00 |
| NNO | Hyena Bomber | 25.00 | 50.00 |
| NNO | Jedi Turbo Speeder | 30.00 | 60.00 |
| NNO | MagnaGuard Fighter | 12.50 | 25.00 |
| NNO | Mandalorian Assault Gunship | 50.00 | 100.00 |
| NNO | Obi-Wan Kenobi's Delta Starfighter | | |
| NNO | Obi-Wan's Jedi Starfighter (Utapau) | | |
| NNO | Plo Koon's Delta Starfighter | 15.00 | 30.00 |
| NNO | Republic Attack Shuttle | 75.00 | 150.00 |
| NNO | Republic AV-7 Mobile Cannon | 30.00 | 75.00 |
| NNO | Republic Fighter Tank | | |
| NNO | Republic Fighter Tank (blue deco) | | |
| NNO | Republic Fighter Tank (green deco) | | |
| NNO | Republic Fighter Tank (Remote Control) | 25.00 | 50.00 |
| NNO | Republic Swamp Speeder | 30.00 | 60.00 |
| NNO | Separatist Droid Gunship | 30.00 | 75.00 |
| NNO | Trade Federation Armored Assault Tank (AAT - brown/blue) | 20.00 | 40.00 |
| NNO | Trade Federation Armored Assault Tank (AAT) | 30.00 | 60.00 |
| NNO | V-19 Torrent Starfighter | | |
| NNO | Vulture Droid | 20.00 | 40.00 |
| NNO | V-Wing Starfighter | 20.00 | 40.00 |
| NNO | Xanadu Blood | 30.00 | 75.00 |
| NNO | Y-Wing Bomber | 75.00 | 150.00 |

### 2008-13 Star Wars The Clone Wars Vehicles Exclusives

| | | | |
|---|---|---|---|
| NNO | ARC-170 Starfighter (flaming wampa) | | |
| | (Toys R Us Exclusive) | | |
| NNO | Hailfire Droid & General Grievous | | |
| | (Toys R Us Exclusive) | | |
| NNO | Kit Fisto's Delta Starfighter | | |
| | (Walmart Exclusive) | | |
| NNO | Octuptarra Droid | 30.00 | 75.00 |
| | (Walmart Exclusive) | | |
| NNO | Republic Gunship (crumb bomber) | | |
| | (Toys R Us Exclusive) | | |
| NNO | Republic Gunship (Lucky Lekku) | 125.00 | 250.00 |
| | (Walmart Exclusive) | | |
| NNO | V-Wing Starfighter & V-Wing Pilot | | |
| | (Toys R Us Exclusive) | | |
| NNO | V-Wing Starfighter (Imperial) | 30.00 | 75.00 |
| | (Toys R Us Exclusive) | | |

### 2008-13 Star Wars The Clone Wars Yoda Pack

| | | | |
|---|---|---|---|
| CW1 | Obi-Wan Kenobi | | |
| CW2 | Savage Opress (armoured apprentice) | | |
| CW3 | Anakin Skywalker | | |
| CW4 | Captain Rex | 15.00 | 30.00 |
| CW5 | R2-D2 | | |
| CW6 | 501st Legion Clone Trooper | 60.00 | 120.00 |
| CW7 | Clone Commander Cody (jet propulsion pack) | | |
| CW8 | Darth Maul | 30.00 | 60.00 |
| CW9 | Battle Droid | 15.00 | 30.00 |

### 1996-99 Star Wars Collector Series

| | | | |
|---|---|---|---|
| 1 | Admiral Ackbar | 20.00 | 40.00 |
| 2 | AT-AT Driver | 15.00 | 30.00 |
| 3 | Boba Fett | 25.00 | 50.00 |
| 4 | C-3PO | 20.00 | 40.00 |
| 5 | Cantina Band - Doikk Na'ts (w/Fizzz) | 12.00 | 25.00 |
| | (Walmart Exclusive) | | |
| 6 | Cantina Band - Figrin D'an (w/Kloo Horn) | 10.00 | 20.00 |
| | (Walmart Exclusive) | | |
| 7 | Cantina Band - Ickabel (w/fanfar) | 12.00 | 25.00 |
| | (Walmart Exclusive) | | |
| 8 | Cantina Band - Nalan (w/Bandfill) | 10.00 | 20.00 |
| | (Walmart Exclusive) | | |
| 9 | Cantina Band - Tech (w/Omni Box) | 12.00 | 25.00 |
| | (Walmart Exclusive) | | |
| 10 | Cantina Band - Tedn (w/fanfar) | 10.00 | 20.00 |
| | (Walmart Exclusive) | | |
| 11 | Chewbacca | 20.00 | 40.00 |
| 12 | Darth Vader | 15.00 | 30.00 |
| 13 | Greedo | 15.00 | 30.00 |
| | (JC Penney Exclusive) | | |
| 14 | Han Solo | 15.00 | 30.00 |
| 15 | Lando Calrissian | 12.00 | 25.00 |
| 16 | Luke Skywalker | 15.00 | 30.00 |
| 17 | Luke Skywalker (Bespin) | 12.00 | 25.00 |
| 18 | Luke Skywalker (X-Wing Pilot) | 20.00 | 40.00 |
| 19 | Obi-Wan Kenobi | 15.00 | 30.00 |
| 20 | Princess Leia | 15.00 | 30.00 |
| 21 | Sandtrooper | 15.00 | 30.00 |
| 22 | Stormtrooper | 15.00 | 30.00 |
| 23 | TIE Fighter Pilot | 20.00 | 40.00 |
| 24 | Tusken Raider (blaster and binoculars) | 12.00 | 25.00 |
| 25 | Tusken Raider (gaderffi stick) | 12.00 | 25.00 |

### 1996-99 Star Wars Collector Series 2-Packs

| | | | |
|---|---|---|---|
| 1 | Grand Moff Tarkin and Imperial Gunner | 25.00 | 50.00 |
| | (FAO Schwarz Exclusive) | | |
| 2 | Han Solo and Luke Skywalker (stormtrooper gear) | 30.00 | 60.00 |
| | (KB Toys Exclusive) | | |
| 3 | Han Solo and Tauntaun | 30.00 | 60.00 |
| 4 | Luke Hoth and Wampa | 25.00 | 50.00 |
| 5 | Luke Jedi and Bib Fortuna | 25.00 | 50.00 |
| | (FAO Schwarz Exclusive) | | |
| 6 | Obi-Wan Kenobi vs. Darth Vader (electronic) | 25.00 | 50.00 |
| | (JC Penney/KB Toys Exclusive) | | |
| 7 | Princess Leia and R2-D2 (Jabba's prisoners) | | |
| | (FAO Schwarz/KB Toys Exclusive) | | |

## 1996-99 Star Wars Collector Series European Exclusives

| | | |
|---|---|---|
| 1 Han Solo (drawing action) | 12.00 | 25.00 |
| 2 Luke Skywalker (drawing action) | | |

## 1996-99 Star Wars Collector Series Masterpiece Edition

| | | |
|---|---|---|
| 1 Anakin Skywalker/Story of Darth Vader | 10.00 | 20.00 |
| 2 Aurra Sing/Dawn of the Bounty Hunters | 12.00 | 25.00 |
| 3 C-3PO/Tales of the Golden Droid | 20.00 | 40.00 |

## 2006 Star Wars Customs

| | | |
|---|---|---|
| NNO Boba Fett's/ Outlaw Chopper | | |
| NNO Darth Vader's/ Imperial Chopper | | |
| NNO Luke Skywalker's/ Rebel Chopper | | |

## 2006 Star Wars Customs International

| | | |
|---|---|---|
| NNO Boba Fett's/ Outlaw Chopper | | |
| NNO Darth Vader's/ Imperial Chopper | | |
| NNO Luke Skywalker's/ Rebel Chopper | | |

## 2008-10 Star Wars Diamond Select

| | | |
|---|---|---|
| 1 Anakin Skywalker | 25.00 | 50.00 |
| 2 Darth Maul | 30.00 | 75.00 |
| 3 Emperor Palpatine | 25.00 | 50.00 |
| 4 Luke Skywalker Jedi Knight | 60.00 | 120.00 |
| 5 Mace Windu | 30.00 | 60.00 |
| 6 Obi-Wan Kenobi (ROTS) | 30.00 | 60.00 |

## 2012-13 Star Wars Discover the Force

| | | |
|---|---|---|
| NNO Aurra Sing | 12.50 | 25.00 |
| NNO Darth Maul | 8.00 | 15.00 |
| NNO Destroyer Droid | 6.00 | 12.00 |
| NNO G8-R3 | 12.00 | 25.00 |
| NNO Gungan Warrior | 8.00 | 15.00 |
| NNO Mawhonic | 6.00 | 12.00 |
| NNO Obi-Wan Kenobi | 8.00 | 15.00 |
| NNO Qui-Gon Jinn | 6.00 | 12.00 |
| NNO Ric Olie | 6.00 | 12.00 |
| NNO Naboo Pilot | 5.00 | 10.00 |
| NNO Tusken Raider | 5.00 | 10.00 |
| NNO Yoda | 8.00 | 15.00 |

## 2012-13 Star Wars Discover the Force Battle Packs

| | | |
|---|---|---|
| NNO Mos Espa Arena | 20.00 | 40.00 |
| (C-3PO/Anakin/Sebulba/2 Pit Droids) | | |
| NNO Royal Starship Droids | | |
| (R2-B1/R2-R9/R2-D2/R2-N3) | | |

## 2012-13 Star Wars Discover the Force Vehicles-Creatures

| | | |
|---|---|---|
| NNO Dewback | 20.00 | 40.00 |
| NNO Vulture Droid | | |

## 2010-15 Star Wars Disney Characters Exclusives

| | | |
|---|---|---|
| NNO Bad Pete as Jango Fett | 20.00 | 40.00 |
| (2015 Star Wars Weekends Exclusive)/2002 | | |
| NNO Donald Duck as Darth Maul | 25.00 | 50.00 |
| (2012 Star Wars Weekends Exclusive) | | |
| NNO Donald Duck as Savage Opress | 25.00 | 50.00 |
| (2012 Star Wars Weekends Exclusive)/2012 | | |
| NNO Donald Duck as Shadow Trooper | 30.00 | 60.00 |
| (2010 Star Wars Celebration Exclusive)/5000 | | |
| NNO Mickey Mouse and Donald Duck as X-Wing Luke and Han Solo | 15.00 | 30.00 |
| (2014 Star Wars Weekends Exclusive)/1980 | | |
| NNO Mickey Mouse/Chip & Dale as Luke Skywalker and Ewoks | 20.00 | 40.00 |
| (2013 Star Wars Weekends Exclusive)/1983 | | |
| NNO Pluto and Minnie Mouse as R2-D2 and Princess Leia | 30.00 | 60.00 |
| (2015 Star Wars Weekends Exclusive)/1977 | | |
| NNO Stitch as Emperor Palpatine | 15.00 | 30.00 |
| (2010 Star Wars Weekends Exclusive)/1980 | | |
| NNO Stitch as Hologram Yoda | 15.00 | 30.00 |
| (2011 Star Tours Opening Exclusive)/2011 | | |

## 2007 Star Wars Disney Characters Series 1

| | | |
|---|---|---|
| NNO Donald Duck as Han Solo | 12.50 | 25.00 |
| NNO Goofy as Darth Vader | 10.00 | 20.00 |
| NNO Mickey Mouse as Luke Skywalker | 12.50 | 25.00 |
| NNO Minnie Mouse as Princess Leia | 7.50 | 15.00 |
| NNO Stitch as Emperor Palpatine | 12.50 | 25.00 |

## 2008 Star Wars Disney Characters Series 2

| | | |
|---|---|---|
| NNO Donald Duck as Darth Maul | | |
| NNO Goofy as Jar Jar Binks | | |
| NNO Mickey Mouse as Anakin Skywalker | | |
| NNO Minnie Mouse as Padme Amidala | | |
| NNO Stitch as Yoda | | |

## 2009 Star Wars Disney Characters Series 3

| | | |
|---|---|---|
| NNO Chip & Dale as Ewoks | 20.00 | 40.00 |
| NNO Donald Duck as Stormtrooper | 12.50 | 25.00 |
| NNO Goofy as Chewbacca | 15.00 | 30.00 |
| NNO Mickey Mouse as Luke Skywalker (X-Wing Pilot) | 12.50 | 25.00 |
| NNO Minnie Mouse as Slave Leia | | |

## 2010 Star Wars Disney Characters Series 4

| | | |
|---|---|---|
| NNO Bad Pete as Boba Fett | 20.00 | 40.00 |
| NNO Donald Duck as Han in Carbonite | 10.00 | 20.00 |
| NNO Goofy as C-3PO | 20.00 | 40.00 |
| NNO Mickey Mouse as Jedi Knight Luke Skywalker | | |
| NNO Minnie Mouse as Princess Leia Boushh | 15.00 | 30.00 |

## 2011 Star Wars Disney Characters Series 5

| | | |
|---|---|---|
| NNO Daisy Duck as Aurra Sing | 15.00 | 30.00 |
| NNO Donald Duck as Commander Cody | | |
| NNO Goofy as Cad Bane | | |
| NNO Dewey/Huey/Louie as Jawas | 20.00 | 40.00 |
| NNO Stitch as General Grievous | 25.00 | 50.00 |

## 2012 Star Wars Disney Characters Series 6

| | | |
|---|---|---|
| NNO Donald Duck as Darth Maul | 20.00 | 40.00 |
| NNO Goofy as TC-14 | 12.50 | 25.00 |
| NNO Mickey Mouse as Anakin Skywalker | 25.00 | 50.00 |
| NNO Minnie Mouse as Queen Amidala | 12.50 | 25.00 |
| NNO Pluto as R2-D2 | 20.00 | 40.00 |
| NNO Stitch as Yoda | | |

## 2015-19 Star Wars Disney Parks Droid Factory

| | | |
|---|---|---|
| NNO BB-8 (2017) | 7.50 | 15.00 |
| NNO C1-10P Chopper | 15.00 | 30.00 |
| NNO R2-BOO | | |
| (2016 Halloween Exclusive) | 20.00 | 40.00 |
| NNO R2-D60 | | |
| (2015 Disneyland 60th Anniversary Exclusive) | 25.00 | 50.00 |
| NNO R2-H15 | | |
| (2015 Holiday Exclusive) | 30.00 | 75.00 |
| NNO R2-H16 | | |
| (2016 Holiday Exclusive) | 15.00 | 30.00 |
| NNO R3-BOO17 (glow-in-the-dark) | | |
| (2017 Halloween Exclusive) | 60.00 | 120.00 |
| NNO R-3D0 | 10.00 | 20.00 |
| NNO R3-H17 | | |
| (2017 Holiday Exclusive) | 20.00 | 40.00 |
| NNO R4-BOO18 | | |
| (2018 Halloween Exclusive) | 12.50 | 25.00 |
| NNO R4-H18 | | |
| (2018 Holiday Exclusive) | 25.00 | 50.00 |
| NNO R5-BOO19 | | |
| (2019 Halloween Exclusive) | 17.50 | 35.00 |
| NNO R5-D23 | | |
| (2017 D23 Expo Exclusive) | 20.00 | 40.00 |
| NNO R5-M4 | | |
| (2016 May 4th Exclusive) | 12.50 | 25.00 |

## 2015-19 Star Wars Disney Parks Droid Factory Multipacks

| | | |
|---|---|---|
| NNO Artoo Detoo (R2-D2)/See-Threepio (C-3PO) | 30.00 | 75.00 |
| (2017 40th Anniversary Exclusive) | | |
| NNO BB-8/2BB-2/BB-4/BB-9E | 25.00 | 50.00 |
| NNO C2-B5/R2-BHD/R3-M2/R5-SK1 | 30.00 | 75.00 |
| NNO R4-X2/Y5-X2 | 20.00 | 40.00 |
| NNO R5-013/R2-C2/R5-S9/R5-P8 | 25.00 | 50.00 |

## 2017-18 Star Wars Disney Store Toybox

| | | |
|---|---|---|
| 1 Kylo Ren | 10.00 | 20.00 |
| 2 Rey | 10.00 | 20.00 |
| 3 Stormtrooper | 7.50 | 15.00 |
| 4 Darth Vader | 7.50 | 15.00 |
| 5 Luke Skywalker | 12.50 | 25.00 |
| 6 Boba Fett | 10.00 | 20.00 |
| 7 Princess Leia Organa | 7.50 | 15.00 |

| | | | |
|---|---|---|---|
| 8 | Han Solo | 10.00 | 20.00 |
| 9 | Chewbacca | | |
| 10 | Yoda/Force Ghost Yoda 2-Pack | | |
| 11 | Poe Dameron (w/BB-8) | | |

## 2017-18 Star Wars Disney Store Toybox Vehicles

| | | |
|---|---|---|
| NNO | TIE Fighter (w/TIE Fighter Pilot) | |

## 2015 Star Wars Elite Series

| | | | |
|---|---|---|---|
| NNO | Anakin Skywalker | 25.00 | 50.00 |
| NNO | Boba Fett (w/cape) | 20.00 | 40.00 |
| NNO | Boba Fett (w/o cape) | 30.00 | 75.00 |
| NNO | Darth Maul | 30.00 | 60.00 |
| NNO | Darth Vader | 20.00 | 40.00 |
| NNO | General Grievous | 50.00 | 100.00 |
| NNO | Prototype Boba Fett | 30.00 | 75.00 |
| NNO | Stormtrooper | 15.00 | 30.00 |

## 2015-16 Star Wars Elite Series

| | | | |
|---|---|---|---|
| NNO | C-3PO | 20.00 | 40.00 |
| NNO | Captain Phasma | 10.00 | 20.00 |
| NNO | Finn | 10.00 | 20.00 |
| NNO | Finn (w/lightsaber) | 10.00 | 20.00 |
| NNO | Flametrooper | 15.00 | 30.00 |
| NNO | FN-2187 (Finn) | 12.50 | 25.00 |
| NNO | Han Solo | 15.00 | 30.00 |
| NNO | Kylo Ren | 10.00 | 20.00 |
| NNO | Kylo Ren (unmasked) | 12.00 | 25.00 |
| NNO | Poe Dameron | 10.00 | 20.00 |
| NNO | R2-D2 | 20.00 | 40.00 |
| NNO | Rey and BB-8 | 12.00 | 25.00 |
| NNO | Rey and BB-8 (w/lightsaber) | 15.00 | 30.00 |
| NNO | Stormtrooper | 10.00 | 20.00 |
| NNO | Stormtrooper (squad leader) | 12.50 | 25.00 |
| NNO | Stormtrooper (w/riot gear) | 12.50 | 25.00 |
| NNO | Stormtrooper Officer | 15.00 | 30.00 |
| NNO | TIE Fighter Pilot | 12.50 | 25.00 |

## 2016-17 Star Wars Elite Series

| | | | |
|---|---|---|---|
| NNO | Baze Malbus | 10.00 | 20.00 |
| NNO | Bodhi Rook | 10.00 | 20.00 |
| NNO | C2-B5 | 12.00 | 25.00 |
| NNO | Captain Cassian Andor | 8.00 | 15.00 |
| NNO | Chirrut Imwe | 10.00 | 20.00 |
| NNO | Imperial Death Trooper | 15.00 | 30.00 |
| NNO | K-2SO | 10.00 | 20.00 |
| NNO | Sergeant Jyn Erso | 10.00 | 20.00 |
| NNO | Stormtrooper | 10.00 | 20.00 |

## 2017-18 Star Wars Elite Series

| | | | |
|---|---|---|---|
| NNO | Elite Praetorian Guard | 15.00 | 30.00 |
| NNO | First Order Judicial | 30.00 | 60.00 |
| NNO | Kylo Ren | 15.00 | 30.00 |
| NNO | Luke Skywalker | 15.00 | 30.00 |
| NNO | R2-D2 | 20.00 | 40.00 |
| NNO | Rey | 20.00 | 40.00 |

## 2018-19 Star Wars Elite Series

| | | | |
|---|---|---|---|
| NNO | Gonk Droid | 15.00 | 30.00 |
| NNO | R2-D2 | 25.00 | 50.00 |

| | | | |
|---|---|---|---|
| NNO | R4-G9 | 20.00 | 40.00 |
| NNO | R5-D4 | 20.00 | 40.00 |
| NNO | TC-14 | 25.00 | 50.00 |

## 2016-17 Star Wars Elite Series 11-Inch

| | | | |
|---|---|---|---|
| NNO | Darth Vader | 20.00 | 40.00 |
| NNO | Death Trooper | 15.00 | 30.00 |
| NNO | Director Orson Krennic | 20.00 | 40.00 |
| NNO | Jyn Erso | 20.00 | 40.00 |
| NNO | Kylo Ren | 15.00 | 30.00 |
| NNO | Princess Leia Organa | 25.00 | 50.00 |
| NNO | Rey | 15.00 | 30.00 |

## 2015-17 Star Wars Elite Series Multipacks and Exclusives

| | | | |
|---|---|---|---|
| NNO | 8-Piece Gift Set | 500.00 | 750.00 |
| Darth Maul/Anakin/Grievous/Stormtrooper#(Vader/C-3PO/R2-D2/Boba Fett)#((2016 D23 Exclusive) | | | |
| NNO | Deluxe Gift Set | 60.00 | 120.00 |
| Stormtrooper/Phasma/Kylo Ren/Finn/Flametrooper | | | |
| NNO | Droid Gift Pack | 25.00 | 50.00 |
| BB-8, C-3PO, R2-D2 | | | |
| NNO | Han Solo & Luke Skywalker w/blond hair (Stormtrooper Disguise) | 50.00 | 100.00 |
| NNO | Han Solo & Luke Skywalker w/brown hair (Stormtrooper Disguise) | 25.00 | 50.00 |
| NNO | Princess Leia & Darth Vader/1000* | 75.00 | 150.00 |
| (2017 D23 Exclusive) | | | |

## 1999-00 Star Wars Episode I 2-Packs

| | | | |
|---|---|---|---|
| 1 | Darth Maul and Sith Infiltrator | 8.00 | 15.00 |
| 2 | Final Jedi Duel (Qui-Gon Jinn/Darth Maul break apart) | 20.00 | 50.00 |

## 1999-00 Star Wars Episode I Accessory Sets

| | | | |
|---|---|---|---|
| 1 | Flash Cannon | 8.00 | 15.00 |
| 2 | Gungan Catapult | 10.00 | 20.00 |
| 3 | Hyperdrive Repair Kit | 25.00 | 50.00 |
| 4 | Naboo Accessory Set | 8.00 | 15.00 |
| 5 | Pod Race Fuel Station | 8.00 | 15.00 |
| 6 | Rappel Line Attach | 12.00 | 25.00 |
| 7 | Sith Accessory Set | 8.00 | 15.00 |
| 8 | Tatooine Accessory Set | 8.00 | 15.00 |
| 9 | Tatooine Disguise Set | 12.00 | 25.00 |
| 10 | Underwater Accessory Set | 8.00 | 15.00 |

## 1999-00 Star Wars Episode I Action Collection 12-Inch

| | | | |
|---|---|---|---|
| 1 | Anakin Skywalker (fully poseable) | 10.00 | 20.00 |
| 2 | Anakin Skywalker (w/Theed Hangar Droid) | 20.00 | 40.00 |
| 3 | Battle Droid (w/blaster rifle) | 15.00 | 30.00 |
| 4 | Battle Droid Commander(#(w/electrobinoculars) | 10.00 | 20.00 |
| 5 | Boss Nass | 15.00 | 30.00 |
| 6 | Chancellor Valorum & Coruscant Guard | 20.00 | 40.00 |
| 7 | Darth Maul (w/lightsaber) | 12.00 | 25.00 |
| 8 | Darth Maul & Sith Speeder | 20.00 | 40.00 |
| (Walmart Exclusive) | | | |
| 9 | Jar Jar Binks (fully poseable) | 12.00 | 25.00 |
| 10 | Mace Windu (w/lightsaber) | 15.00 | 30.00 |
| 11 | Obi-Wan Kenobi (w/lightsaber) | 12.00 | 25.00 |
| 12 | Pit Droids (fully poseable) | 12.00 | 20.00 |

| | | |
|---|---|---|
| 13 Qui-Gon Jinn (w/lightsaber) | 15.00 | 30.00 |
| 14 Qui-Gon Jinn (Tatooine) | 10.00 | 20.00 |
| 15 R2-A6 (metalized dome) | 20.00 | 40.00 |
| 16 Sebulba (w/Chubas) | 12.00 | 25.00 |
| 17 Watto (w/data pad) | 10.00 | 20.00 |

### 1999-00 Star Wars Episode I Battle Bags

| | | |
|---|---|---|
| 1 Sea Creatures I | 6.00 | 12.00 |
| 2 Sea Creatures II | 6.00 | 12.00 |
| 3 Swamp Creatures I | 6.00 | 12.00 |
| 4 Swamp Creatures II | 6.00 | 12.00 |

### 1999-00 Star Wars Episode I Bonus Battle Droid 2-Packs

PADMÉ NABERRIE with bonus BATTLE DROID

| | | |
|---|---|---|
| NNO Anakin Skywalker (Naboo)/Battle Droid (tan clean) | | |
| NNO Anakin Skywalker (Tatooine)/Battle Droid (tan clean) | 10.00 | 20.00 |
| NNO Battle Droid (tan clean)/Battle Droid (tan clean) | | |
| NNO Battle Droid (tan clean)/Battle Droid (gold/dirty) | | |
| NNO Battle Droid (tan clean)/Battle Droid (tan/blast on chest) | | |
| NNO Battle Droid (tan clean)/Battle Droid (tan/slash on chest/burn marks) | | |
| NNO C-3PO/Battle Droid (tan clean) | 15.00 | 30.00 |
| NNO Captain Panaka/Battle Droid (tan clean) | | |
| NNO Darth Maul (Jedi duel)/Battle Droid (tan clean) | 7.50 | 15.00 |
| NNO Darth Maul (Tatooine)/Battle Droid (tan clean) | 7.50 | 15.00 |
| NNO Darth Sidious/Battle Droid (tan clean) | | |
| NNO Destroyer Droid/Battle Droid (tan clean) | 12.50 | 25.00 |
| NNO Jar Jar Binks/Battle Droid (tan clean) | 12.50 | 25.00 |
| NNO Naboo Royal Security/Battle Droid (tan clean) | | |
| NNO Nute Gunray/Battle Droid (tan clean) | 15.00 | 30.00 |
| NNO Obi-Wan Kenobi (Jedi duel)/Battle Droid (tan clean) | 6.00 | 12.00 |
| NNO Obi-Wan Kenobi (Jedi Knight)/Battle Droid (tan clean) | 6.00 | 12.00 |
| NNO Padme Naberrie/Battle Droid (tan clean) | | |
| NNO Queen Amidala (Naboo)/Battle Droid (tan clean) | 6.00 | 12.00 |
| NNO Queen Amidala (red senate gown)/Battle Droid (tan clean) | | |
| NNO Qui-Gon Jinn/Battle Droid (tan clean) | | |
| NNO Qui-Gon Jinn (Jedi Master)/Battle Droid (tan clean) | 12.50 | 25.00 |
| NNO R2-D2/Battle Droid (tan clean) | 15.00 | 30.00 |
| NNO Ric Olie/Battle Droid (tan clean) | | |
| NNO Rune Haako/Battle Droid (tan clean) | | |
| NNO Senator Palpatine/Battle Droid (tan clean) | | |
| NNO Watto/Battle Droid (tan clean) | 20.00 | 40.00 |
| NNO Yoda/Battle Droid (tan clean) | 6.00 | 12.00 |

### 1999-00 Star Wars Episode I Bonus Pit Droid 2-Packs

| | | |
|---|---|---|
| NNO Anakin Skywalker (Tatooine)/Pit Droid (maroon) | | |
| NNO Anakin Skywalker (Tatooine)/Pit Droid (orange) | | |
| NNO Anakin Skywalker (Tatooine)/Pit Droid (white) | | |
| NNO Darth Maul (Jedi duel)/Pit Droid (maroon) | 25.00 | 50.00 |
| NNO Darth Maul (Jedi duel)/Pit Droid (orange) | | |
| NNO Darth Maul (Jedi duel)/Pit Droid (white) | | |
| NNO Darth Sidius (hologram)/Pit Droid (maroon) | | |
| NNO Darth Sidius (hologram)/Pit Droid (orange) | | |
| NNO Darth Sidius (hologram)/Pit Droid (white) | | |
| NNO Naboo Royal Guard/Pit Droid (maroon) | 10.00 | 20.00 |
| NNO Naboo Royal Guard/Pit Droid (orange) | 20.00 | 40.00 |
| NNO Naboo Royal Guard/Pit Droid (white) | 15.00 | 30.00 |
| NNO Obi-Wan Kenobi (Jedi Knight)/Pit Droid (maroon) | | |
| NNO Obi-Wan Kenobi (Jedi Knight)/Pit Droid (orange) | | |
| NNO Obi-Wan Kenobi (Jedi Knight)/Pit Droid (white) | | |

### 1999-00 Star Wars Episode I CommTech Cinema Scenes

| | | |
|---|---|---|
| 1 Mos Espa Encounter (Sebulba/Jar Jar Binks/Anakin Skywalker) | 12.00 | 25.00 |
| 2 Tatooine Showdown (Darth Maul Qui-Gon Jinn Tatooine/Anakin Skywalker Tatooine) | 8.00 | 20.00 |
| 3 Watto's Box (Watto/Graxol Kelvyyn/Shakka) | 25.00 | 50.00 |

### 1999-00 Star Wars Episode I CommTech Collection 1

| | | |
|---|---|---|
| 1a Anakin Skywalker Naboo (new sticker) | 6.00 | 12.00 |
| 1b Anakin Skywalker Naboo (no new sticker) | 12.00 | 25.00 |
| 2a Anakin Skywalker Naboo pilot (new sticker) | 6.00 | 12.00 |
| 2b Anakin Skywalker Naboo pilot (no new sticker) | 3.00 | 6.00 |
| 3a Anakin Skywalker Tatooine (.00) | 10.00 | 20.00 |
| 3b Anakin Skywalker Tatooine (.0100) | 3.00 | 6.00 |
| 3c Anakin Skywalker Tatooine (.01 innovision back) | 3.00 | 6.00 |
| 4a Battle Droid (tan clean .00) | 5.00 | 10.00 |
| 4b Battle Droid (tan clean .01) | 5.00 | 10.00 |
| 4c Battle Droid (tan clean .02 innovision back) | 5.00 | 10.00 |
| 5a Battle Droid (tan slash on chest w/burn marks .00) | 8.00 | 15.00 |
| 5b Battle Droid (tan slash on chest w/burn marks .01) | 4.00 | 8.00 |
| 5c Battle Droid (tan slash on chest w/burn marks .02 innovision back) | 3.00 | 6.00 |
| 6a Battle Droid (tan blast on chest .00) | 4.00 | 8.00 |
| 6b Battle Droid (tan blast on chest .01) | 3.00 | 6.00 |
| 6c Battle Droid (tan blast on chest .02 innovision back) | 6.00 | 12.00 |
| 7a Battle Droid (gold/dirty .00) | 3.00 | 6.00 |
| 7b Battle Droid (gold/dirty .01) | 3.00 | 6.00 |
| 7c Battle Droid (gold/dirty .02 innovision back) | 3.00 | 6.00 |
| 8a Darth Maul Jedi duel (.00) | 8.00 | 15.00 |
| 8b Darth Maul Jedi duel (.01/ innovision back) | 3.00 | 6.00 |
| 8c Darth Maul Jedi duel (.02) | 5.00 | 10.00 |
| 8d Darth Maul Jedi duel (.0000 large eyes different face more red paint on) | 4.00 | 8.00 |
| 8e Darth Maul Jedi duel (white strip on package card instead of yellow) | 3.00 | 6.00 |
| 9a Darth Maul Sith Lord (new sticker) | 5.00 | 10.00 |
| 9b Darth Maul Sith Lord (no new sticker) | 5.00 | 10.00 |
| 10a Darth Maul Tatooine (new sticker) | 4.00 | 8.00 |
| 10b Darth Maul Tatooine (new sticker/hologram chip sticker) | 3.00 | 6.00 |
| 10c Darth Maul Tatooine (no new sticker) | 3.00 | 6.00 |
| 10d Darth Maul Tatooine (no new sticker/hologram chip sticker) | 3.00 | 6.00 |
| 10e Darth Maul Sith Lord (new sticker/white strip on package card) | 3.00 | 6.00 |
| 11a Destroyer Droid battle damaged (new sticker) | 5.00 | 10.00 |
| 11b Destroyer Droid battle damaged (no new sticker) | 3.00 | 6.00 |
| 12a Jar Jar Binks (.00 large package photo) | 12.00 | 25.00 |
| 12b Jar Jar Binks (.0100 small package photo) | 3.00 | 6.00 |
| 12c Jar Jar Binks (.0200/ innovision back) | 3.00 | 6.00 |
| 13 Jar Jar Binks (Naboo swamp) | 4.00 | 8.00 |
| 14a Obi-Wan Kenobi Jedi duel (.00) | 4.00 | 8.00 |
| 14b Obi-Wan Kenobi Jedi duel (.0100) | 3.00 | 6.00 |
| 15a Obi-Wan Kenobi Jedi Knight (new sticker) | 4.00 | 8.00 |
| 15b Obi-Wan Kenobi Jedi Knight (no new sticker) | 3.00 | 6.00 |
| 16a Obi-Wan Kenobi Naboo (new sticker) | 6.00 | 12.00 |
| 16b Obi-Wan Kenobi Naboo (no new sticker) | 3.00 | 6.00 |
| 17a Padme Naberrie (.00) | 10.00 | 20.00 |
| 17b Padme Naberrie (.0100 innovision back) | 3.00 | 6.00 |
| 18a Queen Amidala Coruscant (new sticker) | 4.00 | 8.00 |
| 18b Queen Amidala Coruscant (no new sticker) | 4.00 | 8.00 |
| 19a Queen Amidala Naboo (.00) | 3.00 | 6.00 |
| 19b Queen Amidala Naboo (.0100 innovision back) | 6.00 | 12.00 |
| 20a Qui-Gon Jinn (.00) | 6.00 | 12.00 |
| 20b Qui-Gon Jinn (.0100 innovision back) | 4.00 | 8.00 |
| 21a Qui-Gon Jinn Jedi Master (new sticker) | 3.00 | 6.00 |
| 21b Qui-Gon Jinn Jedi Master (no new sticker) | 3.00 | 6.00 |
| 22a Qui-Gon Jinn Naboo (new sticker) | 5.00 | 10.00 |
| 22b Qui-Gon Jinn Naboo (no new sticker) | 3.00 | 6.00 |

### 1999-00 Star Wars Episode I CommTech Collection 2

| | | |
|---|---|---|
| 1a C-3PO (.00) | 5.00 | 10.00 |
| 1b C-3PO (.01 innovision back) | 20.00 | 40.00 |
| 2a Captain Panaka (wrong chip line on back they need her to sign a treaty) | 5.00 | 10.00 |
| 2b Captain Panaka (correct chip line on back this battle I do not think) | 5.00 | 10.00 |
| 3a Darth Sidious (.00) | 5.00 | 10.00 |
| 3b Darth Sidious (.01/innovision back) | 3.00 | 6.00 |
| 4 Darth Sidious (holograph) | 15.00 | 30.00 |
| 5a Destroyer Droid (new sticker) | 6.00 | 12.00 |
| 5b Destroyer Droid (no new sticker) | 4.00 | 8.00 |
| 6a Naboo Royal Guard | 8.00 | 15.00 |
| 6b Naboo Royal Security | 3.00 | 6.00 |
| 7a Nute Gunray (new sticker) | 5.00 | 10.00 |
| 7b Nute Gunray (no new sticker) | 8.00 | 15.00 |
| 8a R2-B1 (.0000/Astromech back/no space) | 8.00 | 15.00 |
| 8b R2-B1 (.0100/Astromech back/space) | 8.00 | 15.00 |

| | | |
|---|---|---|
| 9a R2-D2 (large packing bubble/new sticker) | 6.00 | 12.00 |
| 9b R2-D2 (small packing bubble) | 6.00 | 12.00 |
| 10 Pit Droids | 5.00 | 10.00 |
| 11 Queen Amidala (battle) | 6.00 | 12.00 |
| 12a Ric Olie (.00) | 3.00 | 6.00 |
| 12b Ric Olie (.0100/innovision back) | 3.00 | 6.00 |
| 13a Rune Haako (new sticker) | 4.00 | 8.00 |
| 13b Rune Haako (no new sticker) | 3.00 | 6.00 |
| 14a Senator Palpatine (.00) | 3.00 | 6.00 |
| 14b Senator Palpatine (.0100/innovision back) | 3.00 | 6.00 |
| 15 Sio Bibble | 10.00 | 20.00 |
| 16a Watto (.00) | 3.00 | 6.00 |
| 16b Watto (.0100 innovision back) | 3.00 | 6.00 |
| 17a Yoda (episode 1 on front) | 3.00 | 6.00 |
| 17b Yoda (no episode 1 on front) | 5.00 | 10.00 |

### 1999-00 Star Wars Episode I CommTech Collection 3

| | | |
|---|---|---|
| 1 Adi Gallia | 4.00 | 8.00 |
| 2a Boss Nass (.00) | 3.00 | 6.00 |
| 2b Boss Nass (.01/innovision back) | 3.00 | 6.00 |
| 3a Captain Tarpals (.00) | 5.00 | 10.00 |
| 3b Captain Tarpals (.01) | 3.00 | 6.00 |
| 4a Chancellor Valorum (.00/warning) | 3.00 | 6.00 |
| 4b Chancellor Valorum (.00/no warning) | 3.00 | 6.00 |
| 4c Chancellor Valorum (.01/no warning) | 3.00 | 6.00 |
| 4d Chancellor Valorum (.02/no warning) | 3.00 | 6.00 |
| 5a Gasgano with Pit Droid (.0100) | 5.00 | 10.00 |
| 5b Gasgano with Pit Droid (.0200) | 3.00 | 6.00 |
| 6a Ki-Adi-Mundi (.0000) | 3.00 | 6.00 |
| 6b Ki-Adi-Mundi (.0100/innovision back) | 3.00 | 6.00 |
| 7a Mace Windu (.0000) | 3.00 | 6.00 |
| 7b Mace Windu (.0100/innovision back) | 3.00 | 6.00 |
| 8a Ody Mandrell and Otoga (222 Pit Droid) | 3.00 | 6.00 |
| 8b Ody Mandrell and Otoga (222 Pit Droid/hologram chip sticker) | 3.00 | 6.00 |
| 9a OOM-9 (binoculars in package) | 3.00 | 6.00 |
| 9b OOM-9 (binoculars in package/hologram chip sticker) | 3.00 | 6.00 |
| 9c OOM-9 (binoculars in right hand) | 3.00 | 6.00 |
| 9d OOM-9 (binoculars in left hand/hologram chip sticker) | 5.00 | 10.00 |
| 10 TC-14 Protocol Droid | 8.00 | 15.00 |

### 1999-00 Star Wars Episode I CommTech Figure Collector 2-Packs

| | | |
|---|---|---|
| 1 Anakin Skywalker naboo/Obi-Wan Kenobi naboo | 12.00 | 25.00 |
| 2 Battle Droid (tan blast on chest)/Darth Maul Tatooine | | |
| 3 Battle Droid (tan slash on chest w/burn marks)/Darth Maul Tatooine | | |
| 4 Darth Maul Jedi duel/Anakin Skywalker Tatooine | 10.00 | 20.00 |

| | | |
|---|---|---|
| 5 Jar Jar Binks/Qui-Gon Jinn | 6.00 | 12.00 |
| 6 Padme Naberrie/Obi-Wan Kenobi Jedi Knight | | |
| 7 Queen Amidala Naboo/Qui-Gon Jinn Jedi Knight | | |

### 1999-00 Star Wars Episode I Creature 2-Packs

| | | |
|---|---|---|
| 1 Ammo Wagon and Falumpaset | 20.00 | 40.00 |
| 2 Eopie (w/Qui-Gon Jinn) | | |
| 3 Fambaa (w/Gungan warrior) | 50.00 | 100.00 |
| 4 Jabba the Hut (w/two-headed announcer) | 10.00 | 20.00 |
| 5 Kaadu and Jar Jar Binks | 10.00 | 20.00 |
| 6 Opee and Qui-Gon Jinn | 10.00 | 20.00 |

### 1999-00 Star Wars Episode I Deluxe

| | | |
|---|---|---|
| 1 Darth Maul | 3.00 | 6.00 |
| 2 Obi-Wan Kenobi | 3.00 | 6.00 |
| 3 Qui-Gon Jinn | 5.00 | 10.00 |

### 1999-00 Star Wars Episode I Electronic Talking 12-Inch

| | | |
|---|---|---|
| 1 C-3PO | 15.00 | 30.00 |
| 2 Darth Maul | 10.00 | 20.00 |
| 3 Jar Jar Binks | 15.00 | 30.00 |
| 4 Qui-Gon Jinn | 12.00 | 25.00 |
| 5 TC-14 | 20.00 | 40.00 |

### 1999-00 Star Wars Episode I Epic Force

| | | |
|---|---|---|
| 1 Darth Maul | 8.00 | 15.00 |
| 2 Obi-Wan Kenobi | 10.00 | 20.00 |
| 3 Qui-Gon Jinn | 8.00 | 15.00 |

### 1999-00 Star Wars Episode I Invasion Force

| | | |
|---|---|---|
| 1 Armored Scout Tank (w/Battle Droid tan clean) | 6.00 | 12.00 |
| 2 Gungan Assault Cannon (w/Jar Jar Binks) | 6.00 | 12.00 |
| 3 Gungan Scout Sub (w/Obi-Wan Kenobi Naboo water) | 8.00 | 15.00 |
| 4 Sith Attack Speeder (w/Darth Maul Tatooine) | 10.00 | 20.00 |

### 1999-00 Star Wars Episode I Jabba Glob

| | | |
|---|---|---|
| 1 Jabba the Hutt | 10.00 | 20.00 |

### 1999-00 Star Wars Episode I Light-Up

| | | |
|---|---|---|
| 1 Darth Maul hologram/ Wal-Mart exclusive | | |
| 2 Qui-Gon Jinn Hologram | 10.00 | 20.00 |
| (Walmart Exclusive) | | |

### 1999-00 Star Wars Episode I Playsets

| | | |
|---|---|---|
| 1 R2-D2 Carryall | 12.00 | 25.00 |
| 2 Theed Generator Complex (w/Battle Droid) | 12.00 | 25.00 |
| 3 Theed Hangar Power Spin Qui-Gon Jinn/Battle Droid break up | 25.00 | 50.00 |

### 1999-00 Star Wars Episode I Portrait Edition 12-Inch

| | | |
|---|---|---|
| 1 Princess Leia (ceremonial dress) | 20.00 | 40.00 |
| 2 Queen Amidala (black travel gown) | 12.00 | 25.00 |
| 3 Queen Amidala (return to Naboo) | 15.00 | 30.00 |
| 4 Queen Amidala (Senate gown) | 15.00 | 30.00 |
| 5 Return to Naboo 2-Pack/Padme/Qui Gon Ginn | | |

### 1999-00 Star Wars Episode I Vehicles

| | | |
|---|---|---|
| 1 Anakin's Podracer | 20.00 | 40.00 |
| 2 Flash Speeder | 15.00 | 30.00 |
| 3 Naboo Fighter | 15.00 | 30.00 |
| 4 Naboo Royal Starship | 100.00 | 200.00 |
| 5 Sith Speeder (w/Darth Maul Jedi duel) | 8.00 | 15.00 |
| 6 Stap and Battle Droid (burn marks on arms and legs) | 8.00 | 15.00 |
| 7 Sebulba's Podracer (w/Sebulba podrace gear) | 15.00 | 30.00 |
| 8 Trade Federation Droid Fighters | 15.00 | 30.00 |
| 9 Trade Federation Tank | 20.00 | 40.00 |

### 2015-16 Star Wars The Force Awakens 12-Inch

| | | |
|---|---|---|
| 1 BB-8 | 10.00 | 20.00 |
| 2 Chewbacca | 20.00 | 40.00 |
| 3 Darth Vader | 12.00 | 25.00 |
| 4 Fifth Brother Inquisitor | 7.50 | 15.00 |
| 5 Finn (Jakku) | 10.00 | 20.00 |
| 6 First Order Flametrooper | 10.00 | 20.00 |
| 7 First Order Stormtrooper | 8.00 | 15.00 |
| 8 First Order TIE Fighter Pilot | 7.50 | 15.00 |
| 9 Kylo Ren | 7.50 | 15.00 |
| 10 R2-D2 | 10.00 | 20.00 |
| 11 Rey (Jakku) | 10.00 | 20.00 |

### 2015-16 Star Wars The Force Awakens 12-Inch Vehicles

| | | |
|---|---|---|
| NNO Assault Walker (w/Riot Control Stormtrooper) | 12.00 | 25.00 |
| NNO Speeder Bike (w/Poe Dameron) | 12.00 | 25.00 |

## 2015-16 Star Wars The Force Awakens Armor Up 1

| | | | |
|---|---|---|---|
| NNO | Boba Fett | 7.50 | 15.00 |
| NNO | Captain Phasma (Epic Battles) | 10.00 | 20.00 |
| (Toys R Us Exclusive) | | | |
| NNO | Chewbacca | 7.50 | 15.00 |
| NNO | Finn (Jakku) | 7.50 | 15.00 |
| NNO | Finn (Starkiller Base) | 6.00 | 12.00 |
| NNO | First Order Flametrooper | 6.00 | 12.00 |
| NNO | First Order Stormtrooper | 10.00 | 20.00 |
| NNO | First Order TIE Fighter Pilot | 10.00 | 20.00 |
| NNO | Kylo Ren | 7.50 | 15.00 |
| NNO | Luke Skywalker | 7.50 | 15.00 |
| NNO | Poe Dameron | 7.50 | 15.00 |
| NNO | Poe Dameron (Epic Battles) | 6.00 | 12.00 |
| (Toys R Us Exclusive) | | | |

## 2015-16 Star Wars The Force Awakens Build-a-Weapon Collection

| | | | |
|---|---|---|---|
| NNO | Admiral Ackbar | 6.00 | 12.00 |
| NNO | Captain Phasma | 7.50 | 15.00 |
| NNO | Captain Rex | 10.00 | 20.00 |
| NNO | Constable Zuvio | 6.00 | 12.00 |
| NNO | Darth Maul | | |
| NNO | Darth Vader | 6.00 | 12.00 |
| NNO | Ezra Bridger | 6.00 | 12.00 |
| NNO | Fifth Brother | 7.50 | 15.00 |
| NNO | Finn (FN-2187) | 7.50 | 15.00 |
| NNO | Finn (Jakku) | 7.50 | 15.00 |
| NNO | First Order Flametrooper | 6.00 | 12.00 |
| NNO | First Order Snowtrooper | 5.00 | 10.00 |
| NNO | First Order Stormtrooper (running image) | 6.00 | 12.00 |
| NNO | First Order Stormtrooper (shooting blaster image) | 6.00 | 12.00 |
| NNO | First Order Stormtrooper Squad Leader | 10.00 | 20.00 |
| NNO | First Order TIE Fighter Pilot | 5.00 | 10.00 |
| NNO | General Hux | 5.00 | 10.00 |
| NNO | Goss Toowers | 5.00 | 10.00 |
| NNO | Guavian Enforcer | 6.00 | 12.00 |
| NNO | Han Solo | 7.50 | 15.00 |
| NNO | Hassk Thug | 5.00 | 10.00 |
| NNO | Inquisitor | 10.00 | 20.00 |
| NNO | Kanan Jarrus | 5.00 | 10.00 |
| NNO | Kanan Jarrus (stormtrooper disguise) | 6.00 | 12.00 |
| NNO | Kylo Ren (Force grip image) | 7.50 | 15.00 |
| NNO | Kylo Ren (lightsaber image) | 6.00 | 12.00 |
| NNO | Kylo Ren Unmasked | 7.50 | 15.00 |
| NNO | Luke Skywalker (Episode V) | 6.00 | 12.00 |
| NNO | Nien Nunb | 6.00 | 12.00 |
| NNO | Poe Dameron | 6.00 | 12.00 |
| NNO | Princess Leia | | |

| | | | |
|---|---|---|---|
| NNO | PZ-4CO | 5.00 | 10.00 |
| NNO | Resistance Trooper | 6.00 | 12.00 |
| NNO | Rey (Resistance fatigues) | 7.50 | 15.00 |
| NNO | Rey (Starkiller Base) | 7.50 | 15.00 |
| NNO | Sabine Wren | 6.00 | 12.00 |
| NNO | Sarco Plank | 6.00 | 12.00 |
| NNO | Seventh Sister | | |
| NNO | Tasu Leech | 6.00 | 12.00 |
| NNO | Unkar Plutt | 6.00 | 12.00 |
| NNO | X-Wing Pilot Asty | 3.00 | 6.00 |

## 2015-16 Star Wars The Force Awakens Multi-Packs

| | | | |
|---|---|---|---|
| 1 | BB-8, Unkar's Thug, Jakku Scavenger 3-Pack | 8.00 | 15.00 |
| 2 | Forest Mission 5-Pack | 20.00 | 40.00 |
| BB-8, Kylo Ren, Chewbacca, Stormtrooper, Resistance Trooper#((Amazon Exclusive) | | | |
| 3 | Takodana Encounter 4-Pack | 12.00 | 25.00 |
| Maz Kanata, Rey, Finn, BB-8 | | | |
| 4 | Troop Builder 7-Pack | 30.00 | 60.00 |
| (Kohl's Exclusive) | | | |

## 2015-16 Star Wars The Force Awakens 2-Packs

| | | | |
|---|---|---|---|
| NNO | Anakin Skywalker & Yoda | 12.00 | 25.00 |
| NNO | Clone Commander Cody & Obi-Wan Kenobi | 8.00 | 15.00 |
| NNO | Darth Vader & Ahsoka Tano | 12.00 | 25.00 |
| NNO | First Order Snowtrooper Officer & Snap Wexley | 8.00 | 15.00 |
| NNO | Garazeb Orrelios & C1-10P Chopper | 8.00 | 20.00 |
| NNO | Han Solo & Princess Leia | 8.00 | 15.00 |
| NNO | R2-D2 & C-3PO | 10.00 | 20.00 |
| NNO | Sidon Ithano & First Mate Quiggold | 6.00 | 12.00 |

## 2015-16 Star Wars The Force Awakens Vehicles

| | | | |
|---|---|---|---|
| 1 | Assault Walker (w/Stormtrooper Sergeant) | 12.50 | 25.00 |
| 2 | Battle Action Millennium Falcon (w/Finn, BB-8, Chewbacca) | 60.00 | 120.00 |
| 3 | Desert Assault Walker (w/Stormtrooper Officer) | 12.50 | 25.00 |
| (2015 Entertainment Earth Exclusive) | | | |
| 4 | Desert Landspeeder (w/Jakku Finn) | 15.00 | 30.00 |
| 5 | Elite Speeder Bike (w/Special Edition Stormtrooper) | 10.00 | 20.00 |
| 6 | First Order Snowspeeder (w/Snowspeeder Officer) | 15.00 | 30.00 |
| 7 | First Order Special Forces TIE Fighter (w/TIE Fighter Pilot) | 12.50 | 25.00 |

| | | | |
|---|---|---|---|
| 8 | Poe Dameron's Black Squadron X-Wing (w/Poe Dameron) | 30.00 | 75.00 |
| 9 | Rey's Speeder (w/Special Edition Rey) | 10.00 | 20.00 |
| 10 | Slave I (w/Boba Fett) | 25.00 | 50.00 |
| 11 | Y-Wing Scout Bomber (w/Kanan Jarrus) | 12.50 | 25.00 |

## 2005 Star Wars Force Battlers

| | | | |
|---|---|---|---|
| 1 | Anakin Skywalker | | |
| 2 | Chewbacca | | |
| 3 | Clone Trooper | | |
| 4 | Darth Vader/ slashing attack | | |
| 5 | Darth Vader/ missle-launching/ glider cape | | |
| 6 | Emperor Palpatine | | |
| 7 | General Grievous | | |
| 8 | Han Solo | | |
| 9 | Luke Skywalker | 12.00 | 25.00 |
| 10 | Mace Windu | 8.00 | 15.00 |
| 11 | Obi-Wan Kenobi | | |
| 12 | Yoda | | |

## 2006 Star Wars Force Battlers

| | |
|---|---|
| NNO | Chewbacca |
| NNO | General Grievous |
| NNO | Jango Fett |
| NNO | Obi-Wan Kenobi |

## 2006 Star Wars Force Battlers International

| | |
|---|---|
| NNO | Darth Vader/ with missle-launching/ glider cape |
| NNO | Emperor Palpatine |

## 2017 Star Wars Forces of Destiny

| | |
|---|---|
| NNO | Ahsoka Tano |
| NNO | Endor Adventure (Princess Leia Organa & Wicket) |
| NNO | Jyn Erso |
| NNO | Luke Skywalker & Yoda |
| NNO | Padme Amidala |
| NNO | Princess Leia & R2-D2 |
| NNO | Princess Leia & R2-D2 (Platinum Edition) |
| NNO | Rey of Jakku |
| NNO | Rey of Jakku & BB-8 |
| NNO | Rey of Jakku & Kylo Ren |
| NNO | Roaring Chewbacca |
| NNO | Sabine Wren |

## 2004-10 Star Wars Galactic Heroes

| | | | |
|---|---|---|---|
| 1 | 4-LOM/Bossk | 8.00 | 15.00 |
| 2 | Ahsoka Tano/Captain Rex | 15.00 | 30.00 |

| | | | | | |
|---|---|---|---|---|---|
| 3 | Ahsoka Tano/R3-S6 Goldie | 8.00 | 15.00 | | |
| 4 | Anakin Skywalker/Clone Trooper (white) | 6.00 | 12.00 | | |
| 5 | Anakin Skywalker/Clone Trooper (blue) | 6.00 | 12.00 | | |
| 6 | Anakin Skywalker/Count Dooku | 6.00 | 12.00 | | |
| 7 | Anakin Skywalker/STAP | | | | |
| 8 | Asajj Ventress/Count Dooku | 12.00 | 25.00 | | |
| 9 | AT-AT Commander/AT-AT Driver | 8.00 | 15.00 | | |
| 10 | Battle Droid/Clone Trooper | 6.00 | 12.00 | | |
| 11 | C-3PO/Chewbacca | 8.00 | 15.00 | | |
| 12 | Chewbacca/Clone Trooper | 6.00 | 12.00 | | |
| 13 | Chewbacca/Death Star Droid/Mouse Droid | 8.00 | 15.00 | | |
| 14 | Chewbacca/Disassembled C-3PO | 10.00 | 20.00 | | |
| 15 | Clone Trooper/Dwarf Spider Droid | 8.00 | 15.00 | | |
| 16 | Clone Trooper/Mace Windu | 8.00 | 15.00 | | |
| 17 | Commander Bly/Aayla Secura | 12.00 | 25.00 | | |
| 18 | Dark Side Anakin/Clone Trooper | 8.00 | 12.00 | | |
| 19 | Darth Maul/Sith Speeder | 8.00 | 15.00 | | |
| 20 | Darth Vader/Holographic Emperor Palpatine | | | | |
| 21 | Death Star Trooper/Imperial Officer | 6.00 | 12.00 | | |
| 22 | Dengar/Boba Fett | 12.00 | 25.00 | | |
| 23 | Duros/Garindan | | | | |
| 24 | Emperor Palpatine/Shock Trooper | | | | |
| 25 | Emperor Palpatine/Yoda | 6.00 | 15.00 | | |
| 26 | Figrin D'an/Hammerhead | 6.00 | 12.00 | | |
| 27 | Grand Moff Tarkin/Imperial Officer | 5.00 | 10.00 | | |
| 28 | Greedo/Han Solo | 15.00 | 30.00 | | |
| 29 | Han Solo/Logray | 8.00 | 15.00 | | |
| 30 | IG-86/Clone Commander Thire | | | | |
| 31 | IG-88/Zuckuss | 6.00 | 12.00 | | |
| 32 | Jango Fett/Obi-Wan Kenobi | 8.00 | 15.00 | | |
| 33 | Jar Jar Binks/Destroyer Droid | | | | |
| 34 | Jawa/Tusken Raider | 6.00 | 12.00 | | |
| 35 | Ki-Adi-Mundi/Commander Bacara | | | | |
| 36 | Kit Fisto/General Grievous | 8.00 | 15.00 | | |
| 37 | Kit Fisto/Mace Windu | 10.00 | 20.00 | | |
| 38 | Luke Skywalker (w/Yoda)/Spirit of Obi-Wan | 6.00 | 12.00 | | |
| 39 | Luke Skywalker Stormtrooper/Han Solo Stormtrooper | 10.00 | 20.00 | | |
| 40 | Luke Skywalker/Darth Vader | 8.00 | 15.00 | | |
| 41 | Luke Skywalker/Gamorrean Guard | 6.00 | 12.00 | | |
| 42 | Luke Skywalker/Han Solo | | | | |
| 43 | Luke Skywalker/Lando Calrissian | 6.00 | 12.00 | | |
| 44 | Luke Skywalker/R2-D2 | 6.00 | 12.00 | | |
| 45 | Luke Skywalker/Speeder | 15.00 | 30.00 | | |
| 46 | Nien Nunb/Admiral Ackbar | 10.00 | 20.00 | | |
| 47 | Obi-Wan Kenobi/Clone Commander Cody | | | | |
| 48 | Obi-Wan Kenobi/Clone Trooper (blue Star Wars logo) | | | | |
| 49 | Obi-Wan Kenobi/Clone Trooper (red Star Wars logo) | | | | |
| 50 | Obi-Wan Kenobi/Darth Maul | 8.00 | 15.00 | | |
| 51 | Obi-Wan Kenobi/Darth Vader | 6.00 | 12.00 | | |
| 52 | Obi-Wan Kenobi/Durge | 6.00 | 12.00 | | |
| 53 | Obi-Wan Kenobi/General Grievous | | | | |
| 54 | Padme Amidala/Anakin Skywalker | 12.00 | 25.00 | | |
| 55 | Padme Amidala/Clone Trooper | | | | |
| 56 | Padme Amidala/Jar Jar Binks | | | | |
| 57 | Plo Koon/Captain Jag | | | | |
| 58 | Ponda Baba/Snaggletooth | | | | |
| 59 | Princess Leia (Endor general)/Rebel Commando (Battle of Endor) | | | | |
| 60 | Princess Leia Boushh/Han Solo | | | | |
| 61 | Princess Leia/Darth Vader | | | | |
| 62 | Princess Leia/Han Solo | 12.00 | 25.00 | | |
| 63 | R2-D2 (serving tray)/Princess Leia (slave) | | | | |
| 64 | R2-D2/Jawas | | | | |
| 65 | Royal Guard/Imperial Gunner | | | | |
| 66 | Saesee Tiin/Agen Kolar | | | | |
| 67 | Sandtrooper/Obi-Wan Kenobi | | | | |
| 68 | Scout Trooper/Speeder Bike | 6.00 | 12.00 | | |
| 69 | Shaak Ti/Magna Guard | | | | |

| | | | |
|---|---|---|---|
| 70 | Skiff Guard/Lando Calrissian | 8.00 | 15.00 |
| 71 | Snowtrooper/Rebel Trooper | | |
| 72 | Stormtrooper/Rebel Trooper | | |
| 73 | Super Battle Droid/Luminara Unduli | | |
| 74 | Super Battle Droid/R2-D2 | | |
| 75 | Tarfful/Commander Gree | | |
| 76 | Wedge/TIE Pilot | | |
| 77 | Weequay/Barada | | |
| 78 | Yoda/Clone Trooper | | |
| 79 | Yoda/Kashyyyk Trooper | | |

### 2004-10 Star Wars Galactic Heroes Backpack Heroes

1 Boba Fett
2 Darth Tater
3 Darth Vader
4 Han Solo
5 Luke Skywalker
6 Yoda

### 2004-10 Star Wars Galactic Heroes Cinema Scenes

1 Assault on Ryloth
2 Assault on the Death Star
3 Assault on the Death Star 2
4 Battle of Geonosis
5 Battle of Hoth
6 Battle of Naboo
7 Battle of Kashyyyk
8 Battle of Mustafar
9 Cantina Band
10 Cantina Encounter
11 Death Star Escape
12 Endor Attack
13 Endor Celebration
14 Escape from Mos Eisley
15 Geonosis Battle Arena
16 Hoth Snowspeeder Assault
17 Jabba's Palace
18 Jabba's Sail Barge
19 Jabba's Skiff The Pit of Carkoon
20 Jedi Starfighter

21 Jedi vs. Sith
22 Kamino Showdown
23 Millennium Falcon
24 Purchase of the Droids
25 Rancor Pit
26 Shadow Squadron Y-Wing
27 Slave I and Boba Fett
28 Speeder Bike Chase
29 Vader's Bounty Hunters
30 Vader's TIE Fighter (w/Darth Vader)
31 X-Wing Dagobah Landing

### 2004-10 Star Wars Galactic Heroes Exclusives

1 Scout Trooper
(2004 SDCC Exclusive)
2 Yoda/R2-D2
(2004 Burger King Exclusive)

### 2004-10 Star Wars Galactic Heroes Singles

1 Anakin Skywalker
2 Battle Droid
3 Boba Fett
4 Bossk
5 C-3PO
6 Chewbacca
7 Clone Trooper
8 Darth Maul
9 Darth Vader
10 Han Solo
11 Luke Skywalker
12 Obi-Wan Kenobi
13 R2-D2

### 2004-10 Star Wars Galactic Heroes Stocking Stuffers

1 Darth Vader/Boba Fett/Stormtrooper
2 Han Solo/Chewbacca/C-3PO
3 Luke Skywalker/Yoda/R2-D2
4 Obi-Wan Kenobi/Anakin Skywalker/Shock Trooper

## 2004-10 Star Wars Galactic Heroes Vehicles

1 Anakin's Delta Starfighter
2 Landspeeder
3 Millennium Falcon
4 Obi-Wan's Starfighter
5 Snowspeeder
6 X-Wing Fighter
7 X-Wing Racer

## 2019 Star Wars Galaxy of Adventures 3.75-Inch

| | | | |
|---|---|---|---|
| NNO | Boba Fett | 10.00 | 20.00 |
| NNO | Chewbacca | 6.00 | 12.00 |
| NNO | Darth Maul | 7.50 | 15.00 |
| NNO | Darth Vader | 10.00 | 20.00 |
| NNO | General Grievous | 7.50 | 15.00 |
| NNO | Han Solo | 7.50 | 15.00 |
| NNO | Kylo Ren | 7.50 | 15.00 |
| NNO | Luke Skywalker | 7.50 | 15.00 |
| NNO | Obi-Wan Kenobi | 6.00 | 12.00 |
| NNO | Princess Leia Organa | 7.50 | 15.00 |
| NNO | R2-D2 | 6.00 | 12.00 |
| NNO | Rey | 10.00 | 20.00 |
| NNO | Stormtrooper | 7.50 | 15.00 |
| NNO | Yoda | 7.50 | 15.00 |

## 2019 Star Wars Galaxy of Adventures 5-Inch

| | | | |
|---|---|---|---|
| NNO | Darth Vader | 12.50 | 25.00 |
| NNO | C-3PO | | |
| NNO | Han Solo | | |
| NNO | Chewbacca | 7.50 | 15.00 |
| NNO | Kylo Ren | 10.00 | 20.00 |
| NNO | Rey | 12.50 | 25.00 |
| NNO | Jet Trooper | 7.50 | 15.00 |
| NNO | Finn | 7.50 | 15.00 |

## 2019 Star Wars Galaxy of Adventures 5-Inch Multipacks

NNO  D-0/BB-8/R2-D2 3-Pack
NNO  Kylo Ren/Rey 2-Pack

## 2019 Star Wars Galaxy of Adventures 5-Inch Vehicle

| | | | |
|---|---|---|---|
| NNO | Treadspeeder (w/First Order Driver) | 20.00 | 40.00 |

## 2015 Star Wars Hero Mashers

| | | | |
|---|---|---|---|
| NNO | Boba Fett | 5.00 | 10.00 |
| NNO | Bossk | 5.00 | 10.00 |
| NNO | Darth Vader | 6.00 | 12.00 |
| NNO | General Grievous | 7.50 | 15.00 |
| NNO | Jar Jar Binks | 5.00 | 10.00 |
| NNO | Kanan Jarrus | 7.50 | 15.00 |
| NNO | Zeb Orrelios | | |

## 2015 Star Wars Hero Mashers Deluxe

| | | | |
|---|---|---|---|
| NNO | Anakin Skywalker with Speeder Bike | 12.50 | 25.00 |
| NNO | Darth Maul with Sith Speeder Bike | 10.00 | 20.00 |
| NNO | Han Solo vs. Boba Fett | 10.00 | 20.00 |
| NNO | Luke Skywalker vs. Darth Vader | 15.00 | 30.00 |
| NNO | Yoda vs. Emperor Palpatine | 15.00 | 30.00 |

## 2019-20 Star Wars HyperReal

NNO  Darth Vader
NNO  Luke Skywalker

## 2004-05 Star Wars Jedi Force Blue

NNO  Anakin Skywalker (w/Jedi Pod)
NNO  Anakin Skywalker (w/rescue glider)
NNO  C-3PO/R2-D2
NNO  Chewbacca (w/Wookiee Action Tool)
NNO  Chewbacca (w/Wookiee Scout Flyer)
NNO  Darth Vader (w/Imperial Claw Droid)
NNO  Han Solo (w/Jet Bike)
NNO  Luke Skywalker (w/Jedi Jet Pack)
NNO  Luke Skywalker (w/Speeder Bike)
NNO  Luke Skywalker (w/Speeder Board)
NNO  Luke's X-Wing
NNO  Mace Windu (w/Jedi Grappling Hook)

NNO  Obi-Wan Kenobi (w/Boga)
NNO  Yoda (w/Swamp Stomper)

## 2004-05 Star Wars Jedi Force White

| | | | |
|---|---|---|---|
| NNO | Anakin Skywalker/Jar Jar Binks | | |
| NNO | Anakin Skywalker's Jedi Starfighter (w/R2-D2) | | |
| NNO | BARC Speeder Bike (w/Anakin Skywalker) | 10.00 | 20.00 |
| NNO | C-3PO/R2-D2 | | |
| NNO | Darth Vader/Stormtrooper | | |
| NNO | Freeco Bike (w/Obi-Wan Kenobi) | | |
| NNO | Han Solo/Chewbacca | | |
| NNO | Landspeeder (w/Luke Skywalker) | | |
| NNO | Millennium Falcon (w/Han Solo/Chewbacca) | | |
| NNO | Obi-Wan Kenobi/Commander Cody | | |
| NNO | Snowspeeder (w/Luke Skywalker/Han Solo) | | |
| NNO | Yoda/Luke Skywalker | | |

## 2017 Star Wars The Last Jedi Big Figs

| | | | |
|---|---|---|---|
| NNO | Captain Phasma | 15.00 | 30.00 |
| NNO | Elite Praetorian Guard | 12.50 | 25.00 |
| NNO | First Order Executioner | 25.00 | 50.00 |
| NNO | First Order Stormtrooper | 10.00 | 20.00 |
| NNO | Kylo Ren | 12.50 | 25.00 |
| NNO | Poe Dameron | 10.00 | 20.00 |
| NNO | Rey | 12.50 | 25.00 |

## 2017 Star Wars The Last Jedi Force Link

| | | | |
|---|---|---|---|
| 1 | C-3PO | 6.00 | 12.00 |
| 2 | C'Ai Threnalli | 6.00 | 12.00 |
| | (Entertainment Earth Exclusive) | | |
| 3 | Chewbacca (w/porg) | 7.50 | 15.00 |
| 4 | DJ (Canto Bight) | 5.00 | 10.00 |
| 5 | Emperor Palpatine | | |
| 6 | Finn (Resistance Fighter) | 6.00 | 12.00 |
| 7 | First Order Flametrooper | 7.50 | 15.00 |
| | (Entertainment Earth Exclusive) | | |
| 8 | First Order Stormtrooper | 7.50 | 15.00 |
| 9 | General Hux (w/mouse droid) | 5.00 | 10.00 |
| 10 | General Leia Organa | 7.50 | 15.00 |
| 11 | Jyn Erso (Jedha) | 6.00 | 12.00 |
| 12 | Kylo Ren | 7.50 | 15.00 |
| 13 | Luke Skywalker (Jedi Exile) | 7.50 | 15.00 |
| 14 | Luke Skywalker (Jedi Master) | 7.50 | 15.00 |
| 15 | Obi-Wan Kenobi | 7.50 | 15.00 |
| 16 | Poe Dameron (Resistance Pilot) | 5.00 | 10.00 |
| 17 | R2-D2 | 6.00 | 12.00 |
| 18 | Resistance Gunner Paige | 6.00 | 12.00 |
| 19 | Resistance Gunner Rose | 6.00 | 12.00 |
| 20 | Rey (Island Journey) | 6.00 | 12.00 |
| 21 | Rey (Jedi Training) | 10.00 | 20.00 |
| 22 | Yoda | 10.00 | 20.00 |

## 2017 Star Wars The Last Jedi Force Link 2-Packs

| | | | |
|---|---|---|---|
| NNO | Bala-Tik (w/Rathtar) | 7.50 | 15.00 |
| NNO | Chirrut Imwe & Baze Malbus | 12.50 | 25.00 |
| NNO | Darth Vader (w/Imperial probe droid) | | |
| NNO | Finn & Captain Phasma | 15.00 | 30.00 |
| | (Entertainment Earth Exclusive) | | |
| NNO | Han Solo & Boba Fett | 10.00 | 20.00 |
| NNO | Rey (Jedi Training) & Elite Praetorian Guard | 7.50 | 15.00 |
| NNO | Rose Tico (w/BB-8 & BB-9E) | 7.50 | 15.00 |

## 2017 Star Wars The Last Jedi Force Link Multipacks

| | | |
|---|---|---|
| NNO Battle on Crait 4-Pack | 15.00 | 30.00 |
| Rey/First Order Walker Driver#{First Order Gunner/Rose | | |
| NNO Emperor Palpatine/Luke Skywalker/Emperor's Royal Guard 3-Pack | 10.00 | 20.00 |
| (Target Exclusive) | | |
| NNO Era of the Force 8-Pack | | |
| Yoda/Luke/Kylo Ren/Rey#{Darth Maul/Mace Windu#{Obi-Wan Kenobi/Darth Vader#{(Target Exclusive) | | |
| NNO Luke Skywalker/Resistance Tech Rose | 20.00 | 40.00 |
| Rey (Jedi Training)/First Order Stormtrooper 4-Pack | | |

## 2017 Star Wars The Last Jedi Force Link Sets

| | | |
|---|---|---|
| NNO BB-8 2-in-1 Mega Playset | 20.00 | 40.00 |
| NNO Starter Set (w/Elite Praetorian Guard) | | |
| (Toys R Us Exclusive) | | |
| NNO Starter Set (w/Kylo Ren) | 7.50 | 15.00 |
| NNO Starter Set (w/Stormtrooper Executioner) | 15.00 | 30.00 |
| (Toys R Us Exclusive) | | |

## 2017 Star Wars The Last Jedi Force Link Vehicles

| | | |
|---|---|---|
| 1 Canto Bight Police Speeder (w/Canto Bight Police) | 10.00 | 20.00 |
| 2 Kylo Ren's TIE Silencer (w/Kylo Ren) | 20.00 | 40.00 |
| 3 Resistance A-Wing Fighter (w/Resistance Pilot Tallie) | 12.50 | 25.00 |
| 4 Ski Speeder (w/Poe Dameron) | | |
| 5 TIE Fighter (w/TIE Fighter Pilot) | 15.00 | 30.00 |
| (Walmart Exclusive) | | |
| 6 X-Wing Fighter (w/Poe Dameron) | 30.00 | 75.00 |
| (Toys R Us Exclusive) | | |

## 2017 Star Wars The Last Jedi S.H. Figuarts

| | | |
|---|---|---|
| NNO Captain Phasma | 30.00 | 60.00 |
| NNO Elite Praetorian Guard (w/dual blades) | 20.00 | 40.00 |
| NNO Elite Praetorian Guard (w/single blade) | 20.00 | 40.00 |
| NNO Elite Praetorian Guard (w/whip staff) | 25.00 | 50.00 |
| NNO First Order Executioner | 25.00 | 50.00 |
| NNO First Order Stormtrooper | 30.00 | 75.00 |
| NNO Kylo Ren | 50.00 | 100.00 |
| NNO Rey | 50.00 | 100.00 |

## 2008-10 Star Wars The Legacy Collection Battle Packs

| | | |
|---|---|---|
| NNO Battle at the Sarlaac Pit (ultimate) | 50.00 | 100.00 |
| (2008 Target Exclusive) | | |
| NNO Battle of Endor | | |
| NNO Birth of Darth Vader | 20.00 | 40.00 |
| NNO Clone Attack on Coruscant | 20.00 | 40.00 |
| NNO Disturbance at Lars Homestead | 75.00 | 150.00 |
| (2008 Toys R Us Exclusive) | | |
| NNO Duel on Mustafar | | |
| NNO Gelagrub Patrol | 20.00 | 50.00 |
| NNO Geonosis Assault | 50.00 | 100.00 |
| NNO Hoth Recon Patrol | 30.00 | 60.00 |
| NNO Hoth Speeder Bike Patrol | 25.00 | 50.00 |

| | | |
|---|---|---|
| NNO Jedi Training on Dagobah | | |
| NNO Jedi vs. Darth Sidious | 15.00 | 30.00 |
| NNO Kamino Conflict | | |
| NNO Resurgence of the Jedi | 20.00 | 40.00 |
| NNO Scramble on Yavin | 100.00 | 175.00 |
| NNO Shield Generator Assault | 25.00 | 50.00 |
| NNO Tatooine Desert Ambush | | |
| NNO Training on the Falcon | 30.00 | 75.00 |

## 2008-10 Star Wars The Legacy Collection Build-A-Droid Wave 1

| | | |
|---|---|---|
| BD1a Han Solo/ with R4-D6 left leg | 6.00 | 12.00 |
| BD1b Han Solo/ with R4-D6 left leg/ first day of issue sticker | | |
| BD2a Luke Skywalker/ with R4-D6 right leg | | |
| BD2b Luke Skywalker/ with R5-A2 head/ and center leg | | |
| BD2c Luke Skywalker/ with R4-D6 right leg/ first day of issue sticker | | |
| BD3a Chewbacca/ with R4-D6 head/ and center leg | | |
| BD3b Chewbacca/ with R4-D6 head/ and center leg/ first day of issue sticker | | |
| BD4a Leektar/Nippet/ with R4-D6 torso | | |
| BD4b Leektar/Nippet/ with R4-D6 torso/ first day of issue sticker | | |
| BD5a Ak-Rev/ with R7-Z0 left leg | | |
| BD5b Ak-Rev/ with R7-Z0 left leg/ first day of issue sticker | 6.00 | 12.00 |
| BD6a Yarna D'Al'Gargan/ with R7-Z0 right leg | 8.00 | 15.00 |
| BD6b Yarna D'Al'Gargan/ with R7-Z0 right leg/ first day of issue sticker | 6.00 | 12.00 |
| BD7a Bane Malar/ with R7-Z0 torso | | |
| BD7b Bane Malar/ with R7-Z0 torso/ first day of issue sticker | | |
| BD8a Darth Vader/ multi-piece helmet/ with R7-Z0 head | | |
| BD8b Darth Vader/ multi-piece helmet/ with R7-Z0 head/ first day of issue sti | | |
| BD8c Darth Vader/ multi-piece helmet/ with MB-RA-7 head | | |

## 2008-10 Star Wars The Legacy Collection Build-A-Droid Wave 2

| | | |
|---|---|---|
| BD9 Obi-Wan Kenobi general/ with R4-J1 left leg | 10.00 | 20.00 |
| BD10 Clone Scuba Trooper/ with R4-J1 head/ and center leg | 6.00 | 12.00 |
| BD11 Saesee Tiin general/ with R7-T1 right leg | | |
| BD12 Padme Amidala snow/ with R7-T1 left leg | | |
| BD13 IG Lancer Droid/ with R4-J1 torso | | |
| BD14 Mon Calimari Warrior/ with R7-T1 Torso | 8.00 | 15.00 |
| BD15 Quarren Soldier/ with R7-T1 head/ and center leg | | |
| BD16 Clone Trooper blue/ with cannon/with R4-J1 right leg | | |

## 2008-10 Star Wars The Legacy Collection Build-A-Droid Wave 3

| | | |
|---|---|---|
| BD17a Clone Trooper coruscant/ landing platform/ with RD6-RA7 torso | 10.00 | 20.00 |
| BD17b Clone Trooper coruscant/ landing platform/ with MB-RA-7 right arm | | |
| BD18a Jodo Kast/ with RD6-RA7 head | 10.00 | 20.00 |
| BD18b Jodo Kast/ with MB-RA-7 left leg | | |
| BD19 Yaddle/Evan Piell/ with RD6-RA7 right leg | 15.00 | 30.00 |
| BD20a Saleucami Trooper/ with 5D6-RA7 left leg | | |
| BD20b Saleucami Trooper/ with MB-RA7 right leg | | |
| BD21 Count Dooku/ holographic transmission/ with RD6-RA7 right arm | | |
| BD22 Imperial Engineer/ with RD6-RA7 left arm | | |

## 2008-10 Star Wars The Legacy Collection Build-A-Droid Wave 4

| | | |
|---|---|---|
| BD23 Stass Allie/ with MB-RA-7 left arm | 12.00 | 25.00 |
| BD24a Commander Faie/ with MB-RA-7 torso | 10.00 | 20.00 |
| BD24b Commander Faie/ with R5-A2 left leg | 10.00 | 20.00 |
| BD25a General Grievous/ with MB-RA-7 head | 12.00 | 25.00 |
| BD25b General Grievous/ with R5-A2 right leg | | |
| BD26a Bail Organa/ light skin/ with MB-RA-7 left arm | | |
| BD26b Bail Organa/ dark skin/ with MB-RA-7 left arm | | |

| | | |
|---|---|---|
| BD27a Breha Organa/ light skin/ with MB-RA-7 left leg | | |
| BD27b Breha Organa/ dark skin/ with MB-RA-7 left leg | | |
| BD28 FX-6/ with MB-RA-7 right leg | 10.00 | 20.00 |
| BD29 Clone Trooper 327th Star/ Corps yellow shoulder/ with MB-RA-7 torso | | |
| BD29a Clone Trooper 327th Star/ Corps yellow shoulder/ with R5-A2 torso | | |
| BD29b Clone Trooper 327th Star/ Corps yellow shoulder/ with MB-RA-7 torso | | |
| BD29c Clone Trooper 327th Star/ Corps yellow shoulder/ with R5-A2 torso | | |

## 2008-10 Star Wars The Legacy Collection Comic Packs Blue and White

| | |
|---|---|
| 1 Asajj Ventress and Tol Skorr | |
| 2 Anakin Skywalker and Durge | |
| 3 Anakin Skywalker and Assassin Droid | |
| 4 Darth Talon and Cade Skywalker | |
| 5 Antares Draco and Ganner Krieg | |
| 6 Fenn Shysa and Dengar | |
| 7 Princess Leia and Tobbi Dala | |
| 8 Leia Organa and Prince Xizor | |
| 9 Grand Admiral Thrawn and Talon Karrde | |
| 10 Darth Vader and Grand Moff Trachta | |
| 11 Darth Vader and Princess Leia | |
| 12 Clone Emperor and Luke Skywalker | |
| 13 Quinlan Vos and Commander Faie | |
| 14 Wedge Antilles and Borsk Fey'lya | |
| 15 Luke Skywalker and Deena Shan | |
| 16 Ki-Adi-Mundi and Sharad Hett | |

## 2008-10 Star Wars The Legacy Collection Comic Packs Blue and White Exclusives

| | | |
|---|---|---|
| NNO Ibtisam and Nrin Vakil | 25.00 | 50.00 |
| (2008 Walmart Exclusive) | | |

NNO Janek Sunber and Amanin 15.00 30.00
(2008 Walmart Exclusive)
NNO Machook/Keoulkeech/Kettch 30.00 60.00
(2008 Walmart Exclusive)

## 2008-10 Star Wars The Legacy Collection Comic Packs Red and White

1 Darth Vader and Rebel Officer
2 Chewbacca and Han Solo
3 Yuuzhan Vong and Kyle Katarn
4 Wedge Antilles and Borsk Fey'lya
5 Luke Skywalker and Deena Shan
6 Ki-Adi-Mundi and Sharad Hett
7 Lumiya and Luke Skywalker
8 Darth Krayt and Sigel Dare
9 Clone Trooper and Clone Commander
10 Clone Trooper Lieutenant and Clone Trooper
11 Ulic Qel-Droma and Exar Kun
12 T'ra Saa and Tholme
13 Stormtrooper and Blackhole Hologram

## 2008-10 Star Wars The Legacy Collection Comic Packs Red and White Exclusives

NNO Baron Soontir Fel and Ysanne Isard (X-Wing Rogue Squadron)
(2010 Entertainment Earth Exclusive)
NNO Deliah Blue and Darth Nihl (Legacy)
(2010 Entertainment Earth Exclusive)
NNO IG-97 and Rom Mohc
(2009 Walmart Exclusive)
NNO Ja  rael and Rohlan Dyre (Knights of the Old Republic)
(2010 Entertainment Earth Exclusive)
NNO Montross and Jaster Mareel (Jango Fett Open Seasons)
(2010 Entertainment Earth Exclusive)
NNO Plourr Ilo and Dllr Nep
(2009 Online Exclusive)
NNO Storm Commando and General Weir
(2009 Walmart Exclusive)

## 2008-10 Star Wars The Legacy Collection Creatures

1 Dewback (w/Imperial sandtrooper) 25.00 50.00
(2009 Walmart Exclusive)
2 Jabba's Rancor (w/Luke Skywalker) 60.00 120.00
(2008 Target Exclusive)

## 2008-10 Star Wars The Legacy Collection Evolutions

1 Clone Commandos 50.00 100.00
(2009 Walmart Exclusive)
2 Imperial Pilot Legacy I 15.00 30.00
3 Imperial Pilot Legacy II 15.00 30.00
(2009 Walmart Exclusive)
4 Rebel Pilot Legacy I 15.00 40.00
5 Rebel Pilot Legacy II 25.00 50.00
6 Rebel Pilot Legacy III 30.00 75.00
(2009 Walmart Exclusive)
7 The Fett Legacy 15.00 40.00
8 The Jedi Legacy
9 The Padme Amidala Legacy 12.00 25.00
10 The Sith Legacy 60.00 120.00
11 Vader's Secret Apprentice 30.00 60.00

## 2008-10 Star Wars The Legacy Collection Geonosis Battle Arena 2009 Edition

1 Coleman Trebor Vs. Jango Fett
2 Kit Fisto Vs. Geonosis Warrior
3 Mace Windu Vs. Battle Droid Commander
4 Joclad Danva Vs. Battle Droid
5 Roth Del Masona Vs. Super Battle Droid
6 Yoda Vs. Destroyer Droid

## 2008-10 Star Wars The Legacy Collection Geonosis Battle Arena 2010 Edition

1 Obi-Wan Kenobi & Super Battle Droid
2 Rodian Jedi & Battle Droid
3 Anakin Skywalker & Droideka
4 Shaak Ti & Geonosian Warrior
5 Nicanas Tassu & Count Dooku
6 C-3PO & R2-D2

## 2008-10 Star Wars The Legacy Collection Greatest Hits 2008

GH1 Commander Gree 6.00 12.00
GH2 Kashyyyk Trooper 6.00 12.00
GH3 Darth Vader (Battle Damage) 10.00 20.00
GH4 Imperial EVO Trooper 6.00 12.00

## 2008-10 Star Wars The Legacy Collection Saga Legends Blue and White

SL1 R2-D2 (electronic)
SL2 Yoda and Kybuck
SL3 Darth Vader (Anakin Skywalker)
SL4 Obi-Wan Kenobi
SL5 Clone Trooper (AOTC)
SL6 C-3PO
SL7 General Grievous
SL8 Mace Windu
SL9 Plo Koon
SL10 Super Battle Droid
SL11 Destroyer Droid
SL13 Darth Vader

SL14 Darth Maul
SL15 Jango Fett
SL16 501st Legion Trooper
SL17 Shock Trooper
SL18 BARC Trooper
SL19 ARC Trooper
SL21 Sandtrooper
SL22 Luke Skywalker (X-Wing pilot)
SL23 ARC trooper Commander (red)
SL24 Tri-Droid
SL25 Snowtrooper
SL26 Saesee Tiin
SL27 Clone Trooper (ROTS)
SL12a Clone Trooper Officer (red)
SL12b Clone Trooper Officer (yellow)
SL12c Clone Trooper Officer (blue)
SL12d Clone Trooper Officer (green)
SL20a Battle Droids (tan)
SL20b Battle Droids (brown)

## 2008-10 Star Wars The Legacy Collection Saga Legends Red and White

SL1 R2-D2 (electronic)
SL2 Darth Vader (Anakin Skywalker)
SL3 Obi-Wan Kenobi
SL4 Clone Trooper (Episode II)
SL5 Super Battle Droid
SL6 Darth Vader
SL7 Darth Maul
SL8 501st Legion Trooper
SL9 Yoda
SL10 Sandtrooper
SL11 Saesee Tiin
SL12 Clone Trooper (Episode III)
SL13 Plo Koon
SL14 Shocktrooper
SL15a Chewbacca I
SL15b Chewbacca II
SL16 Han Solo
SL17 Luke Skywalker

## 2008-10 Star Wars The Legacy Collection Vehicles

1 AT-ST 30.00 75.00
(2009 Walmart Exclusive)
2 Dagger Squadron B-Wing Fighter 50.00 100.00
(2008 Toys R Us Exclusive)
3 Darth Vader's TIE Advanced x1 Starfighter 15.00 30.00
4 Green Leader's A-Wing Fighter 50.00 100.00
(2008 Walmart Exclusive)

| 5 Millennium Falcon | 300.00 | 600.00 |
|---|---|---|
| 6 Speeder Bike (w/biker scout) | 25.00 | 50.00 |
| (Toys R Us Exclusive) | | |
| 7 TIE Fighter | | |
| 8 TIE Fighter Pirate | | |
| (PX Previews Exclusive) | | |
| 9 TIE Fighter Shadows of the Empire | 150.00 | 300.00 |
| (2009 Target Exclusive) | | |
| 10 TIE Interceptor | 30.00 | 60.00 |
| (2009 Toys R Us Exclusive) | | |
| 11 Wedge Antilles' X-Wing Starfighter | 120.00 | 200.00 |
| (2009 Target Exclusive) | | |

### 2008-09 Star Wars Mighty Muggs

| | | |
|---|---|---|
| NNO Anakin Skywalker | | |
| NNO Asajj Ventress | | |
| NNO Boba Fett | 8.00 | 15.00 |
| NNO C-3PO | 8.00 | 15.00 |
| NNO Captain Rex | 6.00 | 12.00 |
| NNO Chewbacca | 8.00 | 15.00 |
| NNO Commander Cody | 12.00 | 25.00 |
| NNO Count Dooku | 6.00 | 12.00 |
| NNO Darth Maul | 6.00 | 12.00 |
| NNO Darth Maul (shirtless) | 6.00 | 12.00 |
| NNO Darth Revan | 10.00 | 20.00 |
| NNO Darth Vader | 8.00 | 15.00 |
| NNO Darth Vader (unmasked) | | |
| NNO Emperor | 5.00 | 10.00 |
| NNO Gamorrean Guard | 5.00 | 10.00 |
| NNO General Grievous | 12.00 | 25.00 |
| NNO Grand Moff Tarkin | | |
| NNO Han Solo | 8.00 | 15.00 |
| NNO Han Solo (Hoth) | 10.00 | 20.00 |
| NNO Jango Fett | 6.00 | 12.00 |
| NNO Lando Calrissian | 8.00 | 15.00 |
| NNO Luke (Bespin) | 8.00 | 15.00 |
| NNO Luke Skywalker | 8.00 | 15.00 |
| NNO Luke Skywalker (Hoth) | 8.00 | 15.00 |
| NNO Mace Windu | | |
| NNO Obi-Wan Kenobi (old) | 6.00 | 12.00 |
| NNO Obi-Wan Kenobi (young) | | |
| NNO Plo Koon | | |
| NNO Princess Leia | | |
| NNO Qui-Gon Jinn | 8.00 | 15.00 |
| NNO Royal Guard | | |
| NNO Stormtrooper | 6.00 | 12.00 |
| NNO Wampa | 5.00 | 10.00 |
| NNO Wicket | 5.00 | 10.00 |
| NNO Yoda | 8.00 | 15.00 |

### 2008-09 Star Wars Mighty Muggs Exclusives

| | | |
|---|---|---|
| 1 Admiral Ackbar | | |
| (2008 PX Previews Exclusive) | | |
| 2 Biggs Darklighter | | |
| (2009 Target Exclusive) | | |
| 3 Bossk | | |
| (2009 Target Exclusive) | | |
| 4 Commander Gree | | |
| (2008 SDCC Exclusive) | | |
| 5 Shadow Trooper | | |
| (2008 PX Previews Exclusive) | | |
| 6 Shock Trooper | 8.00 | 15.00 |
| (2009 Target Exclusive) | | |

| 7 Snowtrooper | 8.00 | 15.00 |
|---|---|---|
| (2009 Target Exclusive) | | |
| 8 Teebo | | |
| (2009 Target Exclusive) | | |

### 2012 Star Wars Movie Heroes

| | | |
|---|---|---|
| MH1 Shock Trooper | 10.00 | 20.00 |
| MH2 Super Battle Droid | 7.50 | 15.00 |
| MH3 R2-D2 | 10.00 | 20.00 |
| MH4 Battle Droid (repaint) | 6.00 | 12.00 |
| MH4 Battle Droid (variant) | 6.00 | 12.00 |
| MH5 Darth Maul (repaint) | | |
| MH6 Darth Vader | 7.50 | 15.00 |
| MH7 General Grievous | 15.00 | 30.00 |
| MH8 Obi-Wan Kenobi | 5.00 | 10.00 |
| MH9 Yoda | 6.00 | 12.00 |
| MH10 Qui-Gon Jinn | 5.00 | 10.00 |
| MH11 Clone Trooper (with Jetpack) | 6.00 | 12.00 |
| MH12 Destroyer Droid | 5.00 | 10.00 |
| MH13 Jar Jar Binks | 5.00 | 10.00 |
| MH14 Anakin Skywalker | 5.00 | 10.00 |
| MH15 Darth Maul (Spinning Action) | | |
| MH16 Obi-Wan Kenobi (Light-Up Lightsaber) | | |
| MH17 Padme Amidala | 6.00 | 12.00 |
| MH18 Qui-Gon Jinn (Light-Up Lightsaber) | 5.00 | 10.00 |
| MH19 Anakin Skywalker (Light-Up Lightsaber) | | |
| MH20 Darth Vader (Light-Up Lightsaber) | 12.50 | 25.00 |
| MH21 Luke Skywalker (zipline backpack) | 7.50 | 15.00 |
| MH22 Battle Droid (The Phantom Menace)(exploding action) | | |
| MH23 Sandtrooper (Light-Up Weapon) | | |
| MH24 Boba Fett (zipline jetpack) | | |

### 2012 Star Wars Movie Heroes Battle Packs

| | | |
|---|---|---|
| NNO Bespin Battle | 20.00 | 40.00 |
| NNO Duel on Naboo | 15.00 | 30.00 |
| NNO Ewok Pack | | |
| NNO Geonosis Arena Battle | | |
| NNO Rebel Heroes | | |
| NNO Rebel Pilots | | |
| NNO Republic Troopers | | |

### 2012 Star Wars Movie Heroes Exclusives

| | | |
|---|---|---|
| NNO Darth Maul Returns | | |
| NNO Podracer Pilots | | |
| (Toys R Us Exclusive) | | |

### 2012 Star Wars Movie Heroes Vehicles

| | | |
|---|---|---|
| NNO Anakin Skywalker's Jedi Starfighter (The Clone Wars) | | |
| NNO Anakin Skywalker's Podracer | 20.00 | 40.00 |
| NNO Attack Recon Fighter with Anakin Skywalker | | |
| NNO BARC Speeder with Clone Trooper | | |
| NNO Naboo Royal Fighter with Obi-Wan Kenobi | | |
| NNO Naboo Starfighter | 60.00 | 120.00 |
| NNO Republic Assault Submarine with Scuba Clone Trooper | | |
| NNO Republic Attack Dropship with Clone Pilot | | |
| NNO Sebulba's Podracer | | |
| NNO Sith Infiltrator | | |
| NNO Sith Speeder with Darth Maul | | |
| NNO Speeder Bike with Scout and Cannon | | |
| (Toys R Us Exclusive) | | |
| NNO STAP with Battle Droid | | |
| NNO Trade Federation AAT (Armored Assault Tank) | | |

### 2005 Star Wars M&M's Chocolate Mpire

| | | |
|---|---|---|
| 1 Chewbacca/Mace Windu | 6.00 | 12.00 |
| 2 Clone Trooper/Darth Vader | 6.00 | 12.00 |
| 3 Count Dooku/Darth Maul | 12.00 | 25.00 |
| 4 Emperor Palpatine/Anakin Skywalker | 12.00 | 25.00 |
| 5 General Grievous/Obi-Wan Kenobi | 8.00 | 15.00 |
| 6 Han Solo/Boba Fett | 10.00 | 20.00 |
| 7 Luke Skywalker/Princess Leia | 8.00 | 15.00 |
| 8 Queen Amidala/R2-D2/C-3PO | 8.00 | 15.00 |

### 2007 Star Wars Order 66 Target Exclusives

| | | |
|---|---|---|
| 1 Emperor Palpatine/Commander Thire | 12.00 | 25.00 |
| 2 Mace Windu/Galactic Marine | 10.00 | 20.00 |
| 3 Darth Vader/Commander Bow | 12.00 | 25.00 |
| 4 Obi-Wan Kenobi/AT-RT Driver | 10.00 | 20.00 |
| 5 Anakin Skywalker/Airborne Trooper | 12.00 | 25.00 |
| 6 Yoda/Kashyyyk Trooper | 10.00 | 20.00 |

### 2008 Star Wars Order 66 Target Exclusives

| | | |
|---|---|---|
| 1 Obi-Wan Kenobi/ARC Trooper Commander | 12.00 | 25.00 |
| 2 Anakin Skywalker/ARC Trooper | 10.00 | 20.00 |
| 3 Tsui Choi/BARC Trooper | 15.00 | 30.00 |
| 4 Emperor Palpatine/Commander Vill | 12.00 | 25.00 |
| 5 Luminara Unduli/AT-RT Driver | 10.00 | 20.00 |
| 6 Master Sev/ARC Trooper | 15.00 | 30.00 |

### 2004-05 Star Wars The Original Trilogy Collection

| | | |
|---|---|---|
| 1 Luke Skywalker (Dagobah training) | 6.00 | 12.00 |
| 2 Yoda (Dagobah training) | 3.00 | 6.00 |
| 3 Spirit Obi-Wan Kenobi | 8.00 | 15.00 |
| 4 R2-D2 (Dagobah training) | 6.00 | 12.00 |
| 5 Luke Skywalker (X-Wing pilot) | 8.00 | 15.00 |
| 6 Luke Skywalker (Jedi Knight) | 8.00 | 15.00 |
| 7 Han Solo (Mos Eisley escape) | 3.00 | 6.00 |
| 8 Chewbacca (Hoth escape) | 6.00 | 12.00 |

| | | | |
|---|---|---|---|
| 9 Princess Leia | | 10.00 | 20.00 |
| 10 Darth Vader (throne room) | | 8.00 | 15.00 |
| 11 Scout Trooper | | 6.00 | 12.00 |
| 12 R2-D2 | | 8.00 | 15.00 |
| 13 C-3PO | | 8.00 | 15.00 |
| 14 Boba Fett | | 12.00 | 25.00 |
| 15 Obi-Wan Kenobi | | 12.00 | 25.00 |
| 16 Stormtrooper (Death Star attack) | | 8.00 | 15.00 |
| 17 Wicket | | 3.00 | 6.00 |
| 18 Princess Leia (Cloud City) | | 8.00 | 15.00 |
| 19 Cloud Car Pilot | | 3.00 | 6.00 |
| 20 Lobot | | 3.00 | 6.00 |
| 21 TIE Fighter Pilot | | 8.00 | 15.00 |
| 22 Greedo | | 6.00 | 12.00 |
| 23 Tusken Raider | | 10.00 | 20.00 |
| 24 Jawas | | 3.00 | 6.00 |
| 25 Snowtrooper | | 6.00 | 12.00 |
| 26 Luke Skywalker (Bespin) | | 8.00 | 15.00 |
| 27 IG-88 | | 12.00 | 25.00 |
| 28 Bossk | | 6.00 | 12.00 |
| 29 Darth Vader (Hoth) | | 10.00 | 20.00 |
| 30 Gamorrean Guard | | 10.00 | 20.00 |
| 31 Bib Fortuna | | 3.00 | 6.00 |
| 32 Darth Vader | | 3.00 | 6.00 |
| 33 Lando Calrissian (skiff guard) | | 6.00 | 12.00 |
| 34 Princess Leia (sail barge) | | 15.00 | 30.00 |
| 35 Han Solo (AT-ST driver uniform) | | 3.00 | 6.00 |
| 36 General Madine | | 3.00 | 6.00 |
| 37 Lando Calrissian (General) | | 8.00 | 15.00 |
| 38a Imperial Trooper (white) | | 3.00 | 6.00 |
| 38b Imperial Trooper (gray) | | 3.00 | 6.00 |

### 2004-05 Star Wars The Original Trilogy Collection 12-Inch

| | | | |
|---|---|---|---|
| 1 Boba Fett | | 30.00 | 60.00 |
| 2 Chewbacca | | 20.00 | 40.00 |
| 3 Luke Skywalker | | 20.00 | 40.00 |
| 4 Stormtrooper | | 15.00 | 30.00 |

### 2004-05 Star Wars The Original Trilogy Collection Cards

| | | | |
|---|---|---|---|
| 1 Pablo-Jill/ genosis arena | | | |
| 2 Yarua (Coruscant Senate) | | | |
| 3 Sly Moore (Coruscant Senate) | | | |
| 4 Queen Amidala (celebration ceremony) | | | |
| 5 Rabe (Queen's chambers) | | | |
| 6 Feltipern Trevagg (cantina encounter) | | | |
| 7 Myo (cantina encounter) | | | |
| 8 Dannik Jerrico (cantina encounter) | | | |
| 9 Luke Skywalker (Dagobah training) | | | |
| 10 Darth Vader (Death Star hangar) | | | |
| 11 Stormtrooper (Death Star attack) | | | |
| 12 Sandtrooper (Tatooine search) | | | |
| 13 Scout Trooper (Endor raid) | | | |
| 14 Han Solo (Mos Eisley escape) | | | |
| 15 Chewbacca (Hoth escape) | | | |
| 16 Yoda (Dagobah training) | | | |

### 2004-05 Star Wars The Original Trilogy Collection DVD Collection

| | | | |
|---|---|---|---|
| 1 A New Hope | | 6.00 | 12.00 |
| 2 Empire Strikes Back | | 10.00 | 20.00 |
| 3 Return of the Jedi | | 8.00 | 15.00 |

### 2004-05 Star Wars The Original Trilogy Collection Exclusives

| | | | |
|---|---|---|---|
| 1 Darth Vader (silver) | | 10.00 | 20.00 |
| (2004 Toys R Us Exclusive) | | | |
| 2 Emperor Palpatine (executor transmission) | | | |
| (2004 StarWarsShop.com Exclusive) | | | |
| 3 Holiday Darth Vader | | 30.00 | 60.00 |
| (2005 StarWarsShop.com Exclusive) | | | |
| 4 Holographic Princess Leia | | 12.00 | 25.00 |
| (2005 SDCC Exclusive) | | | |
| 5 Holiday Edition Jawas | | 15.00 | 30.00 |
| (2004 Entertainment Earth Exclusive) | | | |
| 6 Luke Skywalker's Encounter with Yoda | | | |
| (2004 Encuentros Mexico Exclusive) | | | |
| 7 Wedge Antilles | | | |
| (2005 Internet Exclusive) | | | |

### 2004-05 Star Wars The Original Trilogy Collection Multipacks

| | | | |
|---|---|---|---|
| 1 Clone Trooper/Troop Builder 4-Pack | | 25.00 | 50.00 |
| Clone Trooper/Clone Trooper/Clone Tr | | | |
| 2 Clone Trooper Builder 4-Pack (white w/battle damage) | | 30.00 | 60.00 |
| 3 Clone Trooper Builder 4-Pack (colored) | | | |
| 4 Clone Trooper Builder 4-Pack (colored w/battle damage) | | 20.00 | 40.00 |
| 5 Endor Ambush (Han Solo/Logray/Rebel Trooper/Wicket/Speeder) | | 12.00 | 25.00 |
| 6 Naboo Final Combat (Battle Droid tan | | 20.00 | 40.00 |
| Gungan Soldier/Captain Tarpals/Kaad) | | | |

### 2004-05 Star Wars The Original Trilogy Collection Screen Scenes

| | | | |
|---|---|---|---|
| 1 Mos Eisley Cantina I/Dr. Evanzan/Wuher/Kitik Keed'kak | | 30.00 | 60.00 |
| 2 Mos Eisley Cantina II (Obi-Wan Kenobi/Ponda Baba/Zutton) | | 30.00 | 60.00 |
| 3 Jedi High Council I (Qui-Gon Jinn/Ki-Adi Mundi/Yoda) | | | |
| 4 Jedi High Council II (Plo Koon/Obi-Wan Kenobi/Eeth Koth) | | | |
| 5 Jedi High Council III (Anakin Skywalker/Saesee Tiin/Adi Gallia) | | | |
| 6 Jedi High Council IV (Shaak Ti/Agen Kolar/Stass Alli) | | | |

### 2004-05 Star Wars The Original Trilogy Collection Transitional

| | | | |
|---|---|---|---|
| 1 Pablo-Jill (Geonosis Arena) | | 6.00 | 12.00 |
| 2 Yarua (Wookiee Senator) | | 10.00 | 20.00 |
| 3 Sly Moore | | 5.00 | 10.00 |
| 4 Queen Amidala (Naboo Celebration) | | 5.00 | 10.00 |
| 5 Rabe (Royal Handmaiden) | | 4.00 | 10.00 |
| 6 Feltipern Trevagg (Cantina) | | 8.00 | 15.00 |
| 7 Myo (Cantina) | | 8.00 | 15.00 |
| 8 Dannik Jerriko (Cantina Encounter) | | 8.00 | 15.00 |
| 9 Luke Skywalker (Dagobah Training) | | | |
| 10 Darth Vader (Death Star Hangar) | | 15.00 | 30.00 |
| 11 Stormtrooper (Death Star Attack) | | | |
| 12 Sandtrooper (Tatooine Search) | | | |
| 13 Scout Trooper (Endor Raid) | | | |
| 14 Han Solo (Mos Eisley Escape) | | | |
| 15 Chewbacca (Hoth Escape) | | 12.00 | 25.00 |
| 16 Yoda (Dagobah Training) | | | |

### 2004-05 Star Wars The Original Trilogy Collection Vehicles

| | | | |
|---|---|---|---|
| 1 Darth Vader's TIE Fighter | | 30.00 | 75.00 |
| 2 Millennium Falcon | | | |
| 3 Millennium Falcon (w/Chewbacca/Han/Luke/Obi-Wan/C-3PO/R2-D2) | | | |
| (2004 Sam's Club Exclusive) | | | |
| 4 Sandcrawler (w/RA-7 and Jawas) | | 100.00 | 200.00 |
| 5 Slave I (w/Boba Fett in tan cape) | | 75.00 | 150.00 |
| 6 TIE Fighter | | 30.00 | 75.00 |
| 7 TIE Fighter & X-Wing Fighter | | 30.00 | 75.00 |
| 8 X-Wing Fighter | | | |
| 9 Y-Wing Fighter (w/pilot) | | | |

### 2004-05 Star Wars The Original Trilogy Collection Vintage

| | | | |
|---|---|---|---|
| 1 Boba Fett (ROTJ) | | 15.00 | 30.00 |
| 2 C-3PO (ESB) | | 6.00 | 12.00 |
| 3 Chewbacca (ROTJ) | | 12.00 | 25.00 |
| 4 Darth Vader (ESB) | | 8.00 | 15.00 |
| 5 Han Solo (SW) | | 6.00 | 12.00 |
| 6 Lando Calrissian (ESB) | | 12.00 | 25.00 |
| 7 Luke Skywalker (SW) | | 6.00 | 12.00 |
| 8 Obi-Wan Kenobi (SW) | | 5.00 | 10.00 |
| 9 Princess Leia Organa (SW) | | 5.00 | 10.00 |
| 10 R2-D2 (ROTJ) | | 15.00 | 30.00 |
| 11 Stormtrooper (ROTJ) | | 8.00 | 15.00 |
| 12 Yoda ESB | | 6.00 | 12.00 |

### 2000-02 Star Wars Power of the Jedi Action Collection 12-Inch

| | | | |
|---|---|---|---|
| 1 4-LOM | | 12.00 | 25.00 |
| 2 Bossk | | 15.00 | 30.00 |
| 3 Captain Tarpals (w/Kaadu) | | 20.00 | 40.00 |
| 4 Death Star Droid | | 15.00 | 30.00 |
| 5 Death Star Trooper | | 20.00 | 40.00 |
| 6 Han Solo Stormtrooper | | 15.00 | 30.00 |
| 7 IG-88 | | 8.00 | 15.00 |
| 8 Luke Skywalker & Yoda | | 20.00 | 40.00 |
| 9 Luke Skywalker (100th figure) | | 30.00 | 60.00 |
| 10 Luke Skywalker (w/speeder bike) | | 40.00 | 80.00 |

### 2000-02 Star Wars Power of the Jedi Attack of the Clones Sneak Preview

| | | | |
|---|---|---|---|
| 1 Clone Trooper | | 4.00 | 8.00 |
| 2 Jango Fett | | 5.00 | 10.00 |
| 3 R3-T7 | | 6.00 | 12.00 |
| 4 Zam Wesell | | 4.00 | 8.00 |

### 2000-02 Star Wars Power of the Jedi Collection 1

| | | | |
|---|---|---|---|
| 1 Anakin Skywalker (mechanic) | | 8.00 | 15.00 |
| 2 Aurra Sing (bounty hunter) | | 6.00 | 12.00 |
| 3 Battle Droid (boomer damage) | | 4.00 | 8.00 |
| 4 Ben Obi Wan Kenobi (Jedi Knight) | | 5.00 | 10.00 |

| | | |
|---|---|---|
| 5 Chewbacca (Millennium Falcon mechanic) | 10.00 | 20.00 |
| 6 Darth Maul (final duel) | 6.00 | 12.00 |
| 7 Darth Maul (Sith Apprentice) | 5.00 | 10.00 |
| 8 Darth Vader (Dagobah) | 8.00 | 15.00 |
| 9 Darth Vader (Emperor's wrath) | 5.00 | 10.00 |
| 10 Han Solo (Bespin capture) | 4.00 | 8.00 |
| 11 Han Solo (Death Star escape) | 6.00 | 12.00 |
| 12 Leia Organa (general) | 5.00 | 10.00 |
| 13 Luke Skywalker (X-Wing Pilot) | 4.00 | 8.00 |
| 14 Obi-Wan Kenobi (cold weather gear) | 4.00 | 8.00 |
| 15 Obi-Wan Kenobi (Jedi) | 4.00 | 8.00 |
| 16 Qui-Gon Jinn (Jedi training gear) | 8.00 | 15.00 |
| 17 Qui-Gon Jinn (Mos Espa disguise) | 4.00 | 8.00 |
| 18 R2-D2 (Naboo escape) | 5.00 | 10.00 |
| 19 Sandtrooper (Tatooine patrol) | 6.00 | 12.00 |

### 2000-02 Star Wars Power of the Jedi Collection 2

| | | |
|---|---|---|
| 1 Battle Droid (security) | 4.00 | 8.00 |
| 2 Bespin Guard (cloud city security) | 4.00 | 8.00 |
| 3 BoShek | 8.00 | 15.00 |
| 4 Boss Nass (Gungan sacred place) | 4.00 | 8.00 |
| 5 Chewbacca (Dejarik Champion) | 10.00 | 20.00 |
| 6 Coruscant Guard | 5.00 | 10.00 |
| 7 Eeth Koth (Jedi Master) | 6.00 | 12.00 |
| 8 Ellorrs Madak (Fan's Choice Figure #1) | 5.00 | 10.00 |
| 9 Fode and Beed (pod race announcers) | 5.00 | 10.00 |
| 10 FX-7 (medical droid) | 10.00 | 20.00 |
| 11 Gungan Warrior | 4.00 | 8.00 |
| 12 IG-88 (bounty hunter) | 12.00 | 25.00 |
| 13 Imperial Officer | 4.00 | 8.00 |
| 14 Jar Jar Binks (Tatooine) | 4.00 | 8.00 |
| 15 Jek Porkins (X-Wing pilot) | 10.00 | 20.00 |
| 16 K-3PO (Echo Base protocol droid) | 6.00 | 12.00 |
| 17 Ketwol | 4.00 | 8.00 |
| 18 Lando Calrissian (Bespin escape) | 6.00 | 12.00 |
| 19 Leia Organa (Bespin escape) | 8.00 | 15.00 |
| 20 Mas Amedda | 5.00 | 10.00 |
| 21 Mon Calamari (officer) | 8.00 | 15.00 |
| 22 Obi-Wan Kenobi (Jedi training gear) | 4.00 | 8.00 |
| 23 Plo Koon (Jedi Master) | 4.00 | 8.00 |
| 24 Queen Amidala (royal decoy) | 6.00 | 12.00 |
| 25 Queen Amidala (Theed invasion) | 6.00 | 12.00 |
| 26 R4-M9 | 8.00 | 15.00 |
| 27 R2-Q5 (Imperial astromech droid) | 8.00 | 15.00 |
| 28 Rebel Trooper (Tantive IV defender) | 4.00 | 8.00 |
| 29 Sabe (Queen's decoy) | 5.00 | 10.00 |
| 30 Saesee Tiin (Jedi Master) | 4.00 | 8.00 |
| 31 Scout Trooper (Imperial patrol) | 6.00 | 12.00 |
| 32 Sebulba (Boonta Eve Challenge) | 5.00 | 10.00 |
| 33 Shmi Skywalker | 5.00 | 10.00 |
| 34 Teebo | 6.00 | 12.00 |
| 35 Tessek | 5.00 | 10.00 |
| 36 Tusken Raider (desert sniper) | 6.00 | 12.00 |
| 37 Zutton (Snaggletooth) | 5.00 | 10.00 |

### 2000-02 Star Wars Power of the Jedi Deluxe

| | | |
|---|---|---|
| 1 Amanaman (w/Salacious Crumb) (Fan's Choice Figure #2) | 10.00 | 20.00 |
| 2 Darth Maul (w/Sith Attack Droid) | 8.00 | 15.00 |
| 3 Luke Skywalker (in Echo Base Bacta Tank) | 10.00 | 20.00 |
| 4 Princess Leia (Jabba's prisoner w/sail barge cannon) | 8.00 | 15.00 |

### 2000-02 Star Wars Power of the Jedi Masters of the Darkside

| | | |
|---|---|---|
| 1 Darth Vader and Darth Maul | 6.00 | 30.00 |

### 2000-02 Star Wars Power of the Jedi Mega Action

| | | |
|---|---|---|
| 1 Darth Maul | 12.00 | 25.00 |
| 2 Destroyer Droid | 20.00 | 40.00 |
| 3 Obi-Wan Kenobi | 12.00 | 25.00 |

### 2000-02 Star Wars Power of the Jedi Playsets

| | | |
|---|---|---|
| 1 Carbon Freezing Chamber (w/Bespin guard) | 40.00 | 80.00 |

### 2000-02 Star Wars Power of the Jedi Special Edition

| | | |
|---|---|---|
| 1 Boba Fett (300th figure) | 15.00 | 30.00 |
| 2 Rorworr (Wookiee scout) | 5.00 | 10.00 |

### 2000-02 Star Wars Power of the Jedi Vehicles

| | | |
|---|---|---|
| 1 B-Wing Fighter (w/Sullustan pilot) | 40.00 | 80.00 |
| 2 Imperial AT-ST & Speeder Bike (w/Paploo) | 25.00 | 50.00 |
| 3 Luke Skywalker's Snowspeeder (w/Dack Ralter) | 40.00 | 80.00 |
| 4 TIE Bomber | 25.00 | 50.00 |
| 5 TIE Interceptor (w/Imperial pilot) | 30.00 | 60.00 |

### 1995-00 Star Wars Power of the Force 3-Packs

| | | |
|---|---|---|
| NNO Lando/Chewbacca/Han Solo | 10.00 | 20.00 |
| NNO Lando/Luke Dagobah/TIE Fighter Pilot | 10.00 | 20.00 |
| NNO Luke Jedi/AT-ST Driver/Leia Boushh | 20.00 | 40.00 |
| NNO Luke Stormtrooper/Tusken Raider/Ben Kenobi | 12.50 | 25.00 |
| NNO Luke/Ben Kenobi/Darth Vader | 10.00 | 20.00 |
| NNO Stormtrooper/R2-D2/C-3PO | 10.00 | 20.00 |

### 1995-00 Star Wars Power of the Force Accessories

| | | |
|---|---|---|
| 1 Escape the Death Star Action Figure Game | 10.00 | 20.00 |
| 2 Millennium Falcon Carrying Case (w/Imperial Scanning Trooper) | 20.00 | 40.00 |
| 3 Millennium Falcon Carrying Case (w/Wedge) | 15.00 | 30.00 |
| 4 Power of the Force Carrying Case | 6.00 | 12.00 |
| 5 Talking C-3PO Carrying Case | 25.00 | 50.00 |

### 1995-00 Star Wars Power of the Force Cinema Scenes

| | | |
|---|---|---|
| 1 Cantina Aliens | 10.00 | 20.00 |
| 2a Cantina Showdown (.00) | 6.00 | 12.00 |
| 2b Cantina Showdown (.01) | 6.00 | 12.00 |
| 3a Death Star Escape (.00) | 12.00 | 25.00 |
| 3b Death Star Escape (.01) | 12.00 | 25.00 |
| 4a Final Jedi Duel (.00) | 10.00 | 20.00 |
| 4b Final Jedi Duel (.01) | 12.50 | 25.00 |
| 5 Jabba the Hutt's Dancers | 10.00 | 20.00 |
| 6 Jabba's Skiff Guards | 10.00 | 20.00 |
| 7 Jedi Spirits | 10.00 | 20.00 |
| 8 Mynock Hunt | 15.00 | 30.00 |
| 9 Purchase of the Droids | 8.00 | 15.00 |
| 10 Rebel Pilots | 10.00 | 20.00 |

### 1995-00 Star Wars Power of the Force Comm-Tech

| | | |
|---|---|---|
| 1 Admiral Motti | 20.00 | 40.00 |
| 2a Darth Vader (holographic chip) | 8.00 | 15.00 |
| 2b Darth Vader (white chip) | 8.00 | 15.00 |
| 3 Greedo | 6.00 | 12.00 |
| 4 Han Solo | 6.00 | 12.00 |
| 5a Jawa (w/Gonk Droid holographic chip) | 8.00 | 15.00 |
| 5b Jawa (w/Gonk Droid white chip) | 8.00 | 15.00 |
| 6 Luke Skywalker (w/T16 Skyhopper) | 6.00 | 12.00 |
| 7 Princess Leia | 8.00 | 15.00 |
| 8 R2-D2 (w/Princess Leia) | 12.00 | 25.00 |
| 9 Stormtrooper | 8.00 | 15.00 |
| 10a Wuher (no sticker) (2000 Fan Club Exclusive) | 8.00 | 15.00 |
| 10b Wuher (sticker) (2000 Fan Club Exclusive) | 6.00 | 12.00 |

### 1995-00 Star Wars Power of the Force Complete Galaxy

| | | |
|---|---|---|
| 1 Dagobah (w/Yoda) | 8.00 | 15.00 |
| 2 Death Star (w/Darth Vader) | 12.00 | 25.00 |
| 3a Endor (w/Ewok) (.00) | 15.00 | 30.00 |
| 3b Endor (w/Ewok) (.01) | 15.00 | 30.00 |
| 4 Tatooine (w/Luke) | 10.00 | 20.00 |

## 1995-00 Star Wars Power of the Force Creatures

| | | |
|---|---|---|
| 1 Bantha & Tusken Raider | 30.00 | 60.00 |
| 2 Dewback & Sandtrooper | 20.00 | 40.00 |
| 3a Jabba the Hutt & Han Solo (Han on left) | | |
| 3b Jabba the Hutt & Han Solo (Han on right) | 15.00 | 30.00 |
| 4 Rancor & Luke Skywalker | 30.00 | 60.00 |
| 5 Ronto & Jawa | 12.00 | 25.00 |
| 6 Tauntaun & Han Solo | 25.00 | 50.00 |
| 7 Tauntaun & Luke Skywalker | 12.00 | 25.00 |
| 8 Wampa & Luke Skywalker | 25.00 | 50.00 |

## 1995-00 Star Wars Power of the Force Deluxe

| | | |
|---|---|---|
| NNO Boba Fett (photon torpedo) | 8.00 | 15.00 |
| NNO Boba Fett (proton torpedo) | 10.00 | 20.00 |
| NNO Han Solo (Smuggler's Flight) | 6.00 | 12.00 |
| NNO Hoth Rebel Soldier | 8.00 | 15.00 |
| NNO Luke Skywalker (Desert Sport Skiff) | 25.00 | 50.00 |
| NNO Probe Droid (printed warning/green cardback) | 6.00 | 12.00 |
| NNO Probe Droid (printed warning/red cardback) | 6.00 | 12.00 |
| NNO Probe Droid (warning sticker/red cardback) | 6.00 | 12.00 |
| NNO Snowtrooper (Tripod Cannon) | 6.00 | 12.00 |
| NNO Stormtrooper (Crowd Control)(no sticker) | 5.00 | 10.00 |
| NNO Stormtrooper (Crowd Control)(warning sticker) | 5.00 | 10.00 |

## 1995-00 Star Wars Power of the Force Epic Force

| | | |
|---|---|---|
| 1 Bespin Luke Skywalker | 5.00 | 12.00 |
| 2 Boba Fett | 5.00 | 12.00 |
| 3 C-3PO | 8.00 | 15.00 |
| 4 Chewbacca | 5.00 | 12.00 |
| 5 Darth Vader | 5.00 | 12.00 |
| 6 Han Solo | 5.00 | 12.00 |
| 7 Obi-Wan Kenobi | 5.00 | 12.00 |
| 8 Princess Leia | 4.00 | 8.00 |
| 9 Stormtrooper | 4.00 | 8.00 |

## 1995-00 Star Wars Power of the Force Exclusives

| | | |
|---|---|---|
| 1a B-Omarr Monk (.00) | 12.50 | 25.00 |
| (1997 Online Exclusive) | | |
| 1b B-Omarr Monk (.01) | 12.50 | 25.00 |

| | | |
|---|---|---|
| (1997 Online Exclusive) | | |
| 2 C-3PO (greenish tint) | 15.00 | 30.00 |
| (Japanese Exclusive) | | |
| 3 Cantina Band Member | 6.00 | 15.00 |
| (1997 Fan Club Exclusive) | | |
| 4 Han Solo (w/Tauntaun) | 15.00 | 30.00 |
| (1997 Toys R Us Exclusive) | | |
| 5 Han Solo Stormtrooper | 8.00 | 15.00 |
| (Kellogg's Mail Order Exclusive) | | |
| 6 Kabe and Muftak | 10.00 | 20.00 |
| (1998 Online Exclusive) | | |
| 7 Luke Skywalker Jedi Knight | 10.00 | 20.00 |
| (Theater Edition Exclusive) | | |
| 8 Oola & Salacious Crumb | 12.00 | 25.00 |
| (1998 Fan Club Exclusive) | | |
| 9 Spirit of Obi-Wan Kenobi | 8.00 | 15.00 |
| (Frito-Lay Mail Order Exclusive) | | |
| 10 Spirit of Obi-Wan Kenobi | | |
| (UK Special Edition Exclusive) | | |

## 1995-00 Star Wars Power of the Force Expanded Universe Vehicles

| | | |
|---|---|---|
| 1 Airspeeder (w/pilot) | 20.00 | 40.00 |
| 2 Cloud Car (w/pilot) | 10.00 | 20.00 |
| 3 Rebel Speeder Bike (w/pilot) | 12.00 | 25.00 |

## 1995-00 Star Wars Power of the Force Flashback

| | | |
|---|---|---|
| 1 Anakin Skywalker | 6.00 | 12.00 |
| 2 Aunt Beru | 5.00 | 10.00 |
| 3 C-3PO (removable arm) | 5.00 | 10.00 |
| 4 Darth Vader | 8.00 | 15.00 |
| 5 Emperor Palpatine | 8.00 | 15.00 |
| 6 Hoth Chewbacca | 8.00 | 15.00 |
| 7 Luke Skywalker | 6.00 | 12.00 |
| 8 Obi-Wan Kenobi | 5.00 | 10.00 |
| 9 Princess Leia (ceremonial dress) | 6.00 | 12.00 |
| 10a R2-D2 (pop-up lightsaber)(forward position) | 6.00 | 12.00 |
| 10b R2-D2 (pop-up lightsaber)(slanted) | 4.00 | 8.00 |
| 11 Yoda | 10.00 | 20.00 |

## 1995-00 Star Wars Power of the Force Freeze Frame Collection 1

| | | |
|---|---|---|
| 1 C-3PO (removable limbs) | 7.50 | 15.00 |
| 2a Endor Rebel Commando (.00) | 5.00 | 10.00 |
| 2b Endor Rebel Commando (.01) | 5.00 | 10.00 |
| 3 Garindan (long snoot) | 10.00 | 20.00 |
| 4 Han Solo | 6.00 | 12.00 |
| 5 Han Solo (Bespin) | 6.00 | 12.00 |
| 6a Han Solo (carbonite)(.04) | 7.50 | 15.00 |
| 6b Han Solo (carbonite)(.05) | 7.50 | 15.00 |
| 7a Han Solo (Endor)(.01) | 5.00 | 10.00 |
| 7b Han Solo (Endor)(.02) | 5.00 | 10.00 |
| 8a Hoth Rebel Soldier (.02) | 5.00 | 10.00 |
| 8b Hoth Rebel Soldier (.03) | 5.00 | 10.00 |
| 9a Lando Calrissian (General)(.00) | 5.00 | 10.00 |
| 9b Lando Calrissian (General)(.01) | 5.00 | 10.00 |
| 10a Lando Calrissian (Skiff guard)(.01) | 5.00 | 10.00 |
| 10b Lando Calrissian (Skiff guard)(.02) | 5.00 | 10.00 |
| 11 Lobot | 3.00 | 6.00 |
| 12a Luke Skywalker (Bespin)(w/gold buckle)(.00) | 6.00 | 12.00 |
| 12b Luke Skywalker (Bespin)(w/gold buckle)(.01) | 6.00 | 12.00 |
| 12c Luke Skywalker (Bespin)(w/silver buckle)(.00) | 6.00 | 12.00 |
| 12d Luke Skywalker (Bespin)(w/silver buckle)(.01) | 6.00 | 12.00 |

| | | |
|---|---|---|
| 13 Luke Skywalker (blast shield helmet) | 7.50 | 15.00 |
| 14 Luke Skywalker (ceremonial) | 5.00 | 10.00 |
| 15a Luke Skywalker (stormtrooper disguise)(.03) | 5.00 | 10.00 |
| 15b Luke Skywalker (stormtrooper disguise)(.04) | 5.00 | 10.00 |
| 16 Mon Mothma | 6.00 | 12.00 |
| 17a Obi-Wan Kenobi (.03) | 7.50 | 15.00 |
| 17b Obi-Wan Kenobi (.04) | 7.50 | 15.00 |
| 18 Orrimaarko (Prune Face) | 4.00 | 8.00 |
| 19 Princess Leia Organa (Ewok celebration) | 5.00 | 10.00 |
| 20a Princess Leia Organa (Jabba's prisoner)(.01) | 7.50 | 15.00 |
| 20b Princess Leia Organa (Jabba's prisoner)(.02) | 7.50 | 15.00 |
| 21 Princess Leia Organa (new likeness) | 5.00 | 10.00 |
| 22a R2-D2 (Death Star slide) | 6.00 | 12.00 |
| 22b R2-D2 (Imperial slide) | 6.00 | 12.00 |
| 23a Rebel Fleet Trooper (.01) | 5.00 | 10.00 |
| 23b Rebel Fleet Trooper (.02) | 5.00 | 10.00 |
| 23c Rebel Fleet Trooper (w/sticker)(.01) | 5.00 | 10.00 |

## 1995-00 Star Wars Power of the Force Freeze Frame Collection 2

| | | |
|---|---|---|
| 1 8D8 | 6.00 | 12.00 |
| 2a Admiral Ackbar (comlink wrist blaster) | 6.00 | 12.00 |
| 2b Admiral Ackbar (wrist blaster) | 6.00 | 12.00 |
| 3 Biggs Darklighter | 4.00 | 8.00 |
| 4 EV-9D9 | 5.00 | 10.00 |
| 5 Ewoks Wicket & Logray | 10.00 | 20.00 |
| 6 Gamorrean Guard | 6.00 | 12.00 |
| 7a Han Solo (Bespin)(.02) | 6.00 | 12.00 |
| 7b Han Solo (Bespin)(.03) | 6.00 | 12.00 |
| 8 Lak Sivrak | 6.00 | 12.00 |
| 9 Malakili (Rancor Keeper) | 5.00 | 10.00 |
| 10 Nien Nunb | 5.00 | 10.00 |
| 11 Saelt-Marae (Yak Face) | 5.00 | 10.00 |
| 12 Ugnaughts | 6.00 | 12.00 |

## 1995-00 Star Wars Power of the Force Freeze Frame Collection 3

| | | |
|---|---|---|
| 1 AT-AT Driver | 10.00 | 20.00 |
| (1998 Fan Club Exclusive) | | |
| 2 Boba Fett | 6.00 | 15.00 |
| 3a Captain Piett (baton sticker) | 5.00 | 10.00 |
| 3b Captain Piett (pistol sticker) | 5.00 | 10.00 |
| 4 Darth Vader | 6.00 | 12.00 |
| 5 Darth Vader (removable helmet) | 8.00 | 15.00 |
| 6 Death Star Droid (w/mouse droid) | 8.00 | 15.00 |
| 7 Death Star Trooper | 12.00 | 25.00 |
| 8 Emperor Palpatine | 8.00 | 15.00 |
| 9 Emperor's Royal Guard | 8.00 | 15.00 |
| 10 Grand Moff Tarkin | 6.00 | 12.00 |
| 11a Ishi Tib (brown pouch) | 5.00 | 10.00 |
| 11b Ishi Tib (gray pouch) | 5.00 | 10.00 |
| 12 Pote Snitkin | 12.00 | 25.00 |
| (1999 Internet Exclusive) | | |
| 13 Princess Leia Organa (Hoth) | 8.00 | 15.00 |
| (1999 Fan Club Exclusive) | | |
| 14 Ree-Yees | 6.00 | 12.00 |
| 15 Sandtrooper | 25.00 | 50.00 |
| 16 Snowtrooper | 5.00 | 10.00 |
| 17 Stormtrooper | 5.00 | 10.00 |
| 18 TIE Fighter Pilot | 5.00 | 10.00 |
| 19 Weequay | 90.00 | 175.00 |
| 20 Zuckuss | 4.00 | 8.00 |

## 1995-00 Star Wars Power of the Force Green Collection 1

| | | |
|---|---|---|
| 1a Bib Fortuna (hologram) | 6.00 | 12.00 |
| 1b Bib Fortuna (photo) | 6.00 | 12.00 |
| 2 Boba Fett (hologram) | 15.00 | 30.00 |
| 3 C-3PO (hologram) | 8.00 | 15.00 |
| 4a Chewbacca | 10.00 | 20.00 |
| 4b Chewbacca (hologram) | 4.00 | 8.00 |
| 5a Darth Vader | 6.00 | 12.00 |
| 5b Darth Vader (hologram) | 8.00 | 15.00 |
| 6a Death Star Gunner | 6.00 | 12.00 |
| 6b Death Star Gunner (hologram) | 6.00 | 12.00 |
| 7a Emperor Palpatine | 6.00 | 12.00 |
| 7b Emperor Palpatine (hologram) | 6.00 | 12.00 |
| 8 Garindan (long snoot) | 4.00 | 8.00 |
| 9a Greedo | 6.00 | 12.00 |
| 9b Greedo (hologram) | 6.00 | 12.00 |
| 10a Han Solo | 5.00 | 10.00 |
| 10b Han Solo (hologram) | 6.00 | 12.00 |
| 11a Han Solo (Bespin) | 6.00 | 12.00 |
| 11b Han Solo (Bespin)(hologram) | 6.00 | 12.00 |
| 12a Han Solo (carbonite stand-up bubble) | 8.00 | 15.00 |
| 12b Han Solo (carbonite stand-up bubble)(hologram) | 8.00 | 15.00 |
| 13a Han Solo (Endor blue pants) | 8.00 | 15.00 |
| 13b Han Solo (Endor blue pants)(hologram) | 8.00 | 15.00 |
| 13c Han Solo (Endor brown pants) | 10.00 | 20.00 |
| 14 Hoth Rebel Soldier (hologram) | 5.00 | 10.00 |
| 15 Lando Calrissian | 20.00 | 40.00 |
| 16 Lando Calrissian (Skiff guard)(hologram) | 6.00 | 12.00 |
| 17a Luke Skywalker (ceremonial) | 5.00 | 10.00 |
| 17b Luke Skywalker (ceremonial)(hologram) | 5.00 | 10.00 |
| 18 Luke Skywalker (Hoth)(hologram) | 5.00 | 10.00 |
| 19a Luke Skywalker (Jedi Knight) | 6.00 | 12.00 |
| 19b Luke Skywalker (Jedi Knight)(hologram) | 6.00 | 12.00 |
| 20 Luke Skywalker (stormtrooper disguise)(hologram) | 6.00 | 12.00 |
| 21 Luke Skywalker (X-Wing pilot)(hologram) | 8.00 | 15.00 |
| 22a Obi-Wan Kenobi (hologram) | 5.00 | 10.00 |
| 22b Obi-Wan Kenobi (photo) | 5.00 | 10.00 |
| 23a Princess Leia Organa (Jabba's prisoner) | 5.00 | 10.00 |
| 23b Princess Leia Organa (Jabba's prisoner) (hologram) | 5.00 | 10.00 |
| 24a Princess Leia Organa (photo) | | |
| 24b Princess Leia Organa (three-ring belt) | 10.00 | 20.00 |
| 24c Princess Leia Organa (two-ring belt)(hologram) | 8.00 | 15.00 |
| 25 R2-D2 | 10.00 | 20.00 |
| 26 Rebel Fleet Trooper (hologram) | 5.00 | 10.00 |
| 27a Sandtrooper | 8.00 | 15.00 |
| 27b Sandtrooper (hologram) | 8.00 | 15.00 |
| 28a Yoda | 6.00 | 12.00 |
| 28b Yoda (hologram) | 6.00 | 12.00 |

## 1995-00 Star Wars Power of the Force Green Collection 2

| | | |
|---|---|---|
| 1a 2-1B (.00) | 5.00 | 10.00 |
| 1b 2-1B (.00)(hologram) | 6.00 | 12.00 |
| 1c 2-1B (.01) | 4.00 | 8.00 |
| 1d 2-1B (.01)(hologram) | 6.00 | 12.00 |
| 2a 4-LOM | 6.00 | 12.00 |
| 2b 4-LOM (hologram) | 6.00 | 12.00 |
| 3 Admiral Ackbar | 4.00 | 8.00 |
| 4a ASP-7 (hologram) | 5.00 | 10.00 |
| 4b ASP-7 (photo) | 5.00 | 10.00 |
| 5a AT-ST Driver | 7.50 | 15.00 |

| | | |
|---|---|---|
| 5b AT-ST Driver (hologram) | 5.00 | 10.00 |
| 6a Bib Fortuna (hologram/stand-up bubble) | 4.00 | 8.00 |
| 6b Bib Fortuna (hologram/straight bubble) | 5.00 | 10.00 |
| 7a Bossk (.00)(hologram) | 4.00 | 8.00 |
| 7b Bossk (.00)(photo) | 4.00 | 8.00 |
| 7c Bossk (.01)(photo) | 6.00 | 12.00 |
| 8 Clone Emperor Palpatine (Expanded Universe) | 8.00 | 15.00 |
| 9 Darktrooper (Expanded Universe) | 10.00 | 20.00 |
| 10a Dengar (hologram) | 7.50 | 15.00 |
| 10b Dengar (photo) | 6.00 | 12.00 |
| 11a EV-9D9 (hologram) | 6.00 | 12.00 |
| 11b EV-9D9 (photo) | 6.00 | 12.00 |
| 12 Gamorrean Guard (hologram) | 5.00 | 10.00 |
| 13 Grand Admiral Thrawn (Expanded Universe) | 20.00 | 40.00 |
| 14a Grand Moff Tarkin | 5.00 | 10.00 |
| 14b Grand Moff Tarkin (hologram) | 5.00 | 10.00 |
| 15a Han Solo (carbonite) | 6.00 | 12.00 |
| 15b Han Solo (carbonite)(hologram) | 7.50 | 15.00 |
| 16a Hoth Rebel Soldier | 5.00 | 10.00 |
| 16b Hoth Rebel Soldier (hologram) | 5.00 | 10.00 |
| 17 Imperial Sentinel (Expanded Universe) | 10.00 | 20.00 |
| 18a Jawas | 5.00 | 10.00 |
| 18b Jawas (hologram) | 5.00 | 10.00 |
| 18c Jawas (new bubble) | 6.00 | 12.00 |
| 18d Jawas (new bubble)(hologram) | 6.00 | 12.00 |
| 19 Kyle Katarn (Expanded Universe) | 10.00 | 20.00 |
| 20a Luke Skywalker (ceremonial)(hologram) | 5.00 | 10.00 |
| 20b Luke Skywalker (ceremonial/different head) | | |
| 21 Luke Skywalker (Expanded Universe) | 10.00 | 20.00 |
| 22a Luke Skywalker (Hoth) | 5.00 | 10.00 |
| 22b Luke Skywalker (Hoth)(hologram) | 5.00 | 10.00 |
| 23a Luke Skywalker (Jedi Knight) | 6.00 | 12.00 |
| 23b Luke Skywalker (Jedi Knight)(hologram) | 7.50 | 15.00 |
| 24a Luke Skywalker (stormtrooper disguise) | 7.50 | 15.00 |
| 24b Luke Skywalker (stormtrooper disguise)(hologram) | 6.00 | 12.00 |
| 25 Malakili (Rancor Keeper)(hologram) | 4.00 | 8.00 |
| 26 Mara Jade (Expanded Universe) | 15.00 | 30.00 |
| 27a Momaw Nadon (Hammerhead) | 3.00 | 8.00 |
| 27b Momaw Nadon (Hammerhead)(hologram) | 4.00 | 8.00 |
| 28 Nien Nunb (hologram) | 4.00 | 8.00 |
| 29a Ponda Baba (black beard) (hologram) | 5.00 | 10.00 |
| 29b Ponda Baba (gray beard) (hologram) | 5.00 | 10.00 |
| 30 Princess Leia (Expanded Universe) | 8.00 | 15.00 |
| 31a R5-D4 (no warning sticker/L-latch) | 5.00 | 10.00 |
| 31b R5-D4 (no warning sticker/L-latch)(hologram) | 5.00 | 10.00 |
| 31c R5-D4 (no warning sticker/straight latch) | 5.00 | 10.00 |
| 31d R5-D4 (no warning sticker/straight latch)(hologram) | 5.00 | 10.00 |
| 31e R5-D4 (warning sticker/L-latch) | 5.00 | 10.00 |
| 31f R5-D4 (warning sticker/L-latch)(hologram) | 5.00 | 10.00 |
| 31g R5-D4 (warning sticker/straight latch) | 5.00 | 10.00 |
| 31h R5-D4 (warning sticker/straight latch)(hologram) | 5.00 | 10.00 |
| 32a Rebel Fleet Trooper | | |
| 32b Rebel Fleet Trooper (hologram) | | |
| 33 Saelt-Marae (Yak Face)(hologram) | | |
| 34 Spacetrooper (Expanded Universe) | 8.00 | 15.00 |
| 35 TIE Fighter Pilot (hologram) | | |
| 36 Tusken Raider (hologram) | 4.00 | 8.00 |
| 37 Weequay | | |
| 38a Yoda | | |
| 38b Yoda (hologram) | | |

## 1995-00 Star Wars Power of the Force Green Collection 3

| | | |
|---|---|---|
| 1 AT-ST Driver | 5.00 | 10.00 |
| 2 AT-ST Driver (hologram) | 5.00 | 10.00 |
| 3 Boba Fett (hologram) | 12.00 | 25.00 |
| 4 Darth Vader (hologram) | 4.00 | 8.00 |
| 5a Death Star Gunner | 5.00 | 10.00 |
| 5b Death Star Gunner (hologram) | 5.00 | 10.00 |
| 6 Emperor Palpatine (hologram) | 4.00 | 8.00 |
| 7a Emperor's Royal Guard | 6.00 | 12.00 |
| 7b Emperor's Royal Guard (hologram) | 6.00 | 12.00 |
| 8a Garindan (long snoot)(hologram) | 4.00 | 8.00 |
| 8b Garindan (long snoot)(photo) | 4.00 | 8.00 |
| 9 Grand Moff Tarkin | 4.00 | 8.00 |
| 10a Ponda Baba (black beard) | 5.00 | 10.00 |
| 10b Ponda Baba (gray beard) | 50.00 | 100.00 |
| 11a Sandtrooper | 5.00 | 10.00 |
| 11b Sandtrooper (hologram) | 5.00 | 10.00 |
| 12a Snowtrooper | | |
| 12b Snowtrooper (hologram) | | |
| 13a Stormtrooper | 5.00 | 10.00 |
| 13b Stormtrooper (holosticker) | 5.00 | 10.00 |
| 14 TIE Fighter Pilot (hologram) | 6.00 | 12.00 |
| 15 Weequay (hologram) | 4.00 | 8.00 |

## 1995-00 Star Wars Power of the Force Gunner Stations

| | | |
|---|---|---|
| 1a Gunner Station (Millennium Falcon w/Han Solo)(.00) | 6.00 | 12.00 |
| 1b Gunner Station (Millennium Falcon w/Han Solo)(.01) | 6.00 | 12.00 |
| 2a Gunner Station (Millennium Falcon w/Luke Skywalker)(.00) | 6.00 | 12.00 |
| 2b Gunner Station (Millennium Falcon w/Luke Skywalker)(.01) | 6.00 | 12.00 |
| 3 Gunner Station (TIE Fighter w/Darth Vader) | 8.00 | 15.00 |

ACTION FIGURES AND FIGURINES

## 1995-00 Star Wars Power of the Force Max Rebo Band Pairs

| | | | |
|---|---|---|---|
| 1a Droopy McCool & Barquin D'an (CGI Sy Snootles on back) | 12.00 | 25.00 |
| (1998 Walmart Exclusive) | | |
| 1b Droopy McCool & Barquin D'an (puppet Sy Snootles on back) | 8.00 | 15.00 |
| (1998 Walmart Exclusive) | | |
| 2 Max Rebo & Doda Bodonawieedo | 15.00 | 30.00 |
| 3a Sy Snootles & Joh Yowza (CGI Sy Snootles on back) | 12.00 | 25.00 |
| (1998 Walmart Exclusive) | | |
| 3b Sy Snootles & Joh Yowza (puppet Sy Snootles on back) | 8.00 | 15.00 |
| (1998 Walmart Exclusive) | | |

## 1995-00 Star Wars Power of the Force Millennium Mint

| | | |
|---|---|---|
| 1 C-3PO | 5.00 | 12.00 |
| 2a Chewbacca (.00) | 6.00 | 12.00 |
| (1998 Toys R Us Exclusive) | | |
| 2b Chewbacca (.01/new insert) | 6.00 | 12.00 |
| (1998 Toys R Us Exclusive) | | |
| 3 Emperor Palpatine | 5.00 | 12.00 |
| (1998 Toys R Us Exclusive) | | |
| 4a Han Solo (Bespin)(.00) | 6.00 | 12.00 |
| (1998 Toys R Us Exclusive) | | |
| 4b Han Solo (Bespin)(.01/new insert) | 12.00 | 25.00 |
| (1998 Toys R Us Exclusive) | | |
| 5a Luke Skywalker (Endor gear)(.00) | 10.00 | 20.00 |
| (1998 Toys R Us Exclusive) | | |
| 5b Luke Skywalker (Endor gear)(.01) | 8.00 | 15.00 |
| (1998 Toys R Us Exclusive) | | |
| 6a Princess Leia (Endor gear)(.00) | 12.00 | 25.00 |
| (1998 Toys R Us Exclusive) | | |
| 6b Princess Leia (Endor gear)(.01) | 10.00 | 20.00 |
| (1998 Toys R Us Exclusive) | | |
| 7a Snowtrooper (.00) | 6.00 | 12.00 |
| (1998 Toys R Us Exclusive) | | |
| 7b Snowtrooper (.01) | 8.00 | 15.00 |
| (1998 Toys R Us Exclusive) | | |

## 1995-00 Star Wars Power of the Force Orange

| | | |
|---|---|---|
| 1 Chewbacca | 6.00 | 12.00 |
| 2a Darth Vader (long saber) | 8.00 | 15.00 |
| 2b Darth Vader (short saber/long tray) | 10.00 | 20.00 |
| 2c Darth Vader (short saber/short tray) | 6.00 | 12.00 |
| 3 Han Solo | 6.00 | 12.00 |
| 4a Stormtrooper | 6.00 | 12.00 |
| 4b Stormtrooper (holosticker) | 6.00 | 12.00 |

## 1995-00 Star Wars Power of the Force Playsets

| | | |
|---|---|---|
| 1a Cantina Pop-Up Diorama (w/sandtrooper) | 12.00 | 25.00 |
| (Retail Store Version - 25" sticker correction) | | |
| 1b Cantina Pop-Up Diorama (w/sandtrooper) | 15.00 | 30.00 |
| (Retail Store Version - 25" wide description) | | |
| 1c Cantina Pop-Up Diorama (w/sandtrooper) | | |
| (Retail Store Version - 26" wide description) | | |
| 2 Cantina Pop-Up Diorama | | |
| (1997 Mail Order Exclusive) | | |
| 3 Death Star Escape | 12.50 | 25.00 |
| 4 Detention Block Rescue | 15.00 | 30.00 |
| 5a Endor Attack (no warning sticker) | | |
| 5b Endor Attack (warning sticker) | 30.00 | 60.00 |
| 6a Hoth Battle (no warning sticker) | 25.00 | 50.00 |
| 6b Hoth Battle (warning sticker) | 20.00 | 40.00 |
| 7a Jabba's Palace (w/Han Solo)(podrace arena bio card) | | |
| 7b Jabba's Palace (w/Han Solo)(podracer bio card) | 15.00 | 30.00 |
| 8 Millennium Falcon Cockpit | 20.00 | 40.00 |
| (PC Explorer Game) | | |

## 1995-00 Star Wars Power of the Force Power F/X

| | | |
|---|---|---|
| 1 Ben (Obi-Wan) Kenobi | 5.00 | 10.00 |
| 2 Darth Vader | 5.00 | 10.00 |
| 3a Emperor Palpatine (.00) | 6.00 | 12.00 |
| 3b Emperor Palpatine (.01) | 4.00 | 8.00 |
| 4 Luke Skywalker | 6.00 | 12.00 |
| 5a R2-D2 (.00) | 4.00 | 8.00 |
| 5b R2-D2 (.01) | 4.00 | 8.00 |
| 5c R2-D2 (.02) | 4.00 | 8.00 |
| 5d R2-D2 (.103) | 4.00 | 8.00 |

## 1995-00 Star Wars Power of the Force Princess Leia Collection

| | | |
|---|---|---|
| 1a Princess Leia & Han Solo (gold border) | 4.00 | 8.00 |
| 1b Princess Leia & Han Solo (gray border) | 10.00 | 20.00 |
| 2a Princess Leia & Luke Skywalker (gold border) | 8.00 | 15.00 |
| 2b Princess Leia & Luke Skywalker (gray border) | 10.00 | 20.00 |
| 3a Princess Leia & R2-D2 (gold border) | 25.00 | 50.00 |
| 3b Princess Leia & R2-D2 (gray border) | 10.00 | 20.00 |
| 4a Princess Leia & Wicket (gold border) | 4.00 | 8.00 |
| 4b Princess Leia & Wicket (gray border) | 10.00 | 20.00 |

## 1995-00 Star Wars Power of the Force Red

| | | |
|---|---|---|
| 1a Boba Fett (full circle) | 7.50 | 15.00 |
| 1b Boba Fett (half circle) | 20.00 | 40.00 |
| 1c Boba Fett (no circle) | 12.00 | 25.00 |
| 2 C-3PO (.00) | 6.00 | 12.00 |
| 3 Death Star Gunner | 7.50 | 15.00 |
| 4 Greedo | 5.00 | 10.00 |
| 5a Han Solo (carbonite block) | 7.50 | 15.00 |
| 5b Han Solo (carbonite freezing chamber) | 6.00 | 12.00 |
| 6a Han Solo (Hoth - closed hand) | 6.00 | 12.00 |
| 6b Han Solo (Hoth - open hand) | 6.00 | 12.00 |
| 7 Jawas | 6.00 | 12.00 |
| 8 Lando Calrissian | 3.00 | 6.00 |
| 9a Luke Skywalker (Dagobah - long saber) | 6.00 | 12.00 |
| 9b Luke Skywalker (Dagobah - short saber/long tray) | 10.00 | 20.00 |
| 9c Luke Skywalker (Dagobah - short saber/short tray) | | |
| 10a Luke Skywalker (Jedi Knight - black vest) | 6.00 | 12.00 |
| 10b Luke Skywalker (Jedi Knight - brown vest) | 10.00 | 20.00 |
| 11a Luke Skywalker (long saber) | 8.00 | 15.00 |
| 11b Luke Skywalker (short saber/long tray) | 6.00 | 12.00 |
| 11c Luke Skywalker (short saber/short tray) | 6.00 | 12.00 |
| 12a Luke Skywalker (stormtrooper disguise) | 8.00 | 15.00 |
| 12b Luke Skywalker (stormtrooper disguise)(hologram) | 7.50 | 15.00 |
| 13a Luke Skywalker (X-Wing pilot - long saber) | 10.00 | 20.00 |
| 13b Luke Skywalker (X-Wing pilot - short saber/long tray) | 5.00 | 10.00 |
| 13c Luke Skywalker (X-Wing pilot - short saber/short tray) | | |
| 14 Momaw Nadon (Hammerhead) (warning sticker) | 4.00 | 8.00 |
| 15a Obi-Wan Kenobi (hologram) | 5.00 | 10.00 |
| 15b Obi-Wan Kenobi (short saber/long tray) | 5.00 | 10.00 |
| 15c Obi-Wan Kenobi (short saber/short tray) | 5.00 | 10.00 |
| 15d Obi-Wan Kenobi (long saber) | 15.00 | 30.00 |
| 15e Obi-Wan Kenobi (photo) | | |
| 16a Princess Leia Organa (2-band belt) | 6.00 | 12.00 |
| 16b Princess Leia Organa (3-band belt) | 6.00 | 12.00 |
| 16c Princess Leia Organa (hologram) | | |
| 17a R2-D2 | 12.50 | 25.00 |
| 17b R2-D2 (hologram) | | |
| 18a R5-D4 (no warning sticker/straight latch) | 6.00 | 12.00 |
| 18b R5-D4 (warning sticker/straight latch) | | |
| 19 Sandtrooper | | |
| 20a TIE Fighter Pilot (printed warning) | 4.00 | 8.00 |
| 20b TIE Fighter Pilot (SOTE) | | |
| 20c TIE Fighter Pilot (warning sticker) | | |
| 21a Tusken Raider (closed left hand) | 6.00 | 12.00 |
| 21b Tusken Raider (open left hand) | | |
| 22a Yoda (.00) | 6.00 | 12.00 |
| 22b Yoda (.00)(hologram) | | |
| 22c Yoda (.01) | | |

## 1995-00 Star Wars Power of the Force Vehicles

| | | |
|---|---|---|
| NNO AT-AT Walker (electronic)(no sticker) | 60.00 | 120.00 |
| NNO AT-AT Walker (electronic)(sticker of figure's legs) | | |
| NNO AT-ST Scout Walker | 30.00 | 60.00 |
| NNO A-Wing Fighter | 25.00 | 50.00 |
| NNO Cruisemissile Trooper (.00) | | |
| NNO Cruisemissile Trooper (.01) | | |
| NNO Darth Vader's TIE Fighter | 25.00 | 50.00 |

| | | | |
|---|---|---|---|
| NNO | Landspeeder | 12.00 | 25.00 |
| NNO | Luke Skywalker's Red Five X-Wing Fighter | 50.00 | 100.00 |
| NNO | Millennium Falcon (electronic) | 60.00 | 120.00 |
| NNO | Power Racing Speeder Bike (w/scout) | | |
| NNO | Rebel Snowspeeder (electronic) | 30.00 | 75.00 |
| NNO | Speeder Bike (w/Leia in Endor fatigues)(grassy background) | | |
| NNO | Speeder Bike (w/Leia in Endor fatigues)(rocky background) | 15.00 | 30.00 |
| NNO | Speeder Bike (w/Luke in Endor fatigues glove) | 30.00 | 60.00 |
| NNO | Speeder Bike (w/Luke in Endor fatigues no glove) | 12.50 | 25.00 |
| NNO | Speeder Bike (w/scout)(aggressiveness removed) | | |
| NNO | Speeder Bike (w/scout)(aggressiveness) | | |
| NNO | Speeder Bike (w/scout)(Canadian windowless package) | | |
| NNO | Speeder Bike (w/scout)(Topps Widevision card) | 10.00 | 20.00 |
| NNO | STAP and Battle Droid Sneak Preview (beige rod) | 10.00 | 20.00 |
| NNO | STAP and Battle Droid Sneak Preview (brown rod) | 12.00 | 25.00 |
| NNO | T-16 Skyhopper | | |
| NNO | Tatooine Skiff | 60.00 | 120.00 |
| NNO | TIE Fighter | 25.00 | 50.00 |
| NNO | X-Wing Fighter (electronic green box) | 15.00 | 30.00 |
| NNO | X-Wing Fighter (electronic red box) | 30.00 | 60.00 |
| NNO | Y-Wing Fighter | 40.00 | 80.00 |

### 2014-15 Star Wars Rebels Hero Series

| | | | |
|---|---|---|---|
| 1 | Agent Kallus | 12.00 | 25.00 |
| 2 | Clone Trooper | 6.00 | 12.00 |
| 3 | Darth Vader | 7.50 | 15.00 |
| 4 | Ezra Bridger | 10.00 | 20.00 |
| 5 | Garazeb Orrelios | 15.00 | 30.00 |
| 6 | Heroes and Villains | 20.00 | 50.00 |
| | (2014 Target Exclusive) | | |
| 7 | Kanan Jarrus | 12.00 | 25.00 |
| 8 | Luke Skywalker | 12.00 | 25.00 |
| 9 | Stormtrooper | 10.00 | 20.00 |
| 10 | The Inquisitor | 8.00 | 15.00 |

### 2014-15 Star Wars Rebels Mission Series

| | | | |
|---|---|---|---|
| MS1 | Garazeb Orrelios/Stormtrooper | 8.00 | 15.00 |
| MS2 | R2-D2/C-3PO | 15.00 | 30.00 |
| MS3 | Luke Skywalker/Darth Vader | 10.00 | 20.00 |
| MS4 | Darth Sidious/Yoda | 12.00 | 25.00 |
| MS5 | Boba Fett/Stormtrooper | 12.00 | 25.00 |
| MS7 | Wullffwarro/Wookiee Warrior | 8.00 | 15.00 |
| MS8 | Sabine Wren/Stormtrooper | 20.00 | 40.00 |
| MS9 | Cikatro Vizago/IG-RM | 10.00 | 20.00 |
| MS10 | Wicket/Biker Scout | 8.00 | 15.00 |
| MS11 | Bossk/IG-88 | 10.00 | 20.00 |
| MS15 | Luke Skywalker/Han Solo | 12.00 | 25.00 |
| MS16 | R2-D2/Yoda | 15.00 | 30.00 |
| MS17 | TIE Pilot/Stormtrooper | 8.00 | 15.00 |
| MS18 | Ezra Bridger/Kanan Jarrus | 8.00 | 15.00 |
| MS19 | Stormtrooper Commander/Hera Syndulla | 12.00 | 25.00 |
| MS20 | Princess Leia/Luke Skywalker Stormtrooper | 10.00 | 20.00 |

### 2014-15 Star Wars Rebels Saga Legends

| | | | |
|---|---|---|---|
| SL1 | Stormtrooper | 6.00 | 12.00 |
| SL2 | Ezra Bridger | 8.00 | 15.00 |
| SL3 | The Inquisitor | 7.50 | 15.00 |
| SL4 | Kanan Jarrus | 6.00 | 12.00 |
| SL5 | Agent Kallus | 12.00 | 30.00 |
| SL6 | C1-10P (Chopper) | 12.00 | 30.00 |
| SL7 | Jango Fett | 6.00 | 12.00 |
| SL8 | Clone Trooper | 6.00 | 12.00 |
| SL9 | Darth Vader | 10.00 | 20.00 |
| SL10 | Luke Skywalker (Jedi Knight) | 7.50 | 15.00 |
| SL11 | Obi-Wan Kenobi | 7.50 | 15.00 |
| SL12 | Snowtrooper | 10.00 | 20.00 |
| SL13 | TIE Pilot | 5.00 | 10.00 |
| SL14 | AT-DP Driver | 20.00 | 40.00 |
| SL15 | Clone Commander Gree | 6.00 | 12.00 |
| SL16 | Plo Koon | 5.00 | 10.00 |
| SL17 | Jedi Temple Guard | 30.00 | 75.00 |
| SL18 | AT-AT Driver | 6.00 | 12.00 |
| SL22 | Luke Skywalker (X-Wing Pilot) | 7.50 | 15.00 |
| SL23 | Lando Calrissian | 7.50 | 15.00 |
| SL24 | Han Solo | 8.00 | 15.00 |
| SL25 | Luke Skywalker (Endor) | 7.50 | 15.00 |
| SL26 | Commander Bly | 6.00 | 12.00 |
| SL27 | Han Solo (Endor) | 8.00 | 15.00 |
| SL28 | Princess Leia (Endor) | 6.00 | 12.00 |

### 2018 Star Wars Resistance Collection

| | |
|---|---|
| NNO | Commander Pyre |
| NNO | First Order Stormtrooper |
| NNO | Kaz Xiono |
| NNO | Major Vonreg |
| NNO | Synara San |
| NNO | Torra Doza |

### 2018 Star Wars Resistance Collection 1 2-Packs

| | |
|---|---|
| NNO | Jarek Yeager & Bucket |
| NNO | Poe Dameron & BB-8 |

### 2019 Star Wars Retro Collection

| | |
|---|---|
| NNO | Chewbacca |
| NNO | Darth Vader |
| NNO | Han Solo |
| NNO | Luke Skywalker |
| NNO | Princess Leia Organa |
| NNO | Stormtrooper |

### 2019 Star Wars Retro Collection Multipack

| | |
|---|---|
| NNO | Escape from Death Star Board Game (w/Grand Moff Tarkin) |
| NNO | Promotional Early Bird Certificate/Figure Six-Pack |

### 2005 Star Wars Revenge of the Sith

| | | | |
|---|---|---|---|
| III1 | Obi-Wan Kenobi (slashing attack) | 8.00 | 15.00 |
| III2 | Anakin Skywalker (slashing attack straight saber red) | 6.00 | 12.00 |
| III2a | Anakin Skywalker (slashing attack bent saber red) | 4.00 | 8.00 |
| III2b | Anakin Skywalker (slashing attack bent saber pink) | 4.00 | 8.00 |
| III3 | Yoda (firing cannon) | 4.00 | 8.00 |
| III4 | Super Battle Droid (firing arm blaster) | 10.00 | 20.00 |
| III5 | Chewbacca (Wookiee rage) | 8.00 | 15.00 |
| III6a | Clone Trooper (white - quick draw attack) | 6.00 | 12.00 |
| III6b | Clone Trooper (red - quick draw attack) | 6.00 | 12.00 |
| III7 | R2-D2 (droid attack) | 5.00 | 10.00 |
| III8 | Grievous's Bodyguard (battle attack) | 4.00 | 8.00 |
| III9 | General Grievous (four lightsaber attack) | 4.00 | 8.00 |
| III10 | Mace Windu (Force combat) | 6.00 | 12.00 |
| III11 | Darth Vader (lightsaber attack) | 4.00 | 8.00 |
| III12 | Emperor Palpatine (firing Force lightning) | 5.00 | 10.00 |
| III13 | Count Dooku (Sith Lord) | 5.00 | 10.00 |
| III14 | Chancellor Palpatine (supreme chancellor) | 4.00 | 8.00 |
| III15 | Bail Organa (Republic Senator) | 5.00 | 10.00 |
| III16 | Plo Koon (Jedi Master) | 4.00 | 8.00 |
| III17 | Battle Droid (separatist army) | 5.00 | 10.00 |
| III18 | C-3PO (protocal droid) | 4.00 | 8.00 |
| III19 | Padme republic senator | 10.00 | 20.00 |
| III20 | Agen Kolar (Jedi Master) | 6.00 | 12.00 |
| III21 | Shaak Ti (Jedi Master) | 10.00 | 20.00 |
| III22 | Kit Fisto (Jedi Master) | 6.00 | 12.00 |
| III23a | Royal Guard (blue - senate security) | 6.00 | 12.00 |
| III23b | Royal Guard (red - senate security) | 8.00 | 15.00 |
| III24 | Mon Mothma (Republic Senator) | 6.00 | 12.00 |
| III25 | Tarfful (firing bowcaster) | 4.00 | 8.00 |
| III26 | Yoda (spinning attack) | 6.00 | 12.00 |
| III27 | Obi-Wan Kenobi (Jedi kick) | 4.00 | 8.00 |
| III28 | Anakin Skywalker (slashing attack) | 8.00 | 15.00 |
| III29 | Ki-Adi-Mundi (Jedi Master) | 5.00 | 10.00 |
| III30 | Saesee Tiin (Jedi Master) | 5.00 | 10.00 |
| III31 | Luminara Unduli (Jedi Master) | 6.00 | 12.00 |
| III32 | Aayla Secura (Jedi Knight) | 8.00 | 15.00 |
| III33a | Clone Commander (red - battle gear) | 8.00 | 15.00 |
| III33b | Clone Commander (green - battle gear) | 8.00 | 15.00 |
| III34a | Clone Pilot (firing cannon) | 5.00 | 10.00 |
| III34b | Clone Pilot (black - firing cannon) | 5.00 | 10.00 |
| III35a | Palpatine (red lightsaber - lightsaber attack) | 6.00 | 12.00 |
| III35b | Palpatine (blue lightsaber - lightsaber attack) | 6.00 | 12.00 |
| III36 | General Grievous (exploding body) | 10.00 | 20.00 |

| | | |
|---|---|---|
| III37 | Vader's Medical Droid (chopper droid) | 4.00 | 8.00 |
| III38 | AT-TE Tank Gunner (clone army) | 6.00 | 12.00 |
| III39 | Polis Massan (medic droid) | 4.00 | 8.00 |
| III40 | Mas Amedda (Republic Senator) | 5.00 | 10.00 |
| III41 | Clone Trooper (white - super articulation) | 5.00 | 10.00 |
| III42 | Neimoidian Warrior (Neimoidian weapon attack) | 4.00 | 8.00 |
| III43a | Warrior Wookie (dark - wookie battle bash) | 4.00 | 8.00 |
| III43b | Warrior Wookie (light - wookie battle bash) | 12.00 | 25.00 |
| III44 | Destroyer Droid (firing arm blaster) | 8.00 | 15.00 |
| III45 | Tarkin (Governor) | 4.00 | 8.00 |
| III46 | Ask Aak (Senator) | 6.00 | 12.00 |
| III47 | Meena Tills (Senator) | 4.00 | 8.00 |
| III48 | R2-D2 (try me electronic) | 6.00 | 12.00 |
| III49 | Commander Bacara (quick-draw attack) | 5.00 | 10.00 |
| III50 | Anakin Skywalker (battle damaged) | 8.00 | 15.00 |
| III51 | Captain Antilles (Senate security) | 4.00 | 8.00 |
| III52 | Jett Jukassa (Jedi Padawan) | 4.00 | 8.00 |
| III53 | Utapaun Warrior (Utapaun security) | 5.00 | 10.00 |
| III54 | AT-RT Driver (missile-firing blaster) | 12.00 | 25.00 |
| III55 | Obi-Wan Kenobi (w/pilot gear) | 8.00 | 15.00 |
| III56 | Mustafar Sentury (spinning energy bolt) | 5.00 | 10.00 |
| III57 | Commander Bly (battle gear) | 8.00 | 15.00 |
| III58 | Wookie Commando (Kashyyyk battle gear) | 6.00 | 12.00 |
| III59 | Commander Gree (battle gear) | 10.00 | 20.00 |
| III60 | Grievous's Bodyguard (battle attack) | 6.00 | 12.00 |
| III61 | Passel Argente (separatist leader) | 6.00 | 12.00 |
| III62 | Cat Miin (separatist) | 4.00 | 8.00 |
| III63 | Neimoidian Commander (separatist bodyguard) | 4.00 | 8.00 |
| III64 | R4-P17 (rolling action) | 8.00 | 15.00 |
| III65 | Tactical Ops Trooper (Vader's legion) | 6.00 | 12.00 |
| III66 | Plo Koon (Jedi hologram transmission) | 8.00 | 15.00 |
| III67 | Aayla Secura (Jedi hologram transmission) | 5.00 | 10.00 |
| III68 | Wookiee Heavy Gunner (blast attack) | 5.00 | 10.00 |

### 2005 Star Wars Revenge of the Sith 12-Inch

| | | |
|---|---|---|
| 1 | Anakin Skywalker/Darth Vader (ultimate villain) | 30.00 | 60.00 |
| 2 | Barriss Offee | 15.00 | 30.00 |
| 3 | Chewbacca | 20.00 | 40.00 |
| | (2005 KB Toys Exclusive) | | |
| 4 | Clone Trooper | 12.00 | 25.00 |
| 5 | Darth Sidious | | |
| 6 | General Grievous | 30.00 | 60.00 |
| 7 | Shaak Ti | 15.00 | 30.00 |

### 2005 Star Wars Revenge of the Sith Accessories

| | | |
|---|---|---|
| 10 | Darth Vader Carrying Case (w/Clone Trooper & Anakin Skywalker) | | |
| 20 | Darth Vader Carrying Case (w/Darth Vader & Obi-Wan Kenobi) | | |

### 2005 Star Wars Revenge of the Sith Battle Arena

| | | |
|---|---|---|
| 1 | Bodyguard vs. Obi-Wan (Utapau landing platform) | 8.00 | 15.00 |
| 2 | Dooku vs Anakin (Trade Federation cruiser) | 8.00 | 15.00 |
| 3 | Sidius vs. Mace (Chancellor's office) | 8.00 | 15.00 |

### 2005 Star Wars Revenge of the Sith Battle Packs

| | | |
|---|---|---|
| NNO | Assault on Hoth (General Veers/Probot/3 Snowtroopers) | | |
| NNO | Attack on Coruscant (5 Clone Troopers) | 30.00 | 60.00 |
| NNO | Imperial Throne Room (Emperor Palpatine Imperial Dignitary/2 Royal Guards/Stormtrooper) | | |
| NNO | Jedi Temple Assault (Anakin/Clone Pilot/3 Special Ops Troopers) | | |
| NNO | Jedi vs. Sith (Anakin/Asajj Ventress General Grievous/Obi-Wan/Yoda) | 20.00 | 40.00 |
| NNO | Jedi vs. Separatists (Anakin/Darth Maul Jango Fett/Obi-Wan/Mace Windu) | 15.00 | 30.00 |
| NNO | Rebel vs. Empire (Chewbacca/Vader/Han/Luke/Stormtrooper) | 20.00 | 40.00 |

### 2005 Star Wars Revenge of the Sith Collectible Cup Figures

| | | |
|---|---|---|
| 1 | Boba Fett | 12.00 | 25.00 |
| 2 | Clone Trooper | | |
| 3 | Darth Vader | 10.00 | 20.00 |
| 4 | General Grievous | | |
| 5 | Han Solo | 10.00 | 20.00 |
| 6 | Obi-Wan Kenobi | 10.00 | 20.00 |
| 7 | Princess Leia | | |
| 8 | Stormtrooper | 8.00 | 15.00 |
| 9 | Yoda | 8.00 | 15.00 |

### 2005 Star Wars Revenge of the Sith Commemorative Episode III DVD Collection

| | | |
|---|---|---|
| 1 | Jedi Knights (Anakin Skywalker/Mace Windu/Obi-Wan Kenobi) | 10.00 | 20.00 |
| 2 | Sith Lords (Emperor Palpatine/Darth Vader/Count Dooku) | 10.00 | 20.00 |
| 3 | Clone Troopers (3 Clone Troopers) | 12.00 | 25.00 |

### 2005 Star Wars Revenge of the Sith Creatures

| | | |
|---|---|---|
| 10 | Boga (w/Obi-Wan Kenobi) | 20.00 | 40.00 |

### 2005 Star Wars Revenge of the Sith Deluxe

| | | |
|---|---|---|
| 1 | Anakin Skywalker (changes to Darth Vader) | 15.00 | 30.00 |
| 2 | Clone Trooper (firing jet pack) | 5.00 | 10.00 |
| 3 | Clone Troopers (Build Your Army - 3 white) | 8.00 | 15.00 |
| 4 | Clone Troopers (Build Your Army - 2 white and 1 red) | 10.00 | 20.00 |
| 5 | Clone Troopers (Build Your Army - 2 white and 1 green) | 8.00 | 15.00 |
| 6 | Clone Troopers (Build Your Army - 2 white and 1 blue) | 12.00 | 25.00 |
| 7 | Crab Droid (moving legs/missile launcher) | 12.00 | 25.00 |
| 8 | Darth Vader (rebuild Darth Vader) | 10.00 | 20.00 |
| 9 | Emperor Palpatine (changes to Darth Sidious) | 8.00 | 15.00 |
| 10 | General Grievous (secret lightsaber attack) | 15.00 | 30.00 |
| 11 | Obi-Wan Kenobi (Force jump attack - w/super battle droid) | 5.00 | 10.00 |
| 12 | Spider Droid (firing laser action) | 5.00 | 10.00 |
| 13 | Stass Allie (exploding action - w/BARC speeder) | 5.00 | 10.00 |
| 14 | Vulture Droid (blue - firing missile launcher) | 6.00 | 12.00 |
| 15 | Vulture Droid (brown - firing missile launcher) | 10.00 | 20.00 |
| 16 | Yoda (fly into battle - w/can-cell) | 8.00 | 15.00 |

### 2005 Star Wars Revenge of the Sith Evolutions

| | | |
|---|---|---|
| 1 | Anakin Skywalker to Darth Vader | 12.00 | 25.00 |
| 2 | Clone Trooper (Attack of the Clones Revenge of the Sith/A New Hope) | 15.00 | 30.00 |
| 3 | Clone Trooper (Attack of the Clones Revenge of the Sith - gray/A New Hope - gray) | 15.00 | 30.00 |
| 4 | Sith Lords (Darth Maul/Darth Tyranus/Darth Sidious) | 15.00 | 30.00 |

### 2005 Star Wars Revenge of the Sith Exclusives

| | | |
|---|---|---|
| 1 | Anakin Skywalker Paris-Mai (2005 Star Wars Reunion Convention Exclusive) | | |
| 2 | Clone Trooper (Neyo logo) (2005 Target Exclusive) | | |
| 3 | Clone Trooper (Sith logo) (2005 Target Exclusive) | 12.00 | 25.00 |
| 4 | Covert Ops Clone Trooper (2005 StarWarsShop.com Exclusive) | | |
| 5 | Darth Vader (Duel at Mustafar) (2005 Target Exclusive) | 8.00 | 15.00 |
| 6 | Darth Vader (lava reflection) (2005 Target Exclusive) | 8.00 | 15.00 |
| 7 | Darth Vader (2005 Celebration III Exclusive) | 12.00 | 25.00 |
| 8 | Holographic Emperor (2005 Toys R Us Exclusive) | 6.00 | 12.00 |
| 9 | Holographic Yoda (Kashyyyk transmission) (2005 Toys R Us Exclusive) | 6.00 | 12.00 |
| 10 | Obi-Wan Kenobi (Duel at Mustafar) (2005 Target Exclusive) | 12.00 | 25.00 |
| 11 | R2-D2 (remote control) (2005 Japanese Exclusive) | | |
| 12 | Utapau Shadow Trooper (super articulation) (2005 Target Exclusive) | 10.00 | 20.00 |

### 2005 Star Wars Revenge of the Sith Kay Bee Toys Collector Packs

| | | |
|---|---|---|
| 1 | Luminara Unduli/Count Dooku/Royal Guard/Kit Fisto Darth Vader/Bail Organa/C-3PO/Ki-Adi-Mundi/Chancellor Palpatine | 20.00 | 40.00 |

### 2005 Star Wars Revenge of the Sith Playsets

| | | |
|---|---|---|
| 1 | Mustafar Final Duel/Anakin Skywalker/Obi-Wan Kenobi | | |

| 2 Mustafar Final Duel (w/Obi-Wan Darth Vader/4 Clone Troopers) | 40.00 | 80.00 |
| --- | --- | --- |

## 2005 Star Wars Revenge of the Sith Promos

| | | |
| --- | --- | --- |
| 1 Anakin Skywalker | | |
| 2 Darth Vader | | |

## 2005 Star Wars Revenge of the Sith Sneak Preview

| 1 General Grievous | 8.00 | 15.00 |
| --- | --- | --- |
| 2 Tion Medon | 4.00 | 8.00 |
| 3 Wookie Warrior | 4.00 | 8.00 |
| 4 R4-G9 | 4.00 | 8.00 |
| NNO Anakin's Jedi Starfighter (vehicle) | 15.00 | 30.00 |

## 2005 Star Wars Revenge of the Sith Super Deformed

| 1 Boba Fett | 6.00 | 12.00 |
| --- | --- | --- |
| 2 C-3PO | 6.00 | 12.00 |
| 3 Chewbacca | 6.00 | 12.00 |
| 4 Darth Maul | 6.00 | 12.00 |
| 5 Darth Vader | 6.00 | 12.00 |
| 6 R2-D2 | 6.00 | 12.00 |
| 7 Stormtrooper | 6.00 | 12.00 |
| 8 Yoda | 6.00 | 12.00 |

## 2005 Star Wars Revenge of the Sith Vehicles

| 1 Anakin's Jedi Starfighter (w/Anakin) | 20.00 | 40.00 |
| --- | --- | --- |
| (2005 Toys R Us Exclusive) | | |
| 2 ARC-170 Fighter | 50.00 | 100.00 |
| 3 ARC-170 Fighter (w/4 Troopers) | 75.00 | 150.00 |
| 4 AR-RT/AR-RT Driver | | |
| 5 AR-RT/AR-RT Driver (w/Clone Trooper white) | | |
| 6 Barc Speeder (w/Barc Trooper & Wookiee warrior) | | |
| 7 Barc Speeder (w/Barc Trooper) | | |
| 8 Droid Tri-Fighter | | |
| 9 Grievous's Wheel Bike (w/General Grievous) | 25.00 | 50.00 |
| 10 Millennium Falcon | | |
| 11 Obi-Wan's Jedi Starfighter | 20.00 | 40.00 |
| 12 Obi-Wan's Jedi Starfighter (w/Obi-Wan) | 12.00 | 25.00 |
| (2005 Toys R Us Exclusive) | | |
| 13 Plo Koon's Jedi Starfighter | 15.00 | 30.00 |
| (2005 Target Exclusive) | | |
| 14 Republic Gunship | 100.00 | 200.00 |
| 15 Wookiee Flyer (w/Wookiee warrior) | | |

## 2016 Star Wars Rogue One 2-Packs

| NNO Baze Malbus vs. Imperial Stormtrooper | 7.50 | 15.00 |
| --- | --- | --- |
| NNO Captain Cassian Andor vs. Imperial Stormtrooper | 12.50 | 25.00 |
| NNO First Order Snowtrooper Officer vs. Poe Dameron | 8.00 | 15.00 |
| NNO Moroff vs. Scariff Stormtrooper Squad Leader | 7.50 | 15.00 |
| NNO Rebel Commander Pao vs. Imperial Death Trooper | 10.00 | 20.00 |
| NNO Seventh Sister Inquisitor vs. Darth Maul | 15.00 | 30.00 |
| NNO Captain Phasma vs. Finn | 10.00 | 20.00 |

## 2016 Star Wars Rogue One Big Figs

| NNO Imperial Death Trooper | 15.00 | 30.00 |
| --- | --- | --- |
| NNO Imperial Stormtrooper | 15.00 | 30.00 |
| NNO K-2SO | 15.00 | 30.00 |
| NNO Sergeant Jyn Erso | 12.00 | 25.00 |

## 2016 Star Wars Rogue One Build-A-Weapon

| 1 Admiral Raddus | 10.00 | 20.00 |
| --- | --- | --- |
| 2 Bodhi Rook | 12.00 | 25.00 |
| 3 Captain Cassian Andor (Eadu) | 8.00 | 15.00 |
| 4 Chirrut Imwe | 8.00 | 15.00 |
| 5 Darth Vader | 8.00 | 15.00 |
| 6 Director Krennic | 6.00 | 12.00 |
| 7 Fenn Rau | 60.00 | 120.00 |
| 8 Galen Erso | 12.00 | 25.00 |
| 9 Grand Admiral Thrawn (admiral rank) | 15.00 | 30.00 |
| 10 Grand Admiral Thrawn (director rank) | 30.00 | 60.00 |
| 11 Imperial Death Trooper (Specialist Gear) | 10.00 | 20.00 |
| 12 Imperial Ground Crew | 6.00 | 12.00 |
| 13 Imperial Stormtrooper | 6.00 | 12.00 |
| 14 K-2SO | 6.00 | 12.00 |
| 15 Kanan Jarrus (stormtrooper disguise)(Star Wars Rebels) | 10.00 | 20.00 |
| 16 Kylo Ren (The Force Awakens) | 8.00 | 15.00 |
| 17 Lieutenant Sefla | 6.00 | 12.00 |
| 18 Princess Leia Organa (Star Wars Rebels) | 6.00 | 12.00 |
| 19 Rey (Jakku)(The Force Awakens) | 6.00 | 12.00 |
| 20 Sabine Wren (Star Wars Rebels) | 6.00 | 12.00 |
| 21 Sergeant Jyn Erso (Eadu) | 6.00 | 12.00 |
| 22 Sergeant Jyn Erso (Imperial Ground Crew Disguise) | 8.00 | 15.00 |
| 23 Sergeant Jyn Erso (Jedha) | 6.00 | 12.00 |
| 24 Shoretrooper | 8.00 | 15.00 |

## 2016 Star Wars Rogue One Hero Series

| NNO Captain Cassian Andor | 8.00 | 15.00 |
| --- | --- | --- |
| NNO First Order Stormtrooper | | |
| NNO Imperial Death Trooper | 8.00 | 15.00 |
| NNO Sergeant Jyn Erso | 8.00 | 15.00 |
| NNO Shoretrooper | | |

## 2016 Star Wars Rogue One Multipacks

| NNO Eadu 3-Pack | 12.00 | 25.00 |
| --- | --- | --- |
| Sergeant Jyn Erso/Captain Cassian Andor/K-2SO#((Walmart Exclusive) | | |
| NNO Jedha Revolt 4-Pack | 15.00 | 30.00 |
| Edrio Two Tubes/Saw Gerrera/Sergeant Jyn Erso/Imperial Hovertank Pilot | | |
| NNO Rey vs. Kylo Ren | | |
| Poe Dameron vs. First Order TIE Fighter Pilot#(Finn vs. FN-2199 | | |
| NNO Scarif 4-Pack | 12.00 | 25.00 |
| Rebel Commando Pao/Moroff/Imperial Death Trooper/Imperial Stormtrooper#((Kohl's Exclusive) | | |
| NNO Star Wars 8-Pack | 15.00 | 30.00 |
| Darth Maul/Jango Fett/Obi-Wan/Chewbacca#(Darth Vader/Luke/Rey/BB-8#((Target Exclusive) | | |

## 2016 Star Wars Rogue One Vehicles

| NNO Assault Walker (w/stormtrooper sergeant)(The Force Awakens) | 20.00 | 40.00 |
| --- | --- | --- |
| NNO A-Wing (w/Hera Syndulla)(Star Wars Rebels) | 20.00 | 40.00 |
| NNO Ezra Bridger's Speeder (w/Ezra Bridger)(Star Wars Rebels) | 12.00 | 25.00 |
| NNO First Order Snowspeeder (w/stormtrooper)(The Force Awakens) | 15.00 | 30.00 |
| NNO Imperial AT-ACT Playset (w/Jyn Erso/astromech droid/driver) | 75.00 | 150.00 |
| NNO Imperial Speeder (w/AT-DP pilot)(Star Wars Rebels) | 12.00 | 25.00 |
| NNO Imperial TIE Striker (w/pilot) | 20.00 | 40.00 |
| NNO Imperial TIE Striker (w/pilot) | 10.00 | 20.00 |
| (Toys R Us Exclusive) | | |
| NNO Rebel U-Wing Fighter (w/Cassian Andor) | 20.00 | 40.00 |
| NNO Y-Wing Scout Bomber (w/Kanan Jarrus) | 20.00 | 40.00 |

## 2015-16 Star Wars S.H. Figuarts

| NNO Battle Droid | 30.00 | 60.00 |
| --- | --- | --- |
| NNO Captain Phasma | 30.00 | 60.00 |
| NNO Clone Trooper (Phase 1) | 25.00 | 50.00 |
| NNO Darth Maul | 50.00 | 100.00 |
| NNO Darth Vader (w/display stand) | 80.00 | 150.00 |
| NNO First Order Riot Control Stormtrooper | 30.00 | 60.00 |
| NNO First Order Stormtrooper | 30.00 | 60.00 |
| NNO First Order Stormtrooper Heavy Gunner | 40.00 | 80.00 |
| NNO Jango Fett | 40.00 | 80.00 |
| NNO Kylo Ren | | |
| NNO Luke Skywalker (Episode IV) | 40.00 | 80.00 |
| NNO Luke Skywalker (Episode VI) | 60.00 | 120.00 |
| NNO Mace Windu | 40.00 | 80.00 |
| NNO Obi-Wan Kenobi (Episode I) | 30.00 | 60.00 |
| NNO Scout Trooper and Speeder Bike | 120.00 | 200.00 |
| NNO Shadow Trooper | 40.00 | 80.00 |
| NNO Stormtrooper | 50.00 | 100.00 |

## 2002-04 Star Wars Saga 12-Inch

| NNO Anakin Skywalker | 12.50 | 25.00 |
| --- | --- | --- |
| NNO Anakin Skywalker (w/slashing lightsaber) | 15.00 | 30.00 |
| NNO AT-ST Driver | 15.00 | 30.00 |
| NNO Biker Scout | 30.00 | 75.00 |
| NNO Clone Commander | 8.00 | 15.00 |
| NNO Clone Trooper (black-and-white) | 12.50 | 25.00 |

| | | | |
|---|---|---:|---:|
| NNO | Clone Trooper (red-and-white) | 12.50 | 25.00 |
| NNO | Count Dooku | 25.00 | 50.00 |
| NNO | Dengar | 12.50 | 25.00 |
| NNO | Ewok 2-Pack (Logray & Keoulkeech) | 20.00 | 40.00 |
| NNO | Gamorrean Guard | 25.00 | 50.00 |
| NNO | Garindan | 20.00 | 40.00 |
| NNO | Geonosian Warrior | 12.50 | 25.00 |
| NNO | Han Solo | | |
| NNO | Imperial Officer | 10.00 | 20.00 |
| NNO | Jango Fett | 30.00 | 75.00 |
| NNO | Jango Fett (electronic battling) | 20.00 | 40.00 |
| NNO | Jawas | 25.00 | 50.00 |
| NNO | Ki-Adi-Mundi | 20.00 | 40.00 |
| NNO | Lando Calrissian (Skiff disguise) | 12.00 | 25.00 |
| NNO | Luke Skywalker & Tauntaun | 50.00 | 100.00 |
| NNO | Luke Skywalker (w/slashing lightsaber) | 25.00 | 50.00 |
| NNO | Mace Windu | 15.00 | 30.00 |
| NNO | Obi-Wan Kenobi | 12.00 | 25.00 |
| NNO | Obi-Wan Kenobi (electronic battling) | 10.00 | 20.00 |
| NNO | Obi-Wan Kenobi (Tatooine encounter) | 20.00 | 40.00 |
| NNO | Padme Amidala | 15.00 | 30.00 |
| NNO | Plo Koon | | |
| NNO | Princess Leia (Boushh) & Han Solo (carbonite) | 30.00 | 60.00 |
| NNO | Princess Leia (w/speeder bike) | 30.00 | 75.00 |
| NNO | Super Battle Droid | 12.00 | 25.00 |
| NNO | Yoda (w/hoverchair) | 20.00 | 40.00 |
| NNO | Zam Wesell | 12.00 | 25.00 |
| NNO | Zuckuss | 20.00 | 40.00 |

### 2002-04 Star Wars Saga 12-Inch Character Collectibles

| | | | |
|---|---|---:|---:|
| NNO | Anakin Skywalker | | |
| NNO | Darth Vader | | |
| NNO | Jango Fett | 30.00 | 60.00 |
| NNO | Mace Windu | 10.00 | 20.00 |

### 2002-04 Star Wars Saga Accessory Sets

| | | | |
|---|---|---:|---:|
| NNO | Arena Conflict with/Battle Droid brown | 12.00 | 25.00 |
| NNO | Death Star (w/Death Star trooper and droids) | 10.00 | 20.00 |
| NNO | Endor Victory (w/scout trooper) | 10.00 | 20.00 |
| NNO | Hoth Survival (w/Hoth Rebel soldier) | 7.50 | 15.00 |

### 2002-04 Star Wars Saga Arena Battle Beasts

| | | | |
|---|---|---:|---:|
| NNO | Acklay | 25.00 | 50.00 |
| NNO | Reek | 15.00 | 30.00 |

### 2002-04 Star Wars Saga Cinema Scenes

| | | | |
|---|---|---:|---:|
| NNO | Death Star Trash Compactor (Chewbacca & Princess Leia) | 20.00 | 40.00 |
| NNO | Death Star Trash Compactor (Luke Skywalker & Han Solo) | 25.00 | 50.00 |
| NNO | Geonosian War Chamber (Nute Gunray/Passel Argente/Shu Mai) | 12.00 | 25.00 |
| NNO | Geonosian War Chamber (Poggle the Lesser/Count Dooku/San Hill) | 12.00 | 25.00 |
| NNO | Jedi High Council (Mace Windu Oppo Rancisis/Even Piell) | 20.00 | 40.00 |
| NNO | Jedi High Council (Yarael Poof Depa Billaba/Yaddle) | 10.00 | 20.00 |

### 2002-04 Star Wars Saga Collectible Cup Figures

| | | | |
|---|---|---:|---:|
| NNO | Episode I/Darth Maul | 10.00 | 20.00 |

| | | | |
|---|---|---:|---:|
| NNO | Episode II | 10.00 | 20.00 |
| | Anakin Skywalker | | |
| NNO | Episode IV | 10.00 | 20.00 |
| | Obi-Wan Kenobi | | |
| NNO | Episode V | 10.00 | 20.00 |
| | Luke Skywalker | | |
| NNO | Episode VI | 12.00 | 25.00 |
| | Princess Leia Organa | | |

### 2002-04 Star Wars Saga Collection 1 (2002)

| | | | |
|---|---|---:|---:|
| 1 | Anakin Skywalker (outland peasant disguise) | 6.00 | 12.00 |
| 2 | Padme Amidala (arena escape) | 6.00 | 12.00 |
| 3 | Obi-Wan Kenobi (Coruscant chase) | 6.00 | 12.00 |
| 4 | C-3PO (protocol droid) | 5.00 | 10.00 |
| 5 | Kit Fisto (Jedi Master) | 5.00 | 10.00 |
| 6 | Super Battle Droid | 5.00 | 10.00 |
| 17 | Clone Trooper | 6.00 | 12.00 |
| 18 | Zam Wesell (bounty hunter) | 6.00 | 12.00 |
| 22 | Anakin Skywalker (hangar duel) | 12.00 | 25.00 |
| 23 | Yoda (Jedi Master) | | |
| 27 | Count Dooku (Dark Lord) | 6.00 | 12.00 |
| 28 | Mace Windu (Geonosian rescue) | 8.00 | 15.00 |
| 29 | Luke Skywalker (Bespin duel) | 8.00 | 15.00 |
| 30 | Darth Vader (Bespin duel) | 6.00 | 12.00 |
| 31 | Jango Fett (final battle) | 5.00 | 10.00 |
| 36 | Obi-Wan Kenobi (Jedi starfighter) | 12.00 | 25.00 |
| 37 | Han Solo (Endor bunker) | | |
| 38 | Chewbacca (Cloud City capture w/C-3PO) | 6.00 | 12.00 |
| 40 | Djas Puhr (bounty hunter) | 6.00 | 12.00 |
| 41 | Padme Amidala (Coruscant attack) | 6.00 | 12.00 |
| 43 | Anakin Skywalker (Tatooine attack) | 6.00 | 12.00 |
| 47 | Jango Fett (Slave-1 pilot) | 5.00 | 10.00 |
| 48 | Destroyer Droid (Geonosis battle) | | |
| 49 | Clone Trooper (Republic gunship pilot) | 8.00 | 15.00 |
| 53 | Yoda (Jedi High Council) | | |

### 2002-04 Star Wars Saga Collection 1 (2003)

| | | | |
|---|---|---:|---:|
| 1 | Obi-Wan Kenobi (acklay battle) | 5.00 | 10.00 |
| 2 | Mace Windu (arena confrontation) | 5.00 | 10.00 |
| 3 | Darth Tyranus (Geonosian escape) | 8.00 | 15.00 |
| 7 | Anakin Skywalker (secret ceremony) | 8.00 | 15.00 |
| 8 | Boba Fett (The Pit of Carkoon) | 8.00 | 15.00 |
| 9 | R2-D2 (droid factory) | 6.00 | 12.00 |
| 13 | Han Solo (Hoth rescue) | | |
| 14 | Chewbacca (mynock hunt) | 5.00 | 10.00 |
| 17 | Luke Skywalker (throne room duel) | 5.00 | 10.00 |
| 18 | Darth Vader (throne room duel) | 6.00 | 12.00 |
| 19 | Snowtrooper (The Battle of Hoth) | 8.00 | 15.00 |
| 20 | Jango Fett (Kamino duel) | | |
| 21 | C-3PO (Tatooine attack) | | |

### 2002-04 Star Wars Saga Collection 2 (2002)

| | | | |
|---|---|---:|---:|
| 7 | Boba Fett (Kamino escape) | 8.00 | 15.00 |
| 8 | Tusken Raider Female (w/Tusken child) | 6.00 | 12.00 |
| 9 | Captain Typho (Padme's head of security) | 5.00 | 10.00 |
| 10 | Shaak Ti (Jedi Master) | 5.00 | 10.00 |
| 11a | Battle Droid (arena battle tan) | 5.00 | 10.00 |
| 11b | Battle Droid (arena battle brown) | 12.00 | 25.00 |
| 12 | Plo Koon (arena battle) | | |
| 13 | Jango Fett (Kamino escape) | 8.00 | 15.00 |
| 14 | R2-D2 (Coruscant sentry) | 8.00 | 15.00 |
| 15 | Geonosian Warrior | 5.00 | 10.00 |
| 16 | Dexter Jettster (Coruscant informant) | 5.00 | 10.00 |
| 19 | Royal Guard (Coruscant security) | 6.00 | 12.00 |
| 20 | Saesee Tin (Jedi Master) | 5.00 | 10.00 |
| 21 | Nikto (Jedi Knight) | 6.00 | 12.00 |
| 24 | Jar Jar Binks (Gungan Senator) | 5.00 | 10.00 |
| 25 | Taun We (Kamino cloner) | 6.00 | 12.00 |
| 26 | Luminara Unduli | 5.00 | 10.00 |
| 32 | Qui-Gon Jinn (Jedi Master) | 6.00 | 12.00 |
| 33a | Endor Rebel Soldier (facial hair) | | |
| 33a | Endor Rebel Soldier (no facial hair) | | |
| 34 | Massiff (w/Geonosian handler) | 8.00 | 15.00 |
| 35 | Orn Free Taa (senator) | | |
| 39 | Supreme Chancellor Palpatine | | |
| 42 | Darth Maul (Sith training) | 5.00 | 10.00 |
| 44 | Ki-Adi-Mundi (Jedi Master) | 5.00 | 10.00 |
| 45 | Ephant Man (Jabba's head of security) | | |
| 46 | Teemto Pagalies (pod racer) | | |
| 50 | Watto (Mos Espa junk dealer) | 5.00 | 10.00 |
| 51 | Lott Dod (Neimoidian Senator) | | |
| 52 | Tusken Raider (w/massiff) | 6.00 | 12.00 |
| 54 | Rebel Trooper (Tantive IV defender) | | |
| 55 | Imperial Officer | | |
| 56 | Eeth Koth (Jedi Master) | | |
| 57 | Teebo | | |

### 2002-04 Star Wars Saga Collection 2 (2003)

| | | | |
|---|---|---:|---:|
| 4 | Padme Amidala (droid factory chase) | | |
| 5 | SP-4 & JN-66 (research droids) | 6.00 | 12.00 |
| 6 | Tusken Raider (Tatooine camp ambush) | 5.00 | 10.00 |
| 10 | Lama Su (w/clone child) | 10.00 | 20.00 |
| 11 | Aayla Secura (Battle of Geonosis) | 8.00 | 15.00 |
| 12 | Barriss Offee (Luminara Unduli's Padawan) | 6.00 | 12.00 |
| 15 | Yoda and Chian (Padawan lightsaber training) | | |
| 16 | Ashla & Jempa (Jedi Padawans) | 8.00 | 15.00 |
| 22 | Padme Amidala (secret ceremony) | 10.00 | 20.00 |
| 23 | Wat Tambor (Geonosis war room) | 10.00 | 20.00 |
| 24 | Coleman Trebor (Battle of Geonosis) | | |
| 25 | Darth Maul (Theed hangar duel) | 8.00 | 15.00 |
| 26 | Princess Leia Organa (Imperial captive) | 5.00 | 10.00 |

| | | |
|---|---|---|
| 27 Han Solo (fight to Alderaan) | | |
| 28 WA-7 (Dexter's diner) | 8.00 | 15.00 |
| 29 Lt. Dannl Faytonni (Coruscant Outlander club) | | |
| 30 The Emperor (throne room) | | |
| 31 Luke Skywalker (Tatooine encounter) | 5.00 | 10.00 |
| 32 Darth Vader (Death Star clash) | 8.00 | 15.00 |
| 33 Bail Organa (Alderaan Senator) | 6.00 | 12.00 |
| 34 Stormtrooper (McQuarrie concept) | 8.00 | 15.00 |
| 35 Imperial Dignitary Janus Greejatus | | |
| (Death Star procession) | | |
| 36 Padme Amidala (Lars' homestead) | 15.00 | 30.00 |
| 37 Achk Med-Beq (Coruscant Outlander club) | 6.00 | 12.00 |
| 38 Ayy Vida (Outlander nightclub patron) | 10.00 | 20.00 |
| 39 Obi-Wan Kenobi (Outlander nightclub patron) | 6.00 | 12.00 |
| 40 Elan Sleazebaggano (Outlander nightclub encounter) | 8.00 | 15.00 |
| 41 Imperial Dignitary Kren Blista-Vanee | | |
| (Death Star procession) | | |

### 2002-04 Star Wars Saga Deluxe

| | | |
|---|---|---|
| NNO Anakin Skywalker (w/Force flipping attack) | 4.00 | 8.00 |
| NNO Anakin Skywalker (w/lightsaber slashing action) | 6.00 | 12.00 |
| NNO C-3PO (w/droid factory assembly line) | 4.00 | 8.00 |
| NNO Clone Trooper (w/speeder bike) | 6.00 | 12.00 |
| NNO Darth Tyranus (w/Force flipping attack) | 4.00 | 8.00 |
| NNO Flying Geonosian (w/sonic blaster and attack pod) | 4.00 | 8.00 |
| NNO Jango Fett (Kamino showdown) | 4.00 | 8.00 |
| NNO Jango Fett (w/electronic backpack and snap-on armor) | 4.00 | 8.00 |
| NNO Mace Windu (w/blast apart droid tan) | 4.00 | 8.00 |
| NNO Mace Windu (w/blast apart droid brown) | 4.00 | 8.00 |
| NNO Nexu (w/snapping jaw and attack roar) | 12.00 | 25.00 |
| NNO Obi-Wan Kenobi (Kamino showdown) | 4.00 | 8.00 |
| NNO Obi-Wan Kenobi (w/Force flipping attack) | 4.00 | 8.00 |
| NNO Spider Droid (w/rotating turret and firing cannon) | 4.00 | 8.00 |
| NNO Super Battle Droid Builder (w/droid factory assembly mold) | 4.00 | 8.00 |
| NNO Yoda (w/Force powers) | 10.00 | 20.00 |

### 2002-04 Star Wars Saga Exclusives

| | | |
|---|---|---|
| NNO Boba Fett (silver) | 15.00 | 30.00 |
| (2003 Convention Exclusive) | | |
| NNO C-3PO (Santa) & R2-D2 (reindeer) | 12.00 | 25.00 |
| (2002 Holiday Edition Exclusive) | | |
| NNO Clone Trooper (silver) | 6.00 | 12.00 |
| (2003 Toys R Us Exclusive) | | |
| NNO Clone Trooper/Super Battle Droid | 12.00 | 25.00 |
| (2004 Jedi Con Exclusive) | | |
| NNO Commander Jorg Sacul | 20.00 | 40.00 |
| (2002 Celebration 2 Exclusive) | | |
| NNO Darth Vader (silver) | 30.00 | 60.00 |
| (2002 New York Toy Fair Exclusive) | | |
| NNO R2-D2 (silver) | 15.00 | 30.00 |

| | | |
|---|---|---|
| (2002 Toys R Us Silver Anniversary Exclusive) | | |
| NNO Sandtrooper (silver) | | |
| (2004 SDCC Exclusive) | | |
| NNO Yoda (Santa) | | |
| (2003 Holiday Edition Exclusive) | | |

### 2002-04 Star Wars Saga Mos Eisley Cantina Bar

| | | |
|---|---|---|
| NNO Dr. Evezan | | |
| NNO Greedo | 8.00 | 15.00 |
| NNO Kitik Keed'kak | | |
| NNO Momaw Nadon | | |
| NNO Ponda Baba | | |
| NNO Wuher | | |

### 2002-04 Star Wars Saga Multipacks

| | | |
|---|---|---|
| NNO Endor Soldiers (w/four soldiers paint may vary slightly) | | |
| NNO Imperial Forces (Darth Vader | 15.00 | 30.00 |
| Stormtrooper/AT-ST Driver/R4-I9) | | |
| NNO Jedi Warriors (Obi-Wan Kenobi | 10.00 | 20.00 |
| Saesee Tiin/Plo Koon/Fi-Ek Sirch) | | |
| NNO Light Saber Action Pack | | |
| (Anakin Skywalker/Count Dooku/Yoda) | | |
| NNO Rebel Troopers Builder Set | | |
| NNO Sandtroopers Builder Set | | |
| (orange, black, gray, & white shoulder pad) | | |
| NNO Skirmish at Karkoon | 10.00 | 20.00 |
| (Han Solo/Klaatu/Nikto/Barada) | | |
| NNO Stormtroopers Builder Set | | |
| NNO The Battle of Hoth (Luke | 20.00 | 40.00 |
| Leia/Chewbacca/R3-A2/Tauntaun) | | |
| NNO Ultimate Bounty (Boba Fett | 12.00 | 25.00 |
| Bossk/IG-88/Aurra Sing w/swoop vehicle) | | |
| NNO Value 4-Pack (Zam Wesell | | |
| Battle Droid/Kit Fisto/Super Battle Droid) | | |

### 2002-04 Star Wars Saga Playsets

| | | |
|---|---|---|
| NNO Geonosian Battle Arena | 60.00 | 120.00 |

### 2002-04 Star Wars Saga Playskool

| | | |
|---|---|---|
| NNO Arena Adventure | 12.00 | 25.00 |
| NNO Duel with Darth Maul | 25.00 | 50.00 |
| NNO Fast through the Forest | 8.00 | 15.00 |
| NNO Millennium Falcon Adventure | 20.00 | 40.00 |

| | | |
|---|---|---|
| NNO The Stompin' Wampa | | |
| NNO X-Wing Adventure | 25.00 | 50.00 |

### 2002-04 Star Wars Saga Re-Issues

| | | |
|---|---|---|
| NNO Anakin Skywalker (hangar duel) | 8.00 | 15.00 |
| 2002 Star Wars Saga Collection 1 | | |
| NNO C-3PO (Death Star escape) | | |
| 1997-98 Star Wars Power of the Force Green | | |
| NNO Chewbacca (escape from Hoth) | | |
| 2000-01 Star Wars Power of the Jedi | | |
| NNO Darth Maul (Theed hangar duel) | | |
| 2003 Star Wars Saga Collection 2 | | |
| NNO Darth Vader (Death Star clash) | | |
| 2003 Star Wars Saga Collection 2 | | |
| NNO Han Solo (flight to Alderaan) | | |
| 2003 Star Wars Saga Collection 2 | | |
| NNO Luke Skywalker (Tatooine encounter) | | |
| 2003 Star Wars Saga Collection 2 | | |
| NNO Obi-Wan Kenobi (Coruscant chase) | | |
| 2002 Star Wars Saga Collection 1 | | |
| NNO Princess Leia Organa (Death Star captive) | 10.00 | 20.00 |
| 2003 Star Wars Saga Collection 2 | | |
| NNO R2-D2 (Tatooine mission) | | |
| 2000-01 Star Wars Power of the Jedi | | |
| NNO Stormtrooper (Death Star chase) | 8.00 | 15.00 |
| 1998-99 Star Wars Power of the Force | | |
| NNO Yoda (Battle of Geonosis) | | |
| 2002 Star Wars Saga Collection 1 | | |

### 2002-04 Star Wars Saga Ultra With Accessories

| | | |
|---|---|---|
| NNO C-3PO with Escape Pod | 12.00 | 25.00 |
| NNO Ewok (w/attack glider) | | |
| NNO General Rieekan (w/Hoth tactical screen) | 20.00 | 40.00 |
| NNO Jabba's Palace Court Denizens | | |
| NNO Jabba the Hutt (w/pipe stand) | | |
| NNO Jango Fett (Kamino confrontation) | | |
| NNO Obi-Wan Kenobi (Kamino confrontation) | 15.00 | 30.00 |
| NNO Wampa (w/Hoth cave) | | |

### 2002-04 Star Wars Saga Vehicles

| | | |
|---|---|---|
| NNO Anakin Skywalker's Speeder | 10.00 | 20.00 |
| NNO Anakin Skywalker's Swoop Bike (w/Anakin) | 20.00 | 40.00 |
| NNO A-Wing Fighter | 20.00 | 40.00 |
| NNO Darth Tyranus's Speeder Bike (w/Darth Tyranus) | 15.00 | 30.00 |
| NNO Imperial Dogfight TIE Fighter | 20.00 | 40.00 |
| NNO Imperial Shuttle | 120.00 | 200.00 |
| NNO Jango Fett's Slave 1 | 25.00 | 50.00 |
| NNO Jedi Starfighter | 15.00 | 30.00 |
| NNO Jedi Starfighter (w/Obi-Wan Kenobi) | 20.00 | 40.00 |
| NNO Landspeeder (w/Luke Skywalker) | 20.00 | 40.00 |
| NNO Luke Skywalker's X-Wing Fighter (w/R2-D2) | 60.00 | 120.00 |
| NNO Red Leader's X-Wing Fighter (w/Red Leader) | 30.00 | 60.00 |
| NNO Republic Gunship | 75.00 | 150.00 |
| NNO TIE Bomber | 30.00 | 75.00 |
| NNO Zam Wesell's Speeder | 10.00 | 20.00 |

## 2002-04 Star Wars Saga Wave 1 Hoth

| | | |
|---|---|---|
| 1 Hoth Trooper (Hoth evacuation) | 8.00 | 15.00 |
| 2 R-3PM (Hoth evacuation) | | |
| 3 Luke Skywalker (Hoth attack) | | |

## 2002-04 Star Wars Saga Wave 2 Tatooine

| | | |
|---|---|---|
| 4 Luke Skywalker (Jabba's Palace) | 6.00 | 12.00 |
| 5 R2-D2 (Jabba's sail barge) | 8.00 | 15.00 |
| 6 R1-G4 (Tatooine transaction) | | |

## 2002-04 Star Wars Saga Wave 3 Jabba's Palace

| | | |
|---|---|---|
| 7 Lando Calrissian (Jabba's sail barge) | 5.00 | 10.00 |
| 8 Rappertunie (Jabba's Palace) | | |
| 9 J'Quille (Jabba's sail barge) | 12.00 | 25.00 |
| 10 Tanus Spojek | | |
| 11 TIE Fighter Pildof | | |

## 2002-04 Star Wars Saga Wave 4 Battle of Yavin

| | | |
|---|---|---|
| 12 General Jan Dodonna (Battle of Yavin) | | |
| 13 Dutch Vander Gold Leader (Battle of Yavin) | | |
| 14 TIE Fighter Pilot (Battle of Yavin) | 6.00 | 12.00 |
| 15 Captain Antilles | | |

## 2002-04 Star Wars Saga Wave 5 Star Destroyer

| | | |
|---|---|---|
| 16 Admiral Ozzel | | |
| 17 Dengar (executor meeting) | | |
| 18 Bossk (executor meeting) | | |

## 2002-04 Star Wars Saga Wave 6 Battle of Endor

| | | |
|---|---|---|
| 19 Han Solo (Endor strike) | | |
| 20 General Madine (Imperial shuttle capture) | | |
| 21 Lando Calrissian (Death Star attack) | 6.00 | 12.00 |

## 2006-07 Star Wars The Saga Collection

| | | |
|---|---|---|
| SAGA1 Princess Leia boushh | 7.50 | 15.00 |
| SAGA2 Han Solo carbonite | 7.50 | 15.00 |
| SAGA3 Bib Fortuna | 12.50 | 25.00 |
| SAGA4 Barada skiff | 4.00 | 8.00 |
| SAGA5 Chewbacca/ boushh prisoner | 6.00 | 12.00 |
| SAGA6 Boba Fett | 7.50 | 15.00 |
| SAGA7 General Veers | 12.50 | 25.00 |
| SAGA8 Major Bren Derlin | 6.00 | 12.00 |
| SAGA9 AT-AT Driver | 4.00 | 8.00 |
| SAGA10 R2-D2 | 6.00 | 12.00 |
| SAGA11 Snowtrooper | 5.00 | 10.00 |
| SAGA12 General Rieeken | 4.00 | 8.00 |
| SAGA13 Darth Vader | 7.50 | 15.00 |
| SAGA14 Power Droid | 10.00 | 20.00 |
| SAGA15 Sora Bulq | 6.00 | 12.00 |
| SAGA16 Sun Fac | 10.00 | 20.00 |
| SAGA17 C-3PO with/ battle droid head/ droid head on | 4.00 | 8.00 |
| SAGA18 Poggle the Lesser | 4.00 | 8.00 |
| SAGA19 Yoda | 7.50 | 15.00 |
| SAGA20 Jango Fett | 5.00 | 10.00 |
| SAGA21 Scorch | 15.00 | 30.00 |
| SAGA22 Firespeeder Pilot | 4.00 | 8.00 |
| SAGA23 Lushros Dofine | 6.00 | 12.00 |
| SAGA24 Clone Commander Cody/ orange highlights | 7.50 | 15.00 |
| SAGA25 Anakin Skywalker | 5.00 | 10.00 |
| SAGA26 Utapau Clone Trooper | 7.50 | 15.00 |

| | | |
|---|---|---|
| SAGA27 Holographic Ki-Adi-Mundi | 5.00 | 10.00 |
| SAGA28 Obi-Wan Kenobi beard | 4.00 | 8.00 |
| SAGA29 Faul Maudama | 6.00 | 12.00 |
| SAGA30 General Grievous | 7.50 | 15.00 |
| SAGA31 Momaw Nadon/ clear cup | 5.00 | 10.00 |
| SAGA32 R5-D4 | 4.00 | 8.00 |
| SAGA33 Hem Dazon blue cup | 4.00 | 8.00 |
| SAGA34 Garindan | 10.00 | 20.00 |
| SAGA35 Han Solo | 6.00 | 12.00 |
| SAGA36 Luke Skywalker | 4.00 | 8.00 |
| SAGA37 Sandtrooper | 6.00 | 12.00 |
| SAGA38 Darth Vader bespin/ saber fight | 7.50 | 15.00 |
| SAGA39 Chief Chirpa | 10.00 | 20.00 |
| SAGA40 Moff Jerjerrod | 6.00 | 12.00 |
| SAGA41 Death Star Gunner | 7.50 | 15.00 |
| SAGA42 C-3PO (with/ ewok throne/ unpainted knees) | 10.00 | 20.00 |
| SAGA43 Emperor Palpatine | 6.00 | 12.00 |
| SAGA44 Luke Skywalker | 4.00 | 8.00 |
| SAGA45 Darth Vader/ shocked by emperor | 6.00 | 12.00 |
| SAGA46 Rebel Trooper/ endor black | 4.00 | 8.00 |
| SAGA47 Obi-Wan Kenobi/ no beard | 5.00 | 10.00 |
| SAGA48 Holographic Darth Maul | 4.00 | 8.00 |
| SAGA49 Rep Been | 5.00 | 10.00 |
| SAGA50 Naboo Soldier yellow | 6.00 | 12.00 |
| SAGA51 Dud Bolt & Mars Guo | 5.00 | 10.00 |
| SAGA52 Gragra | 7.50 | 15.00 |
| SAGA53 Sith Training Darth Maul | 7.50 | 15.00 |
| SAGA54 Chewbacca with/ electronic C-3PO | 10.00 | 20.00 |
| SAGA55 Kit Fisto | 4.00 | 8.00 |
| SAGA56 Holographic Clone Commander Cody | 5.00 | 10.00 |
| SAGA57 Clone Trooper 442nd Siege Batallion | 15.00 | 30.00 |
| (green highlights) | | |
| SAGA58 R5-J2 | 12.50 | 25.00 |
| SAGA59 Clone Trooper Fifth Fleet Security/ | 10.00 | 20.00 |
| (blue stripes on head/shoulder) | | |
| SAGA60 Clone Trooper Sergeant | 7.50 | 15.00 |
| SAGA61 Super Battle Droid | 6.00 | 12.00 |
| SAGA62 Battle Droids (green and yellow) | 4.00 | 8.00 |
| SAGA63 Holographic Obi-Wan Kenobi | 7.50 | 15.00 |
| SAGA64 Commander Oppo (blue highlights/ blue shoulder) | 5.00 | 10.00 |
| SAGA65 Elite Corps Clone Commander | 4.00 | 8.00 |
| SAGA66 R4-K5 Darth Vader's Astromech Droid | 4.00 | 8.00 |
| SAGA67 Padme Amidala | 4.00 | 8.00 |
| SAGA68 Combat Engineer Clone Trooper | 4.00 | 8.00 |
| (brown highlights) | | |
| SAGA69 Yarael Poof | 4.00 | 8.00 |
| SAGA70 Aurra Sing | 4.00 | 8.00 |
| SAGA71 Kitik Keed'Kak | 4.00 | 8.00 |
| SAGA72 Nabrun Leids & Kabe | 4.00 | 8.00 |
| SAGA73 Labria | 4.00 | 8.00 |
| SAGA74 R4-M6 Mace Windu's Astromech Droid | 4.00 | 8.00 |
| SAGA17a C-3PO with/ battle droid head/ C-3PO head on | 4.00 | 8.00 |
| SAGA31a Momaw Nadon/ blue cup | 5.00 | 10.00 |
| SAGA33a Hem Dazon white cup | 4.00 | 8.00 |
| SAGA42a C-3PO (with/ ewok throne/ painted knees) | 10.00 | 20.00 |
| SAGA46a Rebel Trooper/ endor white | 4.00 | 8.00 |

## 2006-07 Star Wars The Saga Collection Battle Packs

| | | |
|---|---|---|
| 1 Battle Above the Sarlacc (Boba Fett | 25.00 | 50.00 |
| Lando Calrissian skiff/Han Solo carbonite) | | |
| 2 Jedi vs. Darth Sidious (Darth Sidious | 25.00 | 50.00 |
| Kit Fisto/Mace Windu/Saesee Tiin) | | |
| 3 Sith Lord Attack (Obi-Wan Kenobi | 20.00 | 40.00 |
| Qui-Gon Jinn/Darth Maul/Battle Droid tan) | | |

## 2006-07 Star Wars The Saga Collection Battle Packs Exclusives

| | | |
|---|---|---|
| 1 Mace Windu's Attack Batallion (Mace Windu | 50.00 | 100.00 |
| Clone Trooper purple/ with sk) | | |
| 2 Skirmish in the Senate (Emperor Palpatine | 20.00 | 40.00 |
| Yoda/Clone Trooper red/Clone) | | |
| 3 The Hunt for Grievous (Clone Trooper red | 30.00 | 75.00 |
| Clone Trooper blue/Clone Trooper) | | |

## 2006-07 Star Wars The Saga Collection Commemorative DVD Collection

| | | |
|---|---|---|
| 1 Luke Skywalker/Darth Vader/Obi-Wan Kenobi | 10.00 | 20.00 |
| 2 Han Solo/Chewbacca/Stormtrooper | 10.00 | 20.00 |
| 3 Luke Skywalker/Emperor Palpatine/R2-D2/C-3PO | 15.00 | 30.00 |

## 2006-07 Star Wars The Saga Collection Episode III Greatest Battles Collection

| | | |
|---|---|---|
| 1 501st Legion Trooper | 6.00 | 12.00 |
| (blue with orange feet) | | |
| 2 AT-TE Tank Gunner | 6.00 | 12.00 |
| (gold helmet highlights) | | |
| 3 C-3PO | 4.00 | 8.00 |
| 4 Count Dooku | 10.00 | 20.00 |
| 5 Royal Guard Blue | 5.00 | 10.00 |
| 6 Padme | 5.00 | 10.00 |
| 7 R4-G9 | 4.00 | 8.00 |
| 8 Kit Fisto | 6.00 | 12.00 |
| 9 Wookiee Warrior | 4.00 | 8.00 |
| 10 R2-D2 | 6.00 | 12.00 |
| 11 Shock Trooper | 4.00 | 8.00 |
| 12 Obi-Wan Kenobi (flight helmet) | 4.00 | 8.00 |
| 13 Emperor Palpatine | 4.00 | 8.00 |
| 14a Clone Commander (green with skirt sash) | 7.50 | 15.00 |
| 14b Clone Commander (red with skirt sash) | 10.00 | 20.00 |

## 2006-07 Star Wars The Saga Collection Episode III Heroes & Villains Collection

| | | |
|---|---|---|
| 1 Darth Vader | 4.00 | 8.00 |
| 2 Anakin Skywalker | 4.00 | 8.00 |
| 3 Yoda | 4.00 | 8.00 |
| 4 Commander Bacara | 4.00 | 8.00 |
| 5 Clone Trooper | 4.00 | 8.00 |
| 6 Clone Pilot black | 4.00 | 8.00 |
| 7 Chewbacca | 4.00 | 8.00 |
| 8 Obi-Wan Kenobi | 4.00 | 8.00 |
| 9 General Grievous cape | 4.00 | 8.00 |
| 10 Mace Windu | 4.00 | 8.00 |
| 11 R2-D2 | 4.00 | 8.00 |
| 12 Destroyer Droid | 4.00 | 8.00 |
| 9a General Grievous/ no cape | 4.00 | 8.00 |

## 2006-07 Star Wars The Saga Collection Exclusives

| | | |
|---|---|---|
| 1 501st Stormtrooper | 15.00 | 30.00 |
| (2006 SDCC Exclusive) | | |
| 2 Clone Trooper (Saleucami) | | |
| (2006 Toys R Us French Exclusive) | | |
| 3 Darth Vader | 30.00 | 75.00 |
| (2006 UK Woolworth's Exclusive) | | |
| 4 Demise of General Grievous | 6.00 | 12.00 |
| (2006 Target Exclusive) | | |
| 5 Early Bird Certificate Package | | |
| (2005 Walmart Exclusive) | | |
| 6 Early Bird Kit (Luke Skywalker, Princess Leia, Chewbacca, and R2-D2) 30.00 | | 75.00 |
| (2005 Mailaway Exclusive) | | |
| 7 George Lucas Stormtrooper | 30.00 | 75.00 |
| (2006 Mailaway Exclusive) | | |
| 8 Separation of the Twins Leia Organa (w/Bail Organa) | 15.00 | 30.00 |
| (2005 Walmart Exclusive) | | |
| 9 Separation of the Twins Luke Skywalker (w/Obi-Wan Kenobi) | 12.00 | 25.00 |
| (2005 Walmart Exclusive) | | |
| 10 Shadow Stormtrooper | 12.00 | 25.00 |
| (2006 Starwarsshop.com Exclusive) | | |

## 2006-07 Star Wars The Saga Collection International

| | |
|---|---|
| SAGA1 Princess Leia Boushh | |
| SAGA2 Han Solo (in carbonite) | |
| SAGA3 Bib Fortuna | |
| SAGA4 Barada Skiff Guard | |
| SAGA5 Chewbacca (Boushh Prisoner) | |
| SAGA6 Boba Fett | |

## 2006-07 Star Wars The Saga Collection Multipacks

| | | |
|---|---|---|
| NNO Droid Pack I/R4-A22/R2-C4/R3-T2/R2-Q2/R3-T6 | 30.00 | 60.00 |
| (2006 Entertainment Earth Exclusive) | | |
| NNO Droid Pack II/R4-E1/R2-X2/R2-M5/R2-A6/R3-Y2 | 30.00 | 60.00 |
| (2006 Entertainment Earth Exclusive) | | |
| NNO Episode III Gift Pack/Darth Vader | 20.00 | 40.00 |
| General Grievous/Obi-Wan Kenobi/R2-D2#((2006 UK Woolworth's Exclusive) | | |
| NNO Jedi Knights/Anakin Skywalker | | |
| Mace Windu/Obi-Wan Kenobi#((2005 UK Argos Exclusive) | | |
| NNO Lucas Collector's Set/Zett Jukassa | 12.50 | 25.00 |
| Baron Papanoida/Terr Taneel/Chi Eekway#((2006 Starwarsshop.com Exclusive) | | |
| NNO Revenge of the Sith Collector's Set | | |
| (UK Exclusive) | | |

## 2006-07 Star Wars The Saga Collection Previews Exclusives

| | | |
|---|---|---|
| NNO Death Star Briefing (Darth Vader | 60.00 | 120.00 |
| Grand Moff Tarkin/Admiral Motti/General) | | |
| NNO The Hunt For the Millenium Falcon | 30.00 | 60.00 |
| (Darth Vader/Dengar/IG-88/Boba Fett) | | |
| NNO Republic Commando Delta Squad | | |
| (Delta Three-Eight orange/Scoarch blue) | | |

## 2006-07 Star Wars The Saga Collection Ultimate Galactic Hunt

| | | |
|---|---|---|
| NNO AT-AT Driver (ESB Stand) | 6.00 | 12.00 |
| NNO Anakin Skywalker (ROTS Stand) | 4.00 | 8.00 |
| NNO Boba Fett (ROTJ Stand) | 30.00 | 60.00 |
| NNO Commander Cody (ROTS Stand) | 4.00 | 8.00 |
| NNO Darth Vader (ESB Stand) | 4.00 | 8.00 |
| NNO General Grievous (ROTS Stand) | 6.00 | 12.00 |
| NNO Han Solo Carbonite (ROTJ Stand) | 6.00 | 12.00 |
| NNO Obi-Wan Kenobi (ROTS Stand) | 4.00 | 8.00 |
| NNO Scorch Republic Commando (SW Stand) | 8.00 | 15.00 |
| NNO Snowtrooper (ESB Stand) | 8.00 | 15.00 |

## 2006-07 Star Wars The Saga Collection Ultimate Galactic Hunt Vehicles

| | | |
|---|---|---|
| NNO Republic Gunship | 150.00 | 300.00 |
| (Toys R Us Exclusive) | | |

## 2006-07 Star Wars The Saga Collection Ultimate Galactic Hunt Vintage

| | | |
|---|---|---|
| NNO Bossk | 10.00 | 20.00 |
| NNO IG-88 | 12.50 | 25.00 |
| NNO Han Solo Hoth | 15.00 | 30.00 |
| NNO Luke Skywalker Bespin | 15.00 | 30.00 |
| NNO Princess Leia Organa (Endor combat poncho) | 10.00 | 20.00 |
| NNO Imperial Stormtrooper Hoth | 12.50 | 25.00 |

## 2006-07 Star Wars The Saga Collection Vehicles

| | | |
|---|---|---|
| NNO Anakin's Jedi Starfighter | 20.00 | 40.00 |
| NNO Darth Vader's TIE Advanced X1 Starfighter | | |
| NNO Droid Tri-Fighter | | |
| NNO General Grievous's Wheel Bike | | |
| NNO Obi-Wan's Jedi Starfighter | | |
| NNO Mace Windu's Jedi Starfighter | | |

## 2006-07 Star Wars The Saga Collection Vehicles Exclusives

| | | |
|---|---|---|
| NNO Luke Skywalker's X-Wing (w/Luke Skywalker Dagobah) | 75.00 | 150.00 |
| (Toys R Us Exclusive) | | |
| NNO TIE Fighter (w/Tie Fighter Pilot) | | |
| (Toys R Us Exclusive | | |
| NNO Imperial Shuttle (Royal Guard red/Darth Vader) | 250.00 | 400.00 |
| (Target Exclusive) | | |
| NNO Kit Fisto's Jedi Starfighter | 20.00 | 40.00 |
| (Target Exclusive | | |
| NNO Rogue Two Snowspeeder (w/Zev Senesca) | 50.00 | 100.00 |

## 2006-07 Star Wars The Saga Collection Vintage

| | | |
|---|---|---|
| NNO Biker Scout | 8.00 | 15.00 |
| NNO Greedo | 6.00 | 12.00 |
| NNO Han Solo (w/cape) | 6.00 | 12.00 |
| NNO Luke Skywalker X-Wing Pilot | 10.00 | 20.00 |
| NNO Sand People | 6.00 | 12.00 |

## 2010 Star Wars Saga Legends

| | | |
|---|---|---|
| SL1 Bossk | 12.00 | 25.00 |
| SL2 IG-88 | 10.00 | 20.00 |
| SL3 Zuckuss | 8.00 | 15.00 |
| SL4 Greedo | 8.00 | 15.00 |
| SL5 Jango Fett | 6.00 | 12.00 |
| SL6a Darth Vader | 6.00 | 12.00 |
| SL6b Darth Vader (unmasked) | 8.00 | 15.00 |
| SL7 Princess Leia Boushh | 10.00 | 20.00 |
| SL8 Darth Maul | 6.00 | 12.00 |
| SL9 General Grievous | 10.00 | 20.00 |
| SL10 Clone Trooper | 8.00 | 15.00 |
| SL11 Darth Vader (Anakin Skywalker) | 8.00 | 15.00 |
| SL12 Obi-Wan Kenobi | 6.00 | 12.00 |
| SL13 Yoda | 8.00 | 15.00 |
| SL14 R2-D2 | 8.00 | 15.00 |
| SL15 Shocktrooper | 15.00 | 30.00 |
| SL16 Clone Trooper (Revenge of the Sith) | 8.00 | 15.00 |
| SL17 C-3PO | 8.00 | 15.00 |
| SL18 Chewbacca | 8.00 | 15.00 |
| SL19 501st Legion Trooper | 12.00 | 25.00 |
| SL20 Battle Droid 2-Pack | 6.00 | 12.00 |
| SL21 Luke Skywalker | 8.00 | 15.00 |
| SL22 Han Solo (Hoth) | 8.00 | 15.00 |
| SL23 Snowtrooper | 10.00 | 20.00 |

## 2013 Star Wars Saga Legends

| | | |
|---|---|---|
| SL1 Mace Windu | 6.00 | 12.00 |
| SL2 Clone Trooper | | |
| SL3 Anakin Skywalker | 6.00 | 12.00 |

| | | |
|---|---|---|
| SL4 Obi-Wan Kenobi (ROTS) | 8.00 | 15.00 |
| SL5 Super Battle Droid | 8.00 | 15.00 |
| SL6 R4-P17 | | |
| SL7 Yoda | | |
| SL8 Shock Trooper | | |
| SL9 Boba Fett | | |
| SL10 Captain Rex | | |
| SL11 Stormtrooper | | |
| SL12 Clone Commander Cody | | |
| SL13 Obi-Wan Kenobi (Clone Wars) | | |
| SL14 Luke Skywalker | | |
| SL15 Darth Maul | | |
| SL16 Snowtrooper | | |

## 2013 Star Wars Saga Legends Mission Series

| | | |
|---|---|---|
| MS1 Darth Vader/Seeker Droid (Star Destroyer) | 7.50 | 15.00 |
| MS2 Anakin/501st Legion Trooper (Coruscant) | 6.00 | 12.00 |
| MS3 Battle Droid/Jango Fett (Geonosis) | 10.00 | 20.00 |
| MS4 Battle Droid/212th Battalion Clone Trooper (Utapau) | 15.00 | 30.00 |
| MS5 R2-D2/C-3PO (Tantive IV) | 12.50 | 25.00 |
| MS6 Obi-Wan Kenobi/Darth Maul (Mandalore) | 15.00 | 30.00 |
| MS7 Han Solo/Chewbacca (Death Star) | 10.00 | 20.00 |
| MS8 Obi-Wan Kenobi/General Grievous (Utapau) | 7.50 | 15.00 |
| MS9 Luke Skywalker/Darth Vader (Bespin) | 15.00 | 30.00 |
| MS10 Darth Sidious/Yoda (Senate Duel) | 12.50 | 25.00 |

## 2013 Star Wars Saga Legends Multi-Packs

| | |
|---|---|
| NNO Battle of Geonosis I (Jedi Knights) | |
| (2013 Toys R Us Exclusive) | |
| NNO Battle of Geonosis II (Jedi Knights) | |
| (2013 Toys R Us Exclusive) | |
| NNO The Evolution of Darth Vader | |
| NNO The Rise of Darth Vader | |
| (2013 Target Exclusive) | |

## 2013 Star Wars Saga Legends Vehicles

NNO Obi-Wan's Jedi Starfighter (red)
NNO Obi-Wan's Jedi Starfighter (blue)

## 1996 Star Wars Shadows of the Empire

CHEWBACCA
IN FOURTH HUNTER DISGUISE
VIBRO AXE AND HEAVY BLASTER RIFLE

---

| | | |
|---|---|---|
| 1 Boba Fett vs IG-88/ with comic book | 12.00 | 25.00 |
| 2 Chewbacca/ bounty hunter disguise | 8.00 | 15.00 |
| 3 Darth Vader vs Prince Xizor | 12.00 | 25.00 |
| with comic book | | |
| 4 Dash Rendar | 10.00 | 20.00 |
| 5 Luke Skywalker/ imperial guard | 10.00 | 20.00 |
| 6 Prince Xizor | 6.00 | 12.00 |
| 7 Princess Leia/ boushh disguise | 10.00 | 20.00 |

## 1996 Star Wars Shadows of the Empire European

| | | |
|---|---|---|
| 1 Chewbacca bounty/ hunter disguise | 12.50 | 25.00 |
| 2 Dash Rendar | 10.00 | 20.00 |
| 3 Luke Skywalker/ imperial guard | 15.00 | 30.00 |
| 4 Princess Leia/ boushh disguise | 10.00 | 20.00 |
| 5 Prince Xizor | 15.00 | 30.00 |

## 1996 Star Wars Shadows of the Empire Vehicles

| | | |
|---|---|---|
| 1 Boba Fett's Slave I | 40.00 | 80.00 |
| 2 Dash Rendar's Outrider | 25.00 | 50.00 |
| 3 Swoop with Swoop Trooper | 12.00 | 25.00 |
| 4 Speeder Bike/ with Endor Trooper | 12.00 | 25.00 |

## 2010-12 Star Wars Sideshow

| | | |
|---|---|---|
| NNO Commander Bacara Base Art | 100.00 | 200.00 |
| NNO Tusken Raider | | |
| NNO Tusken Raider (Gaffi weapon) | 120.00 | 250.00 |

## 2010-12 Star Wars Sideshow 12-Inch

| | | |
|---|---|---|
| NNO Commander Praji | 100.00 | 200.00 |
| NNO Grand Admiral Thrawn | | |
| NNO Grand Admiral Thrawn (command chair)/750* | 800.00 | 1200.00 |
| NNO General Obi-Wan Kenobi Clone Wars | 60.00 | 120.00 |
| NNO General Obi-Wan Kenobi Clone Wars (w/Captain Rex hologram)/1500* | 75.00 | 150.00 |

## 2010-12 Star Wars Sideshow 12-Inch Environments

| | | |
|---|---|---|
| NNO Han Solo in Carbonite/2000* | 250.00 | 400.00 |
| NNO Imperial Throne | 175.00 | 350.00 |
| NNO Jabba's Throne | 500.00 | 700.00 |

## 2010-12 Star Wars Sideshow Action Heroes

| | | |
|---|---|---|
| NNO C-3PO | 200.00 | 350.00 |
| NNO R2-D2 | 100.00 | 200.00 |
| NNO TC-14 | | |

## 2010-12 Star Wars Sideshow Heroes of the Rebellion

| | |
|---|---|
| NNO Anakin Skywalker Clone Wars | |
| NNO Anakin Skywalker Clone Wars w/Rotta the Hutt)/750* | |

---

| | | |
|---|---|---|
| NNO Han Solo & Luke Skywalker Stormtroopers | 120.00 | 250.00 |
| (SDCC Exclusive) | | |
| NNO Han Solo Bespin | 60.00 | 120.00 |
| NNO Han Solo Bespin (w/Mynock)/2000* | 50.00 | 100.00 |
| NNO Han Solo Smuggler | 75.00 | 150.00 |
| NNO Han Solo Smuggler Cantina Blaster Pistol/1977* | | |
| NNO Lando Calrissian | | |
| NNO Lando Calrissian (w/Bespin communicator)/750* | | |
| NNO Luke Skywalker Episode IV | | |
| NNO Luke Skywalker Episode IV (hat and googles)/1977* | | |
| NNO Luke Skywalker Rebel Commander | 200.00 | 400.00 |
| NNO Luke Skywalker Rebel Commander (missing hand)/1980* | 120.00 | 250.00 |
| NNO Luke Skywalker Rebel Hero/600* | 30.00 | 75.00 |
| (30th Anniversary Exclusive) | | |
| NNO Padme Amidala Ilum Mission | 30.00 | 75.00 |
| NNO Princess Leia Boushh | 75.00 | 120.00 |
| NNO Princess Leia Boushh (Ubese blaster pistol)/2500* | 60.00 | 120.00 |
| NNO Princess Leia | 50.00 | 100.00 |
| NNO Princess Leia (wrist binders)/1977* | | |

## 2010-12 Star Wars Sideshow Jedi Order

| | | |
|---|---|---|
| NNO Aayla Secura | 120.00 | 200.00 |
| (SDCC Exclusive) | | |
| NNO Anakin Skywalker | 50.00 | 100.00 |
| NNO Anakin Skywalker (w/holographic Sidious)/1750* | 60.00 | 120.00 |
| NNO Ki-Adi-Mundi | 50.00 | 100.00 |
| NNO Kit Fisto | 50.00 | 100.00 |
| NNO Kit Fisto (w/Battle Droid head)/1250* | 60.00 | 120.00 |
| NNO Luke Skywalker Jedi Knight | 50.00 | 100.00 |
| NNO Luke Skywalker Jedi Knight (blaster)/1250* | 60.00 | 120.00 |
| NNO Mace Windu | 50.00 | 100.00 |
| NNO Mace Windu (w/Jango Fett's helmet)/1750* | 60.00 | 120.00 |
| NNO Obi-Wan Kenobi | 50.00 | 100.00 |
| NNO Obi-Wan Kenobi (blaster)/1750* | 60.00 | 120.00 |
| NNO Obi-Wan Kenobi Episode IV | 50.00 | 100.00 |
| NNO Obi-Wan Kenobi Episode IV (holographic Leia)/1977* | 75.00 | 150.00 |
| NNO Obi-Wan Kenobi Jedi Knight | 30.00 | 75.00 |
| NNO Obi-Wan Kenobi Jedi Knight (Kamino dart)/1000* | 50.00 | 100.00 |
| NNO Plo Koon | | |
| NNO Plo Koon (twin-bladed lightsaber gauntlet)/1500* | 60.00 | 120.00 |
| NNO Qui-Gon Jinn | 30.00 | 75.00 |
| NNO Qui-Gon Jinn (poncho)/2000* | 50.00 | 100.00 |

## 2010-12 Star Wars Sideshow Legendary 40-Inch

NNO Darth Maul

## 2010-12 Star Wars Sideshow Lords of the Sith

| | | |
|---|---|---|
| NNO Asajj Ventress | 120.00 | 200.00 |
| NNO Asajj Ventress (eye paint)/2000* | 75.00 | 150.00 |
| NNO Darth Maul | 75.00 | 150.00 |
| NNO Darth Maul (damage saber hilt)/LE | 500.00 | 800.00 |
| NNO Darth Vader Episode IV | | |
| NNO Darth Vader Episode IV (Force choke)/1977* | | |
| NNO Darth Vader Sith Apprentice | | |
| (SDCC Exclusive) | | |
| NNO Emperor Palpatine | | |
| NNO Emperor Palpatine (angry head)/1000* | | |
| NNO Darth Sidious (hologram and mechno-chair)/5000* | 50.00 | 100.00 |
| (SDCC Exclusive) | | |
| NNO Palpatine and Sidious | 120.00 | 250.00 |
| NNO Palpatine and Sidious (statue)/2000* | 100.00 | 200.00 |

## 2010-12 Star Wars Sideshow Militaries

| | | | |
|---|---|---|---|
| NNO | Admiral Piett | 120.00 | 250.00 |
| NNO | Captain Antilles | 100.00 | 200.00 |
| NNO | Clone Trooper Episode II Phase 1 | 100.00 | 200.00 |
| NNO | Coruscant Clone Trooper | | |
| NNO | Coruscant Clone Trooper (41st Elite Corps display base) | 100.00 | 175.00 |
| NNO | Endor Rebel Commando Sergeant | 50.00 | 100.00 |
| NNO | Endor Rebel Infantry | 50.00 | 100.00 |
| NNO | Endor Striker Force Bundle | | |
| NNO | Imperial Shock Trooper | 100.00 | 200.00 |
| NNO | Imperial Shock Trooper (display base)/750* | 100.00 | 200.00 |
| NNO | Nik Sant Endor Rebel Commando Pathfinder | 50.00 | 100.00 |
| NNO | Rebel Fleet Trooper | 120.00 | 200.00 |
| NNO | Sandtrooper | | |
| NNO | Sandtrooper (holding droid piece)/1000* | | |
| NNO | Sandtrooper Corporal | 100.00 | 175.00 |
| NNO | Sandtrooper Squad Leader | | |
| NNO | Stormtrooper | 120.00 | 200.00 |
| NNO | Stormtrooper (stand)/1500* | 100.00 | 200.00 |
| NNO | Stormtrooper Commander | 100.00 | 200.00 |
| NNO | Stormtrooper Commander (base)/1000* | 150.00 | 300.00 |
| NNO | Utapau Clone Trooper | 75.00 | 150.00 |
| NNO | Utapau Clone Trooper (Utapau base)/1500* | 100.00 | 175.00 |

## 2010-12 Star Wars Sideshow Premium Format

| | | | |
|---|---|---|---|
| NNO | Han Solo Carbonite | | |

## 2010-12 Star Wars Sideshow Scum and Villainy

| | | | |
|---|---|---|---|
| NNO | Bib Fortuna | 50.00 | 100.00 |
| NNO | Bib Fortuna (ceremonial staff)/2500* | 60.00 | 120.00 |
| NNO | Boba Fett | 150.00 | 300.00 |
| NNO | Buboicullaar Creature Pack | | |
| NNO | Buboicullaar Creature Pack (scratching womp rat)/1500* | | |
| NNO | Jabba the Hutt | 200.00 | 350.00 |
| NNO | Jabba the Hutt (cup) | 250.00 | 400.00 |
| NNO | Salacious Crumb Creature Pack | | |
| NNO | Salacious Crumb Creature Pack (w/dwarf varactyl) | | |

## 2005 Star Wars Special Edition 500th Figure

1 Darth Vader/ meditation chamber

## 2013 Star Wars Titan Heroes 12-Inch

| | | | |
|---|---|---|---|
| NNO | Anakin Skywalker | 12.50 | 25.00 |
| NNO | Clone Trooper | | |
| NNO | Darth Vader | 12.50 | 25.00 |
| NNO | Luke Skywalker | 7.50 | 15.00 |
| NNO | Obi-Wan Kenobi | | |

## 2005-10 Star Wars Transformers

| | | | |
|---|---|---|---|
| NNO | Anakin Skywalker/Jedi Starfighter | 12.00 | 25.00 |
| NNO | Boba Fett/Slave One | 15.00 | 30.00 |

| | | | |
|---|---|---|---|
| NNO | Clone Pilot/ARC-170 Fighter | 15.00 | 30.00 |
| NNO | Clone Pilot/ARC-170 Fighter (repaint) | 12.00 | 25.00 |
| NNO | Darth Maul/Sith Infiltrator | 10.00 | 20.00 |
| NNO | Darth Vader/Death Star | 30.00 | 60.00 |
| NNO | Darth Vader/Sith Starfighter | 15.00 | 30.00 |
| NNO | Darth Vader/TIE Advanced | 12.00 | 25.00 |
| NNO | Emperor Palpatine/Imperial Shuttle | 10.00 | 20.00 |
| NNO | General Grievous/Wheel Bike | 12.00 | 30.00 |
| NNO | Jango Fett/Slave One | 12.00 | 25.00 |
| NNO | Luke Skywalker/Snowspeeder | 15.00 | 30.00 |
| NNO | Luke Skywalker/X-Wing Fighter | 25.00 | 50.00 |
| NNO | Obi-Wan Kenobi/Jedi Starfighter | 12.00 | 25.00 |

## 2005-10 Star Wars Transformers Crossovers

| | | | |
|---|---|---|---|
| NNO | Anakin Skywalker to Jedi Starfighter | 8.00 | 15.00 |
| NNO | Anakin Skywalker to Y-Wing Bomber | 10.00 | 20.00 |
| NNO | Captain Rex to AT-TE | 12.00 | 25.00 |
| NNO | Darth Vader to TIE Advanced X1 Starfighter | 12.00 | 25.00 |
| NNO | Obi-Wan Kenobi to Jedi Starfighter | 10.00 | 20.00 |
| NNO | Yoda to Republic Attack Shuttle | 12.00 | 25.00 |

## 2005-10 Star Wars Transformers Deluxe

| | | | |
|---|---|---|---|
| NNO | Han Solo and Chewbacca/Millennium Falcon | 30.00 | 75.00 |

## 2002-07 Star Wars Unleashed

| | | | |
|---|---|---|---|
| NNO | Aayla Secura | 15.00 | 30.00 |
| NNO | Anakin Skywalker (2005) | 15.00 | 30.00 |
| NNO | Anakin Skywalker (rage) | 12.00 | 25.00 |
| NNO | Asajj Ventress | 15.00 | 30.00 |
| NNO | Aurra Sing | 15.00 | 30.00 |
| NNO | Boba Fett | 25.00 | 50.00 |
| NNO | Bossk | 15.00 | 30.00 |
| NNO | Chewbacca (2004) | 10.00 | 20.00 |
| NNO | Chewbacca (2006) | 15.00 | 30.00 |
| NNO | Clone Trooper (red) | 15.00 | 30.00 |
| NNO | Clone Trooper (white) | 12.00 | 25.00 |
| NNO | Count Dooku | 15.00 | 30.00 |
| NNO | Darth Maul (fury) | 15.00 | 30.00 |
| NNO | Darth Sidious | 25.00 | 50.00 |
| NNO | Darth Tyranus (dissension) | 6.00 | 12.00 |
| NNO | Darth Vader (2005) | 15.00 | 30.00 |
| NNO | Darth Vader (power) | 12.00 | 25.00 |
| NNO | Darth Vader (redemption) | 30.00 | 75.00 |
| NNO | General Grievous | 15.00 | 30.00 |

| | | | |
|---|---|---|---|
| NNO | General Grievous | 20.00 | 40.00 |
| | (2006 Target Exclusive) | | |
| NNO | Han Solo | 20.00 | 40.00 |
| NNO | Han Solo Stormtrooper | 15.00 | 30.00 |
| NNO | IG-88 | 15.00 | 30.00 |
| NNO | Jango and Boba Fett (intensity) | 15.00 | 30.00 |
| NNO | Luke Skywalker | 20.00 | 40.00 |
| NNO | Luke Skywalker (snowspeeder pilot) | 15.00 | 30.00 |
| NNO | Mace Windu (honor) | 12.00 | 25.00 |
| NNO | Obi-Wan Kenobi (2003) | 15.00 | 30.00 |
| NNO | Obi-Wan Kenobi (2005) | 15.00 | 30.00 |
| NNO | Padme Amidala (courage) | 30.00 | 60.00 |
| NNO | Palpatine vs. Yoda | 20.00 | 40.00 |
| NNO | Princess Leia | 30.00 | 75.00 |
| NNO | Shock Trooper | 15.00 | 30.00 |
| NNO | Stormtrooper | 20.00 | 40.00 |
| NNO | Tusken Raider | 10.00 | 20.00 |
| NNO | Yoda | 15.00 | 30.00 |

## 2006-08 Star Wars Unleashed Battle Packs

| | | | |
|---|---|---|---|
| NNO | Attack on Tantive IV Commanders | | |
| NNO | Attack on Tantive IV Rebel Blockade Troopers | | |
| NNO | Attack on Tantive IV Stormtrooper Boarding Party | | |
| NNO | Battle of Felucia Aayla Secura's 327th Star Corps | | |
| NNO | Battle of Geonosis The Clone Wars | | |
| NNO | Battle of Hoth Evacuation at Echo Base | | |
| NNO | Battle of Hoth Imperial Encounter | | |
| NNO | Battle of Hoth Imperial Invasion | | |
| NNO | Battle of Hoth Imperial Stormtroopers | | |
| NNO | Battle of Hoth Rebel Alliance Troopers | | |
| NNO | Battle of Hoth Snowspeeder Assault | | |
| NNO | Battle of Hoth Snowtrooper Battalion | | |
| NNO | Battle of Hoth Wampa Assault | | |
| NNO | Battle of Kashyyyk Droid Invasion | | |
| NNO | Battle of Kashyyyk and Felucia Heroes | 30.00 | 60.00 |
| NNO | Battle of Kashyyyk Wookiee Warriors | 15.00 | 30.00 |
| NNO | Battle of Kashyyyk Yoda's Elite Clone Troopers | | |
| NNO | Battle of Utapau Battle Droids | | |
| NNO | Battle of Utapau Clone Trooper Attack Battalion | 12.50 | 25.00 |
| NNO | Battle of Utapau Commanders | 12.00 | 25.00 |
| NNO | Battle of Utapau Utapaun Warriors | 10.00 | 20.00 |
| NNO | Clone Wars 501st Legion | | |
| NNO | Clone Wars ARC Troopers | | |
| NNO | Clone Wars Battle of Mon Calamari | | |
| NNO | Clone Wars Clone Pilots and AT-TE Gunners | | |
| NNO | Clone Wars Clone Troopers | | |
| NNO | Clone Wars Jedi Generals | | |
| NNO | Clone Wars Jedi Heroes | | |
| NNO | Clone Wars Jedi vs. Sith | 15.00 | 30.00 |
| NNO | Clone Wars Theed Battle Heroes | | |
| NNO | Clone Wars Vader's Bounty Hunters | | |
| NNO | Death Star Encounters Imperial and Rebel Commanders | | |
| NNO | Death Star Encounters Imperial and Rebel Pilots | | |
| NNO | Death Star Encounters Imperial Troops | | |
| NNO | Order 66 A New Empire | | |
| NNO | Order 66 Jedi Masters | 7.50 | 15.00 |
| NNO | Order 66 Shock Trooper Battalion | | |
| NNO | Order 66 Vader's 501st Legion | | |
| NNO | The Force Unleashed Empire | | |
| NNO | The Force Unleashed Imperial Troopers | | |
| NNO | The Force Unleashed Unleashed Warriors | | |
| NNO | Trouble on Tatooine Cantina Encounter | | |
| NNO | Trouble on Tatooine Jawas and Droids | | |
| NNO | Trouble on Tatooine Sandtrooper Search | | |
| NNO | Trouble on Tatooine The Streets of Mos Eisley | | |
| NNO | Trouble on Tatooine Tusken Raiders | | |

NN0 Ultimate Battles 187th Legion Troopers
NN0 Ultimate Battles Battle Droid Factory
NN0 Ultimate Battles Mygeeto Clone Battalion

## 2007 Star Wars Unleashed Battle Packs Singles

1 Commander Bly
2 Darth Vader
3 Darth Vader (Anakin Skywalker)
4 Han Solo
5 Luke Skywalker
6 Mace Windu
7 Obi-Wan Kenobi
8 Shock Trooper
9 Stormtrooper

## 2005-07 Star Wars Unleashed Tubed Packs

| | | |
|---|---|---|
| NN0 Anakin Skywalker | 25.00 | 50.00 |
| NN0 ARC Heavy Gunner | | |
| NN0 Boba Fett | 25.00 | 50.00 |
| (2006 Target Exclusive) | | |
| NN0 Darth Vader | 12.00 | 25.00 |
| (2005 Best Buy Exclusive) | | |
| NN0 Darth Vader | | |
| (2006 KB Toys Exclusive) | | |
| NN0 Darth Vader | 10.00 | 20.00 |
| (2006 Walmart Exclusive) | | |
| NN0 Luke Skywalker | | |
| (2006 Walmart Exclusive) | | |
| NN0 Obi-Wan Kenobi | 15.00 | 30.00 |
| NN0 Shadow Stormtrooper | 8.00 | 15.00 |

## 2010-19 Star Wars The Vintage Collection

| | | |
|---|---|---|
| VC1a Dengar (age warning on left back) | 20.00 | 40.00 |
| VC1b Dengar (age warning on bottom back) | 30.00 | 60.00 |
| VC2a Leia (Hoth)(age warning on left back) | 25.00 | 50.00 |
| VC2b Leia (Hoth)(age warning on bottom back) | 20.00 | 40.00 |
| VC3a Han Solo (Echo Base)(age warning on left back) | 15.00 | 30.00 |
| VC3b Han Solo (Echo Base)(age warning on bottom back) | 12.50 | 25.00 |
| VC3c Han Solo (Echo Base)(FOIL card) | 15.00 | 30.00 |
| VC4a Luke Skywalker (Bespin)(age warning on left back) | 25.00 | 50.00 |
| VC4b Luke Skywalker (Bespin)(age warning on bottom back) | 50.00 | 100.00 |
| VC4c Luke Skywalker (Bespin)(FOIL card) | 30.00 | 60.00 |
| VC5 AT-AT Commander (age warning on left back) | 20.00 | 40.00 |
| VC5 AT-AT Commander (age warning on bottom back) | 20.00 | 40.00 |
| VC6 See-Threepio (C-3PO)(age warning on left back) | 15.00 | 30.00 |
| VC6 See-Threepio (C-3PO)(age warning on bottom back) | 20.00 | 40.00 |
| VC7 Dack Ralter | 15.00 | 30.00 |
| VC8a Darth Vader (age warning on left back) | 15.00 | 30.00 |
| VC8b Darth Vader (age warning on bottom back) | 12.50 | 25.00 |
| VC8c Darth Vader (Boba Fett sticker/plus shipping and handling) | 20.00 | 40.00 |
| VC8d Darth Vader (barcode #54674 sticker) | 20.00 | 40.00 |
| VC8e Darth Vader (barcode #54674 printed) | 20.00 | 40.00 |
| VC8f Darth Vader (Revenge of the Jedi) | | |
| VC8g Darth Vader (Return of the Jedi) | 25.00 | 50.00 |
| VC8h Darth Vader (Wave 1 ESB figure back) | 15.00 | 30.00 |
| VC8i Darth Vader (FOIL card) | 25.00 | 50.00 |
| VC9aa Boba Fett (age warning on left back) | 30.00 | 60.00 |
| VC9ab Boba Fett (age warning on bottom back) | 20.00 | 40.00 |
| VC9ac Boba Fett (black gun barrel) | 25.00 | 50.00 |
| VC9ad Boba Fett (no warning on card back) | 60.00 | 120.00 |
| VC9ae Boba Fett (FOIL card) | 30.00 | 75.00 |
| VC9ba Boba Fett (Revenge of the Jedi) | 30.00 | 75.00 |
| VC9bb Boba Fett (Return of the Jedi) | 25.00 | 50.00 |

| | | |
|---|---|---|
| VC10a 4-LOM (age warning on left back) | 12.50 | 25.00 |
| VC10b 4-LOM (age warning on bottom back) | 17.50 | 35.00 |
| VC11a (Twin-Pod) Cloud Car Pilot (age warning on left back) | 15.00 | 30.00 |
| VC11b (Twin-Pod) Cloud Car Pilot (age warning on bottom back) | 12.50 | 25.00 |
| VC12 Darth Sidious | 25.00 | 50.00 |
| VC12 Darth Sidious (FOIL card) | 30.00 | 75.00 |
| VC13a Anakin Skywalker (Darth Vader) | | |
| (Boba Fett mailway sticker front) | 30.00 | 60.00 |
| VC13b Anakin Skywalker (Darth Vader) | | |
| (Darth Vader title on front and back) | 20.00 | 40.00 |
| VC13c Anakin Skywalker (Darth Vader) | | |
| (Boba Fett sticker/shipping and handling) | | |
| VC13d Anakin Skywalker (Darth Vader)(barcode #54885) | | |
| VC13e Anakin Skywalker (Darth Vader)(FOIL card) | 30.00 | 60.00 |
| VC14a Sandtrooper (dim photo front) | 10.00 | 20.00 |
| VC14b Sandtrooper (bright photo front) | 10.00 | 20.00 |
| VC14c Sandtrooper (Boba Fett sticker/shipping and handling) | 17.50 | 35.00 |
| VC14d Sandtrooper (barcode #54573 sticker) | 12.50 | 25.00 |
| VC14e Sandtrooper (barcode #54573 printed) | 25.00 | 50.00 |
| VC14e Sandtrooper (FOIL card) | 15.00 | 30.00 |
| VC15a Clone Trooper (dim photo front) | 15.00 | 30.00 |
| VC15b Clone Trooper (bright photo front) | | |
| VC15c Clone Trooper (Boba Fett sticker/shipping and handling) | 12.50 | 25.00 |
| VC15d Clone Trooper (barcode #54888 sticker) | 15.00 | 30.00 |
| VC15e Clone Trooper (barcode #54888 printed) | 12.50 | 25.00 |
| VC15f Clone Trooper (FOIL card) | 20.00 | 40.00 |
| VC16a Obi-Wan Kenobi | 20.00 | 40.00 |
| VC16b Obi-Wan Kenobi (FOIL card) | 30.00 | 60.00 |
| VC17a General Grievous (Boba Fett sticker on front) | 30.00 | 75.00 |
| VC17b General Grievous (barcode #54572 sticker) | 30.00 | 60.00 |
| VC17c General Grievous (barcode #54572 printed) | 30.00 | 60.00 |
| VC17d General Grievous (FOIL card) | 25.00 | 50.00 |
| VC18a MagnaGuard | 25.00 | 50.00 |
| VC18b MagnaGuard (FOIL card) | 30.00 | 75.00 |
| VC19a Clone Commander Cody (dim photo front) | 30.00 | 75.00 |
| VC19b Clone Commander Cody (bright photo front) | 75.00 | 150.00 |
| VC19c Clone Commander Cody (FOIL card) | 30.00 | 60.00 |
| VC20a Yoda | 25.00 | 50.00 |
| VC20b Yoda (Boba Fett sticker front) | 25.00 | 50.00 |
| VC21a Gamorrean Guard (1st Boba Fett rocket sticker) | 25.00 | 50.00 |
| VC21b Gamorrean Guard (2nd Boba Fett rocket sticker) | | |
| VC21c Gamorrean Guard (barcode #54898 sticker) | 30.00 | 60.00 |
| VC21d Gamorrean Guard (barcode #54898 printed) | 20.00 | 40.00 |
| VC21e Gamorrean Guard (Darth Maul sticker front) | 30.00 | 60.00 |
| VC22a Admiral Ackbar (1st Boba Fett rocket sticker) | 12.50 | 25.00 |
| VC22b Admiral Ackbar (2nd Boba Fett rocket sticker) | 15.00 | 30.00 |
| VC22c Admiral Ackbar (barcode #54900) | 15.00 | 30.00 |
| VC22d Admiral Ackbar (barcode #52864) | 15.00 | 30.00 |
| VC23a Luke Skywalker (Jedi Knight Outfit / Endor Captive) | | |
| (1st Boba Fett rocket sticker) | 25.00 | 50.00 |
| VC23b Luke Skywalker (Jedi Knight Outfit / Endor Captive) | | |
| (2nd Boba Fett rocket sticker) | 15.00 | 30.00 |
| VC23c Luke Skywalker (Jedi Knight Outfit / Endor Captive) | | |
| VC23d Luke Skywalker (Jedi Knight Outfit / Endor Captive) | | |
| (barcode #54902) | 20.00 | 40.00 |
| VC23e Luke Skywalker (Jedi Knight Outfit / Endor Captive) | | |
| (portrait back) | | |
| VC23f Luke Skywalker (Jedi Knight Outfit / Endor Captive) | | |
| (no warning on back) | | |
| VC23g Luke Skywalker (Jedi Knight Outfit / Endor Captive) | | |
| (Revenge of the Jedi) | | |
| VC23h Luke Skywalker (Jedi Knight Outfit / Endor Captive) | | |
| (barcode #52867) | 20.00 | 40.00 |
| VC24a Wooof (Klaatu)(1st Boba Fett rocket sticker) | 30.00 | 75.00 |
| VC24b Wooof (Klaatu)(2nd Boba Fett rocket sticker) | 25.00 | 50.00 |
| VC24c Wooof (Klaatu)(barcode #54905) | 20.00 | 40.00 |
| VC24d Wooof (Klaatu)(figures left off backs) | | |

| | | |
|---|---|---|
| VC25a R2-D2 (w/Pop-Up Lightsaber) | | |
| (1st Boba Fett rocket sticker) | 20.00 | 40.00 |
| VC25b R2-D2 (w/Pop-Up Lightsaber) | | |
| (2nd Boba Fett rocket sticker) | 17.50 | 35.00 |
| VC25c R2-D2 (w/Pop-Up Lightsaber) | | |
| (R2-D2 back) | 20.00 | 40.00 |
| VC25d R2-D2 (w/Pop-Up Lightsaber) | | |
| (Revenge of the Jedi) | 17.50 | 35.00 |
| VC25e R2-D2 (w/Pop-Up Lightsaber) | | |
| (no warning on back) | | |
| VC26aa Rebel Commando (1st Boba Fett rocket sticker) | 15.00 | 30.00 |
| VC26ab Rebel Commando (2nd Boba Fett rocket sticker) | 20.00 | 40.00 |
| VC26ac Rebel Commando (barcode #54907) | 15.00 | 30.00 |
| VC26ba Rebel Commando (Version II)(Return of the Jedi logo) | 15.00 | 30.00 |
| VC26bb Rebel Commando (Version II)(Revenge of the Jedi logo) | 30.00 | 75.00 |
| VC27a Wicket (1st Boba Fett rocket sticker) | 25.00 | 50.00 |
| VC27b Wicket (2nd Boba Fett rocket sticker) | 25.00 | 50.00 |
| VC27c Wicket (barcode #54908) | 25.00 | 50.00 |
| VC27d Wicket (barcode #52900) | 25.00 | 50.00 |
| VC27e Wicket (no warning on back) | | |
| VC28a Wedge Antilles (card image on back) | 12.50 | 25.00 |
| VC28b Wedge Antilles (film image on back) | | |
| VC28ca Wedge Antilles (light violet background) | 25.00 | 50.00 |
| VC28cb Wedge Antilles (dark blue to violet background) | | |
| VC29 Kit Fisto | 20.00 | 40.00 |
| VC30 Zam Wesell | 15.00 | 30.00 |
| VC31a Obi-Wan Kenobi (figures left of cardbacks) | 20.00 | 40.00 |
| VC31b Obi-Wan Kenobi (Prototype Boba Fett sticker) | 30.00 | 60.00 |
| VC32a Anakin Skywalker (Peasant Disguise) | 12.50 | 25.00 |
| VC32b Anakin Skywalker (Peasant Disguise)(Boba Fett sticker front) | 12.50 | 25.00 |
| VC33 Padme Amidala (Peasant Disguise) | 17.50 | 35.00 |
| VC34a Jango Fett (figures left of cardbacks) | 25.00 | 50.00 |
| VC34b Jango Fett (no warning on back) | 20.00 | 40.00 |
| VC34c Jango Fett (Prototype Boba Fett sticker) | 25.00 | 50.00 |
| VC35 Mace Windu | 30.00 | 60.00 |
| VC36a Senate Guard (close-up photo front) | 12.50 | 25.00 |
| VC36b Senate Guard (wide photo front) | 10.00 | 20.00 |
| VC37 Super Battle Droid | 15.00 | 30.00 |
| VC38 Clone Trooper (212th Battalion) | 15.00 | 30.00 |
| VC39 Luke Skywalker (Death Star Escape) | 15.00 | 30.00 |
| VC40 R5-D4 | 20.00 | 40.00 |
| VC41a Stormtrooper (barcode #62162 sticker) | 15.00 | 30.00 |
| VC41b Stormtrooper (barcode #62162 printed) | 15.00 | 30.00 |
| VC41c Stormtrooper (warning sticker on front) | | |
| VC41d Stormtrooper (Revenge of the Jedi) | 20.00 | 40.00 |
| VC41e Stormtrooper (Return of the Jedi) | 12.50 | 25.00 |
| VC42 Han Solo (Yavin Ceremony) | 25.00 | 50.00 |
| VC43 Commander Gree (Greatest Hits) | 17.50 | 35.00 |
| VC44 Luke Skywalker (Dagobah Landing) | 50.00 | 100.00 |
| VC45 Clone Trooper (Phase I) | 12.50 | 25.00 |
| VC46 AT-RT Driver | 20.00 | 40.00 |
| VC47 General Lando Calrissian | 15.00 | 30.00 |
| VC48 Weequay (Skiff Master) | 20.00 | 40.00 |
| VC49 Fi-Ek Sirch (Jedi Knight) | 20.00 | 40.00 |
| VC50 Han Solo (Bespin Outfit) | 25.00 | 50.00 |
| VC51 Barriss Offee (Jedi Padawan) | 30.00 | 60.00 |
| VC52 Rebel Fleet Trooper | 30.00 | 60.00 |
| VC53 Bom Vimdin (Cantina Patron) | 12.50 | 25.00 |
| VC54 ARC Trooper Commander (Captain Fordo) | 25.00 | 50.00 |
| VC55 Logray (Ewok Medicine Man) | 12.50 | 25.00 |
| VC56a Kithaba (Skiff Guard)(black headband) | 15.00 | 30.00 |
| VC56b Kithaba (Skiff Guard)(red headband) | 20.00 | 40.00 |
| VC57a Dr. Cornelius Evazan (pink scar) | 20.00 | 40.00 |
| VC57b Dr. Cornelius Evazan (no pink scar) | 12.50 | 25.00 |
| VC58 Aayla Secura | 20.00 | 40.00 |
| VC59 Nom Anor | 12.50 | 25.00 |
| VC60 Clone Trooper (501st Legion) | 25.00 | 50.00 |

**ACTION FIGURES AND FIGURINES**

| | | |
|---|---|---|
| VC61 Prototype Armour Boba Fett | | |
| (2011 Mailaway Exclusive) | 17.50 | 35.00 |
| VC62 Han Solo (In Trench Coat) | 15.00 | 30.00 |
| VC63 B-Wing Pilot (Keyan Farlander) | 12.50 | 25.00 |
| VC64 Princess Leia (Slave Outfit) | 50.00 | 100.00 |
| VC65 TIE Fighter Pilot | 20.00 | 40.00 |
| VC66 Salacious Crumb | | |
| (2011 SDCC Exclusive) | 12.50 | 25.00 |
| VC67 Mouse Droid | | |
| (2011 SDCC Exclusive) | | |
| VC68 Rebel Soldier (Echo Base Battle Gear) | 50.00 | 100.00 |
| VC69 Bastila Shan | 45.00 | 90.00 |
| VC70 Ponda Baba (Walrus Man) | 30.00 | 60.00 |
| VC71 Mawhonic | 12.50 | 25.00 |
| VC72 Naboo Pilot | 12.50 | 25.00 |
| VC73 Aurra Sing | 25.00 | 50.00 |
| VC74 Gungan Warrior | 12.50 | 25.00 |
| VC75 Qui-Gon Jinn | 12.50 | 25.00 |
| VC76 Obi-Wan Kenobi (Jedi Padawan) | 12.50 | 25.00 |
| VC77 Ratts Tyerell & Pit Droid | 12.50 | 25.00 |
| VC78 Battle Droid | 12.50 | 25.00 |
| VC79 Darth Sidious | 15.00 | 30.00 |
| VC80 Anakin Skywalker (Jedi Padawan) | 12.50 | 25.00 |
| VC81 Ben Quadinaros & Pit Droid | 10.00 | 20.00 |
| VC82 Daultay Dofine | 10.00 | 20.00 |
| VC83 Naboo Royal Guard | 10.00 | 20.00 |
| VC84 Queen Amidala (Post-Senate) | 12.50 | 25.00 |
| VC85 Quinlan Vos (Mos Espa) | 10.00 | 20.00 |
| VC86 Darth Maul | 20.00 | 40.00 |
| VC87 Luke Skywalker (Lightsaber Construction) | 20.00 | 40.00 |
| VC88 Princess Leia (Sandstorm Outfit) | 25.00 | 50.00 |
| VC89 Lando Calrissian (Sandstorm Outfit) | 25.00 | 50.00 |
| VC90 Colonel Cracken (Millennium Falcon Crew) | 15.00 | 30.00 |
| VC91 Rebel Pilot (Mon Calamari) | 15.00 | 30.00 |
| VC92 Anakin Skywalker (The Clone Wars) | 20.00 | 40.00 |
| VC93 Darth Vader (A New Hope) | 15.00 | 30.00 |
| VC94 Imperial Navy Commander | 12.50 | 25.00 |
| VC95 Luke Skywalker (Hoth Outfit) | 15.00 | 30.00 |
| VC96 Darth Malgus (The Old Republic) | 20.00 | 40.00 |
| VC97 Clone Pilot Davijaan (Oddball) | 15.00 | 30.00 |
| VC98 Grand Moff Tarkin | 75.00 | 150.00 |
| VC99 Nikto (Vintage) | 25.00 | 50.00 |
| VC100 Galen Marek (The Force Unleashed II) | | |
| VC101 Shae Vizsla | 100.00 | 200.00 |
| VC102 Ahsoka Tano (The Clone Wars) | 125.00 | 250.00 |
| VC103 Obi-Wan Kenobi (The Clone Wars) | 50.00 | 100.00 |
| VC104 Lumat | 30.00 | 60.00 |
| VC105 Emperor's Royal Guard | 30.00 | 75.00 |
| VC106 Nien Nunb | 30.00 | 75.00 |
| VC107 Weequay (Hunter) | 25.00 | 50.00 |
| VC108a Jar Jar Binks | 30.00 | 60.00 |
| VC108b Jar Jar Binks (lost line) | | |
| VC109a Clone Trooper Lieutenant | 20.00 | 40.00 |
| VC109b Clone Trooper Lieutenant (lost line) | | |
| VC110a Shock Trooper | 25.00 | 50.00 |
| VC110b Shock Trooper (lost line) | | |
| VC111a Leia Organa (Bespin) | 25.00 | 50.00 |
| VC111b Leia Organa (Bespin) (lost line) | | |
| VC112a Sandtrooper (with Patrol Droid) | 20.00 | 40.00 |
| VC112b Sandtrooper (with Patrol Droid) (lost line) | | |
| VC113 Republic Trooper | 90.00 | 175.00 |
| VC114 Orrimarko | 20.00 | 40.00 |
| VC115a Darth Vader (Emperor's Wrath) | 30.00 | 75.00 |
| VC115b Darth Vader (Emperor's Wrath) (lost line) | | |
| VC116 Rey (Jakku) | 10.00 | 20.00 |
| VC117 Kylo Ren | 12.50 | 25.00 |
| VC118 First Order Stormtrooper | 10.00 | 20.00 |

| | | |
|---|---|---|
| VC119 Jyn Erso | 7.50 | 15.00 |
| VC120 Rebel Soldier (Hoth) | 7.50 | 15.00 |
| VC121 Supreme Leader Snoke | 6.00 | 12.00 |
| VC122 Rey (Island Journey) | 25.00 | 50.00 |
| VC123 Stormtrooper (Mimban) | 17.50 | 35.00 |
| VC124 Han Solo | 15.00 | 30.00 |
| VC125 Enfys Nest | 15.00 | 30.00 |
| VC126 Imperial Assault Tank Driver | 15.00 | 30.00 |
| VC127 Imperial Death Trooper | 12.50 | 25.00 |
| VC128 Range Trooper | 20.00 | 40.00 |
| VC129 Doctor Aphra | 20.00 | 40.00 |
| VC130 Captain Cassian Andor | 15.00 | 30.00 |
| VC131 Luke Skywalker | 20.00 | 40.00 |
| VC132 Saelt-Marae | 15.00 | 30.00 |
| VC133 Scarif Stormtrooper | 10.00 | 20.00 |
| VC134 Princess Leia Organa (Boushh) | 15.00 | 30.00 |
| VC135 Klaatu (Skiff Guard) | 8.00 | 20.00 |
| VC136 Han Solo (Carbonite) | 20.00 | 40.00 |
| VC137 Ree Yees | 12.50 | 25.00 |
| VC138 Elite Praetorian Guard | 12.50 | 25.00 |
| VC139 Lando Calrissian | 10.00 | 20.00 |
| VC140 Imperial Stormtrooper | 12.50 | 25.00 |
| VC141 Chewbacca | 10.00 | 20.00 |
| VC142 Captain Phasma | 10.00 | 20.00 |
| VC143 Han Solo (Stormtrooper) | 12.50 | 25.00 |
| VC144 Lando Calrissian (Skiff Guard) | 7.50 | 15.00 |
| VC145 41st Elite Corps Clone Trooper | 7.50 | 15.00 |
| VC146 Luke Skywalker (Crait) | 12.50 | 25.00 |
| VC147 Death Star Gunner | 7.50 | 15.00 |
| VC148 Imperial Assault Tank Commander | 7.50 | 15.00 |
| VC149 Artoo-Detoo (R2-D2) | 7.50 | 15.00 |

### 2010-19 Star Wars The Vintage Collection Creatures

| | | |
|---|---|---|
| NNO Luke Skywalker's Tauntaun | 30.00 | 60.00 |
| (Target Exclusive) | | |

### 2010-19 Star Wars The Vintage Collection Exclusives

| | | |
|---|---|---|
| NNO Jocasta Nu | 60.00 | 120.00 |
| (Brian's Toys Exclusive) | | |
| NNO Stewart Storm Trooper/1 | | |
| (2010 Jon Stewart One-of-a-Kind Exclusive) | | |
| VCP3 Boba Fett (rocket-firing) | 30.00 | 75.00 |
| (Mailaway Exclusive) | | |
| VCP12 4-LOM/Zuckuss 2-Pack | 30.00 | 60.00 |
| (TVC Convention Exclusive) | | |

### 2010-19 Star Wars The Vintage Collection Multipacks

| | | |
|---|---|---|
| NNO Android 3-Pack | 30.00 | 75.00 |
| C-3PO, R2-D2, Chewbacca#(Target Exclusive) | | |
| NNO Death Star Scanning Crew | 20.00 | 40.00 |
| (K-Mart Exclusive) | | |
| NNO Doctor Aphra Comic Set | | |
| (2018 SDCC Exclusive) | | |
| NNO Droid 3-Pack | 12.00 | 25.00 |
| R5-D4, Death Star Droid, Power Droid#(Target Exclusive) | | |
| NNO Endor AT-ST Crew 2-Pack | 20.00 | 40.00 |
| (K-Mart Exclusive) | | |
| NNO Ewok Assault Catapult | 25.00 | 50.00 |
| (K-Mart Exclusive) | | |
| NNO Ewok Scouts 2-Pack | 15.00 | 30.00 |

| | | |
|---|---|---|
| (K-Mart Exclusive) | | |
| NNO Hero 3-Pack | 15.00 | 30.00 |
| Luke Skywalker, Ben Kenobi, Han Solo#(Target Exclusive) | | |
| NNO Imperial 3-Pack | 20.00 | 40.00 |
| Imperial Commander, Dengar, AT-AT Driver#(Target Exclusive) | | |
| NNO Imperial Forces 3-Pack | 20.00 | 40.00 |
| Bossk, IG-88, Snowtrooper#(Target Exclusive) | | |
| NNO Imperial Scanning Crew | 20.00 | 40.00 |
| (K-Mart Exclusive) | | |
| NNO Lost Line Carbon Freeze Chamber 7-Figure Set | 120.00 | 200.00 |
| (2012 SDCC Exclusive) | | |
| NNO Rebel 3-Pack | 20.00 | 40.00 |
| 2-1B, Leia (Hoth), Rebel Commander#(Target Exclusive) | | |
| NNO Revenge of the Jedi 14-Figure Death Star Set | 750.00 | 1500.00 |
| (2011 SDCC Exclusive) | | |
| NNO Skiff Guard 3-Pack (Special) | | |
| (Fan Channels Exclusive) | | |
| NNO Special Action Figure Set | 15.00 | 30.00 |
| Han Solo (Hoth), Hoth Rebel Trooper, FX-7#(Target Exclusive) | | |
| NNO Special Action Figure Set | | |
| Jedi Luke, X-Wing Luke, Stormtrooper Luke | | |
| NNO Villain 3-Pack 2012 | 15.00 | 30.00 |
| Sand People, Boba Fett, Snaggletooth#(Target Exclusive) | | |
| NNO Villain 3-Pack | 20.00 | 40.00 |
| Stormtrooper, Darth Vader, Death Star Trooper#(Target Exclusive) | | |

### 2010-19 Star Wars The Vintage Collection Playset

| | | |
|---|---|---|
| NNO Jabba's Palace Adventure Set | | |
| (Walmart Exclusive) | | |

### 2010-19 Star Wars The Vintage Collection Vehicles

| | | |
|---|---|---|
| NNO AT-AP | 30.00 | 75.00 |
| NNO Biggs' Red 3 X-Wing Fighter | 100.00 | 175.00 |
| (Toys R Us Exclusive) | | |
| NNO B-Wing Starfighter | 75.00 | 150.00 |
| (K-Mart Exclusive) | | |
| NNO Imperial AT-AT (ESB) | 250.00 | 400.00 |
| (Toys R Us Exclusive) | | |
| NNO Imperial AT-AT (ROTJ) | 200.00 | 350.00 |
| (Toys R Us Exclusive) | | |
| NNO Imperial Combat Assault Tank | | |
| (2018) | | |
| NNO Imperial TIE Fighter | 50.00 | 100.00 |
| (Target Exclusive) | | |
| NNO Imperial TIE Fighter | | |
| (2018 Walmart Exclusive) | | |
| NNO Jabba's Sail Barge | | |
| (HasLab Exclusive) | | |
| NNO Landspeeder | 60.00 | 120.00 |
| (Target Exclusive) | | |
| NNO Millennium Falcon | 300.00 | 500.00 |
| (Toys R Us Exclusive) | | |
| NNO Obi-Wan Kenobi's Jedi Starfighter | 50.00 | 100.00 |
| NNO Rebel Armored Snowspeeder | 50.00 | 100.00 |
| (Target Exclusive) | | |
| NNO Republic Gunship | 175.00 | 300.00 |
| (Toys R Us Exclusive) | | |
| NNO Scout Walker AT-ST | 60.00 | 120.00 |
| (K-Mart Exclusive) | | |
| NNO Slave I | 120.00 | 200.00 |
| (Amazon Exclusive) | | |
| NNO TIE Interceptor | 50.00 | 100.00 |
| (Amazon Exclusive) | | |
| NNO V-19 Torrent Starfighter | 30.00 | 75.00 |
| NNO Y-Wing Starfighter | 60.00 | 120.00 |
| (Toys R Us Exclusive) | | |

### 2011-12 Funko Blox

| | | | |
|---|---|---|---|
| 23 | Darth Vader | 10.00 | 20.00 |
| 24 | Boba Fett | 8.00 | 15.00 |
| 25 | Stormtrooper | 8.00 | 12.00 |

### 2017-19 Funko Dorbz Star Wars

| | | | |
|---|---|---|---|
| 1 | Luke Skywalker | 7.50 | 15.00 |
| 2 | Princess Leia | 7.50 | 15.00 |
| 3A | Darth Vader | 10.00 | 20.00 |
| | (2017) | | |
| 3B | Darth Vader HOLO CH | 10.00 | 20.00 |
| 4 | Han Solo | 6.00 | 12.00 |
| 5A | Chewbacca | 10.00 | 20.00 |
| 5B | Chewbacca FLK CH | 15.00 | 30.00 |
| 6 | C-3PO | 7.50 | 15.00 |
| 7 | Stormtrooper | 10.00 | 20.00 |
| 8 | Jawa | 7.50 | 15.00 |
| 9 | Luke Skywalker w/Speeder | 20.00 | 40.00 |
| 10 | Tusken Raider w/Bantha | 20.00 | 40.00 |
| 11 | Han Solo | 10.00 | 20.00 |
| | (2018) | | |
| 12A | Chewbacca | 7.50 | 15.00 |
| | (2018) | | |
| 12B | Chewbacca FLK CH | 15.00 | 30.00 |
| 13 | Qi'Ra | 6.00 | 12.00 |
| | (2018) | | |
| 14A | Lando Calrissian | | |
| | (2018) | | |
| 14B | Lando Calrissian White Cape CH | 20.00 | 40.00 |

### 2017-19 Funko Dorbz Star Wars Multi-Pack

COMMON DORBZ

| | | | |
|---|---|---|---|
| NNO | Greedo/Walrus Man/Snaggletooth D23 | 20.00 | 40.00 |

### 2014-16 Funko Fabrikations

| | | | |
|---|---|---|---|
| 2 | Yoda | 8.00 | 15.00 |
| 3 | Boba Fett | 6.00 | 12.00 |
| 4 | Greedo | 6.00 | 12.00 |
| 12 | Darth Vader | 6.00 | 12.00 |
| 13 | Chewbacca | 6.00 | 12.00 |
| 26 | Wicket Warrick | 10.00 | 20.00 |
| 27 | Princess Leia | 12.00 | 25.00 |
| 29 | Stormtrooper | 6.00 | 12.00 |

### 2009 Funko Force Star Wars

COMMON FIGURINE

| | | | |
|---|---|---|---|
| NNO | 501st Clone Trooper/1008* SDCC | 30.00 | 60.00 |
| NNO | Boba Fett | 7.50 | 15.00 |

| | | | |
|---|---|---|---|
| NNO | Chewbacca | 6.00 | 12.00 |
| NNO | Darth Maul | 15.00 | 30.00 |
| NNO | Darth Vader | 7.50 | 15.00 |
| NNO | Emperor Palpatine | 12.50 | 25.00 |
| NNO | Shadow Trooper | 12.50 | 25.00 |
| NNO | Shocktrooper | 20.00 | 40.00 |
| NNO | Stormtrooper | 12.50 | 25.00 |
| NNO | Yoda | 7.50 | 15.00 |

### 2017-18 Funko Galactic Plushies Star Wars

| | | | |
|---|---|---|---|
| NNO | Ahsoka ECCC | 15.00 | 30.00 |
| NNO | Ahsoka SCE | 10.00 | 20.00 |
| NNO | BB-8 | 6.00 | 12.00 |
| NNO | BB-9E | 7.50 | 15.00 |
| NNO | Boba Fett | 5.00 | 10.00 |
| NNO | C-3PO | 5.00 | 10.00 |
| NNO | Chewbacca 12" WG | 7.50 | 15.00 |
| NNO | Chewbacca | 7.50 | 15.00 |
| NNO | Darth Vader | 6.00 | 12.00 |
| NNO | Finn | 6.00 | 12.00 |
| NNO | First Order Executioner | 6.00 | 12.00 |
| NNO | First Order Stormtrooper | 7.50 | 15.00 |
| NNO | Han Solo | 6.00 | 12.00 |
| NNO | Jabba the Hutt & Salacious B. Crumb 2-Pack | | |
| | (2017 Galactic Convention Exclusive) | | |
| NNO | Jabba the Hutt/Salacious Crumb 2Pk SWC | | |
| NNO | Kylo Ren | 5.00 | 10.00 |
| NNO | Luke Skywalker/Wampa 2Pk GS | 7.50 | 15.00 |
| NNO | Luke Skywalker | 6.00 | 12.00 |
| NNO | Maz Kanata | 6.00 | 12.00 |
| NNO | Porg Brown | 12.50 | 25.00 |
| NNO | Porg Gray | 10.00 | 20.00 |
| NNO | Porg (gray/yellow eyes) | 10.00 | 20.00 |
| | (2017) | | |
| NNO | Porg (talking) | 25.00 | 50.00 |
| | (2018) | | |
| NNO | Praetorian Guard WG | 6.00 | 12.00 |
| NNO | Princess Leia | 6.00 | 12.00 |
| NNO | R2-D2 | 7.50 | 15.00 |
| NNO | Resistance BB Unit | 6.00 | 12.00 |
| NNO | Rey | 6.00 | 12.00 |
| NNO | Rey TLJ | 6.00 | 12.00 |
| NNO | Stormtrooper | 7.50 | 15.00 |
| NNO | Supreme Leader Snoke WG | 6.00 | 12.00 |
| NNO | Tusken Raider/Bantha 2Pk TAR | 6.00 | 12.00 |
| NNO | Wampa SB | 5.00 | 10.00 |
| NNO | Wicket | 6.00 | 12.00 |
| NNO | Yoda SB | 5.00 | 10.00 |
| NNO | Yoda | 7.50 | 15.00 |

### 2015-18 Funko Hikari Star Wars

| | | | |
|---|---|---|---|
| NNO | Boba Fett Clear Glitter/750* NYCC | 25.00 | 50.00 |
| NNO | Boba Fett Glitter/1200* | 20.00 | 40.00 |
| NNO | Boba Fett Infrared/1000* SDCC | 25.00 | 50.00 |
| NNO | Boba Fett Infrared/1000* SCE | 25.00 | 50.00 |
| NNO | Boba Fett Midnight/1000* SWC | 60.00 | 120.00 |
| NNO | Boba Fett Prism/750* | 30.00 | 60.00 |
| NNO | Boba Fett Proto/250* FS | 30.00 | 75.00 |
| NNO | Boba Fett/1500* | 20.00 | 40.00 |
| NNO | Bossk MET/1000* | 25.00 | 50.00 |
| NNO | Bossk Planet X/600* | 20.00 | 40.00 |
| NNO | Bossk Prism/500* EE | 25.00 | 50.00 |
| NNO | Bossk Rainbow/550* SLCC | 30.00 | 75.00 |
| NNO | Bossk Starfield/500* NYCC | 30.00 | 75.00 |

| | | | |
|---|---|---|---|
| NNO | Bossk/1000* | 25.00 | 50.00 |
| NNO | C-3PO Clear Glitter/750* SLCC | 30.00 | 60.00 |
| NNO | C-3PO Dirty Penny/500* TT | 30.00 | 75.00 |
| NNO | C-3PO Red/750* SLCC | 25.00 | 50.00 |
| NNO | C-3PO Rusty/500* Gemini | 25.00 | 50.00 |
| NNO | C-3PO/1500* | 20.00 | 40.00 |
| NNO | Captain Phasma Alloy/250* | 30.00 | 60.00 |
| NNO | Captain Phasma Blue Steel/400* | 30.00 | 75.00 |
| NNO | Captain Phasma Classic/500* | 25.00 | 50.00 |
| NNO | Captain Phasma Cold Steel/250* | 30.00 | 60.00 |
| NNO | Captain Phasma Meltdown/100* HT | 100.00 | 175.00 |
| NNO | Clone Trooper Dirty Penny/250* EE | 25.00 | 50.00 |
| NNO | Clone Trooper Rusty White/250* GS | 20.00 | 40.00 |
| NNO | Clone Trooper 442 Siege Glitter/100* | 60.00 | 120.00 |
| NNO | Clone Trooper 442 Siege/900* | 20.00 | 40.00 |
| NNO | Clone Trooper 501st Glitter/250* | 30.00 | 75.00 |
| NNO | Clone Trooper 501st/1500* SDCC | 20.00 | 40.00 |
| NNO | Clone Trooper Starfield/1000* SWC | 25.00 | 50.00 |
| NNO | Clone Trooper Utapau Glitter/100* EE | 50.00 | 100.00 |
| NNO | Clone Trooper Utapau/600* EE | 25.00 | 50.00 |
| NNO | Clone Trooper/1500* | 15.00 | 30.00 |
| NNO | Darth Vader Holographic GITD/300* Gemini | 30.00 | 75.00 |
| NNO | Darth Vader Holographic/750* | 25.00 | 50.00 |
| NNO | Darth Vader Infrared/500* EE | 30.00 | 60.00 |
| NNO | Darth Vader Lightning/1500* | 20.00 | 40.00 |
| NNO | Darth Vader Matte Back/1200* SDCC | 25.00 | 50.00 |
| NNO | Darth Vader Starfield/750*Gemini | 30.00 | 75.00 |
| NNO | Darth Vader/1500* | 20.00 | 40.00 |
| NNO | E-3PO/500* | 20.00 | 40.00 |
| NNO | FO Snowtrooper Ice Storm/500* | 20.00 | 40.00 |
| NNO | FO Snowtrooper Iron Age/250* | 25.00 | 50.00 |
| NNO | Stormtrooper Inferno/250* | 30.00 | 75.00 |
| NNO | FO Stormtrooper Kiln/400* | 30.00 | 75.00 |
| NNO | FO Stormtrooper Nocturne/400* | 30.00 | 60.00 |
| NNO | FO Stormtrooper Phantasm/250* | 30.00 | 60.00 |
| NNO | FO Stormtrooper/500* | 15.00 | 30.00 |
| NNO | Greedo Mystic Powers/750* | 30.00 | 75.00 |
| NNO | Greedo Platinum/600* NYCC | 25.00 | 50.00 |
| NNO | Greedo Sublime/750* | 15.00 | 30.00 |
| NNO | Greedo Verdigris/500* SWC | 30.00 | 60.00 |
| NNO | Greedo Original/2000* | 20.00 | 40.00 |
| NNO | K-3PO/750* | 20.00 | 40.00 |
| NNO | Kylo Ren Alchemy/300* | 25.00 | 50.00 |
| NNO | Kylo Ren Dark Side/500* | 20.00 | 40.00 |
| NNO | Kylo Ren Live Wire/250* | 60.00 | 120.00 |
| NNO | Kylo Ren Onyx/150* HT | 75.00 | 150.00 |
| NNO | Kylo Ren Rage/250* HT | 60.00 | 120.00 |
| NNO | Shadow Trooper/1000* | 20.00 | 40.00 |
| NNO | Snowtrooper Celsius/400* | 30.00 | 60.00 |
| NNO | Snowtrooper Galaxy/250* | 20.00 | 40.00 |
| NNO | Stormtrooper Blue MET/1000* | 20.00 | 40.00 |
| NNO | Stormtrooper Cosmic/2000* SDCC LC | 15.00 | 30.00 |
| NNO | Stormtrooper Green/100* ECCC | 75.00 | 150.00 |
| NNO | Stormtrooper Ice/750* SWC | 60.00 | 120.00 |
| NNO | Stormtrooper Prism/750* TT | 30.00 | 75.00 |
| NNO | Stormtrooper Relic/500* | 20.00 | 40.00 |
| NNO | Stormtrooper Rusty Silver/750* | 25.00 | 50.00 |
| NNO | Stormtrooper Starfield/750* | 20.00 | 40.00 |
| NNO | Stormtrooper/1500* | 30.00 | 60.00 |
| NNO | Wampa Bloody/750* | 20.00 | 40.00 |
| NNO | Wampa Glitter/750* | 20.00 | 40.00 |
| NNO | Wampa Grey Skull/250* EE | 20.00 | 40.00 |
| NNO | Wampa Ice/500* Gemini | 30.00 | 60.00 |

## 2017-18 Funko Hikari XS Star Wars

| | | |
|---|---|---|
| NNO Chopper (black) | 7.50 | 15.00 |
| (2017 Smuggler's Bounty Exclusive) | | |
| NNO Chopper (clear) | 4.00 | 8.00 |
| (2017 Smuggler's Bounty Exclusive) | | |
| NNO Chopper (gold) | 5.00 | 10.00 |
| (2017 Smuggler's Bounty Exclusive) | | |
| NNO Chopper (orange) | 4.00 | 8.00 |
| (2017 Smuggler's Bounty Exclusive) | | |
| NNO Chopper (red) | 4.00 | 8.00 |
| (2017 Smuggler's Bounty Exclusive) | | |
| NNO Darth Vader (black) | 6.00 | 12.00 |
| (2017 Smuggler's Bounty Exclusive) | | |
| NNO Darth Vader (blue) | 4.00 | 8.00 |
| (2017 Smuggler's Bounty Exclusive) | | |
| NNO Darth Vader (gold) | 15.00 | 30.00 |
| (2017 Smuggler's Bounty Exclusive) | | |
| NNO Darth Vader (red) | 5.00 | 10.00 |
| (2017 Smuggler's Bounty Exclusive) | | |
| NNO Darth Vader (silver) | 4.00 | 8.00 |
| (2017 Smuggler's Bounty Exclusive) | | |
| NNO Greedo 2-Pack (blue & clear) | 10.00 | 20.00 |
| (2017 Galactic Convention Exclusive) | | |
| NNO Greedo 2-Pack (blue & clear) | 10.00 | 20.00 |
| (2017 Star Wars Celebration Exclusive) | | |
| NNO Greedo 2-Pack (green & gold) | 6.00 | 12.00 |
| (2017 Galactic Convention Exclusive) | | |
| NNO Greedo 2-Pack (green & gold) | 12.50 | 25.00 |
| (2017 Star Wars Celebration Exclusive) | | |

## 2005-18 Funko Mini Wacky Wobblers Star Wars

| | | |
|---|---|---|
| NNO C-3PO | 12.50 | 25.00 |
| NNO C-3PO/R2-D2 Ulta Mini | 7.50 | 15.00 |
| NNO Chewbacca | 20.00 | 40.00 |
| NNO Darth Vader | 10.00 | 20.00 |
| NNO Darth Vader/Stormtrooper | 7.50 | 15.00 |
| NNO Darth Vader Holiday | 7.50 | 15.00 |
| NNO Jawa Holiday | 12.50 | 25.00 |
| NNO R2-D2 | 7.50 | 15.00 |
| NNO R2-D2 Holiday | 7.50 | 15.00 |
| NNO Star Wars 5Pk | 15.00 | 30.00 |
| NNO Stormtrooper | 7.50 | 15.00 |
| NNO Yoda | 5.00 | 10.00 |
| NNO Yoda & Chewbacca (ultra mini) | 7.50 | 15.00 |
| NNO Yoda (holiday) | 6.00 | 12.00 |

## 2012 Funko Mini Wacky Wobblers Star Wars Monster Mash-Ups

| | | |
|---|---|---|
| NNO Chewbacca | 7.50 | 15.00 |
| NNO Darth Vader | 7.50 | 15.00 |
| NNO Jawa | 12.50 | 25.00 |
| NNO Stormtrooper | 10.00 | 20.00 |
| NNO Tusken Raider | 7.50 | 15.00 |
| NNO Yoda | 7.50 | 15.00 |

## 2017 Funko MyMoji Star Wars

| | | |
|---|---|---|
| COMMON MYMOJI | 2.50 | 5.00 |
| NNO Chewbacca (laughing) | 4.00 | 8.00 |
| NNO Chewbacca (smiling) | 4.00 | 8.00 |
| NNO Chewbacca (surprised) | 2.50 | 5.00 |
| NNO Darth Vader (angry) | 4.00 | 8.00 |
| NNO Darth Vader (sad) | 2.50 | 5.00 |
| NNO Darth Vader (staring) | 2.50 | 5.00 |
| NNO Jabba (bored) | 2.50 | 5.00 |
| NNO Jabba (closed eyes) | 4.00 | 8.00 |

| | | |
|---|---|---|
| NNO Jabba (sad) | 4.00 | 8.00 |
| NNO Luke Skywalker (big smile) | 2.50 | 5.00 |
| NNO Luke Skywalker (closed eyes) | 2.50 | 5.00 |
| NNO Luke Skywalker (sad) | 2.50 | 5.00 |
| NNO Princess Leia (big smile) | 3.00 | 6.00 |
| NNO Princess Leia (closed eyes) | 2.50 | 5.00 |
| NNO Princess Leia (sad) | 2.50 | 5.00 |
| NNO Wampa (angry) | 2.50 | 5.00 |
| NNO Wampa (bored) | 2.50 | 5.00 |
| NNO Wampa (sad) | 2.50 | 5.00 |
| NNO Wicket (laughing) | 2.50 | 5.00 |
| NNO Wicket (sad) | 2.50 | 5.00 |
| NNO Wicket (smiling) | 2.50 | 5.00 |
| NNO Yoda (closed eyes) | 2.50 | 5.00 |
| NNO Yoda (curious) | 2.50 | 5.00 |
| NNO Yoda (smiling) | 4.00 | 8.00 |

## 2018 Funko Mystery Mini Plushies Smuggler's Bounty

| | | |
|---|---|---|
| NNO Ewok | | |

## 2018 Funko Mystery Mini Plushies Keychains Solo A Star Wars Story

| | | |
|---|---|---|
| NNO Chewbacca | 4.00 | 8.00 |
| NNO Han Solo | 4.00 | 8.00 |
| NNO Han Solo (goggles) | 5.00 | 10.00 |
| NNO L3-37 | 7.50 | 15.00 |
| NNO Lando Calrissian | 4.00 | 8.00 |
| NNO Qi'Ra | 5.00 | 10.00 |
| NNO Range Trooper | 4.00 | 8.00 |
| NNO Tobias Beckett | 4.00 | 8.00 |

## 2018 Funko Mystery Mini Plushies Keychains Star Wars Classic

| | | |
|---|---|---|
| NNO Boba Fett | 6.00 | 12.00 |
| NNO C-3PO | 6.00 | 12.00 |
| NNO Darth Vader | 6.00 | 12.00 |
| NNO Ewok | 7.50 | 15.00 |
| NNO Greedo | 12.50 | 25.00 |
| NNO Jawa | 12.50 | 25.00 |
| NNO Princess Leia | 6.00 | 12.00 |
| NNO Yoda | 7.50 | 15.00 |

## 2018 Funko Mystery Mini Plushies Keychains Star Wars The Last Jedi

| | | |
|---|---|---|
| NNO BB-8 | | |
| NNO BB-9E | | |
| NNO Chewbacca | 6.00 | 12.00 |
| NNO Finn | | |
| NNO Kylo Ren | | |
| NNO Porg | | |
| NNO Rey | | |
| NNO Stormtrooper | | |

## 2018 Funko Mystery Minis Solo A Star Wars Story

| | | |
|---|---|---|
| COMMON MYSTERY MINI | 3.00 | 6.00 |
| NNO Chewbacca | 4.00 | 8.00 |
| NNO Chewbacca (prisoner) | 4.00 | 8.00 |
| (Target Exclusive) | | |
| NNO Dryden Voss | 7.50 | 15.00 |
| NNO Enfys Nest | 3.00 | 6.00 |
| NNO Han Solo | 4.00 | 8.00 |
| NNO Han Solo (pilot) | 125.00 | 250.00 |

| | | |
|---|---|---|
| (Target Exclusive) | | |
| NNO Han Solo (prisoner) | 7.50 | 15.00 |
| (Target Exclusive) | | |
| NNO L3-37 | 15.00 | 30.00 |
| NNO Lando Calrissian | 4.00 | 8.00 |
| NNO Patrol Trooper | 6.00 | 12.00 |
| NNO Qi'Ra | 3.00 | 6.00 |
| NNO Qi'Ra (dress) | 7.50 | 15.00 |
| (Target Exclusive) | | |
| NNO Range Trooper | 10.00 | 20.00 |
| (Target Exclusive) | | |
| NNO Rio Durant | 5.00 | 10.00 |
| NNO Tobias Beckett | 4.00 | 8.00 |
| NNO Tobias Beckett (w/rifle) | 15.00 | 30.00 |
| (Target Exclusive) | | |
| NNO Val | 15.00 | 30.00 |
| NNO Weazel | 5.00 | 10.00 |

## 2017 Funko Mystery Minis Star Wars

| | | |
|---|---|---|
| COMPLETE SET (24) | | |
| NNO C-3PO | 3.00 | 6.00 |
| NNO Chewbacca | 4.00 | 8.00 |
| NNO Chewbacca (w/bowcaster) | 10.00 | 20.00 |
| (Walmart Exclusive) | | |
| NNO Darth Vader (Force Choke) | 75.00 | 150.00 |
| (Hot Topic Exclusive) | | |
| NNO Darth Vader (Force Lift) | 15.00 | 30.00 |
| NNO Darth Vader (lightsaber) | 25.00 | 50.00 |
| (GameStop Exclusive) | | |
| NNO Grand Moff Tarkin | 4.00 | 8.00 |
| NNO Greedo | 4.00 | 8.00 |
| NNO Greedo (pistol up) | 20.00 | 40.00 |
| (Hot Topic Exclusive) | | |
| NNO Hammerhead | 4.00 | 8.00 |
| NNO Han Solo | 6.00 | 12.00 |
| NNO Han Solo (stormtrooper) | 12.00 | 25.00 |
| (GameStop Exclusive) | | |
| NNO Jawa | 6.00 | 12.00 |
| NNO Luke Skywalker | 10.00 | 20.00 |
| NNO Luke Skywalker (stormtrooper) | 15.00 | 30.00 |
| (GameStop Exclusive) | | |
| NNO Obi Wan Kenobi | 4.00 | 8.00 |
| NNO Obi Wan Kenobi (Force Ghost) | 30.00 | 75.00 |
| (Walmart Exclusive) | | |
| NNO Ponda Baba | 3.00 | 6.00 |
| NNO Princess Leia | 2.50 | 5.00 |
| NNO Shadow Trooper | 5.00 | 10.00 |
| NNO Snaggletooth | 2.50 | 5.00 |
| NNO Stormtrooper | 4.00 | 8.00 |
| NNO TIE Pilot | 30.00 | 75.00 |
| (Hot Topic Exclusive) | | |
| NNO Tusken Raider | 20.00 | 40.00 |
| (Walmart Exclusive) | | |

## 2018 Funko Mystery Minis Star Wars Empire Strikes Back

| | | |
|---|---|---|
| COMMON MYSTERY MINI | 3.00 | 6.00 |
| NNO 4-LOM | 25.00 | 50.00 |
| (GameStop Exclusive) | | |
| NNO Boba Fett | 30.00 | 60.00 |
| NNO Bossk | 75.00 | 150.00 |
| (Hot Topic Exclusive) | | |
| NNO Chewbacca | 3.00 | 6.00 |
| NNO Darth Vader | 3.00 | 6.00 |
| NNO Dengar | 30.00 | 75.00 |
| NNO Han Solo (Bespin) | 3.00 | 6.00 |
| NNO Han Solo (Hoth) | 12.50 | 25.00 |

(Hot Topic Exclusive)

| | | |
|---|---|---|
| NNO IG-88 | 12.50 | 25.00 |
| NNO Imperial AT-AT Driver | 15.00 | 30.00 |
| (GameStop Exclusive) | | |
| NNO Lando Calrissian | 6.00 | 12.00 |
| NNO Lobot | 25.00 | 50.00 |
| (Target Exclusive) | | |
| NNO Luke Skywalker (Bespin) | 12.50 | 25.00 |
| (Target Exclusive) | | |
| NNO Luke Skywalker (Hoth) | 15.00 | 30.00 |
| NNO Princess Leia (Bespin) | 7.50 | 15.00 |
| (GameStop Exclusive) | | |
| NNO Princess Leia (Hoth) | 7.50 | 15.00 |
| NNO R2-D2 | 3.00 | 6.00 |
| NNO Snowtrooper | 20.00 | 40.00 |
| (Hot Topic Exclusive) | | |
| NNO Wampa | 7.50 | 15.00 |
| NNO Yoda | 4.00 | 8.00 |
| NNO Zuckuss | 60.00 | 120.00 |
| (Target Exclusive) | | |

## 2017 Funko Mystery Minis Star Wars The Last Jedi

COMPLETE SET (24)

| | | |
|---|---|---|
| NNO BB-8 | 2.50 | 5.00 |
| NNO BB-9E | 6.00 | 12.00 |
| NNO C'ai Threnalli | 50.00 | 100.00 |
| (Walgreens Exclusive) | | |
| NNO Captain Phasma | 4.00 | 8.00 |
| NNO Chewbacca (w/porg) | 4.00 | 8.00 |
| NNO DJ | 4.00 | 8.00 |
| NNO Finn | 7.50 | 15.00 |
| NNO Finn (First Order uniform) | 3.00 | 6.00 |
| NNO First Order Executioner | 7.50 | 15.00 |
| (GameStop Exclusive) | | |
| NNO Kylo Ren | 25.00 | 50.00 |
| NNO Kylo Ren (unmasked) | 60.00 | 120.00 |
| (Walmart Exclusive) | | |
| NNO Poe Dameron | 3.00 | 6.00 |
| NNO Porg | 12.00 | 25.00 |
| NNO Porg (wings open) | 15.00 | 30.00 |
| (GameStop Exclusive) | | |
| NNO Praetorian Guard | 5.00 | 10.00 |
| NNO Praetorian Guard (w/staff) | 6.00 | 12.00 |
| (Walgreens Exclusive) | | |
| NNO Praetorian Guard (w/whip) | 12.50 | 25.00 |
| (Walmart Exclusive) | | |
| NNO Princess Leia | 6.00 | 12.00 |
| NNO Resistance BB Unit | 6.00 | 12.00 |
| NNO Rey | 4.00 | 8.00 |
| NNO Rey (cloaked) | 8.00 | 15.00 |
| (GameStop Exclusive) | | |
| NNO Rose | 3.00 | 6.00 |
| NNO Supreme Leader Snoke | 3.00 | 6.00 |
| NNO Supreme Leader Snoke (holographic) | 10.00 | 20.00 |
| (Walgreens Exclusive) | | |

## 2017-19 Funko Mystery Minis Star Wars Smuggler's Bounty

| | | |
|---|---|---|
| NNO Darth Maul | 6.00 | 12.00 |
| NNO Darth Vader (hands on hips) | | |
| (2019) | | |
| NNO Emperor Palpatine | 10.00 | 20.00 |
| NNO Lando Calrissian | 7.50 | 15.00 |
| NNO Luke Skywalker TFA | 7.50 | 15.00 |
| NNO Luke Skywalker TLJ | 10.00 | 20.00 |

## 2018-19 Funko Pop PEZ Star Wars

| | | |
|---|---|---|
| NNO Boba Fett Prototype | 10.00 | 20.00 |
| NNO Boba Fett | 6.00 | 12.00 |
| NNO Bossk | 7.50 | 15.00 |
| NNO Gamorrean Guard SWC | 10.00 | 20.00 |
| NNO Greedo | 6.00 | 12.00 |
| NNO Jabba the Hutt SWC | 7.50 | 15.00 |
| NNO Jawa | 7.50 | 15.00 |
| NNO Ponda Boba Blue Stem CH | 15.00 | 30.00 |
| NNO Ponda Boba | 4.00 | 8.00 |
| NNO Salacious Crumb SWC | 10.00 | 20.00 |
| NNO Snaggletooth Blue Stem CH | 15.00 | 30.00 |
| NNO Snaggletooth | 4.00 | 8.00 |
| NNO Tusken Raider | 5.00 | 10.00 |

## 2015-19 Funko Pop Vinyl Conan O'Brien

| | | |
|---|---|---|
| 6 Stormtrooper Conan COCO SDCC | 50.00 | 100.00 |
| 7 Ghostbuster Conan COCO SDCC | 45.00 | 90.00 |
| 10 Jedi Conan COCO SDCC | 45.00 | 90.00 |
| 14 Rebel Pilot Conan COCO SDCC | 30.00 | 60.00 |

## 2011-19 Funko Pop Vinyl Freddy Funko

| | | |
|---|---|---|
| A9A Clone Trooper/48* SDCC | 800.00 | 1300.00 |
| A9B Cl.Trooper Blue Hair/12* SDCC | 1800.00 | 2200.00 |
| 28A Boba Fett/196* SDCC | 1000.00 | 1500.00 |
| 28B B.Fett Red Hair/24* SDCC | 3000.00 | 3500.00 |
| 46 Kylo Ren/400* FD | 250.00 | 450.00 |
| SE Poe Dameron/200* FD | 250.00 | 400.00 |
| SE Yoda/450* FD | 450.00 | 650.00 |
| SE C-3PO/520* FD | | |

## 2017-19 Funko Pop Vinyl MLB

| | | |
|---|---|---|
| SE Kevin Kiermaier Han Solo RAYS | 12.50 | 25.00 |

## 2011-19 Funko Pop Vinyl Star Wars

| | | |
|---|---|---|
| COMMON FUNKO POP | 5.00 | 10.00 |
| 1A Darth Vader | 5.00 | 10.00 |
| 1B Darth Vader MET HT | 10.00 | 20.00 |
| 2A Yoda | 6.00 | 12.00 |
| 2B Yoda Spirit WG ERR | 6.00 | 12.00 |
| 2C Yoda Spirit WG COR | 6.00 | 12.00 |
| 2C Yoda Spirit WG COR Sticker | 6.00 | 12.00 |
| 3A Han Solo V | 75.00 | 150.00 |
| 3B Han Solo VAULT | 10.00 | 20.00 |
| 4 Princess Leia | 6.00 | 12.00 |
| 5A Stormtrooper | 6.00 | 12.00 |
| 5B Stormtrooper Red TAR | 7.50 | 15.00 |
| 6A Chewbacca | 5.00 | 10.00 |
| 6B Chewbacca FLK/480* SDCC | 800.00 | 1200.00 |
| 6C Chewbacca Hoth GS | 7.50 | 15.00 |
| 7A Greedo V | 125.00 | 250.00 |
| 7B Greedo VAULT | 6.00 | 12.00 |
| 8A Boba Fett | 7.50 | 15.00 |
| 8B Boba Fett Prototype WG ERR | 7.50 | 15.00 |
| 8C Boba Fett Prototype WG COR | 7.50 | 15.00 |
| 8D Boba Fett Prototype WG COR Sticker | 7.50 | 15.00 |
| 9 Darth Maul | 6.00 | 12.00 |
| 10A Obi-Wan Kenobi V | 60.00 | 120.00 |
| 10B Obi-Wan VAULT | 12.50 | 25.00 |
| 11A Luke Skywalker Jedi Knight V | 25.00 | 50.00 |
| 11B Jedi Luke Skywalker VAULT | 15.00 | 30.00 |
| 12A Gamorrean Guard V | 50.00 | 100.00 |
| 12B Gamorrean Guard VAULT | 7.50 | 15.00 |
| 13A C-3PO | 5.00 | 10.00 |
| 13B C-3PO Gold Chrome SDCC | 20.00 | 40.00 |
| 13C C-3PO Gold Chrome SCE | 12.50 | 25.00 |
| 14 Shadow Trooper/480* SDCC | 1000.00 | 1500.00 |
| 15 H.Solo Stormtrooper/1000* ECCC | 300.00 | 500.00 |
| 16 L.Skywalker Stormtrooper/1000* ECCC | 300.00 | 500.00 |
| 17 Luke Skywalker X-Wing | 7.50 | 15.00 |
| 18A Slave Leia V | 25.00 | 50.00 |
| 18B Slave Leia VAULT | 12.50 | 25.00 |
| 19A Tusken Raider V | 20.00 | 40.00 |
| 19B Tusken Raider VAULT | 7.50 | 15.00 |
| 20A Jawa V | 25.00 | 50.00 |
| 20B Jawa VAULT | 7.50 | 15.00 |
| 21A Clone Trooper V | 30.00 | 75.00 |
| 21B Clone Trooper VAULT | 7.50 | 15.00 |
| 22 Jabba the Hutt | 6.00 | 12.00 |
| 23 Darth Maul HOLO/480* SDCC | 2500.00 | 3000.00 |
| 24 Biggs Darklighter/480* SDCC | 500.00 | 750.00 |
| 25 501st Clone Trooper/480* SDCC | 400.00 | 600.00 |
| 26A Wicket the Ewok | 5.00 | 10.00 |
| 26B Wicket the Ewok FLK FT | 60.00 | 120.00 |
| 27 Jar Jar Binks V | 75.00 | 100.00 |
| 28 Admiral Ackbar V | 20.00 | 40.00 |
| 29 Queen Amidala V | 75.00 | 150.00 |
| 30 Lando Calrissian V | 30.00 | 75.00 |
| 31 R2-D2 | 5.00 | 10.00 |
| 32 Boba Fett Droids/480* SDCC | 500.00 | 750.00 |
| 33A Darth Vader HOLO GITD DCC | 250.00 | 400.00 |
| 33B Darth Vader HOLO GITD PE | 250.00 | 400.00 |
| 34 Luke Skywalker Hoth V | 7.50 | 15.00 |
| 35 Bossk V | 30.00 | 60.00 |
| 36 The Emperor V | 25.00 | 50.00 |
| 37 Hammerhead V | 7.50 | 15.00 |
| 38 Biker Scout V | 12.50 | 25.00 |
| 39A 6" Wampa V | 10.00 | 20.00 |
| 39B Wampa 6" FLK HT | 10.00 | 20.00 |
| 40 Emperor HOLO TW | 25.00 | 50.00 |
| 41A R2-Q5 GCE | 15.00 | 30.00 |
| 41B R2-Q5 SWC | 50.00 | 100.00 |
| 42A Shock Trooper GCE | 50.00 | 100.00 |
| 42B Shock Trooper SWC | 60.00 | 120.00 |
| 43A Unmasked Vader GCE | 7.50 | 15.00 |
| 43B Unmasked Vader SWC | 50.00 | 100.00 |
| 44A R2-R9 GCE | 15.00 | 30.00 |
| 44B R2-R9 SWC | 20.00 | 40.00 |
| 45 R2-B1 GS | 6.00 | 12.00 |
| 46A E-3PO GCE | 7.50 | 15.00 |
| 46B E-3PO SWC | 7.50 | 15.00 |
| 47 Han Solo Hoth GS | 6.00 | 12.00 |
| 48 Figrin D'an GS | 6.00 | 12.00 |
| 49 Luke Skywalker Tatooine | 7.50 | 15.00 |
| 50 Princess Leia Boussh | 6.00 | 12.00 |
| 51A TIE Fighter Pilot | 6.00 | 12.00 |
| 51B TIE Pilot MET | 7.50 | 15.00 |
| 52 Nalan Cheel | 5.00 | 10.00 |
| 53 Bib Fortuna | 6.00 | 12.00 |
| 54A Leia Boussh Unmasked SDCC | 300.00 | 450.00 |
| 54B Leia Boussh Unmasked SCE | 300.00 | 450.00 |

| No. | Name | Low | High | No. | Name | Low | High | No. | Name | Low | High |
|---|---|---|---|---|---|---|---|---|---|---|---|
| 55 | K-3PO B&N | 6.00 | 12.00 | 108 | Maz Kanata | 6.00 | 12.00 | 157G | Darth Vader Gold MET WM | | |
| 56A | Snowtrooper WG ERR | 6.00 | 12.00 | 109 | General Hux | 5.00 | 10.00 | 157H | Darth Vader Futura NYCC/TAR | | |
| 56B | Snowtrooper WG COR | 6.00 | 12.00 | 110 | Snap Wexley | 5.00 | 10.00 | 157I | Darth Vader Futura TAR | | |
| 56C | Snowtrooper WG COR Sticker | 6.00 | 12.00 | 111 | FN-2199 V | 5.00 | 10.00 | 158 | Darth Vader Bespin SB | 12.50 | 25.00 |
| 57A | Imperial Guard WG ERR | 6.00 | 12.00 | 112 | Guavian | 5.00 | 10.00 | 159 | Grand Moff Tarkin SB | 7.50 | 15.00 |
| 57B | Imperial Guard WG COR | 6.00 | 12.00 | 113 | ME-8D9 | 5.00 | 10.00 | 160 | Max Rebo SS | 7.50 | 15.00 |
| 57C | Imperial Guard WG COR Sticker | 6.00 | 12.00 | 114 | Rey Jedi Temple WG | 7.50 | 15.00 | 161 | Rey w/Jacket TAR | 6.00 | 12.00 |
| 58A | Rey | 5.00 | 10.00 | 115A | Han Solo w/Bowcaster SDCC | 7.50 | 15.00 | 162 | Young Anakin | 6.00 | 12.00 |
| 59 | Finn | 5.00 | 10.00 | 115B | Han Solo w/Bowcaster SCE | 7.50 | 15.00 | 164 | Captain Rex SB | 7.50 | 15.00 |
| 60 | Kylo Ren | 5.00 | 10.00 | 116A | BB-8 w/Lighter SDCC | 7.50 | 15.00 | 165 | Darth Maul Rebels SB | 15.00 | 30.00 |
| 61 | BB-8 | 5.00 | 10.00 | 116B | BB-8 w/Lighter SCE | 7.50 | 15.00 | 166 | The Inquisitor | 6.00 | 12.00 |
| 62 | Poe Dameron V | 5.00 | 10.00 | 117 | Poe Dameron Jacket/Blaster HT | 6.00 | 12.00 | 167 | Seventh Sister | 5.00 | 10.00 |
| 63A | Chewbacca | 5.00 | 10.00 | 118 | Maz Kanata Goggles Up TAR | 5.00 | 10.00 | 168 | Fifth Brother | 6.00 | 12.00 |
| 63B | Chewbacca FLK SB | 6.00 | 12.00 | 119 | Rey X-Wing Helmet GS | 7.50 | 15.00 | 169A | Han Solo SWC | 20.00 | 40.00 |
| 63C | Chewbacca Blue Chrome SWC | 30.00 | 75.00 | 120 | Poe Dameron X-Wing Jumpsuit FYE | 5.00 | 10.00 | 169B | Han Solo GCE | 7.50 | 15.00 |
| 63D | Chewbacca Gold Chrome GCE | 7.50 | 15.00 | 121 | R2-D2 Jabba's Sail Barge SB | 5.00 | 10.00 | 170A | Grand Admiral Thrawn SWC | 30.00 | 75.00 |
| 64A | C-3PO | 6.00 | 12.00 | 122 | Zuckuss TW | 6.00 | 12.00 | 170B | Grand Admiral Thrawn GCE | 25.00 | 50.00 |
| 64B | C-3PO MET B&N | 5.00 | 10.00 | 123 | Luke Skywalker (Endor) | 6.00 | 12.00 | 171A | 442nd Clone Trooper SWC | 30.00 | 60.00 |
| 65A | Captain Phasma | 7.50 | 15.00 | 124A | Yoda | 6.00 | 12.00 | 171B | 442nd Clone Trooper GCW | 20.00 | 40.00 |
| 65B | Captain Phasma Last Jedi Box | 6.00 | 12.00 | 124B | Yoda Blue Chrome SWC | 30.00 | 75.00 | 172 | Mace Windu WG | 7.50 | 15.00 |
| 66 | First Order Stormtrooper | 5.00 | 10.00 | 124C | Yoda Gold Chrome GCE | 7.50 | 15.00 | 173A | Muftak ECCC | 10.00 | 20.00 |
| 67A | First Order Snowtrooper | 5.00 | 10.00 | 124D | Yoda Green Chrome SDCC | 30.00 | 75.00 | 173B | Muftak SPCE | 10.00 | 20.00 |
| 67B | First Order Snowtrooper Last Jedi Box | 5.00 | 10.00 | 124E | Yoda Green Chrome SCE | 10.00 | 20.00 | 174A | Rey w/Speeder SWC | 20.00 | 40.00 |
| 68A | First Order Flametrooper | 5.00 | 10.00 | A125 | Hoth Han Solo w/Tauntaun SB | 20.00 | 40.00 | 174B | Rey w/Speeder GCE | 20.00 | 40.00 |
| 68B | First Order Flametrooper Last Jedi Box | 5.00 | 10.00 | B125A | Princess Leia Hoth SWC | 20.00 | 40.00 | 175 | Luke w/Speeder SB | 12.50 | 25.00 |
| 69 | Blue Snaggletooth CH SB | 12.50 | 25.00 | B125B | Princess Leia Hoth GCE | 12.50 | 25.00 | A176 | Darth Vader w/TIE Fighter TAR | 12.50 | 25.00 |
| 70 | Red Snaggletooth SB | 5.00 | 10.00 | 126A | Luke Skywalker Hood SWC | 20.00 | 40.00 | B176 | Commander Cody WG | 7.50 | 15.00 |
| 71 | Shadow Guard WG | 7.50 | 15.00 | 126B | Luke Skywalker Hood GCE | 25.00 | 50.00 | 177A | Saw Gerrera w/Hair NYCC | 7.50 | 15.00 |
| 72 | Poe Dameron No Helmet WM | 7.50 | 15.00 | 127A | Garindan SWC | 20.00 | 40.00 | 177B | Saw Gerrera w/Hair FCE | 7.50 | 15.00 |
| 73 | Rey w/Goggles HT | 5.00 | 10.00 | 127B | Garindan GCE | 7.50 | 15.00 | 178A | Jyn Erso w/Helmet NYCC | 12.50 | 25.00 |
| 74 | FO Stormtrooper w/Rifle AMZ | 7.50 | 15.00 | 128A | Qui Gon Jinn NYCC | 200.00 | 350.00 | 178B | Jyn Erso w/Helmet FCE | 7.50 | 15.00 |
| 75 | FO Stormtrooper w/Shield WG | 6.00 | 12.00 | 128B | Qui Gon Jinn HOLO SWC | 30.00 | 75.00 | 179A | K-2SO Action Pose NYCC | 7.50 | 15.00 |
| 76 | Finn Stormtrooper GS | 6.00 | 12.00 | 128C | Qui Gon Jinn HOLO GCE | 20.00 | 40.00 | 179B | K-2SO Action Pose FCE | 7.50 | 15.00 |
| 77 | Kylo Ren Unhooded TAR | 5.00 | 10.00 | 129 | General Grievous WG | 30.00 | 75.00 | 180 | R5-D4 SB | 5.00 | 10.00 |
| 78 | R2-L3 Dorkside Toys | 12.50 | 25.00 | 130A | Ahsoka HT | 7.50 | 15.00 | 181 | C-3PO Unfinished SB | 10.00 | 20.00 |
| 79 | Han Solo | 5.00 | 10.00 | 130B | Ahsoka GITD Comikaze | 7.50 | 15.00 | 182A | Snoke GITD SDCC | 12.50 | 25.00 |
| 80 | Princess Leia | 5.00 | 10.00 | 131 | Sabine Masked WG | 7.50 | 15.00 | 182B | Supreme Leader Snoke GITD SCE | 7.50 | 15.00 |
| 81 | Admiral Ackbar | 5.00 | 10.00 | 132 | Kanan | 5.00 | 10.00 | 183A | Bodhi Rook SDCC | 7.50 | 15.00 |
| 82 | Nien Nunb | 5.00 | 10.00 | 133A | Chopper | 6.00 | 12.00 | 183B | Bodhi Rook SCE | 7.50 | 15.00 |
| 83 | Sidon Ithano | 5.00 | 10.00 | 133B | Chopper Imperial SWC | 5.00 | 10.00 | 184B | Tank Trooper SDCC | 5.00 | 10.00 |
| 84 | Varmik | 5.00 | 10.00 | 133C | Chopper Imperial GCE | 5.00 | 10.00 | 184C | Combat Assault Tank Trooper SCE | 5.00 | 10.00 |
| 85 | Finn w/Lightsaber B&N | 5.00 | 10.00 | 134 | Ezra | 6.00 | 12.00 | 185 | Young Jyn Erso | 5.00 | 10.00 |
| 86 | Han Solo Snow Gear LC | 5.00 | 10.00 | 135 | Sabine | 6.00 | 12.00 | 186 | Galen Erso | 5.00 | 10.00 |
| 87 | Kylo Ren Unmasked WM | 5.00 | 10.00 | 136 | Hera | 7.50 | 15.00 | 187 | Weeteef Cyubee | 6.00 | 12.00 |
| 88 | Nien Nunb w/Helmet GS | 7.50 | 15.00 | 137 | Zeb | 5.00 | 10.00 | 188A | Death Star Droid Rogue One NYCC | 5.00 | 10.00 |
| 89 | TIE Fighter Pilot SB | 5.00 | 10.00 | 138 | Jyn Erso | 5.00 | 10.00 | 188B | Death Star Droid Rogue One FCE | 5.00 | 10.00 |
| A90 | TIE Fighter Pilot Red Stripe SB CH | 12.50 | 25.00 | 139 | Captain Cassian Andor | 5.00 | 10.00 | 189 | Death Star Droid Black | 5.00 | 10.00 |
| B90 | Luke Ceremony SWC | 6.00 | 12.00 | 140 | Chirrut Imwe | 7.50 | 15.00 | 190A | Rey | 5.00 | 10.00 |
| A91 | Captain Phasma MET SB | 6.00 | 12.00 | 141 | Baze Malbus | 5.00 | 10.00 | 190B | Rey GITD COST | 7.50 | 15.00 |
| B91A | Han Ceremony SWC | 7.50 | 15.00 | 142 | Director Orson Krennic | 5.00 | 10.00 | 191 | Finn | 5.00 | 10.00 |
| B91B | Han Ceremony GCE | 7.50 | 15.00 | 143 | Darth Vader | 7.50 | 15.00 | 192 | Poe Dameron | 5.00 | 10.00 |
| 92 | AT-AT Driver WG | 7.50 | 15.00 | 144 | Imperial Death Trooper | 6.00 | 12.00 | 193 | Luke Skywalker | 5.00 | 10.00 |
| 93A | Luke Skywalker Bespin | 6.00 | 12.00 | 145 | Scarif Stormtrooper | 6.00 | 12.00 | 194A | Kylo Ren | 5.00 | 10.00 |
| 93B | Luke Skywalker Bespin Gold WM | 12.50 | 25.00 | 146 | K-2SO | 5.00 | 10.00 | 194B | Kylo Ren GITD COST | 12.50 | 25.00 |
| 94A | Luke Skywalker Bespin SWC | 7.50 | 15.00 | 147 | C2-B5 | 5.00 | 10.00 | 194C | Kylo Ren HOLO TAR OL | 15.00 | 30.00 |
| 94B | Luke Skywalker Bespin GCE | 7.50 | 15.00 | 148 | Jyn Erso Mountain Gear SB | 6.00 | 12.00 | 195A | Chewbacca w/Porg | 6.00 | 12.00 |
| 95 | Ree Yees WG | 5.00 | 10.00 | 149 | Death Trooper Sniper SB | 6.00 | 12.00 | 195B | Chewbacca w/Porg FLK FYE | 7.50 | 15.00 |
| 96 | Kit Fisto WG | 6.00 | 12.00 | 150 | Jyn Erso Hooded HT | 5.00 | 10.00 | 196 | BB-8 | 6.00 | 12.00 |
| 97 | Plo Koon WG | 7.50 | 15.00 | 151 | Capt. C.Andor Brown Jacket TAR | 5.00 | 10.00 | 197 | Rose | 5.00 | 10.00 |
| 98 | Blue Senate Guard SWC | 12.50 | 25.00 | 152 | Jyn Erso Imperial Disguise TAR | 6.00 | 12.00 | 198A | Porg | 5.00 | 10.00 |
| 99 | Old Ben Kenobi SB | 6.00 | 12.00 | 153 | Saw Gerrera WM | 6.00 | 12.00 | 198B | Porg Open Mouth CH | 7.50 | 15.00 |
| 100 | FN-2187 TAR | 12.50 | 25.00 | 154 | Imp. Death Trooper Black MET WM | 7.50 | 15.00 | 198C | Porg FLK HT | 7.50 | 15.00 |
| 101A | 4-LOM SWC | 25.00 | 50.00 | 155 | Bistan NYCC | 6.00 | 12.00 | 198D | Porg Open Mouth FLK HT | 10.00 | 20.00 |
| 101B | 4-LOM GCE | 12.50 | 25.00 | 156 | Scarif Stormtrooper Striped WG | 7.50 | 15.00 | 198E | Porg Wings Open TAR | 7.50 | 15.00 |
| 102 | Bobe Fett Action SB | 20.00 | 40.00 | 157A | Vader Force Choke GS | 12.50 | 25.00 | 198F | Porg 10" TAR | 15.00 | 30.00 |
| 103 | IG-88 SB | 7.50 | 15.00 | 157B | D.Vader Force Choke Blue Chr. SWC | 100.00 | 200.00 | 199 | Supreme Leader Snoke | 5.00 | 10.00 |
| 104 | Rey w/Lightsaber | 6.00 | 12.00 | 157C | D.Vader Force Choke Gold Chr. GCE | 10.00 | 20.00 | 200 | Praetorian Guard | 5.00 | 10.00 |
| 105 | Kylo Ren Unmasked Action | 5.00 | 10.00 | 157D | Darth Vader Red Chrome TAR RC | 12.50 | 25.00 | 201 | First Order Executioner | 6.00 | 12.00 |
| 106 | Luke Skywalker Force Awakens | 7.50 | 15.00 | 157E | Darth Vader Gold Chrome MCM | 7.50 | 15.00 | 202A | BB-9E | 5.00 | 10.00 |
| 107 | General Leia | 7.50 | 15.00 | 157F | Darth Vader Black Chrome SB | 15.00 | 30.00 | 202B | BB-9E Chrome BL | 6.00 | 12.00 |

|  |  | | |
|---|------|---|---|
| 203 | Kylo Ren w/Helmet TRU | 5.00 | 10.00 |
| 205 | Rose SS | 7.50 | 15.00 |
| 207 | DJ GS | 6.00 | 12.00 |
| 208 | Praetorian Guard w/Swords WG | 5.00 | 10.00 |
| 209 | Praetorian Guard w/Whip WG | 5.00 | 10.00 |
| 210 | Resistance BB Unit Orange NBC | 7.50 | 15.00 |
| 211 | Resistance BB Unit WM | 5.00 | 10.00 |
| 212 | Medical Droid WG | 6.00 | 12.00 |
| 213A | Boba Fett w/Slave I NYCC | 25.00 | 50.00 |
| 213B | Boba Fett w/Slave I FCE | 25.00 | 50.00 |
| 214 | Obi-Wan Kenobi ROTS SB | 10.00 | 20.00 |
| 215 | Kylo Ren w/TIE Fighter | 7.50 | 15.00 |
| 217 | Aayla Secura SB | 7.50 | 15.00 |
| 218 | Princess Leia WM | 5.00 | 10.00 |
| 219 | Wedge Antilles w/Snow Speeder WG | 7.50 | 15.00 |
| 220 | BB-8 Baseball and Bat Giants | 20.00 | 40.00 |
| 221 | Tie Fighter w/Tie Pilot | 10.00 | 20.00 |
| A222 | Escape Pod Landing WM | 10.00 | 20.00 |
| 222B | Duel on Mustafar SB | 30.00 | 60.00 |
| 223 | Cantina Faceoff WM | 15.00 | 30.00 |
| 224 | Trash Compactor Escape WM | 10.00 | 20.00 |
| 225 | Death Star Duel WM | 10.00 | 20.00 |
| 226 | Cloud City Duel WG | 15.00 | 30.00 |
| 227 | Poe Dameron w/X-Wing SB | 7.50 | 15.00 |
| 228 | Princess Leia w/Speeder Bike | 6.00 | 12.00 |
| 229 | Luke Skywalker w/Speeder Bike CH | 10.00 | 20.00 |
| 230A | Dengar NYCC | 7.50 | 15.00 |
| 230B | Dengar FCE | 7.50 | 15.00 |
| 231 | Young Anakin Podracing WG | 6.00 | 12.00 |
| 232 | Luke Skywalker w/X-Wing 40th Anniv. | 30.00 | 60.00 |
| 233 | Count Dooku SB | 10.00 | 20.00 |
| 234 | Scout Trooper w/Speeder SB | 12.50 | 25.00 |
| 235 | Vice Admiral Holdo | 5.00 | 10.00 |
| 236 | Chewbacca w/AT-ST | 10.00 | 20.00 |
| 237A | Padme Amidala ECCC | 10.00 | 20.00 |
| 237B | Padme Amidala SCE | 7.50 | 15.00 |
| 238 | Han Solo | 6.00 | 12.00 |
| 239A | Chewbacca | 6.00 | 12.00 |
| 239B | Chewbacca FLK BL | 7.50 | 15.00 |
| 239C | Chewbacca FLK MCM | 12.50 | 25.00 |
| 240 | Lando Calrissian | 6.00 | 12.00 |
| 241 | Qi'Ra | 5.00 | 10.00 |
| 242 | Tobias Beckett | 6.00 | 12.00 |
| 243 | Val | 6.00 | 12.00 |
| 244 | Rio Durant | 5.00 | 10.00 |
| 245 | L3-37 | 6.00 | 12.00 |
| 246 | Range Trooper | 5.00 | 10.00 |
| 247 | Enfys Nest | 6.00 | 12.00 |
| 248A | Han Solo Goggles TAR | 6.00 | 12.00 |
| 248B | Mudtrooper FS | 15.00 | 30.00 |
| 250 | Tobias Beckett WM | 5.00 | 10.00 |
| 251 | Lando Calrissian White Cape HT | 5.00 | 10.00 |
| 252A | Stormtrooper SDCC | 20.00 | 40.00 |
| 252B | Stormtrooper SCE | 7.50 | 15.00 |
| 253 | Dryden Voss FYE | 7.50 | 15.00 |
| 254 | Dryden Gangster TAR | 7.50 | 15.00 |
| 255 | Han Solo Vest WG | 5.00 | 10.00 |
| 256 | Vulptex Crystal Fox | 7.50 | 15.00 |
| 257 | Rematch on the Supremacy | 10.00 | 20.00 |
| 258 | Ewok w/Speeder Bike FS | 25.00 | 50.00 |
| 260 | C'ai Threnalli | 6.00 | 12.00 |
| 261 | Porg Frowning | 5.00 | 10.00 |
| 262A | Cad Bane SDCC | 15.00 | 30.00 |
| 262B | Cad Bane SCE | 6.00 | 12.00 |
| 263 | Caretaker | 6.00 | 12.00 |
| 264 | Clash on the Supremacy Rey | 10.00 | 20.00 |
| 265 | Clash on the Supremacy Kylo | 10.00 | 20.00 |
| 266A | Luke Skywalker | 6.00 | 12.00 |
| 266B | Luke Skywalker Gold/80* FD | 2000.00 | 2500.00 |
| 267 | Paige | 6.00 | 12.00 |
| 268 | Ahsoka | 6.00 | 12.00 |
| 269 | Yoda | 6.00 | 12.00 |
| 270 | Obi-Wan Kenobi | 6.00 | 12.00 |
| 271 | Anakin Skywalker | 5.00 | 10.00 |
| 272 | Ahsoka Force Push HT | 7.50 | 15.00 |
| 273 | Obi-Wan Kenobi Hooded WG | 10.00 | 20.00 |
| 274A | Captain Rex NYCC | 30.00 | 60.00 |
| 274B | Captain Rex FCE | 30.00 | 75.00 |
| 275 | R2-D2 w/Antlers | 5.00 | 10.00 |
| 276 | C-3PO w/Santa Hat | 6.00 | 12.00 |
| 277 | Yoda Santa Outfit | 5.00 | 10.00 |
| 278 | Chewbacca Christmas Lights | 6.00 | 12.00 |
| 279A | Darth Vader Candy Cane Lightsaber | 6.00 | 12.00 |
| 279B | Darth Vader GITD Candy Cane Lightsaber CH | 10.00 | 20.00 |
| 280 | Boba Gets His Bounty SB | 20.00 | 40.00 |
| 281 | Anakin Skywalker Dark Side Eyes WG | 12.50 | 25.00 |
| 282 | Lando Calrissian Skiff SB | 10.00 | 20.00 |
| 283 | Klaatu SB | 7.50 | 15.00 |
| 284 | Dagobah Face-Off SB | 7.50 | 15.00 |
| 285 | Jango Fett Jet Pack WG | 10.00 | 20.00 |
| 286 | Han Solo | 7.50 | 15.00 |
| 287A | Princess Leia | 7.50 | 15.00 |
| 287B | Princess Leia Gold MET WM | | |
| 288A | Darth Vader | 5.00 | 10.00 |
| 288B | Darth Vader GITD CH | 7.50 | 15.00 |
| 289 | Emperor Palpatine Force Lightning | 6.00 | 12.00 |
| 290 | Wicket | 6.00 | 12.00 |
| 291 | Lando Calrissian | 6.00 | 12.00 |
| 292 | Baby Nippet FLK TAR | 7.50 | 15.00 |
| 293 | Wicket 10" TAR | 20.00 | 40.00 |
| 294 | Encounter on Endor | 12.50 | 25.00 |
| 295A | Princess Leia Blue Chrome SWC | 30.00 | 75.00 |
| 295B | Princess Leia Gold Chrome GCE | 7.50 | 15.00 |
| 296A | Stormtrooper Blue Chrome SWC | 30.00 | 75.00 |
| 296B | Stormtrooper Gold Chrome GCE | 10.00 | 20.00 |
| 297A | Boba Fett Blue Chrome SWC | 75.00 | 150.00 |
| 297B | Boba Fett Gold Chrome GCE | 7.50 | 15.00 |
| 297C | Boba Fett Green Chrome SDCC | 25.00 | 50.00 |
| 297D | Boba Fett Green Chrome SCE | 10.00 | 20.00 |
| 297E | Boba Fett Futura TAR | | |
| 297F | Boba Fett Futura Black TAR | | |
| 297G | Boba Fett Futura Red TAR | | |
| 298A | Watto SWC | 12.50 | 25.00 |
| 298B | Watto GCE | 7.50 | 15.00 |
| 299A | Darth Maul SWC | 20.00 | 40.00 |
| 299B | Darth Maul GCE | 10.00 | 20.00 |
| 300 | Chewbacca Oxygen Mask SB | 12.50 | 25.00 |
| 301 | DJ R3X GE | 20.00 | 40.00 |
| 302 | Hondo Ohnaka GE | 25.00 | 50.00 |
| 303 | Aurra Sing SB | 15.00 | 30.00 |
| 304 | Sebulba SB | 15.00 | 30.00 |
| 305 | Boba Fett Animated GSFIC | 10.00 | 20.00 |
| 306A | Sith Trooper SDCC | 200.00 | 350.00 |
| 306B | Sith Trooper | | |
| 307 | Rey | | |
| 308 | Kylo Ren | | |
| 309 | Finn | | |
| 310 | Poe Dameron | | |
| 311 | Zorii Bliss | | |
| 312 | D-0 | | |
| 313 | Lando Calrissian | | |
| 314 | BB-8 | | |
| 315 | Jannah | | |
| 316 | Rose | | |
| 317 | First Order Jet Trooper | | |
| 318 | Sith Jet Trooper | | |
| 319 | Lieutenant Connix | | |
| 320 | First Order Tread Speeder | | |
| 321 | Millennium Falcon w/Han AMZ | | |
| 322A | Sandtrooper NYCC | | |
| 322B | Sandtrooper FCE | | |
| 326A | The Mandalorian | | |
| 326B | The Mandalorian D23 | 75.00 | 150.00 |
| 327 | Cara Dune | | |
| 328 | IG-11 | | |
| 329 | Kuiil | | |
| 330A | The Mandalorian Pistol NYCC | | |
| 330B | The Mandalorian Pistol FCE | | |
| 343 | Darth Vader Electrical | | |

## 2011-19 Funko Pop Vinyl Star Wars Multi-Packs

| | | | |
|---|---|---|---|
| NNO | BB-8/BB-9E BB | 7.50 | 15.00 |
| NNO | BB-8 Gold Dome HT BF | 7.50 | 15.00 |
| NNO | Biggs/Wedge/Porkins WM | 7.50 | 15.00 |
| NNO | Fighting Droids GS | 7.50 | 15.00 |
| NNO | First Order Kylo Ren/Snoke/BB-9E COSTCO | 30.00 | 60.00 |
| NNO | First Order Kylo Ren/Snoke/Executioner/BB-9E COSTCO | 25.00 | 50.00 |
| NNO | Greedo/Hammerhead/Walrus Man WM | 7.50 | 15.00 |
| NNO | Gunner/Officer/Trooper WM | 12.50 | 25.00 |
| NNO | Han Solo/Chewbacca SB | 12.50 | 25.00 |
| NNO | Jabba/Slave Leia/Salacious Crumb WM | 30.00 | 60.00 |
| NNO | Jango Fett GITD/LEGO Star Wars III Bundle | 20.00 | 40.00 |
| NNO | Lobot/Ugnaught/Bespin Guard WM | 7.50 | 15.00 |
| NNO | Luke Skywalker & Wampa SDCC | 100.00 | 175.00 |
| NNO | Praetorian Guards POPCULTCHA | 30.00 | 60.00 |
| NNO | Princess Leia/R2-D2 SDCC | 12.50 | 25.00 |
| NNO | Princess Leia/R2-D2 SCE | 7.50 | 15.00 |
| NNO | R2-D2 Gold Dome HT BF | 7.50 | 15.00 |
| NNO | Rancor/Luke/Slave Oola PX | 20.00 | 40.00 |
| NNO | Rebel Rey/Chewbacca/BB-8 COSTCO | 7.50 | 15.00 |
| NNO | Rebel Rey/Luke/Chewbacca/BB-8 COSTCO | 20.00 | 40.00 |
| NNO | Rogue One Jyn/Cassian/K-2SO/C2-B5/Krennic Vader/Scarif/Death Trooper | 60.00 | 120.00 |
| NNO | Sandtrooper/Dewback WM | 12.50 | 25.00 |
| NNO | Tarfful/Unhooded Emperor/Clone Trooper WM | 7.50 | 15.00 |
| NNO | Teebo/Chirpa/Logray WM | 12.50 | 25.00 |

## 2015-16 Funko Super Shogun

| | | | |
|---|---|---|---|
| 2 | Shadowtrooper SWC | 120.00 | 200.00 |
| 3 | Boba Fett ROTJ SWC | 120.00 | 200.00 |
| 4 | Boba Fett ESB | 60.00 | 120.00 |
| 5 | Boba Fett Proto/400* FS | 150.00 | 250.00 |

## 2017-18 Funko Vynl Star Wars

| | | | |
|---|---|---|---|
| NNO | Chewbacca + C-3PO | 7.50 | 15.00 |
| NNO | Darth Vader + Stormtrooper | 7.50 | 15.00 |
| NNO | Han Solo + Greedo | 6.00 | 12.00 |
| NNO | Han Solo + Lando Calrissian | 6.00 | 12.00 |
| NNO | Luke Skywalker + Darth Vader | 7.50 | 15.00 |
| NNO | Luke Skywalker + Princess Leia | 10.00 | 20.00 |
| NNO | Obi-Wan Kenobi + Darth Maul | 5.00 | 10.00 |

## 2007-16 Funko Wacky Wobblers Star Wars

| | | | |
|---|---|---|---|
| NNO | 4-LOM | 6.00 | 12.00 |
| NNO | 501st Clone Trooper | 15.00 | 30.00 |
| NNO | Admiral Ackbar | 25.00 | 50.00 |
| NNO | Ahsoka Tano | 25.00 | 50.00 |
| NNO | Anakin Skywalker Clone Wars | 7.50 | 15.00 |
| NNO | Battle Droid | 10.00 | 20.00 |
| NNO | Boba Fett | 7.50 | 15.00 |
| NNO | Boba Fett Chrome Base | 15.00 | 30.00 |
| NNO | Bossk | 7.50 | 15.00 |
| NNO | C-3PO | 7.50 | 15.00 |
| NNO | C-3PO TFA | 7.50 | 15.00 |
| NNO | Cantina Band | 10.00 | 20.00 |
| NNO | Captain Phasma | 6.00 | 12.00 |
| NNO | Captain Rex | 10.00 | 20.00 |
| NNO | Captain Red Chrome Base | 12.50 | 25.00 |
| NNO | Chewbacca | 7.50 | 15.00 |
| NNO | Chewbacca Chrome Base | 25.00 | 50.00 |
| NNO | Chewbacca TFA | 5.00 | 10.00 |
| NNO | Clone Trooper | 25.00 | 50.00 |
| NNO | Clone Trooper Utapau AFE | 10.00 | 20.00 |
| NNO | Clone Trooper (yellow) | 15.00 | 30.00 |
| (2008) | | | |
| NNO | Clone Trooper Denal Chrome Base WM | 12.50 | 25.00 |
| NNO | Clone Trooper Sinker | 75.00 | 150.00 |
| NNO | Clone Troooper Denal WM | 7.50 | 15.00 |
| NNO | Commander Gree/1500* DIAMOND | 7.50 | 15.00 |
| NNO | Darth Maul | 15.00 | 30.00 |
| NNO | Darth Maul HOLO Chrome Base/12* SDCC | 90.00 | 175.00 |
| NNO | Darth Maul HOLO/480* SDCC | 60.00 | 120.00 |
| NNO | Darth Vader | 7.50 | 15.00 |
| NNO | Darth Vader (chrome base) | 25.00 | 50.00 |
| NNO | Darth Vader Holiday EE | 7.50 | 15.00 |
| NNO | Darth Vader HOLO SDCC/WWC | 20.00 | 40.00 |
| NNO | Darth Vader HOLO Chrome Base SDCC/WWC | 25.00 | 50.00 |
| NNO | Emperor Palpatine | 25.00 | 50.00 |
| NNO | Emperor Palpatine (chrome base) | 25.00 | 50.00 |
| NNO | Finn | 6.00 | 12.00 |
| NNO | Finn/Kylo Ren HMV | 15.00 | 30.00 |
| NNO | Finn Stormtrooper | 5.00 | 10.00 |
| NNO | First Order Flametrooper | 6.00 | 12.00 |
| NNO | First Order Snowtrooper | 5.00 | 10.00 |
| NNO | First Order Stormtrooper | 6.00 | 12.00 |
| NNO | Gamorrean Guard | 12.50 | 25.00 |
| NNO | General Grievous | 10.00 | 20.00 |
| NNO | Greedo | 7.50 | 15.00 |
| NNO | Greedo Chrome Base | 25.00 | 50.00 |
| NNO | Han Solo | 12.50 | 25.00 |
| NNO | Han Solo Stormtrooper/1008* SDCC | 20.00 | 40.00 |
| NNO | Holiday C-3PO | 7.50 | 15.00 |
| NNO | Holiday Special Boba Fett | 10.00 | 20.00 |
| NNO | Holiday Yoda | 7.50 | 15.00 |
| NNO | Jango Fett | 7.50 | 15.00 |
| NNO | Jawa | 10.00 | 20.00 |
| NNO | K-3PO/1500* | 6.00 | 12.00 |
| NNO | Kylo Ren | 5.00 | 10.00 |
| NNO | Kylor Ren No Hood | 6.00 | 12.00 |
| NNO | Luke Skywalker | 20.00 | 40.00 |
| NNO | Luke Skywalker (stormtrooper) | 25.00 | 50.00 |
| (2008 Entertainment Earth Exclusive) | | | |
| NNO | Luke Skywalker X-Wing Pilot | 20.00 | 40.00 |
| NNO | Obi-Wan Kenobi | 25.00 | 50.00 |
| NNO | Obi-Wan Kenobi (Clone Wars) | 12.50 | 25.00 |
| NNO | Obi-Wan Kenobi Force Ghost NYCC | 15.00 | 30.00 |
| NNO | Obi-Wan Kenobi Force Ghost Chrome Base | 25.00 | 50.00 |
| NNO | Princess Leia | 7.50 | 15.00 |
| NNO | R2-D2 | 7.50 | 15.00 |
| NNO | R2-Q2/756* EE | | |
| NNO | R2-R9/756* EE | 7.50 | 15.00 |
| NNO | R2-X2/756* EE | 20.00 | 40.00 |
| NNO | Rey | 6.00 | 12.00 |

| | | | |
|---|---|---|---|
| NNO | Shadow Stormtrooper SDCC | 12.50 | 25.00 |
| NNO | Shock Trooper/1008* SDCC | 30.00 | 75.00 |
| NNO | Slave Leia | 10.00 | 20.00 |
| NNO | Stormtrooper | 7.50 | 15.00 |
| NNO | TC-14/480* SDCC | 25.00 | 50.00 |
| NNO | TIE Fighter Pilot | 12.50 | 25.00 |
| NNO | Tusken Raider | 7.50 | 15.00 |
| NNO | Wicket | 7.50 | 15.00 |
| NNO | Wicket Chrome Base | 30.00 | 60.00 |
| NNO | Yoda | 6.00 | 12.00 |
| NNO | Yoda Chrome Base | 15.00 | 30.00 |
| NNO | Yoda Force Ghost | 6.00 | 12.00 |
| NNO | Yoda Force Ghost/1500* DIAMOND SDCC | 25.00 | 50.00 |
| NNO | Yoda (holiday) | 6.00 | 12.00 |

## 2010 Funko Wacky Wobblers Star Wars Monster Mash-Ups

| | | | |
|---|---|---|---|
| NNO | Chewbacca | 6.00 | 12.00 |
| NNO | Darth Vader | 6.00 | 12.00 |
| NNO | Stormtrooper | 7.50 | 15.00 |
| NNO | Yoda | 5.00 | 10.00 |

## 2016-18 Funko Wobblers Star Wars

COMMON FIGURINE

| | | | |
|---|---|---|---|
| NNO | Boba Fett (prototype) | 15.00 | 30.00 |
| (2017 Galactic Convention Exclusive) | | | |
| NNO | Boba Fett Proto SWC | 15.00 | 30.00 |
| NNO | Boba Fett | 6.00 | 12.00 |
| NNO | Captain Cassian Andor | 4.00 | 8.00 |
| NNO | Chewbacca | 6.00 | 12.00 |
| NNO | Darth Vader | 7.50 | 15.00 |
| NNO | First Order Executioner | 6.00 | 12.00 |
| NNO | Han Solo (Solo film) | 7.50 | 15.00 |
| (2018) | | | |
| NNO | Imperial Death Trooper | 6.00 | 12.00 |
| NNO | Jyn Erso | 5.00 | 10.00 |
| NNO | Lando Calrissian | 6.00 | 12.00 |
| (2018) | | | |
| NNO | Princess Leia | 7.50 | 15.00 |
| NNO | Rey | 7.50 | 15.00 |
| NNO | Scarif Stormtrooper | 6.00 | 12.00 |

## 2010 Mighty Beanz Star Wars

| | |
|---|---|
| 1 | Luke Skywalker C |
| 2 | Han Solo C |
| 3 | Princess Leia C |
| 4 | Darth Vader C |
| 5 | R2-D2 C |
| 6 | Obi-Wan Kenobi C |
| 7 | Yoda C |
| 8 | Chewbacca C |
| 9 | Jabba the Hutt C |
| 10 | Battle Droid C |
| 11 | C-3PO C |
| 12 | Clone Trooper C |
| 13 | 501st Legion Trooper C |
| 14 | Commander Cody C |
| 15 | Stormtrooper C |
| 16 | Admiral Ackbar C |
| 17 | Gamorrean Guard C |
| 18 | Count Dooku C |
| 19 | Boba Fett C |
| 20 | Greedo C |
| 21 | Sandtrooper C |
| 22 | Anakin Skywalker (child) C |
| 23 | Mace Windu C |
| 24 | AT-AT Driver C |
| 25 | General Grievous C |
| 26 | TIE Pilot C |
| 27 | Snowtrooper C |
| 28 | Wicket C |
| 29 | Jawa C |
| 30 | Tusken Raider C |
| 31 | Padme Amidala R |
| 32 | Darth Maul R |
| 33 | Anakin Skywalker R |
| 34 | 2-1B R |
| 35 | Han Solo (carbonite) R |
| 36 | Cantina Musician R |
| 37 | Bossk R |
| 38 | Lando Calrissian R |
| 39 | Biggs Darklighter R |
| 40 | Jango Fett R |
| 41 | Bib Fortuna R |
| 42 | IG-88 R |
| 43 | Emperor Palpatine R |
| 44 | Qui-Gon Jinn R |
| 45 | Rancor Keeper R |
| 46 | Max Rebo R |
| 47 | Luke Rebel Pilot R |
| 48 | Sebulba R |
| 49 | Rancor R |
| 50 | Ponda Baba R |
| 51 | Princess Leia UR |
| 52 | Jar Jar Binks UR |
| 53 | Dengar UR |
| 54 | Kit Fisto UR |
| 55 | Ki-Adi-Mundi UR |
| 56 | Jek Porkins UR |
| 57 | Nien Nunb UR |
| 58 | Salacious Crumb UR |
| 59 | Watto UR |
| 60 | Queen Amidala UR |

## 2017 Vinylmation Eachez Star Wars The Last Jedi

| | | | |
|---|---|---|---|
| NNO | Praetorian Guard Single Blade | 30.00 | 75.00 |
| NNO | Praetorian Guard Double Blade (chaser) | 50.00 | 100.00 |
| NNO | Praetorian Guard Whip | 12.00 | 25.00 |

## 2012-13 Vinylmation Star Wars Disney Characters

| | | | |
|---|---|---|---|
| NNO | Boba Fett Pete | 6.00 | 12.00 |
| NNO | Chewbacca Goofy | 20.00 | 40.00 |
| (LE 1500) | | | |
| NNO | Darth Vader Goofy | 8.00 | 15.00 |
| NNO | Emperor Stitch | 25.00 | 50.00 |
| (LE 2000) | | | |
| NNO | Ewok Chip | 20.00 | 40.00 |
| (LE 1500) | | | |
| NNO | Ewok Dale | 20.00 | 40.00 |
| (LE 1500) | | | |
| NNO | Han Solo Donald | 30.00 | 60.00 |
| (LE 1500) | | | |
| NNO | Jedi Mickey | 20.00 | 40.00 |
| (LE 2000) | | | |
| NNO | Princess Leia Minnie | 10.00 | 20.00 |

| | | |
|---|---|---|
| NNO Stormtrooper Donald | 6.00 | 12.00 |
| NNO X-Wing Pilot Luke Mickey | 12.00 | 25.00 |
| NNO Yoda Stitch | 20.00 | 40.00 |

### 2016 Vinylmation Star Wars The Force Awakens Series 2

| | | |
|---|---|---|
| NNO Admiral Ackbar | 5.00 | 10.00 |
| NNO Captain Phasma | | |
| NNO Ello Asty (w/ helmet) | 6.00 | 12.00 |
| NNO Ello Asty (helmetless) | | |
| NNO First Mate Guiggold | 4.00 | 8.00 |
| NNO First Order Snowtrooper | 6.00 | 12.00 |
| NNO First Order TIE Fighter Pilot | 8.00 | 15.00 |
| NNO First Order TIE Fighter Pilot (red mark) | | |
| NNO Princess Leia | 12.00 | 25.00 |
| NNO Sidon Ithano | 5.00 | 10.00 |

### 2015 Vinylmation Star Wars The Force Awakens Series 1

| | | |
|---|---|---|
| NNO BB-8 | 10.00 | 20.00 |
| NNO C-3PO | 4.00 | 8.00 |
| NNO Finn (leather jacket) | 5.00 | 10.00 |
| NNO Finn (stormtrooper) | | |
| NNO First Order Stormtrooper | 12.00 | 25.00 |
| NNO Han Solo (chaser) | 15.00 | 30.00 |
| NNO Kylo Ren | 10.00 | 20.00 |
| NNO Poe Dameron | 4.00 | 8.00 |
| NNO Rey | | |
| NNO Rey (desert wear) | 30.00 | 75.00 |

### 2016 Vinylmation Star Wars Rogue One

| | | |
|---|---|---|
| NNO Admiral Raddus | 8.00 | 15.00 |
| NNO Baze Malbus | 6.00 | 12.00 |
| NNO Bistan | 4.00 | 8.00 |
| NNO C2-B5 | 6.00 | 12.00 |
| NNO Cassian Andor | 8.00 | 15.00 |
| NNO Chirrut Imwe | 8.00 | 15.00 |
| NNO Director Orson Krennic | 6.00 | 12.00 |
| NNO Imperial Death Trooper (w/o shoulder pad) | 8.00 | 15.00 |
| NNO Imperial Death Trooper (w/ shoulder pad) | 30.00 | 75.00 |
| NNO Jyn Erso (w/o helm) | 8.00 | 15.00 |
| NNO Jyn Erso (w/ helm) | 60.00 | 120.00 |
| NNO K-2SO | 10.00 | 20.00 |
| NNO Rebel Commando Pao | 8.00 | 15.00 |
| NNO Saw Gererra | 12.00 | 25.00 |

### 2011 Vinylmation Star Wars Series 1

| | | |
|---|---|---|
| NNO Boba Fett | 12.00 | 25.00 |
| NNO C-3PO | 8.00 | 15.00 |
| NNO Chewbacca | 6.00 | 12.00 |
| NNO Darth Vader | 10.00 | 20.00 |
| NNO Han Solo | 12.00 | 25.00 |
| NNO Lando | 10.00 | 20.00 |
| NNO Leia | 6.00 | 12.00 |
| NNO Luke | 6.00 | 12.00 |
| NNO Obi-Wan Kenobi Ghost | 30.00 | 60.00 |
| (super chaser) | | |
| NNO Obi-Wan Kenobi | 8.00 | 15.00 |
| (chaser) | | |
| NNO R2-D2 | 6.00 | 12.00 |
| NNO Stormtrooper | 8.00 | 15.00 |
| NNO Yoda | 8.00 | 15.00 |

### 2012 Vinylmation Star Wars Series 2

| | | |
|---|---|---|
| NNO Darth Vader | 20.00 | 40.00 |
| NNO Garindan | 25.00 | 50.00 |
| (chaser) | | |

| | | |
|---|---|---|
| NNO Grand Moff Tarkin | 6.00 | 12.00 |
| NNO Greedo | 6.00 | 12.00 |
| NNO Han Solo | 6.00 | 12.00 |
| NNO Hologram Princess Leia | 30.00 | 60.00 |
| (LE 2500) Celebration VI Exclusive | | |
| NNO Jawa | 15.00 | 30.00 |
| (LE 2000) | | |
| NNO Luke Skywalker | 8.00 | 15.00 |
| NNO Muftak | 6.00 | 12.00 |
| NNO Obi-Wan Kenobi | 8.00 | 15.00 |
| NNO Ponda Baba | 6.00 | 12.00 |
| NNO Princess Leia | 8.00 | 15.00 |
| NNO R5-D4 | | |
| (LE 2000) | | |
| NNO Tusken Raider | 8.00 | 15.00 |
| NNO Wedge Antilles | 6.00 | 12.00 |

### 2013 Vinylmation Star Wars Series 3

| | | |
|---|---|---|
| NNO Admiral Ackbar | 10.00 | 20.00 |
| NNO Bib Fortuna | 6.00 | 12.00 |
| NNO Biker Scout | 8.00 | 15.00 |
| NNO Emperor Palpatine | 30.00 | 60.00 |
| (chaser) | | |
| NNO Emperor's Royal Guard | 10.00 | 20.00 |
| NNO Gamorrean Guard | 6.00 | 12.00 |
| NNO Helmetless Princess Leia in Boushh Disguise | | |
| (variant) | | |
| NNO Lando Calrissian Skiff Guard Disguise | 8.00 | 15.00 |
| NNO Logray | 10.00 | 20.00 |
| NNO Luke Skywalker Jedi | 8.00 | 15.00 |
| NNO Nien Nunb | 6.00 | 12.00 |
| NNO Princess Leia in Boushh Disguise | 15.00 | 30.00 |
| NNO Wicket | 10.00 | 20.00 |

### 2014 Vinylmation Star Wars Series 4

| | | |
|---|---|---|
| NNO 4-LOM | 6.00 | 12.00 |
| NNO Bespin Princess Leia | 6.00 | 12.00 |
| NNO Boba Fett Concept | 20.00 | 40.00 |
| (combo topper) | | |
| NNO Boba Fett Holiday Special | | |
| (LE 1500) | | |
| NNO Boba Fett | 15.00 | 30.00 |
| (combo topper) | | |
| NNO Bossk | 6.00 | 12.00 |
| NNO Dagobah Luke Skywalker 9-Inch | 30.00 | 60.00 |
| (LE 2000) | | |
| NNO Dengar | 6.00 | 12.00 |
| NNO Han Solo Carbonite | 50.00 | 100.00 |
| (LE 2000) | | |
| NNO Han Solo Hoth | 6.00 | 12.00 |
| NNO Holographic Emperor | 12.00 | 25.00 |
| (LE 2000) | | |
| NNO Jabba the Hutt and Salacious Crumb 9-Inch | 30.00 | 60.00 |
| (LE 2000) | | |
| NNO Luke Skywalker Hoth | 6.00 | 12.00 |
| NNO R2-D2 Dagobah | 12.00 | 25.00 |
| NNO R2-D2 | 15.00 | 30.00 |
| (variant) | | |
| NNO R2-MK | 8.00 | 15.00 |
| NNO Rancor and Malakili 9-and-3-Inch Combo | 40.00 | 80.00 |
| NNO Snowtrooper | 10.00 | 20.00 |
| NNO Tauntaun | 6.00 | 12.00 |
| NNO Ugnaught | 6.00 | 12.00 |
| NNO Wampa Attacked Luke | | |
| (variant) | | |
| NNO Wampa | 15.00 | 30.00 |
| (chaser) | | |
| NNO Yoda 9-Inch | | |
| (LE 2000) | | |
| NNO Zuckuss | 6.00 | 12.00 |

### 2015 Vinylmation Star Wars Series 5

| | | |
|---|---|---|
| NNO Death Star and Trooper 9-and-3-Inch Combo | 40.00 | 80.00 |
| (LE 1000) | | |
| NNO Death Star Droid | 8.00 | 15.00 |
| NNO Dr. Evazan | 6.00 | 12.00 |
| NNO Duros | | |
| NNO Figrin D'an | 15.00 | 30.00 |
| (instrument 1) | | |
| NNO Figrin D'an | 20.00 | 40.00 |
| (instrument 2) | | |
| NNO Figrin D'an | 20.00 | 40.00 |
| (instrument 3) | | |
| NNO Figrin D'an | 15.00 | 30.00 |
| (instrument 4) | | |
| NNO Figrin D'an | 20.00 | 40.00 |
| (instrument 5) | | |
| NNO Han Solo Stormtrooper | 12.00 | 25.00 |
| NNO Heroes of Yavin Han | | |
| (LE 2500) | | |
| NNO Heroes of Yavin Luke | 12.00 | 25.00 |
| (LE 2500) | | |
| NNO Jabba the Hutt | 6.00 | 12.00 |
| NNO Jawa | 20.00 | 40.00 |
| (LE 2500) | | |
| NNO Labria | 6.00 | 12.00 |
| NNO Luke Skywalker Stormtrooper | 50.00 | 100.00 |
| (variant) | | |
| NNO Luke Skywalker X-Wing Pilot | 10.00 | 20.00 |
| (combo topper) | | |
| NNO Momaw Nadon | 6.00 | 12.00 |
| NNO Power Droid | 10.00 | 25.00 |
| (LE 2500) | | |
| NNO Princess Leia | 6.00 | 12.00 |
| NNO Sandtrooper | 8.00 | 15.00 |
| NNO Snaggletooth | 10.00 | 20.00 |
| (chaser) | | |
| NNO Tie Fighter Pilot | 10.00 | 20.00 |

### 2016 Vinylmation Star Wars Series 6

| | | |
|---|---|---|
| NNO Anakin/Yoda/Obi-Wan Spirits | | |
| (LE 2500) | | |
| NNO Han Solo | | |
| NNO Klaatu | | |
| NNO Luke Skywalker | | |
| NNO Luke Skywalker (w/o helmet) | | |
| NNO Max Rebo | | |
| NNO Oola | | |
| NNO Princess Leia | | |
| NNO Princess Leia (chaser) | | |
| NNO Stormtrooper | | |
| NNO Stormtrooper Battle Damaged (variant) | | |
| NNO Teebo | | |
| NNO Wicket 9" | | |
| (LE 1000) | | |

## STAR WARS FILMS

### 1977 Star Wars

Han Solo and Chewbacca

| | | |
|---|---|---|
| COMPLETE SET W/STICKERS (330) | 125.00 | 250.00 |
| COMP.SER.1 SET W/STICKERS (66) | 30.00 | 80.00 |
| COMP.SER.2 SET W/STICKERS (66) | 20.00 | 50.00 |
| COMP.SER.3 SET W/STICKERS (66) | 20.00 | 50.00 |
| COMP.SER.4 SET W/STICKERS (66) | 20.00 | 50.00 |
| COMP.SER.5 SET W/STICKERS (66) | 25.00 | 60.00 |
| UNOPENED SER.1 BOX (36 PACKS) | 1600.00 | 2000.00 |
| UNOPENED SER.1 PACK (7 CARDS+1 STICKER) | | |
| UNOPENED SER.2 BOX (36 PACKS) | 500.00 | 600.00 |
| UNOPENED SER.2 PACK (7 CARDS+1 STICKER) | | |
| UNOPENED SER.3 BOX (36 PACKS) | 400.00 | 500.00 |
| UNOPENED SER.3 PACK (7 CARDS+1 STICKER) | | |
| UNOPENED SER.4 BOX (36 PACKS) | 450.00 | 600.00 |
| UNOPENED SER.4 PACK (7 CARDS+1 STICKER) | | |
| UNOPENED SER.5 BOX (36 PACKS) | 350.00 | 500.00 |
| UNOPENED SER.5 PACK (7 CARDS+1 STICKER) | | |
| COMMON BLUE (1-66) | 0.30 | 0.75 |
| COMMON RED (67-132) | 0.25 | 0.60 |
| COMMON YELLOW (133-198) | 0.25 | 0.60 |
| COMMON GREEN (199-264) | 0.25 | 0.60 |
| COMMON ORANGE (265-330) | 0.25 | 0.60 |
| 207A C-3PO Anthony Daniels ERR Obscene | 30.00 | 80.00 |
| 207B C-3PO Anthony Daniels COR Airbrushed | 0.25 | 0.60 |

### 1977 Star Wars Stickers

| | | |
|---|---|---|
| COMPLETE SET (55) | 40.00 | 80.00 |
| COMPLETE SERIES 1 (11) | 6.00 | 15.00 |
| COMPLETE SERIES 2 (11) | 6.00 | 15.00 |
| COMPLETE SERIES 3 (11) | 6.00 | 15.00 |
| COMPLETE SERIES 4 (11) | 6.00 | 15.00 |
| COMPLETE SERIES 5 (11) | 6.00 | 15.00 |
| COMMON STICKER (1-11) | 0.75 | 2.00 |
| COMMON STICKER (12-22) | 0.60 | 1.50 |
| COMMON STICKER (23-33) | 0.60 | 1.50 |
| COMMON STICKER (34-44) | 0.60 | 1.50 |
| COMMON STICKER (45-55) | 0.60 | 1.50 |
| 1 Luke Skywalker | 1.25 | 3.00 |
| 7 Lord Darth Vader | 1.25 | 3.00 |
| 36 Star Pilot Luke Skywalker | 1.25 | 3.00 |
| 43 Stormtrooper Tool of the Empire | 1.25 | 3.00 |

### 1977 Star Wars Mexican

| | | |
|---|---|---|
| COMPLETE SET (66) | 250.00 | 400.00 |
| UNOPENED PACK (2 CARDS) | 35.00 | 40.00 |
| COMMON CARD (1-66) | 3.00 | 8.00 |

### 1977 Star Wars OPC

| | | |
|---|---|---|
| COMPLETE SET (264) | 200.00 | 400.00 |
| COMPLETE SERIES 1 SET (66) | 100.00 | 200.00 |
| COMPLETE SERIES 2 SET (66) | 60.00 | 120.00 |
| COMPLETE SERIES 3 SET (132) | 50.00 | 100.00 |
| UNOPENED SERIES 1 BOX (36 PACKS) | | |
| UNOPENED SERIES 1 PACK (7 CARDS+1 STICKER) | | |
| UNOPENED SERIES 2 BOX (36 PACKS) | | |
| UNOPENED SERIES 2 PACK (7 CARDS+1 STICKER) | | |
| UNOPENED SERIES 3 BOX (36 PACKS) | | |
| UNOPENED SERIES 3 PACK (7 CARDS+1 STICKER) | | |
| COMMON BLUE (1-66) | 2.50 | 5.00 |
| COMMON RED (67-132) | 1.25 | 3.00 |
| COMMON ORANGE (133-264) | 0.50 | 1.25 |

### 1978 Star Wars General Mills

| | | |
|---|---|---|
| COMPLETE SET (18) | 12.00 | 30.00 |
| COMMON CARD (1-18) | 1.00 | 2.50 |

### 1977 Star Wars Tip Top Ice Cream

| | | |
|---|---|---|
| COMPLETE SET (15) | 80.00 | 150.00 |
| COMMON CARD | 5.00 | 12.00 |
| UNNUMBERED SET LISTED ALPHABETICALLY | | |
| ALSO KNOWN AS R2-D2 SPACE ICE | | |

### 1977 Star Wars Wonder Bread

| | | |
|---|---|---|
| COMPLETE SET (16) | 8.00 | 20.00 |
| COMMON CARD (1-16) | 0.75 | 2.00 |

### 1995 Star Wars Widevision

| | | |
|---|---|---|
| COMPLETE SET (120) | 15.00 | 40.00 |
| UNOPENED BOX (36 PACKS) | 80.00 | 100.00 |
| UNOPENED PACK (10 CARDS) | 2.50 | 3.00 |
| COMMON CARD (1-120) | 0.20 | 0.50 |

### 1995 Star Wars Widevision Finest

| | | |
|---|---|---|
| COMPLETE SET (10) | 40.00 | 100.00 |
| COMMON CARD (1-10) | 5.00 | 12.00 |
| STATED ODDS 1:11 | | |

### 2007 Star Wars 30th Anniversary

A long time ago in a galaxy far, far away...

STAR WARS

| | | |
|---|---|---|
| COMPLETE SET (120) | 5.00 | 12.00 |
| UNOPENED HOBBY BOX (24 PACKS) | 200.00 | 225.00 |
| UNOPENED HOBBY PACK (7 CARDS) | 10.00 | 12.00 |
| UNOPENED RETAIL BOX (24 PACKS) | | |
| UNOPENED RETAIL PACK (7 CARDS) | | |
| COMMON CARD (1-120) | 0.15 | 0.40 |
| *BLUE: 4X TO 10X BASIC CARDS | | |
| *RED: 8X TO 20X BASIC CARDS | | |
| *GOLD/30: 80X TO 150X BASIC CARDS | | |

### 2007 Star Wars 30th Anniversary Animation Cels

| | | |
|---|---|---|
| COMPLETE SET (9) | 6.00 | 15.00 |
| COMMON CARD (1-9) | 1.50 | 4.00 |
| STATED ODDS 1:6 RETAIL | | |

### 2007 Star Wars 30th Anniversary Autographs

| | | |
|---|---|---|
| COMMON AUTO (UNNUMBERED) | 10.00 | 20.00 |
| STATED ODDS 1:43 HOBBY | | |
| NNO Anthony Daniels | 700.00 | 1200.00 |
| NNO Carrie Fisher | 600.00 | 1000.00 |
| NNO Christine Hewett | 12.00 | 30.00 |

| | | | |
|---|---|---|---|
| NNO | Colin Higgins | 15.00 | 40.00 |
| NNO | David Prowse | 300.00 | 600.00 |
| NNO | Gary Kurtz | 30.00 | 75.00 |
| NNO | George Roubichek | 12.00 | 30.00 |
| NNO | Harrison Ford | | |
| NNO | Joe Viskocil | 15.00 | 40.00 |
| NNO | John Dykstra | 20.00 | 50.00 |
| NNO | John Williams | 750.00 | 1200.00 |
| NNO | Jon Berg | 12.00 | 30.00 |
| NNO | Ken Ralston | 15.00 | 40.00 |
| NNO | Kenny Baker | 120.00 | 250.00 |
| NNO | Lorne Peterson | 12.00 | 30.00 |
| NNO | Maria De Aragon | 15.00 | 40.00 |
| NNO | Norman Reynolds | 25.00 | 60.00 |
| NNO | Peter Mayhew | 150.00 | 300.00 |
| NNO | Phil Tippet | 30.00 | 75.00 |
| NNO | Richard Edlund | 15.00 | 40.00 |
| NNO | Richard LeParmentier | 8.00 | 20.00 |
| NNO | Rusty Goffe | 20.00 | 50.00 |

### 2007 Star Wars 30th Anniversary Blister Bonus

| | | |
|---|---|---|
| COMPLETE SET (3) | 3.00 | 8.00 |
| COMMON CARD (1-3) | 1.25 | 3.00 |
| STATED ODDS 1:BLISTER PACK | | |

### 2007 Star Wars 30th Anniversary Magnets

| | | |
|---|---|---|
| COMPLETE SET (9) | 12.00 | 30.00 |
| COMMON CARD (UNNUMBERED) | 1.50 | 4.00 |
| STATED ODDS 1:8 RETAIL | | |

### 2007 Star Wars 30th Anniversary Original Series Box-Toppers

| | | |
|---|---|---|
| SERIES 1 (1-66) BLUE | 12.00 | 30.00 |
| SERIES 2 (67-132) RED | 12.00 | 30.00 |
| SERIES 3 (133-198) YELLOW | 12.00 | 30.00 |
| SERIES 4 (199-264) GREEN | 12.00 | 30.00 |
| SERIES 5 (265-330) ORANGE SP | 30.00 | 80.00 |
| STATED ODDS 1:BOX | | |

### 2007 Star Wars 30th Anniversary Triptych Puzzle

| | | |
|---|---|---|
| COMPLETE SET (27) | 12.00 | 25.00 |
| COMMON CARD (1-27) | 0.75 | 2.00 |
| STATED ODDS 1:3 | | |

### 2017 Star Wars 40th Anniversary

| | | |
|---|---|---|
| COMPLETE SET (200) | 10.00 | 25.00 |
| UNOPENED BOX (24 PACKS) | 120.00 | 150.00 |
| UNOPENED PACK (8 CARDS) | 5.00 | 6.50 |

| | | |
|---|---|---|
| COMMON CARD (1-200) | 0.20 | 0.50 |
| *GREEN: .5X TO 1.2X BASIC CARDS | 0.40 | 1.00 |
| *BLUE: .6X TO 1.5X BASIC CARDS | 0.50 | 1.25 |
| *PURPLE/100: 3X TO 8X BASIC CARDS | 2.50 | 6.00 |
| *GOLD/40: 6X TO 15X BASIC CARDS | 5.00 | 12.00 |
| *RED/1: UNPRICED DUE TO SCARCITY | | |
| *P.P.BLACK/1: UNPRICED DUE TO SCARCITY | | |
| *P.P.CYAN/1: UNPRICED DUE TO SCARCITY | | |
| *P.P.MAGENTA/1: UNPRICED DUE TO SCARCITY | | |
| *P.P.YELLOW/1: UNPRICED DUE TO SCARCITY | | |

### 2017 Star Wars 40th Anniversary Autographed Medallions

STATED PRINT RUN 10 SER.#'d SETS

UNPRICED DUE TO SCARCITY

AD Anthony Daniels
CF Carrie Fisher
HF Harrison Ford
KB Kenny Baker
MH Mark Hamill

### 2017 Star Wars 40th Anniversary Autographs

| | | |
|---|---|---|
| COMMON AUTO | 6.00 | 15.00 |
| *PURPLE/40: .6X TO 1.5X BASIC AUTOS | | |
| *GOLD/10: 1X TO 2.5X BASIC AUTOS | | |
| *RED/1: UNPRICED DUE TO SCARCITY | | |
| *P.P.BLACK/1: UNPRICED DUE TO SCARCITY | | |
| *P.P.CYAN/1: UNPRICED DUE TO SCARCITY | | |
| *P.P.MAGENTA/1: UNPRICED DUE TO SCARCITY | | |
| *P.P.YELLOW/1: UNPRICED DUE TO SCARCITY | | |
| RANDOMLY INSERTED INTO PACKS | | |

| | | | |
|---|---|---|---|
| AAAH | Alan Harris | 6.00 | 15.00 |
| AAAL | Al Lampert | 10.00 | 20.00 |
| AABF | Barbara Frankland | 10.00 | 25.00 |
| AABL | Bai Ling | 8.00 | 20.00 |
| AACR | Clive Revill | 10.00 | 25.00 |
| AADL | Denis Lawson | 10.00 | 25.00 |
| AADR | Deep Roy | 10.00 | 25.00 |
| AAFF | Femi Taylor | 8.00 | 20.00 |
| AAGB | Glyn Baker | 8.00 | 20.00 |
| AAGH | Garrick Hagon | 8.00 | 20.00 |
| AAGR | George Roubicek | 10.00 | 25.00 |
| AAHQ | Hugh Quarshie | 10.00 | 25.00 |
| AAIL | Ian Liston | 10.00 | 25.00 |
| AAJB | Jeremy Bulloch | 15.00 | 40.00 |
| AAJK | Jack Klaff | 10.00 | 25.00 |
| AAKC | Kenneth Colley | 8.00 | 20.00 |
| AAKR | Kipsang Rotich | 10.00 | 25.00 |
| AAMC | Michael Carter | 12.00 | 30.00 |
| AAMW | Matthew Wood | 10.00 | 25.00 |
| AAPS | Paul Springer | 8.00 | 20.00 |
| AARO | Richard Oldfield | 10.00 | 25.00 |
| AASC | Stephen Costantino | 8.00 | 20.00 |
| AATR | Tim Rose | 8.00 | 20.00 |
| AACDW | Corey Dee Williams | 8.00 | 20.00 |
| AAPBL | Paul Blake | 10.00 | 25.00 |
| AAPBR | Paul Brooke | 8.00 | 20.00 |

### 2017 Star Wars 40th Anniversary Celebration Orlando Promos

| | | |
|---|---|---|
| COMPLETE SET (4) | 225.00 | 450.00 |
| COMMON CARD (C1-C4) | 50.00 | 100.00 |
| C1 Luke Skywalker | 80.00 | 150.00 |
| C2 Princess Leia | 80.00 | 150.00 |
| C3 Han Solo | 60.00 | 120.00 |

### 2017 Star Wars 40th Anniversary Classic Stickers

| | | |
|---|---|---|
| COMMON CARD | 12.00 | 30.00 |
| STATED PRINT RUN 100 SER.#'d SETS | | |

### 2017 Star Wars 40th Anniversary Medallions

| | | |
|---|---|---|
| COMMON MEDALLION | 6.00 | 15.00 |
| MILLENNIUM FALCON (1-12) | | |
| DEATH STAR (13-23) | | |
| *BLUE/40: .5X TO 1.2X BASIC MEDALLIONS | 8.00 | 20.00 |
| *PURPLE/25: .6X TO 1.5X BASIC MEDALLIONS | 10.00 | 25.00 |
| *GOLD/10: 1.2X TO 3X BASIC MEDALLIONS | 20.00 | 50.00 |
| *RED/1: UNPRICED DUE TO SCARCITY | | |

### 2017 Star Wars 40th Anniversary Patches

| | | |
|---|---|---|
| COMMON CARD (1-20) | 5.00 | 12.00 |
| *BLUE/40: 6X TO 1.5X BASIC CARDS | 8.00 | 20.00 |
| *PURPLE/25: 1X TO 2.5X BASIC CARDS | 12.00 | 30.00 |
| *GOLD/10: 1.5X TO 4X BASIC CARDS | 20.00 | 50.00 |
| RANDOMLY INSERTED INTO PACKS | | |
| TARGET EXCLUSIVE | | |

### 2017 Star Wars 1978 Sugar Free Wrappers Set

| | | |
|---|---|---|
| COMPLETE SET (49) | 10.00 | 25.00 |
| COMPLETE FACTORY SET (51) | | |
| COMMON CARD (1-49) | 0.30 | 0.75 |
| *BLUE/75: 2X TO 5X BASIC CARDS | 1.50 | 4.00 |
| *GREEN/40: 4X TO 10X BASIC CARDS | 3.00 | 8.00 |
| *GOLD/10: 6X TO 15X BASIC CARDS | 5.00 | 12.00 |
| *RED/1: UNPRICED DUE TO SCARCITY | | |

### 2013 Star Wars Illustrated A New Hope

| | | |
|---|---|---|
| COMPLETE SET (100) | 8.00 | 20.00 |
| COMMON CARD (1-100) | 0.20 | 0.50 |

*PURPLE: 2.5X TO 6X BASIC CARDS
*BRONZE: 5X TO 12X BASIC CARDS
*GOLD/10: 50X TO 120X BASIC CARDS
*P.P.BLACK/1: UNPRICED DUE TO SCARCITY
*P.P.CYAN/1: UNPRICED DUE TO SCARCITY
*P.P.MAGENTA/1: UNPRICED DUE TO SCARCITY
*P.P.YELLOW/1: UNPRICED DUE TO SCARCITY

### 2013 Star Wars Illustrated A New Hope Film Cels

| | | |
|---|---|---|
| COMPLETE SET (20) | 250.00 | 500.00 |
| COMMON CARD (FR1-FR20) | 12.00 | 30.00 |
| FR8  Greedo's Bounty | 15.00 | 40.00 |
| FR14  The Final Encounter | 60.00 | 120.00 |

### 2013 Star Wars Illustrated A New Hope Movie Poster Reinterpretations

| | | |
|---|---|---|
| COMPLETE SET (9) | 5.00 | 12.00 |
| COMMON CARD (MP1-MP9) | 1.25 | 3.00 |

*P.P.BLACK/1: UNPRICED DUE TO SCARCITY
*P.P.CYAN/1: UNPRICED DUE TO SCARCITY
*P.P.MAGENTA/1: UNPRICED DUE TO SCARCITY
*P.P.YELLOW/1: UNPRICED DUE TO SCARCITY
STATED ODDS 1:3

### 2013 Star Wars Illustrated A New Hope One Year Earlier

| | | |
|---|---|---|
| COMPLETE SET (18) | 5.00 | 12.00 |
| COMMON CARD (OY1-OY18) | 0.60 | 1.50 |

*P.P.BLACK/1: UNPRICED DUE TO SCARCITY
*P.P.CYAN/1: UNPRICED DUE TO SCARCITY
*P.P.MAGENTA/1: UNPRICED DUE TO SCARCITY

---

*P.P.YELLOW/1: UNPRICED DUE TO SCARCITY
STATED ODDS 1:2

### 2013 Star Wars Illustrated A New Hope Radio Drama Puzzle

| | | |
|---|---|---|
| COMPLETE SET (6) | 5.00 | 12.00 |
| COMMON CARD (1-6) | 1.50 | 4.00 |

*P.P.BLACK/1: UNPRICED DUE TO SCARCITY
*P.P.CYAN/1: UNPRICED DUE TO SCARCITY
*P.P.MAGENTA/1: UNPRICED DUE TO SCARCITY
*P.P.YELLOW/1: UNPRICED DUE TO SCARCITY
STATED ODDS 1:8

### 2013 Star Wars Illustrated A New Hope The Mission Destroy the Death Star

| | | |
|---|---|---|
| COMPLETE SET (12) | 30.00 | 60.00 |
| COMMON CARD (1-12) | 3.00 | 8.00 |

*P.P.BLACK/1: UNPRICED DUE TO SCARCITY
*P.P.CYAN/1: UNPRICED DUE TO SCARCITY
*P.P.MAGENTA/1: UNPRICED DUE TO SCARCITY
*P.P.YELLOW/1: UNPRICED DUE TO SCARCITY
STATED ODDS 1:12

### 2013 Star Wars Illustrated A New Hope Promos

| | | |
|---|---|---|
| COMPLETE SET (4) | 5.00 | 12.00 |

### 2018 Star Wars A New Hope Black and White

| | | |
|---|---|---|
| COMPLETE SET (140) | 15.00 | 40.00 |
| UNOPENED BOX (7 PACKS) | | |
| UNOPENED PACK (8 CARDS) | | |
| COMMON CARD (1-140) | 0.25 | 0.60 |

*SEPIA: .75X TO 2X BASIC CARDS | 0.50 | 1.25
*BLUE: 1X TO 2.5X BASIC CARDS | 0.60 | 1.50
*GREEN/99: 3X TO 8X BASIC CARDS | 2.00 | 5.00
*PURPLE/25: 8X TO 20X BASIC CARDS | 5.00 | 12.00
*RED/10: UNPRICED DUE TO SCARCITY
*METAL/1: UNPRICED DUE TO SCARCITY

### 2018 Star Wars A New Hope Black and White Autographs

| | | |
|---|---|---|
| COMMON AUTO | 6.00 | 15.00 |

*BLUE/99: .5X TO 1.2X BASIC AUTOS
*GREEN/25: .6X TO 1.5X BASIC AUTOS
*PURPLE/10: UNPRICED DUE TO SCARCITY
*RED/1: UNPRICED DUE TO SCARCITY
STATED ODDS 1:18

| | | |
|---|---|---|
| NNO  Al Lampert | 8.00 | 20.00 |
| NNO  Annette Jones | 8.00 | 20.00 |
| NNO  Barbara Frankland | 8.00 | 20.00 |
| NNO  Denis Lawson | 12.00 | 30.00 |
| NNO  Garrick Hagon | 8.00 | 20.00 |
| NNO  Paul Blake | 10.00 | 25.00 |

### 2018 Star Wars A New Hope Black and White Autographs Blue

*BLUE: .5X TO 1.2X BASIC AUTOS
STATED ODDS 1:62
STATED PRINT RUN 99 SER.#'d SETS

| | | |
|---|---|---|
| NNO  Peter Mayhew | 30.00 | 75.00 |

---

### 2018 Star Wars A New Hope Black and White Autographs Green

*GREEN: .6X TO 1.5X BASIC AUTOS
STATED ODDS 1:202
STATED PRINT RUN 25 SER.#'d SETS

| | | |
|---|---|---|
| NNO  Anthony Daniels | 75.00 | 150.00 |
| NNO  Kenny Baker | 60.00 | 120.00 |

### 2018 Star Wars A New Hope Black and White Behind-the-Scenes

| | | |
|---|---|---|
| COMPLETE SET (41) | 20.00 | 50.00 |
| COMMON CARD (BTS1-BTS41) | 2.00 | 5.00 |
| STATED ODDS 1:2 | | |

### 2018 Star Wars A New Hope Black and White Concept Art

| | | |
|---|---|---|
| COMPLETE SET (12) | 10.00 | 25.00 |
| COMMON CARD (CA1-CA12) | 1.50 | 4.00 |
| STATED ODDS 1:4 | | |

### 2018 Star Wars A New Hope Black and White Iconic Characters

| | | |
|---|---|---|
| COMPLETE SET (12) | 15.00 | 40.00 |
| COMMON CARD (IC1-IC12) | 2.00 | 5.00 |
| STATED ODDS 1:12 | | |
| IC1  Luke Skywalker | 4.00 | 10.00 |
| IC2  Han Solo | 5.00 | 12.00 |
| IC3  Princess Leia Organa | 4.00 | 10.00 |
| IC4  Chewbacca | 2.50 | 6.00 |
| IC5  Ben (Obi-Wan) Kenobi | 4.00 | 10.00 |
| IC7  R2-D2 | 2.50 | 6.00 |
| IC8  Darth Vader | 5.00 | 12.00 |

### 2018 Star Wars A New Hope Black and White Posters

| | | |
|---|---|---|
| COMPLETE SET (12) | 12.00 | 30.00 |
| COMMON CARD (PO1-PO12) | 1.50 | 4.00 |
| STATED ODDS 1:6 | | |

### 1980 Star Wars Empire Strikes Back

"WELCOME, YOUNG LUKE!"

| | | |
|---|---|---|
| COMPLETE SET (352) | 60.00 | 120.00 |
| COMPLETE SET W/STICKERS (440) | 75.00 | 150.00 |
| COMPLETE SERIES 1 SET (132) | 20.00 | 50.00 |
| COMPLETE SERIES 1 SET W/STICKERS (165) | 25.00 | 60.00 |
| COMPLETE SERIES 2 SET (132) | 15.00 | 40.00 |
| COMPLETE SERIES 2 SET W/STICKERS (165) | 20.00 | 50.00 |
| COMPLETE SERIES 3 SET (88) | 12.00 | 30.00 |
| COMPLETE SERIES 3 SET W/STICKERS (110) | 15.00 | 40.00 |
| UNOPENED SERIES 1 BOX (36 PACKS) | 150.00 | 200.00 |
| UNOPENED SERIES 1 PACK (12 CARDS+1 STICKER) | 5.00 | 6.00 |
| UNOPENED SERIES 2 BOX (36 PACKS) | 65.00 | 80.00 |

| | | |
|---|---|---|
| UNOPENED SERIES 2 PACK (12 CARDS+1 STICKER) | 2.50 | 3.00 |
| UNOPENED SERIES 3 BOX (36 PACKS) | 65.00 | 80.00 |
| UNOPENED SERIES 3 PACK (12 CARDS+1 STICKER) | 2.50 | 3.00 |
| COMMON SERIES 1 CARD (1-132) | 0.10 | 0.25 |
| COMMON SERIES 2 CARD (133-264) | 0.06 | 0.15 |
| COMMON SERIES 3 CARD (265-352) | 0.06 | 0.15 |

## 1980 Star Wars Empire Strikes Back Stickers

| | | |
|---|---|---|
| COMPLETE SET (88) | 15.00 | 40.00 |
| COMPLETE SERIES 1 SET (33) | 8.00 | 20.00 |
| COMPLETE SERIES 2 SET (33) | 6.00 | 15.00 |
| COMPLETE SERIES 3 SET (22) | 3.00 | 8.00 |
| COMMON CARD (1-33) | 0.60 | 1.50 |
| COMMON CARD (34-66) | 0.40 | 1.00 |
| COMMON CARD (67-88) | 0.20 | 0.50 |

## 1980 Star Wars Empire Strikes Back 5X7 Photos

| | | |
|---|---|---|
| COMPLETE SET (30) | 12.00 | 30.00 |
| COMMON CARD (1-30) | 1.00 | 2.50 |

## 1980 Star Wars Empire Strikes Back 5X7 Photos Test Issue

| | | |
|---|---|---|
| COMPLETE SET (30) | 100.00 | 200.00 |
| COMMON CARD (1-30) | 3.00 | 8.00 |

## 1980 Star Wars Empire Strikes Back Twinkies New Zealand

| | | |
|---|---|---|
| COMPLETE SET (6) | 15.00 | 40.00 |
| COMMON CARD (UNNUMBERED) | 4.00 | 10.00 |

## 1980 Star Wars Empire Strikes Back York Peanut Butter Discs

| | | |
|---|---|---|
| COMPLETE SET (6) | 12.00 | 30.00 |
| COMMON CARD (1-6) | 3.00 | 8.00 |

## 1995 Star Wars Empire Strikes Back Widevision

| | | |
|---|---|---|
| COMPLETE SET (144) | 12.00 | 30.00 |
| UNOPENED BOX (36 PACKS) | 30.00 | 40.00 |
| UNOPENED PACK (9 CARDS) | 1.00 | 1.25 |
| COMMON CARD (1-144) | 0.25 | 0.60 |

## 1995 Star Wars Empire Strikes Back Widevision Finest

| | | |
|---|---|---|
| COMPLETE SET (10) | 40.00 | 100.00 |
| COMMON CARD (C1-C10) | 4.00 | 10.00 |
| STATED ODDS 1:12 | | |

## 1995 Star Wars Empire Strikes Back Widevision Mini Posters

| | | |
|---|---|---|
| COMPLETE SET (6) | 40.00 | 80.00 |
| COMMON CARD (1-6) | 6.00 | 15.00 |
| STATED ODDS 1:BOX | | |

## 1995 Star Wars Empire Strikes Back Widevision Promos

| | | |
|---|---|---|
| COMMON CARD | 2.00 | 5.00 |
| NNO 3-Card Sheet | 5.00 | 12.00 |
| P1-P3 | | |

## 2010 Star Wars Empire Strikes Back 3-D Widevision

| | | |
|---|---|---|
| COMPLETE SET (48) | 10.00 | 25.00 |
| COMMON CARD (1-48) | 0.40 | 1.00 |
| P1 Luke Skywalker PROMO | 8.00 | 20.00 |

## 2010 Star Wars Empire Strikes Back 3-D Widevision Autographs

| | | |
|---|---|---|
| COMMON CARD | 150.00 | 300.00 |
| STATED ODDS 1:1,055 | | |
| 1 Irvin Kershner | 250.00 | 400.00 |
| 2 Ralph McQuarrie | 500.00 | 800.00 |
| 4 David Prowse | 500.00 | 800.00 |
| 6 Carrie Fisher | 500.00 | 800.00 |
| 8 Mark Hamill | 400.00 | 600.00 |

## 1996 Star Wars Empire Strikes Back 3-Di

| | | |
|---|---|---|
| P1 AT-ATs | 2.00 | 5.00 |

## 2019 Star Wars Empire Strikes Back Black and White

| | | |
|---|---|---|
| COMPLETE SET (150) | 20.00 | 50.00 |
| UNOPENED BOX (7 PACKS) | 55.00 | 70.00 |
| UNOPENED PACK (8 CARDS) | 8.00 | 10.00 |
| COMMON CARD (1-150) | 0.30 | 0.75 |
| *SEPIA: 1X TO 2.5X BASIC CARDS | | |
| *BLUE HUE: 2.5X TO 6X BASIC CARDS | | |
| *GREEN HUE/99: 4X TO 10X BASIC CARDS | | |
| *PURPLE HUE/25: 6X TO 15X BASIC CARDS | | |
| *RED HUE/10: UNPRICED DUE TO SCARCITY | | |
| *ORANGE HUE/5: UNPRICED DUE TO SCARCITY | | |
| *METAL/1: UNPRICED DUE TO SCARCITY | | |

## 2019 Star Wars Empire Strikes Back Black and White Autographs

| | | |
|---|---|---|
| COMMON AUTO | | |
| *BLUE HUE/99: .5X TO 1.2X BASIC AUTOS | | |
| *GREEN HUE/25: .6X TO 1.5X BASIC AUTOS | | |
| *PURPLE HUE/10: UNPRICED DUE TO SCARCITY | | |
| *ORANGE HUE/5: UNPRICED DUE TO SCARCITY | | |
| *RED HUE/1: UNPRICED DUE TO SCARCITY | | |
| STATED ODDS 1:22 | | |
| AAH Alan Harris | 10.00 | 25.00 |
| ACM Cathy Munro | 8.00 | 20.00 |
| ACP Chris Parsons | 8.00 | 20.00 |
| ACR Clive Revill | 6.00 | 15.00 |
| AHW Howie Weed | 8.00 | 20.00 |
| AJB Jeremy Bulloch | 20.00 | 50.00 |
| AJM John Morton/Dak' | 8.00 | 20.00 |
| AJR John Ratzenberger | 15.00 | 40.00 |
| AKC Kenneth Colley | 8.00 | 20.00 |
| AMC Mark Capri | 6.00 | 15.00 |
| AMJ Milton Johns | 10.00 | 25.00 |
| ARO Richard Oldfield | 8.00 | 20.00 |
| AJMB John Morton/Boba Fett's Double | 10.00 | 25.00 |

## 2019 Star Wars Empire Strikes Back Black and White Behind-the-Scenes

| | | |
|---|---|---|
| COMPLETE SET (40) | 25.00 | 60.00 |
| COMMON CARD (BTS1-BTS40) | 1.25 | 3.00 |
| STATED ODDS 1:2 | | |

## 2019 Star Wars Empire Strikes Back Black and White Color Short-Printed Autographs

| | | |
|---|---|---|
| COMMON AUTO | | |
| STATED ODDS 1:3,947 | | |
| NNO Kenny Baker | | |
| NNO Anthony Daniels | | |
| NNO Carrie Fisher | | |
| NNO Harrison Ford | | |
| NNO Peter Mayhew | | |

## 2019 Star Wars Empire Strikes Back Black and White Concept Art

| | | |
|---|---|---|
| COMPLETE SET (10) | 12.00 | 30.00 |
| COMMON CARD (CA1-CA10) | 2.00 | 5.00 |
| STATED ODDS 1:4 | | |

## 2019 Star Wars Empire Strikes Back Black and White Dual Autographs

| | | |
|---|---|---|
| STATED ODDS 1:525 | | |
| UNPRICED DUE TO SCARCITY | | |
| NNO K.Baker/A.Daniels | | |
| NNO J.Bulloch/A.Harris | | |
| NNO B.Williams/P.Mayhew | | |
| NNO H.Ford/C.Fisher | | |
| NNO A.Harris/C.Munroe | | |
| NNO D.Lawson/J.Morton | | |
| NNO D.Lawson/R.Oldfield | | |
| NNO C.Parsons/C.Munroe | | |

## 2019 Star Wars Empire Strikes Back Black and White Iconic Characters

| | | |
|---|---|---|
| COMMON CARD (IC1-IC20) | 5.00 | 12.00 |
| STATED ODDS 1:12 | | |

## 2019 Star Wars Empire Strikes Back Black and White Posters

| | | |
|---|---|---|
| COMPLETE SET (10) | 12.00 | 30.00 |
| COMMON CARD (PO1-PO10) | 2.00 | 5.00 |
| STATED ODDS 1:6 | | |

## 2019 Star Wars Empire Strikes Back Black and White Six-Person Autograph

STATED ODDS 1:74,984
STATED PRINT RUN 1 SER.#'d SET
UNPRICED DUE TO SCARCITY

NNO H.Ford/C.Fisher/B.Williams
A.Daniels/K.Baker/P.Mayhew

## 2019 Star Wars Empire Strikes Back Black and White Triple Autographs

STATED ODDS 1:728
UNPRICED DUE TO SCARCITY

NNO J.Bulloch/C.Munroe/C.Parsons
NNO H.Ford/C.Fisher/B.Williams
NNO D.Lawson/J.Morton/R.Oldfield
NNO P.Mayhew/K.Baker/A.Daniels
NNO C.Munroe/C.Parsons/A.Harris

## 2015 Star Wars Illustrated Empire Strikes Back

| | | |
|---|---|---|
| COMPLETE SET (100) | 10.00 | 25.00 |
| COMMON CARD (1-100) | 0.20 | 0.50 |
| *PURPLE: 5X TO 12X BASIC CARDS | 2.50 | 6.00 |
| *BRONZE: 8X TO 20X BASIC CARDS | 4.00 | 10.00 |
| *GOLD/10: 20X TO 50X BASIC CARDS | 10.00 | 25.00 |
| *P.P.BLACK/1: UNPRICED DUE TO SCARCITY | | |
| *P.P.CYAN/1: UNPRICED DUE TO SCARCITY | | |
| *P.P.MAGENTA/1: UNPRICED DUE TO SCARCITY | | |
| *P.P.YELLOW/1: UNPRICED DUE TO SCARCITY | | |

## 2015 Star Wars Illustrated Empire Strikes Back Celebration VII Promos

| | | |
|---|---|---|
| COMPLETE SET (10) | 10.00 | 25.00 |
| COMMON CARD (1-10) | 1.50 | 4.00 |

## 2015 Star Wars Illustrated Empire Strikes Back Artist Autographs

| | | |
|---|---|---|
| COMMON BUSCH (EVEN #'s) | 5.00 | 12.00 |
| COMMON MARTINEZ (ODD #'s) | 5.00 | 12.00 |

## 2015 Star Wars Illustrated Empire Strikes Back Film Cel Relics

| | | |
|---|---|---|
| COMPLETE SET (25) | 100.00 | 200.00 |
| COMMON CARD (SKIP #'d) | 6.00 | 15.00 |
| FR2 Back at Echo Base | 8.00 | 20.00 |
| FR3 Monster in the Snow | 8.00 | 20.00 |
| FR6 The Imperial Walkers | 10.00 | 25.00 |
| FR7 Luke Vs. the AT-AT | 8.00 | 20.00 |
| FR8 Imperial Pursuit | 10.00 | 25.00 |
| FR9 Asteroid Field | 8.00 | 20.00 |
| FR10 Dagobah Landing | 8.00 | 20.00 |
| FR13 Message From the Emperor | 12.00 | 30.00 |
| FR15 Bounty Hunters Assemble | 8.00 | 20.00 |
| FR16 Failure at the Cave | 10.00 | 25.00 |
| FR20 A Most Gracious Host | 10.00 | 25.00 |
| FR25 You Are not a Jedi Yet | 10.00 | 25.00 |
| FR26 Lando's Redemption | 8.00 | 20.00 |
| FR27 Battle in the Gantry | 10.00 | 25.00 |
| FR28 The Truth Revealed | 8.00 | 20.00 |
| FR29 Rescuing Luke | 15.00 | 40.00 |
| FR30 Saying Farewell | 8.00 | 20.00 |

## 2015 Star Wars Illustrated Empire Strikes Back Movie Poster Reinterpretations

| | | |
|---|---|---|
| COMPLETE SET (10) | 8.00 | 20.00 |
| COMMON CARD (MP1-MP10) | 1.50 | 4.00 |
| *P.P.BLACK/1: UNPRICED DUE TO SCARCITY | | |
| *P.P.CYAN/1: UNPRICED DUE TO SCARCITY | | |
| *P.P.MAGENTA/1: UNPRICED DUE TO SCARCITY | | |
| *P.P.YELLOW/1: UNPRICED DUE TO SCARCITY | | |
| STATED ODDS 1:3 | | |

## 2015 Star Wars Illustrated Empire Strikes Back One Year Earlier

| | | |
|---|---|---|
| COMPLETE SET (18) | 15.00 | 40.00 |
| COMMON CARD (OY1-OY18) | 1.50 | 4.00 |
| *P.P.BLACK/1: UNPRICED DUE TO SCARCITY | | |
| *P.P.CYAN/1: UNPRICED DUE TO SCARCITY | | |
| *P.P.MAGENTA/1: UNPRICED DUE TO SCARCITY | | |
| *P.P.YELLOW/1: UNPRICED DUE TO SCARCITY | | |
| STATED ODDS 1:2 | | |

## 2015 Star Wars Illustrated Empire Strikes Back The Force Awakens Inserts

| | | |
|---|---|---|
| COMPLETE SET (4) | 20.00 | 50.00 |
| COMMON CARD (SKIP #'d) | 8.00 | 20.00 |

## 2015 Star Wars Illustrated Empire Strikes Back The Mission Capture Skywalker

| | | |
|---|---|---|
| COMPLETE SET (10) | 12.00 | 30.00 |
| COMMON CARD (1-10) | 2.50 | 6.00 |
| *P.P.BLACK/1: UNPRICED DUE TO SCARCITY | | |
| *P.P.CYAN/1: UNPRICED DUE TO SCARCITY | | |
| *P.P.MAGENTA/1: UNPRICED DUE TO SCARCITY | | |
| *P.P.YELLOW/1: UNPRICED DUE TO SCARCITY | | |
| STATED ODDS 1:8 | | |
| 3 Han Solo | 3.00 | 8.00 |
| 9 Boba Fett | 4.00 | 10.00 |

## 1983 Star Wars Return of the Jedi

| | | |
|---|---|---|
| COMPLETE SET (220) | 15.00 | 40.00 |
| COMMON CARD (1-220) | 0.15 | 0.40 |

## 1983 Star Wars Return of the Jedi Stickers

| | | |
|---|---|---|
| COMPLETE SET W/O VARIANTS (55) | 6.00 | 15.00 |
| COMMON CARD (1-55) | 0.20 | 0.50 |
| STATED ODDS 1:1 | | |

## 2014 Star Wars Return of the Jedi 3-D Widevision

| | | |
|---|---|---|
| COMPLETE SET (44) | 12.00 | 30.00 |
| COMMON CARD (1-44) | 0.50 | 1.25 |
| TOPPS WEBSITE EXCLUSIVE SET | | |

## 2014 Star Wars Return of the Jedi 3-D Widevision Autographs

| | | |
|---|---|---|
| COMMON AUTO (UNNUMBERED) | 15.00 | 40.00 |
| STATED ODDS 1:SET | | |
| NNO Alan Harris | 25.00 | 60.00 |
| NNO Barrie Holland | 25.00 | 60.00 |
| NNO Carrie Fisher | 600.00 | 1000.00 |
| NNO Jeremy Bulloch | 50.00 | 100.00 |
| NNO Mark Hamill | 500.00 | 800.00 |
| NNO Mike Quinn | 20.00 | 50.00 |
| NNO Peter Mayhew | 50.00 | 100.00 |
| NNO Tim Rose | 20.00 | 50.00 |

## 2014 Star Wars Return of the Jedi 3-D Widevision Manufactured Patches

| | | |
|---|---|---|
| COMPLETE SET (4) | 50.00 | 100.00 |
| COMMON CARD | 10.00 | 25.00 |
| STATED ODDS ONE PATCH/SKETCH PER SET | | |

## 1983 Star Wars Return of the Jedi Kellogg's Stick'R Series

| | | |
|---|---|---|
| COMPLETE SET (10) | 12.00 | 30.00 |
| COMMON CARD (1-10) | 2.00 | 5.00 |

## 1983 Star Wars Return of the Jedi OPC

| | | |
|---|---|---|
| COMPLETE SET (132) | 25.00 | 60.00 |
| UNOPENED BOX (36 PACKS) | 125.00 | 150.00 |
| UNOPENED PACK | 4.00 | 5.00 |
| COMMON CARD (1-132) | 0.30 | 0.75 |

## 1997 Star Wars Return of the Jedi Special Edition

NNO  Crescent City Con XII

## 1996 Star Wars Return of the Jedi Widevision

INT. COCKPIT — MILLENNIUM FALCON

| | | |
|---|---|---|
| COMPLETE SET (144) | 10.00 | 25.00 |
| UNOPENED BOX (24 PACKS) | 50.00 | 60.00 |
| UNOPENED PACK (9 CARDS) | 1.50 | 2.00 |
| COMMON CARD (1-144) | 0.20 | 0.50 |

DIII  Admiral Akbar

## 1996 Star Wars Return of the Jedi Widevision Finest

| | | |
|---|---|---|
| COMPLETE SET (10) | 40.00 | 80.00 |
| COMMON CARD (C1-C10) | 4.00 | 10.00 |
| STATED ODDS 1:12 | | |

## 1996 Star Wars Return of the Jedi Widevision Mini Posters

| | | |
|---|---|---|
| COMPLETE SET (6) | 40.00 | 80.00 |
| COMMON CARD (1-6) | 6.00 | 15.00 |
| STATED ODDS 1:BOX | | |

## 1996 Star Wars Return of the Jedi Widevision Promos

| | | |
|---|---|---|
| COMMON CARD | 2.00 | 5.00 |
| P6  Luke, Han, & Chewbacca in Jabba's Palace | 25.00 | 60.00 |
| NNO  1-Card Sheet | | |
| Complete the Trilogy | | |

## 1999 Star Wars Episode One Widevision Series One

| | | |
|---|---|---|
| COMPLETE SET (80) | 8.00 | 20.00 |
| UNOPENED HOBBY BOX (36 PACKS) | 45.00 | 60.00 |
| UNOPENED HOBBY PACK (8 CARDS) | 1.50 | 2.00 |
| UNOPENED RETAIL BOX (11 PACKS) | 30.00 | 45.00 |
| UNOPENED RETAIL PACK (8 CARDS) | 2.75 | 4.00 |
| COMMON CARD (1-80) | 0.25 | 0.60 |

## 1999 Star Wars Episode One Widevision Series One Chrome

| | | |
|---|---|---|
| COMPLETE SET (8) | 30.00 | 60.00 |
| COMMON CARD (C1-C8) | 4.00 | 10.00 |
| STATED ODDS 1:12 | | |

## 1999 Star Wars Episode One Widevision Series One Expansion

| | | |
|---|---|---|
| COMPLETE SET (40) | 30.00 | 60.00 |
| COMMON CARD (X1-X40) | 1.00 | 2.50 |
| STATED ODDS 1:2 | | |

## 1999 Star Wars Episode One Widevision Series One Foil

| | | |
|---|---|---|
| COMPLETE SET (10) | 30.00 | 60.00 |
| COMMON CARD (F1-F10) | 3.00 | 8.00 |

## 1999 Star Wars Episode One Widevision Series One Stickers

| | | |
|---|---|---|
| COMPLETE SET (16) | 8.00 | 20.00 |
| COMMON CARD (S1-S16) | 0.60 | 1.50 |

## 1999 Star Wars Episode One Widevision Series One Tin Inserts

| | | |
|---|---|---|
| COMPLETE SET (5) | 12.00 | 30.00 |
| COMMON CARD (1-5) | 4.00 | 10.00 |
| STATED ODDS ONE PER RETAIL TIN | | |
| 2  Darth Maul | 5.00 | 12.00 |

## 1999 Star Wars Episode One Widevision Series Two

| | | |
|---|---|---|
| COMPLETE SET (80) | 8.00 | 20.00 |
| UNOPENED HOBBY BOX (36 PACKS) | 40.00 | 50.00 |
| UNOPENED HOBBY PACK (8 CARDS) | 1.25 | 1.50 |
| UNOPENED RETAIL BOX (24 PACKS) | 35.00 | 45.00 |
| UNOPENED RETAIL PACK (8 CARDS) | 1.50 | 1.75 |
| COMMON CARD (1-80) | 0.25 | 0.60 |

## 1999 Star Wars Episode One Widevision Series Two Box-Toppers

| | | |
|---|---|---|
| COMPLETE SET (3) | 10.00 | 20.00 |
| COMMON CARD (1-3) | 4.00 | 10.00 |
| STATED ODDS 1:HOBBY BOX | | |

## 1999 Star Wars Episode One Widevision Series Two Chrome Hobby

| | | |
|---|---|---|
| COMPLETE SET (4) | 12.00 | 25.00 |
| COMMON CARD (HC1-HC4) | 4.00 | 10.00 |
| STATED ODDS 1:18 HOBBY | | |

## 1999 Star Wars Episode One Widevision Series Two Chrome Retail

| | | |
|---|---|---|
| COMPLETE SET (4) | 20.00 | 40.00 |
| COMMON CARD (C1-C4) | 6.00 | 15.00 |
| STATED ODDS 1:18 RETAIL | | |

## 1999 Star Wars Episode One Widevision Series Two Embossed Hobby

| | | |
|---|---|---|
| COMPLETE SET (6) | 8.00 | 20.00 |
| COMMON CARD (HE1-HE6) | 2.50 | 6.00 |
| STATED ODDS 1:12 HOBBY | | |

## 1999 Star Wars Episode One Widevision Series Two Embossed Retail

| | | |
|---|---|---|
| COMPLETE SET (6) | 20.00 | 40.00 |
| COMMON CARD (E1-E6) | 4.00 | 10.00 |
| STATED ODDS 1:12 RETAIL | | |

## 1999 Star Wars Episode One Widevision Series Two Promos

| | | |
|---|---|---|
| COMPLETE SET (2) | 3.00 | 8.00 |
| COMMON CARD (P1-P2) | 2.00 | 5.00 |

## 2000 Star Wars Episode One 3-D

| | | |
|---|---|---|
| COMPLETE SET (46) | 20.00 | 40.00 |
| UNOPENED BOX (36 PACKS) | 45.00 | 60.00 |
| UNOPENED PACK (2 CARDS) | 1.50 | 2.00 |
| COMMON CARD (1-46) | 0.50 | 1.25 |

## 2000 Star Wars Episode One 3-D Multi-Motion

| | | |
|---|---|---|
| COMPLETE SET (2) | 10.00 | 25.00 |
| COMMON CARD (1-2) | 6.00 | 15.00 |

## 1999 Star Wars Episode I Bluebird Potato Chips New Zealand

| | | |
|---|---|---|
| COMPLETE SET (30) | 10.00 | 25.00 |
| COMMON CARD (1-30) | 0.60 | 1.50 |

## 1999 Star Wars Episode I Family Toy

| | | |
|---|---|---|
| COMPLETE SET (3) | 8.00 | 20.00 |
| COMMON CARD | 4.00 | 10.00 |

## 1999 Star Wars Episode I Flip Images

| | | |
|---|---|---|
| COMPLETE SET (6) | 5.00 | 12.00 |
| COMMON CARD | 1.25 | 3.00 |

## 1999 Star Wars Episode I Hallmark

| | | |
|---|---|---|
| H1  Anakin Skywalker and Obi-Wan Kenobi | 2.00 | 5.00 |
| H2  Obi-Wan Kenobi and Yoda | 2.00 | 5.00 |
| H3  Qui-Gon Jinn and Obi-Wan Kenobi | 2.00 | 5.00 |

## 1999 Star Wars Episode I iKon

01. Padmé

| | | |
|---|---|---|
| COMPLETE SET (60) | 6.00 | 15.00 |
| UNOPENED BOX (36 PACKS) | | |
| UNOPENED PACK (6 CARDS) | | |
| COMMON CARD (1-60) | 0.20 | 0.50 |
| *SILVER: 1.5X TO 4X BASIC CARDS | | |
| *GOLD: 2.5X TO 6X BASIC CARDS | | |

## 1999 Star Wars Episode I KFC Australia

| | | |
|---|---|---|
| COMPLETE SET (10) | 3.00 | 8.00 |
| COMMON CARD (1-10) | 0.50 | 1.25 |

### 1999 Star Wars Episode I KFC UK

| | | |
|---|---|---|
| COMPLETE SET (20) | 8.00 | 20.00 |
| COMMON CARD (1-20) | 0.60 | 1.50 |
| STATED ODDS 1: | | |

### 1999 Star Wars Episode I Lay's Minis

| | | |
|---|---|---|
| COMPLETE SET (12) | 6.00 | 15.00 |
| COMMON CARD (1-12) | 0.75 | 2.00 |

### 1999 Star Wars Episode I The Phantom Menace Harmony Foods

| | | |
|---|---|---|
| COMPLETE SET (24) | 50.00 | 100.00 |
| COMMON CARD (1-24) | 2.00 | 5.00 |

### 1999 Star Wars Episode I The Phantom Menace Kentucky Fried Chicken Employee Stickers

| | | |
|---|---|---|
| COMPLETE SET (5) | 6.00 | 15.00 |
| COMMON CARD (UNNUMBERED) | 2.00 | 5.00 |

### 1999 Star Wars Episode I The Phantom Menace Show Promo

| | | |
|---|---|---|
| NNO  DLP Exclusive Presentation | 5.00 | 12.00 |

### 2001 Star Wars Episode I The Phantom Menace Walmart DVD Promos

| | | |
|---|---|---|
| COMPLETE SET (4) | 3.00 | 8.00 |
| COMMON CARD | 1.25 | 3.00 |

### 1999 Star Wars Episode I Star Mart

| | | |
|---|---|---|
| NNO  Anakin Skywalker | 2.00 | 5.00 |
| NNO  C-3PO | 2.00 | 5.00 |
| NNO  Darth Maul | 2.00 | 5.00 |
| NNO  R2-D2 | 2.00 | 5.00 |

### 2019 Star Wars On-Demand Phantom Menace 20th Anniversary

| | | |
|---|---|---|
| COMPLETE SET (25) | 8.00 | 20.00 |
| COMMON CARD (1-25) | 0.60 | 1.50 |
| *SILVER: 1.2X TO 3X BASIC CARDS | | |
| *BLUE/10: UNPRICED DUE TO SCARCITY | | |
| *PURPLE/5: UNPRICED DUE TO SCARCITY | | |
| *GOLD/1: UNPRICED DUE TO SCARCITY | | |

### 2019 Star Wars On-Demand Phantom Menace 20th Anniversary Autographs

| | | |
|---|---|---|
| COMMON AUTO | 6.00 | 15.00 |
| *BLUE/10: UNPRICED DUE TO SCARCITY | | |
| *PURPLE/5: UNPRICED DUE TO SCARCITY | | |
| *GOLD/1: UNPRICED DUE TO SCARCITY | | |
| STATED OVERALL ODDS 1:SET | | |
| 1  Ian McDiarmid | | |
| 2  Samuel L. Jackson | | |
| 3  Ray Park | 30.00 | 75.00 |
| 4  Oliver Ford Davies | 6.00 | 15.00 |
| 5  Anthony Daniels | | |
| 6  Kenny Baker | 75.00 | 150.00 |
| 7  Hugh Quarshie | 6.00 | 15.00 |
| 8  Andy Secombe | 6.00 | 15.00 |
| 9  Lewis MacLeod | 6.00 | 15.00 |
| 10  Michonne Bourriague | 6.00 | 15.00 |
| 11  Matthew Wood | 6.00 | 15.00 |
| 12  Silas Carson | 6.00 | 15.00 |
| 13  Jerome Blake | 6.00 | 15.00 |
| 14  Ralph Brown | 6.00 | 15.00 |

### 2019 Star Wars On-Demand Phantom Menace 20th Anniversary Jedi Council

| | | |
|---|---|---|
| COMPLETE SET (12) | 150.00 | 300.00 |
| COMMON CARD (1-12) | 10.00 | 25.00 |
| STATED ODDS 1:2 | | |

### 2002 Star Wars Attack of the Clones

| | | |
|---|---|---|
| COMPLETE SET (100) | 5.00 | 12.00 |
| UNOPENED BOX (36 PACKS) | 45.00 | 60.00 |
| UNOPENED PACK (7 CARDS) | 1.50 | 2.00 |
| COMMON CARD (1-100) | 0.15 | 0.40 |

### 2002 Star Wars Attack of the Clones Foil

| | | |
|---|---|---|
| COMPLETE SET (10) | 6.00 | 15.00 |
| COMMON CARD (1-10) | 0.75 | 2.00 |

### 2002 Star Wars Attack of the Clones Panoramic Fold-Outs

| | | |
|---|---|---|
| COMPLETE SET (5) | 12.00 | 30.00 |
| COMMON CARD (1-5) | 3.00 | 8.00 |
| STATED ODDS 1:12 | | |

### 2002 Star Wars Attack of the Clones Prisms

| | | |
|---|---|---|
| COMPLETE SET (8) | 8.00 | 20.00 |
| COMMON CARD (1-8) | 1.25 | 3.00 |

### 2002 Star Wars Attack of the Clones Promos

| | | |
|---|---|---|
| COMMON CARD | 1.25 | 3.00 |
| | | |
| B1  UK Distribution | 2.50 | 6.00 |
| (Album Exclusive) | | |
| P4  Star Wars Insider/Star Wars Gamer Exclusive | 3.00 | 8.00 |
| P6  Star Wars Celebration II Exclusive | 3.00 | 8.00 |
| NNO  Best Buy Soundtrack Exclusive | 3.00 | 8.00 |

### 2002 Star Wars Attack of the Clones Widevision

| | | |
|---|---|---|
| COMPLETE SET (80) | 5.00 | 12.00 |
| COMMON CARD (1-80) | 0.15 | 0.40 |

### 2002 Star Wars Attack of the Clones Widevision Autographs

| | | |
|---|---|---|
| COMPLETE SET (24) | 600.00 | 1200.00 |
| COMMON AUTO (UNNUMBERED) | 10.00 | 25.00 |
| STATED ODDS 1:24 | | |
| NNO  Ahmed Best | 30.00 | 75.00 |
| NNO  Alethea McGrath | 25.00 | 60.00 |
| NNO  Amy Allen | 30.00 | 60.00 |
| NNO  Andrew Secombe | 15.00 | 40.00 |
| NNO  Ayesha Dharker | 15.00 | 40.00 |
| NNO  Bodie Taylor | 15.00 | 40.00 |
| NNO  Bonnie Piesse | 40.00 | 80.00 |
| NNO  Daniel Logan | 25.00 | 60.00 |
| NNO  David Bowers | 15.00 | 40.00 |
| NNO  Frank Oz | 250.00 | 400.00 |
| NNO  Jay Laga'aia | 15.00 | 40.00 |
| NNO  Joel Edgerton | 20.00 | 50.00 |
| NNO  Kenny Baker | 100.00 | 200.00 |
| NNO  Leeanna Walsman | 15.00 | 40.00 |
| NNO  Mary Oyaya | 15.00 | 40.00 |
| NNO  Rena Owen | 15.00 | 40.00 |
| NNO  Ronald Falk | 15.00 | 40.00 |
| NNO  Silas Carson/Ki-Adi-Mundi | 25.00 | 50.00 |
| NNO  Silas Carson/Nute Gunray | 25.00 | 50.00 |
| NNO  Zachariah Jensen | 12.00 | 30.00 |

### 2002 Star Wars Attack of the Clones Widevision Promos

| | | |
|---|---|---|
| P1  Spider Droid | 0.60 | 1.50 |
| (Non-Sport Update Exclusive) | | |
| S1  Spider Droid | | |
| (UK Exclusive) | | |

### 2002 Star Wars Attack of the Clones Widevision DVD Promos

| | | |
|---|---|---|
| COMPLETE SET (5) | 3.00 | 8.00 |
| COMMON CARD (W1-W5) | 1.00 | 2.50 |

### 2016 Star Wars Attack of the Clones 3-D Widevision

| | | |
|---|---|---|
| COMPLETE SET (44) | 12.00 | 30.00 |
| COMMON CARD (1-44) | 0.50 | 1.25 |

### 2016 Star Wars Attack of the Clones 3-D Widevision Autographs

| | | |
|---|---|---|
| COMMON AUTO | 12.00 | 30.00 |
| *SILVER/25: UNPRICED DUE TO SCARCITY | | |
| *GOLD/10: UNPRICED DUE TO SCARCITY | | |
| *RED/1: UNPRICED DUE TO SCARCITY | | |

STATED ODDS 1:SET

| | | |
|---|---|---|
| NNO Alan Ruscoe | 15.00 | 40.00 |
| NNO Amy Allen | 12.00 | 30.00 |
| NNO Daniel Logan | 15.00 | 40.00 |
| NNO Jesse Jensen | 15.00 | 40.00 |
| NNO Jett Lucas | 15.00 | 40.00 |
| NNO Kenny Baker | 80.00 | 150.00 |
| NNO Matthew Wood | 25.00 | 60.00 |
| Magaloof | | |
| NNO Oliver Ford | 15.00 | 40.00 |

### 2016 Star Wars Attack of the Clones 3-D Widevision Medallions

| | | |
|---|---|---|
| COMPLETE SET (10) | 175.00 | 350.00 |
| COMMON CARD (MC1-MC10) | 15.00 | 40.00 |

*RED/1: UNPRICED DUE TO SCARCITY
STATED ODDS PATCH OR MEDALLION 1:1

### 2016 Star Wars Attack of the Clones 3-D Widevision Patches

| | | |
|---|---|---|
| COMPLETE SET (12) | 200.00 | 350.00 |
| COMMON CARD (MP1-MP12) | 15.00 | 40.00 |

*RED/1: UNPRICED DUE TO SCARCITY
STATED ODDS PATCH OR MEDALLION 1:1

### 2002 Star Wars Episode II Instant Win

| | | |
|---|---|---|
| COMPLETE SET (5) | 5.00 | 12.00 |
| COMMON CARD (UNNUMBERED) | 1.50 | 4.00 |

### 2002 Star Wars Episode II Jedi Fruit Rolls

| | | |
|---|---|---|
| COMPLETE SET (6) | 5.00 | 12.00 |
| UNNUMBERED SET | | |
| 1 Luke vs. Darth Vader | 3.00 | 8.00 |
| 2 Luke vs. Darth Vader | 3.00 | 8.00 |
| 3 Obi-Wan vs. Count Dooku | 0.75 | 2.00 |
| 4 Obi-Wan vs. Darth Vader | 2.00 | 5.00 |
| 5 Obi-Wan vs. Jango Fett | 0.75 | 2.00 |
| 6 Qui-Gon Jinn vs. Darth Maul | 1.25 | 3.00 |

### 2005 Star Wars Revenge of the Sith

MACE VS. PALPATINE

| | | |
|---|---|---|
| COMPLETE SET (90) | 5.00 | 12.00 |
| UNOPENED HOBBY BOX (36 PACKS) | 65.00 | 80.00 |
| UNOPENED HOBBY PACK (7 CARDS) | 2.00 | 2.50 |
| UNOPENED RETAIL BOX (24 PACKS) | 30.00 | 40.00 |
| UNOPENED RETAIL PACK (7 CARDS) | 1.50 | 1.75 |
| COMMON CARD (1-90) | 0.15 | 0.40 |

### 2005 Star Wars Revenge of the Sith Blister Bonus

| | | |
|---|---|---|
| COMPLETE SET (3) | 6.00 | 15.00 |
| COMMON CARD (B1-B3) | 2.50 | 6.00 |

STATED ODDS ONE PER BLISTER PACK

### 2005 Star Wars Revenge of the Sith Embossed Foil

| | | |
|---|---|---|
| COMPLETE SET (10) | 20.00 | 50.00 |
| COMMON CARD (1-10) | 2.50 | 6.00 |

STATED ODDS 1:6 RETAIL

### 2005 Star Wars Revenge of the Sith Etched Foil Puzzle

| | | |
|---|---|---|
| COMPLETE SET (6) | 12.00 | 30.00 |
| COMMON CARD (1-6) | 2.50 | 6.00 |

STATED ODDS 1:6

### 2005 Star Wars Revenge of the Sith Flix-Pix

| | | |
|---|---|---|
| COMPLETE SET (68) | 50.00 | 100.00 |
| UNOPENED BOX (36 PACKS) | 100.00 | 150.00 |
| UNOPENED PACK | 3.00 | 5.00 |
| COMMON CARD (1-68) | 1.00 | 2.50 |
| CL (TRI-FOLD INSERT) | 0.40 | 1.00 |

### 2005 Star Wars Revenge of the Sith Holograms

| | | |
|---|---|---|
| COMPLETE SET (3) | 5.00 | 12.00 |
| COMMON CARD (1-3) | 2.00 | 5.00 |

STATED ODDS 1:14 RETAIL

### 2005 Star Wars Revenge of the Sith Lenticular Morph Hobby

| | | |
|---|---|---|
| COMPLETE SET (2) | 5.00 | 12.00 |
| COMMON CARD (1-2) | 3.00 | 8.00 |

STATED ODDS 1:24 HOBBY

### 2005 Star Wars Revenge of the Sith Lenticular Morph Retail

| | | |
|---|---|---|
| COMPLETE SET (2) | 5.00 | 12.00 |
| COMMON CARD (1-2) | 3.00 | 8.00 |

STATED ODDS 1:24 RETAIL

### 2005 Star Wars Revenge of the Sith Stickers

| | | |
|---|---|---|
| COMPLETE SET (10) | 2.50 | 6.00 |
| COMMON CARD (1-10) | 0.40 | 1.00 |

STATED ODDS 1:3 RETAIL

### 2005 Star Wars Revenge of the Sith Tattoos

| | | |
|---|---|---|
| COMPLETE SET (10) | 4.00 | 10.00 |
| COMMON CARD (1-10) | 1.00 | 2.50 |

STATED ODDS 1:3 RETAIL

### 2005 Star Wars Revenge of the Sith Tin Gold

| | | |
|---|---|---|
| COMPLETE SET (6) | 5.00 | 12.00 |
| COMMON CARD (A-F) | 1.00 | 2.50 |

STATED ODDS ONE PER TIN

### 2005 Star Wars Revenge of the Sith Tin Story

| | | |
|---|---|---|
| COMPLETE SET (6) | 5.00 | 12.00 |
| COMMON CARD (1-6) | 1.00 | 2.50 |

STATED ODDS ONE PER TIN

### 2005 Star Wars Revenge of the Sith Promos

| | | |
|---|---|---|
| COMMON CARD (P1-P5) | 1.00 | 2.50 |
| P3 The Circle is Complete | 15.00 | 40.00 |
| (Star Wars Shop) | | |

### 2005 Star Wars Revenge of the Sith Medalionz

| | | |
|---|---|---|
| COMPLETE SET (24) | 15.00 | 40.00 |
| COMMON CARD (1-24) | 1.00 | 2.50 |

*GOLD: .8X TO 2X BASIC MED.

| | | |
|---|---|---|
| CL Checklist | 0.20 | 0.50 |

### 2005 Star Wars Revenge of the Sith Widevision

| | | |
|---|---|---|
| COMPLETE SET (80) | 5.00 | 12.00 |
| UNOPENED HOBBY BOX (24 PACKS) | 25.00 | 40.00 |
| UNOPENED HOBBY PACK (6 CARDS) | 1.50 | 2.00 |
| UNOPENED RETAIL BOX (24 PACKS) | 25.00 | 40.00 |
| UNOPENED RETAIL PACK (6 CARDS) | 1.50 | 2.00 |
| COMMON CARD (1-80) | 0.15 | 0.40 |

### 2005 Star Wars Revenge of the Sith Widevision Autographs

| | | |
|---|---|---|
| COMMON CARD (UNNUMBERED) | 25.00 | 50.00 |

STATED ODDS 1:48 HOBBY

| | | |
|---|---|---|
| NNO Matthew Wood | 50.00 | 100.00 |
| NNO Peter Mayhew | 50.00 | 100.00 |
| NNO Samuel L. Jackson | 600.00 | 1000.00 |

### 2005 Star Wars Revenge of the Sith Widevision Chrome Hobby

| | | |
|---|---|---|
| COMPLETE SET (10) | 12.50 | 30.00 |
| COMMON CARD (H1-H10) | 1.50 | 4.00 |

STATED ODDS 1:6 HOBBY

### 2005 Star Wars Revenge of the Sith Widevision Chrome Retail

| | | |
|---|---|---|
| COMPLETE SET (10) | 15.00 | 40.00 |
| COMMON CARD (R1-R10) | 2.00 | 5.00 |

STATED ODDS 1:60 RETAIL

### 2005 Star Wars Revenge of the Sith Widevision Flix-Pix

| | | |
|---|---|---|
| COMPLETE SET (10) | 15.00 | 40.00 |
| COMMON CARD (1-10) | 2.00 | 5.00 |

STATED ODDS 1:6

### 2015 Star Wars Revenge of the Sith 3-D Widevision

| | | |
|---|---|---|
| COMPLETE SET (44) | 10.00 | 25.00 |
| COMPLETE FACTORY SET (46) | 60.00 | 120.00 |
| COMMON CARD (1-44) | 0.40 | 1.00 |

### 2015 Star Wars Revenge of the Sith 3-D Widevision Autographs

| | | |
|---|---|---|
| COMMON AUTO | 15.00 | 40.00 |

*SILVER/15: UNPRICED DUE TO SCARCITY
*GOLD/1: UNPRICED DUE TO SCARCITY

| | | |
|---|---|---|
| NNO Peter Mayhew | 60.00 | 120.00 |
| NNO Jeremy Bulloch | 25.00 | 60.00 |
| NNO Bai Ling | 30.00 | 80.00 |

### 2015 Star Wars Revenge of the Sith 3-D Widevision Medallions

| | | |
|---|---|---|
| COMPLETE SET (8) | 100.00 | 200.00 |
| COMMON MEM | 15.00 | 40.00 |

*SILVER/30: .6X TO 1.5X BASIC MEM
*GOLD/1: UNPRICED DUE TO SCARCITY
STATED PRINT RUN 60 SER.#'d SETS

## 2015 Star Wars Revenge of the Sith 3-D Widevision Patches

AUTHENTIC PATCH CARD

| | | |
|---|---|---|
| COMPLETE SET (4) | 50.00 | 100.00 |
| COMMON MEM | 15.00 | 40.00 |
| *SILVER/30: .6X TO 1.5X BASIC MEM | | |
| *GOLD/1: UNPRICED DUE TO SCARCITY | | |
| STATED PRINT RUN 60 SER.#'d SETS | | |

## 2017 Star Wars The Force Awakens 3-D Widevision

| | | |
|---|---|---|
| COMPLETE SET (44) | 12.00 | 30.00 |
| COMPLETE BOXED SET (46) | | |
| COMMON CARD (1-44) | 0.40 | 1.00 |

## 2017 Star Wars The Force Awakens 3-D Widevision Autographs

| | | |
|---|---|---|
| COMMON AUTO | 6.00 | 15.00 |
| *BLUE/50: UNPRICED DUE TO SCARCITY | | |
| *BLACK/25: UNPRICED DUE TO SCARCITY | | |
| *ORANGE/10: UNPRICED DUE TO SCARCITY | | |
| *GOLD/5: UNPRICED DUE TO SCARCITY | | |
| *RED/1: UNPRICED DUE TO SCARCITY | | |
| STATED ODDS 2:SET | | |
| WVAAJ Andrew Jack | 6.00 | 15.00 |
| WVAASH Arti Shah | 8.00 | 20.00 |
| WVABH Brian Herring | 10.00 | 25.00 |
| WVABV Brian Vernel | 6.00 | 15.00 |
| WVACC Crystal Clarke | 8.00 | 20.00 |
| WVAEE Emun Elliott | 6.00 | 15.00 |
| WVAHW Harriet Walter | 6.00 | 15.00 |
| WVAIU Iko Uwais | 10.00 | 25.00 |
| WVAJH Jessica Henwick | 10.00 | 25.00 |
| WVAKF Kate Fleetwood | 6.00 | 15.00 |
| WVAPW Paul Warren | 6.00 | 15.00 |
| WVATC Tosin Cole | 6.00 | 15.00 |
| WVAYR Yayan Ruhian | 6.00 | 15.00 |

## 2016 Star Wars The Force Awakens Chrome

| | | |
|---|---|---|
| COMPLETE SET (100) | 8.00 | 20.00 |
| UNOPENED BOX (24 PACKS) | 50.00 | 70.00 |
| UNOPENED PACK (6 CARDS) | 3.00 | 3.50 |
| COMMON CARD (1-100) | 0.25 | 0.60 |
| *REFRACTOR: 1.2X TO 3X BASIC CARDS | 0.60 | 1.50 |
| *PRISM REF./99: 5X TO 12X BASIC CARDS | 3.00 | 8.00 |
| *SHIMMER REF./50: 10X TO 25X BASIC CARDS | 6.00 | 15.00 |
| *PULSAR REF./10: 15X TO 40X BASIC CARDS | 10.00 | 25.00 |
| *SUPERFRACTOR/1: UNPRICED DUE TO SCARCITY | | |
| *P.P.BLACK/1: UNPRICED DUE TO SCARCITY | | |
| *P.P.CYAN/1: UNPRICED DUE TO SCARCITY | | |
| *P.P.MAGENTA/1: UNPRICED DUE TO SCARCITY | | |
| *P.P.YELLOW/1: UNPRICED DUE TO SCARCITY | | |

## 2016 Star Wars The Force Awakens Chrome Autographs

| | | |
|---|---|---|
| COMMON CARD | 5.00 | 12.00 |
| *ATOMIC/99: .5X TO 1.2X BASIC CARDS | | |
| *PRISM/50: .6X TO 1.5X BASIC CARDS | | |
| *X-FRACTOR/25: .75X TO 2X BASIC CARDS | | |
| *SHIMMER/10: UNPRICED DUE TO SCARCITY | | |
| *PULSAR/5: UNPRICED DUE TO SCARCITY | | |
| *SUPERFRACTOR/1: UNPRICED DUE TO SCARCITY | | |
| *P.P.BLACK/1: UNPRICED DUE TO SCARCITY | | |
| *P.P.CYAN/1: UNPRICED DUE TO SCARCITY | | |
| *P.P.MAGENTA/1: UNPRICED DUE TO SCARCITY | | |
| *P.P.YELLOW/1: UNPRICED DUE TO SCARCITY | | |
| OVERALL AUTO ODDS 1:24 | | |
| CAAB Anna Brewster | 8.00 | 20.00 |
| CABV Brian Vernel | 10.00 | 25.00 |
| CAGG Greg Grunberg | 10.00 | 25.00 |
| CAJS Joonas Suotamo | 10.00 | 25.00 |
| CAKS Kipsang Rotich | 8.00 | 20.00 |
| CAMD Mark Dodson | 10.00 | 25.00 |
| CAMQ Mike Quinn | 8.00 | 20.00 |
| CAPM Peter Mayhew | 20.00 | 50.00 |
| CASA Sebastian Armesto | 8.00 | 20.00 |
| CAYR Yayan Ruhian | 10.00 | 25.00 |
| CAMWG Matthew Wood | 8.00 | 20.00 |

## 2016 Star Wars The Force Awakens Chrome Autographs Atomic Refractors

| | | |
|---|---|---|
| *ATOMIC/99: .5X TO 1.2X BASIC CARDS | | |
| CAJB John Boyega | 120.00 | 200.00 |
| CAWD Warwick Davis | 12.00 | 30.00 |

## 2016 Star Wars The Force Awakens Chrome Autographs Prism Refractors

| | | |
|---|---|---|
| *PRISM/50: .6X TO 1.5X BASIC CARDS | | |
| CAAD Anthony Daniels | | |
| CAAS Andy Serkis | 120.00 | 200.00 |

## 2016 Star Wars The Force Awakens Chrome Autographs X-fractors

| | | |
|---|---|---|
| *X-FRACTORS: .75X TO 2X BASIC CARDS | | |
| CACF Carrie Fisher | 120.00 | 250.00 |
| CADR Daisy Ridley | 1800.00 | 2200.00 |
| CAEB Erik Bauersfeld | | |
| CAKB Kenny Baker | 150.00 | 300.00 |
| CAMWU Matthew Wood | | |

## 2016 Star Wars The Force Awakens Chrome Behind-the-Scenes

| | | |
|---|---|---|
| COMPLETE SET (12) | 10.00 | 25.00 |
| COMMON CARD (1-12) | 1.25 | 3.00 |
| *SHIMMER REF./50: 1X TO 2.5X BASIC CARDS | 3.00 | 8.00 |
| *PULSAR REF./10: UNPRICED DUE TO SCARCITY | | |
| *SUPERFRACTOR/1: UNPRICED DUE TO SCARCITY | | |
| *P.P.BLACK/1: UNPRICED DUE TO SCARCITY | | |
| *P.P.CYAN/1: UNPRICED DUE TO SCARCITY | | |
| *P.P.MAGENTA/1: UNPRICED DUE TO SCARCITY | | |
| *P.P.YELLOW/1: UNPRICED DUE TO SCARCITY | | |
| STATED ODDS 1:4 | | |

## 2016 Star Wars The Force Awakens Chrome Heroes of the Resistance

PZ-4CO
HEROES OF THE RESISTANCE

| | | |
|---|---|---|
| COMPLETE SET (18) | 10.00 | 25.00 |
| COMMON CARD (1-18) | 0.75 | 2.00 |
| *SHIMMER REF./50:1 X TO 2.5X BASIC CARDS | 2.00 | 5.00 |
| *PULSAR REF./10: UNPRICED DUE TO SCARCITY | | |
| *SUPERFRACTOR/1: UNPRICED DUE TO SCARCITY | | |
| *P.P.BLACK/1: UNPRICED DUE TO SCARCITY | | |
| *P.P.CYAN/1: UNPRICED DUE TO SCARCITY | | |
| *P.P.MAGENTA/1: UNPRICED DUE TO SCARCITY | | |
| *P.P.YELLOW/1: UNPRICED DUE TO SCARCITY | | |
| STATED ODDS 1:2 | | |
| 1 Finn | 1.25 | 3.00 |
| 2 Rey | 1.25 | 3.00 |
| 3 Poe Dameron | 1.00 | 2.50 |
| 9 BB-8 | 1.50 | 4.00 |
| 10 C-3PO | 1.00 | 2.50 |
| 11 R2-D2 | 1.00 | 2.50 |
| 13 Han Solo | 1.50 | 4.00 |
| 14 Chewbacca | 1.00 | 2.50 |
| 18 General Leia Organa | 1.00 | 2.50 |

## 2016 Star Wars The Force Awakens Chrome Medallions

| | | |
|---|---|---|
| COMPLETE SET (25) | 200.00 | 400.00 |
| COMMON CARD | 3.00 | 8.00 |
| *SILVER/25: .5X TO 1.2X BASIC CARDS | | |
| *GOLD/10: UNPRICED DUE TO SCARCITY | | |
| *PLATINUM/1: UNPRICED DUE TO SCARCITY | | |
| M1 Han Solo | 12.00 | 30.00 |
| M2 General Leia Organa | 12.00 | 30.00 |
| M3 Admiral Ackbar | 5.00 | 12.00 |
| M4 Chewbacca | 6.00 | 15.00 |
| M5 Admiral Statura | 5.00 | 12.00 |
| M6 Snap Wexley | 8.00 | 20.00 |
| M7 Jess Testor Pava | 8.00 | 20.00 |
| M10 Poe Dameron | 8.00 | 20.00 |
| M11 Rey | 20.00 | 50.00 |
| M12 Finn | 10.00 | 25.00 |
| M13 BB-8 | 10.00 | 25.00 |
| M14 Riot Control Stormtrooper | 8.00 | 20.00 |
| M16 Colonel Datoo | 6.00 | 15.00 |
| M17 Supreme Leader Snoke | 6.00 | 15.00 |
| M18 Flametrooper | 5.00 | 12.00 |
| M19 Kylo Ren | 8.00 | 20.00 |
| M20 Kylo Ren | 8.00 | 20.00 |
| M21 General Hux | 5.00 | 12.00 |
| M22 Captain Phasma | 8.00 | 20.00 |
| M23 FN-2187 | 10.00 | 25.00 |

## 2016 Star Wars The Force Awakens Chrome Patches

| | | |
|---|---|---|
| COMPLETE SET (27) | 175.00 | 350.00 |
| COMMON CARD (P1-P27) | 5.00 | 12.00 |
| *SHIMMER/199: .5X TO 1.2X BASIC CARDS | | |
| *PULSAR/99: .6X TO 1.5X BASIC CARDS | | |
| *SUPERFRACTOR/5: UNPRICED DUE TO SCARCITY | | |
| P1 Rey/686 | 15.00 | 40.00 |
| P2 Han Solo/299 | 8.00 | 20.00 |
| P4 Finn/686 | 8.00 | 20.00 |
| P7 Kylo Ren/401 | 6.00 | 15.00 |
| P11 General Leia Organa/755 | 8.00 | 20.00 |
| P15 BB-8/686 | 6.00 | 15.00 |
| P16 Poe Dameron & BB-8/686 | 6.00 | 15.00 |
| P17 Rey & BB-8/686 | 12.00 | 30.00 |
| P18 R2-D2/686 | 6.00 | 15.00 |
| P19 Rey/299 | 10.00 | 25.00 |
| P20 Rey/686 | 10.00 | 25.00 |
| P23 Han Solo & Chewbacca/737 | 10.00 | 25.00 |

## 2016 Star Wars The Force Awakens Chrome Power of the First Order

COLONEL DATOO

POWER OF THE FIRST ORDER

| | | |
|---|---|---|
| COMPLETE SET (9) | 6.00 | 15.00 |
| COMMON CARD (1-9) | 0.75 | 2.00 |
| *SHIMMER REF./50: 1X TO 2.5X BASIC CARDS | | |
| *PULSAR REF./10: UNPRICED DUE TO SCARCITY | | |
| *SUPERFRACTOR/1: UNPRICED DUE TO SCARCITY | | |
| *P.P.BLACK/1: UNPRICED DUE TO SCARCITY | | |
| *P.P.CYAN/1: UNPRICED DUE TO SCARCITY | | |
| *P.P.MAGENTA/1: UNPRICED DUE TO SCARCITY | | |
| *P.P.YELLOW/1: UNPRICED DUE TO SCARCITY | | |
| STATED ODDS 1:12 | | |
| 1 Supreme Leader Snoke | 1.50 | 4.00 |
| 2 Kylo Ren | 1.50 | 4.00 |
| 3 General Hux | 1.25 | 3.00 |
| 4 Captain Phasma | 1.25 | 3.00 |

## 2016 Star Wars The Force Awakens Chrome Ships and Vehicles

| | | |
|---|---|---|
| COMPLETE SET (11) | 6.00 | 15.00 |
| COMMON CARD (1-11) | 1.00 | 2.50 |
| *SHIMMER REF./50: 1X TO 2.5X BASIC CARDS | 2.50 | 6.00 |
| *PULSAR REF./10: UNPRICED DUE TO SCARCITY | | |
| *SUPERFRACTOR/1: UNPRICED DUE TO SCARCITY | | |
| *P.P.BLACK/1: UNPRICED DUE TO SCARCITY | | |
| *P.P.CYAN/1: UNPRICED DUE TO SCARCITY | | |
| *P.P.MAGENTA/1: UNPRICED DUE TO SCARCITY | | |
| *P.P.YELLOW/1: UNPRICED DUE TO SCARCITY | | |
| STATED ODDS 1:8 | | |

## 2015 Star Wars The Force Awakens Dog Tags

| | | |
|---|---|---|
| COMPLETE SET (16) | 15.00 | 40.00 |
| COMMON CARD (1-16) | 1.25 | 3.00 |
| *GOLD: 1X TO 2.5X BASIC TAGS | | |
| 1 Kylo Ren | 2.00 | 5.00 |
| 2 Rey | 2.00 | 5.00 |
| 3 Finn | 1.50 | 4.00 |
| 5 Captain Phasma | 1.50 | 4.00 |
| 10 BB-8 | 2.50 | 6.00 |
| 11 Rey | 2.00 | 5.00 |
| 12 Finn | 1.50 | 4.00 |
| 13 Kylo Ren | 2.00 | 5.00 |

## 2015 Star Wars The Force Awakens Dog Tags Target Exclusives

| | | |
|---|---|---|
| COMPLETE SET (2) | 10.00 | 25.00 |
| COMMON CARD (T1-T2) | 5.00 | 12.00 |
| *GOLD: .75X TO 2X BASIC TAGS | | |
| EXCLUSIVE TO TARGET | | |
| T2 BB-8 | 8.00 | 20.00 |

## 2015 Star Wars The Force Awakens Dog Tags Toys 'R' Us Exclusives

| | | |
|---|---|---|
| COMPLETE SET (2) | 10.00 | 25.00 |
| COMMON CARD (TR1-TR2) | 6.00 | 15.00 |
| *GOLD: 1X TO 2.5X BASIC TAGS | | |
| EXCLUSIVE TO TOYS 'R' US | | |

## 2015 Star Wars The Force Awakens Dog Tags Walmart Exclusives

| | | |
|---|---|---|
| COMPLETE SET (2) | 6.00 | 15.00 |
| COMMON CARD (W1-W2) | 4.00 | 10.00 |
| *GOLD: 1X TO 2.5X BASIC TAGS | | |
| EXCLUSIVE TO WALMART | | |

## 2016 Star Wars The Force Awakens Factory Set

| | | |
|---|---|---|
| COMPLETE FACTORY SET (310) | 40.00 | 80.00 |
| COMMON CARD | 0.15 | 0.40 |
| JOURNEY TO TFA (1-110) | | |
| TFA SERIES ONE (1-100) | | |
| TFA SERIES TWO (1-100) | | |
| *LIM.ED./100: 6X TO 15X BASIC CARDS | 2.50 | 6.00 |

## 2015 Star Wars The Force Awakens Glow-in-the-Dark Decals

| | | |
|---|---|---|
| COMPLETE SET (7) | 10.00 | 25.00 |
| COMMON CARD | 1.25 | 3.00 |
| STATED ODDS 1:CEREAL BOX | | |
| INSERTED IN BOXES OF GENERAL MILLS CEREAL | | |
| MILLENNIUM FALCON IS KROGER EXCLUSIVE | | |
| 1 BB-8 | 2.50 | 6.00 |
| 2 C-3PO and R2-D2 | 1.50 | 4.00 |
| 3 Captain Phasma | 2.00 | 5.00 |
| 5 Kylo Ren | 2.00 | 5.00 |
| 6 Millennium Falcon SP | 5.00 | 12.00 |
| Kroger Exclusive | | |

## 2015 Star Wars The Force Awakens Series One

| | | |
|---|---|---|
| COMPLETE SET w/o SP (100) | 10.00 | 25.00 |
| COMMON CARD (1-100) | 0.20 | 0.50 |
| *LTSBR GREEN: .5X TO 1.2X BASIC CARDS | | |
| *LTSBR BLUE: .6X TO 1.5X BASIC CARDS | | |
| *LTSBR PURPLE: .75X TO 2X BASIC CARDS | | |
| *FOIL/250: 4X TO 10X BASIC CARDS | | |
| *GOLD/100: 6X TO 15X BASIC CARDS | | |
| *PLATINUM/1: UNPRICED DUE TO SCARCITY | | |
| *P.P.BLACK/1: UNPRICED DUE TO SCARCITY | | |
| *P.P.CYAN/1: UNPRICED DUE TO SCARCITY | | |
| *P.P.MAGENTA/1: UNPRICED DUE TO SCARCITY | | |
| *P.P.YELLOW/1: UNPRICED DUE TO SCARCITY | | |
| TARGET EXCLUSIVES SP 101-103 | | |

| 100 | Han Solo & Chewbacca return home | 0.75 | 2.00 |
| 101 | Maz Kanata SP | 3.00 | 8.00 |
| 102 | Wollivan SP | 3.00 | 8.00 |
| 103 | Grummgar SP | 3.00 | 8.00 |

### 2015 Star Wars The Force Awakens Series One
### Autographs

| COMMON AUTO | 15.00 | 40.00 |
| *LTSBR PURPLE/25: UNPRICED DUE TO SCARCITY | | |
| *GOLD/10: UNPRICED DUE TO SCARCITY | | |
| *IMP. RED/1: UNPRICED DUE TO SCARCITY | | |
| *P.P.BLACK/1: UNPRICED DUE TO SCARCITY | | |
| *P.P.CYAN/1: UNPRICED DUE TO SCARCITY | | |
| *P.P.MAGENTA/1: UNPRICED DUE TO SCARCITY | | |
| *P.P.YELLOW/1: UNPRICED DUE TO SCARCITY | | |
| STATED ODDS 1:106 H; 1:12,334 R | | |

| NNO | Anthony Daniels | 100.00 | 200.00 |
| NNO | Carrie Fisher | 200.00 | 350.00 |
| NNO | Daisy Ridley | 750.00 | 1500.00 |
| NNO | John Boyega | 100.00 | 200.00 |
| NNO | Peter Mayhew | 50.00 | 100.00 |

### 2015 Star Wars The Force Awakens Series One
### Behind-the-Scenes

| COMPLETE SET (7) | 5.00 | 12.00 |
| COMMON CARD (1-7) | 1.00 | 2.50 |
| *LTSBR GREEN: .5X TO 1.2X BASIC CARDS | | |
| *LTSBR BLUE: .6X TO 1.5X BASIC CARDS | | |
| *LTSBR PURPLE: .75X TO 2X BASIC CARDS | | |
| *FOIL/250: 4X TO 10X BASIC CARDS | | |
| *GOLD/100: 6X TO 15X BASIC CARDS | | |
| *PLATINUM/1: UNPRICED DUE TO SCARCITY | | |
| *P.P.BLACK/1: UNPRICED DUE TO SCARCITY | | |
| *P.P.CYAN/1: UNPRICED DUE TO SCARCITY | | |
| *P.P.MAGENTA/1: UNPRICED DUE TO SCARCITY | | |
| *P.P.YELLOW/1: UNPRICED DUE TO SCARCITY | | |
| STATED ODDS 1:8 H; 1:5 R | | |

### 2015 Star Wars The Force Awakens Series One
### Character Montages

| COMPLETE SET (8) | 4.00 | 10.00 |
| COMMON CARD (1-8) | 0.75 | 2.00 |
| *LTSBR GREEN: .5X TO 1.2X BASIC CARDS | | |
| *LTSBR BLUE: .6X TO 1.5X BASIC CARDS | | |
| *LTSBR PURPLE: .75X TO 2X BASIC CARDS | | |
| *FOIL/250: 4X TO 10X BASIC CARDS | | |
| *GOLD/100: 6X TO 15X BASIC CARDS | | |
| *PLATINUM/1: UNPRICED DUE TO SCARCITY | | |
| *P.P.BLACK/1: UNPRICED DUE TO SCARCITY | | |
| *P.P.CYAN/1: UNPRICED DUE TO SCARCITY | | |
| *P.P.MAGENTA/1: UNPRICED DUE TO SCARCITY | | |
| *P.P.YELLOW/1: UNPRICED DUE TO SCARCITY | | |
| STATED ODDS 1:7 H; 1:4 R | | |
| 1 Rey | 1.50 | 4.00 |
| 5 Captain Phasma | 1.25 | 3.00 |
| 7 BB-8 | 1.50 | 4.00 |

### 2015 Star Wars The Force Awakens Series One
### Character Stickers

| COMPLETE SET (18) | 6.00 | 15.00 |
| COMMON CARD (1-18) | 0.60 | 1.50 |
| *LTSBR GREEN: .5X TO 1.2X BASIC CARDS | | |
| *LTSBR BLUE: .6X TO 1.5X BASIC CARDS | | |
| *LTSBR PURPLE: .75X TO 2X BASIC CARDS | | |
| *FOIL/250: 4X TO 10X BASIC CARDS | | |
| *GOLD/100: 6X TO 15X BASIC CARDS | | |
| *PLATINUM/1: UNPRICED DUE TO SCARCITY | | |
| *P.P.BLACK/1: UNPRICED DUE TO SCARCITY | | |
| *P.P.CYAN/1: UNPRICED DUE TO SCARCITY | | |
| *P.P.MAGENTA/1: UNPRICED DUE TO SCARCITY | | |
| *P.P.YELLOW/1: UNPRICED DUE TO SCARCITY | | |
| STATED ODDS 1:3 H; 1:2 R | | |
| 1 Rey | 1.25 | 3.00 |
| 5 Captain Phasma | 1.00 | 2.50 |
| 8 BB-8 | 1.25 | 3.00 |
| 12 Rey | 1.25 | 3.00 |

### 2015 Star Wars The Force Awakens Series One
### Concept Art

| COMPLETE SET (20) | 8.00 | 20.00 |
| COMMON CARD (1-20) | 0.75 | 2.00 |
| *LTSBR GREEN: .5X TO 1.2X BASIC CARDS | | |
| *LTSBR BLUE: .6X TO 1.5X BASIC CARDS | | |
| *LTSBR PURPLE: .75X TO 2X BASIC CARDS | | |
| *FOIL/250: 4X TO 10X BASIC CARDS | | |
| *GOLD/100: 6X TO 15X BASIC CARDS | | |
| *PLATINUM/1: UNPRICED DUE TO SCARCITY | | |
| *P.P.BLACK/1: UNPRICED DUE TO SCARCITY | | |

| *P.P.CYAN/1: UNPRICED DUE TO SCARCITY | | |
| *P.P.MAGENTA/1: UNPRICED DUE TO SCARCITY | | |
| *P.P.YELLOW/1: UNPRICED DUE TO SCARCITY | | |
| STATED ODDS 1:3 H; 1:2 R | | |

### 2015 Star Wars The Force Awakens Series One
### First Order Rises

| COMPLETE SET (9) | 6.00 | 15.00 |
| COMMON CARD (1-9) | 1.25 | 3.00 |
| *LTSBR GREEN: .5X TO 1.2X BASIC CARDS | | |
| *LTSBR BLUE: .6X TO 1.5X BASIC CARDS | | |
| *LTSBR PURPLE: .75X TO 2X BASIC CARDS | | |
| *FOIL/250: 4X TO 10X BASIC CARDS | | |
| *GOLD/100: 6X TO 15X BASIC CARDS | | |
| *PLATINUM/1: UNPRICED DUE TO SCARCITY | | |
| *P.P.BLACK/1: UNPRICED DUE TO SCARCITY | | |
| *P.P.CYAN/1: UNPRICED DUE TO SCARCITY | | |
| *P.P.MAGENTA/1: UNPRICED DUE TO SCARCITY | | |
| *P.P.YELLOW/1: UNPRICED DUE TO SCARCITY | | |
| STATED ODDS 1:6 H; 1:4 R | | |
| 2 Captain Phasma | 1.50 | 4.00 |

### 2015 Star Wars The Force Awakens Series One
### First Order Stormtrooper Costume Relics

| COMMON CARD | 12.00 | 30.00 |
| *BRONZE/99: .75X TO 2X BASIC CARDS | | |
| *SILVER/50: 1.2X TO 3X BASIC CARDS | | |
| *GOLD/10: 2X TO 5X BASIC CARDS | | |
| *PLATINUM/1: UNPRICED DUE TO SCARCITY | | |

### 2015 Star Wars The Force Awakens Series One
### Locations

| COMPLETE SET (9) | 3.00 | 8.00 |
| COMMON CARD (1-9) | 0.60 | 1.50 |
| *LTSBR GREEN: .5X TO 1.2X BASIC CARDS | | |
| *LTSBR BLUE: .6X TO 1.5X BASIC CARDS | | |
| *LTSBR PURPLE: .75X TO 2X BASIC CARDS | | |
| *FOIL/250: 4X TO 10X BASIC CARDS | | |
| *GOLD/100: 6X TO 15X BASIC CARDS | | |

TRADING CARDS

*PLATINUM/1: UNPRICED DUE TO SCARCITY
*P.P.BLACK/1: UNPRICED DUE TO SCARCITY
*P.P.CYAN/1: UNPRICED DUE TO SCARCITY
*P.P.MAGENTA/1: UNPRICED DUE TO SCARCITY
*P.P.YELLOW/1: UNPRICED DUE TO SCARCITY
STATED ODDS 1:6 H; 1:4 R

### 2015 Star Wars The Force Awakens Series One Medallions

| | | |
|---|---|---|
| COMMON CARD (M1-M66) | 8.00 | 20.00 |
| STATED ODDS 1:BOX | | |

### 2015 Star Wars The Force Awakens Series One Movie Scenes

| | | |
|---|---|---|
| COMPLETE SET (20) | 5.00 | 12.00 |
| COMMON CARD (1-20) | 0.50 | 1.25 |
| *LTSBR GREEN: .5X TO 1.2X BASIC CARDS | | |
| *LTSBR BLUE: .60X TO 1.5X BASIC CARDS | | |
| *LTSBR PURPLE: .75X TO 2X BASIC CARDS | | |
| *FOIL/250: 4X TO 10X BASIC CARDS | | |
| *GOLD/100: 6X TO 15X BASIC CARDS | | |
| *PLATINUM/1: UNPRICED DUE TO SCARCITY | | |
| *P.P.BLACK/1: UNPRICED DUE TO SCARCITY | | |
| *P.P.CYAN/1: UNPRICED DUE TO SCARCITY | | |
| *P.P.MAGENTA/1: UNPRICED DUE TO SCARCITY | | |
| *P.P.YELLOW/1: UNPRICED DUE TO SCARCITY | | |
| STATED ODDS 1:3 H; 1:2 R | | |

### 2015 Star Wars The Force Awakens Series One Weapons

| | | |
|---|---|---|
| COMPLETE SET (10) | 4.00 | 10.00 |
| COMMON CARD (1-10) | 0.60 | 1.50 |
| *LTSBR GREEN: .5X TO 1.2X BASIC CARDS | | |
| *LTSBR BLUE: .6X TO 1.5X BASIC CARDS | | |
| *LTSBR PURPLE: .75X TO 2X BASIC CARDS | | |
| *FOIL/250: 4X TO 10X BASIC CARDS | | |
| *GOLD/100: 6X TO 15X BASIC CARDS | | |
| *PLATINUM/1: UNPRICED DUE TO SCARCITY | | |
| *P.P.BLACK/1: UNPRICED DUE TO SCARCITY | | |
| *P.P.CYAN/1: UNPRICED DUE TO SCARCITY | | |
| *P.P.MAGENTA/1: UNPRICED DUE TO SCARCITY | | |
| *P.P.YELLOW/1: UNPRICED DUE TO SCARCITY | | |
| STATED ODDS 1:6 H; 1:3 R | | |
| 1 Kylo Ren's lightsaber | 1.25 | 3.00 |
| 9 Han Solo's Blaster | 0.75 | 2.00 |

### 2016 Star Wars The Force Awakens Series Two

| | | |
|---|---|---|
| COMPLETE SET W/O SP (100) | 10.00 | 25.00 |
| COMPLETE SET W/SP (102) | 20.00 | 50.00 |
| UNOPENED HOBBY BOX (24 PACKS) | 60.00 | 100.00 |
| UNOPENED HOBBY PACK (8 CARDS) | 2.50 | 4.00 |
| COMMON CARD (1-100) | 0.20 | 0.50 |
| *LTSBR GREEN: .5X TO 1.2X BASIC CARDS | | |
| *LTSBR BLUE: .6X TO 1.5X BASIC CARDS | | |

*LTSBR PURPLE: .75X TO 2X BASIC CARDS
*FOIL: 4X TO 10X BASIC CARDS
*GOLD/100: 6X TO 15X BASIC CARDS
*PLATINUM/1: UNPRICED DUE TO SCARCITY
*P.P.BLACK/1: UNPRICED DUE TO SCARCITY
*P.P.CYAN/1: UNPRICED DUE TO SCARCITY
*P.P.MAGENTA/1: UNPRICED DUE TO SCARCITY
*P.P.YELLOW/1: UNPRICED DUE TO SCARCITY

| | | |
|---|---|---|
| 101 Finding Luke Skywalker SP | 6.00 | 15.00 |
| 102 The Lightsaber Returned SP | 10.00 | 25.00 |

### 2016 Star Wars The Force Awakens Series Two Autographs

| | | |
|---|---|---|
| COMMON CARD | 8.00 | 20.00 |
| *LTSBR PURPLE/50: .5X TO 1.2X BASIC AUTOS | | |
| *FOIL/25: .75X TO 2X BASIC AUTOS | | |
| *GOLD/10: UNPRICED DUE TO SCARCITY | | |
| *IMP. RED/1: UNPRICED DUE TO SCARCITY | | |
| *P.P.BLACK/1: UNPRICED DUE TO SCARCITY | | |
| *P.P.CYAN/1: UNPRICED DUE TO SCARCITY | | |
| *P.P.MAGENTA/1: UNPRICED DUE TO SCARCITY | | |
| *P.P.YELLOW/1: UNPRICED DUE TO SCARCITY | | |
| 1 David Acord | 20.00 | 50.00 |
| FN-2199 | | |
| 2 David Acord | 15.00 | 40.00 |
| Teedo | | |
| 4 Kenny Baker | 50.00 | 100.00 |
| 6 John Boyega | 150.00 | 300.00 |
| 7 Anna Brewster | 12.00 | 30.00 |
| 8 Dante Briggins | 12.00 | 30.00 |
| 9 Thomas Brodie-Sangster | 10.00 | 25.00 |
| 10 Aidan Cook | 12.00 | 30.00 |
| 11 Anthony Daniels | 50.00 | 100.00 |
| 12 Warrick Davis | 10.00 | 25.00 |
| 13 Harrison Ford | | |
| 14 Greg Grunberg | 15.00 | 40.00 |
| 17 Jessica Henwick | 15.00 | 40.00 |
| 18 Brian Herring | 60.00 | 120.00 |
| 19 Andrew Jack | 10.00 | 25.00 |
| 20 Billie Lourd | 15.00 | 40.00 |
| 21 Rocky Marshall | 10.00 | 25.00 |
| 22 Peter Mayhew | 25.00 | 60.00 |
| 25 Arti Shah | 12.00 | 30.00 |
| 26 Kiran Shah | 10.00 | 25.00 |
| 27 Joonas Suotamo | 15.00 | 40.00 |
| 28 Brian Vernel | 10.00 | 25.00 |
| 29 Dame Harriet Walter | 12.00 | 30.00 |
| 30 Paul Warren | 10.00 | 25.00 |

### 2016 Star Wars The Force Awakens Series Two Card Trader Characters

| | | |
|---|---|---|
| COMPLETE SET (9) | | |
| COMMON CARD (1-9) | 50.00 | 100.00 |
| STATED PRINT RUN 100 SER.#'d SETS | | |
| 1 BB-8 | 60.00 | 120.00 |
| 3 Finn | 60.00 | 120.00 |
| 5 Kylo Ren | 80.00 | 150.00 |
| 6 Captain Phasma | 80.00 | 150.00 |
| 7 Poe Dameron | 60.00 | 120.00 |
| 8 Rey | 120.00 | 200.00 |

### 2016 Star Wars The Force Awakens Series Two Character Poster Inserts

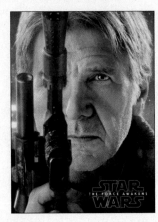

| | | |
|---|---|---|
| COMPLETE SET (5) | 5.00 | 12.00 |
| COMMON CARD (1-5) | 1.50 | 4.00 |
| *P.P.BLACK/1: UNPRICED DUE TO SCARCITY | | |
| *P.P.CYAN/1: UNPRICED DUE TO SCARCITY | | |
| *P.P.MAGENTA/1: UNPRICED DUE TO SCARCITY | | |
| *P.P.YELLOW/1: UNPRICED DUE TO SCARCITY | | |
| STATED ODDS 1:24 | | |
| 1 Rey | 2.50 | 6.00 |
| 2 Finn | 2.50 | 6.00 |
| 5 Han Solo | 2.00 | 5.00 |

### 2016 Star Wars The Force Awakens Series Two Character Stickers

| | | |
|---|---|---|
| COMPLETE SET (18) | 6.00 | 15.00 |
| COMMON CARD (1-18) | 0.50 | 1.25 |
| *P.P.BLACK/1: UNPRICED DUE TO SCARCITY | | |
| *P.P.CYAN/1: UNPRICED DUE TO SCARCITY | | |
| *P.P.MAGENTA/1: UNPRICED DUE TO SCARCITY | | |
| *P.P.YELLOW/1: UNPRICED DUE TO SCARCITY | | |
| 1 Finn | 0.75 | 2.00 |
| 2 Rey | 1.00 | 2.50 |
| 5 Han Solo | 1.00 | 2.50 |
| 6 Leia Organa | 0.75 | 2.00 |
| 8 Poe Dameron | 1.25 | 3.00 |
| 11 BB-8 | 1.25 | 3.00 |
| 12 Unkar Plutt | 0.60 | 1.50 |
| 13 General Hux | 0.75 | 2.00 |
| 15 Admiral Ackbar | 0.60 | 1.50 |
| 16 Stormtrooper | 0.75 | 2.00 |
| 18 Maz Kanata | 0.60 | 1.50 |

### 2016 Star Wars The Force Awakens Series Two Concept Art

| | | |
|---|---|---|
| COMPLETE SET (9) | 5.00 | 12.00 |
| COMMON CARD (1-9) | 1.00 | 2.50 |
| *P.P.BLACK/1: UNPRICED DUE TO SCARCITY | | |
| *P.P.CYAN/1: UNPRICED DUE TO SCARCITY | | |
| *P.P.MAGENTA/1: UNPRICED DUE TO SCARCITY | | |
| *P.P.YELLOW/1: UNPRICED DUE TO SCARCITY | | |

### 2016 Star Wars The Force Awakens Series Two Galactic Connexions

| | | |
|---|---|---|
| COMPLETE SET (5) | 120.00 | 250.00 |
| COMMON CARD (1-5) | 30.00 | 80.00 |
| STATED PRINT RUN 100 ANNCD SETS | | |
| WAL-MART EXCLUSIVE | | |
| 3 BB-8 | 50.00 | 100.00 |

### 2016 Star Wars The Force Awakens Series Two Heroes of the Resistance

| | | |
|---|---|---|
| COMPLETE SET (16) | 8.00 | 20.00 |
| COMMON CARD (1-16) | 0.75 | 2.00 |
| *P.P.BLACK/1: UNPRICED DUE TO SCARCITY | | |
| *P.P.CYAN/1: UNPRICED DUE TO SCARCITY | | |
| *P.P.MAGENTA/1: UNPRICED DUE TO SCARCITY | | |
| *P.P.YELLOW/1: UNPRICED DUE TO SCARCITY | | |
| 2 Poe Dameron | 1.00 | 2.50 |
| 3 Finn | 1.00 | 2.50 |
| 4 Rey | 1.25 | 3.00 |
| 5 Han Solo | 1.50 | 4.00 |
| 16 BB-8 | 1.50 | 4.00 |

### 2016 Star Wars The Force Awakens Series Two Maz's Castle

| | | |
|---|---|---|
| COMPLETE SET (9) | 5.00 | 12.00 |
| COMMON CARD (1-9) | 0.75 | 2.00 |
| *P.P.BLACK/1: UNPRICED DUE TO SCARCITY | | |
| *P.P.CYAN/1: UNPRICED DUE TO SCARCITY | | |
| *P.P.MAGENTA/1: UNPRICED DUE TO SCARCITY | | |
| *P.P.YELLOW/1: UNPRICED DUE TO SCARCITY | | |

### 2016 Star Wars The Force Awakens Series Two Medallions

| | | |
|---|---|---|
| COMMON CARD | 4.00 | 10.00 |
| *SILVER p/r 244-399: .5X TO 1.2X BASIC CARDS | | |
| *SILVER p/r 120-199: .6X TO 1.5X BASIC CARDS | | |
| *SILVER p/r 50-99: 1X TO 2.5X BASIC CARDS | | |
| *GOLD p/r 120-199: .6X TO 1.5X BASIC CARDS | | |

---

| | | |
|---|---|---|
| *GOLD p/r 74-100: .75X TO 2X BASIC CARDS | | |
| *GOLD p/r 25-50: 1.2X TO 3X BASIC CARDS | | |
| *PLATINUM p/r 16-25: X TO X BASIC CARDS | | |
| *PLATINUM p/r 5-15: UNPRICED DUE TO SCARCITY | | |
| *PLATINUM/1: UNPRICED DUE TO SCARCITY | | |
| 1 Kylo Ren | 6.00 | 15.00 |
| 2 General Hux | 5.00 | 12.00 |
| 3 Captain Phasma | 5.00 | 12.00 |
| 4 FN-2187 | 5.00 | 12.00 |
| 6 Kylo Ren | 6.00 | 15.00 |
| 12 Kylo Ren | 6.00 | 15.00 |
| 13 Maz Kanata | 5.00 | 12.00 |
| 14 Rey | 6.00 | 15.00 |
| 15 BB-8 | 5.00 | 12.00 |
| 16 Han Solo | 8.00 | 20.00 |
| 17 Chewbacca | 5.00 | 12.00 |
| 18 Finn | 6.00 | 15.00 |
| 19 Rey | 6.00 | 15.00 |
| 22 Colonel Datoo | 6.00 | 15.00 |
| 23 Captain Phasma | 5.00 | 12.00 |
| 24 Finn | 5.00 | 12.00 |
| 27 BB-8 | 5.00 | 12.00 |
| 28 Resistance X-Wing Fighter | 5.00 | 12.00 |
| 29 Nien Nunb | 6.00 | 15.00 |
| 30 C-3PO | 6.00 | 15.00 |
| 31 R2-D2 | 8.00 | 20.00 |
| 32 Jess Testor Pava | 10.00 | 25.00 |
| 33 Snap Wexley | 6.00 | 15.00 |
| 34 Admiral Statura | 6.00 | 15.00 |
| 35 Admiral Ackbar | 6.00 | 15.00 |
| 36 Major Brance | 5.00 | 12.00 |

### 2016 Star Wars The Force Awakens Series Two Power of the First Order

| | | |
|---|---|---|
| COMPLETE SET (11) | 5.00 | 12.00 |
| COMMON CARD (1-11) | 0.40 | 1.00 |
| *P.P.BLACK/1: UNPRICED DUE TO SCARCITY | | |
| *P.P.CYAN/1: UNPRICED DUE TO SCARCITY | | |
| *P.P.MAGENTA/1: UNPRICED DUE TO SCARCITY | | |
| *P.P.YELLOW/1: UNPRICED DUE TO SCARCITY | | |
| 1 Kylo Ren | 1.25 | 3.00 |
| 2 General Hux | 1.00 | 2.50 |
| 3 Captain Phasma | 1.25 | 3.00 |
| 11 Supreme Leader Snoke | 1.00 | 2.50 |

### 2016 Star Wars Rogue One Series One

| | | |
|---|---|---|
| COMPLETE SET (90) | 8.00 | 20.00 |
| UNOPENED BOX (24 PACKS) | 80.00 | 100.00 |
| UNOPENED PACK (8 CARDS) | 3.00 | 4.00 |
| COMMON CARD (1-90) | 0.25 | 0.60 |
| *DEATH STAR BL.: .6X TO 1.5X BASIC CARDS | | |
| *GREEN SQ.: .75X TO 2X BASIC CARDS | | |
| *BLUE SQ.: 1X TO 2.5X BASIC CARDS | | |

---

| | | |
|---|---|---|
| *GRAY SQ./100: 4X TO 10X BASIC CARDS | | |
| *GOLD SQ./50: 6X TO 15X BASIC CARDS | | |
| *ORANGE SQ./1: UNPRICED DUE TO SCARCITY | | |
| *P.P.BLACK/1: UNPRICED DUE TO SCARCITY | | |
| *P.P.CYAN/1: UNPRICED DUE TO SCARCITY | | |
| *P.P.MAGENTA1/1: UNPRICED DUE TO SCARCITY | | |
| *P.P.YELLOW/1: UNPRICED DUE TO SCARCITY | | |

### 2016 Star Wars Rogue One Series One Autographs

| | | |
|---|---|---|
| COMMON CARD | 10.00 | 25.00 |
| *BLACK/50: .6X TO 1.5X BASIC CARDS | | |
| *GOLD/10: UNPRICED DUE TO SCARCITY | | |
| *P.P.BLACK/1: UNPRICED DUE TO SCARCITY | | |
| *P.P.CYAN/1: UNPRICED DUE TO SCARCITY | | |
| *P.P.MAGENTA/1: UNPRICED DUE TO SCARCITY | | |
| *P.P.YELLOW/1: UNPRICED DUE TO SCARCITY | | |
| RANDOMLY INSERTED INTO PACKS | | |
| 1 Donnie Yen | 100.00 | 200.00 |
| 2 Felicity Jones | 300.00 | 600.00 |
| 3 Forest Whitaker | 100.00 | 200.00 |
| 4 Genevieve O'Reilly | 15.00 | 40.00 |

### 2016 Star Wars Rogue One Series One Blueprints of Ships and Vehicles

| | | |
|---|---|---|
| COMPLETE SET (8) | 5.00 | 12.00 |
| COMMON CARD (BP1-BP8) | 1.00 | 2.50 |
| *P.P.BLACK/1: UNPRICED DUE TO SCARCITY | | |
| *P.P.CYAN/1: UNPRICED DUE TO SCARCITY | | |
| *P.P.MAGENTA/1: UNPRICED DUE TO SCARCITY | | |
| *P.P.YELLOW/1: UNPRICED DUE TO SCARCITY | | |
| RANDOMLY INSERTED INTO PACKS | | |

### 2016 Star Wars Rogue One Series One Character Icons

| | | |
|---|---|---|
| COMPLETE SET (11) | 8.00 | 20.00 |
| COMMON CARD (CI1-CI11) | 1.25 | 3.00 |
| *P.P.BLACK/1: UNPRICED DUE TO SCARCITY | | |
| *P.P.CYAN/1: UNPRICED DUE TO SCARCITY | | |
| *P.P.MAGENTA/1: UNPRICED DUE TO SCARCITY | | |
| *P.P.YELLOW/1: UNPRICED DUE TO SCARCITY | | |
| RANDOMLY INSERTED INTO PACKS | | |

### 2016 Star Wars Rogue One Series One Character Stickers

| | | |
|---|---|---|
| COMPLETE SET (18) | 10.00 | 25.00 |
| COMMON CARD (CS1-CS18) | 0.75 | 2.00 |
| *P.P.BLACK/1: UNPRICED DUE TO SCARCITY | | |
| *P.P.CYAN/1: UNPRICED DUE TO SCARCITY | | |
| *P.P.MAGENTA/1: UNPRICED DUE TO SCARCITY | | |
| *P.P.YELLOW/1: UNPRICED DUE TO SCARCITY | | |
| RANDOMLY INSERTED INTO PACKS | | |

### 2016 Star Wars Rogue One Series One Gallery

| COMPLETE SET (10) | 4.00 | 10.00 |
|---|---|---|
| COMMON CARD (G1-G10) | 0.50 | 1.25 |
| *P.P.BLACK/1: UNPRICED DUE TO SCARCITY | | |
| *P.P.CYAN/1: UNPRICED DUE TO SCARCITY | | |
| *P.P.MAGENTA/1: UNPRICED DUE TO SCARCITY | | |
| *P.P.YELLOW/1: UNPRICED DUE TO SCARCITY | | |
| RANDOMLY INSERTED INTO PACKS | | |
| G1 Jyn Erso | 0.75 | 2.00 |
| G2 Jyn Erso | 0.75 | 2.00 |
| G3 Jyn Erso | 0.75 | 2.00 |
| G4 Jyn Erso | 0.75 | 2.00 |
| G5 Jyn Erso | 0.75 | 2.00 |
| G6 Jyn Erso | 0.75 | 2.00 |
| G7 Jyn Erso | 0.75 | 2.00 |

### 2016 Star Wars Rogue One Series One Heroes of the Rebel Alliance

| COMPLETE SET (14) | 8.00 | 20.00 |
|---|---|---|
| COMMON CARD (HR1-HR14) | 1.00 | 2.50 |
| *P.P.BLACK/1: UNPRICED DUE TO SCARCITY | | |
| *P.P.CYAN/1: UNPRICED DUE TO SCARCITY | | |
| *P.P.MAGENTA/1: UNPRICED DUE TO SCARCITY | | |
| *P.P.YELLOW/1: UNPRICED DUE TO SCARCITY | | |
| RANDOMLY INSERTED INTO PACKS | | |
| HR1 Jyn Erso | 1.50 | 4.00 |
| HR4 Chirrut IMWE | 1.25 | 3.00 |

### 2016 Star Wars Rogue One Series One Medallions

| COMMON CARD | 4.00 | 10.00 |
|---|---|---|
| *BRONZE: SAME VALUE AS BASIC | | |
| *SILVER/99: .5X TO 1.2X BASIC CARDS | | |
| *GOLD/50: .6X TO 1.5X BASIC CARDS | | |
| *PLATINUM/1: UNPRICED DUE TO SCARCITY | | |
| RANDOMLY INSERTED INTO PACKS | | |
| 5 Captain Cassian Andor with X-Wing | 6.00 | 15.00 |
| 6 Captain Cassian Andor with U-Wing | 6.00 | 15.00 |
| 7 Chirrut Imwe with Y-Wing | 6.00 | 15.00 |
| 8 Darth Vader with Death Star | 6.00 | 15.00 |
| 9 Darth Vader with Imperial Star Destroyer | 6.00 | 15.00 |
| 10 Death Trooper with Imperial Star Destroyer | 6.00 | 15.00 |
| 14 Edrio Two Tubes with U-Wing | 6.00 | 15.00 |
| 15 Jyn Erso with X-Wing | 8.00 | 20.00 |
| 16 Jyn Erso with U-Wing | 8.00 | 20.00 |
| 17 Jyn Erso with Death Star | 8.00 | 20.00 |
| 18 K-2SO with X-Wing | 5.00 | 12.00 |
| 20 Moroff with U-Wing | 5.00 | 12.00 |
| 24 Shoretrooper with AT-ACT | 5.00 | 12.00 |
| 25 Stormtrooper with AT-ST | 5.00 | 12.00 |
| 27 TIE Fighter Pilot with TIE Striker | 5.00 | 12.00 |

### 2016 Star Wars Rogue One Series One Montages

| COMPLETE SET (9) | 5.00 | 12.00 |
|---|---|---|
| COMMON CARD (M1-M9) | 1.00 | 2.50 |
| *P.P.BLACK/1: UNPRICED DUE TO SCARCITY | | |
| *P.P.CYAN/1: UNPRICED DUE TO SCARCITY | | |
| *P.P.MAGENTA/1: UNPRICED DUE TO SCARCITY | | |
| *P.P.YELLOW/1: UNPRICED DUE TO SCARCITY | | |
| STATED ODDS 1: | | |

### 2016 Star Wars Rogue One Series One Villains of the Galactic Empire

| COMPLETE SET (8) | 6.00 | 15.00 |
|---|---|---|
| COMMON CARD (VE1-VE8) | 1.00 | 2.50 |
| *P.P.BLACK/1: UNPRICED DUE TO SCARCITY | | |
| *P.P.CYAN/1: UNPRICED DUE TO SCARCITY | | |
| *P.P.MAGENTA/1: UNPRICED DUE TO SCARCITY | | |
| *P.P.YELLOW/1: UNPRICED DUE TO SCARCITY | | |

### 2017 Star Wars Rogue One Series Two

KRENNIC AND TARKIN CONFER

| COMPLETE SET (100) | 6.00 | 15.00 |
|---|---|---|
| UNOPENED BOX (24 PACKS) | 110.00 | 120.00 |
| UNOPENED PACK (8 CARDS) | 5.00 | 6.00 |
| COMMON CARD (1-100) | 0.20 | 0.50 |
| *DTHSTR BLACK: .6X TO 1.5X BASIC CARDS | | |
| *GREEN SQ: .75X TO 2X BASIC CARDS | | |
| *BLUE SQ: 1X TO 2.5X BASIC CARDS | | |
| *GRAY SQ/100: 5X TO 12X BASIC CARDS | | |
| *GOLD SQ/50: 10X TO 25X BASIC CARDS | | |
| *ORANGE/1: UNPRICED DUE TO SCARCITY | | |
| *RED/1: UNPRICED DUE TO SCARCITY | | |
| *P.P.BLACK/1: UNPRICED DUE TO SCARCITY | | |
| *P.P.CYAN/1: UNPRICED DUE TO SCARCITY | | |
| *P.P.MAGENTA/1: UNPRICED DUE TO SCARCITY | | |
| *P.P.YELLOW/1: UNPRICED DUE TO SCARCITY | | |

### 2017 Star Wars Rogue One Series Two Autographs

FELICITY JONES AS JYN ERSO

| COMMON AUTO | 10.00 | 25.00 |
|---|---|---|
| *BLACK/50: .6X TO 1.5X BASIC AUTOS | | |
| *GOLD/10: 1.2X TO 3X BASIC AUTOS | | |
| *ORANGE/1: UNPRICED DUE TO SCARCITY | | |
| *P.P.BLACK/1: UNPRICED DUE TO SCARCITY | | |
| *P.P.CYAN/1: UNPRICED DUE TO SCARCITY | | |
| *P.P.MAGENTA/1: UNPRICED DUE TO SCARCITY | | |

| *P.P.YELLOW/1: UNPRICED DUE TO SCARCITY | | |
|---|---|---|
| STATED ODDS 1:36 | | |
| JONES, WHITAKER, AND KELLINGTON | | |
| DO NOT HAVE BASE AUTOGRAPHS | | |
| DA Derek Arnold | 12.00 | 30.00 |
| DY Donnie Yen | 80.00 | 150.00 |
| GO Genevieve O'Reilly | 8.00 | 20.00 |
| RA Riz Ahmed | 120.00 | 200.00 |
| WD Warwick Davis | 12.00 | 30.00 |
| AC1 Aidan Cook | 10.00 | 25.00 |
| Benthic Two Tubes | | |
| AC2 Aidan Cook | 10.00 | 25.00 |
| Caitken | | |

### 2017 Star Wars Rogue One Series Two Autographs Black

| *BLACK/50: .6X TO 1.5X BASIC AUTOS | | |
|---|---|---|
| STATED ODDS 1:163 | | |
| STATED PRINT RUN 50 SER.#'d SETS | | |
| FJ Felicity Jones | 300.00 | 600.00 |
| FW Forest Whitaker | 100.00 | 200.00 |
| NK Nick Kellington | 20.00 | 50.00 |

### 2017 Star Wars Rogue One Series Two Character Stickers

| COMPLETE SET (18) | 30.00 | 80.00 |
|---|---|---|
| COMMON CARD (CS1-CS18) | 2.50 | 6.00 |
| STATED ODDS 1:12 | | |
| CS1 Jyn Erso | 5.00 | 12.00 |
| CS8 Director Krennic | 3.00 | 8.00 |
| CS9 Darth Vader | 4.00 | 10.00 |
| CS10 K-2SO | 3.00 | 8.00 |
| CS14 Chirrut Imwe | 4.00 | 10.00 |
| CS18 Admiral Raddus | 3.00 | 8.00 |

### 2017 Star Wars Rogue One Series Two Heroes of the Rebel Alliance

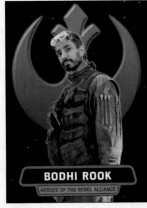

BODHI ROOK
HEROES OF THE REBEL ALLIANCE

| COMPLETE SET (10) | 6.00 | 15.00 |
|---|---|---|
| COMMON CARD (HR1-HR10) | 1.00 | 2.50 |
| *P.P.BLACK/1: UNPRICED DUE TO SCARCITY | | |
| *P.P.CYAN/1: UNPRICED DUE TO SCARCITY | | |
| *P.P.MAGENTA/1: UNPRICED DUE TO SCARCITY | | |
| *P.P.YELLOW/1: UNPRICED DUE TO SCARCITY | | |
| STATED ODDS 1:7 | | |

### 2017 Star Wars Rogue One Series Two Movie Posters

| COMPLETE SET (10) | 30.00 | 80.00 |
|---|---|---|
| COMMON CARD (1-10) | 3.00 | 8.00 |
| *P.P.BLACK/1: UNPRICED DUE TO SCARCITY | | |

*P.P.CYAN/1: UNPRICED DUE TO SCARCITY
*P.P.MAGENTA/1: UNPRICED DUE TO SCARCITY
*P.P.YELLOW/1: UNPRICED DUE TO SCARCITY
STATED ODDS 1:24

| 1 | United States Theatrical Poster | 6.00 | 15.00 |
| 5 | Cassian Andor Character Poster | 4.00 | 10.00 |
| 6 | Bodhi Rook Character Poster | 5.00 | 12.00 |
| 7 | Chirrut Imwe Character Poster | 6.00 | 15.00 |
| 9 | K-2SO Character Poster | 6.00 | 15.00 |

## 2017 Star Wars Rogue One Series Two Patches

LT. ZAL DINNES (RED EIGHT)

| COMMON CARD | 5.00 | 12.00 |
|---|---|---|

*SILVER/100: .5X TO 1.2X BASIC CARDS
*GOLD/50: .6X TO 1.5X BASIC CARDS
*RED/10: 1.2X TO 3X BASIC CARDS
*ORANGE/1: UNPRICED DUE TO SCARCITY

## 2017 Star Wars Rogue One Series Two Prime Forces

| COMPLETE SET (10) | 8.00 | 20.00 |
|---|---|---|
| COMMON CARD (PF1-PF10) | 1.50 | 4.00 |

*P.P.BLACK/1: UNPRICED DUE TO SCARCITY
*P.P.CYAN/1: UNPRICED DUE TO SCARCITY
*P.P.MAGENTA/1: UNPRICED DUE TO SCARCITY
*P.P.YELLOW/1: UNPRICED DUE TO SCARCITY
STATED ODDS 1:2

## 2017 Star Wars Rogue One Series Two Troopers

| COMPLETE SET (10) | 8.00 | 20.00 |
|---|---|---|
| COMMON CARD (TR1-TR10) | 1.50 | 4.00 |

*P.P.BLACK/1: UNPRICED DUE TO SCARCITY
*P.P.CYAN/1: UNPRICED DUE TO SCARCITY
*P.P.MAGENTA/1: UNPRICED DUE TO SCARCITY
*P.P.YELLOW/1: UNPRICED DUE TO SCARCITY
STATED ODDS 1:2

## 2017 Star Wars Rogue One Series Two Villains of the Galactic Empire

| COMPLETE SET (10) | 12.00 | 30.00 |
|---|---|---|
| COMMON CARD (VG1-VG10) | 2.50 | 6.00 |

*P.P.BLACK/1: UNPRICED DUE TO SCARCITY
*P.P.CYAN/1: UNPRICED DUE TO SCARCITY
*P.P.MAGENTA/1: UNPRICED DUE TO SCARCITY
*P.P.YELLOW/1: UNPRICED DUE TO SCARCITY
STATED ODDS 1:7

## 2017 Star Wars The Last Jedi Disney Movie Reward Oversized Theater Promos

| COMPLETE SET (9) | 15.00 | 40.00 |
|---|---|---|
| COMMON CARD (UNNUMBERED) | 2.00 | 5.00 |
| THEATER PROMOTION EXCLUSIVE | | |

## 2017 Star Wars The Last Jedi Series One

FINN

| COMPLETE SET (100) | 6.00 | 15.00 |
|---|---|---|
| UNOPENED BOX (24 PACKS) | 75.00 | 100.00 |
| UNOPENED PACK (8 CARDS) | 4.00 | 5.00 |
| COMMON CARD (1-100) | 0.12 | 0.30 |

*BLUE: 2X TO 5X BASIC CARDS 0.60 1.50
*GREEN: 2.5X TO 6X BASIC CARDS 0.75 2.00
*PURPLE: 3X TO 8X BASIC CARDS 1.00 2.50
*RED: 4X TO 10X BASIC CARDS 1.25 3.00
*SILVER/99: 10X TO 25X BASIC CARDS 3.00 8.00
*GOLD/25: 20X TO 50X BASIC CARDS 6.00 15.00
*BLACK/1: UNPRICED DUE TO SCARCITY
*P.P.BLACK/1: UNPRICED DUE TO SCARCITY
*P.P.CYAN/1: UNPRICED DUE TO SCARCITY
*P.P.MAGENTA/1: UNPRICED DUE TO SCARCITY
*P.P.YELLOW/1: UNPRICED DUE TO SCARCITY

## 2017 Star Wars The Last Jedi Series One Autographs

| COMMON AUTO | 6.00 | 15.00 |
|---|---|---|

*RED/99: .5X TO 1.2X BASIC AUTOS
*SILVER/25: .6X TO 1.5X BASIC AUTOS
*GOLD/10: UNPRICED DUE TO SCARCITY
*BLACK/1: UNPRICED DUE TO SCARCITY
*P.P.BLACK/1: UNPRICED DUE TO SCARCITY
*P.P.CYAN/1: UNPRICED DUE TO SCARCITY
*P.P.MAGENTA/1: UNPRICED DUE TO SCARCITY
*P.P.YELLOW/1: UNPRICED DUE TO SCARCITY

| NNO | Aidan Cook | 8.00 | 20.00 |
| NNO | Andy Serkis TFA AU | 60.00 | 120.00 |
| NNO | Billie Lourd | 60.00 | 120.00 |
| NNO | Brian Herring | 12.00 | 30.00 |
| NNO | Crystal Clarke | 10.00 | 25.00 |
| NNO | Dave Chapman | 12.00 | 30.00 |
| NNO | Ian Whyte | 8.00 | 20.00 |
| NNO | Jimmy Vee | 15.00 | 40.00 |
| NNO | Mike Quinn | 8.00 | 20.00 |
| NNO | Paul Kasey | 10.00 | 25.00 |
| NNO | Tom Kane | 8.00 | 20.00 |
| NNO | Veronica Ngo | 15.00 | 40.00 |

## 2017 Star Wars The Last Jedi Series One Autographs Red

*RED: .5X TO 1.2X BASIC AUTOS
STATED PRINT RUN 99 SER.#'d SETS

| NNO | John Boyega | | 120.00 |
| NNO | Joonas Suotamo | | 75.00 |

## 2017 Star Wars The Last Jedi Series One Autographs Silver

*SILVER: .6X TO 1.5X BASIC AUTOS
STATED PRINT RUN 25 SER.#'d SETS

| NNO | Gwendoline Christie | 100.00 | 200.00 |

## 2017 Star Wars The Last Jedi Series One Blueprints and Schematics

| COMPLETE SET (8) | 6.00 | 15.00 |
|---|---|---|
| COMMON CARD (BP1-BP8) | 1.25 | 3.00 |

*PURPLE/250: .6X TO 1.5X BASIC CARDS 2.00 5.00
*RED/199: .75X TO 2X BASIC CARDS 2.50 6.00
*SILVER/99: 1X TO 2.5X BASIC CARDS 3.00 8.00
*GOLD/25: UNPRICED DUE TO SCARCITY
*BLACK/1: UNPRICED DUE TO SCARCITY
*P.P.BLACK/1: UNPRICED DUE TO SCARCITY
*P.P.CYAN/1: UNPRICED DUE TO SCARCITY
*P.P.MAGENTA/1: UNPRICED DUE TO SCARCITY
*P.P.YELLOW/1: UNPRICED DUE TO SCARCITY

## 2017 Star Wars The Last Jedi Series One Character Portraits

| COMPLETE SET (16) | 12.00 | 30.00 |
|---|---|---|
| COMMON CARD (CP1-CP16) | 1.50 | 4.00 |

*PURPLE/250: .6X TO 1.5X BASIC CARDS 2.50 6.00
*RED/199: .75X TO 2X BASIC CARDS 3.00 8.00
*SILVER/99: 1X TO 2.5X BASIC CARDS 4.00 10.00
*GOLD/25: UNPRICED DUE TO SCARCITY
*BLACK/1: UNPRICED DUE TO SCARCITY
*P.P.BLACK/1: UNPRICED DUE TO SCARCITY
*P.P.CYAN/1: UNPRICED DUE TO SCARCITY
*P.P.MAGENTA/1: UNPRICED DUE TO SCARCITY
*P.P.YELLOW/1: UNPRICED DUE TO SCARCITY
RANDOMLY INSERTED INTO PACKS

## 2017 Star Wars The Last Jedi Series One Character Stickers

| COMPLETE SET (6) | 8.00 | 20.00 |
|---|---|---|
| COMMON CARD (DS1-DS6) | 1.25 | 3.00 |
| RANDOMLY INSERTED INTO PACKS | | |

| | | |
|---|---|---|
| DS1 Kylo Ren | 1.50 | 4.00 |
| DS4 Rey | 3.00 | 8.00 |
| DS5 Finn | 2.50 | 6.00 |
| DS6 Poe Dameron | 2.00 | 5.00 |

### 2017 Star Wars The Last Jedi Series One Illustrated

| | | |
|---|---|---|
| COMPLETE SET (11) | 8.00 | 20.00 |
| COMMON CARD (SWI1-SWI11) | 1.25 | 3.00 |
| *PURPLE/250: .6X TO 1.5X BASIC CARDS | 2.00 | 5.00 |
| *RED/199: .75X TO 2X BASIC CARDS | 2.50 | 6.00 |
| *SILVER/99: 1X TO 2.5X BASIC CARDS | 3.00 | 8.00 |
| *GOLD/25: UNPRICED DUE TO SCARCITY | | |
| *BLACK/1: UNPRICED DUE TO SCARCITY | | |
| *P.P.BLACK/1: UNPRICED DUE TO SCARCITY | | |
| *P.P.CYAN/1: UNPRICED DUE TO SCARCITY | | |
| *P.P.MAGENTA/1: UNPRICED DUE TO SCARCITY | | |
| *P.P.YELLOW/1: UNPRICED DUE TO SCARCITY | | |
| RANDOMLY INSERTED INTO PACKS | | |

### 2017 Star Wars The Last Jedi Series One Medallions

| | | |
|---|---|---|
| COMMON MEDALLION | 4.00 | 10.00 |
| *PURPLE/99: .5X TO 1.2X BASIC MEDALLIONS | 5.00 | 12.00 |
| *RED/25: 1.2X TO 3X BASIC MEDALLIONS | 12.00 | 30.00 |
| *ORANGE/1: UNPRICED DUE TO SCARCITY | | |
| RANDOMLY INSERTED INTO PACKS | | |
| NNO BB-8 / BB-8 | 5.00 | 12.00 |
| NNO BB-8 / Resistance | 6.00 | 15.00 |
| NNO C-3PO / R2-D2 | 5.00 | 12.00 |
| NNO Chewbacca / R2-D2 | 8.00 | 20.00 |
| NNO Executioner Stormtrooper / First Order | 5.00 | 12.00 |
| NNO Finn / BB-8 | 5.00 | 12.00 |
| NNO Finn / Resistance | 6.00 | 15.00 |
| NNO General Hux / First Order | 5.00 | 12.00 |
| NNO General Leia Organa / Resistance | 6.00 | 15.00 |
| NNO Kylo Ren / First Order | 6.00 | 15.00 |
| NNO Luke Skywalker / Millennium Falcon | 10.00 | 25.00 |
| NNO Poe Dameron / BB-8 | 5.00 | 12.00 |
| NNO Poe Dameron / Resistance | 6.00 | 15.00 |
| NNO Porg / Millennium Falcon | 6.00 | 15.00 |
| NNO Porg / R2-D2 | 6.00 | 15.00 |
| NNO Praetorian Guard / First Order | 5.00 | 12.00 |
| NNO R2-D2 / Resistance | 5.00 | 12.00 |
| NNO Rey / BB-8 | 8.00 | 20.00 |
| NNO Rey / Millennium Falcon | 8.00 | 20.00 |
| NNO Rey / Resistance | 8.00 | 20.00 |
| NNO Rose / Resistance | 5.00 | 12.00 |

### 2017 Star Wars The Last Jedi Series One Red Character Illustrations

| | | |
|---|---|---|
| COMPLETE SET (8) | 8.00 | 20.00 |
| COMMON CARD (RL1-RL8) | 1.50 | 4.00 |
| *PURPLE/250: .6X TO 1.5X BASIC CARDS | 2.50 | 6.00 |
| *RED/199: .75X TO 2X BASIC CARDS | 3.00 | 8.00 |
| *SILVER/99: 1X TO 2.5X BASIC CARDS | 4.00 | 10.00 |
| *GOLD/25: UNPRICED DUE TO SCARCITY | | |
| *BLACK/1: UNPRICED DUE TO SCARCITY | | |
| *P.P.BLACK/1: UNPRICED DUE TO SCARCITY | | |
| *P.P.CYAN/1: UNPRICED DUE TO SCARCITY | | |
| *P.P.MAGENTA/1: UNPRICED DUE TO SCARCITY | | |
| *P.P.YELLOW/1: UNPRICED DUE TO SCARCITY | | |
| RANDOMLY INSERTED INTO PACKS | | |

### 2017 Star Wars The Last Jedi Series One Resist!

| | | |
|---|---|---|
| COMPLETE SET (8) | 5.00 | 12.00 |
| COMMON CARD (R1-R8) | 1.00 | 2.50 |
| *PURPLE/250: .6X TO 1.5X BASIC CARDS | 1.50 | 4.00 |
| *RED/199: .75X TO 2X BASIC CARDS | 2.00 | 5.00 |
| *SILVER/99: 1X TO 2.5X BASIC CARDS | 2.50 | 6.00 |
| *GOLD/25: UNPRICED DUE TO SCARCITY | | |
| *BLACK/1: UNPRICED DUE TO SCARCITY | | |
| *P.P.BLACK/1: UNPRICED DUE TO SCARCITY | | |
| *P.P.CYAN/1: UNPRICED DUE TO SCARCITY | | |
| *P.P.MAGENTA/1: UNPRICED DUE TO SCARCITY | | |
| *P.P.YELLOW/1: UNPRICED DUE TO SCARCITY | | |
| RANDOMLY INSERTED INTO PACKS | | |

### 2017 Star Wars The Last Jedi Series One Source Material Fabric Relics

| | | |
|---|---|---|
| COMMON RELIC | 12.00 | 30.00 |
| *SILVER/99: .5X TO 1.2X BASIC RELICS | 15.00 | 40.00 |
| *GOLD/25: UNPRICED DUE TO SCARCITY | | |
| *BLACK/1: UNPRICED DUE TO SCARCITY | | |
| RANDOMLY INSERTED INTO PACKS | | |

### 2018 Star Wars The Last Jedi Series Two

| | | |
|---|---|---|
| COMPLETE SET (100) | 6.00 | 15.00 |
| UNOPENED BOX (24 PACKS) | | |
| UNOPENED PACK (8 CARDS) | | |
| COMMON CARD (1-100) | 0.12 | 0.30 |
| *BLUE: 2X TO 5X BASIC CARDS | 0.60 | 1.50 |
| *PURPLE: 3X TO 8X BASIC CARDS | 1.00 | 2.50 |
| *RED/199: 4X TO 10X BASIC CARDS | 1.25 | 3.00 |
| *BRONZE/99: 10X TO 25X BASIC CARDS | 3.00 | 8.00 |
| *SILVER/25: 20X TO 50X BASIC CARDS | 6.00 | 15.00 |
| *GOLD/10: UNPRICED DUE TO SCARCITY | | |
| *BLACK/1: UNPRICED DUE TO SCARCITY | | |
| *P.P.BLACK/1: UNPRICED DUE TO SCARCITY | | |
| *P.P.CYAN/1: UNPRICED DUE TO SCARCITY | | |

| | | |
|---|---|---|
| *P.P.MAGENTA/1: UNPRICED DUE TO SCARCITY | | |
| *P.P.YELLOW/1: UNPRICED DUE TO SCARCITY | | |

### 2018 Star Wars The Last Jedi Series Two Autographs

| | | |
|---|---|---|
| COMMON AUTO | 6.00 | 15.00 |
| *RED/99: X TO X BASIC AUTOS | | |
| *SILVER/25: X TO X BASIC AUTOS | | |
| *GOLD/10: UNPRICED DUE TO SCARCITY | | |
| *BLACK/1: UNPRICED DUE TO SCARCITY | | |
| *P.P.BLACK/1: UNPRICED DUE TO SCARCITY | | |
| *P.P.CYAN/1: UNPRICED DUE TO SCARCITY | | |
| *P.P.MAGENTA/1: UNPRICED DUE TO SCARCITY | | |
| *P.P.YELLOW/1: UNPRICED DUE TO SCARCITY | | |
| STATED ODDS 1:36 | | |
| NNO Adam Driver | | |
| NNO Adrian Edmondson | 10.00 | 25.00 |
| NNO Amanda Lawrence | 12.00 | 30.00 |
| NNO Andy Serkis | | |
| NNO Anthony Daniels | | |
| NNO Billie Lourd | | |
| NNO Brian Herring | 8.00 | 20.00 |
| NNO Crystal Clarke | 8.00 | 20.00 |
| NNO Daisy Ridley | | |
| NNO Gwendoline Christie | | |
| NNO Hermione Corfield | 20.00 | 50.00 |
| NNO Jimmy Vee | 10.00 | 25.00 |
| NNO John Boyega | 50.00 | 100.00 |
| NNO Joonas Suotamo | | |
| NNO Kiran Shah | 8.00 | 20.00 |
| NNO Laura Dern | | |
| NNO Mike Quinn | | |
| NNO Tom Kane | | |
| NNO Veronica Ngo | 15.00 | 40.00 |

### 2018 Star Wars The Last Jedi Series Two Autographs Red

| | | |
|---|---|---|
| *RED: .5X TO 1.2X BASIC AUTOS | | |
| STATED ODDS 1:127 | | |
| STATED PRINT RUN 99 SER.#'d SETS | | |
| NNO Laura Dern | 75.00 | 150.00 |

### 2018 Star Wars The Last Jedi Series Two Autographs Silver

| | | |
|---|---|---|
| STATED ODDS 1:350 | | |
| STATED PRINT RUN 25 SER.#'d SETS | | |
| NNO Adam Driver | 300.00 | 500.00 |
| NNO Andy Serkis | 60.00 | 120.00 |
| NNO Anthony Daniels | 100.00 | 200.00 |
| NNO Joonas Suotamo | 50.00 | 100.00 |

## 2018 Star Wars The Last Jedi Series Two Character Stickers

| | | |
|---|---|---|
| COMPLETE SET (10) | 15.00 | 40.00 |
| COMMON STICKER (CS1-CS10) | 1.25 | 3.00 |
| STATED ODDS 1:16 | | |
| CS1 Rey | 3.00 | 8.00 |
| CS2 Kylo Ren | 1.50 | 4.00 |
| CS3 Finn | 2.00 | 5.00 |
| CS4 Poe Dameron | 5.00 | 12.00 |
| CS5 Supreme Leader Snoke | 1.50 | 4.00 |
| CS6 Captain Phasma | 2.00 | 5.00 |
| CS8 General Leia Organa | 2.00 | 5.00 |
| CS10 Luke Skywalker | 2.50 | 6.00 |

## 2018 Star Wars The Last Jedi Series Two Commemorative Patches

| | | |
|---|---|---|
| COMMON PATCH | 3.00 | 8.00 |
| *GOLD/25: UNPRICED DUE TO SCARCITY | | |
| *BLACK/1: UNPRICED DUE TO SCARCITY | | |
| STATED ODDS 1:67 | | |
| NNO BB-8 - BB-8 | 5.00 | 12.00 |
| NNO BB-8 - Resist | 5.00 | 12.00 |
| NNO BB-8 - Resistance | 5.00 | 12.00 |
| NNO C-3PO - BB-8 | 4.00 | 10.00 |
| NNO C-3PO - Resist | 4.00 | 10.00 |
| NNO C'ai Threnalli - Resistance Pilots | 5.00 | 12.00 |
| NNO Captain Phasma - BB-9E | 6.00 | 15.00 |
| NNO Captain Phasma - First Order | 6.00 | 15.00 |
| NNO Chewbacca - BB-8 | 4.00 | 10.00 |
| NNO Chewbacca - Resistance | 4.00 | 10.00 |
| NNO Ensign Pamich Nerro Goode - A-Wing | 5.00 | 12.00 |
| NNO Ensign Pamich Nerro Goode - Resistance | 5.00 | 12.00 |
| NNO Finn - A-Wing | 6.00 | 15.00 |
| NNO Finn - BB-8 | 6.00 | 15.00 |
| NNO Finn - Resist | 6.00 | 15.00 |
| NNO General Ematt - A-Wing | 5.00 | 12.00 |
| NNO General Ematt - Resistance | 5.00 | 12.00 |

| | | |
|---|---|---|
| NNO General Leia Organa - Resist | 8.00 | 20.00 |
| NNO General Leia Organa - Resistance | 8.00 | 20.00 |
| NNO Kaydel Ko Connix - A-Wing | 6.00 | 15.00 |
| NNO Kaydel Ko Connix - Resistance | 6.00 | 15.00 |
| NNO Kylo Ren - BB-9E | 6.00 | 15.00 |
| NNO Kylo Ren - First Order | 6.00 | 15.00 |
| NNO Luke Skywalker - BB-8 | 8.00 | 20.00 |
| NNO Luke Skywalker - Resist | 8.00 | 20.00 |
| NNO Poe Dameron - A-Wing | 5.00 | 12.00 |
| NNO Poe Dameron - BB-8 | 5.00 | 12.00 |
| NNO Poe Dameron - Resistance | 5.00 | 12.00 |
| NNO Poe Dameron - Resistance Pilots | 5.00 | 12.00 |
| NNO Praetorian Guard - BB-9E | 6.00 | 15.00 |
| NNO Praetorian Guard - First Order | 6.00 | 15.00 |
| NNO R2-D2 - BB-8 | 5.00 | 12.00 |
| NNO R2-D2 - Resist | 5.00 | 12.00 |
| NNO R2-D2 - Resistance | 5.00 | 12.00 |
| NNO Resistance Gunner Paige Tico - Resistance Pilots | 5.00 | 12.00 |
| NNO Rey - A-Wing | 6.00 | 15.00 |
| NNO Rey - BB-8 | 6.00 | 15.00 |
| NNO Rey - Resist | 6.00 | 15.00 |
| NNO Rose Tico - Resistance | 5.00 | 12.00 |
| NNO Stormtrooper Executioner - First Order | 4.00 | 10.00 |
| NNO Supreme Leader Snoke - BB-9E | 5.00 | 12.00 |
| NNO Supreme Leader Snoke - First Order | 5.00 | 12.00 |
| NNO Vice Admiral Holdo - Resist | 5.00 | 12.00 |

## 2018 Star Wars The Last Jedi Series Two Items and Artifacts

| | | |
|---|---|---|
| COMPLETE SET (20) | 10.00 | 25.00 |
| COMMON CARD (IA1-IA20) | 0.75 | 2.00 |
| *RED/99: .5X TO 1.2X BASIC CARDS | | |
| *BRONZE/50: .75X TO 2X BASIC CARDS | | |
| *SILVER/25: UNPRICED DUE TO SCARCITY | | |
| *GOLD/10: UNPRICED DUE TO SCARCITY | | |
| *BLACK/1: UNPRICED DUE TO SCARCITY | | |
| *P.P.BLACK/1: UNPRICED DUE TO SCARCITY | | |
| *P.P.CYAN/1: UNPRICED DUE TO SCARCITY | | |
| *P.P.MAGENTA/1: UNPRICED DUE TO SCARCITY | | |
| *P.P.YELLOW/1: UNPRICED DUE TO SCARCITY | | |
| STATED ODDS 1:1 | | |
| IA1 Skywalker's Lightsaber | 2.00 | 5.00 |
| IA2 Luke Skywalker's Compass | 2.00 | 5.00 |
| IA4 Proton Bomb | 1.25 | 3.00 |
| IA14 Kylo Ren's Lightsaber | 3.00 | 8.00 |

## 2018 Star Wars The Last Jedi Series Two Leaders of the Resistance

| | | |
|---|---|---|
| COMPLETE SET (10) | 5.00 | 12.00 |
| COMMON CARD (RS1-RS10) | 0.75 | 2.00 |
| *RED/99: .5X TO 1.2X BASIC CARDS | | |
| *BRONZE/50: .75X TO 2X BASIC CARDS | | |
| *SILVER/25: UNPRICED DUE TO SCARCITY | | |
| *GOLD/10: UNPRICED DUE TO SCARCITY | | |
| *BLACK/1: UNPRICED DUE TO SCARCITY | | |
| *P.P.BLACK/1: UNPRICED DUE TO SCARCITY | | |
| *P.P.CYAN/1: UNPRICED DUE TO SCARCITY | | |
| *P.P.MAGENTA/1: UNPRICED DUE TO SCARCITY | | |
| *P.P.YELLOW/1: UNPRICED DUE TO SCARCITY | | |
| STATED ODDS 1:2 | | |

## 2018 Star Wars The Last Jedi Series Two Patrons of Canto Bight

| | | |
|---|---|---|
| COMPLETE SET (10) | 6.00 | 15.00 |
| COMMON CARD (CB1-CB10) | 1.25 | 3.00 |
| *RED/99: .5X TO 1.2X BASIC CARDS | 1.50 | 4.00 |
| *BRONZE/50: .75X TO 2X BASIC CARDS | 2.50 | 6.00 |
| *SILVER/25: UNPRICED DUE TO SCARCITY | | |
| *GOLD/10: UNPRICED DUE TO SCARCITY | | |
| *BLACK/1: UNPRICED DUE TO SCARCITY | | |
| *P.P.BLACK/1: UNPRICED DUE TO SCARCITY | | |
| *P.P.CYAN/1: UNPRICED DUE TO SCARCITY | | |
| *P.P.MAGENTA/1: UNPRICED DUE TO SCARCITY | | |
| *P.P.YELLOW/1: UNPRICED DUE TO SCARCITY | | |
| STATED ODDS 1:6 | | |

## 2018 Star Wars The Last Jedi Series Two Ships and Vehicles

| | | |
|---|---|---|
| COMPLETE SET (10) | 8.00 | 20.00 |
| COMMON CARD (SV1-SV10) | 1.50 | 4.00 |
| *RED/99: .5X TO 1.2X BASIC CARDS | 2.00 | 5.00 |
| *BRONZE/50: .75X TO 2X BASIC CARDS | 3.00 | 8.00 |
| *SILVER/25: UNPRICED DUE TO SCARCITY | | |
| *GOLD/10: UNPRICED DUE TO SCARCITY | | |
| *BLACK/1: UNPRICED DUE TO SCARCITY | | |
| *P.P.BLACK/1: UNPRICED DUE TO SCARCITY | | |
| *P.P.CYAN/1: UNPRICED DUE TO SCARCITY | | |
| *P.P.MAGENTA/1: UNPRICED DUE TO SCARCITY | | |
| *P.P.YELLOW/1: UNPRICED DUE TO SCARCITY | | |
| STATED ODDS 1:8 | | |

## 2018 Star Wars The Last Jedi Series Two Soldiers of the First Order

| | | |
|---|---|---|
| COMPLETE SET (10) | 6.00 | 15.00 |
| COMMON CARD (FO1-FO10) | 1.25 | 3.00 |

| | | |
|---|---|---|
| *RED/99: .5X TO 1.2X BASIC CARDS | 1.50 | 4.00 |
| *BRONZE/50: .75X TO 2X BASIC CARDS | 2.50 | 6.00 |
| *SILVER/25: UNPRICED DUE TO SCARCITY | | |
| *GOLD/10: UNPRICED DUE TO SCARCITY | | |
| *BLACK/1: UNPRICED DUE TO SCARCITY | | |
| *P.P.BLACK/1: UNPRICED DUE TO SCARCITY | | |
| *P.P.CYAN/1: UNPRICED DUE TO SCARCITY | | |
| *P.P.MAGENTA/1: UNPRICED DUE TO SCARCITY | | |
| *P.P.YELLOW/1: UNPRICED DUE TO SCARCITY | | |
| STATED ODDS 1:4 | | |

### 2018 Star Wars The Last Jedi Series Two Source Material Fabric Swatches

| | | |
|---|---|---|
| COMMON MEM | 20.00 | 50.00 |
| *GOLD/10: UNPRICED DUE TO SCARCITY | | |
| STATED ODDS 1:360 | | |
| STATED PRINT RUN 99 SER.#'d SETS | | |
| NNO Captain Peavy's First Order Uniform | 25.00 | 60.00 |
| NNO Caretaker's Smock | 60.00 | 120.00 |
| NNO Praetorian Guard's Ceremonial Battle Skirt | 50.00 | 100.00 |

### 2018 Star Wars The Last Jedi Series Two Teaser Posters

| | | |
|---|---|---|
| COMPLETE SET (6) | 8.00 | 20.00 |
| COMMON CARD (TP1-TP6) | 2.00 | 5.00 |
| STATED ODDS 1:24 | | |
| TP1 Rey | 2.50 | 6.00 |
| TP5 General Leia Organa | 2.50 | 6.00 |

### 2018 Countdown to Solo A Star Wars Story

| | | |
|---|---|---|
| COMPLETE SET (25) | 60.00 | 120.00 |
| COMMON CARD (1-25) | 4.00 | 10.00 |

### 2018 Solo A Star Wars Story

| | | |
|---|---|---|
| COMPLETE SET (100) | 8.00 | 20.00 |
| UNOPENED BOX (24 PACKS) | 50.00 | 60.00 |
| UNOPENED PACK (8 CARDS) | 2.50 | 3.00 |
| COMMON CARD (1-100) | 0.15 | 0.40 |
| *YELLOW: .6X TO 1.5X BASIC CARDS | 0.25 | 0.60 |
| *BLACK: .75X TO 2X BASIC CARDS | 0.30 | 0.75 |
| *SILVER: 1.5X TO 4X BASIC CARDS | 0.60 | 1.50 |
| *PINK/99: 6X TO 15X BASIC CARDS | 2.50 | 6.00 |
| *ORANGE/25: 15X TO 40X BASIC CARDS | 6.00 | 15.00 |
| *GOLD/10: UNPRICED DUE TO SCARCITY | | |
| *IMPERIAL RED/1: UNPRICED DUE TO SCARCITY | | |
| *P.P.BLACK/1: UNPRICED DUE TO SCARCITY | | |
| *P.P.CYAN/1: UNPRICED DUE TO SCARCITY | | |
| *P.P.MAGENTA/1: UNPRICED DUE TO SCARCITY | | |
| *P.P.YELLOW/1: UNPRICED DUE TO SCARCITY | | |

### 2018 Solo A Star Wars Story Autographs

| | | |
|---|---|---|
| COMMON AUTO | 8.00 | 20.00 |
| *PINK/99: .5X TO 1.2X BASIC AUTOS | | |
| *ORANGE/25: .6X TO 1.5X BASIC AUTOS | | |
| *GOLD/10: UNPRICED DUE TO SCARCITY | | |
| *IMPERIAL RED/1: UNPRICED DUE TO SCARCITY | | |

| | | |
|---|---|---|
| *P.P.BLACK/1: UNPRICED DUE TO SCARCITY | | |
| *P.P.CYAN/1: UNPRICED DUE TO SCARCITY | | |
| *P.P.MAGENTA/1: UNPRICED DUE TO SCARCITY | | |
| *P.P.YELLOW/1: UNPRICED DUE TO SCARCITY | | |
| STATED ODDS 1:33 | | |
| AAF Anna Francolini | 12.00 | 30.00 |
| AAJ Andrew Jack | 10.00 | 25.00 |
| AAW Andrew Woodall | 12.00 | 30.00 |
| ADA Derek Arnold | 12.00 | 30.00 |
| ADT Dee Tails | 10.00 | 25.00 |
| AIK Ian Kenny | 10.00 | 25.00 |

### 2018 Solo A Star Wars Story Autographs Pink

| | | |
|---|---|---|
| STATED ODDS 1:231 | | |
| STATED PRINT RUN 99 SER.#'d SETS | | |
| AJS Joonas Suotamo | 50.00 | 100.00 |
| AWD Warwick Davis | 20.00 | 50.00 |
| AJSC Joonas Suotamo | 50.00 | 100.00 |

### 2018 Solo A Star Wars Story Character Stickers

| | | |
|---|---|---|
| COMPLETE SET (7) | 8.00 | 20.00 |
| COMMON CARD (CS1-CS7) | 2.00 | 5.00 |
| STATED ODDS 1:12 | | |

### 2018 Solo A Star Wars Story Icons

| | | |
|---|---|---|
| COMPLETE SET (7) | 5.00 | 12.00 |
| COMMON CARD (I1-I7) | 1.00 | 2.50 |
| *P.P.BLACK/1: UNPRICED DUE TO SCARCITY | | |
| *P.P.CYAN/1: UNPRICED DUE TO SCARCITY | | |
| *P.P.MAGENTA/1: UNPRICED DUE TO SCARCITY | | |
| *P.P.YELLOW/1: UNPRICED DUE TO SCARCITY | | |
| STATED ODDS 1:8 | | |

### 2018 Solo A Star Wars Story Manufactured Patches

| | | |
|---|---|---|
| COMMON PATCH | 3.00 | 8.00 |
| *PINK/99: .5X TO 1.2X BASIC PATCHES | | |
| *ORANGE/25: .6X TO 1.5X BASIC PATCHES | | |
| *GOLD/10: UNPRICED DUE TO SCARCITY | | |
| *IMPERIAL RED/1: UNPRICED DUE TO SCARCITY | | |
| STATED ODDS 1:32 | | |
| MPCC Chewbacca | 5.00 | 12.00 |
| MPCH Chewbacca | 5.00 | 12.00 |
| MPHM Han Solo | 6.00 | 15.00 |
| MPIS Imperial Fleet Trooper | 4.00 | 10.00 |
| MPLH L3-37 | 5.00 | 12.00 |
| MPLM Lando Calrissian | 6.00 | 15.00 |
| MPME Enfys Nest | 5.00 | 12.00 |
| MPMS Mimban Stormtrooper | 6.00 | 15.00 |
| MPQC Qi'ra | 8.00 | 20.00 |
| MPQH Qi'ra | 8.00 | 20.00 |
| MPRS R5-PHT | 4.00 | 10.00 |
| MPSS Stormtrooper | 4.00 | 10.00 |
| MPTS TIE Fighter Pilot | 6.00 | 15.00 |
| MPENH Enfys Nest | 5.00 | 12.00 |
| MPHSC Han Solo | 6.00 | 15.00 |
| MPHSH Han Solo | 6.00 | 15.00 |
| MPLCH Lando Calrissian | 6.00 | 15.00 |

### 2018 Solo A Star Wars Story Ships and Vehicles

| | | |
|---|---|---|
| COMPLETE SET (9) | 4.00 | 10.00 |
| COMMON CARD (SV1-SV9) | 0.60 | 1.50 |
| *P.P.BLACK/1: UNPRICED DUE TO SCARCITY | | |
| *P.P.CYAN/1: UNPRICED DUE TO SCARCITY | | |

| | | |
|---|---|---|
| *P.P.MAGENTA/1: UNPRICED DUE TO SCARCITY | | |
| *P.P.YELLOW/1: UNPRICED DUE TO SCARCITY | | |
| STATED ODDS 1:4 | | |

### 2018 Solo A Star Wars Story Silhouettes

| | | |
|---|---|---|
| COMPLETE SET (11) | 6.00 | 15.00 |
| COMMON CARD (SL1-SL11) | 1.00 | 2.50 |
| *P.P.BLACK/1: UNPRICED DUE TO SCARCITY | | |
| *P.P.CYAN/1: UNPRICED DUE TO SCARCITY | | |
| *P.P.MAGENTA/1: UNPRICED DUE TO SCARCITY | | |
| *P.P.YELLOW/1: UNPRICED DUE TO SCARCITY | | |
| STATED ODDS 1:2 | | |

### 2018 Solo A Star Wars Story Smooth Sayings

| | | |
|---|---|---|
| COMPLETE SET (8) | 8.00 | 20.00 |
| COMMON CARD (SS1-SS8) | 1.50 | 4.00 |
| *P.P.BLACK/1: UNPRICED DUE TO SCARCITY | | |
| *P.P.CYAN/1: UNPRICED DUE TO SCARCITY | | |
| *P.P.MAGENTA/1: UNPRICED DUE TO SCARCITY | | |
| *P.P.YELLOW/1: UNPRICED DUE TO SCARCITY | | |
| STATED ODDS 1:6 | | |
| SS1 I Got This | 1.50 | 4.00 |
| SS2 Chewie Is My Copilot | 1.50 | 4.00 |
| SS3 Just Be Charming | 1.50 | 4.00 |
| SS4 We're Doing This My Way | 1.50 | 4.00 |
| SS5 Kessel Crew | 1.50 | 4.00 |
| SS6 Just Trust Us | 1.50 | 4.00 |
| SS7 Smooth & Sophisticated | 1.50 | 4.00 |
| SS8 Double-Crossing No-Good Swindler | 1.50 | 4.00 |

### 2018 Solo A Star Wars Story Target Exclusive Manufactured Patches

| | | |
|---|---|---|
| COMMON PATCH | 5.00 | 12.00 |
| *PINK/99: .5X TO 1.2X BASIC PATCHES | 6.00 | 15.00 |
| *ORANGE/25: .6X TO 1.5X BASIC PATCHES | 8.00 | 20.00 |
| *GOLD/10: UNPRICED DUE TO SCARCITY | | |
| *IMPERIAL RED/1: UNPRICED DUE TO SCARCITY | | |
| STATED ODDS 1:TARGET BLASTER BOX | | |

### 2018 Solo A Star Wars Story Promo

| | | |
|---|---|---|
| P1 Han Solo | 4.00 | 10.00 |

### 2018 Solo A Star Wars Story Denny's

| | | |
|---|---|---|
| COMPLETE SET (12) | 20.00 | 50.00 |
| UNOPENED PACK (2 CARDS+1 COUPON) | 3.00 | 8.00 |
| COMMON CARD (UNNUMBERED) | 2.00 | 5.00 |
| *FOIL: 6X TO 15X BASIC CARDS | 30.00 | 75.00 |

### 2018 Solo A Star Wars Story Odeon Cinemas

| | | |
|---|---|---|
| COMPLETE SET (4) | 3.00 | 8.00 |
| COMMON CARD (UNNUMBERED) | 1.00 | 2.50 |

### 2019 Star Wars The Rise of Skywalker Trailer

| | | |
|---|---|---|
| COMPLETE SET (10) | 10.00 | 25.00 |
| COMMON CARD (1-10) | 1.50 | 4.00 |
| TOPPS ONLINE EXCLUSIVE | | |

## 2009 Art of Star Wars Comics Postcards

| | | |
|---|---|---|
| COMPLETE SET (100) | 12.00 | 30.00 |
| COMMON CARD (1-100) | .25 | .60 |

## 2014 Disney Store Star Wars North America

| | | |
|---|---|---|
| COMPLETE SET (9) | 10.00 | 25.00 |
| COMMON CARD (1-10) | .75 | 2.00 |
| US/CANADA EXCLUSIVE | | |
| 1 Luke Skywalker | 2.00 | 5.00 |
| 4 Darth Vader | 2.00 | 5.00 |
| 7 Princess Leia | 2.00 | 5.00 |
| 9 Han Solo | 2.00 | 5.00 |

## 2014 Disney Store Star Wars United Kingdom

| | | |
|---|---|---|
| COMPLETE SET (12) | 15.00 | 40.00 |
| COMMON CARD (1-12) | 1.00 | 2.50 |
| UK EXCLUSIVE | | |
| 1 Chewbacca | 1.25 | 3.00 |
| 2 Darth Vader | 4.00 | 10.00 |
| 4 Han Solo | 4.00 | 10.00 |
| 6 Luke Skywalker | 3.00 | 8.00 |
| 8 Obi-Wan Kenobi | 1.25 | 3.00 |
| 9 Princess Leia Organa | 3.00 | 8.00 |
| 10 R2-D2 and C-3PO | 1.25 | 3.00 |
| 11 Stormtrooper | 1.25 | 3.00 |

## 2008 Family Guy Episode IV A New Hope

| | | |
|---|---|---|
| COMPLETE SET (50) | 5.00 | 12.00 |
| COMMON CARD (1-50) | .15 | .40 |

---

| | | |
|---|---|---|
| CL1 ISSUED AS CASE EXCLUSIVE | | |
| CL1 Evil Empire CI | 12.00 | 25.00 |

## 2008 Family Guy Episode IV A New Hope Droid Chat

| | | |
|---|---|---|
| COMPLETE SET (3) | 5.00 | 12.00 |
| COMMON CARD (DC1-DC3) | 2.00 | 5.00 |
| STATED ODDS 1:23 | | |

## 2008 Family Guy Episode IV A New Hope Promos

| | | |
|---|---|---|
| P1 Left half w/Han | 1.00 | 2.50 |
| Pi Right half w/Leia | 1.00 | 2.50 |

## 2008 Family Guy Episode IV A New Hope Puzzle

| | | |
|---|---|---|
| COMPLETE SET (9) | 4.00 | 10.00 |
| COMMON CARD (NH1-NH9) | .75 | 2.00 |
| STATED ODDS 1:7 | | |

## 2008 Family Guy Episode IV A New Hope Scenes from Space

| | | |
|---|---|---|
| COMPLETE SET (6) | 4.00 | 10.00 |
| COMMON CARD (S1-S6) | 1.25 | 3.00 |
| STATED ODDS 1:11 | | |

## 2008 Family Guy Episode IV A New Hope Spaceships and Transports

| | | |
|---|---|---|
| COMPLETE SET (9) | 4.00 | 10.00 |
| COMMON CARD (ST1-ST9) | 1.00 | 2.50 |
| STATED ODDS 1:9 | | |

## 2008 Family Guy Episode IV A New Hope What Happens Next?

| | | |
|---|---|---|
| COMPLETE SET (6) | 4.00 | 10.00 |
| COMMON CARD (WN1-WN6) | 1.25 | 3.00 |
| STATED ODDS 1:11 | | |

## 2017 Funko Pop Buttons Star Wars

| | | |
|---|---|---|
| NNO Boba Fett | 2.00 | 5.00 |
| NNO C-3PO | 2.00 | 5.00 |
| NNO Chewbacca | 2.00 | 5.00 |
| NNO Darth Maul | 2.00 | 5.00 |
| NNO Darth Vader | 4.00 | 10.00 |
| NNO Ewok (Wicket) | 2.00 | 5.00 |
| NNO Greedo | 2.00 | 5.00 |
| NNO Han Solo HT | | |
| NNO Jabba | 2.00 | 5.00 |
| NNO Jabba (vaping) | | |
| (Hot Topic Exclusive) | | |
| NNO Luke Skywalker | | |
| (Hot Topic Exclusive) | | |
| NNO Luke/Han/Leia | 2.00 | 5.00 |
| NNO Princess Leia | 6.00 | 15.00 |
| NNO R2-D2 | 2.00 | 5.00 |
| NNO Stormtroopers | 2.00 | 5.00 |

## 2017 Funko Pop Flair Star Wars

| | | |
|---|---|---|
| NNO Chewbacca | 1.50 | 4.00 |
| NNO Darth Vader | 2.50 | 6.00 |
| NNO Greedo | 1.25 | 3.00 |
| NNO Han Solo | 2.50 | 6.00 |
| NNO Princess Leia | 1.50 | 4.00 |
| NNO Stormtrooper | 1.25 | 3.00 |
| NNO Yoda | 1.50 | 4.00 |

## 2015-17 Funko Star Wars Smuggler's Bounty Patches

| | | |
|---|---|---|
| COMMON PATCH | 2.00 | 5.00 |
| SMUGGLER'S BOUNTY EXCLUSIVE | | |
| NNO BB-8 | 2.50 | 6.00 |
| NNO Darth Vader | 2.50 | 6.00 |

---

## 2015 Star Wars Original Trilogy Series Bikkuriman Stickers

| | | |
|---|---|---|
| COMPLETE SET (24) | 30.00 | 80.00 |
| COMMON CARD | 2.00 | 5.00 |

## 2015 Star Wars Prequel Trilogy Series Bikkuriman Stickers

| | | |
|---|---|---|
| COMPLETE SET (24) | 25.00 | 60.00 |
| COMMON CARD | 1.25 | 3.00 |

## 1996 Star Wars 3-Di Widevision

| | | |
|---|---|---|
| COMPLETE SET (63) | 30.00 | 60.00 |
| COMMON CARD (1-63) | .60 | 1.50 |
| 1M STATED ODDS 1:24 | | |
| 1M Death Star Explosion | 6.00 | 15.00 |

## 1996 Star Wars 3-Di Widevision Promos

| | | |
|---|---|---|
| 3Di1 Darth Vader | 2.50 | 6.00 |
| 3Di2 Luke Skywalker | 12.00 | 30.00 |
| Darth Vader/1000* | | |

## 2015 Star Wars Abrams Promos

| | | |
|---|---|---|
| COMPLETE SET (4) | 10.00 | 25.00 |
| COMMON CARD (1-4) | 3.00 | 8.00 |
| STATED ODDS 1:SET PER BOOK | | |

## 1997 Star Wars Adventure Journal

NNO One of a Kind by Doug Shuler
NNO To Fight Another Day by Mike Vilardi
NNO Mist Encounter by Doug Shuler

## 2018 Star Wars Archives Signature Series Adam Driver

| | |
|---|---|
| 61 Adam Driver 2016 TFA Chrome/2 | |
| 62 Adam Driver 2016 TFA Chrome/2 | |
| 65 Adam Driver 2016 TFA Chrome/2 | |
| 66 Adam Driver 2016 TFA Chrome/1 | |
| 92 Adam Driver 2016 Evolution/4 | |
| P1 Adam Driver 2015 Journey TFA Patches/1 | |

## 2018 Star Wars Archives Signature Series Adrian Edmonson

| | |
|---|---|
| 52 Adrian Edmonson 2017 TLJ S1/86 | |
| 52 Adrian Edmonson 2017 TLJ S1 Red/1 | |
| 52 Adrian Edmonson 2017 TLJ S1 Purple/35 | |
| 52 Adrian Edmonson 2017 TLJ S1 Green/50 | |
| 52 Adrian Edmonson 2017 TLJ S1 Blue/65 | |

## 2018 Star Wars Archives Signature Series Aidan Cook

16 Aidan Cook 2015 TFA S1/9
44 Aidan Cook 2015 TFA S1/9
44 Aidan Cook 2015 TFA S1 Green/2
64 Aidan Cook 2016 Rogue One S1 Blue/4
64 Aidan Cook 2016 Rogue One S1/28

## 2018 Star Wars Archives Signature Series Al Lampert

10 Al Lampert 1977 SW/4
468 Al Lampert 2013 GF2 Blue/56

## 2018 Star Wars Archives Signature Series Alan Harris

13 Alan Harris 2001 Evolution/31
31 Alan Harris 2016 Card Trader/28
31 Alan Harris 2016 Card Trader Blue/7
53 Alan Harris 2015 Journey TFA/51
53 Alan Harris 2015 Journey TFA Green/7
73 Alan Harris 1980 ESB/8
74 Alan Harris 1980 ESB/18
B2 Alan Harris 2016 Card Trader Bounty/6
TC6 Alan Harris 2016 Card Trader Choice/17
ESB4 Alan Harris 2017 GF Reborn/35

## 2018 Star Wars Archives Signature Series Alan Ruscoe

60 Alan Ruscoe 2001 Evolution/35
82 Alan Ruscoe 2012 Galactic Files/35
8J Alan Ruscoe 2015 Chrome JvS/40
8S Alan Ruscoe 2015 Chrome JvS Refractors/13
8S Alan Ruscoe 2015 Chrome JvS/54
426 Alan Ruscoe 2013 GF2/42
TPM21 Alan Ruscoe 2017 GF Reborn/27

## 2018 Star Wars Archives Signature Series Alan Tudyk

18 Alan Tudyk 2017 Rogue One S2 Black/2
19 Alan Tudyk 2017 Rogue One S2/21
29 Alan Tudyk 2017 Rogue One S2/20
51 Alan Tudyk 2017 Rogue One S2/16
56 Alan Tudyk 2017 Rogue One S2/20
57 Alan Tudyk 2017 Rogue One S2/10
71 Alan Tudyk 2017 Rogue One S2/20
76 Alan Tudyk 2017 Rogue One S2/20
C18 Alan Tudyk 2016 Rogue One S1 Icons/13
HR3 Alan Tudyk 2016 Rogue One S1 Heroes/4
HR4 Alan Tudyk 2017 Rogue One S2 Heroes/4
MP2 Alan Tudyk 2016 Rogue One MB Patches/7
PF7 Alan Tudyk 2017 Rogue One S2 PF/15

## 2018 Star Wars Archives Signature Series Alistaire Petrie

10 Alistaire Petrie 2016 Rogue One S1 Green/16

10 Alistaire Petrie 2016 Rogue One S1 Black/19
10 Alistaire Petrie 2016 Rogue One S1/77

## 2018 Star Wars Archives Signature Series Amanda Lawrence

47 Amanda Lawrence 2017 TLJ S1 Purple/35
47 Amanda Lawrence 2017 TLJ S1 Green/50
47 Amanda Lawrence 2017 TLJ S1 Blue/65
47 Amanda Lawrence 2017 TLJ S1/85

## 2018 Star Wars Archives Signature Series Amy Allen

81 Amy Allen 2012 Galactic Files/14
424 Amy Allen 2013 GF2/22
AOTC18 Amy Allen 2017 GF Reborn Orange/2
AOTC18 Amy Allen 2017 GF Reborn/37

## 2018 Star Wars Archives Signature Series Andrew Jack

12 Andrew Jack 2016 TFA S2 Heroes/2
17 Andrew Jack 2015 TFA S1 Blue/1
31 Andrew Jack 2017 TLJ S1 Purple/35
31 Andrew Jack 2017 TLJ S1 Green/50
31 Andrew Jack 2017 TLJ S1 Blue/66
31 Andrew Jack 2017 TLJ S1/85
49 Andrew Jack 2016 Card Trader Blue/8
49 Andrew Jack 2016 Card Trader/22
TFA21 Andrew Jack 2017 GF Reborn/22

## 2018 Star Wars Archives Signature Series Andy Secombe

NNO Andy Secombe

## 2018 Star Wars Archives Signature Series Andy Serkis

1 Andy Serkis 2016 TFA Chrome Power of FO/11
10 Andy Serkis 2017 Journey TLJ/1
14 Andy Serkis 2017 Journey TLJ Characters/4
25 Andy Serkis 2017 TLJ S1/5
26 Andy Serkis 2016 Card Trader/26
30 Andy Serkis 2017 GF Reborn TFA10/30
60 Andy Serkis 2016 Card Trader Red/2
60 Andy Serkis 2016 Card Trader Blue/5
75 Andy Serkis 2016 TFA S2 Blue/4
75 Andy Serkis 2016 TFA S2 Green/5
75 Andy Serkis 2016 TFA Chrome Refractors/15
75 Andy Serkis 2016 TFA S2/16

## 2018 Star Wars Archives Signature Series Angus MacInnes

92 Angus MacInnes 2016 Rogue One MB Blue/1
92 Angus MacInnes 2016 Rogue One MB/47
476 Angus MacInnes 2013 GF 2/33
ANH28 Angus MacInnes 2017 GF Reborn/24

## 2018 Star Wars Archives Signature Series Anthony Forest

31 Anthony Forest 2016 Rogue One MB/36
94 Anthony Forest 1977 Star Wars/7
138 Anthony Forest 1977 Star Wars/9
223 Anthony Forest 2012 Galactic Files/45
WM1 Anthony Forest 2013 GF 2/17

## 2018 Star Wars Archives Signature Series Ashley Eckstein

7 Ashley Eckstein 2010 CW ROTBH/3
8 Ashley Eckstein 2017 Journey TLJ Red/1
8 Ashley Eckstein 2017 Journey TLJ Green/1
8 Ashley Eckstein 2017 Journey TLJ/6
10 Ashley Eckstein 2016 Evolution/59
11 Ashley Eckstein 2016 Evolution/39
12 Ashley Eckstein 2016 Evolution/36
36 Ashley Eckstein 2008 CW/9
42 Ashley Eckstein 2010 CW ROTBH/5
44 Ashley Eckstein 2010 CW ROTBH/5
62 Ashley Eckstein 2017 Journey TLJ/9
70 Ashley Eckstein 2008 CW/6
82 Ashley Eckstein 2008 CW/15
88 Ashley Eckstein 2010 CW ROTBH/5
98 Ashley Eckstein 2016 Card Trader/30
I4 Ashley Eckstein 2013 Jedi Legacy Influencers/24
13J Ashley Eckstein 2015 Chrome JvS Refractors/16
13J Ashley Eckstein 2015 Chrome JvS/55
13S Ashley Eckstein 2015 Chrome JvS/56
231 Ashley Eckstein 2012 Galactic Files/12
ACW1 Ashley Eckstein 2017 GF Reborn/34

## 2018 Star Wars Archives Signature Series Ben Daniels

9 Ben Daniels 2016 Rogue One S1 Black/18
9 Ben Daniels 2016 Rogue One S1/72
9 Ben Daniels 2016 Rogue One S1 Green/15
49 Ben Daniels 2016 Rogue One S1 Blue/8
49 Ben Daniels 2016 Rogue One S1 Green/9
49 Ben Daniels 2016 Rogue One S1/37
63 Ben Daniels 2017 Rogue One S2/10

## 2018 Star Wars Archives Signature Series Ben Mendelsohn

5 Ben Mendelsohn 2016 Rogue One MB Patches/6
13 Ben Mendelsohn 2016 Rogue One S1 Blue/8
13 Ben Mendelsohn 2016 Rogue One S1 Black/9
13 Ben Mendelsohn 2016 Rogue One S1/38
37 Ben Mendelsohn 2017 Rogue One S2 Blue/1
37 Ben Mendelsohn 2017 Rogue One S2/11
52 Ben Mendelsohn 2016 Rogue One S1 Blue/7
52 Ben Mendelsohn 2016 Rogue One S1 Black/10
52 Ben Mendelsohn 2016 Rogue One S1/36
66 Ben Mendelsohn 2016 Rogue One S1 Green/8

66  Ben Mendelsohn 2016 Rogue One S1 Gray/8
66  Ben Mendelsohn 2016 Rogue One S1/37
83  Ben Mendelsohn 2016 Rogue One S1 Black/7
83  Ben Mendelsohn 2016 Rogue One S1 Green/8
83  Ben Mendelsohn 2016 Rogue One S1 Blue/8
83  Ben Mendelsohn 2016 Rogue One S1/39
CI2  Ben Mendelsohn 2016 Rogue One S1 Characters/14
RO6  Ben Mendelsohn 2017 GF Reborn/23
VE3  Ben Mendelsohn 2016 Rogue One S1 Villains/6

### 2018 Star Wars Archives Signature Series Billy Dee Williams

8  Billy Dee Williams 1980 ESB/9
64  Billy Dee Williams 2016 Evolution/1
189  Billy Dee Williams 1980 ESB/2
198  Billy Dee Williams 1980 ESB/2
IL4  Billy Dee Williams 2013 Jedi Legacy Influencers I14/7
ESB3  Billy Dee Williams 2017 GF Reborn/1

### 2018 Star Wars Archives Signature Series Brian Herring

6  Brian Herring 2015 TFA S1/3
6  Brian Herring 2015 TFA S1 Blue/3
7  Brian Herring 2017 40th Ann./3
10  Brian Herring 2016 TFA Chrome Refractors/1
16  Brian Herring 2016 TFA S2 Heroes/6
26  Brian Herring 2016 TFA S2/8
27  Brian Herring 2016 TFA Chrome Refractors/1
27  Brian Herring 2016 TFA S2 Green/1
28  Brian Herring 2016 TFA S2/1
28  Brian Herring 2016 TFA S2 Green/2
30  Brian Herring 2016 TFA Chrome Wave Ref./1
48  Brian Herring 2016 Card Trader/8
78  Brian Herring 2015 TFA S1 Green/1
78  Brian Herring 2015 TFA S1 Blue/1
78  Brian Herring 2015 TFA S1/3
81  Brian Herring 2015 TFA S1 Purple/1
81  Brian Herring 2015 TFA S1/11
82  Brian Herring 2015 TFA S1/5
82  Brian Herring 2015 Journey TFA Green/10
82  Brian Herring 2015 Journey TFA/19
97  Brian Herring 2016 Journey TLJ Green/1
104  Brian Herring 2015 Journey TFA Pink/1
104  Brian Herring 2015 Journey TFA Green/7
104  Brian Herring 2015 Journey TFA/20
TFA4  Brian Herring 2017 GF Reborn/10

### 2018 Star Wars Archives Signature Series Caroline Blakiston

MON MOTHMA™

9  Caroline Blakiston 2016 Rogue One MB Heroes/6
30  Caroline Blakiston 2016 Card Trader Red/2
30  Caroline Blakiston 2016 Card Trader Blue/4
30  Caroline Blakiston 2016 Card Trader/25
63  Caroline Blakiston 1983 ROTJ/11
64  Caroline Blakiston 1983 ROTJ/38
85  Caroline Blakiston 2016 Evolution/47
174  Caroline Blakiston 2012 Galactic Files/14
B15  Caroline Blakiston 2016 Card Trader Bounty/5
ROTJ8  Caroline Blakiston 2017 GF Reborn/25

### 2018 Star Wars Archives Signature Series Cathy Munroe

37  Cathy Munroe 2016 Card Trader/29
37  Cathy Munroe 2016 Card Trader Blue/3
89  Cathy Munroe 2001 Evolution/33
B8  Cathy Munroe 2016 Card Trader Bounty/5
ESB6  Cathy Munroe 2017 GF Reborn Orange/3
ESB6  Cathy Munroe 2017 GF Reborn/25

### 2018 Star Wars Archives Signature Series Chris Parsons

1  Chris Parsons 2001 Evolution/34
38  Chris Parsons 2016 Card Trader Blue/8
38  Chris Parsons 2016 Card Trader/28
53  Chris Parsons 2015 Journey TLA/13
B7  Chris Parsons 2016 Card Trader Bounty/6
136  Chris Parsons 2012 Galactic Files/38
ESB5  Chris Parsons 2017 GF Reborn/24

### 2018 Star Wars Archives Signature Series Corey Dee Williams

40  Corey Dee Williams 2001 Star Wars Evolution/34

### 2018 Star Wars Archives Signature Series Daisy Ridley

23  Daisy Ridley 2016 TFA S2/1
P6  Daisy Ridley 2015 Journey TFA Patches/1
R1  Daisy Ridley 2015 Journey TFA Heroes/1
P15  Daisy Ridley 2015 Journey TFA Patches/1

### 2018 Star Wars Archives Signature Series Daniel Logan

BOBA FETT

41  Daniel Logan 2012 Galactic Files/21
51  Daniel Logan 2016 Evolution Blue/4
51  Daniel Logan 2016 Evolution/48
78  Daniel Logan 2010 CW ROTBH/3
83  Daniel Logan 2010 CW ROTBH/4
408  Daniel Logan 2013 GF2/38
ACW7  Daniel Logan 2017 GF Reborn/24
AOTC5  Daniel Logan 2017 GF Reborn/28

### 2018 Star Wars Archives Signature Series Dave Chapman

6  Dave Chapman 2015 TFA S1/20
6  Dave Chapman 2015 TFA S1 Blue/3
9  Dave Chapman 2016 TFA Chrome Heroes/10
16  Dave Chapman 2016 TFA S2 Heroes/4
19  Dave Chapman 2015 TFA S1 Movie Scenes/6
26  Dave Chapman 2016 TFA Chrome Refractors/3
26  Dave Chapman 2016 TFA S2/16
27  Dave Chapman 2016 TFA S2 Blue/1
28  Dave Chapman 2016 TFA Chrome Refractors/1
28  Dave Chapman 2016 TFA S2/5
30  Dave Chapman 2016 TFA S2/4
30  Dave Chapman 2016 TFA Chrome/7
39  Dave Chapman 2016 TFA Chrome/9
39  Dave Chapman 2016 TFA S2/14
40  Dave Chapman 2016 TFA Chrome/3
48  Dave Chapman 2016 Card Trader Blue/4
48  Dave Chapman 2016 Card Trader/16
49  Dave Chapman 2016 TFA S2/3
49  Dave Chapman 2016 TFA Chrome/5
63  Dave Chapman 2016 TFA S2 Green/3
63  Dave Chapman 2016 TFA S2 Blue/3
63  Dave Chapman 2016 TFA S2/7
63  Dave Chapman 2016 TFA Chrome/23
73  Dave Chapman 2016 TFA S2 Blue/3
73  Dave Chapman 2016 TFA Chrome/7
73  Dave Chapman 2016 TFA S2/14
76  Dave Chapman 2015 TFA S1/25
77  Dave Chapman 2015 TFA S1/12
78  Dave Chapman 2015 TFA S1/6
79  Dave Chapman 2015 TFA S1/7
80  Dave Chapman 2015 TFA S1/6
81  Dave Chapman 2015 TFA S1 Green/3
81  Dave Chapman 2015 TFA S1/23
82  Dave Chapman 2015 Journey TFA Black/3
82  Dave Chapman 2015 Journey TFA/48
83  Dave Chapman 2015 TFA S1/5
97  Dave Chapman 2017 Journey TLJ/1
R4  Dave Chapman 2015 Journey TFA Heroes/7
104  Dave Chapman 2015 Journey TFA Black/3
104  Dave Chapman 2015 Journey to TFA Green/20
104  Dave Chapman 2015 Journey TFA/48
P18  Dave Chapman 2015 Journey TFA Patches/3
TFA4  Dave Chapman 2017 GF Reborn/16

### 2018 Star Wars Archives Signature Series David Acord

7  David Acord 2016 TFA S2 Maz's Castle/2
8  David Acord 2015 TFA S1/13
11  David Acord 2015 TFA S1/10
20  David Acord 2015 TFA S1 Blue/11

20 David Acord 2015 TFA S1 Green/11
20 David Acord 2015 TFA S1/28
25 David Acord 2016 TFA Chrome/4
29 David Acord 2015 TFA S1/26
43 David Acord 2016 TFA Chrome/4
52 David Acord 2016 TFA Chrome Refractors/2
52 David Acord 2015 TFA S1/6
58 David Acord 2016 Card Trader/23
61 David Acord 2016 Card Trader/23
68 David Acord 2016 TFA S2 Blue/5
68 David Acord 2016 TFA S2 Green/10
68 David Acord 2016 TFA S2/25
68 David Acord 2016 TFA Chrome Refractors/30
68 David Acord 2016 TFA Chrome/38
75 David Acord 2015 TFA S1/11
TFA29 David Acord 2017 GF Reborn/22

### 2018 Star Wars Archives Signature Series David Ankrum

19 David Ankrum 2016 Card Trader/13
88 David Ankrum 2016 Rogue One MB Black/1
88 David Ankrum 2016 Rogue One MB/16
9R David Ankrum 2014 Chrome 9R/11
118 David Ankrum 2012 Galactic Files/14
145 David Ankrum 2012 Galactic Files/13
175 David Ankrum 2012 Galactic Files/15
I12 David Ankrum 2013 Jedi Legacy Influencers/19
ANH23 David Ankrum 2017 GF Reborn/21

### 2018 Star Wars Archives Signature Series David Barclay

3 David Barclay 2017 40th Ann. Green/1
9 David Barclay 1980 ESB/10
9 David Barclay 2016 Card Trader/10
10 David Barclay 2016 Card Trader Blue/5
10 David Barclay 2016 Card Trader/19
13 David Barclay 1983 ROTJ/5
14 David Barclay 1983 ROTJ/18
15 David Barclay 1983 ROTJ/7
21 David Barclay 2012 Galactic Files/1
28 David Barclay 2017 40th Ann. Green/1
36 David Barclay 2001 Evolution/11
41 David Barclay 1999 Chrome Archives/1
46 David Barclay 1983 ROTJ/8
49 David Barclay 2015 Journey TFA Green/2
49 David Barclay 2015 Journey TFA/2
58 David Barclay 1980 ESB/7
63 David Barclay 1980 ESB/5
63 David Barclay Journey TFA/22
80 David Barclay 2015 Journey TFA Green/1
82 David Barclay 2016 Evolution/20
83 David Barclay 2016 Evolution Blue/19
83 David Barclay 2016 Evolution/19

163 David Barclay 2012 Galactic Files/11
172 David Barclay 1983 ROTJ/20
34L David Barclay Jedi Legacy/30
35J David Barclay 2015 Chrome JvS/19
35S David Barclay Chrome JvS/31
490 David Barclay 2013 GF2/1
50E David Barclay 2014 Chrome 50E/5
50R David Barclay 2014 Chrome 50R/5
519 David Barclay 2013 GF2/15
C15 David Barclay 2013 Jedi Legacy Connections/10
ESB2 David Barclay 2017 GF Reborn/22

### 2018 Star Wars Archives Signature Series Dee Bradley Baker

6 Dee Baker 2008 CW/6
8 Dee Baker 2010 CW ROTBH/5
94 Dee Baker 2016 Card Trader Blue/7
94 Dee Baker 2016 Card Trader/26
233 Dee Baker 2012 Galactic Files/19
475 Dee Baker 2015 Chrome JvS/8
ACW9 Dee Baker 2017 GF Reborn/1
ACW9 Dee Baker 2017 GF Reborn/27

### 2018 Star Wars Archives Signature Series Deep Roy

21 Deep Roy 1983 ROTJ/14
183 Deep Roy 2012 Galactic Files/32
ROTJ16 Deep Roy 2017 GF Reborn/42

### 2018 Star Wars Archives Signature Series Denis Lawson

19 Denis Lawson 2016 Card Trader Red/1
19 Denis Lawson 2016 Card Trader Blue/4
19 Denis Lawson 2016 Card Trader/11
83 Denis Lawson 2001 Evolution/16
88 Denis Lawson 2016 Rogue One MB/27
9R Denis Lawson 2014 Chrome Refractors/2
9R Denis Lawson 2014 Chrome 9R/12
127 Denis Lawson 1983 ROTJ/9
145 Denis Lawson 2012 Galactic Files/16
175 Denis Lawson 2012 Galactic Files/16
I12 Denis Lawson 2013 Jedi Legacy Influencers/16
ANH23 Denis Lawson 2017 GF Reborn/13
ESB13 Denis Lawson 2017 GF Reborn/15

### 2018 Star Wars Archives Signature Series Derek Arnold

19 Derek Arnold 2016 Rogue One S1 Blue/7
19 Derek Arnold 2016 Rogue One S1/38
34 Derek Arnold 2017 Rogue One S2 Blue/2
34 Derek Arnold 2016 Rogue One S1 Green/8
34 Derek Arnold 2016 Rogue One S1/34
58 Derek Arnold 2017 Rogue One S2 Black/2
58 Derek Arnold 2017 Rogue One S2/10

87 Derek Arnold 2016 Rogue One S1 Green/8
87 Derek Arnold 2016 Rogue One S1/39
HR10 Derek Arnold 2016 Rogue One S1 Heroes/2

### 2018 Star Wars Archives Signature Series Dermot Crowley

39 Dermot Crowley 2016 Card Trader Blue/6
39 Dermot Crowley 2016 Card Trader/24
ROTJ9 Dermot Crowley 2017 GF Reborn/24

### 2018 Star Wars Archives Signature Series Dickey Beer

47 Dickey Beer 1983 ROTJ/7
25L Dickey Beer 2013 Jedi Legacy/14
32L Dickey Beer 2013 Jedi Legacy/20
379 Dickey Beer GF2/44

### 2018 Star Wars Archives Signature Series Dual Autographs

18 Taylor Gray/Tiya Sircar 40th Ann./4
64 Tim Rose/Aidan Cook Rogue One S1/9
71 Tiya Sircar/Vanessa Marshall Rebels Foil/7
78 Tiya Sircar/Vanessa Marshall Rebels Foil/14
92 Tom Kane/James Taylor 40th Ann. Green/1
M5 Nick Kellington/Derek Arnold Rogue One S1 Montages/3
GM3 Taylor Gray/Tiya Sircar Card Trader GM/3
PF6 Nick Kellington/Derek Arnold Rogue One S2 PF/11
GM17 Kane/Taylor Card Trader GM/5

### 2018 Star Wars Archives Signature Series Felicity Jones

1 Felicity Jones 2016 Rogue One S1/6
21 Felicity Jones 2016 Rogue One S1/1
21 Felicity Jones 2016 Rogue One S1/4
24 Felicity Jones 2016 Rogue One S1/1
24 Felicity Jones 2016 Rogue One S1/6
46 Felicity Jones 2016 Rogue One S1/11
51 Felicity Jones 2016 Rogue One S1 Black/2
70 Felicity Jones 2016 Rogue One S1/1
70 Felicity Jones 2016 Rogue One S1/11
79 Felicity Jones 2016 Rogue One S1 Blue/1
79 Felicity Jones 2016 Rogue One S1/21
80 Felicity Jones 2016 Rogue One S1/11
84 Felicity Jones 2016 Rogue One S1/6
G1 Felicity Jones 2016 Rogue One S1 Gallery/1
RO1 Felicity Jones 2017 GF Reborn Blue/2

### 2018 Star Wars Archives Signature Series Femi Taylor

55 Femi Taylor 2001 Evolution/30
177 Femi Taylor 2012 Galactic Files/23
ROTJ5 Femi Taylor 2017 GF Reborn Blue/1
ROTJ5 Femi Taylor GF Reborn/30

### 2018 Star Wars Archives Signature Series Forest Whitaker

6 Forest Whitaker 2016 Rogue One S1 Green/16
6 Forest Whitaker 2016 Rogue One S1 Black/20
6 Forest Whitaker 2016 Rogue One S1/92
8 Forest Whitaker 2017 Rogue One S2 Posters/1
27 Forest Whitaker 2017 Rogue One S2/14
HR8 Forest Whitaker 2016 Rogue One S1 Heroes/4
RO7 Forest Whitaker 2017 GF Reborn/25

### 2018 Star Wars Archives Signature Series Garrick Hagon

10 Garrick Hagon 2001 Evolution/33
36 Garrick Hagon 2016 Card Trader Blue/4
36 Garrick Hagon 2016 Card Trader/25
89 Garrick Hagon 2016 Rogue One MB/32
111 Garrick Hagon 2007 30th Ann./10
119 Garrick Hagon 2012 Galactic Files/32
16E Garrick Hagon 2014 Chrome/5
16R Garrick Hagon 2014 Chrome/8
243 Garrick Hagon 1977 Star Wars/12
I10 Garrick Hagon 2013 Jedi Legacy Influencers I10/37
ANH25 Garrick Hagon 2017 GF Reborn/39

### 2018 Star Wars Archives Signature Series Genevieve O'Reilly

8 Genevieve O'Reilly 2016 Rogue One S1 Blue/15
8 Genevieve O'Reilly 2016 Rogue One S1 Black/19
8 Genevieve O'Reilly 2016 Rogue One S1/99
9 Genevieve O'Reilly 2016 Rogue One MB Heroes/4
10 Genevieve O'Reilly 2017 Rogue One S2 Black/3
10 Genevieve O'Reilly 2017 Rogue One S2/15
41 Genevieve O'Reilly 2017 Rogue One S2/16
60 Genevieve O'Reilly 2017 40th Ann./3
73 Genevieve O'Reilly 2016 Rogue One S1 Green/8
73 Genevieve O'Reilly 2016 Rogue One S1/57
84 Genevieve O'Reilly 2016 Evolution/37
91 Genevieve O'Reilly 2012 Galactic Files/15
102 Genevieve O'Reilly 2016 Rogue One MB/1
102 Genevieve O'Reilly 2016 Rogue One MB/19

### 2018 Star Wars Archives Signature Series Gerald Home

ROTJ15 Gerald Home 2017 GF Reborn/23

### 2018 Star Wars Archives Signature Series Harrison Ford

NNO Harrison Ford

### 2018 Star Wars Archives Signature Series Hayden Christensen

2 Hayden Christensen 2016 Evolution/8
3 Hayden Christensen 2017 Journey TLJ Red/1
3 Hayden Christensen 2016 Evolution/6
3 Hayden Christensen 2017 Journey TLJ/6
4 Hayden Christensen 2017 Journey TLJ/1
6 Hayden Christensen 2017 40th Ann./1
6 Hayden Christensen 2017 Journey TLJ/5
9 Hayden Christensen 2015 Journey TFA Black/1
9 Hayden Christensen 2015 Journey TFA Pink/1
9 Hayden Christensen 2017 Journey TLJ/4
12 Hayden Christensen 2017 Journey TLJ/3
13 Hayden Christensen 2010 CW ROTBH/8
14 Hayden Christensen 2016 Rogue One MB/4
15 Hayden Christensen 2016 Rogue One MB Black/1
17 Hayden Christensen 2015 Journey TFA Black/1
2J Hayden Christensen 2015 Chrome JvS Refractors/5
2J Hayden Christensen 2015 Chrome JvS/8
2S Hayden Christensen 2015 Chrome JvS/6
49 Hayden Christensen 2017 40th Ann. Blue/2
49 Hayden Christensen 2017 40th Ann./5
51 Hayden Christensen 2017 40th Ann./4
52 Hayden Christensen 2017 40th Ann./3
53 Hayden Christensen 2017 40th Ann./5
57 Hayden Christensen 2017 Journey TLJ Red/1
57 Hayden Christensen 2017 Journey TLJ/3
66 Hayden Christensen 2012 Galactic Files/10
71 Hayden Christensen 2016 Card Trader Blue/7
71 Hayden Christensen 2016 Card Trader/24
80 Hayden Christensen 2015 Journey TFA/6
89 Hayden Christensen 2017 40th Ann./1
93 Hayden Christensen 2004 Heritage/2
100 Hayden Christensen 2004 Heritage/1
17A Hayden Christensen 2013 Jedi Legacy/6
19A Hayden Christensen 2013 Jedi Legacy/8
21A Hayden Christensen 2013 Jedi Legacy/4
24A Hayden Christensen 2013 Jedi Legacy/6
27A Hayden Christensen 2013 Jedi Legacy/8
33A Hayden Christensen 2013 Jedi Legacy Blue/1
36A Hayden Christensen 2013 Jedi Legacy/8
38A Hayden Christensen 2013 Jedi Legacy/7
401 Hayden Christensen 2013 GF2/8
45A Hayden Christensen 2013 Jedi Legacy/5
CL7 Hayden Christensen 2012 Galactic Files Classic Lines/3
CL8 Hayden Christensen 2013 GF2/2
ROTS1 Hayden Christensen 2017 GF Reborn/24

### 2018 Star Wars Archives Signature Series Hermione Corfield

49 Hermione Corfield 2017 TLJ S1 Purple/36
49 Hermione Corfield 2017 TLJ S1 Green/50
49 Hermione Corfield 2017 TLJ S1 Blue/65
49 Hermione Corfield 2017 TLJ S1/85

### 2018 Star Wars Archives Signature Series Howie Weed

ESB15 Howie Weed 2017 GF Reborn/22

### 2018 Star Wars Archives Signature Series Ian McDiarmid

NNO Ian McDiarmid

### 2018 Star Wars Archives Signature Series Ian McElhinney

17 Ian McElhinney 2016 Rogue One S1 Green/6
17 Ian McElhinney 2016 Rogue One S1 Black/9
17 Ian McElhinney 2016 Rogue One S1/39

### 2018 Star Wars Archives Signature Series Jack Klaff

90 Jack Klaff 2016 Rogue One MB/48
122 Jack Klaff 2012 Galactic Files/21

### 2018 Star Wars Archives Signature Series James Arnold Taylor

3 James Arnold Taylor CW ROTBH/1
19 James Arnold Taylor CW ROTBH/3
26 James Arnold Taylor CW ROTBH/4
40 James Arnold Taylor CW ROTBH/3

### 2018 Star Wars Archives Signature Series Jason Isaacs

NNO Jason Isaacs

### 2018 Star Wars Archives Signature Series Jason Spisak

ACW15 Jason Spisak 2017 GF Reborn/24

### 2018 Star Wars Archives Signature Series Jeremy Bulloch

11 Jeremy Bulloch 2001 Evolution/19
12 Jeremy Bulloch 2016 Card Trader Blue/4
23 Jeremy Bulloch 1983 ROTJ/38
53 Jeremy Bulloch 2016 Evolution/14
53 Jeremy Bulloch 2016 Evolution/52
54 Jeremy Bulloch 2016 Evolution/48
73 Jeremy Bulloch 1980 ESB/13
75 Jeremy Bulloch 1980 ESB/22
162 Jeremy Bulloch 2012 Galactic Files/10
34J Jeremy Bulloch 2015 Chrome JvS/54
34S Jeremy Bulloch 2015 Chrome JvS/45
474 Jeremy Bulloch 2013 GF2/44
518 Jeremy Bulloch 2013 GF2/21
ESB1 Jeremy Bulloch GF Reborn/23

### 2018 Star Wars Archives Signature Series Jerome Blake

30 Jerome Blake 2012 Galactic Files/37
40 Jerome Blake 2006 Evolution Update/1
57 Jerome Blake 2001 Evolution/36
84 Jerome Blake 2016 Card Trader Blue/8
84 Jerome Blake 2016 Card Trader/25
382 Jerome Blake 2013 GF2/2

41J  Jerome Blake 2015 Chrome JvS Refractors/6
41J  Jerome Blake 2015 Chrome JvS/66
TPM15  Jerome Blake 2017 GF Reborn/23

### 2018 Star Wars Archives Signature Series Jesse Jensen

NNO  Jesse Jensen

### 2018 Star Wars Archives Signature Series Jimmy Vee

13  Jimmy Vee 2017 TLJ S1 Red/1
13  Jimmy Vee 2017 TLJ S1 Purple/35
13  Jimmy Vee 2017 TLJ S1 Green/50
13  Jimmy Vee 2017 TLJ S1 Blue/66
13  Jimmy Vee 2017 TLJ S1/85

### 2018 Star Wars Archives Signature Series John Boyega

2  John Boyega 2015 TFA S1 Montages/1
2  John Boyega 2015 TFA S1 Green/2
4  John Boyega 2015 Journey TFA Silhouette/3
9  John Boyega 2017 Journey TLJ Green/1
9  John Boyega 2016 TFA S2/1
13  John Boyega 2016 Evolution Stained/1
21  John Boyega 2016 TFA S2/1
29  John Boyega 2016 TFA S2/1
29  John Boyega 2016 TFA S2 Blue/2
32  John Boyega 2016 TFA S2/3
38  John Boyega 2016 TFA S2/5
39  John Boyega 2016 TFA S2 Purple/1
40  John Boyega 2015 TFA S1/1
45  John Boyega 2016 TFA S2/1
67  John Boyega 2016 TFA S2/1
70  John Boyega 2016 TFA S2 Blue/1
73  John Boyega 2017 Journey TLJ/28
75  John Boyega 2017 Journey TLJ/29
82  John Boyega 2017 Journey TLJ/26
85  John Boyega 2016 TFA S2/1
89  John Boyega 2016 Evolution/1
90  John Boyega 2016 TFA S1/1
90  John Boyega 2016 TFA S2 Green/3
96  John Boyega 2017 Journey TLJ/25
97  John Boyega 2015 TFA S1/1
99  John Boyega 2015 TFA S1/1
R9  John Boyega 2015 Journey TFA Heroes/1

### 2018 Star Wars Archives Signature Series John Morton

11  John Morton 1980 ESB/12
20  John Morton 2016 Card Trader Blue/6
20  John Morton 2016 Card Trader/33
37  John Morton 2004 Heritage/2
38  John Morton 1980 ESB/14
50  John Morton 1999 Chrome Archives/1
91  John Morton 1980 ESB/23
98  John Morton 1980 ESB/7

C8  John Morton 2013 Jedi Legacy Connections/29
131  John Morton 2012 Galactic Files /11
146  John Morton 2012 Galactic Files/31
210  John Morton 1980 ESB/8
220  John Morton 1980 ESB/38
489  John Morton 2013 GF2/23
FQ3  John Morton 2016 Card Trader Film Quotes/8
CL10  John Morton 2012 Galactic Files Classic Lines/1
ESB14  John Morton 2017 GF Reborn Blue/1
ESB14  John Morton 2017 GF Reborn/25

### 2018 Star Wars Archives Signature Series Joonas Suotamo

10  Joonas Suotamo 2015 TFA S1 Movie Scenes/3
25  Joonas Suotamo 2015 TFA S1/20
41  Joonas Suotamo 2016 TFA Chrome/3
44  Joonas Suotamo 2016 TFA Chrome/1
44  Joonas Suotamo 2016 TFA Chrome/3
59  Joonas Suotamo 2016 Evolution/20
70  Joonas Suotamo 2016 TFA S2 Green/3
70  Joonas Suotamo 2016 TFA Chrome Ref./8
70  Joonas Suotamo 2016 TFA S2/9
70  Joonas Suotamo 2016 TFA S1/11
76  Joonas Suotamo 2016 TFA Chrome Ref./3
76  Joonas Suotamo 2016 TFA S2/5
76  Joonas Suotamo 2016 TFA Chrome/7
P5  Joonas Suotamo 2015 Journey TFA Patches/5
100  Joonas Suotamo 2016 TFA Factory/1
100  Joonas Suotamo 2015 TFA S1/7
109  Joonas Suotamo 2015 Journey TFA Black/2
P13  Joonas Suotamo 2015 Journey TFA Patches/4
TFA11  Joonas Suotamo 2017 GF Reborn/24

### 2018 Star Wars Archives Signature Series Julian Glover

29  Julian Glover 2016 Card Trader/31
31  Julian Glover 2001 Evolution/31
140  Julian Glover 2012 Galactic Files/23
30R  Julian Glover 2014 Chrome/7
ESB11  Julian Glover 2017 GF Reborn/36

### 2018 Star Wars Archives Signature Series Ken Leung

5  Ken Leung 2016 TFA Chrome Heroes/2
15  Ken Leung 2015 TFA S1 Movie Scenes/2
27  Ken Leung 2015 TFA S1/8
51  Ken Leung 2016 Card Trader Blue/7
51  Ken Leung 2016 Card Trader/22
TFA22  Ken Leung 2017 GF Reborn/24

### 2018 Star Wars Archives Signature Series Kenneth Colley

4  Ken Colley 2001 Evolution/38
16  Ken Colley 2016 Card Trader Blue/8
16  Ken Colley 2016 Card Trader/28

141  Ken Colley 2012 Galactic Files/24
29E  Ken Colley 2014 Chrome/1
ESB9  Ken Colley 2017 GF Reborn/26
ROTJ7  Ken Colley 2017 GF Reborn/38

### 2018 Star Wars Archives Signature Series Kiran Shah

35  Kiran Shah 2017 TLJ S1 Purple/35
35  Kiran Shah 2017 TLJ S1 Green/50
35  Kiran Shah 2017 TLJ S1 Blue/65
35  Kiran Shah 2017 TLJ S1/85

### 2018 Star Wars Archives Signature Series Lily Cole

34  Lily Cole 2017 TLJ S1 Red/1
34  Lily Cole 2017 TLJ S1 Purple/34
34  Lily Cole 2017 TLJ S1 Green/50
34  Lily Cole 2017 TLJ S1 Blue/65
34  Lily Cole 2017 TLJ S1/85

### 2018 Star Wars Archives Signature Series Mads Mikkelsen

2  Mads Mikkelsen Rogue One S2 Green/1
2  Mads Mikkelsen Rogue One S2/8
38  Mads Mikkelsen Rogue One S1 Blue/7
38  Mads Mikkelsen Rogue One Black/9
38  Mads Mikkelsen Rogue One S1/33
RO8  Mads Mikkelsen GF Reborn/23

### 2018 Star Wars Archives Signature Series Mark Dodson

16  Mark Dodson 1983 ROTJ/40
34  Mark Dodson 2016 Card Trader Red/1
34  Mark Dodson 2016 Card Trader Blue/7
34  Mark Dodson 2016 Card Trader/29
71  Mark Dodson 2001 Evolution/34
181  Mark Dodson 2012 GF Reborn/28
ROTJ14  Mark Dodson 2017 GF Reborn/42

### 2018 Star Wars Archives Signature Series Matt Lanter

2  Matt Lanter 2008 CW/13
9  Matt Lanter 2016 Rogue One MB/33
10  Matt Lanter 2017 40th Ann./2
10  Matt Lanter 2017 40th Ann./4
10  Matt Lanter 2016 Rogue One MB/5
23  Matt Lanter 2010 CW ROTBH/3
36  Matt Lanter 2010 CW ROTBH/3
71  Matt Lanter 2010 CW ROTBH/4
84  Matt Lanter 2008 CW/5
22A  Matt Lanter 2013 Jedi Legacy/2

### 2018 Star Wars Archives Signature Series Matthew Wood

NNO  Matthew Wood

## 2018 Star Wars Archives Signature Series Michaela Cottrell

25 Michaela Cottrell 2001 Evolution/39
28 Michaela Cottrell 2012 Galactic Files/29
17J Michaela Cottrell 2015 Chrome JvS Ref./24
17J Michaela Cottrell 2015 Chrome JvS/58
TPM22 Michaela Cottrell 2017 GF Reborn/31

## 2018 Star Wars Archives Signature Series Mike Edmonds

44 Mike Edmonds 2001 Evolution/34
82 Mike Edmonds 1983 ROTJ/8
84 Mike Edmonds 1983 ROTJ/16
85 Mike Edmonds 1983 ROTJ/33
92 Mike Edmonds 1983 ROTJ/14
103 Mike Edmonds 1983 ROTJ/4
171 Mike Edmonds 2012 Galactic Files/24

## 2018 Star Wars Archives Signature Series Mike Quinn

15 Mike Quinn 2016 Card Trader/29
16 Mike Quinn 2016 TFA Chrome Heroes/14
20 Mike Quinn 1983 ROTJ/41
22 Mike Quinn 1983 ROTJ/41
33 Mike Quinn 2016 Card Trader/25
39 Mike Quinn 2016 TFA Chrome Ref./4
39 Mike Quinn 2016 TFA Chrome/7
48 Mike Quinn 2016 TFA Factory/2
48 Mike Quinn 2016 TFA S1 Blue/4
48 Mike Quinn 2015 TFA S1 Green/7
48 Mike Quinn 2015 TFA S1/35
52 Mike Quinn 2001 Evolution/39
96 Mike Quinn 2016 TFA Green/4
96 Mike Quinn 2016 TFA Chrome/5
123 Mike Quinn 1983 ROTJ/28
182 Mike Quinn 2012 Galactic Files/12
184 Mike Quinn 1983 ROTJ/25
25R Mike Quinn 2014 Chrome Ref./1
25R Mike Quinn 2014 Chrome 25R/2
ROTJ12 Mike Quinn 2017 GF Reborn/25
ROTJ13 Mike Quinn 2017 GF Reborn/37

## 2018 Star Wars Archives Signature Series Nick Kellington

7 Nick Kellington 2016 Rogue One S1 Blue/15
7 Nick Kellington 2016 Rogue One S1 Black/17
7 Nick Kellington 2016 Rogue One S1/76
88 Nick Kellington 2016 Rogue One S1 Green/7
88 Nick Kellington 2016 Rogue One S1 Blue/8
88 Nick Kellington 2016 Rogue One S1/38
HR9 Nick Kellington 2016 Rogue One S1 Heroes/6

## 2018 Star Wars Archives Signature Series Nika Futterman

93 Nika Futterman 2016 Card Trader Blue/4
93 Nika Futterman 2016 Card Trader/21

30J Nika Futterman 2015 Chrome JvS/5
30S Nika Futterman 2015 Chrome JvS/4
ACW6 Nika Futterman 2017 GF Reborn/24

## 2018 Star Wars Archives Signature Series Oliver Ford Davies

AOTC8 Oliver Ford Davies 2017 GF Reborn/24
TPM10 Oliver Ford Davies 2017 GF Reborn/23

## 2018 Star Wars Archives Signature Series Orli Shoshan

65 Orli Shoshan 2012 Galactic Files/31
6J Orli Shoshan 2015 Chrome JvS/59
6S Orli Shoshan 2015 Chrome JvS/61

## 2018 Star Wars Archives Signature Series Paul Blake

21 Paul Blake 2016 Card Trader Blue/8
21 Paul Blake 2016 Card Trader/26
33 Paul Blake 2001 Evolution/30
73 Paul Blake 2007 30th Ann./11
B1 Paul Blake 2016 Card Trader Bounty/9
104 Paul Blake 2012 Galactic Files/28
ANH19 Paul Blake 2017 GF Reborn Orange/1
ANH19 Paul Blake 2017 GF Reborn/36

## 2018 Star Wars Archives Signature Series Paul Brooke

371 Paul Brooke 2013 GF2/41
ROTJ11 Paul Brooke 2013 GF Reborn Orange/1
ROTJ11 Paul Brooke 2013 GF Reborn/24

## 2018 Star Wars Archives Signature Series Paul Kasey

20 Paul Kasey 2017 TLJ S1 Red/1
20 Paul Kasey 2017 TLJ S1 Purple/40
20 Paul Kasey 2017 TLJ S1 Green/50
20 Paul Kasey 2017 TLJ S1 Blue/67
20 Paul Kasey 2017 TLJ S1/85

## 2018 Star Wars Archives Signature Series Peter Mayhew

7 Peter Mayhew 1983 ROTJ/1
8 Peter Mayhew 2016 Card Trader Blue/7
8 Peter Mayhew 2016 Card Trader/22
33 Peter Mayhew 2015 Journey TFA Black/2
33 Peter Mayhew 2015 Journey TFA/3
40 Peter Mayhew Journey TFA/1
55 Peter Mayhew 2016 Evolution/25
56 Peter Mayhew 2016 Evolution/5
57 Peter Mayhew 2016 Evolution/4
58 Peter Mayhew 2016 Evolution/3
84 Peter Mayhew 1980 ESB/8
89 Peter Mayhew 1980 ESB/5
121 Peter Mayhew 1977 Star Wars/5

128 Peter Mayhew 1977 Star Wars/5
157 Peter Mayhew 2012 Galactic Files/3
217 Peter Mayhew 1980 ESB/2
24S Peter Mayhew 2015 Chrome JvS/8
24S Peter Mayhew 2015 Chrome JvS Ref./10
306 Peter Mayhew 1980 ESB/2
513 Peter Mayhew 2013 Galactic Files/2
FQ12 Peter Mayhew 2016 Card Trader Film Quotes/3
ROTS13 Peter Mayhew 2017 GF Reborn/24

## 2018 Star Wars Archives Signature Series Phil Eason

86 Phil Eason 2001 Evolution/35
393 Phil Eason 2013 GF2/48

## 2018 Star Wars Archives Signature Series Philip Anthony-Rodriguez

96 Philip Anthony-Rodriguez 2016 Card Trader Blue/4
96 Philip Anthony-Rodriguez 2016 Card Trader/22

## 2018 Star Wars Archives Signature Series Ralph Brown

TPM24 Ralph Brown 2017 GF Reborn/23

## 2018 Star Wars Archives Signature Series Ray Park

2 Ray Park 2016 Rogue One MB/6
4 Ray Park 2017 40th Ann./5
6 Ray Park 2012 Galactic Files/3
79 Ray Park 2004 Heritage/2
79 Ray Park 2016 Card Trader/22
94 Ray Park 2016 Evolution/30
B3 Ray Park 2016 Card Trader Bounty/5
285 Ray Park 2015 Chrome JvS/13
28J Ray Park 2015 Chrome JvS/4
FQ10 Ray Park 2016 Card Trader Film Quotes/7
TPM4 Ray Park 2017 GF Reborn/23

## 2018 Star Wars Archives Signature Series Riz Ahmed

NNO Riz Ahmed

## 2018 Star Wars Archives Signature Series Robin Atkin Downes

ACW17 Robin Atkin Downes 2017 GF Reborn/24

## 2018 Star Wars Archives Signature Series Rusty Goffe

11 Rusty Goffe 1977 Star Wars/9
13 Rusty Goffe 1977 Star Wars/16
19 Rusty Goffe 1983 ROTJ/23
24 Rusty Goffe 2015 Journey TFA Green/15
24 Rusty Goffe 2015 Journey TFA/38
27 Rusty Goffe 2016 Card Trader Red/2
27 Rusty Goffe 2016 Card Trader Blue/7
27 Rusty Goffe 2016 Card Trader/25
38 Rusty Goffe 2001 Evolution/36

186 Rusty Goffe 1977 Star Wars/12
203 Rusty Goffe 1977 Star Wars/6
257 Rusty Goffe 1977 Star Wars/12
304 Rusty Goffe 1977 Star Wars/1
314 Rusty Goffe 1977 Star Wars/1
ANH8 Rusty Goffe 2017 GF Reborn Orange/2
ANH8 Rusty Goffe 2017 GF Reborn/25

## 2018 Star Wars Archives Signature Series Sam Witwer

TPM4 Sam Witwer 2017 GF Reborn/23
ACW13 Sam Witwer 2017 GF Reborn/23

## 2018 Star Wars Archives Signature Series Silas Carson

82 Silas Carson 2016 Card Trader Red/1
82 Silas Carson 2016 Card Trader Blue/8
82 Silas Carson 2016 Card Trader/24
14J Silas Carson 2015 Chrome JvS Ref./7
14S Silas Carson 2015 Chrome JvS/7
TPM14 Silas Carson 2017 GF Reborn Orange/2
TPM14 Silas Carson 2017 GF Reborn/25
TPM19 Silas Carson 2017 GF Reborn/24

## 2018 Star Wars Archives Signature Series Simon Williamson

40 Simon Williamson 2016 Card Trader Blue/7
40 Simon Williamson 2016 Card Trader/23

## 2018 Star Wars Archives Signature Series Stephen Stanton

WHEN TARKIN MET ANAKIN

10 Stephen Stanton 2016 Rogue One MB/1
10 Stephen Stanton 2016 Rogue One MB/28
55 Stephen Stanton 2017 Journey TLJ Green/2
55 Stephen Stanton 2017 Journey TLJ/12
60 Stephen Stanton 2016 Evolution/34
42S Stephen Stanton 2015 Chrome JvS Ref./11
42S Stephen Stanton 2015 Chrome JvS/62
HR7 Stephen Stanton 2016 Rogue One S1 Heroes/8
MP4 Stephen Stanton 2016 Rogue One MB Patches/5

## 2018 Star Wars Archives Signature Series Steve Blum

4 Steve Blum 2015 Rebels Foil/7
57 Steve Blum 2015 Rebels/57
74 Steve Blum 2015 Rebels Foil/5
81 Steve Blum 2015 Rebels Foil/7
85 Steve Blum 2015 Rebels/5
90 Steve Blum 2016 Card Trader Red/1
90 Steve Blum 2016 Card Trader Blue/8
90 Steve Blum 2016 Card Trader/26
REB4 Steve Blum 2017 GF Reborn/38

## 2018 Star Wars Archives Signature Series Taylor Gray

1 Taylor Gray 2015 Rebels/5
1 Taylor Gray 2015 Rebels Foil/6
15 Taylor Gray 2017 Journey TLJ Red/1

15 Taylor Gray 2017 Journey TLJ/6
16 Taylor Gray 2017 40th Ann./2
39 Taylor Gray 2015 Rebels/3
50 Taylor Gray 2015 Rebels Foil/5
50 Taylor Gray 2015 Rebels/6
54 Taylor Gray 2015 Rebels/6
61 Taylor Gray 2017 Journey TLJ Green/1
61 Taylor Gray 2015 Rebels/5
61 Taylor Gray 2015 Rebels Foil/7
62 Taylor Gray 2015 Rebels Foil/4
66 Taylor Gray 2015 Rebels/6
67 Taylor Gray 2015 Rebels/5
67 Taylor Gray 2015 Rebels/6
69 Taylor Gray 2015 Rebels Foil/7
69 Taylor Gray 2015 Rebels/8
73 Taylor Gray 2015 Rebels Foil/3
82 Taylor Gray 2015 Rebels Foil/6
86 Taylor Gray 2018 Card Trader Blue/6
86 Taylor Gray 2016 Card Trader/28
96 Taylor Gray 2015 Rebels Foil/6
96 Taylor Gray 2015 Rebels/6
98 Taylor Gray 2017 40th Ann./17
99 Taylor Gray 2015 Rebels/5
EL7 Taylor Gray 2016 Evolution EOTL/8
REB6 Taylor Gray 2017 GF Reborn/37

## 2018 Star Wars Archives Signature Series Temuera Morrison

95 Temuera Morrison 2004 Heritage/4
25A Temuera Morrison 2013 Jedi Legacy/1
25A Temuera Morrison 2013 Jedi Legacy/12
33J Temuera Morrison 2015 Chrome JvS Ref./12
33J Temuera Morrison 2015 Chrome JvS/42
33S Temuera Morrison 2015 Chrome JvS/49
AOTC4 Temuera Morrison 2017 GF Reborn/23

## 2018 Star Wars Archives Signature Series Tim Dry

164 Tim Dry 1983 ROTJ/43

## 2018 Star Wars Archives Signature Series Tim Rose

2 Tim Rose 2016 TFA Chrome BTS/5
3 Tim Rose 2001 Evolution/37
7 Tim Rose 2016 TFA S2 Heroes/7
12 Tim Rose 2017 TLJ S1/35
14 Tim Rose 2016 Card Trader Blue/8
14 Tim Rose 2016 Card Trader/22
15 Tim Rose 2016 TFA Chrome Heroes/14
28 Tim Rose 2015 TFA S1 Blue/6
28 Tim Rose 2015 TFA S1 Green/12
28 Tim Rose 2015 TFA S1/28
35 Tim Rose 2017 Journey TLJ/6
37 Tim Rose 2017 Journey TLJ/7
10E Tim Rose 2015 Chrome/16
10R Tim Rose 2014 Chrome/24
124 Tim Rose 1983 ROTJ/33
167 Tim Rose 2012 Galactic Files/27
FQ16 Tim Rose 2016 Card Trader Film Quotes/8
ROTJ17 Tim Rose 2017 GF Reborn/24

## 2018 Star Wars Archives Signature Series Tiya Sircar

SABINE WREN
STAR WARS REBELS

3 Tiya Sircar 2015 Rebels Foil/6
3 Tiya Sircar 2015 Rebels/7
56 Tiya Sircar 2015 Rebels/6
88 Tiya Sircar 2016 Card Trader/25
REB3 Tiya Sircar 2017 GF Reborn/34

## 2018 Star Wars Archives Signature Series Toby Philpott

3 Toby Philpott 2017 40th Ann. Green/2
3 Toby Philpott 2017 40th Ann./5
9 Toby Philpott 2016 Card Trader Blue/4
9 Toby Philpott 2016 Card Trader/18
14 Toby Philpott 1983 ROTJ/20
15 Toby Philpott 1983 ROTJ/6
36 Toby Philpott 2001 Evolution/20
46 Toby Philpott 1983 ROTJ/15
62 Toby Philpott 1999 Chrome Archives/2
63 Toby Philpott 2015 Journey TFA Green/2
63 Toby Philpott 2015 Journey TFA/25
82 Toby Philpott 2016 Evolution/26
83 Toby Philpott 2016 Evolution/36
83 Toby Philpott 2016 EvolutionBlue /36
86 Toby Philpott 2007 30th Ann./3
163 Toby Philpott Galactic Files/17
172 Toby Philpott 1983 ROTJ/19
34L Toby Philpott 2013 Jedi Legacy/44
35J Toby Philpott 2015 Chrome JvS/29
35S Toby Philpott 2015 Chrome JvS/32
50R Toby Philpott 2014 Chrome/6
519 Toby Philpott 2013 GF2/25
C15 Toby Philpott 2013 Jedi Legacy Connections/26

## 2018 Star Wars Archives Signature Series Tom Kane

9 Tom Kane 2017 40th Ann./6
12 Tom Kane 2017 TLJ S1 Purple/15
12 Tom Kane 2017 TLJ S1 Green/25
12 Tom Kane 2017 TLJ S1 Blue/35
12 Tom Kane 2017 TLJ S1/49
15 Tom Kane 2017 40th Ann. Green/2

15 Tom Kane 2017 40th Ann./10
35 Tom Kane 2010 CW ROTBH/3
61 Tom Kane 2010 CW ROTBH/10
76 Tom Kane 2017 TLJ S1 Red/1
76 Tom Kane 2017 TLJ S1 Purple/15
76 Tom Kane 2017 TLJ S1 Green/25
76 Tom Kane 2017 TLJ S1 Blue/35
76 Tom Kane 2017 TLJ S1/49
92 Tom Kane 2017 40th Ann./2
92 Tom Kane 2017 40th Ann. Green/3

### 2018 Star Wars Archives Signature Series Tom Wilton

14 Tom Wilton 2015 TFA S1 Purple/5
14 Tom Wilton 2015 TFA S1 Blue/12
14 Tom Wilton 2015 TFA S1 Green/13
14 Tom Wilton 2015 TFA S1/36

### 2018 Star Wars Archives Signature Series Vanessa Marshall

6 Vanessa Marshall 2015 Rebels/5
6 Vanessa Marshall 2015 Rebels Foil/6
17 Vanessa Marshall 2016 Rogue One MB Black/1
17 Vanessa Marshall 2016 Rogue One MB/29
53 Vanessa Marshall 2015 Rebels Foil/6
59 Vanessa Marshall 2015 Rebels Foil/5
80 Vanessa Marshall 2015 Rebels/6
84 Vanessa Marshall 2015 Rebels Foil/6
89 Vanessa Marshall 2016 Card Trader Red/2
89 Vanessa Marshall 2016 Card Trader Blue/6
89 Vanessa Marshall 2016 Card Trader/27
97 Vanessa Marshall 2015 Rebels Foil/6
REB2 Vanessa Marshall 2017 GF Reborn Orange/4
REB2 Vanessa Marshall 2017 GF Reborn/39

### 2018 Star Wars Archives Signature Series Warwick Davis

2 Warwick Davis 2016 TFA S2 Maz's Castle/9
24 Warwick Davis 2016 Card Trader Red/2
24 Warwick Davis 2016 Card Trader Blue/5
24 Warwick Davis 2016 Card Trader/24
84 Warwick Davis 2001 Evolution/34
138 Warwick Davis 1983 ROTJ/40
142 Warwick Davis 1983 ROTJ/17
169 Warwick Davis 2012 Galactic Files/12
190 Warwick Davis 1983 ROTJ/22
ROTJ3 Warwick Davis 2017 GF Reborn/24

### 2018 Star Wars Archives Signature Series Zac Jensen

6 Zac Jensen 2015 Chrome JvS/11
58 Zac Jensen 2012 Galactic Files/25
59 Zac Jensen 2017 Journey TLJ/4
78 Zac Jensen 2012 Galactic Files/23
11J Zac Jensen 2015 Chrome JvS/53
11S Zac Jensen 2015 Chrome JvS Ref./12
11S Zac Jensen 2015 Chrome JvS/53
AOTC17 Zac Jensen 2017 GF Reborn/24

### 2019 Star Wars Authentics

| COMPLETE SET (25) | 150.00 | 300.00 |
| --- | --- | --- |
| UNOPENED BOX (1 CARD+1 AUTO'd 8X10) | | |
| COMMON CARD (1-25) | 4.00 | 10.00 |
| *BLUE/25: .6X TO 1.5X BASIC CARDS | | |
| *PURPLE/10: UNPRICED DUE TO SCARCITY | | |
| *ORANGE/5: UNPRICED DUE TO SCARCITY | | |
| *RED/1: UNPRICED DUE TO SCARCITY | | |
| STATED PRINT RUN 75 SER.#'d SETS | | |

| 1 Ahsoka Tano | 10.00 | 25.00 |
| --- | --- | --- |
| 2 Anakin Skywalker | 8.00 | 20.00 |
| 3 BB-8 | 12.00 | 30.00 |
| 5 Captain Tarkin | 6.00 | 15.00 |
| 6 Chancellor Palpatine | 10.00 | 25.00 |
| 7 Chirrut Œmwe | 5.00 | 12.00 |
| 8 Darth Maul | 10.00 | 25.00 |
| 9 Director Krennic | 6.00 | 15.00 |
| 10 Dryden Vos | 6.00 | 15.00 |
| 11 Finn | 6.00 | 15.00 |
| 12 Han Solo | 8.00 | 20.00 |
| 13 Jango Fett | 5.00 | 12.00 |
| 14 Jyn Erso | 6.00 | 15.00 |
| 15 K-2SO | 5.00 | 12.00 |
| 16 Kanan Jarrus | 6.00 | 15.00 |
| 17 Kylo Ren | 10.00 | 25.00 |
| 18 Lando Calrissian | 10.00 | 25.00 |
| 19 Maul (Sam Witwer) | 8.00 | 20.00 |
| 20 Obi-Wan Kenobi | 5.00 | 12.00 |
| 21 Rey | 15.00 | 40.00 |
| 23 Seventh Sister | 5.00 | 12.00 |
| 24 Vice Admiral Holdo | 15.00 | 40.00 |

### 2019 Star Wars Authentics Series Two

| COMPLETE SET (29) | 100.00 | 200.00 |
| --- | --- | --- |
| UNOPENED BOX (1 CARD+1 AUTO'd 8X10) | | |
| COMMON CARD (1-29) | 3.00 | 8.00 |
| *BLUE/25: .5X TO 1.2X BASIC CARDS | | |
| *PURPLE/10: UNPRICED DUE TO SCARCITY | | |
| *ORANGE/5: UNPRICED DUE TO SCARCITY | | |
| *RED/1: UNPRICED DUE TO SCARCITY | | |
| STATED PRINT RUN 99 SER.#'d SETS | | |

| 1 Boba Fett | 4.00 | 10.00 |
| --- | --- | --- |
| 2 Bo-Katan Kryze | 3.00 | 8.00 |
| 3 C'ai Threnalli | 10.00 | 25.00 |
| 4 Captain Needa | 3.00 | 8.00 |
| 5 Chewbacca | 3.00 | 8.00 |
| 6 Ezra Bridger | 3.00 | 8.00 |
| 7 Fode | 3.00 | 8.00 |
| 8 General Hux | 3.00 | 8.00 |
| 9 Han Solo | 6.00 | 15.00 |
| 10 Hera Syndulla | 6.00 | 15.00 |
| 11 Hype Fazon | 3.00 | 8.00 |
| 12 Iden Versio | 3.00 | 8.00 |
| 13 Jan Dodonna | 3.00 | 8.00 |
| 14 Jar Jar Binks | 3.00 | 8.00 |
| 15 Jarek Yeager | 3.00 | 8.00 |
| 16 Kazuda Xiono | 10.00 | 25.00 |
| 17 Major Bren Derlin | 3.00 | 8.00 |
| 18 Moff Jerjerrod | 3.00 | 8.00 |
| 19 Obi-Wan Kenobi | 6.00 | 15.00 |
| 20 Orka | 3.00 | 8.00 |
| 21 Padmé Amidala | 5.00 | 12.00 |
| 22 Rose Tico | 3.00 | 8.00 |
| 23 Sabine Wren | 5.00 | 12.00 |
| 24 Snap Wexley | 3.00 | 8.00 |
| 25 Tallie Lintra | 10.00 | 25.00 |
| 26 Tam Ryvora | 3.00 | 8.00 |
| 27 The Grand Inquisitor | 5.00 | 12.00 |
| 28 Torra Doza | 3.00 | 8.00 |
| 29 Wicket | 4.00 | 10.00 |

### 1984 Star Wars C-3PO's Cereal Masks

| COMPLETE SET (6) | 150.00 | 300.00 |
| --- | --- | --- |
| COMMON CARD | 12.00 | 30.00 |
| STATED ODDS 1:CEREAL BOX | | |
| 1 C-3PO | 60.00 | 120.00 |
| 2 Chewbacca | 25.00 | 60.00 |
| 5 Stormtrooper | 15.00 | 40.00 |
| 6 Yoda | 15.00 | 40.00 |

### 2016 Star Wars Card Trader

SAVAGE OPRESS
STAR WARS: THE CLONE WARS.

| COMPLETE SET (100) | 6.00 | 15.00 |
| --- | --- | --- |
| UNOPENED BOX (24 PACKS) | 35.00 | 50.00 |
| UNOPENED PACK (6 CARDS) | 2.00 | 3.00 |
| COMMON CARD (1-100) | .12 | .30 |
| *BLUE: .6X TO 1.5X BASIC CARDS | .20 | .50 |
| *RED: 1.2X TO 3X BASIC CARDS | .40 | 1.00 |
| *GREEN/99: 6X TO 15X BASIC CARDS | 2.00 | 5.00 |
| *ORANGE/50: 12X TO 30X BASIC CARDS | 4.00 | 10.00 |
| *BAT.DAM./10: 30X TO 80X BASIC CARDS | 10.00 | 25.00 |
| *SLAVE I/5: UNPRICED DUE TO SCARCITY | | |

### 2016 Star Wars Card Trader Actor Digital Autographs

| COMPLETE SET (20) | 150.00 | 300.00 |
| --- | --- | --- |
| COMMON CARD (DA1-DA20) | 8.00 | 20.00 |
| *RED/10: UNPRICED DUE TO SCARCITY | | |
| *GOLD/5: UNPRICED DUE TO SCARCITY | | |
| STATED ODDS 1:788 | | |
| STATED PRINT RUN 25 SER.#'d SETS | | |

### 2016 Star Wars Card Trader Bounty

| COMPLETE SET (20) | 15.00 | 40.00 |
| --- | --- | --- |
| COMMON CARD (B1-B20) | 1.25 | 3.00 |
| STATED ODDS 1:5 | | |

### 2016 Star Wars Card Trader Classic Artwork

CHEWBACCA

| COMPLETE SET (20) | 15.00 | 40.00 |
| COMMON CARD (CA1-CA20)) | 1.25 | 3.00 |
| STATED ODDS 1:5 | | |

## 2016 Star Wars Card Trader Film Quotes

| COMPLETE SET (20) | 10.00 | 25.00 |
| COMMON CARD (FQ1-FQ20) | 1.00 | 2.50 |
| STATED ODDS 1:4 | | |

## 2016 Star Wars Card Trader Galactic Moments

| COMPLETE SET (20) | 15.00 | 40.00 |
| COMMON CARD (GM1-GM20) | 1.25 | 3.00 |
| STATED ODDS 1:5 | | |

## 2016 Star Wars Card Trader Reflections

Darth Vader & Obi-Wan Kenobi

| COMPLETE SET (7) | 12.00 | 30.00 |
| COMMON CARD (R1-R7) | 2.50 | 6.00 |
| STATED ODDS 1:8 | | |

## 2016 Star Wars Card Trader Topps Choice

| COMPLETE SET (13) | 15.00 | 40.00 |
| COMMON CARD (TC1-TC13) | 2.00 | 5.00 |
| STATED ODDS 1:16 | | |
| | | |
| TC4 Kabe | 8.00 | 20.00 |
| TC7 Lak Sivrak | 3.00 | 8.00 |
| TC10 Bo-Katan Kryze | 3.00 | 8.00 |
| TC13 Todo 360 | 2.50 | 6.00 |

## 2015 Star Wars Celebration VII Oversized Vintage Wrappers

| COMPLETE SET (16) | 50.00 | 100.00 |
| COMMON CARD | 3.00 | 8.00 |

## 2017 Star Wars Celebration Orlando Cartamundi Playing Card Promos

| COMPLETE SET (4) | 10.00 | 25.00 |

---

| COMMON CARD (1-4) | 3.00 | 8.00 |
| 2 Luke | 4.00 | 10.00 |
| 3 Darth Vader | 5.00 | 12.00 |
| 4 Boba Fett | 4.00 | 10.00 |

## 1999 Star Wars Chrome Archives

| COMPLETE SET (90) | 10.00 | 25.00 |
| UNOPENED BOX (36 PACKS) | 65.00 | 80.00 |
| UNOPENED PACK (5 CARDS) | 2.00 | 2.50 |
| COMMON CARD (1-90) | .20 | .50 |

## 1999 Star Wars Chrome Archives Clearzone

| COMPLETE SET (4) | 7.50 | 20.00 |
| COMMON CARD (C1-C4) | 2.50 | 6.00 |

## 1999 Star Wars Chrome Archives Double Sided

| COMPLETE SET (9) | 40.00 | 100.00 |
| COMMON CARD (C1-C9) | 6.00 | 15.00 |

## 1999 Star Wars Chrome Archives Promos

| P1 Hate me, Luke! Destroy me! | 1.00 | 2.50 |
| P2 Welcome, young Luke | 1.00 | 2.50 |

## 2019 Star Wars Chrome Legacy

| COMPLETE SET (200) | 75.00 | 150.00 |
| COMMON CARD (1-200) | .60 | 1.50 |
| *REFRACTOR: .75X TO 2X BASIC CARDS | | |
| *BLUE/99: 1.2X TO 3X BASIC CARDS | | |
| *GREEN/50: 1.5X TO 4X BASIC CARDS | | |
| *ORANGE/25: 2X TO 5X BASIC CARDS | | |
| *BLACK/10: 4X TO 10X BASIC CARDS | | |
| *RED/5: UNPRICED DUE TO SCARCITY | | |
| *SUPER/1: UNPRICED DUE TO SCARCITY | | |

## 2019 Star Wars Chrome Legacy Classic Trilogy Autographs

| *BLACK/10: UNPRICED DUE TO SCARCITY | | |
| *RED/5: UNPRICED DUE TO SCARCITY | | |
| *SUPER/1: UNPRICED DUE TO SCARCITY | | |
| STATED ODDS 1:113 | | |
| | | |
| CAAD Anthony Daniels | | |
| CACB Caroline Blakiston | | |
| CACF Carrie Fisher | | |
| CACR Clive Revill | | |
| CADB David Barclay | | |
| CAHF Harrison Ford | | |
| CAJB Jeremy Bulloch | | |
| CAKB Kenny Baker | | |
| CAMQ Mike Quinn | | |
| CARG Rusty Goffe | | |
| CAWD Warwick Davis | | |
| CABDW Billy Dee Williams | | |
| CAIME Ian McDiarmid | | |

## 2019 Star Wars Chrome Legacy Concept Art

CONCEPT ART

---

| COMPLETE SET (20) | 12.00 | 30.00 |
| COMMON CARD (CA1-CA20) | 1.00 | 2.50 |
| *GREEN/50: .5X TO 2X BASIC CARDS | | |
| *ORANGE/25: .6X TO 1.5X BASIC CARDS | | |
| *BLACK/10: UNPRICED DUE TO SCARCITY | | |
| *RED/5: UNPRICED DUE TO SCARCITY | | |
| *SUPER/1: UNPRICED DUE TO SCARCITY | | |
| STATED ODDS 1:3 | | |

## 2019 Star Wars Chrome Legacy Droid Medallions

| COMMON MEM | 5.00 | 12.00 |
| *GREEN/50: .6X TO 1.5X BASIC MEM | | |
| *ORANGE/25: .75X TO 2X BASIC MEM | | |
| *BLACK/10: UNPRICED DUE TO SCARCITY | | |
| *RED/5: UNPRICED DUE TO SCARCITY | | |
| *SUPER/1: UNPRICED DUE TO SCARCITY | | |
| STATED ODDS 1:23 | | |
| | | |
| NNO C-3PO / C-3PO | 5.00 | 12.00 |
| NNO 2-1B / 2-1B | 5.00 | 12.00 |
| NNO 8D8 / EV-9D9 | 5.00 | 12.00 |
| NNO Anakin Skywalker / R2-D2 | 5.00 | 12.00 |
| NNO Battle Droid / Battle Droid | 5.00 | 12.00 |
| NNO Baze Malbus / K-2SO | 5.00 | 12.00 |
| NNO BB-8 / BB-8 | 5.00 | 12.00 |
| NNO Bossk / IG-88 | 5.00 | 12.00 |
| NNO Captain Cassian Andor / K-2SO | 5.00 | 12.00 |
| NNO Chewbacca / C-3PO | 5.00 | 12.00 |
| NNO Chewbacca / L3-37 | 5.00 | 12.00 |
| NNO Chopper / Chopper | 5.00 | 12.00 |
| NNO Count Dooku / Battle Droid | 5.00 | 12.00 |
| NNO Darth Vader / IG-88 | 5.00 | 12.00 |
| NNO Dengar / IG-88 | 5.00 | 12.00 |
| NNO EV-9D9 / EV-9D9 | 5.00 | 12.00 |
| NNO Ezra Bridger / Chopper | 5.00 | 12.00 |
| NNO Finn / BB-8 | 5.00 | 12.00 |
| NNO FX-7 / 2-1B | 5.00 | 12.00 |
| NNO Gamorrean Guard / EV-9D9 | 5.00 | 12.00 |
| NNO Han Solo / 2-1B | 5.00 | 12.00 |
| NNO Han Solo / L3-37 | 5.00 | 12.00 |
| NNO IG-88 / IG-88 | 5.00 | 12.00 |
| NNO Jabba the Hutt / EV-9D9 | 5.00 | 12.00 |
| NNO Jyn Erso / K-2SO | 5.00 | 12.00 |
| NNO K-2SO / K-2SO | 5.00 | 12.00 |
| NNO Kanan Jarrus / Chopper | 5.00 | 12.00 |
| NNO L3-37 / L3-37 | 5.00 | 12.00 |
| NNO Lando Calrissian / L3-37 | 5.00 | 12.00 |
| NNO Luke Skywalker / 2-1B | 5.00 | 12.00 |
| NNO Luke Skywalker / C-3PO | 5.00 | 12.00 |
| NNO Luke SkyWalker / R2-D2 | 5.00 | 12.00 |
| NNO Nute Gunray / Battle Droid | 5.00 | 12.00 |
| NNO Poe Dameron / BB-8 | 5.00 | 12.00 |
| NNO Princess Leia Organa / C-3PO | 5.00 | 12.00 |
| NNO Princess Leia Organa / R2-D2 | 5.00 | 12.00 |
| NNO R2-D2 / C-3PO | 5.00 | 12.00 |
| NNO R2-D2 / R2-D2 | 5.00 | 12.00 |
| NNO Rey / BB-8 | 5.00 | 12.00 |
| NNO Rune Haako / Battle Droid | 5.00 | 12.00 |
| NNO Sabine Wren / Chopper | 5.00 | 12.00 |

## 2019 Star Wars Chrome Legacy Dual Autographs

*BLACK/10: UNPRICED DUE TO SCARCITY
*RED/5: UNPRICED DUE TO SCARCITY
*SUPER/1: UNPRICED DUE TO SCARCITY
STATED ODDS 1:3,502

NNO A.Driver/D.Gleeson
NNO A.Daniels/D.Barclay
NNO A.Daniels/K.Baker
NNO D.Ridley/J.Boyega
NNO S.Jackson/H.Christensen

## 2019 Star Wars Chrome Legacy Marvel Comic Book Covers

| | | |
|---|---|---|
| COMPLETE SET (25) | 15.00 | 40.00 |
| COMMON CARD (MC1-MC25) | 1.25 | 3.00 |

*GREEN/50: .6X TO 1.5X BASIC CARDS
*ORANGE/25: .75X TO 2X BASIC CARDS
*BLACK/10: UNPRICED DUE TO SCARCITY
*RED/5: UNPRICED DUE TO SCARCITY
*SUPER/1: UNPRICED DUE TO SCARCITY
STATED ODDS 1:3

## 2019 Star Wars Chrome Legacy New Trilogy Autographs

*BLACK/10: UNPRICED DUE TO SCARCITY
*RED/5: UNPRICED DUE TO SCARCITY
*SUPER/1: UNPRICED DUE TO SCARCITY
STATED ODDS 1:225

NAAD Adam Driver
NAAL Amanda Lawrence
NAAS Andy Serkis
NABH Brian Herring
NABL Billie Lourd
NADG Domhnall Gleeson
NADR Daisy Ridley
NAJS Joonas Suotamo
NALD Laura Dern
NAJBF John Boyega
NAKMT Kelly Marie Tran

## 2019 Star Wars Chrome Legacy Posters

| | | |
|---|---|---|
| COMPLETE SET (25) | 15.00 | 40.00 |
| COMMON CARD (PC1-PC25) | 1.25 | 3.00 |

*GREEN/50: .6X TO 1.5X BASIC CARDS
*ORANGE/25: .75X TO 2X BASIC CARDS
*BLACK/10: UNPRICED DUE TO SCARCITY
*RED/5: UNPRICED DUE TO SCARCITY
*SUPER/1: UNPRICED DUE TO SCARCITY
STATED ODDS 1:6

## 2019 Star Wars Chrome Legacy Prequel Trilogy Autographs

*BLACK/10: UNPRICED DUE TO SCARCITY

*RED/5: UNPRICED DUE TO SCARCITY
*SUPER/1: UNPRICED DUE TO SCARCITY
STATED ODDS 1:229

PAEM Ewan McGregor
PAGP Greg Proops
PAHC Hayden Christensen
PAHQ Hugh Quarshie
PAJB Jerome Blake
PALM Lewis MacLeod
PAMW Matthew Wood
PARP Ray Park
PATM Temuera Morrison
PASLJ Samuel L. Jackson

## 2014 Star Wars Chrome Perspectives

| | | |
|---|---|---|
| COMPLETE SET (100) | 30.00 | 60.00 |
| UNOPENED BOX (24 PACKS) | 175.00 | 200.00 |
| UNOPENED PACK (6 CARDS) | 8.00 | 10.00 |
| COMMON CARD (1E-50E) | .40 | 1.00 |
| COMMON CARD (1R-50R) | .40 | 1.00 |

*REFRACTOR: 1.2X TO 3X BASIC CARDS
*PRISM: 1.5X TO 4X BASIC CARDS
*X-FRACTOR/99: 3X TO 8X BASIC CARDS
*GOLD REF./50: 6X TO 15X BASIC CARDS
*SUPERFRACTOR/1: UNPRICED DUE TO SCARCITY
*P.P.BLACK/1: UNPRICED DUE TO SCARCITY
*P.P.CYAN/1: UNPRICED DUE TO SCARCITY
*P.P.MAGENTA/1: UNPRICED DUE TO SCARCITY
*P.P.YELLOW/1: UNPRICED DUE TO SCARCITY

## 2014 Star Wars Chrome Perspectives Autographs

| | | |
|---|---|---|
| COMMON AUTO | 8.00 | 20.00 |

*GOLD REF./10: UNPRICED DUE TO SCARCITY
*SUPERFRACTOR/1: UNPRICED DUE TO SCARCITY

*P.P.BLACK/1: UNPRICED DUE TO SCARCITY
*P.P.CYAN/1: UNPRICED DUE TO SCARCITY
*P.P.MAGENTA/1: UNPRICED DUE TO SCARCITY
*P.P.YELLOW/1: UNPRICED DUE TO SCARCITY
STATED ODDS 1 PER BOX W/SKETCHES

| | | |
|---|---|---|
| NNO Angus MacInnes | 15.00 | 40.00 |
| NNO Anthony Daniels | 300.00 | 500.00 |
| NNO Billy Dee Williams | 60.00 | 120.00 |
| NNO Carrie Fisher | 300.00 | 600.00 |
| NNO Harrison Ford | 2500.00 | 4000.00 |
| NNO James Earl Jones | 150.00 | 300.00 |
| NNO Jeremy Bulloch | 30.00 | 60.00 |
| NNO Julian Glover | 15.00 | 40.00 |
| NNO Kenneth Colley | 12.00 | 25.00 |
| NNO Mark Capri | 12.00 | 25.00 |
| NNO Mark Hamill | 600.00 | 900.00 |

## 2014 Star Wars Chrome Perspectives Empire Priority Targets

| | | |
|---|---|---|
| COMPLETE SET (10) | 8.00 | 20.00 |
| COMMON CARD (1-10) | 1.25 | 3.00 |

*P.P.BLACK/1: UNPRICED DUE TO SCARCITY
*P.P.CYAN/1: UNPRICED DUE TO SCARCITY
*P.P.MAGENTA/1: UNPRICED DUE TO SCARCITY
*P.P.YELLOW/1: UNPRICED DUE TO SCARCITY
STATED ODDS 1:4

## 2014 Star Wars Chrome Perspectives Empire Propaganda

| | | |
|---|---|---|
| COMPLETE SET (10) | 15.00 | 40.00 |
| COMMON CARD (1-10) | 3.00 | 8.00 |

*P.P.BLACK/1: UNPRICED DUE TO SCARCITY
*P.P.CYAN/1: UNPRICED DUE TO SCARCITY
*P.P.MAGENTA/1: UNPRICED DUE TO SCARCITY
*P.P.YELLOW/1: UNPRICED DUE TO SCARCITY
STATED ODDS 1:24

## 2014 Star Wars Chrome Perspectives Helmet Medallions

| | | |
|---|---|---|
| COMPLETE SET (30) | 75.00 | 200.00 |
| COMMON CARD (1-30) | 5.00 | 12.00 |

*GOLD/50: 1.2X TO 3X BASIC MEDALLIONS
STATED ODDS 1:24

## 2014 Star Wars Chrome Perspectives Rebel Propaganda

| | | |
|---|---|---|
| COMPLETE SET (10) | 12.00 | 30.00 |
| COMMON CARD (1-10) | 2.00 | 5.00 |

*P.P.BLACK/1: UNPRICED DUE TO SCARCITY
*P.P.CYAN/1: UNPRICED DUE TO SCARCITY
*P.P.MAGENTA/1: UNPRICED DUE TO SCARCITY
*P.P.YELLOW/1: UNPRICED DUE TO SCARCITY
STATED ODDS 1:12

## 2014 Star Wars Chrome Perspectives Rebel Training

| | | |
|---|---|---|
| COMPLETE SET (10) | 6.00 | 15.00 |
| COMMON CARD (1-10) | 1.25 | 3.00 |

*P.P.BLACK/1: UNPRICED DUE TO SCARCITY
*P.P.CYAN/1: UNPRICED DUE TO SCARCITY

## 2014 Star Wars Chrome Perspectives Wanted Posters Rebellion

| | | |
|---|---|---|
| COMPLETE SET (10) | 5.00 | 12.00 |
| COMMON CARD (1-10) | .75 | 2.00 |

*P.P.BLACK/1: UNPRICED DUE TO SCARCITY
*P.P.CYAN/1: UNPRICED DUE TO SCARCITY
*P.P.MAGENTA/1: UNPRICED DUE TO SCARCITY
*P.P.YELLOW/1: UNPRICED DUE TO SCARCITY
STATED ODDS 1:2

## 2015 Star Wars Chrome Perspectives Jedi vs. Sith

| | | |
|---|---|---|
| COMPLETE SET (100) | 25.00 | 60.00 |
| UNOPENED BOX (24 PACKS) | 60.00 | 70.00 |
| UNOPENED PACK (6 CARDS) | 3.00 | 4.00 |
| COMMON CARD | .40 | 1.00 |

*REFRACTOR: 1.2X TO 3X BASIC CARDS
*PRISM REF./199: 1.5X TO 4X BASIC CARDS
*X-FRACTOR/99: 3X TO 8X BASIC CARDS
*GOLD REF./50: 6X TO 15X BASIC CARDS
*P.P.BLACK/1: UNPRICED DUE TO SCARCITY
*P.P.CYAN/1: UNPRICED DUE TO SCARCITY
*P.P.MAGENTA/1: UNPRICED DUE TO SCARCITY
*P.P.YELLOW/1: UNPRICED DUE TO SCARCITY

## 2015 Star Wars Chrome Perspectives Jedi vs. Sith Autographs

| | | |
|---|---|---|
| COMMON AUTO | 6.00 | 15.00 |

*PRISM REF./50: .5X TO 1.2X BASIC AUTOS
* X-FRACTORS/25: .6X TO 1.5X BASIC AUTOS
*GOLD REF./10: UNPRICED DUE TO SCARCITY
*SUPERFRACTOR/1: UNPRICED DUE TO SCARCITY
*P.P.BLACK/1: UNPRICED DUE TO SCARCITY
*P.P.CYAN/1: UNPRICED DUE TO SCARCITY
*P.P.MAGENTA/1: UNPRICED DUE TO SCARCITY
*P.P.YELLOW/1: UNPRICED DUE TO SCARCITY

| | | |
|---|---|---|
| NNO Ashley Eckstein | 10.00 | 25.00 |
| NNO Barbara Goodson | 10.00 | 25.00 |
| NNO Carrie Fisher | 400.00 | 600.00 |
| NNO David Prowse | 50.00 | 100.00 |
| NNO Jerome Blake | 10.00 | 25.00 |
| NNO Matthew Wood | 10.00 | 25.00 |
| NNO Michaela Cottrell | 10.00 | 25.00 |
| NNO Nalini Krishan | 12.00 | 30.00 |
| NNO Olivia D'Abo | 10.00 | 25.00 |
| NNO Peter Mayhew | 25.00 | 60.00 |
| NNO Ray Park | 20.00 | 50.00 |
| NNO Sam Witwer | 10.00 | 25.00 |

## 2015 Star Wars Chrome Perspectives Jedi vs. Sith Jedi Hunt

| | | |
|---|---|---|
| COMPLETE SET (10) | 10.00 | 25.00 |
| COMMON CARD (1-10) | 2.00 | 5.00 |

*P.P.BLACK/1: UNPRICED DUE TO SCARCITY
*P.P.CYAN/1: UNPRICED DUE TO SCARCITY
*P.P.MAGENTA/1: UNPRICED DUE TO SCARCITY
*P.P.YELLOW/1: UNPRICED DUE TO SCARCITY
STATED ODDS 1:4

## 2015 Star Wars Chrome Perspectives Jedi vs. Sith Jedi Information Guide

| | | |
|---|---|---|
| COMPLETE SET (10) | 20.00 | 50.00 |
| COMMON CARD (1-10) | 4.00 | 10.00 |

*P.P.BLACK/1: UNPRICED DUE TO SCARCITY
*P.P.CYAN/1: UNPRICED DUE TO SCARCITY
*P.P.MAGENTA/1: UNPRICED DUE TO SCARCITY
*P.P.YELLOW/1: UNPRICED DUE TO SCARCITY
STATED ODDS 1:12

## 2015 Star Wars Chrome Perspectives Jedi vs. Sith Jedi Training

| | | |
|---|---|---|
| COMPLETE SET (10) | 12.00 | 30.00 |
| COMMON CARD (1-10) | 2.50 | 6.00 |

*P.P.BLACK/1: UNPRICED DUE TO SCARCITY
*P.P.CYAN/1: UNPRICED DUE TO SCARCITY
*P.P.MAGENTA/1: UNPRICED DUE TO SCARCITY
*P.P.YELLOW/1: UNPRICED DUE TO SCARCITY
STATED ODDS 1:24

## 2015 Star Wars Chrome Perspectives Jedi vs. Sith Medallions

| | | |
|---|---|---|
| COMPLETE SET (36) | 120.00 | 250.00 |
| COMMON MEDALLION (1-36) | 5.00 | 10.00 |
| *SILVER/150: .6X TO 1.5X BASIC MEDALLIONS | 6.00 | 15.00 |
| *GOLD/50: .75X TO 2X BASIC MEDALLIONS | 8.00 | 20.00 |
| OVERALL MEDALLION ODDS 1:BOX | | |

## 2015 Star Wars Chrome Perspectives Jedi vs. Sith Rare Dual Autographs

| | | |
|---|---|---|
| COMMON AUTO | 25.00 | 60.00 |

*P.P.BLACK/1: UNPRICED DUE TO SCARCITY
*P.P.CYAN/1: UNPRICED DUE TO SCARCITY
*P.P.MAGENTA/1: UNPRICED DUE TO SCARCITY
*P.P.YELLOW/1: UNPRICED DUE TO SCARCITY
STATED PRINT RUN 200 SER.#'d SETS

| | | |
|---|---|---|
| NNO A.Allen/O.Shoshan | 50.00 | 100.00 |
| NNO A.Eckstein/N.Futterman | 30.00 | 75.00 |
| NNO A.Eckstein/O.D'Abo | 50.00 | 100.00 |
| NNO M.Cottrell/Z.Jensen | 50.00 | 100.00 |

## 2015 Star Wars Chrome Perspectives Jedi vs. Sith Sith Fugitives

| | | |
|---|---|---|
| COMPLETE SET (10) | 8.00 | 20.00 |
| COMMON CARD (1-10) | 1.50 | 4.00 |

## 2015 Star Wars Chrome Perspectives Jedi vs. Sith Sith Propaganda

| | | |
|---|---|---|
| COMPLETE SET (10) | 12.00 | 30.00 |
| COMMON CARD (1-10) | 2.50 | 6.00 |

*P.P.BLACK/1: UNPRICED DUE TO SCARCITY
*P.P.CYAN/1: UNPRICED DUE TO SCARCITY
*P.P.MAGENTA/1: UNPRICED DUE TO SCARCITY
*P.P.YELLOW/1: UNPRICED DUE TO SCARCITY
STATED ODDS 1:8

## 2015 Star Wars Chrome Perspectives Jedi vs. Sith The Force Awakens

Poe Dameron in his X-Wing

| | | |
|---|---|---|
| COMPLETE SET (8) | 20.00 | 50.00 |
| COMMON CARD | 4.00 | 10.00 |

*MATTE BACK: .6X TO1.5X BASIC CARDS
STATED ODDS 1:24

## 2004 Star Wars Clone Wars Cartoon

| | | |
|---|---|---|
| COMPLETE SET (90) | 5.00 | 12.00 |
| UNOPENED HOBBY BOX (36 PACKS) | 50.00 | 60.00 |
| UNOPENED HOBBY PACK (7 CARDS) | 1.50 | 2.00 |
| UNOPENED RETAIL BOX (36 PACKS) | 55.00 | 65.00 |
| UNOPENED RETAIL PACK (7 CARDS) | 1.75 | 2.25 |
| COMMON CARD (1-90) | .15 | .40 |

## 2004 Star Wars Clone Wars Cartoon Autographs

| | | |
|---|---|---|
| COMMON CARD | 12.00 | 30.00 |

## 2004 Star Wars Clone Wars Cartoon Battle Motion

| | | |
|---|---|---|
| COMPLETE SET (10) | 15.00 | 40.00 |
| COMMON CARD (B1-B10) | 2.00 | 5.00 |

## 2004 Star Wars Clone Wars Cartoon Stickers

| | | |
|---|---|---|
| COMPLETE SET (10) | 3.00 | 8.00 |
| COMMON CARD (1-10) | .40 | 1.00 |

## 2008 Star Wars Clone Wars

| | | |
|---|---|---|
| COMPLETE SET (90) | 5.00 | 12.00 |
| UNOPENED BOX (36 PACKS) | 40.00 | 50.00 |
| UNOPENED PACK (7 CARDS) | 1.50 | 2.00 |
| COMMON CARD (1-90) | .15 | .40 |
| *GOLD: 8X TO 20X BASIC CARD | | |

## 2008 Star Wars Clone Wars Foil

| | | |
|---|---|---|
| COMPLETE SET (10) | 12.00 | 25.00 |
| COMMON CARD (1-10) | 2.00 | 5.00 |
| STATED ODDS 1:3 RETAIL | | |

## 2008 Star Wars Clone Wars Animation Cels

| | | |
|---|---|---|
| COMPLETE SET (10) | 7.50 | 15.00 |
| COMMON CARD (1-10) | 1.25 | 3.00 |
| STATED ODDS 1:6 | | |
| ALSO KNOWN AS THE WHITE CELS | | |

## 2008 Star Wars Clone Wars Blue Animation Cels

| | | |
|---|---|---|
| COMPLETE SET (5) | 15.00 | 40.00 |
| COMMON CARD | 4.00 | 10.00 |
| STATED ODDS 1:6 WALMART PACKS | | |

TRADING CARDS

### 2008 Star Wars Clone Wars Red Animation Cels

| | | |
|---|---|---|
| COMPLETE SET (5) | 20.00 | 50.00 |
| COMMON CARD | 5.00 | 12.00 |
| STATED ODDS 1:6 TARGET PACKS | | |

### 2008 Star Wars Clone Wars Coins Purple

| | | |
|---|---|---|
| COMPLETE SET (12) | 15.00 | 40.00 |
| COMMON CARD (1-12) | 2.50 | 6.00 |
| *RED: SAME VALUE | | |
| *YELLOW: SAME VALUE | | |
| PURPLE ODDS 2:WALMART/MEIER BONUS BOX | | |
| RED ODDS 2:TARGET BONUS BOX | | |
| YELLOW ODDS 2:TRU BONUS BOX | | |

### 2008 Star Wars Clone Wars Motion

| | | |
|---|---|---|
| COMPLETE SET (5) | 4.00 | 8.00 |
| COMMON CARD (1-5) | 1.25 | 3.00 |
| STATED ODDS 1:8 RETAIL | | |

### 2008 Star Wars Clone Wars Promos

| | | |
|---|---|---|
| COMPLETE SET (2) | 2.50 | 6.00 |
| COMMON CARD (P1-P2) | 1.50 | 4.00 |

### 2008 Star Wars Clone Wars Stickers

| | | |
|---|---|---|
| COMPLETE SET (90) | 15.00 | 40.00 |
| COMMON CARD (1-90) | .40 | 1.00 |

### 2008 Star Wars Clone Wars Stickers Die-Cut Magnets

| | | |
|---|---|---|
| COMPLETE SET (9) | 10.00 | 25.00 |
| COMMON CARD (1-9) | 2.00 | 5.00 |
| STATED ODDS 1:12 | | |

### 2008 Star Wars Clone Wars Stickers Die-Cut Pop-Ups

| | | |
|---|---|---|
| COMPLETE SET (10) | 3.00 | 8.00 |
| COMMON CARD (1-10) | .60 | 1.50 |
| STATED ODDS 1:3 | | |

### 2008 Star Wars Clone Wars Stickers Foil

| | | |
|---|---|---|
| COMPLETE SET (10) | 5.00 | 12.00 |
| COMMON CARD (1-10) | .75 | 2.00 |
| STATED ODDS 1:3 | | |

### 2008 Star Wars Clone Wars Stickers Temporary Tattoos

| | | |
|---|---|---|
| COMPLETE SET (10) | 6.00 | 15.00 |
| COMMON CARD (1-10) | 1.00 | 2.50 |
| STATED ODDS 1:4 | | |

### 2008 Star Wars Clone Wars Stickers Tin Lid Stickers

| | | |
|---|---|---|
| COMPLETE SET (6) | 12.00 | 30.00 |
| STATED ODDS 1 PER TIN | | |
| 1 Anakin | 3.00 | 8.00 |
| 2 Obi-Wan | 3.00 | 8.00 |
| 3 Anakin and Obi-Wan | 3.00 | 8.00 |
| 4 Clone Troopers | 3.00 | 8.00 |
| 5 Yoda | 3.00 | 8.00 |
| 6 Anakin and Ahsoka | 3.00 | 8.00 |

### 2010 Star Wars Clone Wars Rise of the Bounty Hunters

| | | |
|---|---|---|
| COMPLETE SET (90) | 4.00 | 10.00 |
| UNOPENED BOX (24 PACKS) | 15.00 | 20.00 |
| UNOPENED PACK (7 CARDS) | .75 | 1.00 |
| COMMON CARD (1-90) | .10 | .30 |
| *SILVER/100: 20X TO 50X BASIC CARDS | | |
| *GOLD/1: UNPRICED DUE TO SCARCITY | | |

### 2010 Star Wars Clone Wars Rise of the Bounty Hunters Cels Red

| | | |
|---|---|---|
| COMPLETE SET (5) | 8.00 | 20.00 |
| COMMON CARD (1-5) | 3.00 | 8.00 |

### 2010 Star Wars Clone Wars Rise of the Bounty Hunters Cels Yellow

| | | |
|---|---|---|
| COMPLETE SET (5) | 6.00 | 15.00 |
| COMMON CARD (1-5) | 2.50 | 6.00 |

### 2010 Star Wars Clone Wars Rise of the Bounty Hunters Foil

| | | |
|---|---|---|
| COMPLETE SET (20) | 8.00 | 20.00 |
| COMMON CARD (1-20) | .60 | 1.50 |
| STATED ODDS 1:3 | | |

### 2010 Star Wars Clone Wars Rise of the Bounty Hunters Motion

| | | |
|---|---|---|
| COMPLETE SET (5) | 6.00 | 15.00 |
| COMMON CARD (1-5) | 1.50 | 4.00 |
| STATED ODDS 1:6 | | |

### 2010 Star Wars Clone Wars Rise of the Bounty Hunters Promos

| | | |
|---|---|---|
| P1 Cad Bane and Others | 1.25 | 3.00 |
| P3 Pre Vizsla and Mandalorian Death Watch | 1.25 | 3.00 |

### 2018 Star Wars Clone Wars 10th Anniversary

| | | |
|---|---|---|
| COMPLETE SET (25) | 15.00 | 40.00 |
| COMMON CARD (1-25) | 1.00 | 2.50 |
| *PURPLE: .75X TO 2X BASIC CARDS | | |
| *BLUE/10: UNPRICED DUE TO SCARCITY | | |
| *RED/5: UNPRICED DUE TO SCARCITY | | |
| *GOLD/1: UNPRICED DUE TO SCARCITY | | |

### 2018 Star Wars Clone Wars 10th Anniversary Autographs

| | | |
|---|---|---|
| *BLUE/10: UNPRICED DUE TO SCARCITY | | |
| *RED/5: UNPRICED DUE TO SCARCITY | | |
| *GOLD/1: UNPRICED DUE TO SCARCITY | | |
| STATED OVERALL ODDS 1:SET | | |
| 1A Matt Lanter | | |
| 2A Ashley Eckstein | | |
| 3A James Arnold Taylor | 8.00 | 20.00 |
| 4A Tom Kane | | |
| 6A Tim Curry | | |
| 7A Catherine Taber | | |
| 8A Phil Lamarr | | |
| 9A Nika Futterman | | |
| 10A Meredith Salenger | | |
| 12A Stephen Stanton | | |
| 13A Daniel Logan | | |
| 14A Sam Witwer | | |
| 15A Anna Graves | | |
| 16A Anthony Daniels | | |
| 18A Dee Bradley Baker | | |
| 20A Matthew Wood | | |
| 21A David Tennant | | |
| 22A Blair Bess | | |
| 23A Cas Anvar | | |
| 24A Kathleen Gati | | |
| 25A George Takei | | |

### 2018 Star Wars Clone Wars 10th Anniversary Dual Autographs

| | | |
|---|---|---|
| UNPRICED DUE TO SCARCITY | | |
| NNO J.A.Taylor/M.Lanter | | |

| | | |
|---|---|---|
| NNO J.A.Taylor/S.Witwer | | |
| NNO J.A.Taylor/T.Kane | | |
| NNO M.Lanter/A.Eckstein | | |
| NNO S.Stanton/A.Eckstein | | |

### 2009 Star Wars Clone Wars Widevision

| | | |
|---|---|---|
| COMPLETE SET (80) | 5.00 | 12.00 |
| UNOPENED BOX (24 PACKS) | 60.00 | 70.00 |
| UNOPENED PACK (7 CARDS) | 2.50 | 3.00 |
| COMMON CARD (1-80) | .15 | .40 |
| *SILVER: 5X TO 12X BASIC CARDS | | |

### 2009 Star Wars Clone Wars Widevision Animation Cels

THREEPIO AND JAR JAR

| | | |
|---|---|---|
| COMPLETE SET (10) | 6.00 | 15.00 |
| COMMON CARD (1-10) | .75 | 2.00 |
| STATED ODDS 1:4 | | |

### 2009 Star Wars Clone Wars Widevision Autographs

MATT LANTER
ANAKIN SKYWALKER

| | | |
|---|---|---|
| COMMON AUTO | 8.00 | 20.00 |
| STATED ODDS 1:67 HOBBY; 1:174 RETAIL | | |
| NNO Anthony Daniels | | |
| NNO Matthew Wood/Droids | 15.00 | 40.00 |
| NNO Matthew Wood/Grievous | 10.00 | 25.00 |
| NNO Nika Futterman | 12.00 | 30.00 |
| NNO Tom Kane | 12.00 | 30.00 |

### 2009 Star Wars Clone Wars Widevision Foil Characters

GENERAL GRIEVOUS

| | | |
|---|---|---|
| COMPLETE SET (20) | 15.00 | 40.00 |
| COMMON CARD (1-20) | 1.00 | 2.50 |
| STATED ODDS 1:3 | | |

### 2009 Star Wars Clone Wars Widevision Motion

| | | |
|---|---|---|
| COMPLETE SET (5) | 6.00 | 15.00 |
| COMMON CARD (1-5) | 1.50 | 4.00 |
| STATED ODDS 1:8 | | |

### 2009 Star Wars Clone Wars Widevision Season Two Previews

| | | |
|---|---|---|
| COMPLETE SET (8) | 3.00 | 8.00 |
| COMMON CARD (PV1-PV8) | .50 | 1.25 |
| STATED ODDS 1:2 | | |

## 2019 Star Wars Comic Convention Exclusives

| | | |
|---|---|---|
| 1 Darth Vader SWC | 75.00 | 150.00 |
| 2 Luke Skywalker SWC | | |
| 3 Princess Leia Organa SWC | 25.00 | 60.00 |
| 4 Han Solo SWC | 30.00 | 75.00 |
| 5 Chewbacca SWC | 30.00 | 75.00 |
| 6 Anakin Skywalker SDCC | 12.00 | 30.00 |
| 7 Obi-Wan Kenobi SDCC | 12.00 | 30.00 |
| 8 Padme Amidala SDCC | 10.00 | 25.00 |
| 9 Qui-Gon Jinn SDCC | 10.00 | 25.00 |
| 10 Darth Maul SDCC | 20.00 | 50.00 |
| 11 Rey NYCC | 60.00 | 120.00 |
| 12 Kylo Ren NYCC | 20.00 | 50.00 |
| 13 Finn NYCC | 15.00 | 40.00 |
| 14 Poe Dameron NYCC | 25.00 | 60.00 |
| 15 General Hux NYCC | 20.00 | 50.00 |

## 2017 Star Wars Countdown to The Last Jedi

| | | |
|---|---|---|
| COMPLETE SET (20) | 75.00 | 150.00 |
| COMMON CARD (1-20) | 5.00 | 12.00 |
| 1 Rey Encounters Luke Skywalker/775* | 8.00 | 20.00 |

## 1994 Star Wars Day

| | | |
|---|---|---|
| COMPLETE SET (2) | 6.00 | 15.00 |
| COMMON CARD (SD1-SD2) | 4.00 | 10.00 |

## 1995 Star Wars Day

| | | |
|---|---|---|
| NNO Millennium Falcon w/X-Wings and TIE Fighters | 5.00 | 12.00 |

## 1999 Star Wars Defeat the Dark Side and Win Medallions

| | | |
|---|---|---|
| COMPLETE SET W/O SP (16) | 12.00 | 30.00 |
| COMMON MEDALLION | 1.00 | 2.50 |
| 2 Daultay Dofine/50* | | |
| 4 Yoda/1500* | | |
| 10 Shmi Skywalker/1* | | |
| 13 Battle Droid/1* | | |
| 20 Chancellor Valorum/1* | | |

## 2015 Star Wars Disney Pixar Cars Promos

| | | |
|---|---|---|
| COMPLETE SET (5) | 30.00 | 80.00 |
| COMMON CARD | 10.00 | 25.00 |

## 2015 Star Wars Disney Store The Force Awakens Promos

Finn on the run!

| | | |
|---|---|---|
| COMPLETE SET (8) | 20.00 | 50.00 |
| COMMON CARD (SKIP #'d) | 4.00 | 10.00 |
| 11 BB-8 on the move! | 6.00 | 15.00 |
| 67 Kylo Ren ignites his Lightsaber! | 5.00 | 12.00 |
| 96 The Millennium Falcon | 5.00 | 12.00 |

## 2011 Star Wars Dog Tags

| | | |
|---|---|---|
| COMPLETE SET (24) | 25.00 | 60.00 |
| UNOPENED BOX ( PACKS) | | |
| UNOPENED PACK (1 TAG+1 CARD) | | |
| COMMON TAG (1-24) | 2.00 | 5.00 |
| *SILVER: .5X TO 1.2X BASIC TAGS | 2.50 | 6.00 |
| *RAINBOW: 1.2X TO 3X BASIC TAGS | 6.00 | 15.00 |

## 2001 Star Wars Evolution

| | | |
|---|---|---|
| COMPLETE SET (93) | 5.00 | 12.00 |
| UNOPENED BOX (36 PACKS) | 45.00 | 60.00 |
| UNOPENED PACK (8 CARDS) | 1.50 | 2.00 |
| COMMON CARD (1-93) | .15 | .40 |

## 2001 Star Wars Evolution Autographs

| | | |
|---|---|---|
| COMMON AUTO | 15.00 | 40.00 |
| GROUP A/1000* STATED ODDS 1:37 | | |
| GROUP B/400* STATED ODDS 1:919 | | |
| GROUP C/300* STATED ODDS 1:2450 | | |
| GROUP D/100* STATED ODDS 1:3677 | | |
| NNO Anthony Daniels/100* | 1000.00 | 1500.00 |
| NNO Billy Dee Williams/300* | 200.00 | 400.00 |
| NNO Carrie Fisher/100* | 1000.00 | 1500.00 |
| NNO Ian McDiarmid/400* | 250.00 | 500.00 |
| NNO James Earl Jones/1000* | 200.00 | 350.00 |
| NNO Jeremy Bulloch/1000* | 75.00 | 150.00 |
| NNO Kenny Baker/1000* | 125.00 | 200.00 |
| NNO Lewis MacLeod | 20.00 | 50.00 |
| NNO Michael Culver/1000* | 20.00 | 50.00 |
| NNO Michonne Bourriague/1000* | 20.00 | 50.00 |
| NNO Peter Mayhew/400* | 100.00 | 200.00 |
| NNO Phil Brown/1000* | 25.00 | 60.00 |
| NNO Warwick Davis/1000* | 20.00 | 50.00 |

## 2001 Star Wars Evolution Insert A

| | | |
|---|---|---|
| COMPLETE SET (12) | 15.00 | 30.00 |
| COMMON CARD (1A-12A) | 1.50 | 4.00 |
| STATED ODDS 1:6 | | |

## 2001 Star Wars Evolution Insert B

| | | |
|---|---|---|
| COMPLETE SET (8) | 20.00 | 40.00 |
| COMMON CARD (1B-8B) | 2.50 | 6.00 |
| STATED ODDS 1:12 | | |

## 2001 Star Wars Evolution Promos

| | | |
|---|---|---|
| COMMON CARD | 1.00 | 2.50 |
| P3 Nien Nunb ALPHA CON | 3.00 | 8.00 |
| P4 Anakin Skywalker SDCC | 2.00 | 5.00 |

## 2006 Star Wars Evolution Update

| | | |
|---|---|---|
| COMPLETE SET (90) | 5.00 | 12.00 |
| UNOPENED BOX (24 PACKS) | 40.00 | 50.00 |
| UNOPENED PACK (6 CARDS) | 2.00 | 2.25 |
| COMMON CARD (1-90) | .15 | .40 |
| 1D ISSUED AS DAMAGED AUTO REPLACEMENT | | |
| CL1 Luke Connections CL | .40 | 1.00 |
| CL2 Leia Connections CL | .40 | 1.00 |
| 1D Luke Skywalker SP | 2.00 | 5.00 |
| P1 Obi-Wan Kenobi PROMO | 1.00 | 2.50 |
| P2 Darth Vader PROMO | 1.00 | 2.50 |

## 2006 Star Wars Evolution Update Autographs

| | | |
|---|---|---|
| COMMON AUTO (UNNUMBERED) | 6.00 | 15.00 |
| STATED ODDS 1:24 HOBBY | | |
| GROUP A ODDS 1:2,005 | | |
| GROUP B ODDS 1:231 | | |
| GROUP C ODDS 1:81 | | |
| GROUP D ODDS 1:259 | | |
| GROUP E ODDS 1:48 | | |
| NNO Alec Guinness | | |
| NNO Bob Keen B | 25.00 | 50.00 |
| NNO David Barclay B | 25.00 | 50.00 |
| NNO Garrick Hagon E | 10.00 | 25.00 |
| NNO George Lucas | | |
| NNO Hayden Christensen A | 600.00 | 1000.00 |
| NNO James Earl Jones A | 200.00 | 400.00 |
| NNO John Coppinger B | 15.00 | 40.00 |
| NNO Maria De Aragon C | 10.00 | 25.00 |
| NNO Matt Sloan E | 8.00 | 20.00 |
| NNO Michonne Bourriague C | 10.00 | 25.00 |
| NNO Mike Edmonds B | 15.00 | 40.00 |
| NNO Mike Quinn B | 25.00 | 50.00 |
| NNO Nalini Krishan D | 8.00 | 20.00 |
| NNO Peter Cushing | | |
| NNO Richard LeParmentier C | 10.00 | 25.00 |
| NNO Sandi Finlay C | 8.00 | 20.00 |
| NNO Toby Philpott B | 25.00 | 50.00 |
| NNO Wayne Pygram B | 90.00 | 175.00 |

## 2006 Star Wars Evolution Update Etched Foil Puzzle

| | | |
|---|---|---|
| COMPLETE SET (6) | 6.00 | 15.00 |
| COMMON CARD (1-6) | 1.25 | 3.00 |
| STATED ODDS 1:6 | | |

## 2006 Star Wars Evolution Update Galaxy Crystals

| | | |
|---|---|---|
| COMPLETE SET (10) | 12.50 | 30.00 |
| COMMON CARD (G1-G10) | 1.50 | 4.00 |
| STATED ODDS 1:4 RETAIL | | |

## 2006 Star Wars Evolution Update Insert A

| | | |
|---|---|---|
| COMPLETE SET (20) | 20.00 | 40.00 |
| COMMON CARD (1A-20A) | 1.50 | 4.00 |
| STATED ODDS 1:6 | | |

## 2006 Star Wars Evolution Update Insert B

| | | |
|---|---|---|
| COMPLETE SET (15) | 20.00 | 40.00 |
| COMMON CARD (1B-15B) | 2.00 | 5.00 |
| STATED ODDS 1:12 | | |

## 2006 Star Wars Evolution Update Luke and Leia

| | | |
|---|---|---|
| COMPLETE SET (2) | 1000.00 | 2000.00 |
| COMMON CARD (1-2) | 600.00 | 1200.00 |
| STATED ODDS 1:1975 HOBBY | | |
| STATED PRINT RUN 100 SER. #'d SETS | | |

## 2016 Star Wars Evolution

| | | |
|---|---|---|
| COMPLETE SET (100) | 8.00 | 20.00 |
| UNOPENED BOX (24 PACKS) | 60.00 | 75.00 |
| UNOPENED PACK (8 CARDS) | 2.50 | 3.00 |
| COMMON CARD (1-100) | .15 | .40 |
| *LTSBR BLUE: 4X TO 10X BASIC CARDS | | |
| *LTSBR PURPLE: 8X TO 20X BASIC CARDS | | |
| *GOLD/50: 15X TO 40X BASIC CARDS | | |
| *IMP.RED/1: UNPRICED DUE TO SCARCITY | | |
| *P.P.BLACK/1: UNPRICED DUE TO SCARCITY | | |
| *P.P.CYAN/1: UNPRICED DUE TO SCARCITY | | |
| *P.P.MAGENTA/1: UNPRICED DUE TO SCARCITY | | |
| *P.P.YELLOW/1: UNPRICED DUE TO SCARCITY | | |

## 2016 Star Wars Evolution Autographs

| | | |
|---|---|---|
| COMMON AUTO | 6.00 | 15.00 |
| *PURPLE/25: .6X TO 1.5X BASIC AUTOS | | |
| *GOLD/10: UNPRICED DUE TO SCARCITY | | |
| *IMP.RED/1: UNPRICED DUE TO SCARCITY | | |
| *P.P.BLACK/1: UNPRICED DUE TO SCARCITY | | |
| *P.P.CYAN/1: UNPRICED DUE TO SCARCITY | | |
| *P.P.MAGENTA/1: UNPRICED DUE TO SCARCITY | | |
| *P.P.YELLOW/1: UNPRICED DUE TO SCARCITY | | |
| RANDOMLY INSERTED INTO PACKS | | |
| NNO  Alan Harris | 8.00 | 20.00 |
| NNO  Amy Allen | 10.00 | 25.00 |
| NNO  Andy Serkis | 100.00 | 200.00 |
| NNO  Angus MacInnes | 12.00 | 30.00 |
| NNO  Ashley Eckstein | 20.00 | 50.00 |
| NNO  Clive Revill | 25.00 | 60.00 |
| NNO  Dee Bradley Baker | 8.00 | 20.00 |
| NNO  Deep Roy | 10.00 | 25.00 |
| NNO  Denis Lawson | 15.00 | 40.00 |

| | | |
|---|---|---|
| NNO  Dickey Beer | 12.00 | 30.00 |
| NNO  Freddie Prinze Jr. | 60.00 | 120.00 |
| NNO  George Takei | 15.00 | 40.00 |
| NNO  Greg Grunberg | 15.00 | 40.00 |
| NNO  Harriet Walter | 12.00 | 30.00 |
| NNO  Hugh Quarshie | 20.00 | 50.00 |
| NNO  Jeremy Bulloch | 15.00 | 40.00 |
| NNO  Jerome Blake | 10.00 | 25.00 |
| NNO  John Boyega | 75.00 | 150.00 |
| NNO  John Ratzenberger | 8.00 | 20.00 |
| NNO  Keisha Castle-Hughes | 10.00 | 25.00 |
| NNO  Kenneth Colley | 12.00 | 30.00 |
| NNO  Matthew Wood | 12.00 | 30.00 |
| NNO  Mercedes Ngoh | 20.00 | 50.00 |
| NNO  Michael Carter | 20.00 | 50.00 |
| NNO  Mike Quinn | 8.00 | 20.00 |
| NNO  Orli Shoshan | 8.00 | 20.00 |
| NNO  Paul Blake | 8.00 | 20.00 |
| NNO  Phil Lamarr | 15.00 | 40.00 |
| NNO  Ray Park | 25.00 | 60.00 |
| NNO  Sam Witwer | 8.00 | 20.00 |
| NNO  Stephen Stanton | 10.00 | 25.00 |
| NNO  Taylor Gray | 10.00 | 25.00 |
| NNO  Tim Dry | 12.00 | 30.00 |
| NNO  Tiya Sircar | 8.00 | 20.00 |
| NNO  Tom Kane | 10.00 | 25.00 |
| NNO  Vanessa Marshall | 8.00 | 20.00 |
| NNO  Warwick Davis | 12.00 | 30.00 |

## 2016 Star Wars Evolution Evolution of the Lightsaber

| | | |
|---|---|---|
| COMPLETE SET (9) | 12.00 | 30.00 |
| COMMON CARD (EL1-EL9) | 2.00 | 5.00 |
| *P.P.BLACK/1: UNPRICED DUE TO SCARCITY | | |
| *P.P.CYAN/1: UNPRICED DUE TO SCARCITY | | |
| *P.P.MAGENTA/1: UNPRICED DUE TO SCARCITY | | |
| *P.P.YELLOW/1: UNPRICED DUE TO SCARCITY | | |
| STATED ODDS 1:8 | | |

## 2016 Star Wars Evolution Evolution of Vehicles and Ships

| | | |
|---|---|---|
| COMPLETE SET (18) | 8.00 | 20.00 |
| COMMON CARD (EV1-EV18) | .75 | 2.00 |
| *P.P.BLACK/1: UNPRICED DUE TO SCARCITY | | |
| *P.P.CYAN/1: UNPRICED DUE TO SCARCITY | | |
| *P.P.MAGENTA/1: UNPRICED DUE TO SCARCITY | | |
| *P.P.YELLOW/1: UNPRICED DUE TO SCARCITY | | |
| STATED ODDS 1:2 | | |

## 2016 Star Wars Evolution Lenticular Morph

| | | |
|---|---|---|
| COMPLETE SET (9) | 60.00 | 120.00 |
| COMMON CARD (1-9) | 6.00 | 15.00 |
| STATED ODDS 1:72 | | |
| 1  Darth Vader | 10.00 | 25.00 |
| 2  Luke Skywalker | 10.00 | 25.00 |
| 3  Leia Organa | 8.00 | 20.00 |
| 4  Han Solo | 10.00 | 25.00 |
| 9  Chewbacca | 8.00 | 20.00 |

## 2016 Star Wars Evolution Marvel Star Wars Comics

| | | |
|---|---|---|
| COMPLETE SET (17) | 12.00 | 30.00 |
| COMMON CARD (EC1-EC17) | 1.50 | 4.00 |
| *P.P.BLACK/1: UNPRICED DUE TO SCARCITY | | |
| *P.P.CYAN/1: UNPRICED DUE TO SCARCITY | | |
| *P.P.MAGENTA/1: UNPRICED DUE TO SCARCITY | | |
| *P.P.YELLOW/1: UNPRICED DUE TO SCARCITY | | |
| STATED ODDS 1:4 | | |

## 2016 Star Wars Evolution Patches

| | | |
|---|---|---|
| COMMON CARD | 5.00 | 12.00 |
| *SILVER/50: 5X TO 1.2X BASIC CARDS | | |
| *GOLD/25: .6X TO 1.5X BASIC CARDS | | |
| *IMP.RED/1: UNPRICED DUE TO SCARCITY | | |
| *PLATINUM/10: UNPRICED DUE TO SCARCITY | | |
| NNO  Admiral Ackbar | 6.00 | 15.00 |
| NNO  Ahsoka Tano | 6.00 | 15.00 |
| NNO  BB-8 | 8.00 | 20.00 |
| NNO  Chancellor Palpatine | 6.00 | 15.00 |
| NNO  Clone Trooper | 6.00 | 15.00 |
| NNO  Darth Vader | 6.00 | 15.00 |
| NNO  Ezra Bridger | 6.00 | 15.00 |
| NNO  General Hux | 6.00 | 15.00 |
| NNO  Grand Moff Tarkin | 8.00 | 20.00 |
| NNO  Han Solo | 8.00 | 20.00 |
| NNO  Kylo Ren | 8.00 | 20.00 |
| NNO  Luke Skywalker | 6.00 | 15.00 |
| NNO  Mon Mothma | 6.00 | 15.00 |
| NNO  Poe Dameron | 6.00 | 15.00 |
| NNO  Princess Leia Organa | 6.00 | 15.00 |
| NNO  Qui-Gon Jinn | 6.00 | 15.00 |
| NNO  Rey | 10.00 | 25.00 |
| NNO  Senator Amidala | 6.00 | 15.00 |
| NNO  Supreme Leader Snoke | 6.00 | 15.00 |

## 2016 Star Wars Evolution SP Inserts

| | | |
|---|---|---|
| COMPLETE SET (9) | 250.00 | 500.00 |
| COMMON CARD (1-9) | 25.00 | 60.00 |
| STATED PRINT RUN 100 SER.#'d SETS | | |
| 1  Luke | 30.00 | 80.00 |
| Stormtrooper Disguise | | |
| 2  Leia | 30.00 | 80.00 |
| Boussh Disguise | | |
| 5  Vader | 50.00 | 100.00 |
| Birth of the Dark Lord | | |
| 6  Boba Fett | 30.00 | 80.00 |
| Skiff Battle | | |

## 2016 Star Wars Evolution Stained Glass Pairings

| | | |
|---|---|---|
| COMPLETE SET (9) | 20.00 | 50.00 |
| COMMON CARD (1-9) | 2.50 | 6.00 |
| STATED ODDS 1:24 | | |
| 1 Luke Skywalker | 5.00 | 12.00 |
| Princess Leia | | |
| 2 Han Solo | 4.00 | 10.00 |
| Lando Calrissian | | |
| 4 Darth Sidious | 4.00 | 10.00 |
| Darth Maul | | |
| 5 Darth Vader | 3.00 | 8.00 |
| Grand Moff Tarkin | | |
| 6 Kylo Ren | 3.00 | 8.00 |
| Captain Phasma | | |
| 7 Chewbacca | 3.00 | 8.00 |
| C-3PO | | |
| 9 Rey | 6.00 | 15.00 |
| Finn | | |

## 2007 Star Wars Family Guy Blue Harvest DVD Promos

| | | |
|---|---|---|
| COMPLETE SET (12) | 5.00 | 12.00 |
| COMMON CARD (UNNUMBERED) | .75 | 2.00 |
| *GERMAN: SAME VALUE AS ENGLISH | | |
| *ITALIAN: SAME VALUE AS ENGLISH | | |
| *SPANISH: SAME VALUE AS ENGLISH | | |

## 1996 Star Wars Finest

| | | |
|---|---|---|
| COMPLETE SET (90) | 10.00 | 25.00 |
| UNOPENED BOX (36 PACKS) | 45.00 | 60.00 |
| UNOPENED PACK (5 CARDS) | 1.50 | 2.00 |
| COMMON CARD (1-90) | .20 | .50 |
| *REF.: 5X TO 12X BASIC CARDS | | |

## 1996 Star Wars Finest Embossed

| | | |
|---|---|---|
| COMPLETE SET (6) | 10.00 | 25.00 |
| COMMON CARD (F1-F6) | 2.00 | 5.00 |

## 1996 Star Wars Finest Matrix

| | | |
|---|---|---|
| COMPLETE SET (4) | 6.00 | 15.00 |
| COMMON CARD (M1-M4) | 2.00 | 5.00 |
| NNO Exchange Card | | |

## 1996 Star Wars Finest Promos

| | | |
|---|---|---|
| COMPLETE SET (3) | 2.50 | 6.00 |
| COMMON CARD (SWF1-SWF3) | 1.00 | 2.50 |
| B1 Han Solo & Chewbacca | 3.00 | 8.00 |
| (Album Exclusive) | | |
| NNO 1-Card Sheet | | |
| NNO 1-Card Sheet Refractor | | |
| NNO Star Wars Goes Split Level | 200.00 | 400.00 |

## 2018 Star Wars Finest

| | | |
|---|---|---|
| COMPLETE SET W/SP (120) | 75.00 | 150.00 |
| COMPLETE SET W/O SP (100) | 20.00 | 50.00 |
| COMMON CARD (1-100) | .40 | 1.00 |
| COMMON SP (101-120) | 3.00 | 8.00 |
| *REF.: 1.25X TO 3X BASIC CARDS | | |
| *BLUE/150: 2X TO 5X BASIC CARDS | | |
| *GREEN/99: 3X TO 8X BASIC CARDS | | |
| *GOLD/50: 4X TO 10X BASIC CARDS | | |
| *GOLD SP/50: .5X TO 1.2X BASIC CARDS | | |
| *ORANGE/25: UNPRICED DUE TO SCARCITY | | |
| *BLACK/10: UNPRICED DUE TO SCARCITY | | |
| *RED/5: UNPRICED DUE TO SCARCITY | | |
| *SUPER/1: UNPRICED DUE TO SCARCITY | | |

## 2018 Star Wars Finest Autographs

| | | |
|---|---|---|
| *ORANGE/25: UNPRICED DUE TO SCARCITY | | |
| *BLACK/10: UNPRICED DUE TO SCARCITY | | |
| *RED/5: UNPRICED DUE TO SCARCITY | | |
| *SUPER/1: UNPRICED DUE TO SCARCITY | | |
| FAAL Amanda Lawrence | | |
| FADBB Dee Bradley Baker | 8.00 | 20.00 |
| FAHCT Hermione Corfield | 10.00 | 25.00 |
| FAJAT James Arnold Taylor | | |
| FAJBM Jerome Blake | 5.00 | 12.00 |
| FAMEM Mary Elizabeth McGlynn | 6.00 | 15.00 |
| FAJZ Zac Jensen | | |

## 2018 Star Wars Finest Droids and Vehicles

| | | |
|---|---|---|
| COMPLETE SET (20) | 12.00 | 30.00 |
| COMMON CARD (DV1-DV20) | 1.50 | 4.00 |
| *GOLD/50: .75X TO 2X BASIC CARDS | | |
| *RED/5: UNPRICED DUE TO SCARCITY | | |
| *SUPER/1: UNPRICED DUE TO SCARCITY | | |

## 2018 Star Wars Finest Lightsaber Hilt Medallions

| | | |
|---|---|---|
| COMMON MEM | 5.00 | 12.00 |
| *GOLD/50: .5X TO 1.2X BASIC MEM | | |
| *ORANGE/25: UNPRICED DUE TO SCARCITY | | |
| *BLACK/10: UNPRICED DUE TO SCARCITY | | |
| *RED/5: UNPRICED DUE TO SCARCITY | | |
| *SUPER/1: UNPRICED DUE TO SCARCITY | | |
| NNO Ahsoka Tano | 6.00 | 15.00 |
| CW | | |
| NNO Ahsoka Tano | 6.00 | 15.00 |
| CW | | |
| NNO Ahsoka Tano | 6.00 | 15.00 |
| CW | | |
| NNO Anakin Skywalker | 6.00 | 15.00 |
| AOTC | | |
| NNO Anakin Skywalker | 12.00 | 30.00 |
| ROTS | | |
| NNO Anakin Skywalker | 10.00 | 25.00 |

| | | |
|---|---|---|
| The Skywalker Saber ROTS | | |
| NNO Asajj Ventress | 6.00 | 15.00 |
| CW | | |
| NNO Barriss Offee | 6.00 | 15.00 |
| Asajj Ventress' Lightsaber CW | | |
| NNO Darth Maul | 10.00 | 25.00 |
| TPM | | |
| NNO Darth Sidious | 6.00 | 15.00 |
| ROTS | | |
| NNO Darth Vader | 8.00 | 20.00 |
| ROTS | | |
| NNO Darth Vader | 10.00 | 25.00 |
| RO | | |
| NNO Darth Vader | 10.00 | 25.00 |
| ESB | | |
| NNO Finn | 6.00 | 15.00 |
| TFA | | |
| NNO Kylo Ren | 12.00 | 30.00 |
| TFA | | |
| NNO Kylo Ren | 12.00 | 30.00 |
| TLJ | | |
| NNO Luke Skywalker | 10.00 | 25.00 |
| ANH | | |
| NNO Luke Skywalker | 8.00 | 20.00 |
| ESB | | |
| NNO Luke Skywalker | 10.00 | 25.00 |
| TLJ | | |
| NNO Luke Skywalker | 10.00 | 25.00 |
| ROTJ | | |
| NNO Luke Skywalker | 10.00 | 25.00 |
| ROTJ | | |
| NNO Luke Skywalker | 10.00 | 25.00 |
| The Skywalker Saber ANH | | |
| NNO Mace Windu | 8.00 | 20.00 |
| AOTC | | |
| NNO Obi-Wan Kenobi | 6.00 | 15.00 |
| AOTC | | |
| NNO Rey | 15.00 | 40.00 |
| TFA | | |
| NNO Rey | 15.00 | 40.00 |
| {The Skywalker Lightsaber TFA | | |
| NNO Shaak Ti | 6.00 | 15.00 |
| AOTC | | |
| NNO The Grand Inquisitor | 8.00 | 20.00 |
| REB | | |
| NNO Yoda | 8.00 | 20.00 |
| AOTC | | |
| NNO Yoda | 6.00 | 15.00 |
| CW | | |

## 2018 Star Wars Finest Prime Autographs

| | | |
|---|---|---|
| STATED PRINT RUN 10 SER.#'d SETS | | |
| UNPRICED DUE TO SCARCITY | | |
| PAAD Adam Driver | | |
| PAAS Andy Serkis | | |
| PAADC Anthony Daniels | | |
| PACF Carrie Fisher | | |
| PADR Daisy Ridley | | |
| PAHF Harrison Ford | | |
| PAKB Kenny Baker | | |
| PAPM Peter Mayhew | | |

## 2018 Star Wars Finest Rogue One

| | | |
|---|---|---|
| COMPLETE SET (20) | 20.00 | 50.00 |
| COMMON CARD (RO1-RO20) | 2.00 | 5.00 |
| *GOLD/50: .6X TO 1.5X BASIC CARDS | | |
| *RED/5: UNPRICED DUE TO SCARCITY | | |
| *SUPER/1: UNPRICED DUE TO SCARCITY | | |

## 2018 Star Wars Finest Rogue One Autographs

*ORANGE/25: UNPRICED DUE TO SCARCITY
*BLACK/10: UNPRICED DUE TO SCARCITY
*RED/5: UNPRICED DUE TO SCARCITY
*SUPER/1: UNPRICED DUE TO SCARCITY

RAAP  Alistair Petrie
RAAT  Alan Tudyk
RABD  Ben Daniels
RABM  Ben Mendelsohn
RADA  Derek Arnold
RADY  Donnie Yen
RAFJ  Felicity Jones
RAFW  Forest Whitaker
RAGO  Genevieve O'Reilly
RAIM  Ian McElhinney
RAMM  Mads Mikkelsen
RARA  Riz Ahmed

## 2018 Star Wars Finest Solo A Star Wars Story

| | | |
|---|---|---|
| COMPLETE SET (20) | 15.00 | 40.00 |
| COMMON CARD (SO1-SO20) | 1.25 | 3.00 |

*GOLD/50: .75X TO 2X BASIC CARDS
*RED/5: UNPRICED DUE TO SCARCITY
*SUPER/1: UNPRICED DUE TO SCARCITY

## 2015 Star Wars Galactic Connexions

| | | |
|---|---|---|
| COMPLETE SET (75) | 8.00 | 20.00 |
| COMMON DISC | .20 | .50 |

*FOIL: .6X TO 1.5X BASIC DISCS
*BLK: .75X TO 2X BASIC DISCS
*HOLOFOIL: .75X TO 2X BASIC DISCS
*BLK FOIL: 1.5X TO 4X BASIC DISCS
*CLR: 1.5X TO 4X BASIC DISCS
*PATTERN FOIL: 2X TO 5X BASIC DISCS
*BLK PATTERN FOIL: 2.5X TO 6X BASIC DISCS
*JABBA SLIME GREEN: 3X TO 8X BASIC DISCS
*CLR FOIL: 4X TO 10X BASIC DISCS
*LTSABER RED: 4X TO 10X BASIC DISCS
*CLR PATTERN FOIL: 8X TO 20X BASIC DISCS
*C-3PO GOLD: 10X TO 25X BASIC DISCS
*DEATH STAR SILVER: 12X TO 30X BASIC DISCS
*SOLID GOLD: 20X TO 50X BASIC DISCS

## 2015 Star Wars Galactic Connexions Battle Damaged Border

| | | |
|---|---|---|
| 1  Darth Vader | 250.00 | 500.00 |
| Red | | |
| 2  Han Solo | 150.00 | 300.00 |
| Red | | |
| 3  Luke Skywalker | 120.00 | 250.00 |
| Red | | |
| 4  Obi-Wan Kenobi | | |
| Red | | |
| 5  Princess Leia Organa | | |
| Red | | |

## 2015 Star Wars Galactic Connexions Blue Starfield Exclusives

| | | |
|---|---|---|
| COMPLETE SET (10) | 10.00 | 25.00 |
| COMMON DISC | 1.50 | 4.00 |

## 2015 Star Wars Galactic Connexions SDCC Promos

| | | |
|---|---|---|
| COMPLETE SET (6) | 100.00 | 200.00 |
| COMMON DISC | 12.00 | 30.00 |
| 4  Stormtrooper | 30.00 | 80.00 |
| Red | | |
| 5  Stormtrooper | 20.00 | 50.00 |
| Gold | | |

## 2015 Star Wars Galactic Connexions Series 2

| | | |
|---|---|---|
| COMPLETE SET (75) | 8.00 | 20.00 |
| COMMON DISC | .20 | .50 |

*GRAY FOIL: .6X TO 1.5X BASIC DISCS
*BLK: .75X TO 2X BASIC DISCS
*GRAY: .75X TO 2X BASIC DISCS
*BLK FOIL: 1.5X TO 4X BASIC DISCS
*CLR: 1.5X TO 4X BASIC DISCS
*GRAY PATTERN FOIL: 2X TO 5X BASIC DISCS
*BLK PATTERN FOIL: 2.5X TO 6X BASIC DISCS
*JABBA SLIME GREEN: 3X TO 8X BASIC DISCS
*CLR FOIL: 4X TO 10X BASIC DISCS
*LTSABER PURPLE: 4X TO 10X BASIC DISCS
*LTSABER RED: 4X TO 10X BASIC DISCS
*CLR PATTERN FOIL: 8X TO 20X BASIC DISCS
*C-3PO GOLD: 10X TO 25X BASIC DISCS
*DEATH STAR SILVER: 12X TO 30X BASIC DISCS
*SOLID GOLD: 20X TO 50X BASIC DISCS

## 2012 Star Wars Galactic Files

| | | |
|---|---|---|
| COMPLETE SET (350) | 25.00 | 50.00 |
| UNOPENED BOX (24 PACKS) | 80.00 | 100.00 |
| UNOPENED PACK (12 CARDS) | 4.00 | 5.00 |
| COMMON CARD (1-350) | .15 | .40 |

*BLUE: 8X TO 20X BASIC CARDS
*RED: 20X TO 50X BASIC CARDS
*GOLD/1: UNPRICED DUE TO SCARCITY
*P.P.BLACK/1: UNPRICED DUE TO SCARCITY
*P.P.CYAN/1: UNPRICED DUE TO SCARCITY
*P.P.MAGENTA/1: UNPRICED DUE TO SCARCITY
*P.P.YELLOW/1: UNPRICED DUE TO SCARCITY

| | | |
|---|---|---|
| 76  Darth Vader (Jedi Purge) SP | 12.00 | 30.00 |
| 96  Luke Skywalker (Stormtrooper) SP | 12.00 | 30.00 |
| 125B  Princess Leia (Despair) SP | 12.00 | 30.00 |

## 2012 Star Wars Galactic Files Autographs

| | | |
|---|---|---|
| COMMON AUTO | 10.00 | 25.00 |

STATED ODDS ONE AUTO OR PATCH PER HOBBY BOX

| | | |
|---|---|---|
| NNO  Carrie Fisher | 200.00 | 350.00 |
| NNO  Daniel Logan | 12.00 | 30.00 |
| NNO  Felix Silla | 12.00 | 30.00 |
| NNO  Harrison Ford | 2500.00 | 4000.00 |
| NNO  Irvin Kershner | 600.00 | 1000.00 |
| NNO  Jake Lloyd | 25.00 | 60.00 |
| NNO  James Earl Jones | 200.00 | 350.00 |
| NNO  Jeremy Bulloch | 20.00 | 50.00 |
| NNO  Mark Hamill | 300.00 | 500.00 |
| NNO  Matthew Wood | 15.00 | 40.00 |
| NNO  Michonne Bourrigue | 12.00 | 30.00 |
| NNO  Peter Mayhew | 30.00 | 75.00 |
| NNO  Ray Park | 15.00 | 40.00 |

## 2012 Star Wars Galactic Files Classic Lines

| | | |
|---|---|---|
| COMPLETE SET (10) | 3.00 | 8.00 |
| COMMON CARD (CL1-CL10) | .75 | 2.00 |
| STATED ODDS 1:4 | | |

## 2012 Star Wars Galactic Files Duels of Fate

| | | |
|---|---|---|
| COMPLETE SET (10) | 4.00 | 10.00 |
| COMMON CARD (DF1-DF10) | 1.00 | 2.50 |
| STATED ODDS 1:6 | | |

## 2012 Star Wars Galactic Files Galactic Moments

| | | |
|---|---|---|
| COMPLETE SET (20) | 20.00 | 40.00 |
| COMMON CARD (GM1-GM20) | 1.50 | 4.00 |
| STATED ODDS 1:6 | | |

## 2012 Star Wars Galactic Files Heroes on Both Sides

| | | |
|---|---|---|
| COMPLETE SET (10) | 4.00 | 10.00 |
| COMMON CARD (HB1-HB10) | 1.00 | 2.50 |
| STATED ODDS 1:6 | | |

## 2012 Star Wars Galactic Files I Have a Bad Feeling About This

| | | |
|---|---|---|
| COMPLETE SET (8) | 3.00 | 8.00 |
| COMMON CARD (BF1-BF8) | .75 | 2.00 |
| STATED ODDS 1:4 | | |

## 2012 Star Wars Galactic Files Patches

| | | |
|---|---|---|
| COMMON CARD | 8.00 | 20.00 |

STATED ODDS ONE AUTO OR PATCH PER HOBBY BOX

| | | |
|---|---|---|
| PR1  X-Wing Fighter Pilots: Red Leader | 50.00 | 100.00 |
| Garven Dreis | | |
| PR2  X-Wing Fighter Pilots: Red Two | 50.00 | 100.00 |
| Wedge Antilles | | |
| PR3  X-Wing Fighter Pilots: Red Three | 50.00 | 100.00 |
| Biggs Darklighter | | |
| PR4  X-Wing Fighter Pilots: Red Four | 50.00 | 100.00 |
| John D. Branon | | |
| PR5  X-Wing Fighter Pilots: Red Five | 100.00 | 200.00 |
| Luke Skywalker | | |
| PR6  X-Wing Fighter Pilots: Red Six | 50.00 | 100.00 |
| Jek Porkins | | |
| PR12  Jedi Starfighter Pilots | 12.00 | 30.00 |
| Obi-Wan Kenobi | | |
| PR13  Jedi Starfighter Pilots | 15.00 | 40.00 |
| Anakin Skywalker | | |
| PR14  Jedi Starfighter Pilots | 12.00 | 30.00 |
| Plo Koon | | |
| PR17  Snowspeeder Pilots: Rogue Leader | 75.00 | 150.00 |
| Luke Skywalker | | |
| PR18  Snowspeeder Pilots: Rogue Two | 40.00 | 80.00 |
| Zev Senesca | | |
| PR19  Snowspeeder Pilots: Rogue Three | 40.00 | 80.00 |
| Wedge Antilles | | |
| PR20  Snowspeeder Pilots: Rogue Four | 30.00 | 60.00 |
| Derek Hobbie Kuvian | | |
| PR21  Snowspeeder Pilots: Rogue Leader | 30.00 | 60.00 |
| (Gunner) Dak Ralter | | |
| PR23  Death Star Command | 15.00 | 40.00 |

Grand Moff Tarkin

| | | |
|---|---|---|
| PR24 Death Star Command | 15.00 | 40.00 |
| Darth Vader | | |
| PR25 Millennium Falcon Pilots | 35.00 | 70.00 |
| Han Solo | | |
| PR26 Millennium Falcon Pilots | 15.00 | 40.00 |
| Chewbacca | | |
| PR27 Millennium Falcon Pilots: Gold Leader | 25.00 | 50.00 |
| Lando Calrissian | | |
| PR28 Millennium Falcon Pilots: Gold Leader | 15.00 | 40.00 |
| Nien Numb | | |

## 2013 Star Wars Galactic Files 2

DARTH ZANNAH
SITH APPRENTICE

| | | |
|---|---|---|
| COMPLETE SET (353) | 20.00 | 50.00 |
| COMP.SET W/O SP (350) | 12.00 | 30.00 |
| UNOPENED BOX (24 PACKS) | 70.00 | 80.00 |
| UNOPENED PACK (12 CARDS) | 3.00 | 4.00 |
| COMMON CARD (351-699) | .15 | .40 |
| COMMON SP | 4.00 | 10.00 |
| *BLUE/350: 2X TO 5X BASIC CARDS | | |
| *RED/35: 15X TO 40X BASIC CARDS | | |
| *GOLD/10: 50X TO 120X BASIC CARDS | | |
| *P.P.BLACK/1: UNPRICED DUE TO SCARCITY | | |
| *P.P.CYAN/1: UNPRICED DUE TO SCARCITY | | |
| *P.P.MAGENTA/1: UNPRICED DUE TO SCARCITY | | |
| *P.P.YELLOW/1: UNPRICED DUE TO SCARCITY | | |
| 463b Han Solo Stormtrooper SP | 4.00 | 10.00 |
| 481b Luke Skywalker Bacta Tank SP | 4.00 | 10.00 |
| 510b Princess Leia Slave Girl SP | 4.00 | 10.00 |

## 2013 Star Wars Galactic Files 2 Autographs

| | | |
|---|---|---|
| COMMON AUTO | 12.00 | 30.00 |
| STATED ODDS 1:55 | | |
| NNO Billy Dee Williams | 50.00 | 100.00 |
| NNO Carrie Fisher | 200.00 | 350.00 |
| NNO Ian McDiarmid | 400.00 | 600.00 |
| NNO James Earl Jones | 200.00 | 350.00 |
| NNO Jeremy Bulloch | 15.00 | 40.00 |
| NNO Mark Hamill | 350.00 | 500.00 |
| NNO Peter Mayhew | 30.00 | 75.00 |

## 2013 Star Wars Galactic Files 2 Dual Autographs

HARRISON FORD
HAN SOLO

PETER MAYHEW
CHEWBACCA

| | | |
|---|---|---|
| ANNOUNCED COMBINED PRINT RUN 200 | | |
| NNO A.Eckstein/T.Kane | 100.00 | 200.00 |
| NNO J.Bulloch/A.Harris | 100.00 | 200.00 |
| NNO J.Jones/I.McDiarmid | | |
| NNO C.Fisher/M.Hamill | | |
| NNO H.Ford/P.Mayhew | | |

## 2013 Star Wars Galactic Files 2 Classic Lines

| | | |
|---|---|---|
| COMPLETE SET (10) | 3.00 | 8.00 |
| COMMON CARD (CL1-CL10) | .60 | 1.50 |
| *P.P.BLACK/1: UNPRICED DUE TO SCARCITY | | |
| *P.P.CYAN/1: UNPRICED DUE TO SCARCITY | | |
| *P.P.MAGENTA/1: UNPRICED DUE TO SCARCITY | | |
| *P.P.YELLOW/1: UNPRICED DUE TO SCARCITY | | |
| STATED ODDS 1:4 | | |

## 2013 Star Wars Galactic Files 2 Galactic Moments

| | | |
|---|---|---|
| COMPLETE SET (20) | 30.00 | 60.00 |
| COMMON CARD (GM1-GM20) | 2.00 | 5.00 |
| *P.P.BLACK/1: UNPRICED DUE TO SCARCITY | | |
| *P.P.CYAN/1: UNPRICED DUE TO SCARCITY | | |
| *P.P.MAGENTA/1: UNPRICED DUE TO SCARCITY | | |
| *P.P.YELLOW/1: UNPRICED DUE TO SCARCITY | | |
| STATED ODDS 1:12 | | |

## 2013 Star Wars Galactic Files 2 Honor the Fallen

| | | |
|---|---|---|
| COMPLETE SET (10) | 4.00 | 10.00 |
| COMMON CARD (HF1-HF10) | .75 | 2.00 |
| *P.P.BLACK/1: UNPRICED DUE TO SCARCITY | | |
| *P.P.CYAN/1: UNPRICED DUE TO SCARCITY | | |
| *P.P.MAGENTA/1: UNPRICED DUE TO SCARCITY | | |
| *P.P.YELLOW/1: UNPRICED DUE TO SCARCITY | | |
| STATED ODDS 1:6 | | |

## 2013 Star Wars Galactic Files 2 Medallions

| | | |
|---|---|---|
| COMMON MEDALLION (MD1-MD30) | 8.00 | 20.00 |
| STATED ODDS 1:55 | | |
| MD1 Luke Skywalker | 12.00 | 30.00 |
| MD3 Han Solo | 20.00 | 50.00 |
| MD5 Lando Calrissian | 12.00 | 30.00 |
| MD6 Han Solo | 150.00 | 250.00 |
| MD7 Boba Fett | 30.00 | 75.00 |
| MD9 Princess Leia Organa | 15.00 | 40.00 |
| MD10 Bail Organa | 10.00 | 25.00 |
| MD12 General Veers | 20.00 | 50.00 |
| MD13 Jawa | 20.00 | 50.00 |
| MD14 C-3PO | 30.00 | 75.00 |
| MD15 R2-D2 | 15.00 | 40.00 |
| MD16 R5-D4 | 12.00 | 30.00 |
| MD19 Luke Skywalker | 30.00 | 75.00 |
| MD20 Obi-Wan Kenobi | 12.00 | 30.00 |
| MD21 C-3PO & R2-D2 | 30.00 | 75.00 |
| MD22 TIE Fighter Pilot | 10.00 | 25.00 |
| MD23 Darth Vader | 15.00 | 40.00 |
| MD24 Stormtrooper | 12.00 | 30.00 |
| MD25 Obi-Wan Kenobi | 12.00 | 30.00 |
| MD26 Plo Koon | 12.00 | 30.00 |
| MD27 Captain Panaka | 12.00 | 30.00 |
| MD28 Qui-Gon Jinn | 12.00 | 30.00 |
| MD29 Obi-Wan Kenobi | 15.00 | 40.00 |
| MD30 Queen Amidala | 50.00 | 100.00 |

## 2013 Star Wars Galactic Files 2 Ripples in the Galaxy

| | | |
|---|---|---|
| COMPLETE SET (10) | 4.00 | 10.00 |
| COMMON CARD (RG1-RG10) | .75 | 2.00 |
| *P.P.BLACK/1: UNPRICED DUE TO SCARCITY | | |
| *P.P.CYAN/1: UNPRICED DUE TO SCARCITY | | |
| *P.P.MAGENTA/1: UNPRICED DUE TO SCARCITY | | |
| *P.P.YELLOW/1: UNPRICED DUE TO SCARCITY | | |
| STATED ODDS 1:6 | | |

## 2013 Star Wars Galactic Files 2 The Weak Minded

| | | |
|---|---|---|
| COMPLETE SET (7) | 2.50 | 6.00 |
| COMMON CARD (WM1-WM7) | .60 | 1.50 |
| *P.P.BLACK/1: UNPRICED DUE TO SCARCITY | | |
| *P.P.CYAN/1: UNPRICED DUE TO SCARCITY | | |
| *P.P.MAGENTA/1: UNPRICED DUE TO SCARCITY | | |
| *P.P.YELLOW/1: UNPRICED DUE TO SCARCITY | | |
| STATED ODDS 1:3 | | |

## 2017 Star Wars Galactic Files Reborn

KANAN JARRUS
GHOST TEAM LEADER

| | | |
|---|---|---|
| COMPLETE SET (200) | 10.00 | 25.00 |
| UNOPENED BOX (24 PACKS) | 80.00 | 100.00 |
| UNOPENED PACK (6 CARDS) | 4.00 | 5.00 |
| COMMON CARD | .15 | .40 |
| *ORANGE: .75X TO 2X BASIC CARDS | | |
| *BLUE: 1.2X TO 3X BASIC CARDS | | |
| *GREEN/199: 4X TO 10X BASIC CARDS | | |
| *PURPLE/99: 8X TO 20X BASIC CARDS | | |
| *GOLD/10: 20X TO 50X BASIC CARDS | | |
| *RED/1: UNPRICED DUE TO SCARCITY | | |
| *P.P.BLACK/1: UNPRICED DUE TO SCARCITY | | |
| *P.P.CYAN/1: UNPRICED DUE TO SCARCITY | | |
| *P.P.MAGENTA/1: UNPRICED DUE TO SCARCITY | | |
| *P.P.YELLOW/1: UNPRICED DUE TO SCARCITY | | |

## 2017 Star Wars Galactic Files Reborn Autographs

| | | |
|---|---|---|
| COMMON AUTO | 5.00 | 12.00 |
| *GOLD/5-25: UNPRICED DUE TO SCARCITY | | |
| *RED/1: UNPRICED DUE TO SCARCITY | | |
| *P.P.BLACK/1: UNPRICED DUE TO SCARCITY | | |
| *P.P.CYAN/1: UNPRICED DUE TO SCARCITY | | |
| *P.P.MAGENTA/1: UNPRICED DUE TO SCARCITY | | |
| *P.P.YELLOW/1: UNPRICED DUE TO SCARCITY | | |
| NNO Adrienne Wilkinson | 6.00 | 15.00 |
| NNO Alan Tudyk | 100.00 | 200.00 |
| NNO Anna Graves | 8.00 | 20.00 |
| NNO Ashley Eckstein | 12.00 | 30.00 |
| NNO Bruce Spence | 5.00 | 12.00 |
| NNO Catherine Taber | 15.00 | 40.00 |
| NNO Dave Barclay | 10.00 | 25.00 |
| NNO David Bowers | 6.00 | 15.00 |
| NNO Dee Bradley | 12.00 | 30.00 |
| NNO Denis Lawson | 10.00 | 25.00 |
| NNO Freddie Prinze | | |
| NNO George Takei | 12.00 | 30.00 |
| NNO Hassani Shapi | 8.00 | 20.00 |
| NNO Jeremy Bulloch | 20.00 | 50.00 |
| NNO Jerome Blake | 6.00 | 15.00 |
| NNO Jesse Jensen | 6.00 | 15.00 |
| NNO Jim Cummings | 6.00 | 15.00 |
| NNO Julian Glover | 6.00 | 15.00 |
| NNO Kath Soucie | 8.00 | 20.00 |

| | | | |
|---|---|---|---|
| NNO | Keone Young | 20.00 | 50.00 |
| NNO | Lewis MacLeod | 5.00 | 12.00 |
| NNO | Mary Oyaya | 12.00 | 30.00 |
| NNO | Megan Udall | 6.00 | 15.00 |
| NNO | Michael Carter | 8.00 | 20.00 |
| NNO | Michonne Bourriague | 6.00 | 15.00 |
| NNO | Nika Futterman | 12.00 | 30.00 |
| NNO | Oliver Ford | 8.00 | 20.00 |
| NNO | Oliver Walpole | 10.00 | 25.00 |
| NNO | Olivia D'Abo | 8.00 | 20.00 |
| NNO | Phil Eason | 6.00 | 15.00 |
| NNO | Phil LaMarr | 10.00 | 25.00 |
| NNO | Rajia Baroudi | 8.00 | 20.00 |
| NNO | Rena Owen | 6.00 | 15.00 |
| NNO | Rohan Nichol | 10.00 | 25.00 |
| NNO | Sam Witwer | 15.00 | 40.00 |
| NNO | Stephen Stanton | 25.00 | 60.00 |
| NNO | Tom Kenny | 6.00 | 15.00 |
| NNO | Wayne Pygram | 8.00 | 20.00 |
| NNO | Zac Jensen | 8.00 | 20.00 |

### 2017 Star Wars Galactic Files Reborn Dual Autographs

| | | |
|---|---|---|
| COMMON CARD | 15.00 | 40.00 |
| STATED PRINT RUN 5-50 SER.#'d SETS | | |
| NNO Blakiston/Rose/50 | 20.00 | 50.00 |
| NNO Fisher/Blakiston/5 | | |
| NNO McDiarmid/Carson/5 | | |

### 2017 Star Wars Galactic Files Reborn Famous Quotes

| | | |
|---|---|---|
| COMPLETE SET (15) | 8.00 | 20.00 |
| COMMON CARD (MQ1-MQ15) | 1.00 | 2.50 |
| *GOLD/10: UNPRICED DUE TO SCARCITY | | |
| *RED/1: UNPRICED DUE TO SCARCITY | | |
| *P.P.BLACK/1: UNPRICED DUE TO SCARCITY | | |
| *P.P.CYAN/1: UNPRICED DUE TO SCARCITY | | |
| *P.P.MAGENTA/1: UNPRICED DUE TO SCARCITY | | |
| *P.P.YELLOW/1: UNPRICED DUE TO SCARCITY | | |

### 2017 Star Wars Galactic Files Reborn Galactic Moments

| | | |
|---|---|---|
| COMPLETE SET (9) | 8.00 | 20.00 |
| COMMON CARD (GM1-GM9) | 1.25 | 3.00 |
| *PURPLE/99: X TO X BASIC CARDS | | |
| *GOLD/10: UNPRICED DUE TO SCARCITY | | |
| *RED/1: UNPRICED DUE TO SCARCITY | | |
| *P.P.BLACK/1: UNPRICED DUE TO SCARCITY | | |
| *P.P.CYAN/1: UNPRICED DUE TO SCARCITY | | |

---

| | | |
|---|---|---|
| *P.P.MAGENTA/1: UNPRICED DUE TO SCARCITY | | |
| *P.P.YELLOW/1: UNPRICED DUE TO SCARCITY | | |

### 2017 Star Wars Galactic Files Reborn Locations

| | | |
|---|---|---|
| COMPLETE SET (10) | 6.00 | 15.00 |
| COMMON CARD (L1-L10) | 1.00 | 2.50 |
| *GOLD/10: UNPRICED DUE TO SCARCITY | | |
| *RED/1: UNPRICED DUE TO SCARCITY | | |
| *P.P.BLACK/1: UNPRICED DUE TO SCARCITY | | |
| *P.P.CYAN/1: UNPRICED DUE TO SCARCITY | | |
| *P.P.MAGENTA/1: UNPRICED DUE TO SCARCITY | | |
| *P.P.YELLOW/1: UNPRICED DUE TO SCARCITY | | |

### 2017 Star Wars Galactic Files Reborn Vehicle Medallions

| | | |
|---|---|---|
| COMMON MEM | 5.00 | 12.00 |
| *SILVER/99: .6X TO 1.5X BASIC MEM | | |
| *GOLD/25: 1.2X TO 3X BASIC MEM | | |
| *RED/1: UNPRICED DUE TO SCARCITY | | |

### 2017 Star Wars Galactic Files Reborn Vehicles

| | | |
|---|---|---|
| COMPLETE SET (20) | 10.00 | 25.00 |
| COMMON CARD (V1-V20) | .75 | 2.00 |
| *PURPLE/99: 1.5X TO 4X BASIC CARDS | | |
| *GOLD/10: UNPRICED DUE TO SCARCITY | | |
| *RED/1: UNPRICED DUE TO SCARCITY | | |
| *P.P.BLACK/1: UNPRICED DUE TO SCARCITY | | |
| *P.P.CYAN/1: UNPRICED DUE TO SCARCITY | | |
| *P.P.MAGENTA/1: UNPRICED DUE TO SCARCITY | | |
| *P.P.YELLOW/1: UNPRICED DUE TO SCARCITY | | |

### 2017 Star Wars Galactic Files Reborn Weapons

CHEWBACCA'S BOWCASTER

| | | |
|---|---|---|
| COMPLETE SET (10) | 6.00 | 15.00 |
| COMMON CARD (W1-W10) | 1.00 | 2.50 |
| *PURPLE/99: 1.2X TO 3X BASIC CARDS | | |
| *GOLD/10: UNPRICED DUE TO SCARCITY | | |
| *RED/1: UNPRICED DUE TO SCARCITY | | |
| *P.P.BLACK/1: UNPRICED DUE TO SCARCITY | | |
| *P.P.CYAN/1: UNPRICED DUE TO SCARCITY | | |
| *P.P.MAGENTA/1: UNPRICED DUE TO SCARCITY | | |
| *P.P.YELLOW/1: UNPRICED DUE TO SCARCITY | | |

### 2018 Star Wars Galactic Files

| | | |
|---|---|---|
| COMPLETE SET (200) | 12.00 | 30.00 |
| UNOPENED BOX (24 PACKS) | 60.00 | 90.00 |
| UNOPENED PACK (8 CARDS) | 3.00 | 4.00 |
| COMMON CARD (RO9-ROTS23) | .20 | .50 |
| *ORANGE: .6X TO 1.5X BASIC CARDS | | |
| *BLUE: .75X TO 2X BASIC CARDS | | |
| *GREEN/199: 4X TO 10X BASIC CARDS | | |
| *PURPLE/99: 6X TO 15X BASIC CARDS | | |
| *GOLD/10: UNPRICED DUE TO SCARCITY | | |
| *WHITE/5: UNPRICED DUE TO SCARCITY | | |
| *RED/1: UNPRICED DUE TO SCARCITY | | |
| *P.P.BLACK/1: UNPRICED DUE TO SCARCITY | | |
| *P.P.CYAN/1: UNPRICED DUE TO SCARCITY | | |
| *P.P.MAGENTA/1: UNPRICED DUE TO SCARCITY | | |
| *P.P.YELLOW/1: UNPRICED DUE TO SCARCITY | | |

### 2018 Star Wars Galactic Files Autographs

| | |
|---|---|
| *GOLD/10: UNPRICED DUE TO SCARCITY | |
| *WHITE/5: UNPRICED DUE TO SCARCITY | |

---

| | | |
|---|---|---|
| *RED/1: UNPRICED DUE TO SCARCITY | | |
| *P.P.BLACK/1: UNPRICED DUE TO SCARCITY | | |
| *P.P.CYAN/1: UNPRICED DUE TO SCARCITY | | |
| *P.P.MAGENTA/1: UNPRICED DUE TO SCARCITY | | |
| *P.P.YELLOW/1: UNPRICED DUE TO SCARCITY | | |
| AAB | Ariyon Bakare | 6.00 | 15.00 |
| AAD | Adam Driver | | |
| AAG | Anna Graves | 5.00 | 12.00 |
| AAP | Alistair Petrie | | |
| AAT | Alan Tudyk | | |
| ABG | Barbara Goodson | | |
| ABP | Bonnie Piesse | 5.00 | 12.00 |
| ACA | Cas Anvar | 10.00 | 25.00 |
| ACF | Carrie Fisher | | |
| ACR | Clive Revill | | |
| ADM | Daniel Mays | 6.00 | 15.00 |
| ADR | Daisy Ridley | | |
| ADT | David Tennant | | |
| ADY | Donnie Yen | | |
| AFJ | Felicity Jones | | |
| AFW | Forest Whitaker | | |
| AGC | Gwendoline Christie | | |
| AGG | Greg Grunberg | | |
| AGT | George Takei | | |
| AHC | Hayden Christensen | | |
| AHF | Harrison Ford | | |
| AHS | Hugh Skinner | 8.00 | 20.00 |
| AIM | Ian McDiarmid | | |
| AJB | John Boyega | | |
| AJL | Jett Lucas | 6.00 | 15.00 |
| AKB | Kenny Baker | | |
| AKF | Kate Fleetwood | 5.00 | 12.00 |
| AKR | Kipsang Rotich | 5.00 | 12.00 |
| ALD | Laura Dern | | |
| AMS | Meredith Salenger | 6.00 | 15.00 |
| ARA | Riz Ahmed | | |
| ARD | Robbie Daymond | 5.00 | 12.00 |
| ARN | Robert Nairne | 10.00 | 25.00 |
| ARP | Ray Park | | |
| ATM | Temuera Morrison | | |
| AVK | Valene Kane | 6.00 | 15.00 |
| AADT | Andy De La Tour | 12.00 | 30.00 |
| AAEK | Ashley Eckstein | | |
| AAND | Anthony Daniels | | |
| ABDW | Billy Dee Williams | | |
| AFPJ | Freddie Prinze Jr. | | |
| AJSC | Jordan Stephens | 5.00 | 12.00 |
| AMSA | Marc Silk | 5.00 | 12.00 |
| ASMG | Sarah Michelle Gellar | | |

### 2018 Star Wars Galactic Files Band of Heroes

THE RESISTANCE

| | | |
|---|---|---|
| COMPLETE SET (7) | 5.00 | 12.00 |
| COMMON CARD (BH1-BH7) | 1.25 | 3.00 |
| *PURPLE/99: .6X TO 1.5X BASIC CARDS | | |
| *GOLD/10: UNPRICED DUE TO SCARCITY | | |
| *WHITE/5: UNPRICED DUE TO SCARCITY | | |
| *P.P.BLACK/1: UNPRICED DUE TO SCARCITY | | |
| *P.P.CYAN/1: UNPRICED DUE TO SCARCITY | | |
| *P.P.MAGENTA/1: UNPRICED DUE TO SCARCITY | | |
| *P.P.YELLOW/1: UNPRICED DUE TO SCARCITY | | |

## 2018 Star Wars Galactic Files Galactic Moments

| | | |
|---|---|---|
| COMPLETE SET (10) | 6.00 | 15.00 |
| COMMON CARD (GM1-GM10) | 1.00 | 2.50 |

*PURPLE/99: .75X TO 2X BASIC CARDS
*GOLD/10: UNPRICED DUE TO SCARCITY
*WHITE/5: UNPRICED DUE TO SCARCITY
*P.P.BLACK/1: UNPRICED DUE TO SCARCITY
*P.P.CYAN/1: UNPRICED DUE TO SCARCITY
*P.P.MAGENTA/1: UNPRICED DUE TO SCARCITY
*P.P.YELLOW/1: UNPRICED DUE TO SCARCITY

## 2018 Star Wars Galactic Files Locations

CLOUD CITY GANTRY

| | | |
|---|---|---|
| COMPLETE SET (10) | 8.00 | 20.00 |
| COMMON CARD (L1-L10) | 1.25 | 3.00 |

*PURPLE/99: .75X TO 2X BASIC CARDS
*GOLD/10: UNPRICED DUE TO SCARCITY
*WHITE/5: UNPRICED DUE TO SCARCITY
*P.P.BLACK/1: UNPRICED DUE TO SCARCITY
*P.P.CYAN/1: UNPRICED DUE TO SCARCITY
*P.P.MAGENTA/1: UNPRICED DUE TO SCARCITY
*P.P.YELLOW/1: UNPRICED DUE TO SCARCITY

## 2018 Star Wars Galactic Files Manufactured Movie Poster Patches

DARTH MAUL

| | | |
|---|---|---|
| COMMON PATCH | 6.00 | 15.00 |

*BLUE/99: .5X TO 1.2X BASIC PATCHES
*GREEN/50: .6X TO 1.5X BASIC PATCHES
*PURPLE/25: .75X TO 2X BASIC PATCHES
*GOLD/10: UNPRICED DUE TO SCARCITY
*WHITE/5: UNPRICED DUE TO SCARCITY
*RED/1: UNPRICED DUE TO SCARCITY

| | | |
|---|---|---|
| NNO Admiral Ackbar - Return of the Jedi | | |
| NNO Anakin Skywalker - Attack of the Clones | 8.00 | 20.00 |
| NNO Anakin Skywalker - Revenge of the Sith | 8.00 | 20.00 |
| NNO Anakin Skywalker - The Phantom Menace | 8.00 | 20.00 |
| NNO Baze Malbus - Rogue One | | |
| NNO Boba Fett - The Empire Strikes Back | 10.00 | 25.00 |
| NNO Bodhi Rook - Rogue One | 15.00 | 40.00 |
| NNO C-3PO - A New Hope | 10.00 | 25.00 |
| NNO Captain Phasma - The Force Awakens | | |
| NNO Cassian Andor - Rogue One | | |

| | | |
|---|---|---|
| NNO Chirrut Imwe - Rogue One | 10.00 | 25.00 |
| NNO Count Dooku - Attack of the Clones | | |
| NNO Darth Maul - The Phantom Menace | 10.00 | 25.00 |
| NNO Darth Sidious - Revenge of the Sith | | |
| NNO Darth Vader - Revenge of the Sith | | |
| NNO Darth Vader - The Empire Strikes Back | | |
| NNO Director Krennic - Rogue One | 8.00 | 20.00 |
| NNO Finn - The Force Awakens | | |
| NNO Finn - The Last Jedi | | |
| NNO General Grievous - Revenge of the Sith | 6.00 | 15.00 |
| NNO General Hux - The Last Jedi | 6.00 | 15.00 |
| NNO General Leia Organa - The Force Awakens | 12.00 | 30.00 |
| NNO Grand Moff Tarkin - A New Hope | 8.00 | 20.00 |
| NNO Han Solo - A New Hope | 12.00 | 30.00 |
| NNO Han Solo - Return of the Jedi | 12.00 | 30.00 |
| NNO Han Solo - The Empire Strikes Back | 12.00 | 30.00 |
| NNO Han Solo - The Force Awakens | 12.00 | 30.00 |
| NNO Jabba The Hutt - Return of the Jedi | 6.00 | 15.00 |
| NNO Jango Fett - Attack of the Clones | 6.00 | 15.00 |
| NNO Jyn Erso - Rogue One | | |
| NNO Kylo Ren - The Force Awakens | | |
| NNO Kylo Ren - The Last Jedi | | |
| NNO Lando Calrissian - The Empire Strikes Back | 8.00 | 20.00 |
| NNO Luke Skywalker - A New Hope | 10.00 | 25.00 |
| NNO Luke Skywalker - Return of the Jedi | 10.00 | 25.00 |
| NNO Luke Skywalker - The Empire Strikes Back | 10.00 | 25.00 |
| NNO Luke Skywalker - The Last Jedi | 10.00 | 25.00 |
| NNO Obi-Wan Kenobi - A New Hope | 6.00 | 15.00 |
| NNO Obi-Wan Kenobi - Attack of the Clones | 6.00 | 15.00 |
| NNO Obi-Wan Kenobi - Revenge of the Sith | 12.00 | 30.00 |
| NNO Obi-Wan Kenobi - The Phantom Menace | 6.00 | 15.00 |
| NNO Padme Amidala - Attack of the Clones | 12.00 | 30.00 |
| NNO Poe Dameron - The Force Awakens | | |
| NNO Poe Dameron - The Last Jedi | | |
| NNO Princess Leia - The Empire Strikes Back | 15.00 | 40.00 |
| NNO Princess Leia Organa - A New Hope | 10.00 | 25.00 |
| NNO Princess Leia Organa - Return of the Jedi | 10.00 | 25.00 |
| NNO Queen Amidala - The Phantom Menace | 12.00 | 30.00 |
| NNO Qui-Gon Jinn - The Phantom Menace | 15.00 | 40.00 |
| NNO R2-D2 - A New Hope | 8.00 | 20.00 |
| NNO Rey - The Force Awakens | 10.00 | 25.00 |
| NNO Rey - The Last Jedi | 15.00 | 40.00 |
| NNO Saw Gerrera - Rogue One | 15.00 | 40.00 |
| NNO Supreme Leader Snoke - The Last Jedi | | |
| NNO The Emperor - Return of the Jedi | 15.00 | 40.00 |
| NNO Yoda - The Empire Strikes Back | | |

## 2018 Star Wars Galactic Files Memorable Quotes

| | | |
|---|---|---|
| COMPLETE SET (10) | 6.00 | 15.00 |
| COMMON CARD (MQ1-MQ10) | 1.00 | 2.50 |

*PURPLE/99: .75X TO 2X BASIC CARDS
*GOLD/10: UNPRICED DUE TO SCARCITY
*WHITE/5: UNPRICED DUE TO SCARCITY
*P.P.BLACK/1: UNPRICED DUE TO SCARCITY
*P.P.CYAN/1: UNPRICED DUE TO SCARCITY
*P.P.MAGENTA/1: UNPRICED DUE TO SCARCITY
*P.P.YELLOW/1: UNPRICED DUE TO SCARCITY

## 2018 Star Wars Galactic Files Sinister Syndicates

BLACK SUN

| | | |
|---|---|---|
| COMPLETE SET (15) | 10.00 | 25.00 |
| COMMON CARD (SS1-SS15) | 1.25 | 3.00 |

*PURPLE/99: .75X TO 2X BASIC CARDS
*GOLD/10: UNPRICED DUE TO SCARCITY
*WHITE/5: UNPRICED DUE TO SCARCITY
*P.P.BLACK/1: UNPRICED DUE TO SCARCITY
*P.P.CYAN/1: UNPRICED DUE TO SCARCITY
*P.P.MAGENTA/1: UNPRICED DUE TO SCARCITY
*P.P.YELLOW/1: UNPRICED DUE TO SCARCITY

## 2018 Star Wars Galactic Files Source Material Fabric Swatches

| | | |
|---|---|---|
| COMMON SWATCH | 20.00 | 50.00 |

*PURPLE/25: UNPRICED DUE TO SCARCITY
*GOLD/10: UNPRICED DUE TO SCARCITY
*WHITE/5: UNPRICED DUE TO SCARCITY
*RED/1: UNPRICED DUE TO SCARCITY

| | | |
|---|---|---|
| NNO Galen Erso's Jacket | 25.00 | 60.00 |
| NNO Jyn Erso's Poncho | 50.00 | 100.00 |
| NNO Poe Dameron's Shirt | 25.00 | 60.00 |
| NNO Praetorian Guard's Uniform | 30.00 | 75.00 |
| NNO Rey's Head Wrap | 60.00 | 120.00 |
| NNO Rey's Jacket | 100.00 | 200.00 |

## 2018 Star Wars Galactic Files Vehicles

| | | |
|---|---|---|
| COMPLETE SET (10) | 6.00 | 15.00 |
| COMMON CARD (V1-V10) | 1.00 | 2.50 |

*NO FOIL: .5X TO 1.2X BASIC CARDS
*PURPLE/99: .75X TO 2X BASIC CARDS
*GOLD/10: UNPRICED DUE TO SCARCITY
*WHITE/5: UNPRICED DUE TO SCARCITY
*P.P.BLACK/1: UNPRICED DUE TO SCARCITY
*P.P.CYAN/1: UNPRICED DUE TO SCARCITY
*P.P.MAGENTA/1: UNPRICED DUE TO SCARCITY
*P.P.YELLOW/1: UNPRICED DUE TO SCARCITY

## 2018 Star Wars Galactic Files Weapons

CHIRRUT IMWE'S STAFF

| | | |
|---|---|---|
| COMPLETE SET (10) | 6.00 | 15.00 |
| COMMON CARD (W1-W10) | 1.00 | 2.50 |

*PURPLE/99: .75X TO 2X BASIC CARDS
*GOLD/10: UNPRICED DUE TO SCARCITY
*WHITE/5: UNPRICED DUE TO SCARCITY
*P.P.BLACK/1: UNPRICED DUE TO SCARCITY
*P.P.CYAN/1: UNPRICED DUE TO SCARCITY
*P.P.MAGENTA/1: UNPRICED DUE TO SCARCITY
*P.P.YELLOW/1: UNPRICED DUE TO SCARCITY

## 2018-19 Star Wars Galactic Moments Countdown to Episode 9

| | | |
|---|---|---|
| COMMON CARD | 5.00 | 12.00 |

124 General Leia Organa/280*
125 Paige Tico's Sacrifice/268*
126 Luke Skywalker and the Lightsaber/273*
127 Supreme Leader Snoke/
128 Rey's First Lesson/
129 Escaping Canto Bight/
130 General Hux/
131 The Force Connection/
132 Master and Student Reunited/

## 1993-95 Star Wars Galaxy

| | | |
|---|---|---|
| COMPLETE SET (365) | 15.00 | 40.00 |
| COMP.SER 1 SET (140) | 6.00 | 15.00 |
| COMP.SER 2 SET (135) | 6.00 | 15.00 |
| COMP.SER 3 SET (90) | 6.00 | 15.00 |
| UNOPENED SER.1 BOX (36 PACKS) | 30.00 | 40.00 |
| UNOPENED SER.1 PACK (8 CARDS) | 1.00 | 1.25 |
| UNOPENED SER.2 BOX (36 PACKS) | 20.00 | 30.00 |
| UNOPENED SER.2 PACK (8 CARDS) | .75 | 1.00 |
| UNOPENED SER.3 BOX (36 PACKS) | 20.00 | 30.00 |
| UNOPENED SER.3 PACK (7 CARDS) | .75 | 1.00 |
| COMMON CARD (1-365) | .15 | .40 |
| *MIL.FALCON FOIL: .8X TO 2X BASIC CARDS | | |
| *FIRST DAY: 1X TO 2.5X BASIC CARDS | | |
| DARTH VADER FOIL UNNUMBERED | 4.00 | 10.00 |

## 1993-95 Star Wars Galaxy Clearzone

| | | |
|---|---|---|
| COMPLETE SET (6) | 15.00 | 40.00 |
| COMMON CARD (E1-E6) | 3.00 | 8.00 |

## 1993-95 Star Wars Galaxy Etched Foil

| | | |
|---|---|---|
| COMPLETE SET (18) | 60.00 | 120.00 |
| COMMON CARD (1-18) | 3.00 | 8.00 |

## 1993-95 Star Wars Galaxy LucasArts

| | | |
|---|---|---|
| COMPLETE SET (12) | 6.00 | 15.00 |
| COMMON CARD (L1-L12) | .60 | 1.50 |

## 1993-95 Star Wars Galaxy Promos

| | | |
|---|---|---|
| 0 Ralph McQuarrie (Darth Vader) | 2.50 | 6.00 |
| 0 Drew Sturzan artwork (SW Galaxy Magazine) | 1.25 | 3.00 |
| 0 Ken Steacy Art | | |
| P1 Jae Lee/Rancor Monster(dealer cello pack) | 1.25 | 4.00 |
| P1 Jae Lee/Rancor Monster/AT-AT | | |
| P1 Rancor Card | | |
| AT-AT/Yoda 5X7 | | |
| P2 Chris Sprouse/Luke building lightsaber (NSU) | 2.00 | 5.00 |
| P2 Snowtrooper (Convention exclusive) | 1.50 | 4.00 |
| P3 Yoda Shrine SP | 250.00 | 400.00 |
| P3 Darth Vader on Hoth (NSU) | 1.25 | 3.00 |
| P4 Dave Gibbons/C-3PO and Jawas (SW Galaxy 1 Tin Set) | | |
| P4 Luke on Dagobah/Art Suydam | .60 | 1.50 |
| P5 Joe Phillips/Han and Chewbacca (Cards Illustrated) | 2.00 | 5.00 |
| P5 AT-AT | .75 | 2.00 |
| P6 Tom Taggart/Boba Fett (Hero) | 2.50 | 6.00 |
| P6 Luke with lightsaber (SW Galaxy Magazine) | | |
| P7 Leia with Jacen and Jania (Wizard Magazine) | 2.00 | 5.00 |
| P8 Boba Fett and Darth Vader (Cards Illustrated) | 4.00 | 10.00 |
| 140 Look for Series Two (Bend Ems Toys) | | |
| DH2 Cam Kennedy artwork/BobaFett | 2.00 | 5.00 |
| DH3 Cam Kennedy artwork/Millennium Falcon | 2.00 | 5.00 |
| NNO Jim Starlin/Stormtrooper and Ewoks (Triton #3) | 1.50 | 4.00 |
| NNO Tim Truman/Tuskan Raiders | 3.00 | 8.00 |
| NNO Boba Fett | 3.00 | 8.00 |
| NNO AT-AT 5 x 7 (Previews) | | |
| NNO Boba Fett/Dengar (Classic Star Wars) | 2.00 | 5.00 |
| NNO Jabba the Hutt (NSU/Starlog/Wizard) | 1.25 | 3.00 |
| NNO Princess Leia (NSU) | 1.50 | 4.00 |
| NNO Sandtrooper (Wizard Magazine) | 1.50 | 4.00 |
| NNO Truce at Bakura (Bantam exclusive) | 4.00 | 10.00 |
| NNO Princess Leia/Sandtrooper 2-Card Panel (Advance exclusive) | | |
| NNO Jabba the Hutt, Obi-Wan/Darth Vader 5X7 (Previews exclusive) | | |
| DH1A Cam Kennedy artwork/Battling Robots | | |
| (Dark Lords of the Sith comic) | 2.00 | 5.00 |
| Series at line 8 | | |
| DH1B Cam Kennedy artwork/Battling Robots | | |
| (Dark Lords of the Sith comic) | 2.00 | 5.00 |
| Series at line 9 | | |
| SWB1 Grand Moff Tarkin (album exclusive) | 4.00 | 10.00 |

## 2016 Star Wars Galaxy Bonus Abrams

| | |
|---|---|
| COMPLETE SET (4) | |
| COMMON CARD (1-4) | |

1 Display Box, Series 1, 1993
Art By Ken Steacy
2 A Tribute to George Lucas, Card No. 2, Series 1, 1993
Art By Drew Struzan

3 New Visions, Card No. 110, Series 1, 1993
Art By Mike Mignola
4 Levitating Yoda, Original Art for Topps Galaxy Series 2 Promo Card, 1994
Art By John Rheume

## 1999 Star Wars Galaxy Collector

| | | |
|---|---|---|
| COMPLETE SET W/O SP (9) | 6.00 | 15.00 |
| COMMON CARD (SW0-SW9) | 1.25 | 3.00 |
| SW0 Episode I | 30.00 | 75.00 |
| (Non-Sport Update Gummie Award Exclusive) | | |

## 1996 Star Wars Galaxy Magazine Cover Gallery

| | | |
|---|---|---|
| COMPLETE SET (4) | 3.00 | 8.00 |
| COMMON CARD (C1-C4) | 1.00 | 2.50 |

## 1995 Star Wars Galaxy Magazine Finest Promos

| | | |
|---|---|---|
| COMPLETE SET (4) | 3.00 | 8.00 |
| COMMON CARD (SWGM1-SWGM4) | 1.50 | 4.00 |

## 2009 Star Wars Galaxy Series 4

| | | |
|---|---|---|
| COMPLETE SET (120) | 5.00 | 12.00 |
| UNOPENED BOX (24 PACKS) | 70.00 | 80.00 |
| UNOPENED PACK (7 CARDS) | 3.00 | 4.00 |
| UNOPENED BOX (24 PACKS) | 100.00 | 120.00 |
| UNOPENED PACK (7 CARDS) | 5.00 | 6.00 |
| COMMON CARD (1-120) | .15 | .40 |
| *P.P.BLACK/1: UNPRICED DUE TO SCARCITY | | |
| *P.P.CYAN/1: UNPRICED DUE TO SCARCITY | | |
| *P.P.MAGENTA/1: UNPRICED DUE TO SCARCITY | | |
| *P.P.YELLOW/1: UNPRICED DUE TO SCARCITY | | |

## 2009 Star Wars Galaxy Series 4 Silver Foil

| | | |
|---|---|---|
| COMPLETE SET (15) | 5.00 | 12.00 |
| COMMON CARD (1-15) | .60 | 1.50 |
| *BRONZE: 2X TO 5X BASIC CARDS | | |
| *GOLD: .8X TO 2X BASIC CARDS | | |
| *SILVER REF./1: UNPRICED DUE TO SCARCITY | | |
| STATED ODDS 1:3 | | |

## 2009 Star Wars Galaxy Series 4 Etched Foil

| | | |
|---|---|---|
| COMPLETE SET (6) | 6.00 | 12.00 |
| COMMON CARD (1-6) | 1.50 | 4.00 |
| STATED ODDS 1:6 | | |

## 2009 Star Wars Galaxy Series 4 Galaxy Evolutions

| | | |
|---|---|---|
| COMPLETE SET (6) | 30.00 | 80.00 |
| COMMON CARD (1-6) | 8.00 | 20.00 |
| STATED ODDS 1:24 RETAIL | | |

## 2009 Star Wars Galaxy Series 4 Lost Galaxy

| | | |
|---|---|---|
| COMPLETE SET (5) | 12.00 | 25.00 |
| COMMON CARD (1-5) | 3.00 | 8.00 |
| STATED ODDS 1:24 | | |
| YODA'S WORLD/999 STATED ODDS 1:277 | | |
| JOHN RHEAUME AUTO STATED ODDS 1:2,789 | | |
| NNO Yoda's World/999 | 15.00 | 30.00 |
| NNOAU Yoda's World | | |
| Rheaume AU | | |

## 2009 Star Wars Galaxy Series 4 Promos

| | | |
|---|---|---|
| COMPLETE SET (4) | 8.00 | 20.00 |
| COMMON CARD (P1A-P3) | .75 | 2.00 |
| P1A Ventress | 1.50 | 4.00 |
| Dooku GEN | | |
| P1B Starcruiser crash/ (Fan Club Excl.) | 6.00 | 15.00 |
| P3 Group shot WW | 2.00 | 5.00 |

## 2010 Star Wars Galaxy Series 5

| | | |
|---|---|---|
| COMPLETE SET (120) | 8.00 | 20.00 |
| COMMON CARD (1-120) | .15 | .40 |
| *P.P.BLACK/1: UNPRICED DUE TO SCARCITY | | |
| *P.P.CYAN/1: UNPRICED DUE TO SCARCITY | | |
| *P.P.MAGENTA/1: UNPRICED DUE TO SCARCITY | | |
| *P.P.YELLOW/1: UNPRICED DUE TO SCARCITY | | |

TRADING CARDS

## 2010 Star Wars Galaxy Series 5 Etched Foil

| | | |
|---|---|---|
| COMPLETE SET (6) | 4.00 | 10.00 |
| COMMON CARD (1-6) | 1.25 | 3.00 |
| STATED ODDS 1:6 H/R | | |

## 2010 Star Wars Galaxy Series 5 Silver Foil

| | | |
|---|---|---|
| COMPLETE SET (15) | 6.00 | 15.00 |
| COMMON CARD (1-15) | .60 | 1.50 |
| *BRONZE FOIL: 1.2X TO 3X BASIC CARDS | | |
| *GOLD FOIL/770: 6X TO 15X BASIC CARDS | | |
| *SILVER REFR./1: UNPRICED DUE TO SCARCITY | | |
| STATED ODDS 1:3 H/R | | |

## 2010 Star Wars Galaxy Series 5 Autographs

| | | |
|---|---|---|
| COMMON AUTO | 30.00 | 80.00 |
| STATED ODDS 1:274 HOBBY | | |
| DP David Prowse | 60.00 | 120.00 |
| JB Jeremy Bulloch | 50.00 | 100.00 |
| JJ James Earl Jones | 120.00 | 250.00 |
| KB Kenny Baker | 50.00 | 100.00 |
| MH Mark Hamill | 300.00 | 450.00 |

## 2010 Star Wars Galaxy Series 5 Lost Galaxy

| | | |
|---|---|---|
| COMPLETE SET (5) | 10.00 | 25.00 |
| COMMON CARD (1-5) | 3.00 | 8.00 |
| STATED ODDS 1:24 HOBBY | | |

## 2011 Star Wars Galaxy Series 6

| | | |
|---|---|---|
| COMPLETE SET (120) | 8.00 | 20.00 |
| COMMON CARD (1-120) | .15 | .40 |
| *P.P.BLACK/1: UNPRICED DUE TO SCARCITY | | |
| *P.P.CYAN/1: UNPRICED DUE TO SCARCITY | | |
| *P.P.MAGENTA/1: UNPRICED DUE TO SCARCITY | | |
| *P.P.YELLOW/1: UNPRICED DUE TO SCARCITY | | |

## 2011 Star Wars Galaxy Series 6 Silver Foil

| | | |
|---|---|---|
| COMPLETE SET (10) | 6.00 | 15.00 |
| COMMON CARD (1-10) | 1.00 | 2.50 |
| *BRONZE: 1.2X TO 3X BASIC CARDS | | |
| *GOLD/600: 4X TO 10X BASIC CARDS | | |
| UNPRICED REFR. PRINT RUN 1 | | |
| STATED ODDS 1:3 | | |

## 2011 Star Wars Galaxy Series 6 Animation Cels

| | | |
|---|---|---|
| COMPLETE SET (9) | 20.00 | 40.00 |
| COMMON CARD (1-9) | 3.00 | 8.00 |
| STATED ODDS 1:4 RETAIL | | |

## 2011 Star Wars Galaxy Series 6 Etched Foil

| | | |
|---|---|---|
| COMPLETE SET (6) | 5.00 | 12.00 |
| COMMON CARD (1-6) | 1.25 | 3.00 |
| STATED ODDS 1:6 | | |

## 2012 Star Wars Galaxy Series 7

| | | |
|---|---|---|
| COMPLETE SET (110) | 8.00 | 20.00 |
| UNOPENED BOX (24 PACKS) | 60.00 | 70.00 |
| UNOPENED PACK (7 CARDS) | 2.50 | 3.00 |
| COMMON CARD (1-110) | .15 | .40 |
| *P.P.BLACK/1: UNPRICED DUE TO SCARCITY | | |
| *P.P.CYAN/1: UNPRICED DUE TO SCARCITY | | |
| *P.P.MAGENTA/1: UNPRICED DUE TO SCARCITY | | |
| *P.P.YELLOW/1: UNPRICED DUE TO SCARCITY | | |

## 2012 Star Wars Galaxy Series 7 Silver Foil

| | | |
|---|---|---|
| COMPLETE SET (15) | 6.00 | 15.00 |
| COMMON CARD (1-15) | .75 | 2.00 |
| *BRONZE: 1.5X TO 4X SILVER | | |
| *GOLD: 3X TO 8X SILVER | | |
| *SILVER REF./1: UNPRICED DUE TO SCARCITY | | |
| STATED ODDS 1:3 | | |

## 2012 Star Wars Galaxy Series 7 Cels

| | | |
|---|---|---|
| COMPLETE SET (9) | 35.00 | 70.00 |
| COMMON CARD (1-9) | 4.00 | 10.00 |

## 2012 Star Wars Galaxy Series 7 Etched Foil

| | | |
|---|---|---|
| COMPLETE SET (6) | 5.00 | 12.00 |
| COMMON CARD (1-6) | 1.50 | 4.00 |
| *ORIG.ART/1: UNPRICED DUE TO SCARCITY | | |
| STATED ODDS 1:6 | | |

## 2018 Star Wars Galaxy

| | | |
|---|---|---|
| COMPLETE SET (100) | 15.00 | 40.00 |
| UNOPENED BOX (24 PACKS) | 65.00 | 80.00 |
| UNOPENED PACK (8 CARDS) | 3.00 | 4.00 |
| COMMON CARD (1-100) | .40 | 1.00 |
| *BLUE: .6X TO 1.5X BASIC CARDS | | |
| *GREEN: 1.2X TO 3X BASIC CARDS | | |
| *PURPLE/99: 2.5X TO 6X BASIC CARDS | | |
| *ORANGE/25: 6X TO 15X BASIC CARDS | | |
| *RED/1: UNPRICED DUE TO SCARCITY | | |
| *P.P.BLACK/1: UNPRICED DUE TO SCARCITY | | |
| *P.P.CYAN/1: UNPRICED DUE TO SCARCITY | | |
| *P.P.MAGENTA/1: UNPRICED DUE TO SCARCITY | | |
| *P.P.YELLOW/1: UNPRICED DUE TO SCARCITY | | |

## 2018 Star Wars Galaxy Art Patches

| | | |
|---|---|---|
| *BLUE/199: SAME VALUE AS BASIC | | |
| *GREEN/150: .5X TO 1.2X BASIC MEM | | |
| *PURPLE/99: .6X TO 1.5X BASIC MEM | | |
| *ORANGE/25: .75X TO 2X BASIC MEM | | |
| *GOLD/5: UNPRICED DUE TO SCARCITY | | |
| *RED/1: UNPRICED DUE TO SCARCITY | | |
| MD Droids | 8.00 | 20.00 |
| MDV Darth Vader | 8.00 | 20.00 |

| | | |
|---|---|---|
| MHL Han and Leia | 10.00 | 25.00 |
| MJW Jawas | 6.00 | 15.00 |
| MLL Luke and Leia | 10.00 | 25.00 |
| MLS Luke Skywalker | 8.00 | 20.00 |
| MPL Princess Leia | 8.00 | 20.00 |
| MSC Salacious B. Crumb | 6.00 | 15.00 |
| MTR Tusken Raider | 8.00 | 20.00 |
| MWT Wilhuff Tarkin | 6.00 | 15.00 |
| MWW Wicket W. Warrick | 6.00 | 15.00 |
| MXW X-Wings | 8.00 | 20.00 |

## 2018 Star Wars Galaxy Autographs

| | | |
|---|---|---|
| *PURPLE/10: UNPRICED DUE TO SCARCITY | | |
| *ORANGE/5: UNPRICED DUE TO SCARCITY | | |
| *RED/1: UNPRICED DUE TO SCARCITY | | |
| *P.P.BLACK/1: UNPRICED DUE TO SCARCITY | | |
| *P.P.CYAN/1: UNPRICED DUE TO SCARCITY | | |
| *P.P.MAGENTA/1: UNPRICED DUE TO SCARCITY | | |
| *P.P.YELLOW/1: UNPRICED DUE TO SCARCITY | | |
| RANDOMLY INSERTED INTO PACKS | | |
| NNO Adam Driver | | |
| NNO Alan Tudyk | | |
| NNO Amy Allen | 8.00 | 20.00 |
| NNO Andrew Secombe | | |
| NNO Anthony Daniels | | |
| NNO Ashley Eckstein | | |
| NNO Bai Ling | 6.00 | 15.00 |
| NNO Billy Dee Williams | | |
| NNO Carrie Fisher | | |
| NNO Clive Revill | | |
| NNO Daisy Ridley | | |
| NNO Daniel Logan | 12.00 | 30.00 |
| NNO David Tennant | | |
| NNO Deep Roy | | |
| NNO Donnie Yen | | |
| NNO Eric Lopez | 6.00 | 15.00 |
| NNO Felicity Jones | | |
| NNO Forest Whitaker | | |
| NNO Freddie Prinze Jr. | | |
| NNO George Takei | | |
| NNO Gwendoline Christie | | |
| NNO Harrison Ford | | |
| NNO Hayden Christensen | | |
| NNO Hugh Quarshie | | |
| NNO Ian McDiarmid | | |
| NNO James Arnold Taylor | | |
| NNO Jason Isaacs | | |
| NNO Jim Cummings | 6.00 | 15.00 |

| | | | |
|---|---|---|---|
| NNO | John Boyega | | |
| NNO | John Coppinger | 8.00 | 20.00 |
| NNO | Keisha Castle-Hughes | | |
| NNO | Kenny Baker | | |
| NNO | Lloyd Sherr | | |
| NNO | Mary Oyaya | 5.00 | 12.00 |
| NNO | Michael Kingma | | |
| NNO | Michaela Cottrell | 6.00 | 15.00 |
| NNO | Nalini Krishan | 6.00 | 15.00 |
| NNO | Nika Futterman | | |
| NNO | Olivia d'Abo | | |
| NNO | Paul Warren | 5.00 | 12.00 |
| NNO | Peter Mayhew | | |
| NNO | Philip Anthony-Rodriguez | 5.00 | 12.00 |
| NNO | Raija Baroudi | 6.00 | 15.00 |
| NNO | Ralph Brown | 8.00 | 20.00 |
| NNO | Ray Park | | |
| NNO | Riz Ahmed | | |
| NNO | Rohan Nichol | 5.00 | 12.00 |
| NNO | Sam Witwer | | |
| NNO | Sarah Michelle Gellar | | |
| NNO | Stephen Stanton | | |
| NNO | Steven Blum | 5.00 | 12.00 |
| NNO | Tom Baker | | |
| NNO | Tom Kenny | | |
| NNO | Tosin Cole | 5.00 | 12.00 |

### 2018 Star Wars Galaxy Dual Autographs

*ORANGE/5: UNPRICED DUE TO SCARCITY
*RED/1: UNPRICED DUE TO SCARCITY
STATED PRINT RUN 25 SER.#'d SETS

| | | | |
|---|---|---|---|
| NNO | A.Driver/A.Serkis | | |
| NNO | B.Vernel/Y.Ruhian | 15.00 | 40.00 |
| NNO | D.Barclay/G.Home | 15.00 | 40.00 |
| NNO | F.Jones/R.Ahmed | | |
| NNO | G.Takei/A.Eckstein | | |
| NNO | G.Grunberg/K.Rotich | | |
| NNO | J.Boyega/A.Driver | | |
| NNO | J.Boyega/M.Wood | | |
| NNO | N.Futterman/A.Ventress | | |
| NNO | O.Walpole/M.Udall | 12.00 | 30.00 |

### 2018 Star Wars Galaxy Etched Foil Galaxy Puzzle

| | | |
|---|---|---|
| COMPLETE SET (6) | 15.00 | 40.00 |
| COMMON CARD (GP1-GP6) | 4.00 | 10.00 |
| RANDOMLY INSERTED INTO PACKS | | |

### 2018 Star Wars Galaxy Ghost Crew Wanted Posters

| | | |
|---|---|---|
| COMPLETE SET (6) | 5.00 | 12.00 |
| COMMON CARD (P1-P6) | 1.25 | 3.00 |

*P.P.BLACK/1: UNPRICED DUE TO SCARCITY
*P.P.CYAN/1: UNPRICED DUE TO SCARCITY
*P.P.MAGENTA/1: UNPRICED DUE TO SCARCITY
*P.P.YELLOW/1: UNPRICED DUE TO SCARCITY
RANDOMLY INSERTED INTO PACKS

### 2018 Star Wars Galaxy Journey of Ahsoka

| | | |
|---|---|---|
| COMPLETE SET (10) | 6.00 | 15.00 |
| COMMON CARD (1-10) | 1.00 | 2.50 |

*PURPLE/99: .6X TO 1.5X BASIC CARDS
*ORANGE/25: 1.2X TO 3X BASIC CARDS
*RED/1: UNPRICED DUE TO SCARCITY
*P.P.BLACK/1: UNPRICED DUE TO SCARCITY
*P.P.CYAN/1: UNPRICED DUE TO SCARCITY
*P.P.MAGENTA/1: UNPRICED DUE TO SCARCITY
*P.P.YELLOW/1: UNPRICED DUE TO SCARCITY
RANDOMLY INSERTED INTO PACKS

### 2018 Star Wars Galaxy Legends

| | | |
|---|---|---|
| COMPLETE SET (5) | 10.00 | 25.00 |
| COMMON CARD (C1-C5) | 3.00 | 8.00 |

*PURPLE/99: .6X TO 1.5X BASIC CARDS
*RED/1: UNPRICED DUE TO SCARCITY
*P.P.BLACK/1: UNPRICED DUE TO SCARCITY
*P.P.CYAN/1: UNPRICED DUE TO SCARCITY
*P.P.MAGENTA/1: UNPRICED DUE TO SCARCITY
*P.P.YELLOW/1: UNPRICED DUE TO SCARCITY
RANDOMLY INSERTED INTO PACKS

### 2018 Star Wars Galaxy New Trilogy Propaganda

| | | |
|---|---|---|
| COMPLETE SET (6) | 5.00 | 10.00 |
| COMMON CARD (TP1-TP6) | 1.00 | 2.50 |

*P.P.BLACK/1: UNPRICED DUE TO SCARCITY
*P.P.CYAN/1: UNPRICED DUE TO SCARCITY
*P.P.MAGENTA/1: UNPRICED DUE TO SCARCITY
*P.P.YELLOW/1: UNPRICED DUE TO SCARCITY
RANDOMLY INSERTED INTO PACKS

### 2018 Star Wars Galaxy Rogue One Propaganda

| | | |
|---|---|---|
| COMPLETE SET (9) | 6.00 | 15.00 |
| COMMON CARD (RP1-RP9) | 1.25 | 3.00 |

*P.P.BLACK/1: UNPRICED DUE TO SCARCITY
*P.P.CYAN/1: UNPRICED DUE TO SCARCITY
*P.P.MAGENTA/1: UNPRICED DUE TO SCARCITY
*P.P.YELLOW/1: UNPRICED DUE TO SCARCITY
RANDOMLY INSERTED INTO PACKS

### 2018 Star Wars Galaxy Six-Person Autograph

UNPRICED DUE TO SCARCITY

NNO Ridley/Boyega/Dern
Serkis/Driver/Christie

### 2004 Star Wars Heritage

BLESSINGS FROM BEYOND

| | | |
|---|---|---|
| COMPLETE SET (120) | 8.00 | 20.00 |
| UNOPENED BOX (36 PACKS) | 65.00 | 70.00 |
| UNOPENED PACK (5 CARDS) | 2.00 | 2.50 |
| COMMON CARD (1-120) | .15 | .40 |

### 2004 Star Wars Heritage Alphabet Stickers

| | | |
|---|---|---|
| COMPLETE SET (30) | 12.00 | 30.00 |
| STATED ODDS 1:3 RETAIL | | |

### 2004 Star Wars Heritage Autographs

STATED ODDS 1:578

| | | | |
|---|---|---|---|
| NNO | Carrie Fisher | 300.00 | 500.00 |
| NNO | James Earl Jones | 150.00 | 300.00 |
| NNO | Mark Hamill | 600.00 | 1000.00 |

### 2004 Star Wars Heritage Etched Wave One

| | | |
|---|---|---|
| COMPLETE SET (6) | 6.00 | 15.00 |
| COMMON CARD (1-6) | 1.25 | 3.00 |
| STATED ODDS 1:9 | | |

### 2004 Star Wars Heritage Etched Wave Two

| | | |
|---|---|---|
| COMPLETE SET (6) | 6.00 | 15.00 |
| COMMON CARD (1-6) | 1.25 | 3.00 |
| STATED ODDS 1:9 | | |

### 2004 Star Wars Heritage Promos

| | | |
|---|---|---|
| COMMON CARD (P1-P6, S1) | .75 | 2.00 |
| P1 The Phantom Menace | 2.00 | 5.00 |
| P2 Attack of the Clones | 6.00 | 15.00 |
| P6 Return of the Jedi | 2.00 | 5.00 |
| S1 Empire Strikes Back CT UK | 2.50 | 6.00 |

### 2015 Star Wars High Tek

| | | |
|---|---|---|
| COMPLETE SET w/o SP (112) | 60.00 | 120.00 |
| COMPLETE SET w/SP (127) | 250.00 | 500.00 |
| UNOPENED BOX (8 CARDS) | 100.00 | 120.00 |
| COMMON CARD (1-112) | .40 | 1.00 |

*DS CORE: .5X TO 1.2X BASIC CARDS
*HOTH TAC.: .5X TO 1.2X BASIC CARDS
*TIE FRONT: .6X TO 1.5X BASIC CARDS
*VADER TIE: .6X TO 1.5X BASIC CARDS
*MIL.FALCON: .75X TO 2X BASIC CARDS
*STAR DEST.: .75X TO 2X BASIC CARDS
*CARBON: 1X TO 2.5X BASIC CARDS
*EMP.THRONE: 1X TO 2.5X BASIC CARDS

*DS EXT.: 2X TO 5X BASIC CARDS
*TIE WING: 2X TO 5X BASIC CARDS
TIDAL/99: 1.2X TO 3X BASIC CARDS
GOLD RAINBOW/50: 1.5X TO 4X BASIC CARDS
CLOUDS/25: 2X TO 5X BASIC CARDS
RED ORBIT/5: UNPRICED DUE TO SCARCITY
BLACK GALACTIC/1: UNPRICED DUE TO SCARCITY
*P.P.BLACK/1: UNPRICED DUE TO SCARCITY
*P.P.CYAN/1: UNPRICED DUE TO SCARCITY
*P.P.MAGENTA/1: UNPRICED DUE TO SCARCITY
*P.P.YELLOW/1: UNPRICED DUE TO SCARCITY

| | | |
|---|---|---|
| 1A Luke | 3.00 | 8.00 |
| lightsaber | | |
| 1B Luke | 10.00 | 25.00 |
| blaster SP | | |
| 1C Luke | 12.00 | 30.00 |
| Jedi Knight SP | | |
| 2A Leia | 3.00 | 8.00 |
| A New Hope | | |
| 2B Leia | 15.00 | 40.00 |
| Bespin uniform SP | | |
| 2C Leia | 120.00 | 200.00 |
| Slave SP | | |
| 3A Han Solo | 4.00 | 10.00 |
| blaster | | |
| 3B Han Solo | 20.00 | 50.00 |
| Bespin SP | | |
| 3C Han Solo | 12.00 | 30.00 |
| Endor SP | | |
| 4 Darth Vader | 5.00 | 12.00 |
| 5A The Emperor | 2.00 | 5.00 |
| 5B Sheev Palpatine SP | 4.00 | 10.00 |
| 5C Darth Sidious SP | 12.00 | 30.00 |
| 6 Yoda | 1.25 | 3.00 |
| 7A C-3PO | 4.00 | 10.00 |
| shiny chrome | | |
| 7B C-3PO | 8.00 | 20.00 |
| dirty chrome SP | | |
| 8 R2-D2 | 1.25 | 3.00 |
| 9 Chewbacca | 1.25 | 3.00 |
| 10A Lando | 2.00 | 5.00 |
| cape | | |
| 10B Lando | 8.00 | 20.00 |
| blaster SP | | |
| 11 Boba Fett | 2.00 | 5.00 |
| 36A Anakin Skywalker | 1.25 | 3.00 |
| 36B Anakin | 6.00 | 15.00 |
| two lightsabers SP | | |
| 37A Obi-Wan Kenobi | 1.25 | 3.00 |
| 37B Obi-Wan | 12.00 | 30.00 |
| young SP | | |
| 37C Obi-Wan | 8.00 | 20.00 |
| old SP | | |
| 40A Padme | 1.25 | 3.00 |
| dark dress | | |
| 40B Padme Amidala | 10.00 | 25.00 |
| white outfit SP | | |
| 42 Darth Maul | 1.25 | 3.00 |
| 44B Boba Fett | 25.00 | 60.00 |
| armor SP | | |
| 88 Anakin Skywalker | 1.25 | 3.00 |
| 94 The Inquisitor | .75 | 2.00 |
| 106 Finn | 3.00 | 8.00 |
| 107 Kylo Ren | 3.00 | 8.00 |
| 108 Rey | 5.00 | 12.00 |

| | | |
|---|---|---|
| 109 Poe Dameron | 3.00 | 8.00 |
| 110 BB-8 | 4.00 | 10.00 |
| 111 Captain Phasma | 3.00 | 8.00 |
| 112 Flametrooper | 2.00 | 5.00 |

## 2015 Star Wars High Tek Armor Tek

| | | |
|---|---|---|
| COMPLETE SET (10) | 120.00 | 250.00 |
| COMMON CARD (AT1-AT10) | 8.00 | 20.00 |
| STATED PRINT RUN 50 SER.#'d SETS | | |
| AT1 Boba Fett | 15.00 | 40.00 |
| AT3 Commander Cody | 15.00 | 40.00 |
| AT4 Darth Vader | 20.00 | 50.00 |
| AT5 Jango Fett | 12.00 | 30.00 |
| AT7 Luke Skywalker | 12.00 | 30.00 |
| AT8 Sabine Wren | 10.00 | 25.00 |
| AT9 Poe Dameron | 15.00 | 40.00 |
| AT10 Kylo Ren | 15.00 | 40.00 |

## 2015 Star Wars High Tek Autographs

| | | |
|---|---|---|
| COMMON AUTO | 6.00 | 15.00 |
| *TIDAL/75: .5X TO 1.2X BASIC AUTOS | | |
| *GOLD RAINBOW/50: .6X TO 1.5X BASIC AUTOS | | |
| *CLOUDS/25: .75X TO 2X BASIC AUTOS | | |
| *RED ORBIT/5: UNPRICED DUE TO SCARCITY | | |
| *P.P.BLACK/1: UNPRICED DUE TO SCARCITY | | |
| *P.P.CYAN/1: UNPRICED DUE TO SCARCITY | | |
| *P.P.MAGENTA/1: UNPRICED DUE TO SCARCITY | | |
| *P.P.YELLOW/1: UNPRICED DUE TO SCARCITY | | |
| 2 Carrie Fisher | 200.00 | 400.00 |
| 4 David Prowse | 120.00 | 250.00 |
| 6 Deep Roy | 20.00 | 50.00 |
| 7 Anthony Daniels | 80.00 | 150.00 |
| 9 Peter Mayhew | 25.00 | 60.00 |
| 11 Jeremy Bulloch | 15.00 | 40.00 |
| 12 Paul Blake | 10.00 | 25.00 |
| 14 Alan Harris | 8.00 | 20.00 |
| 16 Tim Rose | 10.00 | 25.00 |
| 20 Warwick Davis | 12.00 | 30.00 |
| 23 Dickey Beer | 10.00 | 25.00 |
| 27 John Ratzenberger | 10.00 | 25.00 |
| 28 Pam Rose | 30.00 | 80.00 |
| 29 Dickey Beer | 15.00 | 40.00 |
| 30 Paul Brooke | 10.00 | 25.00 |
| 42 Ray Park | 20.00 | 50.00 |
| 49 Bai Ling | 8.00 | 20.00 |
| 57 Amy Allen | 10.00 | 25.00 |
| 61 Silas Carson | 10.00 | 25.00 |
| 78 Bruce Spence | 8.00 | 20.00 |
| 79 Wayne Pygram | 10.00 | 25.00 |

| | | |
|---|---|---|
| 80 Silas Carson | 10.00 | 25.00 |
| 90 Andy Secombe | 8.00 | 20.00 |
| 96 Taylor Gray | 10.00 | 25.00 |
| 97 Vanessa Marshall | 8.00 | 20.00 |
| 100 Tiya Sircar | 12.00 | 30.00 |
| 102 Ashley Eckstein | 10.00 | 25.00 |
| 104 George Takei | 20.00 | 50.00 |
| 105 Dee Bradley Baker | 12.00 | 30.00 |

## 2015 Star Wars High Tek Moments of Power

| | | |
|---|---|---|
| COMPLETE SET (15) | 175.00 | 350.00 |
| COMMON CARD (MP1-MP15) | 8.00 | 20.00 |
| STATED PRINT RUN 50 SER.#'d SETS | | |
| MP1 Anakin Skywalker | 10.00 | 25.00 |
| MP2 Darth Maul | 12.00 | 30.00 |
| MP3 Obi-Wan Kenobi | 15.00 | 40.00 |
| MP4 Padme Amidala | 12.00 | 30.00 |
| MP6 Yoda | 12.00 | 30.00 |
| MP7 The Emperor | 10.00 | 25.00 |
| MP8 Han Solo | 20.00 | 50.00 |
| MP9 Luke Skywalker | 15.00 | 40.00 |
| MP10 Boba Fett | 15.00 | 40.00 |
| MP11 Chewbacca | 10.00 | 25.00 |
| MP13 Princess Leia Organa | 15.00 | 40.00 |
| MP15 Darth Vader | 20.00 | 50.00 |

## 2015 Star Wars High Tek Tek Heads

| | | |
|---|---|---|
| COMPLETE SET (15) | 150.00 | 275.00 |
| COMMON CARD (TH1-TH15) | 6.00 | 15.00 |
| STATED PRINT RUN 50 SER.#'d SETS | | |
| TH1 Darth Vader | 20.00 | 50.00 |
| TH2 C-3PO | 10.00 | 25.00 |
| TH3 Luke Skywalker | 10.00 | 25.00 |
| TH4 R2-D2 | 8.00 | 20.00 |
| TH5 IG-88 | 8.00 | 20.00 |
| TH7 BB-8 | 12.00 | 30.00 |
| TH8 FX-7 | 8.00 | 20.00 |
| TH10 2-1B | 10.00 | 25.00 |
| TH12 R7-A7 | 10.00 | 25.00 |
| TH13 General Grievous | 8.00 | 20.00 |
| TH14 Chopper | 10.00 | 25.00 |

## 2016 Star Wars High Tek

| | | |
|---|---|---|
| COMPLETE SET W/O SP (112) | 100.00 | 200.00 |
| COMPLETE SET W/SP (127) | 300.00 | 600.00 |
| UNOPENED BOX (1 PACK/8 CARDS) | 50.00 | 60.00 |
| COMMON CARD (SW1-SW112) | 1.25 | 3.00 |

*F1P1: SAME VALUE AS BASIC
*F1P2: SAME VALUE AS BASIC
*F1P3: .75X TO 2X BASIC CARDS
*F1P4: .75X TO 2X BASIC CARDS
*F1P5: 1.5X TO 4X BASIC CARDS
*F2P1: SAME VALUE AS BASIC
*F2P2: SAME VALUE AS BASIC
*F2P3: .75X TO 2X BASIC CARDS
*F2P4: 1X TO 2.5X BASIC CARDS
*F2P5: 1.50X TO 4X BASIC CARDS
*BLUE RAIN/99: .75X TO 2X BASIC CARDS
*GOLD RAIN/50: 1.5X TO 4X BASIC CARDS
*ORANGE MAGMA/25: 3X TO 6X BASIC CARDS
*GREEN CUBE/10: 4X TO 10X BASIC CARDS
*RED ORBIT/5: 6X TO 15X BASIC CARDS
*BLACK GALACTIC/1: UNPRICED DUE TO SCARCITY
*P.P.BLACK/1: UNPRICED DUE TO SCARCITY
*P.P.CYAN/1: UNPRICED DUE TO SCARCITY
*P.P.MAGENTA/1: UNPRICED DUE TO SCARCITY
*P.P.YELLOW/1: UNPRICED DUE TO SCARCITY

| | | |
|---|---|---|
| SW60A Kylo Ren | 15.00 | 40.00 |
| Dark Side Disciple SP | | |
| SW72A General Leia Organa | 25.00 | 60.00 |
| Resistance Leader SP | | |
| SW75A Rey | 15.00 | 40.00 |
| Jakku Scavenger SP | | |
| SW75B Rey | 80.00 | 150.00 |
| Force Sensitive SP | | |
| SW75C Rey | 60.00 | 120.00 |
| Starkiller Base Duel SP | | |
| SW76A FN-2187 | 30.00 | 80.00 |
| First Order Stormtrooper SP | | |
| SW76B Flametrooper | 12.00 | 30.00 |
| First Order Infantry SP | | |
| SW76C Snowtrooper | 12.00 | 30.00 |
| First Order Infantry SP | | |
| SW76D TIE Pilot | 12.00 | 30.00 |
| First Order Pilot SP | | |
| SW84A Han Solo | 50.00 | 100.00 |
| Smuggler SP | | |
| SW87A Finn | 30.00 | 80.00 |
| Resistance Warrior SP | | |
| SW87B Finn | 20.00 | 50.00 |
| Resistance Fighter SP | | |
| SW88A Chewbacca | 30.00 | 80.00 |
| Millennium Falcon Co-Pilot SP | | |

| | | |
|---|---|---|
| SW100A Poe Dameron | 25.00 | 60.00 |
| Resistance Messenger SP | | |
| SW100B Poe Dameron | 15.00 | 40.00 |
| Resistance Pilot SP | | |

## 2016 Star Wars High Tek Armor Tek

| | | |
|---|---|---|
| COMMON CARD (AT1-AT11) | 8.00 | 20.00 |
| STATED PRINT RUN 50 SER.#'d SETS | | |
| AT1 Kylo Ren | 15.00 | 40.00 |
| AT2 Captain Phasma | 12.00 | 30.00 |
| AT3 Poe Dameron | 10.00 | 25.00 |
| AT6 First Order Tie Fighter Pilot | 12.00 | 30.00 |
| AT7 First Order Stormtrooper | 12.00 | 30.00 |
| AT8 Rey | 20.00 | 50.00 |
| AT9 Stormtrooper (Heavy Gunner) | 10.00 | 25.00 |
| AT11 Sidon Ithano | 12.00 | 30.00 |

## 2016 Star Wars High Tek Autographs

| | | |
|---|---|---|
| COMMON CARD | 5.00 | 12.00 |

*BLUE RAIN/75: .5X TO 1.2X BASIC CARDS
*GOLD RAIN/50: .6X TO 1.5X BASIC CARDS
*ORANGE MAGMA/25: .75X TO 2X BASIC CARDS
*GREEN CUBE/10: UNPRICED DUE TO SCARCITY
*RED ORBIT/5: UNPRICED DUE TO SCARCITY
*BLACK GALACTIC/1: UNPRICED DUE TO SCARCITY
*P.P.BLACK/1: UNPRICED DUE TO SCARCITY
*P.P.CYAN/1: UNPRICED DUE TO SCARCITY
*P.P.MAGENTA/1: UNPRICED DUE TO SCARCITY
*P.P.YELLOW/1: UNPRICED DUE TO SCARCITY

| | | |
|---|---|---|
| 3 Aidan Cook/Cookie Tuggs | 8.00 | 20.00 |
| 4 Alan Ruscoe/Bib Fortuna | 6.00 | 15.00 |
| 6 Amy Allen | 8.00 | 20.00 |
| 8 Anna Brewster | 8.00 | 20.00 |
| 10 Ashley Eckstein | 10.00 | 25.00 |
| 13 Brian Vernel | 6.00 | 15.00 |
| 15 Catherine Taber | 6.00 | 15.00 |
| 17 Cristina da Silva | 8.00 | 20.00 |
| 20 Dave Barclay | 8.00 | 20.00 |
| 21 David Acord/Med.Droid | 6.00 | 15.00 |
| 22 David Acord/Voiceover | 6.00 | 15.00 |
| 23 David Bowers | 6.00 | 15.00 |
| 24 Dee Bradley Baker | 6.00 | 15.00 |
| 26 Dickey Beer | | |
| 30 Harriet Walter | 6.00 | 15.00 |
| 33 Jeremy Bulloch | 12.00 | 30.00 |
| 38 Julie Dolan | 8.00 | 20.00 |
| 39 Kiran Shah | 6.00 | 15.00 |
| 40 Marc Silk | 6.00 | 15.00 |
| 42 Mark Dodson/S.Crumb | 6.00 | 15.00 |
| 45 Michael Kingma | 6.00 | 15.00 |
| 47 Mike Edmonds | 6.00 | 15.00 |
| 48 Mike Quinn | 8.00 | 20.00 |

| | | |
|---|---|---|
| 50 Paul Blake | 6.00 | 15.00 |
| 51 Paul Springer | 6.00 | 15.00 |
| 57 Sam Witwer | 8.00 | 20.00 |
| 59 Sebastian Armesto | 6.00 | 15.00 |
| 60 Silas Carson | 8.00 | 20.00 |
| 62 Taylor Gray | 6.00 | 15.00 |
| 63 Tim Rose | 6.00 | 15.00 |
| 64 Tiya Sircar | 6.00 | 15.00 |
| 66 Tosin Cole | 10.00 | 25.00 |

## 2016 Star Wars High Tek Autographs Gold Rainbow

*GOLD RAINBOW/50: .6X TO 1.5X BASIC CARDS

| | | |
|---|---|---|
| 12 Brian Herring | 25.00 | 60.00 |
| 25 Denis Lawson | 15.00 | 40.00 |
| 67 Warwick Davis | 12.00 | 30.00 |

## 2016 Star Wars High Tek Autographs Orange Magma Diffractor

*ORANGE MAGMA/25: .75X TO 2X BASIC CARDS

| | | |
|---|---|---|
| 14 Carrie Fisher | 250.00 | 500.00 |
| 28 Freddie Prinze Jr. | 30.00 | 80.00 |
| 37 John Boyega | 120.00 | 250.00 |

## 2016 Star Wars High Tek Living Tek

| | | |
|---|---|---|
| COMMON CARD (LT1-LT13) | 6.00 | 15.00 |
| STATED PRINT RUN 50 SER.#'d SETS | | |
| LT1 Crusher Roodown | 10.00 | 25.00 |
| LT2 Luke Skywalker | 15.00 | 40.00 |
| LT3 C-3PO | 8.00 | 20.00 |
| LT4 BB-8 | 12.00 | 30.00 |
| LT5 GA-97 | 8.00 | 20.00 |
| LT6 Luggabeast | 8.00 | 20.00 |
| LT7 PZ-4CO | 8.00 | 20.00 |
| LT9 B-U4D | 12.00 | 30.00 |
| LT11 Sidon Ithano | 12.00 | 30.00 |
| LT12 HURID-327 | 8.00 | 20.00 |
| LT13 R2-D2 | 8.00 | 20.00 |

## 2017 Star Wars High Tek

| | | |
|---|---|---|
| UNOPENED BOX (1 PACK OF 8 CARDS) | 50.00 | 80.00 |
| COMMON FORM 1 (1-56) | 1.00 | 2.50 |
| COMMON FORM 2 (57-112) | 1.50 | 4.00 |
| *F1P1: .75X TO 2X BASIC CARDS | 2.00 | 5.00 |
| *F1P2: .75X TO 2X BASIC CARDS | 2.00 | 5.00 |
| *F1P3: 1X TO 2.5X BASIC CARDS | 2.50 | 6.00 |
| *F2P1: .6X TO 1.5X BASIC CARDS | 2.50 | 6.00 |
| *F2P3: .6X TO 1.5X BASIC CARDS | 2.50 | 6.00 |
| *TIDAL DIFF./99: 1X TO 2.5X BASIC CARDS | 2.50 | 6.00 |
| *F2P2: .75X TO 2X BASIC CARDS | 3.00 | 8.00 |
| *GOLD R.F./50: 1.2X TO 3X BASIC CARDS | 3.00 | 8.00 |
| *F1P4: 2X TO 5X BASIC CARDS | 5.00 | 12.00 |
| *F2P4: 1.2X TO 3X BASIC CARDS | 5.00 | 12.00 |
| *F1P5: 3X TO 8X BASIC CARDS | 8.00 | 20.00 |
| *F2P5: UNPRICED DUE TO SCARCITY | | |
| *ORANGE DIFF./25: UNPRICED DUE TO SCARCITY | | |
| *GREEN DIFF./10: UNPRICED DUE TO SCARCITY | | |
| *RED DIFF./5: UNPRICED DUE TO SCARCITY | | |
| *BLACK DIFF./1: UNPRICED DUE TO SCARCITY | | |
| *P.P.BLACK/1: UNPRICED DUE TO SCARCITY | | |
| *P.P.CYAN/1: UNPRICED DUE TO SCARCITY | | |
| *P.P.MAGENTA/1: UNPRICED DUE TO SCARCITY | | |
| *P.P.YELLOW/1: UNPRICED DUE TO SCARCITY | | |
| 7 Rey | 2.50 | 6.00 |
| 14 Han Solo | 1.50 | 4.00 |
| 15 Luke Skywalker | 1.50 | 4.00 |
| 16 Princess Leia Organa | 3.00 | 8.00 |
| 20 Jango Fett | 2.00 | 5.00 |
| 36 Boba Fett | 1.50 | 4.00 |
| 53 Kylo Ren | 1.25 | 3.00 |
| 56 Yoda | 1.25 | 3.00 |
| 57 Jyn Erso | 4.00 | 10.00 |
| 62 Chirrut Imwe | 2.00 | 5.00 |
| 68 Darth Vader | 2.00 | 5.00 |

### 2017 Star Wars High Tek Autographs

| | | |
|---|---|---|
| *GREEN DIFF./10: UNPRICED DUE TO SCARCITY | | |
| *RED DIFF./5: UNPRICED DUE TO SCARCITY | | |
| *BLACK DIFF./1: UNPRICED DUE TO SCARCITY | | |
| *P.P.BLACK/1: UNPRICED DUE TO SCARCITY | | |
| *P.P.CYAN/1: UNPRICED DUE TO SCARCITY | | |
| *P.P.MAGENTA/1: UNPRICED DUE TO SCARCITY | | |
| *P.P.YELLOW/1: UNPRICED DUE TO SCARCITY | | |
| RANDOMLY INSERTED INTO PACKS | | |
| NNO Adrienne Wilkinson | 6.00 | 15.00 |
| NNO Alistair Petrie | 6.00 | 15.00 |
| NNO Angus MacInnes | 6.00 | 15.00 |
| NNO Anthony Forest | 6.00 | 15.00 |
| NNO Ariyon Bakare | 10.00 | 25.00 |

| | | |
|---|---|---|
| NNO Ashley Eckstein | 10.00 | 25.00 |
| NNO Ben Daniels | 6.00 | 15.00 |
| NNO Brian Herring | 15.00 | 40.00 |
| NNO Cathy Munroe | 12.00 | 30.00 |
| NNO Chris Parsons | 8.00 | 20.00 |
| NNO Daniel Mays | 15.00 | 40.00 |
| NNO David Acord | 6.00 | 15.00 |
| NNO Derek Arnold | 6.00 | 15.00 |
| NNO Duncan Pow | 6.00 | 15.00 |
| NNO Guy Henry | 20.00 | 50.00 |
| NNO Ian McElhinney | 6.00 | 15.00 |
| NNO Ian Whyte | 6.00 | 15.00 |
| NNO Jeremy Bulloch | 15.00 | 40.00 |
| NNO Jordan Stephens | 10.00 | 25.00 |
| NNO Lars Mikkelsen | 10.00 | 25.00 |
| NNO Lloyd Sherr | 6.00 | 15.00 |
| NNO Matthew Wood | 6.00 | 15.00 |
| NNO Olivia d'Abo | 6.00 | 15.00 |
| NNO Stephen Stanton | | |
| NNO Valene Kane | 10.00 | 25.00 |
| NNO Zarene Dallas | 6.00 | 15.00 |

### 2017 Star Wars High Tek Heroes and Villains of The Force Awakens

| | | |
|---|---|---|
| COMPLETE SET (20) | 150.00 | 300.00 |
| COMMON CARD (HV1-HV20) | 6.00 | 15.00 |
| STATED PRINT RUN 50 SER.#'d SETS | | |
| HV1 Han Solo | 10.00 | 25.00 |
| HV2 Luke Skywalker | 10.00 | 25.00 |
| HV4 Kylo Ren | 8.00 | 20.00 |
| HV5 Rey | 20.00 | 50.00 |
| HV6 Finn | 12.00 | 30.00 |
| HV8 Supreme Leader Snoke | 8.00 | 20.00 |
| HV9 R2-D2 | 10.00 | 25.00 |
| HV12 Snap Wexley | 10.00 | 25.00 |
| HV13 Captain Phasma | 8.00 | 20.00 |
| HV14 General Hux | 8.00 | 20.00 |
| HV17 Ello Asty | 8.00 | 20.00 |
| HV18 Unkar Plutt | 8.00 | 20.00 |
| HV19 Chewbacca | 10.00 | 25.00 |
| HV20 Riot Control Stormtrooper | 12.00 | 30.00 |

### 2017 Star Wars High Tek A More Elegant Weapon

| | | |
|---|---|---|
| COMMON CARD (MW1-MW10) | 10.00 | 25.00 |
| STATED PRINT RUN 50 SER.#'d SETS | | |
| MW1 Yoda | 15.00 | 40.00 |
| MW2 Ahsoka Tano | 12.00 | 30.00 |
| MW3 Anakin Skywalker | 12.00 | 30.00 |
| MW5 Rey | 30.00 | 75.00 |
| MW6 Luke Skywalker | 15.00 | 40.00 |
| MW7 Darth Vader | 15.00 | 40.00 |
| MW8 Obi-Wan Kenobi | 12.00 | 30.00 |
| MW10 Mace Windu | 12.00 | 30.00 |

### 2017 Star Wars High Tek Rogue One Vehicles

| | | |
|---|---|---|
| STATED PRINT RUN 50 SER.#'d SETS | | |
| RV1 Jyn Erso/U-wing | 10.00 | 25.00 |
| RV2 Gunner/Death Star | 6.00 | 15.00 |
| RV3 Krennic/Krennic's Shuttle | 12.00 | 30.00 |
| RV4 Tank Commander/Combat Assault Tank | 6.00 | 15.00 |
| RV5 Tarkin/Imperial Star Destroyer | 8.00 | 20.00 |
| RV6 Merrick/X-wing | 12.00 | 30.00 |
| RV7 TIE Striker Pilot/TIE Striker | | |
| RV8 Cassian Andor/U-wing | | |
| RV9 K-2SO/U-wing | | |
| RV10 Bodhi Rook/Imperial Zeta-Class Transport | 6.00 | 15.00 |

### 2017 Star Wars High Tek Troopers

| | | |
|---|---|---|
| COMMON CARD (TR1-TR16) | 6.00 | 15.00 |
| STATED PRINT RUN 50 SER.#'d SETS | | |
| TR1 First Order TIE Fighter Pilot | 10.00 | 25.00 |
| TR2 First Order Stormtrooper | 8.00 | 20.00 |
| TR3 First Order Riot Control Stormtrooper | 10.00 | 25.00 |
| TR9 Imperial Death Trooper | 15.00 | 40.00 |
| TR12 Imperial Sandtrooper | 10.00 | 25.00 |
| TR14 Imperial TIE Fighter Pilot | 8.00 | 20.00 |
| TR15 Galactic Republic Clone Trooper | 8.00 | 20.00 |
| TR16 Galactic Marine | 10.00 | 25.00 |

### 2015 Star Wars Honey Maid

| | | |
|---|---|---|
| COMPLETE SET (12) | 3.00 | 8.00 |
| COMMON CARD | .40 | 1.00 |
| PAN1 Obi-Wan Kenobi | 2.00 | 5.00 |
| Darth Vader#{Han Solo#{Chewbacca#{Storm Trooper#{C-3PO | | |
| PAN2 R2-D2 | 2.00 | 5.00 |
| The Emperor#{Yoda#{Luke Skywalker#{Boba Fett#{Princess Leia Organa | | |

### 2013 Star Wars Jedi Legacy

| | | |
|---|---|---|
| COMPLETE SET (90) | 6.00 | 15.00 |
| UNOPENED BOX (24 PACKS) | 60.00 | 70.00 |
| UNOPENED PACK (8 CARDS) | 2.50 | 3.00 |
| COMMON CARD (1A-45L) | .20 | .50 |
| *BLUE: 1.2X TO 3X BASIC CARDS | | |
| *MAGENTA: 4X TO 10X BASIC CARDS | | |
| *GREEN: 5X TO 12X BASIC CARDS | | |
| *GOLD/10: 50X TO 120X BASIC CARDS | | |
| *P.P.BLACK/1: UNPRICED DUE TO SCARCITY | | |
| *P.P.CYAN/1: UNPRICED DUE TO SCARCITY | | |
| *P.P.MAGENTA/1: UNPRICED DUE TO SCARCITY | | |
| *P.P.YELLOW/1: UNPRICED DUE TO SCARCITY | | |

### 2013 Star Wars Jedi Legacy Autographs

| | | |
|---|---|---|
| COMMON CARD (UNNUMBERED) | 10.00 | 25.00 |
| STATED ODDS 1:72 | | |
| NNO Alan Harris | 20.00 | 50.00 |

| | | | |
|---|---|---|---|
| NNO | Anthony Daniels | 200.00 | 400.00 |
| NNO | Billy Dee Williams | 125.00 | 250.00 |
| NNO | Carrie Fisher | 300.00 | 500.00 |
| NNO | Harrison Ford | 1750.00 | 2500.00 |
| NNO | Ian McDiarmid | 300.00 | 500.00 |
| NNO | James Earl Jones | 150.00 | 300.00 |
| NNO | Jeremy Bulloch | 30.00 | 60.00 |
| NNO | John Morton | 15.00 | 40.00 |
| NNO | Kenneth Colley | 15.00 | 40.00 |
| NNO | Kenny Baker | 30.00 | 60.00 |
| NNO | Mark Hamill | 400.00 | 600.00 |
| NNO | Tim Rose | 15.00 | 40.00 |

### 2013 Star Wars Jedi Legacy Chewbacca Fur Relics

| | | |
|---|---|---|
| COMMON CARD (CR1-CR4) | 75.00 | 150.00 |
| STATED ODDS 1:720 | | |

### 2013 Star Wars Jedi Legacy Connections

| | | |
|---|---|---|
| COMPLETE SET (15) | 5.00 | 12.00 |
| COMMON CARD (C1-C15) | .60 | 1.50 |
| *P.P.BLACK/1: UNPRICED DUE TO SCARCITY | | |
| *P.P.CYAN/1: UNPRICED DUE TO SCARCITY | | |
| *P.P.MAGENTA/1: UNPRICED DUE TO SCARCITY | | |
| *P.P.YELLOW/1: UNPRICED DUE TO SCARCITY | | |
| STATED ODDS 1:2 | | |

### 2013 Star Wars Jedi Legacy Ewok Fur Relics

| | | |
|---|---|---|
| COMMON CARD (ER1-ER4) | 20.00 | 50.00 |
| STATED ODDS 1:120 | | |
| ER1 Wicket W. Warrick | 35.00 | 70.00 |
| ER4 Widdle Warrick | 50.00 | 100.00 |

### 2013 Star Wars Jedi Legacy Film Cels

| | | |
|---|---|---|
| COMMON CARD (FR1-FR30) | 10.00 | 25.00 |
| STATED ODDS 1:BOX | | |
| FR6 Darth Vader | 20.00 | 50.00 |

### 2013 Star Wars Jedi Legacy Dual Film Cels

| | | |
|---|---|---|
| COMPLETE SET (6) | 120.00 | 250.00 |
| COMMON CARD (DFR1-DFR6) | 20.00 | 50.00 |
| STATED ODDS 1:144 | | |
| DFR1 Darth Vader/Luke Skywalker | 30.00 | 60.00 |

### 2013 Star Wars Jedi Legacy Triple Film Cels

| | | |
|---|---|---|
| COMPLETE SET (10) | 250.00 | 500.00 |
| COMMON CARD (TFR1-TFR10) | 30.00 | 60.00 |
| STATED ODDS 1:144 | | |

### 2013 Star Wars Jedi Legacy Influencers

| | | |
|---|---|---|
| COMPLETE SET (18) | 5.00 | 12.00 |
| COMMON CARD (I1-I18) | .50 | 1.25 |

---

| | | |
|---|---|---|
| *P.P.BLACK/1: UNPRICED DUE TO SCARCITY | | |
| *P.P.CYAN/1: UNPRICED DUE TO SCARCITY | | |
| *P.P.MAGENTA/1: UNPRICED DUE TO SCARCITY | | |
| *P.P.YELLOW/1: UNPRICED DUE TO SCARCITY | | |
| STATED ODDS 1:2 | | |

### 2013 Star Wars Jedi Legacy Jabba's Sail Barge Relics

| | | |
|---|---|---|
| COMPLETE SET (5) | 300.00 | 600.00 |
| COMMON CARD (JR1-JR5) | 50.00 | 100.00 |
| STATED ODDS 1:336 | | |
| JR1 Luke Skywalker | 125.00 | 200.00 |
| JR2 Leia Organa | 100.00 | 175.00 |
| JR3 Boba Fett | 75.00 | 150.00 |

### 2013 Star Wars Jedi Legacy The Circle is Now Complete

| | | |
|---|---|---|
| COMPLETE SET (12) | 35.00 | 70.00 |
| COMMON CARD (CC1-CC12) | 4.00 | 10.00 |
| *P.P.BLACK/1: UNPRICED DUE TO SCARCITY | | |
| *P.P.CYAN/1: UNPRICED DUE TO SCARCITY | | |
| *P.P.MAGENTA/1: UNPRICED DUE TO SCARCITY | | |
| *P.P.YELLOW/1: UNPRICED DUE TO SCARCITY | | |
| STATED ODDS 1:12 | | |
| NNO1 Luke Skywalker PROMO | | |

### 2013 Star Wars Jedi Legacy Promos

| | | |
|---|---|---|
| COMMON CARD | 3.00 | 8.00 |
| P1 Battle Through Blood | 8.00 | 20.00 |
| (Darth Vader) | | |
| P2 Battle Through Blood | 8.00 | 20.00 |
| (Luke Skywalker) | | |
| P3 Challenge of a Fallen Jedi | 8.00 | 20.00 |
| (Anakin vs. Count Dooku) | | |
| P4 Challenge of a Fallen Jedi | 8.00 | 20.00 |
| (Luke vs. Vader) | | |
| P5 Death of a Mentor | 3.00 | 8.00 |
| (Qui Gon vs. Darth Maul)#{(Philly Non-Sports Show Exclusive) | | |
| NNO Darth Vader Disc | 1.50 | 4.00 |
| NNO Luke Skywalker Disc | 1.50 | 4.00 |
| NNO Two Paths. Two Journeys. One Destiny | | |
| (5 X 7 Jumbo) | | |

---

### 2015 Star Wars Journey to The Force Awakens

Star Wars: The Force Awakens™

| | | |
|---|---|---|
| COMPLETE SET (110) | 10.00 | 25.00 |
| COMMON CARD (1-110) | .20 | .50 |
| *JABBA SLIME GREEN: .5X TO 1.2X BASIC CARDS | | |
| *BLACK: .6X TO 1.5X BASIC CARDS | | |
| *DEATH STAR SILVER: .75X TO 2X BASIC CARDS | | |
| *LTSBR. NEON PINK: 1.5X TO 4X BASIC CARDS | | |
| *PURPLE: 4X TO 10X BASIC CARDS | | |
| *HOTH ICE/150: 6X TO 15X BASIC CARDS | | |
| *GOLD/50: 10X TO 25X BASIC CARDS | | |
| *HOLOGRAM/25: 15X TO 40X BASIC CARDS | | |
| *RED IMPERIAL/1: UNPRICED DUE TO SCARCITY | | |
| *P.P. BLACK/1: UNPRICED DUE TO SCARCITY | | |
| *P.P. CYAN/1: UNPRICED DUE TO SCARCITY | | |
| *P.P. MAGENTA/1: UNPRICED DUE TO SCARCITY | | |
| *P.P. YELLOW/1: UNPRICED DUE TO SCARCITY | | |

### 2015 Star Wars Journey to The Force Awakens Autographs

Alan Harris

ALAN HARRIS
AUTHENTIC AUTOGRAPH

| | | | |
|---|---|---|---|
| COMMON AUTO | | 8.00 | 20.00 |
| *SILVER/50: .75X TO 2X BASIC AUTOS | | | |
| *GOLD/10: UNPRICED DUE TO SCARCITY | | | |
| *RED/1: UNPRICED DUE TO SCARCITY | | | |
| *P.P.BLACK/1: UNPRICED DUE TO SCARCITY | | | |
| *P.P.CYAN/1: UNPRICED DUE TO SCARCITY | | | |
| *P.P.MAGENTA/1: UNPRICED DUE TO SCARCITY | | | |
| *P.P.YELLOW/1: UNPRICED DUE TO SCARCITY | | | |
| NNO | Alan Harris | 10.00 | 25.00 |
| NNO | Amy Allen | 12.00 | 30.00 |
| NNO | Angus MacInnes | 8.00 | 20.00 |
| NNO | Anthony Daniels | 200.00 | 400.00 |
| NNO | Ashley Eckstein | 15.00 | 40.00 |
| NNO | Bai Ling | 15.00 | 40.00 |
| NNO | Billy Dee Williams | 50.00 | 100.00 |
| NNO | Caroline Blakiston | 10.00 | 25.00 |
| NNO | Carrie Fisher | 120.00 | 250.00 |
| NNO | David Prowse | 80.00 | 150.00 |
| NNO | Dickey Beer | 10.00 | 25.00 |
| NNO | Femi Taylor | 12.00 | 30.00 |
| NNO | Hassani Shapi | 12.00 | 30.00 |

TRADING CARDS

| | | |
|---|---|---|
| NNO Jeremy Bulloch | 25.00 | 60.00 |
| NNO Jerome Blake | 10.00 | 25.00 |
| NNO John Ratzenberger | 12.00 | 30.00 |
| NNO Kenji Oates | 10.00 | 25.00 |
| NNO Kenneth Colley | 10.00 | 25.00 |
| NNO Kenny Baker | 100.00 | 200.00 |
| NNO Mark Hamill | 225.00 | 350.00 |
| NNO Michonne Bourriague | 12.00 | 30.00 |
| NNO Mike Quinn | 25.00 | 60.00 |
| NNO Nika Futterman | 10.00 | 25.00 |
| NNO Olivia d'Abo | 80.00 | 150.00 |
| NNO Orli Shoshan | 10.00 | 25.00 |
| NNO Pam Rose | 10.00 | 25.00 |
| NNO Peter Mayhew | 50.00 | 100.00 |
| NNO Ray Park | 25.00 | 60.00 |
| NNO Rohan Nichol | 12.00 | 30.00 |
| NNO Steven Blum | 10.00 | 25.00 |
| NNO Taylor Gray | 12.00 | 30.00 |
| NNO Tiya Sircar | 25.00 | 60.00 |
| NNO Vanessa Marshall | 15.00 | 40.00 |
| NNO Wayne Pygram | 12.00 | 30.00 |

### 2015 Star Wars Journey to The Force Awakens Behind-the-Scenes

The Birth of 2-1B

| | | |
|---|---|---|
| COMPLETE SET (9) | 5.00 | 12.00 |
| COMMON CARD (BTS1-BTS9) | 1.00 | 2.50 |
| *P.P.BLACK/1: UNPRICED DUE TO SCARCITY | | |
| *P.P.CYAN/1: UNPRICED DUE TO SCARCITY | | |
| *P.P.MAGENTA/1: UNPRICED DUE TO SCARCITY | | |
| *P.P.YELLOW/1: UNPRICED DUE TO SCARCITY | | |

### 2015 Star Wars Journey to The Force Awakens Blueprints

| | | |
|---|---|---|
| COMPLETE SET (8) | 15.00 | 40.00 |
| COMMON CARD (BP1-BP8) | 3.00 | 8.00 |
| BP1 BB-8 | 6.00 | 15.00 |
| BP3 Millennium Falcon | 5.00 | 12.00 |
| BP4 X-Wing Fighter | 4.00 | 10.00 |

### 2015 Star Wars Journey to The Force Awakens Character Stickers

| | | |
|---|---|---|
| COMPLETE SET (18) | 15.00 | 40.00 |
| COMMON CARD (S1-S18) | 1.25 | 3.00 |
| *P.P.BLACK/1: UNPRICED DUE TO SCARCITY | | |
| *P.P.CYAN/1: UNPRICED DUE TO SCARCITY | | |
| *P.P.MAGENTA/1: UNPRICED DUE TO SCARCITY | | |
| *P.P.YELLOW/1: UNPRICED DUE TO SCARCITY | | |
| S1 Luke Skywalker | 1.50 | 4.00 |
| S2 Han Solo | 2.00 | 5.00 |
| S9 BB-8 | 2.50 | 6.00 |
| S10 Captain Phasma | 1.50 | 4.00 |
| S11 Kylo Ren | 2.00 | 5.00 |
| S14 Darth Vader | 2.00 | 5.00 |

| | | |
|---|---|---|
| S15 Boba Fett | 1.50 | 4.00 |
| S17 Kylo Ren | 2.00 | 5.00 |
| S18 Yoda | 1.50 | 4.00 |

### 2015 Star Wars Journey to The Force Awakens Choose Your Destiny

| | | |
|---|---|---|
| COMPLETE SET (9) | 12.00 | 30.00 |
| COMMON CARD (CD1-CD9) | 2.50 | 6.00 |

### 2015 Star Wars Journey to The Force Awakens Classic Captions

| | | |
|---|---|---|
| COMPLETE SET (8) | 15.00 | 40.00 |
| COMMON CARD (CC1-CC8) | 4.00 | 10.00 |

### 2015 Star Wars Journey to The Force Awakens Cloth Stickers

| | | |
|---|---|---|
| COMPLETE SET (9) | 8.00 | 20.00 |
| COMMON CARD (CS1-CS9) | 1.50 | 4.00 |
| CS6 Kylo Ren | 2.00 | 5.00 |
| CS9 Kylo Ren (w/TIE Fighters) | 2.00 | 5.00 |

### 2015 Star Wars Journey to The Force Awakens Concept Art

| | | |
|---|---|---|
| COMPLETE SET (9) | 5.00 | 12.00 |
| COMMON CARD (CA1-CA9) | 1.00 | 2.50 |
| *P.P.BLACK/1: UNPRICED DUE TO SCARCITY | | |
| *P.P.CYAN/1: UNPRICED DUE TO SCARCITY | | |
| *P.P.MAGENTA/1: UNPRICED DUE TO SCARCITY | | |
| *P.P.YELLOW/1: UNPRICED DUE TO SCARCITY | | |

### 2015 Star Wars Journey to The Force Awakens Dual Autographs

STATED PRINT RUN 3 SER.#'d SETS

UNPRICED DUE TO SCARCITY

1 Mark Hamill/Kenny Baker
2 Ian McDiarmid/Wayne Pygram
3 Peter Mayhew/Anthony Daniels
4 Mark Hamill/David Prowse

### 2015 Star Wars Journey to The Force Awakens Family Legacy Matte Backs

| | | |
|---|---|---|
| COMPLETE SET (8) | 10.00 | 25.00 |
| COMMON CARD (FL1-FL8) | 1.50 | 4.00 |
| *GLOSSY: .5X TO 1.2X BASIC CARDS | | |
| *P.P.BLACK/1: UNPRICED DUE TO SCARCITY | | |
| *P.P.CYAN/1: UNPRICED DUE TO SCARCITY | | |
| *P.P.MAGENTA/1: UNPRICED DUE TO SCARCITY | | |
| *P.P.YELLOW/1: UNPRICED DUE TO SCARCITY | | |
| FL1 Boba Fett and Jango Fett | 2.00 | 5.00 |
| FL2 Anakin Skywalker and Luke Skywalker | 2.00 | 5.00 |
| FL3 Padme Amidala and Leia Organa | 2.00 | 5.00 |

### 2015 Star Wars Journey to The Force Awakens Heroes of the Resistance

BB-8

HEROES OF THE RESISTANCE

| | | |
|---|---|---|
| COMPLETE SET (9) | 6.00 | 15.00 |
| COMMON CARD (R1-R9) | 1.25 | 3.00 |
| *P.P.BLACK/1: UNPRICED DUE TO SCARCITY | | |
| *P.P.CYAN/1: UNPRICED DUE TO SCARCITY | | |
| *P.P.MAGENTA/1: UNPRICED DUE TO SCARCITY | | |
| *P.P.YELLOW/1: UNPRICED DUE TO SCARCITY | | |
| R4 BB-8 | 2.00 | 5.00 |
| R8 The Millennium Falcon | 1.50 | 4.00 |

### 2015 Star Wars Journey to The Force Awakens Patches

| | | |
|---|---|---|
| COMPLETE SET (20) | 150.00 | 300.00 |
| COMMON CARD (P1-P20) | 8.00 | 20.00 |
| P1 Kylo Ren | 12.00 | 30.00 |
| P3 Captain Phasma | 12.00 | 30.00 |
| P9 BB-8 | 12.00 | 30.00 |
| P18 BB-8 | 12.00 | 30.00 |

### 2015 Star Wars Journey to The Force Awakens Power of the First Order

| | | |
|---|---|---|
| COMPLETE SET (8) | 6.00 | 15.00 |
| COMMON CARD (FD1-FD8) | 1.25 | 3.00 |
| *P.P.BLACK/1: UNPRICED DUE TO SCARCITY | | |
| *P.P.CYAN/1: UNPRICED DUE TO SCARCITY | | |
| *P.P.MAGENTA/1: UNPRICED DUE TO SCARCITY | | |
| *P.P.YELLOW/1: UNPRICED DUE TO SCARCITY | | |
| FD1 Kylo Ren | 2.00 | 5.00 |
| FD2 Captain Phasma | 1.50 | 4.00 |

### 2015 Star Wars Journey to The Force Awakens Silhouette Foil

| | | |
|---|---|---|
| COMPLETE SET (8) | 4.00 | 10.00 |
| COMMON CARD (1-8) | .75 | 2.00 |
| *P.P.BLACK/1: UNPRICED DUE TO SCARCITY | | |
| *P.P.CYAN/1: UNPRICED DUE TO SCARCITY | | |
| *P.P.MAGENTA/1: UNPRICED DUE TO SCARCITY | | |
| *P.P.YELLOW/1: UNPRICED DUE TO SCARCITY | | |
| ERRONEOUSLY LISTED AS A 9-CARD SET | | |
| ON THE CARD BACKS | | |
| 5 Kylo Ren | 1.50 | 4.00 |
| 7 Captain Phasma | 1.25 | 3.00 |

### 2015 Star Wars Journey to The Force Awakens Promos

| | | |
|---|---|---|
| COMPLETE SET (6) | 10.00 | 25.00 |
| COMMON CARD (P1-P6) | 2.00 | 5.00 |
| P1 Luke Skywalker | 6.00 | 15.00 |
| (SDCC Marvel Star Wars Lando exclusive) | | |
| P6 Kanan Jarrus | 5.00 | 12.00 |
| (NYCC exclusive) | | |

## 2015 Star Wars Journey to The Force Awakens UK

| | | |
|---|---|---|
| COMPLETE SET (208) | 30.00 | 80.00 |
| COMMON CARD | .30 | .75 |
| LEY  Yoda | | |
| LEBF  Boba Fett | | |
| LECH  Chewbacca | | |
| LEHS  Han Solo | | |
| LELC  Lando Calrissian | | |
| LELS  Luke Skywalker | | |
| LEPL  Princess Leia | | |
| LER2  R2-D2 | | |
| LEST  Stormtrooper | | |
| LETE  The Emperor | | |

## 2017 Star Wars Journey to The Last Jedi

| | | |
|---|---|---|
| COMPLETE SET (110) | 12.00 | 30.00 |
| UNOPENED BOX (24 PACKS) | 85.00 | 100.00 |
| UNOPENED PACK (8 CARDS) | 3.00 | 4.00 |
| COMMON CARD (1-110) | .20 | .50 |
| *GREEN STAR.: .5X TO 1.2X BASIC CARDS | .25 | .60 |
| *PINK STAR.: .6X TO 1.5X BASIC CARDS | .30 | .75 |
| *BLACK STAR.: .75X TO 2X BASIC CARDS | .40 | 1.00 |
| *SILVER STAR.: 1.2X TO 3X BASIC CARDS | .60 | 1.50 |
| *PURPLE STAR.: 2X TO 5X BASIC CARDS | 1.00 | 2.50 |
| *WHITE STAR./199: 12X TO 30X BASIC CARDS | 6.00 | 15.00 |
| *ORANGE STAR./50: 15X TO 40X BASIC CARDS | 8.00 | 20.00 |
| *GOLD STAR./25: 25X TO 60X BASIC CARDS | 12.00 | 30.00 |
| *IMP. RED/1: UNPRICED DUE TO SCARCITY | | |
| *P.P.BLACK/1: UNPRICED DUE TO SCARCITY | | |
| *P.P.CYAN/1: UNPRICED DUE TO SCARCITY | | |
| *P.P.MAGENTA/1: UNPRICED DUE TO SCARCITY | | |
| *P.P.YELLOW/1: UNPRICED DUE TO SCARCITY | | |

## 2017 Star Wars Journey to The Last Jedi Allies

| | | |
|---|---|---|
| COMPLETE SET (5) | 50.00 | 100.00 |
| COMMON CARD (1-5) | 10.00 | 25.00 |
| *P.P.BLACK/1: UNPRICED DUE TO SCARCITY | | |
| *P.P.CYAN/1: UNPRICED DUE TO SCARCITY | | |
| *P.P.MAGENTA/1: UNPRICED DUE TO SCARCITY | | |
| *P.P.YELLOW/1: UNPRICED DUE TO SCARCITY | | |
| GAMESTOP EXCLUSIVE | | |

## 2017 Star Wars Journey to The Last Jedi Autographs

| | | |
|---|---|---|
| *GOLD/10: UNPRICED DUE TO SCARCITY | | |
| *IMP. RED/1: UNPRICED DUE TO SCARCITY | | |
| *P.P.BLACK/1: UNPRICED DUE TO SCARCITY | | |
| *P.P.CYAN/1: UNPRICED DUE TO SCARCITY | | |
| *P.P.MAGENTA/1: UNPRICED DUE TO SCARCITY | | |
| *P.P.YELLOW/1: UNPRICED DUE TO SCARCITY | | |
| AAD  Adam Driver | | |
| AAE  Ashley Eckstein | | |
| AAP  Alistair Petrie | | |
| AAS  Andy Serkis | | |
| AAT  Alan Tudyk | | |
| ABD  Ben Daniels | 20.00 | 50.00 |
| ABH  Brian Herring | 12.00 | 30.00 |
| ABL  Billie Lourd | | |
| ABW  Billy Dee Williams | | |
| ACD  Cristina da Silva | 12.00 | 30.00 |
| ACF  Carrie Fisher | | |
| ACR  Clive Revill | | |
| ACT  Catherine Taber | 15.00 | 40.00 |
| ADB  Dee Bradley Baker | 12.00 | 30.00 |
| ADC  Dave Champman | 20.00 | 50.00 |
| ADL  Daniel Logan | 12.00 | 30.00 |
| ADP  Duncan Pow | 8.00 | 20.00 |

| | | |
|---|---|---|
| ADR  Daisy Ridley | | |
| ADY  Donnie Yen | | |
| AFJ  Felicity Jones | | |
| AFP  Freddie Prinze Jr. | | |
| AFW  Forest Whitaker | | |
| AGC  Gwendoline Christie | | |
| AGT  George Takei | | |
| AHC  Hayden Christensen | | |
| AHF  Harrison Ford | | |
| AIU  Iko Uwais | | |
| AIW  Ian Whyte | 10.00 | 25.00 |
| AJB  John Boyega | | |
| AJC  Jim Cummings | 10.00 | 25.00 |
| AJD  Julie Dolan | 10.00 | 25.00 |
| AJI  Jason Isaacs | | |
| AKB  Kenny Baker | | |
| AKF  Kate Fleetwood | | |
| AKY  Keone Young | 15.00 | 40.00 |
| AMH  Mark Hamill | | |
| APB  Paul Blake | 15.00 | 40.00 |
| APM  Peter Mayhew | | |
| APW  Paul Warren | 10.00 | 25.00 |
| ARA  Riz Ahmed | | |
| ARC  Richard Cunningham | 12.00 | 30.00 |
| ARP  Ray Park | | |
| ASG  Stefan Grube | 12.00 | 30.00 |
| ASR  Scott Richardson | 15.00 | 40.00 |
| ASW  Sam Witwer | | |
| ATB  Thomas Brodie-Sangster | | |
| ATC  Tosin Cole | | |
| ATK  Tom Kane | | |
| ATW  Tom Wilton | 12.00 | 30.00 |
| AWP  Wayne Pygram | 10.00 | 25.00 |
| AYR  Yayan Ruhian | | |
| AZD  Zarene Dallas | 12.00 | 30.00 |
| AADA  Anthony Daniels | | |
| AADX  Adam Driver Unmasked | | |
| ACAR  Cecp Arif Rahman | 15.00 | 40.00 |
| ADAR  Derek Arnold | | |
| ADBA  Dave Barclay | 10.00 | 25.00 |
| ADRX  Daisy Ridley Scavenger | | |
| AGGA  Gloria Garcia | 12.00 | 30.00 |
| AGGA  Greg Grunberg | | |
| AIMD  Ian McDiarmid | | |
| AIME  Ian McElhinney | 12.00 | 30.00 |
| AJBL  Jerome Blake | 10.00 | 25.00 |
| AJBU  Jeremy Bulloch | | |
| ASDB  Sharon Duncan-Brewster | 15.00 | 40.00 |

## 2017 Star Wars Journey to The Last Jedi Blueprints

| | | |
|---|---|---|
| COMPLETE SET (7) | 8.00 | 20.00 |
| COMMON CARD (1-7) | 2.00 | 5.00 |
| *P.P.BLACK/1: UNPRICED DUE TO SCARCITY | | |
| *P.P.CYAN/1: UNPRICED DUE TO SCARCITY | | |
| *P.P.MAGENTA/1: UNPRICED DUE TO SCARCITY | | |
| *P.P.YELLOW/1: UNPRICED DUE TO SCARCITY | | |

## 2017 Star Wars Journey to The Last Jedi Character Retro Stickers

| | | |
|---|---|---|
| COMPLETE SET (18) | 100.00 | 200.00 |
| COMMON CARD (1-18) | 6.00 | 15.00 |
| *P.P.BLACK/1: UNPRICED DUE TO SCARCITY | | |
| *P.P.CYAN/1: UNPRICED DUE TO SCARCITY | | |
| *P.P.MAGENTA/1: UNPRICED DUE TO SCARCITY | | |
| *P.P.YELLOW/1: UNPRICED DUE TO SCARCITY | | |

## 2017 Star Wars Journey to The Last Jedi Characters

| | | |
|---|---|---|
| COMPLETE SET (16) | 12.00 | 30.00 |
| COMMON CARD (1-16) | 1.25 | 3.00 |
| *P.P.BLACK/1: UNPRICED DUE TO SCARCITY | | |
| *P.P.CYAN/1: UNPRICED DUE TO SCARCITY | | |
| *P.P.MAGENTA/1: UNPRICED DUE TO SCARCITY | | |
| *P.P.YELLOW/1: UNPRICED DUE TO SCARCITY | | |

## 2017 Star Wars Journey to The Last Jedi Choose Your Destiny

| | | |
|---|---|---|
| COMPLETE SET (10) | 8.00 | 20.00 |
| COMMON CARD (1-10) | 1.25 | 3.00 |
| *P.P.BLACK/1: UNPRICED DUE TO SCARCITY | | |
| *P.P.CYAN/1: UNPRICED DUE TO SCARCITY | | |
| *P.P.MAGENTA/1: UNPRICED DUE TO SCARCITY | | |
| *P.P.YELLOW/1: UNPRICED DUE TO SCARCITY | | |

## 2017 Star Wars Journey to The Last Jedi Darkness Rises

| | | |
|---|---|---|
| COMPLETE SET (6) | 6.00 | 15.00 |
| COMMON CARD (1-6) | 1.50 | 4.00 |

## 2017 Star Wars Journey to The Last Jedi Family Legacy

| | | |
|---|---|---|
| COMPLETE SET (6) | 5.00 | 12.00 |
| COMMON CARD (1-6) | 1.25 | 3.00 |
| *P.P.BLACK/1: UNPRICED DUE TO SCARCITY | | |
| *P.P.CYAN/1: UNPRICED DUE TO SCARCITY | | |
| *P.P.MAGENTA/1: UNPRICED DUE TO SCARCITY | | |
| *P.P.YELLOW/1: UNPRICED DUE TO SCARCITY | | |

## 2017 Star Wars Journey to The Last Jedi Illustrated Characters

PORGS

| | | |
|---|---|---|
| COMPLETE SET (14) | 10.00 | 25.00 |
| COMMON CARD (1-14) | 1.00 | 2.50 |
| *P.P.BLACK/1: UNPRICED DUE TO SCARCITY | | |
| *P.P.CYAN/1: UNPRICED DUE TO SCARCITY | | |
| *P.P.MAGENTA/1: UNPRICED DUE TO SCARCITY | | |
| *P.P.YELLOW/1: UNPRICED DUE TO SCARCITY | | |

## 2017 Star Wars Journey to The Last Jedi Patches

| | | |
|---|---|---|
| COMMON CARD (UNNUMBERED) | 5.00 | 12.00 |
| *ORANGE/99: .75X TO 2X BASIC CARDS | 10.00 | 25.00 |
| *GOLD/25: 1.2X TO 3X BASIC CARDS | 15.00 | 40.00 |
| *IMP. RED/1: UNPRICED DUE TO SCARCITY | | |

## 2017 Star Wars Journey to The Last Jedi Rey Continuity

| | | |
|---|---|---|
| COMPLETE SET (10) | 12.00 | 30.00 |
| COMMON CARD (1-5) | 1.25 | 3.00 |
| COMMON CARD (6-10) | 2.00 | 5.00 |

*P.P.BLACK/1: UNPRICED DUE TO SCARCITY
*P.P.CYAN/1: UNPRICED DUE TO SCARCITY
*P.P.MAGENTA/1: UNPRICED DUE TO SCARCITY
*P.P.YELLOW/1: UNPRICED DUE TO SCARCITY
RANDOMLY INSERTED INTO PACKS
1-5 JOURNEY TO THE LAST JEDI EXCLUSIVE
6-10 THE LAST JEDI SER.1 EXCLUSIVE
11-15 THE LAST JEDI SER.2 EXCLUSIVE

## 2019 Star Wars Journey to The Rise of Skywalker

| | | |
|---|---|---|
| COMPLETE SET (110) | 10.00 | 25.00 |
| COMMON CARD (1-110) | .20 | .50 |

*GREEN: .75X TO 2X BASIC CARDS
*SILVER: 1.2X TO 3X BASIC CARDS
*BLACK/199: 3X TO 8X BASIC CARDS
*ORANGE/50: 6X TO 15X BASIC CARDS
*GOLD/25: 12X TO 30X BASIC CARDS
*RED/1: UNPRICED DUE TO SCARCITY
*P.P.BLACK/1: UNPRICED DUE TO SCARCITY
*P.P.CYAN/1: UNPRICED DUE TO SCARCITY
*P.P.MAGENTA/1: UNPRICED DUE TO SCARCITY
*P.P.YELLOW/1: UNPRICED DUE TO SCARCITY

## 2019 Star Wars Journey to The Rise of Skywalker Six-Person Autographs

UNPRICED DUE TO SCARCITY

NNO Ridley/Boyega/Tran/Serkis/Driver/Gleeson
NNO Ford/Fisher/Ridley/Boyega/Baker/Daniels

## 2019 Star Wars Journey to The Rise of Skywalker Autographed Commemorative Patches

UNPRICED DUE TO SCARCITY

NNO Adam Driver
NNO Andy Serkis
NNO Daisy Ridley
NNO Domhnall Gleeson
NNO Greg Grunberg
NNO John Boyega
NNO Joonas Suotamo
NNO Matthew Wood
NNO Mike Quinn
NNO Paul Kasey

## 2019 Star Wars Journey to The Rise of Skywalker Autographs

*GOLD/25: UNPRICED DUE TO SCARCITY
*RED/1: UNPRICED DUE TO SCARCITY
*P.P.BLACK/1: UNPRICED DUE TO SCARCITY

*P.P.CYAN/1: UNPRICED DUE TO SCARCITY
*P.P.MAGENTA/1: UNPRICED DUE TO SCARCITY
*P.P.YELLOW/1: UNPRICED DUE TO SCARCITY
RANDOMLY INSERTED INTO PACKS

NNO Adam Driver
NNO Adrian Edmondson
NNO Amanda Lawrence
NNO Andrew Jack
NNO Andy Serkis 1
NNO Andy Serkis 2
NNO Anthony Daniels
NNO Arti Shah
NNO Billie Lourd
NNO Brian Vernel
NNO Carrie Fisher
NNO Cavin Cornwall
NNO Cecep Arif Rahman
NNO Crystal Clarke
NNO Daisy Ridley
NNO Dave Chapman
NNO David Acord
NNO Derek Arnold
NNO Domhnall Gleeson
NNO Emun Elliott
NNO Gloria Garcia
NNO Greg Grunberg
NNO Harrison Ford
NNO Hermione Corfield
NNO Hugh Skinner
NNO Ian Whyte
NNO Iko Uwais
NNO Jimmy Vee
NNO John Boyega 1
NNO John Boyega 2
NNO Joonas Suotamo
NNO Kelly Marie Tran
NNO Kenny Baker
NNO Kiran Shah
NNO Laura Dern
NNO Lily Cole
NNO Mike Quinn
NNO Nathalie Cuzner
NNO Paul Kasey
NNO Paul Warren
NNO Rocky Marshall
NNO Sebastian Armesto
NNO Stefan Grube
NNO Thomas Brodie-Sangster
NNO Tim Rose
NNO Tom Kane
NNO Tom Wilton
NNO Warwick Davis

## 2019 Star Wars Journey to The Rise of Skywalker Battle Lines

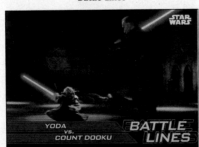

| | | |
|---|---|---|
| COMPLETE SET (10) | 25.00 | 60.00 |
| COMMON CARD (BL1-BL10) | 4.00 | 10.00 |

*P.P.BLACK/1: UNPRICED DUE TO SCARCITY
*P.P.CYAN/1: UNPRICED DUE TO SCARCITY

*P.P.MAGENTA/1: UNPRICED DUE TO SCARCITY
*P.P.YELLOW/1: UNPRICED DUE TO SCARCITY
RANDOMLY INSERTED IN PACKS

## 2019 Star Wars Journey to The Rise of Skywalker Character Foil

| | | |
|---|---|---|
| COMPLETE SET (8) | 6.00 | 15.00 |
| COMMON CARD (FC1-FC8) | 1.00 | 2.50 |

*P.P.BLACK/1: UNPRICED DUE TO SCARCITY
*P.P.CYAN/1: UNPRICED DUE TO SCARCITY
*P.P.MAGENTA/1: UNPRICED DUE TO SCARCITY
*P.P.YELLOW/1: UNPRICED DUE TO SCARCITY
RANDOMLY INSERTED INTO PACKS

## 2019 Star Wars Journey to The Rise of Skywalker Character Stickers

| | | |
|---|---|---|
| COMPLETE SET (19) | 10.00 | 25.00 |
| COMMON CARD (CS1-CS19) | 1.25 | 3.00 |

*P.P.BLACK/1: UNPRICED DUE TO SCARCITY
*P.P.CYAN/1: UNPRICED DUE TO SCARCITY
*P.P.MAGENTA/1: UNPRICED DUE TO SCARCITY
*P.P.YELLOW/1: UNPRICED DUE TO SCARCITY
RANDOMLY INSERTED INTO PACKS

## 2019 Star Wars Journey to The Rise of Skywalker Choose Your Destiny

| | | |
|---|---|---|
| COMPLETE SET (10) | 12.00 | 30.00 |
| COMMON CARD (CD1-CD10) | 2.00 | 5.00 |

*P.P.BLACK/1: UNPRICED DUE TO SCARCITY
*P.P.CYAN/1: UNPRICED DUE TO SCARCITY
*P.P.MAGENTA/1: UNPRICED DUE TO SCARCITY
*P.P.YELLOW/1: UNPRICED DUE TO SCARCITY
RANDOMLY INSERTED INTO PACKS

## 2019 Star Wars Journey to The Rise of Skywalker Commemorative Jumbo Patches

*RED/1: UNPRICED DUE TO SCARCITY
RANDOMLY INSERTED INTO PACKS

JPC Chewbacca
JPF Finn
JPR Rey
JPAA Admiral Ackbar
JPAH Vice Admiral Holdo
JPBB BB-8
JPBO Bail Organa
JPC3 C-3PO
JPCT C'ai Threnalli
JPHS Han Solo
JPKC Lieutenant Connix
JPLC Lando Calrissian
JPLO General Leia Organa
JPLS Luke Skywalker
JPME Major Ematt
JPMM Mon Mothma
JPPA Padmè Amidala
JPPD Poe Dameron
JPR2 R2-D2
JPRT Rose Tico

## 2019 Star Wars Journey to The Rise of Skywalker Commemorative Patches

*RED/1: UNPRICED DUE TO SCARCITY
RANDOMLY INSERTED INTO PACKS

PCCR Chewbacca
PCFR Finn
PCRR Rey
PCCCT Captain Canady
PCCPK Captain Phasma
PCCPT Captain Peavey
PCCTX C'ai Threnalli
PCCXP C'ai Threnalli
PCEAX Ello Asty
PCEXP Ello Asty
PCGHK General Hux
PCHFO General Hux
PCHSR Han Solo
PCKFO Kylo Ren
PCKRK Kylo Ren
PCKRT Kylo Ren
PCLOR General Leia Organa
PCLSR Luke Skywalker
PCNNX Nien Nunb
PCNXP Nien Nunb
PCPDX Poe Dameron
PCPFO Captain Phasma
PCPGK Praetorian Guard
PCPXP Poe Dameron
PCSFO Supreme Leader Snoke
PCSLK Supreme Leader Snoke
PCSWX Snap Wexley
PCSXP Snap Wexley
PCTFO Stormtrooper
PCTFP Tie Fighter Pilot

## 2019 Star Wars Journey to The Rise of Skywalker Dual Autographs

UNPRICED DUE TO SCARCITY

NNO A.Serkis/A.Driver
NNO A.Serkis/D.Gleeson
NNO A.Daniels/K.Baker
NNO D.Ridley/A.Driver
NNO G.Grunberg/H.Corfield
NNO K.Tran/V.Ngo
NNO L.Dern/Hugh Skinner
NNO P.Kasey/T.Rose

## 2019 Star Wars Journey to The Rise of Skywalker Illustrated Characters

COMPLETE SET (16)
COMMON CARD (IC1-IC16)
*P.P.BLACK/1: UNPRICED DUE TO SCARCITY
*P.P.CYAN/1: UNPRICED DUE TO SCARCITY
*P.P.MAGENTA/1: UNPRICED DUE TO SCARCITY
*P.P.YELLOW/1: UNPRICED DUE TO SCARCITY
RANDOMLY INSERTED INTO PACKS

## 2019 Star Wars Journey to The Rise of Skywalker Schematics

| | | |
|---|---|---|
| COMPLETE SET (10) | 5.00 | 12.00 |
| COMMON CARD (S1-S10) | .75 | 2.00 |

*P.P.BLACK/1: UNPRICED DUE TO SCARCITY
*P.P.CYAN/1: UNPRICED DUE TO SCARCITY
*P.P.MAGENTA/1: UNPRICED DUE TO SCARCITY
*P.P.YELLOW/1: UNPRICED DUE TO SCARCITY
RANDOMLY INSERTED INTO PACKS

## 2019 Star Wars Journey to The Rise of Skywalker Triple Autographs

UNPRICED DUE TO SCARCITY

NNO Serkis/Ridley/Driver

---

NNO Daniels/Baker/Mayhew
NNO Davis/Cole/Shah
NNO Dern/Skinner/Lawrence

## 1996 Star Wars Laser

| | | |
|---|---|---|
| 0 Star Wars 20th Anniversary Commemorative Magazine | 3.00 | 8.00 |

## 2016 Star Wars LEGO Droid Tales

| | | |
|---|---|---|
| COMPLETE SET (9) | 15.00 | 40.00 |
| UNOPENED PACK (3 CARDS) | 6.00 | 8.00 |
| COMMON CARD (DT1-DT9) | | |

ONE PACK INSERTED INTO
STAR WARS LEGO DROID TALES DVD

## 2019 Star Wars Living Set

COMMON CARD
TOPPS ONLINE EXCLUSIVE

| | | |
|---|---|---|
| 1 Darth Vader/3,909* | 6.00 | 15.00 |
| 2 Nien Nunb/2,888* | 4.00 | 10.00 |
| 3 R2-D2/2,710* | 3.00 | 8.00 |
| 4 Stormtrooper/2,601* | 3.00 | 8.00 |
| 5 Bossk/2,205* | 3.00 | 8.00 |
| 8 Death Star Gunner/1,922* | 3.00 | 8.00 |
| 9 Grand Admiral Thrawn/1,760* | 4.00 | 10.00 |
| 11 Wedge Antilles/1,662* | 3.00 | 8.00 |
| 15 Orson Krennic/1,385* | 3.00 | 8.00 |
| 17 Lando Calrissian/1,427* | 3.00 | 8.00 |
| 21 Han Solo/2,376* | 4.00 | 10.00 |
| 25 Darth Maul/1,739* | 4.00 | 10.00 |
| 29 BB-8/1,502* | 3.00 | 8.00 |
| 31 Aurra Sing/1,343* | | |
| 32 Tobias Beckett/1,395* | | |
| 33 Wicket W. Warrick/1,390* | | |
| 34 Scout Trooper/1,283* | | |
| 35 General Hux/1,170* | | |
| 36 Dak Ralter/1,164* | | |
| 37 Bail Organa/ | | |
| 38 Gamorrean Guard/ | | |
| 39 Sebulba/ | | |
| 40 Kanan Jarrus/ | | |

## 2019 Star Wars The Mandalorian Trailer Set

| | | |
|---|---|---|
| COMPLETE SET (10) | 10.00 | 25.00 |
| COMMON CARD (1-10) | 2.00 | 5.00 |

STATED PRINT RUN 1,425 SER.#'d SETS

## 1995 Star Wars Mastervisions

| | | |
|---|---|---|
| COMPLETE BOXED SET (36) | 10.00 | 25.00 |
| COMMON CARD (1-36) | .30 | .75 |

---

## 1995 Star Wars Mastervisions Promos

| | | |
|---|---|---|
| COMMON CARD | .75 | 2.00 |
| P2 Luke on Hoth | 1.25 | 3.00 |

(Star Wars Galaxy Magazine Exclusive)

## 2015 Star Wars Masterwork

| | | |
|---|---|---|
| COMPLETE SET w/o SP (50) | 60.00 | 120.00 |
| UNOPENED BOX (4 MINIBOXES) | 300.00 | 350.00 |
| UNOPENED MINIBOX (5 CARDS) | 80.00 | 95.00 |
| COMMON CARD (1-50) | 2.00 | 5.00 |
| COMMON CARD (51-75) | 5.00 | 12.00 |

*BLUE/299: .5X TO 1.2X BASIC CARDS
*BLUE SP/299: .2X TO .50X BASIC CARDS
*SILVER/99: .75X TO 2X BASIC CARDS
*SILVER SP/99: .3X TO .80X BASIC CARDS
*GREEN/50: 1.2X TO 3X BASIC CARDS
*GREEN SP/50: .5X TO 1.2X BASIC CARDS
*P.P.BLACK/1: UNPRICED DUE TO SCARCITY
*P.P.CYAN/1: UNPRICED DUE TO SCARCITY
*P.P.MAGENTA/1: UNPRICED DUE TO SCARCITY
*P.P.YELLOW/1: UNPRICED DUE TO SCARCITY

## 2015 Star Wars Masterwork Autographs

| | | |
|---|---|---|
| COMMON AUTO | 8.00 | 20.00 |

*FRAMED/28: UNPRICED DUE TO SCARCITY
*FOIL/25: UNPRICED DUE TO SCARCITY
*CANVAS/10: UNPRICED DUE TO SCARCITY
*WOOD/1: UNPRICED DUE TO SCARCITY
STATED ODDS 1:4

| | | |
|---|---|---|
| NNO Alan Harris | 10.00 | 25.00 |
| NNO Amy Allen | 12.00 | 30.00 |
| NNO Angus MacInnes | 10.00 | 25.00 |
| NNO Anthony Daniels | 120.00 | 250.00 |
| NNO Ashley Eckstein | 15.00 | 40.00 |
| NNO Billy Dee Williams | 100.00 | 200.00 |
| NNO Carrie Fisher | 600.00 | 1000.00 |
| NNO Chris Parsons | 10.00 | 25.00 |
| NNO Dermot Crowley | 10.00 | 25.00 |
| NNO Dickey Beer | 8.00 | 20.00 |
| NNO Gerald Home | 10.00 | 25.00 |
| NNO Harrison Ford | 1800.00 | 3000.00 |
| NNO James Earl Jones | 300.00 | 450.00 |
| NNO Jeremy Bulloch | 20.00 | 50.00 |
| NNO Jesse Jensen | 10.00 | 25.00 |
| NNO John Morton | 15.00 | 40.00 |
| NNO John Ratzenberger | 12.00 | 30.00 |
| NNO Julian Glover | 12.00 | 30.00 |
| NNO Kenneth Colley | 10.00 | 25.00 |
| NNO Kenny Baker | 150.00 | 300.00 |
| NNO Mark Hamill | 400.00 | 750.00 |
| NNO Michonne Bourriague | 10.00 | 25.00 |
| NNO Mike Quinn | 12.00 | 30.00 |
| NNO Oliver Ford Davies | 10.00 | 25.00 |
| NNO Orli Shoshan | 10.00 | 25.00 |
| NNO Pam Rose | 10.00 | 25.00 |
| NNO Paul Brooke | 12.00 | 30.00 |
| NNO Peter Mayhew | 75.00 | 150.00 |
| NNO Phil Eason | 10.00 | 25.00 |
| NNO Rusty Goffe | 12.00 | 30.00 |
| NNO Tim Rose | 15.00 | 40.00 |
| NNO Wayne Pygram | 10.00 | 25.00 |

## 2015 Star Wars Masterwork Companions

| | | |
|---|---|---|
| COMPLETE SET (10) | 25.00 | 60.00 |
| COMMON CARD (C1-C10) | 10.00 | 10.00 |

*RAINBOW/299: .6X TO 1.5X BASIC CARDS
*CANVAS/99: 1X TO 2.5X BASIC CARDS
*WOOD/50: 1.2X TO 3X BASIC CARDS
*CLEAR ACE./25: 1.5X TO 4X BASIC CARDS
*METAL/10: UNPRICED DUE TO SCARCITY
*GOLDEN METAL/1: UNPRICED DUE TO SCARCITY
*P.P.BLACK/1: UNPRICED DUE TO SCARCITY
*P.P.CYAN/1: UNPRICED DUE TO SCARCITY
*P.P.MAGENTA/1: UNPRICED DUE TO SCARCITY
*P.P.YELLOW/1: UNPRICED DUE TO SCARCITY

| | | |
|---|---|---|
| C1 Han Solo and Chewbacca | 6.00 | 15.00 |
| C2 Luke and Leia | 6.00 | 15.00 |
| C3 Vader and Palpatine | 5.00 | 12.00 |
| C5 C-3PO and R2-D2 | 5.00 | 12.00 |
| C8 R2-D2 and Luke Skywalker | 5.00 | 12.00 |
| C10 Boba Fett and Jango Fett | 5.00 | 12.00 |

## 2015 Star Wars Masterwork Defining Moments

| | | |
|---|---|---|
| COMPLETE SET (10) | 25.00 | 60.00 |
| COMMON CARD (DM1-DM10) | 4.00 | 10.00 |

*RAINBOW/299: .6X TO 1.5X BASIC CARDS
*CANVAS/99: 1X TO 2.5X BASIC CARDS
*WOOD/50: 1.2X TO 3X BASIC CARDS
*CLEAR ACE./25: 1.5X TO 4X BASIC CARDS
*METAL/10: UNPRICED DUE TO SCARCITY
*GOLDEN METAL/1: UNPRICED DUE TO SCARCITY
*P.P.BLACK/1: UNPRICED DUE TO SCARCITY
*P.P.CYAN/1: UNPRICED DUE TO SCARCITY
*P.P.MAGENTA/1: UNPRICED DUE TO SCARCITY
*P.P.YELLOW/1: UNPRICED DUE TO SCARCITY

| | | |
|---|---|---|
| DM1 Darth Vader | 5.00 | 12.00 |
| DM2 Luke Skywalker | 5.00 | 12.00 |
| DM3 Han Solo | 8.00 | 20.00 |
| DM4 Princess Leia Organa | 5.00 | 12.00 |
| DM7 Anakin Skywalker | 5.00 | 12.00 |
| DM8 Obi-Wan Kenobi | 5.00 | 12.00 |
| DM10 Chewbacca | 5.00 | 12.00 |

## 2015 Star Wars Masterwork Return of the Jedi Bunker Relics Bronze

| | | |
|---|---|---|
| COMMON CARD | 12.00 | 30.00 |

*SILVER/77: .75X TO 2X BASIC CARDS
CARDS 1, 2, 3, 4, 10, 12 SER.#'d TO 155
CARDS 5, 6, 7, 8, 9, 11 SER.#'d TO 255

| | | |
|---|---|---|
| 1 Han Solo/155 | 20.00 | 50.00 |
| 2 Princess Leia Organa/155 | 20.00 | 50.00 |
| 3 Chewbacca/155 | 15.00 | 40.00 |
| 4 Luke Skywalker/155 | 25.00 | 60.00 |
| 10 Ewok (frame)/155 | 15.00 | 40.00 |
| 12 Han, Leia & Luke/155 | 20.00 | 50.00 |

## 2015 Star Wars Masterwork Scum and Villainy

| | | |
|---|---|---|
| COMPLETE SET (10) | 25.00 | 60.00 |
| COMMON CARD (SV1-SV10) | 4.00 | 10.00 |

*RAINBOW/299: 1.5X TO 6X BASIC CARDS
*CANVAS/99: 1X TO 2.5X BASIC CARDS
*WOOD/50: 1.2X TO 3X BASIC CARDS
*CLEAR ACE./25: 1.5X TO 4X BASIC CARDS

*METAL/10: UNPRICED DUE TO SCARCITY
*GOLDEN METAL/1: UNPRICED DUE TO SCARCITY
*P.P.BLACK/1: UNPRICED DUE TO SCARCITY
*P.P.CYAN/1: UNPRICED DUE TO SCARCITY
*P.P.MAGENTA/1: UNPRICED DUE TO SCARCITY
*P.P.YELLOW/1: UNPRICED DUE TO SCARCITY

| | | |
|---|---|---|
| SV1 Boba Fett | 6.00 | 15.00 |
| SV2 Jabba the Hutt | 5.00 | 12.00 |
| SV4 General Grievous | 6.00 | 15.00 |
| SV5 Jango Fett | 5.00 | 12.00 |
| SV8 Ponda Baba | 6.00 | 15.00 |
| SV9 Bossk | 5.00 | 12.00 |
| SV10 Tusken Raider | 6.00 | 15.00 |

## 2015 Star Wars Masterwork Stamp Relics

| | | |
|---|---|---|
| COMMON CARD | 20.00 | 50.00 |
| STATED ODDS 1:CASE | | |
| NNO Anakin vs. Obi-Wan | 50.00 | 100.00 |
| NNO Ben (Obi-Wan) Kenobi | 30.00 | 80.00 |
| NNO Boba Fett | 60.00 | 120.00 |
| NNO C-3PO | 25.00 | 60.00 |
| NNO Darth Maul | 50.00 | 100.00 |
| NNO Darth Vader | 30.00 | 80.00 |
| NNO Emperor Palpatine | 30.00 | 80.00 |
| NNO Han Solo and Chewbacca | 50.00 | 100.00 |
| NNO Luke Skywalker | 30.00 | 80.00 |
| NNO The Millennium Falcon | 50.00 | 100.00 |
| NNO X-Wing Fighter | 30.00 | 80.00 |

## 2015 Star Wars Masterwork Triple Autograph

STATED PRINT RUN 2 SER.#'d SETS
UNPRICED DUE TO SCARCITY

1 Mark Hamill
Harrison Ford#|Carrie Fisher

*METAL/10: UNPRICED DUE TO SCARCITY
*GOLDEN METAL/1: UNPRICED DUE TO SCARCITY
*P.P.BLACK/1: UNPRICED DUE TO SCARCITY
*P.P.CYAN/1: UNPRICED DUE TO SCARCITY
*P.P.MAGENTA/1: UNPRICED DUE TO SCARCITY
*P.P.YELLOW/1: UNPRICED DUE TO SCARCITY

| | | |
|---|---|---|
| SV1 Boba Fett | 6.00 | 15.00 |
| SV2 Jabba the Hutt | 5.00 | 12.00 |
| SV4 General Grievous | 6.00 | 15.00 |
| SV5 Jango Fett | 5.00 | 12.00 |
| SV8 Ponda Baba | 6.00 | 15.00 |
| SV9 Bossk | 5.00 | 12.00 |
| SV10 Tusken Raider | 6.00 | 15.00 |

## 2015 Star Wars Masterwork Weapons Lineage Medallions

| | | |
|---|---|---|
| COMPLETE SET (30) | 250.00 | 500.00 |
| COMMON CARD | 8.00 | 20.00 |

*SILVER/50: 1.2X TO 3X BASIC CARDS
*GOLD/10: UNPRICED DUE TO SCARCITY
STATED ODDS 1:6

| | | |
|---|---|---|
| NNO Anakin Skywalker | 10.00 | 25.00 |
| Mace Windu's Lightsaber | | |
| NNO Anakin Skywalker | 12.00 | 30.00 |
| Anakin Skywalker's Lightsaber | | |
| NNO B. Fett's Blaster | 10.00 | 25.00 |
| NNO B. Fett's Blaster | 12.00 | 30.00 |
| NNO Darth Maul's Lightsaber | 10.00 | 25.00 |
| NNO Vader | 10.00 | 25.00 |
| Vader's Lightsaber | | |
| NNO Vader | 10.00 | 25.00 |
| Vader's Lightsaber | | |
| NNO Vader | 10.00 | 25.00 |
| Vader's Lightsaber | | |
| NNO Vader Solo's Blaster | 12.00 | 30.00 |
| NNO Darth Vader | 15.00 | 40.00 |
| Luke Skywalker's Lightsaber | | |
| NNO Han Solo | 12.00 | 30.00 |
| Han Solo's Blaster | | |
| NNO Han Solo | 12.00 | 30.00 |
| Han Solo's Blaster | | |
| NNO Han Solo | 15.00 | 40.00 |
| Luke Skywalker's Lightsaber | | |
| NNO Luke Skywalker | 10.00 | 25.00 |
| Luke Skywalker's Lightsaber | | |
| NNO Luke Skywalker | 10.00 | 25.00 |
| Luke Skywalker's Lightsaber | | |
| NNO Mace Windu | 10.00 | 25.00 |
| Mace Windu's Lightsaber | | |
| NNO Princess Leia Organa | 10.00 | 25.00 |
| Stormtrooper Blaster Rifle | | |
| NNO Leia | 12.00 | 30.00 |
| Leia's Blaster | | |
| NNO R2-D2 | 10.00 | 25.00 |
| Luke's Lightsaber | | |
| NNO Stormtrooper | 12.00 | 30.00 |
| Stormtrooper Blaster Rifle | | |
| NNO Yoda | 15.00 | 40.00 |
| Yoda's Lightsaber | | |

## 2016 Star Wars Masterwork

| | | |
|---|---|---|
| COMPLETE SET W/SP (75) | 200.00 | 400.00 |
| COMPLETE SET W/O SP (50) | 30.00 | 80.00 |
| UNOPENED BOX (4 PACKS) | 150.00 | 200.00 |
| UNOPENED PACK (5 CARDS) | 50.00 | 60.00 |
| COMMON CARD (1-75) | 2.00 | 5.00 |

| | | |
|---|---|---|
| COMMON SP (51-75) | 4.00 | 10.00 |
| *BLUE MET.: SAME VALUE | 2.00 | 5.00 |
| *BLUE MET.SP: SAME VALUE | 4.00 | 10.00 |
| *SILVER MET./99: .75X TO 1.5X BASIC CARDS | 3.00 | 8.00 |
| *SILVER MET.SP/99: .30X TO .75X BASIC CARDS | 3.00 | 8.00 |
| *GREEN MET./50: 1.2X TO 3X BASIC CARDS | 6.00 | 15.00 |
| *GREEN MET.SP/50: .6X TO 1.5X BASIC CARDS | 6.00 | 15.00 |
| *LT.SBR PURP./25: 1.5X TO 4X BASIC CARDS | 8.00 | 20.00 |
| *LT.SBR PURP.SP/25: .75X TO 2X BASIC CARDS | 8.00 | 20.00 |
| *GOLD/1: UNPRICED DUE TO SCARCITY | | |
| *P.P.BLACK/1: UNPRICED DUE TO SCARCITY | | |
| *P.P.CYAN/1: UNPRICED DUE TO SCARCITY | | |
| *P.P.MAGENTA/1: UNPRICED DUE TO SCARCITY | | |
| *P.P.YELLOW/1: UNPRICED DUE TO SCARCITY | | |
| 66 Han Solo SP | 6.00 | 15.00 |
| 71 Rey SP | 8.00 | 20.00 |

## 2016 Star Wars Masterwork Alien Identification Guide

| | | |
|---|---|---|
| COMPLETE SET (10) | 20.00 | 50.00 |
| COMMON CARD (AI1-AI10) | 2.50 | 6.00 |
| *FOIL/299: .6X TO 1.5X BASIC CARDS | 3.00 | 8.00 |
| *CANVAS/99: .75X TO 2X BASIC CARDS | 5.00 | 12.00 |
| *WOOD/50: 1X TO 2.5X BASIC CARDS | 6.00 | 15.00 |
| *SILVER/10: UNPRICED DUE TO SCARCITY | | |
| *GOLD/1: UNPRICED DUE TO SCARCITY | | |
| *P.P.BLACK/1: UNPRICED DUE TO SCARCITY | | |
| *P.P.CYAN/1: UNPRICED DUE TO SCARCITY | | |
| *P.P.MAGENTA/1: UNPRICED DUE TO SCARCITY | | |
| *P.P.YELLOW/1: UNPRICED DUE TO SCARCITY | | |
| STATED ODDS 1:4 | | |

## 2016 Star Wars Masterwork Autographs

| | | |
|---|---|---|
| COMMON CARD | 6.00 | 15.00 |
| *FOIL/50: .6X TO 1.5X BASIC CARDS | | |
| *CANVAS/25: .75X TO 2X BASIC CARDS | | |
| *WOOD/10: UNPRICED DUE TO SCARCITY | | |
| *SILVER/10: UNPRICED DUE TO SCARCITY | | |
| *GOLD/1: UNPRICED DUE TO SCARCITY | | |
| *P.P.BLACK/1: UNPRICED DUE TO SCARCITY | | |
| *P.P.CYAN/1: UNPRICED DUE TO SCARCITY | | |
| *P.P.MAGENTA/1: UNPRICED DUE TO SCARCITY | | |
| *P.P.YELLOW/1: UNPRICED DUE TO SCARCITY | | |
| 5 Andy Serkis | 80.00 | 150.00 |
| 8 Ashley Eckstein | 12.00 | 30.00 |
| 11 Caroline Blakiston | 8.00 | 20.00 |
| 14 Clive Revill | 12.00 | 30.00 |
| 15 Corey Dee Williams | 8.00 | 20.00 |
| 19 David Ankrum | 8.00 | 20.00 |
| 20 David Barclay | 8.00 | 20.00 |
| 24 Dickey Beer | 10.00 | 25.00 |
| 34 Jeremy Bulloch | 15.00 | 40.00 |
| 39 John Coppinger | 8.00 | 20.00 |
| 47 Mark Dodson | 10.00 | 25.00 |
| 50 Matthew Wood | 8.00 | 20.00 |
| 55 Mike Edmonds | 8.00 | 20.00 |
| 56 Mike Quinn | 8.00 | 20.00 |
| 65 Sam Witwer | 8.00 | 20.00 |
| 73 Tim Dry | 8.00 | 20.00 |
| 74 Tim Rose | 8.00 | 20.00 |
| 75 Tiya Sircar | 8.00 | 20.00 |

## 2016 Star Wars Masterwork Autographs Canvas

| | | |
|---|---|---|
| *CANVAS/25: .75X TO 2X BASIC CARDS | | |
| STATED ODDS 1:25 | | |
| STATED PRINT RUN 25 SER.#'d SETS | | |
| 1 Adam Driver | 400.00 | 800.00 |
| 5 Andy Serkis | 150.00 | 300.00 |
| 7 Anthony Daniels | 80.00 | 150.00 |
| 10 Billy Dee Williams | | |
| 12 Carrie Fisher | 300.00 | 600.00 |

| | | |
|---|---|---|
| 16 Daisy Ridley | 1200.00 | 2000.00 |
| 23 Denis Lawson | 25.00 | 60.00 |
| 26 Freddie Prinze Jr. | 30.00 | 80.00 |
| 29 Greg Grunberg | 12.00 | 30.00 |
| 31 Harrison Ford/1 | | |
| 32 Hugh Quarshie | | |
| 38 John Boyega | | |
| 42 Julian Glover | | |
| 43 Keisha Castle-Hughes | | |
| 48 Mark Hamill | 250.00 | 500.00 |
| 52 Michael Carter | 12.00 | 30.00 |
| 60 Peter Mayhew | | |
| 61 Ray Park | | |
| 79 Warwick Davis | 15.00 | 40.00 |

## 2016 Star Wars Masterwork Autographs Foil

| | | |
|---|---|---|
| *FOIL/50: .6X TO 1.5X BASIC CARDS | | |
| STATED ODDS 1:30 | | |
| STATED PRINT RUN 50 SER.#'d SETS | | |
| 3 Alan Harris | | |
| 7 Anthony Daniels | 50.00 | 100.00 |
| 12 Carrie Fisher | | |
| 14 Clive Revill | | |
| 15 Corey Dee Williams | | |
| 19 David Ankrum | | |
| 20 David Barclay | | |
| 23 Denis Lawson | | |
| 25 Femi Taylor | | |
| 26 Freddie Prinze Jr. | | |
| 27 Garrick Hagon | | |
| 28 George Takei | 15.00 | 40.00 |
| 29 Greg Grunberg | 10.00 | 25.00 |
| 32 Hugh Quarshie | 10.00 | 25.00 |
| 33 Jack Klaff | | |
| 38 John Boyega | 120.00 | 250.00 |
| 40 John Morton | | |
| 41 John Ratzenberger | | |
| 43 Keisha Castle-Hughes | | |
| 44 Kenneth Colley | | |
| 47 Mark Dodson | | |
| 51 Mercedes Ngoh | | |
| 52 Michael Carter | | |
| 59 Paul Blake | | |
| 60 Peter Mayhew | 30.00 | 80.00 |
| 61 Ray Park | | |
| 67 Sean Crawford | | |
| 76 Toby Philpott | | |
| 79 Warwick Davis | | |

## 2016 Star Wars Masterwork Dual Autographs

| | | |
|---|---|---|
| STATED ODDS 1:4,658 | | |
| NNO Fisher/Baker | | |
| NNO Barclay/Philpott | 25.00 | 60.00 |
| NNO McDiarmid/Revil | | |
| NNO Blake/Bowers | 20.00 | 50.00 |
| NNO Hamill/Ridley | | |
| NNO Hamill/Baker | | |
| NNO Pygram/Stanton | 15.00 | 40.00 |

## 2016 Star Wars Masterwork Great Rivalries

| | | |
|---|---|---|
| COMPLETE SET (10) | 15.00 | 40.00 |
| COMMON CARD (GR1-GR10) | 2.50 | 6.00 |
| *FOIL/299: .6X TO 1.5X BASIC CARDS | | |
| *CANVAS/99: .75X TO 2X BASIC CARDS | | |
| *WOOD/50: 1X TO 2.5X BASIC CARDS | | |
| *SILVER/10: UNPRICED DUE TO SCARCITY | | |
| *GOLD/1: UNPRICED DUE TO SCARCITY | | |
| *P.P.BLACK/1: UNPRICED DUE TO SCARCITY | | |

| | | |
|---|---|---|
| *P.P.CYAN/1: UNPRICED DUE TO SCARCITY | | |
| *P.P.MAGENTA/1: UNPRICED DUE TO SCARCITY | | |
| *P.P.YELLOW/1: UNPRICED DUE TO SCARCITY | | |
| STATED ODDS 1:2 | | |

## 2016 Star Wars Masterwork Medallion Relics

| | | |
|---|---|---|
| COMMON CARD | 5.00 | 12.00 |
| *SILVER/99: .6X TO 1.5X BASIC CARDS | 8.00 | 20.00 |
| *GOLD/10: 1.5X TO 4X BASIC CARDS | 20.00 | 50.00 |
| *PLATINUM/1: UNPRICED DUE TO SCARCITY | | |
| STATED ODDS 1:7 | | |
| NNO Han Solo Hoth | 6.00 | 15.00 |
| NNO Han Solo Starkiller Base | 6.00 | 15.00 |
| NNO Han Solo Yavin | 6.00 | 15.00 |
| NNO Kylo Ren Starkiller Base | | |
| NNO Rey Starkiller Base | 6.00 | 15.00 |

## 2016 Star Wars Masterwork Show of Force

| | | |
|---|---|---|
| COMPLETE SET (10) | 25.00 | 60.00 |
| COMMON CARD (SF1-SF10) | 3.00 | 8.00 |
| *FOIL/299: .6X TO 1.5X BASIC CARDS | 5.00 | 12.00 |
| *CANVAS/99: .75X TO 2X BASIC CARDS | 6.00 | 15.00 |
| *WOOD/50: 1X TO 2.5X BASIC CARDS | 8.00 | 20.00 |
| *SILVER/10: UNPRICED DUE TO SCARCITY | | |
| *GOLD/1: UNPRICED DUE TO SCARCITY | | |
| *P.P.BLACK/1: UNPRICED DUE TO SCARCITY | | |
| *P.P.CYAN/1: UNPRICED DUE TO SCARCITY | | |
| *P.P.MAGENTA/1: UNPRICED DUE TO SCARCITY | | |
| *P.P.YELLOW/1: UNPRICED DUE TO SCARCITY | | |
| STATED ODDS 1:4 | | |
| SF10 Rey | 4.00 | 10.00 |

## 2016 Star Wars Masterwork Stamp Relics

| | | |
|---|---|---|
| COMPLETE SET (12) | 100.00 | 200.00 |
| COMMON CARD | 8.00 | 20.00 |
| *BRONZE/99: .6X TO 1.5X BASIC CARDS | 12.00 | 30.00 |
| *SILVER/50: .75X TO 2X BASIC CARDS | 15.00 | 40.00 |
| *GOLD/10: UNPRICED DUE TO SCARCITY | | |
| *PLATINUM/1: UNPRICED DUE TO SCARCITY | | |
| STATED ODDS 1:13 | | |
| STATED PRINT RUN 249 SER.#'d SETS | | |
| NNO Han Solo | 10.00 | 25.00 |
| NNO Rey | 12.00 | 30.00 |

## 2017 Star Wars Masterwork

| | | |
|---|---|---|
| COMMON CARD (1-75) | 2.50 | 6.00 |
| COMMON SP (76-100) | 5.00 | 12.00 |
| *BLUE: .5X TO 1.25X BASIC CARDS | 3.00 | 8.00 |
| *GREEN/99: .6X TO 1.5X BASIC CARDS | 4.00 | 10.00 |
| *PURPLE/50: .75X TO 2X BASIC CARDS | 5.00 | 12.00 |
| *GOLD/25: 1X TO 2.5X BASIC CARDS | 6.00 | 15.00 |
| *RED/1: UNPRICED DUE TO SCARCITY | | |
| *P.P.BLACK/1: UNPRICED DUE TO SCARCITY | | |
| *P.P.CYAN/1: UNPRICED DUE TO SCARCITY | | |
| *P.P.MAGENTA/1: UNPRICED DUE TO SCARCITY | | |
| *P.P.YELLOW/1: UNPRICED DUE TO SCARCITY | | |

## 2017 Star Wars Masterwork Adventures of R2-D2

| | | |
|---|---|---|
| COMMON CARD (AR1-AR10) | 2.50 | 6.00 |
| *RAINBOW FOIL: .5X TO 1.25X BASIC CARDS | 3.00 | 8.00 |
| *CANVAS: .6X TO 1.5X BASIC CARDS | 4.00 | 10.00 |
| *WOOD/50: .75X TO 2X BASIC CARDS | 5.00 | 12.00 |
| *METAL/10: UNPRICED DUE TO SCARCITY | | |
| *GOLD TINTED/1: UNPRICED DUE TO SCARCITY | | |
| *P.P.BLACK/1: UNPRICED DUE TO SCARCITY | | |
| *P.P.CYAN/1: UNPRICED DUE TO SCARCITY | | |
| *P.P.MAGENTA/1: UNPRICED DUE TO SCARCITY | | |
| *P.P.YELLOW/1: UNPRICED DUE TO SCARCITY | | |

## 2017 Star Wars Masterwork Autographs

| | | |
|---|---|---|
| COMMON CARD | 6.00 | 15.00 |
| *WOOD/10: UNPRICED DUE TO SCARCITY | | |
| SILVER FRAMED/10>: UNPRICED DUE TO SCARCITY | | |
| *GOLD TINTED/1: UNPRICED DUE TO SCARCITY | | |
| NNO Adam Driver (horizontal) | | |
| NNO Adam Driver (vertical) | | |
| NNO Alan Tudyk | 50.00 | 100.00 |

| | | |
|---|---|---|
| NNO Andy Serkis | | |
| NNO Ashley Eckstein | 15.00 | 40.00 |
| NNO Ben Daniels | 8.00 | 20.00 |
| NNO Billy Dee Williams | | |
| NNO Brian Herring | 15.00 | 40.00 |
| NNO Clive Revill | 8.00 | 20.00 |
| NNO Daisy Ridley | | |
| NNO Dee Bradley Baker | 10.00 | 25.00 |
| NNO Derek Arnold | 8.00 | 20.00 |
| NNO Donnie Yen | 60.00 | 120.00 |
| NNO Felicity Jones (horizontal) | | |
| NNO Felicity Jones (vertical) | | |
| NNO Forest Whitaker (horizontal) | | |
| NNO Forest Whitaker (vertical) | | |
| NNO Freddie Prinze Jr. | | |
| NNO Gwendoline Christie | | |
| NNO Harrison Ford | | |
| NNO Hayden Christensen | 150.00 | 300.00 |
| NNO Ian McDiarmid | | |
| NNO Ian Whyte | 10.00 | 25.00 |
| NNO Jeremy Bulloch | 15.00 | 40.00 |
| NNO John Boyega (horizontal) | | |
| NNO John Boyega (vertical) | 60.00 | 120.00 |
| NNO Julian Glover | 12.00 | 30.00 |
| NNO Lars Mikkelsen | 25.00 | 60.00 |
| NNO Mark Hamill | | |
| NNO Mary Elizabeth McGlynn | 12.00 | 30.00 |
| NNO Matt Lanter | 15.00 | 40.00 |
| NNO Matthew Wood | | |
| NNO Phil LaMarr | 8.00 | 20.00 |
| NNO Ray Park | | |
| NNO Riz Ahmed | | |
| NNO Robbie Daymond | 10.00 | 25.00 |
| NNO Sam Witwer | 10.00 | 25.00 |
| NNO Sarah Michelle Gellar | | |
| NNO Temuera Morrison | 25.00 | 60.00 |
| NNO Tiya Sircar | 8.00 | 20.00 |
| NNO Tom Baker | | |
| NNO Valene Kane | 25.00 | 60.00 |
| NNO Warwick Davis | 10.00 | 25.00 |
| NNO Zarene Dallas | 8.00 | 20.00 |

## 2017 Star Wars Masterwork Droid Medallion Relics

| | | |
|---|---|---|
| COMMON CARD | 5.00 | 12.00 |
| *SILVER/40: .5X TO 1.2X BASIC RELICS | 6.00 | 15.00 |
| *GOLD/25: .6X TO 1.5X BASIC RELICS | 8.00 | 20.00 |
| *BLACK/1: UNPRICED DUE TO SCARCITY | | |
| STATED PRINT RUN 150 SER.#'d SETS | | |

## 2017 Star Wars Masterwork Dual Autographs

| | | |
|---|---|---|
| *PURPLE/10: UNPRICED DUE TO SCARCITY | | |
| *GOLD/5: UNPRICED DUE TO SCARCITY | | |
| *RED/1: UNPRICED DUE TO SCARCITY | | |
| NNO Graves/Taber | 20.00 | 50.00 |
| NNO Daniels/Baker | | |
| NNO Herring/Baker | | |
| NNO Fisher/Baker | | |
| NNO Barclay/Taylor | 15.00 | 40.00 |
| NNO Jones/Tudyk | | |
| NNO Whitaker/Ahmed | | |
| NNO Prinze Jr./Gellar | | |

| | | |
|---|---|---|
| NNO Christie/Boyega | | |
| NNO Christensen/Baker | | |
| NNO Christensen/Wood | | |
| NNO McDiarmid/Christensen | | |
| NNO Uwais/Qin-Fee | 12.00 | 30.00 |
| NNO Isaccs/Gray | 20.00 | 50.00 |
| NNO Ratzenberger/MacInnes | 12.00 | 30.00 |
| NNO Hamill/Christensen | | |
| NNO Hamill/Baker | | |
| NNO Salenger/Futterman | 12.00 | 30.00 |
| NNO Kasey/Stanton | 12.00 | 30.00 |
| NNO Marshall/Fleetwood | | |
| NNO Witwer/Wilkinson | 15.00 | 40.00 |
| NNO Morrison/Logan | 20.00 | 50.00 |
| NNO Cole/Grube | | |

## 2017 Star Wars Masterwork Evolution of the Rebel Alliance

| | | |
|---|---|---|
| COMMON CARD (LP1-LP10) | 2.50 | 6.00 |
| *RAINBOW FOIL/249: .5X TO 1.25X BASIC CARDS | 3.00 | 8.00 |
| *CANVAS/99: .6X TO 1.5X BASIC CARDS | 4.00 | 10.00 |
| *WOOD/50: .75X TO 2X BASIC CARDS | 5.00 | 12.00 |
| *METAL/10: UNPRICED DUE TO SCARCITY | | |
| *GOLD TINTED/1: UNPRICED DUE TO SCARCITY | | |
| *P.P.BLACK/1: UNPRICED DUE TO SCARCITY | | |
| *P.P.CYAN/1: UNPRICED DUE TO SCARCITY | | |
| *P.P.MAGENTA/1: UNPRICED DUE TO SCARCITY | | |
| *P.P.YELLOW/1: UNPRICED DUE TO SCARCITY | | |

## 2017 Star Wars Masterwork Film Strips

| | | |
|---|---|---|
| COMMON CARD (FCR1-FCR40) | 10.00 | 25.00 |

## 2017 Star Wars Masterwork Hall of Heroes

| | | |
|---|---|---|
| COMPLETE SET (10) | 12.00 | 30.00 |
| COMMON CARD (HH1-HH10) | 3.00 | 8.00 |
| *RAINBOW FOIL: .5X TO 1.2X BASIC CARDS | 4.00 | 10.00 |
| *CANVAS: .6X TO 1.5X BASIC CARDS | 5.00 | 12.00 |
| *WOOD: UNPRICED DUE TO SCARCITY | | |
| *METAL: UNPRICED DUE TO SCARCITY | | |
| *GOLD TINTED: UNPRICED DUE TO SCARCITY | | |
| *P.P.BLACK/1: UNPRICED DUE TO SCARCITY | | |
| *P.P.CYAN/1: UNPRICED DUE TO SCARCITY | | |
| *P.P.MAGENTA/1: UNPRICED DUE TO SCARCITY | | |
| *P.P.YELLOW/1: UNPRICED DUE TO SCARCITY | | |

## 2017 Star Wars Masterwork Source Material Jumbo Swatch Relics

| | | |
|---|---|---|
| COMMON CARD | 25.00 | 60.00 |
| JRCAR Admiral Ackbar Resistance Uniform | 30.00 | 75.00 |
| JRCGE Galen Erso Farmer Disguise | 60.00 | 120.00 |
| JRCGF General Hux First Order Uniform | 50.00 | 100.00 |
| JRCRD Rey Desert Tunic | 200.00 | 400.00 |
| JRCRO Rey Outer Garment | 150.00 | 300.00 |

## 2018 Star Wars Masterwork

| | | |
|---|---|---|
| COMPLETE SET W/SP (125) | | |
| COMPLETE SET W/O SP (100) | | |
| UNOPENED BOX (4 PACKS) | 150.00 | 200.00 |

| | | |
|---|---|---|
| UNOPENED PACK (5 CARDS) | 40.00 | 50.00 |
| COMMON CARD (1-100) | 2.50 | 6.00 |
| COMMON SP (101-125) | 6.00 | 15.00 |
| *BLUE: .5 TO 1.2X BASIC CARDS | | |
| *GREEN/99: .6X TO 1.5X BASIC CARDS | | |
| *PURPLE/50: .75X TO 2X BASIC CARDS | | |
| *ORANGE/10: UNPRICED DUE TO SCARCITY | | |
| *BLACK/5: UNPRICED DUE TO SCARCITY | | |
| *GOLD/1: UNPRICED DUE TO SCARCITY | | |
| *P.P.BLACK/1: UNPRICED DUE TO SCARCITY | | |
| *P.P.CYAN/1: UNPRICED DUE TO SCARCITY | | |
| *P.P.MAGENTA/1: UNPRICED DUE TO SCARCITY | | |
| *P.P.YELLOW/1: UNPRICED DUE TO SCARCITY | | |
| 101 Luke Skywalker SP | 8.00 | 20.00 |
| 102 Princess Leia Organa SP | 12.00 | 30.00 |
| 103 Rey SP | 15.00 | 40.00 |
| 104 Finn SP | 10.00 | 25.00 |
| 105 Obi-Wan Kenobi SP | 10.00 | 25.00 |
| 106 Anakin Skywalker SP | 10.00 | 25.00 |
| 108 Darth Vader SP | 8.00 | 20.00 |
| 109 Darth Maul SP | 8.00 | 20.00 |
| 110 Boba Fett SP | 12.00 | 30.00 |
| 111 Han Solo SP | 12.00 | 30.00 |
| 113 Lando Calrissian SP | 10.00 | 25.00 |
| 114 Saw Gerrera SP | 10.00 | 25.00 |
| 115 Jyn Erso SP | 12.00 | 30.00 |
| 116 Captain Cassian Andor SP | 10.00 | 25.00 |
| 119 Kylo Ren SP | 10.00 | 25.00 |
| 121 Ahsoka Tano SP | 8.00 | 20.00 |
| 124 Bo-Katan Kryze SP | 8.00 | 20.00 |

### 2018 Star Wars Masterwork Autographed Commemorative Vehicle Patches

UNPRICED DUE TO SCARCITY

MPAAD Anthony Daniels
MPABH Brian Herring
MPABM Ben Mendelsohn
MPAFJ Felicity Jones
MPAGO Genevieve O'Reilly
MPAHC Hayden Christensen
MPAHQ Hugh Quarshie
MPAIM Ian McDiarmid
MPAJB John Boyega
MPALM Lars Mikkelsen
MPAMQ Mike Quinn
MPARA Riz Ahmed
MPASB Steve Blum
MPATG Taylor Gray
MPATS Tiya Sircar
MPAVM Vanessa Marshall
MPADBB Dee Bradley Baker
MPAFPJ Freddie Prinze Jr.
MPAGMT Guy Henry
MPAMEM Mary Elizabeth McGlynn

### 2018 Star Wars Masterwork Autographs

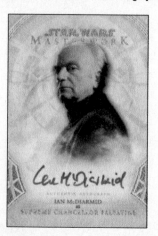

| | | |
|---|---|---|
| COMMON AUTO | 6.00 | 15.00 |
| *BLUE FOIL/99: .5X TO 1.2X BASIC AUTOS | | |
| *WOOD/10: UNPRICED DUE TO SCARCITY | | |
| *SILVER FR./5: UNPRICED DUE TO SCARCITY | | |
| *GOLD FR./1: UNPRICED DUE TO SCARCITY | | |
| *P.P.BLACK/1: UNPRICED DUE TO SCARCITY | | |
| *P.P.CYAN/1: UNPRICED DUE TO SCARCITY | | |
| *P.P.MAGENTA/1: UNPRICED DUE TO SCARCITY | | |
| *P.P.YELLOW/1: UNPRICED DUE TO SCARCITY | | |
| NNO Andrew Kishino | 8.00 | 20.00 |
| NNO Ashley Eckstein | 12.00 | 30.00 |
| NNO Brent Spiner | 12.00 | 30.00 |
| NNO Cavin Cornwall | 12.00 | 30.00 |
| NNO Daniel Mays | 8.00 | 20.00 |
| NNO David Barclay | 10.00 | 25.00 |
| NNO Denis Lawson | 8.00 | 20.00 |
| NNO Guy Henry | 8.00 | 20.00 |
| NNO Howie Weed | 12.00 | 30.00 |
| NNO James Arnold Taylor | 10.00 | 25.00 |
| NNO Jason Spisak | 8.00 | 20.00 |
| NNO Jeremy Bulloch | 15.00 | 40.00 |
| NNO Jimmy Vee | 10.00 | 25.00 |
| NNO Lars Mikkelsen | 10.00 | 25.00 |
| NNO Laura Dern | 100.00 | 200.00 |
| NNO Matt Lanter | 8.00 | 20.00 |
| NNO Matthew Wood | 10.00 | 25.00 |
| NNO Nathalie Cuzner | 8.00 | 20.00 |
| NNO Robert Nairne | 8.00 | 20.00 |
| NNO Sam Witwer | 12.00 | 30.00 |
| NNO Simon Williamson | 12.00 | 30.00 |
| NNO Tom Wilton | 8.00 | 20.00 |

### 2018 Star Wars Masterwork Commemorative Vehicle Patches

| | | |
|---|---|---|
| COMMON PATCH | 4.00 | 10.00 |
| *PURPLE/50: .6X TO 1.5X BASIC PATCHES | | |
| *BLACK/5: UNPRICED DUE TO SCARCITY | | |
| *GOLD/1: UNPRICED DUE TO SCARCITY | | |
| STATED PRINT RUN 175 SER.#'d SETS | | |
| MPBHF Slave I/Boba Fett | 8.00 | 20.00 |
| MPGEA Chimaera/Grand Admiral Thrawn | 6.00 | 15.00 |
| MPGEK Chimaera/Kassius Konstantine | 6.00 | 15.00 |
| MPGEM Krennic's Shuttle/Grand Moff Tarkin | 6.00 | 15.00 |
| MPGEP Chimaera/Governor Arihnda Pryce | 5.00 | 12.00 |
| MPGEV Star Destroyer/Darth Vader | 5.00 | 12.00 |
| MPGRB Radiant VII/Bail Organa | 6.00 | 15.00 |
| MPGRP Radiant VII/PadmÈ Amidala | 8.00 | 20.00 |
| MPJOA Anakin's Fighter/Anakin Skywalker | 5.00 | 12.00 |
| MPJOO Anakin's Fighter/Obi-Wan Kenobi | 6.00 | 15.00 |
| MPJOQ Anakin's Fighter/Qui-Gon Jinn | 5.00 | 12.00 |
| MPPSA The Ghost/Ahsoka Tano | 5.00 | 12.00 |
| MPPSE The Ghost/Ezra Bridger | 5.00 | 12.00 |
| MPPSH The Ghost/Hera Syndulla | 5.00 | 12.00 |
| MPPSZ The Ghost/Zeb Orrelios | 6.00 | 15.00 |
| MPRAB U-Wing/Bodhi Rook | 5.00 | 12.00 |
| MPRAH Y-Wing/Han Solo | 12.00 | 30.00 |
| MPRAJ U-Wing/Jyn Erso | 5.00 | 12.00 |
| MPRAK U-Wing/K-2SO | 5.00 | 12.00 |
| MPRAM U-Wing/Baze Malbus | 6.00 | 15.00 |

| | | |
|---|---|---|
| MPRAP Y-Wing/Princess Leia Organa | 8.00 | 20.00 |
| MPRAR Y-Wing/R2-D2 | 5.00 | 12.00 |
| MPRAS Y-Wing/Luke Skywalker | 6.00 | 15.00 |
| MPRMH The Millennium Falcon/Han Solo | 10.00 | 25.00 |
| MPRML The Millennium Falcon/Lando Calrissian | 5.00 | 12.00 |
| MPRMN The Millennium Falcon/Nien Nunb | 5.00 | 12.00 |
| MPRMP The Millennium Falcon/Princess Leia Organa | 8.00 | 20.00 |
| MPRMS The Millennium Falcon/Luke Skywalker | 6.00 | 15.00 |
| MPTRF Black One/Finn | 6.00 | 15.00 |
| MPTRL Black One/General Leia Organa | 8.00 | 20.00 |
| MPTRR Black One/Rey | 8.00 | 20.00 |

### 2018 Star Wars Masterwork Dual Autographs

| | | |
|---|---|---|
| *WOOD/10: UNPRICED DUE TO SCARCITY | | |
| *BLACK/5: UNPRICED DUE TO SCARCITY | | |
| GOLD/1: UNPRICED DUE TO SCARCITY | | |
| NNO A.Cook/I.Whyte | | |
| NNO B.Mendelsohn/G.Henry | | |
| NNO B.Williams/M.Quinn | | |
| NNO C.Blakiston/G.O'Reilly | | |
| NNO D.Ridley/J.Boyega | | |
| NNO E.Bauersfeld/K.Rotich | 20.00 | 50.00 |
| NNO F.Jones/B.Mendelsohn | | |
| NNO G.Takei/M.Lanter | | |
| NNO H.Christensen/R.Park | | |
| NNO J.Taylor/N.Futterman | | |
| NNO J.Boyega/B.Herring | 75.00 | 150.00 |
| NNO J.Boyega/J.Suotamo | 75.00 | 150.00 |
| NNO K.Leung/G.Grunberg | 15.00 | 40.00 |
| NNO K.Baker/D.Barclay | | |
| NNO L.Mikkelsen/M.McGlynn | 20.00 | 50.00 |
| NNO M.Salenger/O.D'Abo | 30.00 | 75.00 |
| NNO R.Park/M.Wood | | |
| NNO R.Ahmed/A.Tudyk | | |
| NNO S.Witwer/S.Stanton | | |
| NNO S.Gellar/P.Anthony-Rodriguez | | |

### 2018 Star Wars Masterwork History of the Jedi

| | | |
|---|---|---|
| COMPLETE SET (10) | 10.00 | 25.00 |
| COMMON CARD (HJ1-HJ10) | 1.50 | 4.00 |
| *RAINBOW/299: SAME VALUE AS BASIC | | |
| *CANVAS/25: 1.2X TO 3X BASIC CARDS | | |
| *WOOD/10: UNPRICED DUE TO SCARCITY | | |
| *METAL/5: UNPRICED DUE TO SCARCITY | | |
| *GOLD METAL/1: UNPRICED DUE TO SCARCITY | | |
| *P.P.BLACK/1: UNPRICED DUE TO SCARCITY | | |
| *P.P.CYAN/1: UNPRICED DUE TO SCARCITY | | |
| *P.P.MAGENTA/1: UNPRICED DUE TO SCARCITY | | |
| *P.P.YELLOW/1: UNPRICED DUE TO SCARCITY | | |
| HJ1 Yoda | 2.50 | 6.00 |
| HJ2 Mace Windu | 2.50 | 6.00 |
| HJ4 Qui-Gon Jinn | 2.00 | 5.00 |

| | | |
|---|---|---|
| HJ5 Obi-Wan Kenobi | 2.00 | 5.00 |
| HJ6 Anakin Skywalker | 2.00 | 5.00 |
| HJ9 Luke Skywalker | 2.00 | 5.00 |
| HJ10 Rey | 3.00 | 8.00 |

## 2018 Star Wars Masterwork Powerful Partners

| | | |
|---|---|---|
| COMPLETE SET (8) | 10.00 | 25.00 |
| COMMON CARD (PP1-PP8) | 1.50 | 4.00 |
| *RAINBOW/299: SAME VALUE AS BASIC | | |
| *WOOD/10: UNPRICED DUE TO SCARCITY | | |
| *METAL/5: UNPRICED DUE TO SCARCITY | | |
| *GOLD METAL/1: UNPRICED DUE TO SCARCITY | | |
| *P.P.BLACK/1: UNPRICED DUE TO SCARCITY | | |
| *P.P.CYAN/1: UNPRICED DUE TO SCARCITY | | |
| *P.P.MAGENTA/1: UNPRICED DUE TO SCARCITY | | |
| *P.P.YELLOW/1: UNPRICED DUE TO SCARCITY | | |
| PP1 Han Solo & Chewbacca | 2.50 | 6.00 |
| PP3 Luke Skywalker & Princess Leia Organa | 2.50 | 6.00 |
| PP4 Darth Vader & Grand Moff Tarkin | 2.50 | 6.00 |
| PP6 Jyn Erso & Captain Cassian Andor | 3.00 | 8.00 |
| PP7 Rey & Finn | 3.00 | 8.00 |
| PP8 Finn & Rose Tico | 2.00 | 5.00 |

## 2018 Star Wars Masterwork Source Material Fabric Swatches

| | | |
|---|---|---|
| JRGH General Hux Jacket Lining | | |
| JRLP Luke Skywalker Pants | | |
| JRLT Luke Skywalker Tunic | 75.00 | 150.00 |
| JRPD Poe Dameron Jacket Lining | 100.00 | 200.00 |
| JRRG Poe Dameron Shirt | 50.00 | 100.00 |
| JRRS Jyn Erso Poncho | | |
| JRRT Rey Desert Tunic Sleeves | 150.00 | 300.00 |
| JRCRT Rose Tico Ground Crew Flightsuit Lining | 100.00 | 200.00 |

## 2018 Star Wars Masterwork Stamp Relics

| | | |
|---|---|---|
| COMMON MEM | 6.00 | 15.00 |
| *BLACK/5: UNPRICED DUE TO SCARCITY | | |
| *GOLD/1: UNPRICED DUE TO SCARCITY | | |
| RANDOMLY INSERTED INTO PACKS | | |
| SBF Finn | 8.00 | 20.00 |
| BB-8! | | |
| SBP Poe Dameron | 8.00 | 20.00 |
| BB-8! | | |
| SBR Rey | 10.00 | 25.00 |
| BB-8! | | |
| SCC Chewbacca | 8.00 | 20.00 |
| Chewbacca! | | |
| SCH Han Solo | 8.00 | 20.00 |
| Chewbacca! | | |
| SCL Lando Calrissian | 6.00 | 15.00 |
| Chewbacca! | | |
| SCP Princess Leia Organa | 12.00 | 30.00 |
| C-3PO and Jabba the Hutt's Palace | | |
| SCR R2-D2 | 6.00 | 15.00 |
| C-3PO and Jabba the Hutt's Palace | | |
| SCS Luke Skywalker | 6.00 | 15.00 |
| C-3PO and Jabba the Hutt's Palace | | |
| SKC Captain Cassian Andor | 6.00 | 15.00 |
| K-2SO on Scarif! | | |
| SKJ Jyn Erso | 10.00 | 25.00 |
| K-2SO on Scarif! | | |
| SKK K-2SO | 12.00 | 30.00 |
| K-2SO on Scarif! | | |
| SMF Finn | 6.00 | 15.00 |
| Maz Kanata's Castle! | | |
| SMH Han Solo | 8.00 | 20.00 |
| Maz Kanata's Castle! | | |
| SMR Rey | 8.00 | 20.00 |
| Maz Kanata's Castle! | | |
| SPC Chewbacca | 6.00 | 15.00 |
| Ahch-To Island Porgs! | | |
| SPL Luke Skywalker | 6.00 | 15.00 |
| Ahch-To Island Porgs! | | |
| SPR Rey | 12.00 | 30.00 |
| Ahch-To Island Porgs! | | |
| SRA Anakin Skywalker | 6.00 | 15.00 |
| R2-D2! | | |
| SRO Obi-Wan Kenobi | 8.00 | 20.00 |
| R2-D2! | | |
| SRP PadmÈ Amidala | 8.00 | 20.00 |
| R2-D2! | | |
| SSH General Hux | 6.00 | 15.00 |
| Supreme Leader Snoke and the First Order | | |
| SSK Kylo Ren | 10.00 | 25.00 |
| Supreme Leader Snoke and the First Order | | |
| SSP Captain Phasma | 6.00 | 15.00 |
| Supreme Leader Snoke and the First Order | | |

## 2018 Star Wars Masterwork Super Weapons

| | | |
|---|---|---|
| COMPLETE SET (7) | 8.00 | 20.00 |
| COMMON CARD (SW1-SW7) | 2.00 | 5.00 |
| *RAINBOW/299: .5X TO 1.2X BASIC CARDS | | |
| *CANVAS/25: 1.2X TO 3X BASIC CARDS | | |
| *WOOD/10: UNPRICED DUE TO SCARCITY | | |
| *METAL/5: UNPRICED DUE TO SCARCITY | | |
| *GOLD METAL/1: UNPRICED DUE TO SCARCITY | | |
| *P.P.BLACK/1: UNPRICED DUE TO SCARCITY | | |
| *P.P.CYAN/1: UNPRICED DUE TO SCARCITY | | |
| *P.P.MAGENTA/1: UNPRICED DUE TO SCARCITY | | |
| *P.P.YELLOW/1: UNPRICED DUE TO SCARCITY | | |

## 2018 Star Wars Masterwork Triple Autographs

| | |
|---|---|
| *WOOD/10: UNPRICED DUE TO SCARCITY | |
| *BLACK/5: UNPRICED DUE TO SCARCITY | |
| *GOLD/1: UNPRICED DUE TO SCARCITY | |
| UNPRICED DUE TO SCARCITY | |
| NNO A.Serkis/A.Driver/D.Ridley | |
| NNO A.Eckstein/M.Salenger/N.Futterman | |
| NNO B.Williams/P.Mayhew/A.Daniels | |
| NNO D.Ridley/J.Boyega/L.Dern | |
| NNO F.Jones/B.Mendelsohn/F.Whitaker | |
| NNO H.Christensen/T.Morrison/D.Logan | |
| NNO J.Taylor/M.Lanter/A.Eckstein | |
| NNO J.Vee/A.Daniels/D.Chapman | |
| NNO K.Leung/G.Grunberg/T.Rose | |
| NNO T.Baker/F.Prinze Jr./T.Gray | |

## 2017 Star Wars May the 4th Be with You

| | | |
|---|---|---|
| COMPLETE SET (20) | 12.00 | 30.00 |
| COMPLETE FACTORY SET (21) | 40.00 | 80.00 |
| COMMON CARD (1-20) | 1.00 | 2.50 |
| *SILVER/10: 6X TO 15X BASIC CARDS | 15.00 | 40.00 |
| *GOLD/1: UNPRICED DUE TO SCARCITY | | |
| RELEASED 5/4/2017 | | |

## 2017 Star Wars May the 4th Be with You Autographs

| | | |
|---|---|---|
| COMMON AUTO | 10.00 | 25.00 |
| *SILVER/10: .6X TO 1.5X BASIC AUTOS | | |
| *GOLD/1: UNPRICED DUE TO SCARCITY | | |
| STATED ODDS 1:SET | | |
| 1A Harrison Ford | | |
| 2A Mark Hamill | 400.00 | 600.00 |
| 3A Carrie Fisher | | |
| 4A Kenny Baker | | |
| 5A Anthony Daniels | 175.00 | 300.00 |
| 7A Jeremy Bulloch | 25.00 | 60.00 |
| 8A Ian McDiarmid | 250.00 | 400.00 |
| 10A Billy Dee Williams | | |
| 14A Kenneth Colley | 12.00 | 30.00 |
| 16A Erik Bauersfeld | 25.00 | 60.00 |
| 16A Tim Rose | 15.00 | 40.00 |
| 19A Paul Blake | | |

## 1997-98 Star Wars Men Behind the Masks

| | | |
|---|---|---|
| P1 Darth Vader & Boba Fett | 10.00 | 25.00 |
| (Given to Auction Seat Holders) | | |
| P2 Darth Vader & Boba Fett | 10.00 | 25.00 |
| (Given as Admission Ticket) | | |
| P3 Peter Mayhew as Chewbacca | 8.00 | 20.00 |
| (Given to Auction Reserve Seat Holders)/1000* | | |
| P4 Maria de Aragon as Greedo | 10.00 | 25.00 |
| (Show Exclusive)/800* | | |

## 1997-98 Star Wars Men Behind the Masks Test Issue

| | | |
|---|---|---|
| COMPLETE SET (7) | | |
| COMMON CARD | | |
| NNO Chewbacca | 125.00 | 250.00 |
| (prismatic foil/triangles) | | |
| NNO Chewbacca | 125.00 | 250.00 |
| (prismatic foil/vertical lines) | | |
| NNO Chewbacca | 125.00 | 250.00 |
| (refractor foil) | | |
| NNO Greedo | 125.00 | 250.00 |
| (prismatic foil/spotted) | | |
| NNO Greedo | 125.00 | 250.00 |
| (prismatic foil/traingles) | | |
| NNO Greedo | 125.00 | 250.00 |
| (prismatic foil/vertical lines) | | |
| NNO Greedo | 125.00 | 250.00 |
| (refractor foil) | | |

## 1994-96 Star Wars Metal

| | | |
|---|---|---|
| COMPLETE SET (60) | 30.00 | 75.00 |
| COMMON CARD (1-60) | 1.00 | 2.50 |

## 1994-96 Star Wars Metal Promos

| | | |
|---|---|---|
| COMPLETE SET (3) | 12.00 | 30.00 |
| COMMON CARD (P1-P3) | 6.00 | 15.00 |
| P1 Star Wars Episode IV | 6.00 | 15.00 |
| P2 The Empire Strikes Back | 6.00 | 15.00 |
| P3 Return of the Jedi | 6.00 | 15.00 |

## 1996 Star Wars Metal Art of Ralph McQuarrie

| | | |
|---|---|---|
| COMPLETE SET (20) | 10.00 | 25.00 |
| COMMON CARD (1-20) | 1.00 | 2.50 |
| COA Certificate of Authenticity | | |

### 1998 Star Wars Metal Bounty Hunters

| | | |
|---|---|---|
| COMPLETE SET (5) | 2.50 | 6.00 |
| COMMON CARD (1-5) | 1.00 | 2.50 |
| HSJH  Han Solo and Jabba the Hutt SE | | |

### 1995 Star Wars Metal Dark Empire I

| | | |
|---|---|---|
| COMPLETE SET (6) | 3.00 | 8.00 |
| COMMON CARD (1-6) | 1.00 | 2.50 |

### 1996 Star Wars Metal Dark Empire II

| | | |
|---|---|---|
| COMPLETE SET (6) | 3.00 | 8.00 |
| COMMON CARD (1-6) | 1.00 | 2.50 |

### 1998 Star Wars Metal Jedi Knights

| | | |
|---|---|---|
| COMPLETE SET (5) | 3.00 | 8.00 |
| COMMON CARD (1-5) | 1.00 | 2.50 |
| MES  Mos Eisley Spaceport SE | 1.50 | 4.00 |

### 1998 Star Wars Metal Jedi Knights Avon

| | | |
|---|---|---|
| COMPLETE SET (4) | 3.00 | 8.00 |
| COMMON CARD (1-4) | 1.00 | 2.50 |
| WIC  Wampa Ice Creature SE | 1.50 | 4.00 |

### 1997 Star Wars Metal Shadows of the Empire

| | | |
|---|---|---|
| COMPLETE SET (6) | 4.00 | 10.00 |
| COMMON CARD (1-6) | 1.00 | 2.50 |

### 2015 Star Wars Micro Collector Packs

| | | |
|---|---|---|
| COMPLETE SET (36) | 60.00 | 120.00 |
| COMMON CARD (1-36) | 1.50 | 4.00 |
| NNO  3-D Glasses | .40 | 1.00 |

### 2015 Star Wars Micro Collector Packs 3-D Posters

| | | |
|---|---|---|
| COMPLETE SET (6) | 3.00 | 8.00 |
| COMMON CARD | .60 | 1.50 |
| STATED ODDS 1:1 | | |

### 2015 Star Wars Micro Collector Packs Micro-Comics

| | | |
|---|---|---|
| COMPLETE SET (6) | 4.00 | 10.00 |
| COMMON CARD | .75 | 2.00 |
| STATED ODDS 1:1 | | |

### 1996 Star Wars Multimotion

| | | |
|---|---|---|
| 2M  Star Wars 20th Anniversary Commemorative Magazine | 2.50 | 6.00 |

### 1999 Star Wars The New Jedi Order

| | | |
|---|---|---|
| NNO  SDCC Exclusive | 2.00 | 5.00 |

### 2018 Star Wars Nickel City Con Promos

| | | |
|---|---|---|
| COMPLETE SET (3) | 3.00 | 8.00 |
| COMMON CARD (P1-P3) | 1.25 | 3.00 |
| NNO  Darth Vader | 2.00 | 5.00 |
| NNO  Luke Skywalker | 1.50 | 4.00 |

### 2015 Star Wars NYCC Oversized Exclusives

| | | |
|---|---|---|
| COMPLETE SET (70) | 75.00 | 150.00 |
| COMMON CARD (1-70) | 2.00 | 5.00 |

### 2018 Star Wars On-Demand The Last Jedi

| | | |
|---|---|---|
| COMPLETE SET (20) | 15.00 | 40.00 |
| COMMON CARD (1-20) | 1.25 | 3.00 |
| *PURPLE: .75X TO 2X BASIC CARDS | 2.50 | 6.00 |

### 2018 Star Wars On-Demand The Last Jedi Autographs

| | | |
|---|---|---|
| STATED OVERALL ODDS 1:SET | | |
| NNO  Adam Driver | | |
| NNO  Andrew Jack | 10.00 | 25.00 |
| NNO  Andy Serkis | | |
| NNO  Anthony Daniels | | |
| NNO  Billie Lourd | | |
| NNO  Brian Herring | 8.00 | 20.00 |
| NNO  Daisy Ridley | | |
| NNO  Dave Chapman | 8.00 | 20.00 |
| NNO  Gwendoline Christie | | |
| NNO  Jimmy Vee | 10.00 | 25.00 |
| NNO  John Boyega | 50.00 | 100.00 |
| NNO  Mike Quinn | 15.00 | 40.00 |
| NNO  Paul Kasey | 8.00 | 20.00 |
| NNO  Tim Rose | 15.00 | 40.00 |
| NNO  Tom Kane | 8.00 | 20.00 |

### 2019 Star Wars On-Demand The Power of the Dark Side

| | | |
|---|---|---|
| COMPLETE SET W/EXCL. (26) | 15.00 | 40.00 |
| COMPLETE SET W/O EXCL. (25) | 10.00 | 25.00 |
| COMMON CARD (1-26) | 1.25 | 3.00 |
| *BLUE: 1X TO 2.5X BASIC CARDS | | |
| *PURPLE/10: UNPRICED DUE TO SCARCITY | | |
| *GREEN/5: UNPRICED DUE TO SCARCITY | | |
| *GOLD/1: UNPRICED DUE TO SCARCITY | | |
| STATED PRINT RUN 700 SETS | | |
| SDCC SITH TROOPER PRINT RUN 300 CARDS | | |
| 26  Sith Trooper/300* SDCC | 8.00 | 20.00 |

### 2019 Star Wars On-Demand The Power of the Dark Side Autographs

| | |
|---|---|
| *PURPLE/10: UNPRICED DUE TO SCARCITY | |
| *GREEN/5: UNPRICED DUE TO SCARCITY | |
| *GOLD/1: UNPRICED DUE TO SCARCITY | |
| STATED OVERALL ODDS 1:SET | |
| 2A  Ian McDiarmid | |
| 3A  Hayden Christensen | |
| 4A  Guy Henry | |
| 5A  Nika Futterman | |
| 7A  Barbara Goodson | |
| 8A  Matthew Wood | |
| 9A  Ray Park | |
| 10A  Sam Witwer | |
| 11A  Adam Driver | |
| 12A  Domhnall Gleeson | |
| 13A  Andy Serkis | |
| 15A  Jeremy Bulloch | |
| 17A  Ben Mendelsohn | |
| 18A  Paul Bettany | |

| | |
|---|---|
| 20A  Lars Mikkelson | |
| 21A  Jason Isaacs | |
| 22A  Sarah Michelle Gellar | |
| 23A  Philliph Anthony Rodriguez | |
| 24A  Kathleen Gati | |

### 2019 Star Wars On-Demand The Power of the Dark Side Galactic Battles

| | | |
|---|---|---|
| COMPLETE SET (6) | 15.00 | 40.00 |
| COMMON CARD (G1-G6) | 4.00 | 10.00 |
| STATED ODDS 1:SET | | |

### 2019 Star Wars On-Demand The Power of the Light Side

| | | |
|---|---|---|
| COMPLETE SET W/EXCL. (26) | 15.00 | 40.00 |
| COMPLETE SET W/O EXCL.(25) | 10.00 | 25.00 |
| COMMON CARD (1-25) | 1.25 | 3.00 |
| *BLUE: 1X TO 2.5X BASIC CARDS | | |
| *PURPLE/10: UNPRICED DUE TO SCARCITY | | |
| *GREEN/5: UNPRICED DUE TO SCARCITY | | |
| *GOLD/1: UNPRICED DUE TO SCARCITY | | |
| 26  Luke Skywalker NYCC | 12.00 | 30.00 |

### 2019 Star Wars On-Demand The Power of the Light Side Autographs

| | |
|---|---|
| *PURPLE/10: UNPRICED DUE TO SCARCITY | |
| *GREEN/5: UNPRICED DUE TO SCARCITY | |
| *GOLD/1: UNPRICED DUE TO SCARCITY | |
| STATED ODDS 1:SET | |
| 2A  Carrie Fisher | |
| 3A  Harrison Ford | |
| 4A  Peter Mayhew | |
| 5A  Billy Dee Williams | |
| 6A  Kenny Baker | |
| 7A  Anthony Daniels | |
| 8A  Caroline Blakiston | |
| 11A  Tim Rose | |
| 12A  Hayden Christensen | |
| 13A  Samuel L. Jackson | |
| 14A  Ewan McGregor | |
| 17A  Daisy Ridley | |
| 19A  John Boyega | |
| 20A  Felicity Jones | |
| 21A  Hermione Corfield | |
| 22A  Matt Lanter | |
| 23A  James Arnold Taylor | |
| 24A  Ashley Eckstein | |
| 25A  Taylor Gray | |

### 2019 Star Wars On-Demand The Power of the Light Side Galactic Battles

| | | |
|---|---|---|
| COMPLETE SET (6) | 25.00 | 60.00 |
| COMMON CARD (G1-G6) | 4.00 | 10.00 |
| STATED ODDS 1:SET | | |

### 2018 Star Wars On-Demand Rebels Series Finale

| | | |
|---|---|---|
| COMPLETE SET (20) | 15.00 | 40.00 |
| COMMON CARD (1-20) | 1.25 | 3.00 |
| *BLUE: 1X TO 2.5X BASIC CARDS | | |
| *PURPLE/10: UNPRICED DUE TO SCARCITY | | |

*RED/5: UNPRICED DUE TO SCARCITY
*GOLD/1: UNPRICED DUE TO SCARCITY
STATED PRINT RUN 461 SETS

### 2018 Star Wars On-Demand Rebels Series Finale Autographs

*PURPLE/10: UNPRICED DUE TO SCARCITY
*RED/5: UNPRICED DUE TO SCARCITY
*GOLD/1: UNPRICED DUE TO SCARCITY
STATED OVERALL ODDS 1:SET

| | | |
|---|---|---|
| NNO Ashley Eckstein | | |
| NNO Dee Bradley Baker | 12.00 | 30.00 |
| NNO Forest Whitaker | | |
| NNO Freddie Prinze Jr. | | |
| NNO Genevieve O'Reilly | 10.00 | 25.00 |
| NNO Ian McDiarmid | 60.00 | 120.00 |
| NNO Lars Mikkelsen | 30.00 | 75.00 |
| NNO Mary Elizabeth McGlynn | 15.00 | 40.00 |
| NNO Stephen Stanton | 12.00 | 30.00 |
| NNO Steve Blum | 15.00 | 40.00 |
| NNO Taylor Gray | | |
| NNO Tom Baker | | |
| NNO Vanessa Marshall | | |
| NNO Warwick Davis | | |

### 2019 Star Wars On-Demand Women of Star Wars

COMPLETE SET (25)
| COMMON CARD (1-25) | .75 | 2.00 |
|---|---|---|

*PURPLE: 2X TO 5X BASIC CARDS
*BLUE/10: UNPRICED DUE TO SCARCITY
*RED/5: UNPRICED DUE TO SCARCITY
*GOLD/1: UNPRICED DUE TO SCARCITY

### 2019 Star Wars On-Demand Women of Star Wars Autographs

---

| COMMON AUTO | 8.00 | 20.00 |
|---|---|---|

*BLUE/10: UNPRICED DUE TO SCARCITY
*RED/5: UNPRICED DUE TO SCARCITY
*GOLD/1: UNPRICED DUE TO SCARCITY
STATED OVERALL ODDS 1:SET

| 1 Carrie Fisher | | |
|---|---|---|
| 2 Daisy Ridley | 300.00 | 500.00 |
| 3 Felicity Jones | 125.00 | 250.00 |
| 4 Genevieve O'Reilly | 10.00 | 25.00 |
| 5 Ashley Eckstein | 15.00 | 40.00 |
| 6 Sarah Michelle Gellar | 75.00 | 150.00 |
| 7 Vanessa Marshall | 12.00 | 30.00 |
| 8 Tiya Sircar | 10.00 | 25.00 |
| 9 Nika Futterman | 10.00 | 25.00 |
| 10 Laura Dern | | |
| 12 Tovah Feldshuh | 15.00 | 40.00 |
| 13 Orli Shoshan | 12.00 | 30.00 |
| 15 Billie Lourd | 60.00 | 120.00 |
| 16 Gwendoline Christie | | |

### 2019 Star Wars On-Demand Women of Star Wars Evolution of Leia

| COMPLETE SET (8) | 75.00 | 150.00 |
|---|---|---|
| COMMON CARD (EL1-EL8) | 12.00 | 30.00 |

### 2019 Star Wars On-Demand Women of Star Wars Women of the Galaxy

| COMPLETE SET (10) | 75.00 | 150.00 |
|---|---|---|
| COMMON CARD (WG1-WG10) | 10.00 | 25.00 |
RANDOMLY INSERTED INTO SETS

### 1995 Star Wars The Power of the Force

| NNO Luke Skywalker | 2.00 | 5.00 |
|---|---|---|

### 2011 Star Wars Power Plates

| COMPLETE SET W/SP (30) | 75.00 | 150.00 |
|---|---|---|
| COMP.SET W/O SP (24) | 50.00 | 100.00 |
| UNOPENED BOX (48 PACKS) | 120.00 | 150.00 |
| UNOPENED PACK (1 PLATE) | 2.50 | 3.00 |
| COMMON PLATE | 3.00 | 8.00 |
| COMMON PLATE SP | 5.00 | 12.00 |
SP STATED ODDS 1:8

### 1999 Star Wars Preview Guide

| NNO Pod Racers | | 5.00 |
|---|---|---|
(Orange County Register Exclusive)

### 1997 Star Wars Quality Bakers

| COMPLETE SET (10) | 12.00 | 30.00 |
|---|---|---|
| COMMON CARD (1-10) | 2.00 | 5.00 |

### 2016 Star Wars Rancho Obi-Wan Little Debbie

| COMPLETE SET (12) | 20.00 | 50.00 |
|---|---|---|
| COMMON CARD (1-12) | 2.50 | 6.00 |
STATED ODDS 1:1 BOXES OF STAR CRUNCH

### 2015 Star Wars Rebels

| COMPLETE SET (100) | 6.00 | 15.00 |
|---|---|---|
| UNOPENED BOX (24 PACKS) | 40.00 | 50.00 |
| UNOPENED PACK (6 CARDS) | 2.00 | 2.50 |
| COMMON CARD (1-100) | .12 | .30 |
*FOIL: 2X TO 5X BASIC CARDS

### 2015 Star Wars Rebels Stickers

| COMPLETE SET (20) | 5.00 | 12.00 |
|---|---|---|
| COMMON CARD (1-20) | .40 | 1.00 |

### 2015 Star Wars Rebels Tattoos

| COMPLETE SET (10) | 6.00 | 15.00 |
|---|---|---|
| COMMON CARD (1-10) | 1.00 | 2.50 |
STATED ODDS 1:8

### 2017 Star Wars Rebels Season 4 Preview Set

| COMPLETE SET (25) | 30.00 | 80.00 |
|---|---|---|
| UNOPENED BOXED SET (27 CARDS) | | |

---

| COMMON CARD | 2.00 | 5.00 |
|---|---|---|
| *PURPLE/25: 1.2X TO 3X BASIC CARDS | 6.00 | 15.00 |
*SILVER/10: UNPRICED DUE TO SCARCITY
*GOLD/5: UNPRICED DUE TO SCARCITY
*RED/1: UNPRICED DUE TO SCARCITY
RELEASED 10/17/2017

### 2017 Star Wars Rebels Season 4 Preview Set Autographs

*GOLD/5: UNPRICED DUE TO SCARCITY
*RED/1: UNPRICED DUE TO SCARCITY
STATED ODDS 1:1 PER BOX SET

| NNO Freddie Prinze Jr. | | |
|---|---|---|
| NNO Taylor Gray | | |
| NNO Vanessa Marshall | | |
| NNO Tiya Sircar | | |
| NNO Steve Blum | | |
| NNO Ashley Eckstein | | |
| NNO Sam Witwer | | |
| NNO Jason Isaacs | | |
| NNO Philip Anthony Rodriguez | | |
| NNO Sarah Michelle Gellar | | |
| NNO Stephen Stanton | 12.00 | 30.00 |
| NNO Billy Dee Williams | | |
| NNO Forest Whitaker | | |
| NNO Stephen Stanton | | |
| NNO Genevieve O'Reilly | | |
| NNO Mary Elizabeth McGlynn | 12.00 | 30.00 |
| NNO Phil Lamarr | | |
| NNO Tom Baker | | |
| NNO Jim Cummings | | |

### 2014 Star Wars Rebels Subway Promos

| COMPLETE SET (6) | 6.00 | 15.00 |
|---|---|---|
| COMMON CARD | 1.50 | 4.00 |

### 2019 Star Wars Resistance Surprise Packs

| COMPLETE SET (100) | 12.00 | 30.00 |
|---|---|---|
| UNOPENED BOX ( PACKS) | | |
| UNOPENED PACK ( CARDS) | | |
| COMMON CARD (1-100) | .25 | .60 |
*BRONZE/50: 4X TO 10X BASIC CARDS
*SILVER/25: 6X TO 15X BASIC CARDS
*GOLD/10: UNPRICED DUE TO SCARCITY
*RED/1: UNPRICED DUE TO SCARCITY
*P.P.BLACK/1: UNPRICED DUE TO SCARCITY
*P.P.CYAN/1: UNPRICED DUE TO SCARCITY
*P.P.MAGENTA/1: UNPRICED DUE TO SCARCITY
*P.P.YELLOW/1: UNPRICED DUE TO SCARCITY

### 2019 Star Wars Resistance Surprise Packs Character Foil

| COMPLETE SET (25) | 12.00 | 30.00 |
|---|---|---|
| COMMON CARD (1-25) | .75 | 2.00 |

## 2019 Star Wars Resistance Surprise Packs Danglers

| | | |
|---|---|---|
| COMPLETE SET (12) | 12.00 | 30.00 |
| COMMON CARD (1-12) | 2.50 | 6.00 |

## 2019 Star Wars Resistance Surprise Packs Mini Albums

| | | |
|---|---|---|
| COMPLETE SET (4) | 12.00 | 30.00 |
| COMMON ALBUM | 4.00 | 10.00 |

## 2019 Star Wars Resistance Surprise Packs Pop-Ups

| | | |
|---|---|---|
| COMPLETE SET (10) | 6.00 | 15.00 |
| COMMON CARD (1-10) | 1.00 | 2.50 |

## 2019 Star Wars Resistance Surprise Packs Temporary Tattoos

| | | |
|---|---|---|
| COMPLETE SET (10) | 8.00 | 20.00 |
| COMMON CARD (1-10) | 1.25 | 3.00 |

## 2016 Star Wars Rogue One Mission Briefing

JYN ERSO

| | | |
|---|---|---|
| COMPLETE SET (110) | 8.00 | 20.00 |
| UNOPENED BOX (24 PACKS) | 85.00 | 100.00 |
| UNOPENED PACK (8 CARDS) | 4.00 | 5.00 |
| COMMON CARD (1-110) | .20 | .50 |
| *BLACK: .75X TO 2X BASIC CARDS | .40 | 1.00 |
| *GREEN: 1.2X TO 3X BASIC CARDS | .60 | 1.50 |
| *BLUE: 1.5X TO 4X BASIC CARDS | .75 | 2.00 |
| *GRAY/100: 8X TO 20X BASIC CARDS | 4.00 | 10.00 |
| *GOLD/50: 12X TO 30X BASIC CARDS | 6.00 | 15.00 |
| *ORANGE:/1: UNPRICED DUE TO SCARCITY | | |
| *P.P.BLACK/1: UNPRICED DUE TO SCARCITY | | |
| *P.P.CYAN/1: UNPRICED DUE TO SCARCITY | | |
| *P.P.MAGENTA/1: UNPRICED DUE TO SCARCITY | | |
| *P.P.YELLOW/1: UNPRICED DUE TO SCARCITY | | |

## 2016 Star Wars Rogue One Mission Briefing Autographs

| | | |
|---|---|---|
| COMMON CARD | 6.00 | 15.00 |
| *BLACK/50: .6X TO 1.5X BASIC AUTOS | | |
| *BLUE/25: 1.2X TO 3X BASIC AUTOS | | |
| *GOLD/10: UNPRICED DUE TO SCARCITY | | |
| *ORANGE/1: UNPRICED DUE TO SCARCITY | | |
| *P.P.BLACK/1: UNPRICED DUE TO SCARCITY | | |
| *P.P.CYAN/1: UNPRICED DUE TO SCARCITY | | |
| *P.P.MAGENTA/1: UNPRICED DUE TO SCARCITY | | |
| *P.P.YELLOW/1: UNPRICED DUE TO SCARCITY | | |
| RANDOMLY INSERTED INTO PACKS | | |
| NNO Adrienne Wilkinson | 12.00 | 30.00 |
| NNO Al Lampert | 10.00 | 25.00 |
| NNO Anna Graves | 15.00 | 40.00 |
| NNO Barbara Frankland | 10.00 | 25.00 |
| NNO Brian Blessed | 8.00 | 20.00 |
| NNO Candice Orwell | 12.00 | 30.00 |
| NNO Catherine Taber | | |
| NNO Clive Revill | 12.00 | 30.00 |
| NNO Corey Dee Williams | 10.00 | 25.00 |
| NNO Dave Barclay | | |
| NNO David Ankrum | 10.00 | 25.00 |
| NNO Eric Lopez | 10.00 | 25.00 |

| | | |
|---|---|---|
| NNO Femi Taylor | 8.00 | 20.00 |
| NNO Garrick Hagon | 10.00 | 25.00 |
| NNO George Roubicek | 10.00 | 25.00 |
| NNO Glyn Baker | 10.00 | 25.00 |
| NNO Ian Liston | 10.00 | 25.00 |
| NNO Jack Klaff | 8.00 | 20.00 |
| NNO Jim Cummings | 12.00 | 30.00 |
| NNO John Coppinger | 15.00 | 40.00 |
| NNO Kenneth Colley | 8.00 | 20.00 |
| NNO Lloyd Sherr | 10.00 | 25.00 |
| NNO Megan Udall | 10.00 | 25.00 |
| NNO Mercedes Ngoh | 8.00 | 20.00 |
| NNO Michaela Cottrell | 8.00 | 20.00 |
| NNO Mike Edmonds | 12.00 | 30.00 |
| NNO Oliver Walpole | 10.00 | 25.00 |
| NNO Paul Springer | 12.00 | 30.00 |
| NNO Rajia Baroudi | 12.00 | 30.00 |
| NNO Rich Oldfield | 15.00 | 40.00 |
| NNO Rusty Goffe | 10.00 | 25.00 |
| NNO Sam Witwer | 15.00 | 40.00 |
| NNO Scott Capurro | 12.00 | 30.00 |
| NNO Sean Crawford | 10.00 | 25.00 |
| NNO Stephen Stanton | 8.00 | 20.00 |
| NNO Tom Kane | 8.00 | 20.00 |
| NNO Wayne Pygram | 10.00 | 25.00 |

## 2016 Star Wars Rogue One Mission Briefing Character Foil

| | | |
|---|---|---|
| COMPLETE SET (9) | 12.00 | 20.00 |
| COMMON CARD (1-9) | 2.00 | 5.00 |
| *P.P.BLACK/1: UNPRICED DUE TO SCARCITY | | |
| *P.P.CYAN/1: UNPRICED DUE TO SCARCITY | | |
| *P.P.MAGENTA/1: UNPRICED DUE TO SCARCITY | | |
| *P.P.YELLOW/1: UNPRICED DUE TO SCARCITY | | |
| STATED ODDS 1:8 | | |

## 2016 Star Wars Rogue One Mission Briefing Comic Strips Inserts

| | | |
|---|---|---|
| COMPLETE SET (12) | 8.00 | 20.00 |
| COMMON CARD (1-12) | 1.25 | 3.00 |
| *P.P.BLACK/1: UNPRICED DUE TO SCARCITY | | |
| *P.P.CYAN/1: UNPRICED DUE TO SCARCITY | | |
| *P.P.MAGENTA/1: UNPRICED DUE TO SCARCITY | | |
| *P.P.YELLOW/1: UNPRICED DUE TO SCARCITY | | |

## 2016-17 Star Wars Rogue One Darth Vader Continuity

| | | |
|---|---|---|
| COMPLETE SET (15) | 20.00 | 50.00 |
| COMMON CARD (1-15) | 2.50 | 6.00 |
| MISSION BRIEFING (1-5) | | |
| SERIES ONE (6-10) | | |
| SERIES TWO (11-15) | | |
| *P.P.BLACK/1: UNPRICED DUE TO SCARCITY | | |

| | | |
|---|---|---|
| *P.P.CYAN/1: UNPRICED DUE TO SCARCITY | | |
| *P.P.MAGENTA/1: UNPRICED DUE TO SCARCITY | | |
| *P.P.YELLOW/1: UNPRICED DUE TO SCARCITY | | |
| STATED ODDS 1:12 | | |

## 2016 Star Wars Rogue One Mission Briefing The Death Star

SUPERLASER

| | | |
|---|---|---|
| COMPLETE SET (9) | 6.00 | 15.00 |
| COMMON CARD (1-9) | .75 | 2.00 |
| *P.P.BLACK/1: UNPRICED DUE TO SCARCITY | | |
| *P.P.CYAN/1: UNPRICED DUE TO SCARCITY | | |
| *P.P.MAGENTA/1: UNPRICED DUE TO SCARCITY | | |
| *P.P.YELLOW/1: UNPRICED DUE TO SCARCITY | | |
| STATED ODDS 1:4 | | |

## 2016 Star Wars Rogue One Mission Briefing Dual Autographs

STATED PRINT RUN 3 SER.#'d SETS
UNPRICED DUE TO SCARCITY

1 C.Fisher/C.Blakiston
2 M.Hamill/D.Lawson

## 2016 Star Wars Rogue One Mission Briefing Heroes of the Rebel Alliance

| | | |
|---|---|---|
| COMPLETE SET (9) | 10.00 | 25.00 |
| COMMON CARD (1-9) | 1.50 | 3.00 |
| *P.P.BLACK/1: UNPRICED DUE TO SCARCITY | | |
| *P.P.CYAN/1: UNPRICED DUE TO SCARCITY | | |
| *P.P.MAGENTA/1: UNPRICED DUE TO SCARCITY | | |
| *P.P.YELLOW/1: UNPRICED DUE TO SCARCITY | | |
| STATED ODDS 1:8 | | |
| 1 Luke Skywalker | 2.00 | 5.00 |
| 2 Princess Leia | 2.00 | 5.00 |
| 3 Han Solo | 2.00 | 5.00 |
| 4 Chewbacca | 1.50 | 4.00 |
| 6 Obi-Wan Kenobi | 1.50 | 4.00 |
| 7 R2-D2 | 1.50 | 4.00 |

## 2016 Star Wars Rogue One Mission Briefing Mission Briefing Monday

| | | |
|---|---|---|
| COMPLETE SET (36) | 150.00 | 300.00 |
| COMMON CARD | 6.00 | 15.00 |
| NOV.7, 2016 (MBME1-MBME6)/206* | | |
| NOV.14, 2016 (MBM1-MBM5)/226* | | |
| NOV.21, 2016 (MBM6-MBM10)/218* | | |
| NOV.28, 2016 (MBM11-MBM15)/212* | | |
| DEC.5, 2016 (MBM16-MBM20)/224* | | |
| DEC.12, 2016 (MBM21-MBM25)/234* | | |
| DEC.19, 2016 (MBM26-MBM30)/252* | | |

## 2016 Star Wars Rogue One Mission Briefing Montages

| | | |
|---|---|---|
| COMPLETE SET (9) | 15.00 | 40.00 |
| COMMON CARD (1-9) | 3.00 | 8.00 |
| *P.P.BLACK/1: UNPRICED DUE TO SCARCITY | | |
| *P.P.CYAN/1: UNPRICED DUE TO SCARCITY | | |
| *P.P.MAGENTA/1: UNPRICED DUE TO SCARCITY | | |

*P.P.YELLOW/1: UNPRICED DUE TO SCARCITY
STATED ODDS 1:24

| | | |
|---|---|---|
| 3  Jyn Erso | 5.00 | 12.00 |

### 2016 Star Wars Rogue One Mission Briefing NYCC Exclusives

| | | |
|---|---|---|
| COMPLETE SET (10) | 12.00 | 30.00 |
| COMMON CARD (E1-E10) | 2.00 | 5.00 |

2016 NYCC EXCLUSIVE

### 2016 Star Wars Rogue One Mission Briefing Patches

| | | |
|---|---|---|
| COMPLETE SET (12) | 50.00 | 100.00 |
| COMMON CARD (M1-M12) | 3.00 | 8.00 |

*GRAY/100: .75X TO 2X BASIC CARDS
*GOLD/50: 1.5X TO 4X BASIC CARDS
*RED/10: 3X TO 8X BASIC CARDS
STATED ODDS 1:26

| | | |
|---|---|---|
| 1  Jyn Erso | 6.00 | 15.00 |
| 3  L-1 Droid | 5.00 | 12.00 |
| 4  Admiral Raddus | 4.00 | 10.00 |
| 6  TIE Fighter Pilot | 4.00 | 10.00 |
| 7  Shoretrooper | 4.00 | 10.00 |
| 10  Captain Cassian Andor | 5.00 | 12.00 |
| 11  Bistan | 4.00 | 10.00 |

### 2016 Star Wars Rogue One Mission Briefing Stickers

| | | |
|---|---|---|
| COMPLETE SET (18) | 10.00 | 25.00 |
| COMMON CARD (1-18) | 1.00 | 2.50 |

*P.P.BLACK/1: UNPRICED DUE TO SCARCITY
*P.P.CYAN/1: UNPRICED DUE TO SCARCITY
*P.P.MAGENTA/1: UNPRICED DUE TO SCARCITY
*P.P.YELLOW/1: UNPRICED DUE TO SCARCITY
STATED ODDS 1:12

| | | |
|---|---|---|
| 1  Jyn Erso | 1.50 | 4.00 |
| 13  Darth Vader | 2.00 | 5.00 |

### 2016 Star Wars Rogue One Mission Briefing Villains of the Galactic Empire

| | | |
|---|---|---|
| COMPLETE SET (8) | 8.00 | 20.00 |
| COMMON CARD (1-8) | 1.25 | 3.00 |

*P.P.BLACK/1: UNPRICED DUE TO SCARCITY
*P.P.CYAN/1: UNPRICED DUE TO SCARCITY
*P.P.MAGENTA/1: UNPRICED DUE TO SCARCITY
*P.P.YELLOW/1: UNPRICED DUE TO SCARCITY
STATED ODDS 1:8

| | | |
|---|---|---|
| 1  Darth Vader | 1.25 | 5.00 |

### 1999 Star Wars Sci-Fi Expo Celebrity Promos

| | | |
|---|---|---|
| P1  Garrick Hagon | 8.00 | 20.00 |
| (Biggs Darklighter) | | |
| P2  Peter Mayhew | 8.00 | 20.00 |
| (Chewbacca) | | |

### 2015 Star Wars SDCC Oversized Exclusives

| | | |
|---|---|---|
| COMPLETE SET (100) | 120.00 | 250.00 |
| COMMON CARD (1-100) | 2.00 | 5.00 |

### 1997 Star Wars SE Trilogy 3-D Doritos Discs

| | | |
|---|---|---|
| COMPLETE SET (20) | 5.00 | 12.00 |
| COMMON CARD | .40 | 1.00 |

### 1997 Star Wars SE Trilogy 3-D Doritos-Cheetos

| | | |
|---|---|---|
| COMPLETE SET (6) | 3.00 | 8.00 |
| COMMON CARD (1-6) | .75 | 2.00 |

### 1996 Star Wars Shadows of the Empire

| | | |
|---|---|---|
| COMPLETE SET (100) | 15.00 | 40.00 |
| COMMON CARD (1-72, 83-100) | .15 | .40 |
| COMMON ETCHED (73-78) | 2.00 | 5.00 |
| COMMON EMBOSSED (79-82) | 3.00 | 8.00 |

73-78 STATED ODDS 1:9
79-82 STATED ODDS 1:18

### 1996 Star Wars Shadows of the Empire Promos

| | | |
|---|---|---|
| COMMON CARD | 1.00 | 2.50 |
| SOTE1  Xizor | 2.00 | 5.00 |
| SOTE2  Darth Vader | 2.00 | 5.00 |
| SOTE3  Luke Skywalker | 2.00 | 5.00 |
| SOTE4  Dash Rendar & Leebo | 2.00 | 5.00 |
| SOTE5  Boba Fett | 8.00 | 15.00 |
| (Convention Exclusive) | | |
| SOTE6  Guri | 2.00 | 5.00 |
| SOTE7  C-3PO & R2-D2 | 2.00 | 5.00 |
| NNO  SOTE3-SOTE1 (Luke Skywalker/Darth Vader) | | |

### 2019 Star Wars Skywalker Saga

| | | |
|---|---|---|
| COMPLETE SET (100) | 8.00 | 20.00 |
| COMMON CARD (1-100) | .20 | .50 |

*ORANGE: .6X TO 1.5X BASIC CARDS
*BLUE: .75X TO 2X BASIC CARDS
*GREEN/99: 2.5X TO 6X BASIC CARDS
*PURPLE/25: 6X TO 15X BASIC CARDS
*RED/1: UNPRICED DUE TO SCARCITY
*P.P.BLACK/1: UNPRICED DUE TO SCARCITY
*P.P.CYAN/1: UNPRICED DUE TO SCARCITY
*P.P.MAGENTA/1: UNPRICED DUE TO SCARCITY
*P.P.YELLOW/1: UNPRICED DUE TO SCARCITY

### 2019 Star Wars Skywalker Saga Allies

| | | |
|---|---|---|
| COMPLETE SET (10) | 6.00 | 15.00 |
| COMMON CARD (A1-A10) | .75 | 2.00 |

*GREEN/99: 1X TO 2.5X BASIC CARDS
*PURPLE/25: 3X TO 8X BASIC CARDS
*RED/1: UNPRICED DUE TO SCARCITY
*P.P.BLACK/1: UNPRICED DUE TO SCARCITY
*P.P.CYAN/1: UNPRICED DUE TO SCARCITY
*P.P.MAGENTA/1: UNPRICED DUE TO SCARCITY
*P.P.YELLOW/1: UNPRICED DUE TO SCARCITY
STATED ODDS 1:12 HOBBY & BLASTER

### 2019 Star Wars Skywalker Saga Autographs

*PURPLE/5: UNPRICED DUE TO SCARCITY
*RED/1: UNPRICED DUE TO SCARCITY
*P.P.BLACK/1: UNPRICED DUE TO SCARCITY
*P.P.CYAN/1: UNPRICED DUE TO SCARCITY
*P.P.MAGENTA/1: UNPRICED DUE TO SCARCITY
*P.P.YELLOW/1: UNPRICED DUE TO SCARCITY
STATED ODDS 1:39 HOBBY; 1:826 BLASTER

| | |
|---|---|
| AAB  Ahmed Best | |
| AAD  Anthony Daniels | |
| AAS  Andy Serkis | |
| AAT  Alan Tudyk | |
| ABH  Brian Herring | |
| ABL  Billie Lourd | |
| ABM  Ben Mendelsohn | |
| ACF  Carrie Fisher | |

| | |
|---|---|
| ADB  David Barclay | |
| ADG  Domhnall Gleeson | |
| ADL  Daniel Logan | |
| ADR  Daisy Ridley | |
| ADY  Donnie Yen | |
| AEK  Erin Kellyman | |
| AEM  Ewan McGregor | |
| AFJ  Felicity Jones | |
| AFW  Forest Whitaker | |
| AGH  Garrick Hagon | |
| AGO  Genevieve O'Reilly | |
| AHC  Hayden Christensen | |
| AHF  Harrison Ford | |
| AIM  Ian McDiarmid | |
| AJB  Jerome Blake | |
| AKB  Kenny Baker | |
| AKK  Katy Kartwheel | |
| AML  Matt Lanter | |
| AMM  Mads Mikkelsen | |
| ANF  Nika Futterman | |
| APB  Paul Bettany | |
| APL  Phil LaMarr | |
| APM  Peter Mayhew | |
| ARA  Riz Ahmed | |
| ARP  Ray Park | |
| ASC  Silas Carson | |
| ATM  Temuera Morrison | |
| AWD  Warwick Davis | |
| AADK  Adam Driver | |
| AAEH  Alden Ehrenreich | |
| AASW  Andy Secombe | |
| ABDW  Billy Dee Williams | |
| AHCV  Hayden Christensen | |
| AIMS  Ian McDiarmid | |
| AJAT  James Arnold Taylor | |
| AJBF  John Boyega | |
| AJSC  Joonas Suotamo | |
| ASLJ  Samuel L. Jackson | |
| ATKY  Tom Kane | |

### 2019 Star Wars Skywalker Saga Commemorative Blueprint Relics

COMMON MEM
*ORANGE/99: X TO X BASIC MEM
*BLUE/50: X TO X BASIC MEM
*GREEN/25: X TO X BASIC MEM
*PURPLE/5: UNPRICED DUE TO SCARCITY
*RED/1: UNPRICED DUE TO SCARCITY
STATED ODDS 1:64 HOBBY; 1:218 BLASTER

| | |
|---|---|
| BPAT  AT-AT | |
| BPAW  A-wing fighter | |
| BPIS  Imperial Speeder Bike | |
| BPJS  Jawa Sandcrawler | |
| BPMF  Millennium Falcon | |
| BPRS  Rebel Snowspeeder | |
| BPSD  Imperial Star Destroyer | |
| BPSI  Slave I | |
| BPST  AT-ST | |
| BPTB  TIE bomber | |
| BPTF  TIE fighter | |
| BPTI  Tie Interceptor | |
| BPXW  X-wing fighter | |
| BPYW  Y-wing fighter | |

TRADING CARDS

### 2019 Star Wars Skywalker Saga Commemorative Nameplate Patches

COMMON MEM
*ORANGE/99: X TO X BASIC MEM
*BLUE/50: X TO X BASIC MEM
*GREEN/25: X TO X BASIC MEM
*PURPLE/5: UNPRICED DUE TO SCARCITY
*RED/1: UNPRICED DUE TO SCARCITY
STATED ODDS 1:1 BLASTER

NPA  General Leia Organa/A
NPE  Princess Leia Organa/E
NPI  General Leia Organa/I
NPL  Princess Leia Organa/L
NPA2  Anakin Skywalker/A
NPAA  Anakin Skywalker/A
NPAI  Anakin Skywalker/I
NPAK  Anakin Skywalker/K
NPAN  Anakin Skywalker/N
NPKK  Kylo Ren/K
NPKL  Kylo Ren/L
NPKO  Kylo Ren/O
NPKY  Kylo Ren/Y
NPLE  Luke Skywalker/E
NPLK  Luke Skywalker/K
NPLL  Luke Skywalker/L
NPLU  Luke Skywalker/U
NPN2  Anakin Skywalker/N

### 2019 Star Wars Skywalker Saga Enemies

| | | |
|---|---|---|
| COMPLETE SET (10) | 6.00 | 15.00 |
| COMMON CARD (E1-E10) | .75 | 2.00 |

*GREEN/99: 1X TO 2.5X BASIC CARDS
*PURPLE/25: 3X TO 8X BASIC CARDS
*RED/1: UNPRICED DUE TO SCARCITY
*P.P.BLACK/1: UNPRICED DUE TO SCARCITY
*P.P.CYAN/1: UNPRICED DUE TO SCARCITY
*P.P.MAGENTA/1: UNPRICED DUE TO SCARCITY
*P.P.YELLOW/1: UNPRICED DUE TO SCARCITY
STATED ODDS 1:12 HOBBY; 1:12 BLASTER

### 2019 Star Wars Skywalker Saga Iconic Looks

| | | |
|---|---|---|
| COMPLETE SET (10) | 6.00 | 15.00 |
| COMMON CARD (IL1-IL10) | .75 | 2.00 |

*GREEN/99: 1X TO 2.5X BASIC CARDS
*PURPLE/25: 3X TO 8X BASIC CARDS
*RED/1: UNPRICED DUE TO SCARCITY
*P.P.BLACK/1: UNPRICED DUE TO SCARCITY
*P.P.CYAN/1: UNPRICED DUE TO SCARCITY
*P.P.MAGENTA/1: UNPRICED DUE TO SCARCITY
*P.P.YELLOW/1: UNPRICED DUE TO SCARCITY
STATED ODDS 1:4 HOBBY & BLASTER

### 2019 Star Wars Skywalker Saga Path of the Jedi

| | | |
|---|---|---|
| COMPLETE SET (10) | 6.00 | 15.00 |
| COMMON CARD (PJ1-PJ10) | .75 | 2.00 |

*GREEN/99: 1X TO 2.5X BASIC CARDS
*PURPLE/25: 3X TO 8X BASIC CARDS
*RED/1: UNPRICED DUE TO SCARCITY
*P.P.BLACK/1: UNPRICED DUE TO SCARCITY
*P.P.CYAN/1: UNPRICED DUE TO SCARCITY
*P.P.MAGENTA/1: UNPRICED DUE TO SCARCITY
*P.P.YELLOW/1: UNPRICED DUE TO SCARCITY
STATED ODDS 1:2 HOBBY & BLASTER

### 2019 Star Wars Skywalker Saga Skywalker Legacy

| | | |
|---|---|---|
| COMPLETE SET (11) | 6.00 | 15.00 |
| COMMON CARD (FT1-FT11) | 1.00 | 2.50 |

*GREEN/99: 1.5X TO 4X BASIC CARDS
*PURPLE/25: 2.5X TO 6X BASIC CARDS
*RED/1: UNPRICED DUE TO SCARCITY
*P.P.BLACK/1: UNPRICED DUE TO SCARCITY
*P.P.CYAN/1: UNPRICED DUE TO SCARCITY
*P.P.MAGENTA/1: UNPRICED DUE TO SCARCITY
*P.P.YELLOW/1: UNPRICED DUE TO SCARCITY
STATED ODDS 1:12 HOBBY & BLASTER

### 1978 Star Wars Spaceship Hang Gliders

| | | |
|---|---|---|
| COMPLETE SET (4) | 75.00 | 150.00 |
| COMMON GLIDER | 20.00 | 50.00 |

### 2017 Star Wars Stellar Signatures

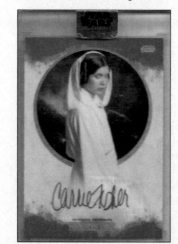

| | | |
|---|---|---|
| COMMON AUTOS | 25.00 | 60.00 |
| *BLUE/25: .5 TO 1.2X BASIC AUTOS | 30.00 | 75.00 |

*GREEN/20: UNPRICED DUE TO SCARCITY
*PURPLE/10: UNPRICED DUE TO SCARCITY
*GOLD/5: UNPRICED DUE TO SCARCITY
*GALACTIC BLACK/1: UNPRICED DUE TO SCARCITY
*IMPERIAL RED/1: UNPRICED DUE TO SCARCITY
*REB.ALL.ORANGE/1: UNPRICED DUE TO SCARCITY
STATED PRINT RUN 40 SER.#'d SETS
100 TOTAL BOXES PRODUCED

| | | |
|---|---|---|
| NNO Adam Driver | 400.00 | 650.00 |
| NNO Alan Tudyk | 100.00 | 175.00 |
| NNO Andy Serkis | 75.00 | 150.00 |
| NNO Ashley Eckstein | 60.00 | 120.00 |
| NNO Ben Mendelsohn EXCH | | |
| NNO Billy Dee Williams | 75.00 | 150.00 |
| NNO Brian Herring | 30.00 | 75.00 |
| NNO Carrie Fisher | 300.00 | 500.00 |
| NNO Daisy Ridley | 800.00 | 1200.00 |
| NNO Donnie Yen | 75.00 | 150.00 |
| NNO Felicity Jones | 300.00 | 500.00 |
| NNO Forest Whitaker | 75.00 | 150.00 |
| NNO Freddie Prinze Jr. | 50.00 | 100.00 |
| NNO Genevieve O'Reilly | 50.00 | 100.00 |
| NNO Gwendoline Christie | 250.00 | 400.00 |
| NNO Harrison Ford | 2500.00 | 4000.00 |
| NNO Hayden Christensen | 250.00 | 400.00 |
| NNO Ian McDiarmid | 250.00 | 400.00 |
| NNO Jeremy Bulloch | 30.00 | 75.00 |
| NNO John Boyega | 120.00 | 250.00 |
| NNO Joonas Suotamo | 30.00 | 75.00 |
| NNO Kenny Baker | 75.00 | 150.00 |
| NNO Lars Mikkelsen | 75.00 | 150.00 |
| NNO Mark Hamill EXCH | | |
| NNO Matthew Wood | 30.00 | 75.00 |
| NNO Peter Mayhew | 75.00 | 150.00 |
| NNO Ray Park | 60.00 | 120.00 |
| NNO Riz Ahmed | 50.00 | 100.00 |
| NNO Sarah Michelle Gellar | 120.00 | 250.00 |
| NNO Stephen Stanton EXCH | | |
| NNO Temuera Morrison | 30.00 | 75.00 |
| NNO Tim Curry | 100.00 | 175.00 |
| NNO Tom Baker | 100.00 | 200.00 |
| NNO Warwick Davis | 50.00 | 100.00 |

### 2018 Star Wars Stellar Signatures

| | | |
|---|---|---|
| COMMON AUTO | 20.00 | 50.00 |

*BLUE/25: SAME VALUE AS BASIC AUTOS
*GREEN/20: UNPRICED DUE TO SCARCITY
*PURPLE/10: UNPRICED DUE TO SCARCITY
*GOLD/5: UNPRICED DUE TO SCARCITY
*BLACK/1: UNPRICED DUE TO SCARCITY
*ORANGE/1: UNPRICED DUE TO SCARCITY
*RED/1: UNPRICED DUE TO SCARCITY

| | | |
|---|---|---|
| AAD Anthony Daniels | 125.00 | 250.00 |
| AAE Ashley Eckstein | 30.00 | 75.00 |
| AAS Andy Serkis | 50.00 | 100.00 |
| AAT Alan Tudyk | 50.00 | 100.00 |
| ABH Brian Herring | 25.00 | 60.00 |
| ACB Caroline Blakiston | 25.00 | 60.00 |
| ADG Domhnall Gleeson | 125.00 | 250.00 |
| ADR Daisy Ridley | 400.00 | 600.00 |
| AEB Erik Bauersfeld | 50.00 | 100.00 |
| AEK Erin Kellyman | 125.00 | 250.00 |
| AFW Forest Whitaker | 60.00 | 120.00 |
| AGG Greg Grunberg | 25.00 | 60.00 |
| AHC Hayden Christensen | 125.00 | 250.00 |

| | | |
|---|---|---|
| AHF Harrison Ford | 800.00 | 1400.00 |
| AIM Ian McDiarmid | 100.00 | 200.00 |
| AJB Jeremy Bulloch | 30.00 | 75.00 |
| AJI Jason Isaacs | 30.00 | 75.00 |
| AJS Joonas Suotamo | 50.00 | 100.00 |
| AKB Kenny Baker | 100.00 | 200.00 |
| ALD Laura Dern | 60.00 | 120.00 |
| AMM Mads Mikkelsen | 125.00 | 250.00 |
| APR Paul Reubens | 75.00 | 150.00 |
| ARA Riz Ahmed | 30.00 | 75.00 |
| ARP Ray Park | 50.00 | 100.00 |
| ATC Tim Curry | 50.00 | 100.00 |
| AADR Adam Driver | 200.00 | 350.00 |
| ABDW Billy Dee Williams | 75.00 | 150.00 |
| ASLJ Samuel L. Jackson | 600.00 | 800.00 |

### 2018 Star Wars Stellar Signatures Autographed Relics

| | | |
|---|---|---|
| COMMON AUTO | 60.00 | 120.00 |
| *BLUE/25: SAME VALUE AS BASIC AUTOS | | |
| *GREEN/20: UNPRICED DUE TO SCARCITY | | |
| *PURPLE/10: UNPRICED DUE TO SCARCITY | | |
| *GOLD/5: UNPRICED DUE TO SCARCITY | | |
| *BLACK/1: UNPRICED DUE TO SCARCITY | | |
| *ORANGE/1: UNPRICED DUE TO SCARCITY | | |
| *RED/1: UNPRICED DUE TO SCARCITY | | |
| ARD Paul Bettany | 150.00 | 300.00 |
| ARJ Felicity Jones | 200.00 | 350.00 |

### 2018 Star Wars Stellar Signatures Dual Autographs

| | | |
|---|---|---|
| COMMON AUTO | | |
| *BLUE/25: X TO X BASIC AUTOS | | |
| *GREEN/20: UNPRICED DUE TO SCARCITY | | |
| *PURPLE/10: UNPRICED DUE TO SCARCITY | | |
| *GOLD/5: UNPRICED DUE TO SCARCITY | | |
| *BLACK/1: UNPRICED DUE TO SCARCITY | | |
| *ORANGE/1: UNPRICED DUE TO SCARCITY | | |
| *RED/1: UNPRICED DUE TO SCARCITY | | |
| DABB J.Bulloch/D.Barclay | | |
| DABM J.Bulloch/T.Morrison | | |
| DABO C.Blakiston/G.O'Reilly | | |
| DACW H.Christensen/M.Wood | | |
| DAFB C.Fisher/K.Baker | | |
| DAMM L.Mikkelsen/M.McGlynn | | |
| DAMP I.McDiarmid/R.Park | | |
| DAOM G.O'Reilly/I.McElhinney | | |
| DARD D.Ridley/A.Driver | | |
| DASV J.Suotamo/J.Vee | | |
| DASW S.Stanton/S.Witwer | | |
| DATL J.Taylor/M.Lanter | | |
| DAWA F.Whitaker/R.Ahmed | | |
| DAWQ B.Williams/M.Quinn | | |

### 1997 Star Wars Stickers US

| | | |
|---|---|---|
| COMPLETE SET (66) | 7.50 | 20.00 |
| COMMON CARD (1-66) | .20 | .50 |
| PRODUCED BY PANINI | | |

### 1997 Star Wars Trilogy The Complete Story

| | | |
|---|---|---|
| COMPLETE SET (72) | 6.00 | 15.00 |
| COMMON CARD (1-72) | .25 | .60 |
| 0 Promo | 1.00 | 2.00 |

### 1997 Star Wars Trilogy The Complete Story Laser

| | | |
|---|---|---|
| COMPLETE SET (6) | 6.00 | 15.00 |
| COMMON CARD (LC1-LC6) | 1.25 | 3.00 |
| STATED ODDS 1:9 | | |

### 1997 Star Wars Trilogy Merlin

| | | |
|---|---|---|
| COMPLETE SET (125) | 10.00 | 25.00 |
| UNOPENED BOX (48 PACKS) | 25.00 | 40.00 |
| UNOPENED PACK (5 CARDS) | 1.00 | 1.25 |
| COMMON CARD (1-125) | .15 | .40 |

### 1997 Star Wars Trilogy Merlin Case-Toppers

| | | |
|---|---|---|
| COMPLETE SET (3) | 20.00 | 50.00 |
| COMMON CARD (P1-P3) | 8.00 | 20.00 |
| STATED ODDS 1:CASE | | |

### 1997 Star Wars Trilogy Special Edition

| | | |
|---|---|---|
| COMPLETE SET (72) | 6.00 | 15.00 |
| UNOPENED BOX (36 PACKS) | 80.00 | 100.00 |
| UNOPENED PACK (9 CARDS) | 2.50 | 3.00 |
| COMMON CARD (1-72) | .15 | .40 |
| 13D ISSUED AS BOX TOPPER | | |
| 13D X-Wings Departing | 6.00 | 15.00 |

### 1997 Star Wars Trilogy Special Edition Holograms

| | | |
|---|---|---|
| COMPLETE SET (2) | 10.00 | 25.00 |
| COMMON CARD (1-2) | 6.00 | 15.00 |
| STATED ODDS 1:18 | | |

### 1997 Star Wars Trilogy Special Edition Laser

| | | |
|---|---|---|
| COMPLETE SET (6) | 6.00 | 15.00 |
| COMMON CARD (LC1-LC6) | 1.25 | 3.00 |
| STATED ODDS 1:9 | | |

### 1997 Star Wars Trilogy Special Edition Promos

| | | |
|---|---|---|
| COMPLETE SET (8) | 10.00 | 25.00 |
| COMMON CARD (P1-P8) | 1.25 | 3.00 |
| P1 Three Stormtroopers | 4.00 | 10.00 |
| P4 Sandcrawler | 3.00 | 8.00 |
| P5 Jawa and Landspeeder | 3.00 | 8.00 |
| P6 Millennium Falcon | 3.00 | 8.00 |

### 1997 Star Wars Trilogy Special Edition Kenner Promos

| | | |
|---|---|---|
| COMPLETE SET (4) | 10.00 | 25.00 |
| COMMON CARD (H1-H4) | 4.00 | 10.00 |

### 1997 Star Wars Trilogy Special Edition Micro Machine Promos

| | | |
|---|---|---|
| COMPLETE SET (5) | 12.00 | 30.00 |
| COMMON CARD (G1-G5) | 4.00 | 10.00 |

### 1997 Star Wars Vehicles

| | | |
|---|---|---|
| COMPLETE SET (72) | 5.00 | 12.00 |
| UNOPENED BOX (36 PACKS) | 40.00 | 50.00 |
| UNOPENED PACK (5 CARDS) | 1.25 | 1.50 |
| COMMON CARD (1-72) | .15 | .40 |

### 1997 Star Wars Vehicles 3-D

| | | |
|---|---|---|
| COMPLETE SET (3) | 25.00 | 60.00 |
| COMMON CARD | 8.00 | 20.00 |
| STATED ODDS 1:36 | | |
| 3 Princess Leia | 15.00 | 40.00 |
| Luke Skywalker | | |

### 1997 Star Wars Vehicles Cut-Away

| | | |
|---|---|---|
| COMPLETE SET (4) | 7.50 | 20.00 |
| COMMON CARD (C1-C4) | 2.50 | 6.00 |
| STATED ODDS 1:18 | | |

### 1997 Star Wars Vehicles Promos

| | | |
|---|---|---|
| P1A Darth Vader & Stormtroopers on Speeder Bikes chromium)/3200* | 12.00 | 30.00 |
| P1B Darth Vader & Stormtroopers on Speeder Bikes (refractor)/320* | 30.00 | 75.00 |
| P2A Stormtroopers on Speeder Bikes (chromium)/1600* | 20.00 | 50.00 |
| P2B Stormtroopers on Speeder Bikes (refractor)/160* | 50.00 | 100.00 |
| NNO 2-Card Sheet | | |

## TCG

### 1995 Star Wars Premiere

| | | |
|---|---|---|
| COMPLETE SET (324) | 75.00 | 150.00 |
| BOOSTER BOX (36 PACKS) | 75.00 | 150.00 |
| BOOSTER PACK (15 CARDS) | 3.00 | 6.00 |
| RELEASED IN DECEMBER 1995 | | |
| 1 5D6-RA-7 (Fivedesix) R1 | 2.00 | 3.00 |
| 2 Admiral Motti R2 | 1.25 | 2.00 |
| 3 Chief Bast U1 | .50 | .75 |
| 4 Colonel Wullf Yularen U1 | .50 | .75 |
| 5 Commander Praji U2 | .50 | .75 |
| 6 Darth Vader R1 | .50 | .75 |
| 7 Dathcha U1 | 5.00 | 8.00 |
| 8 Death Star Trooper C2 | 15.00 | 25.00 |
| 9 Djas Puhr R2 | .50 | .75 |
| 10 Dr. Evazan R2 | .20 | .30 |
| 11 DS-61-2 U1 | 1.25 | 2.00 |
| 12 DS-61-3 R1 | 1.25 | 2.00 |
| 13 EG-6 (Eegee-Six) U2 | .50 | .75 |
| 14 Feltipern Trevagg U1 | .50 | .75 |
| 15 Garindan R2 | 1.25 | 2.00 |
| 16 General Tagge R2 | 1.25 | 2.00 |
| 17 Grand Moff Tarkin R1 | 5.00 | 8.00 |
| 18 Imperial Pilot C2 | .20 | .30 |
| 19 Imperial Trooper Guard C2 | .20 | .30 |
| 20 Jawa DARK C2 | .20 | .30 |
| 21 Kitik Keedkak R1 | 2.00 | 3.00 |
| 22 Labria R2 | .20 | .30 |
| 23 Lieutenant Tanbris U2 | 1.25 | 2.00 |
| 24 LIN-V8M (Elleyein-Veeateemm) C1 | .50 | .75 |
| 25 Miiiyoom Onith U2 | .50 | .75 |
| 26 MSE-6 ëMouseí Droid U1 | .50 | .75 |
| 27 Myo R2 | 1.25 | 2.00 |
| 28 Ponda Baba U1 | .50 | .75 |
| 29 Prophetess U1 | .50 | .75 |
| 30 R1-G4 (Arone-Geefour) C2 | .20 | .30 |
| 31 R4-M9 (Arfour-Emmnine) C2 | .20 | .30 |
| 32 Stormtrooper C3 | .20 | .30 |
| 33 Tonnika Sisters R1 | 2.00 | 3.00 |
| 34 Tusken Raider C2 | .20 | .30 |
| 35 WED-9-M1 ëBanthaí Droid R2 | 1.25 | 2.00 |
| 36 Wuher U2 | .50 | .75 |
| 37 Blaster Scope U1 | .50 | .75 |
| 38 Caller DARK U2 | .50 | .75 |
| 39 Comlink C1 | .20 | .30 |
| 40 Droid Detector C2 | .20 | .30 |
| 41 Fusion Generator Supply Tanks DARK C2 | .20 | .30 |
| 42 Observation Holocam U2 | .50 | .75 |
| 43 Restraining Bolt DARK C2 | .20 | .30 |
| 44 Stormtrooper Backpack C2 | .20 | .30 |
| 45 Stormtrooper Utility Belt C2 | .20 | .30 |
| 46 A Disturbance In The Force U1 | .50 | .75 |
| 47 Baniss Keeg C2 | .20 | .30 |
| 48 Blast Door Controls U2 | .50 | .75 |
| 49 Blaster Rack U1 | .50 | .75 |
| 50 Dark Hours U2 | .50 | .75 |
| 51 Death Star Sentry U1 | .50 | .75 |
| 52 Disarmed DARK R1 | 2.00 | 3.00 |
| 53 Expand The Empire R1 | 2.00 | 3.00 |
| 54 Fear Will Keep Them In Line R2 | 1.25 | 2.00 |
| 55 I Find Your Lack Of Faith Disturbing R1 | 2.00 | 3.00 |
| 56 Iíve Lost Artoo! U1 | .50 | .75 |
| 57 Jawa Pack U1 | .50 | .75 |
| 58 Juri Juice R2 | 1.25 | 2.00 |
| 59 Ket Maliss C2 | .20 | .30 |
| 60 Lateral Damage R2 | 1.25 | 2.00 |
| 61 Luke? Luuuuke! U1 | .50 | .75 |
| 62 Macroscan C2 | .20 | .30 |
| 63 Molator R1 | 2.00 | 3.00 |
| 64 Organaís Ceremonial Necklace R1 | 2.00 | 3.00 |
| 65 Presence Of The Force R1 | 2.00 | 3.00 |
| 66 Reactor Terminal U2 | .50 | .75 |
| 67 Send A Detachment Down R1 | 2.00 | 3.00 |
| 68 Sunsdown U1 | .50 | .75 |
| 69 Tactical Re-Call R2 | 1.25 | 2.00 |
| 70 Wrong Turn U1 | .50 | .75 |
| 71 Your Eyes Can Deceive You U1 | 2.00 | 3.00 |
| 72 Alter DARK U1 | .50 | .75 |
| 73 Boring Conversation Anyway R1 | 2.00 | 3.00 |
| 74 Charming To The Last R2 | 1.25 | 2.00 |
| 75 Collateral Damage C2 | .20 | .30 |
| 76 Counter Assault C1 | .20 | .30 |
| 77 Dark Collaboration R1 | 2.00 | 3.00 |
| 78 Dark Jedi Presence R1 | 6.00 | 10.00 |
| 79 Dark Maneuvers C2 | .20 | .30 |
| 80 Dead Jawa C2 | .20 | .30 |
| 81 Elis Helrot U2 | .50 | .75 |
| 82 Emergency Deployment U1 | .50 | .75 |
| 83 Evacuate? U2 | .50 | .75 |
| 84 Full Scale Alert U2 | .50 | .75 |
| 85 Gravel Storm U2 | .50 | .75 |
| 86 I Have You Now R2 | 1.25 | 2.00 |
| 87 Iíve Got A Problem Here C2 | .20 | .30 |
| 88 Imperial Reinforcements C1 | .20 | .30 |
| 89 Imperial Code Cylinder C2 | .20 | .30 |
| 90 Itís Worse C2 | .20 | .30 |
| 91 Imperial Barrier DARK C2 | .20 | .30 |
| 92 Kintan Strider C1 | .20 | .30 |
| 93 Limited Resources U2 | .50 | .75 |
| 94 Local Trouble R1 | 2.00 | 3.00 |
| 95 Lone Pilot R2 | 1.25 | 2.00 |
| 96 Lone Warrior R2 | 1.25 | 2.00 |
| 97 Look Sir, Droids R1 | 2.00 | 3.00 |
| 98 Moment Of Triumph R2 | 1.25 | 2.00 |
| 99 Nevar Yalnal R2 | 1.25 | 2.00 |
| 100 Ommni Box C2 | .20 | .30 |
| 101 Overload C2 | .20 | .30 |
| 102 Physical Choke R1 | 2.00 | 3.00 |
| 103 Precise Attack C2 | .20 | .30 |
| 104 Scanning Crew C2 | .20 | .30 |
| 105 Sense DARK U1 | .50 | .75 |
| 106 Set For Stun C2 | .20 | .30 |
| 107 Takeel C2 | .20 | .30 |
| 108 Tallon Roll C2 | .20 | .30 |
| 109 The Circle Is Now Complete R1 | 2.00 | 3.00 |
| 110 The Empireís Back U1 | .50 | .75 |
| 111 Trinto Duaba U1 | .50 | .75 |
| 112 Trooper Charge U2 | .50 | .75 |
| 113 Tusken Scavengers C2 | .20 | .30 |
| 114 Utinni! DARK R1 | 2.00 | 3.00 |
| 115 Vaderís Eye R1 | 2.00 | 3.00 |
| 116 Weíre All Gonna Be A Lot Thinner! R1 | 2.00 | 3.00 |
| 117 You Overestimate Their Chances C1 | .50 | .75 |
| 118 Your Powers Are Weak, Old Man R1 | .20 | .30 |
| 119 Alderaan DARK R1 | 2.00 | 3.00 |
| 120 Dantooine DARK U1 | .50 | .75 |
| 121 Death Star: Central Core U2 | .50 | .75 |
| 122 Death Star: Detention Block Corridor C1 | .20 | .30 |
| 123 Death Star: Docking Bay 327 DARK C2 | .20 | .30 |
| 124 Death Star: Level 4 Military Corridor U1 | .50 | .75 |
| 125 Death Star: War Room U2 | .50 | .75 |
| 126 Kessel U2 | 1.25 | 2.00 |
| 127 Tatooine DARK C2 | .20 | .30 |

| # | Card | Price 1 | Price 2 |
|---|---|---|---|
| 128 | Tatooine: Cantina DARK R2 | 1.25 | 2.00 |
| 129 | Tatooine: Docking Bay 94 DARK C2 | .20 | .30 |
| 130 | Tatooine: Jawa Camp DARK C1 | .20 | .30 |
| 131 | Tatooine: Jundland Wastes C1 | .20 | .30 |
| 132 | Tatooine: Larsí Moisture Farm DARK C1 | .20 | .30 |
| 133 | Tatooine: Mos Eisley DARK C1 | .20 | .30 |
| 134 | Yavin 4 DARK C2 | .20 | .30 |
| 135 | Yavin 4: Docking Bay DARK C2 | .20 | .30 |
| 136 | Yavin 4: Jungle DARK U2 | .50 | .75 |
| 137 | Black 2 R1 | 4.00 | 6.00 |
| 138 | Black 3 U1 | .50 | .75 |
| 139 | Devastator R1 | 4.00 | 6.00 |
| 140 | Imperial-Class Star Destroyer U1 | 1.25 | 2.00 |
| 141 | TIE Advanced x1 U2 | .50 | .75 |
| 142 | TIE Fighter C2 | .20 | .30 |
| 143 | TIE Scout C2 | .20 | .30 |
| 144 | Vaderís Custom TIE R1 | 6.00 | 10.00 |
| 145 | Bantha U2 | .50 | .75 |
| 146 | Lift Tube DARK C2 | .20 | .30 |
| 147 | Sandcrawler DARK R2 | 1.25 | 2.00 |
| 148 | Ubrikkian 9000 Z001 C2 | .20 | .30 |
| 149 | Assault Rifle R2 | 1.25 | 2.00 |
| 150 | Blaster Rifle DARK C1 | .20 | .30 |
| 151 | Boosted TIE Cannon U1 | .50 | .75 |
| 152 | Dark Jedi Lightsaber U1 | .60 | 1.00 |
| 153 | Gaderffii Stick C2 | .20 | .30 |
| 154 | Han Seeker R2 | 1.25 | 2.00 |
| 155 | Imperial Blaster DARK C2 | .20 | .30 |
| 156 | Ion Cannon U1 | .50 | .75 |
| 157 | Laser Projector U2 | .50 | .75 |
| 158 | Light Repeating Blaster Rifle R1 | 2.00 | 3.00 |
| 159 | Luke Seeker R2 | 1.25 | 2.00 |
| 160 | Timer Mine DARK C2 | .20 | .30 |
| 161 | Turbolaser Battery R2 | 1.25 | 2.00 |
| 162 | Vaderís Lightsaber R1 | 5.00 | 8.00 |
| 163 | 2X-3KPR (Tooex) U1 | .50 | .75 |
| 164 | Beru Lars U2 | .50 | .75 |
| 165 | Biggs Darklighter R2 | 1.25 | 2.00 |
| 166 | BoShek U1 | .50 | .75 |
| 167 | C-3PO (See-Threepio) R1 | 5.00 | 8.00 |
| 168 | CZ-3 (Seezee-Three) C1 | .20 | .30 |
| 169 | Dice Ibegon R2 | 1.25 | 2.00 |
| 170 | Dutch R1 | 4.00 | 6.00 |
| 171 | Figrin Dían U2 | .50 | .75 |
| 172 | General Dodonna U1 | .50 | .75 |
| 173 | Han Solo R1 | 8.00 | 12.00 |
| 174 | Jawa LIGHT C2 | .20 | .30 |
| 175 | Jek Porkins U1 | .50 | .75 |
| 176 | Kabe U1 | .50 | .75 |
| 177 | KalíFalnl Cíndros R1 | 2.00 | 3.00 |
| 178 | Leesub Sirln R2 | .20 | .30 |
| 179 | Leia Organa R1 | 1.25 | 2.00 |
| 180 | LIN-V8K (Elleyein-Veeatekay) C1 | 6.00 | 10.00 |
| 181 | Luke Skywalker R1 | 10.00 | 15.00 |
| 182 | Momaw Nadon U2 | .50 | .75 |
| 183 | Obi-Wan Kenobi R1 | 6.00 | 10.00 |
| 184 | Owen Lars U1 | .50 | .75 |
| 185 | Pops U1 | .50 | .75 |
| 186 | R2-X2 (Artoo-Extoo) C2 | .20 | .30 |
| 187 | R4-E1 (Arfour-Eeone) C2 | .20 | .30 |
| 188 | Rebel Guard C2 | .20 | .30 |
| 189 | Rebel Pilot C2 | .20 | .30 |
| 190 | Rebel Trooper C3 | .20 | .30 |
| 191 | Red Leader R1 | 4.00 | 6.00 |
| 192 | Shistavanen Wolfman C2 | .20 | .30 |
| 193 | Talz C2 | .20 | .30 |
| 194 | WED-9-M1 'Bantha' Droid R2 | 1.25 | 2.00 |
| 195 | Wioslea U1 | .50 | .75 |
| 196 | Caller LIGHT U2 | .50 | .75 |
| 197 | Electrobinoculars C2 | .20 | .30 |
| 198 | Fusion Generator Supply Tanks LIGHT C2 | .20 | .30 |
| 199 | Hydroponics Station U2 | .50 | .75 |
| 200 | Restraining Bolt LIGHT C2 | .20 | .30 |
| 201 | Targeting Computer U1 | .50 | .75 |
| 202 | Tatooine Utility Belt C2 | .20 | .30 |
| 203 | Vaporator C2 | .20 | .30 |
| 204 | A Tremor In The Force U1 | .50 | .75 |
| 205 | Affect Mind R1 | 2.00 | 3.00 |
| 206 | Beggar R1 | 2.00 | 3.00 |
| 207 | Crash Site Memorial U1 | .50 | .75 |
| 208 | Death Star Plans R1 | 2.00 | 3.00 |
| 209 | Demotion R2 | 1.25 | 2.00 |
| 210 | Disarmed Light R1 | 2.00 | 3.00 |
| 211 | Ellorrs Madak C2 | .20 | .30 |
| 212 | Eyes In The Dark U1 | .50 | .75 |
| 213 | Jawa Siesta U1 | .50 | .75 |
| 214 | Kessel LIGHT U2 | 2.00 | 3.00 |
| 215 | K'lor'slug R1 | .50 | .75 |
| 216 | Lightsaber Proficiency R1 | 2.00 | 3.00 |
| 217 | Mantellian Savrip R2 | 1.25 | 2.00 |
| 218 | Nightfall U1 | .50 | .75 |
| 219 | Obi-Wanís Cape R1 | 2.00 | 3.00 |
| 220 | Our Most Desperate Hour R1 | 2.00 | 3.00 |
| 221 | Plastoid Armor U2 | .50 | .75 |
| 222 | Rebel Planners R2 | 1.25 | 2.00 |
| 223 | Restricted Deployment U1 | .50 | .75 |
| 224 | Revolution R1 | 2.00 | 3.00 |
| 225 | Rycar Ryjerd U1 | .50 | .75 |
| 226 | Saiitorr Kal Fas C2 | .20 | .30 |
| 227 | Special Modifications U1 | .50 | .75 |
| 228 | Traffic Control U2 | .50 | .75 |
| 229 | Tusken Breath Mask U1 | .50 | .75 |
| 230 | Yavin Sentry U2 | .50 | .75 |
| 231 | Yerka Mig U1 | .20 | .30 |
| 232 | A Few Maneuvers C2 | .20 | .30 |
| 233 | Alter LIGHT U1 | .50 | .75 |
| 234 | Beru Stew U2 | .50 | .75 |
| 235 | Cantina Brawl R1 | 2.00 | 3.00 |
| 236 | Collision! C2 | .20 | .30 |
| 237 | Combined Attack C2 | .20 | .30 |
| 238 | Donít Get Cocky R1 | 2.00 | 3.00 |
| 239 | Donít Underestimate Our Chances C1 | .20 | .30 |
| 240 | Droid Shutdown C2 | .20 | .30 |
| 241 | Escape Pod U2 | .50 | .75 |
| 242 | Friendly Fire C2 | .20 | .30 |
| 243 | Full Throttle R2 | 1.25 | 2.00 |
| 244 | Gift Of The Mentor R1 | 2.00 | 3.00 |
| 245 | Hanís Back U2 | .50 | .75 |
| 246 | Hanís Dice C2 | .20 | .30 |
| 247 | Hear Me Baby, Hold Together C2 | .20 | .30 |
| 248 | Help Me Obi-Wan Kenobi R1 | 2.00 | 3.00 |
| 249 | How Did We Get Into This Mess? U2 | .50 | .75 |
| 250 | Hyper Escape C2 | .20 | .30 |
| 251 | I've Got A Bad Feeling About This C2 | .20 | .30 |
| 252 | It Could Be Worse C2 | 1.25 | 2.00 |
| 253 | Into The Garbage Chute, Flyboy R2 | .20 | .30 |
| 254 | Jedi Presence R1 | 2.00 | 3.00 |
| 255 | Krayt Dragon Howl R1 | 2.00 | 3.00 |
| 256 | Leiaís Back U2 | .50 | .75 |
| 257 | Luke's Back U2 | .50 | .75 |
| 258 | Move Along... R1 | 2.00 | 3.00 |
| 259 | Nabrun Leids U2 | .50 | .75 |
| 260 | Narrow Escape C2 | .20 | .30 |
| 261 | Noble Sacrifice R2 | 1.25 | 2.00 |
| 262 | Old Ben C2 | .20 | .30 |
| 263 | On The Edge R2 | 1.25 | 2.00 |
| 264 | Out Of Nowhere U2 | .50 | .75 |
| 265 | Panic U1 | .50 | .75 |
| 266 | Radar Scanner C2 | .20 | .30 |
| 267 | Rebel Barrier C2 | .20 | .30 |
| 268 | Rebel Reinforcements C1 | .20 | .30 |
| 269 | Return Of A Jedi U2 | .50 | .75 |
| 270 | Scomp Link Access C2 | .20 | .30 |
| 271 | Sense LIGHT U1 | .50 | .75 |
| 272 | Skywalkers R1 | 2.00 | 3.00 |
| 273 | Solo Han R2 | 1.25 | 2.00 |
| 274 | Spaceport Speeders U2 | .50 | .75 |
| 275 | Surprise Assault C1 | .20 | .30 |
| 276 | Thank The Maker R2 | 1.25 | 2.00 |
| 277 | The Bith Shuffle C2 | .20 | .30 |
| 278 | The Force Is Strong With This One R2 | 1.25 | 2.00 |
| 279 | This Is All Your Fault U1 | .50 | .75 |
| 280 | Utinni! LIGHT R1 | 2.00 | 3.00 |
| 281 | Warriorís Courage R2 | 1.25 | 2.00 |
| 282 | Weíre Doomed C2 | .20 | .30 |
| 283 | Alderaan LIGHT U2 | 1.25 | 2.00 |
| 284 | Dantooine LIGHT U1 | .50 | .75 |
| 285 | Death Star: Detention Block Control Room U2 | .50 | .75 |
| 286 | Death Star: Docking Bay 327 LIGHT C2 | .20 | .30 |
| 287 | Death Star: Trash Compactor U1 | .50 | .75 |
| 288 | Kessel LIGHT U2 | .50 | .75 |
| 289 | Tatooine LIGHT C2 | .20 | .30 |
| 290 | Tatooine: Cantina LIGHT R2 | 1.25 | 2.00 |
| 291 | Tatooine: Docking Bay 94 LIGHT C2 | .20 | .30 |
| 292 | Tatooine: Dune Sea C1 | .20 | .30 |
| 293 | Tatooine: Jawa Camp LIGHTC1 | .20 | .30 |
| 294 | Tatooine: Larsí Moisture Farm LIGHT U2 | .50 | .75 |
| 295 | Tatooine: Mos Eisley LIGHT C1 | .50 | .75 |
| 296 | Tatooine: Obi-Wanís Hut R1 | 2.00 | 3.00 |
| 297 | Yavin 4: LIGHT C2 | .20 | .30 |
| 298 | Yavin 4: Docking Bay LIGHT C1 | .20 | .30 |
| 299 | Yavin 4: Jungle LIGHT C2 | 2.00 | 3.00 |
| 300 | Yavin 4: Massassi Throne Room R1 | .50 | .75 |
| 301 | Yavin 4: Massassi War Room U2 | .50 | .75 |
| 302 | Corellian Corvette U2 | .60 | 1.00 |
| 303 | Gold 1 R2 | 1.25 | 2.00 |
| 304 | Gold 5 R2 | 1.25 | 2.00 |
| 305 | Millenium Falcon R1 | 5.00 | 8.00 |
| 306 | Red 1 U1 | .50 | .75 |
| 307 | Red 3 R2 | 1.25 | 2.00 |
| 308 | X-wing C2 | .20 | .30 |
| 309 | Y-wing C2 | .20 | .30 |
| 310 | Lift Tube LIGHT C2 | .20 | .30 |
| 311 | Luke's X-34 Landspeeder U2 | .50 | .75 |
| 312 | Sandcrawler LIGHT R2 | 1.25 | 2.00 |
| 313 | SoroSuub V-35 Landspeeder C2 | .20 | .30 |
| 314 | Blaster C2 | .20 | .30 |
| 315 | Blaster Rifle LIGHT C2 | .20 | .30 |
| 316 | Hanís Heavy Blaster Pistol R2 | 1.25 | 2.00 |
| 317 | Jedi Lightsaber U1 | .50 | .75 |
| 318 | Leiaís Sporting Blaster U1 | .50 | .75 |
| 319 | Obi-Wanís Lightsaber R1 | 4.00 | 6.00 |

| | | | |
|---|---|---|---|
| 320 Proton Torpedoes C2 | .20 | .30 |
| 321 Quad Laser Cannon U1 | .50 | .75 |
| 322 Tagge Seeker R2 | 1.25 | 2.00 |
| 323 Tarkin Seeker R2 | 1.25 | 2.00 |
| 324 Timer Mine LIGHT C2 | .20 | .30 |

## 1996 Star Wars Hoth

| | | |
|---|---|---|
| COMPLETE SET (163) | 50.00 | 100.00 |
| BOOSTER BOX (36 PACKS) | 50.00 | 100.00 |
| BOOSTER PACK (15 CARDS) | 2.00 | 4.00 |
| RELEASED IN NOVEMBER 1996 | | |
| 1 AT-AT Driver C2 | .20 | .30 |
| 2 Admiral Ozzel R1 | 2.00 | 3.00 |
| 3 Captain Lennox U1 | .60 | 1.00 |
| 4 Captain Piett R2 | 2.00 | 3.00 |
| 5 FX-10 (Effex-ten) C2 | .20 | .30 |
| 6 General Veers R1 | 5.00 | 8.00 |
| 7 Imperial Gunner C2 | .20 | .30 |
| 8 Lieutenant Cabbel U2 | .60 | 1.00 |
| 9 Probe Droid C2 | .20 | .30 |
| 10 Snowtrooper C3 | .20 | .30 |
| 11 Snowtrooper Officer C1 | .20 | .30 |
| 12 Wampa R2 | 2.00 | 3.00 |
| 13 Deflector Shield Generators U2 | .60 | 1.00 |
| 14 Evacuation Control U1 | .60 | 1.00 |
| 15 Portable Fusion Generator C2 | .20 | .30 |
| 16 Probe Antennae U2 | .60 | 1.00 |
| 17 Breached Defenses U2 | .60 | 1.00 |
| 18 Death Mark R1 | 2.00 | 3.00 |
| 19 Death Squadron U1 | .60 | 1.00 |
| 20 Frostbite LIGHT C2 | .20 | .30 |
| 21 Frozen Dinner R1 | 2.00 | 3.00 |
| 22 High Anxiety R1 | 2.00 | 3.00 |
| 23 Ice Storm LIGHT U1 | .60 | 1.00 |
| 24 Image Of The Dark Lord R2 | 2.00 | 3.00 |
| 25 Imperial Domination U1 | .60 | 1.00 |
| 26 Meteor Impact? R1 | 2.00 | 3.00 |
| 27 Mournful Roar R1 | 2.00 | 3.00 |
| 28 Responsibility Of Command R1 | 2.00 | 3.00 |
| 29 Silence Is Golden U2 | .60 | 1.00 |
| 30 The Shield Doors Must Be Closed U1 | .60 | 1.00 |

| | | |
|---|---|---|
| 31 This Is Just Wrong R1 | 2.00 | 3.00 |
| 32 Too Cold For Speeders U1 | .60 | 1.00 |
| 33 Weapon Malfunction R1 | 2.00 | 3.00 |
| 34 Target The Main Generator R2 | 2.00 | 3.00 |
| 35 A Dark Time For The Rebellion C1 | .20 | .30 |
| 36 Cold Feet C2 | .20 | .30 |
| 37 Collapsing Corridor R2 | 2.00 | 3.00 |
| 38 ComScan Detection C2 | .20 | .30 |
| 39 Crash Landing U1 | .60 | 1.00 |
| 40 Debris Zone R2 | 2.00 | 3.00 |
| 41 Direct Hit U1 | .60 | 1.00 |
| 42 Exhaustion U2 | .60 | 1.00 |
| 43 Exposure U1 | .60 | 1.00 |
| 44 Furry Fury R2 | 2.00 | 3.00 |
| 45 He Hasnìt Come Back Yet C2 | .20 | .30 |
| 46 Iìd Just As Soon Kiss A Wookiee C2 | .20 | .30 |
| 47 Imperial Supply C1 | .20 | .30 |
| 48 Lightsaber Deficiency U1 | .60 | 1.00 |
| 49 Oh, Switch Off C2 | .20 | .30 |
| 50 Our First Catch Of The Day C2 | .20 | .30 |
| 51 Probe Telemetry C2 | .20 | .30 |
| 52 Scruffy-Looking Nerf Herder R2 | 2.00 | 3.00 |
| 53 Self-Destruct Mechanism U1 | .60 | 1.00 |
| 54 Stop Motion C2 | .20 | .30 |
| 55 Tactical Support R2 | 2.00 | 3.00 |
| 56 Thatìs It, The Rebels Are There! U2 | .60 | 1.00 |
| 57 Trample R1 | 2.00 | 3.00 |
| 58 Turn It Off! Turn It Off! C1 | .20 | .30 |
| 59 Walker Barrage U1 | .60 | 1.00 |
| 60 Wall Of Fire U1 | .60 | 1.00 |
| 61 Yaggle Gakkle R2 | 2.00 | 3.00 |
| 62 Hoth DARK U2 | .60 | 1.00 |
| 63 Hoth: Defensive Perimeter LIGHT C2 | .20 | .30 |
| 64 Hoth: Echo Command Center | | |
| (War Room) LIGHT U2 | .60 | 1.00 |
| 65 Hoth: Echo Corridor DARK U2 | .60 | 1.00 |
| 66 Hoth: Echo Docking Bay LIGHT C2 | .20 | .30 |
| 67 Hoth: Ice Plains C2 | .20 | .30 |
| 68 Hoth: North Ridge LIGHT C2 | .20 | .30 |
| 69 Hoth: Wampa Cave R2 | 2.00 | 3.00 |
| 70 Ord Mantell LIGHT U2 | .60 | 1.00 |
| 71 Stalker R1 | 6.00 | 10.00 |
| 72 Tyrant R1 | 5.00 | 8.00 |
| 73 Blizzard 1 R1 | 4.00 | 6.00 |
| 74 Blizzard 2 R2 | 2.00 | 3.00 |
| 75 Blizzard Scout 1 R1 | 4.00 | 6.00 |
| 76 Blizzard Walker U2 | .60 | 1.00 |
| 77 AT-AT Cannon U1 | .60 | 1.00 |
| 78 Echo Base Operations R2 | 2.00 | 3.00 |
| 79 Infantry Mine LIGHT C2 | .20 | .30 |
| 80 Probe Droid Laser U2 | .60 | 1.00 |
| 81 Vehicle Mine LIGHT C2 | .20 | .30 |
| 82 2-1B (Too-Onebee) R1 | 2.00 | 3.00 |
| 83 Cal Alder U2 | .60 | 1.00 |
| 84 Commander Luke Skywalker R1 | 10.00 | 15.00 |
| 85 Dack Ralter R2 | 2.00 | 3.00 |
| 86 Derek ëHobbieí Klivian U1 | .60 | 1.00 |
| 87 Electro-Rangefinder U1 | .60 | 1.00 |
| 88 Echo Base Trooper Officer C1 | .20 | .30 |

| | | |
|---|---|---|
| 89 Echo Trooper Backpack C2 | .20 | .30 |
| 90 FX-7 (Effex-Seven) C2 | .20 | .30 |
| 91 General Carlist Rieekan R2 | 2.00 | 3.00 |
| 92 Jeroen Webb U1 | .60 | 1.00 |
| 93 K-3PO (Kay-Threepio) R1 | 2.00 | 3.00 |
| 94 Major Bren Derlin R2 | 2.00 | 3.00 |
| 95 R2 Sensor Array C2 | .20 | .30 |
| 96 R5-M2 (Arfive-Emmtoo) C2 | .20 | .30 |
| 97 Rebel Scout C1 | .20 | .30 |
| 98 Rogue Gunner C2 | .20 | .30 |
| 99 Romas Lock Navander U2 | .60 | 1.00 |
| 100 Shawn Valdez U1 | .60 | 1.00 |
| 101 Tamizander Rey U2 | .60 | 1.00 |
| 102 Tauntaun Handler C2 | .20 | .30 |
| 103 Tigran Jamiro U1 | .60 | 1.00 |
| 104 Toryn Farr U1 | .60 | 1.00 |
| 105 WED-1016 ëTechieí Droid C1 | .20 | .30 |
| 106 Wes Janson R2 | 2.00 | 3.00 |
| 107 Wyron Serper U2 | .60 | 1.00 |
| 108 Zev Senesca R2 | 2.00 | 3.00 |
| 109 Artillery Remote R2 | 2.00 | 3.00 |
| 110 EG-4 (Eegee-Four) C1 | .20 | .30 |
| 111 Hoth LIGHT U2 | .60 | 1.00 |
| 112 R-3PO (Ar-Threepio) DARK R2 | 2.00 | 3.00 |
| 112 R-3PO (Ar-Threepio) LIGHT R2 | 2.00 | 3.00 |
| 113 Bacta Tank R2 | 3.00 | 5.00 |
| 114 Disarming Creature R1 | 2.00 | 3.00 |
| 115 Echo Base Trooper C3 | .20 | .30 |
| 116 E-web Blaster C1 | .20 | .30 |
| 117 Frostbite DARK C2 | .20 | .30 |
| 118 Ice Storm DARK U1 | .60 | 1.00 |
| 119 Tauntaun Bones U1 | .60 | 1.00 |
| 120 The First Transport Is Away! R1 | 2.00 | 3.00 |
| 121 Attack Pattern Delta U1 | .60 | 1.00 |
| 122 Dark Dissension R1 | 2.00 | 3.00 |
| 123 Fall Back! C2 | .20 | .30 |
| 124 I Thought They Smelled Bad | 2.00 | 3.00 |
| On The Outside R1 | | |
| 125 It Can Wait C2 | .20 | .30 |
| 126 Lucky Shot U1 | .60 | 1.00 |
| 127 Nice Of You Guys To Drop By C2 | .20 | .30 |
| 128 One More Pass U1 | .60 | 1.00 |
| 129 Perimeter Scan C2 | .20 | .30 |
| 130 Rug Hug R1 | 2.00 | 3.00 |
| 131 Under Attack U1 | .60 | 1.00 |
| 132 Walker Sighting U2 | .60 | 1.00 |
| 133 Whoìs Scruffy-Looking? R1 | 2.00 | 3.00 |
| 134 You Have Failed Me | 2.00 | 3.00 |
| For The Last Time R1 | | |
| 135 You Will Go To The Dagobah System R1 | 2.00 | 3.00 |
| 136 Hoth Survival Gear C2 | .20 | .30 |
| 137 Hoth: Defensive Perimeter DARK C2 | .20 | .30 |
| 138 Hoth: Echo Command Center | .60 | 1.00 |
| (War Room) DARK U2 | | |
| 139 Hoth: Echo Corridor LIGHT C2 | .20 | .30 |
| 140 Hoth: Echo Docking Bay DARK C2 | .20 | .30 |
| 141 Hoth: Echo Med Lab C2 | .20 | .30 |
| 142 Hoth: Main Power Generators U2 | .60 | 1.00 |
| 143 Hoth: North Ridge DARK C2 | .20 | .30 |

| | | |
|---|---|---|
| 144 Hoth: Snow Trench C2 | .20 | .30 |
| 145 Ord Mantell DARK C2 | .20 | .30 |
| 146 Medium Transport U2 | .60 | 1.00 |
| 147 Rogue 1 R1 | 4.00 | 6.00 |
| 148 Rogue 2 R2 | 2.00 | 3.00 |
| 149 Rogue 3 R1 | 4.00 | 6.00 |
| 150 Snowspeeder U2 | .60 | 1.00 |
| 151 Tauntaun C2 | .20 | .30 |
| 152 Anakinís Lightsaber R1 | 10.00 | 15.00 |
| 153 Atgar Laser Cannon U2 | .60 | 1.00 |
| 154 Concussion Grenade R1 | 2.00 | 3.00 |
| 155 Dual Laser Cannon U1 | .60 | 1.00 |
| 156 Golan Laser Battery U1 | .60 | 1.00 |
| 157 Infantry Mine DARK C2 | .20 | .30 |
| 158 Medium Repeating Blaster Cannon C1 | .20 | .30 |
| 159 Planet Defender Ion Cannon R2 | 2.00 | 3.00 |
| 160 Power Harpoon U1 | .60 | 1.00 |
| 161 Surface Defense Cannon R2 | 2.00 | 3.00 |
| 162 Vehicle Mine DARK C2 | .20 | .30 |

## 1996 Star Wars Jedi Pack

| | | |
|---|---|---|
| COMPLETE SET (11) | 3.00 | 8.00 |
| RELEASED IN 1996 | | |
| 1 Hyperoute Navigation Chart PM | .60 | 1.00 |
| 2 Dark Forces PM | .60 | 1.00 |
| 3 Eriadu PM | .60 | 1.00 |
| 4 For Luck PM | .60 | 1.00 |
| 5 Gravity Shadow PM | .60 | 1.00 |
| 6 Han PM | .60 | 1.00 |
| 7 Leia PM | .60 | 1.00 |
| 8 Lukeís T-16 Skyhopper PM | .60 | 1.00 |
| 9 Motti PM | .60 | 1.00 |
| 10 Tarkin PM | .60 | 1.00 |
| 11 Tedn Dahai PM | .60 | 1.00 |

## 1996 Star Wars A New Hope

| | | |
|---|---|---|
| COMPLETE SET (162) | 50.00 | 100.00 |
| BOOSTER BOX (36 PACKS) | 50.00 | 100.00 |
| BOOSTER PACK (15 CARDS) | 2.00 | 4.00 |
| RELEASED IN JULY 1996 | | |
| 1 Advosze C2 | .20 | .30 |
| 2 Captain Khurgee U1 | .60 | 1.00 |

| | | |
|---|---|---|
| 3 DS-61-4 R2 | 2.00 | 3.00 |
| 4 Dannik Jerriko R1 | 2.00 | 3.00 |
| 5 Danz Borin U2 | .60 | 1.00 |
| 6 Death Star R2 | 6.00 | 10.00 |
| 7 Defel C2 | .20 | .30 |
| 8 Greedo R1 | 5.00 | 8.00 |
| 9 Hem Dazon R1 | 2.00 | 3.00 |
| 10 IT-O (Eyetee-Oh) R1 | 2.00 | 3.00 |
| 11 Imperial Commander C2 | .20 | .30 |
| 12 Imperial Squad Leader C3 | .20 | .30 |
| 13 Lirin Carín U2 | .60 | 1.00 |
| 14 Lt. Pol Treidum C1 | .20 | .30 |
| 15 Lt. Shann Childsen U1 | .60 | 1.00 |
| 16 Mosep U2 | .60 | 1.00 |
| 17 Officer Evax C1 | .20 | .30 |
| 18 R2-Q2 (Artoo-Kyootoo) C2 | .20 | .30 |
| 19 R3-T6 (Arthree-Teesix) R1 | 2.00 | 3.00 |
| 20 R5-A2 (Arfive-Aytoo) C2 | .20 | .30 |
| 21 Reegesk U2 | .60 | 1.00 |
| 22 Reserve Pilot U1 | .60 | 1.00 |
| 23 Rodian C2 | .20 | .30 |
| 24 Tech Moír U2 | .60 | 1.00 |
| 25 Trooper Davin Felth R2 | 2.00 | 3.00 |
| 26 U-3PO (Yoo-Threepio) R1 | 2.00 | 3.00 |
| 27 URoRRuRiRiR U2 | .60 | 1.00 |
| 28 WED15-I7 éSeptoidí Droid U2 | .60 | 1.00 |
| 29 Dianoga R2 | 2.00 | 3.00 |
| 30 Death Star Tractor Beam R2 | 2.00 | 3.00 |
| 31 Hypo R1 | 2.00 | 3.00 |
| 32 Laser Gate U2 | .60 | 1.00 |
| 33 Maneuver Check R2 | 2.00 | 3.00 |
| 34 Tractor Beam U1 | .60 | 1.00 |
| 35 Astromech Shortage U2 | .60 | 1.00 |
| 36 Besieged R2 | 2.00 | 3.00 |
| 37 Come With Me C2 | .20 | .30 |
| 38 Dark Waters R2 | 2.00 | 3.00 |
| 39 Hyperwave Scan U1 | .60 | 1.00 |
| 40 Imperial Justice C2 | .20 | .30 |
| 41 Krayt Dragon Bones U1 | .60 | 1.00 |
| 42 Merc Sunlet C2 | .20 | .30 |
| 43 Program Trap U1 | .60 | 1.00 |
| 44 Spice Mines Of Kessel R1 | 2.00 | 3.00 |
| 45 Swilla Corey C2 | .20 | .30 |
| 46 Tentacle C2 | .20 | .30 |
| 47 Thereíll Be Hell To Pay U2 | .60 | 1.00 |
| 48 Undercover LIGHT U2 | .60 | 1.00 |
| 49 Commence Primary Ignition R2 | 2.00 | 3.00 |
| 50 Evader U1 | .60 | 1.00 |
| 51 Ghhhk C2 | .20 | .30 |
| 52 Iím On The Leader R1 | 2.00 | 3.00 |
| 53 Informant U1 | .60 | 1.00 |
| 54 Monnok C2 | .20 | .30 |
| 55 Ngiok C2 | .20 | .30 |
| 56 Oo-ta Goo-ta, Solo? C2 | .20 | .30 |
| 57 Retract the Bridge R1 | 2.00 | 3.00 |
| 58 Sniper U1 | .60 | 1.00 |
| 59 Stunning Leader C2 | .20 | .30 |
| 60 This Is Some Rescue! U1 | .60 | 1.00 |
| 61 We Have A Prisoner C2 | .20 | .30 |
| 62 Death Star Gunner C1 | .20 | .30 |

| | | |
|---|---|---|
| 63 Death Star: Conference Room U1 | .60 | 1.00 |
| 64 Imperial Holotable R1 | 2.00 | 3.00 |
| 65 Kashyyyk LIGHTC1 | .20 | .30 |
| 66 Kiffex R1 | 2.00 | 3.00 |
| 67 Ralltiir LIGHT C1 | .20 | .30 |
| 68 Sandcrawler: Droid Junkheap R1 | 2.00 | 3.00 |
| 69 Tatooine: Bluffs R1 | 2.00 | 3.00 |
| 70 Black 4 U2 | .60 | 1.00 |
| 71 Conquest R1 | 6.00 | 10.00 |
| 72 TIE Assault Squadron U1 | .60 | 1.00 |
| 73 TIE Vanguard C2 | .20 | .30 |
| 74 Victory-Class Star Destroyer U1 | .60 | 1.00 |
| 75 Bespin Motors Void Spider THX 1138 C2 | .20 | .30 |
| 76 Mobquet A-1 Deluxe Floater C2 | .20 | .30 |
| 77 Enhanced TIE Laser Cannon C2 | .20 | .30 |
| 78 Jawa Blaster C2 | .20 | .30 |
| 79 Leia Seeker R2 | 2.00 | 3.00 |
| 80 Superlaser R2 | 3.00 | 5.00 |
| 81 URoRRuRiRiRís Hunting Rifle U1 | .60 | 1.00 |
| 82 Arcona C2 | .20 | .30 |
| 83 Brainiac R1 | 4.00 | 6.00 |
| 84 Chewbacca R2 | 10.00 | 15.00 |
| 85 Commander Evram Lajaie C1 | .20 | .30 |
| 86 Commander Vanden Willard U2 | .60 | 1.00 |
| 87 Corellian C2 | .20 | .30 |
| 88 Doikk Naíts U2 | .60 | 1.00 |
| 89 Garouf Lafoe U2 | .60 | 1.00 |
| 90 Het Nkik U2 | .60 | 1.00 |
| 91 Hunchback R1 | 2.00 | 3.00 |
| 92 Ickabel Gíont U2 | .60 | 1.00 |
| 93 Magnetic Suction Tube DARK R2 | 2.00 | 3.00 |
| 94 Nalan Cheel U2 | .60 | 1.00 |
| 95 R2-D2 (Artoo-Detoo) R2 | 10.00 | 15.00 |
| 96 R5-D4 (Arfive-Defour) C2 | .20 | .30 |
| 97 RA-7 (Aray-Seven) C2 | .20 | .30 |
| 98 Rebel Commander C2 | .20 | .30 |
| 99 Rebel Squad Leader C3 | .20 | .30 |
| 100 Rebel Tech C1 | .20 | .30 |
| 101 Saurin C2 | .20 | .30 |
| 102 Tiree U2 | .60 | 1.00 |
| 103 Tzizvvt R2 | 2.00 | 3.00 |
| 104 Wedge Antilles R1 | 10.00 | 15.00 |
| 105 Zutton C1 | .20 | .30 |
| 106 Fire Extinguisher U2 | .60 | 1.00 |
| 107 Magnetic Suction Tube LIGHT R2 | 2.00 | 3.00 |
| 108 Rectenna C2 | .20 | .30 |
| 109 Remote C2 | .20 | .30 |
| 110 Sensor Panel U1 | .60 | 1.00 |
| 111 Cell 2187 R1 | 2.00 | 3.00 |
| 112 Commence Recharging R2 | 2.00 | 3.00 |
| 113 Eject! Eject! C2 | .20 | .30 |
| 114 Grappling Hook C2 | .20 | .30 |
| 115 Logistical Delay U2 | .60 | 1.00 |
| 116 Lukeís Cape R1 | 2.00 | 3.00 |
| 117 M-HYD éBinaryí Droid U1 | .60 | 1.00 |
| 118 Scanner Techs U1 | .60 | 1.00 |
| 119 Solomahal C2 | .20 | .30 |
| 120 Theyíre On Dantooine R1 | 2.00 | 3.00 |
| 121 Undercover DARK U2 | .60 | 1.00 |
| 122 Whatíre You Tryiní To Push On Us? U2 | .60 | 1.00 |

| | | | |
|---|---|---:|---:|
| 123 | Attack Run R2 | 2.00 | 3.00 |
| 124 | Advance Preparation U1 | .60 | 1.00 |
| 125 | Alternatives To Fighting U1 | .60 | 1.00 |
| 126 | Blast The Door, Kid! C2 | .20 | .30 |
| 127 | Blue Milk C2 | .20 | .30 |
| 128 | Corellian Slip C2 | .20 | .30 |
| 129 | Double Agent R2 | 2.00 | 3.00 |
| 130 | Grimtaash C2 | .20 | .30 |
| 131 | Houjix C2 | .20 | .30 |
| 132 | I Have A Very Bad Feeling About This C2 | .20 | .30 |
| 133 | Iím Here To Rescue You U1 | .60 | 1.00 |
| 134 | Let The Wookiee Win R1 | 8.00 | 12.00 |
| 135 | Out Of Commission U2 | .60 | 1.00 |
| 136 | Quite A Mercenary C2 | .20 | .30 |
| 137 | Sabotage U1 | .60 | 1.00 |
| 138 | Sorry About The Mess U1 | .60 | 1.00 |
| 139 | Wookiee Roar R1 | 2.00 | 3.00 |
| 140 | Y-wing Assault Squadron U1 | .60 | 1.00 |
| 141 | Clakidor VII R2 | 2.00 | 3.00 |
| 142 | Corellia R1 | 2.00 | 3.00 |
| 143 | Death Star: Trench R2 | 2.00 | 3.00 |
| 144 | Dejarik Hologameboard R1 | 2.00 | 3.00 |
| 145 | Kashyyyk DARK C1 | .20 | .30 |
| 146 | Ralltiir DARK C1 | .20 | .30 |
| 147 | Sandcrawler: Loading Bay R1 | 2.00 | 3.00 |
| 148 | Yavin 4: Massassi Ruins U1 | .60 | 1.00 |
| 149 | Youíre All Clear Kid! R1 | 2.00 | 3.00 |
| 150 | Gold 2 U1 | .60 | 1.00 |
| 151 | Red 2 R1 | 2.00 | 3.00 |
| 152 | Red 5 R1 | 5.00 | 8.00 |
| 153 | Red 6 U1 | .60 | 1.00 |
| 154 | Tantive IV R1 | 6.00 | 10.00 |
| 155 | Yavin 4: Briefing Room U1 | .60 | 1.00 |
| 156 | Incom T-16 Skyhopper C2 | .20 | .30 |
| 157 | Rogue Bantha U1 | .60 | 1.00 |
| 158 | Bowcaster R2 | 2.00 | 3.00 |
| 159 | Jawa Ion Gun C2 | .20 | .30 |
| 160 | Lukeís Hunting Rifle U1 | .60 | 1.00 |
| 161 | Motti Seeker R2 | 2.00 | 3.00 |
| 162 | SW-4 Ion Cannon R2 | 2.00 | 3.00 |

### 1997 Star Wars Cloud City

| | | | |
|---|---|---:|---:|
| | COMPLETE SET (180) | 50.00 | 100.00 |
| | BOOSTER BOX (60 PACKS) | 50.00 | 100.00 |
| | BOOSTER PACK (9 CARDS) | 2.00 | 4.00 |
| | RELEASED IN NOVEMBER 1997 | | |
| 1 | Ability, Ability, Ability C | .20 | .30 |
| 2 | Abyss U | .60 | 1.00 |
| 3 | Access Denied C | .20 | .30 |
| 4 | Advantage R | 2.00 | 3.00 |
| 5 | Aiiii! Aaa! Agggggggggg! R | 2.00 | 3.00 |
| 6 | All My Urchins R | 2.00 | 3.00 |
| 7 | All Too Easy R | 2.00 | 3.00 |
| 8 | Ambush R | 2.00 | 3.00 |
| 9 | Armed And Dangerous U | .60 | 1.00 |
| 10 | Artoo, Come Back At Once! R | 2.00 | 3.00 |
| 11 | As Good As Gone C | .20 | .30 |
| 12 | Atmospheric Assault R | 2.00 | 3.00 |
| 13 | Beldonís Eye R | 2.00 | 3.00 |
| 14 | Bespin DARK U | .60 | 1.00 |
| 15 | Bespin LIGHT U | .60 | 1.00 |
| 16 | Bespin: Cloud City DARK U | .60 | 1.00 |
| 17 | Bespin: Cloud City LIGHT U | .60 | 1.00 |
| 18 | Binders C | .20 | .30 |
| 19 | Bionic Hand R | 2.00 | 3.00 |
| 20 | Blasted Droid C | .20 | .30 |
| 21 | Blaster Proficiency C | .20 | .30 |
| 22 | Boba Fett R | 12.00 | 20.00 |
| 23 | Boba Fettís Blaster Rifle R | 5.00 | 8.00 |
| 24 | Bounty C | .20 | .30 |
| 25 | Brief Loss Of Control R | 2.00 | 3.00 |
| 26 | Bright Hope R | 2.00 | 3.00 |
| 27 | Captain Bewil R | 2.00 | 3.00 |
| 28 | Captain Han Solo R | 12.00 | 20.00 |
| 29 | Captive Fury U | .60 | 1.00 |
| 30 | Captive Pursuit C | .20 | .30 |
| 31 | Carbon-Freezing U | .60 | 1.00 |
| 32 | Carbonite Chamber Console U | .60 | 1.00 |
| 33 | Chasm U | .60 | 1.00 |
| 34 | Chief Retwin R | 2.00 | 3.00 |
| 35 | Civil Disorder C | .20 | .30 |
| 36 | Clash Of Sabers U | .60 | 1.00 |
| 37 | Cloud Car DARK C | .20 | .30 |
| 38 | Cloud Car LIGHT C | .20 | .30 |
| 39 | Cloud City Blaster DARK C | .20 | .30 |
| 40 | Cloud City Blaster LIGHT C | .20 | .30 |
| 41 | Cloud City Engineer C | .20 | .30 |
| 42 | Cloud City Sabacc DARK U | .60 | 1.00 |
| 43 | Cloud City Sabacc LIGHT U | .60 | 1.00 |
| 44 | Cloud City Technician C | .20 | .30 |
| 45 | Cloud City Trooper DARK C | .20 | .30 |
| 46 | Cloud City Trooper LIGHT C | .20 | .30 |
| 47 | Cloud City: Carbonite Chamber DARK U | .60 | 1.00 |
| 48 | Cloud City: Carbonite Chamber LIGHT U | .60 | 1.00 |
| 49 | Cloud City: Chasm Walkway DARK C | .20 | .30 |
| 50 | Cloud City: Chasm Walkway LIGHT C | .20 | .30 |
| 51 | Cloud City: Dining Room R | 2.00 | 3.00 |
| 52 | Cloud City: East Platform | .20 | .30 |
| | (Docking Bay) C | | |
| 53 | Cloud City: Guest Quarters R | 2.00 | 3.00 |
| 54 | Cloud City: Incinerator DARK C | .20 | .30 |
| 55 | Cloud City: Incinerator LIGHT C | .20 | .30 |

| | | | |
|---|---|---:|---:|
| 56 | Cloud City: Lower Corridor DARK U | .60 | 1.00 |
| 57 | Cloud City: Lower Corridor LIGHT U | .60 | 1.00 |
| 58 | Cloud City: Platform 327 | .20 | .30 |
| | (Docking Bay) C | | |
| 59 | Cloud City: Security Tower C | .20 | .30 |
| 60 | Cloud City: Upper Plaza | .20 | .30 |
| | Corridor DARK C | | |
| 61 | Cloud City: Upper Plaza | .60 | 1.00 |
| | Corridor LIGHT U | | |
| 62 | Clouds DARK C | .20 | .30 |
| 63 | Clouds LIGHT C | .20 | .30 |
| 64 | Commander Desanne U | .60 | 1.00 |
| 65 | Computer Interface C | .20 | .30 |
| 66 | Courage Of A Skywalker R | 2.00 | 3.00 |
| 67 | Crack Shot U | .60 | 1.00 |
| 68 | Cyborg Construct U | .60 | 1.00 |
| 69 | Dark Approach R | 2.00 | 3.00 |
| 70 | Dark Deal R | 2.00 | 3.00 |
| 71 | Dark Strike C | .20 | .30 |
| 72 | Dash C | .20 | .30 |
| 73 | Despair R | 2.00 | 3.00 |
| 74 | Desperate Reach U | .60 | 1.00 |
| 75 | Dismantle On Sight R | 2.00 | 3.00 |
| 76 | Dodge C | .20 | .30 |
| 77 | Double Back U | .60 | 1.00 |
| 78 | Double-Crossing, No-Good Swindler C | .20 | .30 |
| 79 | E Chu Ta C | .20 | .30 |
| 80 | E-3P0 R | 2.00 | 3.00 |
| 81 | End This Destructive Conflict R | 2.00 | 3.00 |
| 82 | Epic Duel R | 3.00 | 5.00 |
| 83 | Fall Of The Empire U | .60 | 1.00 |
| 84 | Fall Of The Legend U | .60 | 1.00 |
| 85 | Flight Escort R | 2.00 | 3.00 |
| 86 | Focused Attack R | 2.00 | 3.00 |
| 87 | Force Field R | 2.00 | 3.00 |
| 88 | Forced Landing R | 2.00 | 3.00 |
| 89 | Frozen Assets R | 2.00 | 3.00 |
| 90 | Gamblerís Luck R | 2.00 | 3.00 |
| 91 | Glancing Blow R | 2.00 | 3.00 |
| 92 | Haven R | 2.00 | 3.00 |
| 93 | Heís All Yours, Bounty Hunter R | 2.00 | 3.00 |
| 94 | Heart Of The Chasm U | .60 | 1.00 |
| 95 | Hero Of A Thousand Devices U | .60 | 1.00 |
| 96 | Higher Ground R | 2.00 | 3.00 |
| 97 | Hindsight R | 2.00 | 3.00 |
| 98 | Hopping Mad R | 2.00 | 3.00 |
| 99 | Human Shield C | .20 | .30 |
| 100 | I Am Your Father R | 2.00 | 3.00 |
| 101 | I Donít Need Their Scum, Either R | 2.00 | 3.00 |
| 102 | I Had No Choice R | 2.00 | 3.00 |
| 103 | Imperial Decree U | .60 | 1.00 |
| 104 | Imperial Trooper Guard Dainsom U | .60 | 1.00 |
| 105 | Impressive, Most Impressive R | 2.00 | 3.00 |
| 106 | Innocent Scoundrel U | .60 | 1.00 |
| 107 | Interrogation Array R | 2.00 | 3.00 |
| 108 | Into The Ventilation Shaft, Lefty R | 2.00 | 3.00 |
| 109 | Itís A Trap! U | .60 | 1.00 |
| 110 | Kebyc U | .60 | 1.00 |
| 111 | Keep Your Eyes Open C | .20 | .30 |
| 112 | Lando Calrissian DARK R | 8.00 | 12.00 |

| # | Card | Low | High |
|---|---|---|---|
| 113 | Lando Calrissian LIGHT R | 8.00 | 12.00 |
| 114 | Lando's Wrist Comlink U | .60 | 1.00 |
| 115 | Leia Of Alderaan R | 3.00 | 5.00 |
| 116 | Levitation Attack U | .60 | 1.00 |
| 117 | Lieutenant Cecius U | .60 | 1.00 |
| 118 | Lieutenant Sheckil R | 2.00 | 3.00 |
| 119 | Lift Tube Escape C | .20 | .30 |
| 120 | Lobot R | 4.00 | 6.00 |
| 121 | Luke's Blaster Pistol R | 2.00 | 3.00 |
| 122 | Mandalorian Armor R | 3.00 | 5.00 |
| 123 | Mostly Armless R | 2.00 | 3.00 |
| 124 | NOOOOOOOOOOOO! R | 2.00 | 3.00 |
| 125 | Obsidian 7 R | 3.00 | 5.00 |
| 126 | Obsidian 8 R | 3.00 | 5.00 |
| 127 | Off The Edge R | 2.00 | 3.00 |
| 128 | Old Pirates R | 2.00 | 3.00 |
| 129 | Out Of Somewhere U | .60 | 1.00 |
| 130 | Path Of Least Resistance C | .20 | .30 |
| 131 | Point Man R | 2.00 | 3.00 |
| 132 | Prepare The Chamber U | .60 | 1.00 |
| 133 | Princess Leia R | 6.00 | 10.00 |
| 134 | Projective Telepathy U | .60 | 1.00 |
| 135 | Protector R | 2.00 | 3.00 |
| 136 | Punch It! R | 2.00 | 3.00 |
| 137 | Put That Down C | .20 | .30 |
| 138 | Redemption R | 4.00 | 6.00 |
| 139 | Release Your Anger R | 2.00 | 3.00 |
| 140 | Rendezvous Point On Tatooine R | 2.00 | 3.00 |
| 141 | Rescue In The Clouds C | .20 | .30 |
| 142 | Restricted Access C | .20 | .30 |
| 143 | Rite Of Passage C | .20 | .30 |
| 144 | Shattered Hope U | .60 | 1.00 |
| 145 | Shocking Information C | .20 | .30 |
| 146 | Shocking Revelation C | .20 | .30 |
| 147 | Slave I R | 6.00 | 10.00 |
| 148 | Slip Sliding Away R | 2.00 | 3.00 |
| 149 | Smoke Screen R | 2.00 | 3.00 |
| 150 | Somersault C | .20 | .30 |
| 151 | Sonic Bombardment U | .60 | 1.00 |
| 152 | Special Delivery C | .20 | .30 |
| 153 | Surprise R | 2.00 | 3.00 |
| 154 | Surreptitious Glance R | 2.00 | 3.00 |
| 155 | Swing-And-A-Miss U | .60 | 1.00 |
| 156 | The Emperor's Prize R | 2.00 | 3.00 |
| 157 | This Is Even Better R | 2.00 | 3.00 |
| 158 | This Is Still Wrong R | 2.00 | 3.00 |
| 159 | Tibanna Gas Miner DARK C | .20 | .30 |
| 160 | Tibanna Gas Miner LIGHT C | .20 | .30 |
| 161 | TIE Sentry Ships C | .20 | .30 |
| 162 | Treva Horme U | .60 | 1.00 |
| 163 | Trooper Assault C | .20 | .30 |
| 164 | Trooper Jerrol Blendin U | .60 | 1.00 |
| 165 | Trooper Utris Mitoc U | .60 | 1.00 |
| 166 | Ugloste R | 2.00 | 3.00 |
| 167 | Ugnaught C | .20 | .30 |
| 168 | Uncontrollable Fury R | 2.00 | 3.00 |
| 169 | Vader's Bounty R | 2.00 | 3.00 |
| 170 | Vader's Cape R | 2.00 | 3.00 |
| 171 | We'll Find Han R | 2.00 | 3.00 |
| 172 | We're The Bait R | 2.00 | 3.00 |
| 173 | Weapon Levitation U | .60 | 1.00 |

| # | Card | Low | High |
|---|---|---|---|
| 174 | Weapon Of An Ungrateful Son U | .60 | 1.00 |
| 175 | Weather Vane DARK U | .60 | 1.00 |
| 176 | Weather Vane LIGHT U | .60 | 1.00 |
| 177 | Why Didn't You Tell Me? R | 2.00 | 3.00 |
| 178 | Wiorkettle U | .60 | 1.00 |
| 179 | Wookiee Strangle R | 2.00 | 3.00 |
| 180 | You Are Beaten U | .60 | 1.00 |

## 1997 Star Wars Dagobah

| | Low | High |
|---|---|---|
| COMPLETE SET (181) | 50.00 | 100.00 |
| BOOSTER BOX (60 PACKS) | 50.00 | 100.00 |
| BOOSTER PACK (9 CARDS) | 1.50 | 3.00 |
| RELEASED ON APRIL 23, 1997 | | |

| # | Card | Low | High |
|---|---|---|---|
| 1 | 3,720 To 1 C | .20 | .30 |
| 2 | 4-LOM R | 4.00 | 6.00 |
| 3 | 4-LOM's Concussion Rifle R | 3.00 | 5.00 |
| 4 | A Dangerous Time C | .20 | .30 |
| 5 | A Jedi's Strength U | .60 | 1.00 |
| 6 | Anger, Fear, Aggression C | .20 | .30 |
| 7 | Anoat DARK U | .60 | 1.00 |
| 8 | Anoat LIGHT U | .60 | 1.00 |
| 9 | Apology Accepted C | .20 | .30 |
| 10 | Asteroid Field DARK C | .20 | .30 |
| 11 | Asteroid Field LIGHT C | .20 | .30 |
| 12 | Asteroid Sanctuary C | .20 | .30 |
| 13 | Asteroids Do Not Concern Me R | 2.00 | 3.00 |
| 14 | Astroid Sanctuary C | .20 | .30 |
| 15 | Astromech Translator C | .20 | .30 |
| 16 | At Peace R | 2.00 | 3.00 |
| 17 | Avenger R | 6.00 | 10.00 |
| 18 | Away Put Your Weapon U | .60 | 1.00 |
| 19 | Awwww, Cannot Get Your Ship Out C | .20 | .30 |
| 20 | Bad Feeling Have I R | 2.00 | 3.00 |
| 21 | Big One DARK U | .60 | 1.00 |
| 22 | Big One LIGHT U | .60 | 1.00 |
| 23 | Big One: Asteroid Cave or Space Slug Belly DARK U | .60 | 1.00 |
| 24 | Big One: Asteroid Cave or Space Slug Belly LIGHT U | .60 | 1.00 |
| 25 | Blasted Varmints C | .20 | .30 |
| 26 | Bog-wing DARK C | .20 | .30 |
| 27 | Bog-wing LIGHT C | .20 | .30 |

| # | Card | Low | High |
|---|---|---|---|
| 28 | Bombing Run R | 2.00 | 3.00 |
| 29 | Bossk R | 5.00 | 8.00 |
| 30 | Bossk's Mortar Gun R | 3.00 | 5.00 |
| 31 | Broken Concentration R | 2.00 | 3.00 |
| 32 | Captain Needa R | 3.00 | 5.00 |
| 33 | Close Call C | .20 | .30 |
| 34 | Closer?! U | .60 | 1.00 |
| 35 | Comm Chief C | .20 | .30 |
| 36 | Commander Brandei U | .60 | 1.00 |
| 37 | Commander Gherant U | .60 | 1.00 |
| 38 | Commander Nemet U | .60 | 1.00 |
| 39 | Control DARK U | .60 | 1.00 |
| 40 | Control LIGHT U | .60 | 1.00 |
| 41 | Corporal Derdram U | .60 | 1.00 |
| 42 | Corporal Vandolay U | .60 | 1.00 |
| 43 | Corrosive Damage R | 2.00 | 3.00 |
| 44 | Dagobah U | .60 | 1.00 |
| 45 | Dagobah: Bog Clearing R | 2.00 | 3.00 |
| 46 | Dagobah: Cave R | 2.00 | 3.00 |
| 47 | Dagobah: Jungle U | .60 | 1.00 |
| 48 | Dagobah: Swamp U | .60 | 1.00 |
| 49 | Dagobah: Training Area C | .20 | .30 |
| 50 | Dagobah: Yoda's Hut R | 3.00 | 5.00 |
| 51 | Defensive Fire C | .20 | .30 |
| 52 | Dengar R | 2.00 | 3.00 |
| 53 | Dengar's Blaster Carbine R | 2.00 | 3.00 |
| 54 | Descent Into The Dark R | 2.00 | 3.00 |
| 55 | Do, Or Do Not C | .20 | .30 |
| 56 | Domain Of Evil U | .60 | 1.00 |
| 57 | Dragonsnake R | 2.00 | 3.00 |
| 58 | Droid Sensorscope C | .20 | .30 |
| 59 | Effective Repairs R | 2.00 | 3.00 |
| 60 | Egregious Pilot Error R | 2.00 | 3.00 |
| 61 | Encampment C | .20 | .30 |
| 62 | Executor R | 12.00 | 20.00 |
| 63 | Executor: Comm Station U | .60 | 1.00 |
| 64 | Executor: Control Station U | .60 | 1.00 |
| 65 | Executor: Holotheatre R | 2.00 | 3.00 |
| 66 | Executor: Main Corridor C | .20 | .30 |
| 67 | Executor: Meditation Chamber R | 2.00 | 3.00 |
| 68 | Failure At The Cave R | 2.00 | 3.00 |
| 69 | Fear C | .20 | .30 |
| 70 | Field Promotion R | 2.00 | 3.00 |
| 71 | Flagship R | 2.00 | 3.00 |
| 72 | Flash Of Insight U | .60 | 1.00 |
| 73 | Found Someone You Have U | .60 | 1.00 |
| 74 | Frustration R | 2.00 | 3.00 |
| 75 | Great Warrior C | .20 | .30 |
| 76 | Grounded Starfighter U | .60 | 1.00 |
| 77 | Han's Toolkit R | 2.00 | 3.00 |
| 78 | He Is Not Ready C | .20 | .30 |
| 79 | Hiding In The Garbage R | 2.00 | 3.00 |
| 80 | HoloNet Transmission U | .60 | 1.00 |
| 81 | Hound's Tooth R | 4.00 | 6.00 |
| 82 | I Have A Bad Feeling About This R | 2.00 | 3.00 |
| 83 | I Want That Ship R | 2.00 | 3.00 |
| 84 | IG-2000 R | 3.00 | 5.00 |
| 85 | IG-88 R | 6.00 | 10.00 |
| 86 | IG-88's Neural Inhibitor R | 3.00 | 5.00 |
| 87 | IG-88's Pulse Cannon R | 3.00 | 5.00 |
| 88 | Imbalance U | .60 | 1.00 |

| | | |
|---|---|---|
| 89 Imperial Helmsman C | .20 | .30 |
| 90 Ineffective Maneuver U | .60 | 1.00 |
| 91 It Is The Future You See R | 2.00 | 3.00 |
| 92 Jedi Levitation R | 2.00 | 3.00 |
| 93 Knowledge And Defense C | .20 | .30 |
| 94 Landing Claw R | 2.00 | 3.00 |
| 95 Lando System? R | 2.00 | 3.00 |
| 96 Levitation U | .60 | 1.00 |
| 97 Lieutenant Commander Ardan U | .60 | 1.00 |
| 98 Lieutenant Suba R | 2.00 | 3.00 |
| 99 Lieutenant Venka U | .60 | 1.00 |
| 100 Light Maneuvers R | 2.00 | 3.00 |
| 101 Location, Location, Location R | 2.00 | 3.00 |
| 102 Lost In Space R | 2.00 | 3.00 |
| 103 Lost Relay C | .20 | .30 |
| 104 Luke's Backpack R | 2.00 | 3.00 |
| 105 Mist Hunter R | 3.00 | 5.00 |
| 106 Moving To Attack Position C | .20 | .30 |
| 107 Much Anger In Him R | 2.00 | 3.00 |
| 108 Mynock DARK C | .20 | .30 |
| 109 Mynock LIGHT C | .20 | .30 |
| 110 Never Tell Me The Odds C | .20 | .30 |
| 111 No Disintegrations! R | 2.00 | 3.00 |
| 112 Nudj C | .20 | .30 |
| 113 Obi-Wan's Apparition R | 2.00 | 3.00 |
| 114 Order To Engage R | 2.00 | 3.00 |
| 115 Polarized Negative Power Coupling R | 2.00 | 3.00 |
| 116 Portable Fusion Generator C | .20 | .30 |
| 117 Precision Targeting U | .60 | 1.00 |
| 118 Proton Bombs U | .60 | 1.00 |
| 119 Punishing One R | 3.00 | 5.00 |
| 120 Quick Draw C | .20 | .30 |
| 121 Raithal DARK R | 2.00 | 3.00 |
| 122 Raithal LIGHT U | .60 | 1.00 |
| 123 Rebel Flight Suit C | .20 | .30 |
| 124 Recoil In Fear C | .20 | .30 |
| 125 Reflection R | 2.00 | 3.00 |
| 126 Report To Lord Vader R | 2.00 | 3.00 |
| 127 Res Luk Ra'auf R | 2.00 | 3.00 |
| 128 Retractable Arm C | .20 | .30 |
| 129 Rogue Asteroid DARK C | .20 | .30 |
| 130 Rogue Asteroid LIGHT C | .20 | .30 |
| 131 Rycar's Run R | 2.00 | 3.00 |
| 132 Scramble U | .60 | 1.00 |
| 133 Shoo! Shoo! U | .60 | 1.00 |
| 134 Shot In The Dark U | .60 | 1.00 |
| 135 Shut Him Up Or Shut Him Down U | .60 | 1.00 |
| 136 Size Matters Not R | 2.00 | 3.00 |
| 137 Sleen C | .20 | .30 |
| 138 Smuggler's Blues R | 2.00 | 3.00 |
| 139 Something Hit Us! U | .60 | 1.00 |
| 140 Son of Skywalker R | 12.00 | 20.00 |
| 141 Space Slug DARK R | 2.00 | 3.00 |
| 142 Space Slug LIGHT U | .60 | 1.00 |
| 143 Star Destroyer: Launch Bay C | .20 | .30 |
| 144 Starship Levitation U | .60 | 1.00 |
| 145 Stone Pile R | 2.00 | 3.00 |
| 146 Sudden Impact U | .60 | 1.00 |
| 147 Take Evasive Action C | .20 | .30 |
| 148 The Dark Path R | 2.00 | 3.00 |
| 149 The Professor R | 2.00 | 3.00 |

| | | |
|---|---|---|
| 150 There Is No Try C | .20 | .30 |
| 151 They'd Be Crazy To Follow Us C | .20 | .30 |
| 152 This Is More Like It R | 2.00 | 3.00 |
| 153 This Is No Cave R | 2.00 | 3.00 |
| 154 Those Rebels Won't Escape Us C | .20 | .30 |
| 155 Through The Force Things | 2.00 | 3.00 |
| You Will See R | | |
| 156 TIE Avenger C | .20 | .30 |
| 157 TIE Bomber U | .60 | 1.00 |
| 158 Tight Squeeze R | 2.00 | 3.00 |
| 159 Transmission Terminated U | .60 | 1.00 |
| 160 Tunnel Vision U | .60 | 1.00 |
| 161 Uncertain Is The Future C | .20 | .30 |
| 162 Unexpected Interruption R | 2.00 | 3.00 |
| 163 Vine Snake DARK C | .20 | .30 |
| 164 Vine Snake LIGHT C | .20 | .30 |
| 165 Visage Of The Emperor R | 2.00 | 3.00 |
| 166 Visored Vision C | .20 | .30 |
| 167 Voyeur C | .20 | .30 |
| 168 Warrant Officer MiKae U | .60 | 1.00 |
| 169 Wars Not Make One Great U | .60 | 1.00 |
| 170 We Can Still Outmaneuver Them R | 2.00 | 3.00 |
| 171 We Don't Need Their Scum R | 2.00 | 3.00 |
| 172 WHAAAAAAAAOOOOW! R | 2.00 | 3.00 |
| 173 What Is Thy Bidding, My Master? R | 2.00 | 3.00 |
| 174 Yoda R | 12.00 | 20.00 |
| 175 Yoda Stew U | .60 | 1.00 |
| 176 Yoda, You Seek Yoda R | 2.00 | 3.00 |
| 177 Yoda's Gimer Stick R | 2.00 | 3.00 |
| 178 Yoda's Hope U | .60 | 1.00 |
| 179 You Do Have Your Moments U | .60 | 1.00 |
| 180 Zuckuss R | 3.00 | 5.00 |
| 181 Zuckuss' Snare Rifle R | 2.00 | 3.00 |

## 1997 Star Wars First Anthology

| | | |
|---|---|---|
| COMPLETE SET (6) | 3.00 | 8.00 |
| RELEASED IN 1997 | | |
| 1 Boba Fett PV | 1.25 | 2.00 |
| 2 Commander Wedge Antilles PV | 1.25 | 2.00 |
| 3 Death Star Assault Squadron PV | 1.25 | 2.00 |
| 4 Hit And Run PV | 1.25 | 2.00 |
| 5 Jabba's Influence PV | 1.25 | 2.00 |
| 6 X-wing Assault Squadron PV | 1.25 | 2.00 |

## 1997 Star Wars Rebel Leaders

| | | |
|---|---|---|
| COMPLETE SET (2) | 1.25 | 3.00 |
| RELEASED IN 1997 | | |
| 1 Gold Leader In Gold 1 PM | 1.50 | 2.50 |
| 2 Red Leader In Red 1 PM | 1.50 | 2.50 |

## 1998 Star Wars Enhanced Premiere

| | | |
|---|---|---|
| COMPLETE SET (6) | 3.00 | 8.00 |
| RELEASED IN 1998 | | |
| 1 Boba Fett With Blaster Rifle PM | 1.25 | 2.00 |
| 2 Darth Vader With Lightsaber PM | 1.25 | 2.00 |
| 3 Han With Heavy Blaster Pistol PM | 1.25 | 2.00 |
| 4 Leia With Blaster Rifle PM | 1.25 | 2.00 |
| 5 Luke With Lightsaber PM | 1.25 | 2.00 |
| 6 Obi-Wan With Lightsaber PM | 1.25 | 2.00 |

## 1998 Star Wars Jabba's Palace

| | | |
|---|---|---|
| COMPLETE SET (180) | 40.00 | 80.00 |
| BOOSTER BOX (60 PACKS) | 40.00 | 80.00 |
| BOOSTER PACK (9 CARDS) | 1.00 | 2.00 |
| RELEASED IN MAY 1998 | | |
| 1 8D8 R | 2.00 | 3.00 |
| 2 A Gift U | .60 | 1.00 |
| 3 Abyssin C | .20 | .30 |
| 4 Abyssin Ornament U | .60 | 1.00 |
| 5 All Wrapped Up U | .60 | 1.00 |
| 6 Amanaman R | 2.00 | 3.00 |

| | | |
|---|---|---|
| 7 Amanin C | .20 | .30 |
| 8 Antipersonnel Laser Cannon U | .60 | 1.00 |
| 9 Aqualish C | .20 | .30 |
| 10 Arc Welder U | .60 | 1.00 |
| 11 Ardon Vapor Crell R | 2.00 | 3.00 |
| 12 Artoo R | 5.00 | 8.00 |
| 13 Artoo, I Have A Bad Feeling About This U | .60 | 1.00 |
| 14 Attark R | 2.00 | 3.00 |
| 15 Aved Luun R | 2.00 | 3.00 |
| 16 Biomarr Monk C | .20 | .30 |
| 17 Bane Malar R | 2.00 | 3.00 |
| 18 Bantha Fodder C | .20 | .30 |
| 19 Barada R | 2.00 | 3.00 |
| 20 Baragwin C | .20 | .30 |
| 21 Bargaining Table U | .60 | 1.00 |
| 22 Beedo R | 2.00 | 3.00 |
| 23 BG-J38 R | 2.00 | 3.00 |
| 24 Bib Fortuna R | 2.00 | 3.00 |
| 25 Blaster Deflection R | 2.00 | 3.00 |
| 26 Bo Shuda U | .60 | 1.00 |
| 27 Bubo U | .60 | 1.00 |
| 28 Cane Adiss U | .60 | 1.00 |
| 29 Chadra-Fan C | .20 | .30 |
| 30 Chevin C | .20 | .30 |
| 31 Choke C | .20 | .30 |
| 32 Corellian Retort U | .60 | 1.00 |
| 33 CZ-4 C | .20 | .30 |
| 34 Den Of Thieves U | .60 | 1.00 |
| 35 Dengar's Modified Riot Gun R | 2.00 | 3.00 |
| 36 Devaronian C | .20 | .30 |
| 37 Don't Forget The Droids C | .20 | .30 |
| 38 Double Laser Cannon R | 2.00 | 3.00 |
| 39 Droopy McCool R | 2.00 | 3.00 |
| 40 Dune Sea Sabacc DARK U | .60 | 1.00 |
| 41 Dune Sea Sabacc LIGHT U | .60 | 1.00 |
| 42 Elom C | .20 | .30 |
| 43 Ephant Mon R | 2.00 | 3.00 |
| 44 EV-9D9 R | 2.00 | 3.00 |
| 45 Fallen Portal U | .60 | 1.00 |
| 46 Florn Lamproid C | .20 | .30 |
| 47 Fozec R | 2.00 | 3.00 |
| 48 Gailid R | 2.00 | 3.00 |
| 49 Gamorrean Ax C | .20 | .30 |
| 50 Gamorrean Guard C | .20 | .30 |
| 51 Garon Nas Tal R | 2.00 | 3.00 |
| 52 Geezum R | 2.00 | 3.00 |
| 53 Ghoel R | 2.00 | 3.00 |
| 54 Giran R | 2.00 | 3.00 |
| 55 Gran C | .20 | .30 |
| 56 Hinemthe C | .20 | .30 |
| 57 Herat R | 2.00 | 3.00 |
| 58 Hermi Odle R | 2.00 | 3.00 |
| 59 Hidden Compartment U | .60 | 1.00 |
| 60 Hidden Weapons U | .60 | 1.00 |
| 61 Holoprojector U | .60 | 1.00 |
| 62 Hutt Bounty R | 2.00 | 3.00 |
| 63 Hutt Smooch U | .60 | 1.00 |
| 64 I Must Be Allowed To Speak R | 2.00 | 3.00 |
| 65 Information Exchange U | .60 | 1.00 |
| 66 Ishi Tib C | .20 | .30 |
| 67 Ithorian C | .20 | .30 |
| 68 JiQuille R | 2.00 | 3.00 |
| 69 Jabba the Hutt R | 6.00 | 10.00 |

| | | |
|---|---|---|
| 70 Jabba's Palace Sabacc DARK U | .60 | 1.00 |
| 71 Jabba's Palace Sabacc LIGHT U | .60 | 1.00 |
| 72 Jabba's Palace: Audience Chamber DARK U | .60 | 1.00 |
| 73 Jabba's Palace: Audience Chamber LIGHT U | | 1.00 |
| 74 Jabba's Palace: Droid Workshop U | .60 | 1.00 |
| 75 Jabba's Palace: Dungeon U | .60 | 1.00 |
| 76 Jabba's Palace: Entrance Cavern DARK U | .60 | 1.00 |
| 77 Jabba's Palace: Entrance Cavern LIGHT U | .60 | 1.00 |
| 78 Jabba's Palace: Rancor Pit U | .60 | 1.00 |
| 79 Jabba's Sail Barge R | 4.00 | 6.00 |
| 80 Jabba's Sail Barge: Passenger Deck R | 2.00 | 3.00 |
| 81 Jedi Mind Trick R | 2.00 | 3.00 |
| 82 Jess R | 2.00 | 3.00 |
| 83 Jet Pack U | .60 | 1.00 |
| 84 Kalit R | 2.00 | 3.00 |
| 85 Ke Chu Ke Kakuta? C | .20 | .30 |
| 86 Kiffex R | 2.00 | 3.00 |
| 87 Kirdo III R | 2.00 | 3.00 |
| 88 Kithaba R | 2.00 | 3.00 |
| 89 Kitonak C | .20 | .30 |
| 90 Klaatu R | 2.00 | 3.00 |
| 91 Klatooinian Revolutionary C | .20 | .30 |
| 92 Laudica R | 2.00 | 3.00 |
| 93 Leslomy Tacema R | 2.00 | 3.00 |
| 94 Life Debt R | 2.00 | 3.00 |
| 95 Loje Nella R | 2.00 | 3.00 |
| 96 Malakili R | 2.00 | 3.00 |
| 97 Mandalorian Mishap U | .60 | 1.00 |
| 98 Max Rebo R | 2.00 | 3.00 |
| 99 Mos Eisley Blaster DARK C | .20 | .30 |
| 100 Mos Eisley Blaster LIGHT C | .20 | .30 |
| 101 Murttoc Yine R | 2.00 | 3.00 |
| 102 Nal Hutta R | 2.00 | 3.00 |
| 103 Nar Shaddaa Wind Chimes U | .60 | 1.00 |
| 104 Nikto C | .20 | .30 |
| 105 Nizuc Bek R | 2.00 | 3.00 |
| 106 None Shall Pass C | .20 | .30 |
| 107 Nysad R | 2.00 | 3.00 |
| 108 Oola R | 2.00 | 3.00 |
| 109 Ortolan C | .20 | .30 |
| 110 Ortugg R | 2.00 | 3.00 |
| 111 Palejo Reshad R | 2.00 | 3.00 |
| 112 Pote Snitkin R | 2.00 | 3.00 |
| 113 Princess Leia Organa R | 5.00 | 8.00 |
| 114 Projection Of A Skywalker U | .60 | 1.00 |
| 115 Pucumir Thryss R | 2.00 | 3.00 |
| 116 Quarren C | .20 | .30 |
| 117 Quick Reflexes C | .20 | .30 |
| 118 Rikik Dinec, Hero Of The Dune Sea R | 2.00 | 3.00 |
| 119 Rancor R | 4.00 | 6.00 |
| 120 Rayc Ryjerd R | 2.00 | 3.00 |
| 121 Ree-Yees R | 2.00 | 3.00 |
| 122 Rennek R | 2.00 | 3.00 |
| 123 Resistance U | .60 | 1.00 |
| 124 Revealed U | .60 | 1.00 |
| 125 Saelt-Marae R | 2.00 | 3.00 |
| 126 Salacious Crumb R | 2.00 | 3.00 |
| 127 Sandwhirl DARK U | .60 | 1.00 |
| 128 Sandwhirl LIGHT U | .60 | 1.00 |
| 129 Scum And Villainy R | 2.00 | 3.00 |

| | | |
|---|---|---|
| 130 Sergeant Doallyn R | 2.00 | 3.00 |
| 131 Shasa Tiel R | 2.00 | 3.00 |
| 132 Sic-Six C | .20 | .30 |
| 133 Skiff DARK C | .20 | .30 |
| 134 Skiff LIGHT C | .20 | .30 |
| 135 Skrilling C | .20 | .30 |
| 136 Skull U | .60 | 1.00 |
| 137 Snivvian C | .20 | .30 |
| 138 Someone Who Loves You U | .60 | 1.00 |
| 139 Strangle R | 2.00 | 3.00 |
| 140 Tamtel Skreej R | 4.00 | 6.00 |
| 141 Tanus Spijek R | 2.00 | 3.00 |
| 142 Tatooine: Desert DARK C | .20 | .30 |
| 143 Tatooine: Desert LIGHT C | .20 | .30 |
| 144 Tatooine: Great Pit Of Carkoon U | .60 | 1.00 |
| 145 Tatooine: Hutt Canyon U | .60 | 1.00 |
| 146 Tatooine: Jabba's Palace U | .60 | 1.00 |
| 147 Taym Dren-garen R | 2.00 | 3.00 |
| 148 Tessek R | 2.00 | 3.00 |
| 149 The Signal C | .20 | .30 |
| 150 Thermal Detonator R | 3.00 | 5.00 |
| 151 Thul Fain R | 2.00 | 3.00 |
| 152 Tibrin R | 2.00 | 3.00 |
| 153 Torture C | .20 | .30 |
| 154 Trandoshan C | .20 | .30 |
| 155 Trap Door U | .60 | 1.00 |
| 156 Twi'lek Advisor C | .20 | .30 |
| 157 Ultimatum U | .60 | 1.00 |
| 158 Unfriendly Fire R | 2.00 | 3.00 |
| 159 Vedain R | 2.00 | 3.00 |
| 160 Velken Tezeri R | 2.00 | 3.00 |
| 161 Vibro-Ax DARK C | .20 | .30 |
| 162 Vibro-Ax LIGHT C | .20 | .30 |
| 163 Vizam R | 2.00 | 3.00 |
| 164 Vul Tazaene R | 2.00 | 3.00 |
| 165 Weapon Levitation U | .60 | 1.00 |
| 166 Weequay Guard C | .20 | .30 |
| 167 Weequay Hunter C | .20 | .30 |
| 168 Weequay Marksman U | .60 | 1.00 |
| 169 Weequay Skiff Master C | .20 | .30 |
| 170 Well Guarded U | .60 | 1.00 |
| 171 Whiphid C | .20 | .30 |
| 172 Wittin R | 2.00 | 3.00 |
| 173 Wooof R | 2.00 | 3.00 |
| 174 Worrt U | .60 | 1.00 |
| 175 Wounded Wookiee U | .60 | 1.00 |
| 176 Yarkora C | .20 | .30 |
| 177 Yarna d'al' Gargan U | .60 | 1.00 |
| 178 You Will Take Me To Jabba Now C | .20 | .30 |
| 179 Yoxgit R | 2.00 | 3.00 |
| 180 Yuzzum C | .20 | .30 |

## 1998 Star Wars Official Tournament Sealed Deck

| | | |
|---|---|---|
| COMPLETE SET (18) | 4.00 | 10.00 |
| RELEASED IN 1998 | | |
| 1 Arleil Schous PM | .60 | 1.00 |
| 2 Black Squadron TIE PM | .60 | 1.00 |
| 3 Chall Bekan PM | .60 | 1.00 |
| 4 Corulag DARK PM | .60 | 1.00 |
| 5 Corulag LIGHT PM | .60 | 1.00 |
| 6 Dreadnaught-Class Heavy Cruiser PM | .60 | 1.00 |
| 7 Faithful Service PM | .60 | 1.00 |
| 8 Forced Servitude PM | .60 | 1.00 |

| 9 Gold Squadron Y-wing PM | .60 | 1.00 |
| 10 Itís a Hit! PM | .60 | 1.00 |
| 11 Obsidian Squadron TIE PM | .60 | 1.00 |
| 12 Rebel Trooper Recruit PM | .60 | 1.00 |
| 13 Red Squadron X-wing PM | .60 | 1.00 |
| 14 Stormtrooper Cadet PM | .60 | 1.00 |
| 15 Tarkinís Orders PM | .60 | 1.00 |
| 16 Tatooine: Jundland Wastes PM | .60 | 1.00 |
| 17 Tatooine: Tusken Canyon PM | .60 | 1.00 |
| 18 Z-95 Headhunter PM | .60 | 1.00 |

### 1998 Star Wars Second Anthology

| COMPLETE SET (6) | 4.00 | 10.00 |
| RELEASED IN 1998 | | |
| 1 Flagship Operations PV | 1.50 | 2.50 |
| 2 Mon Calamari Star Cruiser PV | 1.50 | 2.50 |
| 3 Mon Mothma PV | 1.50 | 2.50 |
| 4 Rapid Deployment PV | 1.50 | 2.50 |
| 5 Sarlacc PV | 1.50 | 2.50 |
| 6 Thunderflare PV | 1.50 | 2.50 |

### 1998 Star Wars Special Edition

| COMPLETE SET (324) | 75.00 | 150.00 |
| BOOSTER BOX (30 PACKS) | 60.00 | 120.00 |
| BOOSTER PACK (9 CARDS) | 3.00 | 6.00 |
| RELEASED IN NOVEMBER 1998 | | |
| 1 ISB Operations / Empireís Sinister Agents R | 1.50 | 2.50 |
| 2 2X-7KPR (Tooex) C | .20 | .30 |

| 3 A Bright Center To The Universe U | .60 | 1.00 |
| 4 A Day Long Remembered U | .60 | 1.00 |
| 5 A Real Hero R | 1.50 | 2.50 |
| 6 Air-2 Racing Swoop C | .20 | .30 |
| 7 Ak-rev U | .60 | 1.00 |
| 8 Alderaan Operative C | .20 | .30 |
| 9 Alert My Star Destroyer! C | .20 | .30 |
| 10 All Power To Weapons C | .20 | .30 |
| 11 All Wings Report In R | 1.50 | 2.50 |
| 12 Anoat Operative DARK C | .20 | .30 |
| 13 Anoat Operative LIGHT C | .20 | .30 |
| 14 Antilles Maneuver C | .20 | .30 |
| 15 ASP-707 (Ayesspee) F | 1.00 | 1.50 |
| 16 Balanced Attack U | .60 | 1.00 |
| 17 Bantha Herd R | 1.25 | 2.00 |
| 18 Barquin Dían U | .60 | 1.00 |
| 19 Ben Kenobi R | 3.00 | 5.00 |
| 20 Blast Points C | .20 | .30 |
| 21 Blown Clear U | .60 | 1.00 |
| 22 Boba Fett R | 2.50 | 4.00 |
| 23 Boelo R | 1.50 | 2.50 |
| 24 Bossk In Houndís Tooth R | 1.50 | 2.50 |
| 25 Bothan Spy C | .20 | .30 |
| 26 Bothawui F | 1.00 | 1.50 |
| 27 Bothawui Operative C | .20 | .30 |
| 28 Brangus Glee R | 1.25 | 2.00 |
| 29 Bren Quersey U | .60 | 1.00 |
| 30 Bron Burs R | 1.25 | 2.00 |
| 31 B-wing Attack Fighter F | 1.00 | 1.50 |
| 32 Camie R | 1.50 | 2.50 |
| 33 Carbon Chamber Testing | 1.50 | 2.50 |
| My Favorite Decoration R | | |
| 34 Chyler U | .60 | 1.00 |
| 35 Clakidor VII Operative U | .60 | 1.00 |
| 36 Cloud City Celebration R | 1.50 | 2.50 |
| 37 Cloud City Occupation R | 2.00 | 3.00 |
| 38 Cloud City: Casino DARK U | .60 | 1.00 |
| 39 Cloud City: Casino LIGHT U | .60 | 1.00 |
| 40 Cloud City: Core Tunnel U | .60 | 1.00 |
| 41 Cloud City: Downtown Plaza DARK R | 1.50 | 2.50 |
| 42 Cloud City: Downtown Plaza LIGHT R | 1.50 | 2.50 |
| 43 Cloud City: Interrogation Room C | .20 | .30 |
| 44 Cloud City: North Corridor C | .20 | .30 |
| 45 Cloud City: Port Town District U | .60 | 1.00 |
| 46 Cloud City: Upper Walkway C | .20 | .30 |
| 47 Cloud City: West Gallery DARK C | .20 | .30 |
| 48 Cloud City: West Gallery LIGHT C | .20 | .30 |
| 49 Colonel Feyn Gospic R | 1.50 | 2.50 |
| 50 Combat Cloud Car F | 1.00 | 1.50 |
| 51 Come Here You Big Coward! C | .20 | .30 |
| 52 Commander Wedge Antilles R | 1.50 | 2.50 |
| 53 Coordinated Attack C | .20 | .30 |
| 54 Corellia Operative U | .60 | 1.00 |
| 55 Corellian Engineering Corporation R | 1.50 | 2.50 |
| 56 Corporal Grenwick R | 1.25 | 2.00 |
| 57 Corporal Prescott U | .60 | 1.00 |
| 58 Corulag Operative C | .20 | .30 |
| 59 Coruscant Celebration R | 1.25 | 2.00 |
| 60 Coruscant DARK R | 4.00 | 6.00 |
| 61 Coruscant LIGHT R | 1.50 | 2.50 |
| 62 Coruscant: Docking Bay C | .20 | .30 |
| 63 Coruscant: Imperial City U | .60 | 1.00 |
| 64 Coruscant: Imperial Square R | 2.00 | 3.00 |
| 65 Counter Surprise Assault R | 1.50 | 2.50 |

| 66 Dagobah U | .60 | 1.00 |
| 67 Dantooine Base Operations | 1.25 | 2.00 |
| More Dangerous Than You Realize R | | |
| 68 Dantooine Operative C | .20 | .30 |
| 69 Darklighter Spin C | .20 | .30 |
| 70 Darth Vader, Dark Lord Of The Sith R | 10.00 | 15.00 |
| 71 Death Squadron Star Destroyer R | 1.50 | 2.50 |
| 72 Death Star Assault Squadron R | 1.50 | 2.50 |
| 73 Death Star R | 2.00 | 3.00 |
| 74 Death Star: Detention Block Control Room C | .20 | .30 |
| 75 Death Star: Detention Block Corridor C | .20 | .30 |
| 76 Debnoli R | 1.50 | 2.50 |
| 77 Desert DARK F | 1.00 | 1.50 |
| 78 Desert LIGHT F | 1.00 | 1.50 |
| 79 Desilijic Tattoo U | .60 | 1.00 |
| 80 Desperate Tactics C | .20 | .30 |
| 81 Destroyed Homestead R | 1.50 | 2.50 |
| 82 Dewback C | .20 | .30 |
| 83 Direct Assault C | .20 | .30 |
| 84 Disruptor Pistol DARK F | 1.00 | 1.50 |
| 85 Disruptor Pistol LIGHT F | 1.00 | 1.50 |
| 86 Docking And Repair Facilities R | 1.50 | 2.50 |
| 87 Dodo Bodonawieedo U | .60 | 1.00 |
| 88 Donít Tread On Me R | 1.50 | 2.50 |
| 89 Down With The Emperor! U | .60 | 1.00 |
| 90 Dr. Evazanís Sawed-off Blaster U | .60 | 1.00 |
| 91 Draw Their Fire U | .60 | 1.00 |
| 92 Dreaded Imperial Starfleet R | 2.00 | 3.00 |
| 93 Droid Merchant C | .20 | .30 |
| 94 Dune Walker R | 2.00 | 3.00 |
| 95 Echo Base Trooper Rifle C | .20 | .30 |
| 96 Elyhek Rue U | .60 | 1.00 |
| 97 Entrenchment R | 1.25 | 2.00 |
| 98 Eriadu Operative C | .20 | .30 |
| 99 Executor: Docking Bay U | .60 | 1.00 |
| 100 Farm F | 1.00 | 1.50 |
| 101 Feltipern Trevaggís Stun Rifle U | .60 | 1.00 |
| 102 Firepower C | .20 | .30 |
| 103 Firin Morett U | .60 | 1.00 |
| 104 First Aid F | 1.00 | 1.50 |
| 105 First Strike U | .60 | 1.00 |
| 106 Flare-S Racing Swoop C | .20 | .30 |
| 107 Flawless Marksmanship C | .20 | .30 |
| 108 Floating Refinery C | .20 | .30 |
| 109 Fondor U | .60 | 1.00 |
| 110 Forest DARK F | 1.00 | 1.50 |
| 111 Forest LIGHT F | 1.00 | 1.50 |
| 112 Gela Yeens U | .60 | 1.00 |
| 113 General McQuarrie R | 1.25 | 2.00 |
| 114 Gold 3 U | .60 | 1.00 |
| 115 Gold 4 U | .60 | 1.00 |
| 116 Gold 6 U | .60 | 1.00 |
| 117 Goo Nee Tay R | 1.50 | 2.50 |
| 118 Greeata U | .60 | 1.00 |
| 119 Grondorn Muse R | 1.25 | 2.00 |
| 120 Harc Seff U | .60 | 1.00 |
| 121 Harvest R | 2.00 | 3.00 |
| 122 Heavy Fire Zone C | .20 | .30 |
| 123 Heroes Of Yavin R | 1.25 | 2.00 |
| 124 Heroic Sacrifice U | .60 | 1.00 |
| 125 Hidden Base | 2.50 | 4.00 |
| Systems Will Slip Through Your Fingers R | | |
| 126 Hit And Run R | 1.25 | 2.00 |
| 127 Hoi Okand U | .60 | 1.00 |

|  |  | | |
|---|---|---|---|
| 128 | Homing Beacon R | 1.50 | 2.50 |
| 129 | Hoth Sentry U | .60 | 1.00 |
| 130 | Hunt Down And Destroy The Jedi | 2.50 | 4.00 |
| | Their Fire Has Gone Out Of The Universe R | | |
| 131 | Hunting Party R | 1.50 | 2.50 |
| 132 | I Canít Shake Him! C | .20 | .30 |
| 133 | Iasa, The Traitor Of Jawa Canyon R | 1.25 | 2.00 |
| 134 | IM4-099 F | 1.00 | 1.50 |
| 135 | Imperial Atrocity R | 5.00 | 8.00 |
| 136 | Imperial Occupation / Imperial Control R | 1.50 | 2.50 |
| 137 | Imperial Propaganda R | 5.00 | 8.00 |
| 138 | In Range C | .20 | .30 |
| 139 | Incom Corporation R | 1.25 | 2.00 |
| 140 | InCom Engineer C | .20 | .30 |
| 141 | Intruder Missile DARK F | 1.00 | 1.50 |
| 142 | Intruder Missile LIGHT F | 1.00 | 1.50 |
| 143 | Itís Not My Fault! F | 1.00 | 1.50 |
| 144 | Jabba R | 1.50 | 2.50 |
| 145 | Jabbaís Influence R | 1.25 | 2.00 |
| 146 | Jabbaís Space Cruiser R | 2.00 | 3.00 |
| 147 | Jabbaís Through With You U | .60 | 1.00 |
| 148 | Jabbaís Twerps U | .60 | 1.00 |
| 149 | Joh Yowza R | 1.25 | 2.00 |
| 150 | Jungle DARK F | 1.00 | 1.50 |
| 151 | Jungle LIGHT F | 1.00 | 1.50 |
| 152 | Kalitís Sandcrawler R | 1.50 | 2.50 |
| 153 | Kashyyyk Operative DARK U | .60 | 1.00 |
| 154 | Kashyyyk Operative LIGHT U | .60 | 1.00 |
| 155 | Kessel Operative U | .60 | 1.00 |
| 156 | Ketwol R | 1.25 | 2.00 |
| 157 | Kiffex Operative DARK U | .60 | 1.00 |
| 158 | Kiffex Operative LIGHT U | .60 | 1.00 |
| 159 | Kirdo III Operative C | .20 | .30 |
| 160 | Koensayr Manufacturing R | 1.50 | 2.50 |
| 161 | Krayt Dragon R | 1.50 | 2.50 |
| 162 | Kuat Drive Yards R | 2.00 | 3.00 |
| 163 | Kuat R | .60 | 1.00 |
| 164 | Landoís Blaster Rifle R | 1.50 | 2.50 |
| 165 | Legendary Starfighter C | .20 | .30 |
| 166 | Leiaís Blaster Rifle R | 1.50 | 2.50 |
| 167 | Lieutenant Lepira U | .60 | 1.00 |
| 168 | Lieutenant Naytaan U | .60 | 1.00 |
| 169 | Lieutenant Tarn Mison R | 1.50 | 2.50 |
| 170 | Lobel C | .20 | .30 |
| 171 | Lobot R | 1.50 | 2.50 |
| 172 | Local Defense U | .60 | 1.00 |
| 173 | Local Uprising / Liberation R | 1.50 | 2.50 |
| 174 | Lyn Me U | .60 | 1.00 |
| 175 | Major Palo Torshan R | 1.50 | 2.50 |
| 176 | Makurth F | 1.00 | 1.50 |
| 177 | Maneuvering Flaps C | .20 | .30 |
| 178 | Masterful Move C | .20 | .30 |
| 179 | Mechanical Failure R | 1.25 | 2.00 |
| 180 | Meditation R | 2.00 | 3.00 |
| 181 | Medium Bulk Freighter U | .60 | 1.00 |
| 182 | Melas R | 1.50 | 2.50 |
| 183 | Mind What You Have Learned | 2.00 | 3.00 |
| | Save You It Can R | | |
| 184 | Moisture Farmer C | .20 | .30 |
| 185 | Nal Hutta Operative C | .20 | .30 |
| 186 | Neb Dulo U | .60 | 1.00 |
| 187 | Nebit R | 1.50 | 2.50 |
| 188 | Niado Duegad U | .60 | 1.00 |
| 189 | Nick Of Time U | .60 | 1.00 |
| 190 | No Bargain U | .60 | 1.00 |
| 191 | Old Times R | 1.25 | 2.00 |
| 192 | On Target C | .20 | .30 |
| 193 | One-Arm R | 1.50 | 2.50 |
| 194 | Oppressive Enforcement U | .60 | 1.00 |
| 195 | Ord Mantell Operative C | .20 | .30 |
| 196 | Organized Attack C | .20 | .30 |
| 197 | OS-72-1 In Obsidian 1 R | 1.50 | 2.50 |
| 198 | OS-72-10 R | 1.50 | 2.50 |
| 199 | OS-72-2 In Obsidian 2 R | 1.50 | 2.50 |
| 200 | Outer Rim Scout R | 2.50 | 4.00 |
| 201 | Overwhelmed C | .20 | .30 |
| 202 | Patrol Craft DARK C | .20 | .30 |
| 203 | Patrol Craft LIGHT C | .20 | .30 |
| 204 | Planetary Subjugation U | .60 | 1.00 |
| 205 | Ponda Babaís Hold-out Blaster U | .60 | 1.00 |
| 206 | Portable Scanner C | .20 | .30 |
| 207 | Power Pivot C | .20 | .30 |
| 208 | Precise Hit C | .20 | .30 |
| 209 | Pride Of The Empire C | .20 | .30 |
| 210 | Princess Organa R | 2.00 | 3.00 |
| 211 | Put All Sections On Alert C | .20 | .30 |
| 212 | R2-A5 (Artoo-Ayfive) U | .60 | 1.00 |
| 213 | R3-A2 (Arthree-Aytoo) U | .60 | 1.00 |
| 214 | R3-T2 (Arthree-Teetoo) R | 1.50 | 2.50 |
| 215 | Raithal Operative C | .20 | .30 |
| 216 | Ralltiir Freighter Captain F | 1.00 | 1.50 |
| 217 | Ralltiir Operations | 2.50 | 4.00 |
| | In The Hands Of The Empire R | | |
| 218 | Ralltiir Operative C | .20 | .30 |
| 219 | Rapid Fire C | .20 | .30 |
| 220 | Rappertunie U | .60 | 1.00 |
| 221 | Rebel Ambush C | .20 | .30 |
| 222 | Rebel Base Occupation R | 1.25 | 2.00 |
| 223 | Rebel Fleet R | 1.50 | 2.50 |
| 224 | Red 10 U | .60 | 1.00 |
| 225 | Red 7 U | .60 | 1.00 |
| 226 | Red 8 U | .60 | 1.00 |
| 227 | Red 9 U | .60 | 1.00 |
| 228 | Relentless Pursuit C | .20 | .30 |
| 229 | Rendezvous Point R | 1.50 | 2.50 |
| 230 | Rendili F | 1.00 | 1.50 |
| 231 | Rendili StarDrive R | 1.25 | 2.00 |
| 232 | Rescue The Princess | 1.50 | 2.50 |
| | Sometimes I Amaze Even Myself R | | |
| 233 | Return To Base R | 1.50 | 2.50 |
| 234 | Roche U | .60 | 1.00 |
| 235 | Rock Wart F | 1.00 | 1.50 |
| 236 | Rogue 4 R | 2.50 | 4.00 |
| 237 | Ronto DARK C | .20 | .30 |
| 238 | Ronto LIGHT C | .20 | .30 |
| 239 | RRiuruurrr R | 1.50 | 2.50 |
| 240 | Ryle Torsyn U | .60 | 1.00 |
| 241 | Rystall R | 2.50 | 4.00 |
| 242 | Sacrifice F | 1.00 | 1.50 |
| 243 | Sandspeeder F | 1.00 | 1.50 |
| 244 | Sandtrooper F | 1.00 | 1.50 |
| 245 | Sarlacc R | 1.50 | 2.50 |
| 246 | Scrambled Transmission U | .60 | 1.00 |
| 247 | Scurrier F | 1.00 | 1.50 |
| 248 | Secret Plans U | .60 | 1.00 |
| 249 | Sentinel-Class Landing Craft F | 1.00 | 1.50 |
| 250 | Sergeant Edian U | .60 | 1.00 |
| 251 | Sergeant Hollis R | 1.50 | 2.50 |
| 252 | Sergeant Major Bursk U | .60 | 1.00 |
| 253 | Sergeant Major Enfield R | 1.25 | 2.00 |
| 254 | Sergeant Merril U | .60 | 1.00 |
| 255 | Sergeant Narthax R | 1.50 | 2.50 |
| 256 | Sergeant Torent R | 1.50 | 2.50 |
| 257 | S-Foils C | .20 | .30 |
| 258 | SFS L-s9.3 Laser Cannons C | .20 | .30 |
| 259 | Short-Range Fighters R | 1.50 | 2.50 |
| 260 | Sienar Fleet Systems R | 1.50 | 2.50 |
| 261 | Slayn and Korpil Facilities R | 1.25 | 2.00 |
| 262 | Slight Weapons Malfunction C | .20 | .30 |
| 263 | Soth Petikkin R | 1.25 | 2.00 |
| 264 | Spaceport City DARK F | 1.00 | 1.50 |
| 265 | Spaceport City LIGHT F | 1.00 | 1.50 |
| 266 | Spaceport Docking Bay DARK F | 1.00 | 1.50 |
| 267 | Spaceport Docking Bay LIGHT F | 1.00 | 1.50 |
| 268 | Spaceport Prefectís Office F | 1.00 | 1.50 |
| 269 | Spaceport Street DARK F | 1.00 | 1.50 |
| 270 | Spaceport Street LIGHT F | 1.00 | 1.50 |
| 271 | Spiral R | 2.00 | 3.00 |
| 272 | Star Destroyer! R | 1.50 | 2.50 |
| 273 | Stay Sharp! U | .60 | 1.00 |
| 274 | Steady Aim C | .20 | .30 |
| 275 | Strategic Reserves R | 1.50 | 2.50 |
| 276 | Suppressive Fire C | .20 | .30 |
| 277 | Surface Defense R | 1.50 | 2.50 |
| 278 | Swamp DARK F | 1.00 | 1.50 |
| 279 | Swamp LIGHT F | 1.00 | 1.50 |
| 280 | Swoop Mercenary F | 1.00 | 1.50 |
| 281 | Sy Snootles R | 1.50 | 2.50 |
| 282 | T-47 Battle Formation R | 1.50 | 2.50 |
| 283 | Tarkinís Bounty U | .60 | 1.00 |
| 284 | Tatooine Celebration R | 2.00 | 3.00 |
| 285 | Tatooine Occupation R | 2.50 | 4.00 |
| 286 | Tatooine: Anchorhead F | 1.00 | 1.50 |
| 287 | Tatooine: Beggarís Canyon R | 1.25 | 2.00 |
| 288 | Tatooine: Jabbaís Palace C | .20 | .30 |
| 289 | Tatooine: Jawa Canyon DARK U | .60 | 1.00 |
| 290 | Tatooine: Jawa Canyon LIGHT U | .60 | 1.00 |
| 291 | Tatooine: Krayt Dragon Pass F | 1.00 | 1.50 |
| 292 | Tatooine: Tosche Station C | .20 | .30 |
| 293 | Tauntaun Skull C | .20 | .30 |
| 294 | Tawss Khaa R | 1.25 | 2.00 |
| 295 | The Planet That Itís Farthest From U | .60 | 1.00 |
| 296 | Thedit R | 1.50 | 2.50 |
| 297 | Theron Nett U | .60 | 1.00 |
| 298 | Theyíre Coming In Too Fast! C | .20 | .30 |
| 299 | Theyíre Tracking Us C | .20 | .30 |
| 300 | Theyíve Shut Down The Main Reactor C | .20 | .30 |
| 301 | Tibrin Operative C | .20 | .30 |
| 302 | TIE Defender Mark I F | 1.00 | 1.50 |
| 303 | TK-422 R | 1.50 | 2.50 |
| 304 | Trooper Sabacc DARK F | 1.00 | 1.50 |
| 305 | Trooper Sabacc LIGHT F | 1.00 | 1.50 |
| 306 | Uh-oh! U | .60 | 1.00 |
| 307 | Umpass-stay R | 1.25 | 2.00 |
| 308 | UriRuír R | 1.50 | 2.50 |
| 309 | URoRRuRiRiRís Bantha R | 1.50 | 2.50 |
| 310 | Uutkik R | 1.50 | 2.50 |
| 311 | Vaderís Personal Shuttle R | 1.50 | 2.50 |
| 312 | Vengeance R | 1.50 | 2.50 |
| 313 | Wakeelmui U | .60 | 1.00 |
| 314 | Watch Your Back! C | .20 | .30 |
| 315 | Weapons Display C | .20 | .30 |

| | | | |
|---|---|---|---|
| 316 Wise Advice U | .60 | 1.00 |
| 317 Wittinís Sandcrawler R | 1.50 | 2.50 |
| 318 Womp Rat C | .20 | .30 |
| 319 Wookiee F | 1.00 | 1.50 |
| 320 Wrist Comlink C | .20 | .30 |
| 321 X-wing Assault Squadron R | 1.50 | 2.50 |
| 322 X-wing Laser Cannon C | .20 | .30 |
| 323 Yavin 4 Trooper F | 1.00 | 1.50 |
| 324 Yavin 4: Massassi Headquarters R | 1.50 | 2.50 |

## 1999 Star Wars Endor

| | | |
|---|---|---|
| COMPLETE SET (180) | 75.00 | 150.00 |
| BOOSTER BOX (30 PACKS) | 75.00 | 150.00 |
| BOOSTER PACK (9 CARDS) | 3.50 | 7.00 |
| RELEASED IN JUNE 1999 | | |

| | | |
|---|---|---|
| 1 AT-ST Pilot C | .20 | .30 |
| 2 Biker Scout Trooper C | .20 | .30 |
| 3 Colonel Dyer R | 2.00 | 3.00 |
| 4 Commander Igar R | 2.00 | 3.00 |
| 5 Corporal Avarik U | .60 | 1.00 |
| 6 Corporal Drazin U | .60 | 1.00 |
| 7 Corporal Drelosyn R | 2.00 | 3.00 |
| 8 Corporal Misik R | 1.50 | 2.50 |
| 9 Corporal Oberk R | 2.00 | 3.00 |
| 10 Elite Squadron Stormtrooper C | .20 | .30 |
| 11 Lieutenant Arnet U | .60 | 1.00 |
| 12 Lieutenant Grond U | .60 | 1.00 |
| 13 Lieutenant Renz R | 1.25 | 2.00 |
| 14 Lieutenant Watts R | 2.00 | 3.00 |
| 15 Major Hewex R | 1.25 | 2.00 |
| 16 Major Marquand R | 2.50 | 4.00 |
| 17 Navy Trooper C | .20 | .30 |
| 18 Navy Trooper Fenson R | 1.50 | 2.50 |
| 19 Navy Trooper Shield Technician C | .20 | .30 |
| 20 Navy Trooper Vesden U | .60 | 1.00 |
| 21 Sergeant Barich R | 3.00 | 5.00 |
| 22 Sergeant Elsek U | .60 | 1.00 |
| 23 Sergeant Irol R | 2.50 | 4.00 |
| 24 Sergeant Tarl U | .60 | 1.00 |
| 25 Sergeant Wallen R | 2.50 | 4.00 |
| 26 An Entire Legion Of My Best Troops U | .60 | 1.00 |
| 27 Aratech Corporation R | 1.50 | 2.50 |
| 28 Battle Order U | .40 | 1.00 |

| | | |
|---|---|---|
| 29 Biker Scout Gear U | .60 | 1.00 |
| 30 Closed Door R | 1.25 | 2.00 |
| 31 Crossfire R | 5.00 | 8.00 |
| 32 Early Warning Network R | 1.25 | 2.00 |
| 33 Empireís New Order R | 1.25 | 2.00 |
| 34 Establish Secret Base R | 2.50 | 4.00 |
| 35 Imperial Academy Training C | .20 | .30 |
| 36 Imperial Arrest Order U | .60 | 1.00 |
| 37 Ominous Rumors R | 1.25 | 2.00 |
| 38 Perimeter Patrol R | 1.50 | 2.50 |
| 39 Pinned Down U | .60 | 1.00 |
| 40 Relentless Tracking R | 1.25 | 2.00 |
| 41 Search And Destroy U | .60 | 1.00 |
| 42 Security Precautions R | 4.00 | 6.00 |
| 43 Well-earned Command R | 1.25 | 2.00 |
| 44 Accelerate C | .20 | .30 |
| 45 Always Thinking With Your Stomach R | 4.00 | 6.00 |
| 46 Combat Readiness C | .20 | .30 |
| 47 Compact Firepower C | .20 | .30 |
| 48 Counterattack R | 1.25 | 2.00 |
| 49 Dead Ewok C | .20 | .30 |
| 50 Donít Move! C | .20 | .30 |
| 51 Eee Chu Wawa! C | .20 | .30 |
| 52 Endor Scout Trooper C | .20 | .30 |
| 53 Freeze! U | .60 | 1.00 |
| 54 Go For Help! C | .20 | .30 |
| 55 High-speed Tactics U | .60 | 1.00 |
| 56 Hot Pursuit C | .20 | .30 |
| 57 Imperial Tyranny C | .20 | .30 |
| 58 Itís An Older Code R | 1.25 | 2.00 |
| 59 Main Course U | .60 | 1.00 |
| 60 Outflank C | .20 | .30 |
| 61 Pitiful Little Band C | .20 | .30 |
| 62 Scout Recon C | .20 | .30 |
| 63 Sneak Attack C | .20 | .30 |
| 64 Wounded Warrior R | 2.50 | 4.00 |
| 65 You Rebel Scum R | 1.50 | 2.50 |
| 66 Carida U | .60 | 1.00 |
| 67 Endor Occupation R | 1.25 | 2.00 |
| 68 Endor: Ancient Forest U | .60 | 1.00 |
| 69 Endor: Back Door LIGHT U | .60 | 1.00 |
| 70 Endor: Bunker LIGHT U | .60 | 1.00 |
| 71 Endor: Dark Forest R | 4.00 | 6.00 |
| 72 Endor: Dense Forest LIGHT C | .20 | .30 |
| 73 Endor: Ewok Village LIGHT U | .60 | 1.00 |
| 74 Endor: Forest Clearing U | .60 | 1.00 |
| 75 Endor: Great Forest LIGHT C | .20 | .30 |
| 76 Endor: Landing Platform (Docking Bay) LIGHT C | .20 | .30 |
| 77 Endor DARK U | .60 | 1.00 |
| 78 Lambda-class Shuttle C | .20 | .30 |
| 79 Speeder Bike LIGHT C | .20 | .30 |
| 80 Tempest 1 R | 1.25 | 2.00 |
| 81 Tempest Scout 1 R | 1.50 | 2.50 |
| 82 Tempest Scout 2 R | 3.00 | 5.00 |
| 83 Tempest Scout 3 R | 1.25 | 2.00 |
| 84 Tempest Scout 4 R | 4.00 | 6.00 |
| 85 Tempest Scout 5 R | 3.00 | 5.00 |
| 86 Tempest Scout 6 R | 4.00 | 6.00 |
| 87 Tempest Scout U | .60 | 1.00 |
| 88 AT-ST Dual Cannon R | 10.00 | 15.00 |
| 89 Scout Blaster C | .20 | .30 |
| 90 Speeder Bike Cannon U | .60 | 1.00 |
| 91 Captain Yutani U | .60 | 1.00 |

| | | |
|---|---|---|
| 92 Chewbacca of Kashyyyk R | 1.25 | 2.00 |
| 93 Chief Chirpa R | 1.50 | 2.50 |
| 94 Corporal Beezer U | .60 | 1.00 |
| 95 Corporal Delevar U | .60 | 1.00 |
| 96 Corporal Janse U | .60 | 1.00 |
| 97 Corporal Kensaric R | 2.00 | 3.00 |
| 98 Daughter of Skywalker R | 12.00 | 20.00 |
| 99 Dresselian Commando C | .20 | .30 |
| 100 Endor LIGHT U | .60 | 1.00 |
| 101 Ewok Sentry C | .20 | .30 |
| 102 Ewok Spearman C | .20 | .30 |
| 103 Ewok Tribesman C | .20 | .30 |
| 104 General Crix Madine R | 1.50 | 2.50 |
| 105 General Solo R | 1.25 | 2.00 |
| 106 Graak R | 1.25 | 2.00 |
| 107 Kazak R | 1.50 | 2.50 |
| 108 Lieutenant Greeve R | 1.25 | 2.00 |
| 109 Lieutenant Page R | 2.50 | 4.00 |
| 110 Logray R | 1.25 | 2.00 |
| 111 Lumat U | .60 | 1.00 |
| 112 Mon Mothma R | 2.00 | 3.00 |
| 113 Orrimaarko R | 1.25 | 2.00 |
| 114 Paploo U | .60 | 1.00 |
| 115 Rabin U | .60 | 1.00 |
| 116 Romba R | 1.25 | 2.00 |
| 117 Sergeant Brooks Carlson R | 1.25 | 2.00 |
| 118 Sergeant Bruckman R | 1.25 | 2.00 |
| 119 Sergeant Junkin U | .60 | 1.00 |
| 120 Teebo R | 1.25 | 2.00 |
| 121 Threepio R | 2.00 | 3.00 |
| 122 Wicket R | 1.25 | 2.00 |
| 123 Wuta U | .60 | 1.00 |
| 124 Aim High R | 1.50 | 2.50 |
| 125 Battle Plan U | .60 | 1.00 |
| 126 Commando Training C | .20 | .30 |
| 127 Count Me In R | 1.25 | 2.00 |
| 128 I Hope Sheís All Right U | .60 | 1.00 |
| 129 I Wonder Who They Found U | .60 | 1.00 |
| 130 Insurrection U | .60 | 1.00 |
| 131 Thatís One R | 1.25 | 2.00 |
| 132 Wokling R | 10.00 | 15.00 |
| 133 Deactivate The Shield Generator R | 2.00 | 3.00 |
| 134 Careful Planning C | .20 | .30 |
| 135 Covert Landing U | .60 | 1.00 |
| 136 Endor Operations / Imperial Outpost R | 4.00 | 6.00 |
| 137 Ewok And Roll C | .20 | .30 |
| 138 Ewok Log Jam C | .20 | .30 |
| 139 Ewok Rescue C | .20 | .30 |
| 140 Firefight C | .20 | .30 |
| 141 Fly Casual R | 1.25 | 2.00 |
| 142 Free Ride U | .60 | 1.00 |
| 143 Get Alongside That One U | .60 | 1.00 |
| 144 Here We Go Again R | 1.25 | 2.00 |
| 145 I Have A Really Bad Feeling About This C | .20 | .30 |
| 146 I Know R | 2.00 | 3.00 |
| 147 Lost In The Wilderness R | 1.25 | 2.00 |
| 148 Rapid Deployment R | 1.25 | 2.00 |
| 149 Sound The Attack C | .20 | .30 |
| 150 Surprise Counter Assault R | 1.25 | 2.00 |
| 151 Take The Initiative C | .20 | .30 |

| | | | |
|---|---|---|---|
| 152 This Is Absolutely Right R | 1.25 | 2.00 | |
| 153 Throw Me Another Charge U | .60 | 1.00 | |
| 154 Were You Looking For Me? R | 6.00 | 10.00 | |
| 155 Wookiee Guide C | .20 | .30 | |
| 156 Yub Yub! C | .20 | .30 | |
| 157 Chandrila U | .60 | 1.00 | |
| 158 Endor Celebration R | 1.25 | 2.00 | |
| 159 Endor: Back Door DARK U | .60 | 1.00 | |
| 160 Endor: Bunker DARK U | .60 | 1.00 | |
| 161 Endor: Chief Chirpaís Hut R | 5.00 | 8.00 | |
| 162 Endor: Dense Forest DARK C | .20 | .30 | |
| 163 Endor: Ewok Village DARK U | .60 | 1.00 | |
| 164 Endor: Great Forest DARK C | .20 | .30 | |
| 165 Endor: Hidden Forest Trail U | .60 | 1.00 | |
| 166 Endor: Landing Platform | .20 | .30 | |
| (Docking Bay) DARK C | | | |
| 167 Endor: Rebel Landing Site (Forest) R | 4.00 | 6.00 | |
| 168 Rebel Strike Team | 2.00 | 3.00 | |
| Garrison Destroyed R | | | |
| 169 Tydirium R | 2.00 | 3.00 | |
| 170 YT-1300 Transport C | .20 | .30 | |
| 171 Chewieís AT-ST R | 5.00 | 8.00 | |
| 172 Ewok Glider C | .20 | .30 | |
| 173 Speeder Bike DARK C | .20 | .30 | |
| 174 A280 Sharpshooter Rifle R | 4.00 | 6.00 | |
| 175 BlasTech E-11B Blaster Rifle C | .20 | .30 | |
| 176 Chewbaccaís Bowcaster R | 4.00 | 6.00 | |
| 177 Ewok Bow C | .20 | .30 | |
| 178 Ewok Catapult U | .60 | 1.00 | |
| 179 Ewok Spear C | .20 | .30 | |
| 180 Explosive Charge U | .60 | 1.00 | |

## 1999 Star Wars Enhanced Cloud City

| | | | |
|---|---|---|---|
| COMPLETE SET (12) | 12.00 | 25.00 | |
| RELEASED IN 1999 | | | |
| 1 4-LOM With Concussion Rifle PM | 2.50 | 4.00 | |
| 2 Any Methods Necessary PM | 3.00 | 5.00 | |
| 3 Boba Fett in Slave I PM | 1.50 | 2.50 | |
| 4 Chewie With Blaster Rifle PM | 1.50 | 2.50 | |
| 5 Crush The Rebellion PM | 2.00 | 3.00 | |
| 6 Dengar In Punishing One PM | 1.50 | 2.50 | |
| 7 IG-88 With Riot Gun PM | 5.00 | 8.00 | |
| 8 Lando In Millennium Falcon PM | 1.50 | 2.50 | |
| 9 Lando With Blaster Pistol PM | 1.50 | 2.50 | |
| 10 Quiet Mining Colony | 1.50 | 2.50 | |
| Independent Operation PM | | | |
| 11 This Deal Is Getting Worse All The Time | 1.50 | 2.50 | |
| Pray I Donít Alter It Any Further | | | |
| 12 Z-95 Bespin Defense Fighter PM | 1.50 | 2.50 | |

## 1999 Star Wars Enhanced Jabba's Palace

| | | | |
|---|---|---|---|
| COMPLETE SET (12) | 20.00 | 40.00 | |
| RELEASE IN 1999 | | | |
| 1 Bossk With Mortar Gun PM | 1.50 | 2.50 | |
| 2 Boushh PM | 2.00 | 3.00 | |
| 3 Court Of The Vile Gangster | 1.50 | 2.50 | |
| I Shall Enjoy Watching You Die PM | | | |
| 4 Dengar With Blaster Carbine PM | 1.50 | 2.50 | |
| 5 IG-88 In IG-2000 PM | 1.50 | 2.50 | |

| | | | |
|---|---|---|---|
| 6 Jodo Kast PM | 2.50 | 4.00 | |
| 7 Mara Jade, The Emperorís Hand PM | 12.00 | 20.00 | |
| 8 Mara Jadeís Lightsaber PM | 2.50 | 4.00 | |
| 9 Master Luke PM | 4.00 | 6.00 | |
| 10 See-Threepio PM | 1.50 | 2.50 | |
| 11 You Can Either Profit By This... | 1.50 | 2.50 | |
| Or Be Destroyed PM | | | |
| 12 Zuckuss In Mist Hunter PM | 2.00 | 3.00 | |

## 2000 Star Wars Death Star II

| | | | |
|---|---|---|---|
| COMPLETE SET (182) | 200.00 | 300.00 | |
| BOOSTER BOX (30 PACKS) | 150.00 | 250.00 | |
| BOOSTER PACK (11 CARDS) | 5.00 | 9.00 | |
| RELEASED IN JULY 2000 | | | |
| 1 Accuser R | 2.00 | 3.00 | |
| 2 Admiral Ackbar XR | 2.00 | 3.00 | |
| 3 Admiral Chiraneau R | 2.50 | 4.00 | |
| 4 Admiral Piett XR | 1.50 | 2.50 | |
| 5 Anakin Skywalker R | 1.50 | 2.50 | |
| 6 Aquaris C | .20 | .30 | |
| 7 A-wing C | .20 | .30 | |
| 8 A-wing Cannon C | .20 | .30 | |
| 9 Baron Soontir Fel R | 2.50 | 4.00 | |
| 10 Battle Deployment R | 2.00 | 3.00 | |
| 11 Black 11 R | 1.50 | 2.50 | |
| 12 Blue Squadron 5 U | .60 | 1.00 | |
| 13 Blue Squadron B-wing R | 2.50 | 4.00 | |
| 14 Bring Him Before Me | 1.50 | 2.50 | |
| Take Your Fatherís Place R | | | |
| 15 B-wing Attack Squadron R | 1.50 | 2.50 | |
| 16 B-wing Bomber C | .20 | .30 | |
| 17 Capital Support R | 1.50 | 2.50 | |
| 18 Captain Godherdt U | .60 | 1.00 | |
| 19 Captain Jonus U | .60 | 1.00 | |
| 20 Captain Sarkli R | 1.50 | 2.50 | |
| 21 Captain Verrack U | .60 | 1.00 | |
| 22 Captain Yorr U | .60 | 1.00 | |
| 23 Chimaera R | 4.00 | 6.00 | |
| 24 Close Air Support C | .20 | .30 | |
| 25 Colonel Cracken R | 1.50 | 2.50 | |
| 26 Colonel Davod Jon U | .60 | 1.00 | |
| 27 Colonel Jendon R | 1.50 | 2.50 | |

| | | | |
|---|---|---|---|
| 28 Colonel Salm U | .60 | 1.00 | |
| 29 Combat Response C | .20 | .30 | |
| 30 Combined Fleet Action R | 1.50 | 2.50 | |
| 31 Commander Merrejk R | 2.00 | 3.00 | |
| 32 Concentrate All Fire R | 1.50 | 2.50 | |
| 33 Concussion Missiles DARK C | .20 | .30 | |
| 34 Concussion Missiles LIGHT C | .20 | .30 | |
| 35 Corporal Marmor U | .60 | 1.00 | |
| 36 Corporal Midge U | .60 | 1.00 | |
| 37 Critical Error Revealed C | .20 | .30 | |
| 38 Darth Vaderís Lightsaber R | 1.50 | 2.50 | |
| 39 Death Star II R | 2.00 | 3.00 | |
| 40 Death Star II: Capacitors C | .20 | .30 | |
| 41 Death Star II: Coolant Shaft C | .20 | .30 | |
| 42 Death Star II: Docking Bay C | .20 | .30 | |
| 43 Death Star II: Reactor Core C | .20 | .30 | |
| 44 Death Star II: Throne Room R | 1.50 | 2.50 | |
| 45 Defiance R | 2.00 | 3.00 | |
| 46 Desperate Counter C | .20 | .30 | |
| 47 Dominator R | 1.50 | 2.50 | |
| 48 DS-181-3 U | .60 | 1.00 | |
| 49 DS-181-4 U | .60 | 1.00 | |
| 50 Emperor Palpatine UR | 40.00 | 60.00 | |
| 51 Emperorís Personal Shuttle R | 1.50 | 2.50 | |
| 52 Emperorís Power U | .60 | 1.00 | |
| 53 Endor Shield U | .60 | 1.00 | |
| 54 Enhanced Proton Torpedoes C | .20 | .30 | |
| 55 Fighter Cover R | 3.00 | 5.00 | |
| 56 Fighters Coming In R | 1.50 | 2.50 | |
| 57 First Officer Thaneespi R | 1.50 | 2.50 | |
| 58 Flagship Executor R | 2.00 | 3.00 | |
| 59 Flagship Operations R | 1.50 | 2.50 | |
| 60 Force Lightning R | 3.00 | 5.00 | |
| 61 Force Pike C | .20 | .30 | |
| 62 Gall C | .20 | .30 | |
| 63 General Calrissian R | 1.50 | 2.50 | |
| 64 General Walex Blissex U | .60 | 1.00 | |
| 65 Gold Squadron 1 R | 1.50 | 2.50 | |
| 66 Gray Squadron 1 U | .60 | 1.00 | |
| 67 Gray Squadron 2 U | .60 | 1.00 | |
| 68 Gray Squadron Y-wing Pilot C | .20 | .30 | |
| 69 Green Leader R | 1.50 | 2.50 | |
| 70 Green Squadron 1 R | 1.50 | 2.50 | |
| 71 Green Squadron 3 R | 1.50 | 2.50 | |
| 72 Green Squadron A-wing R | 2.00 | 3.00 | |
| 73 Green Squadron Pilot C | .20 | .30 | |
| 74 Head Back To The Surface C | .20 | .30 | |
| 75 Heading For The Medical Frigate C | .20 | .30 | |
| 76 Heavy Turbolaser Battery DARK C | .20 | .30 | |
| 77 Heavy Turbolaser Battery LIGHT C | .20 | .30 | |
| 78 Home One R | 6.00 | 10.00 | |
| 79 Home One: Docking Bay C | .20 | .30 | |
| 80 Home One: War Room R | 2.00 | 3.00 | |
| 81 Honor Of The Jedi U | .60 | 1.00 | |
| 82 I Feel The Conflict U | .60 | 1.00 | |
| 83 Iíll Take The Leader R | 4.00 | 6.00 | |
| 84 Iím With You Too R | 2.50 | 4.00 | |
| 85 Imperial Command R | 6.00 | 10.00 | |
| 86 Inconsequential Losses C | .20 | .30 | |
| 87 Independence R | 2.00 | 3.00 | |
| 88 Insertion Planning C | .20 | .30 | |

| 89 Insignificant Rebellion U | .60 | 1.00 |
| 90 Intensify The Forward Batteries R | 1.50 | 2.50 |
| 91 Janus Greejatus R | 1.50 | 2.50 |
| 92 Judicator R | 2.50 | 4.00 |
| 93 Karie Neth U | .60 | 1.00 |
| 94 Keir Santage U | .60 | 1.00 |
| 95 Kin Kian U | .60 | 1.00 |
| 96 Launching The Assault R | 1.50 | 2.50 |
| 97 Leave Them To Me C | .20 | .30 |
| 98 Letís Keep A Little Optimism Here C | .20 | .30 |
| 99 Liberty R | 2.00 | 3.00 |
| 100 Lieutenant Blount R | 1.50 | 2.50 |
| 101 Lieutenant Endicott U | .60 | 1.00 |
| 102 Lieutenant Hebsly U | .60 | 1.00 |
| 103 Lieutenant siToo Vees U | .60 | 1.00 |
| 104 Lieutenant Telsij U | .60 | 1.00 |
| 105 Lord Vader R | 12.00 | 20.00 |
| 106 Luke Skywalker, Jedi Knight UR | 40.00 | 60.00 |
| 107 Lukeís Lightsaber R | 2.50 | 4.00 |
| 108 Luminous U | .60 | 1.00 |
| 109 Major Haashin U | .60 | 1.00 |
| 110 Major Mianda U | .60 | 1.00 |
| 111 Major Olander Brit U | .60 | 1.00 |
| 112 Major Panno U | .60 | 1.00 |
| 113 Major Rhymer U | .60 | 1.00 |
| 114 Major Turr Phennir U | .60 | 1.00 |
| 115 Masanya R | 2.50 | 4.00 |
| 116 Menace Fades C | .20 | .30 |
| 117 Mobilization Points C | .20 | .30 |
| 118 Moff Jerjerrod R | 1.50 | 2.50 |
| 119 Mon Calamari DARK C | .20 | .30 |
| 120 Mon Calamari LIGHT C | .20 | .30 |
| 121 Mon Calamari Star Cruiser R | 2.00 | 3.00 |
| 122 Myn Kyneugh R | 1.50 | 2.50 |
| 123 Nebulon-B Frigate U | .60 | 1.00 |
| 124 Nien Nunb R | 2.00 | 3.00 |
| 125 Obsidian 10 U | .60 | 1.00 |
| 126 Onyx 1 R | 2.00 | 3.00 |
| 127 Onyx 2 U | .60 | 1.00 |
| 128 Operational As Planned C | .20 | .30 |
| 129 Orbital Mine C | .20 | .30 |
| 130 Our Only Hope U | .60 | 1.00 |
| 131 Overseeing It Personally R | 1.50 | 2.50 |
| 132 Prepared Defenses C | .20 | .30 |
| 133 Rebel Leadership R | 5.00 | 8.00 |
| 134 Red Squadron 1 R | 1.50 | 2.50 |
| 135 Red Squadron 4 U | .60 | 1.00 |
| 136 Red Squadron 7 U | .60 | 1.00 |
| 137 Rise, My Friend R | 1.50 | 2.50 |
| 138 Royal Escort C | .20 | .30 |
| 139 Royal Guard C | .20 | .30 |
| 140 Saber 1 R | 10.00 | 15.00 |
| 141 Saber 2 U | .60 | 1.00 |
| 142 Saber 3 U | .60 | 1.00 |
| 143 Saber 4 U | .60 | 1.00 |
| 144 Scimitar 1 U | .60 | 1.00 |
| 145 Scimitar 2 U | .60 | 1.00 |
| 146 Scimitar Squadron TIE C | .20 | .30 |
| 147 Scythe 1 U | .60 | 1.00 |
| 148 Scythe 3 U | .60 | 1.00 |

| 149 Scythe Squadron TIE C | .20 | .30 |
| 150 SFS L-s7.2 TIE Cannon C | .20 | .30 |
| 151 Sim Aloo R | 1.50 | 2.50 |
| 152 Something Special Planned For Them C | .20 | .30 |
| 153 Squadron Assignments C | .20 | .30 |
| 154 Staging Areas C | .20 | .30 |
| 155 Strike Planning R | 1.50 | 2.50 |
| 156 Strikeforce C | .20 | .30 |
| 157 Sullust DARK C | .20 | .30 |
| 158 Sullust LIGHT C | .20 | .30 |
| 159 Superficial Damage C | .20 | .30 |
| 160 Superlaser Mark II U | .60 | 1.00 |
| 161 Taking Them With Us R | 2.00 | 3.00 |
| 162 Tala 1 R | 1.50 | 2.50 |
| 163 Tala 2 R | 1.50 | 2.50 |
| 164 Ten Numb R | 1.50 | 2.50 |
| 165 That Thingís Operational R | 1.50 | 2.50 |
| 166 The Emperorís Shield R | 1.50 | 2.50 |
| 167 The Emperorís Sword R | 1.50 | 2.50 |
| 168 The Time For Our Attack Has Come C | .20 | .30 |
| 169 The Way Of Things U | .60 | 1.00 |
| 170 There Is Good In Him | 1.50 | 2.50 |
| I Can Save Him R | | |
| 171 Thunderflare R | 1.50 | 2.50 |
| 172 TIE Interceptor C | .20 | .30 |
| 173 Twilight Is Upon Me R | 1.50 | 2.50 |
| 174 Tycho Celchu R | 2.00 | 3.00 |
| 175 Visage R | 1.50 | 2.50 |
| 176 Weíre In Attack Position Now R | 4.00 | 6.00 |
| 177 Wedge Antilles, Red Squadron Leader R | 2.50 | 4.00 |
| 178 You Cannot Hide Forever U | .60 | 1.00 |
| 179 You Must Confront Vader R | 2.50 | 4.00 |
| 180 Young Fool R | 1.50 | 2.50 |
| 181 Your Destiny C | .20 | .30 |
| 182 Your Insight Serves You Well U | .60 | 1.00 |

### 2000 Star Wars Jabba's Palace Sealed Deck

| COMPLETE SET (20) | 5.00 | 12.00 |
| RELEASE DATE FALL, 2000 | | |
| 1 Agents In The Court | .60 | 1.00 |
| No Love For The Empire PM | | |
| 2 Hutt Influence PM | .60 | 1.00 |
| 3 Jabbaís Palace: Antechamber PM | .60 | 1.00 |
| 4 Jabbaís Palace: Lower Passages PM | .60 | 1.00 |
| 5 Lando With Vibro-Ax PM | .60 | 1.00 |
| 6 Let Them Make The First Move / My Kind Of Scum | .60 | 1.00 |
| Fearless And Inventive PM | | |
| 7 Mercenary Pilot PM | .60 | 1.00 |
| 8 Mighty Jabba PM | .60 | 1.00 |
| 9 No Escape PM | .60 | 1.00 |
| 10 Ounee Ta PM | .60 | 1.00 |
| 11 Palace Raider PM | .60 | 1.00 |
| 12 Power Of The Hutt PM | .60 | 1.00 |
| 13 Racing Skiff DARK PM | .60 | 1.00 |
| 14 Racing Skiff LIGHT PM | .60 | 1.00 |
| 15 Seeking An Audience PM | .60 | 1.00 |
| 16 Stun Blaster DARK PM | .60 | 1.00 |
| 17 Stun Blaster LIGHT PM | .60 | 1.00 |
| 18 Tatooine: Desert Heart PM | .60 | 1.00 |
| 19 Tatooine: Hutt Trade Route (Desert) PM | .60 | 1.00 |
| 20 Underworld Contacts PM | .60 | 1.00 |

### 2000 Star Wars Reflections II

| COMPLETE SET (54) | 20.00 | 50.00 |
| BOOSTER BOX (30 PACKS) | 150.00 | 250.00 |
| BOOSTER PACK (11 CARDS) | 5.00 | 10.00 |
| RELEASED IN DECEMBER 2000 | | |
| 1 There Is No Try and | 1.00 | 1.50 |
| Oppressive Enforcement PM | | |
| 2 Abyssin Ornament and | .60 | 1.00 |
| Wounded Wookiee PM | | |
| 3 Agents Of Black Sun | .60 | 1.00 |
| Vengence Of The Dark Prince PM | | |
| 4 Alter and Collateral Damage PM | 1.00 | 1.50 |
| 5 Alter and Friendly Fire PM | 1.00 | 1.50 |
| 6 Arica PM | 3.00 | 5.00 |
| 7 Artoo and Threepio PM | 1.00 | 1.50 |
| 8 Black Sun Fleet PM | .60 | 1.00 |
| 9 Captain Gilad Pellaeon PM | 1.00 | 1.50 |
| 10 Chewbacca, Protector PM | 1.00 | 1.50 |
| 11 Control and Set For Stun PM | 1.00 | 1.50 |
| 12 Control and Tunnel Vision PM | 1.50 | 2.50 |
| 13 Corran Horn PM | 2.50 | 4.00 |
| 14 Dark Maneuvers and Tallon Roll PM | 1.50 | 2.50 |
| 15 Dash Rendar PM | 2.00 | 3.00 |
| 16 Defensive Fire and Hutt Smooch PM | .60 | 1.00 |
| 17 Do, Or Do Not and Wise Advice PM | .60 | 1.00 |
| 18 Dr Evazan and Ponda Baba PM | .60 | 1.00 |
| 19 Evader and Monnok PM | 1.00 | 1.50 |
| 20 Ghhhk and Those Rebels | .60 | 1.00 |
| Wonít Escape Us PM | | |
| 21 Grand Admiral Thrawn PM | 4.00 | 6.00 |
| 22 Guri PM | 2.00 | 3.00 |
| 23 Houjix and Out Of Nowhere PM | 1.00 | 1.50 |
| 24 Jabbaís Prize PM | .60 | 1.00 |
| 25 Kir Kanos PM | .60 | 1.00 |
| 26 LE-BO2D9 [Leebo] PM | .60 | 1.00 |
| 27 Luke Skywalker, Rebel Scout PM | 1.50 | 2.50 |
| 28 Mercenary Armor PM | .60 | 1.00 |
| 29 Mirax Terrik PM | 1.00 | 1.50 |
| 30 Nar Shaddaa Wind Chimes | .60 | 1.00 |
| and Out Of Somewhere PM | | |
| 31 No Questions Asked PM | .60 | 1.00 |
| 32 Obi-Wanís Journal PM | .60 | 1.00 |
| 33 Ommni Box and Itís Worse PM | .60 | 1.00 |

| | | |
|---|---|---|
| 34 Out of Commission and | 1.50 | 2.50 |
| Transmission Terminated PM | | |
| 35 Outrider PM | 1.00 | 1.50 |
| 36 Owen Lars and Beru Lars PM | .60 | 1.00 |
| 37 Path Of Least | .60 | 1.00 |
| Resistance and Revealed PM | | |
| 38 Prince Xizor PM | 2.50 | 4.00 |
| 39 Pulsar Skate PM | .60 | 1.00 |
| 40 Sense and Recoil In Fear PM | 1.00 | 1.50 |
| 41 Sense and Uncertain Is The Future PM | 1.00 | 1.50 |
| 42 Shocking Information and Grimtaash PM | .60 | 1.00 |
| 43 Sniper and Dark Strike PM | .60 | 1.00 |
| 44 Snoova PM | 1.50 | 2.50 |
| 45 Sorry About The Mess | 1.00 | 1.50 |
| and Blaster Proficiency PM | | |
| 46 Stinger PM | .60 | 1.00 |
| 47 Sunsdown and | .60 | 1.00 |
| Too Cold For Speeders PM | | |
| 48 Talon Karrde PM | 1.00 | 1.50 |
| 49 The Bith Shuffle and | .60 | 1.00 |
| Desperate Reach PM | | |
| 50 The Emperor PM | 2.50 | 4.00 |
| 51 Vigo PM | 2.50 | 4.00 |
| 52 Virago PM | .60 | 1.00 |
| 53 Watch Your Step | .60 | 1.00 |
| This Place Can Be A Little Rough PM | | |
| 54 Yoda Stew and You Do Have Your Moments PM | .60 | 1.00 |

## 2000 Star Wars Third Anthology

| | | |
|---|---|---|
| COMPLETE SET (6) | 4.00 | 10.00 |
| RELEASED IN 2000 | | |
| 1 A New Secret Base PM | 1.50 | 2.50 |
| 2 Artoo-Detoo In Red 5 PM | 1.50 | 2.50 |
| 3 Echo Base Garrison PM | 1.50 | 2.50 |
| 4 Massassi Base Operations | 1.50 | 2.50 |
| One In A Million PM | | |
| 5 Prisoner 2187 PM | 1.50 | 2.50 |
| 6 Set Your Course For Alderaan | 1.50 | 2.50 |
| The Ultimate Power In The Universe PM | | |

## 2001 Star Wars Coruscant

| | | |
|---|---|---|
| COMPLETE SET (188) | 120.00 | 250.00 |
| BOOSTER BOX (30 PACKS) | 300.00 | 400.00 |
| BOOSTER PACK (11 CARDS) | 12.00 | 15.00 |
| RELEASED IN AUGUST 2001 | | |
| 1 A Tragedy Has Occurred U | .60 | 1.00 |
| 2 A Vergence In The Force U | .60 | 1.00 |
| 3 Accepting Trade Federation Control U | .60 | 1.00 |
| 4 Aks Moe R | 2.00 | 3.00 |
| 5 All Wings Report In and Darklighter Spin R | 10.00 | 15.00 |
| 6 Allegations Of Corruption U | .60 | 1.00 |
| 7 Alter DARK U | .60 | 1.00 |
| 8 Alter LIGHT U | .60 | 1.00 |
| 9 Another Pathetic Lifeform U | .60 | 1.00 |
| 10 Are You Brain Dead?! R | 2.50 | 4.00 |
| 11 Ascertaining The Truth U | .60 | 1.00 |
| 12 Baseless Accusations C | .20 | .30 |
| 13 Baskol Yeesrim U | .60 | 1.00 |
| 14 Battle Droid Blaster Rifle C | .20 | .30 |
| 15 Battle Order and First Strike R | 1.50 | 2.50 |
| 16 Battle Plan and Draw Their Fire R | 2.50 | 4.00 |
| 17 Begin Landing Your Troops U | .60 | 1.00 |
| 18 Blockade Flagship: Bridge R | 5.00 | 8.00 |
| 19 Captain Madakor R | 1.50 | 2.50 |
| 20 Captain Panaka R | 1.50 | 2.50 |
| 21 Chokk U | .60 | 1.00 |
| 22 Control DARK U | .60 | 1.00 |
| 23 Control LIGHT U | .60 | 1.00 |
| 24 Coruscant DARK C | .20 | .30 |
| 25 Coruscant LIGHT C | .20 | .30 |
| 26 Coruscant Guard DARK C | .20 | .30 |
| 27 Coruscant Guard LIGHT C | .20 | .30 |
| 28 Coruscant: Docking Bay DARK C | .20 | .30 |
| 29 Coruscant: Docking Bay LIGHT C | .20 | .30 |
| 30 Coruscant: Galactic Senate DARK C | .20 | .30 |
| 31 Coruscant: Galactic Senate LIGHT C | .20 | .30 |
| 32 Coruscant: Jedi Council Chamber R | 5.00 | 8.00 |
| 33 Credits Will Do Fine C | .20 | .30 |
| 34 Darth Maul, Young Apprentice R | 20.00 | 30.00 |
| 35 Daultay Dofine R | 2.00 | 3.00 |
| 36 Depa Billaba R | 2.00 | 3.00 |
| 37 Destroyer Droid R | 15.00 | 25.00 |
| 38 Dioxis R | 1.50 | 2.50 |

| | | |
|---|---|---|
| 39 Do They Have A Code Clearance? R | 1.50 | 2.50 |
| 40 Droid Starfighter C | .20 | .30 |
| 41 Drop! U | .60 | 1.00 |
| 42 Edcel Bar Gane C | .20 | .30 |
| 43 Enter The Bureaucrat U | .60 | 1.00 |
| 44 Establish Control U | .60 | 1.00 |
| 45 Free Ride and Endor Celebration R | 2.50 | 4.00 |
| 46 Freon Drevan U | .60 | 1.00 |
| 47 Gardulla The Hutt U | .60 | 1.00 |
| 48 Graxol Kelvyyn U | .60 | 1.00 |
| 49 Grotto Werribee R | 2.00 | 3.00 |
| 50 Gungan Warrior C | .20 | .30 |
| 51 Horox Ryyder C | .20 | .30 |
| 52 I Will Not Defer U | .60 | 1.00 |
| 53 Ilve Decided To Go Back C | .20 | .30 |
| 54 Imperial Arrest Order and Secret Plans R | 5.00 | 8.00 |
| 55 Imperial Artillery R | 5.00 | 8.00 |
| 56 Inconsequential Barriers C | .20 | .30 |
| 57 Insurrection and Aim High R | 4.00 | 6.00 |
| 58 Jawa DARK C | .20 | .30 |
| 59 Jawa LIGHT C | .20 | .30 |
| 60 Keder The Black R | 1.50 | 2.50 |
| 61 Ki-Adi-Mundi U | .60 | 1.00 |
| 62 Kill Them Immediately C | .20 | .30 |
| 63 Lana Dobreed U | .60 | 1.00 |
| 64 Laser Cannon Battery U | .60 | 1.00 |
| 65 Liana Merian U | .60 | 1.00 |
| 66 Lieutenant Williams U | .60 | 1.00 |
| 67 Little Real Power C | .20 | .30 |
| 68 Lott Dod R | 2.00 | 3.00 |
| 69 Mace Windu R | 12.00 | 20.00 |
| 70 Malastare DARK U | .60 | 1.00 |
| 71 Malastare LIGHT U | .60 | 1.00 |
| 72 Mas Amedda U | .60 | 1.00 |
| 73 Master Qui-Gon R | 5.00 | 8.00 |
| 74 Masterful Move and Endor Occupation R | 3.00 | 5.00 |
| 75 Maul Strikes R | 3.00 | 5.00 |
| 76 Mauls Sith Infiltrator R | 5.00 | 8.00 |
| 77 Might Of The Republic R | 4.00 | 6.00 |
| 78 Mind Tricks Donìt Work On Me U | .60 | 1.00 |
| 79 Mindful Of The Future R | .20 | .30 |
| 80 Motion Supported U | .60 | 1.00 |
| 81 Murr Danod R | 1.50 | 2.50 |
| 82 My Lord, Is That Legal? | .60 | 1.00 |
| I Will Make It Legal  U | | |
| 83 My Loyal Bodyguard U | .60 | 1.00 |
| 84 Naboo Blaster C | .20 | .30 |
| 85 Naboo Blaster Rifle DARK C | .20 | .30 |
| 86 Naboo Blaster Rifle LIGHT C | .20 | .30 |
| 87 Naboo Defense Fighter C | .20 | .30 |
| 88 Naboo Fighter Pilot C | .20 | .30 |
| 89 Naboo Security Officer Blaster C | .20 | .30 |
| 90 Naboo DARK U | .60 | 1.00 |
| 91 Naboo LIGHT U | .60 | 1.00 |
| 92 Naboo: Battle Plains DARK C | .20 | .30 |
| 93 Naboo: Battle Plains LIGHT C | .20 | .30 |
| 94 Naboo: Swamp DARK C | .20 | .30 |
| 95 Naboo: Swamp LIGHT C | .20 | .30 |
| 96 Naboo: Theed Palace | .20 | .30 |
| Courtyard DARK C | | |
| 97 Naboo: Theed Palace | .20 | .30 |

| | | |
|---|---|---|
| Courtyard LIGHT C | | |
| 98 Naboo: Theed Palace | .20 | .30 |
| Docking Bay DARK C | | |
| 99 Naboo: Theed Palace | .20 | .30 |
| Docking Bay LIGHT C | | |
| 100 Naboo: Theed Palace | .20 | .30 |
| Throne Room DARK C | | |
| 101 Naboo: Theed Palace | .20 | .30 |
| Throne Room LIGHT C | | |
| 102 Neimoidian Advisor U | .60 | 1.00 |
| 103 Neimoidian Pilot C | .20 | .30 |
| 104 New Leadership Is Needed C | .20 | .30 |
| 105 No Civility, Only Politics C | .20 | .30 |
| 106 No Money, No Parts, No Deal! | .60 | 1.00 |
| Youíre A Slave? U | | |
| 107 Nute Gunray R | 1.50 | 2.50 |
| 108 Odin Nesloor U | .60 | 1.00 |
| 109 On The Payroll Of The Trade Federation C | .20 | .30 |
| 110 Orn Free Taa C | .20 | .30 |
| 111 Our Blockade Is Perfectly Legal U | .60 | 1.00 |
| 112 P-59 R | 5.00 | 8.00 |
| 113 P-60 R | 2.50 | 4.00 |
| 114 Panakaís Blaster R | 2.00 | 3.00 |
| 115 Passel Argente C | .20 | .30 |
| 116 Phylo Gandish R | 2.50 | 4.00 |
| 117 Plea To The Court U | .60 | 1.00 |
| 118 Plead My Case To The Senate | .60 | 1.00 |
| Sanity And Compassion U | | |
| 119 Plo Koon R | 5.00 | 8.00 |
| 120 Queen Amidala, Ruler Of Naboo R | 6.00 | 10.00 |
| 121 Queenís Royal Starship R | 2.00 | 3.00 |
| 122 Radiant VII R | 2.50 | 4.00 |
| 123 Rebel Artillery R | 5.00 | 8.00 |
| 124 Republic Cruiser C | .20 | .30 |
| 125 Reveal Ourselves To The Jedi C | .20 | .30 |
| 126 Ric Olie R | 1.50 | 2.50 |
| 127 Rune Haako R | 1.50 | 2.50 |
| 128 Sabe R | 2.00 | 3.00 |
| 129 Sache U | .60 | 1.00 |
| 130 Secure Route U | .60 | 1.00 |
| 131 Security Battle Droid C | .20 | .30 |
| 132 Security Control U | .60 | 1.00 |
| 133 Sei Taria U | .60 | 1.00 |
| 134 Senator Palpatine | 5.00 | 8.00 |
| (head and shoulders) R | | |
| 135 Senator Palpatine (head shot) R | 20.00 | 30.00 |
| 136 Sense DARK U | .60 | 1.00 |
| 137 Sense LIGHT U | .60 | 1.00 |
| 138 Short Range Fighters and | 4.00 | 6.00 |
| Watch Your Back! R | | |
| 139 Speak With The Jedi Council R | 5.00 | 8.00 |
| 140 Squabbling Delegates R | 2.00 | 3.00 |
| 141 Stay Here, Where Itís Safe C | .20 | .30 |
| 142 Supreme Chancellor Valorum R | 1.50 | 2.50 |
| 143 Tatooine DARK U | .60 | 1.00 |
| 144 Tatooine LIGHT U | .60 | 1.00 |
| 145 Tatooine: Marketplace DARK C | .20 | .30 |
| 146 Tatooine: Marketplace LIGHT C | .20 | .30 |
| 147 Tatooine: Mos Espa Docking Bay DARK C | .20 | .30 |
| 148 Tatooine: Mos Espa Docking Bay LIGHT C | .20 | .30 |
| 149 Tatooine: Wattoís Junkyard DARK C | .20 | .30 |
| 150 Tatooine: Wattoís Junkyard LIGHT C | .20 | .30 |

| | | |
|---|---|---|
| 151 TC-14 R | 1.50 | 2.50 |
| 152 Televan Koreyy R | 1.50 | 2.50 |
| 153 Tendau Bendon U | .60 | 1.00 |
| 154 Tey How U | .60 | 1.00 |
| 155 The Gravest Of Circumstances U | .60 | 1.00 |
| 156 The Hyperdrive Generatorís Gone | .60 | 1.00 |
| Weíll Need A New One U | | |
| 157 The Phantom Menace R | 6.00 | 10.00 |
| 158 The Point Is Conceded C | .20 | .30 |
| 159 They Will Be No Match For You R | 1.50 | 2.50 |
| 160 Theyíre Still Coming Through! U | .60 | 1.00 |
| 161 This Is Outrageous! U | .60 | 1.00 |
| 162 Thrown Back C | .20 | .30 |
| 163 Tikkes C | .20 | .30 |
| 164 Toonbuck Toora U | .60 | 1.00 |
| 165 Trade Federation Battleship U | .60 | 1.00 |
| 166 Trade Federation Droid Control Ship R | 2.00 | 3.00 |
| 167 Tusken Raider C | .20 | .30 |
| 168 Vote Now! DARK R | 1.50 | 2.50 |
| 169 Vote Now! LIGHT R | 2.00 | 3.00 |
| 170 We Must Accelerate Our Plans R | 12.00 | 20.00 |
| 171 We Wish To Board At Once R | 3.00 | 5.00 |
| 172 Weíre Leaving C | .20 | .30 |
| 173 Wipe Them Out, All Of Them U | .60 | 1.00 |
| 174 Yade Mírak U | .60 | 1.00 |
| 175 YanÈ U | .60 | 1.00 |
| 176 Yarua U | .60 | 1.00 |
| 177 Yeb Yeb Ademithorn C | .20 | .30 |
| 178 Yoda, Senior Council Member R | 4.00 | 6.00 |
| 179 You Cannot Hide Forever | 4.00 | 6.00 |
| and Mobilization Points R | | |
| 180 You've Got A Lot Of | 2.00 | 3.00 |
| Guts Coming Here R | | |
| 181 Your Insight Serves You Well | 1.50 | 2.50 |
| and Staging Areas R | | |
| 182 Coruscant Dark Side List 1 | .20 | .30 |
| 183 Coruscant Dark Side List 2 | .20 | .30 |
| 184 Coruscant Light Side List 1 | .20 | .30 |
| 185 Coruscant Light Side List 2 | .20 | .30 |
| 186 Coruscant Rule Card 1 | .20 | .30 |
| 187 Coruscant Rule Card 2 | .20 | .30 |
| 188 Coruscant Rule Card 3 | .20 | .30 |

## 2001 Star Wars Reflections III

| | | |
|---|---|---|
| COMPLETE SET (96) | 80.00 | 150.00 |
| BOOSTER BOX (30 PACKS) | 250.00 | 350.00 |
| BOOSTER PACK (11 CARDS) | 7.50 | 15.00 |
| RELEASED IN 2001 | | |
| 1 A Close Race PM | 1.50 | 2.50 |
| 2 A Remote Planet PM | 1.50 | 2.50 |
| 3 A Tragedy Has Occured PM | 2.00 | 3.00 |
| 4 A Useless Gesture PM | 1.50 | 2.50 |
| 5 Aim High PM | 2.00 | 3.00 |
| 6 Allegations of Coruption PM | 1.50 | 2.50 |
| 7 An Unusual Amount Of Fear PM | 1.50 | 2.50 |
| 8 Another Pathetic Lifeform PM | 1.50 | 2.50 |
| 9 Armament Dismantled PM | 1.50 | 2.50 |
| 10 Battle Order PM | 1.50 | 2.50 |
| 11 Battle Plan PM | 2.00 | 3.00 |
| 12 Bib Fortuna PM | 1.50 | 2.50 |
| 13 Blizzard 4 PM | 3.00 | 5.00 |
| 14 Blockade Flagship: Hallway PM | 1.50 | 2.50 |
| 15 Blow Parried PM | 1.50 | 2.50 |
| 16 Boba Fett, Bounty Hunter PM | 8.00 | 12.00 |
| 17 Chewie, Enraged PM | 2.50 | 4.00 |
| 18 Clinging To The Edge PM | 1.50 | 2.50 |
| 19 Colo Claw Fish DARK PM | 1.50 | 2.50 |
| 20 Colo Claw Fish LIGHT PM | 1.50 | 2.50 |
| 21 Come Here You Big Coward PM | 2.00 | 3.00 |
| 22 Conduct Your Search PM | 2.00 | 3.00 |
| 23 Crossfire PM | 1.50 | 2.50 |
| 24 Dark Rage PM | 1.50 | 2.50 |
| 25 Darth Maulís Demise PM | 1.50 | 2.50 |
| 26 Deep Hatred PM | 1.50 | 2.50 |
| 27 Desperate Times PM | 1.50 | 2.50 |
| 28 Diversionary Tactics PM | 1.50 | 2.50 |
| 29 Do They Have A Code Clearance? PM | 2.00 | 3.00 |
| 30 Do, Or Do Not PM | 1.50 | 2.50 |
| 31 Donít Do That Again PM | 1.50 | 2.50 |
| 32 Echo Base Sensors PM | 2.00 | 3.00 |
| 33 Energy Walls DARK PM | 1.50 | 2.50 |
| 34 Energy Walls LIGHT PM | 1.50 | 2.50 |
| 35 Ewok Celebration PM | 1.50 | 2.50 |
| 36 Fall Of A Jedi PM | 1.50 | 2.50 |
| 37 Fanfare PM | 1.50 | 2.50 |
| 38 Fear Is My Ally PM | 1.50 | 2.50 |
| 39 Force Push PM | 2.00 | 3.00 |
| 40 Han, Chewie, and The Falcon PM | 8.00 | 12.00 |
| 41 He Can Go About His Business PM | 1.50 | 2.50 |
| 42 Horace Vancil PM | 1.50 | 2.50 |
| 43 Inner Strength PM | 1.50 | 2.50 |
| 44 Jabba Desilijic Tiure PM | 1.50 | 2.50 |
| 45 Jar Jarís Electropole PM | 1.50 | 2.50 |
| 46 Jedi Leap PM | 1.50 | 2.50 |
| 47 Lando Calrissian, Scoundrel PM | 3.00 | 5.00 |
| 48 Landoís Not A System, Heís A Man PM | 1.50 | 2.50 |
| 49 Leave them to Me PM | 1.50 | 2.50 |
| 50 Leia, Rebel Princess PM | 4.00 | 6.00 |
| 51 Letís Keep A Little Optimism Here PM | 1.50 | 2.50 |
| 52 Lord Maul PM | 10.00 | 15.00 |
| 53 Maulís Double-Bladed Lightsaber PM | 3.00 | 5.00 |
| 54 Naboo: Theed Palace | 1.50 | 2.50 |
| Generator Core DARK PM | | |
| 55 Naboo: Theed Palace | 1.50 | 2.50 |
| Generator Core LIGHT PM | | |
| 56 Naboo: Theed Palace | 1.50 | 2.50 |
| Generator DARK PM | | |

| | | |
|---|---|---|
| 57 Naboo: Theed Palace | 1.50 | 2.50 |
| Generator LIGHT PM | | |
| 58 No Escape PM | 1.50 | 2.50 |
| 59 No Match For A Sith PM | 1.50 | 2.50 |
| 60 Obi-Wan Kenobi, Jedi Knight PM | 2.50 | 4.00 |
| 61 Obi-Wanís Lightsaber PM | 1.50 | 2.50 |
| 62 Only Jedi Carry That Weapon PM | 1.50 | 2.50 |
| 63 Opee Sea Killer DARK PM | 1.50 | 2.50 |
| 64 Opee Sea Killer LIGHT PM | 1.50 | 2.50 |
| 65 Oppressive Enforcement PM | 1.50 | 2.50 |
| 66 Ounee Ta PM | 1.50 | 2.50 |
| 67 Planetary Defenses PM | 1.50 | 2.50 |
| 68 Prepare For A Surface Attack PM | 1.50 | 2.50 |
| 69 Qui-Gon Jinn, Jedi Master PM | 4.00 | 6.00 |
| 70 Qui-Gonís End PM | 2.00 | 3.00 |
| 71 Reistance PM | 1.50 | 2.50 |
| 72 Sando Aqua Monster DARK PM | 1.50 | 2.50 |
| 73 Sando Aqua Monster LIGHT PM | 1.50 | 2.50 |
| 74 Secret Plans PM | 1.50 | 2.50 |
| 75 Sio Bibble PM | 1.50 | 2.50 |
| 76 Stormtrooper Garrison PM | 6.00 | 10.00 |
| 77 Strike Blockaded PM | 1.50 | 2.50 |
| 78 The Ebb Of Battle PM | 1.50 | 2.50 |
| 79 The Hutts Are Gangsters PM | 1.50 | 2.50 |
| 80 There Is No Try PM | 2.00 | 3.00 |
| 81 They Must Never Again | 1.50 | 2.50 |
| Leave This City PM | | |
| 82 Thok and Thug PM | 1.50 | 2.50 |
| 83 Through The Corridor PM | 1.50 | 2.50 |
| 84 Ultimatum PM | 1.50 | 2.50 |
| 85 Unsalvageable PM | 1.50 | 2.50 |
| 86 Weíll Let Fate-a Decide, Huh? PM | 1.50 | 2.50 |
| 87 Weapon Of A Fallen Mentor PM | 1.50 | 2.50 |
| 88 Weapon Of A Sith PM | 1.50 | 2.50 |
| 89 Where Are Those Droidekas?! PM | 1.50 | 2.50 |
| 90 Wipe Them Out, All Of Them PM | 1.50 | 2.50 |
| 91 Wise Advice PM | 1.50 | 2.50 |
| 92 Yoda, Master Of The Force PM | 6.00 | 10.00 |
| 93 You Cannot Hide Forever PM | 1.50 | 2.50 |
| 94 Youíve Never Won A Race? PM | 1.50 | 2.50 |
| 95 Your Insight Serves You Well PM | 1.50 | 2.50 |
| 96 Your Ship? PM | 2.00 | 3.00 |

### 2001 Star Wars Tatooine

| | | |
|---|---|---|
| COMPLETE SET (95) | 25.00 | 60.00 |
| BOOSTER BOX (30 PACKS) | 50.00 | 100.00 |
| BOOSTER PACK (11 CARDS) | 2.50 | 5.00 |
| RELEASED IN MAY 2001 | | |
| 1 A Jediís Concentration C | .20 | .30 |
| 2 A Jediís Focus C | .20 | .30 |
| 3 A Jediís Patience C | .20 | .30 |
| 4 A Jediís Resilience U | .60 | 1.00 |
| 5 A Million Voices Crying Out R | 1.25 | 2.00 |
| 6 A Step Backward U | .60 | 1.00 |
| 7 Anakinís Podracer R | 1.25 | 2.00 |
| 8 Aurra Sing R | 2.50 | 4.00 |
| 9 Ben Quadinarosí Podracer C | .20 | .30 |
| 10 Boonta Eve Podrace DARK R | 1.50 | 2.50 |
| 11 Boonta Eve Podrace LIGHT R | 1.25 | 2.00 |
| 12 Brisky Morning Munchen R | 1.25 | 2.00 |
| 13 Caldera Righim C | .20 | .30 |
| 14 Changing The Odds C | .20 | .30 |
| 15 Daroe R | 1.25 | 2.00 |
| 16 Darth Maul R | 2.50 | 4.00 |
| 17 Deneb Both U | .60 | 1.00 |
| 18 Donít Do That Again C | .20 | .30 |
| 19 Dud Boltís Podracer C | .20 | .30 |
| 20 Either Way, You Win U | .60 | 1.00 |
| 21 End Of A Reign R | 1.25 | 2.00 |
| 22 Entering The Arena U | .60 | 1.00 |
| 23 Eopie C | .20 | .30 |
| 24 Eventually Youíll Lose U | .60 | 1.00 |
| 25 Fanfare C | .20 | .30 |
| 26 Gamall Wironicc U | .60 | 1.00 |
| 27 Ghana Gleemort U | .60 | 1.00 |
| 28 Gragra U | .60 | 1.00 |
| 29 Great Shot, Kid! R | 1.25 | 2.00 |
| 30 Grugnak U | .60 | 1.00 |
| 31 His Name Is Anakin C | .20 | .30 |
| 32 Hit Racer U | .60 | 1.00 |
| 33 I Canít Believe Heís Gone C | .20 | .30 |
| 34 I Did It! R | 1.25 | 2.00 |
| 35 I Will Find Them Quickly, Master R | 1.25 | 2.00 |
| 36 Iím Sorry R | 1.25 | 2.00 |
| 37 If The Trace Was Correct U | .60 | 1.00 |
| 38 Jar Jar Binks R | 1.25 | 2.00 |
| 39 Jedi Escape C | .20 | .30 |
| 40 Join Me! U | .60 | 1.00 |
| 41 Keeping The Empire Out Forever R | 1.25 | 2.00 |
| 42 Lathe U | .60 | 1.00 |
| 43 Lightsaber Parry C | .20 | .30 |
| 44 Loci Rosen U | .60 | 1.00 |
| 45 Losing Track C | .20 | .30 |
| 46 Maulís Electrobinoculars C | .20 | .30 |
| 47 Maulís Lightsaber R | 1.25 | 2.00 |
| 48 Neck And Neck U | .60 | 1.00 |
| 49 Ni Chuba Na?? C | .20 | .30 |
| 50 Obi-wan Kenobi, Padawan Learner R | 1.50 | 2.50 |
| 51 Padme Naberrie R | 3.00 | 5.00 |
| 52 Pit Crews U | .60 | 1.00 |
| 53 Pit Droid C | .20 | .30 |
| 54 Podrace Prep U | .60 | 1.00 |
| 55 Podracer Collision U | .60 | 1.00 |
| 56 Quietly Observing U | .60 | 1.00 |

| | | |
|---|---|---|
| 57 Qui-Gon Jinn R | 2.50 | 4.00 |
| 58 Qui-Gon Jinnís Lightsaber R | 1.50 | 2.50 |
| 59 Rachalt Hyst U | .60 | 1.00 |
| 60 Sebulba R | 1.25 | 2.00 |
| 61 Sebulbaís Podracer R | 1.25 | 2.00 |
| 62 Shmi Skywalker R | 1.25 | 2.00 |
| 63 Sith Fury C | .20 | .30 |
| 64 Sith Probe Droid R | 1.50 | 2.50 |
| 65 Start Your Engines! U | .60 | 1.00 |
| 66 Tatooine: City Outskirts U | .60 | 1.00 |
| 67 Tatooine: Desert Landing Site R | 1.25 | 2.00 |
| 68 Tatooine: Mos Espa DARK C | .20 | .30 |
| 69 Tatooine: Mos Espa LIGHT C | .20 | .30 |
| 70 Tatooine: Podrace Arena DARK C | .20 | .30 |
| 71 Tatooine: Podrace Arena LIGHT C | .20 | .30 |
| 72 Tatooine: Podracer Bay C | .20 | .30 |
| 73 Tatooine: Slave Quarters U | .60 | 1.00 |
| 74 Teemto Pagaliesí Podracer C | .20 | .30 |
| 75 The Camp C | .20 | .30 |
| 76 The Shield Is Down! R | 1.25 | 2.00 |
| 77 There Is No Conflict C | .20 | .30 |
| 78 Threepio With His Parts Showing R | 2.00 | 3.00 |
| 79 Too Close For Comfort U | .60 | 1.00 |
| 80 Vaderís Anger C | .20 | .30 |
| 81 Watto R | 2.00 | 3.00 |
| 82 Wattoís Box C | .20 | .30 |
| 83 Wattoís Chance Cube U | .60 | 1.00 |
| 84 We Shall Double Our Efforts! R | 1.25 | 2.00 |
| 85 What Was It U | .60 | 1.00 |
| 86 Yotts Orren U | .60 | 1.00 |
| 87 You May Start Your Landing R | 1.25 | 2.00 |
| 88 You Swindled Me! U | .60 | 1.00 |
| 89 You Want This, Donít You? C | .20 | .30 |
| 90 Youíll Find Iím Full Of Surprises U | .60 | 1.00 |
| 91 Tatooine Dark Side List | .20 | .30 |
| 92 Tatooine Light Side List | .20 | .30 |
| 93 Tatooine Rule Card 1 | .20 | .30 |
| 94 Tatooine Rule Card 2 | .20 | .30 |
| 95 Tatooine Rule Card 3 | .20 | .30 |

### 2001 Star Wars Theed Palace

| | | |
|---|---|---|
| COMPLETE SET (121) | 80.00 | 150.00 |
| BOOSTER BOX (30 PACKS) | 400.00 | 500.00 |

| | | |
|---|---|---|
| BOOSTER PACK (11 CARDS) | 15.00 | 20.00 |

RELEASED IN DECEMBER 2001

FINAL EXPANSION PRODUCT BY DECIPHER

| | | |
|---|---|---|
| 1 3B3-10 U | .50 | .75 |
| 2 3B3-1204 U | .50 | .75 |
| 3 3B3-21 U | .50 | .75 |
| 4 3B3-888 U | .50 | .75 |
| 5 AAT Assault Leader R | 1.50 | 2.50 |
| 6 AAT Laser Cannon U | .50 | .75 |
| 7 Activate The Droids C | .20 | .30 |
| 8 After Her! R | 1.25 | 2.00 |
| 9 Amidala's Blaster R | 1.25 | 2.00 |
| 10 Armored Attack Tank U | .50 | .75 |
| 11 Artoo, Brave Little Droid R | 2.50 | 4.00 |
| 12 Ascension Guns U | .50 | .75 |
| 13 At Last We Are Getting Results C | .20 | .30 |
| 14 Battle Droid Officer C | .20 | .30 |
| 15 Battle Droid Pilot C | .20 | .30 |
| 16 Big Boomers! C | .20 | .30 |
| 17 Blockade Flaghip R | 2.50 | 4.00 |
| 18 Blockade Flagship: Docking Bay DARK U | .50 | .75 |
| 19 Blockade Flagship: Docking Bay LIGHT U | .50 | .75 |
| 20 Bok Askol U | .50 | .75 |
| 21 Booma C | .20 | .30 |
| 22 Boss Nass R | 2.00 | 3.00 |
| 23 Bravo 1 R | 1.25 | 2.00 |
| 24 Bravo 2 U | .50 | .75 |
| 25 Bravo 3 U | .50 | .75 |
| 26 Bravo 4 U | .50 | .75 |
| 27 Bravo 5 U | .50 | .75 |
| 28 Bravo Fighter R | 1.25 | 2.00 |
| 29 Captain Tarpals R | 1.25 | 2.00 |
| 30 Captain Tarpals' Electropole C | .20 | .30 |
| 31 Captian Daultay Dofine R | 1.25 | 2.00 |
| 32 Cease Fire! C | .20 | .30 |
| 33 Corporal Rushing U | .50 | .75 |
| 34 Dams Denna U | .50 | .75 |
| 35 Darth Maul With Lightsaber R | 15.00 | 25.00 |
| 36 Darth Sidious R | 30.00 | 50.00 |
| 37 DFS Squadron Starfighter C | .20 | .30 |
| 38 DFS-1015 U | .50 | .75 |
| 39 DFS-1308 R | 1.25 | 2.00 |
| 40 DFS-327 C | .20 | .30 |
| 41 Droid Racks R | 2.00 | 3.00 |
| 42 Droid Starfighter Laser Cannons C | .20 | .30 |
| 43 Drop Your Weapons C | .20 | .30 |
| 44 Electropole C | .20 | .30 |
| 45 Energy Shell Launchers C | .20 | .30 |
| 46 Fambaa C | .20 | .30 |
| 47 Fighters Straight Ahead U | .50 | .75 |
| 48 General Jar Jar R | 2.00 | 3.00 |
| 49 Get To Your Ships! C | .20 | .30 |
| 50 Gian Speeder C | .20 | .30 |
| 51 Gimme A Lift! R | 1.25 | 2.00 |
| 52 Gungan Energy Shield C | .20 | .30 |
| 53 Gungan General C | .20 | .30 |
| 54 Gungan Guard C | .20 | .30 |
| 55 Halt! C | .20 | .30 |
| 56 IIII Try Spinning R | 1.25 | 2.00 |
| 57 Infantry Battle Droid C | .20 | .30 |
| 58 Invasion / In Complete Control U | .50 | .75 |

| | | |
|---|---|---|
| 59 It's On Automatic Pilot C | .20 | .30 |
| 60 Jerus Jannick U | .50 | .75 |
| 61 Kaadu C | .20 | .30 |
| 62 Let's Go Left R | 1.25 | 2.00 |
| 63 Lieutenant Arven Wendik U | .50 | .75 |
| 64 Lieutenant Chamberlyn U | .50 | .75 |
| 65 Lieutenant Rya Kirsch U | .50 | .75 |
| 66 Mace Windu, Jedi Master R | 10.00 | 15.00 |
| 67 Master, Destroyers! R | 1.50 | 2.50 |
| 68 Multi Troop Transport U | .50 | .75 |
| 69 Naboo Celebration R | 1.25 | 2.00 |
| 70 Naboo Occupation R | 1.50 | 2.50 |
| 71 Naboo: Boss Nass's Chambers U | .50 | .75 |
| 72 Naboo: Otoh Gunga Entrance U | .50 | .75 |
| 73 Naboo: Theed Palace Hall U | .50 | .75 |
| 74 Naboo: Theed Palace Hallway U | .50 | .75 |
| 75 No Giben Up, General Jar Jar! R | 1.25 | 2.00 |
| 76 Nothing Can Get Through Are Shield R | 1.50 | 2.50 |
| 77 Nute Gunray, Neimoidian Viceroy R | 3.00 | 5.00 |
| 78 Officer Dolphe U | .50 | .75 |
| 79 Officer Ellberger U | .50 | .75 |
| 80 Officer Perosei U | .50 | .75 |
| 81 OOM-9 U | .50 | .75 |
| 82 Open Fire! C | .20 | .30 |
| 83 OWO-1 With Backup R | 2.00 | 3.00 |
| 84 Panaka, Protector Of The Queen R | 4.00 | 6.00 |
| 85 Proton Torpedoes C | .20 | .30 |
| 86 Queen Amidala R | 12.00 | 20.00 |
| 87 Qui-Gon Jinn With Lightsaber R | 10.00 | 15.00 |
| 88 Rayno Vaca U | .50 | .75 |
| 89 Rep Been U | .50 | .75 |
| 90 Ric Olie, Bravo Leader R | 1.25 | 2.00 |
| 91 Rolling, Rolling, Rolling R | 1.50 | 2.50 |
| 92 Royal Naboo Security Officer C | .20 | .30 |
| 93 Rune Haako, Legal Counsel R | 2.00 | 3.00 |
| 94 Senate Hovercam DARK R | 1.50 | 2.50 |
| 95 Senate Hovercam LIGHT R | 1.50 | 2.50 |
| 96 Sil Unch U | .50 | .75 |
| 97 Single Trooper Aerial Platform C | .20 | .30 |
| 98 SSA-1015 U | .50 | .75 |
| 99 SSA-306 U | .50 | .75 |
| 100 SSA-719 R | 2.00 | 3.00 |
| 101 STAP Blaster Cannons C | .20 | .30 |
| 102 Steady, Steady C | .20 | .30 |
| 103 Take Them Away C | .20 | .30 |
| 104 Take This! C | .20 | .30 |
| 105 Tank Commander C | .20 | .30 |
| 106 The Deflector Shield Is Too Strong R | 1.25 | 2.00 |
| 107 There They Are! U | .50 | .75 |
| 108 They Win This Round R | 1.25 | 2.00 |
| 109 This Is Not Good C | .20 | .30 |
| 110 Trade Federation Landing Craft C | .20 | .30 |
| 111 TT-6 R | 1.50 | 2.50 |
| 112 TT-9 R | 1.25 | 2.00 |
| 113 We Didn't Hit It C | .20 | .30 |
| 114 We Don't Have Time For This R | 1.50 | 2.50 |
| 115 We Have A Plan They Will Be Lost And Confused C | .20 | .30 |
| 116 We're Hit Artoo C | .20 | .30 |
| 117 Wesa Gotta Grand Army C | .20 | .30 |
| 118 Wesa Ready To Do Our-sa Part C | .20 | .30 |
| 119 Whoooo! C | .20 | .30 |
| 120 Theed Palace Dark Side List | .20 | .30 |
| 121 Theed Palace Light Side List | .20 | .30 |

## 2002 Star Wars Attack of the Clones

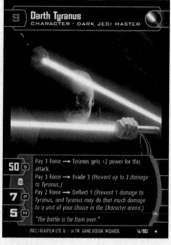

| | | |
|---|---|---|
| COMPLETE SET (180) | 30.00 | 80.00 |
| BOOSTER BOX (36 PACKS) | 20.00 | 40.00 |
| BOOSTER PACK (11 CARDS) | 1.00 | 1.50 |

*FOIL: .75X TO 2X BASIC CARDS

RELEASED IN APRIL 2002

| | | |
|---|---|---|
| 1 Anakin Skywalker (A) R | 1.00 | 1.50 |
| 2 Anakin Skywalker (B) R | 1.00 | 1.50 |
| 3 Assassin Droid ASN-121 (A) R | 1.00 | 1.50 |
| 4 Bail Organa (A) R | 1.00 | 1.50 |
| 5 Battle Fatigue R | 1.00 | 1.50 |
| 6 Boba Fett (A) R | 1.00 | 1.50 |
| 7 Captain Typho (A) R | 1.00 | 1.50 |
| 8 Clear the Skies R | 1.00 | 1.50 |
| 9 Clone Officer R | 1.00 | 1.50 |
| 10 Dark Rendezvous R | 1.00 | 1.50 |
| 11 Dark Side's Command R | 1.00 | 1.50 |
| 12 Dark Side's Compulsion R | 1.00 | 1.50 |
| 13 Darth Sidious (A) R | 1.00 | 1.50 |
| 14 Darth Tyranus (A) R | 1.00 | 1.50 |
| 15 Destruction of Hope R | 1.00 | 1.50 |
| 16 Dexter Jettster (A) R | 1.00 | 1.50 |
| 17 Geonosian Sentry R | 1.00 | 1.50 |
| 18 Hero's Duty R | 1.00 | 1.50 |
| 19 Hero's Flaw R | 1.00 | 1.50 |
| 20 Interference in the Senate R | 1.00 | 1.50 |
| 21 Jango Fett (A) R | 1.00 | 1.50 |
| 22 Jango Fett (B) R | 1.00 | 1.50 |
| 23 Jar Jar Binks (A) R | 1.00 | 1.50 |
| 24 Jedi Call for Help R | 1.00 | 1.50 |
| 25 Jedi Council Summons R | 1.00 | 1.50 |
| 26 Jedi Knight's Deflection R | 1.00 | 1.50 |
| 27 Lama Su (A) R | 1.00 | 1.50 |
| 28 Luxury Airspeeder U | .30 | .50 |
| 29 A Moment's Rest R | 1.00 | 1.50 |
| 30 Naboo Defense Station R | 1.00 | 1.50 |
| 31 Obi-Wan Kenobi (A) R | 1.00 | 1.50 |
| 32 Obi-Wan's Starfighter (A) R | 1.00 | 1.50 |
| 33 Order Here R | 1.00 | 1.50 |
| 34 Padmè Amidala (A) R | 1.00 | 1.50 |
| 35 Padmè Amidala (B) R | 1.00 | 1.50 |
| 36 Padmè's Yacht (A) R | 1.00 | 1.50 |
| 37 Plo Koon (A) R | 1.00 | 1.50 |

| # | Card | | Low | High |
|---|------|---|-----|------|
| 38 | Plot the Secession R | | 1.00 | 1.50 |
| 39 | Power Dive R | | 1.00 | 1.50 |
| 40 | Queen Jamillia (A) R | | 1.00 | 1.50 |
| 41 | R2-D2 (A) R | | 1.00 | 1.50 |
| 42 | San Hill (A) U | | .30 | .50 |
| 43 | Second Effort R | | 1.00 | 1.50 |
| 44 | Seek the Council's Wisdom R | | 1.00 | 1.50 |
| 45 | Shu Mai (A) U | | .30 | .50 |
| 46 | Slave I (A) R | | 1.00 | 1.50 |
| 47 | Spirit of the Fallen R | | 1.00 | 1.50 |
| 48 | Target the Senator R | | 1.00 | 1.50 |
| 49 | Taun We (A) R | | 1.00 | 1.50 |
| 50 | Trade Federation Battleship Core R | | 1.00 | 1.50 |
| 51 | Tyranus's Edict R | | 1.00 | 1.50 |
| 52 | Tyranus's Geonosian Speeder (A) R | | 1.00 | 1.50 |
| 53 | Tyranus's Solar Sailer (A) R | | 1.00 | 1.50 |
| 54 | Tyranus's Wrath R | | 1.00 | 1.50 |
| 55 | War Will Follow R | | 1.00 | 1.50 |
| 56 | Ward of the Jedi R | | 1.00 | 1.50 |
| 57 | Windu's Solution R | | 1.00 | 1.50 |
| 58 | Yoda (A) R | | 1.00 | 1.50 |
| 59 | Yoda's Intervention R | | 1.00 | 1.50 |
| 60 | Zam Wesell (A) R | | 1.00 | 1.50 |
| 61 | Acklay U | | .30 | .50 |
| 62 | Anakin Skywalker (C) U | | .30 | .50 |
| 63 | Anakin's Inspiration U | | .30 | .50 |
| 64 | AT-TE Walker 23X U | | .30 | .50 |
| 65 | AT-TE Walker 71E R | | 1.00 | 1.50 |
| 66 | Attract Enemy Fire U | | .30 | .50 |
| 67 | C-3PO (A) U | | .30 | .50 |
| 68 | Capture Obi-Wan U | | .30 | .50 |
| 69 | Chancellor Palpatine (A) R | | 1.00 | 1.50 |
| 70 | Chase the Villain U | | .30 | .50 |
| 71 | Cheat the Game U | | .30 | .50 |
| 72 | Cliegg Lars (A) U | | .30 | .50 |
| 73 | Clone Warrior 4/163 U | | .30 | .50 |
| 74 | Clone Warrior 5/373 U | | .30 | .50 |
| 75 | Commerce Guild Droid Platoon U | | .30 | .50 |
| 76 | CordÈ (A) U | | .30 | .50 |
| 77 | Coruscant Freighter AA-9 (A) U | | .30 | .50 |
| 78 | Dark Speed U | | .30 | .50 |
| 79 | Darth Tyranus (B) U | | .30 | .50 |
| 80 | Departure Time U | | .30 | .50 |
| 81 | Destroyer Droid, P Series U | | .30 | .50 |
| 82 | Down in Flames U | | .30 | .50 |
| 83 | Droid Control Ship U | | .30 | .50 |
| 84 | Elan Sleazebaggano (A) R | | 1.00 | 1.50 |
| 85 | Geonosian Guard U | | .30 | .50 |
| 86 | Geonosian Warrior U | | .30 | .50 |
| 87 | Go to the Temple U | | .30 | .50 |
| 88 | Infantry Battle Droid, B1 Series U | | .30 | .50 |
| 89 | Jango Fett (C) U | | .30 | .50 |
| 90 | Jawa Sandcrawler U | | .30 | .50 |
| 91 | Jedi Patrol U | | .30 | .50 |
| 92 | Kaminoan Guard U | | .30 | .50 |
| 93 | Kit Fisto (A) U | | .30 | .50 |
| 94 | Master and Apprentice U | | .30 | .50 |
| 95 | Naboo Security Guard U | | .30 | .50 |
| 96 | Naboo Spaceport U | | .30 | .50 |
| 97 | Nexu U | | .30 | .50 |
| 98 | Nute Gunray (A) U | | .30 | .50 |
| 99 | Obi-Wan Kenobi (B) U | | .30 | .50 |
| 100 | PadmÈ Amidala (C) U | | .30 | .50 |
| 101 | Poggle the Lesser (A) U | | .30 | .50 |
| 102 | Reek U | | .30 | .50 |
| 103 | Republic Assault Ship U | | .30 | .50 |
| 104 | Republic Cruiser C | | .15 | .25 |
| 105 | Shaak Ti (A) U | | .30 | .50 |
| 106 | Ship Arrival U | | .30 | .50 |
| 107 | Splinter the Republic U | | .30 | .50 |
| 108 | Strength of Hate U | | .30 | .50 |
| 109 | Subtle Assassination U | | .30 | .50 |
| 110 | Super Battle Droid 8EX U | | .30 | .50 |
| 111 | Trade Federation Battleship U | | .30 | .50 |
| 112 | Trade Federation C-9979 U | | .30 | .50 |
| 113 | Tyranus's Gift U | | .30 | .50 |
| 114 | Underworld Connections U | | .30 | .50 |
| 115 | Wat Tambor (A) U | | .30 | .50 |
| 116 | Watto (A) U | | .30 | .50 |
| 117 | Weapon Response U | | .30 | .50 |
| 118 | Wedding of Destiny U | | .30 | .50 |
| 119 | Yoda (B) U | | .30 | .50 |
| 120 | Zam's Airspeeder (A) U | | .30 | .50 |
| 121 | Anakin Skywalker (D) C | | .15 | .25 |
| 122 | Battle Droid Squad C | | .15 | .25 |
| 123 | Bravo N-1 Starfighter C | | .15 | .25 |
| 124 | Chancellor's Guard Squad C | | .15 | .25 |
| 125 | Clone Platoon C | | .15 | .25 |
| 126 | Clone Squad C | | .15 | .25 |
| 127 | Commerce Guild Droid 81 C | | .15 | .25 |
| 128 | Commerce Guild Starship C | | .15 | .25 |
| 129 | Corellian Star Shuttle C | | .15 | .25 |
| 130 | Darth Tyranus (C) C | | .15 | .25 |
| 131 | Destroyer Droid Squad C | | .15 | .25 |
| 132 | Droid Starfighter DFS-4CT C | | .15 | .25 |
| 133 | Droid Starfighter Squadron C | | .15 | .25 |
| 134 | Droid Starfighter Wing C | | .15 | .25 |
| 135 | Elite Jedi Squad C | | .15 | .25 |
| 136 | Flying Geonosian Squad C | | .15 | .25 |
| 137 | Geonosian Defense Platform C | | .15 | .25 |
| 138 | Geonosian Fighter C | | .15 | .25 |
| 139 | Geonosian Squad C | | .15 | .25 |
| 140 | Gozanti Cruiser C | | .15 | .25 |
| 141 | Hatch a Clone C | | .15 | .25 |
| 142 | Hero's Dodge C | | .15 | .25 |
| 143 | High-Force Dodge C | | .15 | .25 |
| 144 | Hyperdrive Ring C | | .15 | .25 |
| 145 | InterGalactic Banking Clan Starship C | | .15 | .25 |
| 146 | Jango Fett (D) C | | .15 | .25 |
| 147 | Jedi Starfighter 3R3 C | | .15 | .25 |
| 148 | Knockdown C | | .15 | .25 |
| 149 | Lost in the Asteroids C | | .15 | .25 |
| 150 | Lull in the Fighting C | | .15 | .25 |
| 151 | Mending C | | .15 | .25 |
| 152 | N-1 Starfighter C | | .15 | .25 |
| 153 | Naboo Cruiser C | | .15 | .25 |
| 154 | Naboo Royal Starship C | | .15 | .25 |
| 155 | Naboo Senatorial Escort C | | .15 | .25 |
| 156 | Naboo Starfighter Squadron C | | .15 | .25 |
| 157 | Obi-Wan Kenobi (C) C | | .15 | .25 |
| 158 | Padawan's Deflection C | | .15 | .25 |
| 159 | PadmÈ Amidala (D) C | | .15 | .25 |
| 160 | Patrol Speeder C | | .15 | .25 |
| 161 | Peace on Naboo C | | .15 | .25 |
| 162 | Pilot's Dodge C | | .15 | .25 |
| 163 | Recon Speeder U | | .15 | .25 |
| 164 | Republic Attack Gunship UH-478 C | | .15 | .25 |
| 165 | Repulsorlift Malfunction C | | .15 | .25 |
| 166 | Return to Spaceport C | | .15 | .25 |
| 167 | Rickshaw C | | .15 | .25 |
| 168 | Slumming on Coruscant C | | .15 | .25 |
| 169 | Sonic Shockwave C | | .15 | .25 |
| 170 | Speeder Bike Squadron C | | .15 | .25 |
| 171 | Starship Refit C | | .15 | .25 |
| 172 | Surge of Power C | | .15 | .25 |
| 173 | Swoop Bike C | | .15 | .25 |
| 174 | Take the Initiative C | | .15 | .25 |
| 175 | Target Locked C | | .15 | .25 |
| 176 | Taylander Shuttle C | | .15 | .25 |
| 177 | Techno Union Starship C | | .15 | .25 |
| 178 | Trade Federation War Freighter C | | .15 | .25 |
| 179 | Walking Droid Fighter C | | .15 | .25 |
| 180 | Zam Wesell (B) C | | .15 | .25 |

## 2002 Star Wars A New Hope

| | | Low | High |
|---|---|-----|------|
| COMPLETE SET (180) | | 30.00 | 80.00 |
| BOOSTER BOX (36 PACKS) | | 25.00 | 50.00 |
| BOOSTER PACK (11 CARDS) | | 1.50 | 3.00 |

*FOIL: .75X TO 2X BASIC CARDS
RELEASED IN OCTOBER 2002

| # | Card | | Low | High |
|---|------|---|-----|------|
| 1 | Admiral Motti (A) R | | 1.00 | 1.50 |
| 2 | Beru Lars (A) R | | 1.00 | 1.50 |
| 3 | Blaster Barrage R | | 1.00 | 1.50 |
| 4 | Capture the Falcon R | | 1.00 | 1.50 |
| 5 | Contingency Plan R | | 1.00 | 1.50 |
| 6 | Dannik Jerriko (A) R | | 1.00 | 1.50 |
| 7 | Darth Vader (A) R | | 2.00 | 3.00 |
| 8 | Desperate Confrontation R | | 1.25 | 2.00 |
| 9 | Destroy Alderaan R | | 1.00 | 1.50 |
| 10 | Dianoga (A) R | | 1.00 | 1.50 |
| 11 | Disturbance in the Force R | | 1.00 | 1.50 |
| 12 | It's Not Over Yet R | | 1.00 | 1.50 |
| 13 | EG-6 Power Droid R | | 1.00 | 1.50 |
| 14 | Elite Stormtrooper Squad R | | 1.00 | 1.50 |
| 15 | Figrin D'an (A) R | | 1.25 | 2.00 |
| 16 | Greedo (A) R | | 1.00 | 1.50 |
| 17 | Hold 'Em Off R | | 1.00 | 1.50 |
| 18 | Imperial Blockade R | | 1.00 | 1.50 |
| 19 | Imperial Navy Helmsman R | | 1.00 | 1.50 |
| 20 | Imperial Sentry Droid R | | 1.00 | 1.50 |
| 21 | IT-0 Interrogator Droid R | | 1.25 | 2.00 |
| 22 | Jawa Leader R | | 1.00 | 1.50 |
| 23 | Krayt Dragon R | | 1.00 | 1.50 |
| 24 | Leia's Kiss R | | 1.00 | 1.50 |
| 25 | Luke Skywalker (B) R | | 1.00 | 1.50 |
| 26 | Luke Skywalker (A) R | | 1.00 | 1.50 |
| 27 | Luke's Speeder (A) R | | 1.00 | 1.50 |
| 28 | Luke's X-Wing (A) R | | 1.00 | 1.50 |
| 29 | Momaw Nadon (A) R | | 1.50 | 2.50 |
| 30 | Most Desperate Hour R | | 1.00 | 1.50 |
| 31 | No Escape R | | 1.00 | 1.50 |
| 32 | Obi-Wan Kenobi (E) R | | 1.00 | 1.50 |

| | | |
|---|---|---|
| 33 Obi-Wan's Prowess R | 1.00 | 1.50 |
| 34 Obi-Wan's Task R | 1.00 | 1.50 |
| 35 Our Only Hope R | 1.00 | 1.50 |
| 36 Owen Lars (A) R | 1.00 | 1.50 |
| 37 Plan of Attack R | 1.00 | 1.50 |
| 38 Princess Leia (A) R | 1.00 | 1.50 |
| 39 Protection of the Master R | 1.00 | 1.50 |
| 40 R5-D4 (A) R | 1.00 | 1.50 |
| 41 Rebel Crew Chief R | 1.00 | 1.50 |
| 42 Rebel Lieutenant R | 1.00 | 1.50 |
| 43 Regroup on Yavin R | 1.00 | 1.50 |
| 44 Sandtrooper R | 1.00 | 1.50 |
| 45 Starfighter's End R | 1.00 | 1.50 |
| 46 Stormtrooper TK-421 R | 1.00 | 1.50 |
| 47 Strategy Session R | 1.00 | 1.50 |
| 48 Strike Me Down R | 1.00 | 1.50 |
| 49 Surprise Attack R | 1.00 | 1.50 |
| 50 Tantive IV (A) R | 1.00 | 1.50 |
| 51 Tarkin's Stench R | 1.00 | 1.50 |
| 52 TIE Fighter Elite Pilot U | .30 | .50 |
| 53 Tiree (A) R | 1.00 | 1.50 |
| 54 Tractor Beam R | 1.00 | 1.50 |
| 55 URoRRuR'R'R (A) R | 1.00 | 1.50 |
| 56 Imperial Manipulation R | 1.00 | 1.50 |
| 57 Vader's Leadership R | 1.00 | 1.50 |
| 58 Vader's TIE Fighter (A) R | 1.00 | 1.50 |
| 59 Wedge Antilles (A) R | 1.00 | 1.50 |
| 60 Yavin 4 Hangar Base R | 1.00 | 1.50 |
| 61 Astromech Assistance U | .30 | .50 |
| 62 Benefits of Training U | .30 | .50 |
| 63 Biggs Darklighter (A) U | .30 | .50 |
| 64 C-3PO (C) U | .30 | .50 |
| 65 Commander Praji (A) U | .30 | .50 |
| 66 Tatooine Sandcrawler U | .30 | .50 |
| 67 Darth Vader (B) U | .30 | .50 |
| 68 Death Star Hangar Bay U | .30 | .50 |
| 69 Death Star Plans U | .30 | .50 |
| 70 Death Star Scanning Technician U | .30 | .50 |
| 71 Death Star Superlaser Gunner U | .30 | .50 |
| 72 Death Star Turbolaser Gunner U | .30 | .50 |
| 73 Demonstration of Power U | .30 | .50 |
| 74 Devastator (A) U | .30 | .50 |
| 75 Dissolve the Senate U | .30 | .50 |
| 76 Error in Judgment U | .30 | .50 |
| 77 Fate of the Dragon U | .30 | .50 |
| 78 General Dodonna (A) U | .30 | .50 |
| 79 General Tagge (A) U | .30 | .50 |
| 80 Han's Courage U | .30 | .50 |
| 81 Imperial Control Station U | .30 | .50 |
| 82 Imperial Navy Lieutenant U | .30 | .50 |
| 83 Insignificant Power U | .30 | .50 |
| 84 Into the Garbage Chute C | .15 | .25 |
| 85 Jawa U | .30 | .50 |
| 86 Jawa Collection Team U | .30 | .50 |
| 87 Jedi Extinction U | .30 | .50 |
| 88 Jon Dutch Vander (A) U | .30 | .50 |
| 89 Learning the Force U | .30 | .50 |
| 90 Lieutenant Tanbris (A) U | .30 | .50 |
| 91 LIN Demolitionmech U | .30 | .50 |
| 92 Luke Skywalker (C) U | .30 | .50 |
| 93 Luke's Warning U | .30 | .50 |

| | | |
|---|---|---|
| 94 Mounted Stormtrooper U | .30 | .50 |
| 95 Mouse Droid U | .30 | .50 |
| 96 Obi-Wan Kenobi (F) U | .30 | .50 |
| 97 Oil Bath U | .30 | .50 |
| 98 Princess Leia (B) U | .30 | .50 |
| 99 R2-D2 (C) U | .30 | .50 |
| 100 Rebel Blockade Runner U | .30 | .50 |
| 101 Rebel Control Officer U | .30 | .50 |
| 102 Rebel Control Post U | .30 | .50 |
| 103 Rebel Marine U | .30 | .50 |
| 104 Rebel Surrender U | .30 | .50 |
| 105 Rebel Trooper U | .30 | .50 |
| 106 Remote Seeker Droid U | .30 | .50 |
| 107 Press the Advantage U | .30 | .50 |
| 108 Stabilize Deflectors U | .30 | .50 |
| 109 Star Destroyer Commander U | .30 | .50 |
| 110 Stormtrooper Charge U | .30 | .50 |
| 111 Stormtrooper DV-692 U | .30 | .50 |
| 112 Stormtrooper Squad Leader U | .30 | .50 |
| 113 Stormtrooper TK-119 U | .30 | .50 |
| 114 Support in the Senate U | .30 | .50 |
| 115 Disrupt the Power System U | .30 | .50 |
| 116 Tatooine Speeder U | .30 | .50 |
| 117 Tusken Sharpshooter U | .30 | .50 |
| 118 Vader's Interference U | .30 | .50 |
| 119 Vader's TIE Fighter (B) U | 1.00 | 1.50 |
| 120 Wuher (A) U | .30 | .50 |
| 121 Air Cover C | .15 | .25 |
| 122 Precise Blast C | .15 | .25 |
| 123 Stay Sharp C | .15 | .25 |
| 124 Carrack Cruiser C | .15 | .25 |
| 125 Darth Vader (C) C | .15 | .25 |
| 126 Death Star Cannon Tower C | .15 | .25 |
| 127 Death Star Guard Squad C | .15 | .25 |
| 128 Domesticated Bantha C | .15 | .25 |
| 129 Flare-S Swoop C | .15 | .25 |
| 130 Ground Support C | .15 | .25 |
| 131 Imperial Detention Block C | .15 | .25 |
| 132 Imperial Star Destroyer C | .15 | .25 |
| 133 Incom T-16 Skyhopper C | .15 | .25 |
| 134 Into Hiding C | .15 | .25 |
| 135 Jawa Squad C | .15 | .25 |
| 136 Jawa Supply Trip C | .15 | .25 |
| 137 Jump to Lightspeed C | .15 | .25 |
| 138 Luke Skywalker (D) C | .15 | .25 |
| 139 Luke's Repairs C | .15 | .25 |
| 140 Moisture Farm C | .15 | .25 |
| 141 Planetary Defense Turret C | .15 | .25 |
| 142 Nowhere to Run C | .15 | .25 |
| 143 Obi-Wan Kenobi (G) C | .15 | .25 |
| 144 Jedi Intervention C | .15 | .25 |
| 145 Obi-Wan's Plan C | .15 | .25 |
| 146 Penetrate the Shields C | .15 | .25 |
| 147 Preemptive Shot C | .15 | .25 |
| 148 Princess Leia (C) C | .15 | .25 |
| 149 Rebel Fighter Wing C | .15 | .25 |
| 150 Rebel Honor Company C | .15 | .25 |
| 151 Rebel Marine Squad C | .15 | .25 |
| 152 Rebel Pilot C | .15 | .25 |
| 153 Rebel Squad C | .15 | .25 |

| | | |
|---|---|---|
| 154 Rescue C | .15 | .25 |
| 155 Slipping Through C | .15 | .25 |
| 156 SoruSuub V-35 Courier C | .15 | .25 |
| 157 Synchronized Assault C | .15 | .25 |
| 158 Stormtrooper Assault Team C | .15 | .25 |
| 159 Stormtrooper DV-523 C | .15 | .25 |
| 160 Stormtrooper Patrol C | .15 | .25 |
| 161 Stormtrooper Squad C | .15 | .25 |
| 162 TIE Fighter DS-3-12 C | .15 | .25 |
| 163 TIE Fighter DS-73-3 C | .15 | .25 |
| 164 TIE Fighter DS-55-6 C | .15 | .25 |
| 165 TIE Fighter DS-61-9 C | .15 | .25 |
| 166 TIE Fighter Pilot C | .15 | .25 |
| 167 TIE Fighter Squad C | .15 | .25 |
| 168 Tusken Squad C | .15 | .25 |
| 169 Vader's Grip U | .15 | .25 |
| 170 Victory-Class Star Destroyer C | .15 | .25 |
| 171 Well-Aimed Shot C | .15 | .25 |
| 172 X-wing Red One C | .15 | .25 |
| 173 X-wing Red Three C | .15 | .25 |
| 174 X-wing Red Two C | .15 | .25 |
| 175 X-wing Attack Formation C | .15 | .25 |
| 176 Y-wing Gold One C | .15 | .25 |
| 177 Y-wing Gold Squadron C | .15 | .25 |
| 178 YT-1300 Transport C | .15 | .25 |
| 179 YV-664 Light Freighter C | .15 | .25 |
| 180 Z-95 Headhunter C | .15 | .25 |

## 2002 Star Wars Sith Rising

| | | |
|---|---|---|
| COMPLETE SET (90) | 15.00 | 40.00 |
| BOOSTER BOX (36 PACKS) | 25.00 | 50.00 |
| BOOSTER PACK (11 CARDS) | 1.00 | 2.00 |
| *FOIL: .75X TO 2X BASIC CARDS | | |
| RELEASED IN JULY 2002 | | |
| 1 Aayla Secura (A) R | 1.00 | 1.50 |
| 2 Anakin Skywalker (E) R | 1.00 | 1.50 |
| 3 Aurra Sing (A) R | 1.00 | 1.50 |
| 4 Chancellor Palpatine (B) R | 1.00 | 1.50 |
| 5 Clone Captain R | 1.00 | 1.50 |
| 6 Clone Facility R | 1.00 | 1.50 |
| 7 Darth Maul (A) R | 1.00 | 1.50 |
| 8 Darth Maul (C) R | 1.00 | 1.50 |
| 9 Darth Sidious (B) R | 1.00 | 1.50 |

| | | | |
|---|---|---|---|
| 10 Darth Tyranus (D) R | 1.00 | 1.50 | |
| 11 Geonosian Picadors R | 1.00 | 1.50 | |
| 12 Impossible Victory R | 1.00 | 1.50 | |
| 13 Jango Fett (E) R | 1.00 | 1.50 | |
| 14 Jedi Bravery R | 1.00 | 1.50 | |
| 15 Jedi Starfighter Wing R | 1.00 | 1.50 | |
| 16 Jocasta Nu (A) R | 1.00 | 1.50 | |
| 17 Mace Windu (A) R | 1.00 | 1.50 | |
| 18 Mace Windu (C) R | 1.00 | 1.50 | |
| 19 Massiff R | 1.00 | 1.50 | |
| 20 Nute Gunray (B) R | 1.00 | 1.50 | |
| 21 Republic Drop Ship R | 1.00 | 1.50 | |
| 22 Sio Bibble (A) R | 1.00 | 1.50 | |
| 23 Sith Infiltrator (A) R | 1.00 | 1.50 | |
| 24 Slave I (B) R | 1.00 | 1.50 | |
| 25 Super Battle Droid 5TE R | 1.00 | 1.50 | |
| 26 Trade Federation Control Core R | 1.00 | 1.50 | |
| 27 Tusken Camp R | 1.00 | 1.50 | |
| 28 Twilight of the Republic R | 1.00 | 1.50 | |
| 29 Unfriendly Fire R | 1.00 | 1.50 | |
| 30 Yoda (C) R | 1.00 | 1.50 | |
| 31 Aiwha Rider U | .30 | .50 | |
| 32 C-3PO (B) U | .30 | .50 | |
| 33 Careful Targeting U | .30 | .50 | |
| 34 Clever Escape U | .30 | .50 | |
| 35 Clone Trooper 6/298 U | .30 | .50 | |
| 36 Darth Maul (B) U | .30 | .50 | |
| 37 Darth Tyranus (E) U | .30 | .50 | |
| 38 Destroyer Droid, W Series U | .30 | .50 | |
| 39 Female Tusken Raider U | .30 | .50 | |
| 40 Fog of War U | .30 | .50 | |
| 41 Geonosian Scout U | .30 | .50 | |
| 42 Hailfire Droid U | .30 | .50 | |
| 43 Homing Spider Droid U | .30 | .50 | |
| 44 Infantry Battle Droid U | .30 | .50 | |
| 45 Jedi Heroes U | .30 | .50 | |
| 46 Jedi Starfighter Scout U | .30 | .50 | |
| 47 Mace Windu (B) U | .30 | .50 | |
| 48 Moment of Truth U | .30 | .50 | |
| 49 Obi_Wan Kenobi (D) U | .30 | .50 | |
| 50 Out of His Misery U | .30 | .50 | |
| 51 PadmÈ Amidala (E) U | .30 | .50 | |
| 52 Passel Argente (A) U | .30 | .50 | |
| 53 Price of Failure U | .30 | .50 | |
| 54 R2-D2 (B) U | .30 | .50 | |
| 55 Recognition of Valor U | .30 | .50 | |
| 56 Sun Fac (A) U | .30 | .50 | |
| 57 Techno Union Warship U | .30 | .50 | |
| 58 Trade Federation Offensive U | .30 | .50 | |
| 59 Tusken Raider U | .30 | .50 | |
| 60 Visit the Lake Retreat U | .30 | .50 | |
| 61 Acclamator-Class Assault Ship C | .15 | .25 | |
| 62 Aggressive Negotiations C | .15 | .25 | |
| 63 Anakin Skywalker (F) C | .15 | .25 | |
| 64 AT-TE Troop Transport C | .15 | .25 | |
| 65 Battle Droid Assault Squad C | .15 | .25 | |
| 66 Brutal Assault C | .15 | .25 | |
| 67 Clone Trooper Legion C | .15 | .25 | |
| 68 Commerce Guild Cruiser C | .15 | .25 | |
| 69 Commerce Guild Spider Droid C | .15 | .25 | |
| 70 Concentrated Fire C | .15 | .25 | |

| | | |
|---|---|---|
| 71 Corsucant Speeder C | .15 | .25 |
| 72 Darth Maul (D) C | .15 | .25 |
| 73 Diplomatic Cruiser C | .15 | .25 |
| 74 Droid Starfighter DFS-1VR C | .15 | .25 |
| 75 Geonosian Artillery Battery C | .15 | .25 |
| 76 Geonosian Defense Fighter C | .15 | .25 |
| 77 Maul's Strategy C | .15 | .25 |
| 78 Mobile Assault Cannon C | .15 | .25 |
| 79 Naboo Starfighter Wing C | .15 | .25 |
| 80 Nubian Yacht C | .15 | .25 |
| 81 Padawan and Senator C | .15 | .25 |
| 82 Reassemble C-3PO C | .15 | .25 |
| 83 Republic LAAT/i Gunship C | .15 | .25 |
| 84 Retreat Underground R | .15 | .25 |
| 85 Run the Gauntlet C | .15 | .25 |
| 86 Senatorial Cruiser C | .15 | .25 |
| 87 Shoot Her or Something C | .15 | .25 |
| 88 Super Battle Droid Squad C | .15 | .25 |
| 89 Suppressing Fire C | .15 | .25 |
| 90 Trade Federation Warship C | .15 | .25 |

### 2003 Star Wars Battle of Yavin

| | | |
|---|---|---|
| COMPLETE SET (105) | 60.00 | 120.00 |
| BOOSTER BOX (36 PACKS) | 30.00 | 50.00 |
| BOOSTER PACK (11 CARDS) | 2.50 | 5.00 |

*FOIL: .75X TO 2X BASIC CARDS
RELEASED IN MARCH 2003

| | | |
|---|---|---|
| 1 Artoo's Repairs R | 3.00 | 5.00 |
| 2 Blow This Thing R | 2.50 | 4.00 |
| 3 Celebrate the Victory R | 1.25 | 2.00 |
| 4 Chariot Light Assault Vehicle R | 1.25 | 2.00 |
| 5 Chewbacca (B) R | 6.00 | 10.00 |
| 6 Chewbacca (A) R | 6.00 | 10.00 |
| 7 Chief Bast (A) R | 3.00 | 5.00 |
| 8 Colonel Wullf Yularen (A) R | 3.00 | 5.00 |
| 9 Darth Vader (D) R | 6.00 | 10.00 |
| 10 Death Star (A) R | 5.00 | 8.00 |
| 11 Death Star (C) R | 5.00 | 8.00 |
| 12 Garven Dreis (A) R | 2.00 | 3.00 |
| 13 Grand Moff Tarkin (A) R | 5.00 | 8.00 |
| 14 Han Solo (B) R | 8.00 | 12.00 |
| 15 Han Solo (A) R | 6.00 | 10.00 |
| 16 Hero's Potential R | .30 | .50 |

| | | |
|---|---|---|
| 17 Jek Porkins (A) R | 1.00 | 1.50 |
| 18 Lieutenant Shann Childsen (A) R | 2.00 | 3.00 |
| 19 Luke Skywalker (E) R | 6.00 | 10.00 |
| 20 Luke's Skyhopper (A) R | .30 | .50 |
| 21 Luke's X-wing (B) R | 3.00 | 5.00 |
| 22 Millennium Falcon (A) R | 3.00 | 5.00 |
| 23 Millennium Falcon (B) R | 3.00 | 5.00 |
| 24 Millennium Falcon (C) R | 3.00 | 5.00 |
| 25 Obi-Wan Kenobi (H) R | 6.00 | 10.00 |
| 26 Obi-Wan's Guidance R | 1.25 | 2.00 |
| 27 Princess Leia (D) R | 2.00 | 3.00 |
| 28 R2-X2 (A) R | 2.00 | 3.00 |
| 29 R2-Q5 (A) R | 2.00 | 3.00 |
| 30 Rebel Ground Crew Chief R | 1.25 | 2.00 |
| 31 Second Wave R | 2.00 | 3.00 |
| 32 Stormtrooper Commander R | 6.00 | 10.00 |
| 33 Vader's Fury R | 3.00 | 5.00 |
| 34 X-wing Squadron R | 3.00 | 5.00 |
| 35 Your Powers Are Weak R | 2.00 | 3.00 |
| 36 Alien Rage U | .60 | 1.00 |
| 37 C-3PO (D) U | .60 | 1.00 |
| 38 Chewbacca (C) U | .60 | 1.00 |
| 39 Commander Willard (A) U | .60 | 1.00 |
| 40 Countermeasures U | .60 | 1.00 |
| 41 Darth Vader (E) U | .60 | 1.00 |
| 42 Death Star (B) U | .60 | 1.00 |
| 43 Death Star Trooper U | .60 | 1.00 |
| 44 Deflectors Activated U | .60 | 1.00 |
| 45 Grand Moff Tarkin (B) U | .60 | 1.00 |
| 46 Grand Moff Tarkin (C) U | .60 | 1.00 |
| 47 Han Solo (C) U | .60 | 1.00 |
| 48 Heavy Fire Zone U | .60 | 1.00 |
| 49 Imperial Dewback U | .60 | 1.00 |
| 50 Interrogation Droid U | .60 | 1.00 |
| 51 Jawa Crawler U | .60 | 1.00 |
| 52 Jawa Scavenger U | .60 | 1.00 |
| 53 Labria (A) U | .60 | 1.00 |
| 54 Let the Wookiee Win U | .60 | 1.00 |
| 55 Luke Skywalker (F) U | .60 | 1.00 |
| 56 Luke's Speeder (B) U | .60 | 1.00 |
| 57 Mobile Command Base U | .60 | 1.00 |
| 58 Obi-Wan's Handiwork U | .60 | 1.00 |
| 59 Princess Leia (E) U | .60 | 1.00 |
| 60 R2-D2 (D) U | .60 | 1.00 |
| 61 Rebel Armored Freerunner U | .60 | 1.00 |
| 62 Refit on Yavin U | .60 | 1.00 |
| 63 Sabers Locked U | .60 | 1.00 |
| 64 Stormtrooper KE-829 U | .60 | 1.00 |
| 65 Tatooine Hangar U | .60 | 1.00 |
| 66 Tusken Raider Squad U | .60 | 1.00 |
| 67 Tusken War Party U | .60 | 1.00 |
| 68 Untamed Ronto U | .60 | 1.00 |
| 69 WED Treadwell U | .60 | 1.00 |
| 70 Womp Rat U | .60 | 1.00 |
| 71 Accelerate C | .30 | .50 |
| 72 Blast It! C | .30 | .50 |
| 73 Chewbacca (D) C | .30 | .50 |
| 74 Corellian Corvette C | .30 | .50 |
| 75 Creature Attack C | .30 | .50 |
| 76 Luke Skywalker (G) C | .30 | .50 |

| | | | |
|---|---|---|---|
| 77 Darth Vader (F) C | .30 | .50 |
| 78 Death Star Turbolaser Tower C | .30 | .50 |
| 79 Dewback Patrol C | .30 | .50 |
| 80 Escape Pod C | .30 | .50 |
| 81 Greedo's Marksmanship C | .30 | .50 |
| 82 Han Solo (D) C | .30 | .50 |
| 83 Han's Evasion C | .30 | .50 |
| 84 Imperial Landing Craft C | .30 | .50 |
| 85 Jawa Salvage Team C | .30 | .50 |
| 86 Juggernaut U | .30 | .50 |
| 87 Star Destroyer C | .30 | .50 |
| 88 Malfunction C | .30 | .50 |
| 89 Outrun C | .30 | .50 |
| 90 Pilot's Speed C | .30 | .50 |
| 91 Rebel Defense Team C | .30 | .50 |
| 92 Sandtrooper Squad C | .30 | .50 |
| 93 Stormtrooper Assault C | .30 | .50 |
| 94 Stormtrooper TK-875 C | .30 | .50 |
| 95 Stormtrooper Platoon C | .30 | .50 |
| 96 Stormtrooper Regiment C | .30 | .50 |
| 97 TIE Defense Squadron C | .30 | .50 |
| 98 TIE Fighter DS-73-5 C | .30 | .50 |
| 99 TIE Fighter DS-29-4 C | .30 | .50 |
| 100 TIE Fighter DS-55-2 C | .30 | .50 |
| 101 Trust Your Feelings C | .30 | .50 |
| 102 Visit to Mos Eisley C | .30 | .50 |
| 103 X-wing Red Squadron C | .30 | .50 |
| 104 X-wing Red Ten C | .30 | .50 |
| 105 Y-wing Gold Two C | .30 | .50 |

### 2003 Star Wars The Empire Strikes Back

| | | |
|---|---|---|
| COMPLETE SET (210) | 100.00 | 200.00 |
| BOOSTER BOX (36 PACKS) | 400.00 | 550.00 |
| BOOSTER PACK (11 CARDS) | 1.25 | 2.50 |
| *FOIL: .75X TO 2X BASIC CARDS | | |
| RELEASED IN NOVEMBER 2003 | | |
| 1 2-1B Medical Droid (A) R | 2.00 | 3.00 |
| 2 Admiral Firmus Piett (B) R | 2.00 | 3.00 |
| 3 AT-AT Assault Group R | 2.00 | 3.00 |
| 4 Avenger (A) R | 6.00 | 10.00 |
| 5 Blizzard Force Snowtrooper R | 2.00 | 3.00 |
| 6 Blizzard One (A) R | 2.00 | 3.00 |
| 7 C-3PO (E) R | 2.00 | 3.00 |
| 8 Captain Lorth Needa (A) R | 2.00 | 3.00 |
| 9 Carbon Freezing Chamber R | 8.00 | 12.00 |
| 10 Chewbacca (E) U | 2.00 | 3.00 |

| | | |
|---|---|---|
| 11 Chewbacca (G) R | 2.00 | 3.00 |
| 12 Dack Ralter (A) R | 2.00 | 3.00 |
| 13 Dangerous Gamble R | 2.00 | 3.00 |
| 14 Dark Cave R | 2.00 | 3.00 |
| 15 Darth Vader (H) R | 3.00 | 5.00 |
| 16 Darth Vader (I) R | 5.00 | 8.00 |
| 17 Decoy Tactics R | 2.00 | 3.00 |
| 18 Desperate Times R | 2.00 | 3.00 |
| 19 Echo Base R | 5.00 | 8.00 |
| 20 Emperor's Bidding R | 2.00 | 3.00 |
| 21 Emperor's Prize R | 2.00 | 3.00 |
| 22 Executor (A) R | 2.00 | 3.00 |
| 23 Failed for the Last Time R | 2.00 | 3.00 |
| 24 Future Sight R | 2.00 | 3.00 |
| 25 FX-7 Medical Droid (A) R | 2.00 | 3.00 |
| 26 General Carlist Rieekan (A) R | 2.00 | 3.00 |
| 27 General Maximilian Veers (B) R | 2.00 | 3.00 |
| 28 Go for the Legs R | 2.00 | 3.00 |
| 29 Han Solo (G) R | 3.00 | 5.00 |
| 30 Jedi Test R | 2.00 | 3.00 |
| 31 Jedi's Failure R | 2.00 | 3.00 |
| 32 K-3PO (A) R | 2.00 | 3.00 |
| 33 Kiss From Your Sister R | 2.00 | 3.00 |
| 34 Lando Calrissian (A) R | 4.00 | 6.00 |
| 35 Lando Calrissian (D) R | 4.00 | 6.00 |
| 36 Lieutenant Wes Janson (A) R | 3.00 | 5.00 |
| 37 Lobot (A) R | 2.00 | 3.00 |
| 38 Luke Skywalker (J) R | 10.00 | 15.00 |
| 39 Luke Skywalker (K) R | 8.00 | 12.00 |
| 40 Luke's Snowspeeder (A) R | 6.00 | 10.00 |
| 41 Luke's Wrath R | 2.00 | 3.00 |
| 42 Luke's X-wing (c) R | 3.00 | 5.00 |
| 43 Major Bren Derlin (A) R | 2.00 | 3.00 |
| 44 Mara Jade (A) R | 2.00 | 3.00 |
| 45 Millennium Falcon (E) R | 3.00 | 5.00 |
| 46 Millennium Falcon (F) R | 3.00 | 5.00 |
| 47 Millennium Falcon (G) R | 3.00 | 5.00 |
| 48 Obi-Wan's Spirit (A) R | 2.00 | 3.00 |
| 49 Occupation R | 2.00 | 3.00 |
| 50 Parting of Heroes R | 2.00 | 3.00 |
| 51 Planetary Ion Cannon R | 2.00 | 3.00 |
| 52 Princess Leia (G) R | 3.00 | 5.00 |
| 53 Quest for Truth R | 2.00 | 3.00 |
| 54 R2-D2 (G) R | 2.00 | 3.00 |
| 55 R2-D2's Heroism R | 2.00 | 3.00 |
| 56 Rally the Defenders R | 2.00 | 3.00 |
| 57 Sacrifice R | 2.00 | 3.00 |
| 58 Search for the Rebels R | 2.00 | 3.00 |
| 59 Stormtrooper Swarm R | 2.00 | 3.00 |
| 60 Streets of Cloud City R | 2.00 | 3.00 |
| 61 Toryn Farr (A) R | 2.00 | 3.00 |
| 62 Vader's Imperial Shuttle (A) R | 3.00 | 5.00 |
| 63 Wampa Cave R | 2.00 | 3.00 |
| 64 Wedge Antilles (B) R | 6.00 | 10.00 |
| 65 Wedge's Snowspeeder (A) R | 6.00 | 10.00 |
| 66 Yoda (F) R | 2.00 | 3.00 |
| 67 Yoda (G) R | 2.00 | 3.00 |
| 68 Yoda (H) R | 2.00 | 3.00 |
| 69 Yoda's Training R | 2.00 | 3.00 |
| 70 Zev Senesca (A) R | 2.00 | 3.00 |
| 71 3,720 to 1 U | .60 | 1.00 |
| 72 Admiral Firmus Piett (A) U | .60 | 1.00 |
| 73 Admiral Kendal Ozzel (A) U | .60 | 1.00 |
| 74 Outmaneuver Them U | .60 | 1.00 |

| | | |
|---|---|---|
| 75 All Terrain Troop Transport U | .60 | 1.00 |
| 76 Anti-Infantry Laser Battery U | .60 | 1.00 |
| 77 Asteroid Field U | .60 | 1.00 |
| 78 AT-AT Driver U | .60 | 1.00 |
| 79 Blizzard Force AT-ST U | .60 | 1.00 |
| 80 Battle the Wampa U | .60 | 1.00 |
| 81 Cloud City Penthouse U | .60 | 1.00 |
| 82 Cloud City Prison U | .60 | 1.00 |
| 83 Bespin Twin-Pod Cloud Car U | .60 | 1.00 |
| 84 Blockade U | .60 | 1.00 |
| 85 Bright Hope (A) U | .60 | 1.00 |
| 86 C-3PO (F) U | .60 | 1.00 |
| 87 Change in Destiny U | .60 | 1.00 |
| 88 Chewbacca (F) R | .60 | 1.00 |
| 89 Darth Vader (G) R | .60 | 1.00 |
| 90 Darth Vader (K) U | .60 | 1.00 |
| 91 Death Mark U | .60 | 1.00 |
| 92 Derek Hobbie Klivian (A) U | .60 | 1.00 |
| 93 Don't Get All Mushy U | .60 | 1.00 |
| 94 Dragonsnake U | .60 | 1.00 |
| 95 Emergency Repairs U | .60 | 1.00 |
| 96 Carbon Freeze U | .60 | 1.00 |
| 97 Executor Bridge U | .60 | 1.00 |
| 98 Executor Hangar U | .60 | 1.00 |
| 99 Quicker Easier More Seductive U | .60 | 1.00 |
| 100 General Maximilian Veers (A) U | .60 | 1.00 |
| 101 Han Enchained U | .60 | 1.00 |
| 102 Han Solo (F) U | .60 | 1.00 |
| 103 Hoth Icefields U | .60 | 1.00 |
| 104 Imperial Fleet U | .60 | 1.00 |
| 105 Imperial Misdirection U | .60 | 1.00 |
| 106 Jungles of Dagobah U | .60 | 1.00 |
| 107 Lambda-Class Shuttle U | .60 | 1.00 |
| 108 Lando Calrissian (C) U | .60 | 1.00 |
| 109 Leia's Warning U | .60 | 1.00 |
| 110 Luke Skywalker (I) U | .60 | 1.00 |
| 111 Medical Center U | .60 | 1.00 |
| 112 Millennium Falcon (D) U | .60 | 1.00 |
| 113 Mynock U | .60 | 1.00 |
| 114 Painful Reckoning U | .60 | 1.00 |
| 115 Princess Leia (H) U | .60 | 1.00 |
| 116 Probe Droid U | .60 | 1.00 |
| 117 Probot U | .60 | 1.00 |
| 118 R2-D2 (F) U | .60 | 1.00 |
| 119 Rebel Fleet U | .60 | 1.00 |
| 120 Rebel Hoth Army U | .60 | 1.00 |
| 121 Rebel Trenches U | .60 | 1.00 |
| 122 Rebel Troop Cart U | .60 | 1.00 |
| 123 Redemption (A) U | .60 | 1.00 |
| 124 See You In Hell U | .60 | 1.00 |
| 125 Self Destruct U | .60 | 1.00 |
| 126 Shield Generator U | .60 | 1.00 |
| 127 Snowspeeder Rogue Ten U | .60 | 1.00 |
| 128 Snowspeeder Squad U | .60 | 1.00 |
| 129 Snowtrooper Elite Squad U | .60 | 1.00 |
| 130 Stormtrooper Sentry U | .60 | 1.00 |
| 131 Surprise Reinforcements U | .60 | 1.00 |
| 132 TIE Bomber Pilot U | .60 | 1.00 |
| 133 TIE Bomber Squad U | .60 | 1.00 |
| 134 TIE Pursuit Pilot U | .60 | 1.00 |
| 135 Torture Room U | .60 | 1.00 |
| 136 Vader's Call U | .60 | 1.00 |
| 137 Vicious Attack U | .60 | 1.00 |
| 138 Wampa U | .60 | 1.00 |

| | | | |
|---|---|---|---|
| 139 Yoda's Hut U | .60 | 1.00 | |
| 140 725 to 1 C | .30 | .50 | |
| 141 All Terrain Armored Transport C | .30 | .50 | |
| 142 All Terrain Scout Transport C | .30 | .50 | |
| 143 Alter the Deal C | .30 | .50 | |
| 144 Antivehicle Laser Cannon C | .30 | .50 | |
| 145 Armor Plating C | .30 | .50 | |
| 146 Space Slug C | .30 | .50 | |
| 147 Blizzard Force AT-AT C | .30 | .50 | |
| 148 Precise Attack C | .30 | .50 | |
| 149 Belly of the Beast C | .30 | .50 | |
| 150 Cloud City Battleground C | .30 | .50 | |
| 151 Cloud City Dining Hall C | .30 | .50 | |
| 152 Cloud City Landing Platform C | .30 | .50 | |
| 153 Bespin System C | .30 | .50 | |
| 154 Blizzard C | .30 | .50 | |
| 155 Bogwing C | .30 | .50 | |
| 156 Close the Shield Doors C | .30 | .50 | |
| 157 Darth Vader (J) C | .30 | .50 | |
| 158 Vader's Vengeance C | .30 | .50 | |
| 159 Dagobah System C | .30 | .50 | |
| 160 Explore the Swamps C | .30 | .50 | |
| 161 Float Away C | .30 | .50 | |
| 162 Force Throw C | .30 | .50 | |
| 163 Gallofree Medium Transport C | .30 | .50 | |
| 164 Ground Assault C | .30 | .50 | |
| 165 Han Solo (E) C | .30 | .50 | |
| 166 Han's Attack U | .30 | .50 | |
| 167 Han's Promise C | .30 | .50 | |
| 168 Hanging Around C | .30 | .50 | |
| 169 Hope of Another C | .30 | .50 | |
| 170 Hoth Battle Plains C | .30 | .50 | |
| 171 Hoth System C | .30 | .50 | |
| 172 Imperial II-Class Star Destroyer C | .30 | .50 | |
| 173 Jedi Master's Meditation C | .30 | .50 | |
| 174 Jedi Trap C | .30 | .50 | |
| 175 Kuat Lancer-Class Frigate C | .30 | .50 | |
| 176 Kuat Nebulon-B Frigate C | .30 | .50 | |
| 177 Lando Calrissian (B) C | .30 | .50 | |
| 178 Lando's Repairs C | .30 | .50 | |
| 179 Leap into the Chasm C | .30 | .50 | |
| 180 Luke Skywalker (H) C | .30 | .50 | |
| 181 Meditation Chamber C | .30 | .50 | |
| 182 Navy Trooper C | .30 | .50 | |
| 183 Princess Leia (F) C | .30 | .50 | |
| 184 Probe the Galaxy C | .30 | .50 | |
| 185 Rebel Command Center C | .30 | .50 | |
| 186 Rebel Escape Squad C | .30 | .50 | |
| 187 Rebel Hangar C | .30 | .50 | |
| 188 Rebel Trench Defenders C | .30 | .50 | |
| 189 Rebel Assault Frigate C | .30 | .50 | |
| 190 Dreadnaught Heavy Cruiser C | .30 | .50 | |
| 191 Snowspeeder Rogue Two C | .30 | .50 | |
| 192 Snowstorm C | .30 | .50 | |
| 193 Snowtrooper Heavy Weapons Team C | .30 | .50 | |
| 194 Snowtrooper Squad C | .30 | .50 | |
| 195 Snowtrooper Guard C | .30 | .50 | |
| 196 Imperial II Star Destroyer C | .30 | .50 | |
| 197 Strange Lodgings C | .30 | .50 | |
| 198 Swamps of Dagobah C | .30 | .50 | |
| 199 Tauntaun C | .30 | .50 | |
| 200 Tauntaun Mount C | .30 | .50 | |
| 201 TIE Bomber EX-1-2 C | .30 | .50 | |
| 202 TIE Bomber EX-1-8 C | .30 | .50 | |

| | | | |
|---|---|---|---|
| 203 TIE Fighter EX-4-9 C | .30 | .50 | |
| 204 TIE Fighter OS-72-8 C | .30 | .50 | |
| 205 TIE Pursuit Squad C | .30 | .50 | |
| 206 Trust Her Instincts C | .30 | .50 | |
| 207 Visions of the Future C | .30 | .50 | |
| 208 Well-Earned Meal C | .30 | .50 | |
| 209 X-wing Rogue Seven C | .30 | .50 | |
| 210 Y-wing Gold Six C | .30 | .50 | |

## 2003 Star Wars Jedi Guardians

| | | |
|---|---|---|
| COMPLETE SET (105) | 60.00 | 120.00 |
| BOOSTER BOX (36 PACKS) | 120.00 | 250.00 |
| BOOSTER PACK (11 CARDS) | 5.00 | 7.00 |

*FOIL: .75X TO 2X BASIC CARDS

RELEASED IN JULY 2003

| | | |
|---|---|---|
| 1 Adi Gallia (A) R | 2.00 | 3.00 |
| 2 Anakin Skywalker (H) R | 2.00 | 3.00 |
| 3 Aurra Sing (B) R | 2.00 | 3.00 |
| 4 Boba Fett (B) R | 2.00 | 3.00 |
| 5 Coup de Grace U | 2.00 | 3.00 |
| 6 Dark Dreams R | 2.00 | 3.00 |
| 7 Darth Maul (E) R | 5.00 | 8.00 |
| 8 Darth Sidious (C) R | 2.00 | 3.00 |
| 9 Darth Tyranus (F) R | 3.00 | 5.00 |
| 10 Eeth Koth (A) R | 2.00 | 3.00 |
| 11 Even Piell (A) R | 2.00 | 3.00 |
| 12 Furious Charge C | 2.00 | 3.00 |
| 13 Gather the Council R | 2.00 | 3.00 |
| 14 Guidance of the Chancellor C | 2.00 | 3.00 |
| 15 Homing Missile R | 2.00 | 3.00 |
| 16 Jango Fett (G) R | 2.00 | 3.00 |
| 17 Jedi Council Quorum R | 2.00 | 3.00 |
| 18 Jedi Youngling R | 2.00 | 3.00 |
| 19 Ki-Adi-Mundi (A) R | 2.00 | 3.00 |
| 20 Kouhun R | 2.00 | 3.00 |
| 21 Mace Windu (D) R | 4.00 | 6.00 |
| 22 Trade Federation Battle Freighter C | 2.00 | 3.00 |
| 23 Obi-Wan Kenobi (I) R | 2.00 | 3.00 |
| 24 Obi-Wan's Starfighter (B) R | 3.00 | 5.00 |
| 25 Oppo Rancisis (A) R | 2.00 | 3.00 |
| 26 Padme Amidala (F) R | 3.00 | 5.00 |
| 27 Plo Koon (B) R | 2.00 | 3.00 |
| 28 R2-D2 (E) R | 2.00 | 3.00 |

| | | |
|---|---|---|
| 29 Remember the Prophecy R | 2.00 | 3.00 |
| 30 Saesee Tiin (A) R | 3.00 | 5.00 |
| 31 Senator Tikkes (A) R | 2.00 | 3.00 |
| 32 Shaak Ti (B) R | 3.00 | 5.00 |
| 33 Shmi Skywalker (A) R | 3.00 | 5.00 |
| 34 Slave I (C) R | 2.00 | 3.00 |
| 35 Trade Federation Blockade Ship C | 2.00 | 3.00 |
| 36 Rapid Recovery R | 2.00 | 3.00 |
| 37 Tipoca Training Ground R | 2.00 | 3.00 |
| 38 Trade Federation Core Ship C | 2.00 | 3.00 |
| 39 Tyranus's Geonosis Speeder (B) C | 2.00 | 3.00 |
| 40 Unified Attack U | 2.00 | 3.00 |
| 41 Yoda (D) R | 8.00 | 12.00 |
| 42 Zam Wesell (D) R | 2.00 | 3.00 |
| 43 Zam's Airspeeder (B) R | 2.00 | 3.00 |
| 44 Battle Droid Division U | .60 | 1.00 |
| 45 Battle Protocol Droid (A) U | .60 | 1.00 |
| 46 Call for Reinforcements U | .60 | 1.00 |
| 47 Tyranus's Power C | .60 | 1.00 |
| 48 Clone Cadet U | .60 | 1.00 |
| 49 Coleman Trebor (A) U | .60 | 1.00 |
| 50 Corporate Alliance Tank Droid U | .60 | 1.00 |
| 51 Coruscant Air Bus U | .60 | 1.00 |
| 52 Depa Billaba (A) U | .60 | 1.00 |
| 53 Executioner Cart U | .60 | 1.00 |
| 54 FA-4 (A) U | .60 | 1.00 |
| 55 Jango Fett (F) U | .60 | 1.00 |
| 56 Jedi Arrogance U | .60 | 1.00 |
| 57 Jedi Training Exercise U | .60 | 1.00 |
| 58 Jedi Knight's Survival U | .60 | 1.00 |
| 59 Jedi Superiority U | .60 | 1.00 |
| 60 Lightsaber Gift U | .60 | 1.00 |
| 61 Lightsaber Loss U | .60 | 1.00 |
| 62 Neimoidian Shuttle (A) U | .60 | 1.00 |
| 63 Obi-Wan Kenobi (J) U | .60 | 1.00 |
| 64 Orray U | .60 | 1.00 |
| 65 Padme's Yacht (B) U | .60 | 1.00 |
| 66 Underworld Investigations C | .60 | 1.00 |
| 67 Protocol Battle Droid (A) U | .60 | 1.00 |
| 68 Qui-Gon Jinn (B) U | .60 | 1.00 |
| 69 Republic Communications Tower U | .60 | 1.00 |
| 70 RIC-920 U | .60 | 1.00 |
| 71 Sun-Fac (B) U | .60 | 1.00 |
| 72 Tactical leadership U | .60 | 1.00 |
| 73 Tame the Beast U | .60 | 1.00 |
| 74 Train For War U | .60 | 1.00 |
| 75 Tyranus's Return U | .60 | 1.00 |
| 76 Tyranus's Solar Sailer (B) U | .60 | 1.00 |
| 77 Yoda (E) U | .60 | 1.00 |
| 78 Zam Wesell (C) U | .60 | 1.00 |
| 79 Anakin Skywalker (I) C | .30 | .50 |
| 80 Mobile Artillery Division C | .30 | .50 |
| 81 Captured Reek C | .30 | .50 |
| 82 Clone Fire Team C | .30 | .50 |
| 83 Close Pursuit C | .30 | .50 |
| 84 Darth Tyranus (G) C | .30 | .50 |
| 85 Destroyer Droid Team U | .30 | .50 |
| 86 Diplomatic Barge C | .30 | .50 |
| 87 Droid Deactivation C | .30 | .50 |
| 88 Droid Starfighter Assault Wing C | .30 | .50 |
| 89 Trade Federation Droid Bomber C | .30 | .50 |

| | | |
|---|---|---|
| 90 Forward Command Center C | .30 | .50 |
| 91 Geonosian Fighter Escort C | .30 | .50 |
| 92 Gondola Speeder C | .30 | .50 |
| 93 Gunship Offensive C | .30 | .50 |
| 94 Jedi Starfighter Squadron C | .30 | .50 |
| 95 Obi-Wan's Maneuver C | .30 | .50 |
| 96 Plan for the Future C | .30 | .50 |
| 97 Republic Assault Transport C | .30 | .50 |
| 98 Republic Attack Gunship C | .30 | .50 |
| 99 Republic Light Assault Cruiser C | .30 | .50 |
| 100 Republic Hyperdrive Ring C | .30 | .50 |
| 101 Sabaoth Starfighter C | .30 | .50 |
| 102 Scurrier C | .30 | .50 |
| 103 Separatist Battle Droid C | .30 | .50 |
| 104 Shaak C | .30 | .50 |
| 105 Synchronized Systems C | .30 | .50 |

## 2004 Star Wars The Phantom Menace

| | | |
|---|---|---|
| COMPLETE SET (90) | 50.00 | 100.00 |
| BOOSTER BOX (36 PACKS) | 200.00 | 250.00 |
| BOOSTER PACK (11 CARDS) | 1.50 | 3.00 |
| *FOIL: .75X TO 2X BASIC CARDS | | |
| RELEASED IN JULY 2004 | | |
| 1 Ann and Tann Gella (A) R | 3.00 | 5.00 |
| 2 Aurra Sing (C) R | 2.00 | 3.00 |
| 3 Bongo Sub R | 2.00 | 3.00 |
| 4 Boss Nass (A) R | 2.00 | 3.00 |
| 5 C-9979 R | 2.00 | 3.00 |
| 6 Corridors of Power R | 2.00 | 3.00 |
| 7 Dark Woman (A) R | 3.00 | 5.00 |
| 8 Darth Maul (F) R | 3.00 | 5.00 |
| 9 Duel of the Fates R | 2.00 | 3.00 |
| 10 Fambaa Shield Beast R | 2.00 | 3.00 |
| 11 Fight on All Fronts R | 2.00 | 3.00 |
| 12 Gardulla the Hutt (A) R | 2.00 | 3.00 |
| 13 Gas Attack R | 2.00 | 3.00 |
| 14 Gungan Grand Army R | 2.50 | 4.00 |
| 15 Guardian Mantis (A) R | 2.00 | 3.00 |
| 16 In Disguise R | 2.00 | 3.00 |
| 17 Jar Jar Binks (B) R | 2.00 | 3.00 |
| 18 Jedi Temple R | 2.00 | 3.00 |
| 19 Ki-Adi-Mundi (B) R | 3.00 | 5.00 |
| 20 Marauder-Class Corvette R | 2.00 | 3.00 |
| 21 Negotiate the Peace R | 2.00 | 3.00 |
| 22 Nute Gunray (C) R | 2.00 | 3.00 |
| 23 Orn Free Taa (A) R | 2.00 | 3.00 |

| | | |
|---|---|---|
| 24 Otoh Gunga R | 2.00 | 3.00 |
| 25 Podracing Course R | 2.00 | 3.00 |
| 26 Quinlan Vos (A) R | 2.00 | 3.00 |
| 27 Sando Aqua Monster R | 2.00 | 3.00 |
| 28 Sith Infiltrator (B) R | 2.00 | 3.00 |
| 29 Walking Droid Starfighter R | 2.00 | 3.00 |
| 30 Watto's Shop R | 2.00 | 3.00 |
| 31 A'Sharad Hett (A) U | 2.00 | 3.00 |
| 32 Anakin Skywalker (J) U | 5.00 | 8.00 |
| 33 Anakin's Podracer (A) U | 3.00 | 5.00 |
| 34 Bravo Starfighter U | .60 | 1.00 |
| 35 Captain Panaka (A) U | .60 | 1.00 |
| 36 Captain Tarpals (A) U | .60 | 1.00 |
| 37 Citadel Cruiser U | .60 | 1.00 |
| 38 Colo Claw Fish U | .60 | 1.00 |
| 39 Discuss It in Committee U | .60 | 1.00 |
| 40 Durge (A) U | .60 | 1.00 |
| 41 Falumpaset U | .60 | 1.00 |
| 42 Gungan Battle Wagon U | .60 | 1.00 |
| 43 Gungan Catapult U | .60 | 1.00 |
| 44 Inferno (A) U | .60 | 1.00 |
| 45 Kaadu Scout U | .60 | 1.00 |
| 46 Let the Cube Decide U | .60 | 1.00 |
| 47 Modified YV-330 (A) U | .60 | 1.00 |
| 48 Naboo System U | .60 | 1.00 |
| 49 Qui-Gon Jinn (D) U | .60 | 1.00 |
| 50 Ric Olié (A) U | .60 | 1.00 |
| 51 Royal Cruiser U | .60 | 1.00 |
| 52 Rune Haako (A) U | .60 | 1.00 |
| 53 Sebulba (A) U | .60 | 1.00 |
| 54 Sebulba's Podracer (A) U | .60 | 1.00 |
| 55 Streets of Theed U | .60 | 1.00 |
| 56 Trade Federation Hangar U | .60 | 1.00 |
| 57 Trade Federation MTT U | .60 | 1.00 |
| 58 Vilmarh Grahrk (A) U | .60 | 1.00 |
| 59 Watto (B) U | .60 | 1.00 |
| 60 Yaddle (A) U | .60 | 1.00 |
| 61 A Bigger Fish C | .30 | .50 |
| 62 Aayla Secura (B) C | .30 | .50 |
| 63 Blockade (TPM) C | .30 | .50 |
| 64 Blockade Battleship C | .30 | .50 |
| 65 CloakShape Fighter C | .30 | .50 |
| 66 Darth Sidious (D) C | .30 | .50 |
| 67 Delta Six Jedi Starfighter C | .30 | .50 |
| 68 Eopie C | .30 | .50 |
| 69 Finis Valorum (B) C | .30 | .50 |
| 70 Flash Speeder C | .30 | .50 |
| 71 Gian Speeder C | .30 | .50 |
| 72 Gungan Kaadu Squad C | .30 | .50 |
| 73 Jedi Transport C | .30 | .50 |
| 74 Melt Your Way In C | .30 | .50 |
| 75 Mos Espa C | .30 | .50 |
| 76 Naboo Pilot C | .30 | .50 |
| 77 Obi-Wan Kenobi (K) C | .30 | .50 |
| 78 Opee Sea Killer C | .30 | .50 |
| 79 Podrace C | .30 | .50 |
| 80 Qui-Gon Jinn (C) C | .30 | .50 |
| 81 Sith Probe Droid C | .30 | .50 |
| 82 Sneak Attack C | .30 | .50 |
| 83 Swamps of Naboo C | .30 | .50 |
| 84 TC-14 (A) C | .30 | .50 |
| 85 Theed Power Generator C | .30 | .50 |
| 86 Theed Royal Palace C | .30 | .50 |
| 87 Trade Federation AAT C | .30 | .50 |

| | | |
|---|---|---|
| 88 Trade Federation STAP C | .30 | .50 |
| 89 Unconventional Maneuvers C | .30 | .50 |
| 90 Yinchorri Fighter C | .30 | .50 |

## 2004 Star Wars Return of the Jedi

| | | |
|---|---|---|
| COMPLETE SET (109) | 50.00 | 100.00 |
| BOOSTER BOX (36 PACKS) | 100.00 | 200.00 |
| BOOSTER PACK (11 CARDS) | 3.00 | 5.00 |
| *FOIL: .75X TO 2X BASIC CARDS | | |
| RELEASED IN OCTOBER 2004 | | |
| 1 Admiral Ackbar (A) R | 2.00 | 3.00 |
| 2 Anakin Skywalker (K) R | 2.00 | 3.00 |
| 3 Anakin's Spirit (A) R | 2.00 | 3.00 |
| 4 Bargain with Jabba R | 2.00 | 3.00 |
| 5 Bib Fortuna (A) R | 2.00 | 3.00 |
| 6 Chewbacca (J) R | 2.00 | 3.00 |
| 7 Darth Vader (P) R | 2.00 | 3.00 |
| 8 Death Star II (B) R | 2.00 | 3.00 |
| 9 Emperor Palpatine (E) R | 2.00 | 3.00 |
| 10 Endor Imperial Fleet R | 2.00 | 3.00 |
| 11 Endor Rebel Fleet R | 2.00 | 3.00 |
| 12 Endor Shield Generator R | 2.00 | 3.00 |
| 13 Ephant Mon (A) R | 2.00 | 3.00 |
| 14 Endor Regiment R | 2.00 | 3.00 |
| 15 Free Tatooine R | 2.00 | 3.00 |
| 16 Han Solo (K) R | 2.00 | 3.00 |
| 17 Home One (A) R | 2.00 | 3.00 |
| 18 Honor the Fallen R | 2.00 | 3.00 |
| 19 Jabba the Hutt (A) R | 2.00 | 3.00 |
| 20 Jabba's Dancers R | 2.00 | 3.00 |
| 21 Jabba's Palace R | 2.00 | 3.00 |
| 22 Jabba's Spies R | 2.00 | 3.00 |
| 23 Lando Calrissian (H) R | 2.00 | 3.00 |
| 24 Luke Skywalker (N) R | 2.00 | 3.00 |
| 25 Malakili (A) R | 2.00 | 3.00 |
| 26 Max Rebo Band (A) R | 2.00 | 3.00 |
| 27 Mixed Battlegroup R | 2.00 | 3.00 |
| 28 Mon Mothma (A) R | 2.00 | 3.00 |
| 29 Nien Nunb (A) R | 2.00 | 3.00 |
| 30 Occupied Tatooine R | 2.00 | 3.00 |
| 31 Progress Report R | 2.00 | 3.00 |
| 32 Rancor R | 2.00 | 3.00 |
| 33 Reactor Core R | 2.00 | 3.00 |
| 34 Salacious B. Crumb (A) R | 2.00 | 3.00 |
| 35 Sarlacc (A) R | 2.00 | 3.00 |
| 36 Scythe Squadron (A) R | 2.00 | 3.00 |

| | | |
|---|---|---|
| 37 Throne Room R | 2.00 | 3.00 |
| 38 Trap Door! R | 2.00 | 3.00 |
| 39 Vader's Guile R | 2.00 | 3.00 |
| 40 Yoda's Spirit (A) R | 2.00 | 3.00 |
| 41 Baited Trap U | .60 | 1.00 |
| 42 Boba Fett (H) U | .60 | 1.00 |
| 43 C-3PO (H) U | .60 | 1.00 |
| 44 Captain Lennox (A) U | .60 | 1.00 |
| 45 Chief Chirpa (A) U | .60 | 1.00 |
| 46 Darth Vader (N) U | .60 | 1.00 |
| 47 Desperate Bluff U | .60 | 1.00 |
| 48 Emperor Palpatine (D) U | .60 | 1.00 |
| 49 Ewok Village U | .60 | 1.00 |
| 50 Free Bespin U | .60 | 1.00 |
| 51 Free Endor U | .60 | 1.00 |
| 52 Han Solo (J) U | .60 | 1.00 |
| 53 Ionization Weapons U | .60 | 1.00 |
| 55 Jabba the Hutt (C) U | .60 | 1.00 |
| 56 Jabba's Sail Barge (A) U | .60 | 1.00 |
| 57 Lando Calrissian (I) U | .60 | 1.00 |
| 58 Luke Skywalker (O) U | .60 | 1.00 |
| 59 Millennium Falcon (J) U | .60 | 1.00 |
| 60 Occupied Bespin U | .60 | 1.00 |
| 61 Occupied Endor U | .60 | 1.00 |
| 62 Princess Leia (J) U | .60 | 1.00 |
| 63 R2-D2 (I) U | .60 | 1.00 |
| 64 Rancor Pit U | .60 | 1.00 |
| 65 Red Squadron X-wing U | .60 | 1.00 |
| 66 Skiff U | .60 | 1.00 |
| 67 Vader's Summons U | .60 | 1.00 |
| 68 Wicket W. Warrick (A) U | .60 | 1.00 |
| 69 Wookiee Hug U | .60 | 1.00 |
| 70 Worrt U | .60 | 1.00 |
| 71 A-wing C | .30 | .50 |
| 72 B-wing C | .30 | .50 |
| 73 Cantina Bar Mob C | .30 | .50 |
| 74 Chewbacca (K) C | .30 | .50 |
| 75 Close Quarters C | .30 | .50 |
| 76 Elite Royal Guard C | .30 | .50 |
| 77 Darth Vader (O) C | .30 | .50 |
| 78 Death Star Battalion C | .30 | .50 |
| 79 Death Star II (A) C | .30 | .50 |
| 80 Decoy C | .30 | .50 |
| 81 Dune Sea C | .30 | .50 |
| 82 Elite Squad C | .30 | .50 |
| 83 Emperor Palpatine (C) C | .30 | .50 |
| 84 Ewok Artillery C | .30 | .50 |
| 85 Ewok Glider C | .30 | .50 |
| 86 Fly Casual C | .30 | .50 |
| 87 Force Lightning C | .30 | .50 |
| 88 Forest AT-AT C | .30 | .50 |
| 89 Forest AT-ST C | .30 | .50 |
| 90 Endor Attack Squad C | .30 | .50 |
| 91 Forests of Endor C | .30 | .50 |
| 92 Free Coruscant C | .30 | .50 |
| 93 Gray Squadron Y-wing C | .30 | .50 |
| 94 High-Speed Dodge C | .30 | .50 |
| 95 Imperial Speeder Bike C | .30 | .50 |
| 96 Imperial-Class Star Destroyer C | .30 | .50 |
| 97 Jabba's Guards C | .30 | .50 |
| 98 Lightsaber Throw C | .30 | .50 |
| 99 Log Trap C | .30 | .50 |
| 100 Luke Skywalker (M) C | .30 | .50 |
| 101 Mon Calamari Cruiser C | .30 | .50 |
| 102 Occupied Coruscant C | .30 | .50 |
| 103 Oola (A) C | .30 | .50 |
| 104 Princess Leia (K) C | .30 | .50 |
| 105 Rebel Scouts C | .30 | .50 |
| 106 Royal Guards C | .30 | .50 |
| 107 Scout Trooper C | .30 | .50 |
| 108 Surprising Strength C | .30 | .50 |
| 109 TIE Interceptor C | .30 | .50 |
| 110 Savage Attack C | .30 | .50 |

## 2004 Star Wars Rogues and Scoundrels

| | | |
|---|---|---|
| COMPLETE SET (105) | 50.00 | 100.00 |
| BOOSTER BOX (36 PACKS) | 40.00 | 80.00 |
| BOOSTER PACK (11 CARDS) | 1.50 | 3.00 |

*FOIL: .75X TO 2X BASIC CARDS
RELEASED IN APRIL 2004

| | | |
|---|---|---|
| 1 Admiral Firmus Piett (C) R | 2.00 | 3.00 |
| 2 Boba Fett (G) R | 2.00 | 3.00 |
| 3 Bossk (A) R | 2.00 | 3.00 |
| 4 Call For Hunters R | 2.00 | 3.00 |
| 5 Chewbacca (I) R | 2.00 | 3.00 |
| 6 Commander Nemet (A) R | 2.00 | 3.00 |
| 7 Dantooine System R | 2.00 | 3.00 |
| 8 Dark Sacrifice R | 2.00 | 3.00 |
| 9 Dengar (A) R | 2.00 | 3.00 |
| 10 Doctor Evazan (A) R | 2.00 | 3.00 |
| 11 Guri (A) R | 2.00 | 3.00 |
| 12 Han Solo (I) R | 2.00 | 3.00 |
| 13 Het Nkik (A) R | 2.00 | 3.00 |
| 14 Hounds Tooth (A) R | 2.00 | 3.00 |
| 15 IG-2000 (A) R | 2.00 | 3.00 |
| 16 IG-88 (A) R | 2.00 | 3.00 |
| 17 Dune Sea Krayt Dragon R | 2.00 | 3.00 |
| 18 Lando Calrissian (F) R | 2.00 | 3.00 |
| 19 Lando Calrissian (G) R | 2.00 | 3.00 |
| 20 Lando's Influence R | 2.00 | 3.00 |
| 21 Lobot (B) R | 2.00 | 3.00 |
| 22 Mara Jade (B) R | 2.00 | 3.00 |
| 23 Millennium Falcon (I) R | 2.00 | 3.00 |
| 24 Mist Hunter (A) R | 2.00 | 3.00 |
| 25 Modal Nodes (A) R | 2.00 | 3.00 |
| 26 Prince Xizor (A) R | 2.00 | 3.00 |
| 27 Princess Leia (I) R | 2.00 | 3.00 |
| 28 Slave 1 (F) R | 2.00 | 3.00 |

| | | |
|---|---|---|
| 29 Stinger (A) R | 2.00 | 3.00 |
| 30 Take A Prisoner R | 2.00 | 3.00 |
| 31 Trash Compactor R | 2.00 | 3.00 |
| 32 Virago (A) R | 2.00 | 3.00 |
| 33 Yoda (I) R | 2.00 | 3.00 |
| 34 Yoda's Lesson R | 2.00 | 3.00 |
| 35 Zuckuss (A) R | 2.00 | 3.00 |
| 36 4 Lom (A) U | .60 | 1.00 |
| 37 AT-AT U | .60 | 1.00 |
| 38 Bespin Cloud Car Squad U | .60 | 1.00 |
| 39 Big Asteroid U | .60 | 1.00 |
| 40 Boba Fett (F) U | .60 | 1.00 |
| 41 C 3PO (G) U | .60 | 1.00 |
| 42 Chewbacca (H) U | .60 | 1.00 |
| 43 Cloud City Wing Guard U | .60 | 1.00 |
| 44 Darth Vader (M) U | .60 | 1.00 |
| 45 Death Star Control Room U | .60 | 1.00 |
| 46 Garindan (A) U | .60 | 1.00 |
| 47 Greedo (B) U | .60 | 1.00 |
| 48 Han Solo (H) U | .60 | 1.00 |
| 49 Han's Sacrifice U | .60 | 1.00 |
| 50 Holoprojection Chamber U | .60 | 1.00 |
| 51 Human Shield U | .60 | 1.00 |
| 52 Kessel System U | .60 | 1.00 |
| 53 Lando Calrissian (E) U | .60 | 1.00 |
| 54 Lando's Trickery U | .60 | 1.00 |
| 55 Luke Skywalker (L) U | .60 | 1.00 |
| 56 Luke's X-wing (D) U | .60 | 1.00 |
| 57 Millennium Falcon (H) U | .60 | 1.00 |
| 58 Ponda Baba (A) U | .60 | 1.00 |
| 59 Punishing One (A) U | .60 | 1.00 |
| 60 R2-D2 (H) U | .60 | 1.00 |
| 61 Redoubled Effort U | .60 | 1.00 |
| 62 E-3PO (A) U | .60 | 1.00 |
| 63 Slave 1 (E) U | .60 | 1.00 |
| 64 Slave 1 (D) U | .60 | 1.00 |
| 65 Space Slug {RaS} U | .60 | 1.00 |
| 66 Outrider (A) U | .60 | 1.00 |
| 67 Ugnaught U | .60 | 1.00 |
| 68 Vendetta U | .60 | 1.00 |
| 69 Enraged Wampa U | .60 | 1.00 |
| 70 Lars Homestead U | .60 | 1.00 |
| 71 2-1B's Touch C | .30 | .50 |
| 72 Bantha Herd C | .30 | .50 |
| 73 Base Guards C | .30 | .50 |
| 74 Bespin Patrol Cloud Car C | .30 | .50 |
| 75 Boba Fett (C) C | .30 | .50 |
| 76 Boba Fett (D) C | .30 | .50 |
| 77 Boba Fett (E) C | .30 | .50 |
| 78 Darth Vader (L) C | .30 | .50 |
| 79 Dash Rendar (A) C | .30 | .50 |
| 80 Disrupting Strike C | .30 | .50 |
| 81 Falcon's Needs C | .30 | .50 |
| 82 Jabba's Death Mark C | .30 | .50 |
| 83 Kabe (A) C | .30 | .50 |
| 84 Kyle Katarn (A) C | .30 | .50 |
| 85 Lando System? C | .30 | .50 |
| 86 Leebo (A) C | .30 | .50 |
| 87 Luke's Garage C | .30 | .50 |
| 88 Luke's Vow C | .30 | .50 |
| 89 Medium Asteroid C | .30 | .50 |
| 90 Mos Eisley C | .30 | .50 |

| | | | |
|---|---|---|---|
| 91 Mos Eisley Cantina C | | .30 | .50 |
| 92 Muftak C | | .30 | .50 |
| 93 No Good To Me Dead C | | .30 | .50 |
| 94 Ord Mantell System C | | .30 | .50 |
| 95 Sleen C | | .30 | .50 |
| 96 Small Asteroid C | | .30 | .50 |
| 97 Zutton (A) C | | .30 | .50 |
| 98 Star Destroyer (RaS) C | | .30 | .50 |
| 99 Stormtrooper Detachment C | | .30 | .50 |
| 100 Streets Of Tatooine C | | .30 | .50 |
| 101 Tatooine Desert C | | .30 | .50 |
| 102 Tie Fighter C | | .30 | .50 |
| 103 Tusken Warrior C | | .30 | .50 |
| 104 Unmodified Snowspeeder C | | .30 | .50 |
| 105 X Wing Escort C | | .30 | .50 |

### 2005 Star Wars Revenge of the Sith

| | | |
|---|---|---|
| COMPLETE SET (110) | 50.00 | 100.00 |
| BOOSTER BOX (36 PACKS) | 30.00 | 60.00 |
| BOOSTER PACK (11 CARDS) | 1.25 | 2.50 |
| *FOIL: .75X TO 2X BASIC CARDS | | |
| RELEASED IN MAY 2005 | | |

| | | |
|---|---|---|
| 1 Anakin Skywalker (M) R | 2.00 | 3.00 |
| 2 Bail Organa (B) R | 2.00 | 3.00 |
| 3 Chewbacca (M) R | 2.00 | 3.00 |
| 4 Commerce Guild Droid 81-X R | 2.00 | 3.00 |
| 5 Commerce Guild Starship (ROTS) R | 2.00 | 3.00 |
| 6 Coruscant Shuttle R | 2.00 | 3.00 |
| 7 Darth Sidious (G) R | 2.00 | 3.00 |
| 8 Darth Tyranus (I) R | 2.00 | 3.00 |
| 9 Darth Vader (R) R | 2.00 | 3.00 |
| 10 Darth Vader (S) R | 2.00 | 3.00 |
| 11 Dismiss R | 2.00 | 3.00 |
| 12 Droid Security Escort R | 2.00 | 3.00 |
| 13 Engine Upgrade R | 2.00 | 3.00 |
| 14 Foil R | 2.00 | 3.00 |
| 15 Palpatine's Sanctum R | 2.00 | 3.00 |
| 16 Grand Moff Tarkin (D) R | 2.00 | 3.00 |
| 17 It Just Might Work R | 2.00 | 3.00 |
| 18 Jar Jar Binks (C) R | 2.00 | 3.00 |
| 19 Lightsaber Quick Draw R | 2.00 | 3.00 |

| | | |
|---|---|---|
| 20 Mace Windu (F) R | 2.00 | 3.00 |
| 21 Mas Amedda (A) R | 2.00 | 3.00 |
| 22 Mustafar Battle Grounds R | 2.00 | 3.00 |
| 23 Mustafar System R | 2.00 | 3.00 |
| 24 Nos Monster R | 2.00 | 3.00 |
| 25 Obi-Wan Kenobi (N) R | 2.00 | 3.00 |
| 26 PadmÈ Amidala (G) R | 2.00 | 3.00 |
| 27 R4-P17 (A) R | 2.00 | 3.00 |
| 28 Rage of Victory R | 2.00 | 3.00 |
| 29 Recusant-Class Light Destroyer R | 2.00 | 3.00 |
| 30 Republic Fighter Wing R | 2.00 | 3.00 |
| 31 Sacrifice the Expendable R | 2.00 | 3.00 |
| 32 Separatist Fleet R | 2.00 | 3.00 |
| 33 Spinning Slash R | 2.00 | 3.00 |
| 34 Strike with Impunity R | 2.00 | 3.00 |
| 35 Stubborn Personality R | 2.00 | 3.00 |
| 36 Super Battle Droid 7EX R | 2.00 | 3.00 |
| 37 Theta-Class Shuttle R | 2.00 | 3.00 |
| 38 Unexpected Attack R | 2.00 | 3.00 |
| 39 Venator-Class Destroyer R | 2.00 | 3.00 |
| 40 Yoda (K) R | 2.00 | 3.00 |
| 41 Acclamator II-Class Assault Ship U | .60 | 1.00 |
| 42 AT-AP U | .60 | 1.00 |
| 43 C-3PO (I) U | .60 | 1.00 |
| 44 Chancellor's Office U | .60 | 1.00 |
| 45 Combined Squadron Tactics U | .60 | 1.00 |
| 46 Confusion U | .60 | 1.00 |
| 47 Darth Sidious (F) U | .60 | 1.00 |
| 48 Darth Vader (Q) U | .60 | 1.00 |
| 49 Destroyer Droid, Q Series U | .60 | 1.00 |
| 50 Droid Missiles U | .60 | 1.00 |
| 51 Elite Guardian U | .60 | 1.00 |
| 52 Hardcell-Class Transport U | .60 | 1.00 |
| 53 Jedi Concentration U | .60 | 1.00 |
| 54 Jedi Master's Deflection U | .60 | 1.00 |
| 55 Kashyyyk System U | .60 | 1.00 |
| 56 Naboo Star Skiff U | .60 | 1.00 |
| 57 Nute Gunray (D) U | .60 | 1.00 |
| 58 Obi-Wan Kenobi (L) U | .60 | 1.00 |
| 59 PadmÈ Amidala (H) U | .60 | 1.00 |
| 60 Patrol Mode Vulture Droid U | .60 | 1.00 |
| 61 GH-7 Medical Droid U | .60 | 1.00 |
| 62 R2-D2 (J) U | .60 | 1.00 |
| 63 Thread The Needle U | .60 | 1.00 |
| 64 Thwart U | .60 | 1.00 |
| 65 Treachery U | .60 | 1.00 |
| 66 Techno Union Interceptor U | .60 | 1.00 |
| 67 Utapau System U | .60 | 1.00 |
| 68 Vehicle Shields Package U | .60 | 1.00 |
| 69 Vehicle Weapons Package U | .60 | 1.00 |
| 70 Yoda (J) U | .60 | 1.00 |
| 71 Anakin Skywalker (L) C | .30 | .50 |
| 72 Anakin's Starfighter (A) C | .30 | .50 |
| 73 ARC-170 Starfighter C | .30 | .50 |
| 74 AT-RT C | .30 | .50 |
| 75 BARC Speeder C | .30 | .50 |
| 76 Blaster Pistol C | .30 | .50 |
| 77 Blaster Rifle C | .30 | .50 |
| 78 Buzz Droid C | .30 | .50 |
| 79 Chewbacca (L) C | .30 | .50 |

| | | |
|---|---|---|
| 80 Coruscant Emergency Ship C | .30 | .50 |
| 81 Darth Sidious (E) C | .30 | .50 |
| 82 Darth Tyranus (H) C | .30 | .50 |
| 83 DC0052 Intergalactic Airspeeder C | .30 | .50 |
| 84 Diving Attack C | .30 | .50 |
| 85 Droid Battlestaff C | .30 | .50 |
| 86 Droid Tri-Fighter C | .30 | .50 |
| 87 Force Dodge C | .30 | .50 |
| 88 HAVw A6 Juggernaut C | .30 | .50 |
| 89 Homing Missiles Salvo C | .30 | .50 |
| 90 IBC Hailfire Droid C | .30 | .50 |
| 91 Instill Doubt C | .30 | .50 |
| 92 InterGalactic Banking Clan Cruiser C | .30 | .50 |
| 93 Jedi Lightsaber C | .30 | .50 |
| 94 Jedi Piloting C | .30 | .50 |
| 95 Meditate C | .30 | .50 |
| 96 Obi-Wan Kenobi (M) C | .30 | .50 |
| 97 Plo Koon's Starfighter (A) C | .30 | .50 |
| 98 Power Attack C | .30 | .50 |
| 99 Republic Assault Gunboat C | .30 | .50 |
| 100 Security Droid C | .30 | .50 |
| 101 Sith Lightsaber C | .30 | .50 |
| 102 STAP Squad C | .30 | .50 |
| 103 Surge of Strength C | .30 | .50 |
| 104 Tank Droid C | .30 | .50 |
| 105 TF Battle Droid Army C | .30 | .50 |
| 106 Trade Federation Cruiser C | .30 | .50 |
| 107 Unity of the Jedi C | .30 | .50 |
| 108 Utapau Sinkhole C | .30 | .50 |
| 109 Vulture Droid Starfighter C | .30 | .50 |
| 110 V-wing Clone Starfighter C | .30 | .50 |

### 2015 Star Wars Between the Shadows

| | | |
|---|---|---|
| 12710633 A Hero's Trial | 1.25 | 2.00 |
| 12720634 Luke Skywalker | 1.25 | 2.00 |
| 12730635 Speeder Bike | 1.25 | 2.00 |
| 12740636 Luke's Lightsaber | 1.25 | 2.00 |
| 12750637 I Am a Jedi | 1.25 | 2.00 |
| 12760065 Heat of Battle | 1.25 | 2.00 |
| 12810638 The Master's Domain | 1.25 | 2.00 |
| 12820639 Yoda | 1.25 | 2.00 |
| 12830640 Bogwing | 1.25 | 2.00 |
| 12840641 Yoda's Hut | 1.25 | 2.00 |

| | | | |
|---|---|---|---|
| 12850089 Lightsaber Deflection | 1.25 | 2.00 |
| 12860642 The Jedi's Resolve | 1.25 | 2.00 |
| 12910643 Following Fate | 1.25 | 2.00 |
| 12920644 Obi-Wan Kenobi | 1.25 | 2.00 |
| 12930106 R2-D2 | | 2.00 |
| 12940645 Obi-Wan's Lightsaber | 1.25 | 2.00 |
| 12950646 Noble Sacrifice | 1.25 | 2.00 |
| 12960133 Target of Opportunity | 1.25 | 2.00 |
| 13010647 Journey Through the Swamp | 1.25 | 2.00 |
| 13020648 Jubba Bird | 1.25 | 2.00 |
| 13030648 Jubba Bird | 1.25 | 2.00 |
| 13040649 Knobby White Spider | 1.25 | 2.00 |
| 13050650 Life Creates It | 1.25 | 2.00 |
| 13060651 Size Matters Not | 1.25 | 2.00 |
| 13110652 Sacrifice at Endor | 1.25 | 2.00 |
| 13120653 Ewok Hunter | 1.25 | 2.00 |
| 13130653 Ewok Hunter | 1.25 | 2.00 |
| 13140654 Funeral Pyre | 1.25 | 2.00 |
| 13150655 Unexpected Assistance | 1.25 | 2.00 |
| 13160656 Retreat to the Forest | 1.25 | 2.00 |
| 13210657 Commando Raid | 1.25 | 2.00 |
| 13220658 Lieutenant Judder Page | 1.25 | 2.00 |
| 13230659 Page's Commandos | 1.25 | 2.00 |
| 13240659 Page's Commandos | 1.25 | 2.00 |
| 13250065 Heat of Battle | 1.25 | 2.00 |
| 13260133 Target of Opportunity | 1.25 | 2.00 |
| 13310660 Calling In Favors | 1.25 | 2.00 |
| 13320661 Talon Karrde | 1.25 | 2.00 |
| 13330662 Skipray Blastboat | 1.25 | 2.00 |
| 13340662 Skipray Blastboat | 1.25 | 2.00 |
| 13350663 Dirty Secrets | 1.25 | 2.00 |
| 13360664 Clever Ruse | 1.25 | 2.00 |
| 13410665 No Disintegrations | 1.25 | 2.00 |
| 13420666 Boba Fett | 1.25 | 2.00 |
| 13430667 Freelance Hunter | 1.25 | 2.00 |
| 13440668 Flamethrower | 1.25 | 2.00 |
| 13450378 Prized Possession | 1.25 | 2.00 |
| 13460669 Entangled | 1.25 | 2.00 |
| 13510670 Masterful Manipulation | 1.25 | 2.00 |
| 13520671 Prince Xizor | 1.25 | 2.00 |
| 13530672 Black Sun Headhunter | 1.25 | 2.00 |
| 13540673 Debt Collector | 1.25 | 2.00 |
| 13550674 Shadows of the Empire | 1.25 | 2.00 |
| 13560675 The Prince's Scheme | 1.25 | 2.00 |
| 13610676 All Out Brawl | 1.25 | 2.00 |
| 13620677 Zekka Thyne | 1.25 | 2.00 |
| 13630673 Debt Collector | 1.25 | 2.00 |
| 13640678 Armed to the Teeth | 1.25 | 2.00 |
| 13650669 Entangled | 1.25 | 2.00 |
| 13660169 Heat of Battle | 1.25 | 2.00 |
| 13710679 The Best That Credits Can Buy | 1.25 | 2.00 |
| 13720680 Virago | 1.25 | 2.00 |
| 13730672 Black Sun Headhunter | 1.25 | 2.00 |
| 13740681 Rise of the Black Sun | 1.25 | 2.00 |
| 13750682 Warning Shot | 1.25 | 2.00 |
| 13760170 Target of Opportunity | 1.25 | 2.00 |
| 13810683 The Hunters | 1.25 | 2.00 |
| 13820684 Boushh | 1.25 | 2.00 |
| 13830685 Snoova | 1.25 | 2.00 |
| 13840686 A Better Offer | 1.25 | 2.00 |
| 13850542 Pay Out | 1.25 | 2.00 |

| | | | |
|---|---|---|---|
| 13860687 Show of Force | 1.25 | 2.00 |
| 13910688 The Investigation | 1.25 | 2.00 |
| 13920689 Ysanne Isard | 1.25 | 2.00 |
| 13930690 Imperial Intelligence Officer | 1.25 | 2.00 |
| 13940690 Imperial Intelligence Officer | 1.25 | 2.00 |
| 13950691 Confiscation | 1.25 | 2.00 |
| 13960692 Official Inquiry | 1.25 | 2.00 |
| 14010693 Family Connections | 1.25 | 2.00 |
| 14020694 General Tagge | 1.25 | 2.00 |
| 14030695 Security Task Force | 1.25 | 2.00 |
| 14040695 Security Task Force | 1.25 | 2.00 |
| 14050696 Imperial Discipline | 1.25 | 2.00 |
| 14060697 Precision Fire | 1.25 | 2.00 |

### 2015 Star Wars Chain of Command

| | | | |
|---|---|---|---|
| 1611 A Hero's Beginning | 1.25 | 2.00 |
| 1612 Luke's X-34 Landspeeder | 1.25 | 2.00 |
| 1613 Owen Lars | 1.25 | 2.00 |
| 1614 Moisture Vaporator | 1.25 | 2.00 |
| 1615 Unfinished Business | 1.25 | 2.00 |
| 1616 Supporting Fire | 1.25 | 2.00 |
| 1621 Breaking the Blockade | 1.25 | 2.00 |
| 1622 Smuggling Freighter | 1.25 | 2.00 |
| 1623 Smuggling Freighter | 1.25 | 2.00 |
| 1624 Duros Smuggler | 1.25 | 2.00 |
| 1625 Duros Smuggler | 1.25 | 2.00 |
| 1626 Surprising Maneuver | 1.25 | 2.00 |
| 1631 The Imperial Bureaucracy | 1.25 | 2.00 |
| 1632 Sate Pestage | 1.25 | 2.00 |
| 1633 Advisor to the Emperor | 1.25 | 2.00 |
| 1634 Quarren Bureaucrat | 1.25 | 2.00 |
| 1635 Endless Bureaucracy | 1.25 | 2.00 |
| 1636 Supporting Fire | 1.25 | 2.00 |
| 1641 The Last Grand Admiral | 1.25 | 2.00 |
| 1642 Grand Admiral Thrawn | 1.25 | 2.00 |
| 1643 Noghri Bodyguard | 1.25 | 2.00 |
| 1644 Noghri Bodyguard | 1.25 | 2.00 |
| 1645 Chain of Command | 3.00 | 5.00 |
| 1646 Supporting Fire | 1.25 | 2.00 |
| 1651 Nar Shaddaa Drift | 1.25 | 2.00 |
| 1652 Race Circuit Champion | 1.25 | 2.00 |

| | | | |
|---|---|---|---|
| 1653 Racing Swoop | 1.25 | 2.00 |
| 1654 Racing Swoop | 1.25 | 2.00 |
| 1655 Black Market Exchange | 1.25 | 2.00 |
| 1656 Cut Off | 1.25 | 2.00 |

### 2015 Star Wars Draw Their Fire

| | | | |
|---|---|---|---|
| 14610722 The Survivors | 1.25 | 2.00 |
| 14620723 Qu Rahn | 1.25 | 2.00 |
| 14630724 Sulon Sympathizer | 1.25 | 2.00 |
| 14640725 Shien Training | 1.25 | 2.00 |
| 14650061 Force Rejuvenation | 1.25 | 2.00 |
| 14660256 Protection | 1.25 | 2.00 |
| 14710726 Called to Arms | 1.25 | 2.00 |
| 14720727 Gray Squadron Gunner | 1.25 | 2.00 |
| 14730728 Gray Squadron Y-Wing | 1.25 | 2.00 |
| 14740729 Advanced Proton Torpedoes | 1.25 | 2.00 |
| 14750730 Desperation | 1.25 | 2.00 |
| 14760133 Target of Opportunity | 1.25 | 2.00 |
| 14810731 The Daring Escape | 1.25 | 2.00 |
| 14820732 LE-B02D9 | 1.25 | 2.00 |
| 14830733 Outrider | 1.25 | 2.00 |
| 14840734 Spacer Cantina | 1.25 | 2.00 |
| 14850735 Punch It | 1.25 | 2.00 |
| 14860702 Stay on Target | 1.25 | 2.00 |
| 14910736 The Emperor's Sword | 1.25 | 2.00 |
| 14920737 Maarek Stele | 1.25 | 2.00 |
| 14930738 Delta One | 1.25 | 2.00 |
| 14940739 Advanced Concussion Missiles | 1.25 | 2.00 |
| 14950740 Hand of the Emperor | 1.25 | 2.00 |
| 14960169 Heat of Battle | 1.25 | 2.00 |
| 15010741 Guarding the Wing | 1.25 | 2.00 |
| 15020742 DS-61-3 | 1.25 | 2.00 |
| 15030743 Black Squadron Fighter | 1.25 | 2.00 |
| 15040743 Black Squadron Fighter | 1.25 | 2.00 |
| 15050744 Elite Pilot Training | 1.25 | 2.00 |
| 15060170 Target of Opportunity | 1.25 | 2.00 |

## 2015 Star Wars Imperial Entanglement

| | | | |
|---|---|---|---|
| 17110838 House Edge | 1.25 | 2.00 |
| 17120839 Lando Calrissian | 1.25 | 2.00 |
| 17130840 Herglic Sabacc Addict | 1.25 | 2.00 |
| 17140022 Cloud City Casino | 1.25 | 2.00 |
| 17150841 Sabacc Shift | 1.25 | 2.00 |
| 17160842 The Gambler's Trick | 1.25 | 2.00 |
| 17210843 Debt of Honor | 1.25 | 2.00 |
| 17220844 Chewbacca | 1.25 | 2.00 |
| 17230845 Wookiee Defender | 1.25 | 2.00 |
| 17240846 Kashyyyk Resistance Hideout | 1.25 | 2.00 |
| 17250847 Wookiee Rage | 1.25 | 2.00 |
| 17260256 Protection | 1.25 | 2.00 |
| 17310848 Fortune and Fate | 1.25 | 2.00 |
| 17320849 Lady Luck | 1.25 | 2.00 |
| 17330850 Cloud City Technician | 1.25 | 2.00 |
| 17340850 Cloud City Technician | 1.25 | 2.00 |
| 17350851 Central Computer | 1.25 | 2.00 |
| 17360133 Target of Opportunity | 1.25 | 2.00 |
| 17410852 Honor Among Thieves | 1.25 | 2.00 |
| 17420853 Mirax Terrik | 1.25 | 2.00 |
| 17430854 Fringer Captain | 1.25 | 2.00 |
| 17440854 Fringer Captain | 1.25 | 2.00 |
| 17450855 Special Discount | 1.25 | 2.00 |
| 17460856 One Last Trick | 1.25 | 2.00 |
| 17510857 Renegade Reinforcements | 1.25 | 2.00 |
| 17520858 Corporal Dansra Beezer | 1.25 | 2.00 |
| 17530210 Renegade Squadron Operative | 1.25 | 2.00 |
| 17540859 Hidden Backup | 1.25 | 2.00 |
| 17550860 Directed Fire | 1.25 | 2.00 |
| 17560861 Last Minute Reinforcements | 1.25 | 2.00 |
| 17610862 Mysteries of the Rim | 1.25 | 2.00 |
| 17620863 Outer Rim Mystic | 1.25 | 2.00 |
| 17630863 Outer Rim Mystic | 1.25 | 2.00 |
| 17640864 Niman Training | 1.25 | 2.00 |
| 17650864 Niman Training | 1.25 | 2.00 |
| 17660865 Force Illusion | 1.25 | 2.00 |
| 17710866 Planning the Rescue | 1.25 | 2.00 |
| 17720867 General Airen Cracken | 1.25 | 2.00 |
| 17730868 Alliance Infiltrator | 1.25 | 2.00 |
| 17740869 Superior Intelligence | 1.25 | 2.00 |
| 17750870 Undercover | 1.25 | 2.00 |
| 17760117 Rescue Mission | 1.25 | 2.00 |

| | | | |
|---|---|---|---|
| 17810871 The Tarkin Doctrine | 1.25 | 2.00 |
| 17820872 Grand Moff Tarkin | 1.25 | 2.00 |
| 17830873 Stormtrooper Assault Team | 1.25 | 2.00 |
| 17840874 Rule by Fear | 1.25 | 2.00 |
| 17850875 Moment of Triumph | 1.25 | 2.00 |
| 17860171 Twist of Fate | 1.25 | 2.00 |
| 17910876 Might of the Empire | 1.25 | 2.00 |
| 17920877 Chimaera | 1.25 | 2.00 |
| 17930878 DP20 Corellian Gunship | 1.25 | 2.00 |
| 17940879 Fleet Staging Area | 1.25 | 2.00 |
| 17950392 Tractor Beam | 1.25 | 2.00 |
| 17960880 The Empire Strikes Back | 1.25 | 2.00 |
| 18010881 Enforced Loyalty | 1.25 | 2.00 |
| 18020882 Colonel Yularen | 1.25 | 2.00 |
| 18030883 Lieutenant Mithel | 1.25 | 2.00 |
| 18040884 MSE-6 iMouseî Droid | 1.25 | 2.00 |
| 18050024 Control Room | 1.25 | 2.00 |
| 18060885 The Imperial Fist | 1.25 | 2.00 |
| 18110886 Imperial Entanglements | 1.25 | 2.00 |
| 18120887 Imperial Raider | 1.25 | 2.00 |
| 18130888 VT-49 Decimator | 1.25 | 2.00 |
| 18140888 VT-49 Decimator | 1.25 | 2.00 |
| 18150889 Customs Blockade | 1.25 | 2.00 |
| 18160890 Ion Cannon | 1.25 | 2.00 |
| 18210891 Phantoms of Imdaar | 1.25 | 2.00 |
| 18220892 TIE Phantom | 1.25 | 2.00 |
| 18230892 TIE Phantom | 1.25 | 2.00 |
| 18240893 Enhanced Laser Cannon | 1.25 | 2.00 |
| 18250894 Fighters Coming In! | 1.25 | 2.00 |
| 18260169 Heat of Battle | 1.25 | 2.00 |
| 18310895 Brothers of the Sith | 1.25 | 2.00 |
| 18320896 Gorc | 1.25 | 2.00 |
| 18330897 Pic | 1.25 | 2.00 |
| 18340898 Telepathic Connection | 1.25 | 2.00 |
| 18350062 Force Stasis | 1.25 | 2.00 |
| 18360899 Force Invisibility | 1.25 | 2.00 |
| 18410900 The Huttís Menagerie | 1.25 | 2.00 |
| 18420901 Malakili | 1.25 | 2.00 |
| 18430902 Jabbaís Rancor | 1.25 | 2.00 |
| 18440903 Bubo | 1.25 | 2.00 |
| 18450904 Underground Entertainment | 1.25 | 2.00 |
| 18460905 Jabbaís Summons | 1.25 | 2.00 |

## 2015 Star Wars Jump to Lightspeed

## 2015 Star Wars Ready for Takeoff

| | | | |
|---|---|---|---|
| 1661 The Forgotten Masters | 1.25 | 2.00 |
| 1662 Tíra Saa | 1.25 | 2.00 |
| 1663 Lost Master | 1.25 | 2.00 |
| 1664 Lost Master | 1.25 | 2.00 |
| 1665 A Gift from the Past | 1.25 | 2.00 |
| 1666 Echoes of the Force | 1.25 | 2.00 |
| 1671 Heroes of the Rebellion | 1.25 | 2.00 |
| 1672 Tycho Celchu | 1.25 | 2.00 |
| 1673 Wes Janson | 1.25 | 2.00 |
| 1674 Rogue Six | 1.25 | 2.00 |
| 1675 Rogue Nine | 1.25 | 2.00 |
| 1676 Ready for Takeoff | 1.25 | 2.00 |
| 1681 That Bucket of Bolts | 1.25 | 2.00 |
| 1682 Han Solo | 1.25 | 2.00 |
| 1683 Millennium Falcon | 1.25 | 2.00 |
| 1684 Well Paid | 1.25 | 2.00 |
| 1685 Well Paid | 1.25 | 2.00 |
| 1686 Heat of Battle | 1.25 | 2.00 |
| 1691 The Reawakening | 1.25 | 2.00 |
| 1692 Arden Lyn | 1.25 | 2.00 |
| 1693 Dark Side Apprentice | 1.25 | 2.00 |
| 1694 Return to Darkness | 1.25 | 2.00 |
| 1695 Give in to Your Anger | 1.25 | 2.00 |
| 1696 Give in to Your Anger | 1.25 | 2.00 |
| 1701 Behind the Black Sun | 1.25 | 2.00 |
| 1702 Guri | 1.25 | 2.00 |
| 1703 Freelance Assassin | 1.25 | 2.00 |
| 1704 Hidden Vibroknife | 1.25 | 2.00 |
| 1705 Threat Removal | 1.25 | 2.00 |
| 1706 Heat of Battle | 1.25 | 2.00 |

| | | | |
|---|---|---|---|
| 14110698 Rogue Squadron Assault | 1.25 | 2.00 |
| 14120699 Derek iHobbieî Klivian | 1.25 | 2.00 |
| 14130700 Rogue Squadron X-Wing | 1.25 | 2.00 |
| 14140700 Rogue Squadron X-Wing | 1.25 | 2.00 |
| 14150701 Pilot Ready Room | 1.25 | 2.00 |
| 14160702 Stay on Target | 1.25 | 2.00 |
| 14210703 Memories of Taanab | 1.25 | 2.00 |
| 14220704 Lando Calrissian | 1.25 | 2.00 |
| 14230705 System Patrol Craft | 1.25 | 2.00 |
| 14240705 System Patrol Craft | 1.25 | 2.00 |
| 14250706 Conner Net | 1.25 | 2.00 |
| 14260707 A Little Maneuver | 1.25 | 2.00 |
| 14310708 Black Squadron Formation | 1.25 | 2.00 |
| 14320709 iMaulerî Mithel | 1.25 | 2.00 |
| 14330710 Black Two | 1.25 | 2.00 |
| 14340146 TIE Advanced | 1.25 | 2.00 |
| 14350711 Death Star Ready Room | 1.25 | 2.00 |

| | | | |
|---|---|---|---|
| 14360712 | Stay on Target | 1.25 | 2.00 |
| 14410713 | The Empireís Elite | 1.25 | 2.00 |
| 14420714 | Baron Fel | 1.25 | 2.00 |
| 14430715 | 181st TIE Interceptor | 1.25 | 2.00 |
| 14440715 | 181st TIE Interceptor | 1.25 | 2.00 |
| 14450716 | Flight Academy | 1.25 | 2.00 |
| 14460712 | Stay on Target | 1.25 | 2.00 |
| 14510717 | The Grand Heist | 1.25 | 2.00 |
| 14520718 | Niles Ferrier | 1.25 | 2.00 |
| 14530719 | Novice Starship Thief | 1.25 | 2.00 |
| 14540719 | Novice Starship Thief | 1.25 | 2.00 |
| 14550720 | Pirate Hideout | 1.25 | 2.00 |
| 14560721 | Salvage Operation | 1.25 | 2.00 |

## 2016 Star Wars Destiny Awakening

| | | | |
|---|---|---|---|
| COMPLETE SET (174) | | 450.00 | 650.00 |
| BOOSTER BOX (36 PACKS) | | 80.00 | 120.00 |
| BOOSTER PACK (5 CARDS AND 1 DICE) | | 4.00 | 6.00 |
| RELEASED IN NOVEMBER, 2016 | | | |
| 1 | Captain Phasma L | 10.00 | 15.00 |
| 2 | First Order Stormtrooper R | 3.00 | 5.00 |
| 3 | General Grievous R | 3.00 | 5.00 |
| 4 | General Veers R | 3.00 | 5.00 |
| 5 | AT ST L | 8.00 | 12.00 |
| 6 | First Order TIE Fighter R | 3.00 | 5.00 |
| 7 | Commanding Presence L | 10.00 | 15.00 |
| 8 | F 11D Rifle S | 2.00 | 3.00 |
| 9 | Count Dooku R | 3.00 | 5.00 |
| 10 | Darth Vader L | 20.00 | 30.00 |
| 11 | Kylo Ren S | 1.50 | 2.50 |
| 12 | Nightsister R | 3.00 | 5.00 |
| 13 | Force Choke L | 12.00 | 20.00 |
| 14 | Immobilize R | 3.00 | 5.00 |
| 15 | Kylo Rens Lightsaber L | 12.00 | 20.00 |
| 16 | Sith Holocron R | 10.00 | 13.00 |
| 17 | Infantry Grenades R | 3.00 | 5.00 |
| 18 | Speeder Bike Scout R | 3.00 | 5.00 |
| 19 | Bala Tik R | 3.00 | 5.00 |
| 20 | Jabba the Hutt L | 15.00 | 25.00 |
| 21 | Jango Fett R | 3.00 | 5.00 |
| 22 | Tusken Raider R | 3.00 | 5.00 |
| 23 | Crime Lord L | 10.00 | 15.00 |
| 24 | Flame Thrower R | 3.00 | 5.00 |
| 25 | Gaffi Stick R | 3.00 | 5.00 |

| | | | |
|---|---|---|---|
| 26 | On the Hunt R | 3.00 | 5.00 |
| 27 | Admiral Ackbar R | 3.00 | 5.00 |
| 28 | Leia Organa R | 3.00 | 5.00 |
| 29 | Poe Dameron L | 15.00 | 25.00 |
| 30 | Rebel Trooper R | 3.00 | 5.00 |
| 31 | Launch Bay L | 6.00 | 10.00 |
| 32 | Black One L | 5.00 | 8.00 |
| 33 | Scout R | 3.00 | 5.00 |
| 34 | Survival Gear R | 3.00 | 5.00 |
| 35 | Luke Skywalker L | 15.00 | 25.00 |
| 36 | Padawan R | 3.00 | 5.00 |
| 37 | Qui Gon Jinn R | 3.00 | 5.00 |
| 38 | Rey S | 2.00 | 3.00 |
| 39 | Force Protection R | 3.00 | 5.00 |
| 40 | Jedi Robes R | 3.00 | 5.00 |
| 41 | Luke Skywalkers Lightsaber L | 10.00 | 15.00 |
| 42 | One With the Force L | 15.00 | 25.00 |
| 43 | BB 8 R | 3.00 | 5.00 |
| 44 | Reys Staff R | 3.00 | 5.00 |
| 45 | Finn S | 2.00 | 3.00 |
| 46 | Han Solo L | 12.00 | 20.00 |
| 47 | Hired Gun R | 3.00 | 5.00 |
| 48 | Padme Amidala R | 3.00 | 5.00 |
| 49 | Millennium Falcon L | 10.00 | 15.00 |
| 50 | Diplomatic Immunity R | 3.00 | 5.00 |
| 51 | DL 44 Heavy Blaster Pistol R | 3.00 | 5.00 |
| 52 | Infiltrate R | 3.00 | 5.00 |
| 53 | Outpost R | 3.00 | 5.00 |
| 54 | DH 17 Blaster Pistol R | 3.00 | 5.00 |
| 55 | IQA 11 Blaster Rifle R | 3.00 | 5.00 |
| 56 | Promotion R | 3.00 | 5.00 |
| 57 | Force Throw S | 6.00 | 10.00 |
| 58 | Force Training R | 3.00 | 5.00 |
| 59 | Lightsaber S | 2.00 | 3.00 |
| 60 | Mind Probe S | 5.00 | 8.00 |
| 61 | Comlink R | 3.00 | 5.00 |
| 62 | Datapad R | 3.00 | 5.00 |
| 63 | Holdout Blaster R | 12.00 | 20.00 |
| 64 | Black Market R | 3.00 | 5.00 |
| 65 | Cunning R | 3.00 | 5.00 |
| 66 | Jetpack R | 3.00 | 5.00 |
| 67 | Thermal Detonator L | 15.00 | 25.00 |
| 68 | Cannon Fodder C | .15 | .20 |
| 69 | Closing the Net C | .15 | .20 |
| 70 | Endless Ranks U | 1.25 | 2.00 |
| 71 | Occupation C | .15 | .20 |
| 72 | Probe C | .15 | .20 |
| 73 | Sweep the Area C | .15 | .20 |
| 74 | Tactical Mastery U | 2.00 | 3.00 |
| 75 | The Best Defense U | .25 | .40 |
| 76 | Drudge Work C | .15 | .20 |
| 77 | Local Garrison U | .25 | .40 |
| 78 | Personal Escort C | .15 | .20 |
| 79 | Abandon All Hope U | .25 | .40 |
| 80 | Boundless Ambition C | .15 | .20 |
| 81 | Enrage C | .15 | .20 |
| 82 | Feel Your Anger C | .15 | .20 |
| 83 | Force Strike U | .75 | 1.25 |
| 84 | Intimidate C | .15 | .20 |
| 85 | Isolation C | .15 | .20 |
| 86 | No Mercy U | 2.00 | 3.00 |

| | | | |
|---|---|---|---|
| 87 | Pulling the Strings C | .15 | .20 |
| 88 | Emperors Favor U | .25 | .40 |
| 89 | Power of the Dark Side S | .40 | .60 |
| 90 | Hidden in Shadow U | .25 | .40 |
| 91 | Nowhere to Run U | .25 | .40 |
| 92 | Ace in the Hole U | .75 | 1.25 |
| 93 | Armed to the Teeth C | .15 | .20 |
| 94 | Confiscation U | .25 | .40 |
| 95 | Fight Dirty U | .25 | .40 |
| 96 | Go for the Kill C | .15 | .20 |
| 97 | He Doesnt Like You C | .15 | .20 |
| 98 | Lying in Wait C | .15 | .20 |
| 99 | Backup Muscle C | .15 | .20 |
| 100 | My Kind of Scum C | .15 | .20 |
| 101 | Underworld Connections U | 1.00 | 1.50 |
| 102 | Prized Possession U | .25 | .40 |
| 103 | Commando Raid U | .25 | .40 |
| 104 | Defensive Position C | .15 | .20 |
| 105 | Field Medic C | .15 | .20 |
| 106 | Hit and Run C | .15 | .20 |
| 107 | Its a Trap U | .75 | 1.25 |
| 108 | Natural Talent C | .15 | .20 |
| 109 | Rearm U | .25 | .40 |
| 110 | Retreat U | .25 | .40 |
| 111 | Strategic Planning C | .15 | .20 |
| 112 | Surgical Strike C | .15 | .20 |
| 113 | Resistance HQ U | .25 | .40 |
| 114 | Anticipate U | .25 | .40 |
| 115 | Defensive Stance C | .15 | .20 |
| 116 | Force Misdirection C | .15 | .20 |
| 117 | Heroism C | .15 | .20 |
| 118 | Noble Sacrifice C | .15 | .20 |
| 119 | Patience C | .15 | .20 |
| 120 | Return of the Jedi U | .25 | .40 |
| 121 | Riposte C | .15 | .20 |
| 122 | Willpower U | .40 | .60 |
| 123 | Jedi Council U | .25 | .40 |
| 124 | Awakening S | .60 | 1.00 |
| 125 | The Force is Strong C | .15 | .20 |
| 126 | Daring Escape U | .25 | .40 |
| 127 | Dont Get Cocky C | .15 | .20 |
| 128 | Draw Attention C | .15 | .20 |
| 129 | Hyperspace Jump U | .25 | .40 |
| 130 | Let the Wookiee Win U | .25 | .40 |
| 131 | Negotiate C | .15 | .20 |
| 132 | Scavenge C | .15 | .20 |
| 133 | Shoot First U | .25 | .40 |
| 134 | Smuggling C | .15 | .20 |
| 135 | Play the Odds U | .25 | .40 |
| 136 | Street Informants C | .15 | .20 |
| 137 | Second Chance U | 1.50 | 2.50 |
| 138 | Award Ceremony C | .15 | .20 |
| 139 | Dug In U | 2.00 | 3.00 |
| 140 | Firepower C | .15 | .20 |
| 141 | Leadership U | .40 | .60 |
| 142 | Logistics C | .15 | .20 |
| 143 | Squad Tactics C | .15 | .20 |
| 144 | Supporting Fire U | .25 | .40 |
| 145 | Deflect C | .15 | .20 |
| 146 | Disturbance in the Force C | .15 | .20 |
| 147 | Mind Trick U | .40 | .60 |

| | | | |
|---|---|---|---|
| 148 | The Power of the Force C | .15 | .20 |
| 149 | Use the Force S | .75 | 1.25 |
| 150 | It Binds All Things U | 1.25 | 2.00 |
| 151 | Aim S | .50 | .75 |
| 152 | All In U | 1.25 | 2.00 |
| 153 | Block C | .15 | .20 |
| 154 | Close Quarters Assault S | 1.00 | 1.50 |
| 155 | Dodge C | .15 | .20 |
| 156 | Flank U | .25 | .40 |
| 157 | Take Cover C | .15 | .20 |
| 158 | Disarm C | .15 | .20 |
| 159 | Electroshock U | 4.00 | 6.00 |
| 160 | Reversal U | 1.00 | 1.50 |
| 161 | Scramble C | .15 | .20 |
| 162 | Unpredictable C | .15 | .20 |
| 163 | Infamous U | 1.50 | 2.50 |
| 164 | Hunker Down C | .15 | .20 |
| 165 | Command Center U | .25 | .40 |
| 166 | Echo Base U | .25 | .40 |
| 167 | Emperors Throne Room U | .25 | .40 |
| 168 | Frozen Wastes S | .60 | 1.00 |
| 169 | Imperial Armory C | .15 | .20 |
| 170 | Jedi Temple C | .15 | .20 |
| 171 | Rebel War Room C | .15 | .20 |
| 172 | Mos Eisley Spaceport C | .15 | .20 |
| 173 | Separatist Base C | .15 | .20 |
| 174 | Starship Graveyard S | 1.50 | 2.50 |

## 2017 Star Wars Destiny Spirit of Rebellion

| | | | |
|---|---|---|---|
| COMPLETE SET (160) | | 400.00 | 550.00 |
| BOOSTER BOX (36 PACKS) | | 100.00 | 130.00 |
| BOOSTER PACK (5 CARDS AND 1 DICE) | | 4.00 | 6.00 |
| UNLISTED C | | .10 | .20 |
| UNLISTED U | | .25 | .40 |
| UNLISTED R | | 3.00 | 5.00 |
| RELEASED ON APRIL 28, 2017 | | | |
| 1 | Death Trooper R | 4.00 | 6.00 |
| 2 | FN 2199 R | 2.50 | 4.00 |
| 3 | Director Krennic L | 8.00 | 12.00 |
| 4 | TIE Pilot R | 2.50 | 4.00 |
| 5 | E Web Emplacement R | 7.00 | 10.00 |
| 6 | Imperial Discipline R | 2.50 | 4.00 |
| 7 | DT 29 Heavy Blaster Pistol R | 2.50 | 4.00 |

| | | | |
|---|---|---|---|
| 8 | Z6 Riot Control Baton L | 20.00 | 25.00 |
| 9 | Asajj Ventress R | 2.50 | 4.00 |
| 10 | Darth Vader R | 2.50 | 4.00 |
| 11 | Palpatine L | 20.00 | 25.00 |
| 12 | Royal Guard R | 2.50 | 4.00 |
| 13 | Commando Shuttle R | 2.50 | 4.00 |
| 14 | Force Lightning L | 15.00 | 20.00 |
| 15 | Lightsaber Pike R | 7.00 | 10.00 |
| 16 | Lure of Power R | 2.50 | 4.00 |
| 17 | Interrogation Droid R | 2.50 | 4.00 |
| 18 | Aurra Sing R | 2.50 | 4.00 |
| 19 | Guavian Enforcer R | 2.50 | 4.00 |
| 20 | IG 88 L | 8.00 | 12.00 |
| 21 | Unkar Plutt R | 2.50 | 4.00 |
| 22 | Slave I L | 8.00 | 12.00 |
| 23 | Blackmail L | 8.00 | 12.00 |
| 24 | Personal Shield R | 2.50 | 4.00 |
| 25 | Vibroknucklers R | 2.50 | 4.00 |
| 26 | Baze Malbus L | 8.00 | 12.00 |
| 27 | Mon Mothma R | 2.50 | 4.00 |
| 28 | Rebel Commando R | 2.50 | 4.00 |
| 29 | Temmin "Snap" Wexley R | 2.50 | 4.00 |
| 30 | C 3PO R | 2.50 | 4.00 |
| 31 | U Wing L | 8.00 | 12.00 |
| 32 | A180 Blaster R | 2.50 | 4.00 |
| 33 | Overkill R | 2.50 | 4.00 |
| 34 | Jedi Acolyte R | 2.50 | 4.00 |
| 35 | Chirrut Œmwe R | 2.50 | 4.00 |
| 36 | Luminara Unduli R | 2.50 | 4.00 |
| 37 | Obi Wan Kenobi L | 8.00 | 12.00 |
| 38 | Delta 7 Interceptor R | 2.50 | 4.00 |
| 39 | Handcrafted Light Bow L | 8.00 | 12.00 |
| 40 | Force Heal R | 2.50 | 4.00 |
| 41 | Journals of Ben Kenobi R | 2.50 | 4.00 |
| 42 | R2 D2 R | 2.50 | 4.00 |
| 43 | Chewbacca L | 8.00 | 12.00 |
| 44 | Jyn Erso R | 2.50 | 4.00 |
| 45 | Maz Kanata R | 2.50 | 4.00 |
| 46 | Outer Rim Smuggler R | 2.50 | 4.00 |
| 47 | Smuggling Freighter R | 2.50 | 4.00 |
| 48 | Bowcaster L | 8.00 | 12.00 |
| 49 | Lone Operative R | 2.50 | 4.00 |
| 50 | Mazs Goggles L | 8.00 | 12.00 |
| 51 | Supply Line R | 2.50 | 4.00 |
| 52 | Astromech R | 2.50 | 4.00 |
| 53 | Rocket Launcher L | 30.00 | 35.00 |
| 54 | Force Push R | 2.50 | 4.00 |
| 55 | Force Speed L | 50.00 | 65.00 |
| 56 | Makashi Training R | 2.50 | 4.00 |
| 57 | Vibroknife R | 15.00 | 20.00 |
| 58 | Quadjumper L | 8.00 | 12.00 |
| 59 | Ascension Gun R | 7.00 | 10.00 |
| 60 | Con Artist R | 2.50 | 4.00 |
| 61 | Battle Formation C | .10 | .20 |
| 62 | Imperial War Machine U | .25 | .40 |
| 63 | Lockdown C | .10 | .20 |
| 64 | Sustained Fire U | .25 | .40 |
| 65 | Traitor U | .25 | .40 |
| 66 | Trench Warfare C | .10 | .20 |
| 67 | Undying Loyalty C | .10 | .20 |
| 68 | We Have Them Now U | .40 | .60 |
| 69 | Attrition C | .10 | .20 |
| 70 | Imperial Inspection U | .40 | .60 |
| 71 | Anger U | .75 | 1.25 |

| | | | |
|---|---|---|---|
| 72 | Lightsaber Throw U | .60 | 1.00 |
| 73 | Manipulate C | .10 | .20 |
| 74 | No Disintegrations C | .10 | .20 |
| 75 | Now You Will Die C | .10 | .20 |
| 76 | Rise Again U | 1.00 | 1.50 |
| 77 | The Price of Failure C | .10 | .20 |
| 78 | Dark Presence U | 1.00 | 1.50 |
| 79 | Now I Am The Master C | .10 | .20 |
| 80 | Doubt C | .10 | .20 |
| 81 | Arms Deal C | .10 | .20 |
| 82 | Bait and Switch C | .10 | .20 |
| 83 | Friends in High Places U | .25 | .40 |
| 84 | Loose Ends U | .25 | .40 |
| 85 | One Quarter Portion C | .10 | .20 |
| 86 | Relentless Pursuit C | .10 | .20 |
| 87 | Scrap Buy U | .25 | .40 |
| 88 | Salvage Stand C | .10 | .20 |
| 89 | Armor Plating U | .60 | 1.00 |
| 90 | Emergency Evacuation U | .25 | .40 |
| 91 | Friendly Fire U | .25 | .40 |
| 92 | Guerrilla Warfare C | .10 | .20 |
| 93 | Our Only Hope U | .25 | .40 |
| 94 | Rebel Assault C | .10 | .20 |
| 95 | Sensor Placement U | .25 | .40 |
| 96 | Spirit of Rebellion C | .10 | .20 |
| 97 | Planetary Uprising U | .60 | 1.00 |
| 98 | Spy Net C | .10 | .20 |
| 99 | Tactical Aptitude C | .10 | .20 |
| 100 | Caution U | .75 | 1.25 |
| 101 | Destiny C | .10 | .20 |
| 102 | Determination C | .10 | .20 |
| 103 | Guard U | .25 | .40 |
| 104 | Krayt Dragon Howl C | .10 | .20 |
| 105 | My Ally Is The Force U | .60 | 1.00 |
| 106 | Synchronicity C | .10 | .20 |
| 107 | Your Eyes Can Decive You U | .25 | .40 |
| 108 | Protective Mentor C | .10 | .20 |
| 109 | Confidence C | .10 | .20 |
| 110 | Garbagell Do C | .10 | .20 |
| 111 | Hold On C | .10 | .20 |
| 112 | Rebel U | .25 | .40 |
| 113 | Long Con C | .10 | .20 |
| 114 | Loth Cat and Mouse C | .10 | .20 |
| 115 | Never Tell Me the Odds U | .25 | .40 |
| 116 | Planned Explosion U | .25 | .40 |
| 117 | Double Dealing C | .10 | .20 |
| 118 | Life Debt U | .25 | .40 |
| 119 | Bombing Run U | .25 | .40 |
| 120 | Collateral Damage C | .10 | .20 |
| 121 | Salvo U | .40 | .60 |
| 122 | Suppression C | .10 | .20 |
| 123 | Aftermath C | .10 | .20 |
| 124 | Air Superiority C | .10 | .20 |
| 125 | Training U | 2.00 | 2.50 |
| 126 | Wingman C | .10 | .20 |
| 127 | Decisive Blow C | .10 | .20 |
| 128 | High Ground C | .10 | .20 |
| 129 | Momentum Shift U | .25 | .40 |
| 130 | Overconfidence C | .10 | .20 |
| 131 | Premonitions U | .25 | .40 |
| 132 | Rejuvenate C | .10 | .20 |
| 133 | Trust Your Instincts U | 1.25 | 2.00 |
| 134 | Meditate C | .10 | .20 |
| 135 | Force Illusion U | 2.00 | 3.00 |

| | | | |
|---|---|---|---|
| 136 Evade C | .10 | .20 |
| 137 New Orders U | .60 | 1.00 |
| 138 Parry C | .10 | .20 |
| 139 Swiftness C | .10 | .20 |
| 140 Resolve U | .25 | .40 |
| 141 Ammo Belt C | .10 | .20 |
| 142 Bolt Hole C | .10 | .20 |
| 143 Cheat U | .75 | 1.25 |
| 144 Diversion C | .10 | .20 |
| 145 Fair Trade U | .25 | .40 |
| 146 Friends in Low Places C | .10 | .20 |
| 147 Sabotage U | .25 | .40 |
| 148 Improvisation C | .10 | .20 |
| 149 Outmaneuver C | .10 | .20 |
| 150 Fast Hands U | 5.00 | 7.00 |
| 151 Carbon Freezing Chamber U | .25 | .40 |
| 152 Cargo Hold C | .10 | .20 |
| 153 Docking Bay C | .10 | .20 |
| 154 Ewok Village C | .10 | .20 |
| 155 Mazs Castle U | .25 | .40 |
| 156 Moisture Farm U | .25 | .40 |
| 157 Otoh Gunga C | .10 | .20 |
| 158 Secluded Beach C | .10 | .20 |
| 159 Secret Facility U | .25 | .40 |
| 160 War Torn Streets C | .10 | .20 |

## 2017 Star Wars Destiny Empire at War

| | | |
|---|---|---|
| COMPLETE SET (160) | 300.00 | 550.00 |
| BOOSTER BOX (36 PACKS) | 85.00 | 120.00 |
| BOOSTER PACK (5 CARDS) | 3.00 | 5.00 |
| UNLISTED C | .10 | .20 |
| UNLISTED U | .40 | .60 |
| UNLISTED R | 2.00 | 5.00 |
| RELEASED IN FALL 2017 | | |
| 1 †Ciena Ree† Adept Pilot R | 2.00 | 5.00 |
| 2 †General Hux† Aspiring Commander R | 2.00 | 5.00 |
| 3 †MagnaGuard R | 2.00 | 5.00 |
| 4 †Thrawn†Master Strategist L | 15.00 | 20.00 |
| 5 †AT DP R | 2.00 | 5.00 |
| 6 †Probe Droid R | 2.00 | 5.00 |
| 7 †T 7 Ion Disruptor Rifle L | 8.00 | 15.00 |
| 8 †Quinlan Vost† Dark Disciple R | 2.00 | 5.00 |
| 9 †Servant of the Dark Side R | 2.00 | 5.00 |
| 10 †Seventh Sister† Agile Inquisitor L | 8.00 | 15.00 |
| 11 †Grand Inquisitor† Sith Loyalist L | 8.00 | 15.00 |
| 12 †Darth Vaders TIE Advanced R | 2.00 | 5.00 |
| 13 †ID9 Seeker Droid R | 2.00 | 5.00 |

| | | |
|---|---|---|
| 14 †Temptation R | 2.00 | 5.00 |
| 15 †Grand Inquisitors Lightsaber L | 8.00 | 15.00 |
| 16 †Bazine Netal† Master Manipulator R | 2.00 | 5.00 |
| 17 †Bosskt† Wookiee Slayer R | 2.00 | 5.00 |
| 18 †Cad Ban† Vicious Mercenary L | 15.00 | 20.00 |
| 19 †Gamorrean Guard R | 2.00 | 5.00 |
| 20 †Hounds Tooth L | 8.00 | 15.00 |
| 21 †Cable Launcher R | 2.00 | 5.00 |
| 22 †LL 30 Blaster Pistol R | 2.00 | 5.00 |
| 23 †Relby V10 Mortar Gun R | 2.00 | 5.00 |
| 24 †General Rieekan† Defensive Mastermind R | 2.00 | 5.00 |
| 25 †Hera Syndulla† Phoenix Leader R | 2.00 | 5.00 |
| 26 †K 2SO† Reprogrammed Droid L | 8.00 | 15.00 |
| 27 †Rookie Pilot R | 2.00 | 5.00 |
| 28 †Ghost L | 8.00 | 15.00 |
| 29 †Y Wing R | 2.00 | 5.00 |
| 30 †A280 Blaster Rifle R | 2.00 | 5.00 |
| 31 †Ahsoka Tano† Force Operative L | 20.00 | 25.00 |
| 32 †Jedi Instructor R | 2.00 | 5.00 |
| 33 †Kanan Jarrus† Rebel Jedi R | 2.00 | 5.00 |
| 34 †Mace Windu† Jedi Champion L | 8.00 | 15.00 |
| 35 †Training Remote R | 2.00 | 5.00 |
| 36 †Master of the Council L | 8.00 | 15.00 |
| 37 †Coordination R | 2.00 | 5.00 |
| 38 †Ezra Bridger† Force sensitive Thief R | 2.00 | 5.00 |
| 39 †Lando Calrissian† Galactic Entrepreneur R | 2.00 | 5.00 |
| 40 †Sabine Wren† Explosives Expert L | 8.00 | 15.00 |
| 41 †Wookiee Warrior R | 2.00 | 5.00 |
| 42 †Chopper L | 8.00 | 15.00 |
| 43 †Energy Slingshot R | 2.00 | 5.00 |
| 44 †Tough Haggler R | 2.00 | 5.00 |
| 45 †T 47 Airspeeder R | 2.00 | 5.00 |
| 46 †LR1K Sonic Cannon L | 8.00 | 15.00 |
| 47 †Electrostaff R | 2.00 | 5.00 |
| 48 †Natural Pilot R | 2.00 | 5.00 |
| 49 †Ancient Lightsaber L | 35.00 | 45.00 |
| 50 †Psychometry R | 2.00 | 5.00 |
| 51 †Shoto Lightsaber R | 2.00 | 5.00 |
| 52 †Weapons Cache R | 2.00 | 5.00 |
| 53 †BD 1 Cutter Vibro AX R | 2.00 | 5.00 |
| 54 †Extortion R | 2.00 | 5.00 |
| 55 †X 8 Night Sniper L | 8.00 | 15.00 |
| 56 †Z 95 Headhunter R | 2.00 | 5.00 |
| 57 †Chance Cube R | 2.00 | 5.00 |
| 58 †EMP Grenades R | 2.00 | 5.00 |
| 59 †Lead by Example R | 2.00 | 5.00 |
| 60 †Scatterblaster R | 2.00 | 5.00 |
| 61 †Commandeer U | .40 | .60 |
| 62 †Crossfire C | .10 | .20 |
| 63 †Drop Your Weapon! U | .40 | .60 |
| 64 †Imperial Backing U | .40 | .60 |
| 65 †Prepare for War C | .10 | .20 |
| 66 †Red Alert C | .10 | .20 |
| 67 †Ruthless Tactics C | .10 | .20 |
| 68 †Take Prisoner U | .40 | .60 |
| 69 †Imperial HQ C | .10 | .20 |
| 70 †As You Command C | .10 | .20 |
| 71 †Cornered Prey C | .10 | .20 |
| 72 †Indomitable C | .10 | .20 |
| 73 †It Will All Be Mine U | .40 | .60 |
| 74 †Kill Them All C | .10 | .20 |
| 75 †Unyielding U | .40 | .60 |
| 76 †Insidious C | .10 | .20 |
| 77 †Hate U | .40 | .60 |

| | | |
|---|---|---|
| 78 †Anarchy U | .40 | .60 |
| 79 †Bounty Postings C | .10 | .20 |
| 80 †Buy Out U | .40 | .60 |
| 81 †Coercion U | .40 | .60 |
| 82 †Only Business Matters C | .10 | .20 |
| 83 †Pilfered Goods U | .40 | .60 |
| 84 †Twin Shadows U | .40 | .60 |
| 85 †Hutt Ties C | .10 | .20 |
| 86 †Deadly U | .40 | .60 |
| 87 †No Survivors C | .10 | .20 |
| 88 †Detention Center U | .40 | .60 |
| 89 †All Quiet On The Front U | .40 | .60 |
| 90 †Entrenched U | .40 | .60 |
| 91 †Fortuitous Strike C | .10 | .20 |
| 92 †Rearguard C | .10 | .20 |
| 93 †Reckless Reentry U | .40 | .60 |
| 94 †Strike Briefing C | .10 | .20 |
| 95 †Swift Strike C | .10 | .20 |
| 96 †Rally Aid U | .40 | .60 |
| 97 †Shield Generator C | .10 | .20 |
| 98 †At Peace C | .10 | .20 |
| 99 †Bestow C | .10 | .20 |
| 100 †Bring Balance U | .40 | .60 |
| 101 †Reaping The Crystal U | .40 | .60 |
| 102 †Secret Mission C | .10 | .20 |
| 103 †Trust The Force C | .10 | .20 |
| 104 †Funeral Pyre C | .10 | .20 |
| 105 †Yodas Quarters U | .40 | .60 |
| 106 †Fearless U | .40 | .60 |
| 107 †Against The Odds C | .10 | .20 |
| 108 †Appraise C | .10 | .20 |
| 109 †Bad Feeling C | .10 | .20 |
| 110 †Double Cross U | .40 | .60 |
| 111 †Impersonate U | .40 | .60 |
| 112 †Local Patrol C | .10 | .20 |
| 113 †Quick Escape U | .40 | .60 |
| 114 †Tenacity C | .10 | .20 |
| 115 †Running Interference U | .40 | .60 |
| 116 †Thermal Paint C | .10 | .20 |
| 117 †Defiance C | .10 | .20 |
| 118 †Covering Fire C | .10 | .20 |
| 119 †Deploy Squadron C | .10 | .20 |
| 120 †Fall Back U | .40 | .60 |
| 121 †Feint U | .40 | .60 |
| 122 †Flanking Maneuver U | .40 | .60 |
| 123 †Heat Of Battle C | .10 | .20 |
| 124 †Pinned Down C | .10 | .20 |
| 125 †The Day is Ours C | .10 | .20 |
| 126 †Drop Zone U | .40 | .60 |
| 127 †Tech Team C | .10 | .20 |
| 128 †Battle of Wills U | .40 | .60 |
| 129 †Force Vision C | .10 | .20 |
| 130 †Lightsaber Pull C | .10 | .20 |
| 131 †Lightsaber Training C | .10 | .20 |
| 132 †No Surrender C | .10 | .20 |
| 133 †Something familiar U | .40 | .60 |
| 134 †Voices Cry Out C | .10 | .20 |
| 135 †Keen Instincts U | .40 | .60 |
| 136 †Battle Rage C | .10 | .20 |
| 137 †Disable C | .10 | .20 |
| 138 †Persuade C | .10 | .20 |
| 139 †Pickpocket C | .10 | .20 |
| 140 †Threaten U | .40 | .60 |
| 141 †Trickery U | .40 | .60 |

| | | |
|---|---|---|
| 142 †Truce C | .10 | .20 |
| 143 †Stolen Cache C | .10 | .20 |
| 144 †Hidden Agenda U | .40 | .60 |
| 145 †Mandalorian Armor C | .10 | .20 |
| 146 †Dangerous Mission C | .10 | .20 |
| 147 †Endurance U | .40 | .60 |
| 148 †Partnership C | .10 | .20 |
| 149 †Recycle C | .10 | .20 |
| 150 †Rend C | .10 | .20 |
| 151 †Roll On C | .10 | .20 |
| 152 †Plastoid Armor C | .10 | .20 |
| 153 †BOmarr Monastery† Teth C | .10 | .20 |
| 154 †Fort Anaxes† Anaxes U | .40 | .60 |
| 155 †Garel Spaceport† Garel U | .40 | .60 |
| 156 †Imperial Academy† Lothal U | .40 | .60 |
| 157 †Main Plaza† Vashka C | .10 | .20 |
| 158 †Medical Center† Kaliida Shoals U | .40 | .60 |
| 159 †Port District† Bespin U | .40 | .60 |
| 160 †Weapons Factory Alpha† Cymoon 1 U | .40 | .60 |

### 1999 Young Jedi Menace of Darth Maul

Darth Maul
Sith Assassin

6 POWER

5 DAMAGE

Subtracts 2 from his DAMAGE when he is using Darth Maul's Lightsaber.

| | | |
|---|---|---|
| COMPLETE SET (140) | 10.00 | 25.00 |
| BOOSTER BOX (30 PACKS) | 30.00 | 50.00 |
| BOOSTER PACK (11 CARDS) | 1.00 | 2.00 |
| RELEASED ON MAY 12, 1999 | | |
| 1 Obi-Wan Kenobi, Young Jedi R | 3.00 | 5.00 |
| 2 Qui-Gon Jinn, Jedi Master R | 2.50 | 4.00 |
| 3 Jar Jar Binks, Gungan Chuba Thief R | 1.50 | 2.50 |
| 4 Anakin Skywalker, Podracer Pilot R | 1.25 | 2.00 |
| 5 Padme Naberrie, Handmaiden R | 2.00 | 3.00 |
| 6 Captain Panaka, Protector of the Queen R | 1.25 | 2.00 |
| 7 Mace Windu, Jedi Master R | 1.50 | 2.50 |
| 8 Queen Amidala, Ruler of Naboo R | 2.00 | 3.00 |
| 9 Queen Amidala, Royal Leader R | 2.00 | 3.00 |
| 10 Yoda, Jedi Master R | 2.00 | 3.00 |
| 11 R2-D2, Astromech Droid R | 1.50 | 2.50 |
| 12 C-3PO, Anakin's Creation R | 1.50 | 2.50 |
| 13 Boss Nass, Leader of the Gungans U | .50 | .75 |
| 14 Ric Olie, Ace Pilot U | .50 | .75 |
| 15 Captain Tarpals, Gungan Guard U | .50 | .75 |
| 16 Rabe, Handmaiden U | .50 | .75 |
| 17 Rep Been, Gungan U | .50 | .75 |
| 18 Mas Amedda, Vice Chancellor U | .50 | .75 |
| 19 Naboo Officer, Battle Planner U | .50 | .75 |
| 20 Naboo Security, Guard C | .15 | .25 |
| 21 Bravo Pilot, Veteran Flyer C | .15 | .25 |

| | | |
|---|---|---|
| 22 Gungan Official, Bureaucrat C | .15 | .25 |
| 23 Gungan Soldier, Scout C | .15 | .25 |
| 24 Gungan Guard C | .15 | .25 |
| 25 Gungan Warrior, Infantry C | .15 | .25 |
| 26 Gungan Soldier, Veteran C | .15 | .25 |
| 27 Ishi Tib, Warrior C | .15 | .25 |
| 28 Ithorian, Merchant C | .15 | .25 |
| 29 Jawa, Thief C | .15 | .25 |
| 30 Jawa, Bargainer S | .15 | .25 |
| 31 Royal Guard, Leader C | .15 | .25 |
| 32 Royal Guard, Veteran C | .15 | .25 |
| 33 Obi-Wan Kenobi, Jedi Padawan S | .15 | .25 |
| 34 Obi-Wan Kenobi's Lightsaber R | 1.50 | 2.50 |
| 35 Jedi Lightsaber | .50 | .75 |
| Constructed by Ki-Adi-Mundi U | | |
| 36 Anakin Skywalker's Podracer R | 1.25 | 2.00 |
| 37 Captain Panaka's Blaster C | .15 | .25 |
| 38 Jar Jar Binks' Electropole U | .50 | .75 |
| 39 Electropole C | .15 | .25 |
| 40 Eopie C | .15 | .25 |
| 41 Kaadu C | .15 | .25 |
| 42 Flash Speeder C | .15 | .25 |
| 43 Jawa Ion Blaster C | .15 | .25 |
| 44 Naboo Blaster C | .15 | .25 |
| 45 Blaster C | .15 | .25 |
| 46 Blaster Rifle C | .15 | .25 |
| 47 Anakin Skywalker | .50 | .75 |
| Meet Obi-Wan Kenobi U | | |
| 48 Are You An Angel? U | .50 | .75 |
| 49 Cha Skrunee Da Pat, Sleemo C | .15 | .25 |
| 50 Counterparts U | .50 | .75 |
| 51 Da Beings Hereabouts Cawazy C | .15 | .25 |
| 52 Enough Of This Pretense U | .50 | .75 |
| 53 Fear Attracts The Fearful U | .50 | .75 |
| 54 Gungan Curiosity C | .15 | .25 |
| 55 He Was Meant To Help You U | .50 | .75 |
| 56 I Have A Bad Feeling About This U | .50 | .75 |
| 57 I've Been Trained In Defense U | .50 | .75 |
| 58 Security Volunteers C | .15 | .25 |
| 59 Shmi's Pride U | .50 | .75 |
| 60 The Federation Has Gone Too Far C | .15 | .25 |
| 61 The Negotiations Were Short C | .15 | .25 |
| 62 The Queen's Plan C | .15 | .25 |
| 63 We're Not In Trouble Yet U | .50 | .75 |
| 64 Yousa Guys Bombad! R | 1.00 | 1.50 |
| 65 Tatooine Podrace Arena S | .15 | .25 |
| 66 Coruscant Capital City S | .15 | .25 |
| 67 Naboo Theed Palace S | .15 | .25 |
| 68 Bravo 1, Naboo Starfighter U | .50 | .75 |
| 69 Naboo Starfighter C | .15 | .25 |
| 70 Republic Cruiser, Transport C | .15 | .25 |
| 71 Darth Maul, Sith Apprentice R | 4.00 | 6.00 |
| 72 Darth Sidious, Sith Master R | 2.50 | 4.00 |
| 73 Sebulba, Bad-Tempered Dug R | 1.50 | 2.50 |
| 74 Watto, Slave Owner R | 1.25 | 2.00 |
| 75 Aurra Sing, Bounty Hunter R | 2.00 | 3.00 |
| 76 Jabba the Hutt, Vile Crime Lord R | 1.50 | 2.50 |
| 77 Gardulla the Hutt, Crime Lord U | .50 | .75 |
| 78 Destroyer Droid Squad | 1.00 | 1.50 |
| Security Division R | | |
| 79 Battle Droid Squad, Assault Unit R | 1.25 | 2.00 |
| 80 Ben Quadinaros, Podracer Pilot U | .50 | .75 |
| 81 Gasgano, Podracer Pilot U | .50 | .75 |
| 82 Mawhonic, Podracer Pilot U | .50 | .75 |

| | | |
|---|---|---|
| 83 Teemto Pagalies, Podracer Pilot U | .50 | .75 |
| 84 Bib Fortuna, Twi'lek Advisor U | .50 | .75 |
| 85 Ann and Tann Gella | .50 | .75 |
| Sebulba's Attendants U | | |
| 86 Gragra, Chuba Peddler C | .15 | .25 |
| 87 Passel Argente, Senator C | .15 | .25 |
| 88 Trade Federation Tank | 1.25 | 2.00 |
| Armored Division R | | |
| 89 Destroyer Droid, Wheel Droid C | .15 | .25 |
| 90 Destroyer Droid, Defense Droid C | .15 | .25 |
| 91 Sith Probe Droid, Spy Drone C | .15 | .25 |
| 92 Pit Droid, Engineer C | .15 | .25 |
| 93 Pit Droid, Heavy Lifter C | .15 | .25 |
| 94 Pit Droid, Mechanic C | .15 | .25 |
| 95 Tusken Raider, Nomad C | .15 | .25 |
| 96 Tusken Raider, Marksman C | .15 | .25 |
| 97 Battle Droid: Pilot, MTT Division C | .15 | .25 |
| 98 Battle Droid: Security, MTT Division C | .15 | .25 |
| 99 Battle Droid: Infantry, MTT Division C | .15 | .25 |
| 100 Battle Droid: Officer, MTT Division C | .15 | .25 |
| 101 Battle Droid: Pilot, AAT Division C | .15 | .25 |
| 102 Battle Droid: Security, AAT Division C | .15 | .25 |
| 103 Battle Droid: Infantry, AAT Division C | .15 | .25 |
| 104 Battle Droid: Officer, AAT Division C | .15 | .25 |
| 105 Neimoidian, Trade Federation Pilot S | .15 | .25 |
| 106 Darth Maul, Sith Lord S | .60 | 1.00 |
| 107 Sith Lightsaber R | 1.25 | 2.00 |
| 108 Aurra Sing's Blaster Rifle R | 1.00 | 1.50 |
| 109 Sebulba's Podracer R | 1.00 | 1.50 |
| 110 Ben Quadinaros' Podracer U | .50 | .75 |
| 111 Gasgano's Podracer U | .50 | .75 |
| 112 Mawhonic's Podracer U | .50 | .75 |
| 113 Teemto Pagalies' Podracer U | .50 | .75 |
| 114 Trade Federation Tank Laser Cannon U | .50 | .75 |
| 115 Multi Troop Transport U | .50 | .75 |
| 116 STAP U | .50 | .75 |
| 117 Tatooine Thunder Rifle C | .15 | .25 |
| 118 Battle Droid Blaster Rifle C | .15 | .25 |
| 119 Blaster C | .15 | .25 |
| 120 Blaster Rifle C | .15 | .25 |
| 121 At Last We Will Have Revenge R | 1.00 | 1.50 |
| 122 Begin Landing Your Troops C | .15 | .25 |
| 123 Boonta Eve Podrace U | .50 | .75 |
| 124 Grueling Contest U | .50 | .75 |
| 125 In Complete Control C | .15 | .25 |
| 126 Kaa Bazza Kundee Hodrudda! U | .50 | .75 |
| 127 Opee Sea Killer C | .15 | .25 |
| 128 Podrace Preparation U | .50 | .75 |
| 129 Sandstorm C | .15 | .25 |
| 130 Sniper C | .15 | .25 |
| 131 The Invasion Is On Schedule C | .15 | .25 |
| 132 Vile Gangsters U | .50 | .75 |
| 133 Watto's Wager U | .50 | .75 |
| 134 You Have Been Well Trained R | 1.00 | 1.50 |
| 135 Tatooine Desert Landing Site S | .15 | .25 |
| 136 Coruscant Jedi Council Chamber S | .15 | .25 |
| 137 Naboo Gungan Swamp S | .15 | .25 |
| 138 Darth Maul's Starfighter | 1.50 | 2.50 |
| Sith Infiltrator R | | |
| 139 Droid Starfighter C | .15 | .25 |
| 140 Battleship | .15 | .25 |
| Trade Federation Transport C | | |

**1999 Young Jedi Menace of Darth Maul Foil**

| | | |
|---|---|---|
| COMPLETE SET (18) | 6.00 | 15.00 |
| RELEASED ON MAY 12, 1999 | | |
| F1 Obi-Wan Kenobi, Young Jedi R | 4.00 | 6.00 |
| F2 Jar-Jar Binks, Gungan Chuba Thief R | 2.00 | 3.00 |
| F3 Mace Windu, Jedi Master U | 2.00 | 3.00 |
| F4 Queen Amidala, Ruler of Naboo U | 3.00 | 5.00 |
| F5 C-3PO, Anakin's Creation U | 2.00 | 3.00 |
| F6 Obi-Wan Kenobi's Lightsaber C | 1.50 | 2.50 |
| F7 Anakin Skywalker's Podracer C | 1.25 | 2.00 |
| F8 Bravo 1, Naboo Starfighter C | .60 | 1.00 |
| F9 Republic Cruiser, Transport C | .60 | 1.00 |
| F10 Darth Maul, Sith Apprentice R | 5.00 | 8.00 |
| F11 Darth Sidious, Sith Master R | 3.00 | 5.00 |
| F12 Destroyer Droid Squad | 1.00 | 1.50 |
| Security Division U | | |
| F13 Battle Droid Squad, Assault Unit U | 1.00 | 1.50 |
| F14 Sebulba's Podracer U | 1.00 | 1.50 |
| F15 Ben Quadinaros' Podracer C | .60 | 1.00 |
| F16 Gasgano's Podracer C | .60 | 1.00 |
| F17 Mawhonic's Podracer C | .60 | 1.00 |
| F18 Teemto Pagalies' Podracer C | .60 | 1.00 |

## 1999 Young Jedi The Jedi Council

| | | |
|---|---|---|
| COMPLETE SET (140) | 8.00 | 20.00 |
| BOOSTER BOX (30 PACKS) | 20.00 | 30.00 |
| BOOSTER BOX (11 CARDS) | .75 | 1.25 |
| RELEASED ON OCTOBER 27, 1999 | | |
| 1 Obi-Wan Kenobi, Jedi Apprentice R | 2.50 | 4.00 |
| 2 Qui-Gon Jinn, Jedi Protector R | 2.00 | 3.00 |
| 3 Jar-Jar Binks, Gungan Outcast R | 1.25 | 2.00 |
| 4 Anakin Skywalker, Child of Prophecy R | 1.25 | 2.00 |
| 5 Padme Naberrie, Queen's Handmaiden R | 1.50 | 2.50 |
| 6 Captain Panaka, Amidala's Bodyguard R | 1.00 | 1.50 |
| 7 Mace Windu | 1.25 | 2.00 |
| Senior Jedi Council Member R | | |
| 8 Queen Amidala, Representative of Naboo R | 1.50 | 2.50 |
| 9 Queen Amidala, Voice of Her People R | 1.50 | 2.50 |
| 10 Yoda, Jedi Council Member R | 1.50 | 2.50 |
| 11 R2-D2, Loyal Droid R | 1.25 | 2.00 |
| 12 Ki-Adi-Mundi, Cerean Jedi Knight R | 1.25 | 2.00 |
| 13 Adi Gallia, Corellian Jedi Master U | .50 | .75 |
| 14 Depa Billaba, Jedi Master U | .50 | .75 |
| 15 Eeth Koth, Zabrak Jedi Master U | .50 | .75 |
| 16 Even Piell, Lannik Jedi Master U | .50 | .75 |
| 17 Oppo Rancisis, Jedi Master U | .50 | .75 |

| | | |
|---|---|---|
| 18 Plo Koon, Jedi Master U | .50 | .75 |
| 19 Saesee Tiin, Iktotchi Jedi Master U | .50 | .75 |
| 20 Yaddle, Jedi Master U | .50 | .75 |
| 21 Yarael Poof, Quermian Jedi Master U | .50 | .75 |
| 22 Boss Nass, Gungan Leader U | .50 | .75 |
| 23 Ric Olié, Chief Pilot U | .50 | .75 |
| 24 Captain Tarpals, Gungan Battle Leader U | .50 | .75 |
| 25 Eirtae, Handmaiden U | .50 | .75 |
| 26 Valorum, Supreme Chancellor C | .15 | .25 |
| 27 Sci Taria, Chancellor's Aide C | .15 | .25 |
| 28 Naboo Officer, Liberator C | .15 | .25 |
| 29 Bravo Pilot, Naboo Volunteer C | .15 | .25 |
| 30 Naboo Security, Amidala's Guard C | .15 | .25 |
| 31 Republic Captain, Officer C | .15 | .25 |
| 32 Republic Pilot, Veteran C | .15 | .25 |
| 33 Coruscant Guard | .15 | .25 |
| Coruscant Detachment C | | |
| 34 Coruscant Guard, Peacekeeper C | .15 | .25 |
| 35 Coruscant Guard, Officer C | .15 | .25 |
| 36 Coruscant Guard, Chancellor's Guard C | .15 | .25 |
| 37 Wookiee Senator, Representative C | .15 | .25 |
| 38 Galactic Senator, Delegate S | .15 | .25 |
| 39 Obi-Wan Kenobi, Jedi Warrior S | .15 | .25 |
| 40 Qui-Gon Jinn's Lightsaber R | 1.00 | 1.50 |
| 41 Amidala's Blaster R | 1.00 | 1.50 |
| 42 Adi Gallia's Lightsaber U | .50 | .75 |
| 43 Coruscant Guard Blaster Rifle U | .50 | .75 |
| 44 Ascension Gun C | .15 | .25 |
| 45 Electropole C | .15 | .25 |
| 46 Kaadu C | .15 | .25 |
| 47 Flash Speeder C | .15 | .25 |
| 48 Gian Speeder C | .15 | .25 |
| 49 Naboo Blaster C | .15 | .25 |
| 50 Blaster C | .15 | .25 |
| 51 Blaster Rifle C | .15 | .25 |
| 52 Balance To The Force U | .50 | .75 |
| 53 Brave Little Droid U | .50 | .75 |
| 54 Dos Mackineeks No Comen Here! C | .15 | .25 |
| 55 Galactic Chancellor C | .15 | .25 |
| 56 Hate Leads To Suffering U | .50 | .75 |
| 57 I Will Not Cooperate U | .50 | .75 |
| 58 Invasion! C | .15 | .25 |
| 59 May The Force Be With You C | .15 | .25 |
| 60 Senator Palpatine C | .15 | .25 |
| 61 The Might Of The Republic C | .15 | .25 |
| 62 We Don't Have Time For This C | .15 | .25 |
| 63 We Wish To Board At Once C | .15 | .25 |
| 64 Wisdom Of The Council R | 1.00 | 1.50 |
| 65 Tatooine Mos Espa S | .15 | .25 |
| 66 Coruscant Jedi Council Chamber S | .15 | .25 |
| 67 Naboo Gungan Swamp S | .15 | .25 |
| 68 Bravo 2, Naboo Starfighter U | .50 | .75 |
| 69 Naboo Starfighter C | .15 | .25 |
| 70 Radiant VII, Republic Cruiser Transport C | .15 | .25 |
| 71 Darth Maul, Master of Evil R | 3.00 | 5.00 |
| 72 Darth Sidious, Lord of the Sith R | 2.00 | 3.00 |
| 73 Sebulba, Podracer Pilot R | 1.25 | 2.00 |
| 74 Watto, Junk Merchant R | 1.00 | 1.50 |
| 75 Jabba the Hutt, Gangster R | 1.25 | 2.00 |
| 76 Nute Gunray, Neimoidian Viceroy R | 1.00 | 1.50 |
| 77 Rune Haako, Neimoidian Advisor R | 1.00 | 1.50 |
| 78 Destroyer Droid Squad, Defense Division R | 1.00 | 1.50 |
| 79 Battle Droid Squad, Escort Unit R | 1.00 | 1.50 |
| 80 Trade Federation Tank, Assault Division R | 1.00 | 1.50 |

| | | |
|---|---|---|
| 81 Lott Dod, Neimoidian Senator R | 1.00 | 1.50 |
| 82 Fode and Beed, Podrace Announcer R | 1.00 | 1.50 |
| 83 Clegg Holdfast, Podracer Pilot U | .50 | .75 |
| 84 Dud Bolt, Podracer Pilot U | .50 | .75 |
| 85 Mars Guo, Podracer Pilot U | .50 | .75 |
| 86 Ody Mandrell, Podracer Pilot U | .50 | .75 |
| 87 Ratts Tyerell, Podracer Pilot U | .50 | .75 |
| 88 Aks Moe, Senator C | .15 | .25 |
| 89 Horox Ryyder, Senator C | .15 | .25 |
| 90 Edcel Bar Gane, Roona Senator C | .15 | .25 |
| 91 Galactic Delegate, Representative C | .15 | .25 |
| 92 Destroyer Droid, Assault Droid C | .15 | .25 |
| 93 Destroyer Droid, Battleship Security C | .15 | .25 |
| 94 Sith Probe Droid, Hunter Droid C | .15 | .25 |
| 95 Rodian, Mercenary C | .15 | .25 |
| 96 Battle Droid: Pilot, Assault Division C | .15 | .25 |
| 97 Battle Droid: Security, Assault Division C | .15 | .25 |
| 98 Battle Droid: Infantry, Assault Division C | .15 | .25 |
| 99 Battle Droid: Officer, Assault Division C | .15 | .25 |
| 100 Battle Droid: Pilot, Guard Division C | .15 | .25 |
| 101 Battle Droid: Security, Guard Division C | .15 | .25 |
| 102 Battle Droid: Infantry, Guard Division C | .15 | .25 |
| 103 Battle Droid: Officer, Guard Division C | .15 | .25 |
| 104 Neimoidian Aide | .15 | .25 |
| Trade Federation Delegate S | | |
| 105 Darth Maul, Sith Warrior S | .15 | .25 |
| 106 Darth Maul's Lightsaber R | 1.00 | 1.50 |
| 107 Darth Maul's Sith Speeder R | 1.00 | 1.50 |
| 108 Clegg Holdfast's Podracer U | .50 | .75 |
| 109 Dud Bolt's Podracer U | .50 | .75 |
| 110 Mars Guo's Podracer U | .50 | .75 |
| 111 Ody Mandrell's Podracer U | .50 | .75 |
| 112 Ratts Tyerell's Podracer U | .50 | .75 |
| 113 Trade Federation Tank Laser Cannon U | .50 | .75 |
| 114 Multi Troop Transport U | .50 | .75 |
| 115 STAP U | .50 | .75 |
| 116 Thermal Detonator U | .50 | .75 |
| 117 Battle Droid Blaster Rifle C | .15 | .25 |
| 118 Blaster C | .15 | .25 |
| 119 Blaster Rifle C | .15 | .25 |
| 120 I Object! C | .15 | .25 |
| 121 I Will Deal With Them Myself C | .15 | .25 |
| 122 Let Them Make The First Move R | 1.00 | 1.50 |
| 123 Move Against The Jedi First C | .15 | .25 |
| 124 Open Fire! U | .50 | .75 |
| 125 Seal Off The Bridge U | .50 | .75 |
| 126 Start Your Engines! U | .50 | .75 |
| 127 Switch To Bio C | .15 | .25 |
| 128 Take Them To Camp Four C | .15 | .25 |
| 129 Very Unusual C | .15 | .25 |
| 130 Vote Of No Confidence C | .15 | .25 |
| 131 We Are Meeting No Resistance C | .15 | .25 |
| 132 We Have Them On The Run U | .50 | .75 |
| 133 Yoka To Bantha Poodoo C | .15 | .25 |
| 134 Your Little Insurrection Is At An End U | .50 | .75 |
| 135 Tatooine Podrace Arena S | .15 | .25 |
| 136 Coruscant Galactic Senate S | .15 | .25 |
| 137 Naboo Battle Plains S | .15 | .25 |
| 138 Sith Infiltrator, Starfighter U | .50 | .75 |
| 139 Droid Starfighter C | .15 | .25 |
| 140 Battleship, Trade Federation Transport C | .15 | .25 |

### 1999 Young Jedi The Jedi Council Foil

| | | |
|---|---|---|
| COMPLETE SET (18) | 4.00 | 10.00 |
| RELEASED ON OCTOBER 27, 1999 | | |
| F1 Obi-Wan Kenobi, Jedi Apprentice UR | 3.00 | 5.00 |
| F2 Qui-Gon Jinn, Jedi Protector SR | 1.25 | 2.00 |
| F3 PadmÉ Naberrie | 1.25 | 2.00 |
| Queen's Handmaiden SR | | |
| F4 Captain Panaka | 1.00 | 1.50 |
| Amidala's Bodyguard SR | | |
| F5 Mace Windu | 1.50 | 2.50 |
| Senior Jedi Council Member SR | | |
| F6 Queen Amidala | 2.00 | 3.00 |
| Representative of Naboo VR | | |
| F7 R2-D2, Loyal Droid VR | 2.00 | 3.00 |
| F8 Qui-Gon Jinn's Lightsaber VR | .60 | 1.00 |
| F9 Amidala's Blaster VR | .60 | 1.00 |
| F10 Darth Maul, Master of Evil UR | 3.00 | 5.00 |
| F11 Darth Sidious, Lord of the Sith UR | 2.00 | 3.00 |
| F12 Watto, Junk Merchant SR | 1.00 | 1.50 |
| F13 Jabba the Hutt, Gangster SR | 1.00 | 1.50 |
| F14 Nute Gunray, Neimoidian Viceroy SR | 1.00 | 1.50 |
| F15 Rune Haako, Neimoidian Advisor VR | .60 | 1.00 |
| F16 Lott Dod, Neimoidian Senator VR | .60 | 1.00 |
| F17 Darth Maul's Lightsaber VR | .60 | 1.00 |
| F18 Darth Maul's Sith Speeder VR | .60 | 1.00 |

### 2000 Young Jedi Battle of Naboo

| | | |
|---|---|---|
| COMPLETE SET (140) | 8.00 | 20.00 |
| BOOSTER BOX (30 PACKS) | 15.00 | 30.00 |
| BOOSTER PACK (11 CARDS) | .75 | 1.25 |
| RELEASED ON APRIL 5, 2000 | | |
| 1 Obi-Wan Kenobi, Jedi Knight R | 2.50 | 4.00 |
| 2 Qui-Gon Jinn, Jedi Ambassador R | 2.00 | 3.00 |
| 3 Jar Jar Binks, Bombad Gungan General R | 1.25 | 2.00 |
| 4 Anakin Skywalker, Padawan R | 1.25 | 2.00 |
| 5 Padme Naberrie, Amidala's Handmaiden R | 1.50 | 2.50 |
| 6 Captain Panaka, Veteran Leader R | 1.00 | 1.50 |
| 7 Mace Windu, Jedi Speaker R | 1.25 | 2.00 |
| 8 Queen Amidala, Resolute Negotiator R | 1.50 | 2.50 |
| 9 Queen Amidala, Keeper of the Peace R | 1.50 | 2.50 |
| 10 Yoda, Jedi Elder R | 1.50 | 2.50 |
| 11 R2-D2, The Queen's Hero R | 1.25 | 2.00 |
| 12 Boss Nass, Gungan Chief U | .50 | .75 |

| | | |
|---|---|---|
| 13 Ric Olie, Bravo Leader U | .50 | .75 |
| 14 Captain Tarpals, Gungan Officer U | .50 | .75 |
| 15 Sio Bibble, Governor of Naboo U | .50 | .75 |
| 16 Sabe, Handmaiden Decoy Queen U | .50 | .75 |
| 17 Sache, Handmaiden U | .50 | .75 |
| 18 Yane, Handmaiden U | .50 | .75 |
| 19 Naboo Officer, Squad Leader U | .50 | .75 |
| 20 Naboo Officer, Commander C | .15 | .25 |
| 21 Naboo Bureaucrat, Official C | .15 | .25 |
| 22 Naboo Security, Trooper C | .15 | .25 |
| 23 Naboo Security, Defender C | .15 | .25 |
| 24 Bravo Pilot, Ace Flyer C | .15 | .25 |
| 25 Coruscant Guard, Chancellor's Escort C | .15 | .25 |
| 26 Alderaan Diplomat, Senator C | .15 | .25 |
| 27 Council Member, Naboo Governor C | .15 | .25 |
| 28 Gungan Warrior, Veteran C | .15 | .25 |
| 29 Gungan Guard, Lookout C | .15 | .25 |
| 30 Gungan General, Army Leader C | .15 | .25 |
| 31 Gungan Soldier, Infantry C | .15 | .25 |
| 32 Rep Officer, Gungan Diplomat S | .15 | .25 |
| 33 Obi-Wan Kenobi, Jedi Negotiator S | .15 | .25 |
| 34 Mace Windu's Lightsaber R | 1.00 | 1.50 |
| 35 Eeth Koth's Lightsaber U | .50 | .75 |
| 36 Captain Tarpals' Electropole U | .50 | .75 |
| 37 Planetary Shuttle C | .15 | .25 |
| 38 Fambaa C | .15 | .25 |
| 39 Electropole C | .15 | .25 |
| 40 Kaadu C | .15 | .25 |
| 41 Flash Speeder C | .15 | .25 |
| 42 Blaster C | .15 | .25 |
| 43 Heavy Blaster C | .15 | .25 |
| 44 Capture The Viceroy C | .15 | .25 |
| 45 Celebration C | .15 | .25 |
| 46 Guardians Of The Queen U | .50 | .75 |
| 47 Gunga City C | .15 | .25 |
| 48 Gungan Battle Cry U | .50 | .75 |
| 49 How Wude! U | .50 | .75 |
| 50 I Will Take Back What Is Ours C | .15 | .25 |
| 51 Jedi Force Push U | .50 | .75 |
| 52 Meeeesa Lika Dis! C | .15 | .25 |
| 53 NOOOOOOOOOO! R | 1.00 | 1.50 |
| 54 Thanks, Artoo! U | .50 | .75 |
| 55 The Chancellor's Ambassador U | .50 | .75 |
| 56 The Will Of The Force R | 1.00 | 1.50 |
| 57 Young Skywalker U | .50 | .75 |
| 58 Your Occupation Here Has Ended C | .15 | .25 |
| 59 Bombad General U | .50 | .75 |
| 60 Kiss Your Trade Franchise Goodbye U | .50 | .75 |
| 61 There's Always A Bigger Fish C | .15 | .25 |
| 62 Uh-Oh! C | .15 | .25 |
| 63 We Wish To Form An Alliance C | .15 | .25 |
| 64 Tatooine Desert Landing Site S | .15 | .25 |
| 65 Coruscant Galactic Senate S | .15 | .25 |
| 66 Naboo Battle Plains S | .15 | .25 |
| 67 Amidala's Starship, Royal Transport R | 1.00 | 1.50 |
| 68 Bravo 3, Naboo Starfighter U | .50 | .75 |
| 69 Naboo Starfighter C | .15 | .25 |
| 70 Republic Cruiser, Transport C | .15 | .25 |
| 71 Darth Maul, Dark Lord of the Sith R | 3.00 | 5.00 |
| 72 Darth Sidious, Sith Manipulator R | 2.00 | 3.00 |
| 73 Sebulba, Dangerous Podracer Pilot R | 1.00 | 1.50 |
| 74 Watto, Toydarian Gambler R | 1.00 | 1.50 |
| 75 Aurra Sing, Mercenary R | 1.25 | 2.00 |
| 76 Jabba The Hutt, Crime Lord R | 1.00 | 1.50 |

| | | |
|---|---|---|
| 77 Nute Gunray, Neimoidian Despot R | 1.00 | 1.50 |
| 78 Rune Haako, Neimoidian Deputy R | 1.00 | 1.50 |
| 79 Destroyer Droid Squad, Guard Division R | 1.00 | 1.50 |
| 80 Battle Droid Squad, Guard Unit R | 1.00 | 1.50 |
| 81 Trade Federation Tank, Guard Division R | 1.00 | 1.50 |
| 82 Trade Federation Tank, Patrol Division R | 1.00 | 1.50 |
| 83 P-59, Destroyer Droid Commander U | .50 | .75 |
| 84 OOM-9, Battle Droid Commander U | .50 | .75 |
| 85 Daultay Dofine, Neimoidian Attendant U | .50 | .75 |
| 86 Diva Shaliqua, Singer U | .50 | .75 |
| 87 Diva Funquita, Dancer U | .50 | .75 |
| 88 Bith, Musician U | .50 | .75 |
| 89 Quarren, Smuggler U | .50 | .75 |
| 90 Toonbuck Toora, Senator U | .50 | .75 |
| 91 Aqualish, Galactic Senator C | .15 | .25 |
| 92 Twi'lek Diplomat, Senator C | .15 | .25 |
| 93 Weequay, Enforcer C | .15 | .25 |
| 94 Nikto, Slave C | .15 | .25 |
| 95 Pacithhip, Prospector C | .15 | .25 |
| 96 Destroyer Droid, Vanguard Droid C | .15 | .25 |
| 97 Destroyer Droid, MTT Infantry C | .15 | .25 |
| 98 Sith Probe Droid, Remote Tracker C | .15 | .25 |
| 99 Battle Droid: Pilot, Patrol Division C | .15 | .25 |
| 100 Battle Droid: Security, Patrol Division C | .15 | .25 |
| 101 Battle Droid: Infantry, Patrol Division C | .15 | .25 |
| 102 Battle Droid: Officer, Patrol Division C | .15 | .25 |
| 103 Battle Droid: Pilot, Defense Division C | .15 | .25 |
| 104 Battle Droid: Security, Defense Division C | .15 | .25 |
| 105 Battle Droid: Infantry, Defense Division C | .15 | .25 |
| 106 Battle Droid: Officer, Defense Division C | .15 | .25 |
| 107 Neimoidian Advisor, Bureaucrat S | .15 | .25 |
| 108 Darth Maul, Evil Sith Lord S | .15 | .25 |
| 109 Darth Maul's Lightsaber R | 1.25 | 2.00 |
| 110 Sith Lightsaber R | 1.00 | 1.50 |
| 111 Darth Maul's Electrobinoculars U | .50 | .75 |
| 112 Trade Federation Tank Laser Cannon U | .50 | .75 |
| 113 Multi Troop Transport U | .50 | .75 |
| 114 STAP U | .50 | .75 |
| 115 Battle Droid Blaster Rifle C | .15 | .25 |
| 116 Blaster C | .15 | .25 |
| 117 Blaster Rifle C | .15 | .25 |
| 118 A Thousand Terrible Things C | .15 | .25 |
| 119 Armored Assault C | .15 | .25 |
| 120 Death From Above C | .15 | .25 |
| 121 Don't Spect A Werm Welcome C | .15 | .25 |
| 122 I Will Make It Legal C | .15 | .25 |
| 123 Not For A Sith R | 1.00 | 1.50 |
| 124 Now There Are Two Of Them U | .50 | .75 |
| 125 Sith Force Push U | .50 | .75 |
| 126 The Phantom Menace U | .50 | .75 |
| 127 They Win This Round C | .15 | .25 |
| 128 We Are Sending All Troops C | .15 | .25 |
| 129 After Her! C | .15 | .25 |
| 130 Da Dug Chaaa! U | .50 | .75 |
| 131 Sando Aqua Monster C | .15 | .25 |
| 132 They Will Not Stay Hidden For Long C | .15 | .25 |
| 133 This Is Too Close! U | .50 | .75 |
| 134 Tatooine Mos Espa S | .15 | .25 |
| 135 Coruscant Capital City S | .15 | .25 |
| 136 Naboo Theed Palace S | .15 | .25 |
| 137 Droid Control Ship | .50 | .75 |
| Trade Federation Transport U | | |

| | | | |
|---|---|---|---|
| 138 | Sith Infiltrator, Starfighter U | .50 | .75 |
| 139 | Droid Starfighter C | .15 | .25 |
| 140 | Battleship, Trade Federation Transport C | .15 | .25 |

### 2000 Young Jedi Battle of Naboo Foil

| | | | |
|---|---|---|---|
| COMPLETE SET (18) | | 4.00 | 10.00 |
| F1 | Obi-Wan Kenobi, Jedi Knight UR | 2.50 | 4.00 |
| F2 | Qui-Gon Jinn, Jedi Ambassador UR | 1.25 | 2.00 |
| F3 | Queen Amidala, Keeper of the Peace SR | 1.25 | 2.00 |
| F4 | Yoda, Jedi Elder SR | 1.25 | 2.00 |
| F5 | R2-D2, The Queen's Hero SR | 1.25 | 2.00 |
| F6 | Queen Amidala, Resolute Negotiator VR | 1.00 | 1.50 |
| F7 | Mace Windu's Lightsaber VR | .60 | 1.00 |
| F8 | The Will Of The Force VR | .60 | 1.00 |
| F9 | Amidala's Starship, Royal Transport VR | .60 | 1.00 |
| F10 | Darth Maul, Dark Lord of the Sith UR | 2.50 | 4.00 |
| F11 | Aurra Sing, Mercenary UR | 1.25 | 2.00 |
| F12 | Nute Gunray | 1.00 | 1.50 |
| | Neimoidian Despot SR | | |
| F13 | Destroyer Droid Squad | 1.00 | 1.50 |
| | Guard Division SR | | |
| F14 | Trade Federation Tank | 1.00 | 1.50 |
| | Guard Division SR | | |
| F15 | Battle Droid Squad, Guard Unit VR | .60 | 1.00 |
| F16 | Trade Federation Tank | .60 | 1.00 |
| | Patrol Division VR | | |
| F17 | Darth Maul's Lightsaber VR | .60 | 1.00 |
| F18 | Not For A Sith VR | .60 | 1.00 |

### 2000 Young Jedi Duel of the Fates

| | | | |
|---|---|---|---|
| COMPLETE SET (60) | | 5.00 | 12.00 |
| BOOSTER BOX (30 PACKS) | | 30.00 | 40.00 |
| BOOSTER PACK (11 CARDS) | | 1.00 | 1.50 |
| RELEASED ON NOVEMBER 8, 2000 | | | |
| 1 | Obi-Wan Kenobi, Jedi Student R | 2.50 | 4.00 |
| 2 | Qui-Gon Jinn, Jedi Mentor UR | 2.00 | 3.00 |
| 3 | Anakin Skywalker, Rookie Pilot R | 1.25 | 2.00 |
| 4 | Captain Panaka, Security Commander R | 1.00 | 1.50 |
| 5 | Mace Windu, Jedi Councilor R | 1.25 | 2.00 |
| 6 | Queen Amidala, Young Leader R | 1.50 | 2.50 |
| 7 | Yoda, Jedi Philosopher R | 1.50 | 2.50 |
| 8 | R2-D2, Repair Droid R | 1.25 | 2.00 |
| 9 | Ric Olie, Starship Pilot R | 1.00 | 1.50 |
| 10 | Bravo Pilot, Flyer C | .15 | .25 |
| 11 | Valorum, Leader of the Senate C | .15 | .25 |
| 12 | Qui-Gon Jinn's Lightsaber | 1.00 | 1.50 |
| | Wielded by Obi-Wan Kenobi R | | |
| 13 | Booma U | .50 | .75 |
| 14 | A Powerful Opponent C | .15 | .25 |
| 15 | Come On, Move! U | .50 | .75 |
| 16 | Critical Confrontation C | .15 | .25 |
| 17 | Gungan Mounted Troops U | .50 | .75 |
| 18 | Naboo Fighter Attack C | .15 | .25 |
| 19 | Qui-Gon's Final Stand C | .15 | .25 |
| 20 | Run The Blockade C | .15 | .25 |
| 21 | Twist Of Fate C | .15 | .25 |
| 22 | You Are Strong With The Force U | .50 | .75 |
| 23 | Gungan Energy Shield U | .50 | .75 |
| 24 | He Can See Things Before They Happen U | .50 | .75 |
| 25 | Jedi Meditation U | .50 | .75 |
| 26 | Jedi Training U | .50 | .75 |
| 27 | Naboo Royal Security Forces U | .50 | .75 |

| | | | |
|---|---|---|---|
| 28 | Pounded Unto Death C | .15 | .25 |
| 29 | Senate Guard C | .15 | .25 |
| 30 | Naboo Starfighter C | .15 | .25 |
| 31 | Darth Maul, Student of the Dark Side UR | 2.50 | 4.00 |
| 32 | Darth Sidious, Master of the Dark Side R | 1.50 | 2.50 |
| 33 | Aurra Sing, Trophy Collector R | 1.25 | 2.00 |
| 34 | Tey How, Neimoidian Command Officer R | 1.00 | 1.50 |
| 35 | OWO-1, Battle Droid Command Officer R | 1.00 | 1.50 |
| 36 | Rayno Vaca, Taxi Driver R | 1.00 | 1.50 |
| 37 | Baskol Yeesrim, Gran Senator R | 1.00 | 1.50 |
| 38 | Starfighter Droid, DFS-327 R | 1.00 | 1.50 |
| 39 | Starfighter Droid, DFS-1104 R | 1.00 | 1.50 |
| 40 | Starfighter Droid, DFS-1138 R | 1.00 | 1.50 |
| 41 | Jedi Lightsaber, Stolen by Aurra Sing U | .50 | .75 |
| 42 | Coruscant Taxi U | .50 | .75 |
| 43 | Neimoidian Viewscreen C | .15 | .25 |
| 44 | Battle Droid Patrol U | .50 | .75 |
| 45 | Change In Tactics C | .15 | .25 |
| 46 | Dangerous Encounter C | .15 | .25 |
| 47 | Darth Maul Defiant C | .15 | .25 |
| 48 | Impossible! C | .15 | .25 |
| 49 | It's A Standoff! U | .50 | .75 |
| 50 | Mobile Assassin U | .50 | .75 |
| 51 | Power Of The Sith C | .15 | .25 |
| 52 | Starfighter Screen C | .15 | .25 |
| 53 | To The Death C | .15 | .25 |
| 54 | Use Caution U | .50 | .75 |
| 55 | Blockade U | .50 | .75 |
| 56 | End This Pointless Debate U | .50 | .75 |
| 57 | The Duel Begins U | .50 | .75 |
| 58 | The Jedi Are Involved U | .50 | .75 |
| 59 | Where Are Those Droidekas? U | .50 | .75 |
| 60 | Droid Starfighter C | .15 | .25 |

### 2000 Young Jedi Enhanced Menace of Darth Maul

| | | | |
|---|---|---|---|
| P1 | Qui-Gon Jinn, Jedi Protector | 3.00 | 5.00 |
| P2 | Mace Windu, Jedi Warrior | 2.00 | 3.00 |
| P3 | Queen Amidala, Cunning Warrior | 6.00 | 10.00 |
| P4 | Darth Maul, Sith Assassin | 3.00 | 5.00 |
| P5 | Sebulba, Champion Podracer Pilot | 6.00 | 10.00 |
| P6 | Trade Federation Tank, Assault Leader | 4.00 | 6.00 |

### 2001 Young Jedi Boonta Eve Podrace

| | | | |
|---|---|---|---|
| COMPLETE SET (63) | | 4.00 | 10.00 |
| BOOSTER BOX (30 PACKS) | | 30.00 | 40.00 |
| BOOSTER PACK (11 CARDS) | | 1.00 | 1.50 |
| RELEASED ON SEPTEMBER 5, 2001 | | | |
| 1 | Anakin Skywalker, Boonta Eve Podracer Pilot UR | 1.25 | 2.00 |
| 2 | Yoda, Jedi Instructor R | 1.50 | 2.50 |
| 3 | C-3PO, Human-Cyborg Relations Droid R | 1.25 | 2.00 |
| 4 | Jira, Pallie Vendor R | 1.00 | 1.50 |
| 5 | Kitster, Anakin's Friend R | 1.00 | 1.50 |
| 6 | Wald, Anakin's Friend R | 1.00 | 1.50 |
| 7 | Seek, Anakin's Friend U | .50 | .75 |
| 8 | Amee, Anakin's Friend U | .50 | .75 |
| 9 | Melee, Anakin's Friend U | .50 | .75 |
| 10 | Captain Tarpals, Gungan Leader R | 1.00 | 1.50 |
| 11 | Boles Roor, Podracer Pilot U | .50 | .75 |
| 12 | Elan Mak, Podracer Pilot U | .50 | .75 |
| 13 | Neva Kee, Podracer Pilot U | .50 | .75 |
| 14 | Wan Sandage, Podracer Pilot U | .50 | .75 |
| 15 | Shmi Skywalker, Anakin's Mother R | 1.00 | 1.50 |
| 16 | Boles Roor's Podracer U | .50 | .75 |
| 17 | Elan Mak's Podracer U | .50 | .75 |
| 18 | Neva Kee's Podracer U | .50 | .75 |
| 19 | Wan Sandage's Podracer U | .50 | .75 |
| 20 | Comlink C | .15 | .25 |
| 21 | Hold-Out Blaster C | .15 | .25 |
| 22 | Dis Is Nutsen C | .15 | .25 |
| 23 | Masquerade C | .15 | .25 |
| 24 | No Giben Up, General Jar Jar C | .15 | .25 |
| 25 | What Does Your Heart Tell You? C | .15 | .25 |
| 26 | All-Out Defense U | .50 | .75 |
| 27 | Bravo Squadron C | .15 | .25 |
| 28 | Hologram Projector C | .15 | .25 |
| 29 | Boonta Eve Classic R | 1.00 | 1.50 |
| 30 | Amidala's Starship R | 1.00 | 1.50 |
| 31 | Sebulba, Dug Podracer Pilot UR | 1.00 | 1.50 |
| 32 | Watto, Podrace Sponsor R | 1.00 | 1.50 |
| 33 | Aurra Sing, Formidable Adversary R | 1.25 | 2.00 |
| 34 | Jabba The Hutt, O Grandio Lust R | 1.00 | 1.50 |
| 35 | TC-14, Protocol Droid R | 1.00 | 1.50 |
| 36 | Orr'UrRuuR'R, Tusken Raider Leader Rare R | 1.00 | 1.50 |
| 37 | UrrOr'RuuR, Tusken Raider Warrior U | .50 | .75 |
| 38 | RuuR'Ur, Tusken Raider Sniper C | .15 | .25 |
| 39 | Sil Unch, Neimoidian Comm Officer U | .50 | .75 |
| 40 | Graxol Kelvyyn and Shakka U | .50 | .75 |
| 41 | Corix Venne, Bith Musician C | .15 | .25 |
| 42 | Reike Th'san, Arms Smuggler R | 1.00 | 1.50 |
| 43 | Meddun, Nikto Mercenary U | .50 | .75 |
| 44 | Rum Sleg, Bounty Hunter R | 1.00 | 1.50 |
| 45 | Aehrrley Rue, Freelance Pilot U | .50 | .75 |
| 46 | Jedwar Seelah, Explorer Scout U | .50 | .75 |
| 47 | Chokk, Klatooinian Explosives Expert C | .15 | .25 |
| 48 | Tatooine Backpack C | .15 | .25 |
| 49 | Gaderffii Stick C | .15 | .25 |
| 50 | Hold-Out Blaster C | .15 | .25 |
| 51 | Watto's Datapad U | .50 | .75 |
| 52 | Colo Claw Fish C | .15 | .25 |
| 53 | He Always Wins! C | .15 | .25 |
| 54 | Bounty Hunter C | .15 | .25 |
| 55 | Two-Pronged Attack C | .15 | .25 |
| 56 | All-Out Attack U | .50 | .75 |
| 57 | Eventually You'll Lose U | .50 | .75 |
| 58 | Gangster's Paradise U | .50 | .75 |
| 59 | Boonta Eve Classic R | 1.00 | 1.50 |

| | | | |
|---|---|---|---|
| 60 | Viceroy's Battleship R | 1.00 | 1.50 |
| R1 | Rule Card 1 | .15 | .20 |
| R2 | Rule Card 2 | .15 | .20 |
| R3 | Rule Card 3 | .15 | .25 |

## 2001 Young Jedi Enhanced Battle of Naboo

| | | | |
|---|---|---|---|
| COMPLETE SET (12) | | 30.00 | 80.00 |
| RELEASED IN 2001 | | | |
| P8 | Obi-Wan Kenobi, Jedi Avenger | 6.00 | 10.00 |
| P9 | Anakin Skywalker, Tested By The Jedi Council | 15.00 | 25.00 |
| P10 | PadmÈ Naberrie, Loyal Handmaiden | 20.00 | 30.00 |
| P11 | Captain Panaka, Royal Defender | 3.00 | 5.00 |
| P12 | Yoda, Wise Jedi | 6.00 | 10.00 |
| P13 | R2-D2, Starship Maintenance Droid | 8.00 | 12.00 |
| P14 | Darth Sidious, The Phantom Menace | 3.00 | 5.00 |
| P15 | Watto, Risk Taker | 6.00 | 10.00 |
| P16 | Aurra Sing, Scoundrel | 6.00 | 10.00 |
| P17 | Jabba The Hutt | 6.00 | 10.00 |
| P18 | Nute Gunray, Neimoidean Bureaucrat | 4.00 | 6.00 |
| P19 | Rune Haako, Neimoidean Lieutenant | 8.00 | 12.00 |

## 2001 Young Jedi Reflections

| | | | |
|---|---|---|---|
| COMPLETE SET (106) | | 200.00 | 350.00 |
| RELEASED ON JULY 18, 2001 | | | |
| A1 | Jar Jar Binks, Bombad Gungan General | 2.00 | 3.00 |
| | Jar Jar Binks' Electropole | | |
| A2 | Boss Nass, Gungan Chief | 3.00 | 5.00 |
| | Fambaa | | |
| A3 | Adi Gallia, Corellian Jedi Master | 2.50 | 4.00 |
| | Adi Gallia's Lightsaber | | |
| A4 | Eeth Koth, Zabrak Jedi Master | 3.00 | 5.00 |
| | Eeth Koth's Lightsaber | | |
| A5 | Ki-Adi-Mundi, Cerean Jedi Knight | 3.00 | 5.00 |
| | Jedi Lightsaber, Constructed by Ki-Adi-Mundi | | |
| A6 | Valorum, Supreme Chancellor | 2.00 | 3.00 |
| | Planetary Shuttle | | |
| A7 | Aurra Sing, Trophy Collector | 3.00 | 5.00 |
| | Jedi Lightsaber, Stolen by Aurra Sing | | |
| A8 | Nute Gunray, Neimoidian Viceroy | 2.50 | 4.00 |
| | Neimoidian Viewscreen | | |
| A9 | OOM-9, Battle Droid Commander | 2.50 | 4.00 |
| | Battle Droid Blaster Rifle | | |
| A10 | OWO-1, Battle Droid Command Officer | 3.00 | 5.00 |
| | STAP | | |
| A11 | P-59, Destroyer Droid Commander | 2.50 | 4.00 |

| | | | |
|---|---|---|---|
| | Multi Troop Transport | | |
| A12 | Toonbuck Toora, Senator | 3.00 | 5.00 |
| | Coruscant Taxi | | |
| C1 | Are You An Angel? | 1.25 | 2.00 |
| | I've Been Trained In Defense | | |
| C2 | Brave Little Droid | 1.00 | 1.50 |
| | Counterparts | | |
| C3 | Celebration | 1.25 | 2.00 |
| | Gungan Mounted Trooops | | |
| C4 | Enough Of This Pretense | 1.00 | 1.50 |
| | I Will Not Cooperate | | |
| C5 | Fear Attracts The Fearful | 1.25 | 2.00 |
| | How Wude! | | |
| C6 | I Have A Bad Feeling About This | 1.25 | 2.00 |
| | NOOOOOOOOOOO! | | |
| C7 | Jedi Force Push | 1.25 | 2.00 |
| | We're Not In Trouble Yet | | |
| C8 | Dos Mackineeks No Comen Here! | 1.25 | 2.00 |
| | Bombad General | | |
| C9 | At last we will have revenge | .60 | 1.00 |
| | Sith force push | | |
| C10 | The Queen's Plan | 1.25 | 2.00 |
| | Naboo Royal Security Forces | | |
| C11 | The Might Of The Republic | 1.25 | 2.00 |
| | Senate Guard | | |
| C12 | The Negotiations Were Short | 1.25 | 2.00 |
| | Qui-Gon's Final Stand | | |
| C13 | Wisdom Of The Council | 1.25 | 2.00 |
| | Jedi Training | | |
| C14 | Yousa Guys Bombad! | 1.25 | 2.00 |
| | Uh-Oh! | | |
| C15 | A Thousand Terrible Things & We Are Sending All Troops | 1.00 | 1.50 |
| C16 | Battle Droid Patrol & In Complete Control | 1.00 | 1.50 |
| C17 | Boonta Eve Podrace & Kaa Bazza Kundee Hodrudda! | 1.00 | 1.50 |
| C18 | Podrace Preparation & Yoka To Bantha Poodoo | 1.25 | 2.00 |
| C19 | Switch To Bio & Your Little Insurrection Is At An End | .60 | 1.00 |
| C20 | The Phantom Menace & Use Caution | 1.25 | 2.00 |
| D1 | Dos Mackineeks No Comen Here! | 1.25 | 2.00 |
| | Bombad General | | |
| D2 | Gunga City | 1.25 | 2.00 |
| | Gungan Energy Shield | | |
| D3 | The Queen's Plan | 1.25 | 2.00 |
| | Naboo Royal Security Forces | | |
| D4 | The Might Of The Republic | 1.25 | 2.00 |
| | Senate Guard | | |
| D5 | The Negotiations Were Short | 1.25 | 2.00 |
| | Qui-Gon's Final Stand | | |
| D6 | Wisdom Of The Council | 1.25 | 2.00 |
| | Jedi Training | | |
| D7 | Yousa Guys Bombad! | 1.25 | 2.00 |
| | Uh-Oh! | | |
| D8 | Grueling Contest | 1.25 | 2.00 |
| | Da Dug Chaaa! | | |
| D9 | Let Them Make The First Move | .60 | 1.00 |
| | Very Unusual | | |
| D10 | Now There Are Two Of Them | 1.00 | 1.50 |
| | The Duel Begins | | |
| D11 | Opee Sea Killer | 1.25 | 2.00 |
| | To The Death | | |
| D12 | Starfighter Screen | 1.25 | 2.00 |
| | Blockade | | |

| | | | |
|---|---|---|---|
| D13 | We Have Them On The Run | 1.25 | 2.00 |
| | Where Are Those Droidekas? | | |
| D14 | You Have Been Well Trained | .60 | 1.00 |
| | After Her! | | |
| 2BEP | Yoda, Jedi Instructor (foil) | 4.00 | 6.00 |
| 2MDM | Qui-Gon Jinn, Jedi Master (foil) | 15.00 | 25.00 |
| 3BEP | C-3PO, Human-Cyborg Relations Droid (foil) | 4.00 | 6.00 |
| 4BEP | Jira, Pallie Vendor (foil) | 2.00 | 3.00 |
| 4BON | Anakin Skywalker, Padawan (foil) | 5.00 | 8.00 |
| 4TJC | Anakin Skywalker, Child of Prophecy (foil) | 10.00 | 15.00 |
| 5BEP | Kitster, Anakin's Friend (foil) | 3.00 | 5.00 |
| 6BEP | Wald, Anakin's Friend (foil) | 2.50 | 4.00 |
| 7BON | Mace Windu, Jedi Speaker (foil) | 15.00 | 25.00 |
| 9MDM | Queen Amidala, Royal Leader (foil) | 5.00 | 8.00 |
| 9TJC | Queen Amidala, Voice of Her People (foil) | 6.00 | 10.00 |
| 10MDM | Yoda, Jedi Master (foil) | 3.00 | 5.00 |
| 1DOTF | Obi-Wan Kenobi, Jedi Student (foil) | 10.00 | 15.00 |
| 2DOTF | Qui-Gon Jinn, Jedi Mentor (foil) | 5.00 | 8.00 |
| 30BEP | Amidala's Starship, Queen's Transport (foil) | 3.00 | 5.00 |
| 32BEP | Watto, Podrace Sponsor (foil) | 3.00 | 5.00 |
| 33BEP | Aurra Sing, Formidable Adversary (foil) | 6.00 | 10.00 |
| 34BEP | Jabba The Hutt, O Grandio Lust (foil) | 3.00 | 5.00 |
| 35BEP | TC-14, Protocol Droid (foil) | 3.00 | 5.00 |
| 36BEP | Orr'UrRuuR'R, Tusken Raider Leader (foil) | 3.00 | 5.00 |
| 3DOTF | Anakin Skywalker, Rookie Pilot (foil) | 5.00 | 8.00 |
| 4DOTF | Captain Panaka, Security Commander (foil) | 3.00 | 5.00 |
| 5DOTF | Mace Windu, Jedi Councilor (foil) | 4.00 | 6.00 |
| 60BEP | Viceroy's Battleship, Trade Federation Transport (foil) | 2.50 | 4.00 |
| 6DOTF | Queen Amidala, Young Leader (foil) | 5.00 | 8.00 |
| 72BON | Darth Sidious, Sith Manipulator (foil) | 5.00 | 8.00 |
| 73BON | Sebulba, Dangerous Podracer Pilot (foil) | 12.00 | 20.00 |
| 73TJC | Sebulba, Podracer Pilot (foil) | 2.50 | 4.00 |
| 74BON | Watto, Toydarian Gambler (foil) | 1.50 | 2.50 |
| 74MDM | Watto, Slave Owner (foil) | 3.00 | 5.00 |
| 75MDM | Aurra Sing, Bounty Hunter (foil) | 6.00 | 10.00 |
| 76BON | Jabba The Hutt, Crime Lord (foil) | 3.00 | 5.00 |
| 78BON | Rune Haako, Neimoidian Deputy (foil) | 3.00 | 5.00 |
| 78TJC | Destroyer Droid Squad, Defense Division (foil) | 5.00 | 8.00 |
| 79TJC | Battle Droid Squad, Escort Unit (foil) | 3.00 | 5.00 |
| 7DOTF | Yoda, Jedi Philosopher (foil) | 6.00 | 10.00 |
| 80TJC | Trade Federation Tank, Assault Division (foil) | 10.00 | 15.00 |
| 88MDM | Trade Federation Tank, Armored Division (foil) | 3.00 | 5.00 |
| 31DOTF | Darth Maul, Student of the Dark Side (foil) | 5.00 | 8.00 |
| 32DOTF | Darth Sidious, Master of the Dark Side (foil) | 15.00 | 25.00 |
| 33DOTF | Aurra Sing, Trophy Collector (foil) | 2.50 | 4.00 |
| P1EMDM | Qui-Gon Jinn, Jedi Protector (foil) | 6.00 | 10.00 |
| P2EMDM | Mace Windu, Jedi Warrior (foil) | 6.00 | 10.00 |
| P3EMDM | Queen Amidala, Cunning Warrior (foil) | 12.00 | 20.00 |
| P4EMDM | Darth Maul, Sith Assassin (foil) | 12.00 | 20.00 |
| P5EMDM | Sebulba, Champion Podracer Pilot (foil) | 3.00 | 5.00 |
| P6EMDM | Trade Federation Tank, Assault Leader (foil) | 2.50 | 4.00 |
| P7PREM | Shmi Skywalker, Anakin's Mother (foil) | 2.50 | 4.00 |
| P8EBON | Obi-Wan Kenobi, Jedi Avenger (foil) | 5.00 | 8.00 |
| P9EBON | Anakin Skywalker, Tested by the Jedi Council (foil) | 5.00 | 8.00 |
| P10EBON | PadmÈ Naberrie, Loyal Handmaiden (foil) | 3.00 | 5.00 |
| P11EBON | Captain Panaka, Royal Defender (foil) | 3.00 | 5.00 |
| P12EBON | Yoda, Wise Jedi (foil) | 6.00 | 10.00 |
| P13EBON | R2-D2, Starship Maintenance Droid (foil) | 5.00 | 8.00 |
| P14EBON | Darth Sidious, The Phantom Menace (foil) | 5.00 | 8.00 |
| P15EBON | Watto, Risk Taker (foil) | 3.00 | 5.00 |
| P16EBON | Aurra Sing, Scoundrel (foil) | 2.50 | 4.00 |
| P17EBON | Jabba The Hutt, Tatooine Tyrant (foil) | 3.00 | 5.00 |
| P18EBON | Nute Gunray, Neimoidian Bureaucrat (foil) | 2.50 | 4.00 |
| P19EBON | Rune Haako, Neimoidian Lieutenant (foil) | 3.00 | 5.00 |

## 2004 Star Wars Rebel Storm Miniatures

| | | | |
|---|---|---|---|
| COMPLETE SET (60) | | 120.00 | 250.00 |
| RELEASED ON SEPTEMBER 3, 2004 | | | |
| 1 | 4-LOM R | 6.00 | 10.00 |
| 2 | Bespin Guard C | .50 | .75 |
| 3 | Boba Fett VR | 25.00 | 40.00 |
| 4 | Bossk R | 6.00 | 10.00 |
| 5 | Bothan Spy U | 1.00 | 1.50 |
| 6 | C-3PO R | 6.00 | 10.00 |
| 7 | Chewbacca R | 8.00 | 12.00 |
| 8 | Commando on Speeder Bike VR | 15.00 | 25.00 |
| 9 | Darth Vader, Dark Jedi R | 8.00 | 12.00 |
| 10 | Darth Vader, Sith Lord VR | 15.00 | 25.00 |
| 11 | Dengar R | 6.00 | 10.00 |
| 12 | Duros Mercenary U | 1.00 | 1.50 |
| 13 | Elite Hoth Trooper U | 1.00 | 1.50 |
| 14 | Elite Rebel Trooper C | .50 | .75 |
| 15 | Elite Snowtrooper U | 1.00 | 1.50 |
| 16 | Elite Stormtrooper U | 1.00 | 1.50 |
| 17 | Emperor Palpatine VR | 20.00 | 30.00 |
| 18 | Ewok C | .50 | .75 |
| 19 | Gamorrean Guard U | 1.00 | 1.50 |
| 20 | General Veers R | 6.00 | 10.00 |
| 21 | Grand Moff Tarkin R | 6.00 | 10.00 |
| 22 | Greedo R | 6.00 | 10.00 |
| 23 | Han Solo R | 6.00 | 10.00 |
| 24 | Heavy Stormtrooper U | 1.00 | 1.50 |
| 25 | Hoth Trooper C | .50 | .75 |
| 26 | IG-88 R | 6.00 | 10.00 |
| 27 | Imperial Officer U | 1.00 | 1.50 |
| 28 | Ithorian Scout U | 1.00 | 1.50 |
| 29 | Jabba the Hutt VR | 15.00 | 25.00 |
| 30 | Jawa C | .50 | .75 |
| 31 | Lando Calrissian R | 6.00 | 10.00 |
| 32 | Luke Skywalker, Jedi Knight VR | 20.00 | 30.00 |
| 33 | Luke Skywalker, Rebel R | 8.00 | 12.00 |
| 34 | Mara Jade Emperor's Hand R | 6.00 | 10.00 |
| 35 | Mon Calamari Mercenary C | .50 | .75 |
| 36 | Obi-Wan Kenobi VR | 15.00 | 25.00 |
| 37 | Princess Leia, Captive VR | 15.00 | 25.00 |
| 38 | Princess Leia, Senator R | 8.00 | 12.00 |
| 39 | Probe Droid VR | 12.00 | 20.00 |
| 40 | Quarren Assassin U | 1.00 | 1.50 |
| 41 | R2-D2 R | 8.00 | 12.00 |
| 42 | Rebel Commando U | 1.00 | 1.50 |
| 43 | Rebel Officer U | 1.00 | 1.50 |
| 44 | Rebel Pilot C | .50 | .75 |
| 45 | Rebel Trooper C | .50 | .75 |
| 46 | Rebel Trooper C | .50 | .75 |
| 47 | Royal Guard U | 1.00 | 1.50 |
| 48 | Sandtrooper on Dewback VR | 12.00 | 20.00 |
| 49 | Scout Trooper on Bike VR | 12.00 | 20.00 |
| 50 | Scout Trooper U | 1.00 | 1.50 |
| 51 | Snowtrooper C | .50 | .75 |
| 52 | Stormtrooper C | .50 | .75 |
| 53 | Stormtrooper C | .50 | .75 |
| 54 | Stormtrooper C | .50 | .75 |
| 55 | Stormtrooper Officer U | 1.00 | 1.50 |
| 56 | Tusken Raider C | .50 | .75 |
| 57 | Twi'lek Bodyguard U | 1.00 | 1.50 |
| 58 | Twi'lek Scoundrel C | .50 | .75 |
| 59 | Wampa VR | 12.00 | 20.00 |
| 60 | Wookiee Soldier C | .50 | .75 |

## 2004 Star Wars Clone Strike Miniatures

| | | | |
|---|---|---|---|
| COMPLETE SET (60) | | 150.00 | 300.00 |
| RELEASED ON DECEMBER 13, 2004 | | | |
| 1 | 48 Super Battle Droid U | 1.00 | 1.50 |
| 2 | Aayla Secura VR | 12.00 | 20.00 |
| 3 | Aerial Clone Trooper Captain R | 8.00 | 12.00 |
| 4 | Agen Kolar R | 8.00 | 12.00 |
| 5 | Anakin Skywalker VR | 15.00 | 25.00 |
| 6 | Aqualish Spy C | .50 | .75 |
| 7 | ARC Trooper U | 1.00 | 1.50 |
| 8 | Asajj Ventress R | 8.00 | 12.00 |
| 9 | Aurra Sing VR | 20.00 | 30.00 |
| 10 | Battle Droid C | .50 | .75 |
| 11 | Battle Droid C | .50 | .75 |
| 12 | Battle Droid C | .50 | .75 |
| 13 | Battle Droid Officer U | 1.00 | 1.50 |
| 14 | Battle Droid on STAP R | 8.00 | 12.00 |
| 15 | Captain Typho R | 8.00 | 12.00 |
| 16 | Clone Trooper C | .50 | .75 |
| 17 | Clone Trooper C | .50 | .75 |
| 18 | Clone Trooper Commander U | 1.00 | 1.50 |
| 19 | Clone Trooper Grenadier C | .50 | .75 |
| 20 | Clone Trooper Sergeant C | .50 | .75 |
| 21 | Count Dooku VR | 15.00 | 25.00 |
| 22 | Dark Side Acolyte U | 1.00 | 1.50 |
| 23 | Darth Maul VR | 20.00 | 30.00 |
| 24 | Darth Sidious VR | 15.00 | 25.00 |
| 25 | Destroyer Droid R | 8.00 | 12.00 |
| 26 | Devaronian Bounty Hunter C | .50 | .75 |
| 27 | Durge R | 8.00 | 12.00 |
| 28 | Dwarf Spider Droid R | 8.00 | 12.00 |
| 29 | General Grievous VR | 20.00 | 30.00 |
| 30 | General Kenobi R | 8.00 | 12.00 |
| 31 | Geonosian Drone C | .50 | .75 |
| 32 | Geonosian Overseer U | 1.00 | 1.50 |
| 33 | Geonosian Picador on Orray R | 8.00 | 12.00 |
| 34 | Geonosian Soldier U | 1.00 | 1.50 |
| 35 | Gran Raider C | .50 | .75 |
| 36 | Gungan Cavalry on Kaadu R | 8.00 | 12.00 |
| 37 | Gungan Infantry C | .50 | .75 |
| 38 | Ishi Tib Scout U | 1.00 | 1.50 |
| 39 | Jango Fett R | 8.00 | 12.00 |
| 40 | Jedi Guardian U | 1.00 | 1.50 |
| 41 | Ki-Adi-Mundi R | 8.00 | 12.00 |
| 42 | Kit Fisto R | 8.00 | 12.00 |
| 43 | Klatooinian Enforcer C | .50 | .75 |
| 44 | Luminara Unduli R | 8.00 | 12.00 |
| 45 | Mace Windu VR | 15.00 | 25.00 |
| 46 | Naboo Soldier U | 1.00 | 1.50 |
| 47 | Nikto Soldier C | .50 | .75 |
| 48 | Padme Amidala VR | 12.00 | 20.00 |
| 49 | Plo Koon R | 8.00 | 12.00 |
| 50 | Quarren Raider U | 1.00 | 1.50 |
| 51 | Qui-Gon Jinn VR | 12.00 | 20.00 |
| 52 | Quinlan Vos VR | 12.00 | 20.00 |
| 53 | Rodian Mercenary U | 1.00 | 1.50 |
| 54 | Saesee Tiin R | 8.00 | 12.00 |
| 55 | Security Battle Droid C | .50 | .75 |
| 56 | Super Battle Droid U | 1.00 | 1.50 |
| 57 | Weequay Mercenary C | .50 | .75 |
| 58 | Wookiee Commando U | 1.00 | 1.50 |
| 59 | Yoda VR | 20.00 | 30.00 |
| 60 | Zam Wesell R | 8.00 | 12.00 |

## 2005 Star Wars Revenge of the Sith Miniatures

| | | | |
|---|---|---|---|
| COMPLETE SET (61) | | 120.00 | 250.00 |
| RELEASED ON APRIL 2, 2005 | | | |
| 1 | Agen Kolar, Jedi Master R | 8.00 | 12.00 |
| 2 | Alderaan Trooper U | 1.00 | 1.50 |
| 3 | Anakin Skywalker, Jedi Knight R | 8.00 | 12.00 |
| 4 | AT-RT VR | 15.00 | 25.00 |
| 5 | Bail Organa VR | 12.00 | 20.00 |
| 6 | Captain Antilles R | 8.00 | 12.00 |
| 7 | Chewbacca of Kashyyk VR | 15.00 | 25.00 |
| 8 | Clone Trooper C | .50 | .75 |
| 9 | Clone Trooper C | .50 | .75 |
| 10 | Clone Trooper Commander U | 1.00 | 1.50 |
| 11 | Clone Trooper Gunner C | .50 | .75 |
| 12 | Jedi Knight U | 1.00 | 1.50 |
| 13 | Mace Windu, Jedi Master VR | 20.00 | 30.00 |
| 14 | Mon Mothma VR | 12.00 | 20.00 |
| 15 | Obi-Wan Kenobi, Jedi Master R | 8.00 | 12.00 |
| 16 | Polis Massa Medic C | .50 | .75 |
| 17 | R2-D2, Astromech Droid VR | 15.00 | 25.00 |
| 18 | Senate Guard U | 1.00 | 1.50 |
| 19 | Shaak Ti R | 8.00 | 12.00 |
| 20 | Stass Allie R | 8.00 | 12.00 |
| 21 | Tarfful R | 8.00 | 12.00 |
| 22 | Wookiee Berserker C | .50 | .75 |

| | | | |
|---|---|---:|---:|
| 23 | Wookiee Scout U | 1.00 | 1.50 |
| 24 | Yoda, Jedi Master R | 10.00 | 15.00 |
| 25 | Battle Droid C | .50 | .75 |
| 26 | Battle Droid C | .50 | .75 |
| 27 | Bodyguard Droid U | 1.00 | 1.50 |
| 28 | Bodyguard Droid U | 1.00 | 1.50 |
| 29 | Darth Tyranus R | 8.00 | 12.00 |
| 30 | Destroyer Droid R | 8.00 | 12.00 |
| 31 | General Grievous, Jedi Hunter VR | 20.00 | 30.00 |
| 32 | General Grievous, Supreme Commander R | 8.00 | 12.00 |
| 33 | Grievous's Wheel Bike VR | 15.00 | 25.00 |
| 34 | Muun Guard U | 1.00 | 1.50 |
| 35 | Neimoidian Soldier U | 1.00 | 1.50 |
| 36 | Neimoidian Soldier U | 1.00 | 1.50 |
| 37 | San Hill R | 8.00 | 12.00 |
| 38 | Separatist Commando C | .50 | .75 |
| 39 | Super Battle Droid C | .50 | .75 |
| 40 | Super Battle Droid C | .50 | .75 |
| 41 | Wat Tambor R | 8.00 | 12.00 |
| 42 | Boba Fett, Young Mercenary R | 8.00 | 12.00 |
| 43 | Chagrian Mercenary Commander U | 1.00 | 1.50 |
| 44 | Devaronian Soldier C | .50 | .75 |
| 45 | Gotal Fringer U | 1.00 | 1.50 |
| 46 | Human Mercenary U | 1.00 | 1.50 |
| 47 | Iktotchi Tech Specialist U | 1.00 | 1.50 |
| 48 | Medical Droid R | 8.00 | 12.00 |
| 49 | Nautolan Soldier C | .50 | .75 |
| 50 | Sly Moore R | 8.00 | 12.00 |
| 51 | Tion Medon R | 8.00 | 12.00 |
| 52 | Utapaun Soldier C | .50 | .75 |
| 53 | Utapaun Soldier C | .50 | .75 |
| 54 | Yuzzem C | .50 | .75 |
| 55 | Zabrak Fringer C | .50 | .75 |
| 56 | Anakin Skywalker Sith Apprentice VR | 15.00 | 25.00 |
| 57 | Dark Side Adept U | 1.00 | 1.50 |
| 58 | Darth Vader VR | 20.00 | 30.00 |
| 59 | Emperor Palpatine, Sith Lord VR | 20.00 | 30.00 |
| 60 | Royal Guard U | 1.00 | 1.50 |

### 2005 Star Wars Universe Miniatures

| | | | |
|---|---|---:|---:|
| COMPLETE SET (61) | | 150.00 | 300.00 |
| RELEASED ON AUGUST 19, 2005 | | | |
| 1 | Abyssin Black Sun Thug C | .50 | .75 |
| 2 | Acklay U | 1.00 | 1.50 |
| 3 | Admiral Ackbar VR | 12.00 | 20.00 |
| 4 | ASP-7 U | 1.00 | 1.50 |
| 5 | AT-ST R | 10.00 | 15.00 |

| | | | |
|---|---|---:|---:|
| 6 | B'omarr Monk R | 10.00 | 15.00 |
| 7 | Baron Fel VR | 20.00 | 30.00 |
| 8 | Battle Droid U | 1.00 | 1.50 |
| 9 | Battle Droid U | 1.00 | 1.50 |
| 10 | Bith Rebel C | .50 | .75 |
| 11 | Chewbacca, Rebel Hero R | 10.00 | 15.00 |
| 12 | Clone Trooper C | .50 | .75 |
| 13 | Clone Trooper on BARC Speeder R | 12.00 | 20.00 |
| 14 | Dark Side Marauder U | 1.00 | 1.50 |
| 15 | Dark Trooper Phase III U | 1.00 | 1.50 |
| 16 | Darth Maul on Speeder VR | 15.00 | 25.00 |
| 17 | Darth Vader, Jedi Hunter R | 10.00 | 15.00 |
| 18 | Dash Rendar R | 10.00 | 15.00 |
| 19 | Dr. Evazan VR | 12.00 | 20.00 |
| 20 | Dressellian Commando C | .50 | .75 |
| 21 | Elite Clone Trooper U | 1.00 | 1.50 |
| 22 | Flash Speeder U | 1.00 | 1.50 |
| 23 | Gonk Power Droid C | .50 | .75 |
| 24 | Grand Admiral Thrawn VR | 20.00 | 30.00 |
| 25 | Guri R | 10.00 | 15.00 |
| 26 | Hailfire Droid U | 1.00 | 1.50 |
| 27 | Han Solo, Rebel Hero R | 10.00 | 15.00 |
| 28 | Kaminoan Ascetic C | .50 | .75 |
| 29 | Kyle Katarn VR | 12.00 | 20.00 |
| 30 | Lando Calrissian, Hero of Taanab R | 10.00 | 15.00 |
| 31 | Lobot R | 8.00 | 12.00 |
| 32 | Luke Skywalker on Tauntaun R | 12.00 | 20.00 |
| 33 | Luke Skywalker, Jedi Master VR | 20.00 | 30.00 |
| 34 | New Republic Commander U | 1.00 | 1.50 |
| 35 | New Republic Trooper C | .50 | .75 |
| 36 | Nexu U | 1.00 | 1.50 |
| 37 | Nien Nunb R | 8.00 | 12.00 |
| 38 | Nightsister Sith Witch U | 1.00 | 1.50 |
| 39 | Noghri U | 1.00 | 1.50 |
| 40 | Nom Anor R | 10.00 | 15.00 |
| 41 | Nute Gunray R | 8.00 | 12.00 |
| 42 | Obi-Wan on Boga VR | 15.00 | 25.00 |
| 43 | Ponda Baba R | 8.00 | 12.00 |
| 44 | Prince Xizor VR | 12.00 | 20.00 |
| 45 | Princess Leia, Rebel Hero VR | 12.00 | 20.00 |
| 46 | Rancor VR | 20.00 | 30.00 |
| 47 | Reek U | 1.00 | 1.50 |
| 48 | Rodian Black Sun Vigo U | 1.00 | 1.50 |
| 49 | Shistavanen Pilot U | 1.00 | 1.50 |
| 50 | Stormtrooper C | .50 | .75 |
| 51 | Stormtrooper Commander U | 1.00 | 1.50 |
| 52 | Super Battle Droid C | .50 | .75 |
| 53 | Super Battle Droid Commander U | 1.00 | 1.50 |
| 54 | Tusken Raider on Bantha U | 1.00 | 1.50 |
| 55 | Vornskr C | .50 | .75 |
| 56 | Warmaster Tsavong Lah VR | 15.00 | 25.00 |
| 57 | Wedge Antilles R | 10.00 | 15.00 |
| 58 | X-1 Viper Droid U | 1.00 | 1.50 |
| 59 | Young Jedi Knight C | .50 | .75 |
| 60 | Yuuzhan Vong Subaltern U | 1.00 | 1.50 |
| 61 | Yuuzhan Vong Warrior C | .50 | .75 |

### 2006 Star Wars Champions of the Force Miniatures

| | | | |
|---|---|---:|---:|
| COMPLETE SET (61) | | 120.00 | 250.00 |
| RELEASED ON JUNE 6, 2006 | | | |
| 1 | Arcona Smuggler C | .50 | .75 |
| 2 | Barriss Offee R | 8.00 | 12.00 |
| 3 | Bastila Shan VR | 12.00 | 20.00 |
| 5 | Clone Commander Bacara R | 8.00 | 12.00 |
| 6 | Clone Commander Cody R | 10.00 | 15.00 |
| 7 | Clone Commander Gree R | 8.00 | 12.00 |
| 8 | Corran Horn R | 8.00 | 12.00 |
| 9 | Coruscant Guard C | .50 | .75 |
| 10 | Crab Droid U | 1.00 | 1.50 |
| 11 | Dark Jedi U | 1.00 | 1.50 |
| 12 | Dark Jedi Master U | 1.00 | 1.50 |
| 13 | Dark Side Enforcer U | 1.00 | 1.50 |
| 14 | Dark Trooper Phase I C | .50 | .75 |
| 15 | Dark Trooper Phase II U | 1.00 | 1.50 |
| 16 | Dark Trooper Phase II VR | 12.00 | 20.00 |
| 17 | Darth Bane VR | 15.00 | 25.00 |
| 18 | Darth Malak VR | 15.00 | 25.00 |
| 19 | Darth Maul, Champion of the Sith R | 10.00 | 15.00 |
| 20 | Darth Nihilus VR | 12.00 | 20.00 |
| 21 | Darth Sidious, Dark Lord of the Sith R | 8.00 | 12.00 |
| 22 | Depa Billaba R | 8.00 | 12.00 |
| 23 | Even Piell R | 8.00 | 12.00 |
| 24 | Exar Kun VR | 15.00 | 25.00 |
| 25 | General Windu R | 8.00 | 12.00 |
| 26 | Gundark Fringe U | 1.00 | 1.50 |
| 27 | HK-47 VR | 12.00 | 20.00 |
| 28 | Hoth Trooper with Atgar Cannon R | 8.00 | 12.00 |
| 29 | Jacen Solo VR | 12.00 | 20.00 |
| 30 | Jaina Solo VR | 12.00 | 20.00 |
| 31 | Jedi Consular U | 1.00 | 1.50 |
| 32 | Jedi Guardian U | 1.00 | 1.50 |
| 33 | Jedi Padawan U | 1.00 | 1.50 |
| 34 | Jedi Sentinel U | 1.00 | 1.50 |
| 35 | Jedi Weapon Master C | .50 | .75 |
| 36 | Kashyyyk Trooper C | .50 | .75 |
| 37 | Luke Skywalker, Young Jedi VR | 15.00 | 25.00 |
| 38 | Mas Amedda R | 10.00 | 15.00 |
| 39 | Massassi Sith Mutant U | 1.00 | 1.50 |
| 41 | Octuparra Droid R | 8.00 | 12.00 |
| 42 | Old Republic Commander U | 1.00 | 1.50 |
| 43 | Old Republic Trooper U | 1.00 | 1.50 |
| 44 | Old Republic Trooper C | .50 | .75 |

| | | |
|---|---|---|
| 45 Queen Amidala R | 8.00 | 12.00 |
| 46 Qui-Gon Jinn, Jedi Master R | 10.00 | 15.00 |
| 47 R5 Astromech Droid C | .50 | .75 |
| 48 Republic Commando Boss U | 1.00 | 1.50 |
| 49 Republic Commando Fixer C | .50 | .75 |
| 50 Republic Commando Scorch C | .50 | .75 |
| 51 Republic Commando Sev C | .50 | .75 |
| 52 Saleucami Trooper C | .50 | .75 |
| 53 Sandtrooper C | .50 | .75 |
| 54 Sith Assault Droid U | 1.00 | 1.50 |
| 55 Sith Trooper C | .50 | .75 |
| 56 Sith Trooper C | .50 | .75 |
| 57 Sith Trooper Commander U | 1.00 | 1.50 |
| 58 Snowtrooper with E-Web Blaster R | 8.00 | 12.00 |
| 59 Ugnaught Demolitionist C | .50 | .75 |
| 60 Ulic Qel-Droma VR | 10.00 | 15.00 |
| 61 Utapau Trooper C | .50 | .75 |
| 62 Varactyl Wrangler C | .50 | .75 |
| 63 Yoda of Dagobah VR | 15.00 | 25.00 |

## 2006 Star Wars Bounty Hunters Miniatures

| | | |
|---|---|---|
| COMPLETE SET (60) | 150.00 | 300.00 |
| RELEASED ON SEPTEMBER 23, 2006 | | |
| 1 4-LOM, Bounty Hunter R | 8.00 | 12.00 |
| 2 Aqualish Assassin C | .50 | .75 |
| 3 Ayy Vida R | 8.00 | 12.00 |
| 4 Basilisk War Droid U | 1.00 | 1.50 |
| 5 Bib Fortuna R | 8.00 | 12.00 |
| 6 Bith Black Sun Vigo U | 1.00 | 1.50 |
| 7 Boba Fett, Bounty Hunter VR | 25.00 | 40.00 |
| 8 BoShek R | 8.00 | 12.00 |
| 9 Bossk, Bounty Hunter R | 10.00 | 15.00 |
| 10 Boushh R | 8.00 | 12.00 |
| 11 Calo Nord†R | 8.00 | 12.00 |
| 12 Chewbacca w/C-3PO VR | 10.00 | 20.00 |
| 13 Commerce Guild Homing Spider Droid U | 1.00 | 1.50 |
| 14 Corellian Pirate U | 1.00 | 1.50 |
| 15 Corporate Alliance Tank Droid U | 1.00 | 1.50 |
| 16 Dannik Jerriko VR | 10.00 | 15.00 |
| 17 Dark Hellion Marauder on Swoop Bike U | 1.00 | 1.50 |
| 18 Dark Hellion Swoop Gang Member C | .50 | .75 |
| 19 Defel Spy C | .50 | .75 |
| 20 Dengar, Bounty Hunter R | 10.00 | 15.00 |
| 21 Djas Puhr R | 8.00 | 12.00 |
| 22 Droid Starfighter in Walking Mode R | 10.00 | 15.00 |
| 23 E522 Assassin Droid U | 1.00 | 1.50 |
| 24 Gamorrean Thug C | .50 | .75 |
| 25 Garindan R | 8.00 | 12.00 |
| 26 Han Solo, Scoundrel VR | 10.00 | 15.00 |
| 27 Huge Crab Droid U | 1.00 | 1.50 |
| 28 Human Blaster-for-Hire C | .50 | .75 |
| 29 IG-88, Bounty Hunter VR | 15.00 | 25.00 |
| 30 ISP Speeder R | 8.00 | 12.00 |
| 31 Jango Fett, Bounty Hunter VR | 20.00 | 30.00 |
| 32 Klatooinian Hunter C | .50 | .75 |
| 33 Komari Vosa R | 10.00 | 15.00 |
| 34 Lord Vader VR | 12.00 | 20.00 |
| 35 Luke Skywalker of Dagobah R | 10.00 | 15.00 |
| 36 Mandalore the Indomitable VR | 15.00 | 25.00 |
| 37 Mandalorian Blademaster U | 1.00 | 1.50 |
| 38 Mandalorian Commander U | 1.00 | 1.50 |
| 39 Mandalorian Soldier C | .50 | .75 |
| 40 Mandalorian Supercommando C | .50 | .75 |
| 41 Mandalorian Warrior C | .50 | .75 |
| 42 Mistryl Shadow Guard U | 1.00 | 1.50 |
| 43 Mustafarian Flea Rider R | 8.00 | 12.00 |
| 44 Mustafarian Soldier C | .50 | .75 |
| 45 Nikto Gunner on Desert Skiff VR | 12.00 | 20.00 |
| 46 Nym VR | 10.00 | 15.00 |
| 47 Princess Leia, Hoth Commander R | 10.00 | 15.00 |
| 48 Quarren Bounty Hunter C | .50 | .75 |
| 49 Rebel Captain U | 1.00 | 1.50 |
| 50 Rebel Heavy Trooper U | 1.00 | 1.50 |
| 51 Rebel Snowspeeder U | 1.00 | 1.50 |
| 52 Rodian Hunt Master U | 1.00 | 1.50 |
| 53 Talon Karrde VR | 10.00 | 15.00 |
| 54 Tamtel Skreej VR | 10.00 | 15.00 |
| 55 Tusken Raider Sniper C | .50 | .75 |
| 56 Utapaun on Dactillion VR | 10.00 | 15.00 |
| 57 Weequay Leader U | 1.00 | 1.50 |
| 58 Weequay Thug C | .50 | .75 |
| 59 Young Krayt Dragon VR | 12.00 | 20.00 |
| 60 Zuckuss R | 10.00 | 15.00 |

## 2007 Star Wars Alliance and Empire Miniatures

| | | |
|---|---|---|
| COMPLETE SET (60) | 100.00 | 200.00 |
| RELEASED IN MAY 2007 | | |
| 1 Admiral Piett R | 6.00 | 10.00 |
| 2 Advance Agent, Officer U | 1.00 | 1.50 |
| 3 Advance Scout C | .50 | .75 |
| 4 Aurra Sing, Jedi Hunter VR | 12.00 | 20.00 |
| 5 Biggs Darklighter VR | 10.00 | 15.00 |
| 6 Boba Fett, Enforcer VR | 15.00 | 25.00 |
| 7 C-3PO and R2-D2 R | 6.00 | 10.00 |
| 8 Chadra-Fan Pickpocket U | 1.00 | 1.50 |
| 9 Chewbacca, Enraged Wookiee R | 6.00 | 10.00 |
| 10 Darth Vader, Imperial Commander VR | 15.00 | 25.00 |

| | | |
|---|---|---|
| 11 Death Star Gunner U | 1.00 | 1.50 |
| 12 Death Star Trooper C | .50 | .75 |
| 13 Duros Explorer C | .50 | .75 |
| 14 Elite Hoth Trooper C | .50 | .75 |
| 15 Ephant Mon VR | 10.00 | 15.00 |
| 16 Ewok Hang Glider R | 6.00 | 10.00 |
| 17 Ewok Warrior C | .50 | .75 |
| 18 Gamorrean Guard C | .50 | .75 |
| 19 Han Solo in Stormtrooper Armor R | 6.00 | 10.00 |
| 20 Han Solo on Tauntaun VR | 12.00 | 20.00 |
| 21 Han Solo Rogue R | 6.00 | 10.00 |
| 22 Heavy Stormtrooper U | 1.00 | 1.50 |
| 23 Human Force Adept C | .50 | .75 |
| 24 Imperial Governor Tarkin R | 6.00 | 10.00 |
| 25 Imperial Officer U | 1.00 | 1.50 |
| 26 Ithorian Commander U | 1.00 | 1.50 |
| 27 Jabba, Crime Lord VR | 10.00 | 15.00 |
| 28 Jawa on Ronto VR | 10.00 | 15.00 |
| 29 Jawa Trader U | 1.00 | 1.50 |
| 30 Lando Calrissian, Dashing Scoundrel R | 6.00 | 10.00 |
| 31 Luke Skywalker, Champion of the Force VR | 15.00 | 25.00 |
| 32 Luke Skywalker, Hero of Yavin R | 6.00 | 10.00 |
| 33 Luke's Landspeeder VR | 10.00 | 15.00 |
| 34 Mara Jade, Jedi R | 6.00 | 10.00 |
| 35 Mon Calamari Tech Specialist C | .50 | .75 |
| 36 Nikto Soldier C | .50 | .75 |
| 37 Obi-Wan Kenobi, Force Spirit VR | 10.00 | 15.00 |
| 38 Princess Leia R | 6.00 | 10.00 |
| 39 Quinlan Vos, Infiltrator VR | 12.00 | 20.00 |
| 40 Rampaging Wampa VR | 10.00 | 15.00 |
| 41 Rebel Commando C | .50 | .75 |
| 42 Rebel Commando Strike Leader U | 1.00 | 1.50 |
| 43 Rebel Leader U | 1.00 | 1.50 |
| 44 Rebel Pilot C | .50 | .75 |
| 45 Rebel Trooper U | 1.00 | 1.50 |
| 46 Rodian Scoundrel U | 1.00 | 1.50 |
| 47 Scout Trooper U | 1.00 | 1.50 |
| 48 Snivvian Fringer C | .50 | .75 |
| 49 Snowtrooper C | .50 | .75 |
| 50 Storm Commando R | 6.00 | 10.00 |
| 51 Stormtrooper C | .50 | .75 |
| 52 Stormtrooper Officer U | 1.00 | 1.50 |
| 53 Stormtrooper on Repulsor Sled VR | 12.00 | 20.00 |
| 54 Talz Spy Fringe U | 1.00 | 1.50 |
| 55 Trandoshan Mercenary U | 1.00 | 1.50 |
| 56 Tusken Raider C | .50 | .75 |
| 57 Twi'lek Rebel Agent U | 1.00 | 1.50 |
| 58 Wicket R | 6.00 | 10.00 |
| 59 Wookiee Freedom Fighter C | .50 | .75 |
| 60 Yomin Carr R | 8.00 | 12.00 |

## 2007 Star Wars The Force Unleashed Miniatures

| | | |
|---|---|---|
| COMPLETE SET (60) | 350.00 | 800.00 |
| RELEASED IN 2007 | | |
| 1 Darth Revan VR | 50.00 | 75.00 |
| 2 Kazdan Paratus R | 6.00 | 10.00 |
| 3 Shaak Ti, Jedi Master VR | 12.00 | 20.00 |
| 4 Chewbacca of Hoth VR | 6.00 | 10.00 |
| 5 Elite Hoth Trooper C | 6.00 | 10.00 |
| 6 Golan Arms DF-9 Anti-Infantry Battery UC | 6.00 | 10.00 |
| 7 Han Solo in Carbonite VR | 6.00 | 10.00 |
| 8 Han Solo of Hoth VR | 6.00 | 10.00 |
| 9 Hoth Trooper Officer UC | 6.00 | 10.00 |
| 10 Hoth Trooper with Repeating Blaster Cannon UC | 6.00 | 10.00 |
| 11 Juno Eclipse R | 6.00 | 10.00 |
| 12 K-3PO R | 6.00 | 10.00 |
| 13 Luke Skywalker, Hoth Pilot Unleashed R | 6.00 | 10.00 |

| | | | |
|---|---|---|---|
| 14 Luke Skywalker and Yoda VR | 10.00 | 15.00 |
| 15 Luke's Snowspeeder VR | 10.00 | 15.00 |
| 16 Master Kota R | 10.00 | 15.00 |
| 17 Mon Calamari Medic C | 6.00 | 10.00 |
| 18 Obi-Wan Kenobi, Unleashed R | 6.00 | 10.00 |
| 19 Princess Leia of Cloud City R | 6.00 | 10.00 |
| 20 Rebel Marksman UC | 6.00 | 10.00 |
| 21 Rebel Troop Cart UC | 6.00 | 10.00 |
| 22 Rebel Trooper on Tauntaun R | 6.00 | 10.00 |
| 23 Rebel Vanguard UC | 6.00 | 10.00 |
| 24 2-1B R | 6.00 | 10.00 |
| 25 Vader's Secret Apprentice, Redeemed R | 12.00 | 20.00 |
| 26 Verpine Tech Rebel C | 6.00 | 10.00 |
| 27 Wedge Antilles, Red Two Rebel R | 6.00 | 10.00 |
| 28 Wookiee Warrior Rebel C | 6.00 | 10.00 |
| 29 Admiral Ozzel R | 6.00 | 10.00 |
| 30 AT-AT Driver UC | 6.00 | 10.00 |
| 31 Dark trooper UC | 6.00 | 10.00 |
| 32 Darth Vader, Unleashed VR | 6.00 | 10.00 |
| 33 Emperor's Shadow Guard UC | 6.00 | 10.00 |
| 34 Evo Trooper UC | 6.00 | 10.00 |
| 35 Felucian Stormtrooper Officer UC | 6.00 | 10.00 |
| 36 Gotal Imperial Assassin C | 6.00 | 10.00 |
| 37 Imperial Navy trooper C | 6.00 | 10.00 |
| 38 Raxus Prime Trooper C | 6.00 | 10.00 |
| 39 Snowtrooper C | 6.00 | 10.00 |
| 40 Star Destroyer Officer UC | 6.00 | 10.00 |
| 41 Stormtrooper UC | 6.00 | 10.00 |
| 42 TIE Crawler UC | 6.00 | 10.00 |
| 43 Vader's Apprentice, Unleashed VR | 6.00 | 10.00 |
| 44 Wookiee Hunter AT-ST R | 10.00 | 15.00 |
| 45 Garm Bel Iblis R | 6.00 | 10.00 |
| 46 Amanin Scout UC | 6.00 | 10.00 |
| 47 Boba Fett, Mercenary VR | 30.00 | 50.00 |
| 48 Caamasi Noble C | 6.00 | 10.00 |
| 49 Cloud Car Pilot C | 6.00 | 10.00 |
| 50 Felucian Warrior on Rancor VR | 25.00 | 40.00 |
| 51 Junk golem UC | 6.00 | 10.00 |
| 52 Knobby white spider UC | 6.00 | 10.00 |
| 53 Maris Brood VR | 10.00 | 15.00 |
| 54 Muun Tactics Broker C | 6.00 | 10.00 |
| 55 Mynock UC | 6.00 | 10.00 |
| 56 PROXY R | 6.00 | 10.00 |
| 57 Telosian Tank Droid UC | 6.00 | 10.00 |
| 58 Uggernaught R | 6.00 | 10.00 |
| 59 Ugnaught Boss UC | 6.00 | 10.00 |
| 60 Ugnaught Tech UC | 6.00 | 10.00 |

## 2008 Star Wars Knights of the Old Republic Miniatures

| | | | |
|---|---|---|---|
| COMPLETE SET (60) | 330.00 | 800.00 |
| RELEASED ON AUGUST 7, 2008 | | |
| 1 Atton Rand VR | 6.00 | 10.00 |
| 2 Bao-Dur R | 6.00 | 10.00 |
| 3 Carth Onasi VR | 12.00 | 20.00 |
| 4 Juggernaut War Droid C | 6.00 | 10.00 |
| 5 Master Lucien Draay VR | 6.00 | 10.00 |
| 6 Mira VR | 20.00 | 30.00 |
| 7 Old Republic Captain UC | 6.00 | 10.00 |
| 8 Old Republic Guard C | 6.00 | 10.00 |
| 9 Squint VR | 6.00 | 10.00 |
| 10 Visas Marr R | 6.00 | 10.00 |
| 11 Wookiee Elite Warrior C | 6.00 | 10.00 |
| 12 Wookiee Trooper C | 6.00 | 10.00 |
| 13 Darth Malak, Dark Lord of the Sith VR | 6.00 | 10.00 |
| 14 Darth Sion VR | 40.00 | 60.00 |
| 15 Elite Sith Trooper UC | 6.00 | 10.00 |
| 16 Sith Assassin UC | 6.00 | 10.00 |
| 17 Sith Guard C | 15.00 | 25.00 |
| 18 Sith Heavy Assault Droid UC | 6.00 | 10.00 |
| 19 Sith Marauder UC | 6.00 | 10.00 |
| 20 Sith Operative C | 6.00 | 10.00 |
| 21 Sith Trooper Captain UC | 6.00 | 10.00 |
| 22 Captain Panaka R | 6.00 | 10.00 |
| 23 Captain Tarpals R | 6.00 | 10.00 |
| 24 Gungan Artillerist C | 6.00 | 10.00 |
| 25 Gungan Shieldbearer UC | 6.00 | 10.00 |
| 26 Gungan Soldier C | 6.00 | 10.00 |
| 27 Jar Jar Binks VR | 20.00 | 30.00 |
| 28 Obi-Wan Kenobi, Padawan VR | 6.00 | 10.00 |
| 29 Supreme Chancellor Palpatine R | 6.00 | 10.00 |
| 30 Han Solo, Smuggler R | 6.00 | 10.00 |
| 31 Leia Organa, Senator VR | 6.00 | 10.00 |
| 32 Luke Skywalker, Jedi R | 6.00 | 10.00 |
| 33 Darth Vader, Scourge of the Jedi R | 6.00 | 10.00 |
| 34 RA-7 Death Star Protocol Droid UC | 6.00 | 10.00 |
| 35 General Wedge Antilles R | 6.00 | 10.00 |
| 36 ASN Assassin Droid UC | 6.00 | 10.00 |
| 37 Boma UC | 6.00 | 10.00 |
| 38 Czerka Scientist C | 6.00 | 10.00 |
| 39 Echani Handmaiden C | 6.00 | 10.00 |
| 40 GenoHaradan Assassin C | 6.00 | 10.00 |
| 41 Jarael R | 6.00 | 10.00 |
| 42 Jawa Scout C | 6.00 | 10.00 |
| 43 Jolee Bindo VR | 6.00 | 10.00 |
| 44 Juhani VR | 15.00 | 25.00 |
| 45 Kreia VR | 6.00 | 10.00 |
| 46 Massiff UC | 6.00 | 10.00 |
| 47 Mission Vao R | 12.00 | 20.00 |
| 48 Rakghoul UC | 6.00 | 10.00 |
| 49 Shyrack UC | 6.00 | 10.00 |
| 50 T1 Series Bulk Loader Droid UC | 6.00 | 10.00 |
| 51 T3-M4 R | 10.00 | 15.00 |
| 52 Tusken Raider Scout C | 6.00 | 10.00 |
| 53 Zaalbar R | 6.00 | 10.00 |
| 54 Zayne Carrick R | 6.00 | 10.00 |
| 55 Mandalore the Ultimate VR | 30.00 | 50.00 |
| 56 Mandalorian Captain UC | 6.00 | 10.00 |
| 57 Mandalorian Commando C | 6.00 | 10.00 |
| 58 Mandalorian Marauder C | 6.00 | 10.00 |
| 59 Mandalorian Quartermaster UC | 6.00 | 10.00 |
| 60 Mandalorian Scout C | 6.00 | 10.00 |

## 2008 Star Wars Legacy of the Force Miniatures

| | | | |
|---|---|---|---|
| COMPLETE SET (60) | 300.00 | 700.00 |
| RELEASED ON MARCH 28, 2008 | | |
| 1 Nomi Sunrider VR | 10.00 | 15.00 |
| 2 Old Republic Recruit C | 6.00 | 10.00 |
| 3 Old Republic Scout C | 6.00 | 10.00 |
| 4 Darth Caedus VR | 20.00 | 30.00 |
| 5 Darth Krayt VR | 20.00 | 30.00 |
| 6 Darth Nihl VR | 6.00 | 10.00 |
| 7 Darth Talon VR | 30.00 | 50.00 |
| 8 Lumiya, the Dark Lady R | 6.00 | 10.00 |
| 9 Republic Commando Training Sergeant U | 6.00 | 10.00 |
| 10 Darth Tyranus, Legacy of the dark side R | 6.00 | 10.00 |
| 11 Bothan Noble U | 6.00 | 10.00 |
| 12 Deena Shan R | 6.00 | 10.00 |
| 13 Elite Rebel Commando U | 6.00 | 10.00 |
| 14 General Dodonna R | 6.00 | 10.00 |
| 15 Luke Skywalker, Legacy of the Light Side R | 6.00 | 10.00 |
| 16 Rebel Honor Guard C | 6.00 | 10.00 |
| 17 Twi'lek Scout C | 6.00 | 10.00 |
| 18 Antares Draco R | 8.00 | 12.00 |
| 19 Emperor Roan Fel VR | 6.00 | 10.00 |
| 20 Imperial Knight U | 6.00 | 10.00 |
| 21 Imperial Knight U | 6.00 | 10.00 |
| 22 Imperial Pilot C | 6.00 | 10.00 |
| 23 Imperial Security Officer U | 6.00 | 10.00 |
| 24 Jagged Fel R | 6.00 | 10.00 |
| 25 Marasiah Fel R | 6.00 | 10.00 |
| 26 Moff Morlish Veed VR | 6.00 | 10.00 |
| 27 Moff Nyna Calixte R | 6.00 | 10.00 |
| 28 Noghri Commando U | 6.00 | 10.00 |
| 29 Shadow Stormtrooper U | 6.00 | 10.00 |
| 30 Corellian Security Officer U | 6.00 | 10.00 |
| 31 Galactic Alliance Scout C | 6.00 | 10.00 |
| 32 Galactic Alliance Trooper C | 6.00 | 10.00 |
| 33 Han Solo, Galactic Hero R | 6.00 | 10.00 |
| 34 Kyle Katarn, Jedi Battlemaster VR | 6.00 | 10.00 |
| 35 Leia Organa Solo, Jedi Knight VR | 6.00 | 10.00 |
| 36 Luke Skywalker, Force Spirit VR | 6.00 | 10.00 |
| 37 Mara Jade Skywalker VR | 10.00 | 15.00 |
| 38 Shado Vao R | 6.00 | 10.00 |
| 39 Wolf Sazen VR | 6.00 | 10.00 |
| 40 Cade Skywalker, Bounty Hunter VR | 6.00 | 10.00 |
| 41 Deliah Blue R | 6.00 | 10.00 |
| 42 Dug Fringer U | 6.00 | 10.00 |
| 43 Duros Scoundrel C | 6.00 | 10.00 |
| 44 Gotal Mercenary C | 6.00 | 10.00 |
| 45 Guard Droid C | 6.00 | 10.00 |
| 46 Human Bodyguard C | 6.00 | 10.00 |
| 47 Human Scoundrel C | 6.00 | 10.00 |
| 48 Human Scout C | 6.00 | 10.00 |

| | | |
|---|---|---|
| 49 Jariah Syn R | 6.00 | 10.00 |
| 50 Kel Dor Bounty Hunter C | 6.00 | 10.00 |
| 51 Rodian Blaster for Hire U | 6.00 | 10.00 |
| 52 Trandoshan Mercenary C | 6.00 | 10.00 |
| 53 Boba Fett, Mercenary Commander VR | 6.00 | 10.00 |
| 54 Canderous Ordo R | 6.00 | 10.00 |
| 55 Mandalorian Gunslinger U | 6.00 | 10.00 |
| 56 Mandalorian Trooper U | 6.00 | 10.00 |
| 57 Yuuzhan Vong Elite Warrior U | 6.00 | 10.00 |
| 58 Yuuzhan Vong Jedi Hunter U | 6.00 | 10.00 |
| 59 Yuuzhan Vong Shaper U | 6.00 | 10.00 |
| 60 Yuuzhan Vong Warrior C | 6.00 | 10.00 |

## 2008 Star Wars The Clone Wars Miniatures

| | | |
|---|---|---|
| COMPLETE SET (40) | 200.00 | 400.00 |
| RELEASED ON NOVEMBER 4, 2008 | | |
| 1 Darth Sidious Hologram VR | 6.00 | 10.00 |
| 2 Ahsoka Tano VR | 15.00 | 25.00 |
| 3 Anakin Skywalker Champion of Nelvaan R | 6.00 | 10.00 |
| 4 Anakin Skywalker on STAP VR | 6.00 | 10.00 |
| 5 ARC Trooper Sniper U | 6.00 | 10.00 |
| 6 Barriss Offee, Jedi Knight R | 6.00 | 10.00 |
| 7 Captain Rex VR | 6.00 | 10.00 |
| 8 Clone Trooper on Gelagrub R | 6.00 | 10.00 |
| 9 Commander Gree R | 6.00 | 10.00 |
| 10 Elite Clone Trooper Commander U | 6.00 | 10.00 |
| 11 Elite Clone Trooper Grenadier C | 6.00 | 10.00 |
| 12 Galactic Marine U | 6.00 | 10.00 |
| 13 General Aayla Secura R | 10.00 | 15.00 |
| 14 Heavy Clone Trooper C | 6.00 | 10.00 |
| 15 Mon Calamari Knight U | 6.00 | 10.00 |
| 16 Odd Ball R | 6.00 | 10.00 |
| 17 Padmé Amidala Senator VR | 8.00 | 12.00 |
| 18 Star Corps Trooper U | 6.00 | 10.00 |
| 19 Wookiee Scoundrel C | 6.00 | 10.00 |
| 20 Yoda on Kybuck VR | 6.00 | 10.00 |
| 21 Battle Droid C | 6.00 | 10.00 |
| 22 Battle Droid C | 6.00 | 10.00 |
| 23 Battle Droid Sniper U | 6.00 | 10.00 |
| 24 Chameleon Droid R | 6.00 | 10.00 |
| 25 Durge, Jedi Hunter VR | 15.00 | 25.00 |
| 26 General Grievous, Droid Army Commander VR | 6.00 | 10.00 |
| 27 Heavy Super Battle Droid C | 6.00 | 10.00 |
| 28 IG-100 MagnaGuard U | 6.00 | 10.00 |
| 29 Neimoidian Warrior C | 6.00 | 10.00 |
| 30 Quarren Isolationist U | 6.00 | 10.00 |
| 31 Rocket Battle Droid U | 6.00 | 10.00 |
| 32 Super Battle Droid C | 6.00 | 10.00 |
| 33 Techno Union Warrior C | 6.00 | 10.00 |
| 34 Aqualish Warrior C | 6.00 | 10.00 |
| 35 Gha Nachkt R | 6.00 | 10.00 |

| | | |
|---|---|---|
| 36 Human Soldier of Fortune C | 6.00 | 10.00 |
| 37 IG-86 Assassin Droid U | 6.00 | 10.00 |
| 38 Nelvaanian Warrior U | 6.00 | 10.00 |
| 39 Trandoshan Scavenger U | 6.00 | 10.00 |
| 40 Utapaun Warrior C | 6.00 | 10.00 |

### 2008 Star Wars The Clone Wars Miniatures Starter

| | | |
|---|---|---|
| COMPLETE SET (6) | 20.00 | 50.00 |
| RELEASED ON NOVEMBER 4, 2008 | | |
| 1 General Obi-Wan Kenobi | 5.00 | 8.00 |
| 2 Clone Trooper | 5.00 | 8.00 |
| 3 Clone Trooper Commander | 5.00 | 8.00 |
| 4 Count Dooku of Serenno | 5.00 | 8.00 |
| 5 Security Battle Droid | 5.00 | 8.00 |
| 6 Super Battle Droid Commander | 5.00 | 8.00 |

## 2009 Star Wars Galaxy at War Miniatures

| | | |
|---|---|---|
| COMPLETE SET (40) | 60.00 | 160.00 |
| RELEASED ON OCTOBER 27, 2009 | | |
| 1 501st Clone Trooper C | 2.50 | 4.00 |
| 2 A4-Series Lab Droid U | 2.50 | 4.00 |
| 3 Admiral Yularen VR | 2.50 | 4.00 |
| 4 Aqualish Technician C | 2.50 | 4.00 |
| 5 ARF Trooper C | 2.50 | 4.00 |
| 6 Asajj Ventress, Strike Leader R | 2.50 | 4.00 |
| 7 AT-TE Driver C | 2.50 | 4.00 |
| 8 B3 Ultra Battle Droid U | 2.50 | 4.00 |
| 9 Battle Droid C | 2.50 | 4.00 |
| 10 Battle Droid Sergeant U | 2.50 | 4.00 |
| 11 Cad Bane VR | 2.50 | 4.00 |
| 12 Captain Argyus VR | 2.50 | 4.00 |
| 13 Captain Mar Tuuk VR | 2.50 | 4.00 |
| 14 Captain Rex, 501st Commander R | 2.50 | 4.00 |
| 15 Clone Trooper Pilot C | 2.50 | 4.00 |

| | | |
|---|---|---|
| 16 Clone Trooper Sergeant U | 2.50 | 4.00 |
| 17 Clone Trooper with Night Vision C | 2.50 | 4.00 |
| 18 Clone Trooper with Repeating Blaster U | 2.50 | 4.00 |
| 19 Commander Ahsoka R | 2.50 | 4.00 |
| 20 Commander Cody R | 2.50 | 4.00 |
| 21 Commando Droid C | 2.50 | 4.00 |
| 22 Commando Droid C | 2.50 | 4.00 |
| 23 Commando Droid Captain U | 2.50 | 4.00 |
| 24 Elite Senate Guard U | 2.50 | 4.00 |
| 25 General Grievous, Scourge of the Jedi R | 2.50 | 4.00 |
| 26 General Skywalker R | 2.50 | 4.00 |
| 27 General Whorm Loathsom VR | 2.50 | 4.00 |
| 28 Hondo Ohnaka VR | 2.50 | 4.00 |
| 29 IG-100 MagnaGuard Artillerist U | 2.50 | 4.00 |
| 30 IG-100 MagnaGuard U | 2.50 | 4.00 |
| 31 Jedi Master Kit Fisto R | 2.50 | 4.00 |
| 32 LR-57 Combat Droid U | 2.50 | 4.00 |
| 33 Nahdar Vebb VR | 2.50 | 4.00 |
| 34 Obi-Wan Kenobi, Jedi General R | 2.50 | 4.00 |
| 35 R7 Astromech Droid U | 2.50 | 4.00 |
| 36 Rodian Trader C | 2.50 | 4.00 |
| 37 Senate Commando C | 2.50 | 4.00 |
| 38 Treadwell Droid U | 2.50 | 4.00 |
| 39 Wat Tambor, Techno Union Foreman VR | 2.50 | 4.00 |
| 40 Weequay Pirate C | 2.50 | 4.00 |

## 2009 Star Wars Imperial Entanglements Miniatures

| | | |
|---|---|---|
| COMPLETE SET (40) | 180.00 | 450.00 |
| RELEASED ON MARCH 17, 2009 | | |
| 1 Bothan Commando C | 6.00 | 10.00 |
| 2 C-3PO, Ewok Deity VR | 6.00 | 10.00 |
| 3 General Crix Madine R | 6.00 | 10.00 |
| 4 General Rieekan VR | 8.00 | 12.00 |
| 5 Leia, Bounty Hunter VR | 6.00 | 10.00 |
| 6 Luke Skywalker, Rebel Commando VR | 12.00 | 20.00 |
| 7 Rebel Commando Pathfinder U | 6.00 | 10.00 |
| 8 Rebel Trooper C | 6.00 | 10.00 |
| 9 R2-D2 with Extended Sensor R | 6.00 | 10.00 |
| 10 Veteran Rebel Commando C | 6.00 | 10.00 |
| 11 Arica R | 6.00 | 10.00 |
| 12 Darth Vader, Legacy of the Force VR | 12.00 | 20.00 |
| 13 Emperor Palpatine on Throne VR | 15.00 | 25.00 |
| 14 Imperial Dignitary U | 6.00 | 10.00 |
| 15 Moff Tiaan Jerjerrod R | 6.00 | 10.00 |
| 16 181st Imperial Pilot U | 6.00 | 10.00 |
| 17 Sandtrooper C | 6.00 | 10.00 |
| 18 Sandtrooper Officer U | 6.00 | 10.00 |
| 19 Scout Trooper C | 6.00 | 10.00 |
| 20 Shock Trooper U | 6.00 | 10.00 |
| 21 Snowtrooper C | 6.00 | 10.00 |
| 22 Snowtrooper Commander U | 6.00 | 10.00 |
| 23 Stormtrooper C | 6.00 | 10.00 |
| 24 Thrawn Mitth'raw'nuruodo R | 6.00 | 10.00 |

| | | |
|---|---|---|
| 25 Kyp Durron R | 6.00 | 10.00 |
| 26 Bacta Tank U | 6.00 | 10.00 |
| 27 Bespin Guard C | 6.00 | 10.00 |
| 28 Chiss Mercenary C | 6.00 | 10.00 |
| 29 Dash Rendar, Renegade Smuggler VR | 10.00 | 15.00 |
| 30 Duros Scout C | 6.00 | 10.00 |
| 31 Ewok Scout C | 6.00 | 10.00 |
| 32 Jawa Scavenger C | 6.00 | 10.00 |
| 33 Lobot, Computer Liaison Officer R | 6.00 | 10.00 |
| 34 Logray, Ewok Shaman R | 6.00 | 10.00 |
| 35 Mercenary Commander U - resembling Airen Cracken | 6.00 | 10.00 |
| 36 Mouse Droid U | 6.00 | 10.00 |
| 37 Twi'lek Black Sun Vigo U | 6.00 | 10.00 |
| 38 Ugnaught Droid Destroyer U | 6.00 | 10.00 |
| 39 Whiphid Tracker U | 6.00 | 10.00 |
| 40 Xizor VR | 12.00 | 20.00 |

| | | |
|---|---|---|
| 32 Rocket Battle Droid C | 6.00 | 10.00 |
| 33 Sith apprentice UC - resembling Darth Bandon | 6.00 | 10.00 |
| 34 Sith Lord U | 6.00 | 10.00 |
| 35 Stormtrooper C | 6.00 | 10.00 |
| 36 The Dark Woman VR | 12.00 | 20.00 |
| 37 The Jedi ExileVR | 15.00 | 25.00 |
| 38 Vodo-Siosk Baas VR | 10.00 | 15.00 |
| 39 Youngling C | 6.00 | 10.00 |
| 40 Yuuzhan Vong Ossus Guardian UC | 6.00 | 10.00 |

| | | |
|---|---|---|
| 35 Talz Warrior C | 2.50 | 4.00 |
| 36 Togorian Soldier UC | 2.50 | 4.00 |
| 37 Trandoshan Elite Mercenary UC | 6.00 | 10.00 |
| 38 Trianii Scout UC | 2.50 | 4.00 |
| 39 T'Surr C | 2.50 | 4.00 |
| 40 Zuckuss, Bounty Hunter C | 8.00 | 12.00 |

## 2010 Star Wars Masters of the Force Miniatures

## 2010 Star Wars Dark Times Miniatures

## 2009 Star Wars Jedi Academy Miniatures

| | | |
|---|---|---|
| COMPLETE SET (40) | 200.00 | 450.00 |
| RELEASED ON JUNE 30, 2009 | | |
| 1 Anakin Solo R | 6.00 | 10.00 |
| 2 Antarian Ranger C | 6.00 | 10.00 |
| 3 Cade Skywalker, Padawan R | 6.00 | 10.00 |
| 4 Crimson Nova Bounty Hunter UC | 6.00 | 10.00 |
| 5 Darth Maul, Sith apprentice VR | 15.00 | 25.00 |
| 6 Darth Plagueis VR | 15.00 | 25.00 |
| 7 Darth Sidious, Sith Master R | 6.00 | 10.00 |
| 8 Death Watch Raider C | 6.00 | 10.00 |
| 9 Disciples of Ragnos C | 6.00 | 10.00 |
| 10 Exceptional Jedi Apprentice UC | 6.00 | 10.00 |
| 11 Felucian UC | 6.00 | 10.00 |
| 12 Grand Master Luke Skywalker R | 10.00 | 15.00 |
| 13 Grand Master Yoda R | 8.00 | 12.00 |
| 14 Heavy Clone Trooper C | 6.00 | 10.00 |
| 15 HK-50 Series Assassin Droid UC | 6.00 | 10.00 |
| 16 Imperial Sentinel U | 6.00 | 10.00 |
| 17 Jedi Battlemaster UC | 6.00 | 10.00 |
| 18 Jedi Crusader UC | 6.00 | 10.00 |
| 19 Jensaarai Defender UC | 6.00 | 10.00 |
| 20 Kol Skywalker VR | 6.00 | 10.00 |
| 21 Krath War Droid C | 6.00 | 10.00 |
| 22 Kyle Katarn, Combat Instructor R | 6.00 | 10.00 |
| 23 Leia Skywalker, Jedi Knight R | 6.00 | 10.00 |
| 24 Master K'Kruhk VR | 6.00 | 10.00 |
| 25 Naga Sadow VR | 10.00 | 15.00 |
| 26 Peace Brigade Thug C | 6.00 | 10.00 |
| 27 Praetorite Vong Priest UC | 6.00 | 10.00 |
| 28 Praetorite Vong Warrior C | 6.00 | 10.00 |
| 29 Qui-Gon Jinn, Jedi Trainer R | 6.00 | 10.00 |
| 30 R4 Astromech Droid C | 6.00 | 10.00 |
| 31 Reborn C | 6.00 | 10.00 |

| | | |
|---|---|---|
| COMPLETE SET (40) | 75.00 | 200.00 |
| RELEASED ON JANUARY 26, 2010 | | |
| 1 4-LOM, Droid Mercenary R | 2.50 | 4.00 |
| 2 501st Legion Clone Commander UC | 2.50 | 4.00 |
| 3 501st Legion Clone Trooper C | 2.50 | 4.00 |
| 4 501st Legion Stormtrooper C | 2.50 | 4.00 |
| 5 ARF Trooper UC | 2.50 | 4.00 |
| 6 A'Sharad Hett VR | 10.00 | 15.00 |
| 7 Bomo Greenbark VR | 2.50 | 4.00 |
| 8 Bossk, Trandoshan Hunter R | 2.50 | 4.00 |
| 9 Boushh, Ubese Hunter R | 2.50 | 4.00 |
| 10 Chewbacca, Fearless Scout VR | 2.50 | 4.00 |
| 11 Dass Jennir VR | 6.00 | 10.00 |
| 12 Dengar, Hired Killer R | 2.50 | 4.00 |
| 13 EG-5 Jedi Hunter Droid UC | 5.00 | 8.00 |
| 14 Elite Sith Assassin UC | 2.50 | 4.00 |
| 15 Emperor's Hand UC | 2.50 | 4.00 |
| 16 Ferus Olin VR | 2.50 | 4.00 |
| 17 Gungan Bounty Hunter C | 2.50 | 4.00 |
| 18 Human Engineer C | 2.50 | 4.00 |
| 19 IG-88, Assassin Droid | 5.00 | 8.00 |
| 20 Imperial Engineer C | 2.50 | 4.00 |
| 21 Imperial Inquisitor UC | 2.50 | 4.00 |
| 22 Imperial Sovereign Protector UC | 2.50 | 4.00 |
| 23 Jax Pavan VR | 2.50 | 4.00 |
| 24 Jedi Watchman C | 2.50 | 4.00 |
| 25 Kir Kanos VR | 6.00 | 10.00 |
| 26 K'Kruhk VR | 2.50 | 4.00 |
| 27 Kota's Elite Militia UC | 2.50 | 4.00 |
| 28 Kota's Militia C | 2.50 | 4.00 |
| 29 Major Maximilian Veers R | 2.50 | 4.00 |
| 30 Mandalorian Jedi Hunter UC | 2.50 | 4.00 |
| 31 Merumeru R | 2.50 | 4.00 |
| 32 Rodian Brute C | 2.50 | 4.00 |
| 33 Rodian Raider C | 2.50 | 4.00 |
| 34 Talz Chieftain UC | 2.50 | 4.00 |

| | | |
|---|---|---|
| COMPLETE SET (40) | 115.00 | 280.00 |
| RELEASED APRIL 6, 2010 | | |
| 1 Cay Qel-Droma VR | 10.00 | 15.00 |
| 2 Jedi Healer UC | 4.00 | 6.00 |
| 3 Jedi Instructor - resembling Coleman Trebor UC | 4.00 | 6.00 |
| 4 Jedi Sith Hunter UC | 4.00 | 6.00 |
| 5 Lord Hoth VR | 4.00 | 6.00 |
| 6 Freedon Nadd VR | 4.00 | 6.00 |
| 7 Kit Fisto, Jedi Master R | 4.00 | 6.00 |
| 8 Master Windu R | 4.00 | 6.00 |
| 9 Plo Koon, Jedi Master R | 6.00 | 10.00 |
| 10 Rodian Diplomat UC | 4.00 | 6.00 |
| 11 Saesee Tiin, Jedi Master R | 10.00 | 15.00 |
| 12 Voolvif Monn VR | 15.00 | 25.00 |
| 13 Battle Droid Officer C | 4.00 | 6.00 |
| 14 Anakin Skywalker, Force Spirit R | 4.00 | 6.00 |
| 15 General Han Solo R | 4.00 | 6.00 |
| 16 Lando Calrissian, Rebel Leader R | 4.00 | 6.00 |
| 17 Rebel Soldier C | 4.00 | 6.00 |
| 18 Red Hand Trooper UC | 4.00 | 6.00 |
| 19 Yoda, Force Spirit VR | 4.00 | 6.00 |
| 20 Arden Lyn VR | 4.00 | 6.00 |
| 21 Darth Vader, Sith apprentice R | 4.00 | 6.00 |
| 22 Ganner Rhysode VR | 4.00 | 6.00 |
| 23 Blood Carver Assassin C | 4.00 | 6.00 |
| 24 Chiss Trooper UC | 4.00 | 6.00 |
| 25 Ewok Warrior C | 4.00 | 6.00 |
| 26 Gamorrean Bodyguard C | 4.00 | 6.00 |
| 27 Ghhhk UC | 5.00 | 8.00 |
| 28 Grievous, Kaleesh Warlord VR | 4.00 | 6.00 |
| 29 Houjix C | 4.00 | 6.00 |
| 30 K'lor'slug UC | 5.00 | 8.00 |
| 31 Kaminoan Medic UC | 4.00 | 6.00 |
| 32 Kintan Strider C | 4.00 | 6.00 |
| 33 Mantellian Savrip C | 4.00 | 6.00 |
| 34 Molator UC | 4.00 | 6.00 |
| 35 Monnok UC | 4.00 | 6.00 |
| 36 Ng'ok UC | 5.00 | 8.00 |
| 37 Sullustan Scout C | 4.00 | 6.00 |
| 38 Toydarian Soldier C | 4.00 | 6.00 |
| 39 Far-Outsider C | 4.00 | 6.00 |
| 40 Taung Warrior C | 4.00 | 6.00 |

# Miscellaneous
## PRICE GUIDE

## HOT WHEELS

### 2014 Hot Wheels Star Wars Character Cars Black Cards 1:64

| | | |
|---|---|---|
| 1 Darth Vader | 10.00 | 20.00 |
| 2 R2-D2 | 5.00 | 10.00 |
| 3 Luke Skywalker | 5.00 | 10.00 |
| 4 Chewbacca | 4.00 | 8.00 |
| 5 Yoda | 4.00 | 8.00 |
| 6 Tusken Raider | 5.00 | 10.00 |
| 7 501st Clone Trooper | 8.00 | 15.00 |
| 8 Stormtrooper | 4.00 | 8.00 |
| 9 Darth Maul | 4.00 | 8.00 |
| 10 Boba Fett | 6.00 | 12.00 |
| 11 Chopper (Star Wars Rebels) | 5.00 | 10.00 |
| 12 The Inquisitor (Star Wars Rebels) | 4.00 | 8.00 |
| 13 C-3PO | 8.00 | 15.00 |
| 14 Wicket the Ewok | 5.00 | 10.00 |
| 15 Kanan Jarrus (Star Wars Rebels) | 4.00 | 8.00 |
| 16 Zeb (Star Wars Rebels) | 4.00 | 8.00 |
| 17 Kylo Ren | 5.00 | 10.00 |
| 18 BB-8 | 8.00 | 15.00 |
| 19 General Grievous | 6.00 | 12.00 |
| 20 Han Solo (The Force Awakens) | 8.00 | 15.00 |
| 21 First Order Stormtrooper | 6.00 | 12.00 |
| 22 Obi-Wan Kenobi | 12.00 | 25.00 |
| 23 Rey | 8.00 | 15.00 |
| 24 Jabba the Hutt | 5.00 | 10.00 |
| 25 Admiral Ackbar | 5.00 | 10.00 |
| 26 First Order Flametrooper | 6.00 | 12.00 |
| 27 Battle Droid | 6.00 | 12.00 |
| 28 Sabine Wren (Star Wars Rebels) | 12.50 | 25.00 |
| 29 Clone Shock Trooper#I(UER #27) | | |
| 30 C-3PO (The Force Awakens) | 8.00 | 15.00 |
| 31 Sidon Ithano (The Force Awakens) | 8.00 | 15.00 |
| 32 Jango Fett | 6.00 | 12.00 |

### 2014 Hot Wheels Star Wars Character Cars Blue Cards 1:64

| | | |
|---|---|---|
| 1 Darth Vader | 4.00 | 8.00 |
| 2 R2-D2 | 4.00 | 8.00 |
| 3 Luke Skywalker | 4.00 | 8.00 |
| 4 Chewbacca | 6.00 | 12.00 |
| 5 Yoda | 7.50 | 15.00 |
| 6 Tusken Raider | 4.00 | 8.00 |
| 7 501st Clone Trooper | 4.00 | 8.00 |
| 8 Stormtrooper | 4.00 | 8.00 |
| 9 Darth Maul | 5.00 | 10.00 |
| 10 Boba Fett | 4.00 | 8.00 |
| 11 Chopper (Star Wars Rebels) | 4.00 | 8.00 |
| 12 The Inquisitor (Star Wars Rebels) | 3.00 | 6.00 |
| 13 C-3PO | 6.00 | 12.00 |
| 14 Wicket the Ewok | 4.00 | 8.00 |
| 15 Kanan Jarrus (Star Wars Rebels) | 5.00 | 10.00 |
| 16 Zeb (Star Wars Rebels) | | |
| 17 Kylo Ren | | |
| 18 BB-8 | | |
| 19 General Grievous | | |
| 20 Han Solo (The Force Awakens) | | |
| 21 First Order Stormtrooper | 6.00 | 12.00 |
| 22 Obi-Wan Kenobi | | |
| 23 Rey | | |
| 24 Jabba the Hutt | | |
| 25 Admiral Ackbar | | |
| 26 First Order Flametrooper | | |
| 27 Battle Droid | | |
| 28 Sabine Wren (Star Wars Rebels) | | |
| 29 Clone Shock Trooper#I(UER #27) | | |
| 30 C-3PO (The Force Awakens) | | |
| 31 Sidon Ithano (The Force Awakens) | | |
| 32 Jango Fett | | |

### 2014 Hot Wheels Star Wars Saga Walmart Exclusives 1:64

| | | |
|---|---|---|
| 1 Gearonimo (The Phantom Menace) | 5.00 | 10.00 |
| 2 Nitro Scorcher (Attack of the Clones) | 6.00 | 12.00 |
| 3 Duel Fueler (Revenge of the Sith) | 8.00 | 15.00 |
| 4 Motoblade (A New Hope) | | |
| 5 Spectyte (Empire Strikes Back) | 10.00 | 20.00 |
| 6 Ballistik (Return of the Jedi) | 4.00 | 8.00 |
| 7 Brutalistic (The Clone Wars) | 4.00 | 8.00 |
| 8 Jet Threat 3.0 (Star Wars Rebels) | 12.00 | 25.00 |

### 2014-16 Hot Wheels Star Wars Exclusives 1:64

| | | |
|---|---|---|
| 1 Darth Vader (w/lightsaber box)#((2014 SDCC Exclusive) | 80.00 | 150.00 |
| 2 R2-KT#((2015 Star Wars Celebration | | |
| Make-a-Wish Foundation Exclusive) | 40.00 | 80.00 |
| 3 First Order Stormtrooper#((2015 SDCC Exclusive) | 25.00 | 50.00 |
| 4 Carships Trench Run Set#((2016 SDCC Exclusive) | 50.00 | 100.00 |
| 5 Boba Fett Prototype Armor#((2016 Star Wars Celebration Exclusive)25.00 | | 50.00 |

### 2014-16 Hot Wheels Star Wars Target Exclusive 5-Packs 1:64

| | | |
|---|---|---|
| 1 Character Cars (Battle-Damaged Stormtrooper | | |
| Luke Skywalker/Darth Vader/Yoda/Chewbacca) | 25.00 | 50.00 |
| 2 Light Side vs. Dark Side (Luke Skywalker/Obi-Wan Kenobi | | |
| Anakin Skywalker/Emperor Palpatine/Kylo Ren) | 15.00 | 30.00 |
| 3 Heroes of the Resistance (Chewbacca/Han Solo/Rey | | |
| Poe Dameron/Maz Kanata) | 20.00 | 40.00 |

### 2015 Hot Wheels Star Wars Walmart Exclusives 1:64

| | | |
|---|---|---|
| 1 Obi-Wan Kenobi#((Jedi Order Scorcher) | 4.00 | 8.00 |
| 2 Darth Maul#((Sith Scoopa di Fuego) | 5.00 | 10.00 |
| 3 Clone Trooper#((Galactic Republic Impavido 1) | 4.00 | 8.00 |
| 4 General Grievous#((Separatists Sinistra) | 4.00 | 8.00 |
| 5 Luke Skywalker#((Rebel Alliance Enforcer) | 4.00 | 8.00 |
| 6 Darth Vader#((Galactic Empire Prototype H-24) | 5.00 | 10.00 |
| 7 Poe Dameron#((Resistance Fast Felion) | 4.00 | 8.00 |
| 8 Kylo Ren#((First Order Ettorium) | 4.00 | 8.00 |

### 2015-16 Hot Wheels Star Wars Character Cars Black Carded 2-Packs 1:64

| | | |
|---|---|---|
| 1 Chewbacca & Han Solo | 5.00 | 10.00 |
| 2 R2-D2 & C-3PO (weathered) | 4.00 | 8.00 |
| 3 Obi-Wan Kenobi & Darth Vader | 20.00 | 40.00 |
| 4 501st Clone Trooper & Battle Droid | 4.00 | 8.00 |
| 5 Emperor Palpatine vs. Yoda | 8.00 | 15.00 |
| 6 Darth Vader & Princess Leia | 10.00 | 20.00 |
| 7 Captain Phasma & First Order Stormtrooper | 5.00 | 10.00 |
| 8 Rey vs. First Order Flametrooper | 8.00 | 15.00 |
| 9 BB-8 & Poe Dameron | 10.00 | 20.00 |
| 10 Han Solo vs. Greedo | 12.00 | 25.00 |

| | | |
|---|---|---|
| 11 Boba Fett & Bossk | | |
| 12 Luke Skywalker vs. Rancor | | |
| 13 Stormtrooper & Death Trooper (Rogue One) | 8.00 | 15.00 |

### 2015-16 Hot Wheels Star Wars Character Cars Blue Carded 2-Packs 1:64

| | | |
|---|---|---|
| 1 Chewbacca & Han Solo | 6.00 | 12.00 |
| 2 R2-D2 & C-3PO (weathered) | 6.00 | 12.00 |
| 3 Obi-Wan Kenobi & Darth Vader | 6.00 | 12.00 |
| 4 501st Clone Trooper & Battle Droid | 8.00 | 15.00 |
| 5 Emperor Palpatine vs. Yoda | | |
| 6 Darth Vader & Princess Leia | 6.00 | 12.00 |
| 7 Captain Phasma & First Order Stormtrooper | | |
| 8 Rey vs. First Order Flametrooper | | |
| 9 BB-8 & Poe Dameron | | |
| 10 Han Solo vs. Greedo | 8.00 | 15.00 |
| 11 Boba Fett & Bossk | | |
| 12 Luke Skywalker vs. Rancor | | |
| 13 Stormtrooper & Death Trooper (Rogue One) | 10.00 | 20.00 |

### 2015-16 Hot Wheels Star Wars Tracksets 1:64

| | | |
|---|---|---|
| 1 TIE Factory Takedown (w/Ezra Bridger car) | 12.00 | 25.00 |
| 2 Throne Room Raceway (w/Luke Skywalker car) | 12.00 | 25.00 |
| 3 Death Star Battle Blast (w/X-Wing inspired vehicle) | 10.00 | 20.00 |
| 4 Blast & Battle Lightsaber Launcher (w/Darth Vader car) | 8.00 | 15.00 |
| 5 Starkiller Base Battle (w/Finn car) | | |
| 6 Rancor Rumble set (w/Gamorrean Guard car) | 15.00 | 30.00 |

### 2017 Hot Wheels Star Wars 40th Anniversary Carships 1:64

| | | |
|---|---|---|
| NNO Millennium Falcon | 6.00 | 12.00 |
| NNO TIE Advanced XI Prototype | 6.00 | 12.00 |
| NNO TIE Fighter | 5.00 | 10.00 |
| NNO X-Wing Fighter | 5.00 | 10.00 |
| NNO Y-Wing Fighter | 8.00 | 15.00 |

### 2017 Hot Wheels Star Wars 40th Anniversary Character Cars 1:64

| | | |
|---|---|---|
| NNO Biggs Darklighter#((Celebration Exclusive) | 12.00 | 25.00 |
| NNO Chewbacca | 5.00 | 10.00 |
| NNO Darth Vader | 6.00 | 12.00 |
| NNO Luke Skywalker | 4.00 | 8.00 |
| NNO Princess Leia | 5.00 | 10.00 |
| NNO R2-D2 | 4.00 | 8.00 |
| NNO Stormtrooper | 4.00 | 8.00 |

### 2017 Hot Wheels Star Wars 40th Anniversary Starships 1:64

| | | |
|---|---|---|
| NNO Millennium Falcon | 8.00 | 15.00 |
| NNO Star Destroyer | 10.00 | 20.00 |
| NNO TIE Advanced X1 Prototype | 6.00 | 12.00 |
| NNO TIE Fighter | 6.00 | 12.00 |
| NNO X-Wing Fighter | 6.00 | 12.00 |
| NNO Y-Wing Fighter | 8.00 | 15.00 |

### 2017 Hot Wheels Star Wars The Last Jedi 2-Packs 1:64

| | | |
|---|---|---|
| NNO BB-8 & Poe Dameron | 8.00 | 15.00 |
| NNO Boba Fett & Bossk | 6.00 | 12.00 |
| NNO Jabba the Hutt & Han Solo in Carbonite | 12.00 | 25.00 |
| NNO Kylo Ren & Snoke | 15.00 | 30.00 |
| NNO R2-D2 & C-3PO | 8.00 | 15.00 |
| NNO Rey (Jedi Training) & Luke Skywalker | 15.00 | 30.00 |

### 2017 Hot Wheels Star Wars The Last Jedi Carships 1:64

| | | |
|---|---|---|
| NNO First Order TIE Fighter | 6.00 | 12.00 |
| NNO Kylo Ren's TIE Silencer | | |
| NNO Millennium Falcon | | |
| NNO Poe's X-Wing Fighter | | |

NNO Resistance Ski Speeder
NNO Y-Wing Fighter

## 2017 Hot Wheels Star Wars The Last Jedi Character Cars 1:64

| | | |
|---|---|---|
| 7101 | Lightsaber Duel | 25.00 | 50.00 |
| 7111 | Droid Fighter | 15.00 | 30.00 |
| 7121 | Naboo Swamp | 20.00 | 40.00 |
| 7131 | Anakin's Podracer | 25.00 | 50.00 |
| 7141 | Naboo Fighter | 40.00 | 80.00 |
| 7151 | Sith Infiltrator | 30.00 | 60.00 |
| 7161 | Gungan Sub | 60.00 | 120.00 |
| 7171 | Mos Espa Podrace | 80.00 | 150.00 |

### 1999 LEGO Star Wars Episode IV

| | | | |
|---|---|---|---|
| 7110 | Landspeeder | 20.00 | 40.00 |
| 7140 | X-wing Fighter | 60.00 | 120.00 |
| 7150 | TIE Fighter & Y-wing | 80.00 | 150.00 |

### 1999 LEGO Star Wars Episode V

| | | | |
|---|---|---|---|
| 7130 | Snowspeeder | 40.00 | 80.00 |

| NNO | BB-8 | 7.50 | 15.00 |
|---|---|---|---|
| NNO | BB-9E | 6.00 | 12.00 |
| NNO | C-3PO | 4.00 | 8.00 |
| NNO | Captain Phasma | 4.00 | 8.00 |
| NNO | Chewbacca | 4.00 | 8.00 |
| NNO | Darth Vader | 5.00 | 10.00 |
| NNO | Elite Praetorian Guard | 10.00 | 20.00 |
| NNO | Finn | 7.50 | 15.00 |
| NNO | First Order Executioner | 5.00 | 10.00 |
| NNO | First Order Stormtrooper | | |
| NNO | Kylo Ren | 6.00 | 12.00 |
| NNO | Luke Skywalker | 5.00 | 10.00 |
| NNO | R2-D2 | 4.00 | 8.00 |
| NNO | Rey (Jedi Training) | 6.00 | 12.00 |

## LEGO

### 1999 LEGO Star Wars Episode VI

| | | | |
|---|---|---|---|
| 7128 | Speeder Bikes | 25.00 | 50.00 |

### 2000 LEGO Star Wars Episode I

| | | | |
|---|---|---|---|
| 7115 | Gungan Patrol | 25.00 | 50.00 |
| 7124 | Flash Speeder | 15.00 | 30.00 |
| 7155 | Trade Federation AAT | 40.00 | 80.00 |
| 7159 | Star Wars Bucket | 30.00 | 75.00 |
| 7184 | Trade Federation MTT | 30.00 | 75.00 |

### 2000 LEGO Star Wars Episode IV

| | | | |
|---|---|---|---|
| 7190 | Millennium Falcon | 150.00 | 300.00 |

### 2000 LEGO Star Wars Episode V

| | | | |
|---|---|---|---|
| 7144 | Slave I | 50.00 | 100.00 |

### 2000 LEGO Star Wars Episode VI

| | | | |
|---|---|---|---|
| 7104 | Desert Skiff | 20.00 | 40.00 |
| 7134 | A-wing Fighter | 25.00 | 50.00 |
| 7180 | B-wing at Rebel Control Center | 30.00 | 60.00 |

### 2000 LEGO Star Wars Minifigure Pack

| | | | |
|---|---|---|---|
| 3340 | Emperor Palpatine, Darth Maul and Darth Vader Minifig Pack - Star Wars #1 | 40.00 | 80.00 |

## 2017 Hot Wheels Star Wars The Last Jedi Character Cars All-Terrain 1:64

| NNO | BB-8 | 10.00 | 20.00 |
|---|---|---|---|
| NNO | Darth Vader | | |
| NNO | Luke Skywalker | | |
| NNO | Stormtrooper | | |

### 2017 Hot Wheels Star Wars The Last Jedi Starships 1:64

NNO First Order Heavy Assault Walker
NNO First Order Special Forces TIE Fighter
NNO First Order Star Destroyer
NNO Kylo Ren's TIE Silencer
NNO Kylo Ren's TIE Silencer (boxed)#{(SDCC Exclusive)
NNO Millennium Falcon
NNO Poe's Ski Speeder
NNO Resistance Bomber
NNO Resistance X-Wing Fighter

| 3341 | Luke Skywalker, Han Solo and Boba Fett Minifig Pack - Star Wars #2 | 40.00 | 80.00 |
|---|---|---|---|
| 3342 | Chewbacca and 2 Biker Scouts Minifig Pack - Star Wars #3 | 12.00 | 25.00 |
| 3343 | 2 Battle Droids and Command Officer Minifig Pack - Star Wars #4 | 12.00 | 25.00 |

### 2000 LEGO Star Wars Technic

| 8000 | Pit Droid | 20.00 | 40.00 |
|---|---|---|---|
| 8001 | Battle Droid | 25.00 | 50.00 |
| 8002 | Destroyer Droid | 120.00 | 200.00 |

### 2000 LEGO Star Wars Ultimate Collector Series

| 7181 | TIE Interceptor | 300.00 | 600.00 |
|---|---|---|---|
| 7191 | X-wing Fighter | 450.00 | 900.00 |

### 2001 LEGO Star Wars Episode I

| 7126 | Battle Droid Carrier | 20.00 | 40.00 |
|---|---|---|---|
| 7186 | Watto's Junkyard | 50.00 | 100.00 |

### 1999 LEGO Star Wars Episode I

## 2001 LEGO Star Wars Episode IV

| 7106 | Droid Escape | 15.00 | 30.00 |
| 7146 | TIE Fighter | 60.00 | 120.00 |

## 2001 LEGO Star Wars Episode VI

| 7127 | Imperial AT-ST | 20.00 | 40.00 |
| 7166 | Imperial Shuttle | 40.00 | 80.00 |

## 2001 LEGO Star Wars Technic

| 8007 | C-3PO | 50.00 | 100.00 |
| 8008 | Stormtrooper | 20.00 | 50.00 |

## 2001 LEGO Star Wars Ultimate Collector Series

| 10018 | Darth Maul | 200.00 | 400.00 |
| 10019 | Rebel Blockade Runner | 700.00 | 1,400.00 |

## 2002 LEGO Star Wars Episode I

| 7203 | Jedi Defense I | 15.00 | 30.00 |
| 7204 | Jedi Defense II | 20.00 | 40.00 |

## 2002 LEGO Star Wars Episode II

| 7103 | Jedi Duel | 15.00 | 30.00 |
| 7113 | Tusken Raider Encounter | 20.00 | 40.00 |
| 7133 | Bounty Hunter Pursuit | 30.00 | 60.00 |
| 7143 | Jedi Starfighter | 30.00 | 60.00 |
| 7153 | Jango Fett's Slave I | 125.00 | 250.00 |
| 7163 | Republic Gunship | 125.00 | 250.00 |

## 2002 LEGO Star Wars Episode IV

| 7142 | X-wing Fighter | 100.00 | 200.00 |
| 7152 | TIE Fighter & Y-wing | | |

## 2002 LEGO Star Wars Episode V

| 7119 | Twin-Pod Cloud Car | 25.00 | 50.00 |

## 2002 LEGO Star Wars Episode VI

| 7139 | Ewok Attack | 40.00 | 80.00 |
| 7200 | Final Duel I | 30.00 | 60.00 |
| 7201 | Final Duel II | 20.00 | 40.00 |

## 2002 LEGO Star Wars Miniature Building Set

| 3219 | Mini TIE Fighter | 15.00 | 30.00 |

## 2002 LEGO Star Wars Product Collection

| 65081 | R2-D2 & C-3PO Droid Collectors Set | 50.00 | 100.00 |
| 65145 | X-wing Fighter TIE Fighter & Y-wing Fighter Collectors Set | .00 | .00 |
| 65153 | Jango Fett's Slave I with Bonus Cargo Case | .00 | .00 |

## 2002 LEGO Star Wars Technic

| 8009 | R2-D2 | 30.00 | 60.00 |
| 8010 | Darth Vader | 60.00 | 120.00 |
| 8011 | Jango Fett | 40.00 | 80.00 |
| 8012 | Super Battle Droid | 20.00 | 40.00 |

## 2002 LEGO Star Wars Ultimate Collector Series

| 7194 | Yoda | 300.00 | 600.00 |
| 10026 | Naboo Starfighter Special Edition | 300.00 | 600.00 |
| 10030 | Imperial Star Destroyer | 1,200.00 | 2,000.00 |

## 2003 LEGO Star Wars Episode II

| 4482 | AT-TE | 120.00 | 250.00 |
| 4478 | Geonosian Fighter | 90.00 | 150.00 |
| 4481 | Hailfire Droid | 60.00 | 120.00 |

## 2003 LEGO Star Wars Episode IV

| 4477 | T-16 Skyhopper | 20.00 | 40.00 |

## 2003 LEGO Star Wars Episode V

| 4483 | AT-AT | 250.00 | 500.00 |
| 4479 | TIE Bomber | 100.00 | 200.00 |
| 10123 | Cloud City | 600.00 | 1,000.00 |

## 2003 LEGO Star Wars Episode VI

| 4475 | Jabba's Message | 25.00 | 50.00 |
| 4476 | Jabba's Prize | 80.00 | 150.00 |
| 4480 | Jabba's Palace | 100.00 | 200.00 |

## 2003 LEGO Star Wars Miniature Building Set

| 4484 | X-Wing Fighter & TIE Advanced | 20.00 | 40.00 |
| 4485 | Sebulba's Podracer & Anakin's Podracer | 10.00 | 20.00 |
| 4486 | AT-ST & Snowspeeder | 20.00 | 40.00 |
| 4487 | Jedi Starfighter & Slave I | 12.00 | 25.00 |
| 4488 | Millennium Falcon | 25.00 | 50.00 |
| 4489 | AT-AT | 12.00 | 25.00 |
| 4490 | Republic Gunship | 8.00 | 15.00 |
| 4491 | MTT | 10.00 | 20.00 |

## 2003 LEGO Star Wars Product Collection

| 4207901 | Star Wars MINI Bonus Pack | .00 | .00 |

## 2003 LEGO Star Wars Ultimate Collector Series

| 10129 | Rebel Snowspeeder | 600.00 | 1,200.00 |

## 2004 LEGO Star Wars Episode IV

| 4501 | Mos Eisley Cantina | 100.00 | 200.00 |
| 7262 | TIE Fighter and Y-Wing | 30.00 | 60.00 |

## 2004 LEGO Star Wars Episode V

| 4500 | Rebel Snowspeeder | 25.00 | 50.00 |
| 4502 | X-wing Fighter | 100.00 | 200.00 |
| 4504 | Millennium Falcon | 120.00 | 250.00 |

## 2004 LEGO Star Wars Legends

| 10131 | TIE Fighter Collection | 150.00 | 300.00 |

## 2004 LEGO Star Wars Miniature Building Set

| 4492 | Star Destroyer | 20.00 | 40.00 |
| 4493 | Sith Infiltrator | 8.00 | 15.00 |
| 4494 | Imperial Shuttle | 15.00 | 30.00 |
| 4495 | AT-TE | 12.00 | 25.00 |
| 6963 | X-wing Fighter | 15.00 | 30.00 |
| 6964 | Boba Fett's Slave I | 12.00 | 25.00 |
| 6965 | TIE Interceptor | 12.00 | 25.00 |

## 2004 LEGO Star Wars Product Collection

| 65707 | Bonus/Value Pack | .00 | .00 |

## 2004 LEGO Star Wars Ultimate Collector Series

| 10134 | Y-wing Attack Starfighter | 600.00 | 1,000.00 |

## 2005 LEGO Star Wars Episode III

| 6966 | Jedi Starfighter | 8.00 | 15.00 |
| 6967 | ARC Fighter | 8.00 | 15.00 |
| 6968 | Wookiee Attack | .00 | .00 |
| 7250 | Clone Scout Walker | 30.00 | 60.00 |
| 7251 | Darth Vader Transformation | 50.00 | 100.00 |
| 7252 | Droid Tri-Fighter | 20.00 | 40.00 |
| 7255 | General Grievous Chase | 60.00 | 120.00 |
| 7256 | Jedi Starfighter and Vulture Droid | 40.00 | 80.00 |
| 7257 | Ultimate Lightsaber Duel | 100.00 | 200.00 |
| 7258 | Wookiee Attack | 60.00 | 120.00 |
| 7259 | ARC-170 Fighter | 60.00 | 120.00 |
| 7260 | Wookiee Catamaran | 50.00 | 100.00 |
| 7261 | Clone Turbo Tank | 120.00 | 250.00 |
| 7283 | Ultimate Space Battle | 150.00 | 300.00 |

## 2005 LEGO Star Wars Episode IV

| | | | |
|---|---|---|---|
| 7263 | TIE Fighter | 50.00 | 100.00 |
| 10144 | Sandcrawler | 200.00 | 400.00 |

## 2005 LEGO Star Wars Episode VI

| | | | |
|---|---|---|---|
| 7264 | Imperial Inspection | 100.00 | 200.00 |

## 2005 LEGO Star Wars Product Collection

| | | | |
|---|---|---|---|
| 65771 | Episode III Collectors' Set | 100.00 | 200.00 |
| 65828 | Bonus/Value Pack | .00 | .00 |
| 65844 | Bonus/Value Pack | .00 | .00 |
| 65845 | Bonus/Value Pack | .00 | .00 |

## 2005 LEGO Star Wars Exclusives

| | | | |
|---|---|---|---|
| PROMOSW002 | Anakin Skywalker | | |
| | (2005 International Toy Fair Exclusive) | .00 | .00 |
| PROMOSW003 | Luminara Unduli (2005 International Toy Fair Exclusive) | .00 | .00 |
| SW117PROMO | Darth Vader (2005 Nurnberg Toy Fair Exclusive) | .00 | .00 |
| TF05 | Star Wars V.I.P. Gala Set#((2005 International Toy Fair Exclusive) | .00 | .00 |

## 2005 LEGO Star Wars Ultimate Collector Series

| | | | |
|---|---|---|---|
| 10143 | Death Star II | 400.00 | 800.00 |

## 2006 LEGO Star Wars Episode III

| | | | |
|---|---|---|---|
| 6205 | V-wing Fighter | 25.00 | 50.00 |
| 72612 | Clone Turbo Tank (non-light-up edition) | 150.00 | 300.00 |

## 2006 LEGO Star Wars Episode IV

| | | | |
|---|---|---|---|
| 6211 | Imperial Star Destroyer | 150.00 | 300.00 |

## 2006 LEGO Star Wars Episode V

| | | | |
|---|---|---|---|
| 6209 | Slave I | 80.00 | 150.00 |
| 6212 | X-wing Fighter | 80.00 | 150.00 |

## 2006 LEGO Star Wars Episode VI

| | | | |
|---|---|---|---|
| 6206 | TIE Interceptor | 50.00 | 100.00 |
| 6207 | A-wing Fighter | 30.00 | 60.00 |
| 6208 | B-wing Fighter | 30.00 | 60.00 |
| 6210 | Jabba's Sail Barge | 200.00 | 350.00 |

## 2006 LEGO Star Wars Product Collection

| | | | |
|---|---|---|---|
| 66142 | Bonus/Value Pack | .00 | .00 |
| 66150 | Bonus/Value Pack | .00 | .00 |
| 66221 | Bonus/Value Pack | .00 | .00 |

## 2006 LEGO Star Wars Ultimate Collector Series

| | | | |
|---|---|---|---|
| 10174 | Imperial AT-ST | 275.00 | 550.00 |
| 10175 | Vader's TIE Advanced | 350.00 | 700.00 |

## 2007 LEGO Star Wars Episode I

| | | | |
|---|---|---|---|
| 7660 | Naboo N-1 Starfighter with Vulture Droid | 20.00 | 40.00 |
| 7662 | Trade Federation MTT | 150.00 | 300.00 |
| 7663 | Sith Infiltrator | 25.00 | 50.00 |
| 7665 | Republic Cruiser | 100.00 | 200.00 |

## 2007 LEGO Star Wars Episode III

| | | | |
|---|---|---|---|
| 7654 | Droids Battle Pack | 25.00 | 50.00 |
| 7655 | Clone Troopers Battle Pack | 25.00 | 50.00 |
| 7656 | General Grievous Starfighter | 40.00 | 80.00 |
| 7661 | Jedi Starfighter with Hyperdrive Booster Ring | 60.00 | 120.00 |

## 2007 LEGO Star Wars Episode IV

| | | | |
|---|---|---|---|
| 7658 | Y-wing Fighter | 50.00 | 100.00 |
| 7659 | Imperial Landing Craft | 50.00 | 100.00 |

## 2007 LEGO Star Wars Episode V

| | | | |
|---|---|---|---|
| 7666 | Hoth Rebel Base | 100.00 | 200.00 |
| 10178 | Motorised Walking AT-AT | 300.00 | 600.00 |

## 2007 LEGO Star Wars Episode VI

| | | | |
|---|---|---|---|
| 7657 | AT-ST | 80.00 | 150.00 |

## 2007 LEGO Star Wars Legends

| | | | |
|---|---|---|---|
| 7664 | TIE Crawler | 50.00 | 100.00 |

## 2007 LEGO Star Wars Minifigure Pack

| | | | |
|---|---|---|---|
| 4521221 | Gold chrome plated C-3PO | 250.00 | 500.00 |
| PROMOSW004 | Star Wars Celebration IV Exclusive/500* | 600.00 | 1,000.00 |

## 2007 LEGO Star Wars Ultimate Collector Series

| | | | |
|---|---|---|---|
| 10179 | Ultimate Collector's Millennium Falcon | 3,000.00 | 5,000.00 |

## 2008 LEGO Star Wars The Clone Wars

| | | | |
|---|---|---|---|
| 7669 | Anakin's Jedi Starfighter | 40.00 | 80.00 |
| 7670 | Hailfire Droid & Spider Droid | 30.00 | 60.00 |

| | | | |
|---|---|---|---|
| 7673 | MagnaGuard Starfighter | 30.00 | 80.00 |
| 7674 | V-19 Torrent | 80.00 | 150.00 |
| 7675 | AT-TE Walker | 120.00 | 250.00 |
| 7676 | Republic Attack Gunship | 175.00 | 350.00 |
| 7678 | Droid Gunship | 30.00 | 60.00 |
| 7679 | Republic Fighter Tank | 80.00 | 150.00 |
| 7680 | The Twilight | 80.00 | 150.00 |
| 7681 | Separatist Spider Droid | 50.00 | 100.00 |
| 8031 | V-19 Torrent | 10.00 | 20.00 |
| 20006 | Clone Turbo Tank | 20.00 | 40.00 |

## 2008 LEGO Star Wars Episode III

| | | | |
|---|---|---|---|
| 7671 | AT-AP Walker | 40.00 | 80.00 |

## 2008 LEGO Star Wars Episode V

| | | | |
|---|---|---|---|
| 8029 | Mini Snowspeeder | 6.00 | 12.00 |

## 2008 LEGO Star Wars Legends

| | | | |
|---|---|---|---|
| 7667 | Imperial Dropship | 30.00 | 60.00 |
| 7668 | Rebel Scout Speeder | 25.00 | 50.00 |
| 7672 | Rogue Shadow | 120.00 | 250.00 |

## 2008 LEGO Star Wars Miniature Building Set

| | | | |
|---|---|---|---|
| 8028 | TIE Fighter | 6.00 | 15.00 |

## 2008 LEGO Star Wars Miscellaneous

| | | | |
|---|---|---|---|
| COMCON001 | Clone Wars#((2008 SDCC Exclusive) | .00 | .00 |

## 2008 LEGO Star Wars Ultimate Collector Series

| | | | |
|---|---|---|---|
| 10186 | General Grievous | 120.00 | 200.00 |
| 10188 | Death Star | 225.00 | 450.00 |

## 2009 LEGO Star Wars The Clone Wars

| | | | |
|---|---|---|---|
| 7748 | Corporate Alliance Tank Droid | 25.00 | 50.00 |
| 7751 | Ahsoka's Starfighter and Droids | 80.00 | 150.00 |
| 7752 | Count Dooku's Solar Sailer | 40.00 | 80.00 |
| 7753 | Pirate Tank | 50.00 | 100.00 |
| 8014 | Clone Walker Battle Pack | 30.00 | 60.00 |
| 8015 | Assassin Droids Battle Pack | 12.00 | 25.00 |
| 8016 | Hyena Droid Bomber | 25.00 | 50.00 |
| 8018 | Armored Assault Tank (AAT) | 100.00 | 200.00 |
| 8019 | Republic Attack Shuttle | 60.00 | 120.00 |
| 8033 | General Grievous' Starfighter | 8.00 | 15.00 |
| 8036 | Separatist Shuttle | 30.00 | 60.00 |
| 8037 | Anakin's Y-wing Starfighter | 80.00 | 150.00 |
| 8039 | Venator-Class Republic Attack Cruiser | 175.00 | 350.00 |
| 10195 | Republic Dropship with AT-OT Walker | 300.00 | 600.00 |
| 20007 | Republic Attack Cruiser | 12.00 | 25.00 |

| | | | |
|---|---|---|---|
| 20009 | AT-TE Walker | 10.00 | 20.00 |
| 20010 | Republic Gunship | 15.00 | 30.00 |
| 30004 | Battle Droid on STAP | 10.00 | 20.00 |
| 30006 | Clone Walker | 10.00 | 20.00 |
| COMCON010 | Mini Republic Dropship Mini AT-TE Brickmaster Pack#1(SDCC 2009 Exclusive) | .00 | .00 |

### 2009 LEGO Star Wars Episode IV

| | | | |
|---|---|---|---|
| 7778 | Midi-scale Millennium Falcon | 60.00 | 120.00 |
| 8017 | Darth Vader's TIE Fighter | 60.00 | 120.00 |
| 10198 | Tantive IV | 150.00 | 300.00 |

### 2009 LEGO Star Wars Episode V

| | | | |
|---|---|---|---|
| 7749 | Echo Base | 40.00 | 80.00 |

### 2009 LEGO Star Wars Episode VI

| | | | |
|---|---|---|---|
| 7754 | Home One Mon Calamari Star Cruiser | 100.00 | 200.00 |
| 8038 | The Battle of Endor | 100.00 | 200.00 |
| 30005 | Imperial Speeder Bike | 12.00 | 25.00 |

### 2009 LEGO Star Wars Minifigure Pack

| | | | |
|---|---|---|---|
| 4547551 | Chrome Darth Vader | 120.00 | 250.00 |

### 2009 LEGO Star Wars SDCC Exclusives

| | | | |
|---|---|---|---|
| COMCON004 | Collectible Display Set 1 | .00 | .00 |
| COMCON005 | Collectible Display Set 2 | .00 | .00 |
| COMCON006 | Collectible Display Set 4 | .00 | .00 |
| COMCON007 | Collectible Display Set 5 | .00 | .00 |
| COMCON008 | Collectible Display Set 3 | .00 | .00 |
| COMCON009 | Collectible Display Set 6 | .00 | .00 |
| COMCON011 | Holo-Brick Archives | .00 | .00 |

### 2009 LEGO Star Wars Product Collection

| | | | |
|---|---|---|---|
| 66308 | 3 in 1 Superpack | .00 | .00 |

### 2010 LEGO Star Wars The Clone Wars

| | | | |
|---|---|---|---|
| 8085 | Freeco Speeder | 20.00 | 40.00 |
| 8086 | Droid Tri-Fighter | 25.00 | 50.00 |
| 8093 | Plo Koon's Jedi Starfighter | 25.00 | 50.00 |
| 8095 | General Grievous' Starfighter | 40.00 | 80.00 |
| 8098 | Clone Turbo Tank | 120.00 | 250.00 |
| 8128 | Cad Bane's Speeder | 25.00 | 50.00 |
| 30050 | Republic Attack Shuttle | 10.00 | 20.00 |

### 2010 LEGO Star Wars Episode III

| | | | |
|---|---|---|---|
| 8088 | ARC-170 Starfighter | 80.00 | 150.00 |
| 8091 | Republic Swamp Speeder | 30.00 | 60.00 |
| 8096 | Emperor Palpatine's Shuttle | 60.00 | 120.00 |

### 2010 LEGO Star Wars Episode IV

| | | | |
|---|---|---|---|
| 8092 | Luke's Landspeeder | 50.00 | 100.00 |
| 8099 | Midi-Scale Imperial Star Destroyer | 60.00 | 120.00 |

### 2010 LEGO Star Wars Episode V

| | | | |
|---|---|---|---|
| 8083 | Rebel Trooper Battle Pack | 12.00 | 25.00 |
| 8084 | Snowtrooper Battle Pack | 12.00 | 25.00 |
| 8089 | Hoth Wampa Cave | 50.00 | 100.00 |
| 8097 | Slave I | 100.00 | 200.00 |
| 8129 | AT-AT Walker | 150.00 | 300.00 |
| 20018 | AT-AT Walker | 12.00 | 25.00 |

### 2010 LEGO Star Wars Legends

| | | | |
|---|---|---|---|
| 8087 | TIE Defender | 80.00 | 150.00 |

### 2010 LEGO Star Wars Miniature Building Set

| | | | |
|---|---|---|---|
| 20016 | Imperial Shuttle | 10.00 | 20.00 |

### 2010 LEGO Star Wars Minifigure Pack

| | | | |
|---|---|---|---|
| 2853590 | Chrome Stormtrooper | 40.00 | 80.00 |
| 2853835 | White Boba Fett Figure | 60.00 | 120.00 |

### 2010 LEGO Star Wars Miscellaneous

| | | | |
|---|---|---|---|
| BOBAFETT1 | White Boba Fett minifig and Star Wars Book | .00 | .00 |

### 2010 LEGO Star Wars Product Collection

| | | | |
|---|---|---|---|
| 66341 | Star Wars Super Pack 3 in 1 | .00 | .00 |
| 66364 | Star Wars Super Pack 3 in 1 | .00 | .00 |
| 66366 | Star Wars Super Pack 3 in 1 | .00 | .00 |
| 66368 | Star Wars Super Pack 3 in 1 | .00 | .00 |

### 2010 LEGO Star Wars Ultimate Collector Series

| | | | |
|---|---|---|---|
| 10212 | Imperial Shuttle | 350.00 | 700.00 |
| 10215 | Obi-Wan's Jedi Starfighter | 100.00 | 200.00 |

### 2011 LEGO Star Wars The Clone Wars

| | | | |
|---|---|---|---|
| 7868 | Mace Windu's Jedi Starfighter | 60.00 | 120.00 |
| 7869 | Battle for Geonosis | 40.00 | 80.00 |
| 7913 | Clone Trooper Battle Pack | 25.00 | 50.00 |
| 7914 | Mandalorian Battle Pack | 15.00 | 30.00 |
| 7930 | Bounty Hunter Assault Gunship | 50.00 | 100.00 |
| 7931 | T-6 Jedi Shuttle | 40.00 | 80.00 |
| 7957 | Sith Nightspeeder | 25.00 | 50.00 |
| 7959 | Geonosian Starfighter | 40.00 | 80.00 |
| 7964 | Republic Frigate | 120.00 | 250.00 |
| 20021 | Bounty Hunter Assault Gunship | 10.00 | 20.00 |
| 30053 | Republic Attack Cruiser | 8.00 | 15.00 |

### 2011 LEGO Star Wars Episode I

| | | | |
|---|---|---|---|
| 7877 | Naboo Starfighter | 25.00 | 50.00 |
| 7929 | The Battle of Naboo | 20.00 | 40.00 |
| 7961 | Darth Maul's Sith Infiltrator | 50.00 | 100.00 |
| 7962 | Anakin Skywalker and Sebulba's Podracers | 60.00 | 120.00 |
| 30052 | AAT | 8.00 | 15.00 |

### 2011 LEGO Star Wars Episode IV

| | | | |
|---|---|---|---|
| 7965 | Millennium Falcon | 200.00 | 400.00 |

### 2011 LEGO Star Wars Episode V

| | | | |
|---|---|---|---|
| 7879 | Hoth Echo Base | 150.00 | 300.00 |
| 20019 | Slave I | 15.00 | 30.00 |

### 2011 LEGO Star Wars Episode VI

| | | | |
|---|---|---|---|
| 7956 | Ewok Attack | 20.00 | 40.00 |
| 30054 | AT-ST | 10.00 | 20.00 |

### 2011 LEGO Star Wars Legends

| | | | |
|---|---|---|---|
| 7915 | Imperial V-wing Starfighter | 20.00 | 50.00 |

### 2011 LEGO Star Wars Miniature Building Set

| | | | |
|---|---|---|---|
| 30051 | Mini X-wing | 8.00 | 15.00 |
| 30055 | Vulture Droid | 8.00 | 15.00 |

MISCELLANEOUS

## 2011 LEGO Star Wars Minifigure Pack

| | | | |
|---|---|---|---|
| 2856197 | Shadow ARF Trooper | 40.00 | 80.00 |

## 2011 LEGO Star Wars Exclusive

| | | | |
|---|---|---|---|
| PROMOSW007 | Star Wars Miniland Figures | | |
| | (2011 Toy Fair Collector's Party Exclusive) | .00 | .00 |

## 2011 LEGO Star Wars Product Collection

| | | | |
|---|---|---|---|
| 66377 | Star Wars Super Pack 3 in 1 | 60.00 | 120.00 |
| 66378 | Star Wars Super Pack 3 in 1 | .00 | .00 |
| 66395 | Star Wars Super Pack 3 in 1 | 60.00 | 120.00 |
| 66396 | Star Wars Super Pack 3 in 1 | .00 | .00 |

## 2011 LEGO Star Wars Seasonal Set

| | | | |
|---|---|---|---|
| COMCON015 | Advent calendar#{(2011 SDCC Exclusive) | 60.00 | 120.00 |
| 7958 | Star Wars Advent Calendar | 30.00 | 60.00 |

## 2011 LEGO Star Wars Ultimate Collector Series

| | | | |
|---|---|---|---|
| 10221 | Super Star Destroyer | 600.00 | 1,100.00 |

## 2012 LEGO Star Wars The Clone Wars

| | | | |
|---|---|---|---|
| 9488 | Elite Clone Trooper & Commando Droid Battle Pack | 15.00 | 30.00 |
| 9491 | Geonosian Cannon | 25.00 | 50.00 |
| 9498 | Saesee Tiin's Jedi Starfighter | 30.00 | 60.00 |
| 9515 | Malevolence | 120.00 | 250.00 |
| 9525 | Pre Vizsla's Mandalorian Fighter | 60.00 | 120.00 |
| 30059 | MTT | 8.00 | 15.00 |

## 2012 LEGO Star Wars Episode I

| | | | |
|---|---|---|---|
| 9499 | Gungan Sub | 80.00 | 150.00 |
| 30057 | Anakin's Pod Racer | 6.00 | 12.00 |
| 30058 | STAP | 8.00 | 15.00 |
| 5000063 | Chrome TC-14 | 25.00 | 50.00 |
| COMCON019 | Sith Infiltrator#{(2012 SDCC Exclusive) | 80.00 | 150.00 |

## 2012 LEGO Star Wars Episode III

| | | | |
|---|---|---|---|
| 9494 | Anakin's Jedi Interceptor | 60.00 | 120.00 |
| 9526 | Palpatine's Arrest | 80.00 | 150.00 |

## 2012 LEGO Star Wars Episode IV

| | | | |
|---|---|---|---|
| 9490 | Droid Escape | 30.00 | 60.00 |
| 9492 | TIE Fighter | 100.00 | 200.00 |

## 2012 LEGO Star Wars Episode IV (cont.)

| | | | |
|---|---|---|---|
| 9493 | X-wing Starfighter | 100.00 | 200.00 |
| 9495 | Gold Leader's Y-wing Starfighter | 80.00 | 150.00 |
| COMCON024 | Luke Skywalker's Landspeeder Mini | | |
| | (2012 NYCC Exclusive) | 120.00 | 250.00 |

## 2012 LEGO Star Wars Episode V

| | | | |
|---|---|---|---|
| CELEBVI | Mini Slave I#{(2012 Star Wars Celebration VI Exclusive) | 100.00 | 200.00 |

## 2012 LEGO Star Wars Episode VI

| | | | |
|---|---|---|---|
| 9489 | Endor Rebel Trooper & Imperial Trooper Battle Pack | 25.00 | 50.00 |
| 9496 | Desert Skiff | 50.00 | 100.00 |
| 9516 | Jabba's Palace | 100.00 | 200.00 |

## 2012 LEGO Star Wars Miniature Building Set

| | | | |
|---|---|---|---|
| 30056 | Star Destroyer | 8.00 | 15.00 |

## 2012 LEGO Star Wars Minifigure Pack

| | | | |
|---|---|---|---|
| 5000062 | Darth Maul | 15.00 | 30.00 |

## 2012 LEGO Star Wars The Old Republic

| | | | |
|---|---|---|---|
| 9497 | Republic Striker-class Starfighter | 40.00 | 80.00 |
| 9500 | Sith Fury-class Interceptor | 100.00 | 200.00 |

## 2012 LEGO Star Wars Planet Set

| | | | |
|---|---|---|---|
| 9674 | Naboo Starfighter & Naboo | 10.00 | 20.00 |
| 9675 | Sebulba's Podracer & Tatooine | 8.00 | 15.00 |
| 9676 | TIE Interceptor & Death Star | 15.00 | 30.00 |
| 9677 | X-wing Starfighter & Yavin 4 | 10.00 | 20.00 |
| 9678 | Twin-Pod Cloud Car & Bespin | 10.00 | 20.00 |
| 9679 | AT-ST & Endor | 8.00 | 15.00 |

## 2012 LEGO Star Wars Product Collection

| | | | |
|---|---|---|---|
| 66411 | Super Pack 3-in-1 | .00 | .00 |
| 66431 | Super Pack 3-in-1 | .00 | .00 |
| 66432 | Super Pack 3-in-1 | .00 | .00 |

## 2012 LEGO Star Wars Seasonal Set

| | | | |
|---|---|---|---|
| 9509 | Star Wars Advent Calendar | 30.00 | 60.00 |

## 2012 LEGO Star Wars Ultimate Collector Series

| | | | |
|---|---|---|---|
| 10225 | R2-D2 | 200.00 | 400.00 |
| 10227 | B-Wing Starfighter | 175.00 | 350.00 |

## 2013 LEGO Star Wars The Clone Wars

| | | | |
|---|---|---|---|
| 11905 | Brickmaster Star Wars: Battle for the Stolen Crystals parts | .00 | .00 |
| 30240 | Z-95 Headhunter | 8.00 | 15.00 |
| 30241 | Mandalorian Fighter | 8.00 | 15.00 |
| 30242 | Republic Frigate | 8.00 | 15.00 |
| 30243 | Umbaran MHC | 8.00 | 15.00 |
| 75002 | AT-RT | 25.00 | 50.00 |
| 75004 | Z-95 Headhunter | 40.00 | 80.00 |
| 75012 | BARC Speeder with Sidecar | 60.00 | 120.00 |
| 75013 | Umbaran MHC (Mobile Heavy Cannon) | 40.00 | 80.00 |
| 75022 | Mandalorian Speeder | 40.00 | 80.00 |
| 75024 | HH-87 Starhopper | 50.00 | 100.00 |

## 2013 LEGO Star Wars Episode II

| | | | |
|---|---|---|---|
| 75000 | Clone Troopers vs. Droidekas | 20.00 | 40.00 |
| 75015 | Corporate Alliance Tank Droid | 30.00 | 60.00 |
| 75016 | Homing Spider Droid | 25.00 | 50.00 |
| 75017 | Duel on Geonosis | 50.00 | 100.00 |
| 75019 | AT-TE | 100.00 | 200.00 |
| 75021 | Republic Gunship | 150.00 | 300.00 |
| 5001709 | Clone Trooper Lieutenant | 8.00 | 15.00 |

## 2013 LEGO Star Wars Episode V

| | | | |
|---|---|---|---|
| 75014 | Battle of Hoth | 80.00 | 150.00 |
| 5001621 | Han Solo (Hoth) | 8.00 | 15.00 |

## 2013 LEGO Star Wars Episode VI

| | | | |
|---|---|---|---|
| 75003 | A-wing Starfighter | 30.00 | 60.00 |
| 75005 | Rancor Pit | 100.00 | 200.00 |
| 75020 | Jabba's Sail Barge | 120.00 | 250.00 |

## 2013 LEGO Star Wars The Old Republic

| | | | |
|---|---|---|---|
| 75001 | Republic Troopers vs. Sith Troopers | 20.00 | 40.00 |
| 75025 | Jedi Defender-class Cruiser | 60.00 | 120.00 |

### 2013 LEGO Star Wars Originals

| | | | |
|---|---|---|---|
| 75018 | JEK-14's Stealth Starfighter | 80.00 | 150.00 |
| COMCON032 | Jek-14 Mini Stealth Starfighter#((2013 SDCC Exclusive) | 120.00 | 250.00 |
| MAY2013 | Holocron Droid | 12.00 | 25.00 |
| TRU03 | Mini Jek-14 Stealth Fighter#((2013 Toys R Us Exclusive) | 12.00 | 25.00 |
| YODACHRON | Yoda Chronicles Promotional Set | .00 | .00 |

### 2013 LEGO Star Wars Planet Set

| | | | |
|---|---|---|---|
| 75006 | Jedi Starfighter & Planet Kamino | 12.00 | 25.00 |
| 75007 | Republic Assault Ship & Planet Coruscant | 8.00 | 15.00 |
| 75008 | TIE Bomber & Asteroid Field | 12.00 | 25.00 |
| 75009 | Snowspeeder & Hoth | 25.00 | 50.00 |
| 75010 | B-Wing Starfighter & Planet Endor | 20.00 | 40.00 |
| 75011 | Tantive IV & Planet Alderaan | 25.00 | 50.00 |

### 2013 LEGO Star Wars Product Collection

| | | | |
|---|---|---|---|
| 66449 | Super Pack 3-in-1 | 80.00 | 150.00 |
| 66456 | Star Wars Value Pack | 100.00 | 200.00 |
| 66473 | LEGO Star Wars Super Pack | 120.00 | 250.00 |

### 2013 LEGO Star Wars Promotional Set

| | | | |
|---|---|---|---|
| NYCC2013 | Yoda display box#((2013 NYCC Exclusive) | .00 | .00 |
| YODA | Yoda minifig, NY I Heart Torso | 120.00 | 250.00 |

### 2013 LEGO Star Wars Seasonal Set

| | | | |
|---|---|---|---|
| 75023 | Star Wars Advent Calendar | .00 | .00 |

### 2013 LEGO Star Wars Ultimate Collector Series

| | | | |
|---|---|---|---|
| 10236 | Ewok Village | 175.00 | 350.00 |
| 10240 | Red Five X-wing Starfighter | 150.00 | 300.00 |

### 2014 LEGO Star Wars The Clone Wars

| | | | |
|---|---|---|---|
| 75045 | Republic AV-7 Anti-Vehicle Cannon | 50.00 | 100.00 |
| 75046 | Coruscant Police Gunship | 50.00 | 100.00 |

### 2014 LEGO Star Wars Episode I

| | | | |
|---|---|---|---|
| 75058 | MTT | 80.00 | 150.00 |

### 2014 LEGO Star Wars Episode III

| | | | |
|---|---|---|---|
| 30244 | Anakin's Jedi Interceptor | 8.00 | 15.00 |
| 30247 | ARC-170 Starfighter | 8.00 | 15.00 |
| 75035 | Kashyyyk Troopers | 20.00 | 40.00 |
| 75036 | Utapau Troopers | 20.00 | 40.00 |
| 75037 | Battle on Saleucami | 25.00 | 50.00 |
| 75038 | Jedi Interceptor | 50.00 | 100.00 |
| 75039 | V-Wing Starfighter | 30.00 | 60.00 |
| 75040 | General Grievous' Wheel Bike | 40.00 | 80.00 |
| 75041 | Vulture Droid | 40.00 | 80.00 |
| 75042 | Droid Gunship | 60.00 | 120.00 |
| 75043 | AT-AP | 100.00 | 200.00 |
| 75044 | Droid Tri-Fighter | 25.00 | 50.00 |

### 2014 LEGO Star Wars Episode IV

| | | | |
|---|---|---|---|
| 75034 | Death Star Troopers | 25.00 | 50.00 |
| 75052 | Mos Eisley Cantina | 60.00 | 120.00 |
| 75055 | Imperial Star Destroyer | 200.00 | 400.00 |

### 2014 LEGO Star Wars Episode V

| | | | |
|---|---|---|---|
| 75049 | Snowspeeder | 50.00 | 100.00 |
| 75054 | AT-AT | 150.00 | 300.00 |

### 2014 LEGO Star Wars Episode VI

| | | | |
|---|---|---|---|
| 30246 | Imperial Shuttle | 12.00 | 25.00 |
| 75050 | B-Wing | 40.00 | 80.00 |

### 2014 LEGO Star Wars MicroFighters

| | | | |
|---|---|---|---|
| 75029 | AAT | 15.00 | 30.00 |
| 75028 | Clone Turbo Tank | 20.00 | 40.00 |
| 75030 | Millennium Falcon | 25.00 | 50.00 |
| 75031 | TIE Interceptor | 15.00 | 30.00 |
| 75032 | X-Wing Fighter | 15.00 | 30.00 |
| 75033 | Star Destroyer | 12.00 | 25.00 |

### 2014 LEGO Star Wars Minifigure Pack

| | | | |
|---|---|---|---|
| 5002122 | TC-4 | 15.00 | 30.00 |

### 2014 LEGO Star Wars The Old Republic

| | | | |
|---|---|---|---|
| 5002123 | Darth Revan | 25.00 | 50.00 |

### 2014 LEGO Star Wars Original Content

| | | | |
|---|---|---|---|
| 75051 | Jedi Scout Fighter | 60.00 | 120.00 |

### 2014 LEGO Star Wars Product Collection

| | | | |
|---|---|---|---|
| 66479 | Value Pack | .00 | .00 |
| 66495 | Star Wars Value Pack | .00 | .00 |
| 66512 | Rebels Co-Pack | .00 | .00 |
| 66514 | Microfighter Super Pack 3 in 1 | .00 | .00 |
| 66515 | Microfighter Super Pack 3 in 1 | .00 | .00 |

### 2014 LEGO Star Wars Toys R Us Exclusives

| | | | |
|---|---|---|---|
| TRUGHOST | The Ghost micro-model | 10.00 | 20.00 |
| TRUTIE | TIE Fighter | .00 | .00 |
| TRUXWING | X-wing | .00 | .00 |

### 2014 LEGO Star Wars Rebels

| | | | |
|---|---|---|---|
| 75048 | The Phantom | 80.00 | 150.00 |
| 75053 | The Ghost | 100.00 | 200.00 |
| COMCON039 | The Ghost Starship#((2014 SDCC Exclusive) | 80.00 | 150.00 |
| FANEXPO001 | The Ghost Starship#((2014 Fan Expo Exclusive) | 60.00 | 120.00 |

### 2014 LEGO Star Wars Seasonal Set

| | | | |
|---|---|---|---|
| 75056 | Star Wars Advent Calendar | .00 | .00 |

### 2014 LEGO Star Wars Ultimate Collector Series

| | | | |
|---|---|---|---|
| 75059 | Sandcrawler | 175.00 | 350.00 |

### 2015 LEGO Star Wars Buildable Figures

| | | | |
|---|---|---|---|
| 75107 | Jango Fett | 20.00 | 40.00 |
| 75108 | Clone Commander Cody | 12.00 | 25.00 |
| 75109 | Obi-Wan Kenobi | 20.00 | 40.00 |
| 75110 | Luke Skywalker | 25.00 | 50.00 |
| 75111 | Darth Vader | 25.00 | 50.00 |
| 75112 | General Grievous | 40.00 | 80.00 |

### 2015 LEGO Star Wars The Clone Wars

| | | | |
|---|---|---|---|
| 75087 | Anakin's Custom Jedi Starfighter | 25.00 | 50.00 |

## 2015 LEGO Star Wars Episode I

| 75080 | AAT | 20.00 | 40.00 |
| 75086 | Battle Droid Troop Carrier | 30.00 | 60.00 |
| 75091 | Flash Speeder | 20.00 | 40.00 |
| 75092 | Naboo Starfighter | 30.00 | 60.00 |
| 75096 | Sith Infiltrator | 50.00 | 100.00 |

## 2015 LEGO Star Wars Episode II

| 75085 | Hailfire Droid | 25.00 | 50.00 |

## 2015 LEGO Star Wars Episode IV

| 75081 | T-16 Skyhopper | 25.00 | 50.00 |
| 5002947 | Admiral Yularen | 10.00 | 20.00 |

## 2015 LEGO Star Wars Episode VI

| 30272 | A-Wing Starfighter | 10.00 | 20.00 |
| 75093 | Death Star Final Duel | 50.00 | 100.00 |
| 75094 | Imperial Shuttle Tydirium | 60.00 | 120.00 |

## 2015 LEGO Star Wars The Force Awakens

| 30276 | First Order Special Forces TIE Fighter | 6.00 | 12.00 |
| 75099 | Rey's Speeder | 12.00 | 30.00 |
| 75100 | First Order Snowspeeder | 25.00 | 50.00 |
| 75101 | First Order Special Forces TIE Fighter | 40.00 | 80.00 |
| 75102 | Poe's X-wing Fighter | 50.00 | 100.00 |
| 75103 | First Order Transporter | 60.00 | 120.00 |
| 75104 | Kylo Ren's Command Shuttle | 60.00 | 120.00 |
| 75105 | Millennium Falcon | 100.00 | 200.00 |
| 5002948 | C-3PO | 10.00 | 20.00 |
| 30UNIQUE15 | Force Friday Commemorative Brick | .00 | .00 |

## 2015 LEGO Star Wars Legends

| 75079 | Shadow Troopers | 15.00 | 30.00 |
| 75088 | Senate Commando Troopers | 10.00 | 20.00 |
| 75089 | Geonosis Troopers | 20.00 | 40.00 |

## 2015 LEGO Star Wars Magazine Gift

| SW911506 | Snowspeeder | 8.00 | 15.00 |
| SW911508 | Mini Slave I | .00 | .00 |
| SW911509 | Imperial Shooter | 8.00 | 15.00 |
| SW911510 | Micro Star Destroyer and TIE Fighter | .00 | .00 |
| SW911511 | Jedi Weapon Stand | .00 | .00 |
| SWCOMIC1 | Mini X-Wing Starfighter | 15.00 | 30.00 |

## 2015 LEGO Star Wars MicroFighters

| 75072 | ARC-170 Starfighter | 15.00 | 30.00 |
| 75073 | Vulture Droid | 12.00 | 25.00 |

| 75074 | Snowspeeder | 12.00 | 25.00 |
| 75075 | AT-AT | 20.00 | 40.00 |
| 75076 | Republic Gunship | 12.00 | 25.00 |
| 75077 | Homing Spider Droid | 15.00 | 30.00 |

## 2015 LEGO Star Wars Product Collection

| 66533 | Microfighter 3 in 1 Super Pack | 25.00 | 50.00 |
| 66534 | Microfighter 3 in 1 Super Pack | 25.00 | 50.00 |
| 66535 | Battle Pack 2 in 1 | 50.00 | 100.00 |
| 66536 | Luke Skywalker and Darth Vader | 50.00 | 100.00 |

## 2015 LEGO Star Wars Exclusives

| CELEB2015 | Tatooine Mini-build | | |
| | (2015 Star Wars Celebration Exclusive) | 50.00 | 100.00 |
| FANEXPO2015 | Tatooine Mini Build#((2015 Fan Expo Exclusive) | 80.00 | 150.00 |
| SDCC2015 | Dagobah Mini Build#((2015 SDCC Exclusive) | 100.00 | 200.00 |
| TRUWOOKIEE | Wookiee Gunship#((2015 Toys R Us Exclusive) | 8.00 | 15.00 |
| TRUXWING | Poe's X-wing Fighter#((2015 Toys R Us Exclusive) | 10.00 | 20.00 |

## 2015 LEGO Star Wars Rebels

| 30274 | AT-DP | 8.00 | 15.00 |
| 30275 | TIE Advanced Prototype | 8.00 | 15.00 |
| 75078 | Imperial Troop Transport | 12.00 | 25.00 |
| 75082 | TIE Advanced Prototype | 20.00 | 40.00 |
| 75083 | AT-DP | 50.00 | 100.00 |
| 75084 | Wookiee Gunship | 50.00 | 100.00 |
| 75090 | Ezra's Speeder Bike | 15.00 | 30.00 |
| 75106 | Imperial Assault Carrier | 80.00 | 150.00 |
| 5002938 | Stormtrooper Sergeant | 8.00 | 15.00 |
| 5002939 | The Phantom | 8.00 | 15.00 |

## 2015 LEGO Star Wars Seasonal Set

| 75097 | Star Wars Advent Calendar | .00 | .00 |

## 2015 LEGO Star Wars Ultimate Collector Series

| 75060 | Slave I | 120.00 | 250.00 |
| 75095 | TIE Fighter | 100.00 | 200.00 |

## 2016 LEGO Star Wars Battlefront

| 75133 | Rebel Alliance Battle Pack | 20.00 | 40.00 |
| 75134 | Galactic Empire Battle Pack | 15.00 | 30.00 |

## 2016 LEGO Star Wars Buildable Figures

| 75113 | Rey | 12.00 | 25.00 |
| 75114 | First Order Stormtrooper | 12.00 | 25.00 |

| 75115 | Poe Dameron | 12.00 | 25.00 |
| 75116 | Finn | 10.00 | 20.00 |
| 75117 | Kylo Ren | 12.00 | 25.00 |
| 75118 | Captain Phasma | 15.00 | 30.00 |
| 75119 | Sergeant Jyn Erso | 15.00 | 30.00 |
| 75120 | K-2SO | 15.00 | 30.00 |
| 75121 | Imperial Death Trooper | 12.00 | 25.00 |

## 2016 LEGO Star Wars Episode III

| 75135 | Obi-Wan's Jedi Interceptor | 30.00 | 75.00 |
| 75142 | Homing Spider Droid | 25.00 | 50.00 |
| 75151 | Clone Turbo Tank | 50.00 | 100.00 |

## 2016 LEGO Star Wars Episode IV

| 75136 | Droid Escape Pod | 20.00 | 40.00 |

## 2016 LEGO Star Wars Episode V

| 75137 | Carbon-Freezing Chamber | 20.00 | 40.00 |
| 75138 | Hoth Attack | 25.00 | 50.00 |

## 2016 LEGO Star Wars The Force Awakens

| 30277 | First Order Star Destroyer | 8.00 | 15.00 |
| 30278 | Poe's X-wing Fighter | 6.00 | 12.00 |
| 30279 | Kylo Ren's Command Shuttle | 6.00 | 12.00 |
| 30602 | First Order Stormtrooper | 10.00 | 20.00 |
| 30605 | Finn (FN-2187) | 6.00 | 12.00 |
| 75131 | Resistance Trooper Battle Pack | 10.00 | 20.00 |
| 75132 | First Order Battle Pack | 10.00 | 20.00 |
| 75139 | Battle on Takodana | 25.00 | 50.00 |
| 75140 | Resistance Troop Transporter | 30.00 | 75.00 |
| 75148 | Encounter on Jakku | 25.00 | 50.00 |
| 75149 | Resistance X-wing Fighter | 60.00 | 120.00 |
| 5004406 | First Order General | 8.00 | 15.00 |

## 2016 LEGO Star Wars Magazine Gift

| | | | |
|---|---|---|---|
| SW911607 | Millennium Falcon | 6.00 | 12.00 |
| SW911608 | Landspeeder | 6.00 | 12.00 |
| SW911609 | Naboo Starfighter | 6.00 | 12.00 |
| SW911610 | Probe Droid | 6.00 | 12.00 |
| SW911611 | AAT | 6.00 | 12.00 |
| SW911612 | Acklay | 6.00 | 12.00 |
| SW911613 | TIE Bomber | 6.00 | 12.00 |
| SW911614 | Yoda's Hut | 6.00 | 12.00 |
| SW911615 | AT-AT | 6.00 | 12.00 |
| SW911616 | MTT | 6.00 | 12.00 |
| SW911617 | Palpatine's Shuttle | 6.00 | 12.00 |

### 2016 LEGO Star Wars MicroFighters

| | | | |
|---|---|---|---|
| 75125 | Resistance X-wing Fighter | 12.00 | 25.00 |
| 75126 | First Order Snowspeeder | 10.00 | 20.00 |
| 75127 | The Ghost | 12.00 | 25.00 |
| 75128 | TIE Advanced Prototype | 12.00 | 25.00 |
| 75129 | Wookiee Gunship | 8.00 | 15.00 |
| 75130 | AT-DP | 12.00 | 25.00 |

### 2016 LEGO Star Wars Miscellaneous

| | | | |
|---|---|---|---|
| 11912 | Star Wars: Build Your Own Adventure parts | | |

### 2016 LEGO Star Wars Originals

| | | | |
|---|---|---|---|
| 75145 | Eclipse Fighter | 20.00 | 40.00 |
| 75147 | StarScavenger | 20.00 | 40.00 |

### 2016 LEGO Star Wars Product Collection

| | | | |
|---|---|---|---|
| 66542 | Microfighters Super Pack 3 in 1 | 12.00 | 25.00 |
| 66543 | Microfighters Super Pack 3 in 1 | 15.00 | 30.00 |
| 5005217 | Death Star Ultimate Kit | | |

### 2016 LEGO Star Wars Promotional Set

| | | | |
|---|---|---|---|
| 6176782 | Escape the Space Slug | 75.00 | 150.00 |
| TRUFALCON | Millennium Falcon#(2016 Toys R Us Exclusive) | | |

### 2016 LEGO Star Wars Rebels

| | | | |
|---|---|---|---|
| 75141 | Kanan's Speeder Bike | 25.00 | 50.00 |
| 75150 | Vader's TIE Advanced vs. A-wing Starfighter | 50.00 | 100.00 |
| 75157 | Captain Rex's AT-TE | 50.00 | 100.00 |
| 75158 | Rebel Combat Frigate | 60.00 | 120.00 |
| 5004408 | Rebel A-wing Pilot | 6.00 | 12.00 |

### 2016 LEGO Star Wars Rogue One

| | | | |
|---|---|---|---|
| 75152 | Imperial Assault Hovertank | 25.00 | 50.00 |
| 75153 | AT-ST Walker | 30.00 | 60.00 |
| 75154 | TIE Striker | 25.00 | 50.00 |
| 75155 | Rebel U-wing Fighter | 30.00 | 75.00 |
| 75156 | Krennic's Imperial Shuttle | 60.00 | 120.00 |

### 2016 LEGO Star Wars Seasonal Set

| | | | |
|---|---|---|---|
| 75146 | Star Wars Advent Calendar | 30.00 | 75.00 |

### 2016 LEGO Star Wars Ultimate Collector Series

| | | | |
|---|---|---|---|
| 75098 | Assault on Hoth | 200.00 | 400.00 |
| 75159 | Death Star | 250.00 | 500.00 |

### 2017 LEGO Star Wars BrickHeadz

| | | |
|---|---|---|
| 41498 | Boba Fett & Han Solo in Carbonite#(NYCC Exclusive) | |

### 2017 LEGO Star Wars Buildable Figures

| | | | |
|---|---|---|---|
| 75523 | Scarif Stormtrooper | 12.00 | 25.00 |
| 75524 | Chirrut Imwe | 15.00 | 30.00 |
| 75525 | Baze Malbus | 12.00 | 25.00 |
| 75526 | Elite TIE Fighter Pilot | 15.00 | 30.00 |
| 75528 | Rey | 15.00 | 30.00 |
| 75529 | Elite Praetorian Guard | 20.00 | 40.00 |
| 75530 | Chewbacca | 25.00 | 50.00 |
| 75531 | Stormtrooper Commander | 12.00 | 25.00 |
| 75532 | Scout Trooper & Speeder Bike | 20.00 | 40.00 |

### 2017 LEGO Star Wars The Clone Wars

| | | | |
|---|---|---|---|
| 75168 | Yoda's Jedi Starfighter | 20.00 | 40.00 |

### 2017 LEGO Star Wars Episode I

| | | | |
|---|---|---|---|
| 75169 | Duel on Naboo | 12.00 | 25.00 |

### 2017 LEGO Star Wars Episode II

| | | | |
|---|---|---|---|
| 75191 | Jedi Starfighter (w/hyperdrive) | 60.00 | 120.00 |

### 2017 LEGO Star Wars Episode III

| | | | |
|---|---|---|---|
| 75183 | Darth Vader Transformation | 20.00 | 40.00 |

### 2017 LEGO Star Wars Episode IV

| | | | |
|---|---|---|---|
| 75173 | Luke's Landspeeder | 25.00 | 50.00 |

### 2017 LEGO Star Wars Episode VI

| | | | |
|---|---|---|---|
| 75174 | Desert Skiff Escape | 20.00 | 40.00 |

| | | | |
|---|---|---|---|
| 75175 | A-Wing Starfighter | 30.00 | 60.00 |

### 2017 LEGO Star Wars The Force Awakens

| | | | |
|---|---|---|---|
| 75166 | First Order Transport Speeder Battle Pack | 15.00 | 30.00 |
| 75178 | Jakku Quadjumper | 25.00 | 50.00 |
| 75180 | Rathtar Escape | 50.00 | 100.00 |

### 2017 LEGO Star Wars The Last Jedi

| | | | |
|---|---|---|---|
| 30497 | First Order Heavy Assault Walker | 8.00 | 15.00 |
| 75176 | Resistance Transport Pod | 20.00 | 40.00 |
| 75177 | First Order Heavy Scout Walker | 30.00 | 75.00 |
| 75179 | Kylo Ren's TIE Fighter | 50.00 | 100.00 |
| 75187 | BB-8 | 100.00 | 200.00 |
| 75188 | Resistance Bomber | 75.00 | 150.00 |
| 75189 | First Order Heavy Assault Walker | 150.00 | 300.00 |
| 75190 | First Order Star Destroyer | 150.00 | 300.00 |

### 2017 LEGO Star Wars Legends

| | | | |
|---|---|---|---|
| 75182 | Republic Fighter Tank | 15.00 | 30.00 |

### 2017 LEGO Star Wars Magazine Gift

| | |
|---|---|
| SW911618 | Flash Speeder |
| SW911719 | Kanan Jarrus |
| SW911720 | The Ghost |
| SW911721 | Imperial Combat Driver |
| SW911722 | TIE Advanced |
| SW911723 | Vulture Droid |
| SW911724 | A-Wing |
| SW911725 | Sandcrawler |
| SW911726 | Imperial Snowtrooper |
| SW911727 | Rey's Speeder |
| SW911728 | First Order Snowspeeder |
| SW911729 | Droid Gunship |
| SW911730 | Y-Wing |

### 2017 LEGO Star Wars MicroFighters

| 75160 | U-Wing | 7.50 | 15.00 |
| 75161 | TIE Striker | 7.50 | 15.00 |
| 75162 | Y-Wing | 7.50 | 15.00 |
| 75163 | Krennic's Imperial Shuttle | 7.50 | 15.00 |

### 2017 LEGO Star Wars Originals

| 75167 | Bounty Hunter Speeder Bike Battle Pack | 12.00 | 25.00 |
| 75185 | Tracker I | 30.00 | 75.00 |
| 75186 | The Arrowhead | 60.00 | 120.00 |

### 2017 LEGO Star Wars Promotional

| 30611 | R2-D2 | 12.00 | 25.00 |
| CELEB2017 | Detention Block Rescue | 120.00 | 250.00 |
| SWMF | Millennium Falcon | 7.50 | 15.00 |
| TRUBB8 | BB-8 | | |
| TRULEIA | Princess Leia | | |

### 2017 LEGO Star Wars Rebels

| 75170 | The Phantom | 20.00 | 40.00 |

### 2017 LEGO Star Wars Rogue One

| 30496 | U-Wing Fighter | 6.00 | 12.00 |
| 40176 | Scarif Stormtrooper | 12.00 | 25.00 |
| 40268 | R3-M2 | 7.50 | 15.00 |
| 75164 | Rebel Trooper Battle Pack | 15.00 | 30.00 |
| 75165 | Imperial Trooper Battle Pack | 15.00 | 30.00 |
| 75171 | Battle on Scarif | 30.00 | 75.00 |
| 75172 | Y-Wing Starfighter | 30.00 | 75.00 |

### 2017 LEGO Star Wars Seasonal

| 75184 | Star Wars Advent Calendar | 30.00 | 60.00 |

### 2017 LEGO Star Wars Ultimate Collector Series

| 75144 | Snowspeeder | 120.00 | 250.00 |
| 75192 | Millennium Falcon | 500.00 | 1,000.00 |

### 2018 LEGO Star Wars Buildable Figures

| 75533 | Boba Fett | 30.00 | 60.00 |
| 75534 | Darth Vader | 30.00 | 60.00 |
| 75535 | Han Solo | 15.00 | 30.00 |

| 75536 | Range Trooper | 12.50 | 25.00 |
| 75537 | Darth Maul | 20.00 | 40.00 |
| 75538 | Super Battle Droid | | |
| 75539 | 501st Legion Clone Trooper & AT-RT Walker | | |

### 2018 LEGO Star Wars The Clone Wars

| 75199 | General Grievous' Combat Speeder | 15.00 | 30.00 |
| 75214 | Anakin's Jedi Starfighter | 25.00 | 50.00 |

### 2018 LEGO Star Wars Episode II

| 75206 | Jedi and Clone Troopers Battle Pack | | |

### 2018 LEGO Star Wars Episode IV

| 75198 | Tatooine Battle Pack | 25.00 | 50.00 |
| 75205 | Mos Eisley Cantina | 30.00 | 60.00 |
| 75218 | X-Wing Starfighter | 75.00 | 150.00 |
| 75220 | Sandcrawler | 75.00 | 150.00 |
| 75221 | Imperial Landing Craft | 60.00 | 120.00 |

### 2018 LEGO Star Wars Episode V

| 75203 | Hoth Medical Chamber | 30.00 | 75.00 |
| 75208 | Yoda's Hut | 30.00 | 60.00 |

### 2018 LEGO Star Wars The Last Jedi

| 30380 | Kylo Ren's Shuttle | 7.50 | 15.00 |
| 40298 | DJ | 15.00 | 30.00 |
| 75188 | Resistance Bomber (Finch Dallow) | | |
| 75197 | First Order Specialists Battle Pack | 12.50 | 25.00 |
| 75200 | Ahch-To Island Training | 15.00 | 30.00 |
| 75201 | First Order AT-ST | 15.00 | 30.00 |
| 75202 | Defense of Crait | 30.00 | 60.00 |
| 75216 | Snoke's Throne Room | 60.00 | 120.00 |
| 75230 | Porg | 60.00 | 120.00 |

### 2018 LEGO Star Wars Legends

| 75204 | Sandspeeder | 15.00 | 30.00 |

### 2018 LEGO Star Wars Magazine Gift

| SW911831 | Kylo Ren's Shuttle | | |
| SW911832 | Imperial Shuttle Pilot | | |
| SW911833 | Imperial Shuttle | | |
| SW911834 | Finn | | |
| SW911835 | Dwarf Spider Droid | | |
| SW911836 | Quadjumper | | |
| SW911837 | AT-ST | | |
| SW911838 | Probe Droid | | |
| SW911839 | Obi-Wan Kenobi | | |
| SW911840 | Droideka | | |
| SW911841 | Poe Dameron's X-Wing Fighter | | |
| SW911842 | Star Destroyer | | |
| SW911843 | Luke Skywalker | | |

### 2018 LEGO Star Wars Master Builder

| 75222 | Betrayal at Cloud City | 200.00 | 400.00 |

### 2018 LEGO Star Wars Microfighters

| 75193 | Millennium Falcon | 12.50 | 25.00 |
| 75194 | First Order TIE Fighter | 10.00 | 20.00 |
| 75195 | Ski Speeder vs. First Order Walker | 15.00 | 30.00 |
| 75196 | A-Wing vs. TIE Silencer | 15.00 | 30.00 |

### 2018 LEGO Star Wars Promotional

| 40288 | BB-8 | 12.50 | 25.00 |
| 75512 | Millennium Falcon Cockpit (SDCC Exclusive) | 90.00 | 175.00 |
| 5005376 | Star Wars Anniversary Pod | 10.00 | 20.00 |
| 5005747 | Black Card Display Stand | | |
| 6252770 | Leia Organa | | |
| 6252808 | Chewbacca | | |
| 6252810 | Han Solo | | |
| 6252811 | Obi-Wan Kenobi | | |
| 6252812 | Luke Skywalker | | |
| PORG | Porg | | |

### 2018 LEGO Star Wars Seasonal

| 75213 | Star Wars Advent Calendar | 12.50 | 25.00 |

### 2018 LEGO Star Wars Solo

| | | | |
|---|---|---|---|
| 30381 | Imperial TIE Fighter | 7.50 | 15.00 |
| 30498 | Imperial AT-Hauler | 10.00 | 20.00 |
| 40299 | Kessel Mine Worker | 12.50 | 25.00 |
| 40300 | Han Solo Mudtrooper | | |
| 75207 | Imperial Patrol Battle Pack | 10.00 | 20.00 |
| 75209 | Han Solo's Landspeeder | 20.00 | 40.00 |
| 75210 | Moloch's Landspeeder | 20.00 | 40.00 |
| 75211 | Imperial TIE Fighter | 30.00 | 75.00 |
| 75212 | Kessel Run Millennium Falcon | 125.00 | 250.00 |
| 75215 | Cloud-Rider Swoop Bikes | 25.00 | 50.00 |
| 75217 | Imperial Conveyex Transport | 45.00 | 90.00 |
| 75219 | Imperial AT-Hauler | 60.00 | 120.00 |

### 2018 LEGO Star Wars Ultimate Collector Series

| | | | |
|---|---|---|---|
| 75181 | Y-wing Starfighter | 150.00 | 300.00 |

### 2019 LEGO Star Wars

| | | | |
|---|---|---|---|
| 11920 | Parts for Star Wars: Build Your Own Adventure Galactic Missions | | |
| TANTIVEIV | Tantive IV | | |
| XWING | Mini X-Wing Fighter | | |

### 2019 LEGO Star Wars 4-Plus

| | | | |
|---|---|---|---|
| 75235 | X-Wing Starfighter Trench Run | 20.00 | 40.00 |
| 75237 | TIE Fighter Attack | 12.50 | 25.00 |
| 75247 | Rebel A-wing Starfighter | 10.00 | 20.00 |

### 2019 LEGO Star Wars Battlefront

| | | | |
|---|---|---|---|
| 75226 | Inferno Squad Battle Pack | 12.50 | 25.00 |

### 2019 LEGO Star Wars Boost

| | | | |
|---|---|---|---|
| 75253 | Droid Commander | 125.00 | 250.00 |

### 2019 LEGO Star Wars Episode I

| | | | |
|---|---|---|---|
| 30383 | Naboo Starfighter | 5.00 | 10.00 |
| 30461 | Podracer | 7.50 | 15.00 |
| 75258 | Anakin's Podracer ñ 20th Anniversary Edition | 20.00 | 40.00 |

### 2019 LEGO Star Wars Episode III

| | | | |
|---|---|---|---|
| 75233 | Droid Gunship | 30.00 | 60.00 |
| 75234 | AT-AP Walker | 25.00 | 50.00 |
| 75261 | Clone Scout Walker ñ 20th Anniversary Edition | 20.00 | 40.00 |

### 2019 LEGO Star Wars Episode IV

| | | | |
|---|---|---|---|
| 75229 | Death Star Escape | 15.00 | 30.00 |

| | | | |
|---|---|---|---|
| 75244 | Tantive IV | 125.00 | 250.00 |
| 75246 | Death Star Cannon | 25.00 | 50.00 |

### 2019 LEGO Star Wars Episode V

| | | | |
|---|---|---|---|
| 30384 | Snowspeeder | 5.00 | 10.00 |
| 75239 | Hoth Generator Attack | 12.50 | 25.00 |
| 75241 | Action Battle Echo Base Defence | 20.00 | 40.00 |
| 75243 | Slave I ñ 20th Anniversary Edition | 50.00 | 100.00 |
| 75259 | Snowspeeder ñ 20th Anniversary Edition | 25.00 | 50.00 |

### 2019 LEGO Star Wars Episode VI

| | | | |
|---|---|---|---|
| 75238 | Action Battle Endor Assault | 15.00 | 30.00 |

### 2019 LEGO Star Wars The Force Awakens

| | | | |
|---|---|---|---|
| 75236 | Duel on Starkiller Base | 15.00 | 30.00 |

### 2019 LEGO Star Wars The Last Jedi

| | | | |
|---|---|---|---|
| 75225 | Elite Praetorian Guard Battle Pack | 10.00 | 20.00 |

### 2019 Star Wars Legends

| | | | |
|---|---|---|---|
| 75262 | Imperial Dropship ñ 20th Anniversary Edition | 20.00 | 40.00 |

### 2019 Star Wars Magazine Gift

| | | | |
|---|---|---|---|
| 911944 | Resistance Bomber | 4.00 | 8.00 |
| 911945 | Slave I | 3.00 | 6.00 |
| 911946 | U-Wing | 4.00 | 8.00 |
| 911947 | IG-88 | 3.00 | 6.00 |
| 911948 | AT-M6 | 3.00 | 6.00 |
| 911949 | Millennium Falcon | 4.00 | 8.00 |
| 911950 | B-Wing | 3.00 | 6.00 |
| 911951 | First Order Stormtrooper | 3.00 | 6.00 |
| 911952 | Jedi Interceptor | | |

### 2019 LEGO Star Wars The Mandalorian

| | | | |
|---|---|---|---|
| 75254 | AT-ST Raider | 50.00 | 100.00 |

### 2019 LEGO Star Wars Microfighters

| | | | |
|---|---|---|---|
| 75223 | Naboo Starfighter | 7.50 | 15.00 |
| 75224 | Sith Infiltrator | 6.00 | 12.00 |
| 75228 | Escape Pod vs. Dewback | 10.00 | 20.00 |

### 2018 LEGO Star Wars Miscellaneous

| | | | |
|---|---|---|---|
| 75251 | Darth Vader's Castle | 75.00 | 150.00 |
| 75255 | Yoda | 60.00 | 120.00 |

### 2019 LEGO Star Wars Promotional

| | | | |
|---|---|---|---|
| 40333 | Battle of Hoth - 20th Anniversary Edition | 25.00 | 50.00 |
| 40362 | Battle of Endor | 30.00 | 60.00 |
| 75227 | Darth Vader Bust | 50.00 | 100.00 |
| 75522 | Mini Boost Droid Commander | 30.00 | 75.00 |

### 2019 LEGO Star Wars The Rise of Skywalker

| | | | |
|---|---|---|---|
| 75248 | Resistance A-wing Starfighter | 25.00 | 50.00 |
| 75249 | Resistance Y-wing Starfighter | 40.00 | 80.00 |
| 75250 | Pasaana Speeder Chase | 25.00 | 50.00 |
| 75256 | Kylo Ren's Shuttle | 75.00 | 150.00 |
| 75257 | Millennium Falcon | 100.00 | 200.00 |
| 77901 | Sith Trooper Bust SDCC | 100.00 | 200.00 |

### 2019 LEGO Star Wars Seasonal

| | | | |
|---|---|---|---|
| 75245 | Star Wars Advent Calendar | 30.00 | 60.00 |

### 2019 LEGO Star Wars Ultimate Collector Series

| | | | |
|---|---|---|---|
| 75252 | Imperial Star Destroyer | 800.00 | 1,000.00 |

### 1993-97 Micro Machines Star Wars Planet Playsets

| | | |
|---|---|---|
| 65872 Ice Planet Hoth | 15.00 | 40.00 |
| 65995 Cloud City (w/Twin-Pod Cloud Car) | 8.00 | 20.00 |
| 65858A Planet Tatooine (1994) | 10.00 | 25.00 |
| 65858B Planet Tatooine (1996) | 8.00 | 20.00 |
| 65859A Planet Dagobah (1994) | 10.00 | 25.00 |
| 65859B Planet Dagobah (1996) | | |
| 65871A Death Star from a New Hope (1994) | 10.00 | 25.00 |
| 65871B Death Star from a New Hope (1996) | 5.00 | 12.00 |
| 65873A Planet Endor (w/Imperial AT-ST)(1993) | 8.00 | 20.00 |
| 65873B Planet Endor (w/Imperial AT-ST)(1997) | 6.00 | 15.00 |

### 1993-98 Micro Machines Star Wars Vehicle 3-Packs

| | | |
|---|---|---|
| 65123 Imperial Landing Craft/Death Star/S-Swoop | 8.00 | 20.00 |
| 65124 Outrider Tibanna/Gas Refinery/V-35 Landspeeder | 6.00 | 15.00 |
| 65886 Star Wars A New Hope (silver) | | |
| 65886 Star Wars A New Hope #1 | 6.00 | 15.00 |
| 65887 Star Wars Empire Strikes Back #2 | | |
| 65887 Star Wars Empire Strikes Back (silver) | 5.00 | 12.00 |
| 65888 Star Wars Return of the Jedi (silver) | | |
| 65888 Star Wars Return of the Jedi #3 | | |
| 65897 Star Wars A New Hope #4 | | |
| 65898 Star Wars Empire Strikes Back #5 | 5.00 | 12.00 |
| 65899 Star Wars Return of the Jedi #6 | | |
| 66111 TIE Interceptor/Imperial Star Destroyer/Rebel Blockade Runner | 5.00 | 12.00 |
| 66112 Landspeeder/Millennium Falcon/Jawa Sandcrawler | 8.00 | 20.00 |
| 66113 Darth Vader's TIE Fighter/Y-Wing Starfighter/X-Wing Starfighter | 5.00 | 12.00 |
| 66114 Snowspeeder/Imperial AT-AT/Imperial Probot | 15.00 | 40.00 |
| 66115 Rebel Transport/TIE Bomber/Imperial AT-ST | 6.00 | 15.00 |
| 66116 Escort Frigate/Slave I/Twin-Pod Cloud Car | 5.00 | 12.00 |
| 66117 Desert Sail Barge/Mon Calamari Star Cruiser/Speeder Bike and Rebel Pilot | | |
| 66118 Speeder Bike and Imperial Pilot/Imperial Shuttle Tydirium/TIE Starfighter | | |
| 66119 Super Star Destroyer Executor | | |
| A-Wing Starfighter/B-Wing Starfighter | 10.00 | 25.00 |
| 66137 Lars Family Landspeeder/Death Star II/T-16 Skyhopper | 8.00 | 20.00 |
| 66138 Bespin Cloud City/Mon Calamari Rebel Cruiser/Escape Pod | 6.00 | 15.00 |
| 66139 A-Wing Starfighter/Y-Wing Starfighter/TIE Starfighter | 10.00 | 25.00 |
| 66155 2 Red Squad X-Wings/Green Squad X-Wing | | |

### 1994 Micro Machines Star Wars Fan Club Pieces

| | | |
|---|---|---|
| 18279 Han Solo and the Millennium Falcon | 6.00 | 15.00 |
| 28450 Darth Vader and Imperial Star Destroyer | 6.00 | 15.00 |

### 1994-96 Micro Machines Star Wars Gift Sets

| | | |
|---|---|---|
| 64624 Bronze Finish Collector's Gift Set | 12.00 | 30.00 |
| 65836 Rebel Force Gift Set | 6.00 | 15.00 |
| 65837 Imperial Force Gift Set | 5.00 | 12.00 |
| 65847 11-Piece Collector's Gift Set | 10.00 | 25.00 |
| 65851 A New Hope | 5.00 | 12.00 |
| 65852 Empire Strikes Back | | |
| 65853 Return of the Jedi | 8.00 | 20.00 |
| 65856 Rebel Force Gift Set 2nd Edition | 6.00 | 15.00 |
| 65857 Imperial Force Gift Set 2nd Edition | | |
| 67079 Star Wars Trilogy Gift Set | 15.00 | 40.00 |
| 68042 Rebel vs. Imperial Forces | | |

### 1994-97 Micro Machines Star Wars Collector's Sets

| | | |
|---|---|---|
| 64598 Galaxy Battle Collector's Set 2nd Edition | 8.00 | 20.00 |
| 64601 Master Collector's Edition (19 Items) | 15.00 | 40.00 |
| 64602 Galaxy Battle Collector's Set | 10.00 | 25.00 |
| 66090 Droids | 10.00 | 25.00 |
| 68048 Master Collector's Edition (40 Items) | 8.00 | 20.00 |

### 1994-99 Micro Machines Star Wars Transforming Action Sets

| | | |
|---|---|---|
| 65694 TIE Fighter Pilot/Academy | 10.00 | 25.00 |
| 65695 Royal Guard/Death Star II | 15.00 | 40.00 |
| 65811 C-3PO/Cantina | 10.00 | 25.00 |
| 65812 Darth Vader/Bespin | 10.00 | 25.00 |
| 65813 R2-D2/Jabba's Palace | 12.00 | 30.00 |
| 65814 Stormtrooper/Death Star | 12.00 | 30.00 |
| 65815 Chewbacca/Endor | 10.00 | 25.00 |
| 65816 Boba Fett/Cloud City | 15.00 | 40.00 |
| 65817 Luke Skywalker/Hoth | 10.00 | 25.00 |
| 66551 Jar Jar Binks/Naboo | 6.00 | 15.00 |
| 66552 Battle Droid/Trade Federation Droid Control Ship | | |
| 66553 Darth Maul/Theed Generator | 30.00 | 80.00 |
| 66554 Gungan Sub/Otoh Gunga | | |
| 67094 Star Destroyer/Space Fortress | 15.00 | 40.00 |
| 67095 Slave I/Tatooine | 10.00 | 25.00 |
| 68063 Yoda/Dagobah | 12.00 | 30.00 |
| 68064 Jabba/Mos Eisley Spaceport | 15.00 | 40.00 |

### 1995 Micro Machines Star Wars Action Fleet Playsets

| | | |
|---|---|---|
| 67091 Ice Planet Hoth (w/Battle-Damaged Snow Speeder | | |
| Luke Skywalker on Tauntaun | 10.00 | 25.00 |
| Wampa Ice Creature/Rebel Pilot/Princess Leia/2-1B Droid) | | |
| 67092 The Death Star (w/Darth Vader's Battle-Damaged | | |
| TIE Fighter/Imperial Pilot | 10.00 | 25.00 |
| Imperial Gunner/Darth Vader/Stormtrooper/Imperial Royal Guard/Emperor Palpatine) | | |
| 67093 Yavin Rebel Base (w/Battle-Damaged X-Wing | | |
| Wedge Antilles/R2 Unit | 12.00 | 30.00 |
| Luke Skywalker/Han Solo/Princess Leia/Rebel Sentry) | | |
| 68177 Naboo Hangar Final Combat | | |
| (w/Obi-Wan Kenobi/Darth Maul/Qui-Gon Jinn) | 20.00 | 50.00 |

### 1995 Micro Machines Star Wars Gold Classic

| | | |
|---|---|---|
| 67085 X-Wing Fighter and Slave I | 12.00 | 30.00 |
| 67086 Imperial Shuttle | | |
| 67088 Millennium Falcon and TIE Fighter | 30.00 | 80.00 |

### 1995-03 Micro Machines Star Wars Action Fleet Vehicles

| | | |
|---|---|---|
| 46846 AT-TE | | |
| 46848 Solar Sailer | | |
| 46849 Millennium Falcon | 12.00 | 30.00 |
| 46850 X-Wingfighter | | |
| 47045 Luke Skywalker's Snowspeeder | | |
| 47224 Imperial AT-AT | 8.00 | 20.00 |
| 47287 Republic Gunship | | |
| 47305 Slave I | 5.00 | 12.00 |
| 47356 TIE Advance X1 | | |
| 47414 Naboo N-1 Starfighter | | |
| 47425 Republic Assault Ship | 30.00 | 80.00 |
| 47766 Anakin's Speeder | | |
| 47767 Zam Wessel Speeder | | |
| 47768 Homing Spider Droid | 4.00 | 10.00 |

| | | |
|---|---|---|
| 47994 Jedi Starfighter | 8.00 | 20.00 |
| 47995 Star Destroyer | | |
| 47997 Mon Calamari Cruiser | 8.00 | 20.00 |
| 66989 Rancor (w/Gamorrean Guard and Luke Skywalker) | 10.00 | 25.00 |
| 66990 Virago (w/Prince Xizor and Guri) | 10.00 | 25.00 |
| 66991 X-Wing Starfighter (w/Wedge and R2 Unit) | | |
| 66992 Y-Wing Starfighter (red)(w/Gold Leader and R2 Unit) | | |
| 66993 A-Wing Starfighter (green)(w/Rebel pilot and Mon Mothma) | 8.00 | 20.00 |
| 66994 B-Wing Starfighter (w/Rebel pilot and Admiral Ackbar) | 10.00 | 25.00 |
| 66995 TIE Fighter (w/Imperial pilot and Grand Moff Tarkin) | | |
| 66996 Bespin Twin-Pod Cloud Car (w/Cloud Car pilot and Lobot) | | |
| 66997 Y-Wing Starfighter (blue)(w/Blue Leader and R2 Unit) | 10.00 | 25.00 |
| 66998 X-Wing Starfighter (w/Jek Porkins and R2 Unit) | | |
| 67014 Jabba's Sail Barge (w/Jabba the Hutt/Saelt Marae and R2-D2 | 12.00 | 30.00 |
| 67031 Luke's X-Wing Starfighter (w/Luke and R2-D2) | 15.00 | 40.00 |
| 67032 Darth Vader's TIE Fighter (w/Darth Vader and Imperial pilot) | | |
| 67033 Imperial AT-AT (w/Imperial drive and snowtrooper) | 10.00 | 25.00 |
| 67034 A-Wing Starfighter (w/C-3PO and Rebel pilot) | 6.00 | 15.00 |
| 67035 Imperial Shuttle Tydirium (w/Han Solo and Chewbacca) | | |
| 67036 Rebel Snowspeeder (w/Luke Skywalker and Rebel gunner) | | |
| 67039 Jawa Sandcrawler (w/Jawa and scavenger droid) | 8.00 | 20.00 |
| 67040 Y-Wing Starfighter (w/Gold Leader and R2 Unit) | 8.00 | 20.00 |
| 67041 Slave I (w/Boba Fett and Han Solo) | 12.00 | 30.00 |
| 67058 TIE Interceptor (w/2 Imperial pilots) | 8.00 | 20.00 |
| 67059 TIE Bomber (w/Imperial pilot and Imperial Naval pilot) | 10.00 | 25.00 |
| 67077 Landspeeder and Imperial AT-ST 2-Pack | 10.00 | 25.00 |
| (w/Luke Skywalker/Obi-Wan Kenobi/Imperial Driver/Stormtrooper) | | |
| 67098 Luke's X-Wing from Dagobah (w/Luke Skywalker and R2-D2) | 8.00 | 20.00 |
| (1998 Toy Fair Magazine Exclusive) | | |
| 67100 Millennium Falcon (w/Han Solo and Chewbacca) | | |
| 67101 Rebel Blockade Runner (w/Princess Leia and Rebel trooper) | 8.00 | 20.00 |
| 67102 Incom T-16 Skyhopper (w/Luke Skywalker and Biggs Darklighter) | 6.00 | 15.00 |
| 67103 Imperial Landing Craft (w/Sandtrooper and Imperial Officer) | 15.00 | 40.00 |
| 67105 TIE Defender (w/Imperial pilot and Moff Jerjerrod) | 30.00 | 80.00 |
| 67106 E-Wing Starfighter (w/Rebel pilot and R7 Unit) | | |
| 68131 Naboo Starfighter (w/Anakin) | | |
| 68132 Trade Federation MTT (w/Battle Droid) | 25.00 | 60.00 |
| 68133 Sebulba's Pod Racer (w/Sebulba) | | |
| 68134 Republic Cruiser (w/Qui-Gon Jinn) | 12.00 | 30.00 |
| 68135 Droid Fighter (w/Daultry Dofine) | | |
| 68136 Gungan Sub (w/Qui-Gon Jinn) | 4.00 | 10.00 |
| 68137 Flash Speeder (w/Naboo Royal Guard) | | |
| 68138 Trade Federation Landing Ship (w/Battle Droid) | | |
| 68140 Mars Guo's Pod Racer (w/Mars Guo) | | |
| 68180 Gian Speeder and Theed Palace | | |
| (w/Captain Panaka/Naboo Foot Soldier/2 Battle Droids) | | |
| 79050 Anakin's Pod Racer (w/Anakin) | | |
| 79967 Royal Starship (w/Rick Olie) | 25.00 | 60.00 |
| 79968 Droid Control Ship (w/Neimoidian Commander) | | |
| 79971 Trade Federation Tank (w/Battle Droid) | 12.00 | 30.00 |
| 79972 Sith Infiltrator (w/Darth Maul) | 30.00 | 80.00 |
| 1327CM6 Darth Vader's TIE Fighter (w/Darth Vader and Imperial pilot) | | |

## 1996 Micro Machines Star Wars Adventure Gear

| | | |
|---|---|---|
| 68031 Vader's Lightsaber (w/Death Star Trench/X-Wing | 8.00 | 20.00 |
| Imperial Gunner/Grand Moff Tarkin/Darth Vader | | |

| | | |
|---|---|---|
| 68032 Luke's Binoculars (w/Yavin Rebel Base/Y-Wing | 8.00 | 20.00 |
| Luke Skywalker/R5 Droid/Wedge Antilles | | |

## 1996 Micro Machines Star Wars Epic Collections

| | | |
|---|---|---|
| 66281 Heir to the Empire | 8.00 | 20.00 |
| 66282 Jedi Search | 6.00 | 15.00 |
| 66283 The Truce at Bakura | 8.00 | 20.00 |

## 1996 Micro Machines Star Wars Exclusives

| | | |
|---|---|---|
| 66091 Balance of Power (Special Offer) | | |
| 68060 Star Wars Trilogy (Special Giveaway) | 20.00 | 50.00 |

## 1996 Micro Machines Star Wars Shadows of the Empire

| | | |
|---|---|---|
| 66194 Stinger/IG-2000/Guri/Darth Vader/Asp | 5.00 | 12.00 |
| 66195 Virago/Swoop with Rider/Prince Xizor/Emperor Palpatine | 6.00 | 15.00 |
| 66196 Outrider/Hound's Tooth/Dash Rendar/LE-B02D9 | 10.00 | 25.00 |

## 1996 Micro Machines Star Wars X-Ray Fleet

| | | |
|---|---|---|
| 67071 Darth Vader's TIE Fighter/A-Wing Starfighter | | |
| 67072 X-Wing Starfighter/Imperial AT-AT | | |
| 67073 Millennium Falcon/Jawa Sandcrawler | 6.00 | 15.00 |
| 67074 Boba Fett's Slave I/Y-Wing Starfighter | | |

## 1996-97 Micro Machines Star Wars Action Sets

| | | |
|---|---|---|
| 65878 Millennium Falcon (w/Y-Wing/Mynock/Han Solo/Chewbacca | 20.00 | 50.00 |
| Lando Calrissian/Nien Nunb/Leia | | |
| 65996 Rebel Transport (w/X-Wing/Rebel mechanic/General Rieekan/Major Derlin | | |

## 1996-98 Micro Machines Star Wars Character Sets

| | | |
|---|---|---|
| 66081 Imperial Stormtroopers | 10.00 | 25.00 |
| 66082 Ewoks | 10.00 | 25.00 |
| 66083 Rebel Pilots | 6.00 | 15.00 |
| 66084 Imperial Pilots | 6.00 | 15.00 |
| 66096 Jawas | 5.00 | 12.00 |
| 66097 Imperial Officers | 6.00 | 15.00 |
| 66098 Echo Base Troops | 5.00 | 12.00 |
| 66099 Imperial Naval Troops | 8.00 | 20.00 |
| 66108 Rebel Fleet Troops | 8.00 | 20.00 |
| 66109 Tusken Raiders | 6.00 | 15.00 |
| 66158 Classic Characters | 8.00 | 20.00 |
| 67112 Endor Rebel Strike Force | 10.00 | 25.00 |
| 67113 Imperial Scout Troopers | 5.00 | 12.00 |
| 67114 Bounty Hunters | 10.00 | 25.00 |

## 1996-98 Micro Machines Star Wars Mini Heads

| | | |
|---|---|---|
| 68021 Boba Fett/Admiral Ackbar/Gamorrean Guard | 5.00 | 12.00 |
| 68022 Greedo/Nien Nunb/Tusken Raider | 5.00 | 12.00 |
| 68023 Jawa/Yoda/Leia | 5.00 | 12.00 |
| 68024 Bib Fortuna/Figrin D'an/Scout Trooper | 4.00 | 10.00 |
| 68038 Darth Vader Set | 5.00 | 10.00 |
| 68046 C-3PO Set | | |
| NNO Pizza Hut Set | | |

## 1996-99 Micro Machines Star Wars Battle Packs

| | | |
|---|---|---|
| 68011 Rebel Alliance | 6.00 | 15.00 |
| 68012 Galactic Empire | 6.00 | 15.00 |
| 68013 Aliens and Creatures | 6.00 | 15.00 |
| 68014 Galactic Hunters | 6.00 | 15.00 |
| 68015 Shadow of the Empire | 6.00 | 15.00 |
| 68016 Dune Sea | 6.00 | 15.00 |
| 68017 Droid Escape | 6.00 | 15.00 |
| 68018 Desert Palace | 6.00 | 15.00 |
| 68035 Endor Adventure | 8.00 | 20.00 |
| 68036 Mos Eisley Spaceport | 12.00 | 30.00 |
| 68037 Cantina Encounter | 6.00 | 15.00 |
| 68090 Cantina Smugglers and Spies | 8.00 | 20.00 |
| 68091 Hoth Attack | 10.00 | 25.00 |
| 68092 Death Star Escape | 6.00 | 15.00 |
| 68093 Endor Victory | 12.00 | 30.00 |
| 68094 Lars Family Homestead | 8.00 | 20.00 |
| 68095 Imperial Troops | 15.00 | 40.00 |
| 68096 Rebel Troops | 10.00 | 25.00 |

## 1996-99 Micro Machines Star Wars Die-Cast Vehicles

| | | |
|---|---|---|
| 66267 Death Star | 10.00 | 25.00 |
| 66268 A-Wing Starfighter | | |
| 66269 Snowspeeder | | |
| 66270 TIE Bomber | 8.00 | 20.00 |
| 66271 Landspeeder | | |
| 66272 Executor (w/Star Destroyer) | 6.00 | 15.00 |
| 66273 Slave I | | |
| 66520 Royal Starship | 5.00 | 12.00 |
| 66523 Gian Speeder | | |
| 66524 Trade Federation Battleship | 6.00 | 15.00 |
| 66525 Sith Infiltrator | 4.00 | 10.00 |
| 66526 Republic Cruiser | | |
| 66527 Trade Federation Tank | 6.00 | 15.00 |
| 66528 Sebulba's Pod Racer | | |
| 79021 Trade Federation Droid Starfighter | | |
| 66261A X-Wing Starfighter (bubble) | | |
| 66261B X-Wing Starfighter (stripe) | | |
| 66262A Millennium Falcon (bubble) | 5.00 | 12.00 |
| 66262B Millennium Falcon (stripe) | 8.00 | 20.00 |
| 66263A Imperial Star Destroyer (bubble) | 4.00 | 10.00 |
| 66263B Imperial Star Destroyer (stripe) | 4.00 | 10.00 |
| 66264A TIE Fighter (bubble) | | |

| | | |
|---|---|---|
| 66264B | TIE Fighter (stripe) | | |
| 66265A | Y-Wing Starfighter (bubble) | | |
| 66265B | Y-Wing Starfighter (stripe) | | |
| 66266A | Jawa Sandcrawler (bubble) | 6.00 | 15.00 |
| 66266B | Jawa Sandcrawler (stripe) | 4.00 | 10.00 |

## 1996-99 Micro Machines Star Wars Electronic Action Fleet Vehicles

| | | | |
|---|---|---|---|
| 73419 | AT-AT (w/Snowtrooper and Imperial Driver) | 15.00 | 40.00 |
| 79072 | FAMBAA | | |
| 79073 | Trade Federation Tank | | |

## 1996-99 Micro Machines Star Wars Series Alpha

| | | | |
|---|---|---|---|
| 73421 | X-Wing Starfighter | 8.00 | 20.00 |
| 73422 | Imperial Shuttle | 10.00 | 25.00 |
| 73423 | Rebel Snowspeeder | 6.00 | 15.00 |
| 73424 | Imperial AT-AT | 8.00 | 20.00 |
| 73430 | Twin-Pod Cloud Car | | |
| 73431 | Y-Wing Starfighter | | |
| 73432 | B-Wing Starfighter | | |
| 97033 | Naboo Fighter | | |
| 97034 | Droid Fighter | | |
| 97035 | Sith Infiltrator | 25.00 | 60.00 |
| 97036 | Royal Starship | | |

## 1997 Micro Machines Star Wars Classic Duels

| | | |
|---|---|---|
| 68301 | TIE Fighter vs. X-Wing Starfighter | |
| 68302 | TIE Interceptor vs. Millennium Falcon | |

## 1997 Micro Machines Star Wars Double Takes

| | | | |
|---|---|---|---|
| 75118 | Death Star (w/Millennium Falcon/Obi-Wan Kenobi/Owen Lars30.00 | | 80.00 |
| | Ronto and Jawas/Beru Lars/2 Scurriers | | |

## 1997-98 Micro Machines Star Wars Flight Controllers

| | | | |
|---|---|---|---|
| 73417 | Luke Skywalker's X-Wing Starfighter | | |
| 73418 | Darth Vader's TIE Fighter | 10.00 | 25.00 |
| 73440 | Y-Wing Starfighter | 8.00 | 20.00 |
| 73441 | TIE Interceptor | 8.00 | 20.00 |

## 1998-99 Micro Machines Star Wars Action Fleet Mini Scenes

| | | | |
|---|---|---|---|
| 68121 | STAP Invasion (w/STAP/Jar Jar Binks/Battle Droid) | 5.00 | 12.00 |
| 68122 | Destroyer Droid Ambush | | |

| | | | |
|---|---|---|---|
| | (w/Destroyer Droid/Obi-Wan Kenobi/TC-14) | 4.00 | 10.00 |
| 68123 | Gungan Assault (w/Gungan/Kaadu/Battle Droid) | 4.00 | 10.00 |
| 68124 | Sith Pursuit (w/Sith speeder/Darth Maul/Qui-Gon Jinn) | | |
| 79025 | Trade Federation Raid | | |
| | (w/Trade Federation MTT/Ikopi/Jar Jar Binks/Qui-Gon Jinn) | 5.00 | 12.00 |
| 79026 | Throne Room Reception | | |
| | (w/Throne Room/Sio Bibble/Nute Gunray) | 6.00 | 15.00 |
| 79027 | Watto's Deal (w/Watto's Shop/Anakin/Pit droid) | | |
| 79028 | Generator Core Duel | | |
| | (w/generator core/Darth Maul/Obi-Wan Kenobi | 8.00 | 20.00 |

## 1998-99 Micro Machines Star Wars Platform Action Sets

| | | | |
|---|---|---|---|
| 66541 | Pod Race Arena | 8.00 | 20.00 |
| 66542 | Naboo Temple Ruins | 6.00 | 15.00 |
| 66543 | Galactic Senate | 6.00 | 15.00 |
| 66544 | Galactic Dogfight | 10.00 | 25.00 |
| 66545 | Theed Palace | | |
| 66546 | Tatooine Desert | | |

## 1999 Micro Machines Star Wars Deluxe Platform Action Sets

| | | | |
|---|---|---|---|
| 66561 | Royal Starship Repair | 30.00 | 80.00 |
| 66562 | Theed Palace Assault | 100.00 | 200.00 |

## 1999 Micro Machines Star Wars Deluxe Action Sets

| | | | |
|---|---|---|---|
| 68156 | Pod Racer Hangar Bay (w/pit droid and pit mechanic) | | |
| 68157 | Mos Espa Market (w/Anakin Skywalker and C-3PO) | 8.00 | 20.00 |
| 68158 | Otoh Gunga (w/Obi-Wan Kenobi and Jar Jar Binks) | | |
| 68159 | Theed Palace | | |

## 1999 Micro Machines Star Wars Mega Platform Set

| | | | |
|---|---|---|---|
| 66566 | Trade Federation MTT/Naboo Battlefield | 25.00 | 60.00 |

## 1999 Micro Machines Star Wars Pod Racer

| | | | |
|---|---|---|---|
| 66531 | Pack 1 (w/Anakin and Ratts Tyrell) | 5.00 | 12.00 |
| 66532 | Pack 2 (w/Sebulba and Clegg Holdfast) | 5.00 | 12.00 |
| 66533 | Pack 3 (w/Dud Bolt and Mars Guo) | 5.00 | 12.00 |

| | | | |
|---|---|---|---|
| 66534 | Pack 4 (w/Boles Roor and Neva Kee) | 5.00 | 12.00 |
| 66548A | Build Your Own Pod Racer Green (Galoob) | 5.00 | 12.00 |
| 66548B | Build Your Own Pod Racer Yellow (Galoob) | 5.00 | 12.00 |
| 97023A | Build Your Own Pod Racer Black (Hasbro) | 5.00 | 12.00 |
| 97023B | Build Your Own Pod Racer Blue (Hasbro) | 5.00 | 12.00 |

## 1999 Micro Machines Star Wars Pod Racing Gravity Track

| | | | |
|---|---|---|---|
| 66566 | Beggar's Canyon Challenge | | |
| 66570 | Boonta Eve Challenge | 15.00 | 40.00 |
| 66577 | Arch Canyon Adventure | | |

## 1999 Micro Machines Star Wars Turbo Pod Racers

| | | |
|---|---|---|
| 68148 | Gasgano | |
| 68149 | Ody Mandrell | |

## 2002 Micro Machines Star Wars Action Fleet Movie Scenes

| | | | |
|---|---|---|---|
| 32549 | Dune Sea Ambush (w/Tusken Raider/Bantha/Luke's Landspeeder)5.00 | | 12.00 |
| 32553 | Tatooine Droid Hunter (w/Dewback/Sandtrooper/Escape Pod) 6.00 | | 15.00 |
| 32554 | Imperial Endor Pursuit | | |
| | (w/Luke Skywalker/Scout Trooper/2 speeder bikes/AT-ST) | 6.00 | 15.00 |
| 32557 | Mos Eisley Encounter (w/Ranto/Jawa/Black Landspeeder) | 5.00 | 12.00 |

## 2005-09 Star Wars Titanium Series 3-Inch Die-Cast

| | |
|---|---|
| 1 | A-Wing Fighter |
| 2 | A-Wing Fighter (blue) |
| 3 | A-Wing Fighter (green) |
| 4 | Aayla Secura's Jedi Starfighter |
| 5 | Amidala's Star Skiff |
| 6 | Anakin Skywalker's Pod Racer |
| 7 | Anakin's Jedi Starfighter (Coruscant) |
| 8 | Anakin's Jedi Starfighter (Mustafar) |
| 9 | Anakin's Jedi Starfighter with Hyperspace Ring |
| 10 | Anakin Skywalker's Jedi Starfighter (The Clone Wars) |
| 11 | Anakin's Modified Jedi Starfighter (Clone Wars) |
| 12 | ARC-170 Fighter |
| 13 | ARC-170 Fighter (green) |
| 14 | ARC-170 Fighter (Clone Wars deco) |
| 15 | ARC-170 Starfighter (The Clone Wars) |
| 16 | ARC-170 Fighter (Flaming Wampa) |
| 17 | ARC-170 Starfighter (Lucky Lekku) |
| 18 | AT-AP |
| 19 | AT-AP (The Clone Wars) |
| 20 | AT-AT Walker |
| 21 | AT-AT Walker (Endor) |
| 22 | AT-AT Walker (Shadow) |
| 23 | AT-OT |
| 24 | AT-OT (The Clone Wars) |
| 25 | AT-RT |
| 26 | AT-RT (Kashyyyk) |
| 27 | AT-RT (Utapau) |
| 28 | AT-ST |
| 29 | AT-ST (Hoth deco) |
| 30 | AT-ST (dirty) |
| 31 | AT-TE |
| 32 | AT-TE (The Clone Wars) |
| 33 | Jedi Starfighter with Hyperdrive Ring (green/black) |

34 Jedi Starfighter with Hyperdrive Ring (green/blue)
35 B-Wing Starfighter
36 B-Wing Starfighter (orange)
37 B-Wing Starfighter (Dagger Squadron)
38 BARC Speeder
39 Clone Turbo Tank
40 Clone Turbo Tank (Snow deco)
41 Cloud Car
42 Darth Maul's Sith Speeder
43 Darth Vader's Sith Starfighter
44 Darth Vader's TIE Advanced x1 Starfighter
45 Darth Vader's TIE Advanced x1 Starfighter (white)
46 Death Star
47 Dewback with Stormtrooper
48 Droid Gunship
49 Droid Tri-Fighter
50 Droid Tri-Fighter (Battle Damage)
51 Executor
52 Firespray Interceptor
53 General Grievous' Starfighter
54 Hailfire Droid
55 Hound's Tooth
56 Hyena Droid Bomber
57 IG-2000
58 Imperial Attack Cruiser
59 Imperial Landing Craft
60 Imperial Shuttle
61 Imperial Shuttle (Emperor's Hand)
62 Invisible Hand
63 Jabba's Desert Skiff
64 Jabba's Sail Barge
65 Jedi Starfighter (Hot Rod)
66 Kit Fisto's Jedi Starfighter
67 Landspeeder
68 Mace Windu's Jedi Starfighter
69 Mace Windu's Jedi Starfighter (repaint)
70 Mace Windu's Jedi Starfighter with Hyperdrive Ring
71 Malevolence
72 Millennium Falcon
73 Millennium Falcon (Battle Ravaged)
74 Millennium Falcon (Episode III)
75 Mist Hunter
76 Mon Calamari Star Cruiser
77 Naboo Fighter
78 Naboo Patrol Fighter
79 Naboo Royal Cruiser
80 Naboo Royal Starship
81 Nebulon-B Escort Frigate
82 Neimoidian Shuttle
83 Obi-Wan's Jedi Starfighter (Coruscant)
84 Obi-Wan's Jedi Starfighter (Utapau)
85 Obi-Wan's Jedi Starfighter with Hyperspace Ring
86 Obi-Wan's Jedi Starfighter (The Clone Wars)
87 Outrider
88 P-38 Starfighter / Magnaguard Starfighter
89 Plo Koon's Jedi Starfighter with Hyperspace Ring
90 Punishing One
91 Rebel Blockade Runner
92 Rebel Transport
93 Republic Attack Cruiser
94 Republic Attack Cruiser (The Clone Wars)
95 Republic Attack Shuttle
96 Republic Cruiser

97 Republic Fighter Tank
98 Republic Gunship
99 Republic Gunship – Clone Wars (Titanium Limited)
100 Republic Gunship (Closed Doors)
101 Republic Gunship (Command Gunship deco)
102 Republic Gunship (The Clone Wars)
103 Republic Gunship (Lucky Lekku)
104 Republic V-Wing Fighter
105 Rogue Shadow
106 Saesee Tiin's Jedi Starfighter with Hyperspace Ring
107 Sandcrawler
108 Sandspeeder
109 Sebulba's Pod Racer
110 Shadow Scout on Speeder Bike
111 Shadow Trooper Gunship
112 Sith Infiltrator
113 Slave 1 - Boba Fett
114 Slave 1 – Jango Fett
115 Slave 1 – Jango Fett (Battle Damage)
116 Slave 1 - Silver (Titanium Limited)
117 Snowspeeder
118 Snowspeeder (Luke's)
119 Snowspeeder (Vintage deco)
120 Speeder Bike - Blizzard Force
121 Speeder Bike - Kashyyyk
122 Speeder Bike - Leia
123 Speeder Bike - Luke Skywalker
124 Speeder Bike - Paploo
125 Speeder Bike - Scout Trooper
126 Star Destroyer
127 Star Destroyer (repaint)
128 Swamp Speeder
129 Swamp Speeder (Dirty deco)
130 T-16 Skyhopper
131 TIE Bomber
132 TIE Bomber (Battle Damage)
133 TIE Defender
134 TIE Fighter
135 TIE Fighter (Battle Damage)
136 TIE Fighter – White (Titanium Limited)
137 TIE Fighter (Ecliptic Evader)
138 TIE Interceptor
139 TIE Interceptor (Royal Guard)
140 TIE Interceptor (Baron Fel)
141 Tantive IV
142 Trade Federation AAT
143 Trade Federation AAT (Clone Wars deco)
144 Trade Federation AAT (The Clone Wars)
145 Trade Federation Battleship
146 Trade Federation Landing Craft
147 Trade Federation MTT
148 The Twilight
149 V-19 Torrent Starfighter
150 V-Wing Starfighter
151 V-Wing Starfighter (Imperial)
152 Virago
153 Vulture Droid
154 Vulture Droid (The Clone Wars)
155 Wookiee Flyer
156 X-Wing Fighter
157 X-Wing Starfighter (Biggs Darklighter's Red 3)
158 X-Wing Fighter (Dagobah)
159 X-Wing Starfighter (John Branon's Red 4)

160 X-Wing Fighter (Luke Skywalker's Red 5)
161 X-Wing Starfighter (Red Leader's Red 1)
162 X-Wing Fighter (Wedge Antilles)
163 X-Wing Starfighter (Wedge Antilles' Red 2)
164 Xanadu Blood
165 XP-34 Landspeeder
166 Y-Wing Bomber
167 Y-Wing Bomber (Anakin's)
168 Y-Wing Fighter
169 Y-Wing Fighter (Davish Krail's Gold 5)
170 Y-Wing Fighter (Gold Leader)
171 Y-Wing Starfighter (green deco)
172 Y-Wing Fighter (Red deco)
173 Z-95 Headhunter

## 2015 Micro Machines Star Wars The Force Awakens Playsets

| | | |
|---|---|---|
| 1 First Order Stormtrooper (w/Poe Dameron and transport) | 6.00 | 15.00 |
| 2 Millennium Falcon (w/smaller Millennium Falcon and stormtrooper) | 8.00 | 20.00 |
| 3 R2-D2 (w/Chewbacca/2 snowtroopers and transport) | 5.00 | 12.00 |
| 4 Star Destroyer (w/Kylo Ren/Finn/X-Wing/TIE Fighter) | 12.00 | 30.00 |

## 2015 Micro Machines Star Wars The Force Awakens Vehicles

| | | |
|---|---|---|
| 1 Battle of Hoth (ESB) | 5.00 | 12.00 |
| 2 Clone Army Raid (AOTC) | 4.00 | 10.00 |
| 3 Desert Invasion | 4.00 | 10.00 |
| 4 Droid Army (ROTS) | 5.00 | 12.00 |
| 5 Endor Forest Battle (ROTJ) | 6.00 | 15.00 |
| 6 First Order Attacks | 4.00 | 10.00 |
| 7 First Order TIE Fighter Attack | 4.00 | 10.00 |
| 8 Galactic Showdown | 5.00 | 12.00 |
| 9 Imperial Pursuit (ANH) | 4.00 | 10.00 |
| 10 Inquisitor's Hunt (Rebels) | 4.00 | 10.00 |
| 11 Speeder Chase | 5.00 | 12.00 |
| 12 Trench Run (ANH) | 6.00 | 15.00 |

# Comics

## PRICE GUIDE

### Marvel STAR WARS (1977-1986)

| | | | |
|---|---|---|---|
| 1 | July 1977#{"Star Wars: A New Hope" adaptation Part 1 | 75.00 | 200.00 |
| 1 | July 1977#{Star Wars 35-cent price variant | 3,000.00 | 6,000.00 |
| 2 | August 1977#{"Star Wars: A New Hope" adaptation Part 2 | 20.00 | 50.00 |
| 2 | August 1977#{Star Wars 35-cent price variant | 1,000.00 | 3,000.00 |
| 3 | September 1977#{"Star Wars: A New Hope" adaptation Part 3 | 15.00 | 40.00 |
| 3 | September 1977#{Star Wars 35-cent price variant | 1,000.00 | 3,000.00 |
| 4 | October 1977#{"Star Wars: A New Hope" adaptation Part 4 | 15.00 | 40.00 |
| 4 | October 1977#{Star Wars 35-cent price variant | 1,000.00 | 3,000.00 |
| 5 | November 1977#{"Star Wars: A New Hope" adaptation Part 5 | 15.00 | 40.00 |
| 6 | December 1977#{"Star Wars: A New Hope" adaptation Part 6 | 15.00 | 40.00 |
| 7 | January 1978 | 8.00 | 20.00 |
| 8 | February 1978 | 8.00 | 20.00 |
| 9 | March 1978 | 8.00 | 20.00 |
| 10 | April 1978 | 8.00 | 20.00 |
| 11 | May 1978 | 8.00 | 20.00 |
| 12 | June 1978#{1st appearance of Governor Quarg | 8.00 | 20.00 |
| 13 | July 1978#{John Byrne & Terry Austin cover | 10.00 | 25.00 |
| 14 | August 1978 | 8.00 | 20.00 |
| 15 | September 1978 | 8.00 | 20.00 |
| 16 | October 1978#{1st appearance of Valance | 6.00 | 15.00 |
| 17 | November 1978 | 6.00 | 15.00 |
| 18 | December 1978 | 6.00 | 15.00 |
| 19 | January 1979 | 6.00 | 15.00 |
| 20 | February 1979 | 6.00 | 15.00 |
| 21 | March 1979 | 6.00 | 15.00 |
| 22 | April 1979 | 6.00 | 15.00 |
| 23 | May 1979#{Darth Vader appearance | 6.00 | 15.00 |
| 24 | June 1979 | 6.00 | 15.00 |
| 25 | July 1979 | 6.00 | 15.00 |
| 26 | August 1979 | 6.00 | 15.00 |
| 27 | September 1979 | 6.00 | 15.00 |
| 28 | October 1979 | 6.00 | 15.00 |
| 29 | November 1979#{1st appearance of Tyler Lucian | 6.00 | 15.00 |
| 30 | December 1979 | 5.00 | 12.00 |
| 31 | January 1980 | 5.00 | 12.00 |
| 32 | February 1980 | 5.00 | 12.00 |
| 33 | March 1980 | 5.00 | 12.00 |
| 34 | April 1980 | 5.00 | 12.00 |
| 35 | May 1980#{Darth Vader cover | 6.00 | 15.00 |
| 36 | June 1980 | 5.00 | 12.00 |
| 37 | July 1980 | 5.00 | 12.00 |
| 38 | August 1980 | 5.00 | 12.00 |
| 39 | September 1980#{"The Empire Strikes Back" adaptation - Part 1 | 8.00 | 20.00 |
| 40 | October 1980#{"The Empire Strikes Back" adaptation - Part 2 | 8.00 | 20.00 |
| 41 | November 1980#{"The Empire Strikes Back" adaptation - Part 3 | 8.00 | 20.00 |
| 42 | December 1980#{"The Empire Strikes Back" adaptation - Part 4, "Bounty Hunters" cover w/Boba Fett | 30.00 | 80.00 |
| 43 | January 1981#{"The Empire Strikes Back" adaptation - Part 5 | 8.00 | 20.00 |
| 44 | February 1981#{"The Empire Strikes Back" adaptation - Part 6 | 8.00 | 20.00 |
| 45 | March 1981 | 5.00 | 12.00 |
| 46 | April 1981 | 5.00 | 12.00 |
| 47 | May 1981#{1st appearance Captain Kligson | 5.00 | 12.00 |
| 48 | June 1981#{Princess Leia vs. Darth Vader | 8.00 | 20.00 |
| 49 | July 1981#{"The Last Jedi" story title on cover | 12.00 | 30.00 |
| 50 | August 1981#{Giant-Size issue | 6.00 | 15.00 |
| 51 | September 1981 | 5.00 | 12.00 |
| 52 | October 1981#{Darth Vader cover | 6.00 | 15.00 |
| 53 | November 1981 | 5.00 | 12.00 |
| 54 | December 1981 | 5.00 | 12.00 |
| 55 | January 1982#{1st appearance Plif | 5.00 | 12.00 |
| 56 | February 1982 | 5.00 | 12.00 |
| 57 | March 1982 | 5.00 | 12.00 |
| 58 | April 1982 | 5.00 | 12.00 |
| 59 | May 1982 | 5.00 | 12.00 |
| 60 | June 1982 | 5.00 | 12.00 |
| 61 | July 1982 | 5.00 | 12.00 |
| 62 | August 1982 | 5.00 | 12.00 |
| 63 | September 1982 | 5.00 | 12.00 |
| 64 | October 1982 | 5.00 | 12.00 |
| 65 | November 1982 | 5.00 | 12.00 |
| 66 | December 1982 | 5.00 | 12.00 |
| 67 | January 1983 | 5.00 | 12.00 |
| 68 | February 1983#{Boba Fett cover | 30.00 | 80.00 |
| 69 | March 1983 | 5.00 | 12.00 |
| 70 | April 1983 | 5.00 | 12.00 |
| 71 | May 1983 | 5.00 | 12.00 |
| 72 | June 1983 | 5.00 | 12.00 |
| 73 | July 1983 | 5.00 | 12.00 |
| 74 | August 1983 | 5.00 | 12.00 |
| 75 | September 1983 | 5.00 | 12.00 |
| 76 | October 1983 | 5.00 | 12.00 |
| 77 | November 1983 | 5.00 | 12.00 |
| 78 | December 1983 | 5.00 | 12.00 |
| 79 | January 1984 | 5.00 | 12.00 |
| 80 | February 1984 | 5.00 | 12.00 |
| 81 | March 1984#{Boba Fett appearance | 12.00 | 30.00 |
| 82 | April 1984 | 5.00 | 12.00 |
| 83 | May 1984 | 5.00 | 12.00 |
| 84 | June 1984 | 5.00 | 12.00 |
| 85 | July 1984 | 5.00 | 12.00 |
| 86 | August 1984 | 5.00 | 12.00 |
| 87 | September 1984 | 5.00 | 12.00 |
| 88 | October 1984#{1st appearance of Lumiya | 6.00 | 15.00 |
| 89 | November 1984 | 5.00 | 12.00 |
| 90 | December 1984 | 5.00 | 12.00 |
| 91 | January 1985 | 6.00 | 15.00 |
| 92 | February 1985#{Giant-Size issue | 8.00 | 20.00 |
| 93 | March 1985 | 6.00 | 15.00 |
| 94 | April 1985 | 6.00 | 15.00 |
| 95 | May 1985 | 6.00 | 15.00 |
| 96 | June 1985 | 6.00 | 15.00 |
| 97 | July 1985 | 6.00 | 15.00 |
| 98 | August 1985 | 6.00 | 15.00 |
| 99 | September 1985 | 6.00 | 15.00 |
| 100 | October 1985#{Giant-Size issue | 10.00 | 25.00 |
| 101 | November 1985 | 8.00 | 20.00 |
| 102 | December 1985 | 8.00 | 20.00 |
| 103 | January 1986 | 8.00 | 20.00 |
| 104 | March 1986 | 8.00 | 20.00 |
| 105 | May 1986 | 8.00 | 20.00 |
| 106 | July 1986 | 10.00 | 25.00 |
| 107 | September 1986#{Final issue | 30.00 | 80.00 |

### Marvel STAR WARS Annual

| | | | |
|---|---|---:|---:|
| 1 | Star Wars Annual 1979 | 6.00 | 15.00 |
| 2 | Star Wars Annual 1982 | 6.00 | 15.00 |
| 3 | Star Wars Annual 1983 | 6.00 | 15.00 |

### STAR WARS: RETURN OF THE JEDI MINI-SERIES (1983-1984)

| | | | |
|---|---|---:|---:|
| 1 | October 1983#{"Return of the Jedi" adaptation Part 1 | 4.00 | 10.00 |
| 2 | November 1983#{"Return of the Jedi" adaptation Part 2 | 3.00 | 8.00 |
| 3 | December 1983#{"Return of the Jedi" adaptation Part 3 | 3.00 | 8.00 |
| 4 | January 1984#{"Return of the Jedi" adaptation Part 4 | 3.00 | 8.00 |

### JOURNEY TO STAR WARS: THE FORCE AWAKENS - SHATTERED EMPIRE (2015)

| | | | |
|---|---|---:|---:|
| 1 | November 2015 | 1.50 | 4.00 |
| 1 | November 2015#{Blank Cover Variant | 3.00 | 8.00 |
| 1 | November 2015#{1:20 Hyperspace Variant | 3.00 | 8.00 |
| 1 | November 2015#{1:25 Movie Photo Variant | 3.00 | 8.00 |
| 1 | November 2015#{1:25 Marco Checchetto Variant | 5.00 | 12.00 |
| 2 | December 2015 | 1.50 | 4.00 |
| 2 | December 2015#{1:25 Movie Photo Variant | 4.00 | 10.00 |
| 2 | December 2015#{1:25 Kris Anka Variant | 4.00 | 10.00 |
| 3 | December 2015 | 1.50 | 4.00 |
| 3 | December 2015#{1:25 Movie Photo Variant | 4.00 | 10.00 |
| 3 | December 2015#{1:25 Mike Deodato Jr. Variant | 4.00 | 10.00 |
| 4 | December 2015 | 1.50 | 4.00 |
| 4 | December 2015#{1:25 Movie Photo Variant | 4.00 | 10.00 |
| 4 | December 2015#{1:25 Sara Pichelli Variant | 4.00 | 10.00 |

### Marvel STAR WARS (2015-)

| | | | |
|---|---|---:|---:|
| 1 | March 2015 | 3.00 | 8.00 |
| 1 | March 2015#{Blank Cover Variant | 4.00 | 10.00 |
| 1 | March 2015#{Skottie Young "Baby" Variant | 3.00 | 8.00 |
| 1 | March 2015#{Luke Skywalker Action Figure Variant | 6.00 | 15.00 |
| 1 | March 2015#{1:15 Movie Photo Variant | 4.00 | 10.00 |
| 1 | March 2015#{1:20 Sara Pichelli Variant | 4.00 | 10.00 |
| 1 | March 2015#{1:25 "Two Suns" Variant | 3.00 | 8.00 |
| 1 | March 2015#{1:25 Bob McLeod Variant | 4.00 | 10.00 |
| 1 | March 2015#{1:50 Alex Ross Variant | 20.00 | 50.00 |
| 1 | March 2015#{1:50 J. Scott Campbell Variant | 15.00 | 40.00 |
| 1 | March 2015#{1:100 Joe Quesada Variant | 15.00 | 40.00 |
| 1 | March 2015#{1:200 Alex Ross Sketch Variant | 30.00 | 80.00 |
| 1 | March 2015#{1:500 Joe Quesada Sketch Variant | 75.00 | 200.00 |
| 1 | April 2015#{2nd printing | 4.00 | 10.00 |
| 1 | April 2015#{3rd printing | 4.00 | 10.00 |
| 1 | June 2015#{4th printing | 4.00 | 10.00 |
| 1 | July 2015#{5th printing | 4.00 | 10.00 |
| 1 | September 2015#{6th printing (double cover) | 6.00 | 15.00 |
| 1 | 7th printing | 4.00 | 10.00 |
| 2 | April 2015 | 4.00 | 10.00 |
| 2 | April 2015#{Han Solo Action Figure Variant | 30.00 | 80.00 |
| 2 | April 2015#{Sergio Aragones Variant | 3.00 | 8.00 |
| 2 | April 2015#{1:25 Leinil Francis Yu Variant | 6.00 | 15.00 |
| 2 | April 2015#{1:25 Howard Chaykin Variant | 6.00 | 15.00 |
| 2 | April 2015#{1:100 John Cassaday Sketch Variant | 20.00 | 50.00 |
| 2 | May 2015#{2nd printing | 4.00 | 10.00 |
| 2 | June 2015#{3rd printing | 3.00 | 8.00 |
| 2 | July 2015#{4th printing | 3.00 | 8.00 |
| 2 | August 2015#{5th printing | 3.00 | 8.00 |
| 2 | 6th printing | 3.00 | 8.00 |
| 3 | May 2015 | 2.50 | 6.00 |
| 3 | May 2015#{Obi-Wan Kenobi Action Figure Variant | 2.50 | 6.00 |
| 3 | May 2015#{1:25 Leinil Francis Yu Variant | 6.00 | 15.00 |
| 3 | May 2015#{1:100 John Cassaday Sketch Variant | 15.00 | 40.00 |
| 3 | July 2015#{2nd printing | 2.00 | 5.00 |
| 3 | July 2015#{3rd printing | 2.00 | 5.00 |
| 3 | 4th printing | 2.00 | 5.00 |
| 4 | June 2015 | 2.50 | 6.00 |
| 4 | June 2015#{Chewbacca Action Figure Variant | 2.50 | 6.00 |
| 4 | June 2015#{1:25 Giuseppe Camuncoli Variant | 5.00 | 12.00 |
| 4 | June 2015#{1:100 John Cassaday Sketch Variant | 15.00 | 40.00 |
| 4 | 2nd printing | 2.00 | 5.00 |
| 5 | July 2015 | 2.00 | 5.00 |
| 5 | July 2015#{C-3PO Action Figure Variant | 2.50 | 6.00 |
| 5 | July 2015#{1:100 John Cassaday Sketch Variant | 15.00 | 40.00 |
| 5 | 2nd printing | 2.00 | 5.00 |
| 6 | August 2015 | 2.00 | 5.00 |
| 6 | August 2015#{R2-D2 Action Figure Variant | 3.00 | 8.00 |
| 6 | 2nd printing | 2.00 | 5.00 |
| 6 | 3rd printing | 2.00 | 5.00 |
| 7 | September 2015 | 2.00 | 5.00 |
| 7 | September 2015#{Stormtrooper Action Figure Variant | 2.50 | 6.00 |
| 7 | September 2015#{1:25 Simone Bianchi Variant Cover | 3.00 | 8.00 |
| 7 | September 2015#{1:25 Tony Moore Variant Cover | 3.00 | 8.00 |
| 7 | September 2015#{1:100 John Cassaday Sketch Variant | 15.00 | 40.00 |
| 8 | October 2015 | 2.00 | 5.00 |
| 8 | October 2015#{Tusken Raider Action Figure Variant | 2.50 | 6.00 |
| 8 | October 2015#{1:50 John Cassaday Variant | 6.00 | 15.00 |
| 8 | October 2015#{1:100 Stuart Immonen Sketch Variant | 15.00 | 40.00 |
| 9 | November 2015 | 2.00 | 5.00 |
| 9 | November 2015#{Star Destroyer Commander Action Figure Variant | 2.50 | 6.00 |
| 9 | November 2015#{1:100 Stuart Immonen Sketch Variant | 15.00 | 40.00 |
| 10 | December 2015 | 2.00 | 5.00 |
| 10 | December 2015#{Jawa Action Figure Variant | 2.50 | 6.00 |
| 10 | December 2015#{1:100 Stuart Immonen Sketch Variant | 15.00 | 40.00 |
| 11 | January 2016 | 2.00 | 5.00 |
| 11 | January 2016#{Luke Skywalker: X-Wing Pilot Action Figure Variant | 2.50 | 6.00 |
| 11 | January 2016#{1:100 Stuart Immonen Sketch Variant | 15.00 | 40.00 |
| 12 | January 2016 | 2.00 | 5.00 |
| 12 | January 2016#{Greedo Action Figure Variant | 2.50 | 6.00 |
| 12 | January 2016#{1:100 Stuart Immonen Sketch Variant | 15.00 | 40.00 |
| 13 | February 2016 | 2.00 | 5.00 |
| 13 | February 2016#{R5-D4 Action Figure Variant | 2.50 | 6.00 |
| 13 | February 2016#{Clay Mann Variant | 2.50 | 6.00 |
| 13 | March 2016#{2nd printing | 2.00 | 5.00 |
| 14 | March 2016 | 2.00 | 5.00 |
| 14 | March 2016#{Hammerhead Action Figure Variant | 2.50 | 6.00 |
| 14 | March 2016#{Clay Mann Variant | 2.50 | 6.00 |
| 14 | April 2016#{2nd printing | 2.00 | 5.00 |
| 15 | March 2016 | 2.00 | 5.00 |
| 15 | March 2016#{Snaggletooth Action Figure Variant | 2.50 | 6.00 |
| 15 | March 2016#{1:100 Mike Mayhew Sketch Variant | 15.00 | 40.00 |
| 15 | May 2016#{2nd printing | 2.00 | 5.00 |
| 16 | April 2016 | 2.00 | 5.00 |
| 16 | April 2016#{Death Star Droid Action Figure Variant | 2.50 | 6.00 |
| 16 | April 2016#{1:25 Stuart Immonen Variant | 4.00 | 10.00 |
| 16 | April 2016#{1:25 Leinil Francis Yu Variant | 4.00 | 10.00 |
| 16 | April 2016#{1:100 Terry Dodson Sketch Variant | 15.00 | 40.00 |
| 17 | May 2016 | 2.00 | 5.00 |
| 17 | May 2016#{Walrus Man Action Figure Variant | 2.50 | 6.00 |
| 17 | May 2016#{1:25 Leinil Francis Yu Variant | 4.00 | 10.00 |
| 17 | May 2016#{1:100 Terry Dodson Sketch Variant | 15.00 | 40.00 |
| 18 | June 2016 | 2.00 | 5.00 |
| 18 | June 2016#{Power Droid Action Figure Variant | 2.50 | 6.00 |
| 18 | June 2016#{1:100 Leinil Francis Yu Sketch Variant | 20.00 | 50.00 |
| 19 | July 2016 | 2.00 | 5.00 |
| 19 | July 2016#{Leia Organa: Bespin Gown Action Figure Variant | 3.00 | 8.00 |
| 19 | July 2016#{1:100 Leinil Francis Yu Sketch Variant | 15.00 | 40.00 |
| 20 | August 2016 | 2.00 | 5.00 |
| 20 | August 2016#{Yoda Action Figure Variant | 4.00 | 10.00 |
| 20 | August 2016#{1:100 Mike Mayhew Sketch Variant | 15.00 | 40.00 |
| 21 | September 2016 | 2.00 | 5.00 |
| 21 | September 2016#{Stormtrooper: Hoth Battle Gear Action Figure Variant | 3.00 | 8.00 |
| 21 | September 2016#{1:100 David Aja Sketch Variant | 20.00 | 50.00 |
| 22 | October 2016 | 2.00 | 5.00 |
| 22 | October 2016#{Dengar Action Figure Variant | 2.50 | 6.00 |
| 22 | October 2016#{1:100 Mike Deodato Sketch Variant | 20.00 | 50.00 |
| 23 | November 2016 | 2.00 | 5.00 |
| 23 | November 2016#{Rebel Soldier: Hoth Battle Gear Action Figure Variant | 2.50 | 6.00 |

| 23 November 2016#{1:25 Jorge Molina Variant | 5.00 | 12.00 |
| 23 November 2016#{1:100 Mike Deodato Sketch Variant | 20.00 | 50.00 |
| 24 December 2016' | 2.00 | 5.00 |
| 24 December 2016#{Lobot Action Figure Variant | 2.50 | 6.00 |
| 24 December 2016#{1:100 Mike Deodato Sketch Variant | 20.00 | 50.00 |
| 25 January 2017 | 2.00 | 5.00 |
| 25 January 2017#{IG-88 Action Figure Variant | 2.50 | 6.00 |
| 25 January 2017#{1:100 Mike Deodato Sketch Variant | 20.00 | 50.00 |
| 26 February 2017' | 2.00 | 5.00 |
| 26 February 2017#{2-1B Action Figure Variant | 2.50 | 6.00 |
| 26 February 2017#{Qui-Gon Jinn Action Figure Variant | 20.00 | 50.00 |
| 26 February 2017#{1:100 Mike Deodato Sketch Variant | 20.00 | 50.00 |
| 27 March 2017' | 2.00 | 5.00 |
| 27 March 2017#{R2-D2 with Sensorscope Action Figure Variant | 2.50 | 6.00 |
| 27 March 2017#{Star Wars 40th Anniversary Variant | 4.00 | 10.00 |
| 28 April 2017' | 2.00 | 5.00 |
| 28 April 2017#{C-3PO Removable Limbs Action Figure Variant | 2.50 | 6.00 |
| 28 April 2017#{Star Wars 40th Anniversary Variant | 4.00 | 10.00 |
| 29 May 2017' | 2.00 | 5.00 |
| 29 May 2017#{Luke Skywalker: Hoth Battle Gear Action Figure Variant | 2.50 | 6.00 |
| 29 May 2017#{Star Wars 40th Anniversary Variant | 3.00 | 8.00 |
| 30 June 2017' | 2.00 | 5.00 |
| 30 June 2017#{AT-AT Commander Action Figure Variant | 2.50 | 6.00 |
| 30 June 2017#{Star Wars 40th Anniversary Variant | 3.00 | 8.00 |
| 31 July 2017' | 2.00 | 5.00 |
| 31 July 2017#{Luke Skywalker: Bespin Fatigues Action Figure Variant | 2.50 | 6.00 |
| 31 July 2017#{Star Wars 40th Anniversary Variant | 3.00 | 8.00 |
| 32 August 2017' | 2.00 | 5.00 |
| 32 August 2017#{FX-7 Medical Droid Action Figure Variant | 2.50 | 6.00 |
| 32 August 2017#{Star Wars 40th Anniversary Variant | 3.00 | 8.00 |
| 33 September 2017' | 2.00 | 5.00 |
| 33 September 2017#{Bespin Security Guard Action Figure Variant | 2.50 | 6.00 |
| 33 September 2017#{Star Wars 40th Anniversary Variant | 3.00 | 8.00 |
| 34 October 2017' | 2.00 | 5.00 |
| 34 October 2017#{Han Solo: Hoth Outfit Action Figure Variant | 2.50 | 6.00 |
| 34 October 2017#{Star Wars 40th Anniversary Variant | 3.00 | 8.00 |
| 35 October 2017' | 2.00 | 5.00 |
| 35 October 2017#{Ugnaught Action Figure Variant | 2.50 | 6.00 |
| 35 October 2017#{Star Wars 40th Anniversary Variant | 3.00 | 8.00 |
| 36 November 2017' | 2.00 | 5.00 |
| 36 November 2017#{Leia Organa: Hoth Outfit Action Figure Variant | 3.00 | 8.00 |
| 36 November 2017#{Star Wars 40th Anniversary Variant | 3.00 | 8.00 |
| 37 December 2017' | 2.00 | 5.00 |
| 37 December 2017#{Rebel Commander Action Figure Variant | 2.50 | 6.00 |
| 37 December 2017#{Star Wars 40th Anniversary Variant | 3.00 | 8.00 |
| 38 January 2018' | 2.00 | 5.00 |
| 38 January 2018#{Michael Walsh Variant | 2.00 | 5.00 |
| 38 January 2018#{AT-AT Driver Action Figure Variant | 3.00 | 8.00 |
| 38 January 2018#{1:25 Pepe Larraz Variant | 5.00 | 12.00 |
| 38 January 2018#{1:50 Terry Dodson Variant | 12.00 | 30.00 |
| 38 January 2018#{Star Wars 40th Anniversary Variant | 3.00 | 8.00 |
| 39 January 2018' | 2.00 | 5.00 |
| 39 January 2018#{Imperial Commander Action Figure Variant | 3.00 | 8.00 |
| 40 February 2018' | 2.00 | 5.00 |
| 40 February 2018#{Star Wars 40th Anniversary Variant | 3.00 | 8.00 |
| 40 February 2018#{Luke Skywalker: Yavin Fatigues Action Figure Variant | 20.00 | 50.00 |
| 41 March 2018' | 2.00 | 5.00 |
| 41 March 2018#{Zuckuss Action Figure Variant | 3.00 | 8.00 |
| 41 March 2018#{Rey Galactic Icons Variant | 6.00 | 15.00 |
| 42 March 2018' | 2.00 | 5.00 |
| 42 March 2018#{4-LOM Action Figure Variant | 3.00 | 8.00 |
| 43 April 2018' | 2.00 | 5.00 |
| 43 April 2018#{Imperial TIE Fighter Pilot Action Figure Variant | 3.00 | 8.00 |
| 43 April 2018#{Poe Dameron Galactic Icons Variant | 2.50 | 6.00 |
| 44 May 2018' | 2.00 | 5.00 |
| 44 May 2018#{(Twin Pod) Cloud Car Pilot Action Figure Variant | 3.00 | 8.00 |
| 44 May 2018#{Captain Phasma Galactic Icons Variant | 2.50 | 6.00 |
| 45 May 2018' | 2.00 | 5.00 |
| 45 May 2018#{Bib Fortune Action Figure Variant | 3.00 | 8.00 |
| 46 June 2018' | 2.00 | 5.00 |
| 46 June 2018#{Ree-Yees Action Figure Variant | 3.00 | 8.00 |
| 46 June 2018#{Han Solo Galactic Icons Variant | 2.50 | 6.00 |
| 47 July 2018' | 2.00 | 5.00 |
| 47 July 2018#{Weequay Action Figure Variant | 3.00 | 8.00 |
| 47 July 2018#{Qi'ra Galactic Icons Variant | 2.50 | 6.00 |
| 48 July 2018' | 2.00 | 5.00 |
| 48 July 2018#{Bespin Security Guard Action Figure Variant | 3.00 | 8.00 |
| 49 August 2018' | 2.00 | 5.00 |
| 49 August 2018#{Emperor's Royal Guard Action Figure Variant | 3.00 | 8.00 |
| 49 August 2018#{Sheev Palpatine Galactic Icons Variant | 2.50 | 6.00 |
| 50 September 2018' | 2.50 | 6.00 |
| 50 September 2018#{David Marquez Variant | 2.50 | 6.00 |
| 50 September 2018#{The Emperor Action Figure Variant | 4.00 | 10.00 |
| 50 September 2018#{Thrawn Galactic Icons Variant | 4.00 | 10.00 |
| 50 September 2018#{1:25 Phil Noto Variant | 5.00 | 12.00 |
| 50 September 2018#{1:50 Terry Dodson Variant | 12.00 | 30.00 |
| 50 September 2018#{1:100 Terry Dodson Virgin Variant | 30.00 | 80.00 |
| 50 October 2018#{2nd printing | 2.50 | 6.00 |
| 51 September 2018' | 2.00 | 5.00 |
| 51 September 2018#{Chief Chirpa Action Figure Variant | 3.00 | 8.00 |
| 51 September 2018#{Jabba the Hutt Action Figure Variant | 20.00 | 50.00 |
| 52 October 2018' | 2.00 | 5.00 |
| 52 October 2018#{Lando Calrissian: Skiff Guard Disguise Action Figure Variant | 3.00 | 8.00 |
| 52 October 2018#{Ben Kenobi Galactic Icons Variant | 2.50 | 6.00 |
| 53 November 2018' | 2.00 | 5.00 |
| 53 November 2018#{Logray (Ewok Shaman) Action Figure Variant | 3.00 | 8.00 |
| 54 November 2018' | 2.00 | 5.00 |
| 54 November 2018#{Squid Head Action Figure Variant | 3.00 | 8.00 |
| 55 December 2018' | 2.00 | 5.00 |
| 55 December 2018#{Klaatu Action Figure Variant | 3.00 | 8.00 |
| 55 December 2018#{Cad Bane Galactic Icons Variant | 2.50 | 6.00 |

### Marvel STAR WARS ANNUAL (2015-)

| 1 February 2016 | 2.00 | 5.00 |
| 1 February 2016#{Blank Cover Variant | 3.00 | 8.00 |
| 2 January 2017' | 2.00 | 5.00 |
| 2 January 2017#{Elsa Charretier Variant | 2.00 | 5.00 |
| 3 November 2017' | 2.00 | 5.00 |
| 3 November 2017#{Rod Reis Variant | 2.00 | 5.00 |
| 4 July 2018' | 2.50 | 6.00 |
| 4 July 2018#{1:25 John Tyler Christopher Variant | 15.00 | 40.00 |

### Marvel DARTH VADER (2015-2016)

| 1 April 2015 | 4.00 | 10.00 |
| 1 April 2015#{Blank Cover Variant | 3.00 | 8.00 |
| 1 April 2015#{Skottie Young "Baby" Variant | 2.50 | 6.00 |
| 1 April 2015#{Darth Vader Action Figure Variant | 3.00 | 8.00 |
| 1 April 2015#{1:15 Movie Photo Variant | 4.00 | 10.00 |
| 1 April 2015#{1:25 John Cassaday Variant | 5.00 | 12.00 |
| 1 April 2015#{1:25 Whilce Portacio Variant | 6.00 | 15.00 |
| 1 April 2015#{1:25 Mike Del Mundo Variant | 8.00 | 20.00 |
| 1 April 2015#{1:50 J. Scott Campbell Variant | 15.00 | 40.00 |
| 1 April 2015#{1:50 Alex Ross Variant | 20.00 | 50.00 |
| 1 April 2015#{1:200 Alex Ross Sketch Variant | 75.00 | 200.00 |
| 1 2nd printing | 2.00 | 5.00 |

| | | |
|---|---|---|
| 1 3rd printing | 2.00 | 5.00 |
| 1 4th printing | 2.00 | 5.00 |
| 1 5th printing | 2.00 | 5.00 |
| 2 April 2015 | 4.00 | 10.00 |
| 2 April 2015#{1:25 Dave Dorman Variant | 5.00 | 12.00 |
| 2 April 2015#{1:25 Salvador Larroca Variant | 5.00 | 12.00 |
| 2 2nd printing | 4.00 | 10.00 |
| 2 3rd printing | 4.00 | 10.00 |
| 2 4th printing | 3.00 | 8.00 |
| 2 5th printing | 3.00 | 8.00 |
| 3 May 2015#{1st appearance of Dr. Aphra, 0-0-0 & BT-1 | 10.00 | 25.00 |
| 3 May 2015#{1:25 Salvador Larroca Variant | 40.00 | 100.00 |
| 3 2nd printing | 4.00 | 10.00 |
| 3 3rd printing | 4.00 | 10.00 |
| 3 4th printing | 4.00 | 10.00 |
| 4 June 2015 | 2.50 | 6.00 |
| 4 June 2015#{1:25 Salvador Larroca Variant | 6.00 | 15.00 |
| 4 2nd printing | 2.00 | 5.00 |
| 4 3rd printing | 2.00 | 5.00 |
| 4 4th printing | 2.00 | 5.00 |
| 5 July 2015 | 2.50 | 6.00 |
| 5 July 2015#{1:25 Salvador Larroca Variant | 4.00 | 10.00 |
| 5 2nd printing | 2.00 | 5.00 |
| 6 August 2015 | 2.50 | 6.00 |
| 6 2nd printing | 2.00 | 5.00 |
| 7 September 2015 | 2.50 | 6.00 |
| 8 October 2015 | 2.50 | 6.00 |
| 9 November 2015 | 2.50 | 6.00 |
| 9 November 2015#{1:25 Adi Granov Variant | 6.00 | 15.00 |
| 10 December 2015 | 2.50 | 6.00 |
| 11 December 2015 | 2.50 | 6.00 |
| 12 January 2016 | 2.50 | 6.00 |
| 13 January 2016 | 2.50 | 6.00 |
| 13 January 2016#{Clay Mann Variant | 2.50 | 6.00 |
| 13 2nd printing | 2.50 | 6.00 |
| 14 February 2016 | 2.50 | 6.00 |
| 14 February 2016#{Clay Mann Variant | 2.50 | 6.00 |
| 14 2nd printing | 2.50 | 6.00 |
| 15 March 2016 | 2.50 | 6.00 |
| 15 April 2016#{Clay Mann Variant | 2.50 | 6.00 |
| 15 May 2016#{1:25 Francesco Francavilla Variant | 6.00 | 15.00 |
| 15 June 2016#{1:100 Mark Brooks Sketch Variant | 20.00 | 50.00 |
| 15 2nd printing | 2.50 | 6.00 |
| 16 April 2016 | 2.50 | 6.00 |
| 16 2nd printing | 2.00 | 5.00 |
| 17 May 2016 | 2.50 | 6.00 |
| 18 May 2016 | 2.50 | 6.00 |
| 19 June 2016 | 2.50 | 6.00 |

| | | |
|---|---|---|
| 20 July 2016 | 2.50 | 6.00 |
| 20 July 2016#{Inspector Thanoth Action Figure Variant | 2.50 | 6.00 |
| 20 July 2016#{"The Story Thus Far" Reilly Brown Variant | 2.50 | 6.00 |
| 20 2nd printing | 2.00 | 5.00 |
| 21 August 2016 | 2.50 | 6.00 |
| 21 August 2016#{Tulon Action Figure Variant | 2.50 | 6.00 |
| 21 2nd printing | 2.00 | 5.00 |
| 22 August 2016 | 2.50 | 6.00 |
| 22 August 2016#{Cylo Action Figure Variant | 2.50 | 6.00 |
| 22 2nd printing | 2.00 | 5.00 |
| 23 September 2016 | 2.50 | 6.00 |
| 23 September 2016#{BT-1 Action Figure Variant | 2.50 | 6.00 |
| 23 2nd printing | 2.00 | 5.00 |
| 24 October 2016 | 2.50 | 6.00 |
| 24 0-0-0 (Triple-Zero) Action Figure Variant | 2.50 | 6.00 |
| 25 December 2016#{final issue | 2.50 | 6.00 |
| 25 December 2016#{Doctor Aphra Action Figure Variant | 4.00 | 10.00 |
| 25 December 2016#{Adi Granov Variant | 2.50 | 6.00 |
| 25 December 2016#{Jamie McKelvie Variant | 3.00 | 8.00 |
| 25 December 2016#{Karmome Shirahama Variant | 3.00 | 8.00 |
| 25 December 2016#{Salvador Larroca Variant | 2.50 | 6.00 |
| 25 December 2016#{1:25 Chris Samnee Variant | 6.00 | 15.00 |
| 25 December 2016#{1:25 Sara Pichelli Variant | 6.00 | 15.00 |
| 25 December 2016#{1:25 Cliff Chiang Variant | 8.00 | 20.00 |
| 25 December 2016#{1:50 Michael Cho Variant | 20.00 | 50.00 |
| 25 December 2016#{1:100 Joe Quesada Variant | 40.00 | 100.00 |
| 25 December 2016#{1:200 Joe Quesada Sketch Variant | 75.00 | 200.00 |

## Marvel DARTH VADER ANNUAL (2015-2016)

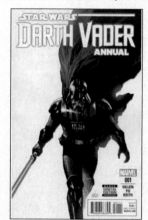

| | | |
|---|---|---|
| 1 February 2015 | 3.00 | 8.00 |
| 1 February 2015#{Blank Cover Variant | 3.00 | 8.00 |

## Marvel STAR WARS: THE FORCE AWAKENS (2016-2017)

| | | |
|---|---|---|
| 1 August 2016#{"Star Wars: The Force Awakens " adaptation Part 1 | 2.00 | 5.00 |
| 1 August 2016#{Blank Cover Variant | 4.00 | 10.00 |
| 1 August 2016#{1:15 Movie Photo Variant | 5.00 | 12.00 |
| 1 August 2016#{1:25 Phil Noto Variant | 10.00 | 25.00 |
| 1 August 2016#{1:50 John Cassaday Variant | 12.00 | 30.00 |
| 1 August 2016#{1:75 Esad Ribic Sketch Variant | 20.00 | 50.00 |
| 1 August 2016#{1:100 Joe Quesada Variant | 125.00 | 300.00 |
| 1 August 2016#{1:200 John Cassaday Sketch Variant | 20.00 | 50.00 |
| 1 August 2016#{1:300 Joe Quesada Sketch Variant | 200.00 | 500.00 |
| 2 September 2016#{"Star Wars: The Force Awakens " adaptation Part 2 | 1.50 | 4.00 |
| 2 September 2016#{1:15 Movie Photo Variant | 4.00 | 10.00 |
| 2 September 2016#{1:25 Chris Samnee Variant | 6.00 | 15.00 |
| 2 September 2016#{1:75 Mike Mayhew Sketch Variant | 30.00 | 80.00 |
| 3 October 2016#{"Star Wars: The Force Awakens" adaptation Part 3 | 1.50 | 4.00 |
| 3 October 2016#{1:15 Movie Photo Variant | 4.00 | 10.00 |
| 3 October 2016#{1:75 Mike Deodato Jr. Sketch Variant | 30.00 | 80.00 |
| 4 November 2016#{"Star Wars: The Force Awakens" adaptation Part 4 | 1.50 | 4.00 |
| 4 November 2016#{1:15 Movie Photo Variant | 4.00 | 10.00 |
| 4 November 2016#{1:75 Mike Del Mundo Sketch Variant | 30.00 | 80.00 |
| 5 December 2016#{"Star Wars: The Force Awakens" adaptation Part 5 | 1.50 | 4.00 |
| 5 December 2016#{1:15 Movie Photo Variant | 6.00 | 15.00 |
| 5 December 2016#{1:75 Rafael Albuquerque Sketch Variant | 50.00 | 120.00 |
| 6 January 2017#{"Star Wars: The Force Awakens" adaptation Part 6 | 1.50 | 4.00 |
| 6 January 2017#{1:15 Movie Photo Variant | 8.00 | 20.00 |
| 6 January 2017#{1:25 Esad Ribic Variant | 10.00 | 25.00 |
| 6 January 2017#{1:75 Paolo Rivera Variant | 30.00 | 80.00 |